Lecture Notes in Computer Science   12100

More information about this series at http://www.springer.com/series/7410

Jintai Ding · Jean-Pierre Tillich (Eds.)

Post-Quantum Cryptography

11th International Conference, PQCrypto 2020
Paris, France, April 15–17, 2020
Proceedings

 Springer

Editors
Jintai Ding 🆔
University of Cincinnati
Cincinnati, OH, USA

Jean-Pierre Tillich 🆔
Inria
Paris, France

ISSN 0302-9743   ISSN 1611-3349   (electronic)
Lecture Notes in Computer Science
ISBN 978-3-030-44222-4   ISBN 978-3-030-44223-1   (eBook)
https://doi.org/10.1007/978-3-030-44223-1

LNCS Sublibrary: SL4 – Security and Cryptology

This Springer imprint is published by the registered company Springer Nature Switzerland AG
The registered company address is: Gewerbestrasse 11, 6330 Cham, Switzerland

Preface

PQCrypto 2020, the 11th International Conference on Post-Quantum Cryptography, was held in Paris, France, during April 15–17, 2020. The aim of the PQCrypto conference series is to serve as a forum for researchers to present results and exchange ideas on cryptography in an era with large-scale quantum computers. Following the same model as its predecessors, PQCrypto 2020 adopted a two-stage submission process in which authors registered their paper one week before the final submission deadline. The conference received 91 submissions with authors from 25 countries. Each paper (that had not been withdrawn by the authors) was reviewed in private by at least three Program Committee members. The private review phase was followed by an intensive discussion phase, conducted online. At the end of this process, the Program Committee selected 29 papers for inclusion in the technical program and publication in these proceedings. The accepted papers cover a broad spectrum of research within the conference's scope, including code-, hash-, isogeny-, and lattice-based cryptography, multivariate cryptography, and quantum cryptanalysis. Along with the 29 contributed technical presentations, the program featured outstanding invited talks and a presentation on NIST's post-quantum cryptography standardization. Organizing and running this year's edition of the PQCrypto conference series was a team effort and we are indebted to everyone who helped make PQCrypto 2020 a success. In particular, we would like thank all members of the Program Committee and the external reviewers who were vital in compiling the technical program. Evaluating and discussing the submissions was a labor-intensive task and we truly appreciate the work that went into this. In the name of the community, let us say that we are all indebted to Antoine Joux from Sorbonne University and Nicolas Sendrier from Inria for organizing this meeting.

February 2020

Jintai Ding
Jean-Pierre Tillich

Organization

General Chairs

Antoine Joux   Sorbonne University, France
Nicolas Sendrier   Inria, France

Program Chairs

Jintai Ding   University of Cincinnati, USA
Jean-Pierre Tillich   Inria, France

Steering Committee

Daniel J. Bernstein   University Illinois at Chicago, USA, and Ruhr
                           University Bochum, Germany
Johannes Buchmann   Technische Universität Darmstadt, Germany
Claude Crépeau   McGill University, Canada
Jintai Ding   University of Cincinnati, USA
Philippe Gaborit   University of Limoges, France
Tanja Lange   Technische Universiteit Eindhoven, The Netherlands
Daniele Micciancio   University of California at San Diego, USA
Michele Mosca   Waterloo University and Perimeter Institute, Canada
Nicolas Sendrier   Inria, France
Tsuyoshi Takagi   University of Tokyo, Japan
Bo-Yin Yang   Academia Sinica, Taiwan

Program Committee

Reza Azarderakhsh   Florida Atlantic University and PQSecure
                           Technologies, USA
Jean-Philippe Aumasson   Teserakt AG, Switzerland
Yoshinori Aono   National Institute of Communication Technology,
                           Japan
Magali Bardet   University of Rouen, France
Daniel J. Bernstein   University Illinois at Chicago, USA, and Ruhr
                           University Bochum, Germany
Olivier Blazy   University of Limoges, France
André Chailloux   Inria, France
Chen-Mou Cheng   Osaka University and Kanazawa University, Japan
Jung Hee Cheon   Seoul National University, South Korea
Tung Chou   Osaka University, Japan, and Academia Sinica, Taiwan
Dung Duong   University of Wollongong, Australia

Scott Fluhrer	Cisco Systems, USA
Philippe Gaborit	University of Limoges, France
Tommaso Gagliardoni	Kudelski Security, Switzerland
Steven Galbraith	The University of Auckland, New Zealand
Xiao-Shan Gao	Chinese Academy of Sciences, China
Tim Güneysu	Ruhr University Bochum and DFKI, Germany
David Jao	University of Waterloo and evolutionQ, Canada
Jiwu Jing	Chinese Academy of Sciences, China
Thomas Johansson	Lund University, Sweden
Antoine Joux	Sorbonne University, France
Kwangjo Kim	KAIST, South Korea
Elena Kirshanova	I. Kant Baltic Federal University, Russia
Yi-Kai Liu	NIST and University of Maryland, USA
Prabhat Mishra	University of Florida, USA
Michele Mosca	Waterloo University and Perimeter Institute, Canada
María Naya-Plasencia	Inria, France
Khoa Nguyen	Nanyang Technological University, Singapore
Ruben Niederhagen	Fraunhofer SIT, Germany
Ray Perlner	NIST, USA
Christophe Petit	University of Birmingham, UK
Rachel Player	University of London, UK
Thomas Pöppelmann	Infineon Technologies, Germany
Thomas Prest	PQShield, UK
Nicolas Sendrier	Inria, France
Junji Shikata	Yokohama National University, Japan
Daniel Smith-Tone	NIST and University of Louisville, USA
Rainer Steinwandt	Florida Atlantic University, USA
Damien Stehlé	ENS de Lyon, France
Tsuyoshi Takagi	University of Tokyo, Japan
Routo Terada	University of São Paulo, Brasil
Serge Vaudenay	EPFL, Switzerland
Keita Xagawa	NTT Secure Platform Laboratories, Japan
Bo-Yin Yang	Academia Sinica, Taiwan
Zhenfeng Zhang	Institute of Software, Chinese Academy of Sciences, China

Additional Reviewers

Nicolas Aragon	Wouter Castryck	Benjamin Curtis
Florian Bache	Ming-Shing Chen	Bernardo David
Subhadeep Banik	Ding-Yuan Cheng	Luca De Feo
Khashayar Barooti	Ilaria Chillotti	Rafael Pablo Del Pino
Loic Bidoux	Wonhee Cho	Amit Deo
Nina Bindel	Gwangbae Choi	Hülya Evkan
Xavier Bonnetain	Alain Couvreur	Xiutao Feng

Tim Fritzmann
Leon Groot Bruinderink
Qian Guo
Yasufumi Hashimoto
Minki Hhan
Seungwan Hong
James Howe
Zhenyu Huang
Loïs Huguenin-Dumittan
Aaron Hutchinson
Yasuhiko Ikematsu
Mitsugu Iwamoto
Saqib A. Kakvi
Elif Bilge Kavun
Duhyeong Kim
Brian Koziel
Peter Kutas
Norman Lahr

Georg Land
Keewoo Lee
Seungbeom Lee
Matthieu Lequesne
Sarah McCarthy
Romy Minko
Erik Mårtensson
Alexander Nilsson
Richard Petri
Ben Pring
Renato Renner
Jan Richter-Brockmann
Yolan Romailler
Miruna Rosca
Rei Safavi-Naini
Amin Sakzad
John Schanck
André Schrottenloher

Hwajeong Seo
Arnaud Sipasseuth
Yongha Son
Junichi Tomida
David Urbanik
Valentin Vasseur
Javier Verbel
Reynaldo Villena
Fernando Virdia
Daniel Volya
Yacheng Wang
Yuntao Wang
Yohei Watanabe
Julian Wälde
Haiyang Xue
Masaya Yasuda
Greg Zaverucha

Organization and Sponsors

The conference was organized by Inria and Sorbonne University, with the support of the ERC Almacrypt[1].
The organizers thank the following companies and institutions for their generous financial support:

Amazon Web Services, USA
Cisco Systems, USA
Infineon Technologies, Germany
PQShield, UK
Worldline, France

---

[1] European Union's H2020 Program under grant agreement number ERC-669891.

Contents

Quantum Algorithms

Security Proofs

Code-Based Cryptography

Randomized Decoding of Gabidulin Codes Beyond the Unique Decoding Radius

Julian Renner[1]([✉]), Thomas Jerkovits[2], Hannes Bartz[2], Sven Puchinger[3], Pierre Loidreau[4], and Antonia Wachter-Zeh[1]

[1] Technical University of Munich (TUM), Munich, Germany
{julian.renner,antonia.wachter-zeh}@tum.de
[2] German Aerospace Center (DLR), Oberpfaffenhofen-Wessling, Germany
{thomas.jerkovits,hannes.bartz}@dlr.de
[3] Technical University of Denmark (DTU), Lyngby, Denmark
svepu@dtu.dk
[4] Univ Rennes, DGA MI, CNRS, IRMAR - UMR 6625, 35000 Rennes, France
pierre.loidreau@univ-rennes1.fr

Abstract. We address the problem of decoding Gabidulin codes beyond their unique error-correction radius. The complexity of this problem is of importance to assess the security of some rank-metric code-based cryptosystems. We propose an approach that introduces row or column erasures to decrease the rank of the error in order to use any proper polynomial-time Gabidulin code error-erasure decoding algorithm. The expected work factor of this new randomized decoding approach is a polynomial term times $q^{m(n-k)-w(n+m)+w^2+\min\{2\xi(\frac{n+k}{2}-\xi),wk\}}$, where n is the code length, q the size of the base field, m the extension degree of the field, k the code dimension, w the number of errors, and $\xi := w - \frac{n-k}{2}$. It improves upon generic rank-metric decoders by an exponential factor.

Keywords: Gabidulin codes · Decoding · Rank metric · Code-based cryptography

1 Introduction

Code-based cryptography relies on the hardness of certain coding-theoretic problems, e.g., decoding a random code up to its unique decoding radius or, as considered in this paper, decoding more errors than the unique decoding radius and

The work of J. Renner and A. Wachter-Zeh was supported by the European Research Council (ERC) under the European Union's Horizon 2020 research and innovation programme (grant agreement No. 801434).
Sven Puchinger has received funding from the European Union's Horizon 2020 research and innovation program under the Marie Sklodowska-Curie grant agreement no. 713683 (COFUNDfellowsDTU).

J. Ding and J.-P. Tillich (Eds.): PQCrypto 2020, LNCS 12100, pp. 3–19, 2020.
https://doi.org/10.1007/978-3-030-44223-1_1

beyond the capabilities of all known polynomial-time decoding algorithms. Rank-metric schemes that rely on the latter problem have the promising potential to achieve key sizes that are *linear* in the security parameter and are for instance the (modified) Faure–Loidreau system [9,33] or the RAMESSES system [21].

In the Hamming metric as well as in the rank metric, it is well-known that the problem of decoding beyond the unique decoding radius, in particular *Maximum-Likelihood* (ML) decoding, is a difficult problem concerning the complexity. In Hamming metric, many works have analyzed how hard it actually is, cf. [6,27], and it was finally shown for general linear codes that ML decoding is NP-hard by Vardy in [29]. For the rank metric, some complexity results were obtained more recently in [15], emphasizing the difficulty of ML decoding. This potential hardness was also corroborated by the existing practical complexities of the generic rank metric decoding algorithms [14].

For specific well-known families of codes such as *Reed–Solomon* (RS) codes in the Hamming metric, (ML or list) decoding can be done efficiently up to a certain radius. Given a received word, an ML decoder returns *the* (or one if there is more than one) *closest codeword* to the received word whereas a list decoder returns *all codewords* up to a fixed radius. The existence of an efficient list decoder up to a certain radius therefore implies an efficient ML decoder up to the same radius. Vice versa, this is however not necessarily true, but we cannot apply a list decoder to solve the ML decoding problem efficiently.

In particular, for an RS code of length n and dimension k, the following is known, depending on the Hamming weight w of the error:

- If $w \leq \lfloor \frac{n-k}{2} \rfloor$, the (ML and list) decoding result is unique and can be found in quasi-linear time,
- If $w < n - \sqrt{n(k-1)}$, i.e., the weight of the error is less than the Johnson bound, list decoding and therefore also ML decoding can be done efficiently by Guruswami–Sudan's list decoding algorithm [16],
- The renewed interest in RS codes after the design of the Guruswami–Sudan list decoder [16] motivated new studies of the theoretical complexity of ML and list decoding of RS codes. In [17] it was shown that ML decoding of RS codes is indeed NP-hard when $w \geq d - 2$, even with some pre-processing.
- Between the Johnson radius and $d - 2$, it has been shown in [5] that the number of codewords in radius w around the received word might become a number that grows super-polynomially in n which makes list decoding of RS codes a hard problem.

Gabidulin codes [7,10,24] can be seen as the rank-metric analog of RS codes. ML decoding of Gabidulin codes is in the focus of this paper which is much less investigated than for RS codes (see the following discussion). However, both problems (ML decoding of RS and Gabidulin codes) are of cryptographic interest. The security of the Augot–Finiasz public-key cryptosystem from [3] relied on the hardness of ML decoding of RS codes but was broken by a structural attack. More recently, some public-key cryptosystems based their security partly upon the difficulty of solving the problem Dec-Gab (Decisional-Gabidulin defined in the following) and Search-Gab (Search-Gabidulin), i.e., decoding Gabidulin codes beyond the unique decoding radius or derived instances of this problem [9,21,33].

Dec-Gab has not been well investigated so far. Therefore, we are interested in designing efficient algorithms to solve Dec-Gab which in turn assesses the security of several public-key cryptosystems. We deal with analyzing the problem of decoding Gabidulin codes beyond the unique radius where a Gabidulin code of length n and dimension k is denoted by $Gab_k(\boldsymbol{g})$ and $\boldsymbol{g} = (g_0, g_1, \ldots, g_{n-1})$ denotes the vector of linearly independent code locators.

Problem 1 (Dec-Gab)

- *Instance: $Gab_k(\boldsymbol{g}) \subset \mathbb{F}_{q^m}^n$, $\boldsymbol{r} \in \mathbb{F}_{q^m}^n$ and an integer $w > 0$.*
- *Query: Is there a codeword $\boldsymbol{c} \in Gab_k(\boldsymbol{g})$, such that $\mathrm{rk}(\boldsymbol{r} - \boldsymbol{c}) \leq w$?*

It is trivial that Dec-Gab($Gab_k(\boldsymbol{g})$, $\boldsymbol{r}$, w) can be solved in deterministic polynomial time whenever:

- $w \leq \lfloor \frac{n-k}{2} \rfloor$, with applying a deterministic polynomial-time decoding algorithm for Gabidulin codes to $\boldsymbol{r}$.
- $w \geq n - k$: In this case the answer is always **yes** since this just tantamounts to finding a solution to an overdetermined full rank linear system (Gabidulin codes are *Maximum Rank Distance* codes).

However, between $\lfloor \frac{n-k}{2} \rfloor$ and $n - k$, the situation for Dec-Gab is less clear than for RS codes (which was analyzed above).

For instance, concerning RS codes, the results from [17] and [5] state that there is a point in the interval $[\lfloor \frac{n-k}{2} \rfloor, n - k]$ where the situation is not solvable in polynomial-time unless the polynomial hierarchy collapses. For RS codes, we can refine the interval to $[n - \sqrt{n(k-1)}, n-k]$, because of the Guruswami-Sudan polynomial-time list decoder up to Johnson bound [16].

On the contrary, for Gabidulin codes, there is no such a refinement. In [31], it was shown that for *all* Gabidulin codes, the list size grows exponentially in n when $w > n - \sqrt{n(k-1)}$. Further, [22] showed that the size of the list is exponential for some Gabidulin codes as soon as $w = \lfloor \frac{n-k}{2} \rfloor + 1$. This result was recently generalized in [28] to other classes of Gabidulin codes (e.g., twisted Gabidulin codes) and, more importantly, it showed that any Gabidulin code of dimension at least two can have an exponentially-growing list size for $w \geq \lfloor \frac{n-k}{2} \rfloor + 1$.

To solve the decisional problem Dec-Gab we do not know a better approach than trying to solve the associated *search* problem, which is usually done for all decoding-based problems.

Problem 2 (Search-Gab)

- *Instance: $Gab_k(\boldsymbol{g}) \subset \mathbb{F}_{q^m}^n$, $\boldsymbol{r} \in \mathbb{F}_{q^m}^n$ and an integer $w > 0$.*
- *Objective: Search for a codeword $\boldsymbol{c} \in Gab_k(\boldsymbol{g})$, such that $\mathrm{rk}(\boldsymbol{r} - \boldsymbol{c}) \leq w$.*

Since Dec-Gab and Search-Gab form the security core of some rank-metric based cryptosystems, it is necessary to evaluate the effective complexity of solving these problems to be able to parameterize the systems in terms of security.

In particular, the problems Dec-Gab and Search-Gab are related to the NIST submission RQC [1], the (modified) Faure–Loidreau (FL) cryptosystem [9,33], and RAMESSES [21].

A part of the security of the newly proposed RAMESSES system [21] directly relies on the hardness of Search-Gab as solving Search-Gab for the public key directly reveals an alternative private key.

The (modified) FL cryptosystem [9,33] is based on the hardness of decoding Gabidulin codes beyond their unique decoding radius. Both, the security of the public key as well as the security of the ciphertext are based on this assumption. The public key can be seen as a corrupted word of an interleaved Gabidulin code whose decoders enabled a structural attack on the original system [13]. In the modified FL system [33], only public keys for which all known interleaved decoders fail are chosen, therefore making the structural attack from [13] impossible. As shown in [19], the component codewords of the public key as well as the ciphertext are a Gabidulin codeword that is corrupted by an error of large weight. Therefore, solving Search-Gab has to be considered when determining the security level of the system.

The NIST submission RQC is based on a similar problem. Here, the ciphertext is also the sum of a Gabidulin codeword and an error of weight larger than the unique decoding radius. The error in this setting has a special structure. However, our problem cannot be applied directly to assess the security level of RQC since the error weight is much larger than in the FL and RAMESSES systems and solving Search-Gab for the RQC setting would return a codeword that is close to the error and therefore not the one that was encoded from the plaintext. It is not clear how to modify our algorithm to be applicable to RQC since we would have to be able to find exactly the encoded codeword and not just *any* codeword. We are not aware of how this can be done but want to emphasize that the underlying problem of RQC is very similar to Problem 2.

In this paper, we propose a randomized approach to solve Search-Gab and analyze its work factor. The new algorithm consists of repeatedly guessing a subspace that should have a large intersection with the error row and/or column space. Then the guessed space is used as erasures in an Gabidulin error-erasure decoder, e.g., [26,32]. The algorithm terminates when the intersection of the guessed space and the error row and/or column space is large enough such that the decoder outputs a codeword that is close enough to the received word r.

This paper is structured as follows. In Sect. 2, we introduce the used notation and define Gabidulin codes as well as the channel model. In Sect. 3, we recall known algorithms to solve Search-Gab and state their work factors. We propose and analyze the new algorithm to solve Problem 2 in Sect. 4. Further, numerical examples and simulation results are given in Sect. 5. Open questions are stated in Sect. 6.

2   Preliminaries

2.1   Notation

Let q be a power of a prime and let $\mathbb{F}_q$ denote the finite field of order q and $\mathbb{F}_{q^m}$ its extension field of order q^m. This definition includes the important cases for cryptographic applications $q = 2$ or $q = 2^r$ for a small positive integer r. It is well-known that any element of $\mathbb{F}_q$ can be seen as an element of $\mathbb{F}_{q^m}$ and that $\mathbb{F}_{q^m}$ is an m-dimensional vector space over $\mathbb{F}_q$.

We use $\mathbb{F}_q^{m \times n}$ to denote the set of all $m \times n$ matrices over $\mathbb{F}_q$ and $\mathbb{F}_{q^m}^n = \mathbb{F}_{q^m}^{1 \times n}$ for the set of all row vectors of length n over $\mathbb{F}_{q^m}$. Rows and columns of $m \times n$-matrices are indexed by $1, \dots, m$ and $1, \dots, n$, where $A_{i,j}$ is the element in the i-th row and j-th column of the matrix $\boldsymbol{A}$. In the following of the paper, we will always consider that $n \leq m$. This is the necessary and sufficient condition to design Gabidulin codes.

For a vector $\boldsymbol{a} \in \mathbb{F}_{q^m}^n$, we define its ($\mathbb{F}_q$-)rank by $\mathrm{rk}(\boldsymbol{a}) := \dim_{\mathbb{F}_q} \langle a_1, \dots, a_n \rangle_{\mathbb{F}_q}$, where $\langle a_1, \dots, a_n \rangle_{\mathbb{F}_q}$ is the $\mathbb{F}_q$-vector space spanned by the entries $a_i \in \mathbb{F}_{q^m}$ of $\boldsymbol{a}$. Note that this rank equals the rank of the matrix representation of $\boldsymbol{a}$, where the i-th entry of $\boldsymbol{a}$ is column-wise expanded into a vector in $\mathbb{F}_q^m$ w.r.t. a basis of $\mathbb{F}_{q^m}$ over $\mathbb{F}_q$.

The Grassmannian $\mathcal{G}(\mathcal{V}, k)$ of a vector space $\mathcal{V}$ is the set of all k-dimensional subspaces of $\mathcal{V}$.

A linear code over $\mathbb{F}_{q^m}$ of length n and dimension k is a k-dimensional subspace of $\mathbb{F}_{q^m}^n$ and denoted by $[n, k]_{q^m}$.

2.2   Gabidulin Codes and Channel Model

Gabidulin codes are a special class of rank-metric codes and can be defined by a generator matrix as follows.

Definition 1 (Gabidulin Code [10]). *A linear $Gab_k(\boldsymbol{g})$ code over $\mathbb{F}_{q^m}$ of length $n \leq m$ and dimension k is defined by its $k \times n$ generator matrix*

$$\boldsymbol{G}_{\mathrm{Gab}} = \begin{pmatrix} g_1 & g_2 & \cdots & g_n \\ g_1^q & g_2^q & \cdots & g_n^q \\ \vdots & \vdots & \ddots & \vdots \\ g_1^{q^{k-1}} & g_2^{q^{k-1}} & \cdots & g_n^{q^{k-1}} \end{pmatrix} \in \mathbb{F}_{q^m}^{k \times n},$$

where $g_1, g_2, \dots, g_n \in \mathbb{F}_{q^m}$ are linearly independent over $\mathbb{F}_q$.

The codes are maximum rank distance (MRD) codes, i.e., they attain the maximal possible minimum distance $d = n - k + 1$ for a given length n and dimension k [10].

Let $\boldsymbol{r} \in \mathbb{F}_{q^m}^n$ be a codeword of a Gabidulin code of length $n \leq m$ and dimension k that is corrupted by an error of rank weight w, i.e.,

$$\boldsymbol{r} = \boldsymbol{m} \boldsymbol{G}_{\mathrm{Gab}} + \boldsymbol{e},$$

where $m \in \mathbb{F}_{q^m}^k$, $G_{\text{Gab}} \in \mathbb{F}_{q^m}^{k \times n}$ is a generator matrix of an $[n,k]_{q^m}$ Gabidulin code and $e \in \mathbb{F}_{q^m}^n$ with $\text{rk}(e) = w > \frac{n-k}{2}$. Each error e of rank weight w can be decomposed into

$$e = aB,$$

where $a \in \mathbb{F}_{q^m}^w$ and $B \in \mathbb{F}_q^{w \times n}$. The subspace $\langle a_1, \ldots, a_w \rangle_{\mathbb{F}_q}$ is called the column space of the error and the subspace spanned by the rows of B, i.e. $\mathcal{R}_{\mathbb{F}_q}(B)$, is called the row space of the error.

We define the excess of the error weight w over the unique decoding radius as

$$\xi := w - \frac{n-k}{2}.$$

Note that 2ξ is always an integer, but ξ does not necessarily need to be one.

The error e can be further decomposed into

$$e = a_C B_C + a_R B_R + a_E B_E, \tag{1}$$

where $a_C \in \mathbb{F}_{q^m}^\gamma$, $B_C \in \mathbb{F}_q^{\gamma \times n}$, $a_R \in \mathbb{F}_{q^m}^\rho$, $B_R \in \mathbb{F}_q^{\rho \times n}$, $a_E \in \mathbb{F}_{q^m}^t$ and $B_E \in \mathbb{F}_q^{t \times n}$.

Assuming neither a_E nor B_E are known, the term $a_E B_E$ is called full rank errors. Further, if a_C is unknown but B_C is known, the product $a_C B_C$ is called column erasures and assuming a_R is known but B_R is unknown, the vector $a_R B_R$ is called row erasures, see [26,32]. There exist efficient algorithms for Gabidulin codes [11,23,25,32] that can correct $\delta := \rho + \gamma$ erasures (sum of row and column erasures) and t errors if

$$2t + \delta \le n - k. \tag{2}$$

3   Solving Problem 2 Using Known Algorithms

3.1   Generic Decoding

Problem 3 (Search-RSD)

  - *Instance: Linear code $\mathcal{C} \subset \mathbb{F}_{q^m}^n$, $r \in \mathbb{F}_{q^m}^n$ and an integer $w > 0$.*
  - *Objective: Search for a codeword $c \in \mathcal{C}$, such that $\text{rk}(r-c) \le w$.*

A generic rank syndrome decoding (RSD) algorithm is an algorithm solving Problem 3. There are potentially many solutions to Problem 3 but for our consideration it is sufficient to find only one of them.

Given a target vector r to Problem 3, the probability that $c \in \mathcal{C}$ is such that $\text{rk}(r-c) \le w$ is given by

$$\Pr_{c \in \mathcal{C}}[\text{rk}(r-c) \le w] = \frac{\sum_{i=0}^{w-1} \left[\prod_{j=0}^{i-1} (q^m - q^j) \right] \begin{bmatrix} n \\ i \end{bmatrix}_q}{q^{mk}}.$$

There are two standard approaches for solving Problem 3. The first method is *combinatorial decoding* which consists of enumerating vector spaces. If there is only one solution to the problem, the complexity of decoding an error of rank w in an $[n, k]_{q^m}$ code is equal to

$$\mathcal{W}_{Comb} = P(n, k)q^{w\lceil (k+1)m/n \rceil - m},$$

where $P(n, k)$ is a cubic polynomial [2]. In the security evaluations, this polynomial is often neglected and only the exponential term is taken into account. Note that in the case where $m > n$ there might be a better combinatorial bound [14]. Since we do not address this setting, we do not consider this case.

For the evaluation of the post-quantum security, Grover's algorithm has to be taken into account which reduces the complexity of enumeration by a factor of 0.5 in the exponent. Thus, the estimated complexity is

$$\mathcal{W}_{PQ\_Comb} = P(n, k)q^{0.5(w\lceil (k+1)m/n \rceil - m)}.$$

Since this is an enumerative approach, the work factors for solving the problem with input r have to be divided by $\mathcal{N} = \max(|\mathcal{C}| \cdot \Pr_{c \in \mathcal{C}}[\mathrm{rk}(r - c) \le w], 1)$, corresponding to the estimated number of candidates.

The second approach is *algebraic decoding*. It consists of expressing the problem in the form of a multivariate polynomial system and computing a Gröbner basis to solve it. A very recent result [4] estimates rather precisely the cost of the attack and gives generally much better estimations than the combinatorial approach. In case there is a unique solution to the system, then the work factor of the algorithm is

$$\mathcal{W}_{Alg} = \begin{cases} O\left(\left[\frac{((m+n)w)^w}{w!} \right]^{\mu} \right) & \text{if } m\binom{n-k-1}{w} \le \binom{n}{w} \\ O\left(\left[\frac{((m+n)w)^{w+1}}{(w+1)!} \right]^{\mu} \right) & \text{otherwise,} \end{cases}$$

where $\mu = 2.807$ is the linear algebra constant. For algebraic decoding, it is neither known how to improve the complexity by using the fact that there are multiple solutions, nor is it known how to speed up the algorithm in the quantum world.

Problem 2 is a special instance of Problem 3, where the linear code is a Gabidulin code. In the following, we will show how to reduce the complexity of solving Problem 2 by using that fact.

3.2 Key Equation Based Decoding

In [10], a decoding algorithm of Gabidulin codes is presented that is based on solving a linear system of $n - k - w$ equations and w unknowns (called the key equation [10, Lemma 4]). If $w > \lfloor \frac{n-k}{2} \rfloor$, there are $w - (n - k - w) = 2\xi$ solutions to this linear system of equations [30, Lemma 4], which include all $c \in Gab_k(g)$ such that $\mathrm{rk}(r - c) \le w$. Brute-force search through all solutions of the key equation solution space for a valid solution to Problem 2 has a work factor of

$$\mathcal{W}_{Key} = \frac{n^2 q^{m2\xi}}{\mathcal{N}},$$

where checking one solution of the key equation solution space is in $O(n^2)$.

4   A New Algorithm Solving Problem 2

In the considered problem, $\mathrm{rk}(\boldsymbol{e}) = w > \frac{n-k}{2}$ and we do not have any knowledge about the row space or the column space of the error, i.e., $\delta = 0$ and $t > \frac{n-k}{2}$, meaning that the known decoders are not able to decode $\boldsymbol{r}$ efficiently.

The idea of the proposed algorithm is to guess parts of the row space and/or the column space of the error and use a basis for the guessed spaces to solve the corresponding error and column/row erasures (see (1)). This approach is a generalization of the algorithm presented in [19], where only criss-cross erasures are used to decode certain error patterns beyond the unique decoding radius.

The proposed algorithm is given in Algorithm 1. The function $\mathsf{Dec}(\boldsymbol{r}, \boldsymbol{a}_R, \boldsymbol{B}_C)$ denotes a row/column error-erasure decoder for the Gabidulin code $\mathrm{Gab}_k(\boldsymbol{g})$ that returns a codeword $\hat{\boldsymbol{c}}$ (if $\mathrm{rk}(\boldsymbol{r} - \hat{\boldsymbol{c}}) \leq t + \rho + \gamma$) or $\emptyset$ (decoding failure) and δ is the total number of guessed dimensions (sum of guessed dimensions of the row space and the column space).

Algorithm 1. Column-Erasure-Aided Randomized Decoder

Input: Received word $\boldsymbol{r} \in \mathbb{F}_{q^m}^n$,
Gabidulin error/erasure decoder $\mathsf{Dec}(\cdot, \cdot, \cdot)$,
Dimension of guessed row space δ,
Error weight w,
Maximum number of iterations N_{max}
Output: $\hat{\boldsymbol{c}} \in \mathbb{F}_{q^m}^n : \mathrm{rk}(\boldsymbol{r} - \hat{\boldsymbol{c}}) \leq w$ or $\emptyset$ (failure)

1 **foreach** $i \in [1, N_{max}]$ **do**
2       $\mathcal{U} \xleftarrow{\$} \mathcal{G}(\mathbb{F}_q^n, \delta)$ // guess δ-dimensional subspace of $\mathbb{F}_q^n$
3       $\boldsymbol{B}_C \leftarrow$ full-rank matrix whose row space equals $\mathcal{U}$
4       $\hat{\boldsymbol{c}} \leftarrow \mathsf{Dec}(\boldsymbol{r}, \boldsymbol{0}, \boldsymbol{B}_C)$ // error and row erasure decoding
5   **if** $\hat{\boldsymbol{c}} \neq \emptyset$ **then**
6   **if** $\mathrm{rk}(\boldsymbol{r} - \hat{\boldsymbol{c}}) \leq w$ **then**
7   **return** $\hat{\boldsymbol{c}}$

8 **return** $\emptyset$ *(failure)*

In the following, we derive the work factor of the proposed algorithm. By ϵ, we denote the dimension of the intersection of our guess and the true error subspaces. As stated above, if

$$2(w - \epsilon) + \delta \leq n - k, \tag{3}$$

any Gabidulin error-erasure decoder is able to correct the error, e.g., [26,32].

Lemma 1. *Let $\mathcal{U}$ be a fixed u-dimensional $\mathbb{F}_q$-linear subspace of $\mathbb{F}_{q^\ell}$. Let $\mathcal{V}$ be chosen uniformly at random from $\mathcal{G}(\mathbb{F}_{q^\ell}, v)$. Then, the probability that the intersection of $\mathcal{U}$ and $\mathcal{V}$ has dimension at least ω is*

$$\Pr[\dim(\mathcal{U} \cap \mathcal{V}) \geq \omega] = \frac{\sum_{i=\omega}^{\min\{u,v\}} \begin{bmatrix} \ell - u \\ v - i \end{bmatrix}_q \begin{bmatrix} u \\ i \end{bmatrix}_q q^{(u-i)(v-i)}}{\begin{bmatrix} \ell \\ v \end{bmatrix}_q}$$

$$\leq 16(\min\{u,v\} + 1 - \omega)q^{(j^*-v)(\ell-u-j^*)},$$

where $j^* := \min\{v - \omega, \frac{1}{2}(\ell + v - u)\}$.

Proof. See Appendix A.

In the following, we analyze guessing only the row space of the error, i.e., $\delta = \gamma$ and $\rho = 0$.

Lemma 2. *Let $r' = mG_{\mathrm{Gab}} + e' \in \mathbb{F}_{q^m}^n$, where $\mathrm{rk}(e') = j$, $e' = a'B'$ with $a' \in \mathbb{F}_{q^m}^j$, $B' \in \mathbb{F}_q^{j \times n}$ and neither parts of the error row space nor column space are known, i.e., $\gamma = \rho = 0$ and $t = j$. For $\delta \in [2\xi, n - k]$, the probability that an error-erasure decoder using a random δ-dimensional guess of the error row space outputs mG_{Gab} is*

$$P_{n,k,\delta,j} := \frac{\sum_{i=\lceil j-\frac{n-k}{2}+\frac{\delta}{2}\rceil}^{\min\{\delta,j\}} \begin{bmatrix} n - j \\ \delta - i \end{bmatrix}_q \begin{bmatrix} j \\ i \end{bmatrix}_q q^{(j-i)(\delta-i)}}{\begin{bmatrix} n \\ \delta \end{bmatrix}_q}$$

$$\leq 16nq^{-(\lceil\frac{\delta}{2}\rceil+j-\frac{n-k}{2})(\frac{n+k}{2}-\lceil\frac{\delta}{2}\rceil)},$$

if $2j + \delta > n - k$ and $P_{n,k,\delta,j} := 1$ else.

Proof. First, consider the case where $2j + \delta > n - k$ and define $\xi' := j - \frac{n-k}{2}$. Let the rows of $\hat{B}_C \in \mathbb{F}_q^{\delta \times n}$ be a basis of the random guess. From (3) follows that if

$$n - k \geq 2j - 2\epsilon + \delta = n - k + 2\xi' - 2\epsilon + \delta, \tag{4}$$

where ϵ is the dimension of the intersection of the $\mathbb{F}_q$-row spaces of $\hat{B}_C$ and B', an error and erasure decoder is able to decode efficiently. Since $\epsilon \leq \delta$, equation (4) gives a lower bound on the dimension δ of the subspace that we have to estimate:

$$2\xi' \leq 2\epsilon - \delta \leq \delta \leq n - k. \tag{5}$$

From (4) follows further that the estimated space doesn't have to be a subspace of the row space of the error. In fact, it is sufficient that the dimension of the intersection of the estimated column space and the true column space has dimension $\epsilon \geq \xi' + \frac{\delta}{2}$. This condition is equivalent to the condition that the subspace distance (see [20]) between $\mathcal{U}$ and $\mathcal{V}$ satisfies $d_s(\mathcal{U}, \mathcal{V}) := \dim(\mathcal{U}) + \dim(\mathcal{V}) - 2\dim(\mathcal{U} \cap \mathcal{V}) \geq j - 2\xi'$.

From Lemma 1 follows that the probability that the randomly guessed space intersects in enough dimensions such that an error-erasure decoder can decode to one particular codeword in distance j to $\boldsymbol{r}$ is

$$
\frac{\sum_{i=\lceil \xi'+\frac{\delta}{2}\rceil}^{\min\{\delta,j\}} \begin{bmatrix} n-j \\ \delta-i \end{bmatrix}_q \begin{bmatrix} j \\ i \end{bmatrix}_q q^{(j-i)(\delta-i)}}{\begin{bmatrix} n \\ \delta \end{bmatrix}_q}
$$

$$
\leq 16\left(\min\{j,\delta\}+1-\left(\xi'+\frac{\delta}{2}\right)\right) q^{-(\lceil\frac{\delta}{2}+\xi'\rceil)(\frac{n+k}{2}-\lceil\frac{\delta}{2}\rceil)}
$$

$$
\leq 16nq^{-(\lceil\frac{\delta}{2}+\xi'\rceil)(\frac{n+k}{2}-\lceil\frac{\delta}{2}\rceil)}.
$$

For the case $2j+\delta \leq n-k$, it is well known that that an error erasure decoder always outputs $\boldsymbol{m}\boldsymbol{G}_{\mathrm{Gab}}$. $\qquad\square$

Lemma 2 gives the probability that the error-erasure decoder outputs exactly the codeword $\boldsymbol{m}\boldsymbol{G}_{\mathrm{Gab}}$. Depending on the application, it might not be necessary to find exactly $\boldsymbol{m}\boldsymbol{G}_{\mathrm{Gab}}$ but any codeword $\boldsymbol{c} \in Gab_k(\boldsymbol{g})$ such that $\mathrm{rk}(\boldsymbol{r}-\boldsymbol{c}) \leq w$, which corresponds to Problem 2. In the following lemma, we derive an upper bound on the success probability of solving Problem 2 using the proposed algorithm.

Lemma 3. *Let $\boldsymbol{r}$ be a uniformly distributed random element of $\mathbb{F}_{q^m}^n$. Then, for $\delta \in [2\xi, n-k]$ the probability that an error-erasure decoder using a random δ-dimensional guess of the error row space outputs $\boldsymbol{c} \in Gab_k(\boldsymbol{g})$ such that $\mathrm{rk}(\boldsymbol{r}-\boldsymbol{c}) \leq w$ is at most*

$$
\sum_{j=0}^{w} \bar{A}_j P_{n,k,\delta,j} \leq 64nq^{m(k-n)+w(n+m)-w^2-(\lceil\frac{\delta}{2}+w-\frac{n-k}{2}\rceil)(\frac{n+k}{2}-\lceil\frac{\delta}{2}\rceil)},
$$

where $\bar{A}_j = q^{m(k-n)} \prod_{i=0}^{j-1} \frac{(q^m-q^i)(q^n-q^i)}{q^j-q^i}$.

Proof. Let $\hat{\mathcal{C}}$ be the set of codewords that have rank distance at most w from the received word, i.e.,

$$
\hat{\mathcal{C}} := \{\boldsymbol{c} \in Gab_k(\boldsymbol{g}) : \mathrm{rk}(\boldsymbol{r}-\boldsymbol{c}) \leq w\} = \{\hat{\boldsymbol{c}}_1, \ldots, \hat{\boldsymbol{c}}_{\mathcal{N}}\}.
$$

Further, let X_i be the event that the error-erasure decoder outputs $\hat{\boldsymbol{c}}_i$ for $i = 1, \ldots, \mathcal{N}$ and $\mathcal{A}_j := \{i : \mathrm{rk}(\boldsymbol{r}-\hat{\boldsymbol{c}}_i) = j\}$. Observe that $P_{n,k,\delta,j} = \Pr[X_i]$ for $i \in \mathcal{A}_j$, where $\Pr[X_i]$ is the probability that the error-erasure decoder outputs $\hat{\boldsymbol{c}}_i$ and $P_{n,k,\delta,j}$ is defined as in Lemma 2. Then we can write

$$
\Pr[success] = \Pr\left[\bigcup_{i=1}^{\mathcal{N}} X_i\right] \leq \sum_{i=1}^{\mathcal{N}} \Pr[X_i] = \sum_{j=0}^{w} |\mathcal{A}_j| P_{n,k,\delta,j}.
$$

Let $\bar{A}_j$ be the average cardinality of the set $\mathcal{A}_j$, we have that

$$\bar{A}_j = q^{m(k-n)} \prod_{i=0}^{j-1} \frac{(q^m - q^i)(q^n - q^i)}{q^j - q^i} \leq 4q^{m(k-n)+j(n+m)-j^2}.$$

Since $\bar{A}_w$ is exponentially larger than $\bar{A}_{w-i}$ for $i > 0$, one can approximate

$$\Pr[success] = \bar{A}_w P_{n,k,\delta,w}$$

$$\leq 64nq^{m(k-n)+w(n+m)-w^2-(\lceil \frac{\delta}{2} \rceil + w - \frac{n-k}{2} \rceil)(\frac{n+k}{2} - \lceil \frac{\delta}{2} \rceil)}. \quad \Box$$

Based on Lemma 3, we can derive a lower bound on the average work factor of Algorithm 1.

Theorem 1. *Let r be a uniformly distributed random element of $\mathbb{F}_{q^m}^n$. Then, Algorithm 1 requires on average at least*

$$\mathcal{W}_{RD} = \min_{\delta \in [2\xi, n-k]} \left\{ \frac{n^2}{\sum_{j=0}^{w} \bar{A}_j P_{n,k,\delta,j}} \right\}$$

$$= \min_{\delta \in [2\xi, n-k]} \left\{ \frac{n^2 \begin{bmatrix} n \\ \delta \end{bmatrix}_q}{\sum_{j=0}^{\lfloor \frac{n-k-\delta}{2} \rfloor} q^{m(k-n)} \prod_{\ell=0}^{j-1} \frac{(q^m - q^\ell)(q^n - q^\ell)}{q^j - q^\ell} + \sum_{j=\lfloor \frac{n-k-\delta}{2} \rfloor +1}^{w} q^{m(k-n)}} \right.$$

$$\cdots \left. \left(\prod_{\ell=0}^{j-1} \frac{(q^m - q^\ell)(q^n - q^\ell)}{q^j - q^\ell} \right) \left(\sum_{i=\lceil j - \frac{n-k}{2} + \frac{\delta}{2} \rceil}^{\min\{\delta,j\}} \begin{bmatrix} n-j \\ \delta-i \end{bmatrix}_q \begin{bmatrix} j \\ i \end{bmatrix}_q q^{(j-i)(\delta-i)} \right) \right\}$$

operations over $\mathbb{F}_{q^m}$ to output $c \in Gab_k(g)$, such that $\mathrm{rk}(r - c) \leq w$, where $\bar{A}_j$ and $P_{n,k,\delta,j}$ are defined as in Lemma 3.

Proof. Lemma 3 gives the probability that an error-erasure decoder using a δ dimensional guess of the row space finds $c \in Gab_k(g)$ such that $\mathrm{rk}(r - c) \leq w$. This means that one has to estimate on average at least

$$\min_{\delta \in [2\xi, n-k]} \left\{ \frac{1}{\sum_{j=0}^{w} \bar{A}_j P_{n,k,\delta,j}} \right\}$$

row spaces in order to output $c \in Gab_k(g)$. Since the complexity of error-erasure decoding is in $O(n^2)$, we get a work factor of

$$\mathcal{W}_{RD} = \min_{\delta \in [2\xi, n-k]} \left\{ \frac{n^2}{\sum_{j=0}^{w} \bar{A}_j P_{n,k,\delta,j}} \right\}. \quad \Box$$

Notice that the upper bound on the probability given in Lemma 3 is a convex function in δ and maximized for either 2ξ or $n - k$. Thus, we get the following lower bound on the work factor.

Corollary 1. *Let r be a uniformly distributed random element of $\mathbb{F}_{q^m}^n$. Then, Algorithm 1 requires on average at least*

$$\mathcal{W}_{RD} \geq \frac{n}{64} \cdot q^{m(n-k)-w(n+m)+w^2+\min\{2\xi(\frac{n+k}{2}-\xi),wk\}}$$

operations over $\mathbb{F}_{q^m}$.

Remark 1. We obtain a rough upper bound of on the expected work factor,

$$\mathcal{W}_{RD} \leq n^2 q^{m(n-k)-w(n+m)+w^2+\min\{2\xi(\frac{n+k}{2}-\xi),wk\}},$$

by the same arguments as in Lemmas 2, 3, and Theorem 1, using

- lower bounds on the Gaussian binomial coefficient in [20, Lemma 4],
- taking the maximal terms in the sums and
- taking the maximal probability of events instead of union-bound arguments.

If $r \in \mathbb{F}_{q^m}^n$ is defined as in Sect. 2.2, where neither parts of the error row space nor column space are known, i.e., $\gamma = \rho = 0$ and $t = w$, the vector r can be seen as a uniformly distributed random element of $\mathbb{F}_{q^m}^n$. Thus, Theorem 1 gives an estimation of the work factor of the proposed algorithm to solve Problem 2. To verify this assumption, we conducted simulations which show that the estimation is very accurate, see Sect. 5.

Remark 2. In Theorem 1, we give a lower bound on the work factor of the proposed algorithm. One observes that especially for small parameters, this bound is not tight which is mainly caused by the approximations of the Gaussian binomials. For larger values, the relative difference to the true work factor becomes smaller.

Another idea is to guess only the column space or the row and column space jointly. Guessing the column space is never advantageous over guessing the row space for Gabidulin codes since we always have $n \leq m$. Hence, replacing n by m in the formulas of Lemma 2 and in the expression of the probability P_j inside the proof of Theorem 1 will only increase the resulting work factor. For joint guessing, some examples indicate that it is not advantageous, either. See Appendix B for more details.

5   Examples and Simulation Results

We validated the bounds on the work factor of the proposed algorithm in Sect. 4 by simulations. The simulations were performed with the row/column error-erasure decoder from [32] that can correct t rank errors, ρ row erasures and γ column erasures up to $2t+\rho+\gamma \leq d-1$. Alternatively, the decoders in [12, 26] may be considered. One can also observe that the derived lower bounds on the work factor give a good estimate of the actual runtime of the algorithm denoted by $\mathcal{W}_{Sim}$. The results in Table 1 show further, that for parameters proposed in [21, 33], the new algorithm solves Problem 2 (Search-Gab) with a significantly lower computational complexity than the approaches based on the known algorithms.

Therefore, for the RAMESSES system, our algorithm determines the work factor of recovering the private key for all sets of parameters given in [21]. For the modified Faure–Loidreau system, our algorithm provides the most efficient key recovery attack for one set of parameters, shown in Line 5 of Table 1. Notice however that there is a message attack (called *Algebraic Attack* in [33]) which has smaller complexity.

Table 1. Comparison of different work factors for several parameter sets including simulation results for one specific parameter set.
$\mathcal{W}_{Sim}$: work factor of the new randomized decoder (simulations).
$\mathcal{W}_{RD}$: work factor of the new randomized decoder (theoretical lower bound).
$\mathcal{W}_{Comb}/\mathcal{N}$: work factor of the combinatorial RSD algorithm.
$\mathcal{W}_{Alg}$: work factor of the algebraic RSD algorithm.
$\mathcal{W}_{Key}$: work factor of the naïve key equation based decoding.

q	m	n	k	w	ξ	δ	Iterations	Success	$\mathcal{W}_{Sim}$	$\mathcal{W}_{RD}$	$\frac{\mathcal{W}_{Comb}}{\mathcal{N}}$	$\mathcal{W}_{Alg}$	$\mathcal{W}_{Key}$
2	24	24	16	6	2	4	6844700	4488	$2^{19.74}$	$2^{19.65}$	$2^{38.99}$	$2^{126.01}$	$2^{43.40}$
2	64	64	32	19	3	6	–	–	–	$2^{257.20}$	$2^{571.21}$	$2^{460.01}$	$2^{371.21}$
2	80	80	40	23	3	6	–	–	–	$2^{401.85}$	$2^{897.93}$	$2^{576.15}$	$2^{492.64}$
2	96	96	48	27	3	6	–	–	–	$2^{578.38}$	$2^{1263.51}$	$2^{694.93}$	$2^{589.17}$
2	82	82	48	20	3	6	–	–	–	$2^{290.92}$	$2^{838.54}$	$2^{504.70}$	$2^{410.92}$

6   Open Problems

There is a list decoding algorithm for Gabidulin codes based on Gröbner bases that allows to correct errors beyond the unique decoding radius [18]. However, there is no upper bound on the list size and the complexity of the decoding algorithm. In future work, the algorithm from [18] should be adapted to solve Problem 2 which could allow for estimating the complexity of the resulting algorithm.

A   Proof of Lemma 1

The number of q-vector spaces of dimension v, which intersections with $\mathcal{U}$ have dimension at least ω, is equal to

$$\sum_{i=\omega}^{\min\{u,v\}} \begin{bmatrix} \ell - u \\ v - i \end{bmatrix}_q \begin{bmatrix} u \\ i \end{bmatrix}_q q^{(u-i)(v-i)} = \sum_{j=\max\{0,v-u\}}^{v-\omega} \begin{bmatrix} \ell - u \\ j \end{bmatrix}_q \begin{bmatrix} u \\ v-j \end{bmatrix}_q q^{j(u-v+j)},$$

see [8]. Since the total number of v-dimensional subspaces of a ℓ-dimensional space is equal to $\begin{bmatrix} \ell \\ v \end{bmatrix}_q$, the probability

$$\Pr[\dim(\mathcal{U} \cap \mathcal{V}) \geq \omega] = \frac{\sum_{i=\omega}^{\min\{u,v\}} \begin{bmatrix} \ell - u \\ v - i \end{bmatrix}_q \begin{bmatrix} u \\ i \end{bmatrix}_q q^{(u-i)(v-i)}}{\begin{bmatrix} \ell \\ v \end{bmatrix}_q}$$

$$= \frac{\sum_{j=\max\{0,v-u\}}^{v-\omega} \begin{bmatrix} \ell - u \\ j \end{bmatrix}_q \begin{bmatrix} u \\ v - j \end{bmatrix}_q q^{j(u-v+j)}}{\begin{bmatrix} \ell \\ v \end{bmatrix}_q}.$$

Using the upper bound on the Gaussian coefficient derived in [20, Lemma 4], it follows that

$$\Pr[\dim(\mathcal{U} \cap \mathcal{V}) \geq \omega] \leq 16 \sum_{j=\max\{0,v-u\}}^{v-\omega} q^{j(\ell-u-j)+v(u-v+j)-v(\ell-v)}$$

$$= 16 \sum_{j=\max\{0,v-u\}}^{v-\omega} q^{(j-v)(\ell-u-j)}$$

$$\leq 16 \, (\min\{u,v\} + 1 - \omega) q^{(j^*-v)(\ell-u-j^*)},$$

where $j^* := \min\{v - \omega, \frac{1}{2}(\ell + v - u)\}$. The latter inequality follows from the fact that the term $(j - v)(\ell - u - j)$ is a concave function in j and is maximum for $j = \frac{1}{2}(\ell + v - u)$. $\square$

B Guessing Jointly the Column and Row Space of the Error

We analyze the success probability of decoding to a specific codeword (i.e., the analog of Lemma 2) for guessing jointly the row and the column space of the error.

Lemma 4. *Let $r \in \mathbb{F}_{q^m}^n$ be defined as in Sect. 2.2, where neither parts of the error row space nor column space are known, i.e., $\gamma = \rho = 0$ and $t = w$. The probability that an error-erasure decoder using a random*

- *δ_r-dimensional guess of the error row space and a*
- *δ_c-dimensional guess of the error column space,*

where $\delta_r + \delta_c =: \delta \in [2\xi, n - k]$, outputs mG_{Gab} is upper-bounded by

$$\frac{\displaystyle\sum_{i=\lceil\xi+\frac{\delta}{2}\rceil}^{\min\{\delta,w\}} \sum_{\substack{0\le w_r,w_c\le i\\ w_r+w_c=i}} \begin{bmatrix} n-w\\ \delta_r-w_r\end{bmatrix}_q \begin{bmatrix} w\\ w_r\end{bmatrix}_q q^{(w-w_r)(\delta_r-w_r)} \begin{bmatrix} m-w\\ \delta_c-w_c\end{bmatrix}_q \begin{bmatrix} w\\ w_c\end{bmatrix}_q q^{(w-w_c)(\delta_c-w_c)}}{\begin{bmatrix} n\\ \delta_r\end{bmatrix}_q \begin{bmatrix} m\\ \delta_c\end{bmatrix}_q}.$$

Proof. The statement follows by the same arguments as Lemma 2, where we computed the probability that the row space of a random vector space of dimension δ intersects with the w-dimensional row space of the error in i dimensions (where i must be sufficiently large to apply the error erasure decoder successfully). Here, we want that a random guess of δ_r- and δ_c-dimensional vector spaces intersect with the row and column space of the error in exactly w_r and w_c dimensions, respectively. We sum up over all choices of w_r and w_c that sum up to an i that is sufficiently large to successfully apply the error erasure decoder. This is an optimistic argument since guessing correctly w_r dimensions of the row and w_c dimensions of the column space of the error might not reduce the rank of the error by $w_r + w_c$. However, this gives an upper bound on the success probability.   □

Example 1 shows that guessing row and column space jointly is not advantageous for some specific parameters.

Example 1. Consider the example $q = 2$, $m = n = 24$, $k = 16$, $w = 6$. Guessing only the row space of the error with $\delta = 4$ succeeds with probability $1.66 \cdot 10^{-22}$ and joint guessing with $\delta_r = \delta_c = 2$ succeeds with probability $1.93 \cdot 10^{-22}$. Hence, it is advantageous to guess only the row space (or due to $m = n$ only the column space). For a larger example with $m = n = 64$, $k = 16$, and $w = 19$, the two probabilities are almost the same, $\approx 5.27 \cdot 10^{-82}$ (for $\delta = 32$ and $\delta_r = \delta_c = 16$).

References

1. Aguilar Melchor, C., et al.: Rank quasi cyclic (RQC). Second round submission to the NIST post-quantum cryptography call (2019). https://pqc-rqc.org
2. Aragon, N., Gaborit, P., Hauteville, A., Tillich, J.: A new algorithm for solving the rank syndrome decoding problem. In: IEEE International Symposium on Information Theory (ISIT), pp. 2421–2425, June 2018. https://doi.org/10.1109/ISIT.2018.8437464
3. Augot, D., Finiasz, M.: A public key encryption scheme based on the polynomial reconstruction problem. In: Biham, E. (ed.) EUROCRYPT 2003. LNCS, vol. 2656, pp. 229–240. Springer, Heidelberg (2003). https://doi.org/10.1007/3-540-39200-9_14
4. Bardet, M., et al.: An algebraic attack on rank metric code-based cryptosystems. Technical report (2019). arXiv:1910.00810v1
5. Ben-Sasson, E., Kopparty, S., Radhakrishnan, J.: Subspace polynomials and limits to list decoding of Reed-Solomon codes. IEEE Trans. Inf. Theory **56**(1), 113–120 (2010). https://doi.org/10.1109/TIT.2009.2034780
6. Berlekamp, E., McEliece, R.J., van Tilborg, H.: On the inherent intractability of certain coding problems. IEEE Trans. Inf. Theory **24**(3), 384–386 (1978)

7. Delsarte, P.: Bilinear forms over a finite field with applications to coding theory. J. Comb. Theory Ser. A **25**(3), 226–241 (1978)
8. Etzion, T., Vardy, A.: Error-correcting codes in projective space. IEEE Trans. Inf. Theory **57**(2), 1165–1173 (2011)
9. Faure, C., Loidreau, P.: A new public-key cryptosystem based on the problem of reconstructing p–polynomials. In: Ytrehus, Ø. (ed.) WCC 2005. LNCS, vol. 3969, pp. 304–315. Springer, Heidelberg (2006). https://doi.org/10.1007/11779360_24
10. Gabidulin, E.M.: Theory of codes with maximum rank distance. Probl. Inf. Transm. **21**(1), 3–16 (1985)
11. Gabidulin, E.M., Paramonov, A.V., Tretjakov, O.V.: Rank errors and rank erasures correction. In: 4th International Colloquium on Coding Theory (1991)
12. Gabidulin, E.M., Pilipchuk, N.I.: Error and erasure correcting algorithms for rank codes. Des. Codes Cryptogr. **49**(1–3), 105–122 (2008)
13. Gaborit, P., Otmani, A., Talé Kalachi, H.: Polynomial-time key recovery attack on the Faure-Loidreau scheme based on Gabidulin codes. Des. Codes Cryptogr. **86**, 1391–1403 (2018)
14. Gaborit, P., Ruatta, O., Schrek, J.: On the complexity of the rank syndrome decoding problem. IEEE Trans. Inf. Theory **62**(2), 1006–1019 (2016). https://doi.org/10.1109/TIT.2015.2511786
15. Gaborit, P., Zémor, G.: On the hardness of the decoding and the minimum distance problems for rank codes. IEEE Trans. Inf. Theory **62**(12), 7245–7252 (2015)
16. Guruswami, V., Sudan, M.: Improved decoding of Reed-Solomon and algebraic-geometry codes. IEEE Trans. Inf. Theory **45**(6), 1757–1767 (1999)
17. Guruswami, V., Vardy, A.: Maximum-likelihood decoding of Reed-Solomon codes is NP-hard. IEEE Trans. Inf. Theory **51**, 2249–2256 (2005)
18. Horlemann-Trautmann, A.L., Kuijper, M.: A module minimization approach to Gabidulin decoding via interpolation. J. Algebra Comb. Discrete Struct. Appl. **5**(1), 29–43 (2017)
19. Jerkovits, T., Bartz, H.: Weak keys in the Faure-Loidreau cryptosystem. In: Baldi, M., Persichetti, E., Santini, P. (eds.) CBC 2019. LNCS, vol. 11666, pp. 102–114. Springer, Cham (2019). https://doi.org/10.1007/978-3-030-25922-8_6
20. Koetter, R., Kschischang, F.R.: Coding for errors and erasures in random network coding. IEEE Trans. Inf. Theory **54**(8), 3579–3591 (2008)
21. Lavauzelle, J., Loidreau, P., Pham, B.D.: Ramesses, a rank metric encryption scheme with short keys. preprint (2019). https://arxiv.org/abs/1911.13119
22. Raviv, N., Wachter-Zeh, A.: Some Gabidulin codes cannot be list decoded efficiently at any radius. IEEE Trans. Inf. Theory **62**(4), 1605–1615 (2016)
23. Richter, G., Plass, S.: Error and erasure decoding of rank-codes with a modified Berlekamp-Massey algorithm. In: International ITG Conference on Systems, Communications and Coding 2004 (SCC) (2004)
24. Roth, R.M.: Maximum-rank array codes and their application to crisscross error correction. IEEE Trans. Inf. Theory **37**(2), 328–336 (1991)
25. Silva, D.: Error control for network coding. Ph.D. thesis (2009)
26. Silva, D., Kschischang, F.R., Koetter, R.: A rank-metric approach to error control in random network coding. IEEE Trans. Inf. Theory **54**(9), 3951–3967 (2008)
27. Stern, J.: Approximating the number of error locations within a constant ratio is NP-complete. In: Cohen, G., Mora, T., Moreno, O. (eds.) AAECC 1993. LNCS, vol. 673, pp. 325–331. Springer, Heidelberg (1993). https://doi.org/10.1007/3-540-56686-4_54
28. Trombetti, R., Zullo, F.: On the list decodability of Rank Metric codes. preprint (2019). https://arxiv.org/abs/1907.01289

29. Vardy, A.: The intractability of computing the minimum distance of a code. IEEE Trans. Inf. Theory **43**(6), 1757–1766 (1997)
30. Wachter, A., Sidorenko, V., Bossert, M.: A basis for all solutions of the key equation for Gabidulin codes. In: IEEE International Symposium on Information Theory (ISIT), pp. 1143–1147, June 2010. https://doi.org/10.1109/ISIT.2010.5513681
31. Wachter-Zeh, A.: Bounds on list decoding of rank-metric codes. IEEE Trans. Inf. Theory **59**(11), 7268–7277 (2013)
32. Wachter-Zeh, A.: Decoding of block and convolutional codes in rank metric. Ph.D. thesis, Ulm University and Université Rennes 1 (2013)
33. Wachter-Zeh, A., Puchinger, S., Renner, J.: Repairing the Faure-Loidreau public-key cryptosystem. In: IEEE International Symposium on Information Theory (ISIT) (2018)

About Low DFR for QC-MDPC Decoding

Nicolas Sendrier[1(✉)] and Valentin Vasseur[1,2]

[1] Inria, Paris, France
{Nicolas.Sendrier,Valentin.Vasseur}@inria.fr
[2] Université de Paris, Paris, France

Abstract. McEliece-like code-based key exchange mechanisms using QC-MDPC codes can reach IND-CPA security under hardness assumptions from coding theory, namely quasi-cyclic syndrome decoding and quasi-cyclic codeword finding. To reach higher security requirements, like IND-CCA security, it is necessary in addition to prove that the decoding failure rate (DFR) is negligible, for some decoding algorithm and a proper choice of parameters. Getting a formal proof of a low DFR is a difficult task. Instead, we propose to ensure this low DFR under some additional security assumption on the decoder. This assumption relates to the asymptotic behavior of the decoder and is supported by several other works. We define a new decoder, Backflip, which features a low DFR. We evaluate the Backflip decoder by simulation and extrapolate its DFR under the decoder security assumption. We also measure the accuracy of our simulation data, in the form of confidence intervals, using standard techniques from communication systems.

1 Introduction

Moderate Density Parity Check (MDPC) codes were introduced for cryptography[1] in [17]. They are related to Low Density Parity Check (LDPC) codes, but instead of admitting a sparse parity check matrix (with rows of small constant weight) they admit a somewhat sparse parity check matrix, typically with rows of Hamming weight $O(\sqrt{n})$ and length n. Together with a quasi-cyclic structure they allow the design of a McEliece-like public-key encryption scheme [16] with reasonable key size and a security that provably reduces to generic hard problems over quasi-cyclic codes, namely the hardness of decoding and the hardness of finding low weight codewords.

Because of these features, QC-MDPC have attracted a lot of interest from the cryptographic community. In particular, the BIKE suite of key exchange mechanisms has been selected to the second round of the NIST call for standardization of quantum safe cryptographic primitives[2]. The second round BIKE

---

[1] MDPC were previously defined, in a different context, by Ouzan and Be'ery in 2009, http://arxiv.org/abs/0911.3262.

[2] https://csrc.nist.gov/Projects/Post-Quantum-Cryptography.

This work was supported by the ANR CBCRYPT project, grant ANR-17-CE39-0007 of the French Agence Nationale de la Recherche.

© Springer Nature Switzerland AG 2020
J. Ding and J.-P. Tillich (Eds.): PQCrypto 2020, LNCS 12100, pp. 20–34, 2020.
https://doi.org/10.1007/978-3-030-44223-1_2

document [1] mentions the Backflip decoder, a new variant of bit flipping decoding, as well as claims about its DFR. The low DFR is an essential feature to achieve IND-CCA security, and incidentally to resist to the GJS key recovery attack [11] which exploits decoding failures.

The Backflip algorithm and its DFR claims were never fully described in an academic work. We provide here the rationale and a precise description of Backflip as well as a justification and a description of the simulation methodology and assumptions that were used for estimating the DFR.

The decoding of MDPC codes can be achieved, as for LDPC codes, with iterative decoders [10] and in particular with the (hard decision) bit flipping algorithm. The Backflip algorithm will introduce soft information (*i.e.* reliability information) by flipping coordinates for a limited time which depends on the confidence we have in each flipping decision. This confidence is measured from quantities that were already computed in bit flipping decoders and are thus available at no extra cost. This way, the new decoder will use soft decision decoding, as in [2, 14] for instance, while keeping the very simple logic and arithmetic which makes it suited to hardware and embedded device implementations [13].

No theoretical argument is known to guaranty a low DFR for the Backflip decoder. We will resort to simulation. However proving a very low DFR (*e.g.* 2^{-128}) cannot be achieved by simulation alone. Instead, we will use simulation data to extrapolate the DFR in a region of parameters where it is too small to be estimated by simulation. This extrapolation technique for the DFR is valid under an additional assumption on the asymptotic behavior of the decoder.

The paper is organized as follows. The Sect. 2 will state and comment the security assumption related to decoding. The Sect. 3 will describe the Backflip algorithm and explain its rationale. The Sect. 4 will explain, under the decoder security assumption, how to obtain DFR estimates with accurate simulation data.

Notation. For any binary vector v, we denote v_i its i-th coordinate and $|v|$ its Hamming weight. Moreover, we will identify v with its support, that is $i \in v$ if and only if $v_i = 1$. Given two binary vectors u and v of same length, we will denote $u \cap v$ the set of all indices that belong to both u and v, or equivalently their component-wise product as vectors.

1.1 Previous Works

A binary Quasi-Cyclic Moderate Density Parity Check (QC-MDPC) code, is a quasi-cyclic code which admits a parity check matrix of density proportional to $1/\sqrt{n}$ where n is the code length. A QC-MDPC code can efficiently correct an error of Hamming weight t proportional to $\sqrt{n}$ thanks to bit flipping decoding (Algorithm 1). A $(2r, r, w, t)$-QC-MDPC-McEliece is an instance of the McEliece scheme [16] using an QC-MDPC code of index 2 correcting t errors. Such a code admits a parity check matrix consisting of two sparse circulant blocks of size $r \times r$ and row weight $w/2$ proportional to $\sqrt{n}$.

We denote $\mathcal{R} = \mathbb{F}_2[x]/(x^r - 1)$. The ring $\mathcal{R}$ is isomorphic to $r \times r$ circulant matrices. The scheme is fully described by the knowledge of the error weight t and of two polynomials h_0, h_1 of $\mathcal{R}$ of Hamming weight $w/2$. Its security relates to the following hard problems.

Problem 1. $(2,1)$-QC Syndrome Decoding
Instance: s, h in $\mathcal{R}$, an integer $t > 0$.
Property: There exists e_0, e_1 in $\mathcal{R}$ such that $|e_0| + |e_1| \leq t$ and $e_0 + e_1 h = s$.

Problem 2. $(2,1)$-QC Codeword Finding
Instance: h in $\mathcal{R}$, an integer $w > 0$.
Property: There exists h_0, h_1 in $\mathcal{R}$ such that $|h_0| + |h_1| = w$ and $h_1 + h_0 h = 0$.

In the rest of Sect. 1.1 we will consider an instance of a $(2r, r, w, t)$-QC-MDPC-McEliece scheme. The code length is $n = 2r$, its dimension is $k = r$, and we will denote $d = w/2$.

Security Assumptions. The security of QC-MDPC-McEliece for QC codes of index 2 (and rate 1/2) relies on two assumptions.

Assumption 1. *Problem 1 is hard on average over s, h in $\mathcal{R}$.*

Assumption 2. *Problem 2 is hard on average over h in $\mathcal{R}$.*

The above assumptions are enough to guaranty the one-wayness of the underlying encryption primitive. With the ad-hoc conversion they will also be enough to prove that the related Key Encapsulation Mechanism (KEM) is IND-CPA (see [1]). To go further and design and prove an IND-CCA KEM, a further assumption on the decoding failure rate (DFR) is required. This will be examined later in the paper.

Tightness and Best Known Attacks. The security proofs for QC-MDPC code-based schemes are tight in the following sense: the proofs require the decisional versions of Problem 1 and 2 to be hard on average for the size (r, t) and (r, w) while the best known attacks only require to solve the search version of either Problem 1 or 2 for the same size (r, t) or (r, w). Note that there is a search to decision reduction for Syndrome Decoding [9] but it has not been transferred so far to the quasi-cyclic case. The best solvers for Problem 1 and 2 use Information Set Decoding (ISD). As explained in [17], it is possible to make use of the quasi-cyclicity together with the multitarget variant of ISD [20] to slightly improve the decoding. If $\mathrm{WF}(n, k, t)$ is the expected cost of the best ISD solver for the decoding t errors in a binary linear $[n, k]$ code, the cost of the best solver for Problem 1 and Problem 2 is upper bounded respectively by $\frac{\mathrm{WF}(2r,r,t)}{\sqrt{r}}$ and $\frac{\mathrm{WF}(2r,r,w)}{r}$. When $t \ll r$, which is the case here, it was shown in [4] that asymptotically the complexity exponent of all variants of ISD was equivalent to the complexity exponent of Prange algorithm [18], that is $\mathrm{WF}(n, k, t) = 2^{t \log_2 \frac{n}{n-k}(1+o(1))}$.

In particular, the value $\mathrm{WF}(2r, r, t) = 2^{t(1+o(1))}$ does not depend, for its first order term, on the block size r.

QC-MDPC-McEliece Practical Security. The security of an instance of the $(2r, r, w, t)$-QC-MDPC-McEliece scheme reduces to Problem 1 with parameters (r, t) and Problem 2 with parameters (r, w). We give in Table 1 the security exponents for the message and key securities, respectively $\frac{\mathrm{WF}(2r,r,t)}{\sqrt{r}}$ and $\frac{\mathrm{WF}(2r,r,w)}{r}$ when the workfactor is computed for the BJMM variant of ISD [3] using the methodology described in [12]. We remark that, as expected, the security exponent grows very slowly with the block size r. The parameters of Table 1 are those of the NIST proposal BIKE [1]. For each security level, the first and second rows correspond respectively to the IND-CPA and IND-CCA variants.

Table 1. Security exponent of $(2r, r, w, t)$-QC-MDPC-McEliece (BIKE parameters)

	(r, w, t)	Problem 2	Problem 1
		Key security	Message security
BIKE level 1	$(10163, 142, 134)$	129.5	128.6
	$(11779, 142, 134)$	129.8	128.9
BIKE level 3	$(19853, 206, 199)$	191.6	192.1
	$(24821, 206, 199)$	192.4	193.0
BIKE level 5	$(32749, 274, 264)$	258.0	255.9
	$(40597, 274, 264)$	258.8	256.9

Bit Flipping Decoding. All decoders for QC-MDPC codes derive from the bit flipping decoder given in Algorithm 1 in its syndrome decoding variant. In Algorithm 1, the counter $|s' \cap h_j|$ is the number of unsatisfied equations involving j. Positions with high counter values are flipped. If $s' = s - eH^\mathsf{T}$ for some (e, s'), with H, s' and e sparse enough, then the algorithm return e with high probability.

Algorithm 1. Bit Flipping Algorithm, (Noisy-)Syndrome Decoding Variant

---

Require: $H \in \mathbb{F}_2^{(n-k) \times n}$, $s \in \mathbb{F}_2^{n-k}$, integer $u \geq 0$ //$u > 0$ *for noisy syndrome*
Ensure: $|s - e'H^\mathsf{T}| \leq u$ or time $>$ max_time
  $e' \leftarrow 0$; time $\leftarrow 1$
  while $|s - e'H^\mathsf{T}| > u$ **and** time $\leq$ max_time **do**
    time $\leftarrow$ time $+ 1$
    $s' \leftarrow s - e'H^\mathsf{T}$
    $T \leftarrow \mathtt{threshold}(context)$
    for $j \in \{0, \dots, n-1\}$ **do**
      if $|s' \cap h_j| \geq T$ **then**   //h_j *the j-th column of* H
        $e'_j \leftarrow 1 - e'_j$
  return e'

The variant presented allows noisy syndrome with $u > 0$ (as needed for BIKE-3), else if $u = 0$, it defines the usual QC-MDPC decoding (used by BIKE-1/2).

Threshold Selection. Selecting the proper threshold is an essential step of the bit flipping algorithm. In the current state of the art [5,21] the optimal threshold is given as a function of the syndrome weight and of the error weight. We consider an execution of Algorithm 1. At any time, let e denote the (remaining) error vector, the syndrome is $s' = eH^T = s - e'H^T$. The optimal threshold is defined as in Fig. 1 with the call `threshold(|eH^T|, |e|)`. Note that the syndrome weight $S = |eH^T| = |s - e'H^T|$ is always known by the the decoder while the error weight $t' = |e|$ is only known at the first iteration, since $|e| = t$ by design. Later on the exact error weight is unknown and a value for t' has to be chosen somehow. One possibility is to guess it by using the fact that the expected value of S is a function of t', $\mathbb{E}(S) = r \sum \rho_{2\ell+1}(t')$. Though this identity is only exact at the first iteration, it provides a good enough estimate of t' as a function of S. Finally, even though the procedure for computing the threshold seems involved, it is not the case in practice. For a given set of parameters, the threshold is a function of S which can be precomputed and is usually well approximated by an affine function.

$T = \mathtt{threshold}(S, t')$ is the smallest integer T such that

$$(n - t')\binom{d}{T}\pi_0^T(1 - \pi_0)^{d-T} \leq \begin{cases} t'\binom{d}{T}\pi_1^T(1 - \pi_1)^{d-T} & \text{if } \pi_1 < 1 \\ 1 & \text{else} \end{cases}$$

where

$$\pi_1 = \frac{S + X(S, t')}{t'd}, \pi_0 = \frac{(w - 1)S - X(S, t')}{(n - t')d}$$

and

$$X(S, t') = \frac{S \sum_{\ell \text{ odd}} (\ell - 1)\rho_\ell(t')}{\sum_{\ell \text{ odd}} \rho_\ell(t')} \text{ with } \rho_\ell(t') = \frac{\binom{w}{\ell}\binom{n-w}{t'-\ell}}{\binom{n}{t'}}.$$

Fig. 1. Threshold function

Attacks on the Decoder. The bit flipping algorithm is iterative and probabilistic. In particular, it has a small but positive Decoding Failure Rate (DFR). This is not an issue if the scheme uses ephemeral keys (*e.g.* TLS using BIKE specification) but creates a threat when static keys are used. It was shown in [11] how to exploit the decoding failures to recover the secret key. This stresses the importance of reducing the DFR to a negligible value. This is mandatory to reach CCA security and requires an evolution of the decoder, an increase of the parameters, an accurate estimate of the DFR, and arguments to support the accuracy of this estimate.

The GJS technique was later extended [8] to efficiently recover the secret key if the adversary has access to the number of effective decoding iterations. The latter attack stresses the need of a constant-time implementation when static keys are used. Allowing constant-time implementation may in turn require an evolution of the decoder and of the system parameters.

1.2 Related Works

The Backflip decoding algorithm and claims about its DFR were given in [1]. The purpose of this work is to detail and support those claims. A simplified bit flipping variant, the step-by-step decoder, is modelled with a Markov chain in [21], the model has a DFR which decreases provably exponentially with the block size. The asymptotic analysis of [22] of QC-MPDC also predicts an exponential decrease in the range of interest for cryptography, but the analysis is made in a specific setting and cannot be directly applied to practical BIKE decoder and parameters. Another recent work [7] explores another decoder variant for BIKE to reach simultaneously a low DFR and a constant-time implementation.

2 An Additional Security Assumption

Preliminary: Tangent Extrapolation. When observing the plot of the logarithm of the simulated DFR versus the block size r (the other parameters w and t are fixed), one observes that it is always concave. It seems rather natural to assume that it will remain so and to extrapolate the DFR accordingly. The strategy will then consist in making a simulation for the largest possible r to accurately measure the tangent of the lowest possible point of the curve. For instance in Fig. 2, suppose the low curve (blue) is giving the $\log_2(\text{DFR})$ and we are able to make accurate simulation as long as the DFR is above 2^{-25} (black dots). Taking the tangent at the last point gives us the red line from which we derive an upper bound r' for a block size with a DFR below 2^{-128} as well as an upper bound 2^{-s} for the DFR for a given block size r.

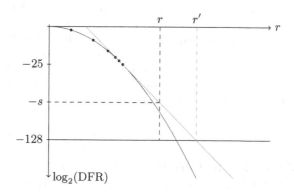

Fig. 2. DFR tangent extrapolation (Color figure online)

2.1 Target Parameters

We will consider here three levels of security named according to the NIST postquantum security nomenclature. For each security level λ below, we denote r_λ^{CPA} the block size of the IND-CPA variants of BIKE (1 and 2).

Level 1: $(w,t) = (142,134)$ for $\lambda = 128$ bits of classical security, $r_\lambda^{\mathrm{CPA}} = 10\,163$
Level 3: $(w,t) = (206,199)$ for $\lambda = 192$ bits of classical security, $r_\lambda^{\mathrm{CPA}} = 19\,853$
Level 5: $(w,t) = (274,264)$ for $\lambda = 256$ bits of classical security, $r_\lambda^{\mathrm{CPA}} = 32\,749$

As mentioned previously, the security of the $(2r,r,w,t)$-QC-MDPC-McEliece scheme only marginally depends of the block size r. To reach IND-CCA security the block size must be increased slightly, at most 25% [1]. To allow constant-time implementation, the current state-of-art [7] suggests an extra 10%. We thus expect that for any security level λ the values of interest for the block size r lie in the interval $[r_\lambda^{\mathrm{CPA}}, 2r_\lambda^{\mathrm{CPA}}]$.

2.2 The Decoder Security Assumption

By decoder, say we denote it $\mathcal{D}$, we mean a family of decoding algorithms which can be applied to QC-MDPC codes corresponding to various security levels λ, including the three levels above, and to any block size $r_\lambda^{\mathrm{CPA}}/2 \leq r \leq 2r_\lambda^{\mathrm{CPA}}$. For a given security level λ, corresponding to a value of (w,t), we will denote $\mathrm{DFR}_{\mathcal{D},\lambda}(r)$ the decoding failure rate when the decoder $\mathcal{D}$ is applied to an instance of $(2r,r,w,t)$-QC-MDPC-McEliece.

Assumption 3. *For a given decoder $\mathcal{D}$, and a given security level λ, the function $r \mapsto \log(\mathrm{DFR}_{\mathcal{D},\lambda}(r))$ is decreasing and is concave if $\mathrm{DFR}_{\mathcal{D},\lambda}(r) \geq 2^{-\lambda}$.*

2.3 Validity of the Concavity Assumption

Error Floors for QC-MDPC. The mapping $r \mapsto \log(\mathrm{DFR}_{\mathcal{D},\lambda}(r))$ cannot be concave in the whole range $r \in [0,\infty)$. As explained in appendix, there is an additive term $P_\lambda(r)$ in $\mathrm{DFR}_{\mathcal{D},\lambda}(r)$, coming from the code weight distribution, whose logarithm is asymptotically equivalent to $C_\lambda - (w/2-1)\log_2 r$. This term will dominate when r grows but only for very large values of r. We have

$$\lambda = 128, \log_2 P_\lambda(r_\lambda^{\mathrm{CPA}}) = -396.8, \text{ and } \log_2 P_\lambda(r) \approx 535.0 - 70\log_2 r$$
$$\lambda = 192, \log_2 P_\lambda(r_\lambda^{\mathrm{CPA}}) = -618.5, \text{ and } \log_2 P_\lambda(r) \approx 837.8 - 102\log_2 r$$
$$\lambda = 256, \log_2 P_\lambda(r_\lambda^{\mathrm{CPA}}) = -868.7, \text{ and } \log_2 P_\lambda(r) \approx 1171.2 - 136\log_2 r$$

and this will not affect the DFR for values of r relevant for Assumption 3.

Theoretical Models for the Decoder. In [21] A Markovian model is given for a simple variant of bit flipping, the step-by-step decoder. This decoder corrects less errors than other bit flipping variants, however it uses the same ingredients: computing counters and flipping the corresponding positions if they are above some threshold. The model can be computed for arbitrary large values of r and we observe that in the range of interest for r the log(DFR) is first strictly concave and eventually decreases linearly with r. This observation is consistent with Assumption 3. Note that the model does not capture the contribution of the weight distribution to the DFR.

Another work explores the asymptotic behavior of QC-MDPC decoding [22]. The asymptotic formula it provides for the DFR cannot be used directly because the setting is different (w and t vary with r), and also the conditions under which it can be proven are not relevant for decoders and parameters of practical interest. However the indication provided by the formula is consistent, the dominant term in the exponent decreases linearly with r.

To conclude this section, the Assumption 3 is and remains an assumption in the current state-of-the-art. We point out though that, for all variants of bit flipping decoding, every related theoretical and simulation results are consistent with it.

3   Backflip: A New Decoder for QC-MDPC Codes Using Reliability

Design Rationale: Positions with higher counters in Algorithm 1 have higher probabilities to be erroneous. Positions are flipped when the counter is above a threshold, how much above doesn't matter and a part of the reliability information is lost. Better performance are achieved with soft-decision decoders such as the belief propagation algorithm for LDPC codes. These decoders work by propagating probabilities back and forth between variable nodes and check nodes in the Tanner graph until the confidence on all values is high enough. Their logic and arithmetic are more complex though. See [2, 14] for examples of soft-decision MDPC decoding. The idea of Backflip is to use the reliability information while keeping the simplicity of the bit flipping decoder.

Among the flip decisions, most are good (an error is removed) and some are bad (an error is added). Bad decisions tend to induce more bad decisions and may lead to a failure. To exploit the reliability information a decoder could lessen the impact of the least reliable decisions and strengthen the impact of the most reliable ones. We propose Backflip, a new bit flipping algorithm which uses time to leverage the reliability information given by the counters on each flip. Every flip gets a (finite) time-to-live (an iteration count). When its time is over, the flip is canceled. Positions with a higher counter stay flipped for a longer time than positions with a counter just above the threshold. The design of Backflip is based on the following principles:

- the most reliable decisions will have more influence in the decoding process,
- all bad decisions will be cancelled at some point,
- conservative threshold selection hinders bad decisions in cascade.

In addition, it is readily seen that, compared to Algorithm 1, the Algorithm 2 only requires a few more operations to manage a delay table D. Moreover, as for the `threshold`, the `ttl` is very well approximated by an affine function for any fixed set of parameters and its computation has a negligible cost in practice.

Algorithm 2. Backflipping Algorithm

Require: $\mathbf{H} \in \mathbb{F}_2^{(n-k) \times n}$, $s \in \mathbb{F}_2^{n-k}$, integer $u \geq 0$ //$u > 0$ for noisy syndrome
Ensure: $|s - e'\mathbf{H}^\mathsf{T}| \leq u$ or time > max_time
    $e' \leftarrow \mathbf{0}$; time $\leftarrow 1$; $D \leftarrow \mathbf{0}$ //D_j = time-of-death of j
    while $|s - e'\mathbf{H}^\mathsf{T}| > u$ **and** time $\leq$ max_time **do**   //here max_time is 100, 10 or 11
       for j such that D_j = time **do** $e'_j \leftarrow 0$ //Undo flips at time-of-death
       time $\leftarrow$ time $+ 1$
       $s' \leftarrow s - e'\mathbf{H}^\mathsf{T}$
       $T \leftarrow$ threshold$(|s'|, t - |e'|)$
       for $j \in \{0, \ldots, n-1\}$ **do**
          if $|s' \cap h_j| \geq T$ **then**   //h_j the j-th column of $\mathbf{H}$
             $e'_j \leftarrow 1 - e'_j$; $D_j \leftarrow$ time $+$ ttl$(|s' \cap h_j| - T)$
    return e'

Threshold Selection Rule threshold(S, t'). As the time-to-live of a flip is always finite, a bad flip will always be canceled eventually. However, it is necessary to avoid adding more bad flips during the period during which it remains flipped. To achieve this, thresholds from Fig. 1 are used with $S = |s'|$ and $t' = t - |e'|$. This is the best case estimate for the error weight, it supposes that every flip removed an error. When many errors were added, the corresponding threshold is higher than for the usual bit flipping algorithm, this will slow down the decoding process, leaving time to cancel the bad decisions while making only very reliable new flips. In the typical case, most flip decisions were good, the threshold is close to optimal, and the decoding converges quickly.

Time-to-Live Rule ttl(δ). Empirically, it appears that the time-to-live should be increasing with the difference δ between the position's counter and the iteration threshold. It should also be finite because otherwise outlier counter values could lead to adding errors that are harder to detect: correct positions with a high counter will become errors with a low counter once flipped, their counter will have to change drastically before it is corrected by an algorithm relying solely on a threshold. The ttl function depends on the code parameters (especially w and t) as well as the maximum number of iterations of the decoder. In practice, a saturating affine function in δ can be used.

$$\text{ttl}(\delta) = \max(1, \min(\text{max\_ttl}, \lfloor \alpha \delta + \beta \rfloor)).$$

To determine a suitable function, w, t, and the number of iterations are fixed. The block size r is chosen so that a sufficiently precise measure of the DFR can be made with a reasonable number of samples ($\approx 10^8$). A nonlinear optimization method (such as Nelder-Mead's) is then used to find values for α and β that minimize the DFR.

Table 2. ttl function parameters

Iteration count	λ	(w,t)	(α,β)	max_ttl
100	128	$(142,134)$	$(0.45,1.1)$	5
	192	$(206,199)$	$(0.36,1.41)$	5
	256	$(274,264)$	$(0.45,1)$	5
10,11	128	$(142,134)$	$(1,1)$	5
	192	$(206,199)$	$(1,1)$	5
	256	$(274,264)$	$(1,1)$	5

Complexity and Constant Time Implementation. Backflip was primarily designed to work with a maximum of 100 iterations. Reducing this number to 10 is possible and requires an adjustment to the ttl function. However it increases significantly the estimated DFR (see Sect. 4). Nevertheless, in both cases, the average number of iterations is much smaller, between 2.03 for $(r,w,t) = (24821,206,199)$ and 4.38 for $(r,w,t) = (32749,274,264)$.

The interest of reducing max_time is to allow constant time implementation. The Backflip iteration can be implemented in constant time [7], but to mask the effective number of iterations and keep the DFR claims, the algorithm has to execute exactly max_time iterations.

4   Estimating the DFR from Simulation

Under Assumption 3 for a decoder $\mathcal{D}$ and a security level λ, we may extrapolate the DFR by accurately estimating the tangent of the function $r \mapsto \log_2(\mathrm{DFR}(r))$ for some value of r. We obtain an estimate of the tangent by taking the line joining the values for two points $r_1 < r_2$. Note that, except for a possible lack of accuracy (discussed below), this will provide upper bounds for the extrapolated DFRs. Results are presented in Table 3, we denote $r_{\mathcal{D},\lambda}$ the smallest r such that $\mathrm{DFR}_{\mathcal{D},\lambda}(r) \leq 2^{-\lambda}$. We denote r_λ^{CPA} and r_λ^{CCA} the blocks sizes in BIKE for CPA and CCA security. Known asymptotic analysis [21,22] indicate that the $\log_2(\mathrm{DFR})$ is ultimately decreasing linearly, but this linear regime probably starts much beyond the simulated region. Thus it is best to choose r_1, r_2 as large as possible, but not too large else we would decrease the accuracy.

Finally note that a significant computational effort was needed to compute the data of Table 4, a total of several years of CPU time (on a single core).

Table 3. DFR estimation for Backflip limited to max_time iterations.

#iter	λ	r_1	r_2	$\log_2(p_1)$	$\log_2(p_2)$	$r_{\mathcal{D},\lambda}$	r_λ^{CCA}	$\log_2(r_\lambda^{\mathrm{CCA}})$	r_λ^{CPA}	$\log_2(r_\lambda^{\mathrm{CPA}})$
100	128	9200	9350	−21.4	−27.7	11717	11779	−130.7	10163	−62.2
	192	18200	18300	−23.0	−25.6	24665	24821	−196.1	19853	−66.2
	256	30250	30400	−23.3	−26.2	42418	40597	−221.2	32749	−71.1
10	128	10000	10050	−22.7	−24.6	12816	11779	−89.2	10163	−28.8
	192	19550	19650	−23.5	−25.7	26939	24821	−143.7	19853	−30.4
	256	32250	32450	−22.9	−26.6	44638	40597	−180.0	32749	−32.3
11	128	10000	10050	−25.1	−27.1	12573	11779	−96.3	10163	−31.6
	192	19550	19650	−25.9	−28.6	25580	24821	−171.1	19853	−34.2
	256	32250	32450	−25.1	−29.5	42706	40597	−209.4	32749	−36.1

Accurary of Simulated DFRs. The decoding failure is a Bernoulli trial of probability p. If we observe F failures out of N trials our estimate is $\hat{p} = F/N$. The normal distribution gives a good approximation of this distribution in which the standard deviation for F is $\sqrt{p(1-p)N}$. For $p \ll 1$ (the case of interest) we have $\left|\frac{\hat{p}-p}{p}\right| \le \varepsilon = z/\sqrt{pN}$ with probability $1-\alpha \approx 0.68, 0.95, 0.997$ for $z = 1, 2, 3$ respectively. We observe that the precision decreases as $z/\sqrt{F}$ where F is the number of failures observed and z will be determined by the confidence we wish to achieve. Note that for the same confidence, $|\log \hat{p} - \log p| \le \varepsilon$. In our case, we use Clopper–Pearson intervals [6] which are exact (they use the correct binomial distribution and not an approximation). Those intervals are not symmetric, the confidence interval is ε^- below and ε^+ above the measured values. In the simulation for max_time $= 10$ we let the decoder run up to 50 iterations and store the number of effective iterations. We are thus able to measure the DFR for 11 iterations of Backflip. We observe in Table 3 a significant improvement in the DFR, but a lower confidence (Table 4) because the block sizes were chosen for 10 iterations. Nevertheless, this suggests that increasing max_time could

Table 4. Raw simulation data with confidence intervals ($\alpha = 0.01$)

#iter	λ	r_1	F_1	N_1	$\log_2 p_1$	ε^-	ε^+	r_2	F_2	N_2	$\log_2 p_2$	ε^-	ε^+
100	128	9200	1253	$3.45\,10^9$	−21.4	0.107	0.104	9350	102	$2.30\,10^{10}$	−27.7	0.390	0.361
	192	18200	499	$4.13\,10^9$	−23.0	0.171	0.165	18300	90	$4.57\,10^9$	−25.6	0.416	0.383
	256	30250	282	$2.96\,10^9$	−23.3	0.229	0.219	30400	80	$6.14\,10^9$	−25.3	0.443	0.407
10	128	10000	1074	$7.29\,10^9$	−22.7	0.115	0.113	10050	282	$6.99\,10^9$	−24.6	0.229	0.219
	192	19550	440	$5.08\,10^9$	−23.5	0.182	0.176	19650	81	$4.55\,10^9$	−25.7	0.440	0.404
	256	32250	513	$3.91\,10^9$	−22.9	0.168	0.163	32450	37	$3.83\,10^9$	−26.6	0.673	0.591
11	128	10000	200	$7.29\,10^9$	−25.1	0.274	0.259	10050	48	$6.99\,10^9$	−27.1	0.584	0.522
	192	19550	83	$5.08\,10^9$	−25.9	0.435	0.399	19650	11	$4.55\,10^9$	−28.6	1.348	1.054
	256	32250	109	$3.91\,10^9$	−25.1	0.376	0.350	32450	5	$3.83\,10^9$	−29.5	2.214	1.501

provide interesting trade-offs between complexity and DFR for constant time implementations.

Additional Comments. In [21], the BIKE round 1 algorithm was estimated to have a DFR around $2^{-47.5}$ for $(r, w, t) = (32\,749, 274, 264)$. A significant improvement is made with Backflip as its DFR is estimated around $2^{-71.1}$ for the same parameters, with a smaller complexity on average.

Finally, note that the suggested parameters for the CCA variant of BIKE Level 5 ($\lambda = 256$) have not been correctly estimated. The extrapolated block size to reach a DFR of 2^{-256} is 42418 rather than 40597 in [1]. This is due to the imprecision of the measures at the time. To mitigate this issue, it is very likely that the tangent we are using is pessimistic and that the actual DFR is much lower than the extrapolated value given here.

5   Conclusion

We have given in this paper the description and the rationale of the Backflip decoder of BIKE [1]. We also explain how the DFR claims were obtained by extrapolating simulation data. To justify the extrapolation technique we introduce a new security assumption, related to the decoder, under which the DFR claims are valid. The assumption is supported by other works analyzing the asymptotic behavior of the bit flipping decoding for QC-MDPC codes. Under this additional assumption, it is possible to prove that the BIKE KEMs, derived from QC-MDPC codes, are IND-CCA. Doing this requires extensive simulations in order to obtain accurate simulation data.

Backflip with 100 iterations would hardly produce efficient constant time implementations. Reducing the number of iterations to 10 increases the DFR and would require larger block size to reach a low enough DFR for IND-CCA security. This was remarked in another independent work [7] which considers another variant of the bit flipping algorithm, closer to the round 1 BIKE decoder, and which is more efficient when the number of iterations is bounded to a small number. The methodology we develop here is valid for other variants of bit flipping and can be used to justify the conclusions of [7]: we may produce efficient constant time variants of BIKE with provably low DFR (under Assumption 3) but it requires a small increase of the block size, in the order of 5% to 10%.

Finally, there is one extra feature of the tangent extrapolation technique. With a larger amount a computational effort for the simulation, it should be possible, under the same assumptions, to get the same security guaranty (*e.g.* IND-CCA) for a smaller block size.

A   Error Floors for QC-MDPC

The DFR study we are making here differs from what is done for communication systems where the code is fixed and the signal to noise ratio increases (*i.e.* the bit error probability decreases). We expect to observe the same kind of DFR behavior here for QC-MDPC when we fix (w, t) and let r grow. Some classes of error correcting codes, namely turbo-codes and LDPC codes to which MDPC codes are akin, suffer from a phenomenon known as error floor. The $\log(\text{DFR})$ curve is first concave and quickly decreasing (the *waterfall*). Then at some point the concavity changes and the DFR decreases much more slowly, this is known as the *error floor* [15,19]. This could contradict the Assumption 3, but fortunately error floors usually occur very low in DFR curves. The error floors are due to the existence of low weight codewords, in the case of turbo codes, or, for LDPC codes, to the existence of specific error configurations known as *near-codewords*. An (u, v)-near-codeword is an error pattern of relatively small weight u with a syndrome of small weight v (the syndrome is computed with the sparse parity check matrix). Intuitively, it can be seen as a cluster of errors which are less visible because, together, they only invalidate a few parity equations. If the initial error pattern contains a near-codeword the decoder is more prone to fail. If many near-codewords exist it may cause an error floor.

Error Floors From Near-Codewords. To affect decoding in a $(2r, r, w, t)$-QC-MDPC-McEliece scheme, an (u, v)-near-codewords (see definition above) must be such that u is smaller than t, and v significantly smaller than the typical syndrome weight. The probability that such a near-codeword exists when the QC-MDPC is chosen at random is extremely small. A very small number of QC-MDPC codes may admit such words, but if they do there will be few of them. Moreover, the decoding of the few error patterns containing near-codewords will not automatically fail, the DFR will just increase a bit, with little impact on the average DFR. Unless there is an algebraic structure which is not immediately apparent, we do not expect near-codewords to have an impact on QC-MDPC DFR.

Error Floors from Low Weight Codewords. Regardless of the algorithm, the decoding of a noisy codeword will almost certainly fail if the noisy codeword comes closer to a codeword c_1 different from the original one c_0. For a given error e of weight t, and two codewords c_0 and c_1 at distance w from one another, the decoding will fail if $|c_0 + e - c_1| \leq |e|$, which happens with probability

$$P_w = \sum_{i=w/2}^{w} \frac{\binom{w}{i}\binom{n-w}{t-i}}{\binom{n}{t}}. \tag{1}$$

An index 2 QC-MDPC code with block size r and parity check matrix row weight w will generally have exactly r codewords of weight w. If $\mathbf{H} = (\mathbf{H}_0 \mid \mathbf{H}_1)$ is the sparse parity check matrix, with two circulant blocks $\mathbf{H}_0, \mathbf{H}_1$, then $\mathbf{G} = (\mathbf{H}_1^\mathsf{T} \mid \mathbf{H}_0^\mathsf{T})$ is a generator matrix of the code. With overwhelming probability, the r rows of that generator matrix are the only minimal weight codewords. Let us denote $P_\lambda(r) \approx r P_w$ the failure probability due to those codewords. A simple analysis shows that $\log_2 P_\lambda(r) \sim_{r \to \infty} C_\lambda - (w/2 - 1)\log_2 r$ where C_λ only depends of w and t. We have $\text{DFR}_{\mathcal{D},\lambda}(r) \geq P_\lambda(r)$ for any decoder, this term will dominate when r grows and thus the logarithm of the DFR is *not concave* in the whole range $r \in [0, \infty[$. However the change of slope only happens for very large values of r. We have

$$\lambda = 128,\ \log_2 P_\lambda(r_\lambda^{\mathrm{CPA}}) = -396.8,\ \text{and}\ \log_2 P_\lambda(r) \approx 535.0 - 70\log_2 r$$
$$\lambda = 192,\ \log_2 P_\lambda(r_\lambda^{\mathrm{CPA}}) = -618.5,\ \text{and}\ \log_2 P_\lambda(r) \approx 837.8 - 102\log_2 r$$
$$\lambda = 256,\ \log_2 P_\lambda(r_\lambda^{\mathrm{CPA}}) = -868.7,\ \text{and}\ \log_2 P_\lambda(r) \approx 1171.2 - 136\log_2 r$$

and this will not affect the DFR for values of r relevant for Assumption 3. Finally note that the sum of two (or more) rows of $\mathbf{G}$ may also contribute to the DFR. However, it is easily observed that the contribution of those codewords is even smaller.

Additional Comment. The error floor issue is new for QC-MDPC codes. As far as this work is concerned, we assume through Assumption 3 that the error floor occurs below the required $2^{-\lambda}$, validating the DFR estimation method. We give above some arguments to support the assumption. We agree, as suggested by one of the reviewers, that the matter needs to be more thoroughly studied, but this goes beyond the scope of the present work.

References

1. Melchor, C.A., et al.: BIKE. Second round submission to the NIST post-quantum cryptography call, April 2019
2. Baldi, M., Santini, P., Chiaraluce, F.: Soft McEliece: MDPC code-based mceliece cryptosystems with very compact keys through real-valued intentional errors. In: Proceedings of IEEE International Symposium on Information Theory - ISIT, pp. 795–799. IEEE Press (2016)
3. Becker, A., Joux, A., May, A., Meurer, A.: Decoding random binary linear codes in $2^{n/20}$: How $1 + 1 = 0$ improves information set decoding. In: Pointcheval, D., Johansson, T. (eds.) EUROCRYPT 2012. LNCS, vol. 7237, pp. 520–536. Springer, Heidelberg (2012). https://doi.org/10.1007/978-3-642-29011-4_31
4. Canto Torres, R., Sendrier, N.: Analysis of information set decoding for a sub-linear error weight. In: Takagi, T. (ed.) PQCrypto 2016. LNCS, vol. 9606, pp. 144–161. Springer, Cham (2016). https://doi.org/10.1007/978-3-319-29360-8_10
5. Chaulet, J.: Étude de cryptosystèmes à clé publique basés sur les codes MDPC quasi-cycliques. Ph.D. thesis, University Pierre et Marie Curie, March 2017
6. Clopper, C.J., Pearson, E.S.: The use of confidence or fiducial limits illustrated in the case of the binomial. Biometrika **26**(4), 404–413 (1934)
7. Drucker, N., Gueron, S., Kostic, D.: On constant-time QC-MDPC decoding with negligible failure rate. Cryptology ePrint Archive, Report 2019/1289 (2019). https://eprint.iacr.org/2019/1289
8. Eaton, E., Lequesne, M., Parent, A., Sendrier, N.: QC-MDPC: a timing attack and a CCA2 KEM. In: Proceedings of Post-Quantum Cryptography - 9th International Conference, PQCrypto 2018, Fort Lauderdale, FL, USA, 9–11 April 2018, pp. 47–76 (2018)
9. Fischer, J.-B., Stern, J.: An efficient pseudo-random generator provably as secure as syndrome decoding. In: Maurer, U. (ed.) EUROCRYPT 1996. LNCS, vol. 1070, pp. 245–255. Springer, Heidelberg (1996). https://doi.org/10.1007/3-540-68339-9_22

10. Gallager, R.G.: Low Density Parity Check Codes. MIT Press, Cambridge (1963)
11. Guo, Q., Johansson, T., Stankovski, P.: A key recovery attack on MDPC with CCA security using decoding errors. In: Cheon, J.H., Takagi, T. (eds.) ASIACRYPT 2016. LNCS, vol. 10031, pp. 789–815. Springer, Heidelberg (2016). https://doi.org/10.1007/978-3-662-53887-6_29
12. Hamdaoui, Y., Sendrier, N.: A non asymptotic analysis of information set decoding. IACR Cryptology ePrint Archive, Report 2013/162 (2013). http://eprint.iacr.org/2013/162
13. Heyse, S., von Maurich, I., Güneysu, T.: Smaller keys for code-based cryptography: QC-MDPC McEliece implementations on embedded devices. In: Bertoni, G., Coron, J.-S. (eds.) CHES 2013. LNCS, vol. 8086, pp. 273–292. Springer, Heidelberg (2013). https://doi.org/10.1007/978-3-642-40349-1_16
14. Liva, G., Bartz, H.: Protograph-based quasi-cyclic MDPC codes for mceliece cryptosystems. In: ISTC, Hong Kong, China, pp. 1–5. IEEE, December 2018
15. MacKay, D.J.C., Postol, M.S.: Weaknesses of margulis and ramanujan-margulis low-density parity-check codes. Electr. Notes Theor. Comput. Sci. **74**, 97–104 (2002)
16. McEliece, R.J.: A public-key system based on algebraic coding theory. DSN Progress Report 44, pp. 114–116. Jet Propulsion Lab (1978)
17. Misoczki, R., Tillich, J.P., Sendrier, N., Barreto, P.S.L.M.: MDPC-McEliece: new McEliece variants from moderate density parity-check codes. In: Proceedings of IEEE International Symposium on Information Theory - ISIT, pp. 2069–2073 (2013)
18. Prange, E.: The use of information sets in decoding cyclic codes. IRE Trans. Inf. Theory **8**(5), 5–9 (1962)
19. Richardson, T.: Error floors of LDPC codes. In: Proceedings of the 41th Annual Allerton Conference on Communication, Control, and Computing (2003)
20. Sendrier, N.: Decoding one out of many. In: Yang, B.-Y. (ed.) PQCrypto 2011. LNCS, vol. 7071, pp. 51–67. Springer, Heidelberg (2011). https://doi.org/10.1007/978-3-642-25405-5_4
21. Sendrier, N., Vasseur, V.: On the decoding failure rate of QC-MDPC bit-flipping decoders. In: Ding, J., Steinwandt, R. (eds.) PQCrypto 2019. LNCS, vol. 11505, pp. 404–416. Springer, Cham (2019). https://doi.org/10.1007/978-3-030-25510-7_22
22. Tillich, J.P.: The decoding failure probability of MDPC codes. In: 2018 IEEE International Symposium on Information Theory, ISIT 2018, Vail, CO, USA, 17–22 June 2018, pp. 941–945 (2018)

QC-MDPC Decoders with Several Shades of Gray

Nir Drucker[1,2(✉)], Shay Gueron[1,2], and Dusan Kostic[3]

[1] University of Haifa, Haifa, Israel
drucker.nir@gmail.com
[2] Amazon, Seattle, USA
[3] EPFL, Lausanne, Switzerland

Abstract. QC-MDPC code-based KEMs rely on decoders that have a small or even negligible Decoding Failure Rate (DFR). These decoders should be efficient and implementable in constant-time. One example for a QC-MDPC KEM is the Round-2 candidate of the NIST PQC standardization project, "BIKE". We have recently shown that the Black-Gray decoder achieves the required properties. In this paper, we define several new variants of the Black-Gray decoder. One of them, called Black-Gray-Flip, needs only 7 steps to achieve a smaller DFR than Black-Gray with 9 steps, for the same block size. On current AVX512 platforms, our BIKE-1 (Level-1) constant-time decapsulation is 1.9× faster than the previous decapsulation with Black-Gray. We also report an additional 1.25× decapsulating speedup using the new AVX512-VBMI2 and vector-PCLMULQDQ instructions available on "Ice-Lake" micro-architecture.

Keywords: BIKE · QC-MDPC codes · Constant-time implementation · QC-MDPC decoders

1 Introduction

The Key Encapsulation Mechanism (KEM) called Bit Flipping Key Encapsulation (BIKE) [2] is based on Quasi-Cyclic Moderate-Density Parity-Check (QC-MDPC) codes, and is one of the Round-2 candidates of the NIST PQC Standardization Project [15]. The submission includes several variants of the KEM and we focus here on BIKE-1-CCA Level-1 and Level-3.

The common QC-MDPC decoding algorithms are derived from the Bit-Flipping algorithm [12] and come in two main variants.

- "Step-by-Step": it recalculates the threshold every time that a bit is flipped. This is an enhancement of the "in-place" decoder described in [11].
- "Simple-Parallel": a parallel algorithm similar to that of [12]. It first calculates some thresholds for flipping bits and then flips the bits in all of the relevant positions, in parallel.

© Springer Nature Switzerland AG 2020
J. Ding and J.-P. Tillich (Eds.): PQCrypto 2020, LNCS 12100, pp. 35–50, 2020.
https://doi.org/10.1007/978-3-030-44223-1_3

BIKE uses a decoder for the decapsulation phase. The specific decoding algorithm is a choice shaped by the target DFR, security, and performance. The IND-CCA version of BIKE Round-2 [2] is specified with the "BackFlip" decoder, which is derived from Simple-Parallel. The IND-CPA version is specified with the "One-Round" decoder, which combines the Simple-Parallel and the Step-By-Step decoders. In the "additional implementation" [7] we chose to use the "Black-Gray" decoder (BG) [5,8], with the thresholds defined in [2]. This decoder (with different thresholds) appears in the BIKE pre-Round-1 submission "CAKE" and is due to N. Sendrier and R. Misoczki.

This paper explores a new family of decoders that combine the BG and the Bit-Flipping algorithms in different ways. Some combinations achieve the same or even better DFR compared to BG with the same block size, and at the same time also have better performance.

For better security we replace the mock-bits technique of the additional implementation [5] with a constant-time implementation that applies rotation and bit-slice-adder as proposed in [3] (and vectorized in [13]), and enhance it with further optimizations. We also report the first measurements of BIKE-1 on the new Intel "Ice-Lake" micro-architecture, leveraging the new AVX512-VBMI2, vector-AESENC and vector-PCLMULQDQ instructions [1] (see also [4,10]).

The paper is organized as follows. Section 2 defines notation and offers some background. The Bit-Flipping and the BG algorithms are given in Sect. 3. In Sect. 4 we define new decoders (BGF, B and BGB) and report our DFR per block size studies in Sect. 5. We discuss our new constant-time QC-MDPC implementation in Sect. 6. Section 7 reports the resulting performance. Section 8 concludes the paper.

2 Preliminaries and Notation

Let $\mathbb{F}_2$ be the finite field of characteristic 2. Let $\mathcal{R}$ be the polynomial ring $\mathbb{F}_2[X]/\langle X^r - 1\rangle$. For every element $v \in \mathcal{R}$ its Hamming weight is denoted by $wt(v)$, its bits length by $|v|$, and its support (i.e., the positions of its set bits) by $supp(v)$. Polynomials in $\mathcal{R}$ are viewed, interchangeably, also as square circulant matrices in $\mathbb{F}_2^{r\times r}$. For a matrix $H \in \mathbb{F}_2^{r\times r}$, let H_i denote its i-th column written as a row vector. We denote a failure by the symbol $\perp$. Uniform random sampling from a set W is denoted by $w \xleftarrow{\$} W$. For an algorithm A, we denote its output by $out = A()$ if A is deterministic, and by $out \leftarrow A()$ otherwise. Hereafter, we use the notation $x.ye-z$ to denote the number $(x + \frac{y}{10}) \cdot 10^{-z}$ (e.g., $1.2e-3 = 1.2 \cdot 10^{-3}$).

BIKE-1 IND-CCA. BIKE-1 (IND-CCA) flows are shown in Table 1. The computations are executed over $\mathcal{R}$, and the block size r is a parameter. The weights of the secret key $h = (h_0, h_1, \sigma_0, \sigma_1)$ and the errors vector $e = (e_0, e_1)$, are w and t, respectively, the public key, ciphertext, and shared secret are $f = (f_0, f_1)$, $c = (c_0, c_1)$, and k, respectively. **H, K** denote hash functions (as in [2]). Currently, the parameters of BIKE-1 IND-CCA for NIST Level-1 are: $r = 11,779$, $|f| = |c| = 23,558$, $|k| = 256$, $w = 142$, $d = w/2 = 71$ and $t = 134$.

Table 1. BIKE-1-CCA

Key generation	• $h_0, h_1 \xleftarrow{\$} \mathcal{R}$ of odd weight $wt(h_0) = wt(h_1) = w/2$
	• $\sigma_0, \sigma_1 \xleftarrow{\$} \mathcal{R}$
	• $g \xleftarrow{\$} \mathcal{R}$ of odd weight (so $wt(g) \approx r/2$)
	• $(f_0, f_1) = (gh_1, gh_0)$
Encapsulation	• $m \xleftarrow{\$} \mathcal{R}$
	• $(e_0, e_1) = \mathbf{H}(mf_0, mf_1)$ where $wt(e_0) + wt(e_1) = t$
	• $(c_0, c_1) = (mf_0 + e_0, mf_1 + e_1)$
	• $k = \mathbf{K}(mf_0, mf_1, c_0, c_1)$
Decapsulation	• Compute the syndrome $s = c_0 h_0 + c_1 h_1$
	• $(e'_o, e'_1) \leftarrow \text{decode}(s, h_0, h_1)$
	• If $wt((e'_0, e'_1)) \neq t$ or decoding failed then $k = \mathbf{K}(\sigma_0, \sigma_1, c)$
	• else $k = \mathbf{K}(c_0 + e'_0, c_1 + e'_1, c_0, c_1)$

3   The Bit-Flipping and the Black-Gray Decoders

Algorithm 1 describes the Bit-Flipping decoder [12]. The `computeThreshold` step computes the relevant threshold according to the syndrome, the errors vector, or the Unsatisfied Parity-Check (UPC) values. The original definition of [12] takes the maximal UPC as its threshold.

Algorithm 1. e=Bit-Flipping(c, H)

Input: $H \in \mathbb{F}_2^{r \times n}$ (parity-check matrix), $c \in \mathbb{F}_2^n$ (ciphertext), X (Maximal number of iterations), u (Maximal syndrome weight)
Output: $e \in \mathbb{F}_2^n$ (errors vector)
Exception: A "decoding failure" returns $\perp$
1: **procedure** BIT-FLIPPING(c, H)
2:     $s = Hc^T$, $e = 0$, $\text{upc}[\text{n-1:0}] = 0^n$
3:     **for** $itr = 0 \ldots X$ **do**
4:         $th = \text{computeThreshold}(s, e)$
5:         **for** i in $0 \ldots n - 1$ **do**
6:             $upc[i] = H_i \cdot s$
7:             **if** $upc[i] > th$ **then** $e[i] = e[i] \oplus 1$ ▷ Flip an error bit
8:         $s = H(c^T + e^T)$ ▷ Update the syndrome
9:     **if** $(wt(s) = u)$ **then return** e
10:     **else return** $\perp$

Algorithm 2 describes the BG decoder. It is implemented in BIKE additional code package [7]. Every iteration of BG involves three main steps. Step I calls `BitFlipIter` to perform one Bit-Flipping iteration and sets the black and gray arrays. Steps II and III call `BitFlipMaskedIter`. Here, another Bit-Flipping iteration is executed, but the errors vector e is updated according to the `black`/`gray` masks, respectively.

In Step I the decoder uses some threshold (th) to decide whether or not a certain bit is an error bit. The probability that the bit is indeed an error bit increases as a function of the gap ($upc[i]$ - th). The algorithm records bits with a small gap in the `black`/`gray` masks so that the subsequent Step II and Step III can use the masks in order to gain more confidence in the flipped bits. In this paper $\delta = 4$.

Algorithm 2. e=BG(c, H)

Input: $H \in \mathbb{F}_2^{r \times n}$ (parity-check matrix), $c \in \mathbb{F}_2^n$ (ciphertext), X_{BG} (maximal number of iterations)
Output: $e \in \mathbb{F}_2^n$ (errors vector)
Exception: A "decoding failure" returns $\perp$

1: **procedure** BITFLIPITER(s, e, th, H)
2:     $black[n-1:0] = gray[n-1:0] = 0^n$
3:     **for** i in $0 \ldots n-1$ **do**
4:         $upc[i] = H_i \cdot s$
5:         **if** $upc[i] \geq th$ **then**
6:             $e[i] = e[i] \oplus 1$ ▷ Flip an error bit
7:             $black[i] = 1$ ▷ Update the Black set
8:         **else if** $upc_i >= th - \delta$ **then**
9:             $gray[i] = 1$ ▷ Update the Gray set
10:     $s = H(c^T + e^T)$ ▷ Update the syndrome
11:     **return** $(s, e, black, gray)$

12: **procedure** BITFLIPMASKEDITER(s, e, $mask$, th, H)
13:     **for** i in $0 \ldots n-1$ **do**
14:         $upc[i] = H_i \cdot s$
15:         **if** $upc[i] \geq th$ **then**
16:             $e[i] = e[i] \oplus mask[i]$ ▷ Flip an error bit
17:     $s = H(c^T + e^T)$ ▷ Update the syndrome
18:     **return** (s, e)

19: **procedure** BLACK-GRAY(c, H)
20:     $s = Hc^T$, $e[n-1:0] = 0^n$, $\delta = 4$
21:     **for** itr in $1 \ldots X_{BG}$ **do**
22:         $th = \text{computeThreshold}(s)$
23:         $(s, e, black, gray) = \text{BitFlipIter}(s, e, th, H)$ ▷ Step I
24:         $(s, e) = \text{BitFlipMaskedIter}(s, e, black, ((d+1)/2), H)$ ▷ Step II
25:         $(s, e) = \text{BitFlipMaskedIter}(s, e, gray, ((d+1)/2), H)$ ▷ Step III
26:     **if** $(wt(s) \neq 0)$ **then**
27:         **return** $\perp$
28:     **else**
29:         **return** e

---

4   New Decoders with Different Shades of Gray

In cases where Algorithm 2 can safely run without a constant-time implementation, Step II and Step III are fast. The reason is that the UPC values are calculated only for indices in $supp(black)/supp(gray)$, and the number of these indices is at most the number of bits that were flipped in Step I (certainly less than n). By contrast, if constant-time and constant memory-access are required, the implementation needs to access all of the n positions uniformly. In such case the performance of Step II and Step III is similar to the performance of Step I. Thus, the overall decoding time of the BG decoder with X_{BG} iterations, where each iteration is executing steps I, II, and III, is proportional to $3 \cdot X_{BG}$.

The decoders that are based on Bit-Flipping are not perfect - they can erroneously flip a bit that is not an error bit. The probability to erroneously flip a "non-error" bit is an increasing function of $wt(e)/n$ and also depends on the threshold (note that $wt(e)$ is changing during the execution). Step II and Step III of BG are designed to fix some erroneously flipped bits and therefore decrease $wt(e)$ compared to $wt(e)$ after one iteration of Simple-Parallel (without the black/gray masks). Apparently, when $wt(e)/n$ becomes sufficiently small the black/gray technique is no longer needed because erroneous flips have low probabilities. This observation leads us to propose several new variations of the BG decoder (see Appendix A for their pseudo-code).

1. A Black decoder (B): every iteration consists of only Steps I, II (i.e., there is no gray mask).
2. A Black-Gray-Flip decoder (BGF): it starts with one BG iteration and continues with several Bit-Flipping iterations.
3. A Black-Gray-Black decoder (BGB): it starts with one BG iteration and continues with several B-iterations.

Example 1 (Counting the number of steps). Consider BG with 3 iterations. Here, every iteration involves 3 steps (I, II, and III). The total number of practically identical steps is 9. Consider, BGF with 3 iterations. Here, the first iteration involves 3 steps (I, II, and III) and the rest of the iterations involve only one step. The total number of practically identical steps is $3 + 1 + 1 = 5$.

5   DFR Evaluations for Different Decoders

In this section we evaluate and compare the B, BG, BGB, and BGF decoders under two criteria.

1. The DFR for a given number of iterations and a given value of r.
2. The value of r that is required to achieve a target DFR with a given number of iterations.

In order to approximate the DFR we use the extrapolation method [16], and apply two forms of extrapolation: "best linear fit" [8] and "two large r's fit" (as in [8][Appendix C]). We point out that the extrapolation method relies on the assumption that the dependence of the DFR on the block size r is a concave function in the relevant range of r. Table 2 summarizes our results. It shows the r-value required for achieving a DFR of $2^{-23} (\approx 10^{-8})$, 2^{-64}, and 2^{-128}. It also shows the approximated DFR for $r = 11,779$ (which is the value used for BIKE-1 Level-1 CCA). Appendix B provides the full information on the experiments and the extrapolation analysis.

Table 2. The DFR achieved by different decoders. Two extrapolation methods are shown: "best linear fit" (as in [8]), "two large r's fit" (as in [8][Appendix C]). The second column shows the number of iterations for each decoder. The third column shows the total number of (time-wise identical) executed steps.

			Best linear fit				Two large r's fit			
Decoder	#I	#S	DFR = 2^{-23}	2^{-64}	2^{-128}	DFR at 11,779	DFR = 2^{-23}	2^{-64}	2^{-128}	DFR at 11,779
BG	3	9	10,253	11,213	12,739	2^{-88}	10,253	11,171	12,619	2^{-90}
	4	12	10,163	11,003	12,347	2^{-100}	10,163	10,909	12,107	2^{-110}
	5	15	10,133	10,909	12,107	2^{-111}	10,133	10,853	11,987	2^{-116}
BGB	4	9	10,253	11,093	12,491	2^{-95}	10,253	11,083	12,491	2^{-96}
	5	11	10,163	10,973	12,227	2^{-105}	10,163	11,027	12,413	2^{-99}
	6	13	10,133	10,973	12,269	2^{-104}	10,133	10,949	12,197	2^{-107}
BGF	5	7	10,301	11,171	12,539	2^{-92}	10,301	11,131	12,491	2^{-95}
	6	8	10,253	11,027	12,277	2^{-102}	10,253	10,973	12,197	2^{-107}
	7	9	10,181	10,949	12,149	2^{-108}	10,181	10,949	12,107	2^{-112}
B	4	8	10,259	11,699	13,901	2^{-67}	10,301	11,813	14,221	2^{-63}
	5	10	10,133	11,437	13,229	2^{-79}	10,133	11,437	13,451	2^{-76}
	6	12	10,067	11,213	13,037	2^{-84}	10,067	11,437	13,397	2^{-78}

Interpreting the Results of Table 2. The conclusions from Table 2 indicate that it is possible to trade BG with 3 iterations for BGF with 6 iterations. This achieves a better DFR and also a $\frac{9}{8} = 1.125\times$ speedup. Moreover, if the required DFR is at most 2^{-64}, it suffices to use BGF with only 5 iterations (and get the same DFR as BG with 3 iterations). This achieves a factor of $\frac{9}{7} = 1.28\times$ speedup. The situation is similar for BG with 4 iterations compared to BGB with 5 iterations: this achieves a $\frac{12}{11} = 1.09\times$ speedup. If a DFR of 2^{-128} is required it is possible to trade BG with 4 iterations for BGF with 7 iterations and achieve a $\frac{12}{9} = 1.33\times$ speedup. Another interesting trade off is available if we are willing to slightly increase the value of r. Compare BG with 4 iterations (i. e., 12 steps) and BGF with 6 iterations (i. e., 8 steps). For a DFR of 2^{-64} we have $r_{BG} = 11,003$ and $r_{BGF} = 11,027$. A very small relative increase in the block size, namely $(r_{BGF} - r_{BG})/r_{BG} = 0.0022$, gives a $\frac{12}{8} = 1.5\times$ speedup.

Example 2 (BGF versus BG with 3 iterations). Fig. 1 shows a qualitative comparison (the precise details are provided in Appendix B). The left panel indicates that BGF has a better DFR than BG for the same number of (9) steps when $r > 9,970$. Similarly, The right panel shows the same phenomenon even with a smaller number of BGF steps (7) when $r > 10,726$ (with the best linear fit method) and $r > 10,734$ (with the two large r's method) that correspond to a DFR of 2^{-43} and 2^{-45}, respectively. Both panels show that that crossover point appears for values of r below the range that is relevant for BIKE.

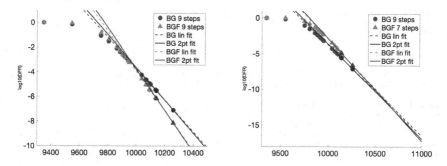

Fig. 1. DFR comparison of BG with 3 iterations (9 steps) to BGF with: (Left panel) 7 iterations (9 steps); (Right panel) 5 iterations (7 steps). See the text for details.

6   Constant-Time Implementation of the Decoders

The mock-bits technique was introduced in [5] for side-channel protection in order to obfuscate the (secret) $supp(h_0), supp(h_1)$. Let M_i denote the mock-bits used for obfuscating $supp(h_i)$ and let $\overline{M_i} = M_i \sqcup supp(h_i)$. For example, the implementation of BIKE-1 Level-1 used $|M_i| = 62$ mock-bits and thus $|\overline{M_i}| = 133$. The probability to correctly guess the secret 71 bits of h_i if the whole set $|\overline{M_i}|$ is given is $\binom{133}{71}^{-1} \approx 2^{-128}$. This technique was designed for ephemeral keys but may leak information on the private key if it is used multiple times (i. e., if most of $|\overline{M_i}|$ can be trapped). By knowing that $supp(h_i) \subset \overline{M_i}$, an adversary can learn that all the other $(r - |\overline{M_i}|)$ bits of h_i are zero. Subsequently, it can generate the following system of linear equations $(h_0, h_1)^T \cdot (f_0, f_1) = 0$, set the relevant variables to zero and solve it. To avoid this, $|\overline{M_i}|$ needs to be at least $r/2$ (probably more) so the system is sufficiently undetermined. However, using more than M_i mock-bits makes this method impractical (it was used as an optimization to begin with).

Therefore, to allow multiple usages of the private key we modify our implementation and use some of the optimizations suggested in [3] that were later vectorized in [13][1]. Specifically, we leverage the (array) rotation technique (which was also used in [14] for FPGAs). Here, the syndrome is rotated, d times, by $supp(h_i)$. The rotated syndrome is then accumulated in the upc array, using a bit-slice technique that implements a Carry Save Adder (CSA).

---

[1] The paper [13] does not point to publicly available code.

6.1   Optimizing the Rotation of an Array

Consider the rotation of the syndrome s (of r bits) by e. g., $1,100$ positions. It starts with "Barrel shifting" by the word size of the underlying architecture (e. g., for AVX512 the words size is 512-bits), here twice ($1,024$ positions). It then continues with internal shifting here by 76 positions. Reference [13] shows a code snippet (for the core functionality) for rotating by a number of positions that is less than the word size. Figure 2 presents our optimized and simplified snippet for the same functionality using the _mm512_permutex2var_epi64 instruction instead of the BLENDV and the VPALIGND.

```
__m512i previous, current, a0, a1, idx, idx1, num_full_qw, one;    1
uint64_t count64 = bitscount & 0x3f;                               2
                                                                  3
num_full_qw = _mm512_set1_epi8(bitscount >> 6);                   4
one         = _mm512_set1_epi64(1);                               5
previous    = _mm512_setzero_si512();                             6
idx         = _mm512_setr_epi64(0x0, 0x1, 0x2, 0x3, 0x4, 0x5, 0x6, 0x7);  7
idx         = _mm512_add_epi64(idx, num_full_qw);                 8
idx1        = _mm512_add_epi64(idx, one);                         9
                                                                  10
for(int i = R_ZMM; i >= 0; i--)                                   11
{                                                                 12
  current = _mm512_loadu_si512(in[i]);                            13
  a0 = _mm512_permutex2var_epi64(current, idx, previous);         14
  a1 = _mm512_permutex2var_epi64(current, idx1, previous);        15
  a0 = _mm512_srli_epi64(a0, count64);                            16
  a1 = _mm512_slli_epi64(a1, 64 - count64);                       17
  _mm512_storeu_si512(out[i], _mm512_or_si512(a0, a1));           18
  previous = current;                                             19
}                                                                 20
```

Fig. 2. Right rotate of 512-bit R_ZMM registers using AVX512 instructions.

The latest Intel micro-architecture "Ice-Lake" introduces a new instruction VPSHRDVQ as part of the new AVX512-VBMI2 set. This instruction receives two 512-bit (ZMM) registers (a, b) together with another 512-bit index register (c) and outputs in dst the following results:

```
For j = 0 to 7                                                    1
    i = j*64                                                      2
    dst[i+63:i] := concat(b[i+63:i], a[i+63:i]) >> (c[i+63:i] & 63)  3
```

Figure 3 shows how VPSHRDVQ can be used in order to replace the three instructions in lines 16–18 of Fig. 2.

Remark 1. Reference [13] remarks on using tables for some syndrome rotations but mentions that it does not yield significant speedup (and in some cases even shows a performance penalty). This is due to two bottlenecks in a constant-time implementation: (a) extensive memory access; (b) pressure on the execution port that the shift operations are using. In our case, the bottleneck is (a) so using tables to reduce the number of shifts is not a remedy. For completeness, we describe a new table method that can be implemented using Ice-Lake CPUs. The new VPERMI2B (_mm512_permutex2var_epi8) instruction [1] allows to permute two ZMMs at a granularity of bytes, and therefore to perform the rotation in lines 16–18 of Fig. 2 at a granularity of 8 bits (instead of 64). To use tables for caching: (a) initialize a table with $i = 0, \ldots, 7$ right-shifts of the syndrome (only 8 rows); (b) modify lines 14–15 to use VPERMI2B; (c) load (in constant-time) the relevant row before calling the Barrel-shifter. As a result, lines 16–18 can be removed to avoid all the shift operations. As explained above, this technique does not improve the performance of the rotation.

```
__m512i count64 = _mm512_set1_epi64(bitscount & 0x3f);          1
                                                                 2
for(int i = R_ZMM; i >= 0; i--)                                  3
{                                                                4
    data = _mm512_loadu_si512(&in->qw[8 * i]);                   5
    a0 = _mm512_permutex2var_epi64(current, idx, previous);      6
    a1 = _mm512_permutex2var_epi64(current, idx1, previous);     7
    a0 = _mm512_shrdv_epi64(a0, a1, count64);                    8
    _mm512_storeu_si512(&out->qw[8 * i], a0);                    9
    previous = current;                                         10
}                                                               11
```

Fig. 3. Right rotate of 512-bit R_ZMM registers using AVX512-VBMI2 instructions. The initialization in Fig. 2 (lines 1–10) is omitted.

6.2   Using Vector-PCLMULQDQ and vector-AESENC

The Ice-Lake processors support the new vectorized PCLMULQDQ and AESENC instructions [1]. We used the multiplication code presented in [9][Figure 2], and the CTR DRBG code of [6,10], in order to improve our BIKE implementation. We also used larger caching of random values (1,024 bytes instead of 16) to fully leverage the DRBG. The results are given in Sect. 7.

7   Performance Studies

We start with describing our experimentation platforms and measurements methodology. The experiments were carried out on two platforms, (Intel® Turbo Boost Technology was turned off on both):

- **EC2 Server:** An AWS EC2 m5.metal instance with the 6th Intel®Core^{TM} Generation (Micro architecture Codename "Sky Lake" [SKL]) Xeon®Platinum 8175M CPU 2.50 GHz. This platform has 384 GB RAM, 32K L1d and L1i cache, 1MiB L2 cache, and 32MiB L3 cache.
- **Ice-Lake:** Dell XPS 13 7390 2-in-1 with the 10th Intel®Core^{TM} Generation (Micro architecture Codename "Ice Lake" [ICL]) Intel®Core^{TM} i7-1065G7 CPU 1.30 GHz. This platform has 16 GB RAM, 48K L1d and 32K L1i cache, 512K L2 cache, and 8MiB L3 cache.

The Code. The code is written in C and x86-64 assembly. The implementations use the (vector) PCLMULQDQ, AES-NI, AVX2, AVX512 and AVX512-VBMI2 instructions when available. The code was compiled with gcc (version 8.3.0) in 64-bit mode, using the "O3" Optimization level with the "-funroll-all-loops" flag, and run on a Linux (Ubuntu 18.04.2 LTS) OS.

Measurements Methodology. The performance measurements reported hereafter are measured in processor cycles (per single core), where lower count is better. All the results were obtained using the same measurement methodology, as follows. Each measured function was isolated, run 25 times (warm-up), followed by 100 iterations that were clocked (using the RDTSC instruction) and averaged. To minimize the effect of background tasks running on the system, every experiment was repeated 10 times, and the minimum result was recorded.

7.1 Decoding and Decapsulation: Performance Studies

Performance of BG. Table 3 shows the performance of our implementation which uses the rotation and bit-slice-adder techniques of [3,13], and compares the results to the additional implementation of BIKE [7]. The results show a speedup of $3.75\times - 6.03\times$ for the portable (C code) of the decoder, $1.1\times$ speedup for the AVX512 implementations but a $0.66\times$ slowdown for the AVX2 implementation. The AVX512 implementation leverages the masked store and load operations that do not exist in the AVX2 architecture. Note that key generation is faster because generation of mock-bits is no longer needed.

Table 4 compares our implementations with different instruction sets (AVX512F, AVX512-VBMI2, vector-PCLMULQDQ, and vector-AES). The results for BIKE-1 Level-1 show speedups of $1.47\times$, $1.28\times$, and $1.26\times$ for key generation, encapsulation, and decapsulation, respectively. Even better speedups are shown for BIKE-1 Level-3 of $1.58\times$, $1.39\times$, and $1.24\times$, respectively.

Consider the 6th column and the BIKE-1 Level-1 results. The $\sim 94K$ $(93,521)$ cycles of the key generation consists of 13K, 13K, 1K, 1K, 5.5K, 26K, 26K cycles for generating $h_0, h_1, \sigma_0, \sigma_1, g, f_0, f_1$, respectively (and some additional overheads). Compared to the 3rd column of this table (with only AVX512F implementation): 13.6K, 13.6K, 2K, 2K, 6K, 46K, 46K, respectively. Indeed, as reported in [9], the use of vector-PCLMULQDQ contributes a $2\times$ speedup to the polynomial multiplication. Note that the vector-AES does not contribute much, because the bottleneck in generating h_0, h_1 is the constant-time rejection sampling check (if a bit is set) and not the AES calculations.

Table 5 compares our right-rotation method to the snippet shown in [13]. To accurately measure these "short" functionalities, we ported them into separate compilation units and compiled them separately using the "-c" flag. In addition, the number of repetitions was increased to $10,000$. This small change improves the rotation significantly (by $2.3\times$) and contributes $\sim 2\%$ to the overall decoding performance.

8 Discussion

Our study shows an unexpected shades-of-gray combination decoders: BGF offers the most favorable DFR-efficiency trade off. Indeed (see Table 2), it is possible to trade BG, which was our leading option so far, for another decoder and have the same or even better DFR for the same block size. The advantage

Table 3. The EC2 server performance of BIKE-1 Level-1 when using the BG decoder with 3 iterations. The cycles (in columns 4, 5) are counted in millions.

Implementation	Level	Op	Additional Implementation [7]	This paper	Speedup
C-portable stand-alone	Level-1	Keygen	1.67	1.37	1.22
		Decaps	60	15.99	3.75
	Level-3	Keygen	4.75	4.03	1.18
		Decaps	242.72	64.09	3.79
C-portable + OpenSSL	Level-1	Keygen	0.86	0.56	1.54
		Decaps	52.38	8.68	6.03
	Level-3	Keygen	2.71	1.98	1.37
		Decaps	218.42	39.82	5.48
AVX2	Level-1	Keygen	0.27	0.15	1.81
		Decaps	3.03	3.62	0.84
	Level-3	Keygen	0.62	0.38	1.64
		Decaps	10.46	15.84	0.66
AVX512	Level-1	Keygen	0.26	0.15	1.79
		Decaps	2.59	1.83	1.42
	Level-3	Keygen	0.57	0.37	1.57
		Decaps	8.97	8.14	1.10

Table 4. BIKE-1 Level-1 using the BG decoder with 3 iterations. Performance on Ice-Lake using various instruction sets.

Level	Op	AVX512F	AVX512F AVX512-VBMI2 VPCLMULQDQ	Speedup	AVX512F AVX512-VBMI2 VPCLMULQDQ, VAES	Speedup
Level-1	Keygen	137,095	95,068	1.44	93,521	1.47
	Encaps	192,123	150,860	1.27	150,612	1.28
	Decaps	2,192,433	1,711,127	1.28	1,737,912	1.26
Level-3	Keygen	375,604	240,350	1.56	238,198	1.58
	Encaps	432,577	310,908	1.39	310,533	1.39
	Decaps	9,019,103	7,201,222	1.25	7,277,357	1.24

Table 5. Rotation performance, comparison of our impl. and the snippet of [13].

Level	$\|R\|$	Platform	Snippet of [13]	Fig. 2	Fig. 3	AVX512 Speedup	AVX512-VBMI Speedup
L1	11,779	EC2 server	128	105	–	1.21	–
L1	11,779	Ice-Lake	149	120	63.97	1.24	2.33
L3	24,821	EC2 server	250	205	–	1.22	–
L3	24,821	Ice-Lake	296	236	121.72	1.25	2.43
L5	40,597	EC2 server	404	329	–	1.23	–
L5	40,597	Ice-Lake	475	382	194.46	1.24	2.44

is either in performance (e. g., BGF with 6 iterations is $\frac{12}{8} = 1.5\times$ faster than BG with 4 iterations) or in implementation simplicity (e. g., the B decoder that does not involve gray steps).

A Comment on the Backflip Decoder. In [8] we compared Backflip with BG and showed that it requires a few more steps to achieve the same DFR (in the relevant range of r). We note that a Backflip iteration is practically equivalent to Step I of BG plus the Time-To-Live (TTL) handling. It is possible to improve the constant-time TTL handling with the bit-slicing techniques and reduce this gap. However, this would not change the DFR-efficiency properties reported here.

Further Optimizations. The performance of BIKE's constant-time implementation is dominated by three primitives: (a) polynomial multiplication (it remains a significant portion of the computations even after using the vector-PCLMULQDQ instructions); (b) polynomial rotation (that requires extensive memory access); (c) the rejection sampling (approximately 25% of the key generation). This paper showed how some of the new Ice-Lake features can already be used for performance improvement. Further optimizations are an interesting challenge.

Parameter Choice Recommendations for BIKE. BIKE-1 Level-1 (IND-CCA) [2] uses $r = 11,779$ with a target DFR of 2^{-128}, and uses the Backflip decoder. Our paper [8] shows some problems with this decoder and therefore recommends to use BG instead. It also shows that even if DFR $= 2^{-128}$ there is still a gap to be addressed, in order to claim IND-CCA security (roughly speaking - a bound on the number of weak keys). We set aside this gap for now and consider a non-weak key. If we limit the number of usages of this key to Q and choose r such that $Q \cdot DFR < 2^{-\mu}$ (for some target margin μ), then the probability that an adversary with at most Q queries sees a decoding failure is at most $2^{-\mu}$. We suggest that KEMs should use ephemeral keys (i. e., $Q = 1$) for forward secrecy, and this usage does not mandate IND-CCA security (IND-CPA suffices). Here, from the practical view-point, we only need to target a sufficiently small DFR such that decapsulation failures would be a significant operability impediment. However, an important property that *is* desired, even with ephemeral keys, is some guarantee that an inadvertent $1 \leq \alpha$ times key reuse (where α is presumably not too large) would not crash the security. This suggests the option for selecting r so that $\alpha \cdot DFR < 2^{-\mu}$. For example, taking $\mu = 32$ and $\alpha = 2^{32}$ (an extremely large number of "inadvertent" reuses), we can target a DFR of 2^{-64}. Using BGF with 5 iterations, we can use $r = 11,171$, which is smaller than $11,779$ that is currently used for BIKE.

Acknowledgments. We thank Ray Perlner from NIST for pointing out that the mock-bits technique is not sufficient for security when using static keys, which drove us to change our BIKE implementation. This research was partly supported by: The Israel Science Foundation (grant No. 3380/19); The BIU Center for Research in Applied Cryptography and Cyber Security, and the Center for Cyber Law and Policy at the University of Haifa, both in conjunction with the Israel National Cyber Bureau in the Prime Minister's Office.

A   Pseudo-Code for B, BG, BGB, BGF

A description of the B, BG, BGB, BGF decoders is given in Sect. 4. Algorithm 3 provides a formal definition of them.

Algorithm 3. e=decoder(D, c, H)

Input: D (decoder type one of {B, BG, BGB, BGF}), $H \in \mathbb{F}_2^{r \times n}$ (parity-check matrix), $c \in \mathbb{F}_2^n$ (ciphertext), X (maximal number of iterations)
Output: $e \in \mathbb{F}_2^n$ (errors vector)
Exception: A "decoding failure" returns $\perp$

```
 1: procedure DECODER(D, c, H)
 2:     s = Hc^T, e[n-1:0] = 0^n, δ = 3
 3:     for itr in 1...X do
 4:         th = computeThreshold(s)
 5:         (s, e, black, gray) = BitFlipIter(s, e, th, H)                    ▷ Step I
 6:         if (D ∈ {B, BG, BGB}) or (D = BGF and it = 1) then
 7:             (s, e) = BitFlipMaskedIter(s, e, black, ((d+1)/2), H)        ▷ Step II
 8:         if (D ∈ {BG, BGB, BGF} and itr = 1) then
 9:             (s, e) = BitFlipMaskedIter(s, e, gray, ((d+1)/2), H)         ▷ Step III
10:     if (wt(s) ≠ 0) then
11:         return ⊥
12:     else
13:         return e
```

B   Additional Information on the Experiments and Results

The following values of r were used by the *best linear fit* extrapolation method:

- BIKE-1 Level-1: 9349, 9547, 9749, 9803, 9859, 9883, 9901, 9907, 9923, 9941, 9949, 10037, 10067, 10069, 10091, 10093, 10099, 10133, 10139.

Table 6. The *best linear* and the *two points* extrapolation equations, and the estimated r values for three target DFRs. Level is abbreviated to Lvl, the number of iterations is abbreviated to iter, linear is abbreviated to lin., equation is abbreviated to eq. The Lin. start column indicates the index of the first value of r where the linear fit starts. The 5 column (number of steps) is the indication for the overall performance of the decoder (lower is better).

KEM	Lvl	Decoder	Iter	Steps	Lin. start	Best lin. fit eq. s.t $\log_{10}\text{DFR} = ar + b =$	2^{-23}	2^{-64}	2^{-128}	Two points line eq. (a,b) $\log_{10}\text{DFR} = ar + b =$	2^{-23}	2^{-64}	2^{-128}
BIKE-1	1	BG	3	9	15	(−1.27e−2, 124)	10,253	11,213	12,739	(−1.33e−2, 129)	10,253	11,171	12,619
BIKE-1	1	BG	4	12	8	(−1.45e−2, 140)	10,163	11,003	12,347	(−1.63e−2, 158)	10,163	10,909	12,107
BIKE-1	1	BG	5	15	13	(−1.61e−2, 156)	10,133	10,909	12,107	(−1.70e−2, 165)	10,133	10,853	11,987
BIKE-1	1	BGB	4	9	13	(−1.38e−2, 134)	10,253	11,093	12,491	(−1.40e−2, 136)	10,253	11,083	12,491
BIKE-1	1	BGB	5	11	13	(−1.52e−2, 147)	10,163	10,973	12,227	(−1.41e−2, 136)	10,163	11,027	12,413
BIKE-1	1	BGB	6	13	7	(−1.48e−2, 143)	10,133	10,973	12,269	(−1.54e−2, 149)	10,133	10,949	12,197
BIKE-1	1	BGF	5	7	14	(−1.40e−2, 137)	10,301	11,171	12,539	(−1.44e−2, 141)	10,301	11,131	12,491
BIKE-1	1	BGF	6	8	13	(−1.53e−2, 149)	10,253	11,027	12,277	(−1.61e−2, 157)	10,253	10,973	12,197
BIKE-1	1	BGF	7	9	13	(−1.61e−2, 157)	10,181	10,949	12,149	(−1.68e−2, 164)	10,181	10,949	12,107
BIKE-1	1	B	4	8	15	(−8.69e−3, 82.4)	10,259	11,699	13,901	(−8.05e−3, 75.8)	10,301	11,813	14,221
BIKE-1	1	B	5	10	15	(−1.02e−2, 96.3)	10,133	11,437	13,229	(−9.56e−3, 89.9)	10,133	11,437	13,451
BIKE-1	1	B	6	12	14	(−1.08e−2, 101)	10,067	11,213	13,037	(−9.52e−3, 88.8)	10,067	11,437	13,397

For Level-1 studies the number of tests for every value of r is $3.84M$ for $r \in [9349, 9901]$ and $384M$ for (larger) $r \in [9907, 10139]$. For the *line through two large points* extrapolation method (see [8][Appendix C] and Level-1, we chose: $r = 10141$ running $384M$ tests, and $r = 10259$ running ~ 7.3 (technically 7.296) billion tests (Table 6).

References

1. Intel®64 and IA-32 architectures software developer's manual. Combined volumes: 1, 2A, 2B, 2C, 2D, 3A, 3B, 3C, 3D, and 4, November 2019. http://www.intel.com/content/www/us/en/processors/architectures-software-developer-manuals.html
2. Aragon, N., et al.: BIKE: Bit Flipping Key Encapsulation (2017). https://bikesuite.org/files/round2/spec/BIKE-Spec-2019.06.30.1.pdf
3. Chou, T.: QcBits: constant-time small-key code-based cryptography. In: Gierlichs, B., Poschmann, A.Y. (eds.) Cryptographic Hardware and Embedded Systems - CHES 2016, pp. 280–300. Springer, Heidelberg (2016). https://doi.org/10.1007/978-3-662-53140-2_14
4. Drucker, N., Gueron, S.: Fast multiplication of binary polynomials with the forthcoming vectorized VPCLMULQDQ instruction. In: 2018 IEEE 25th Symposium on Computer Arithmetic (ARITH), June 2018
5. Drucker, N., Gueron, S.: A toolbox for software optimization of QC-MDPC code-based cryptosystems. J. Cryptographic Eng. **9**, 1–17 (2019). https://doi.org/10.1007/s13389-018-00200-4
6. Drucker, N., Gueron, S.: Fast CTR DRBG for x86 platforms, March 2019. https://github.com/aws-samples/ctr-drbg-with-vector-aes-ni
7. Drucker, N., Gueron, S., Dusan, K.: Additional implementation of BIKE (2019). https://bikesuite.org/additional.html
8. Drucker, N., Gueron, S., Kostic, D.: On constant-time QC-MDPC decoding with negligible failure rate. Technical report 2019/1289, November 2019. https://eprint.iacr.org/2019/1289
9. Drucker, N., Gueron, S., Krasnov, V.: Fast multiplication of binary polynomials with the forthcoming vectorized VPCLMULQDQ instruction. In: 2018 IEEE 25th Symposium on Computer Arithmetic (ARITH), pp. 115–119, June 2018. https://doi.org/10.1109/ARITH.2018.8464777
10. Drucker, N., Gueron, S., Krasnov, V.: Making AES great again: the forthcoming vectorized AES instruction. In: Latifi, S. (ed.) 16th International Conference on Information Technology-New Generations. (ITNG 2019), pp. 37–41. Springer, Cham (2019). https://doi.org/10.1007/978-3-030-14070-0_6
11. Eaton, E., Lequesne, M., Parent, A., Sendrier, N.: QC-MDPC: a timing attack and a CCA2 KEM. In: Lange, T., Steinwandt, R. (eds.) PQCrypto 2018. LNCS, vol. 10786, pp. 47–76. Springer, Cham (2018). https://doi.org/10.1007/978-3-319-79063-3_3
12. Gallager, R.: Low-density parity-check codes. IRE Trans. Inf. Theory **8**(1), 21–28 (1962). https://doi.org/10.1109/TIT.1962.1057683
13. Guimarães, A., Aranha, D.F., Borin, E.: Optimized implementation of QC-MDPC code-based cryptography **31**(18), e5089 (2019). https://onlinelibrary.wiley.com/doi/abs/10.1002/cpe.5089
14. Maurich, I.V., Oder, T., Güneysu, T.: Implementing QC-MDPC McEliece encryption. ACM Trans. Embed. Comput. Syst. **14**(3), 441–4427 (2015). https://doi.org/10.1145/2700102

15. NIST: Post-Quantum Cryptography (2019). https://csrc.nist.gov/projects/post-quantum-cryptography. Accessed 20 Aug 2019
16. Sendrier, N., Vasseur, V.: On the decoding failure rate of QC-MDPC bit-flipping decoders. In: Ding, J., Steinwandt, R. (eds.) PQCrypto 2019. LNCS, vol. 11505, pp. 404–416. Springer, Cham (2019). https://doi.org/10.1007/978-3-030-25510-7_22

Implementation

Isochronous Gaussian Sampling: From Inception to Implementation
With Applications to the **Falcon** Signature Scheme

James Howe[1], Thomas Prest[1], Thomas Ricosset[2], and Mélissa Rossi[2,3,4,5](✉)

[1] PQShield, Oxford, UK
{james.howe,thomas.prest}@pqshield.com
[2] Thales, Gennevilliers, France
thomas.ricosset@thalesgroup.com
[3] ANSSI, Paris, France
[4] École normale supérieure, CNRS, PSL University, Paris, France
melissa.rossi@ens.fr
[5] Inria, Paris, France

Abstract. Gaussian sampling over the integers is a crucial tool in lattice-based cryptography, but has proven over the recent years to be surprisingly challenging to perform in a generic, efficient and provable secure manner. In this work, we present a modular framework for generating discrete Gaussians with arbitrary center and standard deviation. Our framework is extremely simple, and it is precisely this simplicity that allowed us to make it easy to implement, provably secure, portable, efficient, and provably resistant against timing attacks. Our sampler is a good candidate for any trapdoor sampling and it is actually the one that has been recently implemented in the Falcon signature scheme. Our second contribution aims at systematizing the detection of implementation errors in Gaussian samplers. We provide a statistical testing suite for discrete Gaussians called SAGA (Statistically Acceptable GAussian). In a nutshell, our two contributions take a step towards trustable and robust Gaussian sampling real-world implementations.

Keywords: Lattice based cryptography · Gaussian sampling · Isochrony · Statistical verification tools

1 Introduction

Gaussian sampling over the integers is a central building block of lattice-based cryptography, in theory as well as in practice. It is also notoriously difficult to perform efficiently and securely, as illustrated by numerous side-channel attacks exploiting BLISS' Gaussian sampler [9,21,49,56]. For this reason, some schemes limit or proscribe the use of Gaussians [6,36]. However, in some situations, Gaussians are unavoidable. The most prominent example is trapdoor sampling [26,40,48]: performing it with other distributions is an open question, except in limited cases [37] which entail a growth $O(\sqrt{n})$ to $O(n)$ of the output, resulting in dwindling security levels. Given the countless applications of trapdoor sampling (full-domain hash signatures [26,53], identity-based encryption (or IBE) [18,26], hierarchical IBE [1,11], etc.), it is important to come up with Gaussian samplers over the integers which are not only efficient, but also provably secure, resistant to timing attacks, and in general easy to deploy.

Our first contribution is to propose a Gaussian sampler over the integers with all the properties which are expected of a sampler for widespread deployment. It is simple and modular, making analysis and subsequent improvements easy. It is efficient and portable, making it amenable to a variety of scenarios. Finally, we formally prove its security and resistance against timing attacks. We detail below different aspects of our sampler:

- **Simplicity and Modularity.** At a high level, our framework only requires two ingredients (a base sampler and a rejection sampler) and combines them in a simple and black-box way. Not only does it make the description of our sampler modular (as one can replace any of the ingredients), this simplicity and modularity also infuses all aspects of its analysis.
- **Genericity.** Our sampler is fully generic as it works with arbitrary center μ and standard deviation σ. In addition, it does not incur hidden precomputation costs: given a fixed base sampler of parameter $\sigma_{\max}$, our framework allows to sample from $D_{\mathbb{Z},\sigma,\mu}$ for any $\eta_\epsilon(\mathbb{Z}^n) \leq \sigma \leq \sigma_{\max}$. In comparison, [42] implicitly requires a different base sampler for each different value of σ; this limits its applicability for use cases such as Falcon [53], which has up to 2048 different σ's, all computed at key generation.
- **Efficiency and Portability.** Our sampler is instantiated with competitive parameters which make it very efficient in time and memory usage. For $\sigma_{\max} = 1.8205$ and SHAKE256 used as PRNG, our sampler uses only 512 bytes of memory and achieved 1,848,428 samples per second on an Intel i7-6500U clocked at 2.5 GHz. Moreover, our sampler can be instantiated in a way that uses only integer operations, making it highly portable.
- **Provable Security.** A security analysis based on the statistical distance would either provide very weak security guarantees or require to increase the running time by an order of magnitude. We instead rely on the Rényi divergence, a tool which in the recent years has allowed dramatic efficiency gains for lattice-based schemes [3,52]. We carefully selected our parameters as to make them as amenable to a Rényi divergence-based analysis.
- **Isochrony.** We formally show that our sampler is isochronous: its running time is independent of the inputs σ, μ and of the output z. Isochrony is weaker than being constant-time, but it nevertheless suffices to argue security against timing attacks. Interestingly, our proof of isochrony relies on techniques and notions that are common in lattice-based cryptography: the smoothing parameter, the Rényi divergence, etc. In particular, the isochrony of our sampler is implied by parameters dictated by the current state of the art for *black-box* security of lattice-based schemes.

One second contribution stems from a simple observation: implementations of otherwise perfectly secure schemes have failed in spectacular ways by introducing weaknesses, a common one being randomness failure: this is epitomized by nonce reuses in ECDSA, leading to jailbreaking Sony PS3 consoles[1] and exposing Bitcoin wallets [8]. The post-quantum community is aware of this point of failure but does not seem to have converged on a systematic way to mitigate it [46]. Randomness failures have been manually discovered and fixed in implementations of Dilithium [45], Falcon [47,51] and other schemes; the case of Falcon is particularly relevant to us because the sampler implemented was the one described in this document!

Our second contribution is a first step at systematically detecting such failures: we propose a statistical test suite called SAGA for validating discrete Gaussians. This test suite can check univariate samples; we therefore use it to validate our own implementation of our sampler. In addition, our test suite can check multivariate Gaussians as well; this enables validation at a higher level: if the base sampler over the integers is validated, but the output of the high-level scheme does not behave like a multivariate Gaussian even though the theory predicts it should, then this is indicative of an implementation mistake somewhere else in the implementation (or, at the worst case, that the theory is deficient). We illustrate that with a simple example of a (purportedly) deficient implementation of Falcon [53], however it can be used for any other scheme sampling multivariate discrete Gaussians, including but not limited to [5,12,18,25,40]. The test suite is publicly available at: https://github.com/PQShield/SAGA.

2   Related Works

In the recent years, there has been a surge of works related to Gaussian sampling over the integers. Building on convolution techniques from [42,50] proposed an arbitrary-center Gaussian sampler base, as well as a statistical tool (the max-log distance) to analyse it. [3,39,52] revisited classical techniques with the Rényi divergence. Polynomial-based methods were further studied by [4,52,60]. The use of rounded Gaussians was proposed in [31]. Knuth-Yao's DDG trees have been considered in [20,32].[2] Lazy floating-point precision was studied in [16,19]. We note that techniques dating back to von Neumann [57] allow to generate (continuous) Gaussians elegantly using finite automata [2,24,33]. While these have been considered in the context of lattice-based cryptography [15,17] they are also notoriously hard to make isochronous. Finally, [58] studied previously cited techniques with the goal of minimizing their relative error.

---

[1] https://media.ccc.de/v/27c3-4087-en-console_hacking_2010.

[2] We note that one could use [32] to speed up our base sampler; however this results in a huge code size (more than 50 kB). Since the running time of the base sampler was not a bottleneck for the usecase we considered, we instead relied on a straightforward, slightly less efficient CDT-based method.

3   Preliminaries

3.1   Gaussians

For $\sigma, \mu \in \mathbb{R}$ with $\sigma > 0$, we call Gaussian function of parameters σ, μ and denote by $\rho_{\sigma,\mu}$ the function defined over $\mathbb{R}$ as $\rho_{\sigma,\mu}(x) = \exp\left(-\frac{(x-\mu)^2}{2\sigma^2}\right)$. Note that when $\mu = 0$ we omit it in index notation, e.g. $\rho_\sigma(x) = \rho_{\sigma,0}(x)$. The parameter σ (resp. μ) is often called the standard deviation (resp. center) of the Gaussian. In addition, for any countable set $S \subsetneq \mathbb{R}$ we abusively denote by $\rho_{\sigma,\mu}(S)$ the sum $\sum_{z \in S} \rho_{\sigma,\mu}(z)$. When $\sum_{z \in S} \rho_{\sigma,\mu}(z)$ is finite, we denote by $D_{S,\sigma,\mu}$ and call Gaussian distribution of parameters σ, μ the distribution over S defined by $D_{S,\sigma,\mu}(z) = \rho_{\sigma,\mu}(z)/\rho_{\sigma,\mu}(S)$. Here too, when $\mu = 0$ we omit it in index notation, e.g. $D_{S,\sigma,\mu}(z) = D_{S,\sigma}(z)$. We use the notation $\mathcal{B}_p$ to denote the Bernoulli distribution of parameter p.

3.2   Renyi Divergence

We recall the definition of the Rényi divergence, which we will use massively in our security proofs.

Definition 1 (Rényi Divergence). *Let $\mathcal{P}, \mathcal{Q}$ be two distributions such that $Supp(\mathcal{P}) \subseteq Supp(\mathcal{Q})$. For $a \in (1, +\infty)$, we define the Rényi divergence of order a by*

$$R_a(\mathcal{P}, \mathcal{Q}) = \left(\sum_{x \in Supp(\mathcal{P})} \frac{\mathcal{P}(x)^a}{\mathcal{Q}(x)^{a-1}} \right)^{\frac{1}{a-1}} .$$

In addition, we define the Rényi divergence of order $+\infty$ by

$$R_\infty(\mathcal{P}, \mathcal{Q}) = \max_{x \in Supp(\mathcal{P})} \frac{\mathcal{P}(x)}{\mathcal{Q}(x)} .$$

The Rényi divergence is not a distance; for example, it is neither symmetric nor does it verify the triangle inequality, which makes it less convenient than the statistical distance. On the other hand, it does verify cryptographically useful properties, including a few listed below.

Lemma 1 ([3]). *For two distributions $\mathcal{P}, \mathcal{Q}$ and two families of distributions $(\mathcal{P}_i)_i, (\mathcal{Q}_i)_i$, the Rényi divergence verifies these properties:*

- **Data processing inequality.** *For any function f, $R_a(f(\mathcal{P}), f(\mathcal{Q})) \le R_a(\mathcal{P}, \mathcal{Q})$.*
- **Multiplicativity.** $R_a(\prod_i \mathcal{P}_i, \prod_i \mathcal{Q}_i) = \prod_i R_a(\mathcal{P}_i, \mathcal{Q}_i)$.
- **Probability preservation.** *For any event $E \subseteq Supp(\mathcal{Q})$ and $a \in (1, +\infty)$,*

$$\mathcal{Q}(E) \ge \mathcal{P}(E)^{\frac{a}{a-1}} / R_a(\mathcal{P}, \mathcal{Q}), \tag{1}$$
$$\mathcal{Q}(E) \ge \mathcal{P}(E) / R_\infty(\mathcal{P}, \mathcal{Q}). \tag{2}$$

The following lemma shows that a bound of δ on the relative error between two distributions implies a bound $O(a\delta^2)$ on the log of the Rényi divergence (as opposed to a bound $O(\delta)$ on the statistical distance).

Lemma 2 (Lemma 3 of [52]). *Let $\mathcal{P}, \mathcal{Q}$ be two distributions of same support Ω. Suppose that the relative error between $\mathcal{P}$ and $\mathcal{Q}$ is bounded: $\exists \delta > 0$ such that $\left|\frac{\mathcal{P}}{\mathcal{Q}} - 1\right| \leq \delta$ over Ω. Then, for $a \in (1, +\infty)$:*

$$R_a(\mathcal{P}, \mathcal{Q}) \leq \left(1 + \frac{a(a-1)\delta^2}{2(1-\delta)^{a+1}}\right)^{\frac{1}{a-1}} \underset{\delta \to 0}{\sim} 1 + \frac{a\delta^2}{2}$$

3.3 Smoothing Parameter

For $\epsilon > 0$, the smoothing parameter $\eta_\epsilon(\Lambda)$ of a lattice Λ is the smallest value $\sigma > 0$ such that $\rho_{\frac{1}{\sigma\sqrt{2\pi}}}(\Lambda^\star \backslash \{\mathbf{0}\}) \leq \epsilon$, where $\Lambda^\star$ denotes the dual of Λ. In the literature, some definitions of the smoothing parameter scale our definition by a factor $\sqrt{2\pi}$. It is shown in [41] that $\eta_\epsilon(\mathbb{Z}^n) \leq \eta_\epsilon^+(\mathbb{Z}^n)$, where:

$$\eta_\epsilon^+(\mathbb{Z}^n) = \frac{1}{\pi}\sqrt{\frac{1}{2}\log\left(2n\left(1 + \frac{1}{\epsilon}\right)\right)}. \tag{3}$$

3.4 Isochronous Algorithms

We now give a semi-formal definition of isochronous algorithms.

Definition 2. *Let $\mathcal{A}$ be a (probabilistic or deterministic) algorithm with set of input variables $\mathcal{I}$, set of output variables $\mathcal{O}$, and let $\mathcal{S} \subseteq \mathcal{I} \cup \mathcal{O}$ be the set of sensitive variables. We say that $\mathcal{A}$ is perfectly isochronous with respect to $\mathcal{S}$ if its running time is independent of any variable in $\mathcal{S}$.*

In addition, we say that $\mathcal{A}$ statistically isochronous with respect to $\mathcal{S}$ if there exists a distribution $\mathcal{D}$ independent of all the variables in $\mathcal{S}$, such that the running time of $\mathcal{A}$ is statistically close (for a clearly identified divergence) to $\mathcal{D}$.

We note that we can define a notion of computationally isochronous algorithm. For such an algorithm, it is computationally it hard to recover the sensitive variables even given the distribution of the running time of the algorithm. We can even come up with a contrived example of such an algorithm: let $\mathcal{A}()$ select in an isochronous manner an x uniformly in a space of min-entropy $\geq \lambda$, compute $y = H(x)$ and wait a time y before outputting x. One can show that recovering x given the running time of $\mathcal{A}$ is hard if H is a one-way function.

4 The Sampler

In this section, we describe our new sampler with arbitrary standard deviation and center. The main assumption of our setting is to consider that all

Algorithm 1. SamplerZ(σ, μ)
Require: $\mu \in [0,1]$, $\sigma \leq \sigma_{\max}$
Ensure: $z \sim D_{\mathbb{Z},\sigma,\mu}$
1: **while** True **do**
2:    $z_0 \leftarrow$ BaseSampler()
3:    $b \leftarrow \{0,1\}$ uniformly
4:    $z := (2b - 1) \cdot z_0 + b$
5:    $x := \frac{z_0^2}{2\sigma_{\max}^2} - \frac{(z-\mu)^2}{2\sigma^2}$
6:    **if** AcceptSample(σ, x) **then**
7:        **return** z

Algorithm 2. AcceptSample(σ, x)
Require: $\sigma_{\min} \leq \sigma \leq \sigma_{\max}, x < 0$
Ensure: $b \sim \mathcal{B}_{\frac{\sigma_{\min}}{\sigma} \cdot \exp(x)}$
1: $p := \frac{\sigma_{\min}}{\sigma} \cdot$ ApproxExp(x)
Lazy Bernoulli sampling
2: $i := 1$
3: **do**
4:    $i := i \cdot 2^8$
5:    $u \leftarrow [\![0, 2^8 - 1]\!]$ uniformly
6:    $v := \lfloor p \cdot i \rfloor$ & 0xff
7: **while** $u = v$
8: **return** $(u < v)$

the standard deviations are bounded and that the center is in $[0,1]$. In other words, denoting the upper bound and lower bound on the standard deviation as $\sigma_{\max} > \sigma_{\min} > 0$, we present an algorithm that samples the distribution $D_{\mathbb{Z},\sigma,\mu}$ for any $\mu \in [0,1]$ and $\sigma_{\min} \leq \sigma \leq \sigma_{\max}$.

Our sampling algorithm is called SamplerZ and is described in Algorithm 1. We denote by BaseSampler an algorithm that samples an element with the fixed half Gaussian distribution $D_{\mathbb{Z}^+,\sigma_{\max}}$. The first step consists in using BaseSampler. The obtained z_0 sample is then transformed into $z := (2b - 1) \cdot z_0 + b$ where b is a bit drawn uniformly in $\{0,1\}$. Let us denote by $BG_{\sigma_{\max}}$ the distribution of z. The distribution of z is a discrete bimodal half-Gaussian of centers 0 and 1. More formally,

$$BG_{\sigma_{\max}}(z) = \frac{1}{2} \begin{cases} D_{\mathbb{Z}^+,\sigma_{\max}}(-z) & \text{if } z \leq 0 \\ D_{\mathbb{Z}^+,\sigma_{\max}}(z - 1) & \text{if } z \geq 1. \end{cases} \tag{4}$$

Then, to recover the desired distribution $D_{\mathbb{Z},\sigma,\mu}$ for the inputs (σ, μ), one might want to apply the classical rejection sampling technique applied to lattice based schemes [35] and accept z with probability

$$\frac{D_{\mathbb{Z},\sigma,\mu}(z)}{BG_{\sigma_{\max}}(z)} = \begin{cases} \exp\left(\frac{z^2}{2\sigma_{\max}^2} - \frac{(z-\mu)^2}{2\sigma^2}\right) & \text{if } z \leq 0 \\ \exp\left(\frac{(z-1)^2}{2\sigma_{\max}^2} - \frac{(z-\mu)^2}{2\sigma^2}\right) & \text{if } z \geq 1 \end{cases}$$

$$= \exp\left(\frac{z_0^2}{2\sigma_{\max}^2} - \frac{(z-\mu)^2}{2\sigma^2}\right).$$

The element inside the exp is computed in step 5. Next, we also introduce an algorithm denoted AcceptSample. The latter performs the rejection sampling (Algorithm 2): using ApproxExp an algorithm that returns $\exp(\cdot)$, it returns a Bernoulli sample with the according probability. Actually, for isochrony matters, detailed in Sect. 6, the latter acceptance probability is rescaled by a factor $\frac{\sigma_{\min}}{\sigma}$. As z follows the $BG_{\sigma_{\max}}$ distribution, after the rejection sampling, the final distribution of SamplerZ(σ, μ) is then proportional to $\frac{\sigma_{\min}}{\sigma} \cdot D_{\mathbb{Z},\sigma,\mu}$ which is, after

Table 1. Number of calls to SamplerZ, BaseSampler and ApproxExp

	Notation	Value for Falcon
Calls to sign (as per NIST)	Q_{s}	$\leq 2^{64}$
Calls to SamplerZ	Q_{samplZ}	$Q_{\mathrm{s}} \cdot 2 \cdot n \leq 2^{75}$
Calls to BaseSampler	Q_{bs}	$\mathcal{N}_{\mathrm{iter}} \cdot Q_{\mathrm{samplZ}} \leq 2^{76}$
Calls to ApproxExp	Q_{exp}	$Q_{\mathrm{bs}} \leq 2^{76}$

normalization exactly equal to $D_{\mathbb{Z},\sigma,\mu}$. Thus, with this construction, one can derive the following proposition.

Proposition 1 (Correctness). *Assume that all the uniform distributions are perfect and that* BaseSampler $= D_{\mathbb{Z}^+,\sigma_{\max}}$ *and* ApproxExp $= \exp$, *then the construction of* SamplerZ *(in Algorithms 1 and 2) is such that* SamplerZ$(\sigma,\mu) = D_{\mathbb{Z},\sigma,\mu}$.

In practical implementations, one cannot achieve perfect distributions. Only achieving BaseSampler $\approx D_{\mathbb{Z}^+,\sigma_{\max}}$ and ApproxExp $\approx \exp$ is possible. Section 6 proves that, under certain conditions on BaseSampler and ApproxExp and on the number of sampling queries, the final distribution remains indistinguishable from $D_{\mathbb{Z},\sigma,\mu}$.

5 Proof of Security

Table 1 gives the notations for the number of calls to SamplerZ, BaseSampler and ApproxExp and the considered values when the sampler is instanciated for Falcon. Due to the rejection sampling in step 6, there will be a (potentially infinite) number of iterations of the **while** loop. We will show later in Lemma 3, that the number of iterations follows a geometric law of parameter $\approx \frac{\sigma_{\min} \cdot \sqrt{2\pi}}{2 \cdot \rho_{\sigma_{\max}}(\mathbb{Z}^+)}$. We note $\mathcal{N}_{\mathrm{iter}}$ a heuristic considered maximum number of iterations. By a central limit argument, $\mathcal{N}_{\mathrm{iter}}$ will only be marginally higher than the expected number of iterations. To instantiate the values $Q_{\mathrm{exp}} = Q_{\mathrm{bs}} = \mathcal{N}_{\mathrm{iter}} \cdot Q_{\mathrm{samplZ}}$ for the example of Falcon, we take $\mathcal{N}_{\mathrm{iter}} = 2$. In fact, $\frac{\sigma_{\min} \cdot \sqrt{2\pi}}{2 \cdot \rho_{\sigma_{\max}}(\mathbb{Z}^+)} \leq 2$ for Falcon's parameters.

The following Theorem estimates the security of SamplerZ, it is independant of the chosen values for the number of calls.

Theorem 1 (Security of SamplerZ). *Let λ_{IDEAL} (resp. λ_{REAL}) be the security parameter of an implementation using the perfect distribution $D_{\mathbb{Z},\sigma,\mu}$ (resp. the real distribution* SamplerZ*). If both following conditions are respected, at most two bits of security are lost. In other words, $\Delta\lambda := \lambda_{\mathrm{IDEAL}} - \lambda_{\mathrm{REAL}} \leq 2$.*

$$\forall x < 0, \quad \left| \frac{\mathsf{ApproxExp}(x) - \exp(x)}{\exp(x)} \right| \leq \sqrt{\frac{2 \cdot \lambda_{\mathrm{REAL}}}{2 \cdot (2 \cdot \lambda_{\mathrm{REAL}} + 1)^2 \cdot Q_{\mathrm{exp}}}} \qquad \text{(Cond. (1))}$$

$$R_{2 \cdot \lambda_{\mathrm{REAL}} + 1}\left(\mathsf{BaseSampler}, D_{\mathbb{Z}^+,\sigma_{\max}}\right) \leq 1 + \frac{1}{4 \cdot Q_{\mathrm{bs}}} \qquad \text{(Cond. (2))}$$

The proof of this Theorem is given in the full version of our paper [30].

To get concrete numerical values, we assume that 256 bits are claimed on the original scheme, thus 254 bits of security are claimed for the real implementation. Then for an implementation of Falcon, the numerical values are

$$\sqrt{\frac{2 \cdot \lambda_{\text{REAL}}}{2 \cdot (2 \cdot \lambda_{\text{REAL}} + 1)^2 \cdot Q_{\exp}}} \approx 2^{-43} \quad \text{and} \quad \frac{1}{4 \cdot Q_{\text{bs}}} \approx 2^{-78}.$$

5.1 Instanciating the ApproxExp

To achieve condition (1) with ApproxExp, we use a polynomial approximation of the exponential on $[-\ln(2), 0]$. In fact, one can reduce the parameter x modulo $\ln(2)$ such that $x = -r - s\ln(2)$. Compute the exponential remains to compute $\exp(x) = 2^{-s} \exp(-r)$. Noting that $s \geq 64$ happen very rarely, thus s can be saturated at 63 to avoid overflow without loss in precision.

We use the polynomial approximation tool provided in GALACTICS [4]. This tool generates polynomial approximations that allow a computation in fixed precision with chosen size of coefficients and degree. As an example, for 32-bit coefficients and a degree 10, we obtain a polynomial $P_{\text{gal}}(x) := \sum_{i=0}^{10} a_i \cdot x^i$, with:

- $a_0 = 1$;
- $a_1 = 1$;
- $a_2 = 2^{-1}$;
- $a_3 = 2863311530 \cdot 2^{-34}$;
- $a_4 = 2863311481 \cdot 2^{-36}$;
- $a_5 = 2290647631 \cdot 2^{-38}$;

- $a_6 = 3054141714 \cdot 2^{-41}$;
- $a_7 = 3489252544 \cdot 2^{-44}$;
- $a_8 = 3473028713 \cdot 2^{-47}$;
- $a_9 = 2952269371 \cdot 2^{-50}$;
- $a_{10} = 3466184740 \cdot 2^{-54}$.

For any $x \in [-\ln(2), 0]$, P_{gal} verifies $\left| \frac{P_{\text{gal}}(x) - \exp(x)}{\exp(x)} \right| \leq 2^{-47}$, which is sufficient to verify condition (1) for Falcon implementation.

Flexibility on the Implementation of the Polynomial. Depending on the platform and the requirement for the signature, one can adapt the polynomial to fit their constraints. For example, if one wants to minimize the number of multiplications, implementing the polynomial with Horner's form is the best option. The polynomial is written in the following form:

$$P_{\text{gal}}(x) = a_0 + x(a_1 + x(a_2 + x(a_3 + x(a_4 + x(a_5 + x(a_6 + x(a_7 + x(a_8 + x(a_9 + xa_{10}))))))))).$$

Evaluating P_{gal} is then done serially as follows:

$$y \leftarrow a_{10}$$
$$y \leftarrow a_9 + y \times x$$
$$\vdots$$
$$y \leftarrow a_1 + y \times x$$
$$y \leftarrow a_0 + y \times x$$

Some architectures with small register sizes may be faster if the size of the coefficients of the polynomial is minimized, thus GALACTICS tool can be used to generate a polynomial with smaller coefficients. For example, we propose an alternative polynomial approximation on $[0, \frac{ln(2)}{64}]$ with 25 bits coefficients.

$$P = 1 + x + 2^{-1}x^2 + 699051 \cdot 2^{-22} \cdot x^3 + 699299 \cdot 2^{-24} \cdot x^4 + 605552 \cdot 2^{-26} \cdot x^5$$

To recover the polynomial approximation on $[0, ln(2)]$, we compute $P(\frac{x}{64})^{64}$.

Some architectures enjoy some level of parallelism, in which case it is desirable to minimise the depth of the circuit computing the polynomial[3]. Writing P_{gal} in Estrin's form [22] is helpful in this regard.

$$
\begin{aligned}
x_2 \quad &\leftarrow x \times x \\
x_4 \quad &\leftarrow x_2 \times x_2 \\
P_{\text{gal}}(x) \leftarrow &(x_4 \times x_4) \times ((a_8 + a_9 \times x) + x_2 \times a_{10}) \\
+ &(((a_0 + a_1 \times x) + x_2 \times (a_2 + a_3 \times x)) + x_4 \times ((a_4 + a_5 \times x) + x_2 \times (a_6 + a_7 \times x)))
\end{aligned}
$$

5.2 Instanciating the BaseSampler

To achieve condition (2) with BaseSampler, we rely on a cumulative distribution table (CDT). We precompute a table of the cumulative distribution function of $D_{\mathbb{Z}^+,\sigma_{\max}}$ with a certain precision; then, to produce a sample, we generate a random value in $[0, 1]$ with the same precision, and return the index of the last entry in the table that is greater than that value. In variable time, the sampling can be done rather efficiently with a binary search, but a constant-time implementation has essentially no choice but to read the entire table each time and carry out each comparison. This process is summed up in Algorithm 3. The parameters w and θ are respectively the number of elements of the CDT and the precision of its coefficients. Let $a = 2 \cdot \lambda_{\text{REAL}} + 1$. To derive the parameters w and θ we use a simple script that, given $\sigma_{\max}$ and θ as inputs:

1. Computes the smallest tailcut w such that the Renyi divergence R_a between the ideal distribution $D_{\mathbb{Z}^+,\sigma_{\max}}$ and its restriction to $\{0, \ldots, w\}$ (noted $D_{[w],\sigma_{\max}}$) verifies $R_a(D_{[w],\sigma_{\max}}, D_{\mathbb{Z}^+,\sigma_{\max}}) \leq 1 + 1/(4Q_{\text{bs}})$;
2. Rounds the probability density table (PDT) of $D_{[w],\sigma_{\max}}$ with θ bits of absolute precision. This rounding is done "cleverly" by truncating all the PDT values except the largest:
   - for $z \geq 1$, the value $D_{[w],\sigma_{\max}}(z)$ is truncated: $PDT(z) = 2^{-\theta} \lfloor 2^\theta D_{[w],\sigma_{\max}}(z) \rfloor$.
   - in order to have a probability distribution, $PDT(0) = 1 - \sum_{z \geq 1} PDT(z)$.
3. Derives the CDT from the PDT and computes the final $R_a(\text{SampleCDT}_{w=19,\theta=72}, D_{\mathbb{Z}^+,\sigma_{\max}})$.

---

[3] We are thankful to Thomas Pornin for bringing up this fact.

Algorithm 3. SampleCDT: full-table access CDT

$z \leftarrow 0$
$u \leftarrow [0,1)$ uniformly with θ bits of absolute precision
for $0 \leq i \leq w$ **do**
    $b \leftarrow (\text{CDT}[w] \geq u)$ $\triangleright$ $b = 1$ if it is true and 0 otherwise
    $z \leftarrow z + b$
return z

Taking $\sigma_{\max} = 1.8205$ and $\theta = 72$ as inputs, we found $w = 19$.

- $\circ$ PDT(0) $= 2^{-72} \times 1697680241746640300030$
- $\circ$ PDT(1) $= 2^{-72} \times 1459943456642912959616$
- $\circ$ PDT(2) $= 2^{-72} \times 928488355018011056515$
- $\circ$ PDT(3) $= 2^{-72} \times 436693944817054414619$
- $\circ$ PDT(4) $= 2^{-72} \times 151893140790369201013$
- $\circ$ PDT(5) $= 2^{-72} \times 39071441848292237840$
- $\circ$ PDT(6) $= 2^{-72} \times 7432604049020375675$
- $\circ$ PDT(7) $= 2^{-72} \times 1045641569992574730$
- $\circ$ PDT(8) $= 2^{-72} \times 108788995549429682$
- $\circ$ PDT(9) $= 2^{-72} \times 8370422445201343$
- $\circ$ PDT(10) $= 2^{-72} \times 476288472308334$
- $\circ$ PDT(11) $= 2^{-72} \times 20042553305308$
- $\circ$ PDT(12) $= 2^{-72} \times 623729532807$
- $\circ$ PDT(13) $= 2^{-72} \times 14354889437$
- $\circ$ PDT(14) $= 2^{-72} \times 244322621$
- $\circ$ PDT(15) $= 2^{-72} \times 3075302$
- $\circ$ PDT(16) $= 2^{-72} \times 28626$
- $\circ$ PDT(17) $= 2^{-72} \times 197$
- $\circ$ PDT(18) $= 2^{-72} \times 1$

Our experiment showed that for any $a \geq 509$, $R_a(\text{SampleCDT}_{w=19,\theta=72}, D_{\mathbb{Z}^+,\sigma_{\max}}) \leq 1 + 2^{-80} \leq 1 + \frac{1}{4Q_{\mathrm{bs}}}$, which validates condition (2) for Falcon implementation.

6   Analysis of Resistance Against Timing Attacks

In this section, we show that Algorithm 1 is impervious against timing attacks. We formally prove that it is isochronous with respect to σ, μ and the output z (in the sense of Definition 2). We first prove a technical lemma which shows that the number of iterations in the **while** loop of Algorithm 1 is (almost) independent of σ, μ, z.

Lemma 3. *Let $\epsilon \in (0,1)$, $\mu \in [0,1]$ and let $\sigma_{\min}, \sigma, \sigma_0$ be standard deviations such that $\eta_\epsilon^+(\mathbb{Z}^n) = \sigma_{\min} \leq \sigma \leq \sigma_0$. Let $p = \frac{\sigma_{\min} \cdot \sqrt{2\pi}}{2 \cdot \rho_{\sigma_{\max}}(\mathbb{Z}^+)}$. The number of iterations of the **while** loop in SamplerZ(σ, μ) follows a geometric law of parameter*

$$P_{\mathbf{true}}(\sigma, \mu) \in p \cdot \left[1, 1 + \frac{(1 + 2^{-80})\epsilon}{n}\right].$$

The proof of Lemma 3 can be found in the full version of our paper [30].

Next, we show that Algorithm 1 is perfectly isochronous with respect to z and statistically isochronous (for the Rényi divergence) with respect to σ, μ.

Theorem 2. *Let $\epsilon \in (0,1)$, $\mu \in \mathbb{R}$, let $\sigma_{\min}, \sigma, \sigma_0$ be standard deviations such that $\eta_\epsilon^+(\mathbb{Z}^n) = \sigma_{\min} \leq \sigma \leq \sigma_0$, and let $p = \frac{\sigma_{\min} \cdot \sqrt{2\pi}}{2 \cdot \rho_{\sigma_{\max}}(\mathbb{Z}^+)}$ be a constant in $(0,1)$.*

Suppose that the elementary operations $\{+, -, \times, /\}$ over integer and floating-point numbers are isochronous. The running time of Algorithm 1 follows a distribution $T_{\sigma,\mu}$ such that:

$$R_a(T_{\sigma,\mu}\|T) \lesssim 1 + \frac{a\epsilon^2 \max(1, \frac{1-p}{p})^2}{n^2(1-p)} = 1 + O\left(\frac{a\epsilon^2}{n^2}\right)$$

for some distribution T independent of its inputs σ, μ and its output z.

Finally, we leverage Theorem 2 to prove that the running time of SamplerZ(σ, μ) does not help an adversary to break a cryptographic scheme. We consider that the adversary has access to some function $g(\text{SamplerZ}(\sigma, \mu))$ as well as the running time of SamplerZ(σ, μ): this is intended to capture the fact that in practice the output of SamplerZ(σ, μ) is not given directly to the adversary, but processed by some function before. For example, in the signature scheme Falcon, samples are processed by algorithms depending on the signer's private key. On the other hand, we consider that the adversary has powerful timing attack capabilities by allowing him to learn the exact runtime of each call to SamplerZ(σ, μ).

Corollary 1. *Consider an adversary $\mathcal{A}$ making Q_s queries to $g(\text{SamplerZ}(\sigma, \mu))$ for some randomized function g, and solving a search problem with success probability $2^{-\lambda}$ for some $\lambda \geq 1$. With the notations of Theorem 2, suppose that $\max(1, \frac{1-p}{p})^2 \leq n(1-p)$ and $\epsilon \leq \frac{1}{\sqrt{\lambda Q_s}}$. Learning the running time of each call to SamplerZ(σ, μ) does not increase the success probability of $\mathcal{A}$ by more than a constant factor.*

The proof of Corollary 1 can be found in the full version of our paper [30]. A nice thing about Corollary 1 is that the conditions required to make it effective are *already met in practice* since they are also required for black-box security of cryptographic schemes. For example, it is systematic to set $\sigma \geq \eta_\epsilon^+(\mathbb{Z}^n)$.

Impact of the Scaling Factor. The scaling factor $\frac{\sigma_{\min}}{\sigma} \leq \frac{\sigma_{\min}}{\sigma_{\max}}$ is crucial in making our sampler isochronous, as it decorrelates the running time $T_{\sigma,\mu}$ from σ. However, it also impacts the $T_{\sigma,\mu}$, as one can easily show that $T_{\sigma,\mu}$ is proportional to the scaling factor. It is therefore desirable to make it as small as possible. The maximal value of the scaling factor is actually dependent on the cryptographic scheme in which our sampler is used. In the full version of our paper [30], we show that for the case of the signature scheme Falcon, $\frac{\sigma_{\min}}{\sigma_{\max}} \leq 1.17^{-2} \approx 0.73$ and the impact of the scaling factor is limited. Moreover, one can easily show that for Peikert's sampler [48], the scaling factor is equal to 1 and has no impact.

7 "Err on the Side of Gaussian"

This section focuses on ensuring correct and verified implementations of our proposed isochronous Gaussian sampler. The motivation for this section is to minimize implementation bugs, such as implementation issues with Falcon [47,51] or the famous Heartbleed (CVE-2014-0160) or ROCA vulnerabilities [44] (CVE-2017-15361). We propose a test suite named SAGA (Statistically Acceptable GAussians) in order to verify correct univariate or multivariate Gaussian variables. At the very least, SAGA can act as a "sanity check" for implementers and practitioners. Furthermore, SAGA is designed to run in a generic fashion, agnostic to the technique used, by only requiring as input a list of univariate (i.e., outputs of SamplerZ) or multivariate (i.e. a set of signatures) Gaussian samples. Although we evaluate SAGA by applying it to Falcon, SAGA is applicable to any lattice-based cryptographic scheme requiring Gaussian sampling, such as other GPV-based signatures [5,12], FrodoKEM [43], identity-based encryption [10,18], and in fully homomorphic encryption [54].

7.1 Univariate Tests

The statistical tests we implement here are inspired by a previous test suite proposal called GLITCH [29]. We use standard statistical tools to validate a Gaussian sampler is operating with the correct mean, standard deviation, skewness, and kurtosis, and finally we check whether it passes a chi-square normality test. Skewness and kurtosis are descriptors of a normal distribution that respectively measure the symmetry and peakedness of a distribution. To view the full statistical analysis of these tests we created a Python class, UnivariateSamples, which take as initialization arguments the expected mean (mu), expected standard deviation (sigma), and the list of observed univariate Gaussian samples (data). An example of how this works, as well as its output, is shown in the full version of our paper [30].

7.2 Multivariate Tests

This section details multivariate normality tests. The motivation for these tests is to detect situations where the base Gaussian sampler over the integers is correctly implemented, yet the high-level scheme (e.g. a signature scheme) uses it incorrectly way and ends up with a defective multivariate Gaussian.

Multivariate Normality. There are a number of statistical tests which evaluate the normality of multivariate distributions. We found that multivariate normality tests predominantly used in other fields [13,28,38] suffer with size and scaling issues. That is, the large sample sizes we expect to use and the poor power properties of these tests will make a type II error highly likely[4]. In fact, we implemented the Mardia [38] and Henze-Zirkler [28] tests and found, although they worked for small sample sizes, they diverged to produce false negatives for sample sizes ≥ 50 even in small dimensions $n = 64$.

However, the Doornik-Hansen test [14] minimises these issues by using transformed versions of the skewness and kurtosis of the multivariate data, increasing

---

[4] Type I and type II errors are, respectively, rejection of a true null hypothesis and the non-rejection of a false null hypothesis.

the test's power. We also note that it is much faster (essentially linear in the sample size) than [28, 38] (essentially quadratic in the sample size). As with the univariate tests, we created a Python class, denoted `MultivariateSamples`, which outputs four results; two based on the covariance matrix, and two based on the data's normality. An example of how this works, as well as its output, is shown in the full version of our paper [30].

A Glitch in the (Covariance) Matrix. Our second multivariate test asks the following question: *how could someone implement correctly the base sampler, yet subsequently fail to use it properly?* There is no universal answer to that, and one usually has to rely on context, experience and common sense to establish the most likely way this could happen.

For example, in Falcon, univariate samples are linearly combined according to node values of a balanced binary tree computed at key generation (the Falcon tree). If there is an implementation mistake in the procedure computing the tree (during key generation) or when combining the samples (during signing), this effectively results in nodes of the Falcon tree being incorrect or omitted. Such mistakes have a very recognizable effect on the empiric covariance matrix of Falcon signatures: they make them look like block Toeplitz matrices (Fig. 1a) instead of (scaled) identity matrices in the nominal case (Fig. 1b).

We devised a test which discriminates block Toeplitz covariance matrices against the ones expected from spherical Gaussians. The key idea is rather simple: when adding $O(n)$ coefficients over a (block-)subdiagonal of the empiric covariance matrix, the absolute value of the sum will grow in $O(\sqrt{n})$ if the empiric covariance matrix converges to a scaled identity matrix, and in $O(n)$ if it is block Toeplitz. We use this difference in growth to detect defective Gaussians. While we do not provide a formal proof of our test, in practice it detects reasonably well Gaussians induced by defective Falcon trees. We see proving our test and providing analogues for other GPV-based schemes as interesting questions.

Supplementary Tests. In the case where normality has been rejected, SAGA also provides a number of extra tests to aid in finding the issues. More details for this can be found in the full version of our paper [30].

8   Application and Limitations

Our sampler has been implemented by Pornin as part of the new isochronous implementation of Falcon [51]. This implementation can use floating-point hardware or AVX2 instructions when available, but also includes floating-point emulation code that uses only usual integer operations. On ARM Cortex M4 CPUs, which can only support single-precision floating-point instructions, this implementation provides assembly implementations for the core double-precision floating-point operations more than twice faster than the generic emulation. As a result, our sampler can be efficiently implemented on embedded platforms as

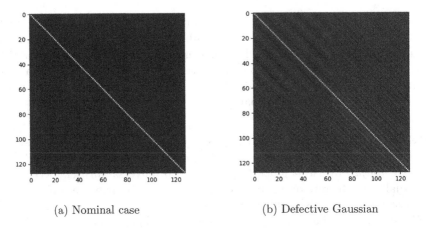

(a) Nominal case   (b) Defective Gaussian

Fig. 1. Empiric covariance matrices of Falcon signatures. Figure 1a corresponds to a correct implementation of Falcon. Figure 1b corresponds to an implementation where there is a mistake when constructing the Falcon tree.

Table 2. Number of samples per second at 2.5 GHz for our sampler and [59].

Algorithm	Number of samples
This work[a]	1.84×10^6/sec
This work (AVX2)[b]	7.74×10^6/sec
[59] (AVX2)[c]	5.43×10^6/sec

[a][51] standard double-precision floating-point (IEEE 754) with SHAKE256.
[b][51] AVX2 implementation with eight ChaCha20 instances in parallel (AVX2).
[c][59] constant-time implementation with hardware AES256 (AES-NI).

limited as Cortex M4 CPUs, while some other samplers (e.g. [32] due to a huge code size) are not compact enough to fit embedded platforms.

We perform benchmarks of this sampler implementation on a single Intel Core i7-6500U CPU core clocked at 2.5 GHz. In Table 2 we present the running times of our isochronous sampler. To compare with [59], we scale the numbers to be based on 2.5 GHz. Note that for our sampler the number of samples per second is on average for $1.2915 < \sigma \leq 1.8502$ while for [59] $\sigma = 2$ is fixed.

In Table 3 we present the running times of the Falcon isochronous implementation [51] that contains our sampler and compare it with a second non-isochronous implementation nearly identical excepting the base sampler which is a faster lazy CDT sampler, and the rejection sampling which is not scaled by a constant. Compared to the non-isochronous implementation, the isochronous one is about 22% slower, but remains very competitive speed-wise.

Table 3. Falcon signature generation time at 2.5 GHz.

Degree	Non-isochronous (using AVX2)	isochronous (using AVX2)
512	210.88 μs (153.64 μs)	257.33 μs (180.04 μs)
1024	418.76 μs (311.33 μs)	515.28 μs (361.39 μs)

Cache-Timing Protection. Following this implementation of the proposed sampler also ensures cache-timing protection [23], as the design *should*[5] bypass conditional branches by using a consistant access pattern (using linear searching of the table) and have isochronous runtime. This has been shown to be sufficient in implementations of Gaussian samplers in Frodo [7,43].

Adapting to Other Schemes. A natural question is how our algorithms could be adapted for other schemes than Falcon, for example [5,12,18,25,40]. An obvious bottleneck seems to be the size of the CDT used in SampleCDT, which is linear in the standard deviation. For larger standard deviations, where linear searching becomes impractical, convolutions can be used to reduce σ, and thus the runtime of the search algorithm [34,50]. It would also be interesting to see if the DDG tree-based method of [32] has better scalability than our CDT-based method, in which case we would recommend it for larger standard deviations. On the other hand, once the base sampler is implemented, we do not see any obvious obstacle for implementing our whole framework. For example, [12] or using Peikert's sampler [48] (in Falcon) entail a small constant number of standard deviations, therefore the rejection step would be very efficient once a base sampler for each standard deviation is implemented.

Advantages and Limitations. Our sampler has an acceptance rate $\approx \frac{\sigma_{\min}}{\sigma_{\max}+0.4}$ making it especially suitable when $\sigma_{\min}$ and $\sigma_{\max}$ are close. In particular, our sampler is, so far, the fastest isochronous sampler for the parameters in Falcon. However, the larger the gap between $\sigma_{\min}$ and $\sigma_{\max}$, the lower the acceptance rate. In addition, our sampler uses a cummulative distribution table (CDT) which is accessed in an isochronous way. This table grows when $\sigma_{\max}$ grows, while making both running time and memory usage larger. When $\sigma_{\max}$ is large or far from $\sigma_{\min}$, there exist faster isochronous samplers based on convolution [42] and rejection sampling [59][6] techniques.

Acknowledgements. We thank Léo Ducas for helpful suggestions. We also thank Thomas Pornin and Mehdi Tibouchi for useful discussions. The first and second authors were supported by the project PQ Cybersecurity (Innovate UK research grant 104423). The third and fourth authors were supported by BPI-France in the context of the national project RISQ (P141580), and by the European Union PROMETHEUS project (Horizon 2020 Research and Innovation Program, grant 780701). The fourth author was also supported by ANRT under the program CIFRE N2016/1583.

---

[5] Compilers may alter the design, thus one should always verify the design post-compilation.

[6] The constant-time sampler in [59] may still reveal σ.

References

1. Agrawal, S., Boneh, D., Boyen, X.: Efficient lattice (H)IBE in the standard model. In: Gilbert, H. (ed.) EUROCRYPT 2010. LNCS, vol. 6110, pp. 553–572. Springer, Heidelberg (2010). https://doi.org/10.1007/978-3-642-13190-5_28
2. Ahrens, J., Dieter, U.: Extension of Forsythe's method for random sampling from the normal distribution. Math. Comput. **27**, 927–937 (1973)
3. Bai, S., Langlois, A., Lepoint, T., Stehlé, D., Steinfeld, R.: Improved security proofs in lattice-based cryptography: using the Rényi divergence rather than the statistical distance. In: Iwata, T., Cheon, J.H. (eds.) ASIACRYPT 2015, vol. 9452. LNCS, pp. 3–24. Springer, Heidelberg (2015). https://doi.org/10.1007/978-3-662-48797-6_1
4. Barthe, G., Belaïd, S., Espitau, T., Fouque, P.A., Rossi, M., Tibouchi, M.: GALACTICS: Gaussian sampling for lattice-based constant-time implementation of cryptographic signatures, revisited. Cryptology ePrint Archive, Report 2019/511 (2019)
5. Bert, P., Fouque, P.-A., Roux-Langlois, A., Sabt, M.: Practical implementation of ring-SIS/LWE based signature and IBE. In: Lange, T., Steinwandt, R. (eds.) Post-Quantum Cryptography - 9th International Conference. PQCrypto 2018, pp. 271–291. Springer, Heidelberg (2018)
6. Bindel, N., et al.: qTESLA. Technical report, National Institute of Standards and Technology (2019). https://csrc.nist.gov/projects/post-quantum-cryptography/round-2-submissions
7. Bos, J.W., et al.: Frodo: take off the ring! Practical, quantum-secure key exchange from LWE. In: Weippl, E.R., Katzenbeisser, S., Kruegel, C., Myers, A.C., Halevi, S. (eds.) ACM CCS 2016, pp. 1006–1018. ACM Press, October 2016
8. Breitner, J., Heninger, N.: Biased nonce sense: lattice attacks against weak ECDSA signatures in cryptocurrencies. In: Goldberg, I., Moore, T. (eds.) FC 2019. LNCS, vol. 11598, pp. 3–20. Springer, Cham (2019). https://doi.org/10.1007/978-3-030-32101-7_1
9. Groot Bruinderink, L., Hülsing, A., Lange, T., Yarom, Y.: Flush, gauss, and reload – a cache attack on the BLISS lattice-based signature scheme. In: Gierlichs, B., Poschmann, A.Y. (eds.) CHES 2016. LNCS, vol. 9813, pp. 323–345. Springer, Heidelberg (2016). https://doi.org/10.1007/978-3-662-53140-2_16
10. Campbell, P., Groves, M.: Practical post-quantum hierarchical identity-based encryption. In: 16th IMA International Conference on Cryptography and Coding (2017)
11. Cash, D., Hofheinz, D., Kiltz, E., Peikert, C.: Bonsai trees, or how to delegate a lattice basis. In: Gilbert, H. (ed.) EUROCRYPT 2010. LNCS, vol. 6110, pp. 523–552. Springer, Heidelberg (2010). https://doi.org/10.1007/978-3-642-13190-5_27
12. Chen, Y., Genise, N., Mukherjee, P.: Approximate trapdoors for lattices and smaller hash-and-sign signatures. In: Galbraith, S.D., Moriai, S. (eds.) ASIACRYPT 2019. LNCS, vol. 11923, pp. 3–32. Springer, Cham (2019). https://doi.org/10.1007/978-3-030-34618-8_1
13. Cox, D.R., Small, N.J.H.: Testing multivariate normality. Biometrika **65**(2), 263–272 (1978)
14. Doornik, J.A., Hansen, H.: An omnibus test for univariate and multivariate normality. Oxford Bull. Econ. Stat. **70**, 927–939 (2008)
15. Yusong, D., Wei, B., Zhang, H.: A rejection sampling algorithm for off-centered discrete Gaussian distributions over the integers. Sci. China Inf. Sci. **62**(3), 39103 (2018)

16. Ducas, L.: Signatures fondées sur les réseaux euclidiens: attaques, analyses et optimisations. Theses, École Normale Supérieure (2013)
17. Ducas, L., Durmus, A., Lepoint, T., Lyubashevsky, V.: Lattice signatures and bimodal Gaussians. In: Canetti, R., Garay, J.A. (eds.) CRYPTO 2013. LNCS, vol. 8042, pp. 40–56. Springer, Heidelberg (2013). https://doi.org/10.1007/978-3-642-40041-4_3
18. Ducas, L., Lyubashevsky, V., Prest, T.: Efficient identity-based encryption over NTRU lattices. In: Sarkar, P., Iwata, T. (eds.) ASIACRYPT 2014. LNCS, vol. 8874, pp. 22–41. Springer, Heidelberg (2014). https://doi.org/10.1007/978-3-662-45608-8_2
19. Ducas, L., Nguyen, P.Q.: Faster Gaussian lattice sampling using lazy floating-point arithmetic. In: Wang, X., Sako, K. (eds.) ASIACRYPT 2012. LNCS, vol. 7658, pp. 415–432. Springer, Heidelberg (2012). https://doi.org/10.1007/978-3-642-34961-4_26
20. Dwarakanath, N.C., Galbraith, S.D.: Sampling from discrete Gaussians for lattice-based cryptography on a constrained device. Appl. Algebra Eng. Commun. Comput. 25(3), 159–180 (2014)
21. Espitau, T., Fouque, P.A., Gérard, B., Tibouchi, M.: Side-channel attacks on BLISS lattice-based signatures: exploiting branch tracing against strongSwan and electromagnetic emanations in microcontrollers. In: Thuraisingham et al. [56], pp. 1857–1874 (2017)
22. Estrin, G.: Organization of computer systems: the fixed plus variable structure computer. In: Western Joint IRE-AIEE-ACM Computer Conference, IRE-AIEE-ACM 1960 (Western), 3–5 May 1960, pp. 33–40. ACM, New York (1960)
23. Facon, A., Guilley, S., Lec'Hvien, M., Schaub, A., Souissi, Y.: Detecting cache-timing vulnerabilities in post-quantum cryptography algorithms. In: 2018 IEEE 3rd International Verification and Security Workshop (IVSW), pp. 7–12. IEEE (2018)
24. Forsythe, G.E.: Von Neumann's comparison method for random sampling from the normal and other distributions. Math. Comput. 26(120), 817–826 (1972)
25. Genise, N., Micciancio, D.: Faster Gaussian sampling for trapdoor lattices with arbitrary modulus. In: Nielsen, J.B., Rijmen, V. (eds.) EUROCRYPT 2018. LNCS, vol. 10820, pp. 174–203. Springer, Cham (2018). https://doi.org/10.1007/978-3-319-78381-9_7
26. Gentry, C., Peikert, C., Vaikuntanathan, V.: Trapdoors for hard lattices and new cryptographic constructions. In: Ladner, R.E., Dwork, C. (eds.) 40th ACM STOC, pp. 197–206. ACM Press, May 2008
27. Gilbert, H. (ed.): EUROCRYPT 2010. LNCS, vol. 6110. Springer, Heidelberg (2010). https://doi.org/10.1007/978-3-642-13190-5
28. Henze, N., Zirkler, B.: A class of invariant consistent tests for multivariate normality. Commun. Stat.-Theory Methods 19(10), 3595–3617 (1990)
29. Howe, J., O'Neill, M.: GLITCH: a discrete gaussian testing suite for lattice-based cryptography. In: Proceedings of the 14th International Joint Conference on e-Business and Telecommunications (ICETE 2017), SECRYPT, Madrid, Spain, 24–26 July 2017, vol. 4, pp. 413–419 (2017)
30. Howe, J., Prest, T., Ricosset, T., Rossi, M.: Isochronous Gaussian sampling: From inception to implementation. Cryptology ePrint Archive, Report 2019/1411 (2019)
31. Hülsing, A., Lange, T., Smeets, K.: Rounded Gaussians - fast and secure constant-time sampling for lattice-based crypto. In: Abdalla, M., Dahab, R. (eds.) PKC 2018. LNCS, vol. 10770, pp. 728–757. Springer, Heidelberg (2018)

32. Karmakar, A., Roy, S.S., Vercauteren, F., Verbauwhede, I.: Pushing the speed limit of constant-time discrete Gaussian sampling. A case study on the Falcon signature scheme. In: Proceedings of the 56th Annual Design Automation Conference, pp. 1–6 (2019)
33. Karney, C.F.F.: Sampling exactly from the normal distribution. ACM Trans. Math. Softw. **42**(1), 3:1–3:14 (2016)
34. Khalid, A., Howe, J., Rafferty, C., Regazzoni, F., O'Neill, M.: Compact, scalable, and efficient discrete Gaussian samplers for lattice-based cryptography. In: 2018 IEEE International Symposium on Circuits and Systems (ISCAS), pp. 1–5. IEEE (2018)
35. Lyubashevsky, V.: Fiat-Shamir with aborts: applications to lattice and factoring-based signatures. In: Matsui, M. (ed.) ASIACRYPT 2009. LNCS, vol. 5912, pp. 598–616. Springer, Heidelberg (2009). https://doi.org/10.1007/978-3-642-10366-7_35
36. Lyubashevsky, V., et al.: Crystals-dilithium. Technical report, National Institute of Standards and Technology (2019). https://csrc.nist.gov/projects/post-quantum-cryptography/round-2-submissions
37. Lyubashevsky, V., Wichs, D.: Simple lattice trapdoor sampling from a broad class of distributions. In: Katz, J. (ed.) PKC 2015. LNCS, vol. 9020, pp. 716–730. Springer, Heidelberg (2015). https://doi.org/10.1007/978-3-662-46447-2_32
38. Mardia, K.V.: Measures of multivariate skewness and kurtosis with applications. Biometrika **57**(3), 519–530 (1970)
39. Melchor, C.A., Ricosset, T.: CDT-based Gaussian sampling: from multi to double precision. IEEE Trans. Comput. **67**(11), 1610–1621 (2018)
40. Micciancio, D., Peikert, C.: Trapdoors for lattices: simpler, tighter, faster, smaller. In: Pointcheval, D., Johansson, T. (eds.) EUROCRYPT 2012. LNCS, vol. 7237, pp. 700–718. Springer, Heidelberg (2012). https://doi.org/10.1007/978-3-642-29011-4_41
41. Micciancio, D., Regev, O.: Worst-case to average-case reductions based on Gaussian measures. SIAM J. Comput. **37**(1), 267–302 (2007)
42. Micciancio, D., Walter, M.: Gaussian sampling over the integers: efficient, generic, constant-time. In: Katz, J., Shacham, H. (eds.) CRYPTO 2017. LNCS, vol. 10402, pp. 455–485. Springer, Cham (2017). https://doi.org/10.1007/978-3-319-63715-0_16
43. Naehrig, M., et al.: FrodoKEM. Technical report, National Institute of Standards and Technology (2019). https://csrc.nist.gov/projects/post-quantum-cryptography/round-2-submissions
44. Nemec, M., Sý, M., Svenda, P., Klinec, D., Matyas, V.: The return of coppersmith's attack: practical factorization of widely used RSA moduli. In: Thuraisingham et al. [56], pp. 1631–1648 (2017)
45. NIST et al.: Official Comment: Crystals-dilithium (2018). https://groups.google.com/a/list.nist.gov/d/msg/pqc-forum/aWxC2ynJDLE/YOsMJ2ewAAAJ
46. NIST et al.: Footguns as an axis for security analysis (2019). https://groups.google.com/a/list.nist.gov/forum/#!topic/pqc-forum/l2iYk-8sGnI. Accessed 23 Oct 2019
47. NIST et al.: Official Comment: Falcon (bug & fixes) (2019). https://groups.google.com/a/list.nist.gov/forum/#!topic/pqc-forum/7Z8x5AMXy8s. Accessed 23 Oct 2019
48. Peikert, C.: An efficient and parallel Gaussian sampler for lattices. In: Rabin, T. (ed.) CRYPTO 2010. LNCS, vol. 6223, pp. 80–97. Springer, Heidelberg (2010). https://doi.org/10.1007/978-3-642-14623-7_5

49. Pessl, P., Bruinderink, L.G., Yarom, Y.: To BLISS-B or not to be: attacking strongSwan's implementation of post-quantum signatures. In: Thuraisingham et al. [56], pp. 1843–1855 (2017)

50. Pöppelmann, T., Ducas, L., Güneysu, T.: Enhanced lattice-based signatures on reconfigurable hardware. In: Batina, L., Robshaw, M. (eds.) CHES 2014. LNCS, vol. 8731, pp. 353–370. Springer, Heidelberg (2014). https://doi.org/10.1007/978-3-662-44709-3_20

51. Pornin, T.: New Efficient, Constant-Time Implementations of Falcon. Cryptology ePrint Archive, Report 2019/893 (2019)

52. Prest, T.: Sharper bounds in lattice-based cryptography using the Rényi divergence. In: Takagi, T., Peyrin, T. (eds.) ASIACRYPT 2017. LNCS, vol. 10624, pp. 347–374. Springer, Cham (2017). https://doi.org/10.1007/978-3-319-70694-8_13

53. Prest, T., et al.: FALCON. Technical report, National Institute of Standards and Technology (2019). https://csrc.nist.gov/projects/post-quantum-cryptography/round-2-submissions

54. Microsoft SEAL (release 3.4), October 2019. Microsoft Research, Redmond, WA. https://github.com/Microsoft/SEAL

55. Thuraisingham, B.M., Evans, D., Malkin, T., Dongyan, X. (eds.): ACM CCS 2017. ACM Press, New York (2017)

56. Tibouchi, M., Wallet, A.: One bit is all it takes: a devastating timing attack on BLISS's non-constant time sign flips. In: MathCrypt 2019 (2019)

57. von Neumann, J.: Various techniques used in connection with random digits. Natl. Bureau Standards Appl. Math Ser. **12**, 36–38 (1950)

58. Walter, M.: Sampling the integers with low relative error. In: Buchmann, J., Nitaj, A., Rachidi, T. (eds.) AFRICACRYPT 2019. LNCS, vol. 11627, pp. 157–180. Springer, Cham (2019). https://doi.org/10.1007/978-3-030-23696-0_9

59. Zhao, R.K., Steinfeld, R., Sakzad, A.: Compact and scalable arbitrary-centered discrete Gaussian sampling over integers. Cryptology ePrint Archive, Report 2019/1011 (2019)

60. Zhao, R.K., Steinfeld, R., Sakzad, A.: Facct: fast, compact, and constant-time discrete Gaussian sampler over integers. IEEE Trans. Comput. (2019)

Benchmarking Post-quantum Cryptography in TLS

Christian Paquin[1], Douglas Stebila[2]([✉]), and Goutam Tamvada[2]

[1] Microsoft Research, Redmond, USA
cpaquin@microsoft.com
[2] University of Waterloo, Waterloo, Canada
dstebila@uwaterloo.ca, gtamvada@edu.uwaterloo.ca

Abstract. Post-quantum cryptographic primitives have a range of trade-offs compared to traditional public key algorithms, either having slower computation or larger public keys and ciphertexts/signatures, or both. While the performance of these algorithms in isolation is easy to measure and has been a focus of optimization techniques, performance in realistic network conditions has been less studied. Google and Cloudflare have reported results from running experiments with post-quantum key exchange algorithms in the Transport Layer Security (TLS) protocol with real users' network traffic. Such experiments are highly realistic, but cannot be replicated without access to Internet-scale infrastructure, and do not allow for isolating the effect of individual network characteristics.

In this work, we develop and make use of a framework for running such experiments in TLS cheaply by *emulating* network conditions using the networking features of the Linux kernel. Our testbed allows us to independently control variables such as link latency and packet loss rate, and then examine the performance impact of various post-quantum-primitives on TLS connection establishment, specifically hybrid elliptic curve/post-quantum key exchange and post-quantum digital signatures, based on implementations from the Open Quantum Safe project. Among our key results, we observe that packet loss rates above 3–5% start to have a significant impact on post-quantum algorithms that fragment across many packets, such as those based on unstructured lattices. The results from this emulation framework are also complemented by results on the latency of loading entire web pages over TLS in real network conditions, which show that network latency hides most of the impact from algorithms with slower computations (such as supersingular isogenies).

Keywords: Post-quantum key exchange · Post-quantum authentication · Transport Layer Security (TLS) · Network performance · Emulation

1 Introduction

Compared to traditional public key algorithms, post-quantum key encapsulation mechanisms (KEMs) and digital signature schemes have a range of

© Springer Nature Switzerland AG 2020
J. Ding and J.-P. Tillich (Eds.): PQCrypto 2020, LNCS 12100, pp. 72–91, 2020.
https://doi.org/10.1007/978-3-030-44223-1_5

trade-offs, either having slower computation, or larger public keys and cipher-texts/signatures, or both. Measuring the performance of these algorithms in isolation is easy; doing so accurately in the broader context of Internet proto-cols such as the Transport Layer Security (TLS) protocol, and under realistic network traffic conditions, is more difficult.

Alongside the development and standardization of post-quantum algorithms in the NIST Post-Quantum Cryptography Standardization project, there have been various efforts to begin preparing the TLS ecosystem for post-quantum cryptography. We can see at least three major lines of work: (draft) specifica-tions of how post-quantum algorithms could be integrated into existing proto-col formats and message flows [9,17,33,34,37,41]; prototype implementations demonstrating such integrations can be done [6–8,15,19,20,30,31] and whether they would meet existing constraints in protocols and software [10]; and per-formance evaluations in either basic laboratory network settings [6,7] or more realistic network settings [8,15,19,21,22]. This paper focuses on the last of these issues, trying to understand how post-quantum cryptography's slower computa-tion and larger communication sizes impact the performance of TLS.

A line of work starting with initial experiments by Google [8,21], with follow-up collaborations between Google, Cloudflare, and others [19,22], has involved Internet companies running experiments to measure the performance of real con-nections using post-quantum key exchange (combined with traditional elliptic curve Diffie–Hellman, resulting in so-called "hybrid" key exchange), by modi-fying client browsers and edge servers to support select hybrid key exchange schemes in TLS 1.3. Such experiments are highly realistic, but cannot be repli-cated without access to commensurate infrastructure, and do not allow for iso-lating the effect of individual network characteristics: it is neither possible to precisely quantify the effect of just a change in (say) packet loss on a network route on the latency of TLS connection establishment, nor is it possible to (say) increase just the packet loss on a route and analyze the resulting effects.

Contributions. In this paper, we develop an experimental framework for mea-suring the performance of the TLS protocol under a variety of network condi-tions. Our framework is inspired by the NetMirage [40] and Mininet [23] network emulation software, and uses the Linux kernel's networking stack to precisely and independently tune characteristics such as link latency and packet loss rate. This allows for emulation of client–server network experiments on a single machine.

Using this framework, we analyze the impact that post-quantum cryptog-raphy has on TLS 1.3 handshake completion time (i.e., until application data can be sent), specifically in the context of hybrid post-quantum key exchange using structured and unstructured lattices and supersingular isogenies; and post-quantum authentication using structured lattices and symmetric-based signa-tures. Our emulated experiments are run at 4 different latencies (emulating round-trip times between real-world data centres), and at packet loss rates rang-ing from 0–20%.

Some of our key observations from the network emulation experiments mea-suring TLS handshake completion time are as follows. For the median connection, handshake completion time is significantly impacted by substantially slower algorithms (for example, supersingular isogenies (SIKE p434) has a significant performance floor compared to the faster structured and unstructured lattice algorithms), although this effect disappears at the 95th percentile. For algorithms with larger messages that result in fragmentation across multiple packets, performance degrades as packet loss rate increases: for example, median connection time for unstructured lattice key exchange (Frodo-640-AES) matches structured lattice performance at 5–10% packet loss, then begins to degrade; at the 95th percentile, this effect is less pronounced until around 15% packet loss. We see similar trends for post-quantum digital signatures, although with degraded performance for larger schemes starting around 3–5% packet loss since a TLS connection includes multiple public keys and signatures in certificates.

We also carry out experiments across real networks, measuring page load time over TLS using geographically scattered virtual machines communication over the Internet. From these, we observe that, as page size or network latency increases, the overhead of slower TLS connection establishment diminishes as a proportion of the overall page load time.

Our key exchange results complement those of Google, Cloudflare, and others [19,22]: they provide a holistic look at how post-quantum key exchange algorithms perform for users on real network connections of whatever characteristic the users happened to have, whereas our results show the independent effect of each network characteristic, and our techniques can be applied without access to commensurate Internet-scale client and edge server infrastructure.

Closely related to our post-quantum signature experiments are the recent works [15,36] on the performance of post-quantum signatures in TLS 1.3. They measure how handshake time varies with server distance (measured in number of hops) and how handshake time and failure rate varies with throughput. Our experiments complement theirs by measuring the impact of other network characteristics: connection latency and packet loss rates.

Organization. In Sect. 2, we describe how we integrated post-quantum algorithms into TLS. Section 3 describes the network emulation framework, and Sect. 4 describes the setup for our two experiments (emulated; and over the real Internet, data-centre-to-data-centre). Section 5 presents and discusses results from the two experiments. Section 6 concludes. Additional data appears in the appendix. Code and complete result data for all the experiments can be found at our GitHub repository: https://github.com/xvzcf/pq-tls-benchmark.

2   Post-quantum Cryptography in TLS

There have been a variety of proposed specifications, implementations, and experiments involving post-quantum cryptography in TLS 1.2 and TLS 1.3.

In the context of TLS 1.2, Schanck, Whyte, and Zhang [34] and Campagna and Crockett [9] submitted Internet-Drafts to the Internet Engineering Task Force (IETF) with proposals for adding post-quantum and hybrid key exchange to TLS 1.2; implementations of these drafts (or ad hoc specifications) in TLS

1.2 include experiments by Google [8] and Amazon [1], in research papers [6,7], as well as the Open Quantum Safe project's OQS-OpenSSL 1.0.2 [30,38].

For hybrid and post-quantum key exchange in TLS 1.3, there have been Internet-Drafts by Kiefer and Kwiatowski [17], Whyte et al. [41], Schanck and Stebila [33], and Stebila et al. [37]. Experimental demonstrations include earlier experiments by Google [20,22], more recent experiments by a team involving Cloudflare, Google, and others [19], as well as the Open Quantum Safe project's OQS-OpenSSL 1.1.1 [10,31], a fork of OpenSSL 1.1.1. There has also been some work on experiments involving post-quantum and hybrid authentication in TLS 1.3, including OQS-OpenSSL 1.1.1 [31] and experiments based on it [15,36].

The experiments in this paper are based on the implementation of hybrid key exchange and post-quantum authentication in TLS 1.3 in OQS-OpenSSL 1.1.1. We now describe the mechanisms used in this particular instantiation of post-quantum cryptography in TLS 1.3. For a broader discussion of design choices and issues in engineering post-quantum cryptography in TLS 1.3, see [37].

2.1 Hybrid Key Exchange in TLS 1.3

Our experiments focused on hybrid key exchange, based on the perspective that early adopters of post-quantum cryptography may want post-quantum long-term forward secrecy while still using ECDH key exchange either because of a lack of confidence in newer post-quantum assumptions, or due to regulatory compliance.

The primary way to negotiate an ephemeral key in TLS 1.3 [32] is to use elliptic-curve Diffie-Hellman (ECDH). To do so, a client, in its `ClientHello` message, can send a `supported_groups` extension that names its supported elliptic curve groups; the client can then also provide corresponding `keyshares`, which are the public cryptographic values used to initiate key exchange. By defining new "groups" for each post-quantum and hybrid method, this framework can also be used in a straightforward manner to support the use of post-quantum key-exchange algorithms. Mapping these on to key encapsulation mechanisms, the client uses a KEM ephemeral public key as its `keyshare`, and the server encapsulates against the public key and sends the corresponding ciphertext as its `keyshare`. Despite performing ephemeral key exchange, we only use the IND-CCA versions of the post-quantum KEMs[1].

In the instantiation of hybrid methods in OQS-OpenSSL 1.1.1, the number of algorithms combined are restricted to two at a time, and a "group" identifier is assigned to each such pair; as a result, combinations are negotiated together, rather than individually. Moreover, in such a hybrid method, the public keys and ciphertexts for the hybrid scheme are simply concatenations of the elliptic curve and post-quantum algorithms' values in the `keyshare` provided by the

---

[1] It may be possible that IND-CPA KEMs suffice for ephemeral key exchange, but this is an open question. Proofs of Diffie–Hellman key exchange in TLS 1.2 [13,18] showed that security against active attacks is required; existing proofs of TLS 1.3 [11] also use an "active" Diffie–Hellman assumption, but whether an active assumption is necessary has not yet been resolved.

`ClientHello` and `ServerHello` messages. For computing the shared secret, individual shared secrets are concatenated and used in place of the ECDH shared secret in the TLS 1.3 key schedule. As OpenSSL does not have a generic KEM or key exchange API in its `libcrypto` component, the modified OpenSSL implementation primarily involves changes in OpenSSL's `ssl` directory, and calls into OpenSSL's `libcrypto` for the ECDH algorithms and into the Open Quantum Safe project's `liboqs` for the post-quantum KEMs.

2.2 Post-quantum Authentication in TLS 1.3

Our experiments focused on post-quantum-only authentication, rather than hybrid authentication. We made this choice because, with respect to authenticating connection establishment, the argument for a hybrid mode is less clear: authentication only needs to be secure at the time a connection is established (rather than for the lifetime of the data as with confidentiality). Moreover, in TLS 1.3 there is no need for a server to have a hybrid certificate that can be used with both post-quantum-aware and non-post-quantum aware clients, as algorithm negotiation will be complete before the server needs to send its certificate.

In TLS 1.3, public key authentication is done via signatures, and public keys are usually conveyed via `X.509` certificates. There are two relevant negotiation mechanisms in TLS 1.3: the `signature_algorithms_cert` extension which is used to negotiate which algorithms are supported for signatures in certificates; and the `signature_algorithms` extension for which algorithms are supported in the protocol itself. Both of these extensions are a list of algorithm identifiers [32].

In the instantiation in OQS-OpenSSL 1.1.1, new algorithm identifiers are added for each post-quantum signature algorithm to be used, and the algorithms themselves are added to OpenSSL's generic "envelope public key" object (`EVP_PKEY`) in `libcrypto`, which then percolate upwards to the X.509 certificate generation and management and TLS authentication, with relatively few changes required at these higher levels.

3   The Network Emulation Framework

To carry out experiments with full control over network characteristics, we rely on features available in Linux to implement a network emulation framework.

The Linux kernel provides the ability to create *network namespaces* [3], which are independent, isolated copies of the kernel's network stack; each namespace has its own routes, network addresses, firewall rules, ports, and network devices. Network namespaces can thus emulate separate network participants on a single system.

Two namespaces can be linked using pairs of *virtual ethernet* (`veth`) devices [4]: `veth` devices are always created in interconnected pairs, and packets transmitted on one device are immediately received on the other device in the pair.

Table 1. Key exchange algorithm communication size and runtime

Algorithm	Public key (bytes)	Ciphertext (bytes)	Key gen. (ms)	Encaps. (ms)	Decaps. (ms)
ECDH NIST P-256	64	64	0.072	0.072	0.072
SIKE p434	330	346	13.763	22.120	23.734
Kyber512-90s	800	736	0.007	0.009	0.006
FrodoKEM-640-AES	9,616	9,720	1.929	1.048	1.064

Table 2. Signature scheme communication size and runtime

Algorithm	Public key (bytes)	Signature (bytes)	Sign (ms)	Verify (ms)
ECDSA NIST P-256	64	64	0.031	0.096
Dilithium2	1,184	2,044	0.050	0.036
qTESLA-P-I	14,880	2,592	1.055	0.312
Picnic-L1-FS	33	34,036	3.429	2.584

Outgoing traffic on these virtual devices can be controlled by the network emulation (**netem**) kernel module [24], which offers the ability to instruct the kernel to apply, among other characteristics, a delay, an independent or correlated packet loss probability, and a rate-limit to all outgoing packets from the device.

To give the link a minimum round trip time of x ms, **netem** can be used to instruct the kernel to apply on both **veth** devices a delay of $\frac{x}{2}$ ms to each outgoing packet. Similarly, to give the link a desired packet loss rate $y\%$, **netem** can instruct the kernel to drop on both devices outgoing packets with (independent or correlated) probability $y\%$. While **netem** can be used to specify other traffic characteristics, such as network jitter or packet duplication, we consider varying the round-trip time and packet loss probability to be sufficient to model a wide variety of network conditions. If the round-trip time on a link connecting a server and client conveys the geographical distance between them, then, for example, a low packet loss can model a high-quality and/or wired ethernet connection. Moderate to high packet losses can model low-quality connections or congested networks, such as when the server experiences heavy traffic, or when a client connects to a website using a heavily loaded WiFi network.

Tools such as NetMirage [40] and Mininet [23] offer the ability to emulate larger, more sophisticated, and more realistic networks where, for example, namespaces can serve as autonomous systems (AS) that group clients, and packets can be routed within an AS or between two ASes. We carried out our experiments over a single link (client–server topology) with direct control over network characteristics using **netem** to enable us to isolate the effect of individual network characteristics on the performance of post-quantum cryptography in TLS 1.3.

4   Experimental Setup

In this section we describe the two experimental setups employed – the emulated network experiment, and the Internet data-centre-to-data-centre experiment.

Table 3. Key exchange and signature algorithms used in our experiments

Notation	Hybrid	Family	Variant	Implementation
Key exchange				
ecdh-p256	✗	Elliptic-curve	NIST P-256	OpenSSL optimized
ecdh-p256-sike-p434	✓	Supersingular isogeny	SIKE p434 [14]	Assembly optimized
ecdh-p256-kyber512_90s	✓	Module LWE	Kyber 90s level 1 [35]	AVX2 optimized
ecdh-p256-frodo640aes	✓	Plain LWE	Frodo-640-AES [27]	C with AES-NI
Signatures				
ecdsa-p256	✗	Elliptic curve	NIST P-256	OpenSSL optimized
dilithium2	✗	Module LWE/SIS	Dilithium2 [25]	AVX2 optimized
qtesla-p-i	✗	Ring LWE/SIS	qTESLA provable 1 [5]	AVX2 optimized
picnic-l1-fs	✗	Symmetric	Picnic-L1-FS [42]	AVX2 optimized

4.1 Cryptographic Scenarios

We consider the two cryptographic scenarios in TLS 1.3: hybrid key exchange and post-quantum authentication. Table 3 shows the four key exchange algorithms and four signature algorithms used in our experiments[2]. Their integration into TLS 1.3 was as described in Sect. 2. We used liboqs for the implementations of the post-quantum algorithms; liboqs takes its implementations directly from teams' submissions to NIST or via the PQClean project [16]. Tables 1 and 2 show public key/ciphertext/signature size and raw performance on the machine used in our network emulation experiments.

For the key exchange scenario, the rest of the algorithms in the TLS connection were as follows: server-to-client authentication was performed using an ECDSA certificate over the NIST P-256 curve using the SHA-384 hash function. For the signature scenario, key exchange was using ecdh-p256-kyber512_90s; the hash function used was SHA-384. In both cases, application data was protected using AES-256 in Galois/counter mode, and the certificate chain was root → server, all of which were using the same algorithms.

4.2 Emulated Network Experiment Setup

The goal of the emulated network experiments was to measure the time elapsed until completion of the TLS handshake under various network conditions.

Following the procedure in Sect. 3, we created two network namespaces and connected them using a veth pair, one namespace representing a client, and the other a server. In the client namespace, we ran a modified version of OpenSSL's

---

[2] Our Internet data-centre-to-data-centre experiment actually included all Level 1 algorithms supported by liboqs (additionally bike1l1cpa, newhope512cca, ntru_hps2048509, lightsaber, and picnic2l1fs) and additionally hybrid authentication with RSA-3072. The network emulation experiments take much longer to run than the Internet experiments, so we did not have time to collect corresponding network emulation results. For parity, in this paper we only present the results obtained using the same algorithms as in the network emulation experiment. The additional data collected can be found on our GitHub repository.

s_time program, which measures TLS performance by making, in a given time period, as many synchronous (TCP) connections as it could to a remote host using TLS; our modified version (which we've called s_timer), for a given number of repetitions, synchronously establishes a TLS connection using a given post-quantum algorithm, closes the connection as soon as the handshake is complete, and records only the time taken to complete the handshake. In the server namespace, we ran the nginx [28] web server, built against OQS-OpenSSL 1.1.1 so that it is post-quantum aware.

We chose 4 round-trip times to model the geographical distance to servers at different locations: the values were chosen to be similar to the round-trip times in the Internet data-centre network experiment (see Sect. 4.3), but are not exactly the same, partly because netem internally converts a given latency to an integral number of kernel packet scheduler "ticks", which results in a slight (and negligible) accuracy loss. For each round-trip time, the packet loss probability was varied from 0% to 20% (the probability applies to each packet independently). For context, telemetry collected by Mozilla on dropped packets in Firefox (nightly 71) in September and October 2019, indicate that, on desktop computers, packet loss rates above 5% are rare: for example, in the distribution of WEBRTC_AUDIO_QUALITY_OUTBOUND_PACKETLOSS_RATE, 67% of the 35.5 million samples collected had packet loss less than 0.1%, 89% had packet loss less than 1%, 95% had packet loss less than 4.3%, and 97% had packet loss less than 20% [26].

Finally, for each combination of round-trip time and packet loss rate, and for each algorithm under test, 40 independent s_timer "client" processes were run, each making repeated synchronous connections to 21 nginx worker processes, each of which was instructed to handle 1024 connections[3].

The experiments were run on a Linux (Ubuntu 18.04) Azure D64s v3 virtual machine, which has 64 vCPUs (2.60 GHz Intel Xeon Platinum 8171M, bursting to 3.7 GHz) and 256 GiB of RAM, in order to give each process its "own" core so as to minimize noise from CPU process scheduling and make the client and server processes as independent of each other as possible.

4.3   Internet Data-Centre-To-Data-Centre Experiment Setup

The emulated network experiment concerned itself only with handshake times. In practice, the latency of establishing TLS might not be noticeable when compared to the latency of retrieving application data over the connection. Accordingly, we conducted a set of experiments that involved a client cloud VM requesting web pages of different sizes from various server VMs over the Internet, and measured the total time to receive the complete file.

We set up one client VM and four server VMs in various cloud data centres using Azure, ranging from the server being close to the client to the server being on the other side of the planet. Table 4 shows the data centre locations and gives the round-trip times between the client and server.

---

[3] nginx worker processes handle connections using an asynchronous, event-driven approach.

Table 4. Client and server locations and network characteristics observed for the Internet data-centre-to-data-centre experiments; packet loss rates were observed to be 0%

Virtual machine	Azure region	Round-trip time
Client	East US 2 (Virginia)	–
Server – near	East US (Virginia)	6.193 ms
Server – medium	Central US (Iowa)	30.906 ms
Server – far	North Europe (Ireland)	70.335 ms
Server – worst-case	Australia East (New South Wales)	198.707 ms

It should be noted that the RTT times between any two VMs depend on the state of the network between them, which is highly variable; our values in Table 4 are one snapshot. Given that these are data-centre-to-data-centre links, the packet loss on these links is practically zero. The VMs were all Linux (Ubuntu 18.04) Azure D8s virtual machines, which each have 8 vCPUs (either 2.4 GHz Intel Xeon E5-2673 v3 (Haswell) or 2.3 GHz Intel Xeon E5-2673 v4 (Broadwell), depending on provisioning, bursting to 3.5 GHz) and 32 GiB of RAM. The Apache Benchmark (ab) tool [2] was installed on the client VM to measure connection time; it was modified to use TLS 1.3 via OQS-OpenSSL 1.1.1 and verify the server certificate.

We installed nginx (compiled against OQS-OpenSSL 1.1.1) on all server VMs, and we configured it to listen on multiple ports (each one offering a certificate with one of the signature algorithms under test) and to serve HTML pages of various sizes (1 kB, 10 kB, 100 kB, 1000 kB). (The http archive [12] reports that the median desktop and mobile page weight is close to 1950 kB and 1750 kB respectively. Experiments with files as large as 2000 kB took an inordinate amount of time, and all the relevant trends can also be seen at the 1000 kB page size.)

All C code in both experiments was built using the GCC compiler.

5   Results and Discussion

5.1   Emulated Network Experiment Results

Key Exchange. Figure 1 shows handshake completion times at the 50th (median) and 95th percentile for different round trip times for the four key exchange mechanisms under test. For each key exchange scenario, we collected 4500 samples[4]. Most of the charts we show report observations at the 50th and 95th percentile comparing across all algorithms under test. Figures 5 and 6 show

---

[4] The slight downward slope for the first few packet loss rates in the median results for ecdh-p256-sike-p434 is an artifact of the experiment setup used: at low packet loss rates, the setup results in many connection requests arriving simultaneously, causing a slight denial-of-service-like effect while the server queues some calculations.

observations at a more granular range of percentiles for each key exchange mechanism and round-trip time; the full data set is available at https://github.com/xvzcf/pq-tls-benchmark.

At the median, over high quality network links (packet loss rates $\leq 1\%$), we observe that public key and ciphertext size have little impact on handshake completion time, and the predominant factor is cryptographic computation time: ECDH, Kyber512-90s, and Frodo-640-AES have raw cryptographic processing times less than 2 ms resulting in comparable handshake completion times; the slower computation of SIKE p434, where the full cryptographic sequence takes approximately 60 ms, results in a higher latency floor.

As packet loss rates increase, especially above 5%, key exchange mechanisms with larger public keys / ciphertexts, by inducing more packets, bring about longer completion times. For example, at the 31.2 ms RTT, we observe that median Frodo-640-AES completion time starts falling behind. This is to be expected since the maximum transmission unit (MTU) of an ethernet connection is 1500 bytes whereas Frodo-640-AES public key and ciphertext sizes are 9616 bytes and 9720 bytes respectively, resulting in fragmentation across multiple packets. Using the packet analyzer `tcpdump`, we determined that 16 IP packets must be sent by the client to establish a TLS connection using `ecdh-p256-frodo640aes`. If the packet loss loss probability is $p = 5\%$, the probability of at least one packet getting dropped is already $1 - (1 - p)^{16} \approx 58\%$, so the median `ecdh-p256-frodo640aes` has required a retransmission. In contrast, only 5 IP packets are required to establish a TLS connection with `ecdh-p256` and `ecdh-p256-sike-p434`, and 6 packets for `ecdh-p256-kyber512_90s`, which explains why SIKE p434's small public-key and ciphertext sizes do not offset its computational demand.

At the 95th percentile, we see the impact of raw cryptographic processing times nearly eliminated. Up to 10% packet loss, the performance of the 4 key exchange algorithms are quite close. Past 15% packet loss, the much larger number of packets causes `ecdh-p256-frodo640aes` completion times to spike.

At the 5.6 ms and 31.2 ms RTTs, the median `ecdh-p256-kyber512_90s` connection briefly outperforms the median `ecdh-p256` connection at packet loss rates above 15%. This is noise due to the high variability inherent in our measurement process.

Digital Signatures. Figure 2 shows handshake completion times at the 50th (median) and 95th percentile for different round trip times for the four key exchange mechanisms under test. For each point, we collected 6000 samples. As with the key-exchange results, some noise is still present, especially at the 95th percentile.

The trends here are similar to key exchange, with respect to impact of computation costs and number of packets: at the median, `dilithium2` imposes the least slowdown of all post-quantum signature schemes, and is commensurate with `ecdsa-p256` at low latencies and packet loss rates. `qtesla-p-i` results in a higher latency floor. `picnic-l1-fs`, which produces 34,036-byte signatures, also degrades rapidly as the link latency and packet loss probability increases.

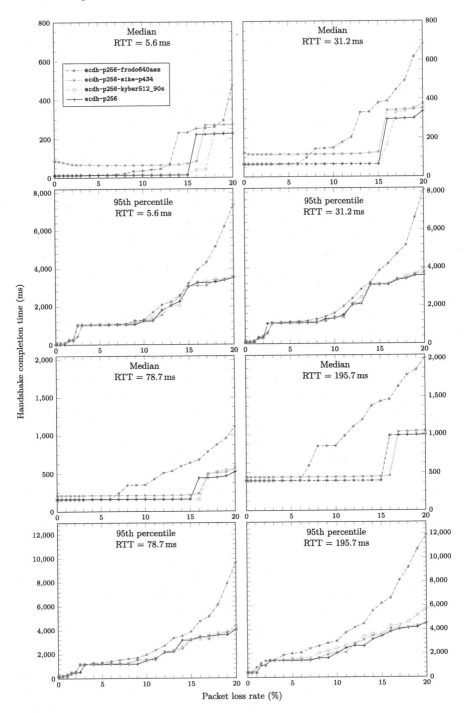

Fig. 1. Network emulation experiment, key exchange scenario: handshake completion time (median & 95th percentile) vs. packet loss, at different round trip times

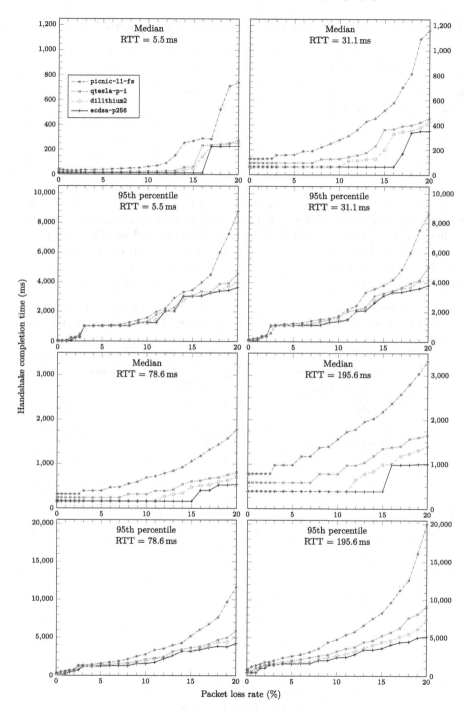

Fig. 2. Network emulation experiment, signature scenario: Handshake completion time (median & 95th percentile) vs. packet loss at different round trip times

5.2   Internet Data-Centre-To-Data-Centre Experiment Results

For each post-quantum scenario, we collected data points by running the `ab` tool for 3 min, resulting in between 100 and 1000 samples for each scenario.

Key Exchange. Figure 3 (left) shows the results for median page download times from our four data centres. Figure 4 in the appendix shows results for the 95th percentile; behaviour at the 95th percentile is not too different from median behaviour, likely due to the extremely low packet loss rate on our connections.

For small-RTT connections and small web pages, the TLS handshake constitutes a significant portion of the overall connection time; faster algorithms perform better. As page size and RTT time increase, the handshake becomes less significant. For example, for the near server (US East, 6.2 ms RTT), in comparing `ecdh-p256` with `ecdh-p256-sikep434`, we observe that, at the median, `ecdh-p256` is 3.12 times faster than `ecdh-p256-sikep434` for 1 kB web pages. However this ratio decreases as page sizes increase to 100 or 1000 kB, and as round trip time increases; for example decreasing to 1.07× and 1.03× for the worst-case server (Australia, 198.7 ms RTT) at 1 and 1000 KB.

Digital Signatures. Fig. 3 (right) shows the results for median round-trip times to the four data centres; Fig. 4 in the appendix shows results for the 95th

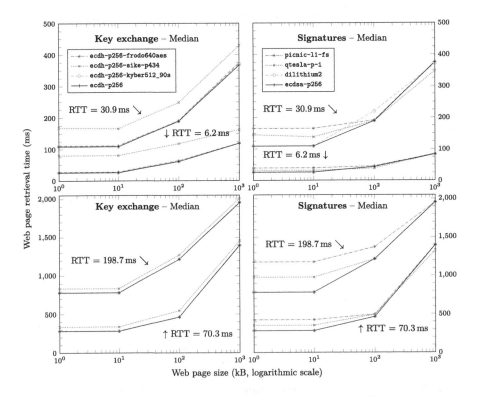

Fig. 3. Internet data-centre-to-data-centre experiment: median retrieval time for various web page sizes from 4 data centres; key exchange (left), signatures (right)

percentile. Just like with the emulated experiment, we observe similar trends between the signature and the key encapsulation mechanisms tests. While the TLS handshake represents a significant portion of the connection establishment time, over increasingly long distances or with increasingly larger payloads, the proportion of time spent on handshake cryptographic processing diminishes.

We do observe some variability in the comparisons between signature algorithms in the Internet experiment in Fig. 3 (especially at 100 and 1000 kB, and for the more distant data centres) that we believe may be due to real-world network conditions changing when running different batches sequentially. This effect, expected to a degree due to the nature of internet routing, might be reduced by interweaving batches and collecting a larger number of samples, which we would like to try in future experimental runs.

6   Conclusion and Future Work

Our experimental results show under which conditions various characteristics of post-quantum algorithms affect performance. In general, on fast, reliable network links, TLS handshake completion time of the median connection is dominated by the cost of public key cryptography, whereas the 95th percentile completion time is not substantially affected. On unreliable network links with packet loss rates of 3–5% or higher, communication sizes come to govern handshake completion time. As application data sizes grow, the relative cost of TLS handshake establishment diminishes compared to application data transmission.

With respect to the effect of communication sizes, it is clear that the maximum transmission unit (MTU) size imposed by the link layer significantly affects the TLS establishment performance of a scheme. Large MTUs may be able to improve TLS establishment performance for post-quantum primitives with large messages. Some ethernet devices provide (non-standard) support for "jumbo frames", which are frames sized anywhere from 1500 to 9000 bytes [39]. Since the feature is non-standard, it is not suitable for use in Internet-facing applications, which cannot make assumptions about the link-layer MTUs of other servers/intermediaries, but may help in local or private networks where every link can be accounted for.

Future work obviously includes extending these experiments to cover more algorithms and more security levels; we intend to continue our experiments and will post future results to our repository at https://github.com/xvzcf/pq-tls-benchmark. It would be interesting to extend the emulation results to bigger networks that aim to emulate multiple network conditions simultaneously using NetMirage or Mininet. On the topic of post-quantum authentication, our experiments focused on a certificate chain where the root CA and endpoint used the same algorithms (resulting in transmission of one public key and two signatures); it would be interesting to experiment with different chain sizes, and with multi-algorithm chains, perhaps optimized for overall public key + signature size. It would also be possible to measure throughput of a server under load from many clients. Finally, our emulation framework could be applied to investigate other protocols, such as SSH, IPsec, Wireguard, and others.

Acknowledgements. We would like to thank Eric Crockett for helpful discussions in the early parts of this work. We are grateful to Geovandro C. C. F. Pereira, Justin Tracey, and Nik Unger for their help with the network emulation experiments. We also thank the anonymous reviewers for their helpful suggestions.

Contributors to the Open Quantum Safe project are listed on the project website [29]. The Open Quantum Safe project has received funding from Amazon Web Services and the Tutte Institute for Mathematics and Computing, and in-kind contributions of developer time from Amazon Web Services, Cisco Systems, evolutionQ, IBM Research, and Microsoft Research. The post-quantum algorithm implementations used in the experiments are directly or indirectly from the original NIST submission teams. Some implementations have been provided by the PQClean project [16].

D.S. is supported in part by Natural Sciences and Engineering Research Council (NSERC) of Canada Discovery grant RGPIN-2016-05146 and a NSERC Discovery Accelerator Supplement. Computation time on Azure was donated by Microsoft Research.

A   Additional Charts

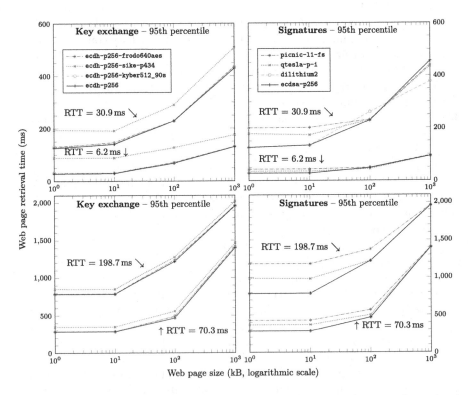

Fig. 4. Internet data-centre-to-data-centre experiment: 95th percentile retrieval time for various web page sizes from four data centres; key exchange scenario (left), signature scenario (right)

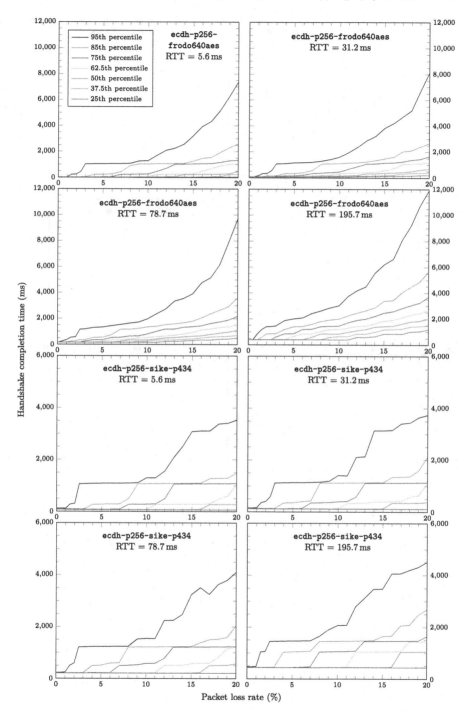

Fig. 5. Network emulation experiment, key exchange scenario: handshake completion time versus packet loss rate at various percentiles, part 1

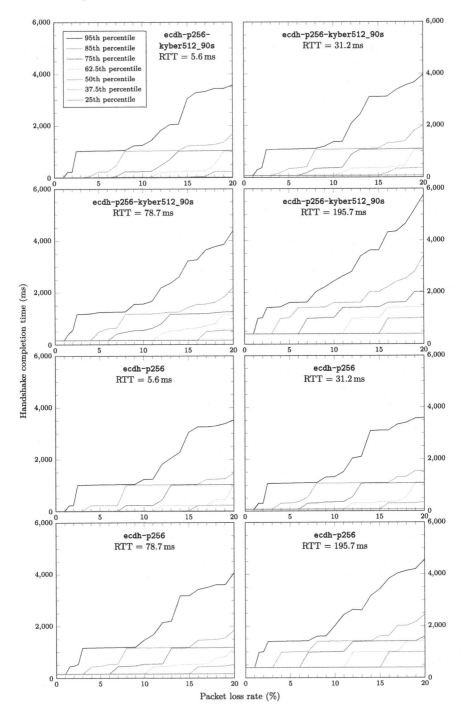

Fig. 6. Network emulation experiment, key exchange scenario: handshake completion time versus packet loss rate at various percentiles, part 2

References

1. Amazon Web Services. s2n (2014). https://github.com/awslabs/s2n
2. Apache Software Foundation. ab - Apache HTTP server benchmarking tool (2019). https://httpd.apache.org/docs/current/programs/ab.html
3. Biederman, E.W.: IP-NETNS(8), January 2013. http://man7.org/linux/man-pages/man8/ip-netns.8.html
4. Biederman, E.W., Pospíšek, T.: VETH(4), February 2018. http://man7.org/linux/man-pages/man4/veth.4.html
5. Bindel, N., Akleylek, S., Alkim, E., Barreto, P.S.L.M., Buchmann, J., Eaton, E., Gutoski, G., Kramer, J., Longa, P., Polat, H., Ricardini, J.E., Zanon, G.: qTESLA. Technical report, National Institute of Standards and Technology (2019). https://csrc.nist.gov/projects/post-quantum-cryptography/round-2-submissions
6. Bos, J.W., Costello, C., Ducas, L., Mironov, I., Naehrig, M., Nikolaenko, V., Raghunathan, A., Stebila, D.: Frodo: take off the ring! practical, quantum-secure key exchange from LWE. In: Weippl, E.R., Katzenbeisser, S., Kruegel, C., Myers, A.C., Halevi, S. (eds.) ACM CCS 2016, pp. 1006–1018. ACM Press, October 2016. https://doi.org/10.1145/2976749.2978425
7. Bos, J.W., Costello, C., Naehrig, M., Stebila, D.: Post-quantum key exchange for the TLS protocol from the ring learning with errors problem. In: 2015 IEEE Symposium on Security and Privacy, pp. 553–570. IEEE Computer Society Press, May 2015. https://doi.org/10.1109/SP.2015.40
8. Braithwaite, M.: Experimenting with post-quantum cryptography, July 2016. https://security.googleblog.com/2016/07/experimenting-with-post-quantum.html
9. Campagna, M., Crockett, E.: Hybrid Post-Quantum Key Encapsulation Methods (PQ KEM) for Transport Layer Security 1.2 (TLS). Internet-Draft draft-campagna-tls-bike-sike-hybrid-01, Internet Engineering Task Force, May 2019. Work in Progress. https://datatracker.ietf.org/doc/html/draft-campagna-tls-bike-sike-hybrid-01
10. Crockett, E., Paquin, C., Stebila, D.: Prototyping post-quantum and hybrid key exchange and authentication in TLS and SSH. In: NIST 2nd Post-Quantum Cryptography Standardization Conference 2019, August 2019
11. Dowling, B., Fischlin, M., Günther, F., Stebila, D.: A cryptographic analysis of the TLS 1.3 handshake protocol candidates. In: Ray, I., Li, N., Kruegel, C. (eds.) ACM CCS 2015, pp. 1197–1210. ACM Press, October 2015. https://doi.org/10.1145/2810103.2813653
12. http archive. Page weight, Novober 2019. https://httparchive.org/reports/page-weight
13. Jager, T., Kohlar, F., Schäge, S., Schwenk, J.: On the security of TLS-DHE in the standard model. In: Safavi-Naini, R., Canetti, R. (eds.) CRYPTO 2012. LNCS, vol. 7417, pp. 273–293. Springer, Heidelberg (2012). https://doi.org/10.1007/978-3-642-32009-5_17
14. Jao, D., Azarderakhsh, R., Campagna, M., Costello, C., De Feo, L., Hess, B., Jalali, A., Koziel, B., LaMacchia, B., Longa, P., Naehrig, M., Renes, J., Soukharev, V., Urbanik, D., Pereira, G.: SIKE. Technical report, National Institute of Standards and Technology (2019). https://csrc.nist.gov/projects/post-quantum-cryptography/round-2-submissions
15. Kampanakis, P., Sikeridis, D.: Two post-quantum signature use-cases: Non-issues, challenges and potential solutions. Cryptology ePrint Archive, Report 2019/1276 (2019). https://eprint.iacr.org/2019/1276

16. Kannwischer, M.J., Rijneveld, J., Schwabe, P., Stebila, D., Wiggers, T.: The PQClean project, November 2019. https://github.com/PQClean/PQClean

17. Kiefer, F., Kwiatkowski, K.: Hybrid ECDHE-SIDH key exchange for TLS. Internet-Draft draft-kiefer-tls-ecdhe-sidh-00, Internet Engineering Task Force, November 2018. Work in Progress. https://datatracker.ietf.org/doc/html/draft-kiefer-tls-ecdhe-sidh-00

18. Krawczyk, H., Paterson, K.G., Wee, H.: On the security of the TLS protocol: a systematic analysis. In: Canetti, R., Garay, J.A. (eds.) CRYPTO 2013. LNCS, vol. 8042, pp. 429–448. Springer, Heidelberg (2013). https://doi.org/10.1007/978-3-642-40041-4_24

19. Kwiatkowski, K., Langley, A., Sullivan, N., Levin, D., Mislove, A., Valenta, L.: Measuring TLS key exchange with post-quantum KEM. In: NIST 2nd Post-Quantum Cryptography Standardization Conference 2019, Auguest 2019

20. Langley, A.: CECPQ2, December 2018. https://www.imperialviolet.org/2018/12/12/cecpq2.html

21. Langley, A.: Post-quantum confidentiality for TLS, April 2018. https://www.imperialviolet.org/2018/04/11/pqconftls.html

22. Langley, A.: Real-world measurements of structured-lattices and supersingular isogenies in TLS, October 2019. https://www.imperialviolet.org/2019/10/30/pqsivssl.html

23. Lantz, B., Heller, B., Handigol, N., Jeyakumar, V., O'Connor, B., Burkard, C.: Mininet, November 2019. http://mininet.org/

24. Ludovici, F., Pfeifer, H.P.: NETEM(4), November 2011. http://man7.org/linux/man-pages/man8/tc-netem.8.html

25. Lyubashevsky, V., Ducas, L., Kiltz, E., Lepoint, T., Schwabe, P., Seiler, G., Stehlé, D.: CRYSTALS-DILITHIUM. Technical report, National Institute of Standards and Technology (2019). https://csrc.nist.gov/projects/post-quantum-cryptography/round-2-submissions

26. Mozilla. Telemetry portal, February 2020. https://telemetry.mozilla.org/

27. Naehrig, M., Alkim, E., Bos, J., Ducas, L., Easterbrook, K., LaMacchia, B., Longa, P., Mironov, I., Nikolaenko, V., Peikert, C., Raghunathan, A., Stebila, D.: FrodoKEM. Technical report, National Institute of Standards and Technology (2019). https://csrc.nist.gov/projects/post-quantum-cryptography/round-2-submissions

28. NGINX, Inc.: NGINX — High Performance Load Balancer, Web Server, & Reverse Proxy (2019). https://www.nginx.com/

29. Open Quantum Safe Project. Open Quantum Safe, November 2019. https://openquantumsafe.org/

30. Open Quantum Safe Project. OQS-OpenSSL_1_0_2-stable, November 2019. https://github.com/open-quantum-safe/openssl/tree/OQS-OpenSSL_1_0_2-stable

31. Open Quantum Safe Project. OQS-OpenSSL_1_1_1-stable, November 2019. https://github.com/open-quantum-safe/openssl/tree/OQS-OpenSSL_1_1_1-stable

32. Rescorla, E.: The Transport Layer Security (TLS) protocol version 1.3. RFC 8446, August 2018. https://rfc-editor.org/rfc/rfc8446.txt

33. Schanck, J.M., Stebila, D.: A Transport Layer Security (TLS) extension for establishing an additional shared secret. Internet-Draft draft-schanck-tls-additional-keyshare-00, Internet Engineering Task Force, April 2017. Work in Progress. https://datatracker.ietf.org/doc/html/draft-schanck-tls-additional-keyshare-00

34. Schanck, J.M., Whyte, W., Zhang, Z.: Quantum-safe hybrid (QSH) ciphersuite for Transport Layer Security (TLS) version 1.2. Internet-Draft draft-whyte-qsh-tls12-02, Internet Engineering Task Force, July 2016. Work in Progress.https://datatracker.ietf.org/doc/html/draft-whyte-qsh-tls12-02
35. Schwabe, P., Avanzi, R., Bos, J., Ducas, L., Kiltz, E., Lepoint, T., Lyubashevsky, V., Schanck, J.M., Seiler, G., Stehlé, D.: CRYSTALS-KYBER. Technical report, National Institute of Standards and Technology (2019). https://csrc.nist.gov/projects/post-quantum-cryptography/round-2-submissions
36. Sikeridis, D., Kampanakis, P., Devetsikiotis, M.: Post-quantum authentication in TLS 1.3: a performance study. Cryptology ePrint Archive, Report 2020/071 (2020). https://eprint.iacr.org/2020/071
37. Stebila, D., Fluhrer, S., Gueron, S.: Design issues for hybrid key exchange in TLS 1.3. Internet-Draft draft-stebila-tls-hybrid-design-01, Internet Engineering Task Force, July 2019. Work in Progress. https://datatracker.ietf.org/doc/html/draft-stebila-tls-hybrid-design-01
38. Stebila, D., Mosca, M.: Post-quantum key exchange for the internet and the Open Quantum Safe project. In: Avanzi, R., Heys, H. (eds.) SAC 2016. LNCS, vol. 10532, pp. 14–37. Springer, Cham (2017). https://doi.org/10.1007/978-3-319-69453-5_2
39. The Ethernet Alliance. Ethernet jumbo frames, November 2009. http://ethernetalliance.org/wp-content/uploads/2011/10/EA-Ethernet-Jumbo-Frames-v0-1.pdf
40. Unger, N., Goldberg, I.: Qatar University, and the Qatar Foundation for Education, Science and Community Development. Netmirage, November 2019. https://crysp.uwaterloo.ca/software/netmirage/
41. Whyte, W., Zhang, Z., Fluhrer, S., Garcia-Morchon, O.: Quantum-safe hybrid (QSH) key exchange for Transport Layer Security (TLS) version 1.3. Internet-Draft draft-whyte-qsh-tls13-06, Internet Engineering Task Force, October 2017. Work in Progress. https://datatracker.ietf.org/doc/html/draft-whyte-qsh-tls13-06
42. Zaverucha, G., Chase, M., Derler, D., Goldfeder, S., Orlandi, C., Ramacher, S., Rechberger, C., Slamanig, D., Katz, J., Wang, X., Kolesnikov, V.: Picnic. Technical report, National Institute of Standards and Technology (2019). https://csrc.nist.gov/projects/post-quantum-cryptography/round-2-submissions

Efficient Key Generation for Rainbow

Albrecht Petzoldt[(⊠)]

FAU Erlangen-Nuremberg, Erlangen, Germany
albrecht.petzoldt@gmail.com

Abstract. Multivariate Cryptography is one of the main candidates for securing communication in a post-quantum world. One of the most promising schemes from this area is the Rainbow signature scheme. While this scheme provides very fast signature generation and verification, the key generation process of Rainbow is relatively slow. In this paper, we propose an algorithm which speeds up the key generation process of the standard Rainbow signature scheme by up to two orders of magnitude, such eliminating one of the few drawbacks of this scheme. Furthermore, we present an improved key generation algorithm for the CyclicRainbow signature scheme. This algorithm allows to generate a key pair for Cyclic Rainbow in essentially the same time as a key pair for standard Rainbow, thus making CyclicRainbow a practical alternative to the standard scheme. Our algorithms are implemented in the Rainbow proposal for the second round of the NIST standardization process for post-quantum cryptosystems.

Keywords: Multivariate cryptography · Rainbow · CyclicRainbow · Efficient key generation · NIST standardization process for post-quantum cryptosystems

1 Introduction

In our modern digital world, cryptographic techniques are an indispensable building block to guarantee the security of our communication systems. Besides encryption, the second important cryptographic primitive are digital signature schemes, which guarantee the authenticity and integrity of signed data such as emails and software updates. The currently used schemes for this purpose are the factoring based RSA cryptosystem [16] and the discrete logarithm based Digital Signature Algorithm (DSA) [11]. However, due to Shor's algorithm [17], the mathematical problems underlying the security of these schemes can be efficiently solved on a large scale quantum computer. In order to preserve the security of communication in an era where quantum computer exist, we therefore need cryptographic schemes which are resistant against such attacks. Especially in the area of digital signature schemes, multivariate cryptography is one of

© Springer Nature Switzerland AG 2020
J. Ding and J.-P. Tillich (Eds.): PQCrypto 2020, LNCS 12100, pp. 92–107, 2020.
https://doi.org/10.1007/978-3-030-44223-1_6

the most promising candidates for this. Multivariate digital signature schemes mainly come in two flavours. On the one hand, we have the BigField schemes such as HFEv- or the NIST candidate GeMSS [3]. On the other hand, there are the SingleField schemes such as UOV and Rainbow. In this paper, we concentrate on these schemes.

UOV and Rainbow. The research in this field was initiated in 1997 by Patarin with his (balanced) Oil and Vinegar signature scheme [12], which was itself inspired by his Linearization Equations attack against the Matsumoto-Imai cryptosystem. After this original proposal was broken by a linear algebra attack by Kipnis and Shamir [9], it was recommended in [8] to choose $v > o$ (Unbalanced Oil and Vinegar (UOV)). In order to increase the efficiency of this scheme, Ding and Schmidt proposed in [6] the Rainbow signature scheme, which can be seen as a multilayer version of UOV. In the following years, Petzoldt et al. proposed in a series of papers [13–15] a number of improvements to this scheme. Compared to the standard Rainbow scheme, their CyclicRainbow signature scheme offers a much smaller public key as well as a faster verification process. However, since existing key generation algorithms for the scheme were very slow, the CyclicRainbow scheme was far from being practical.

Together with (some of) these improvements, Rainbow was accepted as a second round candidate for the NIST standardization process of post-quantum public key cryptosystems [10]. While the signature generation and verification processes of Rainbow are very fast, the key generation process of the scheme was, in the first round proposal, relatively slow.

In this paper we propose two new algorithms for the key generation of the standard and the CyclicRainbow signature schemes. For the standard scheme, our algorithm outperforms existing algorithms (such as that of the first round submission) by up to two orders of magnitude, such eliminating one of the few drawbacks of the scheme. For the CyclicRainbow scheme, our new algorithm is less than 10% slower than that of the standard scheme, such making Cyclic Rainbow a practical alternative to the standard scheme. Furthermore, we show how our techniques could be used to reduce the private key size of the Cyclic Rainbow scheme as well. Our algorithms are inspired by the work of Beullens et al. to create the LUOV signature scheme [2].

The rest of this paper is organized as follows. In Sect. 2, we give a short introduction into the field of multivariate cryptography and present the Rainbow signature scheme of [6]. Section 3 describes our improved key generation algorithm for the standard Rainbow scheme, while Sect. 4 deals with the CyclicRainbow signature scheme of [14]. Section 5 shows the results of our implementation and Sect. 6 sketches a technique to reduce the private key size of CyclicRainbow. Finally, Sect. 7 concludes this paper.

2 Multivariate Public Key Cryptography

The public key of a multivariate public key cryptosystem (MPKC) is a system $\mathcal{P}$ of m quadratic polynomials in n variables over a finite field $\mathbb{F}$ (see Eq. (1)).

$$p^{(1)}(x_1,\ldots,x_n) = \sum_{i,j=1}^{n} p_{ij}^{(1)} x_i x_j + \sum_{i=1}^{n} p_i^{(1)} x_i + p_0^{(1)}$$

$$p^{(2)}(x_1,\ldots,x_n) = \sum_{i,j=1}^{n} p_{ij}^{(2)} x_i x_j + \sum_{i=1}^{n} p_i^{(2)} x_i + p_0^{(2)}$$

$$\vdots$$

$$p^{(m)}(x_1,\ldots,x_n) = \sum_{i,j=1}^{n} p_{ij}^{(m)} x_i x_j + \sum_{i=1}^{n} p_i^{(m)} x_i + p_0^{(m)} \tag{1}$$

The security of MPKC's is based on the

MQ-Problem: Given a system of m quadratic equations $p^{(1)}(\mathbf{x}),\ldots,p^{(m)}(\mathbf{x})$ in n variables as shown in Eq. (1), find a vector $\bar{\mathbf{x}} = (\bar{x}_1,\ldots,\bar{x}_n)$ such that $p^{(1)}(\bar{\mathbf{x}}) = \ldots = p^{(m)}(\bar{\mathbf{x}}) = 0$ holds.

The MQ-Problem (for $m \sim n$) has been proven to be NP-hard, even for polynomials over GF(2) [7] and is believed to be hard on average (for both classical and quantum computers).

In order to create a public key cryptosystem on the basis of the MQ-Problem, one starts with an easily invertible quadratic map $\mathcal{F} : \mathbb{F}^n \to \mathbb{F}^m$ (*central map*). To hide the structure of $\mathcal{F}$ in the public key, one composes it with two affine (or linear) invertible maps $\mathcal{S}$ and $\mathcal{T}$. The *public key* of the cryptosystem is the composed quadratic map $\mathcal{P} = \mathcal{S} \circ \mathcal{F} \circ \mathcal{T}$ which is (hopefully) difficult to invert. The *private key* consists of $\mathcal{S}$, $\mathcal{F}$ and $\mathcal{T}$ and therefore allows to invert $\mathcal{P}$.

In this paper we concentrate on multivariate signature schemes. For such a scheme we have $n \geq m$, which ensures that every message has a signature. The standard process for signature generation and verification works as shown in Fig. 1.

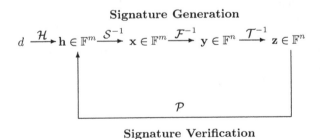

Fig. 1. Workflow of multivariate signature schemes

Signature Generation: In order to generate a signature for a document $d \in \{0,1\}^*$, we use a hash function $\mathcal{H} : \{0,1\}^* \to \mathbb{F}^m$ to compute the hash value $\mathbf{h} = \mathcal{H}(d) \in \mathbb{F}^m$. Then we compute $\mathbf{x} = \mathcal{S}^{-1}(\mathbf{h})$, $\mathbf{y} = \mathcal{F}^{-1}(\mathbf{x})$ and $\mathbf{z} = \mathcal{T}^{-1}(\mathbf{y})$. The signature of the document d is $\mathbf{z} \in \mathbb{F}^n$. Here, $\mathcal{F}^{-1}(\mathbf{x})$ means finding one (of possibly many) pre-image of $\mathbf{x}$ under the central map $\mathcal{F}$.

Signature Verification: To check the authenticity of a document d, one simply computes $\mathbf{h}' = \mathcal{P}(\mathbf{z})$ and the hash value $\mathbf{h} = \mathcal{H}(d)$ of the document. If $\mathbf{h}' = \mathbf{h}$ holds, the signature is accepted, otherwise it is rejected.

2.1 The Rainbow Signature Scheme

In [6], Ding and Schmidt proposed a signature scheme called Rainbow, which is based on the idea of (unbalanced) Oil and Vinegar [8].

Let $\mathbb{F}$ be a finite field and V be the set $\{1, \ldots, n\}$. Let $v_1, \ldots, v_{u+1}, u \geq 1$ be integers such that $0 < v_1 < v_2 < \ldots < v_u < v_{u+1} = n$ and define the sets of integers $V_i = \{1, \ldots, v_i\}$ for $i = 1, \ldots, u$. We set $o_i = v_{i+1} - v_i$ and $O_i = \{v_i + 1, \ldots, v_{i+1}\}$ $(i = 1, \ldots, u)$. The number of elements in V_i is v_i and we have $|O_i| = o_i$. For $k = v_1 + 1, \ldots, n$ we define multivariate quadratic polynomials in the n variables $x_1, \ldots, x_n$ by

$$f^{(k)}(\mathbf{x}) = \sum_{i,j \in V_l, \ i \leq j} \alpha_{ij}^{(k)} x_i x_j + \sum_{i \in O_l, \ j \in V_l} \beta_{ij}^{(k)} x_i x_j + \sum_{i \in V_l \cup O_l} \gamma_i^{(k)} x_i + \eta^{(k)}, \quad (2)$$

where l is the only integer such that $k \in O_l$.

The map $\mathcal{F}(\mathbf{x}) = (f^{(v_1+1)}(\mathbf{x}), \ldots, f^{(n)}(\mathbf{x}))$ can be inverted as follows. First, we choose $x_1, \ldots, x_{v_1}$ at random and substitute these values into the polynomials $f^{(v_1+1)}, \ldots, f^{(n)}$. Thus we get a system of o_1 linear equations (given by the polynomials $f^{(k)}$ $(k \in O_1)$) in the o_1 unknowns $x_{v_1+1}, \ldots, x_{v_2}$, which can be solved by Gaussian elimination. The so computed values of x_i $(i \in O_1)$ are plugged into the polynomials $f^{(k)}(\mathbf{x})$ $(k > v_2)$ and a system of o_2 linear equations (given by the polynomials $f^{(k)}$ $(k \in O_2)$) in the o_2 unknowns x_i $(i \in O_2)$ is obtained. By repeating this process we can compute the values of all the variables x_i $(i = 1, \ldots, n)$.[1]

In order to hide the structure of $\mathcal{F}$ in the public key, we combine it with two invertible affine maps $\mathcal{S} : \mathbb{F}^m \to \mathbb{F}^m$ and $\mathcal{T} : \mathbb{F}^n \to \mathbb{F}^n$. The *public key* $\mathcal{P}$ of the scheme is given as the composed map $\mathcal{P} = \mathcal{S} \circ \mathcal{F} \circ \mathcal{T}$. The *private key* consists of $\mathcal{S}$, $\mathcal{F}$ and $\mathcal{T}$ and therefore allows to invert the public key.

---

[1] It may happen, that one of the linear systems does not have a solution. If so, one has to choose other values for the Vinegar variables $x_1, \ldots x_{v_1}$ and try again.

3   Efficient Key Generation of Rainbow

In the following we restrict to Rainbow schemes with two layers. Note that this is the standard design of Rainbow and also corresponds to the parameter proposals used in the NIST submission. Thus, the scheme is determined by the parameters v_1, o_1 and o_2 and we have $m = o_1 + o_2$ equations and $n = v_1 + m$ variables. We furthermore restrict to homogeneous maps $\mathcal{S}$, $\mathcal{F}$ and $\mathcal{T}$. Note that, due to this choice, the public key $\mathcal{P}$ is a homogeneous quadratic map from $\mathbb{F}^n$ to $\mathbb{F}^m$.

We choose the matrices S and T representing the linear maps $\mathcal{S}$ and $\mathcal{T}$ to be of the form

$$S = \begin{pmatrix} I_{o_1 \times o_1} & S'_{o_1 \times o_2} \\ 0_{o_2 \times o_1} & I_{o_2 \times o_2} \end{pmatrix}, \quad T = \begin{pmatrix} I_{v_1 \times v_1} & T^{(1)}_{v_1 \times o_1} & T^{(2)}_{v_1 \times o_2} \\ 0_{o_1 \times v_1} & I_{o_1 \times o_1} & T^{(3)}_{o_1 \times o_2} \\ 0_{o_2 \times v_1} & 0_{o_2 \times o_1} & I_{o_2 \times o_2} \end{pmatrix}. \tag{3}$$

Note that, for every Rainbow public key $\mathcal{P}$, there exists a corresponding private key $(\mathcal{S}, \mathcal{F}, \mathcal{T})$ with $\mathcal{S}$ and $\mathcal{T}$ being of form (3) [18]. So, the above restriction does not weaken the security of our scheme.

For our special choice of S and T we have $\det(S) = \det(T) = 1$ and (for fields of characteristic 2)

$$S^{-1} = \begin{pmatrix} I_{o_1 \times o_1} & S'_{o_1 \times o_2} \\ 0_{o_2 \times o_1} & I_{o_2 \times o_2} \end{pmatrix} = S, \quad T^{-1} = \begin{pmatrix} I & T^{(1)} & T^{(1)} \cdot T^{(3)} + T^{(2)} \\ 0 & I & T^{(3)} \\ 0 & 0 & I \end{pmatrix}. \tag{4}$$

For abbreviation, we set $T^{(4)} := T^{(1)} \cdot T^{(3)} + T^{(2)}$.

We introduce an intermediate map $\mathcal{Q} = \mathcal{F} \circ \mathcal{T}$. Note that we can write the components of the two maps $\mathcal{F}$ and $\mathcal{Q}$ as quadratic forms

$$f^{(i)}(\mathbf{x}) = \mathbf{x}^T \cdot F^{(i)} \cdot \mathbf{x} \tag{5}$$
$$q^{(i)}(\mathbf{x}) = \mathbf{x}^T \cdot Q^{(i)} \cdot \mathbf{x} \tag{6}$$

with upper triangular matrices $F^{(i)}$ and $Q^{(i)}$. Note that, due to the relation $\mathcal{Q} = \mathcal{F} \circ \mathcal{T}$, we get

$$Q^{(i)} = T^T \cdot F^{(i)} \cdot T \quad (i = v_1 + 1, \ldots, n). \tag{7}$$

Note further that, due to the special form of the Rainbow central map, the matrices $F^{(i)}$ look as shown in Fig. 2. The matrices $Q^{(i)}$ $(i = v_1 + 1, \ldots, n)$ are divided into submatrices $Q^{(i)}_1, \ldots, Q^{(i)}_9$ analogously.

In order to generate a Rainbow key pair, we choose the non zero elements of the matrices S, T and $F^{(v_1+1)}, \ldots, F^{(n)}$ uniformly at random from the field $\mathbb{F}$ and perform the following three steps.

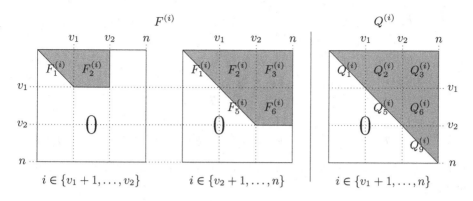

Fig. 2. Matrices $F^{(i)}$ (left) and $Q^{(i)}$ (right) representing the polynomials of the Rainbow central and intermediate maps. The only non-zero elements are contained in the gray spaces.

First Step: Compute the Matrices $Q^{(i)}$ of the First Layer

In the first step, we compute from the matrices $F^{(v_1+1)}, \ldots, F^{(v_2)}$ the matrices $Q^{(v_1+1)}, \ldots, Q^{(v_2)}$. Since the only non zero elements of the matrices $F^{(i)}$ ($i = v_1 + 1, \ldots, v_2$) are contained in the submatrices $F_1^{(i)}$ and $F_2^{(i)}$, we obtain from $Q^{(i)} = T^T \cdot F^{(i)} \cdot T$

$$
\begin{aligned}
Q_1^{(i)} &= F_1^{(i)}, \\
Q_2^{(i)} &= (F_1^{(i)} + (F_1^{(i)})^T) \cdot T_1 + F_2^{(i)}, \\
Q_3^{(i)} &= (F_1^{(i)} + (F_1^{(i)})^T) \cdot T_2 + F_2^{(i)} \cdot T_3, \\
Q_5^{(i)} &= \mathrm{UT}(T_1^T \cdot F_1^{(i)} \cdot T_1 + T_1^T \cdot F_2^{(i)}), \\
Q_6^{(i)} &= T_1^T (F_1^{(i)} + (F_1^{(i)})^T) \cdot T_2 + T_1^T \cdot F_2^{(i)} \cdot T_3 + (F_2^{(i)})^T \cdot T_2, \\
Q_9^{(i)} &= \mathrm{UT}(T_2^T \cdot F_1^{(i)} \cdot T_2 + T_2^T \cdot F_2^{(i)} \cdot T_3).
\end{aligned} \tag{8}
$$

Here, $\mathrm{UT}(A)$ transforms a matrix A into an equivalent upper triangular matrix (i.e. $a_{ij} = a_{ij} + a_{ji}$ for $i < j$, $a_{ij} = 0$ for $i > j$).

Step 2: Compute the Matrices $Q^{(i)}$ of the Second Layer

In the second step, we compute from the matrices $F^{(v_2+1)}, \ldots, F^{(n)}$ the matrices $Q^{(v_2+1)}, \ldots, Q^{(n)}$. Since the only non zero elements of the matrices $F^{(i)}$ ($i = v_2 + 1, \ldots, n$) are contained in the submatrices $F_1^{(i)}, F_2^{(i)}, F_3^{(i)}, F_5^{(i)}$ and $F_6^{(i)}$, we obtain from $Q^{(i)} = T^T \cdot F^{(i)} \cdot T$

$$Q_1^{(i)} = F_1^{(i)},$$
$$Q_2^{(i)} = (F_1^{(i)} + (F_1^{(i)})^T) \cdot T_1 + F_2^{(i)},$$
$$Q_3^{(i)} = (F_1^{(i)} + (F_1^{(i)})^T) \cdot T_2 + F_2^{(i)} \cdot T_3 + F_3^{(i)},$$
$$Q_5^{(i)} = \mathrm{UT}(T_1^T \cdot F_1^{(i)} \cdot T_1 + T_1^T \cdot F_2^{(i)} + F_5^{(i)}), \qquad (9)$$
$$Q_6^{(i)} = T_1^T \cdot (F_1^{(i)} + (F_1^{(i)})^T) \cdot T_2 + T_1^T \cdot F_2^{(i)} \cdot T_3$$
$$+ T_1^T \cdot F_3^{(i)} + (F_2^{(i)})^T \cdot T_2 + (F_5^{(i)} + (F_5^{(i)})^T) \cdot T_3 + F_6^{(i)},$$
$$Q_9^{(i)} = \mathrm{UT}(T_2^T \cdot F_1^{(i)} \cdot T_2 + T_2^T \cdot F_2^{(i)} \cdot T_3 + T_3^T \cdot F_5^{(i)} \cdot T_3 + T_2^T \cdot F_3^{(i)} + T_3^T \cdot F_6^{(i)}).$$

Here, again, $\mathrm{UT}(A)$ transforms the matrix A into an equivalent upper triangular matrix.

Step 3: Compute the Public Key

In the third step, we compute from the matrices $Q^{(i)}$ $(i = v_1 + 1, \ldots, n)$ the public key $\mathcal{P}$ of the scheme. To do this, we first transform the matrices $Q^{(i)}$ into a Macaulay matrix MQ. For $i = v_1 + 1, \ldots, v_2$, we copy the $\frac{n \cdot (n+1)}{2}$ non-zero entries of the matrix $Q^{(i)}$ into the $(i - v_1)$-th row of the matrix MQ_1 (from left to right and top to bottom). Similarly, we copy the elements of the matrices $Q^{(i)}$ of the second layer into the matrix MQ_2. After this, we compute the Macaulay matrix MP of the public key as $MP = S \cdot MQ$ or

$$MP_1 = MQ_1 + S' \cdot MQ_2$$
$$MP_2 = MQ_2 \qquad (10)$$

By following this strategy, the monomials in the Macaulay matrix MP will be ordered according to the lexicographical order. The whole process of computing the matrices MP_1 and MP_2 from $Q^{(v_1+1)}, \ldots, Q^{(n)}$ is illustrated by Fig. 3.

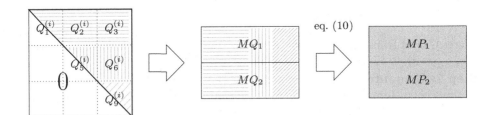

Fig. 3. Computing the public key

Algorithm 1 shows our key generation algorithm for the standard Rainbow scheme in compact form.

4   Key Generation of CyclicRainbow

4.1   The CyclicRainbow Signature Scheme

In [14], Petzoldt et al. proposed the CyclicRainbow signature scheme, which reduces the public key size of the standard Rainbow signature scheme by up to 70%. The idea of the scheme is illustrated in Fig. 4. We set $D_1 = \frac{v_1 \cdot (v_1+1)}{2} + v_1 o_1$, $D_2 = \frac{v_2 \cdot (v_2+1)}{2} + v_2 o_2$ and $D_3 = \frac{n \cdot (n+1)}{2}$. As in the previous chapter, we restrict to Rainbow schemes with two layers, homogeneous maps $\mathcal{S}$, $\mathcal{F}$ and $\mathcal{T}$ and assume that the matrices S and T representing the linear maps $\mathcal{S}$ and $\mathcal{T}$ are of the form (3).

Instead of computing the public key out of the private key, we generate major parts of the public key by a PRNG (using a public seed s_p) and compute the central map from the public key. In particular, we generate the elements of the three matrices B_1, B_2 and B_3 as well as the matrices representing the linear maps S and T (using a private seed s_{ST}). From this, we can compute the matrices F_1, F_2 and F_3 (i.e. the non-zero parts of the central map $\mathcal{F}$) by solving systems of linear equations. Finally, we compute from $\mathcal{F}$ the missing parts of the public key $\mathcal{P}$ (i.e. the matrices C_1, C_2 and C_3).

Note that the monomials in the Macaulay matrices of $\mathcal{F}$, $\mathcal{Q}$ and $\mathcal{P}$ are ordered according to a special monomial order. In this order, we first have a block containing the D_1 quadratic monomials $x_i x_j$ ($1 \leq i \leq v_1$, $i \leq j \leq v_2$). After that, we have a second block containing the quadratic monomials $x_i x_j$ ($1 \leq i \leq v_1$, $v_2 + 1 \leq j \leq n$ or $v_1 + 1 \leq i \leq v_2$, $i \leq j \leq n$). The third block contains the remaining $D_3 - D_2$ quadratic monomials. Inside the blocks, the monomials are ordered according to the lexicographical order. Similar to the matrices MP and MF of Fig. 4, we divide the Macaulay matrix of the map $\mathcal{Q}$ into 6 submatrices, which we denote by $MQ_{i,j}$ ($i \in \{1, 2\}$, $j \in \{1, 2, 3\}$).

In the original proposal [14], the matrices B_1, B_2 and B_3 where chosen as cyclic matrices (hence the name of the scheme). Besides the significant reduction of the public key size, this choice enabled the authors to design a special technique of evaluating the public polynomials, which lead to a speed up of the verification process of up to 60% [15]. However, in order to simplify the security analysis of the scheme, the NIST propsal follows the above strategy using a PRNG. Furthermore, it seems that the above mentioned speed up of the verification procees is hard to realize when using vector instructions to speed up the evaluation of the public polynomials.

The key generation process of CyclicRainbow proposed in [14] required the inversion of a large $D_3 \times D_3$ matrix and therefore was very inefficient, which prevented the CyclicRainbow scheme from being used in practice. Our new key generation algorithm for the CyclicRainbow scheme as presented in the next section is essentially as fast as the key generation process for the standard Rainbow scheme and therefore solves this problem.

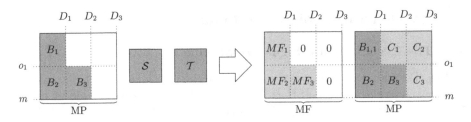

Fig. 4. Key generation of the CyclicRainbow signature scheme. The dark gray parts are chosen by the user, while the light gray parts are computed from them.

4.2   Efficient Key Generation of CyclicRainbow

We generate the entries of the matrices S and T representing the linear maps $\mathcal{S}$ and $\mathcal{T}$ of form (3) and the three matrices B_1, B_2 and B_3 of Fig. 4 using the PRNG (using the seeds s_{ST} and s_p respectively). Our algorithm performs the key generation process of CyclicRainbow as illustrated in Fig. 4 following four steps.

Step 1: Compute the Matrices $MQ_{1,1}$, $MQ_{2,1}$ and $MQ_{2,2}$
Due to the special form of the matrix S, the relation $\mathcal{P} = \mathcal{S} \circ \mathcal{Q}$ yields

$$MQ_{1,1} = B_1 + S' \cdot B_2,$$
$$MQ_{2,1} = B_2, \tag{11}$$
$$MQ_{2,2} = B_3.$$

Step 2: Compute the Central Polynomials of the First Rainbow Layer
For this, we represent the first o_1 components of the maps $\mathcal{Q}$ and $\mathcal{F}$ as upper triangular matrices $Q^{(i)}$ and $F^{(i)}$ respectively (see Fig. 2).

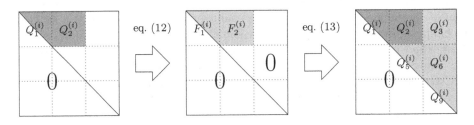

Fig. 5. Computing the central polynomials of the first layer

We insert the D_1 elements of the i-th row of $MQ_{1,1}$ into the dark gray parts of the matrices $Q_1^{(i)}$ and $Q_2^{(i)}$ (from left to right and top to bottom; see Fig. 5 (left)). The corresponding matrices $F^{(i)}$ representing the i-th central polynomial look as shown in Fig. 5 (middle). Note that the only non-zero elements are located in the submatrices $F_1^{(i)}$ and $F_2^{(i)}$. Due to the special form of the map $\mathcal{T}$ of our scheme, the relation $F^{(i)} = (T^{-1})^T \cdot Q^{(i)} \cdot T^{-1}$ yields

$$
\begin{aligned}
F_1^{(i)} &= Q_1^{(i)}, \\
F_2^{(i)} &= (Q_1^{(i)} + (Q_1^{(i)})^T) \cdot T_1 + Q_2^{(i)}. \quad\quad (12)
\end{aligned}
$$

All the other elements of the matrices $F^{(i)}$ ($i \in \{1, \ldots, o_1\}$) are zero. So, after having determined the elements of $F_1^{(i)}$ and $F_2^{(i)}$, we can use the inverse relation $Q^{(i)} = T^T \cdot F^{(i)} \cdot T$ to compute the light gray parts of the matrices $Q^{(i)}$. We find

$$
\begin{aligned}
Q_3^{(i)} &= (F_1^{(i)} + (F_1^{(i)})^T) \cdot T_2 + F_2 \cdot T_3, \\
Q_5^{(i)} &= \mathrm{UT}(T_1^T \cdot F_1^{(i)} \cdot T_1 + T_1^T \cdot F_2^{(i)}), \\
Q_6^{(i)} &= T_1^T(F_1^{(i)} + (F_1^{(i)})^T) \cdot T_2 + T_1^T \cdot F_2^{(i)} \cdot T_3 + (F_2^{(i)})^T \cdot T_2, \\
Q_9^{(i)} &= \mathrm{UT}(T_2^T \cdot F_1^{(i)} \cdot T_2 + T_2^T \cdot F_2^{(i)} \cdot T_3). \quad\quad (13)
\end{aligned}
$$

(see Fig. 5 (right)). Here, $\mathrm{UT}(A)$ again denotes the transformation of the matrix A into an equivalent upper triangular matrix.

Step 3: Compute the Central Polynomials of the Second Rainbow Layer

For this, we insert the D_1 elements of the i-th row of $MQ_{2,1}$ into the dark gray parts of the matrices $Q_1^{(i+v_2)}$ and $Q_2^{(i+v_2)}$ (from left to right and top to bottom). The $D_2 - D_1$ elements of the i-th row of the matrix $MQ_{2,2}$ are inserted into the dark gray parts of the matrices $Q_3^{(i)}, Q_5^{(i)}$ and $Q_6^{(i)}$ (again from left to right and top to bottom; i.e. we fill the matrix $Q_3^{(i)}$ first). Therefore, the matrices $Q^{(i)}$ ($i \in \{v_2 + 1, \ldots, n\}$) look as shown in Fig. 6 (left).

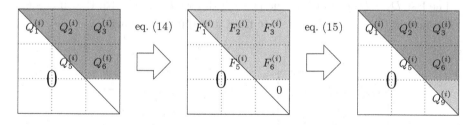

Fig. 6. Computing the central polynomials of the second layer

Due to the special form of the matrix T and the relation $F^{(i)} = (T^{-1})^T \cdot Q^{(i)} \cdot T^{-1}$ we can compute the non-zero parts of the matrices $F^{(i)}$ ($i = v_2 + 1, \ldots, n$) as

$$
\begin{aligned}
F_1^{(i)} &= Q_1^{(i)}, \\
F_2^{(i)} &= (Q_1^{(i)} + (Q_1^{(i)})^T) \cdot T_1 + Q_2^{(i)}, \\
F_3^{(i)} &= (Q_1^{(i)} + (Q_1^{(i)})^T) \cdot T_4 + Q_2^{(i)} \cdot T_3 + Q_3^{(i)}, \\
F_5^{(i)} &= \mathrm{UT}(T_1^T \cdot Q_1^{(i)} \cdot T_1 + T_1^T \cdot Q_2^{(i)} + Q_5^{(i)}), \\
F_6^{(i)} &= T_1^T \cdot (Q_1^{(i)} + (Q_1^{(i)})^T) \cdot T_4 + T_1^T \cdot Q_2^{(i)} \cdot T_3 \\
&\quad + T_1^T \cdot Q_3^{(i)} + (Q_2^{(i)})^T \cdot T_4 + (Q_5^{(i)} + (Q_5^{(i)})^T) \cdot T_3 + Q_6^{(i)}.
\end{aligned} \tag{14}
$$

After this, we can use the inverse relation $Q^{(i)} = T^T \cdot F^{(i)} \cdot T$ to compute the matrices $Q_9^{(i)}$ ($i = v_2 + 1, \ldots, n$). We get

$$
Q_9^{(i)} = \mathrm{UT}(T_2^T \cdot F_1^{(i)} \cdot T_2 + T_2^T \cdot F_2^{(i)} \cdot T_3 + T_3^T \cdot F_5^{(i)} \cdot T_3 + T_2^T \cdot F_3^{(i)} + T_3^T \cdot F_6^{(i)}). \tag{15}
$$

Step 4: Compute the Remaining Parts of the Public Key
For this last step, we transform the matrices $Q^{(i)}$ ($i = v_1 + 1, \ldots, n$) back into a Macaulay matrix MQ. This is done as shown in Fig. 7. For $i = v_1, \ldots, n$, we perform the following 4 steps

- First, we write the D_1 elements of the submatrix $(Q_1^{(i)} \| Q_2^{(i)})$ into the $(i - v_1)$-th row of the matrix MQ (from left to right and top to bottom).
- The following $v_1 o_2$ columns of the $(i - v_1)$-th row of the matrix MQ are filled with the elements of the matrix $Q_3^{(i)}$. Again, these are read from left to right and top to bottom.
- We continue with the elements of the submatrix $(Q_5^{(i)} \| Q_6^{(i)})$.
- The last $D_3 - D_2$ columns of the $(i - v_1)$-th row are filled with the entries of the matrix $Q_9^{(i)}$ (again from left to right and top to bottom).

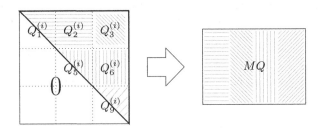

Fig. 7. Building the matrix MQ of CyclicRainbow

The matrix MQ is divided into submatrices as described in Sect. 4.1.

Finally, we compute the matrix MP by $MP = S \cdot MQ$ or, with the special form of our matrix $\mathcal{S}$,

$$C_1 = MQ_{1,2} + S' \cdot MQ_{2,2},$$
$$C_2 = MQ_{1,3} + S' \cdot MQ_{2,3},$$
$$C_3 = MQ_{2,3}. \tag{16}$$

Note that the coefficients in MP are ordered according to the special monomial order defined in Sect. 4.1.

Algorithm 2 presents this key generation algorithm in compact form.

5   Results

Table 1 shows the running time of our key generation algorithms for the standard and the CyclicRainbow signature schemes. The numbers in brackets denote the corresponding timings of the algorithm used in the first round submission to the NIST Standardization Process.

Table 1. Running times of our key generation algorithms on an Intel Xeon @ 3.6 GHz (Skylake) using AVX2 vector instructions. The numbers in brackets give the running times of the first round submission of Rainbow.

NIST security category	I/II		III/IV		V/VI	
Parameter set	(GF(16),32,32,32)		(GF(256),68,36,36)		(GF(256),92,48,48)	
	Standard	Cyclic	Standard	Cyclic	Standard	Cyclic
Mcycles	8.29 (1,081)	9.28	94.8 (1,430)	110	126 (4,633)	137
Time (ms)	2.30 (328)	2.58	26.3 (433)	30.5	34.9 (1,404)	38.0
Memory (MB)	3.5 (3.5)	3.5	4.6 (4.6)	4.6	7.0 (7.0)	7.0

As the table shows, our algorithm for the standard scheme is up to 100 times faster than the algorithm used in the first round submission. The algorithm for the cyclic scheme is only about 10% slower than that for the standard scheme, thus making CyclicRainbow to be a practical alternative to the standard scheme.

6   Reducing the Private Key Size of CyclicRainbow

The simple structure of the equations shown in the previous sections makes it possible to store parts of the central map $\mathcal{F}$ of CyclicRainbow in the form of a random seed, too. In particular, we can generate (parts of) the central map $\mathcal{F}$ on demand during the signature generation process using the seed s_p, the PRNG and (a subset of the) Eqs. (11), (12) and (14). In the following we show that this leads to a tradeoff between the size of the private key and the running time of the signature generation process of CyclicRainbow.

Algorithm 1. Key Generation Algorithm for the standard Rainbow Signature Scheme

---

Input: matrices S, T of form (3), Rainbow central map $\mathcal{F}$
 (given as matrices $F^{(i)}$ $(i = v_1 + 1, \ldots, n)$; see Figure 2)
Output: Rainbow public key $\mathcal{P}$ (consisting of the matrices MP_1 and MP_2)
 1: **for** $i = v_1 + 1$ to v_2 **do**
 2:     Compute the matrices $Q_1^{(i)}, Q_2^{(i)}, Q_3^{(i)}, Q_5^{(i)}, Q_6^{(i)}$ and $Q_9^{(i)}$ using equation (8).
 3: **end for**
 4: **for** $i = v_2 + 1$ to n **do**
 5:     Compute the matrices $Q_1^{(i)}, Q_2^{(i)}, Q_3^{(i)}, Q_5^{(i)}, Q_6^{(i)}$ and $Q_9^{(i)}$ using equation (9).
 6: **end for**
 7: **for** $i = v_1 + 1$ to n **do**
 8:     Insert the elements of the matrix $Q^{(i)}$ into the $(i - v_1)$-th row of the matrix MQ (as described in the text)
 9: **end for**
10: Compute the Rainbow public key using equation (10).
11: **return** MP_1, MP_2.

As a first step, we see from Eqs. (11) and (14) directly, that the entries of the matrices $P_1^{(i)}$ and $F_1^{(i)}$ $(i = v_2 + 1, \ldots, n)$ are identical $(i = v_2 + 1, \ldots, n)$. This allows us to generate this part of the central map using the PRNG and the seed s_P. By doing so, we can reduce the size of the private key by up to 9% nearly without slowing down the signature generation process of our scheme.

The matrices $F_1^{(i)}$ corresponding to the polynomials of the first layer can be computed by generating the matrices B_1 and B_2 from the seed s_p and applying the first equation of (11). By doing so, we can reduce the size of the private key by another 9%. However, we have to compute a large matrix product each time we create a signature, which will slow down the signature generation process of the CyclicRainbow scheme significantly.

As a second example, we can compute the whole second layer of the central map $\mathcal{F}$ by generating the matrices B_2 and B_3 from the seed s_P and using Eq. (14) to compute the matrices $F_1^{(i)}, F_2^{(i)}, F_3^{(i)}, F_5^{(i)}$ and $F_6^{(i)}$ $(i = v_2 + 1, \ldots, n)$. For the parameters recommended in the NIST submission, this reduces the private key size of CyclicRainbow by 65–71%, but delegates a large number of computations to the signature generation process.

Finally, by using the complete equation set, we can generate the whole private key on demand from the seed s_P. However, in order to recover the central map $\mathcal{F}$ as needed to generate a signature, we have to perform the computation of Eqs. (11), (12) and (14) during the signature generation process, which slows down this process drastically.

Since the speed of the signature generation process is one of the main selling points of Rainbow, generating the whole private key from the seed s_p seems, in general, not to be promising. On the other hand, on memory constraint devices, using the above mentioned tradeoff might lead to interesting results. However, since it is not completely clear yet how these techniques will influence the running time of the signature generation process of Rainbow, more research is needed to find an optimal tradeoff between the size of the private key and the speed of the signature generation algorithm.

Algorithm 2. Our Key Generation Algorithm for the CyclicRainbow Signature Scheme

---

Input: Random seeds s_p and s_{ST}.
Output: Rainbow central map $\mathcal{F}$, matrices C_1, C_2 and C_3 (see Figure 4).
 1: Use a PRNG to generate from s_{ST} matrices S and T of form (3).
 2: Use the PRNG to generate from s_p the matrices B_1, B_2 and B_3 of Figure 4.
 3: Compute the matrices $MQ_{1,1}$, $MQ_{2,1}$ and $MQ_{2,2}$ using equation (11).
 4: **for** $i = v_1 + 1$ to v_2 **do**
 5:      Insert the coefficients of the $(i - v_1)$-th row of the matrix $MQ_{1,1}$ into the submatrices $Q_1^{(i)}$ and $Q_2^{(i)}$.
 6:      Set $F_1^{(i)} = Q_1^{(i)}$ and $F_2^{(i)} = (Q_1^{(i)} + (Q_1^{(i)})^T) \cdot T_1 + Q_2^{(i)}$.
 7:      Compute the matrices $Q_3^{(i)}, Q_5^{(i)}, Q_6^{(i)}$ and $Q_9^{(i)}$ using equation (13).
 8: **end for**
 9: **for** $i = v_2 + 1$ to n **do**
10:      Insert the coefficients of the $(i - v_2)$-th row of the matrix $MQ_{2,1}$ into the submatrices $Q_1^{(i)}$ and $Q_2^{(i)}$.
11:      Insert the coefficients of the $(i - v_2)$-th row of the matrix $MQ_{2,2}$ into the submatrices $Q_3^{(i)}, Q_5^{(i)}$ and $Q_6^{(i)}$.
12:      Compute the matrices $F_1^{(i)}, F_2^{(i)}, F_3^{(i)}, F_5^{(i)}$ and $F_6^{(i)}$ using equation (14).
13:      Compute the matrix $Q_9^{(i)}$ using equation (15).
14: **end for**
15: **for** $i = v_1 + 1$ to n **do**
16:      Insert the elements of the matrix $Q^{(i)}$ into the $(i - v_1)$-th row of the matrix MQ (as described in the text)
17: **end for**
18: Compute the matrices C_1, C_2 and C_3 by equation (16).
19: **return** $F^{(v_1+1)}, \dots, F^{(n)}, C_1, C_2, C_3$.

---

7 Conclusion

In this paper we proposed new efficient algorithms for the key generation of the standard and the CyclicRainbow signature schemes. With regard to the standard scheme, our algorithm speeds up the running time of the key generation process by up to two orders of magnitude (compared to the timings of the first round submission to the NIST post-quantum standardization process). Using our algorithm for CyclicRainbow, the key generation process of this scheme is only about 10% slower than that of standard Rainbow, which makes CyclicRainbow to be a practical alternative to the standard scheme. Furthermore we show how our techniques can also be used to reduce the size of the private key of CyclicRainbow, leading to a tradeoff between private key size and signature generation time. However, since it is not yet clear how these techniques influence the speed of the signature generation process, more research in this direction is required.

Acknowledgments. We want to thank Ming-Shing Chen and Bo-Yin Yang for implementing of our algorithms.

References

1. Bernstein, D., Buchmann, J., Dahmen, E.: Post Quantum Cryptography. Springer, Heidelberg (2009). https://doi.org/10.1007/978-3-540-88702-7
2. Beullens, W., Preneel, B.: Field lifting for smaller UOV public keys. In: Patra, A., Smart, N.P. (eds.) INDOCRYPT 2017. LNCS, vol. 10698, pp. 227–246. Springer, Cham (2017). https://doi.org/10.1007/978-3-319-71667-1_12
3. Casanova, A., Faugère, J., Macario-Rat, G., Patarin, J., Perret, L., Ryckeghem, J.: GeMSS: a great multivariate short signature, January 2019. https://csrc.nist.gov/Projects/Post-Quantum-Cryptography/Round-2-Submissions
4. Ding, J., Cheng, M.S., Petzoldt, A., Schmidt, D., Yang, B.Y.: Rainbow: algorithm specification and documentation, December 2017. https://csrc.nist.gov/Projects/Post-Quantum-Cryptography/Round-1-Submissions
5. Ding, J., Cheng, M.S., Petzoldt, A., Schmidt, D., Yang, B.Y.: Rainbow: algorithm specification and documentation, January 2019. https://csrc.nist.gov/Projects/Post-Quantum-Cryptography/Round-2-Submissions
6. Ding, J., Schmidt, D.: Rainbow, a new multivariable polynomial signature scheme. In: Ioannidis, J., Keromytis, A., Yung, M. (eds.) ACNS 2005. LNCS, vol. 3531, pp. 164–175. Springer, Heidelberg (2005). https://doi.org/10.1007/11496137_12
7. Garey, M.R., Johnson, D.S.: Computers and Intractability: A Guide to the Theory of NP-Completeness. W.H. Freeman and Company, New York (1979)
8. Kipnis, A., Patarin, J., Goubin, L.: Unbalanced oil and vinegar signature schemes. In: Stern, J. (ed.) EUROCRYPT 1999. LNCS, vol. 1592, pp. 206–222. Springer, Heidelberg (1999). https://doi.org/10.1007/3-540-48910-X_15
9. Kipnis, A., Shamir, A.: Cryptanalysis of the oil and vinegar signature scheme. In: Krawczyk, H. (ed.) CRYPTO 1998. LNCS, vol. 1462, pp. 257–266. Springer, Heidelberg (1998). https://doi.org/10.1007/BFb0055733
10. National Institute for Standards and Technology: Post-Quantum Cryptography Standardization, December 2016. https://csrc.nist.gov/Projects/Post-Quantum-Cryptography/Post-Quantum-Cryptography-Standardization
11. National Institute of Standards and Technology: Digital Signature Standard (DSS). FIPS 186-4 (2013)
12. Patarin, J.: The oil and vinegar signature scheme, presented at the Dagstuhl Workshop on Cryptography, September 1997
13. Petzoldt, A.: Selecting and reducing key sizes for multivariate cryptography. PhD thesis. TU Darmstadt, July 2013. http://tuprints.ulb.tu-darmstadt.de/3523/
14. Petzoldt, A., Bulygin, S., Buchmann, J.: CyclicRainbow – a multivariate signature scheme with a partially cyclic public key. In: Gong, G., Gupta, K.C. (eds.) INDOCRYPT 2010. LNCS, vol. 6498, pp. 33–48. Springer, Heidelberg (2010). https://doi.org/10.1007/978-3-642-17401-8_4

15. Petzoldt, A., Bulygin, S., Buchmann, J.: Fast verification for improved versions of the UOV and rainbow signature schemes. In: Gaborit, P. (ed.) PQCrypto 2013. LNCS, vol. 7932, pp. 188–202. Springer, Heidelberg (2013). https://doi.org/10.1007/978-3-642-38616-9_13

16. Rivest, R., Shamir, A., Adleman, L.: A method for obtaining digital signatures and public-key cryptosystems. Commun. ACM **21**(2), 120–126 (1978)

17. Shor, P.: Polynomial-time algorithms for prime factorization and discrete logarithms on a quantum computer. SIAM J. Comput. **26**(5), 1484–1509 (1997)

18. Wolf, C., Preneel, B.: Equivalent keys in HFE, C^*, and variations. In: Dawson, E., Vaudenay, S. (eds.) Mycrypt 2005. LNCS, vol. 3715, pp. 33–49. Springer, Heidelberg (2005). https://doi.org/10.1007/11554868_4

Isogeny-Based Cryptography

CSIDH on the Surface

Wouter Castryck and Thomas Decru[(✉)]

Cosic, Research Group at Imec and KU Leuven, Leuven, Belgium
{wouter.castryck,thomas.decru}@esat.kuleuven.be

Abstract. For primes $p \equiv 3 \bmod 4$, we show that setting up CSIDH on the surface, i.e., using supersingular elliptic curves with endomorphism ring $\mathbf{Z}[(1 + \sqrt{-p})/2]$, amounts to just a few sign switches in the underlying arithmetic. If $p \equiv 7 \bmod 8$ then horizontal 2-isogenies can be used to help compute the class group action. The formulas we derive for these 2-isogenies are very efficient (they basically amount to a single exponentiation in $\mathbf{F}_p$) and allow for a noticeable speed-up, e.g., our resulting CSURF-512 protocol runs about 5.68% faster than CSIDH-512. This improvement is completely orthogonal to all previous speed-ups, constant-time measures and construction of cryptographic primitives that have appeared in the literature so far. At the same time, moving to the surface gets rid of the redundant factor $\mathbf{Z}_3$ of the acting ideal-class group, which is present in the case of CSIDH and offers no extra security.

Keywords: Isogeny-based cryptography · Hard homogeneous spaces · CSIDH · Montgomery curves

1 Introduction

A hard homogeneous space [10] is an efficiently computable free and transitive action $\star : G \times S \to S$ of a finite commutative group G on a set S, for which the parallelization problem is hard: given $s_0, s_1, s_2 \in S$, it should be infeasible to find $g_1 g_2 \star s_0$, where $g_1, g_2 \in G$ are such that $s_1 = g_1 \star s_0$ and $s_2 = g_2 \star s_0$. This generalizes the notion of a cyclic group C in which the Diffie–Hellman problem is hard, as can be seen by considering the set S of generators of C, acted upon by $G = (\mathbf{Z}_{|C|})^{\times}$ through exponentiation. The main appeal of hard homogeneous spaces lies in their potential for post-quantum cryptography: while exponentiation-based Diffie–Hellman succumbs to Shor's polynomial-time quantum algorithm [22], in this more general setting the best attack available is Kuperberg's subexponential-time algorithm for finding hidden shifts [16]. This line of research has led to a number of efficient post-quantum cryptographic primitives, such as non-interactive key exchange [7] and digital signatures [4], which stand out in terms of bandwidth requirements, and verifiable delay functions [11].

Unfortunately, we only know of one source of candidate hard homogeneous spaces that are not based on exponentiation. They descend from CM theory,

© Springer Nature Switzerland AG 2020
J. Ding and J.-P. Tillich (Eds.): PQCrypto 2020, LNCS 12100, pp. 111–129, 2020.
https://doi.org/10.1007/978-3-030-44223-1_7

which yields a family of isogeny-wise actions by ideal-class groups on sets of elliptic curves over finite fields, whose use in cryptography was proposed independently by Couveignes [10] and Rostovtsev–Stolbunov [20,23,24]. The current paper revisits CSIDH [7], which is an incarnation of this idea, using supersingular elliptic curves rather than ordinary elliptic curves (as originally suggested), thereby speeding up the resulting protocols by several orders of magnitude.

Concretely, we focus on the following design choice of CSIDH: as put forward in [7], it works over a large finite prime field $\mathbf{F}_p$ with $p \equiv 3 \bmod 8$, and it acts by $G = \mathcal{C}\ell(\mathbf{Z}[\sqrt{-p}])$ on the set S of $\mathbf{F}_p$-isomorphism classes of elliptic curves with endomorphism ring $\mathbf{Z}[\sqrt{-p}]$ — such curves are said to live on the *floor*. The motivation for this choice comes from [7, Prop. 8], which identifies S with

$$S_p^+ = \{\, a \in \mathbf{F}_p \,|\, y^2 = x^3 + ax^2 + x \text{ is supersingular}\,\},$$

i.e., every curve on the floor has a unique representative in Montgomery form and, conversely, every supersingular Montgomery curve over $\mathbf{F}_p$ has endomorphism ring $\mathbf{Z}[\sqrt{-p}]$. This convenient fact allows for compact and easily verifiable public keys. Furthermore $0 \in S_p^+$ makes for a natural choice of s_0.

Contributions

The main contributions of this paper are as follows.

(a) One of our main observations is that for $p \equiv 7 \bmod 8$, a very similar statement applies to the *surface*, consisting of $\mathbf{F}_p$-isomorphism classes of elliptic curves with endomorphism ring $\mathbf{Z}[(1 + \sqrt{-p})/2]$. Concretely, we show that this set can be identified with

$$S_p^- = \{\, A \in \mathbf{F}_p \,|\, y^2 = x^3 + Ax^2 - x \text{ is supersingular}\,\}, \qquad (1)$$

which again contains 0 as a convenient instance of s_0. The tweaked Montgomery form $y^2 = x^3 + Ax^2 - x$ does not seem to have been studied before. From the viewpoint of efficient arithmetic, it is equivalent with the standard Montgomery form: we will show that the required adaptations to the Montgomery ladder and to Vélu's isogeny formulae (in the version of Renes [19]) just amount to a few sign flips, with the exception of 2-isogenies, which require a separate treatment. Therefore, the protocols built from the action of $\mathcal{C}\ell(\mathbf{Z}[(1 + \sqrt{-p})/2])$ on S_p^- are near-copies of those built from CSIDH.[1]

(b) If $p \equiv 7 \bmod 8$ then the prime 2 splits in $\mathbf{Q}(\sqrt{-p})$, which allows for the use of horizontal 2-isogenies. We show that computing 2-isogenies is an order of magnitude faster than computing ℓ-isogenies for odd ℓ. The cost of a 2-isogeny is dominated by a single exponentiation over $\mathbf{F}_p$, leading to a noticeable speed-up (e.g., our CSURF-512 protocol below performs about 5.68% faster than CSIDH-512). We stress that this improvement is totally orthogonal to all previous speed-ups, constant-time measures (see e.g. [9,15]) and cryptographic applications (see e.g. [4,7,11]) that have appeared in the literature so far.

---

[1] Moreover, if $p \equiv 3 \bmod 4$ then $x^3 + Ax^2 - x$ is automatically square-free, allowing for a marginally simpler key validation. But this deserves a footnote, at most.

We note along the way that, by working on the surface, we naturally get rid of the factor $\mathbf{Z}_3$ that is present in $\mathcal{C}\ell(\mathbf{Z}[\sqrt{-p}])$ when $p \equiv 3 \bmod 8$. Because of the interplay between floor and surface, this factor does not give extra security (see Remark 2). Furthermore, it provides a possible hindrance for isogeny-based threshold schemes: when using more than two parties one must map the problem into $\mathcal{C}\ell(\mathbf{Z}[\sqrt{-p}])^3$, which comes at a small cost if the group structure is unknown [12].

Apart from these benefits, given the limited pool of hard homogeneous spaces available, having the complete supersingular picture at our disposal adds freedom to the parameter selection and leads to a better understanding of the interplay between floor and surface. This being said, primes $p \equiv 1 \bmod 4$ are omitted from our discussion, the main reason being Lemma 1 below: for such p, supersingular elliptic curves over $\mathbf{F}_p$ never admit a model of the form $y^2 = x^3 + Ax^2 \pm x$. This complicates comparison with [7]. It is possible that other elliptic curve models can fill this gap, but we leave that for future research.

Acknowledgments

A partial proof of Theorem 3 below can be found in Berre Baelen's master thesis [1], which was the direct inspiration for this research. We thank Luca De Feo for pointing out the relevance to isogeny-based threshold schemes [12], and Frederik Vercauteren for helpful feedback regarding the proof of Lemma 4. We also note that independent and near-simultaneous work by Fan, Tian, Li and Xu [14] largely overlaps with the material in Sect. 3. This work was supported in part by the Research Council KU Leuven grants C14/18/067 and STG/17/019 and by CyberSecurity Research Flanders with reference number VR20192203.

2   Background, and Formulation of Our Main Theorem

Consider a prime number $p > 3$ and a supersingular elliptic curve $E/\mathbf{F}_p$. Its Frobenius endomorphism π_E satisfies $\pi_E \circ \pi_E = -p$, hence $\mathbf{Z}[\sqrt{-p}]$ can be viewed as a subring of the ring $\mathrm{End}_p(E)$ of $\mathbf{F}_p$-rational endomorphisms of E. If $p \equiv 1 \bmod 4$ then this leaves us with one option for $\mathrm{End}_p(E)$, namely $\mathbf{Z}[\sqrt{-p}]$ itself. If $p \equiv 3 \bmod 4$, which is our main case of interest, then we are left with two options for $\mathrm{End}_p(E)$, namely $\mathbf{Z}[\sqrt{-p}]$ and $\mathbf{Z}[(1 + \sqrt{-p})/2]$.

For each such option $\mathcal{O}$, we let $\mathcal{E}\ell\ell_p(\mathcal{O})$ denote the set of $\mathbf{F}_p$-isomorphism classes of elliptic curves $E/\mathbf{F}_p$ for which $\mathrm{End}_p(E) \cong \mathcal{O}$. If $p \equiv 3 \bmod 4$ then $\mathcal{E}\ell\ell_p(\mathbf{Z}[\sqrt{-p}])$ is called the *floor*, whereas $\mathcal{E}\ell\ell_p(\mathbf{Z}[(1 + \sqrt{-p})/2])$ is called the *surface*; this terminology stems from the structure of the 2-isogeny graph of supersingular elliptic curves over $\mathbf{F}_p$, see Delfs–Galbraith [13].

Remark 1. If $p \equiv 3 \bmod 4$ then it is easy to decide whether a given supersingular elliptic curve $E/\mathbf{F}_p$ is located on the floor or on the surface: in the former case $|E(\mathbf{F}_p)[2]| = 2$ while in the latter case $|E(\mathbf{F}_p)[2]| = 4$. If $p \equiv 3 \bmod 8$ then the 3 outgoing 2-isogenies from a curve on the surface all go *down*, that is, the codomain curves all live on the floor. If $p \equiv 7 \bmod 8$ then only one of the codomain curves is located on the floor.

Recall that S_p^- denotes the set of all coefficients $A \in \mathbf{F}_p$ such that $E_A^- : y^2 = x^3 + Ax^2 - x$ is a supersingular elliptic curve. The elements of S_p^- will be called Montgomery$^-$ coefficients and the corresponding elliptic curves *Montgomery$^-$ curves*. As we will see below, such curves are always located on the surface. Mutatis mutandis, the set S_p^+ contains the Montgomery$^+$ coefficients $a \in \mathbf{F}_p \setminus \{\pm 2\}$ such that the *Montgomery$^+$ curve* $E_a^+ : y^2 = x^3 + ax^2 + x$ is supersingular. If $p \equiv 3 \bmod 8$ then such curves are necessarily located on the floor. However, this is not true if $p \equiv 7 \bmod 8$, in which case we will occasionally write $S_{p,\mathcal{O}}^+$ to denote the subset of S_p^+ corresponding to curves with endomorphism ring $\mathcal{O}$.

To every $E \in \mathcal{Ell}_p(\mathcal{O})$ and every $\mathfrak{a} \subseteq \mathcal{O}$ we can associate the subgroup

$$E[\mathfrak{a}] = \bigcap_{\phi \in \mathfrak{a}} \{P \in E \mid \phi(P) = \infty\} \subseteq E,$$

where, of course, ϕ should be viewed as an endomorphism of E through the isomorphism $\mathrm{End}_p(E) \cong \mathcal{O}$ identifying π_E with $\sqrt{-p}$. We then have:

Theorem 1. *The map* $\rho : \mathcal{Cl}(\mathcal{O}) \times \mathcal{Ell}_p(\mathcal{O}) \to \mathcal{Ell}_p(\mathcal{O})$ *sending* $([\mathfrak{a}], E)$ *to* $\mathfrak{a} \star E := E/E[\mathfrak{a}]$ *is a well-defined free and transitive group action.*

Proof. See [21, Thm. 4.5] and its proof. □

Here $\mathcal{Cl}(\mathcal{O})$ denotes the ideal-class group of $\mathcal{O}$, and $[\mathfrak{a}]$ denotes the class of an invertible ideal $\mathfrak{a} \subseteq \mathcal{O}$.

The assumption underlying CSIDH is that this is a hard homogeneous space, as soon as p is large enough. From a constructive point of view, the following version of Theorem 1, obtained by incorporating [7, Prop. 8] and Vélu's isogeny formulas (in the version of [19, Prop. 1]), forms its backbone.

Theorem 2. *If* $p \equiv 3 \bmod 8$ *then the map* $\rho^+ : \mathcal{Cl}(\mathbf{Z}[\sqrt{-p}]) \times S_p^+ \to S_p^+$ *sending* $([\mathfrak{a}], a)$ *to*

$$[\mathfrak{a}] \star a := \left(a - 3 \sum_{\substack{P \in E_a^+[\mathfrak{a}] \\ P \neq \infty}} \left(x(P) - \frac{1}{x(P)} \right) \right) \cdot \prod_{\substack{P \in E_a^+[\mathfrak{a}] \\ P \neq \infty}} x(P)$$

is a well-defined free and transitive group action. Here we assume $(0,0) \notin E_a^+[\mathfrak{a}]$.

The assumption $(0,0) \notin E_a^+[\mathfrak{a}]$ is not a restriction since $\mathcal{Cl}(\mathbf{Z}[\sqrt{-p}])$ is generated by ideals of odd norm, and by design CSIDH acts by such ideals only.[2]

Our main theoretical tool is the following variant of Theorem 2, on which our CSURF-512 protocol from Sect. 6 relies:

---

[2] It has been pointed out, e.g. in [8,17], that allowing for the action of $(4, \sqrt{-p} - 1)$ could lead to a minor improvement. See also Remark 2.

Theorem 3. *If $p \equiv 3 \bmod 4$ then the maps*

$$\rho^- : \begin{cases} \mathcal{C}\ell(\mathbf{Z}[\sqrt{-p}]) \times S_p^- \to S_p^- & \text{if } p \equiv 3 \bmod 8, \\ \mathcal{C}\ell(\mathbf{Z}[(1+\sqrt{-p})/2]) \times S_p^- \to S_p^- & \text{if } p \equiv 7 \bmod 8 \end{cases}$$

sending $([\mathfrak{a}], A)$ to

$$[\mathfrak{a}] \star A := \left(A - 3 \sum_{\substack{P \in E_A^-[\mathfrak{a}] \\ P \neq \infty}} \left(x(P) + \frac{1}{x(P)} \right) \right) \cdot \prod_{\substack{P \in E_A^-[\mathfrak{a}] \\ P \neq \infty}} x(P)$$

are well-defined free and transitive group actions. Here, we assume that the ideal $\mathfrak{a}$ representing $[\mathfrak{a}]$ has odd norm.

We again note that the class group is generated by ideals of odd norm. However, if $p \equiv 7 \bmod 8$ then $\mathcal{C}\ell(\mathbf{Z}[(1+\sqrt{-p})/2])$ also admits invertible ideals of norm 2, which can be used to speed up the evaluation of ρ^- significantly. These require a separate treatment, which is outlined in Sect. 4.

Apart from a striking analogy with Theorem 2, the reader might notice that Theorem 3 is in seeming conflict with Theorem 1 when $p \equiv 3 \bmod 8$. Indeed, since the curves E_A^- always have endomorphism ring $\mathbf{Z}[(1+\sqrt{-p})/2]$, it seems that ρ^- is acting by the wrong class group! However, in Sect. 3 we will see that every curve on the surface has *three* representants in S_p^-, and at the same time $|\mathcal{C}\ell(\mathbf{Z}[\sqrt{-p}])| = 3|\mathcal{C}\ell(\mathbf{Z}[(1+\sqrt{-p})/2])|$. It turns out that, somewhat surprisingly, Vélu's formulas consistently link both factors 3 to each other.

We note that Theorem 2 can be extended to cover $p \equiv 7 \bmod 8$ as well, by merely adding a subscript $\mathbf{Z}[\sqrt{-p}]$ to S_p^+. But for such p there is also a surface version of Theorem 2, which is more subtle and will be discussed in Sect. 5.

Further Notation and Terminology

The identity element of an elliptic curve E will be denoted by ∞ and context will make it clear to which curve it belongs. An **important convention** is that if $p \equiv 3 \bmod 4$, then for a a square in $\mathbf{F}_p$ we denote by $\sqrt{a}$ the unique square root which is again a square; this can be computed as $a^{(p+1)/4}$. Finally, for $B \in \mathbf{Z}_{>0}$ we write $[-B; B]$ for the set of integers $[-B, B] \cap \mathbf{Z}$.

3 Properties of Montgomery⁻ Curves

3.1 Montgomery⁻ Arithmetic: Just a Few Sign Flips

One of the advantages of Montgomery⁺ curves is that arithmetic on them can be done very efficiently. Fortunately, this can easily be adjusted to work for Montgomery⁻ curves. E.g., the formulas for point doubling and differential addition, for use in the Montgomery ladder, take the following form.

Proposition 1. *Let $E_A^- : y^2 = x^3 + Ax^2 - x$ be an elliptic curve over a field K of characteristic different from two, with $P, Q \in E_A^-(K)$.*

1. *If $P = \infty$ or $x(P)^3 + Ax(P)^2 - x(P) = 0$, then $2P = \infty$. Else*

$$x(2P) = \frac{(x(P)^2 + 1)^2}{4(x(P)^3 + Ax(P)^2 - x(P))}.$$

2. *If $\{P, Q, P+Q, P-Q\} \cap \{\infty\} = \emptyset$, then*

$$x(P+Q)x(P-Q) = \frac{(x(P)x(Q) + 1)^2}{(x(P) - x(Q))^2}.$$

Proof. This is almost a copy of the corresponding proofs in [2].   □

Likewise, computing odd degree isogenies between Montgomery⁻ curves just amounts to a few sign changes with respect to the formulas from [19, Prop. 1], leading to the following statement (we will treat 2-isogenies separately in Sect. 4).

Proposition 2. *Let $E_A^- : y^2 = x^3 + Ax^2 - x$ be an elliptic curve over a field of characteristic not two. Let $G \subseteq E_A^-(K)$ be a finite subgroup such that $|G|$ is odd, and let ϕ be a separable isogeny such that $\ker(\phi) = G$. Then there exists a curve $E_B^- : y^2 = x^3 + Bx^2 - x$ such that, up to composition with an isomorphism,*

$$\phi : E_A^- \to E_B^-$$
$$(x, y) \mapsto (f(x), c_0 y f'(x)),$$

where

$$f(x) = x \prod_{T \in G \setminus \{\infty\}} \frac{xx_T + 1}{x - x_T}.$$

Writing

$$\pi = \prod_{T \in G \setminus \{\infty\}} x_T, \qquad \sigma = \sum_{T \in G \setminus \{\infty\}} \left(x_T + \frac{1}{x_T} \right),$$

we also have that $B = \pi(A - 3\sigma)$, $c_0^2 = \pi$.

Proof. Let $i, \theta \in \bar{K}$ be such that $i^2 = -1$ and $\theta^2 = i$, and let $\ell = |G|$. We will construct the isogeny ϕ as the concatenation $\phi_3 \circ \phi_2 \circ \phi_1$ as illustrated in the following diagram,

$$\begin{array}{ccc} E_A^- & \xrightarrow{\phi} & E_B^- \\ \downarrow{\phi_1} & & \uparrow{\phi_3} \\ E_a^+ & \xrightarrow{\phi_2} & E_b^+ \end{array}$$

where $\phi_2 : E_a^+ \to E_b^+$ is the isogeny from [19, Prop. 1], and the elliptic curves are given by the Montgomery⁺ forms $E_a^+ : y^2 = x^3 + ax^2 + x$ and $E_b^+ : y^2 = x^3 + bx^2 + x$.

The isogenies ϕ_1 and ϕ_3 are in fact isomorphisms (over an extension field) given by

$$\phi_1 : E_A^- \to E_a^+$$
$$(x,y) \mapsto (-ix, \theta y)$$

and

$$\phi_3 : E_b^+ \to E_B^-$$
$$(x,y) \mapsto (ix, -i\theta y).$$

It is easy to verify that $a = -iA$ and $B = ib$. The rest of the proof is just a straightforward calculation. With the formulas from [19] we can compute the coefficient b as $\tilde{\pi}(a - 3\tilde{\sigma}) = (-i)^\ell \pi(A - 3\sigma)$ where

$$\tilde{\pi} = \prod_{T \in \phi_1(G)\backslash\{\infty\}} x_T = \prod_{T \in G\backslash\{\infty\}} -ix_T = (-i)^{\ell-1}\pi,$$

$$\tilde{\sigma} = \sum_{T \in \phi_1(G)\backslash\{\infty\}} \left(x_T - \frac{1}{x_T}\right) = \sum_{T \in G\backslash\{\infty\}} \left(-ix_T + \frac{1}{ix_T}\right) = -i\sigma.$$

Similarly if we define

$$\tilde{f} = x \left(\prod_{T \in \phi_1(G)\backslash\{\infty\}} \left(\frac{xx_T - 1}{x - x_T}\right) \right),$$

then with $\tilde{c}_0{}^2 = \tilde{\pi} = (-i)^{\ell-1}\pi$, we have

$$(\phi_2 \circ \phi_1)(x,y) = \left(\tilde{f}(-ix), \tilde{c}_0 \theta y \tilde{f}'(-ix) \right)$$

$$= \left(-ix \prod_{T \in \phi_1(G)\backslash\{\infty\}} \left(\frac{-ixx_T - 1}{-ix - x_T}\right), \tilde{c}_0 \theta y \tilde{f}'(-ix) \right)$$

$$= \left(-ix \prod_{T \in G\backslash\{\infty\}} \left(\frac{-xx_T - 1}{-ix + ix_T}\right), \tilde{c}_0 \theta y \tilde{f}'(-ix) \right)$$

$$= \left(-i^\ell f(x), \tilde{c}_0 \theta y \tilde{f}'(-ix) \right)$$

$$= \left(-i^\ell f(x), \tilde{c}_0 \theta y (-i)^{\ell-1} f'(x) \right).$$

If we assume $\ell \equiv 1 \bmod 4$ then $(-i)^{\ell-1} = 1$ such that $\tilde{c}_0$ is just a square root of π. Composing this with $\phi_3(x,y) = (ix, -i\theta y)$ we get that

$$\phi(x,y) = (f(x), \tilde{c}_0 y f'(x)),$$

as well as $B = \pi(A - 3\sigma)$. In this case we let $c_0 = \tilde{c}_0$.

If $\ell \equiv 3 \bmod 4$ then $\tilde{c_0}^2 = -\pi$ and the isogeny may not be defined over K. Post-composing it with the isomorphism $\tau : (x, y) \mapsto (-x, iy)$ fixes this if needed. In this case we find

$$\phi(x, y) = (f(x), -i\tilde{c_0}yf'(x)),$$

and again $B = \pi(A - 3\sigma)$. Defining $c_0 = -i\tilde{c_0}$ finishes the proof. $\qquad\square$

As usual, it is better to use projective coordinates to avoid costly field inversions, i.e., to represent the x-coordinate of a projective point $P = (X : Y : Z)$ as $x(P) = X/Z$; the required adaptations are straightforward.

3.2 Locating Supersingular Montgomery$^\pm$ Curves

We now switch to curves over finite prime fields $\mathbf{F}_p$. The lemma below shows that supersingular Montgomery$^-$ curves over $\mathbf{F}_p$ are always located on the surface.

Lemma 1. *Let $p > 3$ be a prime number and let $A \in \mathbf{F}_p$ be such that $E_A^- : y^2 = x^3 + Ax^2 - x$ is supersingular. Then $p \equiv 3 \bmod 4$, and there is no $P \in E_A^-(\mathbf{F}_p)$ such that $2P = (0,0)$; in particular, $\mathrm{End}_p(E_A^-) \cong \mathbf{Z}[(1 + \sqrt{-p})/2]$.*

Proof. Let P be a point doubling to $(0,0)$; note that, necessarily, both coordinates are non-zero. The tangent line at P has slope

$$\frac{3x(P)^2 + 2Ax(P) - 1}{2y(P)}.$$

But, since the line should pass through $(0,0)$, a simpler expression for this slope is $y(P)/x(P)$. Equating both expressions leads to $x(P)^2 + 1 = 0$. Now:

- If $p \equiv 1 \bmod 4$ then we conclude $x(P) = \pm i \in \mathbf{F}_p$ and hence $y(P)^2 = -A \mp 2i$. If both expressions on the right-hand side are non-squares then their product $A^2 + 4$ is a square, but then $x^3 + Ax^2 - x$ factors completely over $\mathbf{F}_p$. We conclude that in any case $4 \mid |E_A^-(\mathbf{F}_p)| = p + 1$, which is a contradiction.
- If $p \equiv 3 \bmod 4$ then this shows that such a point P cannot be $\mathbf{F}_p$-rational. But then $E_A^-(\mathbf{F}_p)[2^\infty] \cong \mathbf{Z}/(2^e) \times \mathbf{Z}/(2)$ for some $e \geq 1$, since $|E_A^-(\mathbf{F}_p)| = p + 1 \equiv 0 \bmod 4$. Thus there are 3 outgoing $\mathbf{F}_p$-rational 2-isogenies, hence in view of [13, Thm. 2.7] our curve must be located on the surface. $\qquad\square$

The conclusion $p \equiv 3 \bmod 4$ also applies to supersingular Montgomery$^+$ curves, since it is known [2] that these always carry an $\mathbf{F}_p$-rational point of order 4.

So, from now on, let us assume that $p \equiv 3 \bmod 4$. Then the above lemma settles the 'if' part of Proposition 4 below, which can be viewed as the surface version of the following statement:

Proposition 3. *Let $p > 3$ be a prime number such that $p \equiv 3 \bmod 4$ and let E be a supersingular elliptic curve over $\mathbf{F}_p$. If $\mathrm{End}_p(E) \cong \mathbf{Z}[\sqrt{-p}]$ then there exists a coefficient $a \in \mathbf{F}_p \setminus \{\pm 2\}$ for which E is $\mathbf{F}_p$-isomorphic to the curve $E_a^+ : y^2 = x^3 + ax^2 + x$. Furthermore,*

– *this coefficient is always unique,*
– *if $p \equiv 3 \bmod 8$ then the converse implication holds as well.*

Proof. If $p \equiv 3 \bmod 8$ then this is [7, Prop. 8]. If $p \equiv 7 \bmod 8$ then the relevant part of the proof of [7, Prop. 8] still applies.   □

Proposition 4. *Let $p > 3$ be a prime number such that $p \equiv 3 \bmod 4$ and let E be a supersingular elliptic curve over $\mathbf{F}_p$. Then $\mathrm{End}_p(E) \cong \mathbf{Z}[(1 + \sqrt{-p})/2]$ if and only if there exists a coefficient $A \in \mathbf{F}_p$ for which E is $\mathbf{F}_p$-isomorphic to the curve $E_A^- : y^2 = x^3 + Ax^2 - x$. Furthermore,*

– *if $p \equiv 3 \bmod 8$ then there exist exactly three such coefficients,*
– *if $p \equiv 7 \bmod 8$ then this coefficient is unique.*

We will prove this proposition by means of the following convenient tool, connecting floor and surface:

Lemma 2. *Let $p > 3$ be a prime number such that $p \equiv 3 \bmod 4$. Then*

$$\tau : S_{p,\mathbf{Z}[\sqrt{-p}]}^+ \to S_p^- : a \mapsto -2a/\sqrt{4 - a^2}$$

is a well-defined bijection.

Proof. For $a, b \in \mathbf{F}_p$ with $a^2 - 4b \neq 0$ let us write $E_{a,b}$ for the elliptic curve $y^2 = x^3 + ax^2 + bx$, which admits the well-known 2-isogeny

$$E_{a,b} \to E_{-2a,a^2-4b} : P \mapsto \begin{cases} \left(\frac{y(P)^2}{x(P)^2}, y(P)(1 - \frac{b}{x(P)^2}) \right) & \text{if } P \neq (0,0), \infty \\ \infty & \text{if } P \in \{(0,0), \infty\}. \end{cases} \quad (2)$$

If $a \in S_{p,\mathbf{Z}[\sqrt{-p}]}^+$ then we find that $E_a^+ = E_{a,1}$ is 2-isogenous to the curve

$$E_{-2a,a^2-4} : y^2 = x^3 - 2ax^2 + (a^2 - 4)x,$$

which is necessarily supersingular. Since E_a^+ lives on the floor we see that $a^2 - 4$ is not a square in $\mathbf{F}_p$, hence $4 - a^2$ is a square and letting $\delta = \sqrt{4 - a^2}$, the substitution $x \leftarrow \delta x$, $y \leftarrow \delta^{3/2}y$ transforms the above equation into $y^2 = x^3 - 2a/\sqrt{4 - a^2}x^2 - x$. We conclude that τ is indeed well-defined.

Conversely, if $A \in S_p^-$ then we find that $E_A^- = E_{A,-1}$ is 2-isogenous to

$$E_{-2A,A^2+4} : y^2 = x^3 - 2Ax^2 + (A^2 + 4)x.$$

Since E_A^- lives on the surface by Lemma 1, we have that $A^2 + 4$ is a square in $\mathbf{F}_p$. Letting $\delta = \sqrt{A^2 + 4}$, the same substitution transforms our equation into $y^2 = x^3 - 2A/\sqrt{A^2 + 4}x^2 + x$. It is easily checked that this curve has no $\mathbf{F}_p$-rational points of order 2 besides $(0,0)$, hence the map

$$S_p^- \to S_{p,\mathbf{Z}[\sqrt{-p}]}^+ : A \mapsto -2A/\sqrt{A^2 + 4} \quad (3)$$

is also well-defined. An easy calculation shows that it is an inverse of τ.   □

Proof of Proposition 4. By Proposition 3 each $\mathbf{F}_p$-isomorphism class of elliptic curves on the floor is represented by a unique Montgomery$^+$ curve. Since such curves have a unique $\mathbf{F}_p$-rational point of order 2, the proof of Lemma 2 shows that $\mathbf{F}_p$-rational 2-isogenies give a 1-to-1 correspondence between $\mathcal{E}\ell\ell_p(\mathbf{Z}[\sqrt{-p}])$ and S_p^-. But on the level of $\mathbf{F}_p$-isomorphism classes, by [13, Thm. 2.7] this correspondence is 3-to-1 if $p \equiv 3 \bmod 8$ and 1-to-1 if $p \equiv 7 \bmod 8$. $\qquad\square$

If $p \equiv 7 \bmod 8$ then Proposition 3 leaves open whether or not there exist $a \in S_p^+$ such that E_a^+ is located on the surface. To answer this, we rely on the following lemma.

Lemma 3. *If $p \equiv 7 \bmod 8$ then every $E \in \mathcal{E}\ell\ell_p(\mathbf{Z}[(1 + \sqrt{-p})/2])$ comes with three distinguished points of order 2:*

- *P^-, the x-coordinates of whose halves are not defined over $\mathbf{F}_p$,*
- *P_1^+, whose halves are not defined over $\mathbf{F}_p$, but their x-coordinates are,*
- *P_2^+, whose halves are defined over $\mathbf{F}_p$.*

Proof. From the structure of $E(\mathbf{F}_p)[2^\infty]$ one sees that there is indeed a unique point P_2^+ of order 2 whose halves are $\mathbf{F}_p$-rational. If we position P_2^+ at $(0,0)$ we find a model $y^2 = x^3 + ax^2 + bx$, where necessarily b is a square, as can be seen by mimicking the proof of Lemma 1. When translating the other points of order 2 to the origin we get similar equations, of which the coefficients at x become $\delta(\delta \pm a)/2$ with $\delta = \sqrt{a^2 - 4b}$. The product of these coefficients equals $-b\delta^2$, hence we conclude that one coefficient is a non-square and one coefficient is a square. So, again as in the proof of Lemma 1, we see that the former translated point equals P^-, while the latter translated point equals P_1^+. $\qquad\square$

Corollary 1. *If $p \equiv 7 \bmod 8$ then each $E \in \mathcal{E}\ell\ell_p(\mathbf{Z}[(1 + \sqrt{-p})/2])$ admits exactly 2 coefficients $a \in \mathbf{F}_p \setminus \{\pm 2\}$ for which E is $\mathbf{F}_p$-isomorphic to the curve $E_a^+ : y^2 = x^3 + ax^2 + x$.*

Proof. By Proposition 4, such curves admit a unique Montgomery$^-$ model. Note that, for this model, P^- is positioned at $(0,0)$. The two Montgomery$^+$ models are obtained by translating P_1^+ or P_2^+ to $(0,0)$ and scaling down the resulting b-coefficient (which is a square) to 1, by means of a coordinate change. $\qquad\square$

Table 1 summarizes how and with what frequency Montgomery$^\pm$ curves show up as representatives of $\mathbf{F}_p$-isomorphism classes of supersingular elliptic curves. Figures 1 and 2 give an accompanying visual representation.

4   2-Isogenies Between Montgomery$^-$ Curves

In this section we assume that $p \equiv 7 \bmod 8$ and we consider the maximal order $\mathbf{Z}[(1 + \sqrt{-p})/2]$, in which $(2) = (2, (\sqrt{-p} - 1)/2)(2, (\sqrt{-p} + 1)/2)$. We describe a fast method for computing the repeated action of one of the factors as a chain of 2-isogenies. This relies on the following remarkably precise statement (recall our convention on square roots!):

Table 1. The ratio of the number of Montgomery$\pm$ coefficients to the number of $\mathbf{F}_p$-isomorphism classes of supersingular elliptic curves.

		$(|S_{p,\mathcal{O}}^+| : |\mathcal{E}\ell\ell_p(\mathcal{O})|)$	$(|S_p^-| : |\mathcal{E}\ell\ell_p(\mathcal{O})|)$
$p \equiv 3 \bmod 8$	$\mathcal{O} = \mathbf{Z}\left[\frac{1+\sqrt{-p}}{2}\right]$	0	$(3:1)$
	$\mathcal{O} = \mathbf{Z}[\sqrt{-p}]$	$(1:1)$	0
$p \equiv 7 \bmod 8$	$\mathcal{O} = \mathbf{Z}\left[\frac{1+\sqrt{-p}}{2}\right]$	$(2:1)$	$(1:1)$
	$\mathcal{O} = \mathbf{Z}[\sqrt{-p}]$	$(1:1)$	0
$p \equiv 1 \bmod 4$		0	0

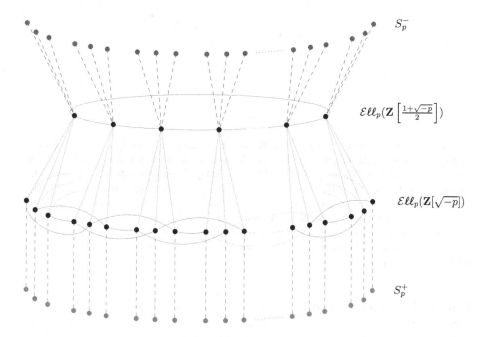

Fig. 1. The supersingular isogeny graph over $\mathbf{F}_p$ with $p \equiv 3 \bmod 8$. The black dots represent supersingular elliptic curves up to $\mathbf{F}_p$-isomorphism. The yellow lines represent the 2-isogenies, which are necessarily between the surface and the floor. The purple lines represent the ℓ-isogenies for some fixed ℓ such that $(\ell, \pi - 1)$ generates $\mathcal{C}\ell(\mathbf{Z}[\sqrt{-p}])$. This implies that the ℓ-isogenies on the floor create one big cycle which we need to depict as spiraling around three times. Indeed, the action of $(\ell, \pi - 1)$ on the surface should result in the same $\mathbf{F}_p$-isomorphism class as first computing a vertical 2-isogeny taking us to the floor, then performing the action of $(\ell, \pi - 1)$, and finally computing a vertical 2-isogeny back to the surface. The red dots and lines represent the Montgomery$^+$ coefficients, which are 1-to-1 with the isomorphism classes on the floor. This correspondence forms the basis for the original CSIDH setting described in [7]. The blue dots and lines represent the Montgomery$^-$ coefficients, which are 3-to-1 with the isomorphism classes on the surface. (Color figure online)

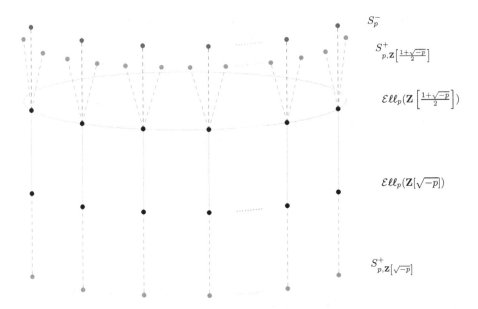

S_p^-

$S_{p,\mathbf{Z}\left[\frac{1+\sqrt{-p}}{2}\right]}^+$

$\mathcal{E}\ell\ell_p\left(\mathbf{Z}\left[\frac{1+\sqrt{-p}}{2}\right]\right)$

$\mathcal{E}\ell\ell_p(\mathbf{Z}[\sqrt{-p}])$

$S_{p,\mathbf{Z}[\sqrt{-p}]}^+$

Fig. 2. The supersingular isogeny graph over $\mathbf{F}_p$ with $p \equiv 7 \bmod 8$. The black dots represent supersingular elliptic curves up to $\mathbf{F}_p$-isomorphism. The yellow lines represent the 2-isogenies, where we assumed that $(2, (\sqrt{-p}-1)/2)$ generates the class group. The red dots and lines represent the Montgomery$^+$ coefficients, which are 2-to-1 with the isomorphism classes on the surface and 1-to-1 with the isomorphism classes on the floor. The blue dots and lines represent the Montgomery$^-$ coefficients, which are 1-to-1 with the isomorphism classes on the surface. Unlike in Fig. 2, no ℓ-isogenies for odd ℓ are depicted here since it is more natural to draw the cycle of 2-isogenies on the surface. (Color figure online)

Lemma 4 (Addendum to Lemma 3). *Assume* $p \equiv 7 \bmod 8$ *and consider an elliptic curve* $E : y^2 = x^3 + ax^2 + bx \in \mathcal{E}\ell\ell_p(\mathbf{Z}[(1 + \sqrt{-p})/2])$. *Let* $\delta = \sqrt{a^2 - 4b}$ *and* $T_1 = ((-a + \delta)/2, 0)$, $T_2 = ((-a - \delta)/2, 0)$. *Then:*

1. *if* $(0,0) = P^-$ *then* $T_1 = P_2^+$ *and* $T_1 = P_1^+$,
2. *if* $(0,0) = P_1^+$ *then* $T_1 = P_2^+$ *and* $T_2 = P^-$,
3. *if* $(0,0) = P_2^+$ *then* $T_1 = P^-$ *and* $T_2 = P_1^+$.

Proof. The change of coordinates $x \leftarrow x + (-a + \delta)/2$ yields

$$y^2 = x\left(x + \frac{-a+\delta}{2}\right)(x+\delta) = x^3 + \frac{-a+3\delta}{2}x^2 + \frac{\delta(-a+\delta)}{2}x \qquad (4)$$

and positions T_1 at the origin. As in the proof of Lemma 1 we see that $T_1 = P_1^+$ or $T_1 = P_2^+$ if and only if the coefficient $\delta(-a+\delta)/2$ is a square, i.e., if and only if $-a + \delta$ is a square.

In particular, for case 2 it suffices to show that $-a + \delta$ is a square. To this end, note that the 2-isogeny from the proof of Lemma 2 takes our input curve

$E : y^2 = x^3 + ax^2 + bx$ to $y^2 = x^3 - 2ax^2 + \delta^2 x$, while mapping P_2^+ to $(0,0)$. But then an $\mathbf{F}_p$-rational half of P_2^+ is mapped to an $\mathbf{F}_p$-rational half of $(0,0)$, which is necessarily of the form $(\pm\delta, \sqrt{2\delta^2(-a\pm\delta)})$. We conclude that at least one of $-a + \delta$ or $-a - \delta$ is a square, but then both elements are squares since their product equals the square $4b$.

Similarly, for case 3 it suffices to prove that $-a + \delta$ is not a square. We can consider the same 2-isogeny, which now maps P_1^+ to $(0,0)$. Using that any point $Q \in E(\mathbf{F}_{p^2} \setminus \mathbf{F}_p)$ doubling to P_1^+ satisfies $\pi_E(Q) = -Q$, which is different from both Q and $Q + (0,0)$, we conclude that the image of P_1^+ cannot be $\mathbf{F}_p$-halvable. From this the desired conclusion follows.

Finally, to settle case 1, consider the curve (4), whose point $(0,0)$ is either P_1^+ or P_2^+. Also note that the first non-trivial factor in (4) corresponds to P^-. But using the identity

$$\left(\frac{-a + 3\delta}{2}\right)^2 - 4\frac{\delta(-a+\delta)}{2} = \left(\frac{a+\delta}{2}\right)^2,$$

we can rewrite (4) as

$$y^2 = x\left(x - \frac{-\frac{-a+3\delta}{2} + \frac{a+\delta}{2}}{2}\right)\left(x - \frac{-\frac{-a+3\delta}{2} - \frac{a+\delta}{2}}{2}\right).$$

Using 2 and the fact that $(a + \delta)/2$ is a square, we see that if $(0,0) = P_1^+$, then the first non-trivial factor of (4) would instead correspond to P_2^+. We conclude that $(0,0) = P_2^+$, from which the lemma follows.   □

This will be combined with the following fact:

Lemma 5. *Assume that $p \equiv 7 \bmod 8$ and let $E \in \mathcal{E}\ell\ell_p(\mathbf{Z}[(1 + \sqrt{-p})/2])$. Then*

$$E\left[\left(2, \frac{\sqrt{-p}-1}{2}\right)\right] = \langle P_2^+\rangle \qquad and \qquad E\left[\left(2, \frac{\sqrt{-p}+1}{2}\right)\right] = \langle P_1^+\rangle.$$

Proof. As in the proof of Lemma 2 one checks that P^- takes us down to the floor, so it suffices to prove the first equality. Let $Q \in E(\mathbf{F}_p)$ be such that $2Q = P_2^+$ and let ϕ denote the endomorphism $\frac{\pi_E - 1}{2}$, then $\phi(P_2^+) = \phi(2Q) = 2\phi(Q) = \pi_E(Q) - Q = \infty$, from which the statement follows.   □

The formulas to compute 2-isogenies between Montgomery$^-$ curves seem easiest if we perform almost all of them on isomorphic Montgomery$^+$ curves. We formulate the procedure in the form of an algorithm.

Sketch of the Proof of Algorithm 1. Note that quadratic twisting swaps the roles of P_1^+ and P_2^+, so with Lemma 5 in mind, we can simply flip the sign of A at the start and the end of the algorithm and focus on P_2^+. Line 4 constitutes a translation $x \leftarrow x + (-a + \delta)/2$, which by Lemma 4 positions $T_1 = P_2^+$ at the origin, followed by the 2-isogeny from (2) and a rescaling to obtain a Montgomery$^+$ curve.

Algorithm 1. Computing the action of $(2, (\sqrt{-p} - 1)/2)^e$ on $A \in S_p^-$, with $p \equiv 7 \bmod 8$

1: **if** $e = 0$ **then return** A
2: **else**
3:     $A \leftarrow \text{sign}(e) \cdot A$
4:     $A \leftarrow 2\dfrac{A - 3\sqrt{A^2 + 4}}{A + \sqrt{A^2 + 4}}$
5: **for** i from 2 to e **do**
6:     $A \leftarrow 2(3 + A(\sqrt{A^2 - 4} - A))$
7: $A \leftarrow \dfrac{A + 3\sqrt{A^2 - 4}}{\sqrt{2\sqrt{A^2 - 4}\left(A + \sqrt{A^2 - 4}\right)}}$
8: **return** $\text{sign}(e) \cdot A$

Line 6 is immediate from [19, Proposition 2], where it should be noted that, due to our choice of canonical square root, $x(P_2^+)$ is always a square so that we do not need to consider possible twists. Line 7 is just a translation followed by a rescaling to put everything back in Montgomery$^-$ form. $\qquad\square$

5 'New' Hard Homogeneous Spaces

For each non-zero entry of Table 1 we obtain a specialization of Theorem 1. For instance, Theorem 2 corresponds to the entry covering Montgomery$^+$ curves, primes $p \equiv 3 \bmod 8$ and endomorphism ring $\mathcal{O} = \mathbf{Z}[\sqrt{-p}]$. The main goal of this section is to prove Theorem 3, which takes care of two further entries, namely those corresponding to Montgomery$^-$ curves, primes $p \equiv 3, 7 \bmod 8$ and endomorphism ring $\mathcal{O} = \mathbf{Z}[(1 + \sqrt{-p})/2]$:

Proof of Theorem 3. If $p \equiv 7 \bmod 8$ then this follows immediately from Theorem 1, along with Proposition 2 and the fact that each $\mathbf{F}_p$-isomorphism class on the surface is represented by exactly one Montgomery$^-$ curve.

If $p \equiv 3 \bmod 8$ then consider the bijection τ from Lemma 2, and let ρ^+ be the group action from Theorem 2. We then define

$$\mathcal{Cl}(\mathbf{Z}[\sqrt{-p}]) \times S_p^- \to S_p^- \; : \; ([\mathfrak{a}], A) \mapsto \tau(\rho^+([\mathfrak{a}], \tau^{-1}(A))),$$

which is clearly a well-defined free and transitive group action, simply because τ is a bijection. So it suffices to show that this matches with ρ^-. For this, consider a Montgomery$^-$ coefficient A and an invertible ideal $\mathfrak{a} \subseteq \mathbf{Z}[\sqrt{-p}]$ having odd norm, along with the subgroup of E_A^- spanned by $E_A^-[\mathfrak{a}]$ and $(0, 0)$. We quotient out this subgroup in the following two ways:

- We first quotient out by $E_A^-[\mathfrak{a}]$, using the formulas from Proposition 2, yielding a Montgomery$^-$ curve E_B^-. Let us abusingly denote the corresponding isogeny by ρ^-, and note that it maps $(0, 0)$ to $(0, 0)$. So we can continue by applying the 2-isogeny from (2), in order to arrive at the Montgomery$^+$ curve $E_{\tau^{-1}(B)}^+$ on the floor.

– Conversely, we apply the 2-isogeny from (2), taking us to the Montgomery$^+$ curve $E^+_{\tau^{-1}(A)}$. Note that this maps $E^-_A[\mathfrak{a}]$ to $E^+_{\tau^{-1}(A)}[\mathfrak{a}]$, which we quotient out in turn, by means of the formulas from [19, Prop. 1]. By the same abuse of notation, we denote the latter isogeny by ρ^+. Because every curve on the floor is represented by a unique Montgomery$^+$ coefficient, this necessarily takes us to $E^+_{\tau^{-1}(B)}$.

Thus we obtain the diagram

$$
\begin{array}{ccc}
E^-_A & \xrightarrow{\;\rho^-\;} & E^-_B \\
\downarrow{\scriptstyle\theta_A} & & \downarrow{\scriptstyle\theta_B} \\
E^+_{\tau^{-1}(A)} & \xrightarrow{\;\rho^+\;} & E^+_{\tau^{-1}(B)}
\end{array}
$$

with θ_A and θ_B denoting the above 2-isogenies, where our reasoning in fact shows that $[\pm 1] \circ \theta_B \circ \rho^- = \rho^+ \circ \theta_A$. This implies that $[\pm 2] \circ \rho^- = \hat{\theta}_B \circ \rho^+ \circ \theta_A$. Multiplication by ± 2 does not change the curve E^-_B, so we are done.   □

Remark 2. Here are two examples of how the surface can help in understanding the floor. We assume $p \equiv 3 \bmod 8$.

– Let $a, a' \in S^+_p$ be given and let $[\mathfrak{a}] \in \mathcal{C}\ell(\mathbf{Z}[\sqrt{-p}])$ be an unknown ideal class such that $a' = [\mathfrak{a}] \star a$ (action by ρ^+ on the floor). By the foregoing proof this is equivalent with $\tau(a') = [\mathfrak{a}] \star \tau(a)$ (action by ρ^- on the surface), which on the level of $\mathbf{F}_p$-isomorphism classes implies that

$$ E^-_{\tau(a')} \cong [\tilde{\mathfrak{a}}] \star E^-_{\tau(a)}, $$

where $\tilde{\mathfrak{a}}$ is the ideal of $\mathbf{Z}[(1 + \sqrt{-p})/2]$ generated by $\mathfrak{a}$. Clearly, in order to find $[\mathfrak{a}]$ it suffices to find $[\tilde{\mathfrak{a}}]$, and then simply try the 3 corresponding possibilities for $\mathfrak{a}$. This confirms that the factor 3 in $|\mathcal{C}\ell(\mathbf{Z}[\sqrt{-p}])|$ offers little extra security to CSIDH.

– If we want a fast evaluation of the action of $[(4, \sqrt{-p} - 1)] \in \mathcal{C}\ell(\mathbf{Z}[\sqrt{-p}])$ on S^+_p, this can be done by composing two 2-isogenies, thereby passing through the surface using τ and τ^{-1}. We leave it as an exercise to verify that this leads to the simple formula $[(4, \sqrt{-p} - 1)] \star a = 2(a - 6)/(a + 2)$, which was first derived in [17, §4.2].

This leaves us with the two entries corresponding to Montgomery$^+$ curves and primes $p \equiv 7 \bmod 8$. This behaves less uniformly since some curves live on the surface and some live on the floor, and in any case these entries seem of lesser cryptographic interest.

If $p \equiv 7 \bmod 8$ then $|\mathcal{C}\ell(\mathbf{Z}[\sqrt{-p}])| = |\mathcal{C}\ell(\mathbf{Z}[(1 + \sqrt{-p})/2])|$. Hence in view of Table 1 there are exactly 3 times as many supersingular Montgomery$^+$ coefficients $a \in \mathbf{F}_p \backslash \{\pm 2\}$ as there are $\mathbf{F}_p$-isomorphism classes of supersingular elliptic curves:

– Under the map $a \mapsto E_a^+$, one third of these are in a 1-to-1 correspondence with $\mathcal{E}\ell\ell_p(\mathbf{Z}[\sqrt{-p}])$. In particular, Theorem 2 remains valid for $p \equiv 7 \bmod 8$, provided that we replace S_p^+ with $S_{p,\mathbf{Z}[\sqrt{-p}]}^+$.

– According to the proof of Corollary 1, the other two thirds split into

$$S_{p,\mathbf{Z}[(1+\sqrt{-p})/2],1}^+ = \{\, a \in S_{p,\mathbf{Z}[(1+\sqrt{-p})/2]}^+ \mid (0,0) \notin 2E_a^+(\mathbf{F}_p) \,\}$$

and

$$S_{p,\mathbf{Z}[(1+\sqrt{-p})/2],2}^+ = \{\, a \in S_{p,\mathbf{Z}[(1+\sqrt{-p})/2]}^+ \mid (0,0) \in 2E_a^+(\mathbf{F}_p) \,\},$$

and both sets are in a 1-to-1 correspondence with $\mathcal{E}\ell\ell_p(\mathbf{Z}[(1 + \sqrt{-p})/2])$. Since the instantiated versions of Vélu's formulae map $(0,0)$ to $(0,0)$, in the statement of Theorem 2 we are equally allowed to replace $\mathbf{Z}[\sqrt{-p}]$ with $\mathbf{Z}[(1 + \sqrt{-p})/2]$ and S_p^+ with $S_{p,\mathbf{Z}[(1+\sqrt{-p})/2],i}^+$, for any choice of $i = 1, 2$.

Remark 3. The latter setting again allows for horizontal 2-isogenies, therefore it should give rise to very similar timings as those reported upon in Sect. 6. One minor drawback is that Alice and Bob should agree on the value of i and validate each other's public keys as such; moreover 0 can no longer be used as a starting coefficient.

Remark 4. Alternatively, it is natural to view

$$S_{p,\mathbf{Z}[(1+\sqrt{-p})/2],1}^+ \qquad \text{and} \qquad S_{p,\mathbf{Z}[(1+\sqrt{-p})/2],2}^+$$

as two orbits under the free but *non-transitive* action

$$\rho^+ : \mathcal{C}\ell(\mathbf{Z}[(1 + \sqrt{-p})]) \times S_{p,\mathbf{Z}[(1+\sqrt{-p})/2]}^+ \to S_{p,\mathbf{Z}[(1+\sqrt{-p})/2]}^+$$

described by the same formulae. Using that the quadratic twisting map $E_a^+ \mapsto E_{-a}^+$ jumps back and forth between the two orbits, along with the fact that $[\mathfrak{a}] \star E^t \cong ([\mathfrak{a}]^{-1} \star E)^t$ (see e.g. [8, Lem. 5]), the two orbits can be glued together into a single orbit under an action by the dihedral group $\text{Dih}\,\mathcal{C}\ell(\mathbf{Z}[(1+\sqrt{-p})/2])$.

6 Implementation

We assume that the reader is familiar with how CSIDH is being set up in practice [7]. In this section we use Theorem 3 and Algorithm 1 to design a variant of CSIDH acting on S_p^- rather than S_p^+. Recall from [7] that CSIDH-512 uses the prime

$$p = 4 \cdot \underbrace{(3 \cdot \ldots \cdot 373)}_{\text{73 first odd primes}} \cdot 587 - 1 \approx 2^{510.668},$$

and then samples exponents from the range $[-5; 5]^{74}$ to represent an element in the class group and let it act on $0 \in S_p^+$, for a conjectured 128 bits of classical security. Concretely, the exponent vector $(e_1, \ldots, e_{74})$ in this case represents the class group element $(3, \sqrt{-p} - 1)^{e_1} \cdots (587, \sqrt{-p} - 1)^{e_{74}}$. For the sake of comparison, we propose CSURF-512 which works over $\mathbf{F}_p$ where

$$p = 2^3 \cdot 3 \cdot \underbrace{(3 \cdot \ldots \cdot 389)}_{\substack{74 \text{ consecutive primes,} \\ \text{skip 347 and 359}}} - 1 \approx 2^{512.880}.$$

This prime will speed up the computation of a class group action in multiple ways. First of all, the largest isogeny we need to compute is of degree 389 instead of 587. Secondly, $p+1$ carries an extra factor 3 that can help with sampling points of order 3 to compute 3-isogenies. Indeed, finding an ℓ-torsion point typically amounts to sampling a random point P and multiplying it by $(p+1)/\ell$, which has a $1/\ell$ chance of failure (i. e. we end up in ∞). For CSURF-512 we can multiply a random point P by both $(p+1)/9$ and $(p+1)/3$ to try and find a point of order 3, improving our chance of failure to only $1/9$.

The biggest speed-up however stems from the fact that $p \equiv 7 \bmod 8$, so we now have 2 as a 75th prime to use. Furthermore 2-isogenies are very fast due to their simple and explicit formulae, see Algorithm 1, so we can sample the exponent for 2 from a much larger interval. In practice we evaluate these 2-isogenies first, without pushing through points, and then proceed with the other primes as in CSIDH.

We implemented both CSIDH-512 and CSURF-512 in Magma [6] to compare their performance. With the exception of 2-isogenies, both implementations are totally similar, making use of the (projective) Montgomery ladder, the pushing through of points, etc., the only differences being the sign switches discussed in Sect. 3.1. However, we did not implement any of the constant-time measures since these are orthogonal to the speed-up we described. Based on experiments, a near-optimal set to sample exponent vectors from seems to be

$$I = [-137; 137] \times [-4; 4]^3 \times [-5; 5]^{46} \times [-4; 4]^{25},$$

which results in $275 \cdot 9^{28} \cdot 11^{46} \approx 2^{255.995}$ distinct secret vectors. As in CSIDH-512, we heuristically expect that these vectors represent the elements in the class group quasi-uniformly, by mimicking the reasoning from [7, §7.1]. Note that for 3-, 5- and 7-isogenies we sample from a smaller interval, since the ease of computing the isogeny is outweighed by the high failure probability of finding the needed torsion points. Sampling from this specific set of exponent vectors gives CSURF-512 a speed-up of about 5.68% compared to CSIDH-512; this estimate is based on an experiment generating 25 000 public keys in both settings. Our source code can be found at https://github.com/TDecru/CSURF.

As a final remark, we note that the advantage of working on the surface is expected to diminish when the underlying prime p becomes larger, since the relative contribution of 2-isogenies will decrease. This is especially relevant given the ongoing discussion about the conjectured quantum security of the protocol, see for example [3,5,18]. However, if $p \equiv 7 \bmod 8$ then the surface will always outperform the floor to *some* extent. This means that setting up these larger instantiations of the CSIDH protocol should preferably be done on the surface, in any case.

References

1. Baelen, B.: Post-quantum key-exchange: using group actions from supersingular elliptic curve isogenies. Master's thesis, KU Leuven (2019)
2. Bernstein, D.J., Lange, T.: Montgomery curves and the Montgomery ladder. In: Bos, J.W., Lenstra, A.K. (eds.) Topics in Computational Number Theory Inspired by Peter L. Montgomery, pp. 82–115. Cambridge University Press, Cambridge (2017)
3. Bernstein, D.J., Lange, T., Martindale, C., Panny, L.: Quantum circuits for the CSIDH: optimizing quantum evaluation of isogenies. In: Ishai, Y., Rijmen, V. (eds.) EUROCRYPT 2019. Part II. LNCS, vol. 11477, pp. 409–441. Springer, Cham (2019). https://doi.org/10.1007/978-3-030-17656-3_15
4. Beullens, W., Kleinjung, T., Vercauteren, F.: CSI-FiSh: efficient isogeny based signatures through class group computations. In: Galbraith, S.D., Moriai, S. (eds.) ASIACRYPT 2019. Part I. LNCS, vol. 11921, pp. 227–247. Springer, Cham (2019). https://doi.org/10.1007/978-3-030-34578-5_9
5. Bonnetain, X., Schrottenloher, A.: Submerging CSIDH. IACR Cryptology ePrint Archive, p. 537 (2018)
6. Bosma, W., Cannon, J., Playoust, C.: The Magma algebra system I. The user language. J. Symbolic Comput. **24**(3–4), 235–265 (1997). Computational algebra and number theory (London, 1993)
7. Castryck, W., Lange, T., Martindale, C., Panny, L., Renes, J.: CSIDH: an efficient post-quantum commutative group action. In: Peyrin, T., Galbraith, S. (eds.) ASIACRYPT 2018. Part III. LNCS, vol. 11274, pp. 395–427. Springer, Cham (2018). https://doi.org/10.1007/978-3-030-03332-3_15
8. Castryck, W., Panny, L., Vercauteren, F.: Rational isogenies from irrational endomorphisms. IACR Cryptology ePrint Archive, 2019:1202 (2019)
9. Cervantes-Vázquez, D., Chenu, M., Chi-Domínguez, J.-J., De Feo, L., Rodríguez-Henríquez, F., Smith, B.: Stronger and faster side-channel protections for CSIDH. In: Schwabe, P., Thériault, N. (eds.) LATINCRYPT 2019. LNCS, vol. 11774, pp. 173–193. Springer, Cham (2019). https://doi.org/10.1007/978-3-030-30530-7_9
10. Couveignes, J.-M.: Hard homogeneous spaces. IACR Cryptology ePrint Archive, 2006:291 (2006)
11. De Feo, L., Masson, S., Petit, C., Sanso, A.: Verifiable delay functions from supersingular isogenies and pairings. IACR Cryptology ePrint Archive, 2019:166 (2019)
12. De Feo, L., Meyer, M.: Threshold schemes from isogeny assumptions. IACR Cryptology ePrint Archive, 2019:1288 (2019)
13. Delfs, C., Galbraith, S.D.: Computing isogenies between supersingular elliptic curves over $\mathbf{F}_p$. Des. Codes Crypt. **78**(2), 425–440 (2016)
14. Fan, X., Tian, S., Li, B., Xiu, X.: CSIDH on other form of elliptic curves. IACR Cryptology ePrint Archive, 2019:1417 (2019)
15. Hutchinson, A., LeGrow, J., Koziel, B., Azarderakhsh, R.: Further optimizations of CSIDH: a systematic approach to efficient strategies, permutations, and bound vectors. IACR Cryptology ePrint Archive, 2019:1121 (2019)
16. Kuperberg, G.: Another subexponential-time quantum algorithm for the dihedral hidden subgroup problem. In: 8th Conference on the Theory of Quantum Computation, Communication and Cryptography. LIPIcs, Leibniz International Proceedings in Informatics, vol. 22, pp. 20–34 (2013)
17. Onuki, H., Takagi, T.: On collisions related to an ideal class of order 3 in CSIDH. IACR Cryptology ePrint Archive, 2019:1209 (2019)

18. Peikert, C.: He gives C-sieves on the CSIDH. IACR Cryptology ePrint Archive, 2019:725 (2019)

19. Renes, J.: Computing isogenies between montgomery curves using the action of (0, 0). In: Lange, T., Steinwandt, R. (eds.) PQCrypto 2018. LNCS, vol. 10786, pp. 229–247. Springer, Cham (2018). https://doi.org/10.1007/978-3-319-79063-3_11

20. Rostovtsev, A., Stolbunov, A.: Public-key cryptosystem based on isogenies. IACR Cryptology ePrint Archive, 2006:145 (2006)

21. Schoof, R.: Nonsingular plane cubic curves over finite fields. J. Combin. Theor. Ser. A **46**(2), 183–211 (1987)

22. Shor, P.W.: Polynomial-time algorithms for prime factorization and discrete logarithms on a quantum computer. SIAM Rev. **41**(2), 303–332 (1999)

23. Stolbunov, A.: Public-key encryption based on cycles of isogenous elliptic curves. Master's thesis, Saint-Petersburg State Polytechnical University (2004). (in Russian)

24. Stolbunov, A.: Cryptographic schemes based on isogenies. Ph.D. thesis, Norwegian University of Science and Technology (2011)

LegRoast: Efficient Post-quantum Signatures from the Legendre PRF

Ward Beullens[1(✉)] and Cyprien Delpech de Saint Guilhem[1,2]

[1] imec-COSIC, KU Leuven, Leuven, Belgium
ward.beullens@esat.kuleuven.be
[2] Department of Computer Science, University of Bristol, Bristol, UK

Abstract. We introduce an efficient post-quantum signature scheme that relies on the one-wayness of the Legendre PRF. This "LEGendRe One-wAyness SignaTure" (LegRoast) builds upon the MPC-in-the-head technique to construct an efficient zero-knowledge proof, which is then turned into a signature scheme with the Fiat-Shamir transform. Unlike many other Fiat-Shamir signatures, the security of LegRoast can be proven without using the forking lemma, and this leads to a tight (classical) ROM proof. We also introduce a generalization that relies on the one-wayness of higher-power residue characters; the "POwer Residue ChaRacter One-wAyness SignaTure" (PorcRoast).

LegRoast outperforms existing MPC-in-the-head-based signatures (most notably Picnic/Picnic2) in terms of signature size and speed. Moreover, PorcRoast outperforms LegRoast by a factor of 2 in both signature size and signing time. For example, one of our parameter sets targeting NIST security level I results in a signature size of 7.2 KB and a signing time of 2.8ms. This makes PorcRoast the most efficient signature scheme based on symmetric primitives in terms of signature size and signing time.

Keywords: Post-quantum signatures · Legendre PRF · MPC-in-the-head

1 Introduction

In 1994, Shor discovered a quantum algorithm for factoring integers and solving discrete logarithms in polynomial time [26]. This implies that an adversary with access to a sufficiently powerful quantum computer can break nearly all public-key cryptography that is deployed today. Therefore, it is important to

This work was supported in part by the Research Council KU Leuven grants C14/18/067 and STG/17/019, by CyberSecurity Research Flanders with reference number VR20192203, by the ERC Advanced Grant ERC-2015-AdG-IMPaCT and by the Defense Advanced Research Projects Agency (DARPA) and Space and Naval Warfare Systems Center, Pacific (SSC Pacific) under contract No. N66001-15-C-4070. Ward Beullens is funded by an FWO fellowship.

© Springer Nature Switzerland AG 2020
J. Ding and J.-P. Tillich (Eds.): PQCrypto 2020, LNCS 12100, pp. 130–150, 2020.
https://doi.org/10.1007/978-3-030-44223-1_8

look for alternative public-key cryptography algorithms that can resist attacks from quantum adversaries. Recently, the US National Institute of Standards and Technology (NIST) has initiated a process to solicit, evaluate, and standardize one or more quantum-resistant public-key cryptographic algorithms [22]. One of the 9 signature schemes that advanced to the second round of the NIST project is Picnic [7,19,27], a signature scheme whose security only relies on symmetric-key primitives.

Indeed, a key pair for Picnic consists of a random secret key sk and the corresponding public key pk = $F($sk$)$, where F is a one-way function which can be computed with a low number of non-linear binary gates [7]. To sign a message m the signer then produces a non-interactive zero-knowledge proof of knowledge of sk such that $F($sk$) = $ pk in a way that binds the message m to the proof. These zero-knowledge proofs (whose security relies additionally only on a secure commitment scheme) are constructed using the MPC-in-the-head paradigm [17]. This results in a signature scheme whose signatures are 33 KB large for 128 bits of security. Later, Katz et al. developed Picnic2 [19], which reduces the signature size to only 14 KB by moving from a 3-party MPC protocol in the honest majority setting to an n-party protocol with preprocessing secure in the dishonest majority setting. However, this increased number of parties slows down the signing and verification algorithms. Picnic and Picnic2 are round 2 candidates in the NIST project [27]. To study the effect of selecting a different function F, Delpech de Saint Guilhem et al. constructed the BBQ scheme using MPC protocols for arithmetic secret sharing to base the signatures on the security of the AES algorithm instead of the less scrutinized block cipher LowMC [24].

Contributions. In this work we propose to use the Legendre PRF [9], denoted by $\mathcal{L}_K(\cdot)$, as one-way function, instead of LowMC or AES. The Legendre PRF is a promising alternative since it can be computed very efficiently in the MPC setting [15]. However, a major limitation of the Legendre PRF is that it only produces one bit of output, which means that the public key should consist of many PRF evaluations $\mathcal{L}_K(i_1), \ldots, \mathcal{L}_K(i_L)$, at some fixed arbitrary list $\mathcal{I} = (i_1, \cdots, i_L)$ of L elements of $\mathbb{F}_p$, to uniquely determine the secret key K. Hence, the zero-knowledge proof needs to prove knowledge of a value K' such that $\mathcal{L}_{K'}(i) = \mathcal{L}_K(i)$ for all $i \in \mathcal{I}$ simultaneously, which results in prohibitively large signatures. Luckily, we can relax the relation to overcome this problem. Instead of proving that the signer knows a K' such that $\mathcal{L}_{K'}(i) = \mathcal{L}_K(i)$ for all $i \in \mathcal{I}$, we let a prover prove knowledge of a K' such that this holds for a large fraction of the i in $\mathcal{I}$. We show that the relaxed statement allows for a much more efficient zero-knowledge proof. This allows us to establish LegRoast, an MPC-in-the-head based scheme with a signature size of 12.2 KB and with much faster signing and verification algorithms than the Picnic2 and BBQ schemes. To further improve the efficiency of LegRoast, we propose to use higher-power residuosity symbols instead of just the quadratic one (i.e. the Legendre symbol) in a second scheme called PorcRoast. This results in signatures that are only 6.3 KB large and in signing and verification times that are twice faster than LegRoast.

A comparison between the signature size and signing time of LegRoast and PorcRoast versus existing signatures based on symmetric primitives (Picnic [27] and SPHINCS+ [16]) is shown in Fig. 1. Even though LegRoast and PorcRoast do not have an AVX optimized implementation yet, we see that LegRoast has faster signing times than both Picnic and SPHINCS+, and that PorcRoast is even faster than LegRoast. We conclude that PorcRoast is the most efficient post-quantum signature scheme based on symmetric primitives in terms of signature size and signing time.

However, note that there are several other branches of post-quantum signatures, such as lattice-based (e.g. Dilithium and Falcon [12,21,23]), Multivariate signatures (e.g., Rainbow, LUOV, MQDSS, MUDFISH [2,5,6,10,11,25]) and isogeny-based signatures (e.g. CSI-FISH [4]), some of which result in more efficient signature schemes.

Roadmap. After some preliminaries in Sect. 2, we introduce a relaxed PRF relation in Sect. 3. We then sketch an identification scheme in Sect. 4 which we formalize as a signature scheme in Sect. 5. We finally discuss parameter choices and implementation results in Sect. 6.

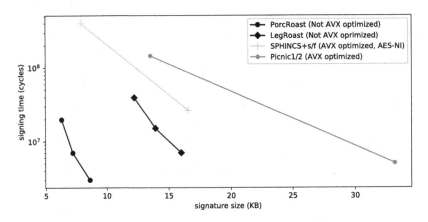

Fig. 1. Signature sizes and timings of post-quantum signature schemes based only on symmetric primitives.

2 Preliminaries - The Legendre and Power Residue PRFs

For an odd prime p the Legendre PRF is conjectured to be a pseudorandom function family, indexed by a key $K \in \mathbb{Z}_p$, such that $\mathcal{L}_K$ takes as input an element $a \in \mathbb{F}_p$ and outputs the bit

$$\mathcal{L}_K(a) = \left\lfloor \frac{1}{2}\left(1 - \left(\frac{K+a}{p}\right)\right)\right\rfloor \in \mathbb{Z}_2,$$

where $\left(\frac{a}{p}\right) \in \{-1, 0, 1\}$ denotes the quadratic residuosity symbol of $a \bmod p$. We note that the function $\mathcal{L}_K$ above is defined such that $\mathcal{L}_0(a \cdot b) = \mathcal{L}_0(a) + \mathcal{L}_0(b)$ for all $a, b \in \mathbb{F}_p^\times$. (Note also that $\mathcal{L}_K(a) = \mathcal{L}_0(K + a)$.)

The seemingly random properties of quadratic residues have been the subject of study for number theorists at least since the early twentieth century, which is why Damgård proposed to use this construction in cryptography [9]. Since then, the security of the Legendre PRF has been studied in several attack models. In the very strong model where a quantum adversary is allowed to query the PRF in superposition, a key can be recovered in quantum polynomial time [8]. If the adversary is only allowed to query the PRF classically, there is a memoryless classical attack that requires computing $O(p^{1/2} \log p)$ Legendre symbols and making $O(p^{1/2} \log p)$ queries to the PRF [20]. Finally, if the adversary is restricted to querying only L Legendre symbols, the best known attack requires computing $O(p \log^2 p / L^2)$ Legendre symbols [3].

Damgård also considers a generalisation of the Legendre PRF, where instead of using the quadratic residue symbol $\left(\frac{a}{p}\right) = a^{\frac{p-1}{2}} \bmod p$, the PRF uses the k-th power residue symbol defined as $\left(\frac{a}{p}\right)_k = a^{\frac{p-1}{k}} \bmod p$, for some k that divides $p - 1$. We define the power residue PRF, analogous to the Legendre PRF, as the keyed function $\mathcal{L}_K^k : \mathbb{F}_p \to \mathbb{Z}_k$, where for an odd prime $p \equiv 1 \bmod k$, $\mathcal{L}_K^k(a)$ is defined as

$$\mathcal{L}_K^k(a) = \begin{cases} i & \text{if } (a + K)/g^i \equiv h^k \bmod p \text{ for some } h \in \mathbb{F}_p^\times \\ 0 & \text{if } (a + K) \equiv 0 \bmod p \end{cases},$$

where g is a fixed generator of $\mathbb{F}_p^\times$. We see that the function $\mathcal{L}_0^k$ is a homomorphism of groups from $\mathbb{F}_p^\times$ to $\mathbb{Z}_k$.

Note that for $k = 2$, this notation coincides with the original Legendre PRF. In this paper, we use the generic notation and we separate the $k = 2$ and $k > 2$ cases only in the experimental sections to highlight the advantages gained by using $k > 2$. One advantage of the power residue PRF is that it yields $\log k$ bits of output, instead of a single bit. The best known attack against the power residue PRF in the setting where an attacker is allowed to query the PRF L times requires computing $O(p \log^2 p / (kL \log^2 k))$ power residue symbols [3].

3   The (Relaxed) Power Residue PRF Relation

In this section, we define the Legendre and power residue PRF NP-languages $R_{\mathcal{L}^k}$, for $k \geq 2$, which consist of the symbol strings of outputs of the $\mathcal{L}^k$ PRF for a given set of inputs. We also define a relaxed version of these languages $R_{\beta \mathcal{L}^k}$, which consist of the strings that are very close (up to addition by a scalar in $\mathbb{Z}_k$) to a word in $R_{\mathcal{L}^k}$, where the Hamming distance d_H is used and β parameterizes the slack.

For properly chosen parameters, it follows from the Weil bound that the relaxed version is as hard as the exact relation, but the relaxed relation will lead to much more efficient signature schemes. To simplify notation, for a list

$\mathcal{I} = (i_1, \cdots, i_L)$ of L arbitrary elements of $\mathbb{Z}_p$, we denote a length-L Legendre/k-th power residue PRF as:

$$F_{\mathcal{I}}^k : \mathbb{F}_p \rightarrow \mathbb{Z}_k^L$$
$$K \mapsto (\mathcal{L}_K^k(i_1), \ldots, \mathcal{L}_K^k(i_L)).$$

Definition 1 (Legendre/k-th power residue PRF relation). *For an odd prime p, a positive integer $k \mid p-1$ and a list $\mathcal{I}$ of L elements of $\mathbb{Z}_p$ we define the Legendre/k-th power residue PRF relation $R_{\mathcal{L}^k}$ with output length L as*

$$R_{\mathcal{L}^k} = \{(F_{\mathcal{I}}^k(K), K) \in \mathbb{Z}_k^L \times \mathbb{F}_p \mid K \in \mathbb{F}_p\}.$$

Definition 2 (β-approximate PRF relation). *For $\beta \in [0,1]$, an odd prime p, a positive integer $k \mid p-1$ and a list $\mathcal{I}$ of L elements of $\mathbb{Z}_p$ we define the β-approximate PRF relation $R_{\beta\mathcal{L}^k}$ with output length L as*

$$R_{\beta\mathcal{L}^k} = \{(s, K) \in \mathbb{Z}_k^L \times \mathbb{F}_p \mid \exists a \in \mathbb{Z}_k : d_H(s + (a, \ldots, a), F_{\mathcal{I}}^k(K)) \leq \beta L\}$$

where $d_H(\cdot, \cdot)$ denotes the Hamming distance.

It follows from the Weil bound for character sums that if β is sufficiently small and L is sufficiently large, then the β-relaxed power residue relation is equally hard as the exact power residue relation, simply because with overwhelming probability over the choice of $\mathcal{I} = (i_1, \cdots, i_L)$ every witness for the relaxed relation is also a witness for the exact relation. The proof is given in Appendix A.

Theorem 1. *Let $\mathcal{B}(n, q)$ denote the binomial distribution with n samples each with success probability q. Take $K \in \mathbb{F}_p$, and take $s = F_{\mathcal{I}}^k(K)$. Then with probability at least $1 - kp \cdot \Pr\left[\mathcal{B}(L, 1/k + 1/\sqrt{p} + 2/p) \geq (1 - \beta)L\right]$ over the choice of $\mathcal{I}$, there exist only one witness for $s \in R_{\beta\mathcal{L}^k}$, namely K, which is also a witness for the exact relation $R_{\mathcal{L}^k}$.*

4   Identification Scheme

In this section, we establish a Picnic-style identification scheme from the Legendre/k-th power residue PRF. We first sketch a scheme very close to the original Picnic construction [7] and gradually add more optimizations, presenting each in turn. Even though the final goal is to construct a signature scheme, we use the language of identification schemes in this section to relate the scheme to existing constructions. We delay the security proof to the next section, where we first apply the Fiat-Shamir transform [13] before we prove that the resulting signature scheme is tightly secure in the ROM. The proof of security of the interactive identification scheme presented here can be derived from the one provided in the next section.

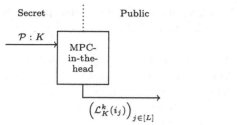

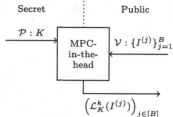

Fig. 2. Picnic-stye identification scheme

Fig. 3. Checking only B symbols

Starting Point. To begin, we take the Picnic2 identification scheme and replace the LowMC block-cipher by the PRF $F_{\mathcal{I}}^k$. The key pair is then $\mathsf{sk} = K$ and $\mathsf{pk} = F_{\mathcal{I}}^k(K) \in \mathbb{Z}_k^L$. From a high-level view, the protocol can be sketched as in Fig. 2 where the prover runs an MPC-in-the-head proof with N parties on a secret sharing of K, to prove to the verifier that he knows K such that $((\frac{K+i_1}{p}),\ldots,(\frac{K+i_L}{p}))$ is equal to the public key. We also use the more efficient method recently proposed by Baum and Nof [1] based on sacrificing rather than the cut-and-choose technique.

Relaxing the PRF Relation. As a first optimization, rather than computing all of the L residue symbols with the MPC protocol, we only check a fixed number B of them. To do so, the verifier chooses random inputs $I^{(1)},\ldots,I^{(B)}$ in $\mathcal{I}$ at which the $\mathcal{L}^k$ PRF is evaluated to check the witness. It is crucial that the verifier sends his choice of $I^{(j)}$s after the prover has committed to his sharing of K, because if a malicious prover knows beforehand which symbols are going to be checked, he can use a fake key K' such that $(\frac{K'+I^{(j)}}{p}) = \mathsf{pk}_{I^{(j)}}$ only for $j \in [B]$. This probabilistic method of selecting which circuit will be executed with the MPC-in-the-head technique is similar to the "sampling circuits on the fly" technique of Baum and Nof [1].

This is now an identification scheme for the β-approximate Legendre PRF relation; a prover that convinces the verifier with probability greater than $(1 - \beta)^B + (1-(1-\beta)^B)/N$ could be used to extract a β-approximate witness following the formalism presented in [1, Section 4]. This protocol is sketched in Fig. 3.

Computing Residue Symbols in the Clear. Since computing residue symbols is relatively expensive, we avoid doing it within the MPC protocol. We use an idea similar to that of Grassi et al. to make this possible [15]. First, we let the prover create sharings of B uniformly random values $r^{(1)},\ldots,r^{(B)} \in \mathbb{F}_p^\times$ and commit to their residue symbols by sending $s^{(j)} = \mathcal{L}_0^k(r^{(j)})$ to the verifier. Then, the MPC protocol only outputs $o^{(j)} = (K + I^{(j)})r^{(j)}$. Since $K + I^{(j)}$ is masked with a uniformly random value with known residue symbol, $o^{(j)}$ does not leak information about K (except for the residue symbol of $K+I^{(j)}$). The verifier then computes $\mathcal{L}_0^k(o^{(j)})$ himself in the clear, and verifies whether it equals $\mathsf{pk}_{I^{(j)}} + s^{(j)}$. The correctness of this check follows from the facts that $\mathcal{L}_0^k : \mathbb{F}_p^\times \to \mathbb{Z}_k$ is a group homomorphism.

Note that the prover can lie about the values of $s^{(j)} = \mathcal{L}_0^k(r^{(j)})$ that he sends to the prover. This is not an issue because he has to commit to these values before the choice of $I^{(j)}$ is revealed. This is the reason why we defined K' to be an β-approximate witness for pk if $F_{\mathcal{I}}^k(K')$ is close to $\mathsf{pk} = F_{\mathcal{I}}^k(K)$ *up to addition by a scalar*. This identification protocol is sketched in Fig. 4.

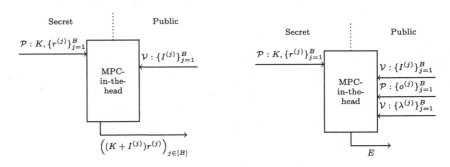

Fig. 4. Computations in the clear.   **Fig. 5.** The final scheme.

Verifying Instead of Computing Multiplications. Instead of using the MPC protocol to *compute* the products $o^{(j)}$, the prover can just send these products directly to verifier. We then use the MPC-in-the-head protocol to instead *verify* that $o^{(j)} = (K + I^{(j)}) \cdot r^{(j)}$ for all $j \in [B]$. A big optimization here is that rather than verifying these B equations separately, it is possible to just check a random linear combination of these equations:

After the prover sends the $o^{(j)}$ values, the verifier chooses random coefficients $\lambda^{(1)}, \ldots, \lambda^{(B)}$ for the linear combination. Then, the MPC protocol is used to compute the error term E defined as

$$E = \sum_{j=1}^{B} \lambda^{(j)} \left((K + I^{(j)}) r^{(j)} - o^{(j)} \right) = K \cdot \sum_{j=1}^{B} \lambda^{(j)} r^{(j)} + \sum_{j=1}^{B} \lambda^{(j)} (I^{(j)} r^{(j)} - o^{(j)}).$$

Clearly, if all the $o^{(j)}$ are correct, then $E = 0$. Otherwise, if one or more of the $o^{(j)}$ are wrong, then E will be a uniformly random value. Therefore, checking if $E = 0$ proves to the verifier that all the $o^{(j)}$ are correct, with a soundness error of $1/p$. Moreover, since the $\lambda^{(j)}, o^{(j)}$ and $I^{(j)}$ are public values, we see that E can be computed with only a single nonlinear operation! This means we can compute E extremely efficiently in MPC. The identification scheme with this final optimization is sketched in Fig. 5.

We note that a single execution of the interactive identification scheme is not enough to achieve negligible soundness error (e.g. the prover has probability

$1/N$ to cheat in the MPC verification protocol). To resolve this, M executions must be run in parallel.

5   LegRoast and PorcRoast Signature Schemes

We now formalize the signature schemes LegRoast (with $k = 2$) and PorcRoast (with $k > 2$) which are constructed from the identification scheme of Sect. 4 with the Fiat-Shamir transform [13], by generating the challenges using three random oracles $\mathcal{H}_1, \mathcal{H}_2$ and $\mathcal{H}_3$. The message is combined with a 2λ-bit salt and bound to the proof by hashing it together with the messages of the prover.

Parameters. Our new signature schemes are parametrized by the following values. Let p be a prime number and let $k \geq 2$ be an integer such that $k \mid p-1$. Let L be an integer determining the length of the public key, $\mathcal{I}$ a pseudo-randomly chosen list of L elements of $\mathbb{Z}_p$ and let $B \leq L$ denote the number of k-th power residue symbols in the public key that will be checked at random. Let N denote the number of parties in the MPC verification protocol and let M denote the number of parallel executions of the identification scheme. These values are grouped under the term params.

Key Generation, Signing and Verifying. The KGen(1^λ, params) algorithm samples sk $= K \xleftarrow{\$} \mathbb{F}_p$ uniformly at random and computes the public key pk $= F_{\mathcal{I}}^k(K)$. The Sign(params, sk, m) algorithm, for message $m \in \{0,1\}^*$ is presented in Fig. 6. The Vf(params, pk, m, σ) algorithm is presented in Fig. 7.

Security. The EUF-CMA security [14] of the LegRoast and PorcRoast signature schemes follows from a *tight* reduction from the problem of finding a witness for the $R_{\beta\mathcal{L}^k}$-relation, which is equally hard as a key recovery on the power residue PRF for our parameters. The proof of Theorem 2 is included in Appendix B.

Theorem 2. *In the classical random oracle model, the LegRoast and PorcRoast signature schemes defined as above are EUF-CMA-secure under the assumption that computing β-approximate witnesses for a given public key is hard.*

6   Parameter Choices and Implementation

This section shows how to choose secure parameters for the LegRoast and PorcRoast signature schemes, and what the resulting key and signature sizes are. We also go over some of the implementation details and the performance of our implementation.

Sign(params, sk, m) :

Phase 1: Commitment to sharings of K, randomness and triples

1: Pick a random salt: salt $\leftarrow \{0,1\}^{2\lambda}$.
2: **for** e from 1 to M **do**
3:     Sample a root seed: $\mathsf{sd}_e \stackrel{\$}{\leftarrow} \{0,1\}^\lambda$.
4:     Build binary tree from sd_e with leaves $\mathsf{sd}_{e,1}, \ldots, \mathsf{sd}_{e,N}$.
5:     **for** i from 1 to N **do**
6:         Sample shares: $K_{e,i}, r_{e,i}^{(1)}, \ldots, r_{e,i}^{(B)}, a_{e,i}, b_{e,i}, c_{e,i} \leftarrow \mathsf{Expand}(\mathsf{sd}_{e,i})$.
7:         Commit to seed: $C_{e,i} \leftarrow \mathcal{H}_{\mathsf{sd}}(\mathsf{salt}, e, i, \mathsf{sd}_{e,i})$.
8:     Compute witness offset: $\Delta K_e \leftarrow K - \sum_{i=1}^{N} K_{e,i}$.
9:     Adjust first share: $K_{e,1} \leftarrow K_{e,1} + \Delta K_e$.
10:    Compute triple: $a_e \leftarrow \sum_{i=1}^{N} a_{e,i}$, $b_e \leftarrow \sum_{i=1}^{N} b_{e,i}$ and $c_e \leftarrow a_e \cdot b_e$.
11:    Compute triple offset: $\Delta c_e \leftarrow c_e - \sum_{i=1}^{N} c_{e,i}$.
12:    Adjust first share: $c_{e,1} \leftarrow c_{e,1} + \Delta c_e$.
13:    **for** j from 1 to B **do**
14:        Compute residuosity symbol: $s_e^{(j)} \leftarrow \mathcal{L}_0^k(r_e^{(j)})$ where $r_e^{(j)} \leftarrow \sum_{i=1}^{N} r_{e,i}^{(j)}$.
15: Set $\sigma_1 \leftarrow ((C_{e,i})_{i\in[N]}, (s_e^{(j)})_{j\in[B]}, \Delta K_e, \Delta c_e)_{e\in[M]}$.

Phase 2: Challenge on public key symbols

1: Compute challenge hash: $h_1 \leftarrow \mathcal{H}_1(m, \mathsf{salt}, \sigma_1)$.
2: Expand hash: $(I_e^{(j)})_{e\in[M], j\in[B]} \leftarrow \mathsf{Expand}(h_1)$, where $I_e^{(j)} \in \mathcal{I}$.

Phase 3: Computation of output values

1: **for** e from 1 to M and **for** j from 1 to B **do**
2:     Compute output value: $o_e^{(j)} \leftarrow (K + I_e^{(j)}) \cdot r_e^{(j)}$.
3: Set $\sigma_2 \leftarrow (o_e^{(1)}, \ldots, o_e^{(B)})_{e\in[M]}$.

Phase 4: Challenge for sacrificing-based verification

1: Compute challenge hash: $h_2 \leftarrow \mathcal{H}_2(h_1, \sigma_2)$.
2: Expand hash $(\epsilon_e, \lambda_e^{(1)}, \ldots, \lambda_e^{(B)})_{e\in[M]} \leftarrow \mathsf{Expand}(h_2)$, where $\epsilon_e, \lambda_e^{(j)} \in \mathbb{Z}_p$.

Phase 5: Commitment to views of sacrificing protocol

1: **for** e from 1 to M **do**
2:     **for** i from 1 to N **do**
3:         Compute shares: $\alpha_{e,i} \leftarrow a_{e,i} + \epsilon_e K_{e,i}$ and $\beta_{e,i} \leftarrow b_{e,i} + \sum_{j=1}^{B} \lambda_e^{(j)} r_{e,i}^{(j)}$.
4:     Compute values: $\alpha_e \leftarrow \sum_{i=1}^{N} \alpha_{e,i}$ and $\beta_e \leftarrow \sum_{i=1}^{N} \beta_{e,i}$.
5:     **for** i from 1 to N **do**
6:         Compute product shares: $z_{e,i} \leftarrow \sum_{j=1}^{B} -\lambda_e^{(j)} r_{e,i}^{(j)} I_e^{(j)}$.
7:         **if** $i \stackrel{?}{=} 1$ **then** $z_{e,i} \leftarrow z_{e,i} + \sum_{j=1}^{B} \lambda_e^{(j)} o_e^{(j)}$.
8:         Compute check value shares: $\gamma_{e,i} \leftarrow \alpha_e b_{e,i} + \beta_e a_{e,i} - c_{e,i} + \epsilon_e z_{e,i}$.
9: Set $\sigma_3 \leftarrow (\alpha_e, \beta_e, (\alpha_{e,i}, \beta_{e,i}, \gamma_{e,i})_{i\in[N]})_{e\in[M]}$.

Phase 6: Challenge on sacrificing protocol

1: Compute challenge hash $h_3 \leftarrow \mathcal{H}_3(h_2, \sigma_3)$.
2: Expand hash $(\bar{i}_e)_{e\in[M]} \leftarrow \mathsf{Expand}(h_3)$, where $\bar{i}_e \in [N]$.

Phase 7: Opening the views of sacrificing protocol

1: **for** e from 1 to M **do**
2:     $\mathsf{seeds}_e \leftarrow \{\log_2(N)$ nodes in tree needed to compute $\mathsf{sd}_{e,i}$ for $i \in [N] \setminus \bar{i}\}$.
3: Output: $\sigma = (\mathsf{salt}, h_1, h_3, (\Delta K_e, \Delta c_e, o_e^{(1)}, \ldots, o_e^{(B)}, \alpha_e, \beta_e, \mathsf{seeds}_e, C_{e,\bar{i}_e})_{e\in[M]})$.

Fig. 6. Signature scheme from proof of knowledge of k-th power residue PRF pre-image.

$\mathsf{Vf}(\mathsf{params}, \mathsf{pk}, m, \sigma)$:

1: Parse $\sigma = (\mathsf{salt}, h_1, h_3, (\Delta K_e, \Delta c_e, o_e^{(1)}, \ldots, o_e^{(B)}, \alpha_e, \beta_e, \mathsf{seeds}_e, \mathsf{C}_{e,\bar{i}_e})_{e \in [M]})$.

2: Compute $h_2 \leftarrow \mathcal{H}_2(h_1, (o_e^{(j)})_{e \in [M], j \in [B]})$.

3: Expand challenge hash 1: $(I_e^{(1)}, \ldots, I_e^{(B)})_{e \in [M]} \leftarrow \mathsf{Expand}(h_1)$, where $I_e^{(j)} \in \mathcal{I}$.

4: Expand challenge hash 2: $(\epsilon_e, \lambda_e^{(1)}, \ldots, \lambda_e^{(B)})_{e \in [M]} \leftarrow \mathsf{Expand}(h_2)$.

5: Expand challenge hash 3: $(\bar{i}_e)_{e \in [M]} \leftarrow \mathsf{Expand}(h_3)$.

6: **for** e from 1 to M **do**

7:     Use seeds_e to compute $\mathsf{sd}_{e,i}$ for $i \in [N] \setminus \bar{i}_e$.

8:     **for** i from 1 to $\bar{i}_e - 1$ and from $\bar{i}_e + 1$ to N **do**

9:         Sample shares: $K_{e,i}, r_{e,i}^{(1)}, \ldots, r_{e,i}^{(B)}, a_{e,i}, b_{e,i}, c_{e,i} \leftarrow \mathsf{Expand}(\mathsf{sd}_{e,i})$.

10:         **if** $i \stackrel{?}{=} 1$ **then**

11:             Adjust shares: $K_{e,i} \leftarrow K_{e,i} + \Delta K_e$ and $c_{e,i} \leftarrow c_{e,i} + \Delta c_e$.

12:         Recompute commitments: $\mathsf{C}_{e,i}^* \leftarrow \mathcal{H}(\mathsf{salt}, e, i, \mathsf{sd}_{e,i})$

13:         Recompute shares: $\alpha_{e,i}^* \leftarrow a_{e,i} + \epsilon_e K_{e,i}$ and $\beta_{e,i}^* \leftarrow b_{e,i} + \sum_{j=1}^{B} \lambda_e^{(j)} r_{e,i}^{(j)}$.

14:         Recompute product shares: $z_{e,i} \leftarrow \sum_{j=1}^{B} -\lambda_e^{(j)} r_{e,i}^{(j)} I_e^{(j)}$.

15:         **if** $i \stackrel{?}{=} 1$ **then**

16:             $z_{e,i} \leftarrow z_{e,i} + \sum_{j=1}^{B} \lambda_e^{(j)} o_e^{(j)}$.

17:         Recompute check value shares: $\gamma_{e,i}^* \leftarrow \alpha_e b_{e,i} + \beta_e a_{e,i} - c_{e,i} + \epsilon_e z_{e,i}$.

18:     Compute missing shares: $\alpha_{e,\bar{i}_e}^* \leftarrow \alpha_e - \sum_{i \neq \bar{i}} \alpha_{e,i}^*$ and $\beta_{e,\bar{i}_e}^* \leftarrow \beta_e - \sum_{i \neq \bar{i}} \beta_{e,i}^*$.

19:     Compute missing check value share: $\gamma_{e,\bar{i}_e}^* = \alpha_e \beta_e - \sum_{i \neq \bar{i}} \gamma_{e,i}^*$.

20:     **for** j from 1 to B **do**

21:         Recompute residuosity symbols: $s_e^{(j)*} \leftarrow \mathcal{L}_0^k(o_e^{(j)}) - \mathsf{pk}_{I_e^{(j)}}$.

22: Check 1: $h_1 \stackrel{?}{=} \mathcal{H}_1(m, \mathsf{salt}, ((\mathsf{C}_{e,i}^*)_{i \in [N]}, (s_e^{(j)*})_{j \in [B]}, \Delta K_e, \Delta c_e)_{e \in [M]})$

23: Check 2: $h_3 \stackrel{?}{=} \mathcal{H}_3(h_2, (\alpha_e, \beta_e, (\alpha_{e,i}^*, \beta_{e,i}^*, \gamma_{e,i}^*)_{i \in [N]})_{e \in [M]})$

24: Output **accept** if both checks pass.

Fig. 7. Verifying algorithm for LegRoast and PorcRoast.

6.1 Parameter Choices

Choosing p, L and $\mathcal{I}$. We choose p and L such that the problem of finding a β-approximate witness for the PRF relation has the required security level. To do this, we first choose p and L such that the problem of recovering the exact key from L symbols of output is hard. For our proposed parameters we choose L such that the public key size is $4\,\mathrm{KB}$, (i.e. $L = 32768/\log(k)$). Different trade-offs are possible (see Remark 1). Then, we set β such that

$$k \cdot p \cdot \Pr[B(L, 1/k + 1/\sqrt(p) + 2/p) > (1 - \beta)l] \leq 2^{-\lambda}.$$

With this choice, Theorem 1 says that with overwhelming probability, finding a β-approximate key is equivalent to finding the exact key. Section 2 gives a short overview of attacks on the Legendre PRF for various attack models. However, in the setting of attacking LegRoast and PorcRoast, the adversary is restricted even more than in the weakest attacker model considered in the literature: an attacker learns only a few evaluations of the Legendre PRF on pseudorandom inputs over which the attacker has no control. If the L inputs are chosen at random, the best known attack is a brute force search which requires computing $O(p/k)$ power residue symbols, and the attack complexity becomes independent of L. For Legroast, we propose to use a prime p of size roughly 2^λ, where λ is the required security level. We choose the Mersenne prime $p = 2^{127} - 1$ to speed up the arithmetic. For PorcRoast, we use the same prime and $k = 254$ such that a power residue symbol can efficiently be represented by a single byte. For $k > 2$, computing a power residue symbol corresponds to a modular exponentiation, which is much more expensive than an AES operation, so even though an attacker has on average only to compute $2^{127}/k \approx 2^{119}$ power residue symbols, we claim that this still provides approximately 128-bits of security. We stress that the quantum polynomial-time key recovery attack on the Legendre PRF does not apply on our scheme, because the adversary can not make queries to the instance of the Legendre PRF (and certainly no quantum queries) [8].

Choosing B, N and M. Our security proof shows that, unless an attacker can produce a β-approximate witness, his best strategy is to query $\mathcal{H}_1$ on many inputs and then choose the query for which

$$\mathcal{L}_0^k((K_e + I_e^{(j)})r_e^{(j)}) = s_e^{(j)} + \mathsf{pk}_{I_e^{(j)}} \text{ for all } j \in [B]$$

holds for the most executions. Say this is the case for M' out of M executions. He then makes one of the parties cheat in the MPC protocol in each of the $M - M'$ remaining executions and queries $\mathcal{H}_3$ in the hope of getting an output $\{\bar{i}_e\}_{e \in [M]}$ that asks him to open all the other non-cheating parties; i.e. the attacker attempts to guess $\bar{i}_e$ for each e. This succeeds with probability $N^{-M+M'}$.

Therefore, to achieve λ bits of security, we take parameters $B, N = 2^n$ and M such that

$$\min_{M' \in \{0, \dots, M\}} \left(\Pr[\mathcal{B}(M, (1 - \beta)^B) \geq M_1]^{-1} + N^{M-M'} \right) \geq 2^\lambda, \tag{1}$$

which says that for each value of M', the adversary is expected to do at least 2^λ hash function evalutations for the attack to succeed. To choose parameters, we fix N to a certain value and compute which values of B and M minimize the signature size while satisfying Eq. (1). The choice of N controls a trade-off between signing time and signature size. If N is large, the soundness error will be small, which results in a smaller signature size, but the signer and the verifier need to simulate an MPC protocol with a large number of parties, which is slow. On the other hand, if N is small, then the signature size will be larger, but signing and verifying will be faster. Some trade-offs achieving 128-bits of security for LegRoast and PorcRoast are displayed in Table 1.

Remark 1. The parameter L controls a trade-off between public key size and signature size. For example, we can decrease the public key size by a factor 8 (to 0.5 KB), at the cost of an increase in signature size by 21% (to 7.6 KB). ($L = 512, k = 254, \beta = 0.871, n = 256, B = 10, M = 20$).

Table 1. Parameter sets for LegRoast and PorcRoast for NIST security level I. For all parameter sets we have $p = 2^{127} - 1$, a secret key size of 16 Bytes and a public key size of 4 KB ($L = 32768$ and 4096 for LegRoast and PorcRoast respectively). The verification time is similar to the signing time.

	Parameters			Signature size	Signing time
	N	M	B	(KB)	(ms)
LegRoast	16	54	9	16.0	2.8
$k = 2$	64	37	12	13.9	6.0
$\beta = 0.449$	256	26	16	12.2	15.7
PorcRoast	16	39	4	8.6	1.2
$k = 254$	64	27	5	7.2	2.8
$\beta = 0.967$	256	19	6	6.3	7.9

6.2 Implementation

In our implementation, we replace the random oracles and the Expand function by SHA-3 and SHAKE128. The signing algorithm is inherently constant time, except for computing Legendre symbols, which when implemented with the usual GCD strategy, leaks timing information on its argument. Therefore, in our implementation, we chose to adopt the slower approach of computing Legendre symbols as an exponentiation with fixed exponent $(p-1)/2$, which is an inherently constant time operation. Higher-power residue symbols are also calculated as an exponentiation with fixed exponent $(p-1)/k$. The signing-time of our implementation, measured on an Intel i5-8400H CPU, running at 2.50 GHz, is displayed in Table 1.

A   Proof of Theorem 1

We will use the following version of the Weil bound for character sums [18].

Theorem 3. Let p be a prime and χ a non-trivial multiplicative character of $\mathbb{F}_p^\times$ of order $d > 1$. If $f \in \mathbb{F}_p[X]$ has m distinct roots and is not a d-th power, then

$$\left| \sum_{x \in \mathbb{F}_p} \chi(f(x)) \right| \leq (m-1)\sqrt{p}.$$

The following lemma immediately follows:

Lemma 1. Let p be a prime and $k \mid p-1$. For any $K \neq K' \in \mathbb{F}_p$ and $a \in \mathbb{Z}_k$, let $I_{K,K',a}$ be the set of indices i such that $\mathcal{L}^k(K+i) = \mathcal{L}^k(K'+i) + a$. Then we have

$$\frac{p}{k} - \sqrt{p} - 1 \leq \#I_{K,K',a} \leq \frac{p}{k} + \sqrt{p} + 2.$$

Proof. Let $\chi : \mathbb{F}_p^\times \to \mathbb{Z}_p$ be the restriction of $\mathcal{L}^k$ to $\mathbb{F}^\times$. Note that (unlike $\mathcal{L}^k$) χ is a group homomorphism. Define $f(i) = (i + K)(i + K')^{k-1}$ and let $\phi(a)$ be the number of i such that $i + K$ and $i + K'$ are non-zero and $\chi(f(i)) = a$. Clearly we have $\phi(a) \le \#I_{K,K',a} \le \phi(a) + 2$. Let $\hat{\phi} : \hat{\mathbb{Z}}_k \to \mathbb{C}$ be the Fourier transform of ϕ. Then we have

$$\hat{\phi}(\rho) = \sum_{a \in \mathbb{Z}_k} \rho(a)\phi(a) = \sum_{a \in \mathbb{Z}_k} \rho(a) \sum_{i \in \mathbb{F}_p, i \ne K, i \ne K'} \begin{cases} 1 \text{ if } \chi(f(i)) = a \\ 0 \text{ otherwise} \end{cases}$$

$$= \sum_{i \in \mathbb{F}_p, i \ne K, i \ne K'} \rho \circ \chi(f(i))$$

Observe that $\rho \circ \chi$ is a multiplicative character of $\mathbb{F}_p^\times$, and that $\rho \circ \chi$ is trivial if and only if ρ is trivial. Clearly $\hat{\phi}(1) = p - 2$, and for non-trivial ρ, the Weil bound says that $|\hat{\phi}(\rho)| \le \sqrt{p}$. Therefore, if follows from the inverse Fourier transform formula that

$$\phi(a) = \frac{1}{|\mathbb{Z}_k|} \sum_{\rho \in \hat{\mathbb{Z}}_k} \rho(a)\hat{\phi}(\rho) \le \frac{p-2}{k} + \frac{k-1}{k}\sqrt{p} \le \frac{p}{k} + \sqrt{p}.$$

and similarly that $\frac{p}{k} - \sqrt{p} - 1 \le \phi(a)$. $\qquad\qquad\square$

Now we can prove Theorem 1.

Proof. According to lemma 1, For any $K' \ne K$ and $a \in \mathbb{Z}_k$, for a uniformly random set of inputs $\mathcal{I}$, the distance $d_H(F_{\mathcal{I}}^k(K') + (a, \dots, a), s)$ is distributed as $\mathcal{B}(L, 1 - \alpha)$, for some $\alpha \in [1/k - \frac{1}{\sqrt{p}} - \frac{1}{p}, 1/k + \frac{1}{\sqrt{p}} + \frac{2}{p}]$. Therefore, the probability that for a tuple (K', a) we have $d_H(F_{\mathcal{I}}^k(K') + (a, \dots, a), s) \le \beta L$ is at most

$$\Pr[\mathcal{B}(L, 1/k + \frac{1}{\sqrt{p} + 2/p}) > (1 - \beta)L].$$

Since there exists only $(p - 1)k$ possibile values for (K', a), the probability that there exists a non-trivial witness for the β-relaxed relation is at most $\Pr[\mathcal{B}(L, 1/k + \frac{1}{\sqrt{p}+2/p}) > (1 - \beta)L](p - 1)k$. $\qquad\square$

B   Security Proof

To prove Theorem 2, we first reduce the EUF-KO security to the β-approximate PRF relation (Lemma 2); we then reduce the EUF-CMA security to the EUF-KO security (Lemma 3). For two real random variables A, B, we write $A \prec B$ if for all $x \in (-\infty, +\infty)$ we have $\Pr[A > x] \le \Pr[B > x]$.

Lemma 2 (EUF-KO security). *Let $\mathcal{H}_{\mathsf{sd}}, \mathcal{H}_1, \mathcal{H}_2$ and $\mathcal{H}_3$ be modeled as random oracles and fix a constant $\beta \in [0, 1]$. If there exists a PPT adversary $\mathcal{A}$ that makes $q_{\mathsf{sd}}, q_1, q_2$ and q_3 queries to the respective oracles, then there exists a*

PPT $\mathcal{B}$ *which, given* $\mathsf{pk} = F_L^k(K)$ *for a random* $K \in \mathbb{F}_p$ *outputs a* β-*approximate witness for* pk *with probability at least* $\mathbf{Adv}_{\mathcal{A}}^{EUF\text{-}KO}(1^\lambda) - e(q_{sd}, q_1, q_2, q_3)$, *with*

$$e(q_{sd}, q_1, q_2, q_3) = \frac{MN(q_{sd} + q_1 + q_2 + q_3)^2}{2^{2\lambda}} + \Pr[X + Y + Z = M],$$

where $X = \max(X_1, \ldots, X_{q_1})$, $Y = \max(Y_1, \ldots, Y_{q_2})$ *and* $Z = \max(Z_1, \ldots, Z_{q_3})$, *the* X_i *are i.i.d as* $\mathcal{B}(M, (1-\beta)^B)$, *the* Y_i *are i.i.d. as* $\mathcal{B}(M - X, \frac{2}{p})$ *and the* Z_i *are i.i.d. as* $\mathcal{B}(M - X - Y, \frac{1}{N})$.

Proof. The algorithm $\mathcal{B}$ receives a statement $s = F_L^k(K)$ and forwards it to $\mathcal{A}$ as pk. Then, $\mathcal{B}$ simulates the random oracles $\mathcal{H}_{sd}, \mathcal{H}_1, \mathcal{H}_2$ and $\mathcal{H}_3$ by maintaining initially empty lists of queries $\mathcal{Q}_{sd}, \mathcal{Q}_1, \mathcal{Q}_2, \mathcal{Q}_3$. Moreover, $\mathcal{B}$ keeps initially empty tables $\mathcal{T}_s, \mathcal{T}_i$ and $\mathcal{T}_o$ for shares, inputs, and openings. If $\mathcal{A}$ queries one of the random oracles on an input that it has queried before, $\mathcal{B}$ responds as before; otherwise $\mathcal{B}$ does the following:

- $\mathcal{H}_{sd}$: On new input $(\mathsf{salt}, \mathsf{sd})$, $\mathcal{B}$ samples $x \xleftarrow{\$} \{0,1\}^{2\lambda}$. If $x \in \mathsf{Bad_H}$, then $\mathcal{B}$ aborts. Otherwise, $\mathcal{B}$ adds x to $\mathsf{Bad_H}$, $((\mathsf{salt}, \mathsf{sd}), x)$ to $\mathcal{Q}_{sd}$ and returns x.
- $\mathcal{H}_1$: On new input $Q = (m, \mathsf{salt}, \sigma_1)$, with $\sigma_1 = ((C_{e,i})_{i \in [N]}, (s_e^{(j)})_{j \in [B]}, \Delta K_e, \Delta c_e)_{e \in [M]})$, then $\mathcal{B}$ adds $C_{e,i}$ to $\mathsf{Bad_H}$ for all $e \in [M]$ and $i \in [N]$. For any $(e, i) \in [M] \times [N]$ for which there exist $\mathsf{sd}_{e,i}$ such that $((\mathsf{salt}, \mathsf{sd}_{e,i}), C_{e,i}) \in \mathcal{Q}_{sd}$ define

$$k_{e,i}, a_{e,i}, b_{e,i}, c_{e,i}, r_{e,i}^{(1)}, \cdots, r_{e,i}^{(B)} \leftarrow \mathsf{Expand}(\mathsf{sd}_{e,i}) \text{ for all } j \in [N]$$

and add $\mathcal{T}_s[Q, e, i] = (k_{e,i}, a_{e,i}, b_{e,i}, c_{e,i}, r_{e,i}^{(1)}, \ldots, r_{e,i}^{(B)})_{j \in [N]}$. If $\mathcal{T}_s[Q, e, i]$ is defined for all $i \in [N]$ for some $e \in [M]$, then we define

$$(k_e, a_e, b_e, c_e, r_e^{(1)}, \ldots, r_e^{(B)}) \leftarrow \sum_{i \in [N]} (k_{e,i}, a_{e_i}, b_{e,i}, c_{e,i}, r_{e,i}^{(1)}, \ldots, r_{e,i}^{(B)})$$

$$(k_e, c_e) \leftarrow (k_e + \Delta k_e, c_e + \Delta c_e)$$

and add $\mathcal{T}_i[Q, e] = (k_{e,i}, a_{e_i}, b_{e,i}, c_{e,i}, r_{e,i}^{(1)}, \ldots, r_{e,i}^{(B)})$. Finally, $\mathcal{B}$ samples $x \xleftarrow{\$} \{0,1\}^{2\lambda}$. If $x \in \mathsf{Bad_H}$ then abort. Otherwise, $\mathcal{B}$ adds (Q, x) to $\mathcal{Q}_1$ and x to $\mathsf{Bad_H}$ and returns x.
- $\mathcal{H}_2$: On new input $Q = (h_1, \sigma_2)$, where $\sigma_2 = (o_e^{(j)})_{e \in [M], j \in [B]}$, $\mathcal{B}$ adds h_1 to $\mathsf{Bad_H}$ and samples $x \xleftarrow{\$} \{0,1\}^{2\lambda}$. If $x \in \mathsf{Bad_H}$ then abort. Otherwise, $\mathcal{B}$ adds (Q, x) to $\mathcal{Q}_2$ and x to $\mathsf{Bad_H}$. If there exists $(Q_1, h_1) \in \mathcal{Q}_1$, then $\mathcal{B}$ does the following: let $(\epsilon_e, \lambda_e^{(1)}, \ldots, \lambda_e^{(B)})_{e \in [M]} \leftarrow \mathsf{Expand}(x)$. For each $e \in [M]$ such that $\mathcal{T}_i(Q_1, e)$ is defined, compute

$$\alpha_e = a_e + \epsilon_e k_e, \qquad \beta_e = b_e + \sum_{j \in [B]} \lambda_e^{(j)} r_e^{(j)} \text{ and}$$

$$\gamma_e = -c_e + \alpha_e b_e + \beta_e a_e + \epsilon_i \sum_{k \in [B]} \lambda_i^{(k)} (o_e^{(j)} - I_e^{(j)} r_e^{(j)})$$

and add $\mathcal{T}_o[Q_2, e] = (\alpha_e, \beta_e, \gamma_e)$. Finally $\mathcal{B}$ returns x.

- $\mathcal{H}_3$: On new input $Q = (h_2, \sigma_3)$, $\mathcal{B}$ adds h_2 to $\mathsf{Bad_H}$ and samples $x \xleftarrow{\$} \{0,1\}^{2\lambda}$. If $x \in \mathsf{Bad_H}$ then $\mathcal{B}$ aborts. Otherwise, $\mathcal{B}$ adds (Q, x) to $\mathcal{Q}_3$, x to $\mathsf{Bad_H}$ and returns x.

When $\mathcal{A}$ terminates, $\mathcal{B}$ goes through $\mathcal{T}_i$ and for each $(K_e, \dots) \in \mathcal{T}_i$, $\mathcal{B}$ checks if K_e is a β-approximate witness. If it is, then $\mathcal{B}$ outputs K_e. If no entry in $\mathcal{T}_i$ contains a witness, $\mathcal{B}$ outputs $\bot$. Clearly, if $\mathcal{A}$ runs in time T, then $\mathcal{B}$ runs in time $T + O(q_{\mathsf{sd}} + q_1 + q_2 + q_3)$.

In the rest of the proof, we show that if $\mathcal{A}$ wins the EUF-KO game with probability ϵ, then $\mathcal{B}$ outputs a β-approximate witness with probability at least $\epsilon - e(q_{\mathsf{sd}}, q_1, q_2, q_3)$ as defined in the statement of Lemma 2.

Cheating in the First Phase. Let $(Q_{\mathsf{best}_1}, h_{\mathsf{best}_1}) \in \mathcal{Q}_1$ be the "best" query-response pair that $\mathcal{A}$ received from $\mathcal{H}_1$, by which we mean the pair that maximizes $\#\mathsf{G}_1((Q, h))$ over all $(Q, h) \in \mathcal{Q}_1$, where $\mathsf{G}_1(Q, h = \{I_e^{(j)}\}_{e \in [M], j \in [B]})$ is defined as the set of "good executions" $e \in [M]$ such that $\mathcal{T}_i(Q, e)$ is defined and

$$\mathcal{L}^k((K_e + I_e^{(j)})r_e^{(j)}) = s_e^{(j)} + \mathsf{pk}_{I_e^{(j)}} \text{ for all } j \in [B]. \tag{2}$$

We show that, if $\mathcal{B}$ outputs $\bot$, then the number of good indices is bounded. More precisely, we prove that $\#\mathsf{G}_1(\sigma_{\mathsf{best}_1}, h_{\mathsf{best}_1})|_{\bot} \prec X$, where X is as defined in the statement of Lemma 2.

Indeed, for each distinct query to $\mathcal{H}_1$ of the form $Q = (m, \mathsf{salt}, \sigma_1)$, with $\sigma_1 = ((C_{e,i})_{i \in [N]}, (s_e^{(j)})_{j \in [B]}, \Delta K_e, \Delta c_e)_{e \in [M]})$ and for all $e \in [M]$, let $\beta_e^{(j)}(Q) = d_H(F_L^k(K_e) + (\mathcal{L}^k(r_e^{(j)}), \dots, \mathcal{L}^k(r_e^{(j)})), s_i^{(j)} + \mathsf{pk})$ if $\mathcal{T}_i(Q, e)$ is defined and $\beta_e^{(j)}(Q) = 1$ otherwise. The event $\bot$ implies that none of the K_e in $\mathcal{T}_i$ is a β-approximate witness, which means that $\beta_e^{(j)}(Q) > \beta$ for all $Q \in \mathcal{Q}_1, e \in [M]$ and $j \in [B]$.

Since the response $h = \{I_e^{(j)}\}_{e \in [M], j \in [B]}$ is uniform, the probability that for a certain e, Eq. (2) holds is $\prod_{k \in [B]}(1 - \beta_i^{(k)}) \leq (1 - \beta)^B$. Therefore, we have that $\#\mathsf{G}_1(Q, h)|_{\bot} \prec X_Q$, where $X_Q \sim \mathcal{B}(M, (1 - \beta)^B)$. Finally, since $\mathsf{G}_1(Q_{\mathsf{best}_1}, h_{\mathsf{best}_1})$ is the maximum over at most q_1 values of $\mathsf{G}_1(Q, h)$, it follows that $\#\mathsf{G}_1(Q_{\mathsf{best}_1}, h_{\mathsf{best}_1})|_{\bot} \prec X$, with X as in the statement of Lemma 2.

Cheating in the Second Round. We now look at the best query-response pair $(Q_{\mathsf{best}_2}, h_{\mathsf{best}_2})$ that $\mathcal{A}$ received from $\mathcal{H}_2$. This is the pair for which $\#\mathsf{G}_2(Q_2, h_2)$ is maximum, where $\mathsf{G}_2(Q_2 = (h_1, (o_e^{(j)})_{e \in [M], j \in [B]}), h_2)$ is the set of "good" executions defined as follows: if there exists no Q_1, such that $(Q_1, h_1) \in \mathcal{Q}_1$, then all indices are bad (because this query can not lead to a valid signature). Otherwise, let $Q_1 = (m, \mathsf{salt}, ((C_{e,i})_{i \in [N]}, (s_e^{(j)})_{j \in [B]}, \Delta K_e, \Delta c_e)_{e \in [M]}))$. If there exist $(e, j) \in [M] \times [B]$ such that

$$\mathcal{L}^k(o_e^{(j)}) \neq s_s^{(j)} + \mathsf{pk}_{I_e^{(j)}}, \tag{3}$$

then this query can also not result in a valid signature, so we define $G_2(Q_2, h_2) = \{\}$. Otherwise, we say $G_2(Q_2, h_2)$ is the set of executions $e \in [M]$ for which $\mathcal{T}_o[Q_2, e] = (\alpha_e, \beta_e, \gamma_e)$ is defined and such that $\alpha_e \beta_e = \gamma_e$.

Again, we prove that in the case that $\mathcal{B}$ outputs $\bot$, the number of good indices is bounded: $\#G_2(Q_{best_2}, h_{best_2})|_\bot \prec X + Y$, where Y is defined as in the statement of Lemma 2.

Note that for fixed $a_e, b_e, c_e, K_e, r_e^{(1)}, \dots, r_e^{(B)}$ and $o_e^{(1)}, \dots, o_e^{(B)}$ the function $\alpha_e(\epsilon_e)\beta_e(\lambda_e^{(j)}) - \gamma_e(\epsilon_e, \lambda_e^{(j)})$ is a quadratic polynomial in $\epsilon_e, \lambda_e^{(1)}, \dots, \lambda_e^{(B)}$. Moreover, this is the zero-polynomial if and only if $c_e = a_e b_e$ and $o_e^{(j)} = (K_e + I_e^{(j)})r_e^{(j)}$ for all $j \in [B]$.

Let $Q = (h_1, \{o_e^{(j)}\}_{e \in [M], j \in [B]})$ be a query to $\mathcal{H}_2$. If there exists no $(Q_1, h_1) \in \mathcal{Q}_1$ then $G_2(Q, h_2) = \{\}$ with probability 1. Otherwise, either $e \notin G_1(\sigma_1, h_1)$, then either $o_e^{(j)} = (K_e + I_e^{(j)})r_e^{(j)}$ for all $(e, j) \in [M] \times [B]$, in which case Eq. (3) does not hold, so $G_2(Q, h_2) = \{\}$ with probability 1, or $o_e^{(j)} \neq (K_e + I_e^{(j)})r_e^{(j)}$ for some $j \in [B]$ in which case $\alpha_e \beta_e - \gamma_e$ is a non-zero quadratic polynomial in ϵ_e and $\lambda_e^{(j)}$, so the Schwartz-Zippel lemma says that for a uniformly random choice of $h_2 = \{\epsilon_e, \lambda_e^{(j)}\}_{e \in [M], j \in [B]} \in \mathbb{F}_p^{M(1+B)}$ the probability that $e \in G_2(Q_2, h_2)$ is at most $2/p$. Therefore, we have that $\#G_2(\sigma_2, h_2)|_{\#G_1(\sigma_1, h_1) = M_1'} \prec M_1 + Y_Q'$, where $Y_q' \sim \mathcal{B}(M - M_1', 2/p)$. Since for integers $a \leq b$ and $p \in [0, 1]$ we have $\mathcal{B}(b, p) \prec a + \mathcal{B}(b - a, p)$, this implies that $\#G_2(\sigma_2, h_2)|_{\#G_1(state_{best}, 1) = M_1} \prec M_1 + Y_Q$, where $Y_Q \sim \mathcal{B}(M - M_1, 2/p)$. Since $\#G_2(state_{best}, 2)$ is the maximum over at most q_2 values of $\#G_2(state)$ it follows that $\#G_2(state_{best}, 2)|_{M_1 = \#G_1(state_{best}, 1)} \prec M_1 + Y$. Finally, by conditioning on $\bot$ and summing over all M_1, we get

$$\#G_2(state_{best, 2})|_\bot \prec \#G_1(state_{best, 1})|_\bot + Y \prec X + Y.$$

Cheating in the Third Round. Finally, we can bound the probability that $\mathcal{A}$ wins the EUF-KO game, conditioned on $\mathcal{B}$ outputting $\bot$. Without loss of generality, we can assume that $\mathcal{A}$ outputs a signature σ such that, if Q_1, Q_2 and Q_3 are the queries that the verifier makes to $\mathcal{H}_1, \mathcal{H}_2$ and $\mathcal{H}_3$ to verify σ, then $\mathcal{A}$ has made these queries as well. (If this is not the case, then we can define $\mathcal{A}'$ that only outputs a signature after running the verification algorithm on $\mathcal{A}$'s output.) Now, for each query $Q = (h_2, (\{\alpha_e, \beta_e\}_{e \in M}, \{\alpha_{e,i}, \beta_{e,i}, \gamma_{e,i}\}_{e \in [M], i \in [N]}))$ that $\mathcal{A}$ makes to $\mathcal{H}_3$, we study the probability that this leads $\mathcal{A}$ to win the EUF-KO game. If there does not exist $Q' = (o_e^{(j)})_{e \in [M], j \in [B]}$ such that $(Q', h_2) \in \mathcal{Q}_2$ then this query cannot result in a win for $\mathcal{A}$, because $\mathcal{A}$ would need to find such a Q' at a later point, and $\mathcal{B}$ would abort if this happens. Take $e \in [M] \setminus G_2(Q', h_2)$, then either $e \notin G_2(Q', h_2)$ because there exists $(e', j) \in [M] \times [B]$ such that $\ell^k o_{e'}^{(j)} \neq s_{e'}^{(j)} + pk_{I_{e'}^{(j)}}$, in which case, independent of h_3, σ_4, we have that $\mathsf{Vf}(\sigma) = 0$. Or otherwise $e \notin G_2(Q', h_2)$ because α_e, β_e and γ_e are not defined or $\alpha_e \beta_e \neq \gamma_e$. In this case, the query can only result in a win if exactly $N - 1$ of the parties "behave honestly" in the MPC protocol. By this we mean that for exactly $N - 1$ values of $i \in [N]$ we have that there exists $sd_{e,i}$ such that $(sd_{e,i}, C_{e,i}) \in \mathcal{Q}_{sd}$ and, if we put $K_{e,i}, a_{e,i}, b_{e,i}, c_{e,i}, \{r_{e,i}^{(j)}\}_{j \in [B]} = \mathsf{Expand}(sd_{e,i})$, then

$$\alpha_{e,i} = a_{e,i} + \epsilon_e K_{e,i}, \qquad \beta_{e,i} = b_{e,i} + \sum_k \lambda_e^{(j)} r_{e,i}^{(j)},$$

$$\gamma_{e,i} = -c_{e,i} + \alpha_e b_{e,i} + \beta_e a_{e,i} + \epsilon_e \sum_{j \in [B]} \lambda_e^{(j)} (o_e^{(j)} - I_e^{(j)} r_{e,i}^{(j)}).$$

Indeed, if there are less than $N-1$ honest parties, σ_4 cannot reveal $N-1$ honest views. In contrast if all the N parties act honestly, then we have $\gamma_e \neq \alpha_e \beta_e$, so the signature verification will also fail. The state $(\sigma_1, h_1, \sigma_2, h_2, \sigma_3)$ can only result in a win if $h_3 = \{\bar{i}_e\}_{e \in N}$ is such that $\bar{i}_e$ is the index of the dishonest party. Since $h_3 \in [N]^M$ is chosen uniformly at random, the probability that this happens for all the $e \notin \mathsf{G}_2(Q, h_3)$ is

$$\left(\frac{1}{N}\right)^{M - \#\mathsf{G}_2(Q', h_2)} \leq \left(\frac{1}{N}\right)^{M - \#\mathsf{G}_2(Q_{\mathsf{best}, 2}, h_{\mathsf{best}, 2})}.$$

The probability that this happens for at least one of the at most q_3 queries is

$$\Pr[\mathcal{A} \, \mathsf{Wins} | \#\mathsf{G}_2(\mathsf{state}_{best,2}) = M_2] \leq 1 - \left(1 - \left(\frac{1}{N}\right)^{M - M_2}\right)^{q_3}.$$

Conditioning on $\mathcal{B}$ outputting $\perp$ and summing over all values of M_2 yields

$$\Pr[\mathcal{A} \, \mathsf{Wins} \, | \perp] \leq \Pr[X + Y + Z = M].$$

To Conclude. We now show that if $\mathcal{A}$ wins the EUF-KO game with probability ϵ, then $\mathcal{B}$ outputs a β-approximate witness with probability $\epsilon - e(q_{\mathsf{sd}}, q_1, q_2, q_3)$. Indeed, $\mathcal{B}$ either aborts outputs $\perp$ or outputs a β-approximate witness. The reduction $\mathcal{B}$ only aborts if one of the random oracles outputs one of the at most $q_{\mathsf{sd}} + MNq_1 + q_2 + q_3$ bad values. Therefore, we have

$$\Pr[\mathcal{E} \text{ aborts }] \leq \frac{MN(q_{\mathsf{sd}} + q_1 + q_2 + q_3)^2}{2^{2\lambda}}.$$

By the law of total probability we have

$$\begin{aligned}
\Pr[\mathcal{A} \text{ wins}] &= \Pr[\mathcal{A} \text{ wins} \wedge \mathcal{B} \text{ aborts}] + \Pr[\mathcal{A} \text{ wins} \wedge \perp] \\
&\quad + \Pr[\mathcal{A} \text{ wins} \wedge \mathcal{B} \text{ outputs witness}] \\
&\leq \Pr[\mathcal{B} \text{ aborts}] + \Pr[\mathcal{A} \text{ wins} | \perp] + \Pr[\mathcal{B} \text{ outputs witness}] \\
&\leq e(q_{\mathsf{sd}}, q_1, q_2, q_3) + \Pr[\mathcal{B} \text{ outputs witness}].
\end{aligned}$$

Lemma 3. *Modeling the commitment scheme as a random oracle, if there is an adversary $\mathcal{A}$ that wins the EUF-CMA security game against LegRoast with advantage ϵ, then there exists an adversary $\mathcal{B}$ that, given oracle access to $\mathcal{A}$, and with a constant overhead factor, wins the EUF-KO security game against LegRoast with probability at least $\epsilon - \frac{q_s(q_s + q_3)}{2^{2\lambda}} - \frac{q_{\mathsf{sd}}}{2^\lambda}$, where q_s, q_{sd} and q_3 are the number of queries that $\mathcal{A}$ makes to the signing oracle, $\mathcal{H}_{\mathsf{sd}}$ and $\mathcal{H}_3$ respectively.*

Proof. Let $\mathcal{A}$ be an adversary against the EUF-CMA security of LegRoast, we construct an adversary $\mathcal{B}$ against its EUF-KO security. When $\mathcal{B}$ is run on input pk, it starts $\mathcal{A}$ also on input pk. We first describe how $\mathcal{B}$ deals with random oracle queries and signature queries, then argue that its signature simulations are indistinguishable from real ones, and finally show that EUF-KO security implies EUF-CMA security.

Simulating Random Oracles. For each random oracle $\mathcal{B}$ maintains a table of input output pairs. When $\mathcal{A}$ queries one of the random oracles, $\mathcal{B}$ first checks if that query has been made before. If this is the case, $\mathcal{B}$ responds to $\mathcal{A}$ with the corresponding recorded output. If not, $\mathcal{B}$ returns a uniformly random output and records the new input-output pair in the table.

Signing Oracle Simulation. When $\mathcal{A}$ queries the signing oracle, $\mathcal{B}$ simulates a signature σ by sampling a random witness and cheating in the MPC verification phase to hide the fact it has sampled the witness as random. It then programs the last random oracle to always hide the party for which it has cheated. Formally, $\mathcal{B}$ simulates the signing oracle as follows:

1. To simulate σ_1, $\mathcal{B}$ follows Phase 1 as in the scheme with one difference: For each $e \in [M]$, it samples ΔK_e uniformly, effectively sampling K_e at random. $\mathcal{B}$ aborts if it picked a salt that was used in one of the earlier simulated signatures.
2. $\mathcal{B}$ simulates the random oracle to obtain $h_1 \leftarrow \mathcal{H}_1(m, \mathsf{salt}, \sigma_1)$.
3. To simulate σ_2, $\mathcal{B}$ samples $o_e^{(j)} \in \mathbb{F}_p^*$ for each $j \in [B]$ and $e \in [M]$ in such a way that $\mathcal{L}^k(o_e^{(j)}) - s_e^{(j)} = \mathsf{pk}_{I_e^{(j)}}$.
4. $\mathcal{B}$ simulates the random oracle to obtain $h_2 \leftarrow \mathcal{H}_2(h_1, \sigma_2)$.
5. To simulate σ_3, $\mathcal{B}$ must cheat during the sacrificing protocol to ensure that $\gamma_e = \alpha_e \beta_e$ for all executions. To do so, for each $e \in [M]$, $\mathcal{B}$ first samples $\bar{i}_e \in [N]$ at random. Then it computes Phase 5 honestly except for $\gamma_{e,\bar{i}_e}$; for that value, it instead sets $\gamma_{e,\bar{i}_e} \leftarrow \alpha_e \beta_e - \sum_{i \neq \bar{i}_e} \gamma_{e,i}$. Finally it sets σ_3 as in the scheme using the alternative $\gamma_{e,\bar{i}_e}$ value.
6. If (h_2, σ_3) has already been queried to $\mathcal{H}_3$, then $\mathcal{B}$ aborts. If not, $\mathcal{B}$ sets $h_3 = (\bar{i}_1, \ldots, \bar{i}_M)$ with the values it sampled previously and then programs its own random oracle $\mathcal{H}_3$ such that $h_3 \leftarrow \mathcal{H}_3(h_2, \sigma_3)$.
7. $\mathcal{B}$ follows the scheme to simulate σ_4 and the final signature σ.

Finally, when $\mathcal{A}$ outputs a forgery for its EUF-CMA game, $\mathcal{B}$ forwards it as its forgery for the EUF-KO game.

Simulation Indistinguishability. If $\mathcal{B}$ doesn't abort, the simulation of the random oracles is perfect. Moreover, if $\mathcal{B}$ doesn't abort we show that $\mathcal{A}$'s can only distinguish a real signing oracle from the simulated oracle with advantage $q_{\mathsf{sd}}/2^\lambda$, where q_{sd} is the number of queries to $\mathcal{H}_{\mathsf{sd}}$.

The simulated signatures follow the exact same distribution as genuine signatures, with the only exception that in a genuine signature the $(C_{e,\bar{i}_e})_{e \in [m]}$ are equal to $\mathcal{H}_{\sf sd}({\sf salt}, e, \bar{i}_e, {\sf sd}_{e,\bar{i}_e})$ for a value of ${\sf sd}_{e,\bar{i}_e}$ that expands to a consistent view of a party in the MPC protocol, whereas in the simulated case, ${\sf sd}_{e,\bar{i}_e}$ expands to the view of a cheating party. Since $\mathcal{H}_{\sf sd}$ is modelled as a random oracle, each of the $q_s \cdot M$ values of $\mathsf{C}_{e,\bar{i}_e}$ that $\mathcal{A}$ gets to see is just a random value, uncorrelated with the rest of the view of $\mathcal{A}$, *unless* $\mathcal{A}$ *has queried* $\mathcal{H}_{\sf sd}$ *on* $({\sf salt}, e, \bar{i}_e, {\sf sd}_{e,\bar{i}_e})$. Since the $({\sf salt}, e, \bar{i}_e)$ is unique per commitment ($\mathcal{B}$ aborts if a salt is repeated) and each seed has λ bits of min-entropy each query that $\mathcal{A}$ makes to $\mathcal{H}_{\sf sd}$ has a probability of at most $2^{-\lambda}$ of distinguishing the simulated signature oracle form a genuine signing oracle. Therefore, an adversary that makes $q_{\sf sd}$ queries to $\mathcal{H}_{\sf sd}$ has a distinguishing advantage bounded by $q_{\sf sd}/2^{\lambda}$.

EUF-KO Security Implies EUF-CMA Security. Finally, we establish $\mathcal{B}$'s advantage against the EUF-KO security game. There are two moments at which $\mathcal{B}$ could abort: In phase 1 if a salt is repeated which happens with probability bounded by $q_s^2/2^{2\lambda}$ (recall that a salt consists of 2λ random bits) and in phase 6, if $\mathcal{B}$ fails to program the oracle $\mathcal{H}_3$, which happens with probability bounded by $q_s q_3/2^{2\lambda}$, since h_2 has 2λ bits of min entropy. Therefore, we have $\Pr[\mathcal{B} \text{ aborts}] \leq \frac{q_s(q_s+q_3)}{2^{2\lambda}}$, where q_s and q_3 denotes the number of signing queries and queries to $\mathcal{H}_3$ made by $\mathcal{A}$ respectively. Conditional on $\mathcal{B}$ not aborting, replacing the genuine oracles for the simulated oracles decreases the winning probability of $\mathcal{A}$ by at most $q_{\sf sd}/2^{\lambda}$. Therefore, given that the winning conditions for the EUF-KO and EUF-CMA games are identical, we have:

$$\mathbf{Adv}_{\mathcal{B}}^{\text{EUF-KO}}(1^{\lambda}) \geq \mathbf{Adv}_{\mathcal{A}}^{\text{EUF-CMA}}(1^{\lambda}) - \frac{q_s(q_s+q_3)}{2^{2\lambda}} - \frac{q_{\sf sd}}{2^{\lambda}}.$$

References

1. Baum, C., Nof, A.: Concretely-efficient zero-knowledge arguments for arithmetic circuits and their application to lattice-based cryptography. Cryptology ePrint Archive, Report 2019/532 (2019). https://eprint.iacr.org/2019/532
2. Beullens, W.: Sigma protocols for MQ, PKP and SIS, and fishy signature schemes. Cryptology ePrint Archive, Report 2019/490 (2019). https://eprint.iacr.org/2019/490
3. Beullens, W., Beyne, T., Udovenko, A., Vitto, G.: Cryptanalysis of the legendre PRF and generalizations. Cryptology ePrint Archive, Report 2019/1357 (2019). https://eprint.iacr.org/2019/1357
4. Beullens, W., Kleinjung, T., Vercauteren, F.: CSI-FiSh: efficient isogeny based signatures through class group computations. In: Galbraith, S.D., Moriai, S. (eds.) ASIACRYPT 2019. LNCS, vol. 11921, pp. 227–247. Springer, Cham (2019). https://doi.org/10.1007/978-3-030-34578-5_9
5. Beullens, W., Preneel, B.: Field lifting for smaller UOV public keys. In: Patra, A., Smart, N.P. (eds.) INDOCRYPT 2017. LNCS, vol. 10698, pp. 227–246. Springer, Cham (2017). https://doi.org/10.1007/978-3-319-71667-1_12
6. Beullens, W., Preneel, B., Szepieniec, A., Vercauteren, F.: LUOV. Technical report, National Institute of Standards and Technology (2019). https://csrc.nist.gov/projects/post-quantum-cryptography/round-2-submissions

7. Chase, M., et al.: Post-quantum zero-knowledge and signatures from symmetric-key primitives. In: Thuraisingham, B.M., Evans, D., Malkin, T., Xu, D. (eds.) ACM CCS 2017, pp. 1825–1842. ACM Press, New York (2017)

8. van Dam, W., Hallgren, S.: Efficient quantum algorithms for shifted quadratic character problems. arXiv preprint arXiv:quant-ph/0011067 (2000)

9. Damgård, I.B.: On the randomness of Legendre and Jacobi sequences. In: Goldwasser, S. (ed.) CRYPTO 1988. LNCS, vol. 403, pp. 163–172. Springer, New York (1990). https://doi.org/10.1007/0-387-34799-2_13

10. Ding, J., Chen, M.S., Petzoldt, A., Schmidt, D., Yang, B.Y.: Rainbow. Technical report, National Institute of Standards and Technology (2019). https://csrc.nist.gov/projects/post-quantum-cryptography/round-2-submissions

11. Ding, J., Schmidt, D.: Rainbow, a new multivariable polynomial signature scheme. In: Ioannidis, J., Keromytis, A., Yung, M. (eds.) ACNS 2005. LNCS, vol. 3531, pp. 164–175. Springer, Heidelberg (2005). https://doi.org/10.1007/11496137_12

12. Ducas, L., et al.: CRYSTALS-Dilithium: a lattice-based digital signature scheme. IACR TCHES **2018**(1), 238–268 (2018). https://tches.iacr.org/index.php/TCHES/article/view/839

13. Fiat, A., Shamir, A.: How to prove yourself: practical solutions to identification and signature problems. In: Odlyzko, A.M. (ed.) CRYPTO 1986. LNCS, vol. 263, pp. 186–194. Springer, Heidelberg (1987). https://doi.org/10.1007/3-540-47721-7_12

14. Goldwasser, S., Micali, S., Rivest, R.L.: A digital signature scheme secure against adaptive chosen-message attacks. SIAM J. Comput. **17**(2), 281–308 (1988)

15. Grassi, L., Rechberger, C., Rotaru, D., Scholl, P., Smart, N.P.: MPC-friendly symmetric key primitives. In: Weippl, E.R., Katzenbeisser, S., Kruegel, C., Myers, A.C., Halevi, S. (eds.) ACM CCS 2016, pp. 430–443. ACM Press, New York (2016)

16. Hulsing, A., et al.: SPHINCS+. Technical report, National Institute of Standards and Technology (2019). https://csrc.nist.gov/projects/post-quantum-cryptography/round-2-submissions

17. Ishai, Y., Kushilevitz, E., Ostrovsky, R., Sahai, A.: Zero-knowledge proofs from secure multiparty computation. SIAM J. Comput. **39**(3), 1121–1152 (2009)

18. Iwaniec, H., Kowalski, E.: Analytic Number Theory, vol. 53. American Mathematical Society, Providence (2004)

19. Katz, J., Kolesnikov, V., Wang, X.: Improved non-interactive zero knowledge with applications to post-quantum signatures. In: Lie, D., Mannan, M., Backes, M., Wang, X. (eds.) ACM CCS 2018, pp. 525–537. ACM Press, Toronto (2018)

20. Khovratovich, D.: Key recovery attacks on the Legendre PRFs within the birthday bound. Cryptology ePrint Archive, Report 2019/862 (2019). https://eprint.iacr.org/2019/862

21. Lyubashevsky, V., et al.: CRYSTALS-DILITHIUM. Technical report, National Institute of Standards and Technology (2019). https://csrc.nist.gov/projects/post-quantum-cryptography/round-2-submissions

22. National Institute of Standards and Technology: Post-quantum cryptography project (2016). https://csrc.nist.gov/projects/post-quantum-cryptography

23. Prest, T., et al.: FALCON. Technical report, National Institute of Standards and Technology (2019). https://csrc.nist.gov/projects/post-quantum-cryptography/round-2-submissions

24. de Saint Guilhem, D.C., De Meyer, L., Orsini, E., Smart, N.P.: BBQ: using AES in picnic signatures. Cryptology ePrint Archive, Report 2019/781 (2019). https://eprint.iacr.org/2019/781

25. Samardjiska, S., Chen, M.S., Hulsing, A., Rijneveld, J., Schwabe, P.: MQDSS. Technical report, National Institute of Standards and Technology (2019). https:// csrc.nist.gov/projects/post-quantum-cryptography/round-2-submissions
26. Shor, P.W.: Algorithms for quantum computation: discrete logarithms and factoring. In: Proceedings 35th Annual Symposium on Foundations of Computer Science, pp. 124–134. IEEE (1994)
27. The Picnic team: The picnic signature algorithm specification (2019). https:// github.com/microsoft/Picnic/blob/master/spec/spec-v2.1.pdf

The Supersingular Isogeny Problem in Genus 2 and Beyond

Craig Costello[1] and Benjamin Smith[2(✉)]

[1] Microsoft Research, Redmond, USA
craigco@microsoft.com
[2] Inria and École Polytechnique, Institut Polytechnique de Paris, Palaiseau, France
smith@lix.polytechnique.fr

Abstract. Let $A/\overline{\mathbb{F}}_p$ and $A'/\overline{\mathbb{F}}_p$ be superspecial principally polarized abelian varieties of dimension $g > 1$. For any prime $\ell \neq p$, we give an algorithm that finds a path $\phi: A \to A'$ in the $(\ell, \dots, \ell)$-isogeny graph in $\widetilde{O}(p^{g-1})$ group operations on a classical computer, and $\widetilde{O}(\sqrt{p^{g-1}})$ calls to the Grover oracle on a quantum computer. The idea is to find paths from A and A' to nodes that correspond to products of lower dimensional abelian varieties, and to recurse down in dimension until an elliptic path-finding algorithm (such as Delfs–Galbraith) can be invoked to connect the paths in dimension $g = 1$. In the general case where A and A' are any two nodes in the graph, this algorithm presents an asymptotic improvement over all of the algorithms in the current literature. In the special case where A and A' are a known and relatively small number of steps away from each other (as is the case in higher dimensional analogues of SIDH), it gives an asymptotic improvement over the quantum claw finding algorithms and an asymptotic improvement over the classical van Oorschot–Wiener algorithm.

1 Introduction

Isogenies of supersingular elliptic curves are now well-established in cryptography, from the Charles–Goren–Lauter Hash Function [10] to Jao and De Feo's SIDH key exchange [27] and beyond [2,12,13,21]. While the security of isogeny-based cryptosystems depend on the difficulty of a range of computational problems, the fundamental one is the *isogeny problem*: given supersingular elliptic curves $\mathcal{E}_1$ and $\mathcal{E}_2$ over $\mathbb{F}_{p^2}$, find a walk in the ℓ-isogeny graph connecting them.

One intriguing aspect of isogeny-based cryptography is the transfer of elliptic-curve techniques from classic discrete-log-based cryptography into the post-quantum arena. In this spirit, it is natural to consider cryptosystems based on isogeny graphs of higher-dimensional abelian varieties, mirroring the transition from elliptic (ECC) to hyperelliptic-curve cryptography (HECC). Compared with elliptic supersingular isogeny graphs, the higher-dimensional graphs have more vertices and higher degrees for a given p, which allows some interesting tradeoffs (for example: in dimension $g = 2$, we get the same number of vertices with a p of one-third the bitlength).

© Springer Nature Switzerland AG 2020
J. Ding and J.-P. Tillich (Eds.): PQCrypto 2020, LNCS 12100, pp. 151–168, 2020.
https://doi.org/10.1007/978-3-030-44223-1_9

For $g = 2$, Takashima [36] and Castryck, Decru, and Smith [7] have defined CGL-style hash functions, while Costello [11] and Flynn and Ti [19] have already proposed SIDH-like key exchanges. Generalizations to dimensions $g > 2$, using isogeny algorithms such as those in [4], are easy to anticipate; for example, a family of hash functions on isogeny graphs of superspecial abelian varieties with real multiplication was hinted at in [9].

So far, when estimating security levels, these generalizations assume that the higher-dimensional supersingular isogeny problem is basically as hard as the elliptic supersingular isogeny problem in graphs of the same size. In this article, we show that this assumption is false. The general supersingular isogeny problem can be partially reduced to a series of lower-dimensional isogeny problems, and thus recursively to a series of elliptic isogeny problems.

Theorem 1. *There exists a classical algorithm which, given a prime ℓ and superspecial abelian varieties $\mathcal{A}_1$ and $\mathcal{A}_2$ of dimension g over $\overline{\mathbb{F}}_p$ with $p \neq \ell$, succeeds with probability $\geq 1/2^{g-1}$ in computing a composition of $(\ell, \ldots, \ell)$-isogenies from $\mathcal{A}_1$ to $\mathcal{A}_2$, running in expected time $\widetilde{O}((p^{g-1}/P))$ on P processors as $p \to \infty$ (with ℓ fixed).*

Given that these graphs have $O(p^{g(g+1)/2})$ vertices, the expected runtime for generic random-walk algorithms is $\widetilde{O}(p^{g(g+1)/4}/P)$. Our algorithm therefore represents a substantial speedup, with nontrivial consequences for cryptographic parameter selection.[1] We also see an improvement in quantum algorithms:

Theorem 2. *There exists a quantum algorithm which, given a prime ℓ and superspecial abelian varieties $\mathcal{A}_1$ and $\mathcal{A}_2$ of dimension g over $\overline{\mathbb{F}}_p$ with $p \neq \ell$, computes a composition of $(\ell, \ldots, \ell)$-isogenies from $\mathcal{A}_1$ to $\mathcal{A}_2$ running in expected time $\widetilde{O}(\sqrt{p^{g-1}})$ as $p \to \infty$ (with ℓ fixed).*

This reflects the general pattern seen in the passage from ECC to HECC: the dimension grows, the base field shrinks—and the mathematical structures become more complicated, which can ultimately reduce claimed security levels. Just as index calculus attacks on discrete logarithms become more powerful in higher genus, where useful structures appear in Jacobians [15,22,23,34], so interesting structures in higher-dimensional isogeny graphs provide attacks that become more powerful as the dimension grows. Here, the interesting structures are (relatively large) subgraphs corresponding to increasing numbers of elliptic factors in (polarized) abelian varieties. These subgraphs are relatively large, and so random-walking into them is relatively easy. We can then glue together elliptic isogenies, found with an elliptic path-finding algorithm, to form product isogenies between products of elliptic curves, and thus to solve the original isogeny problem. We will see that the path-finding problem in the superspecial graph gets asymptotically easier as the dimension grows.

---

[1] Our algorithms apply to the full superspecial graph; we do not claim any impact on cryptosystems that run in small and special subgraphs, such as CSIDH [8].

Notation and Conventions. Throughout, p denotes a prime ≥ 3, and ℓ a prime not equal to p. Typically, p is large, and $\ell \ll \log(p)$ is small enough that computing $(\ell, \dots, \ell)$-isogenies of g-dimensional principally polarized abelian varieties (PPAVs) is polynomial in $\log(p)$. Similarly, we work with PPAVs in dimensions $g \ll \log p$; in our asymptotics and complexities, g and ℓ are fixed. We say a function $f(X)$ is in $\tilde{O}(g(X))$ if $f(X) = O(h(\log X)g(X))$ for some polynomial h.

2   The Elliptic Supersingular Isogeny Graph

An elliptic curve $\mathcal{E}/\overline{\mathbb{F}}_p$ is *supersingular* if $\mathcal{E}[p](\overline{\mathbb{F}}_p) = 0$. We have a number of efficient algorithms for testing supersingularity: see Sutherland [35] for discussion.

Supersingularity is isomorphism-invariant, and any supersingular $\mathcal{E}$ has j-invariant $j(\mathcal{E})$ in $\mathbb{F}_{p^2}$; and in fact the curve $\mathcal{E}$ can be defined over $\mathbb{F}_{p^2}$. We let

$$S_1(p) := \left\{ j(\mathcal{E}) : \mathcal{E}/\mathbb{F}_{p^2} \text{ is supersingular} \right\} \subset \mathbb{F}_{p^2}$$

be the set of isomorphism classes of supersingular elliptic curves over $\overline{\mathbb{F}}_p$. It is well-known that

$$\#S_1(p) = \left\lfloor \frac{p}{12} \right\rfloor + \epsilon_p \tag{1}$$

where $\epsilon_p = 0$ if $p \equiv 1 \pmod{12}$, 2 if $p \equiv -1 \pmod{12}$, and 1 otherwise.

Now fix a prime $\ell \neq p$, and consider the directed multigraph $\Gamma_1(\ell; p)$ whose vertex set is $S_1(p)$, and whose edges correspond to ℓ-isogenies between curves (again, up to isomorphism). The graph $\Gamma_1(\ell; p)$ is $(\ell+1)$-regular: there are (up to isomorphism) $\ell + 1$ distinct ℓ-isogenies from a supersingular elliptic curve $\mathcal{E}/\mathbb{F}_{p^2}$ to other elliptic curves, corresponding to the $\ell+1$ order-ℓ subgroups of $\mathcal{E}[\ell](\overline{\mathbb{F}}_p) \cong (\mathbb{Z}/\ell\mathbb{Z})^2$ that form their kernels. But since supersingularity is isogeny-invariant, the codomain of each isogeny is again supersingular; that is, the $\ell + 1$ order-ℓ subgroups of $\mathcal{E}[\ell]$ are in bijection with the edges out of $j(\mathcal{E})$ in $\Gamma_1(\ell; p)$.

Definition 1. *A* walk *of length n in $\Gamma_1(\ell; p)$ is a sequence of edges $j_0 \to j_1 \to \cdots \to j_n$. A* path *in $\Gamma_1(\ell; p)$ is an acyclic (and, in particular, non-backtracking) walk: that is, a walk $j_0 \to j_1 \to \cdots \to j_n$ such that $j_i = j_{i'}$ if and only if $i = i'$.*

Pizer [32] proved that $\Gamma_1(\ell; p)$ is Ramanujan: in particular, $\Gamma_1(\ell; p)$ is a connected expander graph, and its diameter is $O(\log p)$. We therefore expect the end-points of short random walks from any given vertex j_0 to quickly yield a uniform distribution on $S_1(p)$. Indeed, if j_0 is fixed and j_n is the end-point of an n-step random walk from j_0 in $\Gamma_1(\ell; p)$, then [21, Theorem 1] shows that

$$\left| \Pr[j_n = j] - \frac{1}{\#S_1(p)} \right| \leq \left(\frac{2\sqrt{\ell}}{\ell + 1} \right)^n \qquad \text{for all } j \in S_1(p). \tag{2}$$

The *isogeny problem* in $\Gamma_1(\ell; p)$ is, given j_0 and j in $S_1(p)$, to find a path (of any length) from j_0 to j in $\Gamma_1(\ell; p)$. The difficulty of the isogeny problem underpins the security of the Charles–Goren–Lauter hash function (see Sect. 3 below).

The isogeny problem is supposed to be hard. Our best generic classical path-finding algorithms look for collisions in random walks, and run in expected time the square root of the graph size: in this case, $\widetilde{O}(\sqrt{p})$. In the special case of supersingular isogeny graphs, we can make some practical improvements but the asymptotic complexity remains the same: given j_0 and j in $F_1(p; \ell)$, we can compute a path $j_0 \to j$ in $\widetilde{O}(\sqrt{p})$ classical operations (see [14]).

The best known quantum algorithm for path-finding [3] instead searches for paths from $j_0 \to j_0'$ and from $j \to j'$, where j_0' and j' are both in $\mathbb{F}_p$. Of the $O(p)$ elements in $S_1(p)$, there are $O(\sqrt{p})$ elements contained in $\mathbb{F}_p$; while a classical search for elements this sparse would therefore run in time $O(\sqrt{p})$, Grover's quantum algorithm [24] completes the search in expected time $O(\sqrt[4]{p})$. It remains to find a path from j_0' to j'. This could be computed classically in time $\widetilde{O}(\sqrt[4]{p})$ using the Delfs–Galbraith algorithm, but Biasse, Jao and Sankar [3] show that a quantum computer can find paths between subfield curves in subexponential time, yielding an overall algorithm that runs in expected time $O(\sqrt[4]{p})$.

We can also consider the problem of finding paths of a fixed (and typically *short*) length: for example, given $e > 0$ and j_0 and j in $S_1(p)$ such that there exists a path $\phi : j_0 \to \cdots \to j$ of length e, find ϕ. This problem arises in the security analysis of SIDH, for example.

3   Cryptosystems in the Elliptic Supersingular Graph

The Charles–Goren–Lauter Hash Function (CGL). Supersingular isogenies appeared in cryptography with the CGL hash function, which operates in $\Gamma_1(2; p)$. Fix a base point j_0 in $S_1(p)$, and one of the three edges in $\Gamma_1(2; p)$ leading into it: $j_{-1} \to j_0$, say. To hash an n-bit message $m = (m_0, m_1, \ldots, m_{n-1})$, we let m drive a non-backtracking walk $j_0 \to \cdots \to j_n$ on $\Gamma_1(2; p)$: for each $0 \le i < n$, we compute the two roots α_0 and α_1 of $\Phi_2(j_i, X)/(j_{i-1} - X)$ to determine the neighbours of j_i that are not j_{i-1}, numbering the roots with respect to some ordering of $\mathbb{F}_{p^2}$ (here $\Phi_2(Y, X)$ is the classical modular polynomial), and set $j_{i+1} = \alpha_{m_i}$.

Once we have computed the entire walk $j_0 \to \cdots \to j_n$, we can derive a $\log_2 p$-bit hash value $H(m)$ from the end-point j_n; we call this step *finalisation*. Charles, Goren, and Lauter suggest applying a linear function $f : \mathbb{F}_{p^2} \to \mathbb{F}_p$ to map j_n to $H(m) = f(j_n)$. For example, if $\mathbb{F}_{p^2} = \mathbb{F}_p(\omega)$ then we can map $j_n = j_{n,0} + j_{n,1}\omega$ (with $j_{n,0}$ and $j_{n,1}$ in $\mathbb{F}_p$) to $H(m) = aj_{n,0} + bj_{n,1}$ for some fixed random choice of a and b in $\mathbb{F}_p$. Heuristically, for general f, if we suppose $S_1(p)$ is distributed uniformly in $\mathbb{F}_{p^2}$, then roughly one in twelve elements of $\mathbb{F}_p$ appear as hash values, and each of those has only one expected preimage in $S_1(p)$.

Finding a preimage for a given hash value h in $\mathbb{F}_p$ amounts to finding a path $j_0 \to \cdots \to j$ such that $f(j) = h$: that is, solving the isogeny problem. We note that inverting the finalisation seems hard: for linear $f : \mathbb{F}_p^2 \to \mathbb{F}_p$, we know of no efficient method which given h in $\mathbb{F}_p$ computes a supersingular j such that $f(j) = h$. (Brute force search requires $O(p)$ trials.) Finalisation thus gives us some protection against meet-in-the-middle isogeny algorithms. Finding collisions and second preimages for H amounts to finding cycles in $\Gamma_1(2;p)$. For well-chosen p and j_0, this is roughly as hard as the isogeny problem [10, §5].

SIDH. Jao and De Feo's SIDH key exchange [27] begins with a supersingular curve $\mathcal{E}_0/\mathbb{F}_{p^2}$, where p is in the form $c \cdot 2^a 3^b - 1$, with fixed torsion bases $\langle P_2, Q_2 \rangle = \mathcal{E}_0[2^a]$ and $\langle P_3, Q_3 \rangle = \mathcal{E}_0[3^b]$ (which are rational because of the special form of p). Alice computes a secret walk $\phi_A : \mathcal{E}_0 \to \cdots \to \mathcal{E}_A$ of length a in $\Gamma_1(2;p)$, publishing $\mathcal{E}_A$, $\phi_A(P_3)$, and $\phi_A(Q_3)$; similarly, Bob computes a secret walk $\phi_B : \mathcal{E}_0 \to \cdots \to \mathcal{E}_B$ of length b in $\Gamma_1(3;p)$, publishing $\mathcal{E}_B$, $\phi_B(P_2)$, and $\phi_B(Q_2)$. The basis images allow Alice to compute $\phi_B(\ker \phi_A)$, and Bob $\phi_A(\ker \phi_B)$; Alice can thus "repeat" her walk starting from $\mathcal{E}_B$, and Bob his walk from $\mathcal{E}_A$, to arrive at curves representing the same point in $S_1(p)$, which is their shared secret.

Breaking Alice's public key amounts to solving an isogeny problem in $\Gamma_1(2;p)$ subject to the constraint that the walk have length a (which is particularly short). The 3^b-torsion basis may give some useful information here, though so far this is only exploited in attacks on artificial variants of SIDH [31]. Similarly, breaking Bob's public key amounts to solving a length-b isogeny problem in $\Gamma_1(3;p)$. Alternatively, we can compute these short paths by computing endomorphism rings: [20, Theorem 4.1] states that if $\mathcal{E}$ and $\mathcal{E}'$ are in $S_1(p)$ and we have *explicit descriptions* of $\mathrm{End}(\mathcal{E})$ and $\mathrm{End}(\mathcal{E}')$, then we can efficiently compute the *shortest* path from $\mathcal{E}$ to $\mathcal{E}'$ in $\Gamma_1(\ell;p)$ (see [17,20,29] for further details on this approach).

4 Abelian Varieties and Polarizations

An abelian variety is a smooth projective algebraic group variety. An isogeny of abelian varieties is a surjective finite morphism $\phi : \mathcal{A} \to \mathcal{A}'$ such that $\phi(0_\mathcal{A}) = 0_{\mathcal{A}'}$. In dimension $g = 1$, these definitions coincide with those for elliptic curves.

The proper higher-dimensional generalization of an elliptic curve is a *principally polarized abelian variety* (PPAV). A *polarization* of $\mathcal{A}$ is an isogeny $\lambda : \mathcal{A} \to \widehat{\mathcal{A}}$, where $\widehat{\mathcal{A}} \cong \mathrm{Pic}^0(\mathcal{A})$ is the *dual* abelian variety; λ is *principal* if it is an isomorphism. If $\mathcal{A} = \mathcal{E}$ is an elliptic curve, then there is a canonical principal polarization $\lambda : P \mapsto [(P) - (\infty)]$, and every other principal polarization is isomorphic to λ (via composition with a suitable translation and automorphism). The Jacobian $\mathcal{J}_\mathcal{C}$ of a curve $\mathcal{C}$ also has a canonical principal polarization defined by the theta divisor, which essentially corresponds to an embedding of $\mathcal{C}$ in $\mathcal{J}_\mathcal{C}$, and thus connects $\mathcal{J}_\mathcal{C}$ with the divisor class group of $\mathcal{C}$.

We need a notion of compatibility between isogenies and principal polarizations. First, recall that every isogeny $\phi : \mathcal{A} \to \mathcal{A}'$ has a dual isogeny $\widehat{\phi} : \widehat{\mathcal{A}'} \to \widehat{\mathcal{A}}$. Now, if $(\mathcal{A}, \lambda)$ and $(\mathcal{A}', \lambda')$ are PPAVs, then $\phi : \mathcal{A} \to \mathcal{A}'$ is an *isogeny of PPAVs* if $\widehat{\phi} \circ \lambda' \circ \phi = [d]\lambda$ for some integer d. We then have $\phi^\dagger \circ \phi = [d]$ on $\mathcal{A}$ (and $\phi \circ \phi^\dagger = [d]$ on $\mathcal{A}'$), where $\phi^\dagger := \lambda^{-1} \circ \widehat{\phi} \circ \lambda'$ is the *Rosati dual*. Intuitively, ϕ will be defined by homogeneous polynomials of degree d with respect to projective coordinate systems on $\mathcal{A}$ and $\mathcal{A}'$ corresponding to λ and λ', respectively. There is a simple criterion on subgroups $S \subset \mathcal{A}[d]$ to determine when an isogeny with kernel S is an isogeny of PPAVs: the subgroup should be *Lagrangian*.[2]

Definition 2. *Let $\mathcal{A}/\overline{\mathbb{F}}_p$ be a PPAV and let m be an integer prime to p. A Lagrangian subgroup of $\mathcal{A}[m]$ is a maximal m-Weil isotropic subgroup of $\mathcal{A}[m]$.*

If $\ell \neq p$ is prime, then $\mathcal{A}[\ell^n] \cong (\mathbb{Z}/\ell^n\mathbb{Z})^{2g}$ for all $n > 0$. If $S \subset \mathcal{A}[\ell]$ is Lagrangian, then $S \cong (\mathbb{Z}/\ell\mathbb{Z})^g$. Any Lagrangian subgroup of $\mathcal{A}[\ell^n]$ is isomorphic to $(\mathbb{Z}/\ell\mathbb{Z})^{n_1} \times \cdots \times (\mathbb{Z}/\ell\mathbb{Z})^{n_g}$ for some $n_1 \geq \cdots \geq n_g$ with $\sum_i n_i = gn$ (though not every $(n_1, \ldots, n_g)$ with $\sum_i n_i = gn$ occurs in this way).

We now have almost everything we need to generalize supersingular isogeny graphs from elliptic curves to higher dimension. The elliptic curves will be replaced by PPAVs; ℓ-isogenies will be replaced by isogenies with Lagrangian kernels in the ℓ-torsion—called $(\ell, \ldots, \ell)$-isogenies—and the elliptic dual isogeny will be replaced by the Rosati dual. It remains to define the right analogue of supersingularity in higher dimension, and study the resulting graphs.

5   The Superspecial Isogeny Graph in Dimension g

We need an appropriate generalization of elliptic supersingularity to $g > 1$. As explained in [7], it does not suffice to simply take the PPAVs $\mathcal{A}/\overline{\mathbb{F}}_p$ with $\mathcal{A}[p] = 0$.

Definition 3. *A PPAV $\mathcal{A}$ is **supersingular** if the Newton polygon of its Frobenius endomorphism has all slopes equal to $1/2$, and **superspecial** if Frobenius acts as 0 on $H^1(\mathcal{A}, \mathcal{O}_\mathcal{A})$. Superspecial implies supersingular; in dimension $g = 1$, the definitions coincide.*

All supersingular PPAVs are isogenous to a product of supersingular elliptic curves. Superspecial abelian varieties are isomorphic to a product of supersingular elliptic curves, though generally only as *unpolarized* abelian varieties. The special case of Jacobians is particularly relevant for us when constructing examples: $\mathcal{J}_\mathcal{C}$ is superspecial if and only if the Hasse–Witt matrix of $\mathcal{C}$ vanishes.

It is argued in [7] that the world of superspecial (and not supersingular) PPAVs is the correct setting for supersingular isogeny-based cryptography. We will not repeat this argument here; but in any case, every higher-dimensional "supersingular" cryptosystem proposed so far has in fact been superspecial.

In analogy with the elliptic supersingular graph, then, we define

$$S_g(p) := \left\{ \mathcal{A} : \mathcal{A}/\mathbb{F}_{p^2} \text{ is a superspecial } g\text{-dimensional PPAV} \right\} / \cong .$$

Our first task is to estimate the size of $S_g(p)$.

Lemma 1. *We have $\#S_g(p) = O(p^{g(g+1)/2})$.*

---

[2] Isogenies with strictly smaller kernels exist—isogenies with cyclic kernel are treated algorithmically in [16]—but these isogenies are not relevant to this investigation.

Proof. See [18, §5]. This follows from the Hashimoto–Ibukiyama mass formula

$$\sum_{A \in S_g(p)} \frac{1}{\#\mathrm{Aut}(A)} = \prod_{i=1}^{g} \frac{B_{2i}}{4i}(1 + (-p)^i),$$

where B_{2i} is the $2i$-th Bernoulli number. In particular, $\#S_g(p)$ is a polynomial in p of degree $\sum_{i=1}^{g} i = g(g+1)/2$.   □

Note that $\#S_g(p)$ grows *quadratically* in g (and exponentially in $\log p$): we have $\#S_1(p) = O(p)$, $\#S_2(p) = O(p^3)$, $\#S_3(p) = O(p^6)$, and $\#S_4(p) = O(p^{10})$.

For each prime $\ell \neq p$, we let $\Gamma_g(\ell; p)$ denote the (directed) graph on $S_g(p)$ whose edges are $\overline{\mathbb{F}}_p$-isomorphism classes of $(\ell, \cdots, \ell)$-isogenies of PPAVs: that is, isogenies whose kernels are Lagrangian subgroups of the ℓ-torsion. Superspeciality is invariant under $(\ell, \ldots, \ell)$-isogeny, so to determine the degree of the vertices of $\Gamma_g(\ell; p)$ it suffices to enumerate the Lagrangian subgroups of a g-dimensional PPAV. A simple counting argument yields Lemma 2.

Lemma 2. *If $A/\overline{\mathbb{F}}_p$ is a g-dimensional PPAV, then the number of Lagrangian subgroups of $A[\ell]$, and hence the number of edges leaving A in $\Gamma_g(\ell; p)$, is*

$$N_g(\ell) := \sum_{d=0}^{g} \begin{bmatrix} g \\ d \end{bmatrix}_\ell \cdot \ell^{\binom{g-d+1}{2}}.$$

(The ℓ-binomial coefficient $\begin{bmatrix} n \\ k \end{bmatrix}_\ell := \frac{(n)_\ell \cdots (n-k+1)_\ell}{(k)_\ell \cdots (1)_\ell}$, where $(i)_\ell := \frac{\ell^i - 1}{\ell - 1}$, counts the k-dimensional subspaces of $\mathbb{F}_\ell^n$.) In particular, $\Gamma_g(\ell; p)$ is $N_g(\ell)$-regular; and $N_g(\ell)$ is a polynomial in ℓ of degree $g(g+1)/2$.

We do not yet have analogues of Pizer's theorem to guarantee that $\Gamma_g(\ell; p)$ is Ramanujan when $g > 1$, though this is proven for superspecial abelian varieties with real multiplication [26]. We therefore work on the following hypothesis:

Hypothesis 1. *The graph $\Gamma_g(\ell; p)$ is Ramanujan.*

We need Hypothesis 1 in order to obtain the following analogue of Eq. 2 (a standard random walk theorem, as in [25, §3]): if we fix a vertex A_0 and consider n-step random walks $A_0 \to \cdots \to A_n$, then

$$\left| \Pr[A_n \cong A] - \frac{1}{\#S_g(p)} \right| \leq \left(\frac{2\sqrt{N_g(\ell) - 1}}{N_g(\ell)} \right)^n \qquad \text{for all } A \in S_g(p). \qquad (3)$$

That is, random walks in $\Gamma_g(\ell; p)$ converge exponentially quickly to the uniform distribution: after $O(\log p)$ steps in $\Gamma_g(\ell; p)$ we are uniformly distributed over $S_g(p)$. Given specific ℓ and g, we can explicitly derive the constant hidden by the big-O to bound the minimum n yielding a distribution within $1/\#S_g(p)$ of uniform.

Remark 1. Existing proposals of higher-dimensional supersingular isogeny-based cryptosystems all implicitly assume (special cases of) Hypothesis 1. For the purposes of attacking their underlying hard problems, we are comfortable making the same hypothesis. After all, if our algorithms are less effective because the expansion properties of $\Gamma_g(\ell; p)$ are less than ideal, then the cryptosystems built on $\Gamma_g(\ell; p)$ will fail to be effective by the same measure.

6   Superspecial Cryptosystems in Dimension $g = 2$

Before attacking the isogeny problem in $\Gamma_g(\ell; p)$, we consider some of the cryptosystems that have recently been defined in $\Gamma_2(\ell; p)$. This will also illustrate some methods for computing in these graphs, and as well as special cases of the general phenomena that can help us solve the isogeny problem more efficiently. For the rest of this section, therefore, we restrict to dimension $g = 2$.

Every 2-dimensional PPAV is isomorphic (as a PPAV) to either the Jacobian of a genus-2 curve, or to a product of two elliptic curves. We can therefore split $S_2(p)$ naturally into two disjoint subsets: $S_2(p) = S_2(p)^J \sqcup S_2(p)^E$, where

$$S_2(p)^J := \{\mathcal{A} \in S_2(p) : \mathcal{A} \cong \mathcal{J}_{\mathcal{C}} \text{ with } g(\mathcal{C}) = 2\} \quad \text{and}$$
$$S_2(p)^E := \{\mathcal{A} \in S_2(p) : \mathcal{A} \cong \mathcal{E}_1 \times \mathcal{E}_2 \text{ with } \mathcal{E}_1, \mathcal{E}_2 \in S_1(p)\} .$$

Vertices in $S_2(p)^J$ are "general", while vertices in $S_2(p)^E$ are "special". We can make the estimates implied by Lemma 1 more precise: if $p > 5$, then

$$\#S_2(p)^J = \frac{1}{2880}p^3 + \frac{1}{120}p^2 \quad \text{and} \quad \#S_2(p)^E = \frac{1}{288}p^2 + O(p)$$

(see e.g. [7, Proposition 2]). In particular, $\#S_2(p)^E / \#S_2(p) = 10/p + o(1)$.

Takashima's Hash Function. Takashima [36] was the first to generalize CGL to $g = 2$. We start with a distinguished vertex $\mathcal{A}_0$ in $S_2(p)$, and a distinguished incoming edge $\mathcal{A}_{-1} \to \mathcal{A}_0$ in $\Gamma_2(\ell; p)$. Each message m then drives a walk in $\Gamma_2(\ell; p)$: at each vertex we have a choice of 14 forward isogenies (the 15th is the dual of the previous, which is a prohibited backtracking step). The message m is therefore coded in base 14. While traversing the graph, the vertices are handled as concrete genus-2 curves representing the isomorphism classes of their Jacobians. Lagrangian subgroups correspond to factorizations of the hyperelliptic polynomials into a set of three quadratics, and the isogenies are computed using Richelot's formulæ (see [6, Chapters 9–10] and [33, Chapter 8]). We derive a hash value From the final vertex $\mathcal{A}_n$ as the Igusa–Clebsch invariants of the Jacobian, in $\mathbb{F}_{p^2}^3$; Takashima does not define a finalisation map (into $\mathbb{F}_p^3$, for example).

Flynn and Ti observe in [19] that this hash function has a fatal weakness: it is trivial to compute length-4 cycles starting from any vertex in $\Gamma_2(2; p)$, as in Example 1. Every cycle produces infinitely many hash collisions.

Example 1. Given some $\mathcal{A}_0$ in $S_2(p)$, choose a point P of order 4 on $\mathcal{A}_0$. There exist Q and R in $\mathcal{A}_0[2]$ such that $e_2([2]P, Q) = 1$ and $e_2([2]P, R) = 1$, but $e_2(Q, R) \neq 1$. The Lagrangian subgroups $K_0 := \langle [2]P, Q \rangle$ and $K_0' := \langle [2]P, R \rangle$ of $\mathcal{A}_0[2]$ are kernels of $(2,2)$-isogenies $\phi_0 : \mathcal{A}_0 \to \mathcal{A}_1 \cong \mathcal{A}_0/K_0$ and $\phi_0' : \mathcal{A}_0 \to \mathcal{A}_1' \cong \mathcal{A}_0/K_0'$; and in general, $\mathcal{A}_1 \not\cong \mathcal{A}_1'$. Now $K_1 := \phi_0(K_0')$ and $K_1' := \phi_0'(K_0)$ are Lagrangian subgroups of $\mathcal{A}_1[2]$. Writing $I_1 = \ker \phi_1{}^\dagger$ and $I_1' = \ker (\phi_1')^\dagger$, we see that $K_1 \cap I_1 = \langle \phi_1(R) \rangle$ and $K_1' \cap I_1' = \langle \phi_1(Q) \rangle$. We thus define another pair of $(2,2)$-isogenies, $\phi_1 : \mathcal{A}_1 \to \mathcal{A}_2 \cong \mathcal{A}_1/K_1$ and $\phi_1' : \mathcal{A}_1' \to \mathcal{A}_2' \cong \mathcal{A}_1'/K_1'$. We have $\ker(\phi_1 \circ \phi_0) = \ker(\phi_1' \circ \phi_0')$, so $\mathcal{A}_2 \cong \mathcal{A}_2'$. Now let $\psi := (\phi_0')^\dagger \circ (\phi_1')^\dagger \circ \phi_1 \circ \phi_0$. We have $\psi \cong [4]_{\mathcal{A}_0}$, but ψ does not factor over $[2]_{\mathcal{A}_0}$ (since $\mathcal{A}_1 \not\cong \mathcal{A}_1'$). Hence ψ represents a nontrivial cycle of length 4 in the graph.

The ubiquity of these length-4 cycles does not mean that $\Gamma_2(2; p)$ is no use for hashing: it just means that we must use a stronger rule than backtrack-avoidance when selecting steps in a walk. The following hash function does just this.

The Castryck–Decru–Smith Hash Function (CDS). Another generalization of CGL from $\Gamma_1(2; p)$ to $\Gamma_2(2; p)$, neatly avoiding the length-4 cycles of Example 1, is defined in [7]. Again, we fix a vertex $\mathcal{A}_0$ and an isogeny $\phi_{-1} : \mathcal{A}_{-1} \to \mathcal{A}_0$; we let $I_0 \subset \mathcal{A}_0[2]$ be the kernel of the Rosati dual $\phi_{-1}^\dagger$. Now, let $m = (m_0, \ldots, m_{n-1})$ be a $3n$-bit message, with each $0 \leq m_i < 8$. The sequence $(m_0, \ldots, m_{n-1})$ drives a path through $\Gamma_2(2; p)$ as follows: our starting point is $\mathcal{A}_0$, with its distinguished subgroup I_0 corresponding to the edge $\mathcal{A}_{-1} \to \mathcal{A}_0$. For each $0 \leq i < n$, we compute the set of eight Lagrangian subgroups $\{S_{i,0}, \ldots, S_{i,7}\}$ of $\mathcal{A}_i[2]$ such that $S_{i,j} \cap I_i = 0$, numbering them according to some fixed ordering on the encodings of Lagrangian subgroups. Then we compute $\phi_i : \mathcal{A}_i \to \mathcal{A}_{i+1} \cong \mathcal{A}_i/S_{i,m_i}$, and let $I_{i+1} := \phi_i(\mathcal{A}_i[2]) = \ker \phi_i{}^\dagger$. Once we have computed the entire walk $\mathcal{A}_0 \to \cdots \to \mathcal{A}_n$, we can derive a $3 \log_2 p$-bit hash value $H(m)$ from the isomorphism class of $\mathcal{A}_n$ (though such a finalisation is unspecified in [7]). The subgroup intersection condition ensures that the composition of the isogenies in the walk is a $(2^n, \ldots, 2^n)$-isogeny, thus protecting us from the small cycles of Example 1.

Putting this into practice reveals an ugly technicality. As in Takashima's hash function, we compute with vertices as genus-2 curves, encoded by their hyperelliptic polynomials, with $(2,2)$-isogenies computed using Richelot's formulæ. Walk endpoints are mapped to Igusa–Clebsch invariants in $\mathbb{F}_{p^2}^3$. But these curves, formulæ, and invariants only exist for vertices in $S_2(p)^J$. We can handle vertices in $S_2(p)^E$ as pairs of elliptic curves, with pairs of j-invariants for endpoints, and there are explicit formulæ to compute isogenies in to and out of $S_2(p)^E$ (see e.g. [7, §3]). Switching between representations and algorithms (to say nothing of finalisation, where $S_2(p)^E$ would have a smaller, easily distinguishable, and easier-to-invert image) seems like needless fiddle when the probability of stepping onto a vertex in $S_2(p)^E$ is only $O(1/p)$, which is negligible for cryptographic p.

In [7], this issue was swept under the rug by defining simpler algorithms which efficiently walk in the subgraph of $\Gamma_2(2; p)$ supported on $S_2(p)^J$, and simply fail if they walk into $S_2(p)^E$. This happens with probability $O(1/p)$, which may seem acceptable—however, this also means that *it is exponentially easier to find a message where the hash fails than it is to find a preimage* with a square-root algorithm. The former requires $O(p)$ work, the latter $O(p^{3/2})$. In this, as we will see, the simplified CDS hash function contains the seeds of its own destruction.

Genus-2 SIDH. Flynn and Ti [19] defined an SIDH analogue in dimension $g = 2$. As in the hash functions above, Richelot isogenies are used for Alice's steps in $\Gamma_2(2;p)$, while explicit formulæ for $(3,3)$-isogenies on Kummer surfaces are used for Bob's steps in $\Gamma_2(3;p)$. Walks may (improbably) run into $S_2(p)^E$, as with the hash functions above; but the same work-arounds apply without affecting security. (Further, if we generate a public key in $S_2(p)^E$, then we can discard it and generate a new one in $S_2(p)^J$.) As with SIDH, breaking public keys amounts to computing *short* solutions to the isogeny problem in $\Gamma_2(2;p)$ or $\Gamma_2(3;p)$, though presumably endomorphism attacks generalizing [17] also exist.

7   Attacking the Isogeny Problem in Superspecial Graphs

We want to solve the isogeny problem in $\Gamma_g(\ell;p)$. We can always do this using random walks in $O(\sqrt{\#S_g(p)}) = O(p^{g(g+1)/4})$ classical steps.

Our idea is that $S_{g-1}(p) \times S_1(p)$ maps into $S_g(p)$ by mapping a pair of PPAVs to their product equipped with the product polarization, and the image of $S_{g-1}(p) \times S_1(p)$ represents a large set of easily-identifiable "distinguished vertices" in $\Gamma_g(\ell;p)$. Indeed, since the map $S_{g-1}(p) \times S_1(p) \to S_g(p)$ is generically finite, of degree independent of p, Lemma 1 implies that

$$\#S_g(p)/\#(\text{image of } S_{g-1}(p) \times S_1(p)) = O(p^{g-1}) \qquad \text{for } g > 1. \qquad (4)$$

We can efficiently detect such a step into a product PPAV in a manner analogous to that of the failure of the CDS hash function: for example, by the breakdown of a higher-dimensional analogue of Richelot's formulæ such as [30].

We can walk into this subset, then recursively solve the path-finding problem in the subgraphs $\Gamma_{g-1}(\ell;p), \ldots, \Gamma_1(\ell;p)$ (each time walking from $\Gamma_i(\ell;p)$ into $\Gamma_{i-1}(\ell;p) \times \Gamma_1(\ell;p)$) before gluing the results together to obtain a path in $\Gamma_g(\ell;p)$.

Lemma 3. *Let $\alpha : A \to A'$ and $\beta : B \to B'$ be walks in $\Gamma_i(\ell;p)$ and $\Gamma_j(\ell;p)$ of lengths a and b, respectively. If $a \equiv b \pmod 2$, then we can efficiently compute a path of length $\max(a,b)$ from $A \times B$ to $A' \times B'$ in $\Gamma_{i+j}(\ell;p)$.*

Proof. Write $\alpha = \alpha_1 \circ \cdots \circ \alpha_a$ and $\beta = \beta_1 \circ \cdots \circ \beta_b$ as compositions of $(\ell, \cdots, \ell)$-isogenies. WLOG, suppose $a \geq b$. Set $\beta_{b+1} = \beta_b{}^\dagger$, $\beta_{b+2} = \beta_b$, ..., $\beta_{a-1} = \beta_b{}^\dagger$, $\beta_a = \beta_b$; then $\alpha \times \beta : (\alpha_1 \times \beta_1) \circ \cdots \circ (\alpha_a \times \beta_a)$ is a path from $A \times B$ to $A' \times B'$.   □

Equations 3 and 4 show that a walk of length $O(\log p)$ lands in the image of $S_{g-1}(p) \times S_1(p)$ with probability $O(1/p^{g-1})$, and after $O(p^{g-1})$ such short walks we are in $S_{g-1}(p) \times S_1(p)$ with probability bounded away from zero. More

---

Algorithm 1. Computing isogeny paths in $\Gamma_g(\ell; p)$

Input: $\mathcal{A}$ and $\mathcal{A}'$ in $S_g(p)$

Output: A path $\phi : \mathcal{A} \to \mathcal{A}'$ in $\Gamma_g(\ell; p)$

1 Find a path ψ from $\mathcal{A}$ to some point $\mathcal{B} \times \mathcal{E}$ in $S_{g-1}(p) \times S_1(p)$
2 Find a path ψ' from $\mathcal{A}'$ to some point $\mathcal{B}' \times \mathcal{E}'$ in $S_{g-1}(p) \times S_1(p)$
3 Find a path $\beta : \mathcal{B} \to \mathcal{B}'$ in $\Gamma_{g-1}(\ell; p)$ using Algorithm 1 recursively if
   $g - 1 > 1$, or elliptic path-finding if $g - 1 = 1$
4 Find a path $\eta : \mathcal{E} \to \mathcal{E}'$ in $\Gamma_1(\ell; p)$ using elliptic path-finding
5 Let $b = \text{length}(\beta)$ and $e = \text{length}(\eta)$. If $b \not\equiv e \pmod 2$, then fail and return $\perp$
   (or try again with another ψ and/or ψ', β, or η).
6 Construct the product path $\pi : \mathcal{B} \times \mathcal{E} \to \mathcal{B}' \times \mathcal{E}'$ defined by Lemma 3.
7 **return** the path $\phi := \psi'^\dagger \circ \pi \circ \psi$ from $\mathcal{A}$ to $\mathcal{A}'$.

---

generally, we can walk into the image of $S_{g-i}(p) \times S_i(p)$ for any $0 < i < g$; but the probability of this is $O(1/p^{i(g-i)})$, which is maximised by $i = 1$ and $g - 1$.

Proof of Theorem 1. Algorithm 1 implements the approach above, and proves Theorem 1. Step 1 computes ψ by taking $O(p^{g-1})$ non-backtracking random walks of length $O(\log(p))$ which can be trivially parallelized, so with P processors we expect $\widetilde{O}(p^{g-1}/P)$ steps before finding ψ. (If $\mathcal{A}$ is a fixed public base point then we can assume ψ is already known). Likewise, Step 2 takes $\widetilde{O}(p^{g-1}/P)$ steps to compute ψ'. After $g - 1$ recursive calls, we have reduced to the problem of computing paths in $\Gamma_1(\ell; p)$ in Step 4, which can be done in time $O(\sqrt{p}/P)$. Step 7 applies Lemma 3 to compute the final path in polynomial time. At each level of the recursion, we have a $1/2$ chance of having the same walk-length parity; hence, Algorithm 1 succeeds with probability $1/2^{g-1}$. This could be improved by computing more walks when the parities do not match, but $1/2^{g-1}$ suffices to prove the theorem. The total runtime is $\widetilde{O}(p^{g-1}/P)$ isogeny steps.

Proof of Theorem 2. Algorithm 1 can be run in a quantum computation model as follows. First, recall from the proof of Theorem 1 that Steps 1 and 2 find product varieties by taking $O(p^{g-1})$ walks of length $O(\log(p))$. Here we proceed following Biasse, Jao and Sankar [3, §4]. Let N be the number of walks in $O(p^{g-1})$ of length λ (in $O(\log(p))$). To compute ψ, we define an injection

$$f : [1, \ldots, N] \longrightarrow \{\text{nodes of distance } \lambda \text{ starting from } \mathcal{A}\},$$

and a function $C_f : [1, \ldots, N] \to \{0, 1\}$ by $C_f(x) = 1$ if $f(x)$ is in $S_{g-1}(p) \times S_1(p)$, and 0 otherwise. If there is precisely one x with $C_f(x) = 1$, Grover's algorithm [24] will find it (with probability $\geq 1/2$) in $O(\sqrt{N})$ iterations. If there are an unknown $t \geq 1$ such solutions, then Boyer–Brassard–Høyer–Tapp [5] finds one in $O(\sqrt{N/t})$ iterations. Hence, if we take λ large enough to expect at least one solution, then we will find it in $O(\sqrt{p^{g-1}})$ Grover iterations. We compute ψ' (and any recursive invocations of Steps 1 and 2) similarly.

For the elliptic path finding in Steps 3 and 4, we can apply (classical) Pollard-style pseudorandom walks which require $\widetilde{O}(\sqrt{p})$ memory and $\widetilde{O}(\sqrt{p})$ operations to find an ℓ-isogeny path. Alternatively, we can reduce storage costs by applying Grover's algorithm to the full graph $\Gamma_1(\ell; p)$ to find an ℓ-isogeny path in expected time $O(\sqrt{p})$. Finally, Step 7 applies Lemma 3 to compute the final path.

Remark 2. We can use the same approach as Algorithm 1 to compute explicit endomorphism rings of superspecial PPAVs. Suppose we want to compute $\text{End}(\mathcal{A})$ for some g-dimensional $\mathcal{A}$ in $S_g(p)$. Following the first steps of Algorithm 1, we compute a walk ϕ from $\mathcal{A}$ into $S_{g-1}(p) \times S_1(p)$, classically or quantumly, recursing until we end up at some $\mathcal{E}_1 \times \cdots \times \mathcal{E}_g$ in $S_1(p)^g$. Now we apply an elliptic endomorphism-ring-computing algorithm to each of the $\mathcal{E}_i$; this is equivalent to solving the isogeny problem in $\Gamma_1(\ell; p)$ (see [17, §5]), so its cost is in $\widetilde{O}(\sqrt{p})$. The products of the generators for the $\text{End}(\mathcal{E}_i)$ form generators for $\text{End}(\mathcal{E}_1 \times \cdots \times \mathcal{E}_g)$, which we can then pull back through ϕ to compute a finite-index subring of $\text{End}(\mathcal{A})$ that is maximal away from ℓ. The total cost is a classical $\widetilde{O}(p^{g-1}/P)$ (on P processors), or a quantum $\widetilde{O}(\sqrt{p^{g-1}})$, plus the cost of the pullback.

Remark 3. Algorithm 1 computes compositions of $(\ell, \dots, \ell)$-isogenies. If we relax and allow arbitrary-degree isogenies, not just paths in $\Gamma_g(\ell; p)$ for fixed ℓ, then the elliptic path-finding steps can use the classical Delfs–Galbraith [14] or quantum Biasse–Jao–Sankar [3] algorithms. While this would not change the asymptotic runtime of Algorithm 1 (under the reasonable assumption that the appropriate analogue of vertices "defined over $\mathbb{F}_p$" with commutative endomorphism rings form a subset of size $O(\sqrt{\#S_g(p)})$), both of these algorithms have low memory requirements and are arguably more implementation-friendly than Pollard-style pseudorandom walks [14, §4].

8   Cryptographic Implications

Table 1 compares Algorithm 1 with the best known attacks for dimensions $g \leq 6$. For general path-finding, the best known algorithms are classical Pollard-style pseudorandom walks and quantum Grover search [5,24]. As noted in Remark 3, higher-dimensional analogues of Delfs–Galbraith [14] or Biasse–Jao–Sankar [3] might yield practical improvements, without changing the asymptotic runtime.

Table 1. Logarithms (base p) of asymptotic complexities of algorithms for solving the isogeny problems in $\Gamma_g(\ell; p)$ for $1 \leq g \leq 6$. Further explanation in text.

	Dimension g	1	2	3	4	5	6
Classical	**Algorithm 1**	–	**1**	**2**	**3**	**4**	**5**
	Pollard/Delfs–Galbraith [14]	0.5	1.5	3	5	7.5	10.5
Quantum	**Algorithm 1**	–	**0.5**	**1**	**1.5**	**2**	**2.5**
	Grover/Biasse–Jao–Sankar [3]	0.25	0.75	1.5	2.5	3.75	4.25

The paths in $\Gamma_g(\ell; p)$ constructed by Algorithm 1 are generally too long to be private keys for SIDH analogues, which are paths of a fixed and typically shorter length. Extrapolating from $g = 1$ [27] and $g = 2$ [19], we suppose that the secret keyspace has size $O(\sqrt{\#S_g(p)}) = O(p^{g(g+1)/4})$ and the target isogeny has degree in $O(\sqrt{p})$, corresponding to a path of length roughly $\log_\ell(p)/2$ in $\Gamma_g(\ell; p)$. On the surface, therefore, Algorithm 1 does not yield a direct attack on SIDH-style protocols; or, at least, not a direct attack that succeeds with high probability. (Indeed, to resist direct attacks from Algorithm 1, it would suffice to abort any key generations passing through vertices in $S_{g-1}(p) \times S_1(p)$.)

However, we can anticipate an attack via endomorphism rings, generalizing the attack described at the end of Sect. 3, using the algorithm outlined in Remark 2. If we assume that what is polynomial-time for elliptic endomorphisms remains so for (fixed) $g > 1$, then we can break g-dimensional SIDH keys by computing shortest paths in $\Gamma_g(\ell; p)$ with the same complexity as Algorithm 1: that is, classical $\widetilde{O}(p^{g-1}/P)$ and quantum $\widetilde{O}(p^{(g-1)/2})$ for $g > 1$.

This conjectural cost compares very favourably against the best known classical and quantum attacks on g-dimensional SIDH. In the classical paradigm, a meet-in-the-middle attack would run in $\widetilde{O}(p^{g(g+1)/8})$, with similar storage requirements. In practice the best attack is the golden-collision van Oorschot–Wiener (vOW) algorithm [38] investigated in [1], which given storage w runs in expected time $\widetilde{O}(p^{3g(g+1)/16}/(P\sqrt{w}))$. For fixed w, the attack envisioned above gives an asymptotic improvement over vOW for all $g > 1$. If an adversary has access to a large amount of storage, then vOW may still be the best classical algorithm for $g \leq 5$, particularly when smaller primes are used to target lower security levels. (vOW becomes strictly worse for all $g > 5$, even if we assume unbounded storage.) In the quantum paradigm, Tani's algorithm [37] would succeed in $\widetilde{O}(p^{g(g+1)/12})$, meaning we get the same asymptotic complexities for dimensions 2 and 3, and an asymptotic improvement for all $g > 3$. Moreover, Jaques and Schanck [28] suggest a significant gap between the asymptotic runtime of Tani's algorithm and its actual efficacy in any meaningful model of quantum computation. On the other hand, the bottleneck of the quantum attack forecasted above is a relatively straightforward invocation of Grover search, and the gap between its asymptotic and concrete complexities is likely to be much closer.

Like the size of $S_g(p)$, the exponents in the runtime complexities of all of the algorithms above are quadratic in g. Indeed, this was the practical motivation for instantiating isogeny-based cryptosystems in $g > 1$. In contrast, the exponents for Algorithm 1 and our proposed SIDH attack are linear in g. This makes the potential trade-offs for cryptosystems based on higher-dimensional supersingular isogeny problems appear significantly less favourable, particularly as g grows and the gap between the previous best attacks and Algorithm 1 widens.

A   A Proof-of-Concept Implementation

We include a naive Magma implementation of the product finding stage (i.e. Steps 1–3) of Algorithm 1 in dimension $g = 2$ with $\ell = 2$. First, it generates a challenge by walking from the known superspecial node corresponding to the curve $\mathcal{C}\colon y^2 = x^5 + x$ over a given $\mathbb{F}_{p^2}$ to a random abelian surface in $\Gamma_2(2; p)$, which becomes the target $\mathcal{A}$. Then it starts computing random walks of length slightly larger than $\log_2(p)$, whose steps correspond to $(2, 2)$-isogenies. As each step is taken, it checks whether we have landed on a product of two elliptic curves (at which point it will terminate) before continuing.

Magma's built-in functionality for $(2, 2)$-isogenies makes this rather straightforward. At a given node, the function `RichelotIsogenousSurfaces` computes all 15 of its neighbours, so our random walks are simply a matter of generating enough entropy to choose one of these neighbours at each of the $O(\log(p))$ steps. For the sake of replicability, we have used Magma's inbuilt implementation of SHA-1 to produce pseudo-random walks that are deterministically generated by an input seed. SHA-1 produces 160-bit strings, which correspond to 40 integers in $[0, 1, \ldots, 15]$; this gives a straightforward way to take 40 pseudo-random steps in $\Gamma_2(2; p)$, where no step is taken if the integer is 0, and otherwise the index is used to choose one of the 15 neighbours.

The seed `processor` can be used to generate independent walks across multiple processors. We always used the seed "0" to generate the target surface, and set `processor` to be the string "1" to kickstart a single process for very small primes. For the second and third largest primes, we used the strings "1", "2", ..., "16" as seeds to 16 different deterministic processes. For the largest prime, we seeded 128 different processes.

For the prime $p = \mathbf{127} = 2^7 - 1$, the seed "0" walks us to the starting node corresponding to $C_0/\mathbb{F}_{p^2}\colon y^2 = (41i + 63)x^6 + \cdots + (6i + 12)x + 70$. The single processor seeded with "1" found a product variety $E_1 \times E_2$ on its second walk after taking **53 steps** in total, with $E_1/\mathbb{F}_{p^2}\colon y^2 = x^3 + (93i + 43)x^2 + (23i + 93)x + (2i + 31)$ and $E_2/\mathbb{F}_{p^2}\colon y^2 = x^3 + (98i + 73)x^2 + (30i + 61)x + (41i + 8)$.

For the prime $p = \mathbf{8191} = 2^{13} - 1$, the single processor seeded with "1" found a product variety on its 175-th walk after taking **6554 steps** in total.

For the prime $p = \mathbf{524287} = 2^{19} - 1$, all 16 processors were used. The processor seeded with "2" was the first to find a product variety on its 311-th walk after taking 11680 steps in total. Given that all processors walk at roughly the same pace, at this stage we would have walked close to $16 \cdot 11680 = \mathbf{186880}$ **steps**.

For the 25-bit prime $p = \mathbf{17915903} = 2^{13}3^7 - 1$, the processor seeded with "13" found a product variety after taking 341 walks and a total of 12698 steps. At this stage the 16 processors would have collectively taken around **203168** **steps**.

The largest experiment that we have conducted to date is with the prime $p = \mathbf{2147483647} = 2^{31} - 1$, where 128 processors walked in parallel. Here the processor seeded with "95" found a product variety after taking 10025 walks and a total of 375703 steps. At this stage the processors would have collectively taken around **48089984 steps**.

In all of the above cases we see that product varieties are found with around p steps. The Magma script that follows can be used to verify the experiments[3], or to experiment with other primes.

```
///////////////////////////////////////////////////
clear;

processor:="1";

p:=2^13-1;
Fp:=GF(p);
Fp2<i>:=ExtensionField<Fp,x|x^2+1>;
_<x>:=PolynomialRing(Fp2);

///////////////////////////////////////////////////

Next_Walk := function(str)
    H := SHA1(str);
        steps := [ StringToInteger(x, 16): x in ElementToSequence(H) | x ne "0"];
    return steps ,H;
end function;

///////////////////////////////////////////////////

Walk_To_Starting_Jacobian:=function(str)

        steps,H:= Next_Walk(str);

        C0:=HyperellipticCurve(x^5+x);
        J0:=Jacobian(C0);
        for i:=1 to #steps do
                neighbours:=RichelotIsogenousSurfaces(J0);
                if Type(neighbours[steps[i]]) ne SetCart then
                        J0:=neighbours[steps[i]];
                end if;
        end for;

        return J0;

end function;

///////////////////////////////////////////////////

Walk_Until_Found:=function(seed,J0);

        found:=false;
        H:=seed;
        found:=false;
        walks_done:=0;
        steps_done:=0;

        while not found do

                walks_done+:=1;
                walks_done, "walks and",steps_done, "steps on core", processor, "for p=",p;
                J:=J0;
                steps,H:=Next_Walk(H);

                for i:=1 to #steps do
                        steps_done+:=1;
                        J:=RichelotIsogenousSurfaces(J)[steps[i]];
                        if Type(J) eq SetCart then
                                found:=true;
                                index:=i;
                                break;
                        end if;
                end for;

        end while;

        return steps,index,walks_done,steps_done,J;

end function;

///////////////////////////////////////////////////
```

---

[3] Readers without access to Magma can make use of the free online calculator at http://magma.maths.usyd.edu.au/calc/, omitting the "Write" functions at the end that are used to print to local files.

```
file_name:="p" cat IntegerToString(p)   cat "-" cat processor cat ".txt";
J0:=Walk_To_Starting_Jacobian("0");
steps,index,walks_done,steps_done,J:=Walk_Until_Found(processor,J0);

Write(file_name, "walks done =");
Write(file_name, walks_done);
Write(file_name, "steps_done =");
Write(file_name, steps_done);
Write(file_name, "steps=");
Write(file_name, steps);
Write(file_name, "index=");
Write(file_name, index);
Write(file_name, "Elliptic Product=");
Write(file_name, J);
```

//

References

1. Adj, G., Cervantes-Vázquez, D., Chi-Domínguez, J.-J., Menezes, A., Rodríguez-Henríquez, F.: On the cost of computing isogenies between supersingular elliptic curves. In: Cid, C., Jacobson Jr., M. (eds.) SAC 2018. LNCS, vol. 11349, pp. 322–343. Springer, Cham (2019). https://doi.org/10.1007/978-3-030-10970-7_15. https://eprint.iacr.org/2018/313
2. Azarderakhsh, R., et al.: Supersingular isogeny key encapsulation (2017)
3. Biasse, J.-F., Jao, D., Sankar, A.: A quantum algorithm for computing isogenies between supersingular elliptic curves. In: Meier, W., Mukhopadhyay, D. (eds.) INDOCRYPT 2014. LNCS, vol. 8885, pp. 428–442. Springer, Cham (2014). https://doi.org/10.1007/978-3-319-13039-2_25
4. Bisson, G., Cosset, R., Robert, D.: AVIsogenies - a library for computing isogenies between abelian varieties, November 2012. http://avisogenies.gforge.inria.fr
5. Boyer, M., Brassard, G., Høyer, P., Tapp, A.: Tight bounds on quantum searching. Fortschritte der Physik Progress Phys. 46(4–5), 493–505 (1998)
6. Cassels, J.W.S., Flynn, E.V.: Prolegomena to a Middlebrow Arithmetic of Curves of Genus 2. London Mathematical Society Lecture Note Series, vol. 230. Cambridge University Press, New York (1996)
7. Castryck, W., Decru, T., Smith, B.: Hash functions from superspecial genus-2 curves using Richelot isogenies. Cryptology ePrint Archive, Report 2019/296 (2019). To appear in the Proceedings of NuTMiC 2019
8. Castryck, W., Lange, T., Martindale, C., Panny, L., Renes, J.: CSIDH: an efficient post-quantum commutative group action. In: Peyrin, T., Galbraith, S. (eds.) ASIACRYPT 2018, Part III. LNCS, vol. 11274, pp. 395–427. Springer, Cham (2018). https://doi.org/10.1007/978-3-030-03332-3_15
9. Charles, D.X., Goren, E.Z., Lauter, K.E.: Families of Ramanujan graphs and quaternion algebras. In: Harnad, J., Winternitz, P. (eds.) Groups and Symmetries, From Neolithic Scots to John McKay, pp. 53–80. AMS, Providence (2009)
10. Charles, D.X., Lauter, K.E., Goren, E.Z.: Cryptographic hash functions from expander graphs. J. Cryptol. 22(1), 93–113 (2009). https://doi.org/10.1007/s00145-007-9002-x
11. Costello, C.: Computing supersingular isogenies on Kummer surfaces. In: Peyrin, T., Galbraith, S. (eds.) ASIACRYPT 2018. LNCS, vol. 11274, pp. 428–456. Springer, Cham (2018). https://doi.org/10.1007/978-3-030-03332-3_16
12. De Feo, L., Galbraith, S.D.: SeaSign: compact isogeny signatures from class group actions. In: Ishai, Y., Rijmen, V. (eds.) EUROCRYPT 2019. LNCS, vol. 11478, pp. 759–789. Springer, Cham (2019). https://doi.org/10.1007/978-3-030-17659-4_26

13. De Feo, L., Masson, S., Petit, C., Sanso, A.: Verifiable delay functions from supersingular isogenies and pairings. In: Galbraith, S.D., Moriai, S. (eds.) ASIACRYPT 2019, Part I. LNCS, vol. 11921, pp. 248–277. Springer, Cham (2019). https://doi.org/10.1007/978-3-030-34578-5_10

14. Delfs, C., Galbraith, S.D.: Computing isogenies between supersingular elliptic curves over $\mathbb{F}_p$. Des. Codes Crypt. **78**(2), 425–440 (2016). https://doi.org/10.1007/s10623-014-0010-1

15. Diem, C.: An index calculus algorithm for plane curves of small degree. In: Hess, F., Pauli, S., Pohst, M. (eds.) ANTS 2006. LNCS, vol. 4076, pp. 543–557. Springer, Heidelberg (2006). https://doi.org/10.1007/11792086_38

16. Dudeanu, A., Jetchev, D., Robert, D., Vuille, M.: Cyclic isogenies for abelian varieties with real multiplication. Preprint, November 2017

17. Eisenträger, K., Hallgren, S., Lauter, K., Morrison, T., Petit, C.: Supersingular isogeny graphs and endomorphism rings: reductions and solutions. In: Nielsen, J.B., Rijmen, V. (eds.) EUROCRYPT 2018, Part III. LNCS, vol. 10822, pp. 329–368. Springer, Cham (2018). https://doi.org/10.1007/978-3-319-78372-7_11

18. Ekedahl, T.: On supersingular curves and Abelian varieties. Mathematica Scandinavica **60**, 151–178 (1987)

19. Flynn, E.V., Ti, Y.B.: Genus two isogeny cryptography. In: Ding, J., Steinwandt, R. (eds.) PQCrypto 2019. LNCS, vol. 11505, pp. 286–306. Springer, Cham (2019). https://doi.org/10.1007/978-3-030-25510-7_16

20. Galbraith, S.D., Petit, C., Shani, B., Ti, Y.B.: On the security of supersingular isogeny cryptosystems. In: Cheon, J.H., Takagi, T. (eds.) ASIACRYPT 2016, Part I. LNCS, vol. 10031, pp. 63–91. Springer, Heidelberg (2016). https://doi.org/10.1007/978-3-662-53887-6_3

21. Galbraith, S.D., Petit, C., Silva, J.: Identification protocols and signature schemes based on supersingular isogeny problems. In: Takagi, T., Peyrin, T. (eds.) ASIACRYPT 2017, Part I. LNCS, vol. 10624, pp. 3–33. Springer, Cham (2017). https://doi.org/10.1007/978-3-319-70694-8_1

22. Gaudry, P.: Index calculus for abelian varieties of small dimension and the elliptic curve discrete logarithm problem. J. Symb. Comput. **44**(12), 1690–1702 (2009)

23. Gaudry, P., Thomé, E., Thériault, N., Diem, C.: A double large prime variation for small genus hyperelliptic index calculus. Math. Comput. **76**(257), 475–492 (2007)

24. Grover, L.K.: A fast quantum mechanical algorithm for database search. In: Miller, G.L. (ed.) Proceedings of the Twenty-Eighth Annual ACM Symposium on the Theory of Computing, Philadelphia, Pennsylvania, USA, 22–24 May 1996, pp. 212–219. ACM (1996)

25. Hoory, S., Linial, N., Wigderson, A.: Expander graphs and their applications. Bull. (New Series) Am. Math. Soc. **43**(4), 439–561 (2006)

26. Hubert, M.-N.: Superspecial abelian varieties, theta series and the Jacquet-Langlands correspondence. Ph.D. thesis, McGill University (2005)

27. Jao, D., De Feo, L.: Towards quantum-resistant cryptosystems from supersingular elliptic curve isogenies. In: Yang, B.-Y. (ed.) PQCrypto 2011. LNCS, vol. 7071, pp. 19–34. Springer, Heidelberg (2011). https://doi.org/10.1007/978-3-642-25405-5_2

28. Jaques, S., Schanck, J.M.: Quantum cryptanalysis in the RAM model: claw-finding attacks on SIKE. In: Boldyreva, A., Micciancio, D. (eds.) CRYPTO 2019, Part I. LNCS, vol. 11692, pp. 32–61. Springer, Cham (2019). https://doi.org/10.1007/978-3-030-26948-7_2

29. Kohel, D., Lauter, K., Petit, C., Tignol, J.-P.: On the quaternion ℓ-isogeny path problem. LMS J. Comput. Math. **17**(suppl. A), 418–432 (2014)

30. Lubicz, D., Robert, D.: Arithmetic on abelian and Kummer varieties. Finite Fields Appl. **39**, 130–158 (2016)

31. Petit, C.: Faster algorithms for isogeny problems using torsion point images. In: Takagi, T., Peyrin, T. (eds.) ASIACRYPT 2017, Part II. LNCS, vol. 10625, pp. 330–353. Springer, Cham (2017). https://doi.org/10.1007/978-3-319-70697-9_12

32. Pizer, A.K.: Ramanujan graphs and Hecke operators. Bull. Am. Math. Soc. **23**(1), 127–137 (1990)

33. Smith, B.: Explicit endomorphisms and correspondences. Ph.D. thesis, University of Sydney (2005)

34. Smith, B.: Isogenies and the discrete logarithm problem in Jacobians of genus 3 hyperelliptic curves. J. Cryptol. **22**(4), 505–529 (2009). https://doi.org/10.1007/s00145-009-9038-1

35. Sutherland, A.V.: Identifying supersingular elliptic curves. LMS J. Comput. Math. **15**, 317–325 (2012)

36. Takashima, K.: Efficient algorithms for isogeny sequences and their cryptographic applications. In: Takagi, T., Wakayama, M., Tanaka, K., Kunihiro, N., Kimoto, K., Duong, D.H. (eds.) Mathematical Modelling for Next-Generation Cryptography: CREST Crypto-Math Project. MI, vol. 29, pp. 97–114. Springer, Singapore (2018). https://doi.org/10.1007/978-981-10-5065-7_6

37. Tani, S.: Claw finding algorithms using quantum walk. Theor. Comput. Sci. **410**(50), 5285–5297 (2009)

38. van Oorschot, P.C., Wiener, M.J.: Parallel collision search with cryptanalytic applications. J. Cryptol. **12**(1), 1–28 (1999). https://doi.org/10.1007/PL00003816

Sashimi: Cutting up CSI-FiSh Secret Keys to Produce an Actively Secure Distributed Signing Protocol

Daniele Cozzo[1] and Nigel P. Smart[1,2(✉)]

[1] imec-COSIC, KU Leuven, Leuven, Belgium
{daniele.cozzo,nigel.smart}@kuleuven.be
[2] University of Bristol, Bristol, UK

Abstract. We present the first actively secure variant of a distributed signature scheme based on isogenies. The protocol produces signatures from the recent CSI-FiSh signature scheme. Our scheme works for any access structure, as we use a replicated secret sharing scheme to define the underlying secret sharing; as such it is only practical when the number of maximally unqualified sets is relatively small. This, however, includes the important case of full threshold, and (n, t)-threshold schemes when n is small.

1 Introduction

Threshold signature schemes have recently received more and more attention due to applications in blockchain and other scenarios where high value signatures are produced. Apart from early work on threshold RSA signatures [8,21] and DSA/EC-DSA signatures [15,19], we have seen renewed interest in methods to produce EC-DSA signatures [4,11,13,14,16–18], and interest in threshold schemes from standards bodies such as NIST [2].

In the post-quantum world there has obviously been less work on this problem. In [6] Cozzo and Smart discuss the possibilities for threshold-izing the Round 2 candidate signature schemes in the NIST post-quantum 'competition'. The authors conclude that virtually all proposed signature schemes, with the possible exception of those based on the MQ-like problems, are hard to efficiently turn into threshold variants. However, the NIST candidates do not include any submission based on isogenies; mainly because isogeny based signature schemes did not become efficient until *after* the NIST 'competition' started.

Isogeny based cryptography goes back to the work of Couveignes, Rostovtsev and Stolbunov [5,20]. The first isogeny based signature scheme was created by Stolbunov in his thesis [22]. The basic construction was a Fiat-Shamir transform applied to a standard three-round isogeny-based identification scheme. The problem with Stolbunov's scheme is that one required an efficient method to sample in the class group, and that each class group member should have an efficiently computable unique representation.

© Springer Nature Switzerland AG 2020
J. Ding and J.-P. Tillich (Eds.): PQCrypto 2020, LNCS 12100, pp. 169–186, 2020.
https://doi.org/10.1007/978-3-030-44223-1_10

To solve these problems De Feo and Galbraith used the Fiat-Shamir with aborts method to produce a new signature scheme, based on Stolbunov's, called SeaSign [9]. The SeaSign scheme was further improved by Decru et al. [10]. However, the algorithm still required two minutes to sign a single message.

Recently, Beullens et al. [1] returned to Stolbunov's original method and by calculating the ideal class group of an imaginary quadratic number field with large discriminant were able to instantiate the signature scheme efficiently. This instantiation of Stolbunov's scheme, called CSI-FiSh, requires only 390ms to sign or verify a message, and has signature sizes of only 263 bytes. Thus with CSI-FiSh isogeny based signatures are truly practical.

In [12] De Feo and Meyer consider the case of making CSI-FiSh into a threshold scheme, by distributing the secret key using the Shamir secret sharing scheme. Their resulting protocol is efficient, but only *passively* secure. The main trick that De Feo and Meyer use is to overcome the difficulty that isogenies can be composed, but do not form a group. As a result, performing the calculation of the signature will be more challenging than in the classic setting of distributed signatures based on discrete logarithms. Distributed signing protocols typically have each signer producing a partial signature which is then combined non-interactively into the final signature. Instead, in both the protocol of De Feo and Meyer and our protocol, the signature is produced more in the fashion of a ring signature, with each signer needing to accept and receive a message. A major simplification in our presentation is that we use a Replicated Secret Sharing Scheme. This means that, for a given qualified set, we can treat the resulting sharing as a full threshold sharing.

Just as CSI-FiSh follows the Fiat-Shamir paradigm in defining a signature scheme from isogenies, in much the same way as Schnorr signatures are created from discrete logarithms, we can follow the same paradigm in creating an actively secure threshold variant as is done in the standard case of actively secure distributed Schnorr signatures. Each signer, in the qualified set being used to sign, attaches a zero-knowledge proof to their partial signatures. This ensures the signer has followed the protocol, and importantly for our simulation proof it allows the simulator to extract the underlying secret witness. A similar strategy is used for simulating the key generation.

As just indicated, we prove our protocol secure in a simulation paradigm, but not in a the Universal Composability setting. This is because our protocol makes extensive use of Σ-protocols and the simulator needs to rewind the adversary in order to perform knowledge extraction from the special soundness of the underlying Σ-protocols. Thus our protocol should only be considered 'stand-alone' secure.

We estimate that our protocol will require just under five minutes to execute for the important cases of two party signing, or threshold signing with $(n, t) = (3, 1)$. This cost is mainly due to the zero-knowledge proofs needed to provide active security for our signing protocol.

Improvements to our work could be performed in a number of directions. On a theoretical front a fully UC protocol and proof would be interesting. A method to produce active security, in the standalone setting, without recourse to our zero-knowledge proofs would obviously have a big affect on performance. Extending our method to create an actively secure variant of the Shamir based protocol of De Feo and Meyer should be relatively easy. A change to our zero-knowledge proof technique would be of great interest, although this seems particularly hard, as any improvement to that would likely result in a major performance improvement in the basic CSI-FiSh signature scheme as well.

2 Preliminaries

2.1 Notation

We assume that all involved parties are probabilistic polynomial time Turing machines. Given a positive integer n, we denote by $[n]$ the set $\{1, \ldots, n\}$. We let $x \leftarrow X$ denote the uniformly random assignment to the variable x from the set X, assuming a uniform distribution over X. We also write $x \leftarrow y$ as shorthand for $x \leftarrow \{y\}$. If $\mathcal{D}$ is a probability distribution over a set X, then we let $x \leftarrow \mathcal{D}$ denote sampling from X with respect to the distribution $\mathcal{D}$. If A is a (probabilistic) algorithm then we denote by $a \leftarrow A$ the assignment of the output of A where the probability distribution is over the random tape of A.

2.2 Replicated Secret Sharing

Let $\mathcal{P} = \{P_i\}_{i=1,\ldots,n}$ be the set of parties and let $\Gamma \subset 2^{\mathcal{P}}$ be a monotone family for the relation of inclusion, that is if $Q \in \Gamma$ and $Q \subset Q'$ then $Q' \in \Gamma$. Similarly, let $\Delta \subset 2^{\mathcal{P}}$ be a monotone family with respect to the relation of subsets, that is if $U \in \Delta$ and $U' \subset U$ then $U' \in \Delta$. The pair (Δ, Γ) is called a *monotone access structure* if it holds that $\Delta \cap \Gamma = \emptyset$. We will only consider access structures where Δ and Γ are complementary to each other. The sets inside Γ are called *qualified sets* while the one in Δ are called *unqualified sets*. We denote by Γ^- the family of minimally qualified sets in Γ with respect to the inclusion relation, that is

$$\Gamma^- = \{Q \in \Gamma : Q' \in \Gamma, Q' \subset Q \Rightarrow Q' = Q\}.$$

Similarly, we define the family of maximally unqualified sets Δ^+ as

$$\Delta^+ = \{U \in \Gamma : U' \in \Delta, U \subset U' \Rightarrow U' = U\}.$$

Let Γ be a general monotone access structure and let R be a ring. The replicated scheme for Γ is defined as in Fig. 1. To define the replicated scheme we first define a set $\mathcal{B} = \{B \in 2^{\mathcal{P}} : \mathcal{P} \setminus B \in \Delta^+\}$, then to share a secret $s \in R$ the dealer first additively shares $s = s_{B_1} + \ldots + s_{B_t}$ for $B_i \in \mathcal{B}$. To open a secret is straightforward. For each qualified set Q we define a mapping $\Psi_Q : \mathcal{B} \longrightarrow \mathcal{P}$ which allows the parties in Q to *uniquely* treat their shares as a full threshold sharing of the secret. In particular for each Q we require

$$s = \sum_{P_i \in Q} \left(\sum_{\Psi_Q(B) = P_i} s_B \right),$$

i.e. Ψ_Q partitions the shares s_B for $B \in \mathcal{B}$ between the parties in Q. Such replicated secret sharing schemes are clearly linear, and we will denote sharing an element by this secret sharing scheme by $\langle s \rangle$.

For a set of adversarys $\mathcal{A} \in \Delta$ we can divide the sets $B \in \mathcal{B}$, and hence shares s_B, into three disjoint sets $\mathcal{B}_A$, $\mathcal{B}_M$ and $\mathcal{B}_H$; $\mathcal{B} = \mathcal{B}_A \cup \mathcal{B}_M \cup \mathcal{B}_H$. The sets B in $\mathcal{B}_A$ correspond to shares s_B that are held *only* by the adversary, those in $\mathcal{B}_H$ are those held *only* by honest parties, whist those in $\mathcal{B}_M$ are held by *a mixture* of honest and adversarial parties. For all secret sharing schemes we have $\mathcal{B}_H \neq \emptyset$, otherwise we would have $\mathcal{A} = \mathcal{P}$. In the case of full-threshold sharing we always have $\mathcal{B}_M = \emptyset$.

Replicated Secret Sharing over the ring R

Input: For party to share a secret input $s \in R$, it performs
- Sample $s_B \leftarrow R$ for $B \in \mathcal{B}$ subject to $\sum_{B \in \mathcal{B}} s_B = s$
- For each $B \in \mathcal{B}$ and each $P_j \in B$ give s_B to party P_j.

Open: For a qualified set of parties Q to open a secret s
- For each $B \in \mathcal{B}$ if $P_j \in Q$ and $P_j \notin B$ then all parties $P_i \in B$ send s_B to party P_j
- Each party computes $s = \sum_{B \in \mathcal{B}} s_B$.

ToFullThreshold: For a qualified set of parties Q
- For $P_i \in Q$ define $z_{P_i} \leftarrow \sum_{\Psi_Q(B) = P_i} s_B$.

Fig. 1. Replicated secret sharing over the ring R

2.3   Commitment Schemes

Our protocols require access to a commitment functionality $\mathcal{F}_{\mathsf{Commit}}$. The commitment functionality is a standard functionality allowing one party to first commit, and then decommit, to a value towards another set of parties. We assume that the opened commitment is only available to the receiving parties (i.e. it is sent over a secure channel). The functionality is given in Fig. 2, and it is known to be easily implemented in the random oracle model.

2.4   PRSSs

In our protocols we utilize the fact that, after a key distribution phase, parties can generate non-interactively sharings in a replicated scheme; namely we can define a so-called PRSS. In particular, we require the parties to engage in a pre-processing phase in which they share keys for a Pseudo-Random Function (PRF) in order to generate Pseudo-Random Secret Sharings (PRSSs) for the replicated scheme $\langle v \rangle$. In particular, we make black-box use of the functionality given in Fig. 3. PRSSs for arbitrary access structures can involve a set-up phase requiring

---

The Functionality $\mathcal{F}_{\mathsf{Commit}}$

Init: On input of (Init, P_i, B) from all players, this initializes a commitment functionality from player P_i to the players in B. We write this as $\mathcal{F}_{\mathsf{Commit}}^{i,B}$, if B is a singleton set $B = \{j\}$ then we write $\mathcal{F}_{\mathsf{Commit}}^{i,j}$, and if $B = \mathcal{P} \setminus \{i\}$ then we write $\mathcal{F}_{\mathsf{Commit}}^{P_i}$.

Commit: On input of $(\mathsf{Commit}, \mathsf{id}, \mathsf{data})$ from player P_i and $(\mathsf{Commit}, \mathsf{id}, \perp)$ from all players in B the functionality stores $(\mathsf{id}, \perp)$.

Open: On input of $(\mathsf{Commit}, \mathsf{id})$ from all players in $B \cup \{i\}$ the functionality retrieves the entry $(\mathsf{id}, \mathsf{data})$ and returns data to all parties in B.

Fig. 2. The functionality $\mathcal{F}_{\mathsf{Commit}}$

the agreement of exponentially-many keys in general. The general protocol is given in [7]. To set up the PRSS in the case of our replicated scheme we use the method described in Fig. 4, where $F_k(\cdot)$ is a PRF with codomain equal to R.

The Functionality $\mathcal{F}_{\mathsf{Rand}}$

Init: The functionality accepts Init or **abort** from all parties and the adversary. If any party inputs **abort**, the functionality sends the message **abort** to all parties.

PRSS: On input $\mathsf{PRSS}(\mathsf{cnt})$ from all parties, if the counter value is the same for all parties and has not been used before, the functionality samples a set $\{r_B\}_{B \in \mathcal{B}} \leftarrow R$ and for each $B \in \mathcal{B}$ sends r_B to all $i \in B$.

Fig. 3. The functionality $\mathcal{F}_{\mathsf{Rand}}$

Theorem 2.1. *Assuming F is a pseudo-random function, the protocol Π_{Rand} securely realises $\mathcal{F}_{\mathsf{Rand}}$ in the $\mathcal{F}_{\mathsf{Commit}}$-hybrid model.*

Proof. The Init procedure is clearly secure assuming an secure commitment functionality. As there is no interaction after Init, the protocol is clearly secure if it is correct and passively secure. Correctness follows from basic algebra, and security follows from the fact that F is assumed to be a PRF and from the fact that there is at least one B not held by the adversary (by definition of the access structure). □

2.5 Elliptic Curves and Isogenies

In what follows E denotes an elliptic curve over a finite field $\mathbb{F}_p$ where p is a large prime. An elliptic curve is called supersingular if its number of rational points satisfies the equation $\#E(\mathbb{F}_p) \equiv 1 \pmod{p}$. An elliptic curve is called ordinary if this does not happen. An isogeny between two elliptic curves E and E' is a rational

---

Protocol Π_{Rand}

Init: The parties initialise by doing the following:

1. For each $i \in \mathcal{P}$, for each $j \in \mathcal{P} \setminus \{i\}$, party i samples $\kappa_{i,j} \leftarrow \{0,1\}^\lambda$.
2. Each pair of parties initialises an instance of $\mathcal{F}_{\mathsf{Commit}}$; call it $\mathcal{F}_{\mathsf{Commit}}^{i,j}$.
3. For each $i \in \mathcal{P}$, for each $j \in \mathcal{P} \setminus \{i\}$, the parties call $\mathcal{F}_{\mathsf{Commit}}^{i,j}$ where i submits input $(\mathsf{Commit}, \mathsf{id}_{i,j}, \kappa_{i,j})$ and j gives $(\mathsf{Commit}, \mathsf{id}_{i,j}, \bot)$.
4. For each $i \in \mathcal{P}$, for each $j \in \mathcal{P} \setminus \{i\}$, the parties execute $\mathcal{F}_{\mathsf{Commit}}^{i,j}$ with input $(\mathsf{Open}, \mathsf{id}_{i,j})$ and abort if $\mathcal{F}_{\mathsf{Commit}}$ returns **abort**.
5. For each $B \in \mathcal{B}$, each party $i \in B$ samples $\kappa_{B,i} \leftarrow \{0,1\}^\lambda$.
6. Each set of parties $B \in \mathcal{B}$ initialises an instance of $\mathcal{F}_{\mathsf{Commit}}$; call it $\mathcal{F}_{\mathsf{Commit}}^{i,B}$.
7. For each $B \in \mathcal{B}$, for each $i \in B$, the parties call $\mathcal{F}_{\mathsf{Commit}}^{i,B}$ where i submits input $(\mathsf{Commit}, \mathsf{id}_{B,i}, \kappa_{B,i})$ and all $j \in B \setminus \{i\}$ give $(\mathsf{Commit}, \mathsf{id}_{B,i}, \bot)$.
8. For each $B \in \mathcal{B}$ and for each $i,j \in \mathcal{P}$ with $i,j \in B$, the parties i and j call $\mathcal{F}_{\mathsf{Commit}}^{i,B}$ with input $(\mathsf{Open}, \mathsf{id}_{B,i})$ and abort if $\mathcal{F}_{\mathsf{Commit}}^B$ returns **abort**.
9. Each party i sets $\kappa_B \leftarrow \oplus_{j \in B} \kappa_{B,j}$ for each B containing i.
10. Finally, each party i sets $\mathsf{cnt} \leftarrow 0$, and $\mathsf{cnt}_B \leftarrow 0$ for all $B \in \mathcal{B}$ where $i \in B$.

PRSS: For each $B \in \mathcal{B}$ containing i, party i computes

$$r_B \leftarrow F_{\kappa_B}(\mathsf{cnt}_B)$$

and increments cnt_B.

Fig. 4. Protocol Π_{Rand}

map $\varphi : E \to E'$ which is also a homomorphism with respect to the natural group structure of E and E'. An isomorphism between two ellliptic curves is an injective isogeny. The j-invariant of an elliptic curve is an algebraic invariant under isomorphism. As isogenies are group homomorphisms, any isogeny comes with a subgroup of E, which is its kernel. On the other hand, any subgroup $G \subset E\left(\mathbb{F}_{p^k}\right)$ yields a unique (up to automorphism) separable isogeny $\varphi : E \to E/G$ having G as kernel. It can be shown that the quotient E is an elliptic curve and its equation can be computed using standard formulae [23].

The set $\mathsf{End}(E)$ of all the isogenies of an elliptic curve E form a ring under the composition operator. The isogenies that can be written with coefficients in $\mathbb{F}_p$ forms a subring of $\mathsf{End}(E)$ and is denoted by $\mathsf{End}_{\mathbb{F}_p}(E)$. For supersingular elliptic curves this happens to be a proper subset. In particular, for supersingular elliptic curves the ring $\mathsf{End}(E)$ is an order of a quarternion algebra defined over $\mathbb{Q}$, while $\mathsf{End}_{\mathbb{F}_p}(E)$ is isomorphic to an order of the imaginary quadratic field $\mathbb{Q}(\sqrt{-p})$. By abuse of notation we will identify $\mathsf{End}_{\mathbb{F}_p}(E)$ with the isomorphic order which we will denote by $\mathcal{O}$. The quotient of the fractional invertible ideals by the principal ideals in $\mathcal{O}$, denoted by $\mathsf{Cl}(\mathcal{O})$ of $\mathcal{O}$, is a group called class group of $\mathcal{O}$. There is a natural action of the class group on the class of elliptic curves defined over $\mathbb{F}_p$ with order $\mathcal{O}$. Given an ideal $\mathfrak{a} \subset \mathcal{O}$ one can define the subgroup $S_\mathfrak{a} = \cap_{\alpha \in \mathfrak{a}} \mathsf{Ker}(\alpha)$. As this is a subgroup of E one gets an isogenous elliptic curve $E/S_\mathfrak{a}$ defined up to $\mathbb{F}_p$-automorphism. We will denote the action of an element $\mathfrak{a} \subset \mathcal{O}$ on an elliptic curve E by $\mathfrak{a} \star E$. This action is free and transitive. This action is believed to be hard to invert, even for a quantum computer. Specifically, constructions based on the following problems are believed to be quantum secure:

Definition 2.1 (Group action inverse problem (GAIP) [9]). *Given two elliptic curves E and E' over the same finite field and with* $\mathsf{End}(E) = \mathsf{End}(E') = \mathcal{O}$, *find an ideal* $\mathfrak{a} \subset \mathcal{O}$ *such that* $E' = \mathfrak{a} \star E$.

There is a obvious decisional version of this problem, which we refer to as the decisional-GAIP, see [22].

The CSI-FiSh signature scheme relies on the hardness of random instance of a multi-target version of GAIP, called MT-GAIP. In [9] it is shown that MT-GAIP reduces to GAIP when the class group structure is known.

Definition 2.2 (MT-GAIP). *Given k elliptic curves $E_1, \ldots, E_k$ over the same field, with* $\mathsf{End}(E_1) = \cdots = \mathsf{End}(E_k) = \mathcal{O}$, *find an ideal* $\mathfrak{a} \subset \mathcal{O}$ *such that* $E_i = \mathfrak{a} \star E_j$ *for some* $i, j \in \{0, \ldots, k\}$ *with* $i \neq j$.

2.6 Digital Signature Schemes

As is standard digital signature schemes are defined by

Definition 2.3. *A* digital signature scheme *is given by a tuple of probabilistic algorithms* (KeyGen, Sign, Verify):

- KeyGen (1^λ) *is a randomized algorithm that takes as input the security parameter and returns the public key* pk *and the private key* sk.
- Sign (sk, μ) *is a randomized signing algorithm that takes as inputs the private key and a message and returns a signature on the message.*
- Verify $(\mathsf{pk}, (\sigma, \mu))$ *is a deterministic verification algorithm that takes as inputs the public key and a signature σ on a message μ and outputs a bit which is equal to one if and only if the signature on μ is valid.*

Correctness and security (EU-CMA) are defined in the usual way.

Definition 2.4. *Let $\mathcal{A}$ be an adversary that is given the public key* pk *and oracle access to the signing oracle* $\mathsf{Sign}_{\mathsf{sk}}$. *In its interaction with the oracle it can receive signatures on messages it adaptively chooses. Let $\mathcal{Q}$ be the set of of messages queried by $\mathcal{A}$. A digital signature scheme $\Pi = $ (KeyGen, Sign, Verify) is said to be* existentially unforgeable *if there exists no such an adversary that can produce a signature on a message $m \notin \mathcal{Q}$, except with negligible probability in λ.*

2.7   Distributed Signature Schemes

We assume the existence of secure point-to-point channels and synchronous channels, so parties receive data at the same time in a given round. For our adversarial model, we assume a malicious adversary that might deviate arbitrarily from the protocol. Given our access structure (Δ, Γ), the adversary can statically corrupt any non-qualified set. For a corrupted party, the adversary learns all the internal variables and controls both the input and the output ports of that party. Informally, our security requirement is that such an adversary will learn nothing about the underlying secret signing key, and that deviations from the protocol will result in an abort signal being sent to the honest parties.

Formally we define the ideal functionality given in Fig. 5, and security is defined by requiring that for every adversary there is a simulator such that the adversary cannot tell if it is interacting in the real protocol, or if it is interacting with a simulator which has access to the ideal functionality. The ideal functionality is designed for a signature scheme in which the secret key is a vector of T elements in R, and the secret sharing of such keys is done via a replicated scheme. Note that, the ideal functionality allows the adversary to alter the sharing provided by the ideal functionality to a different secret key; however the ideal functionality then fixes this change to correspond to the public key initially generated.

Distributed Signature Functionality: $\mathcal{F}_{\mathsf{DSign}}$

We let $\mathcal{A}$ denote the set of parties controlled by the adversary.

KeyGen: This proceeds as follows:
1. The functionality generates a public/private key pair; let the private key (say) be $\mathsf{sk} \in R^T$ and let the public key be pk.
2. The functionality shares sk via the replicated scheme as $\langle \mathsf{sk}_i \rangle'$, with $\mathsf{sk}_i = \sum_{B \in \mathcal{B}} s'_{i,B}$.
3. The values $s'_{i,B}$ are sent to player P_j for $P_j \in B$ for every $B \in \mathcal{B}_A \cup \mathcal{B}_M$.
4. The adversary enters shares $s_{i,B}$ for all share components in $\mathcal{B}_A$.
5. The functionality now defines $s_{i,B} = s'_{i,B}$ for all share components in $\mathcal{B}_M$.
6. The functionality completes the sharing so that it still shares sk_i by fixing the shares in $\mathcal{B}_H$ appropriately.
7. The value pk is output to the adversary.
8. The adversary returns with either **abort** or **deliver**. If **deliver** the functionality returns pk to the honest parties, otherwise it aborts.

Sign: On input of a message m the functionality proceeds as follows:
1. The functionality adversary waits for an input from the adversary.
2. If the input is not **abort** then the functionality generates a signature σ on the message m.
3. The signature is returned to the adversary, and the functionality again waits for inpit. If the input is again not **abort** then the functionality returns σ to the honest players.

Fig. 5. Distributed signature functionality: $\mathcal{F}_{\mathsf{DSign}}$

This cannot be detected by the adversary as the adversary does not see the public key until after it has made the change. This is consistent with how the adversary could attack an initial key distribution based on using a PRSS.

3   The CSI-FiSh Signature Scheme

In this section we recap on the basic CSI-FiSh signature scheme from [1]. The scheme is defined in the isogeny graph of the public supersingular elliptic curve

$$E_0(\mathbb{F}_p) : y^2 = x^3 + x$$

where p is a prime of the form $p = 4 \cdot \ell_1 \cdots \cdots \ell_n - 1$, with ℓ_i being distinct small odd primes. For the set of primes $\ell_1, \ldots, \ell_{74}$, chosen in [3] for the CSIDH-512 parameter set, the authors of [1] determine that the associated class group of the endomorphism ring is cyclic, generated by $\mathfrak{g}$, and has cardinality $N = \#\mathsf{Cl}\,(\mathcal{O})$ given by

$$N = 3 \times 37 \times 1407181 \times 51593604295295867744293584889$$
$$\times 31599414504681995853008278745587832204909.$$

For any ideal $\mathfrak{a} \in \mathsf{Cl}\,(\mathcal{O})$ we can write $\mathfrak{a} = \mathfrak{g}^a$, where $a \in \mathbb{Z}/N\mathbb{Z}$, since the group is cyclic. Therefore we can identify uniquely the ideal $\mathfrak{a}$ with the integer a. To simplify notation we write, for an elliptic curve E' isogenous to E_0, $\mathfrak{a} \star E' = [a]E'$. With this notation we have $[a]([b]E) = [a + b]E$. For the elliptic curve E_0 it is also very easy to compute the quadratic twists. The quadratic twist E^t of the elliptic curve $E = [a]E_0$ is isomorphic over $\mathbb{F}_p$ to the elliptic curve $[-a]E_0$.

The basic identification scheme on which CSI-FiSh is built on starts with a public key being the action of a on the elliptic curve E_0, that is $E_1 := a \star E_0 = [a]E_0$. The prover starts by sampling a random element $b \in \mathbb{Z}/N\mathbb{Z}$, and sends the resulting commitment $[b]E_0$ to the verifier. This computation, according to [1], takes around 40 ms to compute per value of b. The verifier then samples a random challenge *bit* $c \in \{0,1\}$ and returns it to the prover. The prover then responds with $r = b$ modulo N if $c = 0$ and with $r = b - a$ modulo N if $c = 1$. The verifier then checks that $[r]E_0 = E$ if $c = 0$ or $[r]E_1 = E$ if $c = 1$. This can then be turned into a signature scheme in the standard manner.

Having a binary challenge spaces gives an adversary a one in two chance of producing an invalid proof. One way to fix this is to enlarge the challenge space. This is done in [1] as follows, which improves soundness, but increases the size of the public key. A positive integer S is chosen, with the secret key being a vector of dimension $S - 1$, say $(a_1, \ldots, a_{S-1})$ and with public key $(E_0, E_1 = [a_1]E_0, \ldots, E_{S-1} = [a_{S-1}]E_0)$. The prover now must prove that it knows a secret $s \in \mathbb{Z}/N\mathbb{Z}$ such that $E_j = [s]E_i$ for some pair of elliptic curves appearing in the public key list. The prover again chooses a random mask $b \in \mathbb{Z}/N\mathbb{Z}$ and commits to it via $E' = [b]E_0$. The verifier now samples the challenge c uniformly from the set $\{-S + 1, \ldots, S - 1\}$ and the prover responds with $r = b - a_c \pmod{N}$.

Verification consists in checking that $[r]E_c = E'$, where we use the notation $E_{-c} = E_c^t$, for negative values. This variant of CSI-FiSh achieves soundness security $\frac{1}{2 \cdot S - 1}$. Thus to obtain $2^{-\text{sec}}$ soundness security overall we need to repeat the basic protocol $t_S = \text{sec} / \log_2(2 \cdot S - 1)$ times, although one can reduce t_S a little bit by choosing a 'slow' hash function[1].

When combined with the Fiat–Shamir heuristic this gives the signature scheme presented in Fig. 6, where $H : \{0, 1\}^* \longrightarrow [-S + 1, \ldots, S - 1]^{t_S}$. This signature scheme is EU-CMA secure under the MT-GAIP assumption, when H is modelled as a random oracle.

3.1   Zero-Knowledge Proof

Our goal is to define a distributed signing protocol which is secure against malicious adversaries. To guarantee that the parties behave correctly, they are asked to commit to their secrets using the class group action and prove that what they are committing to is of the correct form. Clearly, to prove knowledge of a secret isogeny is sufficient to run an instance of the underlying basic CSI-FiSh identification scheme described above. However, we require to prove something a little more general, namely a witness s to the following relation, which we define

---

The CSI-FiSh Signature Algorithm

KeyGen: Key generation proceeds as follows:
1. For $i \in [1, \ldots, S - 1]$ do
   (a) $a_i \leftarrow \mathbb{Z}/N\mathbb{Z}$.
   (b) $E_i \leftarrow [a_i]E_0$.
2. sk $\leftarrow (a_1, \ldots, a_{S-1})$.
3. pk $\leftarrow (E_0, E_1, \ldots, E_{S-1})$.
Sign(m, sk): To sign a message m, the signer performs
1. For $i = 1, \ldots, t_S$
   (a) $b_i \leftarrow \mathbb{Z}/N\mathbb{Z}$.
   (b) $E_i' \leftarrow [b_i]E_0$.
2. $(c_1, \ldots, c_{t_S}) \leftarrow H(E_1' \| \ldots \| E_{t_S}' \| m)$.
3. For $i = 1, \ldots, t_S$
   (a) $r_i \leftarrow b_i - \text{sign}(c_i) \cdot a_{|c_i|} \pmod{N}$.
4. Output $\{(r_i, c_i)\}_{i=1}^{t_S}$.
Verify($\{(r_i, c_i)\}_{i=1}^{t_S}, m$, pk): To verify a signature $\{(r, c)\}_{i=1}^{t_S}$ on a message m one performs
1. For $i = 1, \ldots, t_S$ execute $E_i' \leftarrow [r_i]E_{c_i}$.
2. $(c_1', \ldots, c_{t_S}') \leftarrow H(E_1' \| \ldots \| E_{t_S}' \| m)$.
3. If $((c_1, \ldots, c_{t_S}) = (c_1', \ldots, c_{t_S}'))$ then output one, else output zero.

Fig. 6. The CSI-FiSh signature algorithm

---

[1] For highest computational efficiency [1] selects, for sec $= 128$, the values $S = 2^{15}$ and $t_S = 7$, using a hash function which is 2^{16} times slower than SHA-3.

a useful sub-protocol for performing a full-threshold variant of the group action computation at the heart of isogeny based cryptography. See Fig. 8 for the details; we defer the relevant proof of security till later. It uses the abstract (standard) commitment functionality $\mathcal{F}_{\mathsf{Commit}}$ given earlier. For later use we denote this sub-protocol by $\mathsf{GrpAction}(E_0, Q, [s])$, which for our fixed elliptic curve produces the group action $[s]Q$ in an actively secure manner.

Group Action Computation for a Full Threshold Secret Sharing

Input: The fixed elliptic curve E_0, a set of parties Q, a secret shared element $s \in \mathbb{Z}/N\mathbb{Z}$ held via a full threshold sharing, i.e. $P \in Q$ holds s_P such that $s = \sum_{P \in Q} s_P$.

Output: $[s]E_0$

1. Define an ordering the players in $Q = \{P_1, \ldots, P_t\}$.
2. Each party P_j initialises an instance of $\mathcal{F}_{\mathsf{Commit}}$; call it $\mathcal{F}^{P_j}_{\mathsf{Commit}}$.
3. For $j = 1, \ldots, t$.
   - $E_{P_j} \leftarrow [s_{P_j}]E_0$.
   - $\pi^1_{P_j} \leftarrow \mathsf{ZK}.P((E_0, E_{P_j}), s_{P_j})$.
   - The parties call $\mathcal{F}^{P_j}_{\mathsf{Commit}}$ where P_j submits input $(\mathsf{Commit}, \mathsf{id}_{P_j}, (E_{P_j}, \pi^1_{P_j}))$ and all other parties input $(\mathsf{Commit}, \mathsf{id}_{P_j}, \bot)$
4. For $j = 1, \ldots, t$
   - The parties execute $\mathcal{F}^{P_j}_{\mathsf{Commit}}$ with input $(\mathsf{Open}, \mathsf{id}_{P_j})$ and abort if $\mathcal{F}^{P_j}_{\mathsf{Commit}}$ returns **abort**.
   - For all $P_j \neq P_i$ party P_j executes $\mathsf{ZK}.V((E_0, E_{P_i}), \pi^1_{P_i})$ and aborts if the verification algorithm fails.
5. $E^0 \leftarrow E_0$.
6. For $j = 1, \ldots, t$ do
   - Party P_j computes $E^j \leftarrow [s_{P_j}]E^{j-1}$.
   - $\pi^2_P \leftarrow \mathsf{ZK}.P((E_0, E_{P_j}, E^{j-1}, E^j), s_{P_j})$.
   - Broadcast $(E^j, \pi^2_{P_j})$ to all players.
   - All players execute $\mathsf{ZK}.V((E_0, E_{P_j}, E^{j-1}, E^j), \pi^2_{P_j})$ and abort if the verification algorithm fails.
7. Return E^t.

Fig. 8. Group action computation for a full threshold secret sharing

Note that $\mathsf{GrpAction}(E_0, Q, [s])$ requires two zero-knowledge proofs of two isogenies to be computed per player. And each player needs to verify $2 \cdot (|Q| - 1)$ zero-knowledge proofs. However, the latency is $O(|Q|)$ due to the second loop.

If s is shared by our replicated scheme $\langle s \rangle$ we can use $\mathsf{GrpAction}(E, Q, [s])$, for a qualified set Q, to compute $\langle s \rangle E_0$ as well. The resulting operation we will denote by $\mathsf{GrpAction}(E_0, Q, \langle s \rangle)$. The modifications needed are as follows: Recall we have $s = \sum_{B \in \mathcal{B}} s_B$, and for a qualified set Q we can assign each s_B to a given player P via the function $\Psi_Q(B)$. Thus we can represent $\langle s \rangle$ as a full threshold scheme over the players in Q, where potentially each player plays the part of a set of players. Then we can execute the protocol as above, except that in line 4 we perform an additional check in that if $P' \in B$ then player P' checks whether $E_P = [s_P]E_0$. This check is performed by all players in $\mathcal{P}$, including those not in Q. This copes with the situations where $\mathcal{B}_M \neq \emptyset$, and we need to check consistency of the sharing.

Note, there is a trival optimization of the protocol for $\mathsf{GrpAction}(E_0, Q, \langle s \rangle)$ which does not expand the number of players artificially to $|\mathcal{B}|$ but keeps it at size $|Q|$. However, the above (less efficient) variant is what we will require for our protocol.

4.1 The Distributed Key Generation and Signing Protocols

We can now define our distributed key generation and signing protocols. The key generation protocol and the protocol to execute the signing operation in a distributed manner are given in Fig. 9. The protocols are defined in the $(\mathcal{F}_{\mathsf{Rand}}, \mathcal{F}_{\mathsf{Commit}})$-hybrid models.

To estimate the cost of signing we use the estimate of 40 ms from [1] to compute a single isogency calculation $[b]E$ for a random $b \in \mathbb{Z}/N\mathbb{Z}$. By counting the number of such operations we can determine an approximate value for the execution time of our distributed signing protocol. The main cost is in computing $E' \leftarrow \mathsf{GrpAction}(E_0, Q, [b])$ a total of t_S times. We estimate the cost in terms of the number of parties $t = |Q|$ in the qualified set Q. Note, that one of the

---

The Distributed Key Generation and Signing Protocols $\Pi_{\mathsf{KeyGen}}, \Pi_{\mathsf{Sign}}$

KeyGen: To generate a distributed key we execute:
1. Call $\mathcal{F}_{\mathsf{Rand}}.\mathsf{Init}()$.
2. For $i \in [1, \ldots, S-1]$ do
   (a) $\langle a_i \rangle \leftarrow \mathcal{F}_{\mathsf{Rand}}.\mathsf{PRSS}()$.
   (b) $E_i \leftarrow \mathsf{GrpAction}(E_0, Q, \langle a_i \rangle)$ for some qualified set Q. If this protocol aborts, then abort.
3. Output $\langle a_1 \rangle, \ldots, \langle a_{S-1} \rangle$ and $E_1, \ldots, E_{S-1}$.

Sign($m, \langle s \rangle$): For a set of qualified parties Q to sign a message m they execute:
1. Write $Q = \{P_1, \ldots, P_t\} \subset \mathcal{P}$.
2. For $i = 1, \ldots, t_S$
   (a) Party P_j generates $b_{i,j} \leftarrow \mathbb{Z}/N\mathbb{Z}$, so as to form a full threshold sharing $[b_i]$ over the t parties.
   (b) The parties execute $E'_i \leftarrow \mathsf{GrpAction}(E_0, Q, [b_i])$.
3. The parties locally compute $(c_1, \ldots, c_{t_S}) \leftarrow H(E'_1 \| \ldots \| E'_{t_S} \| m)$.
4. For $i = 1, \ldots, t_S$ party P_j computes $r_{i,j} \leftarrow b_{i,j} - \mathsf{sign}(c_i) \cdot \sum_{\Psi_Q(B)=P_j} a_{|c_i|, B}$.
5. The parties broadcast their values $r_{i,j}$ and locally compute $r_i \leftarrow \sum_{j=1}^{t} r_{i,j}$.
6. Output $\{(r_i, c_i)\}_{i=1}^{t_S}$.

Fig. 9. The distributed key generation and signing protocols $\Pi_{\mathsf{KeyGen}}, \Pi_{\mathsf{Sign}}$

zero-knowledge proofs executed in Step 6 is Special, whereas all others in this step are General. Due to the sequential nature of the calculation this will have a latency of approximately $|Q| \cdot (1 + t_{\mathsf{ZK}}^{\mathsf{Special}})$ isogeny calculations for Step 3, $|Q| \cdot t_{\mathsf{ZK}}^{\mathsf{Special}}$ isogeny calculations for Step 4, and $\left(1 + 4 \cdot \left((|Q| - 1) \cdot t_{\mathsf{ZK}}^{\mathsf{General}} + t_{\mathsf{ZK}}^{\mathsf{Special}}\right)\right)$ isogeny calculations for Step 6, of Fig. 8. Thus the *rough* total execution time is about

$$t_{\mathsf{S}} \cdot \left(|Q| \cdot (1 + 2 \cdot \mathsf{ZK}^{\mathsf{Special}} + 4 \cdot \mathsf{ZK}^{\mathsf{General}}) + 4 \cdot \mathsf{ZK}^{\mathsf{Special}} - 4 \cdot \mathsf{ZK}^{\mathsf{General}} + 1\right)$$

isogeny calculations.

Taking the specimen parameters of $t_{\mathsf{ZK}}^{\mathsf{General}} = 112$ and $t_{\mathsf{ZK}}^{\mathsf{Special}} = 70$ and $t_{\mathsf{S}} = 7$, and considering the case of a set Q with two members, this gives a latency of about $7 \cdot (2 \cdot (1 + 2 \cdot 70 + 4 \cdot 112) + 4 \cdot 70 - 4 \cdot 112 + 1) \cdot 0.040 = 283$ seconds per party. Which is just under five minutes per party.

4.2 Proofs of Security

To prove the distributed key generation and signing protocols secure we present a simulation of the environment to the adversary. The simulator has access to a signing functionality for some unknown secret key, via the functionality in Fig. 5. For security to hold the adversary must not be able to distinguish between executing in the real environment and executing with the simulation. Our simulation requires rewinding of the adversary in order to extract the witnesses for the associated zero-knowledge proofs. Thus our security proof does not provide a UC-proof of the security of the protocol. Thus our protocol should only be considered 'stand-alone' secure.

KeyGen Simulation: The simulator first calls the functionality $\mathcal{F}_{\mathsf{DSign}}$, which outputs a replicated secret sharing of the associated secret keys $\langle a_i \rangle$ for the adversary, i.e. the simulator learns the values $a'_{i,B}$ for all $B \in \mathcal{B}_A \cup \mathcal{B}_M$, but not for those values in $\mathcal{B}_H$. The simulator now passes the values $a'_{i,B}$ for $B \in \mathcal{B}_A \cup \mathcal{B}_M$ to the adversary by simulating the $\mathcal{F}_{\mathsf{Rand}}.\mathsf{PRSS}()$ protocol.

For each $i \in [1, \ldots, S - 1]$ the adversary now engages in an execution of $\mathsf{GrpAction}(E_0, Q, \langle a_i \rangle)$; note E_0 is fixed across all public keys and hence known to the simulator ahead of time. From the committed zero-knowledge proofs π_P^1 the simulator is able to extract the value $a_{i,B}$ entered by the adversary in the first round of proofs. Note, this value may be different from the values returned by the PRSS, but that is allowed in our security model, as long as it does not contradict a value corresponding to an element in $\mathcal{B}_M$ (if there is a contradiction we will be able to abort later when the real system will abort during the check for this fact). The extracted values $a_{i,B}$ are now passed to the functionality, which completes them to a valid set of shares of the secrets and returns the corresponding public key $E_0, \ldots, E_{S-1}$.

The simulator picks a single honest sharing $B^* \in \mathcal{B}_H$ and generates $a_{i,B}$ for $B \in \mathcal{B}_H \setminus \{B^*\}$ at random. Thus a_{i,B^*} will be the secret key values which are unknown to the simulator. We let j denote the player index corresponding to the element B^*. We let the curve E_{P_j} in Step 3 of Fig. 8 denote a random element of the isogeny graph. We can now fake the associated zero-knowledge proof $\pi^1_{P_j}$ using the simulator for the zero-knowledge proof the commitments can now be opened.

Now look at Step 6 of Fig. 8. All steps for honest players can be simulated exactly by following the real protocol, bar that for the party P_j which holds the unknown share $a_{i,B*}$. The input to this party in execution i will be

$$E_i^{j-1} = \left[\sum_{k=1}^{j-1} s_{P_k} \right] E_0,$$

whilst the output needs to be

$$E_i^j = \left[- \sum_{k=j+1}^{t} s_{P_k} \right] E_i,$$

so as to create the correct output public key E_i. The value E_i^j can thus be computed by the simulator in Step 6 of Fig. 8, and the associated zero-knowledge proof can hence be simulated as well.

If the adversary deviates from the protocol in any way, bar changing the values of $a_{i,B}$ for $B \in \mathcal{B}_A$ in the first phase, this is caught be the zero-knowledge proofs and the simulator will be able to abort. Thus the protocol, assuming no abort occurs, will output the same public key as provided by the ideal functionality.

Sign Simulation: The signing simulation is roughly the same as the key generation simulation. For the qualified set Q, the adversarial inputs can be derived from the initial commitments in $\mathsf{GrpAction}(E_0, Q, [b])$. We let j now be the player for which $\Psi_Q(B*) = P_j$. In our simulation of $\mathsf{GrpAction}(E_0, Q, [b])$ we can defined b_i for $P_i \in \mathcal{B}_H \setminus \{P_j\}$ at random, leaving the value b_j unknown and 'fixed' by the implicit equation given by the signature (r, c) returned by the functionality which gives us $E' = [b]E_0 = [r]E_c$.

The final part of the signature which needs simulating is the output of the r_i for the honest players in Q. For $i \neq j$ this is done exactly as one would in the real protocol. For party j, we know what the adversary *should* output and hence can define $r_j = r - \sum_{i \neq j} r_i$.

If the adversary deviates from the protocol in the final step, and uses an invalid value of r_i. Then the adversary will learn the signature, but the honest players will abort; which is exactly the behaviour required by the ideal functionality.

Acknowledgments. We would like to thank Frederik Vercauteren for the numerous and useful discussions on the arithmetic of isogenies. This work has been supported in part by ERC Advanced Grant ERC-2015-AdG-IMPaCT, by the FWO under an Odysseus project GOH9718N and by CyberSecurity Research Flanders with reference number VR20192203. Any opinions, findings and conclusions or recommendations expressed in this material are those of the author(s) and do not necessarily reflect the views of the ERC or FWO.

References

1. Beullens, W., Kleinjung, T., Vercauteren, F.: CSI-FiSh: efficient isogeny based signatures through class group computations. IACR Cryptology ePrint Archive 2019, 498 (2019). https://eprint.iacr.org/2019/498
2. Brandao, L.T.A.N., Davidson, M., Vassilev, A.: NIST 8214A (Draft): towards NIST standards for threshold schemes for cryptographic primitives: a preliminary roadmap (2019). https://nvlpubs.nist.gov/nistpubs/ir/2019/NIST.IR.8214A-draft.pdf
3. Castryck, W., Lange, T., Martindale, C., Panny, L., Renes, J.: CSIDH: an efficient post-quantum commutative group action. In: Peyrin, T., Galbraith, S. (eds.) ASIACRYPT 2018, Part III. LNCS, vol. 11274, pp. 395–427. Springer, Cham (2018). https://doi.org/10.1007/978-3-030-03332-3_15
4. Cogliati, B., et al.: Provable security of (tweakable) block ciphers based on substitution-permutation networks. In: Shacham, H., Boldyreva, A. (eds.) CRYPTO 2018, Part I. LNCS, vol. 10991, pp. 722–753. Springer, Cham (2018). https://doi.org/10.1007/978-3-319-96884-1_24
5. Couveignes, J.M.: Hard homogeneous spaces. Cryptology ePrint Archive, Report 2006/291 (2006). http://eprint.iacr.org/2006/291
6. Cozzo, D., Smart, N.P.: Sharing the LUOV: threshold post-quantum signatures. IACR Cryptology ePrint Archive 2019, 1060 (2019). https://eprint.iacr.org/2019/1060
7. Cramer, R., Damgård, I., Ishai, Y.: Share conversion, pseudorandom secret-sharing and applications to secure computation. In: Kilian, J. (ed.) TCC 2005. LNCS, vol. 3378, pp. 342–362. Springer, Heidelberg (2005). https://doi.org/10.1007/978-3-540-30576-7_19
8. Damgård, I., Koprowski, M.: Practical threshold RSA signatures without a trusted dealer. In: Pfitzmann, B. (ed.) EUROCRYPT 2001. LNCS, vol. 2045, pp. 152–165. Springer, Heidelberg (2001). https://doi.org/10.1007/3-540-44987-6_10
9. De Feo, L., Galbraith, S.D.: SeaSign: compact isogeny signatures from class group actions. In: Ishai, Y., Rijmen, V. (eds.) EUROCRYPT 2019, Part III. LNCS, vol. 11478, pp. 759–789. Springer, Cham (2019). https://doi.org/10.1007/978-3-030-17659-4_26
10. Decru, T., Panny, L., Vercauteren, F.: Faster SeaSign signatures through improved rejection sampling. In: Ding, J., Steinwandt, R. (eds.) PQCrypto 2019. LNCS, vol. 11505, pp. 271–285. Springer, Cham (2019). https://doi.org/10.1007/978-3-030-25510-7_15
11. Doerner, J., Kondi, Y., Lee, E., Shelat, A.: Secure two-party threshold ECDSA from ECDSA assumptions. In: 2018 IEEE Symposium on Security and Privacy, pp. 980–997. IEEE Computer Society Press, May 2018
12. Feo, L.D., Meyer, M.: Threshold schemes from isogeny assumptions. IACR Cryptology ePrint Archive 2019, 1288 (2019). https://eprint.iacr.org/2019/1288
13. Gennaro, R., Goldfeder, S.: Fast multiparty threshold ECDSA with fast trustless setup. In: Lie, D., Mannan, M., Backes, M., Wang, X. (eds.) ACM CCS 2018, pp. 1179–1194. ACM Press, October 2018
14. Gennaro, R., Goldfeder, S., Narayanan, A.: Threshold-optimal DSA/ECDSA signatures and an application to bitcoin wallet security. In: Manulis, M., Sadeghi, A.-R., Schneider, S. (eds.) ACNS 2016. LNCS, vol. 9696, pp. 156–174. Springer, Cham (2016). https://doi.org/10.1007/978-3-319-39555-5_9

15. Gennaro, R., Jarecki, S., Krawczyk, H., Rabin, T.: Robust threshold DSS signatures. In: Maurer, U. (ed.) EUROCRYPT 1996. LNCS, vol. 1070, pp. 354–371. Springer, Heidelberg (1996). https://doi.org/10.1007/3-540-68339-9_31
16. Lindell, Y.: Fast secure two-party ECDSA signing. In: Katz, J., Shacham, H. (eds.) CRYPTO 2017, Part II. LNCS, vol. 10402, pp. 613–644. Springer, Cham (2017). https://doi.org/10.1007/978-3-319-63715-0_21
17. Lindell, Y., Nof, A.: Fast secure multiparty ECDSA with practical distributed key generation and applications to cryptocurrency custody. In: Lie, D., Mannan, M., Backes, M., Wang, X. (eds.) ACM CCS 2018, pp. 1837–1854. ACM Press, October 2018
18. Lindell, Y., Nof, A., Ranellucci, S.: Fast secure multiparty ECDSA with practical distributed key generation and applications to cryptocurrency custody. IACR Cryptology ePrint Archive 2018, 987 (2018). https://eprint.iacr.org/2018/987
19. MacKenzie, P., Reiter, M.K.: Two-party generation of DSA signatures. In: Kilian, J. (ed.) CRYPTO 2001. LNCS, vol. 2139, pp. 137–154. Springer, Heidelberg (2001). https://doi.org/10.1007/3-540-44647-8_8
20. Rostovtsev, A., Stolbunov, A.: Public-key cryptosystem based on isogenies. Cryptology ePrint Archive, Report 2006/145 (2006). http://eprint.iacr.org/2006/145
21. Shoup, V.: Practical threshold signatures. In: Preneel, B. (ed.) EUROCRYPT 2000. LNCS, vol. 1807, pp. 207–220. Springer, Heidelberg (2000). https://doi.org/10.1007/3-540-45539-6_15
22. Stolbunov, A.: Cryptographic schemes based on isogenies. Ph.D. thesis, NTNU (2012)
23. Vélu, J.: Isogènies entre courbes elliptiques. C.R. Acad. Sc. Paris, Série **273**, 238–241 (1971)

Lattice-Based Cryptography

Defeating NewHope with a Single Trace

Dorian Amiet[1]([✉]), Andreas Curiger[2], Lukas Leuenberger[1], and Paul Zbinden[1]

[1] IMES Institute for Microelectronics and Embedded Systems,
HSR Hochschule für Technik Rapperswil, Rapperswil-Jona, Switzerland
{dorian.amiet,lukas.leuenberger,paul.zbinden}@hsr.ch
[2] Securosys SA, Zürich, Switzerland
curiger@securosys.ch

Abstract. The key encapsulation method "NEWHOPE" allows two parties to agree on a secret key. The scheme includes a private and a public key. While the public key is used to encipher a random shared secret, the private key enables to decipher the ciphertext. NEWHOPE is a candidate in the NIST post-quantum project, whose aim is to standardize cryptographic systems that are secure against attacks originating from both quantum and classical computers. While NEWHOPE relies on the theory of quantum-resistant lattice problems, practical implementations have shown vulnerabilities against side-channel attacks targeting the extraction of the private key. In this paper, we demonstrate a new attack on the shared secret. The target consists of the C reference implementation as submitted to the NIST contest, being executed on a Cortex-M4 processor. Based on power measurement, the complete shared secret can be extracted from data of one single trace only. Further, we analyze the impact of different compiler directives. When the code is compiled with optimization turned off, the shared secret can be read from an oscilloscope display directly with the naked eye. When optimizations are enabled, the attack requires some more sophisticated techniques, but the attack still works on single power traces.

Keywords: Post-quantum cryptography · Side-channel attack · NEWHOPE · Message encoding

1 Introduction

A key encapsulation mechanism (KEM) is a scheme including public and private keys, where the public key is used to create a ciphertext (encapsulation) containing a randomly chosen symmetric key. The private key is used to decrypt the ciphertext. This allows two parties to share a secret key. Traditional KEMs such as RSA [1] rely on the difficulty of factoring large integer numbers. This problem is widely regarded to be infeasible for large numbers with classical computers. The factoring problem can be solved in polynomial time with quantum computers [2]. It is, however, not yet clear, whether quantum computer with enough computation power to break current cryptographic schemes may ever be

© Springer Nature Switzerland AG 2020
J. Ding and J.-P. Tillich (Eds.): PQCrypto 2020, LNCS 12100, pp. 189–205, 2020.
https://doi.org/10.1007/978-3-030-44223-1_11

built [3]. However, the sole risk that such a machine may eventually be built justifies the effort in finding alternatives to today's cryptography [4].

In 2017, the National Institute of Standards and Technology (NIST) started a standardization process [5] for post-quantum algorithms, i.e. cryptographic algorithms able to withstand attacks that would benefit from the processing power of quantum computers. Proposed algorithms in this process include digital signature schemes, key exchange mechanisms and asymmetric encryption. In 2019, 26 of the primary 69 candidates were selected to move to the second round [6]. A remaining KEM candidate is NEWHOPE [7], which was submitted by Thomas Pöppelmann et al. Compared to other key-establishment candidates in the NIST process, NEWHOPE has competitive performance in terms of bandwidth (amount of bits needed to be transmitted between both parties) and clock cycles (time required for computing).

The NEWHOPE submission to NIST is based on NEWHOPE-Simple [8], which is a variant of the prior work NEWHOPE-Usenix [9]. All these NEWHOPE schemes are based on the assumption that the ring-learning with errors (RLWE) problem is hard. RLWE first came to prominence with the paper by Lyubashevsky et al. [10]. It is a speed-up of an earlier scheme, i.e. the learning with errors (LWE) problem, which allows for a security reduction from the shortest vector problem (SVP) on arbitrary lattices [11]. Cryptosystems based on LWE typically require key sizes in the order of n^2. In contrast, RLWE-based cryptosystems have significantly smaller key sizes of almost linear size n [12]. Besides shrinking of the key size, the computation speeds up. For NEWHOPE, the variables are polynomials of degree n. The parameters are chosen in such a way that computations can be performed in the domain of the number-theoretic transform (NTT). The price is being payed with a reduction in security, because RLWE adds some algebraic structures into the lattice that might be utilized by an attacker. However, it is reasonable to conjecture that lattice problems on such lattices are still hard. There is currently no known way to take advantage of that extra structure [12].

Whenever an algorithm is executed on any sort of processor, the device will consume electrical power. Depending on the algorithm and input data, the consumed power will fluctuate. This power variation might be used to attack the algorithm running on the device. To apply such an attack, a time-resolved measurement of the executed instructions is required. Information collected by such measurements are often referred to as side channels and may reflect the timing of the processed instructions [13], the power consumption [14], the electromagnetic emission [15], or any other measurement carrying information about the processed operations. One can then draw conclusions about this side channel. Usually this information includes private data, but it may also contain other information, for example how the algorithm is implemented. These kinds of attacks are often referred to as passive side-channel attacks.

There exist some publications addressing side-channel attacks related to NEWHOPE. Some of them require only a single power trace measurement. Primas et al. introduced an attack on the NTT computation [16], which relies on timing information. However, the NEWHOPE reference implementation submitted to the NIST process (we call it "refC" in this paper) executes the NTT in constant time. Therefore, this attack will not work on refC. Another attack that requires only a single power trace is introduced by Aysu et al. [17]. The attack targets the polynomial multiplication implemented in schoolbook manner. The refC implementation speeds up the polynomial multiplication by making use of the NTT. Instead of n multiplications per value, only one multiplication per value remains during polynomial multiplication. This makes the attack, as described in [17], infeasible for the refC implementation.

In this paper, we demonstrate that the refC implementation is vulnerable to a simple power attack. It might be the first documented passive attack on refC which requires only one power trace to be performed. Another difference to previous attacks is the target. Instead of identifying the private key, our attack addresses the message. In the case of KEM, the attack will leak the shared secret. The side channel is measured during message encoding, i.e. when the shared secret is translated from a bit string into its polynomial representation.

In the next Section, we recall the NEWHOPE KEM and summarize existing attacks. Section 3 consists of the attack description and demonstration including power trace measurements. Finally, possible mitigations are discussed in Sect. 4.

2   Background

The main idea behind RLWE is based on the idea of *small* and *big* polynomial rings of integers modulo q. In NEWHOPE, the polynomials have $n \in \{512, 1204\}$ dimensions, and the modulus is $q = 12289$. *Small* polynomials have coefficients in the range $-8 \leq c \leq 8 \pmod{q}$ in every dimension. *Big* polynomials can have equally distributed coefficients between 0 and $q - 1$. The polynomials can be added, subtracted and multiplied. The effect of the polynomial ring on multiplication is as follows: After (schoolbook) polynomial multiplication, the coefficients of all dimensions $i \geq n$ are added to the coefficient in dimension $i \mod n$. E.g. for $n = 2$, the product $(ax+b) \circ (cx+d)$ will result in $(ad+bc \mod q)x + (ac+bd \mod q)$.

In the following demonstration of the RLWE principle, upper-case letters represent big polynomials and lower-case letters represent small polynomials. To generate a key pair, the server randomly samples A, s, and e. The server calculates

$$B = As + e. \tag{1}$$

Both big polynomials A and B form the public key, and s is the private key. The client side randomly samples the message μ and the small polynomials t, e' and e''. The message μ is encoded into the big polynomial V. The client calculates

$$U = At + e' \tag{2}$$

and

$$V' = Bt + e'' + V. \tag{3}$$

U and V' are then sent to the server. The final calculation on the server side is

$$V' - Us = Bt + e'' + V - Ats - e's \tag{4}$$
$$= Ats + et + e'' + V - Ats - e's \tag{5}$$
$$= et + e'' + V - e's. \tag{6}$$

Because V is the only remaining big polynomial, the server can decode μ, as long as the other polynomials remain small enough.

2.1   NewHope-CPA

The passively secure NewHope version (CPA) implements RLWE as described above. Beside RLWE, an important concept in NewHope includes the NTT. It is somehow related to the FFT. The main advantage of the NTT is calculation speedup. A polynomial multiplication implemented in schoolbook manner requires n^2 single coefficient multiplications. In the NTT domain, the polynomial multiplication requires n coefficient multiplications only. Further, the domain transformation requires $n \log_2(n)$ coefficient multiplications. Even for a single polynomial multiplication, the way through the NTT domain results in a speedup. NewHope forces all implementations to use the NTT, as parts of the public key and ciphertext are defined in the NTT domain only.

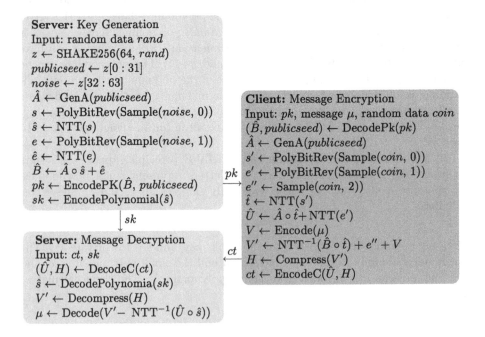

Fig. 1. NewHope-CPA message encapsulation.

Figure 1 shows the NEWHOPE CPA message encapsulation. From an attacker perspective with access to a device and the possibility to measure power traces, the processing of several parts in the scheme are somehow affected by private data. The following parts are potential targets for a passive side-channel attack:

- Random data generation
- SHAKE256
- Generation of s and e (e.g. PolyBitRev(Sample($seed$, 0)))
- Polynomial multiplication and addition (e.g. $\hat{A} \circ \hat{s} + \hat{e}$)
- Both NTT and NTT^{-1}
- Message encoding and decoding.

2.2 Known Attacks

Some of the potential targets have already been exploited and corresponding attacks were already published. Passive side-channel attacks that require only single measurements are the most interesting from a practical view, because such attacks work on ephemeral keys (a fresh NEWHOPE key pair is generated for all key encapsulations) and masking does not prevent these attacks.

[17] introduces a horizontal attack on the polynomial multiplication $a \circ s$ on NEWHOPE-Usenix and Frodo [18]. The target in [17] is the polynomial multiplication implemented in a schoolbook manner: Each coefficient of s is multiplied n times. The attack extracts the coefficients of s out of these n multiplications. It is unclear, if the attack would work on refC with single measurement traces, because in the NTT domain, only one multiplication per coefficient remains.

Another publication describes an attack on the NTT transformation [16]. In this attack, an NTT implementation is exploited that does not execute in constant time. The NEWHOPE refC implementation, however, does not have such a timing leakage. Other related passive attacks on lattice-based key encapsulation schemes include [19–21]. However, we are not aware of any publication that directly targets the message encoding in any lattice-based scheme.

This fact reflects also in publications that cover countermeasures against passive attacks. [22] and [23] introduce masked decryption. The masked operations are NTT^{-1}, polynomial arithmetic operations, and message decoding. Further masking includes also encryption on client side [24]. This scheme masks also message encoding. The message m is split into two shares $m = m' \oplus m''$, and the encoding function is executed on both shares m' and m''.

An active attack that might be applicable on all RLWE schemes in CPA mode uses several forged ciphertexts to reconstruct the private key [25–28]. Because NEWHOPE-CPA is prone to these active attacks, the CPA version is only eligible for ephemeral keys. For all other applications, NEWHOPE-CCA should be used. NEWHOPE-CCA is a superset of NEWHOPE-CPA. The main difference is an additional encryption step after the decryption on the server side. The server calculates the ciphertext by itself and compares it to the ciphertext received from the client side. A forged ciphertext from the client will then be detected.

IND-CCA2 security is traded off with processing time (mainly on server side) and a ciphertext whose size is slightly increased (by 3% or 1.4%, respectively, depending on n).

3   Attack Description

The attack is performed during message encoding. If an active secure NEWHOPE-CCA instance is chosen, the attack works on both server and client side. Concerning the NEWHOPE-CPA instances, message encoding is called on client side only.

The message encoding function translates a 256-bit message or an encapsulated key into its polynomial representation. This encoded polynomial V has a zero in every dimension i, if the corresponding message bit $\mu_{i-k\cdot256}$ is zero. Otherwise, if the message bit $\mu_{i-k\cdot256}$ is one, the corresponding polynomial coefficients are set to $q/2 = 6144$.

A straightforward implementation might use a for-loop over all message bits containing an if-condition which sets the polynomial coefficients to either 0 or $q/2$. Such an implementation would be susceptible to timing attacks. The refC implements the message encoding in a way that the code inside the for-loop always runs in constant time. Listing 1 shows the corresponding function from refC.

```
1  // Name:          poly_frommsg
2  // Description:   Convert 32-byte message to polynomial
3  // Arguments:     - poly *r: pointer to output polynomial
4  //                - const unsigned char *msg: input message
5
6  void poly_frommsg(poly *r, const unsigned char *msg)
7  {
8      unsigned int i,j,mask;
9      for(i=0;i<32;i++)
10     {
11         for(j=0;j<8;j++)
12         {
13             mask = -((msg[i] >> j)&1);
14             r->coeffs[8*i+j+   0] = mask & (NEWHOPE_Q/2);
15             r->coeffs[8*i+j+256] = mask & (NEWHOPE_Q/2);
16 #if (NEWHOPE_N == 1024)//If clause dissolved at compile time
17             r->coeffs[8*i+j+512] = mask & (NEWHOPE_Q/2);
18             r->coeffs[8*i+j+768] = mask & (NEWHOPE_Q/2);
19 #endif
20         }
21     }
22 }
```

Listing 1. Message encoding in refC

A mask, containing 0 or -1 (= 0xFFFF...), replaces the if-condition. The mask calculation is shown in Listing 1 at line 13. The processed message bit is leaked neither in a branch, nor in an address-index look-up nor in differences in execution time. However, power consumption might differ between processing a logical zero or logical one, especially because the mask either contains ones or zeroes only. Chances that processed values can be detected by analyzing the power consumption of the device are high.

A side-channel measurement can be used to differentiate between processed ones and zeroes. If a single trace is sufficient to do so, the attack would be applicable on ephemeral keys. In the case of CPA or message encryption, the attack does not require any public data (i.e. monitoring of the insecure channel is not required), as the attack directly leaks the shared secret.

Note that this type of attack not only works on message encoding of NewHope. A check of NIST submissions indicates several candidates, especially other lattice-based KEMs. Crystals-Kyber [29], for example, uses an almost identical approach to encode the message.

3.1 Experimental Analysis

In this section, we demonstrate a successful attack based on current measurements on a Cortex M4 processor. We use the publicly available platform CW308-STM32F4 from NewAE Technology to execute all our attacks. A 40 Gsps WaveRunner 640Zi oscilloscope from LeCroy was used to record power traces. The processor core runs at 59 MHz.

The STM32CubeIDE together with an ST programmer from STMicroelectronics was used to compile and program the device. The underlying C compiler is gcc. When the message encoding function according to Listing 1 is compiled, the resulting assembler code and thus the program execution differs depending on compiler settings, in particular on the chosen optimization strategy. To cover various cases, we present results for the case when optimization is disabled ($-$O0), and when maximum optimization is applied ($-$O3). All measurements are recorded as follows:

1. A test message is generated in which byte 1 is set to a test value. All other bytes contain random data.
2. A loop, covering test values from 0 to 255, is executed. In this loop, the message encoding function is called and the voltage at the shunt resistor is recorded.

3.2 No Optimization

Message encoding requires 109 clock cycles per bit (Listing 1, lines 13–18) when the code is compiled with optimization turned off. The resulting assembly code is shown in Appendix 1.

As mentioned before, the power consumption should depend on the processed message bits. The question is, however, whether the differences in power consumption are big enough to be exploited. To answer this question, all possible values for message byte 1 have been recorded and plotted on top of each other. To obtain a clear and sharp image, 100 traces per value have been averaged.

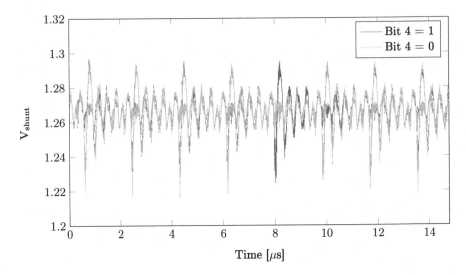

Fig. 2. Measurement traces on top of each other. Every trace is 100 times averaged. Code compiled with optimization disabled.

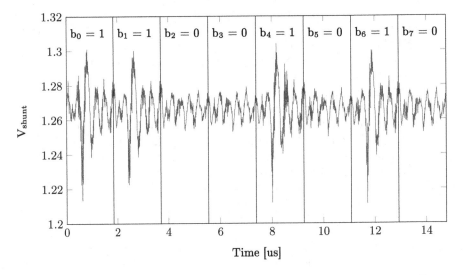

Fig. 3. A single trace measurement where message byte 1 is set to the value 83 (binary 0101 0011). Code compiled with optimization disabled.

The plot in Fig. 2 shows the power traces during processing of message byte 1. The traces are color-separated by the two possible values of bit 4. The fluctuation of the amplitude is significantly higher when the value of the processed message bit is one. The difference is so large that it is even possible to read the processed message bit directly from the oscilloscope's display. Hence, the attack can be classified as a simple power attack (SPA). Figure 3 shows a single power trace. The message byte 83 can directly be read out.

3.3 Optimization Enabled

Message encoding requires 9 clock cycles per bit (Listing 1, lines 13–18) when the code is compiled with maximum optimization setting O3. The assembly code is provided in Appendix 2.

We use the same approach as before to estimate the differences in power consumption depending on individual message bits. Figure 4 shows traces of different test values on top of each other. The power traces still differ, but less obvious than before, when optimization was turned off. A direct read-out of the bit values might be hard to accomplish. Note that the traces plotted in Fig. 4 are 1000 times averaged in order to reduce the noise. In a single-trace setting, the additional noise would make it even more difficult to read out the message bits directly.

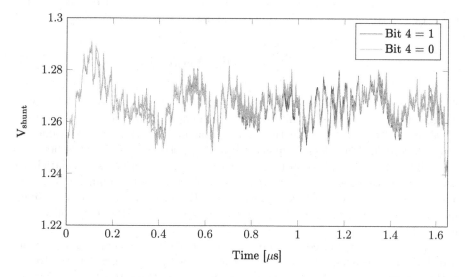

Fig. 4. All measurement traces on top of each other. Every trace is 1000 times averaged. Code compiled with optimization enabled (O3).

Because an SPA might not be applicable, a differential-power attack (DPA) might work. The attack requires a two-stage process. Before the actual attack can start, reference traces are required. These traces are the same power measurements as within the attack, but with known message values. To obtain these traces, an attacker has two possibilities: If the device under attack works as server, the attack is only applicable to NEWHOPE-CCA. The upside for the attacker is that he can perform the attack as client. The attacker creates valid ciphertexts for which he can choose the messages. When the device under attack performs the re-encryption step, the attacker obtains such reference traces. In the reversed case, where the device under attack is the client and the attacker is the server, the attacker is unable to choose the messages: The client executes message encoding with random messages. However, since the attacker performs as server, he knows the private key and can therefore calculate the messages in use. In the following, the attacker can repeat these steps until he has obtained enough reference traces.

For all 256 possible values that a message byte can take on, we record 1,000 reference traces and average them to reduce the impact of noise. After collecting the reference traces, the actual attack is ready to begin. Our treat model assumes that the message changes on every call. Therefore, we try to extract the message byte values from a single power trace only. When an attack trace is available, the trace is cut into 32 power traces, each containing the processing of one message byte. These sliced traces are then compared to all 256 reference traces. The known value of the reference trace which is most similar to the attack trace will then be taken as the corresponding value for the message byte.

One method to calculate the similarity S between a reference trace V_{ref} and the attacked trace V_{attack} is the sum of squares

$$S = \sum_{i=0}^{n_{\text{samples}}-1} (V_{\text{ref}}[i] - V_{\text{attack}}[i])^2. \tag{7}$$

Although the attack will work like this, the signal-to-noise ratio (SNR) may be increased when the noise is filtered out. A single measurement trace contains noise in all frequencies while the information about the processed value lies somewhere below the clock frequency. In our experiment, the SNR is better, if a bandpass filter is applied on both, V_{ref} and V_{attack}, before S is calculated. We used a bandpass filter at 1.5–10 MHz (with the core clock running at 59 MHz). The frequencies were heuristically evaluated. Because the encoding of a single message bit takes 9 clock cycles, a passband around 59 MHz/9 = 6.56 MHz is reasonable.

Equation 7 is calculated 256 times (once per reference trace) to get an S per possible message byte. The smallest S corresponds to the correct byte. To test if the attack works with all possible messages, the attack has been performed over all possible values. The result is illustrated in Fig. 5. The diagram can be read as follows: On the x-axis are the reference traces, whereas on the y-axis traces from the attack can be found. For instance, the horizontal line at $y = 50$ represents all similarities S from the attacked byte value 50 compared to the reference traces. Blue represents high similarity or a small S, respectively. Since S is the smallest at $x = 50$, the attack worked for this message value, because the correct value could be identified. The diagonal blue line indicates that the attack works for (almost) all message values.

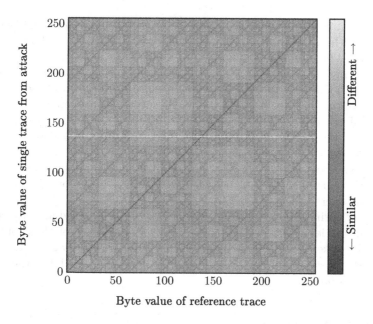

Fig. 5. Similarity between a single power trace compared to the reference traces. (Color figure online)

In Fig. 5, an outlier can be identified. The attacked message value 138 is the only one where the smallest S is not the correct guess. Generally, value 138 sticks out as indicated by the yellow horizontal line. The corresponding power trace, when inspected in the time domain, shows a disturbance pulse with an amplitude of $\approx 150\,\text{mV}$. The pulse has a duration of roughly 250 ns plus some reflections during another 500 ns. The pulse disturbs side-channel information for approximately four message bits. All our measurements contain some of these pulses. They must be somehow related to our measurement setup, because the frequency of these pulses decreases with the time our system is turned on. At start-up, the pulse frequency is $\approx 50\,\text{kHz}$ and falls down to $\approx 1\,\text{kHz}$ within a second. The origin of the pulses is not fully clear. Due to the observations, we suspect the supply voltage regulator as the culprit.

3.4   Success Rate

When all measurements containing disturbing pulses are excluded, the attack success rate gets very close to 100% (we did not find any measurement without outlier and false message bit guess).

When optimization is enabled, about 4% of the attacked message encodings contain an outlier. Depending on timing, this results in one or two false message byte guesses. The minimum similarity S of a faulty key byte guess is more than 1,000 times higher than S of a correct key byte guesses. Therefore, outliers can easily be identified. In the case where a pulse provokes two false message-byte guesses, the message value of the two suspected bytes can be determined by a brute-force attack. The requirement to execute the brute-force attack is knowledge of the public data, public key and ciphertext. The computational effort is $2^{16} = 65,536$ message encryptions in the worst case. To sum up, the attack has a success rate of $\geq 96\%$ in our setup. When the public data is known, most of the remaining 4% can be calculated with a brute-force attack. This results in an overall success rate of $>99\%$.

In case of optimization turned off, about 47% of the attacked message encodings contain at least one outlier pulse. However, the effect of these pulses is marginal. Even key guesses that contain such a pulse are mostly guessed correct. Without any post-processing (brute-force of potentially false bits), the overall success rate is 99.5%.

4   Countermeasures

An approach to make the attack more difficult is to decrease the number of bits that change their value during encryption. This can be achieved by removing the mask calculation. The coefficient in the encoded message can be calculated by a multiplication of the message bit to $q/2$. Lines 13 and 14 from Listing 1 are replaced by Listing 2.

```
13  tmp = (NEWHOPE_Q/2) * ((msg[i] >> j)&1);
14  r->coeffs[8*i+j+  0] = tmp;
```

Listing 2. Message encoding with multiplication

Compiled with optimization enabled, this results in assembly code (see Appendix 3) in which only two bits are set at a time (in contrast to 32 bits in the reference code). Nevertheless, the single power trace DPA from Sect. 3.3 is still applicable, though the SNR is approximately cut in half. Therefore, this small change is not sufficient to prevent the attack. Note that even if a way to hide the message bit to $q/2$ encoding was found, there would still be leakage from storing (lines 4 to 7 in Appendix 2).

Oder et al. [24] introduced a masking scheme for encryption. Instead of using one message, two different messages μ' and μ'' are encrypted. These messages are later xored, or rather summed together in the $\mathcal{R}_q$ space, thus forming the final message μ. However, this approach only makes the presented attack slightly more difficult, as the message encoding must be attacked twice.

A more promising countermeasure which is mentioned in [24] is the use of the Fisher-Yates algorithm [30]. It generates a random list, different for every encryption, which contains all values between 0 and 255. This list then determines the order in which the individual bits of the message are encoded. The initial two `for` loops are further replaced with one for loop, counting from 0 to 255. In Listing 3, the updated mask calculation (line 13 from Listing 1) is shown.

```
13  mask = −((msg[fyList[i] >> 3] >> (fyList[i]&7))&1)
```

Listing 3. Message encoding with Fisher-Yates shuffle

The proposed attack can still be performed. However, as the bits are encoded in a random order, an attacker can only determine the total number of ones and zeroes in a message, but not which value would correspond to which bit. To accomplish this, both the message encoding as well as the shuffling must be attacked to recover the message. Combining the shuffling algorithm together with masking might provide adequate side-channel protection: An attacker would have to attack the message encoding on two shares and twice the shuffling algorithm to determine the message, all on a single side-channel trace.

In reference to existing side-channel attacks on lattice-based encryption schemes [31], not only message encoding, but all linear processed parts of NewHope that contain somehow sensitive data should be protected.

5   Conclusion

The NewHope reference C implementation execution time does not depend on private data. However, our experiments show that constant time execution does not prevent power attacks. The complete shared secret can be extracted from data of one single trace only. Depending on the compiler directive, even simple-power attacks are possible. Prior work about passive side-channel attacks on lattice-based key encapsulations mechanisms usually have the private key as target. We demonstrated that an implementation, which protects all parts of the algorithm in which the private key is processed, is not secure. All parts in the NewHope algorithms that process somehow private data, including the message, must be protected in order to obtain a secured NewHope implementation.

Acknowledgment. We thank the anonymous reviewers for their accurate reviews and valuable comments. This work was supported by Innosuisse, the federal agency responsible for encouraging science-based innovation in Switzerland.

Appendix 1

```
 1 ; mask = -((msg[i] >> j)&1):
 2 ldr     r2, [r7, #0]   ; r2 = memory[r7]
 3 ldr     r3, [r7, #20]  ; r3 = memory[r7 + 20]
 4 add     r3, r2         ; r3 = r2 + r3
 5 ldrb    r3, [r3, #0]   ; r3 = memory[r3]
 6 mov     r2, r3         ; r2 = r3
 7 ldr     r3, [r7, #16]  ; r3 = memory[r3 + 16]
 8 asr.w   r3, r2, r3     ; r3 = r2 >> r3: shift rigth r2 by r3
 9 and.w   r3, r3, #1     ; r3 = r3 & 1
10 negs    r3, r3         ; r3 = (-1)*r3
11 str     r3, [r7, #12]  ; memory(r7 + #12) = r3;
12 ; r->coeffs[8*i+j+  0] = mask & (NEWHOPE_Q/2):
13 ldr     r3, [r7, #12]  ; r3 = memory[r7 + 12)]
14 uxth    r3, r3         ; r3 = zero-extend r3[15:0] to 32
        bits
15 ldr     r2, [r7, #20]  ; r2 = memory[r7 + 20]
16 lsls    r1, r2, #3     ; r1 = r2 << 3: shift left by 3 bits
17 ldr     r2, [r7, #16]  ; r2 = memory[r7 + 16]
18 add     r2, r1         ; r2 = r2 + r1
19 and.w   r3, r3, #6144  ; r3 = r3 & 6144
20 uxth    r1, r3         ; r1 = zero-extend r3[15:0] to 32
        bits
21 ldr     r3, [r7, #4]   ; r3 = memory[r7 + 4]
22 strh.w  r1, [r3, r2, lsl #1] ; memory[r3 + 2 * r2] = r1
23 ; r->coeffs[8*i+j+256] = mask & (NEWHOPE_Q/2):
24 ldr     r3, [r7, #12]  ; r3 = memory[r7 + 12)]
25 uxth    r3, r3         ; r3 = zero-extend r3[15:0] to 32
        bits
26 ldr     r2, [r7, #20]  ; r2 = memory[r7 + 20]
27 lsls    r1, r2, #3     ; r1 = r2 << 3: shift left by 3 bits
28 ldr     r2, [r7, #16]  ; r2 = memory[r7 + 16]
29 add     r2, r1         ; r2 = r2 + r1
30 add.w   r2, r2, #256   ; r2 = r2 + 256
31 and.w   r3, r3, #6144  ; r3 = r3 & 6144
32 uxth    r1, r3         ; r1 = zero-extend r3[15:0] to 32
        bits
33 ldr     r3, [r7, #4]   ; r3 = memory[r7 + 4]
34 strh.w  r1, [r3, r2, lsl #1] ; memory[r3 + 2 * r2] = r1
35 ; line 24 - 34 repeats twice (immediate value at line 30 is
        replaced by 512 and 768)
```

Listing 4. Assembly with optimization turned off (O0), original refC

Appendix 2

```
1 ldrb     r2, [r3, #0]     ; r2 = memory[r3]
2 sbfx     r2, r2, #0, #1   ; r2 = extract bit 0 (1 bit) of r2
     and sign−extend it to 32 bits (if bit 0 (r2) == 0, then
     r2 = 0x0000..., else r2 = 0xffff...)
3 and.w    r2, r2, #6144    ; r2 = r2 & 6144
4 strh     r2, [r0, #0]     ; memory[r0] = r2
5 strh.w   r2, [r0, #512]   ; memory[r0 + 512] = r2
6 strh.w   r2, [r0, #1024]  ; memory[r0 + 1024] = r2
7 strh.w   r2, [r0, #1536]  ; memory[r0 + 1536] = r2
```

Listing 5. Assembly with maximal optimization O3, original refC

Appendix 3

```
1 ldrb     r2, [r3, #0]     ; r2 = memory[r3]
2 ubfx     r4, r2, #0, #1   ; r4 = extract bit 0 (1 bit) of r2
     and zero−extend it to 32 bits
3 lsls     r2, r4, #1       ; r2 = r4 << 1: shift left by 1 bit
4 add      r2, r4           ; r2 = r2 + r4
5 lsls     r2, r2, #11      ; r2 = r3 << 11 (now we have r2 =
     6144 when bit 0 was 1, else r2 remains 0)
6 strh     r2, [r0, #0]     ; memory[r0] = r2
7 strh.w   r2, [r0, #512]   ; memory[r0 + 512] = r2
8 strh.w   r2, [r0, #1024]  ; memory[r0 + 1024] = r2
9 strh.w   r2, [r0, #1536]  ; memory[r0 + 1536] = r2
```

Listing 6. Assembly with maximal optimization O3, mask construction replaced by multiplication

References

1. Rivest, R.L., Shamir, A., Adleman, L.M.: A method for obtaining digital signatures and public-key cryptosystems. Commun. ACM **21**(2), 120–126 (1978). https://doi.org/10.1145/359340.359342
2. Shor, P.W.: Polynomial-time algorithms for prime factorization and discrete logarithms on a quantum computer. SIAM J. Comput. **26**(5), 1484–1509 (1997). https://doi.org/10.1137/S0097539795293172
3. Dyakonov, M.: The case against quantum computing. IEEE Spectr. **56**(3), 24–29 (2019)
4. Mosca, M.: Cybersecurity in an era with quantum computers: will we be ready? IEEE Secur. Priv. **16**(5), 38–41 (2018). https://doi.org/10.1109/MSP.2018.3761723
5. National Institute of Standards and Technology: Submission requirements and evaluation criteria for the post-quantum cryptography standardization process (2016)

6. Alagic, G., et al.: Status report on the first round of the NIST post-quantum cryptography standardization process. NISTIR 8240 (2019). https://doi.org/10. 6028/NIST.IR.8240

7. Alkim, E., et al.: NewHope - algorithm specifications and supporting documentation. Version 1.02 (2019)

8. Alkim, E., Ducas, L., Pöppelmann, T., Schwabe, P.: NewHope without reconciliation. IACR Cryptology ePrint Archive, p. 1157 (2016). http://eprint.iacr.org/2016/1157

9. Alkim, E., Ducas, L., Pöppelmann, T., Schwabe, P.: Post-quantum key exchange - a new hope. In: 25th USENIX Security Symposium, USENIX Security 2016, Austin, TX, USA, 10–12 August 2016, pp. 327–343 (2016)

10. Lyubashevsky, V., Peikert, C., Regev, O.: On ideal lattices and learning with errors over rings. In: Gilbert, H. (ed.) EUROCRYPT 2010. LNCS, vol. 6110, pp. 1–23. Springer, Heidelberg (2010). https://doi.org/10.1007/978-3-642-13190-5_1

11. Regev, O.: On lattices, learning with errors, random linear codes, and cryptography. In: Proceedings of the 37th Annual ACM Symposium on Theory of Computing, Baltimore, MD, USA, 22–24 May 2005, pp. 84–93 (2005). https://doi.org/10. 1145/1060590.1060603

12. Regev, O.: The learning with errors problem (invited survey). In: Proceedings of the 25th Annual IEEE Conference on Computational Complexity, CCC 2010, Cambridge, Massachusetts, USA, 9–12 June 2010, pp. 191–204 (2010). https://doi. org/10.1109/CCC.2010.26

13. Kocher, P.C.: Timing attacks on implementations of Diffie-Hellman, RSA, DSS, and other systems. In: Koblitz, N. (ed.) CRYPTO 1996. LNCS, vol. 1109, pp. 104–113. Springer, Heidelberg (1996). https://doi.org/10.1007/3-540-68697-5_9

14. Kocher, P., Jaffe, J., Jun, B.: Differential power analysis. In: Wiener, M. (ed.) CRYPTO 1999. LNCS, vol. 1666, pp. 388–397. Springer, Heidelberg (1999). https://doi.org/10.1007/3-540-48405-1_25

15. Mulder, E.D., et al.: Electromagnetic analysis attack on an FPGA implementation of an elliptic curve cryptosystem. In: EUROCON 2005 - The International Conference on "Computer as a Tool", vol. 2, pp. 1879–1882 (2005). https://doi.org/10.1109/EURCON.2005.1630348

16. Primas, R., Pessl, P., Mangard, S.: Single-trace side-channel attacks on masked lattice-based encryption. In: Fischer, W., Homma, N. (eds.) CHES 2017. LNCS, vol. 10529, pp. 513–533. Springer, Cham (2017). https://doi.org/10.1007/978-3-319-66787-4_25

17. Aysu, A., Tobah, Y., Tiwari, M., Gerstlauer, A., Orshansky, M.: Horizontal side-channel vulnerabilities of post-quantum key exchange protocols. In: 2018 IEEE International Symposium on Hardware Oriented Security and Trust, HOST 2018, Washington, DC, USA, 30 April–4 May 2018, pp. 81–88 (2018). https://doi.org/10.1109/HST.2018.8383894

18. Bos, J.W., et al.: Frodo: take off the ring! practical, quantum-secure key exchange from LWE. In: Proceedings of the 2016 ACM SIGSAC Conference on Computer and Communications Security, Vienna, Austria, 24–28 October 2016, pp. 1006–1018 (2016). https://doi.org/10.1145/2976749.2978425

19. Park, A., Han, D.: Chosen ciphertext simple power analysis on software 8-bit implementation of ring-LWE encryption. In: 2016 IEEE Asian Hardware-Oriented Security and Trust, AsianHOST 2016, Yilan, Taiwan, 19–20 December 2016, pp. 1–6 (2016). https://doi.org/10.1109/AsianHOST.2016.7835555

20. Huang, W., Chen, J., Yang, B.: Correlation power analysis on NTRU prime and related countermeasures. IACR Cryptology ePrint Archive, p. 100 (2019). https://eprint.iacr.org/2019/100

21. Zheng, X., Wang, A., Wei, W.: First-order collision attack on protected NTRU cryptosystem. Microprocess. Microsyst. Embed. Hardw. Design **37**(6–7), 601–609 (2013). https://doi.org/10.1016/j.micpro.2013.04.008

22. Reparaz, O., Roy, S.S., de Clercq, R., Vercauteren, F., Verbauwhede, I.: Masking ring-LWE. J. Cryptogr. Eng. **6**(2), 139–153 (2016). https://doi.org/10.1007/s13389-016-0126-5

23. Reparaz, O., de Clercq, R., Roy, S.S., Vercauteren, F., Verbauwhede, I.: Additively homomorphic ring-LWE masking. In: Takagi, T. (ed.) PQCrypto 2016. LNCS, vol. 9606, pp. 233–244. Springer, Cham (2016). https://doi.org/10.1007/978-3-319-29360-8_15

24. Oder, T., Schneider, T., Pöppelmann, T., Güneysu, T.: Practical CCA2-secure and masked ring-LWE implementation. IACR Trans. Cryptogr. Hardw. Embed. Syst., 142–174 (2018). https://doi.org/10.13154/tches.v2018.i1.142-174

25. Fluhrer, S.R.: Cryptanalysis of ring-LWE based key exchange with key share reuse. IACR Cryptology ePrint Archive, p. 85 (2016). http://eprint.iacr.org/2016/085

26. Ding, J., Alsayigh, S., Saraswathy, R.V., Fluhrer, S.R., Lin, X.: Leakage of signal function with reused keys in RLWE key exchange. In: IEEE International Conference on Communications, ICC 2017, Paris, France, 21–25 May 2017, pp. 1–6 (2017). https://doi.org/10.1109/ICC.2017.7996806

27. Bauer, A., Gilbert, H., Renault, G., Rossi, M.: Assessment of the key-reuse resilience of NewHope. In: Matsui, M. (ed.) CT-RSA 2019. LNCS, vol. 11405, pp. 272–292. Springer, Cham (2019). https://doi.org/10.1007/978-3-030-12612-4_14

28. Qin, Y., Cheng, C., Ding, J.: A complete and optimized key mismatch attack on NIST candidate NewHope. In: Sako, K., Schneider, S., Ryan, P.Y.A. (eds.) ESORICS 2019, Part II. LNCS, vol. 11736, pp. 504–520. Springer, Cham (2019). https://doi.org/10.1007/978-3-030-29962-0_24

29. Avanzi, R., et al.: CRYSTALS-Kyber algorithm specifications and supporting documentation. Version 2.0 (2019)

30. Fisher, R.A., Yates, F., et al.: Statistical tables for biological, agricultural and medical research (1963). http://hdl.handle.net/2440/10701

31. Khalid, A., Oder, T., Valencia, F., O'Neill, M., Güneysu, T., Regazzoni, F.: Physical protection of lattice-based cryptography: challenges and solutions. In: Proceedings of the 2018 on Great Lakes Symposium on VLSI, GLSVLSI 2018, Chicago, IL, USA, 23–25 May 2018, pp. 365–370 (2018). https://doi.org/10.1145/3194554.3194616

Decryption Failure Is More Likely After Success

Nina Bindel$^{(\boxtimes)}$ and John M. Schanck$^{(\boxtimes)}$

Institute for Quantum Computing, University of Waterloo, Waterloo, Canada
{nlbindel,jschanck}@uwaterloo.ca

Abstract. The user of an imperfectly correct lattice-based public-key encryption scheme leaks information about their secret key with each decryption query that they answer—even if they answer all queries successfully. Through a refinement of the D'Anvers–Guo–Johansson–Nilsson–Vercauteren–Verbauwhede failure boosting attack, we show that an adversary can use this information to improve his odds of finding a decryption failure. We also propose a new definition of δ-correctness, and we re-assess the correctness of several submissions to NIST's post-quantum standardization effort.

Keywords: Public-key cryptography · Lattice-based cryptography · Decryption failure

1 Introduction

Imperfectly correct lattice-based encryption schemes carry risks that perfectly correct schemes do not. Namely, whenever the decryption procedure fails it indicates "some correlation between the secret key and the encryption randomness" that reveals "information about the secret key" [20]. This is widely acknowledged. And yet, if one notes that *successful* decryption indicates a *lack* of correlation in precisely the same way, the consequence is startling: the user of an imperfectly correct lattice-based encryption scheme leaks information about their secret key with each decryption query that they answer. In this work, we show that an adversary can use information from successful decryptions to improve his odds of causing a decryption failure.

First, let us head off some objections. One might object that "[non-failing ciphertexts] will contain negligible information about the secret" [8]. For many schemes, we agree. However, even if a single ciphertext provides negligible information, an adversary might submit *many* non-failing ciphertexts.

One might also object that the risk of imperfect correctness can be mitigated using existing analyses. Indeed, when the Fujisaki–Okamoto transformation [12] is applied to a δ-correct passively secure encryption scheme, the result is an actively secure scheme with a failure probability of no more than $C\delta$ relative to an adversary who generates C ciphertexts [17, Theorem 3.1]. If the designers of an encryption scheme account for this factor of C loss of correctness, they can

J. Ding and J.-P. Tillich (Eds.): PQCrypto 2020, LNCS 12100, pp. 206–225, 2020.
https://doi.org/10.1007/978-3-030-44223-1_12

argue that decryption failures are not a risk. However, when designers rely on a conservative analysis of correctness, they may choose sub-optimal parameters.

We have seen several attempts to plot lattice-based encryption schemes along axes of size and security. These plots mask differences in correctness, even when they accurately represent tradeoffs between size and security against known attacks (c.f. [3]). We believe that an *accurate* and *concrete* assessment of correctness will enable a more fair comparison of the candidates.

Contributions. Our main contributions are: (1) a refinement of the D'Anvers–Guo–Johansson–Nilsson–Vercauteren–Verbauwhede *failure boosting* attack [5]; and (2) a new definition of correctness that is tailored for de-randomized encryption schemes. We also provide software[1] to calculate the correctness of FrodoKEM [20], Saber [6], Kyber [24], and (some parameter sets of) Round5 [13]. We partially validate our calculations with experiments on FrodoKEM.

Our Refinement of Failure Boosting. We focus on the Lindner–Peikert encryption scheme [18], as it underlies all of the imperfectly correct lattice-based public-key encryption schemes that have been submitted to NIST. The correctness condition of these schemes can be stated as

$$-t \leq \langle s, e \rangle \leq t \tag{1}$$

where s is a vector related to the secret key, e is a vector related to the ciphertext randomness, and t is a system parameter.

An instantiation of the Lindner–Peikert scheme is said to be δ-correct if the probability that Eq. (1) is violated for a random honestly generated s and a random honestly generated e is at most δ. The condition that e is honestly generated is reasonable when the scheme is *de-randomized*, e.g. when the Fujisaki–Okamoto transformation is used. In this case, the adversary needs the help of a random oracle to generate a valid ciphertext. The random oracle severely limits the adversary's ability to cause a decryption failure: if the adversary generates C ciphertexts, then his probability of causing a decryption failure is no more than $C\delta$, by a union bound.

The adversary's success probability may be far lower than $C\delta$. A key observation is that if Eq. (1) is satisfied for some e, then it is likely to be satisfied for all e' that are *close* to e. One can quantify the *overlap* between queries and, in doing so, show that a sequence of queries with small overlap are more likely to cause a decryption failure than a sequence of queries with large overlap. An adversary cannot hope to achieve a success probability of $C\delta$ (on average) unless he submits sequences of queries with no overlap. We depict the overlap of a sequence of queries in Fig. 1 and give a precise definition in Sect. 4.

In a *failure boosting attack*, the adversary improves his odds of triggering a decryption failure by searching for values of e that are of large norm. More precisely, the failure boosting adversary generates ciphertexts $c^{(i)}$, $1 \leq i \leq C$,

---

[1] https://jmschanck.info/code/20200203-decfail.tar.gz.

with the help of the random oracle, and selects $Q \leq C$ ciphertexts to query. Previous analyses of failure boosting [5,8,15] assume that the adversary decides whether to query $c^{(i)}$ by looking only at $c^{(i)}$. In effect, previous analyses ignore the overlap between queries. In contrast, we allow the adversary to minimize the overlap between his queries.

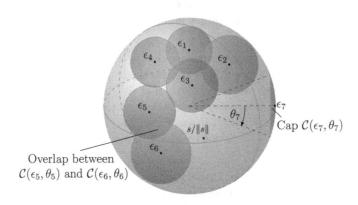

Fig. 1. A user who successfully decrypts ciphertexts $c^{(1)}, \ldots, c^{(7)}$ reveals that their secret, s, does not lie in the blue region. The ciphertext randomness determines the points $\epsilon_i := e^{(i)}/\|e^{(i)}\|_2$. The cap angle θ_i is determined by $\|e^{(i)}\|_2$ and $\|s\|_2$. The probability that a further query, $c^{(8)}$, causes a decryption failure depends on the extent to which the cap of angle θ_8 about ϵ_8 intersects the blue region. (Color figure online)

Our focus here is on finding one decryption failure. After observing a decryption failure, the adversary should switch to a different strategy such as the recently proposed *directional failure boosting* of D'Anvers, Rossi, and Virdia [7]. We will not discuss the process of estimating the secret from a collection of failures. For further background on failure boosting, and reaction attacks on lattice-based schemes more generally, see [5,8,15].

Correctness Definition. We propose an alternative definition of δ-correctness to the one by Hofheinz–Hövelmanns–Kiltz [17]. The correctness experiment in [17] provides the adversary with the secret key. In contrast, our experiment provides the adversary only with the public key and a decryption oracle, and can therefore be run inside an IND-CCA experiment. More importantly, our definition allows a more fine-grained analysis of the impact of adaptive decryption queries on de-randomized encryption schemes. We give our formal definition in Sect. 3.

2   Preliminaries

Notation. For a finite set $\mathcal{X}$ we write $x \leftarrow_\$ \mathcal{X}$ to say that x is sampled uniformly from $\mathcal{X}$. For a distribution χ on $\mathcal{X}$, we write $x \leftarrow \chi$ to say that x is sampled according to χ. We denote the joint distribution of $x \leftarrow \chi_1$ and $y \leftarrow \chi_2$ by $\chi_1 \times \chi_2$.

If χ_1 and χ_2 are distributions on an abelian group, and $(x,y) \leftarrow \chi_1 \times \chi_2$, then we denote the distribution of $x + y$ by $\chi_1 * \chi_2$ where $(\chi_1 * \chi_2)(z) = \sum_{w \in \mathcal{X}} \chi_1(w) \chi_2(z - w)$.

2.1 Definition of PKEs and KEMs

A public-key encryption scheme $\mathsf{P} = (\mathsf{Keygen}, \mathsf{Encr}, \mathsf{Decr})$ is defined over a finite message space $\mathcal{M}$, a ciphertext space $\mathcal{C}$, a secret key space $\mathcal{SK}$ and a public key space $\mathcal{PK}$. In particular, Keygen is a randomized algorithm returning $\mathrm{sk} \in \mathcal{SK}$ and $\mathrm{pk} \in \mathcal{PK}$; Encr is a randomized, or de-randomized, algorithm that takes as input a public key pk and a message $\mathrm{msg} \in \mathcal{M}$ and outputs a ciphertext $c \in \mathcal{C}$; Decr is a deterministic algorithm that takes as input $\mathrm{sk} \in \mathcal{SK}$ and $c \in \mathcal{C}$ and returns either a message $\mathrm{msg} \in \mathcal{M}$ or a special symbol $\perp \notin \mathcal{M}$ indicating failure.

A key encapsulation mechanism (KEM) $\mathsf{K} = (\mathsf{Keygen}, \mathsf{Encaps}, \mathsf{Decaps})$ is defined over a ciphertext space $\mathcal{C}$, the secret key space $\mathcal{SK}$, a public key space $\mathcal{PK}$, and the key space $\mathcal{K}$. In particular, Keygen is a randomized algorithm that returns $\mathrm{pk} \in \mathcal{PK}$ and $\mathrm{sk} \in \mathcal{SK}$; Encaps is a randomized algorithm that takes as input $\mathrm{pk} \in \mathcal{PK}$ and outputs $c \in \mathcal{C}$ and $k \in K$; $\mathsf{Decaps}(\mathrm{sk}, c)$ is a deterministic algorithm that upon input $\mathrm{sk} \in \mathcal{SK}$ and $c \in \mathcal{C}$, returns $\kappa \in K$ or a special symbol $\perp \notin K$ indicating that c is not a valid ciphertext.

Fujisaki–Okamoto Transform. The Fujisaki–Okamoto (FO) transform [9,11, 12] can be used to construct an adaptively secure KEM from passively secure public-key encryption (PKE). Hofheinz, Hövelmanns, and Kiltz provide a decomposition of the FO transform into a sequence of simpler transformations [17]; Bernstein and Persichetti provide a complementary analysis [4]. These works emphasize that the FO transform performs three tasks:

- Derandomization: A probabilistic PKE is transformed into a deterministic PKE by fixing the coins used in encryption to a hash of the message.
- Reencryption: A deterministic PKE is transformed into a rigid[2] deterministic PKE that returns an error symbol, $\perp$, whenever the message obtained by decrypting c does not reencrypt to c.
- Hashing: A rigid deterministic PKE is transformed into an IND-CCA KEM that encrypts a random message and outputs a hash of this message as the session key.

Hofheinz, Hövelmanns, and Kiltz handle the derandomization and reencryption with a single transformation called T. Suppose that $\mathsf{P} = (\mathsf{Keygen}, \mathsf{Encr}, \mathsf{Decr})$ is a probabilistic PKE, that $G : \mathcal{M} \to \mathcal{R}$ and $H : \mathcal{M} \times \mathcal{C} \to \mathcal{K}$ are random oracles, and that $F : \mathcal{K}_F \times \mathcal{C} \to \mathcal{K}$ is a pseudorandom function family. Then $\mathsf{P}_1 = \mathsf{T}[\mathsf{P}, G] = (\mathsf{Keygen}, \mathsf{Encr}_1, \mathsf{Decr})$ is a derandomized PKE with $\mathsf{Encr}_1(\mathrm{pk}, \mathrm{msg}) := \mathsf{Encr}(\mathrm{pk}, \mathrm{msg};\ G(\mathrm{msg}))$.

---

[2] The term "rigid" is due to Bernstein and Persichetti. See [4, Section 6].

Hofheinz, Hövelmanns, and Kiltz provide variants of the hashing step called $U^{\not\perp}$ and $U^{\not\perp}_{\mathrm{msg}}$. The $U^{\not\perp}$ transformation is defined in Fig. 2. The $U^{\not\perp}_{\mathrm{msg}}$ transformation is defined similarly but with the encapsulation key equal to $H(\mathrm{msg})$ rather than $H(\mathrm{msg}, c)$.

Keygen():	Encaps(pk):	Decaps $((\mathrm{sk}_1, \mathrm{sk}_2), c)$:
1 $(\mathrm{pk}, \mathrm{sk}_1) \leftarrow \mathsf{Keygen}()$	1 $\mathrm{msg} \leftarrow_\$ \mathcal{M}$	1 $\mathrm{msg} \leftarrow \mathsf{Decr}_1(\mathrm{sk}_1, c)$
2 $\mathrm{sk}_2 \leftarrow_\$ \mathcal{K}_F$	2 $c \leftarrow \mathsf{Encr}_1(\mathrm{pk}, \mathrm{msg})$	2 if $\mathrm{msg} = \perp$:
3 $\mathrm{sk} \leftarrow (\mathrm{sk}_1, \mathrm{sk}_2)$	3 $K \leftarrow H(\mathrm{msg}, c)$	3 return $F(\mathrm{sk}_2, c)$
4 return $(\mathrm{pk}, \mathrm{sk})$	4 return (K, c)	4 return $H(\mathrm{msg}, c)$

Fig. 2. The algorithms of the $U^{\not\perp}[\mathsf{P}_1, H, F] = (\mathsf{Keygen}, \mathsf{Encaps}, \mathsf{Decaps})$ KEM.

δ-correctness. Hofheinz, Hövelmanns, and Kiltz [17, Section 2.1] define δ-correctness for a PKE as follows.

Definition 1 (δ-correctness for PKEs). *A public-key encryption scheme* $\mathsf{P} = (\mathsf{Keygen}, \mathsf{Encr}, \mathsf{Decr})$ *is δ-correct if*

$$\mathbf{E}\left[\max_{msg \in \mathcal{M}} \Pr[\mathsf{Decr}(sk, c) \neq msg \mid c \leftarrow \mathsf{Encr}(pk, msg)]\right] \leq \delta, \qquad (2)$$

where the expectation is taken over $(pk, sk) \leftarrow \mathsf{Keygen}()$. *Equivalently, δ-correctness means that for all (possibly unbounded) adversaries $\mathcal{A}$, $\Pr[\mathsf{COR}_\mathsf{P}^\mathcal{A}] \leq \delta$, where the correctness game COR is defined in Fig. 3.*

The definition is carefully crafted to obtain a security proof of the T transform—the derandomization step during the Fujisaki–Okamoto transformation [9,11,12] (cf. Appendix 2.1). Moreover, Theorem 3.1 of [17] states (in part) that if P is δ-correct, then $\mathsf{T}[\mathsf{P}, \mathsf{G}]$ is δ_1-correct where $\delta_1(q_\mathsf{G}) \leq q_\mathsf{G} \cdot \delta$ and q_G is the number of queries that the adversary makes to G.

2.2 Lindner–Peikert Encryption Scheme

The Lindner–Peikert scheme [18] is a passively secure public-key encryption scheme based on the learning with errors (LWE) problem [23]. It obtains smaller keys and ciphertexts than earlier LWE encryption schemes [14,23] by using the LWE hardness assumption twice in its security reduction.

Parameters. The system parameters are $(R, q, k, \chi_s, \chi_e, \chi_{e'})$ where R is the *base ring*, q is the integer modulus, k is the R-module rank, χ_s and χ_e are probability distributions supported on R^k, and $\chi_{e'}$ is a probability distribution supported on R. The base ring must have the additive structure of $\mathbb{Z}^m$ for some positive integer m. The $\mathbb{Z}$-module rank, or dimension, of the system is $n = km$. We refer to χ_s as the *secret distribution*, and to χ_e and $\chi_{e'}$ as the *error distributions*. Another important derived parameter is the error threshold t, cf. Sect. 4.

Rings. Commonly used base rings are $R = \mathbb{Z}$ and $R = \mathbb{Z}[x]/(x^m + 1)$ with m a power of two. In the latter case, we view elements of R as vectors in $\mathbb{R}^m$ by expressing them over the power basis $\{1, x, x^2, \cdots, x^{m-1}\}$, i.e. we use the *coefficient embedding*. We identify the power basis with the standard basis of $\mathbb{R}^m$. For $a \in R$, we write $\|a\|_1 = \sum_i |\langle x^i, a \rangle|$, $\|a\|_2 = \sqrt{\langle a, a \rangle}$, and $\|a\|_\infty = \max_i |\langle x^i, a \rangle|$. For elements $a = (a_1, \ldots, a_k)$ and $b = (b_1, \ldots, b_k)$ of a rank k module over R we write $\langle a, b \rangle = \langle a_1, b_1 \rangle + \cdots + \langle a_k, b_k \rangle$. We write $\bar{r}$ for the adjoint of the "multiplication by r" map, i.e. $\langle a, rb \rangle = \langle \bar{r}a, b \rangle$. With $R = \mathbb{Z}$ we have $r = \bar{r}$. With $R = \mathbb{Z}[x]/(x^m + 1)$ we have that $\bar{r}$ is the image of r under $x \mapsto -x^{m-1}$.

Message Encoding. The message space is a subset of R that is defined by maps encode and decode. These maps must satisfy $\mathsf{decode}(\mathsf{encode}(\mathrm{msg})) = \mathrm{msg}$ for all bit strings msg in the domain of encode. A typical choice for a plain LWE system is $\mathsf{encode} : \{0, 1\} \to \mathbb{Z}$ and $\mathsf{decode} : \mathbb{Z} \to \{0, 1\}$ with $\mathsf{encode}(\mathrm{msg}) = \mathrm{msg} \cdot \lfloor q/2 \rfloor$ and $\mathsf{decode}(\mathrm{msg}) = \{0$ if $|\mathrm{msg} \bmod q| \in [0, q/4); \ 1 \text{ otherwise}\}$. We call this the *standard encoding*. Observe that $\mathsf{decode}(\mathsf{encode}(\mathrm{msg}) + \delta) = \mathrm{msg}$ if $|\delta| < q/4$, so we say that the standard encoding has an error threshold of $t = q/4$. The *standard b-bit encoding* is defined similarly: it divides $[0, q/2)$ into 2^b intervals and has an error threshold of $q/2^{b+1}$. Elements of $\{0, 1\}^{b \cdot \mathrm{msg}}$ can be encoded into elements of R by extending the standard b-bit encoding component wise on the power basis.

Algorithms. The key generation, encryption and decryption routines of the passively secure encryption scheme are as follows.

- Keygen(): Sample a $k \times k$ matrix A with each coefficient chosen independently from the uniform distribution on R/q. Sample $k \times 1$ vectors s_1 and s_2 independently from χ_s. Compute $b = (s_1 - As_2) \bmod q$. The public key is (A, b). The secret key is (s_1, s_2).
- Encr (msg, (A, b)): Sample $1 \times k$ vectors e_1 and e_2 independently from χ_e. Sample e_3 from $\chi_{e'}$. Compute the ciphertext (c_1, c_2) with

$$c_1 = (e_1 A + e_2) \bmod q, \quad c_2 = (e_1 b + e_3 + \mathsf{encode}(\mathrm{msg})) \bmod q.$$

- Decr $((c_1, c_2), (s_1, s_2))$: To decrypt (c_1, c_2) using the secret key (s_1, s_2), let $v = (c_1 s_2 + c_2) \bmod q$ and output $\mathsf{decode}(v)$.

3   Correctness in an Adaptive Setting

The Hofheinz–Hövelmanns–Kiltz (HHK) definition of δ-correctness (Definition 1 in Sect. 2.1) involves an expectation over keys and ciphertexts. Care must be taken when the key is fixed (as in an IND-CCA setting) or when the ciphertext is determined by the message (as in a derandomized encryption scheme). For derandomized schemes that use a random oracle G during encryption, HHK define a notion of $\delta(q_G)$-correctness which is stated in terms of the number of queries q_G that the adversary makes to G. They prove that a δ-correct scheme that is derandomized using their T transformation has a correctness error of $\delta(q_G) \leq q_G \cdot \delta$ [17, Theorem 3.1].

The loss of correctness caused by derandomization is often ignored in practice. For example, the authors of the FrodoKEM NIST submission correctly calculate the *one-shot* correctness (the probability of decryption failure for a random key and random ciphertext) of their IND-CPA PKE [20, Section 2.2.7]. They note that the one-shot correctness is equal to the δ-correctness [20, Equation 2]. They then apply the T transformation and claim that the correctness of the resulting IND-CCA PKE is equal to the one-shot correctness of the underlying IND-CPA PKE [20, Section 2.2.10]. This claim is not justified.

And yet, a full factor q_G loss of correctness does not seem realistic. To address this, we propose the following alternative to the $\delta(q_G)$-correctness. This definition restricts the adversary's time, t, and number of decryption queries, q_d.

Definition 2 ($\delta(q_d, t)$-correctness for PKEs). *Let* P *be a derandomized PKE against a (classical or quantum) adversary* $\mathcal{A}$ *making at most* q_d *(classical) queries to its decryption oracle* D *and running in time* t. *We say,* P *is* $\delta(q_d, t)$-*correct if*

$$\Pr[\text{COR-ad}_{\text{PKE}}^{\mathcal{A}} \to 1] \leq \delta(q_d, t),$$

where the correctness game COR-ad *is defined in Fig. 3.*

In contrast to the HHK correctness experiment (COR in Fig. 3), our correctness experiment (COR-ad in Fig. 3) does not provide the adversary with the user's secret key, and can be run as part of the IND-CCA security experiment[3] In this case we call it COR-ad-CCA.

It is important to note that running COR-ad-CCA inside the IND-CCA experiment does not change the power of the IND-CCA adversary; in particular, the number of decryption queries q_d' in COR-ad-CCA is no more than the number of decryption queries q_d in IND-CCA. As such, one can obtain an upper bound on the IND-CCA security of a scheme given the $\delta(q_d, t)$-correctness of a scheme and an attack that violates IND-CCA security using decryption failures.

4   Correctness of the Lindner–Peikert Scheme

Suppose that (c_1, c_2) is an honest encryption of msg to a user with public key (A, b) and secret key $s = (s_1, s_2)$. Let (e_1, e_2, e_3) be the noise that was used to generate (c_1, c_2), and let $e = (e_1, e_2)$. Decryption will be successful, i.e., the decrypting party will recover msg exactly, as long as

$$\|e_1 s_1 + e_2 s_2 + e_3\|_\infty < t, \tag{3}$$

---

[3] A slight modification is necessary, as the IND-CCA decryption oracle gives special treatment to the challenge ciphertext.

where t is the error threshold. The exact one-shot probability of failure can be calculated from Eq. 3 (our software does this). However, we will use a slightly weaker condition to analyze the probability of failure in an adaptive setting. First, an application of the triangle inequality gives

$$\|e_1 s_1 + e_2 s_2\|_\infty < t - \|e_3\|_\infty. \tag{4}$$

Then, by fixing some $\gamma \geq \|e_3\|_\infty$ and using properties of the max-norm and inner product that we discussed in Sect. 2.2, we have

$$\|e_1 s_1 + e_2 s_2\|_\infty = \max_{0 \leq i < m} |\langle \bar{s}, x^i e \rangle| < t - \gamma. \tag{5}$$

$\text{Expt}_P^{\text{COR}}(\mathcal{A}):$

1. $(pk, sk) \leftarrow \text{Keygen}()$
2. $\text{msg} \leftarrow A(sk, pk)$
3. $c \leftarrow \text{Encr}(pk, \text{msg})$
4. return $[\text{Dec}(sk, c) \neq \text{msg}]$

$\text{Expt}_P^{\text{COR-ad-CCA}}(\mathcal{A}, c^*, q_d, L_d, H):$

1. $(pk, sk) \leftarrow \text{Keygen}()$
2. $\text{msg} \leftarrow \mathcal{A}^{H,D}(pk, c^*)$
3. $c \leftarrow \text{Encr}(pk, \text{msg})$
4. return $[\text{Decr}(sk, c) \neq \text{msg}]$

Decryption oracle $D(c)$:

1. $q_d \leftarrow q_d + 1$
2. if $(c = c^*)$: $r \leftarrow \perp$, $L_d = L_d \cup (c, r)$
3. else: $r \leftarrow \text{Decr}(sk, c)$, $L_d = L_d \cup (c, r)$
4. return r

$\text{Expt}_P^{\text{IND-CCA}}((\mathcal{A}_1, \mathcal{A}_2)):$

1. $H \xleftarrow{\$} \mathcal{H}$
2. $q_d \leftarrow 0$
3. $L_d = \{\}$
4. $(pk, sk) \leftarrow \text{Keygen}()$
5. $\text{msg}_0, \text{msg}_1 \leftarrow \mathcal{A}_1^H(pk)$
6. $b \xleftarrow{\$} \{0, 1\}$
7. $c^* \leftarrow \text{Encr}(pk, \text{msg}_b^*)$
8. $b' \leftarrow \mathcal{A}_2^{H,D}(pk, c^*)$
9. return $[b = b']$

Fig. 3. COR and IND-CCA experiment for any PKE P;COR-ad-CCA experiment for a (derandomized) PKE P.

A Geometric Interpretation. Let $\mathcal{S}$ be the unit sphere in $\mathbb{R}^d$. We denote the *angular distance* between points u and v in $\mathbb{R}^d$ by

$$\theta(u, v) = \arccos \left(\frac{\langle u, v \rangle}{\|u\|_2 \cdot \|v\|_2} \right), \tag{6}$$

where $\arccos(x) \in [0, \pi]$. The *spherical cap* of angle θ about u is

$$\mathcal{C}(u, \theta) = \{v \in \mathcal{S} : \theta(u, v) \leq \theta\}. \tag{7}$$

Equation (5) tells us that each *successful* decryption reveals some geometric information about s, as explained next. By restating the condition $\langle \bar{s}, e \rangle < t - \gamma$ (without the absolute value bars that appear in Eq. (5)) in terms of the angular distance,

$$\theta(\bar{s}, e) = \arccos \left(\frac{\langle \bar{s}, e \rangle}{\|s\|_2 \cdot \|e\|_2} \right) > \arccos \left(\frac{t - \gamma}{\|s\|_2 \cdot \|e\|_2} \right) = \theta^*, \tag{8}$$

we see that $\langle \bar{s}, e \rangle < t - \gamma$ implies that $\bar{s}/\|s\|_2$ *does not* lie in the cap of angle θ^* about $e/\|e\|_2$. The full condition, $|\langle \bar{s}, e \rangle| < t - \gamma$, also says that $\bar{s}/\|s\|_2$ does not lie in the cap of angle θ^* about $-e/\|e\|_2$. An adversary can use this information to improve his odds of triggering a decryption failure.

A Heuristic Assumption. We measure the volume of subsets of $\mathcal{S} \subset \mathbb{R}^d$ using the $(d-1)$-dimensional spherical probability measure, σ. This measure is normalized such that $\sigma(\mathcal{S}) = 1$. If u is a point on $\mathcal{S}$ and v is drawn uniformly from $\mathcal{S}$, then the probability that $\theta(u, v) \leq \theta$ is $C(\theta) = \sigma(\mathcal{C}(u, \theta))$. It is important to note that $C(\theta)$ does not depend on u. We assume the following heuristic in our analysis.

Heuristic 1 (Spherical symmetry). *For fixed $\bar{s}$ and $e \leftarrow \chi_e \times \chi_e$, the probability that $\theta(\bar{s}, e) \leq \varphi$, for any $0 < \varphi < \pi/2$, is $C(\varphi)$. Equivalently, $e/\|e\|_2$ "looks like" a uniformly random point on $\mathcal{S}$.*

If Heuristic 1 holds true, the probability that e causes a decryption failure is at least $2C(\theta^*)$. It may even be as large as $2mC(\theta^*)$, due to the maximization over i in Eq. (5).

Remark 1. Previous analyses of failure boosting [5] have modeled the distribution of $\chi_e \times \chi_e$ with a spherically symmetric Gaussian distribution. In contrast, our software uses the exact distribution of $\chi_e \times \chi_e$. Our experiments in Sect. 6 indicate that the spherical symmetry assumption is reasonable for Frodo640. Further experiments are needed for other schemes.

4.1 The Efficacy of a Query Set

Recall θ^* of the previous section. We write $\theta_\alpha^*(\beta; z) = \arccos(z/\alpha\beta)$ with $0 \leq \theta_\alpha^*(\beta; z) \leq \frac{\pi}{2}$. We are primarily interested in the case $\alpha = \|s\|_2$ and $\beta = \|e\|_2$. In later sections we will take α to be an approximation to $\|s\|_2$. We write $\theta_\alpha^*(e; z)$ in place of the cumbersome notation $\theta_\alpha^*(\|e\|_2; z)$, and we suppress the dependence on z when it is clear.

We refer to $e = (e_1, e_2)$ as the "query", rather than (c_1, c_2). We also ignore both the absolute value bars and the maximization over i in Eq. (5). This way queries are one-to-one with spherical caps, and each query can be thought of as "exploring" some cap; by querying e the adversary learns whether or not $\bar{s}$ lies in $C(\theta_\alpha^*(e))$.

We define the *efficacy* of a set E of queries to be the fraction of the sphere that the corresponding caps cover:

$$\text{Eff}_\alpha(E) = \sigma\left(\bigcup_{e \in E} \mathcal{C}\left(e, \theta_\alpha^*(e)\right)\right). \tag{9}$$

Under the spherical symmetry heuristic, the probability that an adversary causes a decryption failure is proportional to the efficacy of his queries. An intelligent adversary will maximize the efficacy of his queries while minimizing the number of queries that he makes. Adversaries are constrained both by their computational power and by the need to collaborate with a random oracle.

In the notation of Definition 2, an instantiation of the Lindner–Peikert scheme is $\delta(q_d, t)$-correct if

$$\delta(q_d, t) \geq 2m\,\text{Eff}_\alpha(E) \tag{10}$$

for all E of size $|E| \leq q_d$ that an adversary can produce in time t. It is important to note that some instantiations exchange more than one element of R; for instance, FrodoKEM exchanges 64 elements of $\mathbb{Z}$. For such instantiations the right hand side of Eq. (10) should be $2\ell m \, \mathrm{Eff}_\alpha(E)$ where ℓ is the number of coefficients exchanged. Assuming spherical symmetry, the actual correctness error can be anywhere between $2 \, \mathrm{Eff}_\alpha(E)$ and $2\ell m \, \mathrm{Eff}_\alpha(E)$, as the failure events may not be independent.

4.2   Approximating the Efficacy

The efficacy of a query set may be difficult to compute exactly. Using the principle of inclusion-exclusion, we can write a k-th order approximation to $\mathrm{Eff}_\alpha(E)$ as

$$\mathrm{Eff}_\alpha^{(k)}(E) = \sum_{\substack{F \subseteq E \\ 0 < |F| \leq k}} (-1)^{|F|+1} \cdot \sigma \left(\bigcap_{e \in F} \mathcal{C}\left(e, \theta_\alpha^*(e)\right) \right). \tag{11}$$

Maximizing the second-order approximation,

$$\mathrm{Eff}_\alpha^{(2)}(E) = \sum_{e \in E} C(\theta_\alpha^*(e)) - \sum_{\{e,e'\} \subset E} \sigma \left(\mathcal{C}(e, \theta_\alpha^*(e)) \cap \mathcal{C}(e', \theta_\alpha^*(e')) \right), \tag{12}$$

already presents quite a challenge. We do not consider algorithms for approximating the efficacy here, but we note that techniques from the near-neighbor search literature, e.g. [2], may be useful for producing high-efficacy query sets.

4.3   The Efficacy of a Random Query Set

A first-order approximation to the efficacy of a random query set, normalized by the query set size N, is

$$Q_\alpha(\chi_1, \chi_2) = \lim_{N \to \infty} \frac{1}{N} \mathbb{E}\left[\mathrm{Eff}_\alpha^{(1)}(V) \right] \tag{13}$$

where the expectation is taken over sets V of N elements drawn independently from $\chi_1 \times \chi_2$. Equation (13) can also be written as the expected size of a cap with respect to the 2-norm distribution of v drawn from $\chi_1 \times \chi_2$,

$$Q_\alpha(\chi_1, \chi_2) = \sum_{j > 0} \Pr\left[\|v\|_2 = j \right] \cdot C\left(\theta_\alpha^*(j) \right). \tag{14}$$

5   Heuristic Analysis of NIST Candidates

In this section we calculate *first-order approximations* to the efficacy of *random query sets* drawn from distributions that come from concrete instantiations of the Lindner–Peikert encryption scheme. It is important to note that a first-order approximation to the efficacy ignores the overlap between queries; it thereby overestimates efficacy and underestimate correctness. Since we are ignoring the overlap, we expect our results to closely mirror those of D'Anvers, Guo, Johansson, Nilsson, Vercauteren, and Verbauwhede from [5]. The calculations that we perform are quite different and serve as an independent check on their results.

We analyze Saber [6], the R5ND_PKE_0d and R5N1_PKE_0d parameter sets of Round5 [13], Frodo [20], and Kyber [24]; all of which are second round candidates in NIST's post-quantum standardization effort.

5.1 Overview

We caution the reader that the following sketch of our analysis is only accurate for Frodo. The treatment of the other schemes is described in Appendix A.

Let χ be a distribution on R. We write $\|\chi\|_2$ and $|\langle 1, \chi \rangle|$, respectively, for the distribution of $\|r\|_2$ and $|\langle 1, r \rangle|$ when $r \leftarrow \chi$. The top u-th quantile of $\|\chi\|_2$ is the largest $\beta \in \mathbb{Z}_+$ for which $\Pr_{r \leftarrow \chi}[\|r\|_2 \geq \beta] \geq 1/u$. We write $\chi(u)$ for the distribution of $r \leftarrow \chi$ conditioned on the event that $\|r\|_2 \geq \beta$. It is important to note that $\chi(1) = \chi$.

We assume that the user has drawn a secret key s from $\chi_s(v) \times \chi_s(v)$, for some $v \geq 1$. A random user does so with probability $1/v^2$. Unless otherwise stated we take $v = 2$, i.e., we assume that the user has a key of above-median length in both components. We evaluate correctness using $Q_\alpha(\cdot, \cdot)$ which depends on the γ of Eq. (5) through θ_α^*. We take α equal to the expected norm of s, and we take γ equal to the top 100-th quantile[4] of $|\langle 1, \chi_{e'} \rangle|$. We account for the absolute value bars in Eq. (5) but ignore the maximization over $0 \leq i < m$. By doing so, we are estimating the *per-coordinate* failure rate: the probability of a failure in the first coordinate of the coefficient embedding.

To first order, an adversary who samples (e_1, e_2) from $\chi_e(u) \times \chi_e(u)$ and who discards all ciphertexts with $|\langle 1, e_3 \rangle| < \gamma$ can expect a query set of size $1/(2\, Q_\alpha(\chi_e(u), \chi_e(u)))$ to include a query that causes a decryption failure (cf. Eq. (10)). A classical adversary expects to make approximately $100u^2$ queries to the random oracle per sample. A quantum adversary, using Grover's algorithm, expects to make approximately $10u$ superposition queries to the random oracle per sample.

5.2 Comparison with One-Shot Failure Rate

Before presenting the results of our analysis, we recall that the *one-shot* failure probability is the probability that Eq. (3) is violated for $(s_1, s_2) \leftarrow \chi_s \times \chi_s$, $(e_1, e_2) \leftarrow \chi_e \times \chi_e$, and $e_3 \leftarrow \chi_{e'}$. Theorem 3.1 of [17] states that a de-randomized scheme with a one-shot failure rate of δ is $\delta_1 \leq q_G \cdot \delta$ correct against an adversary who generates q_G ciphertexts. Table 1 lists the one-shot failure probabilities for Kyber512, R5ND1PKE0d, Frodo640, R5N11PKE0d, and LightSaber[5]. Each

---

[4] The constant 100 is arbitrary. Our software can produce an optimized value if needed.

[5] Note that our analysis should roughly coincide with the one-shot failure probability when $u = v = 1$. We expect some discrepancy due to our treatment of e_3 and the fact that we fix an estimate, α, for the norm of the secret. In contrast, the one-shot failure probabilities are averaged over all keys.

parameter set is advertised as meeting NIST's level 1 security category, so it is reasonable to assume that generating, say, $q_G = 2^{128}$ ciphertexts has lower cost than breaking the scheme. The corresponding values of δ_1 are all larger than 2^{-60}. We find this concerning, as Section 3.3 (resp. Section 4.4 against quantum adversaries) of [17] states potentially large integer multiple of δ_1 in the upper bound on the adversary's success probability in the IND-CCA game.

5.3   Comparison of NIST Candidates

The results of our analyses of Kyber512, R5ND1PKE0d, Frodo640, R5N11PKE0d, and LightSaber are shown in Fig. 4. There are subtleties to each analysis, but one can largely imagine that the lines on the left and right of Fig. 4 plot $u \mapsto 1/(2\,Q_\alpha(\chi_e(u), \chi_e(u)))$ and $u \mapsto 10u/(2\,Q_\alpha(\chi_e(u), \chi_e(u)))$ respectively. We give more details in Appendix A.

An adversary who is not constrained in the number of queries that he can submit will minimize cost. As can be seen from Fig. 4 and Table 1, after minimizing the cost of the attack, the number of queries in an effective query set ranges from $2^{106.7}$ for LightSaber to $2^{152.1}$ for Kyber512. The attacks differ in cost per query. Of course, an honest user will not answer so many queries.

Table 1. Adversary $\mathcal{A}$ sends random queries to random users. Adversaries $\mathcal{B}$ and $\mathcal{C}$ target a fixed user that has a random, above-median norm, key. Adversary $\mathcal{B}$ sends queries of above-median norm to the user. Adversary $\mathcal{C}$ sends queries with norm in the top u-quantile for the value of u that minimizes his total quantum cost, i.e. he chooses u based on the local minima in Fig. 4 (Plot b, d and f). Adversary $\mathcal{D}$ is restricted to 2^{64} queries and 2^{128} quantum operations. Rows $\mathcal{A}$, $\mathcal{B}$, and $\mathcal{C}$ give the expected number of queries that the adversary submits before causing a decryption failure. Row $\mathcal{A}$ is the reciprocal of the one-shot failure probability for a single coordinate. Rows $\mathcal{B}$ and $\mathcal{C}$ are values of $1/(2\,Q_\alpha(\cdot, \cdot))$. Row $\mathcal{D}$ gives the value of $\delta(2^{64}, 2^{128})$ under the assumptions of Sect. 5.3. The impact of m and ℓ are suppressed throughout.

	kyber512	frodo640	r5nd1pke	r5n11pke	lightsaber
$\mathcal{A}$	$2^{186.9}$	$2^{144.8}$	$2^{155.1}$	$2^{126.9}$	$2^{128.4}$
$\mathcal{B}$	$2^{187.1}$	$2^{145.8}$	$2^{152.5}$	$2^{138.5}$	$2^{123.3}$
$\mathcal{C}$	$2^{152.1}$	$2^{124.7}$	$2^{142.8}$	$2^{133.9}$	$2^{106.7}$
$\mathcal{D}$	$2^{-63.5}$	$2^{-34.1}$	$2^{-52.6}$	$2^{-49.4}$	$2^{-20.7}$

	kyber768	frodo976	r5nd3pke	r5n13pke	saber
$\mathcal{A}$	$2^{173.2}$	$2^{205.6}$	$2^{131.0}$	$2^{143.9}$	$2^{144.2}$
$\mathcal{B}$	$2^{169.0}$	$2^{209.0}$	$2^{145.3}$	$2^{144.0}$	$2^{139.1}$
$\mathcal{C}$	$2^{141.0}$	$2^{185.3}$	$2^{137.3}$	$2^{139.9}$	$2^{123.7}$
$\mathcal{D}$	2^{-58}	$2^{-87.6}$	$2^{-51.8}$	$2^{-57.8}$	$2^{-38.3}$

	kyber1024	frodo1344	r5nd5pke	r5n15pke	firesaber
$\mathcal{A}$	$2^{183.2}$	$2^{258.7}$	$2^{144.5}$	$2^{127.3}$	$2^{173.4}$
$\mathcal{B}$	$2^{178.1}$	$2^{263.1}$	$2^{141.6}$	$2^{143.8}$	$2^{170.3}$
$\mathcal{C}$	$2^{151.9}$	$2^{238.1}$	$2^{134.8}$	$2^{140.2}$	$2^{154.0}$
$\mathcal{D}$	$2^{-69.9}$	$2^{-136.4}$	$2^{-52.8}$	$2^{-60.2}$	$2^{-66.6}$

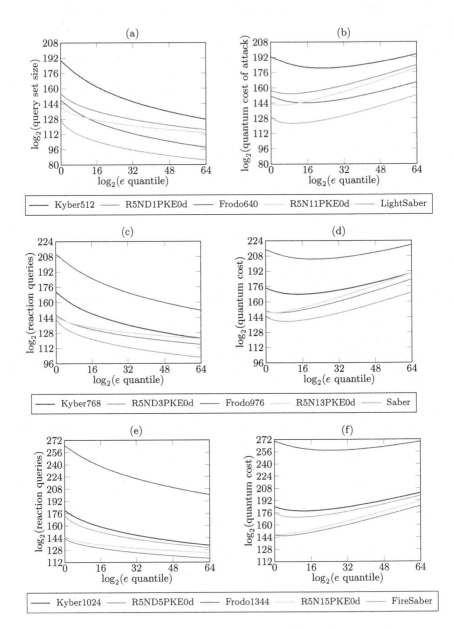

Fig. 4. The predicted size of a query set of unit efficacy (a, c, e) and the quantum cost of producing such a query set (b, d, f). "Quantum cost" is based on Grover's algorithm and has units of "superposition queries to a random oracle". Plots (a) and (b) are NIST level 1 schemes. Plots (c) and (d) are NIST level 3 schemes. Plots (e) and (f) are NIST level 5 schemes.

NIST suggests that "[f]or the purpose of estimating security strengths, it may be assumed that the attacker has access to the decryptions of no more than 2^{64} chosen ciphertexts" [21]. An adversary with this constraint will spend more time per query to improve the efficacy of a smaller query set.

An attacker who can perform a total of 2^{128} quantum operations will perform roughly 2^{64} operations per query and submit 2^{64} queries. Let us briefly assume that our first-order approximation to the efficacy is accurate. Our experiment in the following section provides some indication that the overlap between random queries may be negligible, and supports this assumption. The attaker may then be thought of as randomly sampling from a query set of size $1/(2\,Q_\alpha(\chi_e(2^{64}), \chi_e(2^{64})))$, which is the right-most point in Fig. 4. Let us also briefly assume that the elements of the adversary's query set are equally likely to cause a decryption failure. Under these assumptions, the $\delta(2^{64}, 2^{128})$-correctness of LightSaber is $2^{64}/2^{84.7} = 2^{-20.7}$. This should be compared with the δ_1 correctness of $2^{-0.4}$ that we alluded to in Sect. 5.2. The $\delta(2^{64}, 2^{128})$-correctness of the other schemes, under the same assumptions, is given in Table 1.

6 Experiments

Both the spherical symmetry heuristic and the accuracy of the first-order approximation to the efficacy need to be examined further. As a first step, we have performed experiments with a variant of Frodo640. Since the decryption failure rate of Frodo640 is too small for us to observe experimentally, we have used $q = 2^{13}$ rather than $q = 2^{15}$. We have kept the rest of the parameters the same. This variant has a one-shot failure rate of $2^{-11.7}$.

In the notation of Sect. 5.1, we take α to be the expected value of $\|s\|_2$ when s is drawn from $\chi_s(v) \times \chi_s(v)$. The "Predicted" row in Table 2 gives $1/(2\,Q_\alpha(\chi_1(u), \chi_1(u)))$. The "Observed" row gives $1/f$ where f is the fraction of failures that we observed.

Frodo640 replaces the $k \times 1$ vectors s_1, s_2, e_1 and e_2 by $k \times 8$ matrices. It replaces the scalar e_3 by an 8×8 matrix. The session key is split across 64 approximately agreed upon scalars. In one run of the experiment, we generate 512 keys and 64 key encapsulations per key. For each encapsulation, we draw 16 samples from $\chi_s(v)$, 16 samples from $\chi_e(u)$, and 64 samples from $\chi_{e'}(100)$. We count the total number of coordinates with errors, not the number of encapsulations that fail. In other words f is the fraction of errors observed in $512 \cdot 64 \cdot 64 = 2^{21}$ coordinates.

If $1/(2\,Q_\alpha(\chi_1(u), \chi_1(u)))$ is a good approximation to the size of an effective query set, and each element of an effective query set is equally likely to cause a failure, then we expect $1/f$ to tend to $1/(2\,Q_\alpha(\chi_1(u), \chi_1(u)))$ as we average over many keys and encapsulations. As can be seen in Table 2, we observed a fraction of failures such that $f/(2\,Q_\alpha(\chi_1(u), \chi_1(u))) \approx 2^{-0.4}$ in each case. This provides some indication that our heuristics are reasonable for Frodo640. Further experiments are needed for the other schemes.

Table 2. Results of the experiment of Sect. 6. We did not run the experiment to completion for the columns with $\|\chi_e\| = 2^{20}$. The values reported in those columns are averages over $\approx 2^{18}$, rather than 2^{21}, coordinates.

$\|\chi_s\|$ quantile	2^0			2^{10}			2^{20}		
$\|\chi_e\|$ quantile	2^0	2^{10}	2^{20}	2^0	2^{10}	2^{20}	2^0	2^{10}	2^{20}
Predicted	$2^{11.4}$	$2^{9.8}$	$2^{9.1}$	$2^{9.8}$	$2^{8.4}$	$2^{7.8}$	$2^{9.1}$	$2^{7.8}$	$2^{7.3}$
Observed	$2^{11.1}$	$2^{9.4}$	$2^{8.7}$	$2^{9.4}$	$2^{8.0}$	$2^{7.4}$	$2^{8.8}$	$2^{7.4}$	$2^{6.9}$

7   Conclusion and Future Work

We have presented a decryption failure attack on the Lindner–Peikert scheme that exploits dependencies between failure events. In contrast with previous attacks, our attack leverages information from adaptive queries. The adversary improves his odds of causing a decryption failure by choosing his next query as a function of his past queries—even those queries that were answered successfully.

Our results do not necessarily call for a re-parametrization of the schemes that we have analyzed. However, like previous analyses of failure boosting, they show that the one-shot failure probability is not a reliable indicator of the difficulty of causing decryption failures. We hope that our work stimulates discussion on what an acceptable $\delta(q_d, t)$-correctness is for various security levels.

Future Work. Both the spherical symmetry heuristic and the accuracy of the first-order approximation need further confirmation, either experimentally or theoretically. Beyond this, it is an interesting question to extend our approach to schemes that use error-correction such as ThreeBears [16], NewHope [22], LAC [19], and other parameter sets of Round5 [13]. In a more speculative direction, we wonder whether the information revealed by successful decryptions might be useful in other attacks. Perhaps the knowledge that the secret key does not lie in a particular direction can help an adversary prune an enumeration tree.

The general message that successful queries can leak information about the secret key may be applicable to other constructions as well. Drucker–Gueron–Kostic [10] have already pointed out the risk of ignoring the factor q_G loss of tightness in de-randomizing the code-based scheme BIKE [1].

Acknowledgements. Special thanks to Kathrin Hövelmanns for insights on the correctness definition for PKEs, Jan-Pieter D'Anvers for helpful discussions and for providing us with a copy of [7], and Steve Weiss for computer systems support. NB is supported by NSERC Discovery Accelerator Supplement grant RGPIN-2016-05146. This work was supported by IQC. IQC is supported in part by the Government of Canada and the Province of Ontario.

A   Details of Our Analysis for Each Scheme

A.1   Secret and Error Distributions

Definition 3 (Modulus switching function). *The modulus switching function is defined by $[\![x]\!]_q^r = \lfloor x\frac{r}{q} \rceil \bmod r$ with $\lfloor x\frac{r}{q} \rceil$ computed over $\mathbb{R}$. It is also extended component-wise to vectors and matrices.*

Definition 4 (Compression artifact distribution). *The compression artifact distribution with parameters r and q is the distribution of $y - [\![z]\!]_r^q$ when y is drawn uniformly from $\mathbb{Z}/q$ and $z = [\![y]\!]_q^r$.*

Definition 5 (Centered binomial distribution). *The centered binomial distribution of parameter w assigns probability $\frac{1}{2^{2w}}\binom{2w}{x+w}$ to $x \in \mathbb{Z}$.*

Definition 6 (Fixed weight distribution). *The fixed weight trinary distribution of parameter w in dimension d is the uniform distribution on all $2^w\binom{d}{w}$ vectors in $\mathbb{Z}^d$ that have exactly $\lceil w/2 \rceil$ coefficients equal to $+1$, exactly $\lfloor w/2 \rfloor$ coefficients equal to -1, and the remaining $d - w$ coefficients equal to 0.*

A.2   Compression and Learning with Rounding

Some variants of the Lindner–Peikert scheme have additional *rounding parameters* r_0, r_1, and r_2. They compress the public key to $(A, [\![b]\!]_q^{r_0})$ and the ciphertext to $([\![c_1]\!]_q^{r_1}, [\![c_2]\!]_q^{r_2})$. Note that if $r_i = q$ then no compression occurs in the corresponding component. If $b' = [\![b]\!]_q^{r_0}$ then there is some $v_1 \in \mathbb{Z}/q$ such that $[\![b']\!]_{r_0}^q = (v_1 - As_2) \bmod q$. Likewise, if $c_1' = [\![c_1]\!]_q^{r_1}$ then there is some $v_2 \in \mathbb{Z}/q$ such that $[\![c_1']\!]_{r_1}^q = (e_1 A + v_2) \bmod q$, and if $c_2' = [\![c_2]\!]_q^{r_1}$ then there is some $v_3 \in \mathbb{Z}/q$ such that $[\![c_2']\!]_{r_2}^q = (e_1 A + v_3 + \mathsf{encode}(\mathrm{msg})) \bmod q$. Variants that use well chosen rounding parameters can omit the s_1, e_2, and e_3 terms in key generation and encryption; the *compression artifacts* v_1, v_2, and v_3 take their place. Such schemes are said to be based on the Learning With Rounding problem (LWR). The difference between LWE and LWR is immaterial for our purposes; we simply incorporate the compression artifact noise into the distributions of s_1, e_2, and e_3.

A.3   Frodo

Frodo is an instantiation of the Lindner–Peikert scheme with $R = \mathbb{Z}$. The FrodoKEM NIST submission [20] defines three parameter sets frodo640 ($n = 670$, $q = 2^{15}$, $t = 2^{12}$), frodo976 ($n = 976$, $q = 2^{16}$, $t = 2^{12}$), and frodo1344 ($n = 1344$, $q = 2^{16}$, $t = 2^{11}$). All three use the standard b-bit encoding, and therefore have an error threshold of $t = q/2^{b+1}$. Each parameter set takes $\chi_s = \chi_e = \chi^{\times n}$ where χ is an approximation to a discrete Gaussian distribution on $\mathbb{Z}$. We refer to [20, Table 2] for the exact definition of χ. Our analysis is as described in Sect. 5.1.

A.4   Kyber (Second Round)

Kyber is an instantiation of the Lindner–Peikert scheme over $R = \mathbb{Z}[x]/(x^{256}+1)$. The second round NIST submission [24] includes three parameter sets kyber512 ($m = 256$, $k = 2$, $n = 512$, $q = 3329$, $r_0 = q$, $r_1 = 2^{10}$, $r_2 = 2^3$), kyber768 ($m = 256$, $k = 3$, $n = 768$, $q = 3329$, $r_0 = q$, $r_1 = 2^{10}$, $r_2 = 2^4$), and kyber1024 ($m = 256$, $k = 4$, $n = 1024$, $q = 3329$, $r_0 = q$, $r_1 = 2^{11}$, $r_2 = 2^5$). All three use the standard 1-bit encoding. All three parameter sets sample s_1, s_2, e_1, and e_2 from $\eta_2^{\times n}$, where η_2 is the centered binomial distribution of parameter 2.

We write ρ_r for the compression artifact distribution with parameters r and q. We model e_1 as being drawn from $\eta_2^{\times n}$; we model e_2 as being drawn from $(\eta_2 * \rho_{r_1})^{\times n}$; and we model e_3 as being drawn from $(\eta_2 * \rho_{r_2})^{\times m}$. Due to the difference in size between the coefficients of e_1 and e_2, it seems unlikely that the spherical symmetry heuristic is reasonable. We adapt our analysis as follows.

Let $\chi_1 \times \chi_2$ be the distribution from which the adversary draws $e = (e_1, e_2)$. We will assume that χ_1 and χ_2 (viewed as distributions on the coefficient embedding of R^k) are invariant under permutations of the standard basis. Let z_1 and z_2 be the expected values of $\|e_1\|_2$ and $\|e_2\|_2$ respectively. Let $w = \sqrt{z_2/z_1}$, $e^* = (e_1 \cdot w, e_2/w)$, $s^* = (s_1/w, s_2 \cdot w)$, and observe that $\langle s^*, e^* \rangle = \langle \bar{s}, e \rangle$. We apply the analysis of Sect. 5.1, but we take α to be the expected value of $\|s^*\|_2$ and we compute Q_α with respect to the scaled distributions $\chi_1 \cdot w$ and χ_2/w. The expected values of $\|e_1 \cdot w\|_2$ and $\|e_2/w\|_2$ are both $\sqrt{z_1 z_2}$. By assumption on χ_1 and χ_2, this implies that all $2n$ coefficients of e^* have the same expected size. While this does not imply that the distributions are spherically symmetric, it does make the assumption of spherical symmetry more plausible.

A.5   Saber

Saber is a learning with rounding variant of the Lindner–Peikert scheme that uses the base ring $R = \mathbb{Z}[x]/(x^{256}+1)$. The submission proposes three parameter sets lightsaber ($m = 256$, $k = 2$, $q = 2^{13}$, $r_0 = 2^{10}$, $r_1 = 2^{10}$, $r_2 = 2^3$, $w = 10$), saber ($m = 256$, $k = 3$, $q = 2^{13}$, $r_0 = 2^{10}$, $r_1 = 2^{10}$, $r_2 = 2^4$, $w = 8$), and firesaber ($m = 256$, $k = 4$, $q = 2^{13}$, $r_0 = 2^{10}$, $r_1 = 2^{10}$, $r_2 = 2^6$). All three parameter sets sample s_2 and e_1 from the centered binomial distribution of parameter μ, $\eta_\mu^{\times n}$, for the μ listed in [6, Table 1]. Recall that $s_1 = e_2 = e_3 = 0$ for learning with rounding variants.

We write ρ_r for the compression artifact distribution with parameters q and r. The correctness condition can be rewritten as an inner product between $(\bar{v}_1, \bar{s}_2)$ and (e_1, v_2), where v_1 is drawn from ρ_{r_0} and v_2 is drawn from ρ_{r_1}. The distributions of v_1 and s_2 are invariant under taking adjoints. Note that $r_0 = r_1$ for all of the proposed parameter sets. The coefficients of (e_1, v_2) are not identically distributed, so the spherical symmetry assumption is suspect. However, the inner product is unchanged if we write $\bar{s} = (\bar{v}_1, \bar{v}_2)$ and $e = (e_1, s_2)$. Moreover, unlike the original vectors, the coefficients of s and e are identically distributed. There is still a slight complication: the adversary has control over one component of s and one component of e. If the adversary chooses particularly large values of

e_1 and v_2, then the spherical symmetry assumption will again be violated. We compensate for this by applying the same re-scaling trick from our analysis of Kyber.

A.6   Round5 (R5N1*PKE_0d)

Round5 is a collection of learning with rounding instantiations of the Lindner–Peikert scheme. The R5N1_*_PKE_0d parameter sets of Round5 take $R = \mathbb{Z}$. The second round NIST submission includes three parameter sets [13, Table 13] **r5n1lpke0d** ($n = 636$, $q = 2^{12}$, $b = 2$, $r_0 = 2^9$, $r_1 = 2^9$, $r_3 = 2^6$, $w = 114$), **r5n13pke0d** ($n = 876$, $q = 2^{15}$, $b = 3$, $r_0 = 2^{11}$, $r_1 = 2^{11}$, $r_3 = 2^7$, $w = 446$), and **r5n15pke0d** ($n = 1217$, $q = 2^{15}$, $b = 4$, $r_0 = 2^{12}$, $r_1 = 2^{12}$, $r_3 = 2^9$, $w = 462$). All three use fixed weight w vectors for e_1 and s_2. Since there are no large values of e_1, the adversary will invest all of his effort in finding large values of v_2, As with Saber, we swap components between vectors and apply the re-scaling trick from our analysis of Kyber. The only difference is that we compute Q_α with respect the honest distribution of e_1 and the u^2-th quantile of $\|v_2\|$.

A.7   Round5 (R5ND*0d)

The R5ND_*_0d parameter sets of Round5 take $R = \mathbb{Z}[x]/(1+x+\cdots+x^m)$. The specification includes three parameter sets [13, Table 11] **r5nd1pke0d** ($m = 586$, $q = 2^{13}$, $b = 1$, $r_0 = 2^9$, $r_1 = 2^9$, $r_3 = 2^4$, $w = 182$), **r5nd3pke0d** ($m = 852$, $q = 2^{12}$, $b = 1$, $r_0 = 2^9$, $r_1 = 2^9$, $r_3 = 2^5$, $w = 212$), and **r5nd5pke0d** ($m = 1170$, $q = 2^{13}$, $b = 1$, $r_0 = 2^9$, $r_1 = 2^9$, $r_3 = 2^5$, $w = 222$). We apply essentially the same analysis as for R5ND_*_0d. However, the choice of ring presents a slight obstacle as the adjoint does not preserve spherical symmetry.

Multiplication by a fixed element of R, say $a = a_0 + a_1x + a_2x^2 + \cdots + a_{m-1}x^{m-1}$, is a linear operation on the coefficient embedding. Specifically, it corresponds to left multiplication by the $m \times m$ matrix $[a]_{i,j} = a_{i-j} - a_{-(j+1)}$ where the index arithmetic is modulo $m + 1$ and $a_m = 0$. It follows that the adjoint of multiplication by a is multiplication by $\bar{a}$ where $\bar{a} = a_0 + (a_m - a_{m-1})x + (a_{m-1} - a_{m-2})x^2 + \cdots + (a_1 - a_0)x^{m-1}$. Note that the x^0 and x^1 coefficients are expected to be smaller than the rest. Since only two out of m coefficients are affected, we simply ignore the issue. We re-write the correctness condition as an inner product between $(v_1, \bar{v}_2)$ and $(\bar{e}_1, s_2)$. Since e_1 and v_2 have i.i.d. coefficients, we can easily compute the distributions of $\bar{e}_1$ and $\bar{v}_2$.

References

1. Aragon, N., et al.: BIKE. Technical report, National Institute of Standards and Technology (2019). https://csrc.nist.gov/projects/post-quantum-cryptography/round-2-submissions
2. Becker, A., Ducas, L., Gama, N., Laarhoven, T.: New directions in nearest neighbor searching with applications to lattice sieving. In: Krauthgamer, R. (ed.) 27th SODA, pp. 10–24. ACM-SIAM, January 2016

3. Bernstein, D.J.: Visualizing size-security tradeoffs for lattice-based encryption. Cryptology ePrint Archive, Report 2019/655 (2019). https://eprint.iacr.org/2019/655

4. Bernstein, D.J., Persichetti, E.: Towards KEM unification. Cryptology ePrint Archive, Report 2018/526 (2018). https://eprint.iacr.org/2018/526

5. D'Anvers, J.-P., Guo, Q., Johansson, T., Nilsson, A., Vercauteren, F., Verbauwhede, I.: Decryption failure attacks on IND-CCA secure lattice-based schemes. In: Lin, D., Sako, K. (eds.) PKC 2019. LNCS, vol. 11443, pp. 565–598. Springer, Cham (2019). https://doi.org/10.1007/978-3-030-17259-6_19

6. D'Anvers, J.P., Karmakar, A., Roy, S.S., Vercauteren, F.: SABER. Technical report, National Institute of Standards and Technology (2019). https://csrc.nist.gov/projects/post-quantum-cryptography/round-2-submissions

7. D'Anvers, J.P., Rossi, M., Virdia, F.: (One) failure is not an option: Bootstrapping the search for failures in lattice-based encryption schemes. Cryptology ePrint Archive, Report 2019/1399. EUROCrypt2020 (2019). https://eprint.iacr.org/2019/1399

8. D'Anvers, J.P., Vercauteren, F., Verbauwhede, I.: On the impact of decryption failures on the security of LWE/LWR based schemes. Cryptology ePrint Archive, Report 2018/1089 (2018). https://eprint.iacr.org/2018/1089

9. Dent, A.W.: A designer's guide to KEMs. Cryptology ePrint Archive, Report 2002/174 (2002). http://eprint.iacr.org/2002/174

10. Drucker, N., Gueron, S., Kostic, D.: On constant-time QC-MDPC decoding with negligible failure rate. Cryptology ePrint Archive, Report 2019/1289 (2019). https://eprint.iacr.org/2019/1289

11. Fujisaki, E., Okamoto, T.: Secure integration of asymmetric and symmetric encryption schemes. In: Wiener, M. (ed.) CRYPTO 1999. LNCS, vol. 1666, pp. 537–554. Springer, Heidelberg (1999). https://doi.org/10.1007/3-540-48405-1_34

12. Fujisaki, E., Okamoto, T.: Secure integration of asymmetric and symmetric encryption schemes. J. Cryptol. **26**(1), 80–101 (2013)

13. Garcia-Morchon, O., et al.: Round5. Technical report, National Institute of Standards and Technology (2019). https://csrc.nist.gov/projects/post-quantum-cryptography/round-2-submissions

14. Gentry, C., Peikert, C., Vaikuntanathan, V.: Trapdoors for hard lattices and new cryptographic constructions. In: Ladner, R.E., Dwork, C. (eds.) 40th ACM STOC, pp. 197–206. ACM Press, May 2008

15. Guo, Q., Johansson, T., Nilsson, A.: A generic attack on lattice-based schemes using decryption errors with application to ss-ntru-pke. Cryptology ePrint Archive, Report 2019/043 (2019). https://eprint.iacr.org/2019/043

16. Hamburg, M.: Three bears. Technical report, National Institute of Standards and Technology (2019). https://csrc.nist.gov/projects/post-quantum-cryptography/round-2-submissions

17. Hofheinz, D., Hövelmanns, K., Kiltz, E.: A modular analysis of the Fujisaki-Okamoto transformation. In: Kalai, Y., Reyzin, L. (eds.) TCC 2017. LNCS, vol. 10677, pp. 341–371. Springer, Cham (2017). https://doi.org/10.1007/978-3-319-70500-2_12

18. Lindner, R., Peikert, C.: Better key sizes (and attacks) for LWE-based encryption. In: Kiayias, A. (ed.) CT-RSA 2011. LNCS, vol. 6558, pp. 319–339. Springer, Heidelberg (2011). https://doi.org/10.1007/978-3-642-19074-2_21

19. Lu, X., et al.: LAC. Technical report, National Institute of Standards and Technology (2019). https://csrc.nist.gov/projects/post-quantum-cryptography/round-2-submissions

20. Naehrig, M., et al.: FrodoKEM. Technical report, National Institute of Standards and Technology (2019). https://csrc.nist.gov/projects/post-quantum-cryptography/round-2-submissions
21. National Institute of Standards and Technology (NIST): Submission requirements and evaluation criteria or the post-quantum cryptography standardization process (2017). https://csrc.nist.gov/csrc/media/projects/post-quantum-cryptography/documents/call-for-proposals-final-dec-2016.pdf
22. Poppelmann, T., et al.: NewHope. Technical report, National Institute of Standards and Technology (2019). https://csrc.nist.gov/projects/post-quantum-cryptography/round-2-submissions
23. Regev, O.: On lattices, learning with errors, random linear codes, and cryptography. In: Gabow, H.N., Fagin, R. (eds.) 37th ACM STOC, pp. 84–93. ACM Press, May 2005
24. Schwabe, P., et al.: CRYSTALS-KYBER. Technical report, National Institute of Standards and Technology (2019). https://csrc.nist.gov/projects/post-quantum-cryptography/round-2-submissions

Compact Privacy Protocols from Post-quantum and Timed Classical Assumptions

Jonathan Bootle[1(✉)], Anja Lehmann[2(✉)], Vadim Lyubashevsky[1(✉)], and Gregor Seiler[1,3(✉)]

[1] IBM Research – Zurich, Rüschlikon, Switzerland
{jbt,vad,grs}@zurich.ibm.com
[2] Hasso Plattner Institute, University of Potsdam, Potsdam, Germany
anja.lehmann@hpi.de
[3] ETH Zurich, Zurich, Switzerland

Abstract. While basic lattice-based primitives like encryption and digital signature schemes are already fairly short, more advanced privacy-preserving protocols (e.g. group signatures) that are believed to be post-quantum secure have outputs of at least several hundred kilobytes. In this paper, we propose a framework for building privacy protocols with significantly smaller parameter sizes whose secrecy is based on post-quantum assumptions, but soundness additionally assumes that some classical assumption, e.g., the discrete logarithm problem (DLP), is hard to break within a short amount of time.

The main ingredients of our constructions are statistical zero-knowledge proofs of knowledge for certain relations, whose soundness rely on the hardness of solving the discrete logarithm problem for a *fresh* DLP instance per proof. This notion has recently been described by the term *quantum annoyance*. Using such proofs, while also enforcing that they be completed in a fixed amount of time, we then show how to construct privacy-preserving primitives such as (dynamic) group signatures and DAA schemes, where soundness is based on the hardness of the "timed" discrete logarithm problem and SIS. The outputs of our schemes are significantly shorter ($\approx 30X$) than purely lattice-based schemes.

1 Introduction

Lattice cryptography is a particularly attractive post-quantum alternative to classical cryptographic schemes based on factoring and discrete log. Its main appeal is that one can build basic primitives, such as encryption and digital signature schemes, with relatively short outputs (1–3 KB) with the added bonus of sometimes being faster than the classical analogues. When one looks at more advanced privacy-preserving primitives such as group signatures, verifiable encryption, etc., the situation is considerably less attractive. For example, while

A. Lehmann—Work done while being at IBM Research – Zurich.

© Springer Nature Switzerland AG 2020
J. Ding and J.-P. Tillich (Eds.): PQCrypto 2020, LNCS 12100, pp. 226–246, 2020.
https://doi.org/10.1007/978-3-030-44223-1_13

group signatures based on elliptic curve pairings are only 160 Bytes [34], the smallest lattice-based group signatures, in which keys don't grow linearly with the number of group members, are approximately 600 KB [16].

Despite a considerable amount of research, it's looking very unlikely that even basic privacy-preserving primitives will be reduced to sizes of less than a few hundred kilobytes. This is due to the general approach used in constructing privacy-preserving schemes, such as group signatures, which lacks efficient lattice-based building blocks. The authority gives out a secret key to a particular user by signing the user's identity. To authenticate himself, the user then produces a ZKPoK of the signature on his identity.[1] Because creating an efficient zero-knowledge proof generally requires algebraic structure in the underlying statement, one generally uses standard-model (rather than one secure in the random oracle model) digital signature schemes for the authority's signature rather than rely on schemes that use a hash function modeled as a random oracle. And it is this requirement of a standard-model signature scheme that is the main culprit in the large output sizes of privacy-preserving schemes constructed in the above manner.

In this work we propose a framework for a middle-ground solution which addresses some of the main security problems posed by the eventual coming of quantum computers. One of the biggest concerns today is that communication in the pre-quantum world can be harvested and then eventually decrypted when quantum computers are eventually built. The main result of this paper is a framework for constructing compact privacy schemes where secrecy is either information-theoretic or based on post-quantum assumptions, while soundness is based on classical ones. Because only the soundness is classical, our schemes are not susceptible to the aforementioned harvesting attacks, and are therefore safe to use in the pre-quantum era.

If full-fledged quantum computers arrive and there are still no acceptably compact fully quantum-safe privacy schemes, then one can still continue using our schemes in certain situations. Firstly, they are *quantum annoying* (c.f. [22]), in the sense that breaking soundness requires solving a fresh discrete logarithm instance for each new forgery. This may be good enough in instances where the forgery payoff is less than the cost to use a quantum computer for the attack. In addition, we show that our schemes can be made to satisfy a stronger security notion by relying on "timed" versions of classical assumptions in which the prover must produce a response in a limited amount of time. This implies that a successful cheating prover can be used to solve the underlying problem in a fixed time interval, which may remain a difficult problem well into the post-quantum era (see the discussions in e.g. [23,25,29]).

1.1   Our Techniques

Since the main culprit for inefficient lattice-based privacy schemes are standard-model signatures, we propose avoiding them altogether, and instead construct a

---

[1] If the user wants to sign a message, then he transforms the interactive authentication protocol into a non-interactive one via the Fiat-Shamir framework and uses the message to create the challenge.

proof of knowledge of (possibly short) vectors x, y, s, when given public matrices/vectors A, B, C, z over some polynomial ring, satisfying

$$[A\ B] \cdot \begin{bmatrix} x \\ \tilde{F}(y) \end{bmatrix} = z \land H(F(y)) = Cs. \tag{1}$$

We then show that such proofs are enough for constructing privacy-preserving primitives such as group signatures and DAA schemes. In some constructions, $F = \tilde{F}$ will be (the same) one-way functions, while in others F will be a one-way function while $\tilde{F}$ will just be the identity. The function H is a cryptographic hash function.

The soundness of our proof is based on the assumed intractability of the discrete logarithm problem. More precisely, the prover shows that he either knows the (short) solution x, y, s satisfying the above relation (which means he knows a solution to a lattice problem), or he is able to find $e_i \in \mathbb{Z}$ satisfying $\prod g_i^{e_i} = 1$ for random generators g_i of some group.[2] While the discrete logarithm problem is not quantum secure, the only place in which it is used in our constructions is for guaranteeing the soundness of the zero-knowledge proofs. The zero-knowledge property itself is statistical and hence the privacy of the secrets is not affected by the (quantum) power of the adversary.

By letting the generators g_i be freshly chosen by the verifier (or some randomness beacon) at the time the proof is started, the ZKP already becomes "quantum annoying" as for each forgery the (quantum) adversary must solve a new DLP instance. Moreover, if the running-time of the proof is restricted, i.e. the verifier will not accept the proof if it takes more than Δ time, then one can base the soundness of the proof on the "timed" discrete logarithm assumption, in which the relation $\prod g_i^{e_i} = 1$ must be solved in a fixed amount of time. If this amount of time is short, then this problem may remain hard even for quantum computers.

Proof Approach. Our zero-knowledge proof of (1) builds on the works in [12, 13,17]. One of the contributions of [12,13] was showing an efficient proof of the pre-image y satisfying $H(y) = z$, where H is an arbitrary circuit, based on the hardness of discrete log. These works also showed how to prove linear relations (in the exponent) of Pedersen commitments and applications to range proofs. The work of [17] utilized these techniques to give faster proofs of knowledge of a short vector x satisfying $Ax = z$ for a public matrix A and vector z over the polynomial ring $R_q = \mathbb{Z}_q[X]/(X^d + 1)$.

When $F = \tilde{F}$, we can rewrite (1) as

$$[A\ B] \cdot \begin{bmatrix} x \\ r \end{bmatrix} = z \land F(y) = r \land H(r) = t \land Cs = t, \tag{2}$$

and then proving (1) is equivalent to proving knowledge of x, y, s, r, t, with some of these needing to have coefficients in a certain range, satisfying the above.

---

[2] We will use multiplicative notation for discrete log.

Similarly, if $\tilde{F}$ is the identity, then one can rewrite (1) as

$$[A \; B] \cdot \begin{bmatrix} x \\ y \end{bmatrix} = z \wedge F(y) = r \wedge H(r) = t \wedge Cs = t, \tag{3}$$

The first part of the conjunction in both (2) and (3) can be proven using [17], while the last one is similar except the t is also secret. The other two parts can be proven using the techniques from [12,13] applied to general circuits.

While the proofs in [13] are very compact, their main drawback is that the proof and verification time grows (more than) linearly in the number of gates in the circuit and proving the knowledge of a pre-image of a SHA-256 function (mapping 512 to 256 bits) takes approximately 20 s. In contrast, our schemes will require hash functions that map onto the space of a polynomial ring, which is around ten thousand bits. The proofs in [13] are based on the discrete logarithm assumption, which naturally lend themselves to proving statements over fields of large prime order. Therefore, we would like to use a hash-function built around arithmetic over such fields. MiMC [3] is a family of hash functions designed with precisely this in mind and we analyze the number of multiplication gates required for their evaluation.

Applications. We then show that proving (1) is enough for constructing schemes like group signatures and DAA schemes. While we only provide a few examples of what privacy-preserving schemes can be built from (1), there should be numerous other related schemes that can be constructed using this approach. Intuitively, constructing privacy-preserving primitives can be done by obtaining a signature on an identity from an issuer and proving knowledge of this signature in conjunction with supplementary information connected to the identity (c.f. [14]). One can then view the right part of (1) as a GPV-type signature scheme where the signature of the message (identity) $F(y)$ is s, and then the left side of the conjunction is a relation involving the message/identity y and some supplementary data x. The intuitive reason for why one may want to use $F(y)$ instead of y as the message is that one may wish to sometimes expose $F(y)$ but never expose her secret y. Using the image of the secret $F(y)$ as her identity, and then proving relations about the pre-image, allows the user to ascertain her knowledge of the secret without ever having to reveal it.

Our construction of a group signature scheme results in signatures of approximately 20 KB based on the hardness of standard lattice problems (i.e. NTRU and LWE) and the timed DL assumption. We also give a construction of a DAA scheme in the full version of this paper, where the proofs are tweaked for the setting where attestation are generated jointly by a resource-constrained TPM and powerful host.

1.2   Related Work

In this paper, we demonstrate the feasibility of our framework by giving a concrete construction of a group signature scheme. Since the foundational work of

[5], there have been many constructions of such schemes with security based on various problems. The schemes based on the hardness of the discrete logarithm problem are compact, but not quantum-safe, while those based on the hardness of lattice problems are quantum-safe, but have large signatures and/or public keys. We give a comparison to our scheme in Table 1.

Table 1. Output sizes (in KB) of discrete log, lattice-based, and our group signatures. For pairing based schemes using CP5-663 pairing curve (128 bit security level, 256 bit order curve). The public key size (and opening time) in [21] grows linearly with the number of users. The size given in the table is for 1000 users.

Scheme	Size		(Security) Properties		
	gpk	sign.	Dynamic	Non-frameability	Quantum-safe
DS18 [18]	1.29	1.96	✓	✓	✗
BBS04 [11]	1.05	0.43	✗	✓	✗
dPLS [16]	120	580	✗	✗	✓
ESSLL [21]	9000	48	✓	✗	✓
This work	5.5	20	✓	✓	(✓)

1.3 Open Problems

The main result of our work is a framework for constructing privacy-preserving primitives based on lattice assumptions and the timed discrete logarithm problem. The advantage of this approach is that our protocols enjoy significantly shorter outputs than purely lattice-based (or any purely quantum-safe) schemes. The main drawback of our concrete instantiation of this framework, which uses Bulletproofs along with the MiMC hash function, is that the proofs require millions of group operations, which would take a substantial amount of time for an honest prover.

The most interesting open question is thus to obtain faster solutions which may involve constructing different hash functions along with compatible discrete-log proof systems. There is currently related work, sponsored by the Ethereum Foundation, to create a STARK-friendly hash function [1,7], with several proposals already offering significant improvements over MiMC (e.g. [2,4,26]). Research into such hash functions is still in its infancy and there is reason to believe that we could eventually have hash functions which are very amenable to Bullet-proof style zero-knowledge proofs.

2 Preliminaries

In this section we introduce the building blocks needed for our privacy protocols.

Lattices. For $x, c \in \mathbb{R}^d$ and $\sigma \in \mathbb{R}^+$, we define the Gaussian function $\rho_{c,\sigma}(x) = \exp\left(\frac{-\|x-c\|^2}{2\sigma^2}\right)$, and for a lattice $\mathcal{L}$, we define the distribution $D_{\mathcal{L},c,\sigma}(x)$ to be 0 whenever $x \notin \mathcal{L}$ and $D_{\mathcal{L},c,\sigma}(x) = \frac{\rho_{c,\sigma}(x)}{\sum\limits_{v \in \mathcal{L}} \rho_{c,\sigma}(v)}$. when $x \in \mathcal{L}$. When we omit the $\mathcal{L}$ from the above equation, it is assumed that the lattice is $\mathbb{Z}^d$ (where d is evident from context). Omitting the c implies that $c = 0$.

We will denote by R_q the polynomial ring $\mathbb{Z}_q[X]/(X^d + 1)$ and define the norm of elements in R_q as the norm of its coefficients. As an additive group, the polynomial ring $R = \mathbb{Z}[X]/(X^d + 1)$ has an obvious mapping to $\mathbb{Z}^d$ and so we can write $v \leftarrow D_\sigma$ to signify sampling a random centered element from R.

For polynomials $a, t \in R$, we can define a $2d$-dimensional shifted lattice[3]

$$\mathcal{L}^{\perp}_{a,t} = \{(s_1, s_2) \in R^2 \; : \; as_1 + s_2 = t \bmod q\}$$

and we define the distribution $D^{\perp}_{a,t,\sigma}(x)$ to be 0 whenever $x \notin \mathcal{L}^{\perp}_{a,t}$ and

$$D^{\perp}_{a,t,\sigma}(x) = \frac{\rho_\sigma(x)}{\sum\limits_{v \in \mathcal{L}^{\perp}_{a,t}} \rho_\sigma(v)} \tag{4}$$

In general, given a random $a, t \in R_q$, it is hard (as hard as the Ring-SIS problem [32,33]) to sample according to $D^{\perp}_{a,t,\sigma}$ for small σ. One can do such sampling, however, when given a special trapdoor basis for the lattice $\mathcal{L}^{\perp}_{a,0}$. The smaller the vectors in the trapdoor, the smaller the σ can be in the distribution. A way to create a particularly small trapdoor can be done over NTRU lattices, in particular when $a = f/g$ for two polynomials f, g with small coefficients [19,27,35]. In particular, one can create an a, together with a trapdoor matrix T_a that allows one to sample (using a sampling algorithm from [20,24]) from $D^{\perp}_{a,t,\sigma}$, for any $t \in R_q$, for $\sigma \approx 1.5\sqrt{q}$.

NTRU Signature. This trapdoor sampling algorithm almost directly leads to a rather compact digital signature scheme, in the random oracle model, based on the hardness of finding short vectors in NTRU lattices. The public key is $a = f/g$, while the signing key is T_a. If we model the hash function H_{R_q} as a random oracle, then to sign a message m, the signer samples $s_1, s_2 \leftarrow D^{\perp}_{a,H_{R_q}(m),\sigma}$ and outputs s_1, s_2 (or just s_1 since s_2 can be computed from s_1 and m) as the signature. The signature is valid if $\|s_1\|, \|s_2\| \leq 1.1\sigma\sqrt{d} = 1.65\sqrt{qd}$. In this paper, we will use MiMC as the cryptographic hash function.

NTRU Encryption. The key generation procedure of the NTRU encryption scheme [28] consists of creating two polynomials with small $(-1/0/1)$ coefficients $f, g \in R_q$ and outputting the public key as $h = f/g$ and secret key g. Encryption of a message m with $0/1$ coefficients involves generating an $r, e \in R_q$ with small coefficients and outputting the ciphertext $v = 2(hr + e) + m$. To decrypt v, one would compute $m = (vg \bmod q)/g \bmod 2$.

---

[3] A *shifted lattice* is a lattice shifted by some vector v. Note that a shifted lattice does not have the property that the sum of any two vectors is in the shifted lattice.

Lattice-Based Zero-Knowledge Proofs. Our protocols will use a combination of various lattice and discrete-log based zero-knowledge proofs from the literature.

In general, for a public $A \in R_q^{n \times m}$ and $t \in R_q^n$, the prover knows a secret $s \in R_q^m$ with small coefficients such that $As = t$. Ideally, he would like to give a proof of this s, but such proofs are rather costly in their communication complexity. In some scenarios, however, the high cost may be acceptable. For example, joining a group (or registering a TPM) only needs to be done once and there are generally no strict restrictions on the time of communication complexity. An example of a proof in which a vector s is taken from a set with $\|s\|_\infty \leq \alpha$ and the prover can produce a proof

$$\pi = \mathsf{ZKP}\{s \ : \ As = t, \|s\|_\infty \leq \alpha\} \tag{5}$$

is given in [30]. The proof is a variation of Stern's proof of knowledge of a near codeword [37] and each iteration of the scheme has soundness error $2/3$. A more efficient proof that has soundness error $1/2d$ was introduced by Benhamouda et al. [8] where the prover uses his knowledge of s to prove the knowledge of a vector $\bar{s}$ satisfying $A\bar{s} = 2t$ where $\|\bar{s}\| > \|s\|$. In particular, given an $s = \begin{bmatrix} s_1 \\ \ldots \\ s_m \end{bmatrix}$ such that $\|s_i\| \leq \alpha$, it produces a zero-knowledge proof

$$\pi = \mathsf{ZKP}\{\bar{s} \ : \ A\bar{s} = 2t, \|\bar{s}\| \leq 33\alpha d^{1.5} m\sqrt{\lambda}\} \tag{6}$$

In Appendix A we explicitly provide the prover and verifier algorithms for this relation since they were only given for an interactive, asymptotic version in [8].

Hash Functions with Efficient Proofs. For our privacy protocols we need a hash function that allows for efficient zero-knowledge proofs that a hash was correctly computed and that the prover knows a pre-image of the hash value. We will use zero-knowledge proofs based on the DL assumption, which naturally lend themselves to proving statements over fields of large prime order. Thus, we would like to use a hash function built around arithmetic over such fields.

MiMC [3] is a family of hash functions designed with precisely this in mind. MiMC hash functions are based on the sponge construction [10]. The construction works by cubing the input over the field, adding randomly chosen constant values, and repeating the process many times. We give a more detailed overview of the MiMC hash function and our parameter choices in Appendix B.

3   Timed Zero-Knowledge Proofs

In this section we describe our idea of quantum-annoying and timed zero-knowledge proofs (ZKP), describe how they can be made non-interactive via a beacon service, and realized using a combination of lattice/bulletproofs.

More precisely, we consider ZKPs for generalized statements that prove an exact relation as in (5), but follow the proof system recently introduced in [17]. The proof system uses a CRS made up of random group elements $g_1, \ldots, g_n$, and assuming the DL problem is hard, it allows to prove knowledge of a witness for various NP statements. For example, the protocol of [17] actually proves is that the prover knows a SIS solution s or a non-trivial discrete logarithm relation between $g_1, \ldots, g_n$. The advantage of this technique is that the proofs can be very short, but the disadvantage is that the running time of the prover and verifier is long (e.g. for typical parameters in [17] it was 10–20 s). Formally, the proof in [17] gives a proof of a disjunction

$$\pi = \mathsf{ZKP}\{s, \{r_i\} \ : \ \mathsf{DLR}\,(\{g_i\}, \{r_i\}) = 1 \vee As = t, \ \|s\|_\infty \leq \alpha\}. \tag{7}$$

where g_i are public elements of some group G and A, t are as before.

Generalizing the proof system of [17], we obtain zero-knowledge proofs of the following form in which the prover proves that they know a witness w for relation $\mathcal{R}_q$ or for relation $\mathcal{R}_c$: $\mathsf{ZKP}\{(w) : (x_c, w) \in \mathcal{R}_c \ \vee \ (x_q, w) \in \mathcal{R}_q\}$. In our proof systems, a witness for $\mathcal{R}_c$ will always be a non-trivial DL relation, and $\mathcal{R}_q$ will be the collection of statements and witnesses we are actually interested in.

Quantum Annoying and Timed Proofs. In this plain form, the soundness of the above proof relies on the weaker of both relations, i.e., the DL assumption even though it also proves a lattice relation. We can transform the proof into a quantum annoying version [22] by simply letting the verifier freshly choose g_i when the proof starts. As g_i are not longer long-term parameters, this forces the adversary to solve a fresh DL instance for every proof it wants to forge.

By requiring the prover to produce a proof within a short amount of time, we can further strengthen this approach such that the problem likely remains hard even for quantum computers (or is at least prohibitively expensive to solve). That is, the verifier only accepts a proof when the prover correctly responds within some fixed short time Δ. The soundness of our ZKP then even holds against a quantum adversary under the additional assumption that the DL problem is hard to solve within a short amount of time. We will refer to such an assumption as Δ-hardness. In Appendix C we provide a more formal treatment of such timed ZKPs and discuss their relation to quantum annoyance.

Non-interactive Timed Proofs. Finally, in our privacy protocols we want to use signature proofs of knowledge, i.e., non-interactive ZKPs that follow the Fiat-Shamir paradigm and "sign" a message m by including m in the challenge hash of the NIZK. To maintain the short-term validity aspect in this non-interactive form, we will rely on a beacon and time-stamp service $\mathcal{T}$.

This trusted entity $\mathcal{T}$ has a signing key pair (ssk, spk) and serves a double purpose: First, it regularly publishes signed tuples (t, b, σ) with $\sigma \xleftarrow{\$} \mathsf{Sign}(ssk, (t, b))$ for a time t and random beacon b. We will use b to deterministically generate fresh DL instances $(g_1, \ldots, g_n) \leftarrow G(b, m)$ where G is simply a hash function that outputs group elements of some group $\mathcal{C}$.

The prover first obtains such a timed beacon (t, b, σ), derives fresh DL instances and computes $\pi = \mathsf{NIZK}\{w, \{r_i\} \ : \ \mathsf{DLR}\,(\{g_i\}, \{r_i\}) = 1 \vee (x_q, w) \in \mathcal{R}_q\}(m)$. It then sends $h \leftarrow H(\pi)$ to $\mathcal{T}$ which will return $t', \sigma' \xleftarrow{\$} \mathsf{Sign}(ssk, (t', h))$, i.e., $\mathcal{T}$ time-stamps the hash h for time t'. The non-interactive timed proof output by the prover consists of $(\pi, t, t', b, \sigma, \sigma')$.

For the sake of brevity we use the following shorthand to refer to non-interactive timed proofs of such a form and with running time Δ:

$$\mathsf{ZKP}^{\Delta}_{\mathsf{DLR}}\{w_q : (x_q, w_q) \in \mathcal{R}_q\}.$$

Finally, we stress that while soundness is quantum-annoying or timed, we require the zero-knowledge property of the proof to hold statistically.

Building Timed ZKPs. To build our timed ZKPs needed for our group signature and DAA scheme, we use Bulletproofs [13] (instantiated with MiMC) and the proof system from [17] in a mostly black-box manner. The algorithms in our privacy protocols rely on complex relations made up of combinations of the DL, SIS and pre-image relations of the form $Func(f) := \{\mathbf{u} \in \{0,1\}^m, \mathbf{v} \in \{0,1\}^n : f(\mathbf{u}) = \mathbf{v}\}$. We describe how to realize such proofs from the mentioned proofs systems, and the tweaks that should be made, in Appendix D.

4   Group Signature Scheme

A dynamic group signature allows users to sign messages on behalf of a group without revealing their individual identity. Group membership is managed by an issuer $\mathcal{I}$ that lets users $\mathcal{U}$ dynamically join the group. The anonymity of a user can be lifted through a dedicated opening authority $\mathcal{O}$ that can reveal the identity of the signer behind a particular signature in a verifiable manner. More precisely, a group signature Π_{GS} consists of the following algorithms:

$\mathsf{GKg}(1^{\lambda}) \rightarrow (gpk, isk, osk)$: On input the security parameter 1^{λ} it outputs a group public key gpk, and the secret keys isk, osk for the issuer and opener.

$\mathsf{UKg}(1^{\lambda}) \rightarrow (upk, usk)$: Outputs the private and public key of a user.

$\langle \mathsf{Join}(gpk, upk, usk), \mathsf{Issue}(isk, reg) \rangle \rightarrow (gsk, reg')$: A user can join the group by running an interactive join protocol with the issuer. The user's output is his signing key gsk, and the issuer outputs an updated registration table reg'.

$\mathsf{Sign}(gpk, gsk, \mu) \rightarrow \Sigma$: On input a group public key gpk, a user's secret signing key gsk and a message μ outputs a signature Σ.

$\mathsf{Verify}(gpk, \mu, \Sigma) \rightarrow 1/0$: Verifies a signature Σ against the group public key gpk.

$\mathsf{Open}(gpk, osk, reg, \Sigma, \mu) \rightarrow (upk, \tau)/\bot$: This algorithms uses the opener's secret key osk to recover the identity of the signer of Σ for message μ. It outputs a claimed signer upk and proof τ, or $\bot$ to indicate failure.

$\mathsf{Judge}(gpk, upk, \Sigma, \mu, \tau) \rightarrow 1/0$: This deterministic judge algorithm verifies the proof τ, i.e., whether the user with public key upk is the signer of Σ.

Table 2. Proposed parameters for our group signature

Ring	R_q	$\mathbb{Z}_q[X]/(X^d+1)$
Ring modulus	q	12289
Ring dimension	d	1024
Standard deviation	$\sigma = 1.5\sqrt{q}$	
usk space	$\mathcal{N}$	$\{0,1\}^{2\lambda}$
Encryption randomness	$R_\pm$	$\{-1,0,1\}^d \subset R_q$
upk space	R_+	$\{0,1\}^d \subset R_q$
Credential (gsk) space	$\mathcal{S}$	$s \in \mathbb{Z}_q[X]/(X^d+1)$, s.t. $\|s\| \leq 1.5\sigma\sqrt{d}$
Signature size	$|\Sigma|$	19.86 KB

The user secret keys will be uniformly random 2λ-bit strings from the set $\mathcal{N}$. We define a one-way function $F : \mathcal{N} \to R_+$ which maps a user's secret key ρ to his public key $upk \in R_+$. We will assume that inverting this function (for random input $\rho \in \mathcal{N}$) is λ-hard. A part of the signature will be an encryption of the user identity (and nonce), and we will use the Naor-Yung approach of encrypting the same message under two different public NTRU keys (or where one of the public keys is indistinguishable from random), and provide a zero-knowledge proof of this fact.

Key Generation: The issuer's key consists of a public $a \in R_q$ together with a secret trapdoor T_a that will allow him to sample $s_1, s_2 \sim D_{a,t,\sigma}^{\perp}$ with $\sigma = 1.5\sqrt{q}$. The reference for this algorithm as well as the construction of the trapdoor T_a is discussed in Sect. 2. The opener's public key will be $h = f/g$ where $f, g \leftarrow R_\pm$ and his secret opening key will be (f, g).

A user's key is as described above, i.e. it sets $usk = \rho$ chosen uniformly at random from $\mathcal{N}$, and will define $upk = F_{R_+}(\rho)$ as his public key where F is a λ-hard one-way function.

Algorithm 1. $\mathsf{GKg}(1^\lambda)$

Output: $gpk := (a, h, h')$, $isk := T_a$, $osk := (f, g)$.

1: $(a, T_a) \leftarrow$ NTRUTrapdoor.
2: $f, g, f', g' \leftarrow R_\pm$. If g, g' is not invertible mod q or mod 2, re-sample it.
3: $h := f/g$, $h' := f'/g'$.

Join: When a user with keys $usk = \rho$, $upk = F_{R_+}(\rho)$ wants to join the group, it send upk to the issuer. This upk is the value to which all of his actions can be traced to by the opener. The issuer then samples $s_1, s_2 \leftarrow D_{a,t,\sigma}$, for $t = H_{R_q}(F_{R_+}(\rho))$ and sends s_1, s_2 to the group member. The member will use ρ and the polynomials s_1, s_2 as his signing credentials. Observe that s_1, s_2 is the GPV signature of the message $F_{R_+}(\rho)$ when the GPV signature is instantiated with the concrete hash function H_{R_q}.

Algorithm 2. $\langle$Join$(gpk, upk, usk),$ Issue$(isk, reg)\rangle$

Input: $usk = \rho$, $upk = F_{R_+}(\rho)$, $gpk = (a, h, h')$, $isk = T_a$, reg
Output: User: $gsk = (s_1, s_2, \rho)$, Issuer: updated registr. table reg'.
1: <u>User</u>: Send upk to the Issuer
2: <u>Issuer</u>: Check that $upk \notin reg$. Sample $s_1, s_2 \leftarrow D_{a,t,\sigma}^{\perp}$ for $t := H_{R_q}(upk)$. Send s_1, s_2
    to the User, output $reg' = reg \cup \{upk\}$.
3: <u>User</u>: If $as_1 + s_2 = H_{R_q}(F_{R_+}(\rho))$, output $gsk = (s_1, s_2 \in \mathcal{S}^2, \rho)$.

Algorithm 3. Sign(gpk, gsk, μ):

Input: $gsk = (s_1, s_2, \rho)$ s.t. $as_1 + s_2 = H_{R_q}(\rho)$, $gpk = (a, h, h')$, μ
Output: Signature $\Sigma := (u, u', \pi)$
1: $e_1, e_2, e_1', e_2' \leftarrow R_{\pm}$
2: $u := 2(he_1 + e_2) + F_{R_+}(\rho)$, $u' := 2(he_1' + e_2') + F_{R_+}(\rho)$
3: $\pi := \mathsf{ZKP}_{\mathsf{DLR}}^{\triangle}\{(s_1, s_2, e_1, e_2, e_1', e_2', \rho) : as_1 + s_2 = H_{R_q}(F_{R_+}(\rho)) \wedge 2(he_1 + e_2) + $
    $F_{R_+}(\rho) = u \wedge 2(h'e_1' + e_2') + F_{R_+}(\rho) = u' \wedge s_1, s_2 \in \mathcal{S} \wedge e_1, e_2, e_1', e_2' \in R_{\pm} \wedge \rho \in$
    $\mathcal{N}\}(\mu)$
4: **return** $\Sigma := (u, u', \pi)$

Sign: If a member with credentials (ρ, s_1, s_2), as above, wishes to sign μ, he creates two NTRU encryptions of the message $F_{R_+}(\rho)$ with respect to the public keys h and h' and gives a zero-knowledge proof that he knows the randomness and the message underlying the ciphertexts, as well as the knowledge of ρ, s_1, s_2 satisfying $as_1 + s_2 = H_{R_q}(F_{R_+}(\rho))$ and the fact that $F_{R_+}(\rho)$ is the message in the ciphertext. The μ is signed via its insertion in the random oracle during the Fiat-Shamir transform.

The reason that we need two NTRU "encryptions" is to achieve CCA security via the Naor-Yung transform. While the Naor-Yung approach is usually not the most practical way of building CCA-secure schemes, it actually incurs little overhead in our case because providing proofs of ciphertext correctness would be necessary even if we were only aiming for CPA security. For CCA security, we just need to prove two equations instead of one.

Verify: For verification, the Verifier simply checks the validity of the proof.

Open: The opener checks the proof in the signature and performs NTRU decryption of the ciphertext u using his secret key g. If the decrypted public key is contained in the registration table, he gives a zero-knowledge proof that the opening is correct. In particular, he proves that he knows the secret keys g, f that form the public key h (i.e. $f/g = h$) and also that the multiplication $gu = 2v + gm$ where v is a polynomial with coefficients less than $q/4 - d/2$. If this is satisfied, then decryption is indeed valid because $gu \bmod q = 2v + gm$ in $\mathcal{R}$, which follows from the smallness of v and the fact that all the coefficients of gm are at most d. Therefore decryption, which requires reducing the above modulo 2 guarantees that $gu \bmod q \bmod 2 = gm$. Hence the correct decryption of u is m.

Algorithm 4. Verify(gpk, Σ, μ):

Input: $\Sigma = (u, u', \pi)$, $gpk = (a, h, h')$, μ
Output: Output 1 iff the verification passes
1: **return** 1 iff π is valid wrt u, u', gpk and μ.

Algorithm 5. Open($gpk, osk, reg, \Sigma, \mu$):

Input: $\Sigma = (u, u', \pi)$, message μ, $gpk = (a, h, h')$, $osk = (f, g)$, registration table reg.
Output: Identity $upk = m$, and proof of valid decryption τ, or $\perp$.
1: $m := (gu \bmod q)/g \bmod 2$.
2: **return** $\perp$ if Verify(gpk, Σ, μ) $\neq 1$ or $m \notin reg$
3: $\tau := \mathsf{ZKP}^{\Delta}_{\mathsf{DLR}}\{(f, g, v) \ : \ hg - f = 0 \ \wedge \ ug = 2v + gm \ \wedge \ f, g \in R_{\pm} \ \wedge \ v \in R$ s.t. $\|v\|_{\infty} < q/4 - d/2\}$
4: **return** (m, τ)

Judge: The Judge checks that the opener's proofs are valid. If it is, he concludes that the opener revealed the correct identity.

4.1 Security of the Group Signature Scheme

We now show that our dynamic group signature scheme is secure according to the established notions by Bellare et al. [6], i.e., it satisfies *anonymity*, *traceability* and *non-frameability*. The detailed proof of the following theorem is given in the full version.

Theorem 1. *Our group signature is fully anonymous, traceable and non-frameable when the underlying NTRU encryption scheme is CPA secure, the underlying GPV signature scheme is unforgeable, F is one-way, the proof system* $\mathsf{ZKP}^{\Delta}_{\mathsf{DLR}}$ *is special sound and zero-knowledge, and* DLR *is* Δ-*hard.*

Hardness. We now briefly analyze the concrete security of the underlying lattice schemes in our group signature scheme for the parameters given in Table 2. This means we assess the complexity of some known lattice attacks on our instantiations of the NTRU encryption scheme and the GPV signature scheme.

For NTRU we focus on the primal key recovery attack, see [9] for more details and an overview of other attacks, in particular meet-in-the-middle and hybrid attacks. Given $h \in R_q$, the problem is to find two short polynomials $f, g \in R_q$ such that $gh = f$ in R_q. By lifting the equation to R, this gives a lattice of dimension $2d$ and volume q^d. Now one can hope that certain coefficients of g are zero, say k many, $0 \leq k < d$, and search for a solution in the corresponding sublattice of dimension $2d - k$. This gives a speed-up despite the reduced success probability. Furthermore, we can restrict the search to the sublattice corresponding to only $m \leq d$ of the equations over $\mathbb{Z}^d$, leaving us with a lattice of dimension $d - k + m$ and volume q^m. The general strategy then is to apply the BKZ basis reduction algorithm to the basis of an optimally chosen sublattice with a large

---

Algorithm 6. Judge($gpk, upk, \Sigma, \mu, \tau$):

Input: $\Sigma = (u, u', \pi), \mu, gpk = (a, h, h'), upk = m$, and the opener's proof τ
Output: Output 1 iff the user with upk is the signer of Σ
1: **return** 1 iff Verify(gpk, Σ, μ) = 1 and τ is valid wrt gpk, upk, u.

---

enough block size β so that our target solution will be found. When using John Schanck's estimation scripts [36], we find that for $m = 889$ we would require a block size $\beta = 712$. Costing only one call to an SVP algorithm in dimensions 712 in the so-called Core-SVP methodology gives a time complexity of about 2^{208} when using the best known classical sieving algorithms and a complexity of 2^{188} when also considering quantum speed-ups.

For the GPV signature scheme we focus on the forgery attack. Here the adversary needs to find a short solution $s_1, s_2 \in R_q$ such that $\|s_i\| \leq 1.5\sigma\sqrt{d}$ and $as_1 + s_2 = t$ for a random t. This gives a lattice of dimension $2d + 1$ and volume q^d. But unlike in the case of NTRU we do not search for a particular very short solution. Any solution fulfilling the bound is fine and it is clearly sufficient to search in a sublattice of dimension $n \leq 2d + 1$. The BKZ algorithm with blocksize β finds a solution of length $\delta^n q^{d/n}$ where heuristically $\delta = (\beta(\pi\beta)^{1/\beta}/(2\pi e))^{1/(2(\beta-1))}$. We find that we need $\delta < 1.00226$ and hence a block size of $\beta \geq 875$. Finding a shortest vector in dimension 875 costs 2^{255} classically and 2^{232} quantumly.

4.2 Costs and Sizes

We want to analyze the sizes of the signatures Σ in our group signature scheme and the cost of computing and verifying them in terms of numbers of elliptic curve scalar multiplications. By far the largest element of a signature Σ is the proof π. This proof essentially consists of two parts. In the first part the linear equations for u, u' and $H(upk)$ are proven. The second part is concerned with the nonlinear equations $\|s_i\| \leq 1.5\sigma\sqrt{d}$, $upk = F(\rho)$ and $t = H(upk)$. For the first part we use the proof system from [17] but we further split the proof into two parts involving secret polynomials with coefficients in $\{-1, 0, 1\}$ and $\{-(q-1)/2, \ldots, (q-1)/2\}$, respectively. Note that the 12-norm bound on s_1, s_2 is proven separately and hence it is sufficient for the linear proof of $as_1 + s_2 = H(upk)$ to only include the bound $\|s_i\|_\infty \leq (q-1)/2$. From the formulas in [17] we find that the two linear proofs have combined size 75 group elements plus 6 elements in $\mathbb{Z}_p$. The non-linear proof has size 48 group elements and 5 field elements. Since we use a 521-bit curve, for example NIST P-521, the three proofs have a combined size of about 16.36 KB. The two NTRU encryptions consist of two uniform elements in R_q with size 1.75 KB each. So in total a signature Σ has size 19.86 KB. See Appendix D for more explicit details on how the proofs are conducted.

For the number of exponentiations we find from the formulas in [17] and [13] that the prover has to compute 2.047.271 scalar multiplications for the linear proofs and 11.620.232 scalar multiplications for the non-linear proof. So in total the prover needs to compute 13.7 million scalar multiplications. The verifier has to compute at total number of 4 million scalar multiplications.

Acknowledgements. This work was supported by the SNSF ERC starting transfer grant FELICITY and the EU Horizon 2020 project FutureTPM (No. 779391).

A   Lattice-Based ZKP for Relation 6

Below we provide the prover and verifier algorithms for relation 6 adapted from [8].

If $R_q = \mathbb{Z}_q[X]/(X^d+1)$, then we define the set $\mathcal{M} = \{0, \pm x^i\ 0 \le i < d\}$. The size of $\mathcal{M}$ is $2d+1$. We also define a parameter λ which controls the soundness error of the proof. The soundness error will be $|\mathcal{M}|^{-\lambda} \approx d^{-\lambda-1}$. For example, if $d = 2048$, then to get the soundness error to be less than 2^{-128}, we need to set $\lambda = 11$.

Algorithm 7. Prover

Input: Secret $s = \begin{bmatrix} s_1 \\ \cdots \\ s_m \end{bmatrix} \in R_q^m$ s.t. $\|s_i\| \le \alpha$ and public $A \in R_q^{n \times m}, t = As \in R_q^n$.

Output: $\pi = (z \in R_q^\lambda, (c_1, \ldots, c_\lambda) \in \mathcal{M}^\lambda)$

1: $\sigma := 11\alpha\sqrt{m\lambda}$; for $i = 1$ to λ, $y_i \leftarrow D_\sigma$, $w_i := Ay_i$

2: $(c_1, \ldots, c_\lambda) := H_{\mathcal{M}^\lambda}(A, t, w_1, \ldots, w_\lambda)$; $v := \begin{bmatrix} c_1 s \\ \cdots \\ c_\lambda s \end{bmatrix} \in R_q^{m\lambda}$

3: $z = \begin{bmatrix} z_1 \\ \cdots \\ z_\lambda \end{bmatrix} := \begin{bmatrix} y_1 \\ \cdots \\ y_\lambda \end{bmatrix} + v \in R_q^{m\lambda}$

4: with probability $1 - \frac{D_\sigma(z)}{3D_{v,\sigma}(z)}$, goto 1

5: **return** $z, (c_1, \ldots, c_\lambda)$

Algorithm 8. Verifier

Input: $A \in R_q^{n \times m}, t = As \in R_q^n, \pi = (z \in R_q^\lambda, (c_1, \ldots, c_\lambda) \in \mathcal{M}^\lambda)$

Output: Output 1 iff $\pi = \text{ZKP}\{\bar{s}\ :\ A\bar{s} = 2t, \|\bar{s}\| \le 3\sigma d^{1.5}\sqrt{m} = 33\alpha d^{1.5} m\sqrt{\lambda}\}$

write $\begin{bmatrix} w_1 \\ \cdots \\ w_\lambda \end{bmatrix} := \begin{bmatrix} Az_1 - c_1 t \\ \cdots \\ Az_\lambda - c_\lambda t \end{bmatrix}$

Accept iff $(c_1, \ldots, c_\lambda) = H_{\mathcal{M}^\lambda}(A, t, w_1, \ldots, w_\lambda)$ and $\|z_i\| \le 1.5\sigma\sqrt{dm}$

The proof in Algorithm 7 uses Gaussian-based rejection sampling and can be shown to be zero-knowledge, and requiring 3 iterations on average, using

[31, Theorem 4.6]. If $|\mathcal{M}|^\lambda > 2^{128}$, then a prover succeeding with probability greater than $\approx 2^{-128}$ can be rewound to produce two solutions $\boldsymbol{A}\boldsymbol{z}_i = \boldsymbol{w}_i + c_i\boldsymbol{t}$ and $\boldsymbol{A}\boldsymbol{z}_i' = \boldsymbol{w}_i + c_i'\boldsymbol{t}$ for distinct $c_i \in \mathcal{M}$. These can be combined to form the solution

$$\boldsymbol{A}(\boldsymbol{z}_i - \boldsymbol{z}_i')/(c_i - c_i') = \boldsymbol{t}.$$

By [8, Lemma 3.1], we know that for $c_i \neq c_i' \in \mathcal{M}$, the quotient $2/(c_i - c_i')$ is a polynomial with coefficients in $\{-1, 0, 1\}$ and therefore has ℓ_2-norm at most $\sqrt{d}$. The parameters for the size of $\bar{s}$ in (6) then follow from the parameters in Algorithms 7 and 8.

B   Hash Functions with Efficient Proofs

In our group signature and DAA scheme, we need to use a hash function that allows for efficient zero-knowledge proofs that a hash was correctly computed and that the prover knows a pre-image of the hash value. We will use zero-knowledge proofs based on the discrete logarithm assumption, which naturally lend themselves to proving statements over fields of large prime order. Therefore, we would like to use a hash-function built around arithmetic over such fields.

The MiMC Hash Function Family. MiMC [3] is a family of hash functions designed with precisely this in mind. MiMC hash functions are based on the sponge construction [10]. The construction works by cubing the input over the field, adding randomly chosen constant values, and repeating the process many times.

For fixed input size, output size, and security level, the MiMC family includes a range of hash functions with a trade-off between the size of the prime field used and the number of multiplication gates in a circuit which verifies correct computing of the hash function. Later, in our choices of zero-knowledge proof-system, we will see that for every multiplication in the circuit, the prover must perform some exponentiations over a cryptographic group. Therefore, in the two cases below, we have carefully selected the parameters of the MiMC hash functions in order to minimise the computational burden on the prover. To specify an MiMC hash function, one must give the desired security level and the 'rate' of the round function, which determines the prime field to be used.

As part of our schemes, we will use a pre-image resistant function (later referred to as F_{R_+}) to protect the user's secret key. We instantiate this function with an MiMC hash function with an input length of 256 bits and an output length of 1,024 bits. The circuit used to prove knowledge of a hash pre-image has 60,192 multiplication gates. We will also use a hash-function, modelled as a random oracle, which maps the output of the previous function onto a ring element from $\mathbb{Z}_q[X]/(X^d + 1)$. In this case, we use an MiMC hash function with an input length of 1,024 bits and an output length of 14,336 bits. For the new, larger input and output sizes, the circuit used to prove knowledge of a hash pre-image has 831,577 multiplication gates.

In both cases, we use MiMC hash functions with capacity 512, and a 521-bit prime. This choice of parameters comes from our requirement that the hash function has 256 bits of classical security and therefore 128 bits of quantum security against collision-finding attacks. For 256 bits of classical security, the internal workings of the hash function force us to use a prime of at least 512 bits. Hence, we use a 521-bit prime so that we can use a standardised NIST elliptic curve, for which we expect highly optimised implementations of curve operations compared with unstandardised curves.

C   Quantum Annoying and Timed ZKPs

The core observation behind our timed ZKPs is that while certain hard problems, such as the discrete logarithm problem, can be solved in polynomial-time by (sufficiently sized) quantum computers, it is likely that solving them won't be instantaneous or at least prohibitively expensive. Thus, forcing the adversary to solve a *fresh* DLP instance for each proof might render the attack infeasible.

This property has recently been described as *quantum annoyance* [22] and formalized through a two stage adversary. Roughly, in an offline pre-computation phase the adversary is granted full quantum power, but gets restricted to be classical when turning to an online phase.

We now apply this concept to zero-knowledge proofs, more precisely, we consider ZKPs for generalized statements following the form of Eq. (7) of the proof system recently introduced in [17]. The proof system uses a CRS made up of random group elements $g_1, \ldots, g_n$, and assuming the DL problem is hard, it allows to prove knowledge of a witness for various NP statements. For example, the protocol of [17] actually proves is that the prover knows a SIS solution $\mathbf{s}$ *or* a non-trivial discrete logarithm relation between $g_1, \ldots, g_n$. Generalizing this idea we consider proofs of the form: $\mathsf{ZKP}\{(w) : (x_q, w) \in \mathcal{R}_q \ \lor \ (x_c, w) \in \mathcal{R}_c\}$, where $\mathcal{R}$ denotes a NP relation and w is a witness for a statement x if $(x, w) \in \mathcal{R}$.

In this plain form, the soundness of the proof relies on the weaker of both relations, i.e., the DL assumption in the case of [17] even though it also proves a lattice relation. We can transform the proof into a quantum annoying (and later timed) version by simply letting the verifier freshly choose x_c (i.e., g_i in our concrete scheme) when the proof starts.

Let $x \xleftarrow{\$} \mathsf{Gen}(1^\lambda, \mathcal{L})$ be a generator that produces a random instance $x \in \mathcal{L}$ for security parameter 1^λ and language $\mathcal{L} = \{x \mid \exists w : (x, w) \in \mathcal{R}\}$. We can then formulate quantum-annoying soundness for an interactive proof protocol $(\mathcal{P}, \mathcal{V})$ for statements $(x_q, w) \in \mathcal{R}_q \ \lor \ (x_c, w) \in \mathcal{R}_c$ as follows: For any efficient adversary $(\mathcal{A}_1, \mathcal{A}_2)$—where $\mathcal{A}_1$ is quantum, and $\mathcal{A}_2$ is classical—running the following game

1. sample random $x_q \xleftarrow{\$} \mathsf{Gen}(1^\lambda, \mathcal{L}_q)$
2. $\mathsf{st} \xleftarrow{\$} \mathcal{A}_1(x_q)$
3. sample random $x_c \xleftarrow{\$} \mathsf{Gen}(1^\lambda, \mathcal{L}_c)$
4. where $\Pr\left[\langle \mathcal{A}_2(\mathsf{st}, x_q, x_c), \mathcal{V}(x_q, x_c) \rangle = 1\right] > \epsilon$

there exist an efficient extractor $\mathcal{E}$ with rewindable black-box access to $\mathcal{A}_2$ that outputs w s.t. $(x_q, w) \in \mathcal{R}_q \vee (x_c, w) \in \mathcal{R}_c$ with probability $\geq \epsilon/\mathsf{poly}(1^\lambda)$.

Generally, the online adversary $\mathcal{A}_2$ can be seen as a resource-restricted adversary that cannot break the classical problem. While quantum-annoyance models the resource restriction by simply limiting $\mathcal{A}_2$ to be classical, we can also be more generous and give $\mathcal{A}_2$ quantum power, yet restrict its running time.

That is, the verifier only accepts a proof when the prover correctly responds within some fixed short time Δ. The soundness of our ZKP then even holds against a full quantum adversary under the additional assumption that the problem $\mathcal{R}_c$ is hard to solve within a short amount of time. We will refer to such an assumption as Δ-hardness.

Note that there are subtle constraints on how to choose the time Δ for a concrete ZKP instantiation based on a Δ'-hard problem. For satisfying completeness, Δ must be chosen large enough, such that honest provers can still complete the proof (for $\mathcal{L}_q$) in time. For soundness, Δ depends on the loss in the reduction, i.e., the running time of the extractor that will be used to break the Δ'-hard problem needs to be taken into account. We leave a more formal treatment of these relations as interesting future work.

D   Zero-Knowledge Proofs for Group Signature Algorithms

In this section, we explain how to give the zero-knowledge proofs for the group signature algorithms of Sect. 4 in terms of the proof systems of [17] for SIS relations and [13] for more complicated relations with less special structure available.

Both proof systems rely on the discrete logarithm assumption.

Definition 1 (Discrete Log Relation). *For all PPT adversaries $\mathcal{A}$ and for all $n \geq 2$ there exists a negligible function $\mu(\lambda)$ such that*

$$P\left[\begin{array}{l} \mathcal{C} = \mathcal{G}(1^\lambda),\ g_1, \ldots, g_n \leftarrow \mathcal{C}; \\ a_1, \ldots, a_n \in \mathbb{Z} \leftarrow \mathcal{A}(G, g_1, \ldots, g_n) \end{array} : \exists a_i \neq 0 \wedge \prod_{i=1}^{n} g_i^{a_i} = 1\right] \leq \mu(\lambda)$$

For $n \geq 2$, this is equivalent to the discrete logarithm assumption.

Sign: A zero-knowledge proof of the following statement is computed:

$$\mathsf{ZKP}_{\mathsf{DLR}}^{\Delta} \left\{ \begin{array}{l} s_1, s_2, \\ e_1, e_2, e_1', e_2', \rho \end{array} : \begin{array}{l} as_1 + s_2 = H_{R_q}(F_{R_+}(\rho)) \\ \wedge\ 2(he_1 + e_2) + F_{R_+}(\rho) = u \\ \wedge\ 2(h'e_1' + e_2') + F_{R_+}(\rho) = u' \\ \wedge\ s_1, s_2 \in \mathcal{S}\ \wedge\ \rho \in \mathcal{N} \\ \wedge\ e_1, e_2, e_1', e_2' \in R_\pm \end{array} \right\} (\mu)$$

The conditions in this relation can be rewritten as follows, with appropriate size bounds on different elements. Set $k = F_{R_\pm}(\rho)$ and $l = H_{R_q}(k)$.

$$
\begin{bmatrix} 2h & 2 & 0 & 0 & 1 \\ 0 & 0 & 2h' & 2 & 1 \end{bmatrix} \cdot \begin{bmatrix} e_1 \\ e_2 \\ e_1' \\ e_2' \\ k \end{bmatrix} = \begin{bmatrix} u \\ u' \end{bmatrix} \wedge \begin{bmatrix} a & 1 & -1 \end{bmatrix} \cdot \begin{bmatrix} s_1 \\ s_2 \\ l \end{bmatrix} = 0
$$

$$
\wedge \ \ k = F_{R_\pm}(\rho) \ \wedge \ l = H_{R_q}(k)
$$

We prove the necessary conditions as follows. We use the proof system of [17] to give a zero knowledge proof for the first linear equation, which has an infinity norm bound of 1 on e_1, e_2, e_1', e_2' and k. The size of this proof is roughly 76 group elements and 6 field elements for the parameters that we have chosen. We also use the same proof system from [17] to give a zero-knowledge proof for the second linear equation, with an infinity norm bound of q on s_1, s_2 and l.

The remaining conditions that we have to check are the conditions $k = F_{R_\pm}(\rho)$, $l = H_{R_q}(k)$, and the fact that the ℓ_2-norms of s_1 and s_2 are bounded by $1.5\sigma\sqrt{d}$. We use the proof system of [13] to achieve this. This proof system works with general arithmetic circuits. The number of multiplication gates in the circuit required to prove these conditions is the sum of the sizes of the circuits for $F_{R_\pm}$ and H_{R_q}, plus roughly 2096 extra multiplications which are used for checking that the norms of s_1 and s_2 are bounded correctly. The extra multiplication gates compute the squares of the ℓ_2 norms of each of s_1 and s_2, using 2048 multiplications, check that roughly 48 values are bits by checking that when multiplying them with their complements, the result is zero, and then show that the squares of the ℓ_2 norms are represented by the binary values, so that the norms must be in the correct range. Since we have already used the proof system [17] to check that the infinity norms of s_1 and s_2 are bounded, and we work over a prime field with a much larger modulus than the base ring of s_1 and s_2, we need not worry about overflow when computing the squares of the ℓ_2 norms. We give zero-knowledge proofs of arithmetic circuit satisfiability and prove all of these things using one single proof from [13]. This proof contributes 48 group elements and 5 finite field elements.

In order to use these proof systems, and be sure that certain secret values are consistent across the different proofs, we need to make some adjustments. The first tweak is to split some of the long commitments made in the protocols into several parts, to allow values to be shared between the two proof systems. This is described in the full version. Separate commitments to k and s_1, s_2, l allow these values to be shared between the first two proofs for linear relations and the third proof for non-linear relations.

The second tweak is to modify the protocol of [17] so that it works even if we are proving that the entries of the secret vector lie in an interval whose width is not a power of 2. This is easily achieved using techniques from [15]. The idea is that a binary expansion of the form $\sum_i x_i 2^i$ uniquely expresses every integer in a given interval whose width is a power of 2, but if we change the powers of two in the expression to other values, we can obtain (possibly non-unique) binary expansions for other intervals which suffice for the purpose of giving range proofs. This change has no impact on proof size.

Open: The following zero-knowledge proof is needed:

$$\mathsf{ZKP}_{\mathsf{DLR}}^{\triangle}\left\{(f,g,v) \; : \; \begin{array}{l} hg - f = 0 \;\wedge\; ug = 2v + gm \\ \wedge\; f,g \in R_{\pm} \;\wedge\; v \in \mathcal{R} \text{ s.t. } \|v\|_{\infty} < q/4 - d/2 \end{array}\right\}$$

The conditions in this relation can be rewritten as follows, with appropriate size bounds on different elements.

$$\begin{bmatrix} h & 1 & 0 \\ u & 0 & 2 \end{bmatrix} \cdot \begin{bmatrix} g \\ -f \\ -v \end{bmatrix} = \begin{bmatrix} 0 \\ m \end{bmatrix}$$

This relation is proved by using the proof system from [17] twice. The first proof proves the linear relation from the first row of the matrix, which does not include v. Therefore, the proof system can be used with norm bound 1. The second proof proves the linear relation from the second row of the matrix, which does include v, and therefore works with norm bound $q/4 - d_2$. As with the signing algorithm, we use the adjustments described to make sure that the preimage values are consistent across the two proofs.

References

1. STARK-friendly hash challenge (2019). https://starkware.co/hash-challenge/
2. Albrecht, M.R., et al.: Feistel structures for MPC, and more. Cryptology ePrint Archive, Report 2019/397 (2019). https://eprint.iacr.org/2019/397
3. Albrecht, M., Grassi, L., Rechberger, C., Roy, A., Tiessen, T.: MiMC: efficient encryption and cryptographic hashing with minimal multiplicative complexity. In: Cheon, J.H., Takagi, T. (eds.) ASIACRYPT 2016. LNCS, vol. 10031, pp. 191–219. Springer, Heidelberg (2016). https://doi.org/10.1007/978-3-662-53887-6_7
4. Aly, A., Ashur, T., Ben-Sasson, E., Dhooghe, S., Szepieniec, A.: Design of symmetric-key primitives for advanced cryptographic protocols. Cryptology ePrint Archive, Report 2019/426 (2019). https://eprint.iacr.org/2019/426
5. Bellare, M., Micciancio, D., Warinschi, B.: Foundations of group signatures: formal definitions, simplified requirements, and a construction based on general assumptions. In: Biham, E. (ed.) EUROCRYPT 2003. LNCS, vol. 2656, pp. 614–629. Springer, Heidelberg (2003). https://doi.org/10.1007/3-540-39200-9_38
6. Bellare, M., Shi, H., Zhang, C.: Foundations of group signatures: the case of dynamic groups. In: Menezes, A. (ed.) CT-RSA 2005. LNCS, vol. 3376, pp. 136–153. Springer, Heidelberg (2005). https://doi.org/10.1007/978-3-540-30574-3_11
7. Ben-Sasson, E.: Stark-friendly hash (2019). https://medium.com/starkware/stark-friendly-hash-tire-kicking-8087e8d9a246
8. Benhamouda, F., Camenisch, J., Krenn, S., Lyubashevsky, V., Neven, G.: Better zero-knowledge proofs for lattice encryption and their application to group signatures. In: Sarkar, P., Iwata, T. (eds.) ASIACRYPT 2014. LNCS, vol. 8873, pp. 551–572. Springer, Heidelberg (2014). https://doi.org/10.1007/978-3-662-45611-8_29

9. Bernstein, D.J., Chuengsatiansup, C., Lange, T., van Vredendaal, C.: NTRU prime: reducing attack surface at low cost. In: Adams, C., Camenisch, J. (eds.) SAC 2017. LNCS, vol. 10719, pp. 235–260. Springer, Cham (2018). https://doi.org/10.1007/978-3-319-72565-9_12

10. Bertoni, G., Daemen, J., Peeters, M., Van Assche, G.: On the indifferentiability of the sponge construction. In: Smart, N. (ed.) EUROCRYPT 2008. LNCS, vol. 4965, pp. 181–197. Springer, Heidelberg (2008). https://doi.org/10.1007/978-3-540-78967-3_11

11. Boneh, D., Boyen, X., Shacham, H.: Short group signatures. In: Franklin, M. (ed.) CRYPTO 2004. LNCS, vol. 3152, pp. 41–55. Springer, Heidelberg (2004). https://doi.org/10.1007/978-3-540-28628-8_3

12. Bootle, J., Cerulli, A., Chaidos, P., Groth, J., Petit, C.: Efficient zero-knowledge arguments for arithmetic circuits in the discrete log setting. In: Fischlin, M., Coron, J.-S. (eds.) EUROCRYPT 2016. LNCS, vol. 9666, pp. 327–357. Springer, Heidelberg (2016). https://doi.org/10.1007/978-3-662-49896-5_12

13. Bünz, B., Bootle, J., Boneh, D., Poelstra, A., Wuille, P., Maxwell, G.: Bulletproofs: short proofs for confidential transactions and more. In: IEEE Symposium on Security and Privacy, SP, pp. 315–334 (2018)

14. Camenisch, J., Lysyanskaya, A.: A signature scheme with efficient protocols. In: Cimato, S., Persiano, G., Galdi, C. (eds.) SCN 2002. LNCS, vol. 2576, pp. 268–289. Springer, Heidelberg (2003). https://doi.org/10.1007/3-540-36413-7_20

15. Chaabouni, R., Lipmaa, H., Shelat, A.: Additive combinatorics and discrete logarithm based range protocols. In: Steinfeld, R., Hawkes, P. (eds.) ACISP 2010. LNCS, vol. 6168, pp. 336–351. Springer, Heidelberg (2010). https://doi.org/10.1007/978-3-642-14081-5_21

16. del Pino, R., Lyubashevsky, V., Seiler, G.: Lattice-based group signatures and zero-knowledge proofs of automorphism stability. In: CCS, pp. 574–591 (2018)

17. del Pino, R., Lyubashevsky, V., Seiler, G.: Short discrete log proofs for FHE and ring-LWE ciphertexts. In: Lin, D., Sako, K. (eds.) PKC 2019. LNCS, vol. 11442, pp. 344–373. Springer, Cham (2019). https://doi.org/10.1007/978-3-030-17253-4_12

18. Derler, D., Slamanig, D.: Highly-efficient fully-anonymous dynamic group signatures. In: AsiaCCS, pp. 551–565 (2018)

19. Ducas, L., Lyubashevsky, V., Prest, T.: Efficient identity-based encryption over NTRU lattices. In: Sarkar, P., Iwata, T. (eds.) ASIACRYPT 2014. LNCS, vol. 8874, pp. 22–41. Springer, Heidelberg (2014). https://doi.org/10.1007/978-3-662-45608-8_2

20. Ducas, L., Prest, T.: Fast Fourier orthogonalization. In: ISSAC, pp. 191–198 (2016)

21. Esgin, M.F., Zhao, R.K., Steinfeld, R., Liu, J.K., Liu, D.: MatRiCT: efficient, scalable and post-quantum blockchain confidential transactions protocol. In: CCS, pp. 567–584. ACM (2019)

22. De Feo, L., Masson, S., Petit, C., Sanso, A.: Verifiable delay functions from supersingular isogenies and pairings. In: Galbraith, S.D., Moriai, S. (eds.) ASIACRYPT 2019. LNCS, vol. 11921, pp. 248–277. Springer, Cham (2019). https://doi.org/10.1007/978-3-030-34578-5_10

23. Fowler, A.G., Mariantoni, M., Martinis, J.M., Cleland, A.N.: Surface codes: towards practical large-scale quantum computation. Phys. Rev. A **86**, 032324 (2012)

24. Gentry, C., Peikert, C., Vaikuntanathan, V.: Trapdoors for hard lattices and new cryptographic constructions. In: STOC, pp. 197–206 (2008)

25. Gidney, C.: Why will quantum computers be slow? (2018). http://algassert.com/post/1800. Accessed 22 Feb 2020

26. Grassi, L., Kales, D., Khovratovich, D., Roy, A., Rechberger, C., Schofnegger, M.: Starkad and Poseidon: new hash functions for zero knowledge proof systems. Cryptology ePrint Archive, Report 2019/458 (2019). https://eprint.iacr.org/2019/458

27. Hoffstein, J., Howgrave-Graham, N., Pipher, J., Silverman, J.H., Whyte, W.: NTRUSign: digital signatures using the NTRU lattice. In: Joye, M. (ed.) CT-RSA 2003. LNCS, vol. 2612, pp. 122–140. Springer, Heidelberg (2003). https://doi.org/10.1007/3-540-36563-X_9

28. Hoffstein, J., Pipher, J., Silverman, J.H.: NTRU: a ring-based public key cryptosystem. In: Buhler, J.P. (ed.) ANTS 1998. LNCS, vol. 1423, pp. 267–288. Springer, Heidelberg (1998). https://doi.org/10.1007/BFb0054868

29. Lekitsch, B., et al.: Blueprint for a microwave trapped ion quantum computer. Sci. Adv. **3**(2), e1601540 (2017)

30. Ling, S., Nguyen, K., Stehlé, D., Wang, H.: Improved zero-knowledge proofs of knowledge for the ISIS problem, and applications. In: Kurosawa, K., Hanaoka, G. (eds.) PKC 2013. LNCS, vol. 7778, pp. 107–124. Springer, Heidelberg (2013). https://doi.org/10.1007/978-3-642-36362-7_8

31. Lyubashevsky, V.: Lattice signatures without trapdoors. In: Pointcheval, D., Johansson, T. (eds.) EUROCRYPT 2012. LNCS, vol. 7237, pp. 738–755. Springer, Heidelberg (2012). https://doi.org/10.1007/978-3-642-29011-4_43

32. Lyubashevsky, V., Micciancio, D.: Generalized compact knapsacks are collision resistant. In: Bugliesi, M., Preneel, B., Sassone, V., Wegener, I. (eds.) ICALP 2006, Part II. LNCS, vol. 4052, pp. 144–155. Springer, Heidelberg (2006). https://doi.org/10.1007/11787006_13

33. Peikert, C., Rosen, A.: Efficient collision-resistant hashing from worst-case assumptions on cyclic lattices. In: Halevi, S., Rabin, T. (eds.) TCC 2006. LNCS, vol. 3876, pp. 145–166. Springer, Heidelberg (2006). https://doi.org/10.1007/11681878_8

34. Pointcheval, D., Sanders, O.: Short randomizable signatures. In: Sako, K. (ed.) CT-RSA 2016. LNCS, vol. 9610, pp. 111–126. Springer, Cham (2016). https://doi.org/10.1007/978-3-319-29485-8_7

35. Prest, T., et al.: FALCON. Technical report, National Institute of Standards and Technology (2017). https://csrc.nist.gov/projects/post-quantum-cryptography/round-1-submissions

36. Schanck, J.M.: Security estimator for lattice based cryptosystems (2019). https://github.com/jschanck/estimator

37. Stern, J.: A new identification scheme based on syndrome decoding. In: Stinson, D.R. (ed.) CRYPTO 1993. LNCS, vol. 773, pp. 13–21. Springer, Heidelberg (1994). https://doi.org/10.1007/3-540-48329-2_2

Efficient Post-quantum SNARKs for RSIS and RLWE and Their Applications to Privacy

Cecilia Boschini[1,2]([✉]), Jan Camenisch[3], Max Ovsiankin[4],
and Nicholas Spooner[4]

[1] IBM Research - Zurich, Rüschlikon, Switzerland
[2] Università della Svizzera Italiana, Lugano, Switzerland
cecilia.boschini@gmail.com
[3] Dfinity, Zürich, Switzerland
[4] UC Berkeley, Berkeley, USA

Abstract. In this paper we give efficient statistical zero-knowledge proofs (SNARKs) for Module/Ring LWE and Module/Ring SIS relations, providing the remaining ingredient for building efficient cryptographic protocols from lattice-based hardness assumptions. We achieve our results by exploiting the linear-algebraic nature of the statements supported by the Aurora proof system (Ben-Sasson et al.), which allows us to easily and efficiently encode the linear-algebraic statements that arise in lattice schemes and to side-step the issue of "relaxed extractors", meaning extractors that only recover a witness for a larger relation than the one for which completeness is guaranteed. We apply our approach to the example use case of partially dynamic group signatures and obtain a lattice-based group signature that protects users against corrupted issuers, and that produces signatures smaller than the state of the art, with signature sizes of less than 300 KB for the comparably secure version of the scheme. To obtain our argument size estimates for proof of knowledge of RLWE secret, we implemented the NIZK using libiop.

Keywords: Zero-knowledge proofs · Group signatures · Lattice-based cryptography · Post-quantum cryptography

1 Introduction

We present non-interactive zero knowledge (NIZK) proofs for Module/Ring-LWE and Module/Ring-SIS relations, that have size of the order of 70 kB for 128 bits of security. These proofs rely on Aurora, a SNARK designed by Ben-Sasson et al. [5]. From it, our proofs inherit statistical zero-knowledge and soundness, post-quantum security, exact extractability (that is, the extraction guarantee is for the same relation as the protocol completeness), and transparent setup (no need for a trusted authority to generate the system parameters). Such proofs support

© Springer Nature Switzerland AG 2020
J. Ding and J.-P. Tillich (Eds.): PQCrypto 2020, LNCS 12100, pp. 247–267, 2020.
https://doi.org/10.1007/978-3-030-44223-1_14

algebraic circuits, and therefore can be combined with lattice based building blocks. We show that it is possible to combine this protocol with (the ring version of) Boyen's signature [9], to prove knowledge of a signature on a publicly known message, or knowledge of a valid pair message-signature, and an RLWE-based encryption scheme [21], to prove knowledge of a valid decryption of a given ciphertext. To showcase their efficiency we construct a (partially) dynamic group signature [4], and we compare it with the most efficient NIZK-based group signature to date [12] in Table 1. Differently from ours, the scheme by del Pino et al. does not protect honest users from framing attempts by corrupted issuers (the non-frameability property). Therefore, we compare it with two variants of our scheme: $\mathcal{GS}$, that does not guarantee non-frameability, and $\mathcal{GS}_{\text{full}}$, that also has non-frameability. To compare the security levels of the schemes we consider the Hermite Root Factors (denoted by δ_{HRF}); a smaller delta implies higher security guarantees. In both cases, the NIZK proof is of size less than 250 KB, improving upon the state of the art. The group signature is proven secure in the ROM under RSIS and RLWE. Security in the QROM follows also from [11]; to achieve 128 bits of QROM security requires a three-fold increase in proof size.

Table 1. Comparison for around 90 bits of security.

	Partially dynamic	Anonymous	Traceable	Non-frameable	Users	δ_{HRF}	Signature (MB)
[12]	✓	✓	✓		2^{80}	1.002	0.581
$\mathcal{GS}$	✓	✓	✓		2^{26}	1.0007	0.3
$\mathcal{GS}_{\text{full}}$	✓	✓	✓	✓	2^{26}	1.0007	1.44

We demonstrate the effectiveness of our NIZKs with an implementation. We are able to produce a Ring-LWE proof in around 40 s on a laptop (cf. Sect. 3.7). In comparison, the scheme of [12] produces proofs in under a second. Nonetheless, we consider our NIZK and group signature a benchmark for evaluating efficiency claims for (existing and future) NIZK proofs for lattice relations. In particular, it shows what can be achieved using 'generic' tools.

1.1   Our Techniques

In their simplest form, lattice problems can be generically described as finding a vector $s \in \mathbb{Z}_q^n$ with small coefficients (i.e., $|s_i| \leq \beta$ for all i) such that $Ms = u \bmod q$ for given matrix $M \in \mathbb{Z}_q^{m \times n}$ and vector $u \in \mathbb{Z}_q^m$, q being a prime.

The SNARK Aurora allows to prove knowledge of a witness for a given instance of the *Rank-1 Constraint Satisfaction* (R1CS), i.e., of a vector $z \in \mathbb{F}^{n+1}$ such that, given a vector $v \in \mathbb{F}^k$ and three matrices $A, B, C \in \mathbb{F}^{m \times (n+1)}$, $k < n$, the vector z extends v to satisfy $Az \circ Bz = Cz$, where $\circ$ denotes the entry-wise product. The entries of v are the unknowns of the problem, while the equations they satisfy are called constraints (and are derived from the general equation $Az \circ Bz = Cz$). Hence, we say that the previous R1CS system has

n unknowns and m constraints. Aurora provides proofs of length $O_\lambda(\log^2 N)$, where $f = O_\lambda(\log^2 N)$ means $f = O(\lambda^c \log^2 N)$ for some $c > 0$, and N is the total number of nonzero entries of A, B, C. The conversion of an instance (s, M, u) of the above problem to an instance of R1CS is quite natural. We set $\mathbb{F} := \mathbb{Z}_q$ so that to prove that $Ms = u \bmod q$ holds, it is enough to set $A := [0_{m \times 1}\ M]$, $B := [1_{m \times 1}\ 0_{m \times n}]$, $C := [u\ 0_{m \times n}]$, and $z := [1\ s^T]^T$, where $0_{m \times n}$ (resp. $1_{m \times n}$) is a matrix with m rows and n columns with all components equal to 0 (resp. 1), and the parameter k of the R1CS problem is set to be $k = n$. The number of constraints of this system is m, and the number of variables is n. To prove that the secret vector s has also a small norm, we use binary decomposition. In particular, to prove that a component s_j of s is smaller than $\beta = 2^h$, it is enough to verify that its binary representation is at most h bits long, i.e., $s_j = c_j \sum_{i=0}^{h-1} 2^i b_{i,j}$, with $c_j \in \{\pm 1\}$ and $b_{i,j} \in \{0,1\}\ \forall i$. This is equivalent to proving that $b_{0,j}, \ldots, b_{h-1,j}, s_j$ satisfy the following constraints:

$$ b_{i,j}(1 - b_{i,j}) = 0 \quad \forall i \quad \wedge \quad \left(\sum_{i=0}^{h-1} b_{i,j} 2^i - s_j\right)\left(\sum_{i=0}^{h-1} b_{i,j} 2^i + s_j\right) = 0 . $$

These correspond to the R1CS instance (A_j, B_j, C_j) and witness z_j, with

$$ A_j := \begin{bmatrix} 0 & & 0 \\ \vdots & \mathbb{I}_h & \vdots \\ 0 & & 0 \\ 0\ 1\ 2 \ldots 2^{h-1} & & -1 \end{bmatrix}, \quad B_j := \begin{bmatrix} 1 & & 0 \\ \vdots & -\mathbb{I}_h & \vdots \\ 1 & & 0 \\ 0\ 1\ 2 \ldots 2^{h-1} & & 1 \end{bmatrix}, \quad z_j := \begin{bmatrix} 1 \\ b_{0,j} \\ \vdots \\ b_{h-1,j} \\ s_j \end{bmatrix}, $$

and C_j the all-zero matrix, where $\mathbb{I}_h$ is the identity matrix of dimension h. Thus proving that s has a small norm adds $n(h+1)$ constraints and nh unknowns to the proof (i.e., the coefficients of the bit decomposition of each component of s). Hence, expanding A, B, C, z with all the A_j, B_j, C_j, z_j (taking care not to repeat entries in z) yields the full instance. This includes $m+n(h+1)$ constraints, and the nonzero entries of the matrices A, B, C are $N = nm + 2m + (5h+1)n$, and outputs proofs of length $O(\log^2(n(m+5h+1)+2m))$ (where we recall that h is the logarithm of the bound on the norm of the solution to the lattice problem). The R1CS formalism allows us to prove knowledge of a message-signature pair in Boyen's signature scheme [9] in a natural way (cf. Sect. 3.4).

1.2   Related Work

Both Libert et al. [17] and Baum et al. [3] introduce ZK proof to prove knowledge of solutions of lattice problems that are linear in the length of the secret and in $\log \beta$ respectively (where β is the bound of the norm of the secret vector). Our scheme improves these in that the proof length depends *polylogarithmically* on the length of the secret vector and $\log \beta$. Moreover, we give concrete estimates for parameters that guarantee 128 bits of security. The lattice-based SNARK of [14] relies on the qDH assumption (among others), hence unlike our scheme this is not post-quantum secure, and needs a trusted setup, which prevents to use it to build group signatures with the non-frameability property. Regarding group signature construction, a new construction was published by Katsumata and Yamada [15], that builds group signatures without using NIZK proofs in the standard model. Their construction is of a different form, and, in particular, sidesteps the problem of building NIZKs for lattices, hence we can only compare the signature lengths. Differently from ours, their signature sizes still depend linearly on the number of users (while ours depend polylogarithmically on the number of users) when security is based on standard LWE/SIS. They are able to remove this dependency assuming subexponential hardness for SIS.

2   Preliminaries

We denote vectors and matrices with upper-case letters. Column vectors are denoted as $V = [v_1 ; \ldots ; v_n]$ and row vectors as $V = [v_1 \ldots v_n]$. Sampling and element x from a distribution $\mathcal{D}$ are denoted as $x \xleftarrow{\$} \mathcal{D}$. If x is sampled uniformly over a set A, we write $x \xleftarrow{\$} A$. With $x \leftarrow a$ we denote that x is assigned the value a. When necessary, we denote the uniform distribution over a set S as $\mathcal{U}(S)$. We denote by log the logarithm with base 2. We use the standard Landau notation (i.e., $O(\cdot)$, $\omega(\cdot)$, ...) plus the notation $O_\lambda(\cdot)$, where $f = O_\lambda(g)$ means that there exists $c > 0$ such that $f = O(\lambda^c g)$.

2.1   Preliminaries: Ideal Lattices

Let $\mathbb{Z}[X]$ be the ring of polynomials with integer coefficients, $\mathbf{f} \in \mathbb{Z}[X]$ be a monic, irreducible polynomial of degree n, and $\mathcal{R}$ be the quotient ring $\mathcal{R} := \mathbb{Z}[X]/\langle \mathbf{f} \rangle$. Ring elements are represented with the standard set of representatives $\{\mathbf{g} \bmod \mathbf{f} : \mathbf{g} \in \mathbb{Z}[X]\}$, corresponding to vectors in $\mathbb{Z}^n$ through the standard group homomorphism h that sends $\mathbf{a} = \sum_{i=0}^{n-1} a_i x^i$ to the vector of its coefficients $(a_0, \ldots, a_{n-1})$. Let $\mathcal{R}_q = \mathbb{Z}_q[X]/\langle X^n + 1 \rangle$ for a prime q. Elements in the ring are polynomials of degree at most $n-1$ with coefficients in $[0, q-1]$ and operations between them are done modulo q. For an element $\mathbf{a} = \sum_{i=0}^{n-1} a_i \mathbf{x}^i$, the norms are computed as $\|\mathbf{a}\|_1 = \sum_i |a_i|$, $\|\mathbf{a}\| = \sqrt{\sum_i a_i^2}$ and $\|\mathbf{a}\|_\infty = \max |a_i|$. For a vector $\mathbf{S} = [\mathbf{s}_1, \ldots, \mathbf{s}_m] \in \mathcal{R}^m$, the norm $\|\mathbf{S}\|_p$ is defined as $\max_{i=1}^m \|\mathbf{s}_i\|_p$. Let $\mathcal{S}_1$ be the subset of elements of $\mathcal{R}_q$ with coefficients in $\{0, \pm 1\}$. BitD($\mathbf{a}$) is an algorithm that on input elements $\mathbf{a}_i \in \mathcal{R}_q$, outputs vectors $\vec{a}_i$ containing the binary expansion of the coefficients of $\mathbf{a}_i$. Let deg($\mathbf{a}$) be the degree of the polynomial $\mathbf{a}$. Ideals in $\mathcal{R}$ and $\mathcal{R}_q$ corresponds to lattices in $\mathbb{Z}^n$ and $\mathbb{Z}_q^n$ respectively, through the homomorphism h. A sample $\mathbf{z}$ from a discrete Gaussian $\mathcal{D}_{\mathcal{R}_q, \mathbf{u}, \sigma}$ centered in $\mathbf{u}$ and with std. deviation σ, is generated as a sample from a discrete Gaussian over $\mathbb{Z}^n$ and then map it into $\mathcal{R}_q$ using the obvious embedding of coordinates into coefficients of the polynomials. Similarly, we omit the $\mathbf{0}$ and write $[\mathbf{y}_1 \ldots \mathbf{y}_k] \xleftarrow{\$} \mathcal{D}_{\mathcal{R}_q, \sigma}^k$ to mean that a vector $\mathbf{y}$ is generated according to $\mathcal{D}_{\mathbb{Z}^{kn}, 0, \sigma}$ and then gets interpreted as k polynomials $\mathbf{y}_i$. With an abuse of notation, we denote by $\mathcal{D}^{\perp}_{\mathbf{A},\mathbf{u},s}$ the distribution of the vectors $\mathbf{V} \in \mathcal{R}^m$ such that $\mathbf{V} \sim \mathcal{D}^m_{\mathcal{R},\mathbf{0},s}$ conditioned on $\mathbf{AV} = \mathbf{u} \bmod q$.

Lemma 2.1 (cf. [2, Lemma 1.5], [19, Lemma 4.4]). *Let $m > 0$. The following bounds hold:*

(1) $\Pr_{\mathbf{S} \xleftarrow{\$} \mathcal{D}^m_{\sigma}}(\|\mathbf{S}\| > 1.05\sigma\sqrt{m}) < (0.998)^m$

(2) $\Pr_{\mathbf{S} \xleftarrow{\$} \mathcal{D}^m_{\sigma}}(\|\mathbf{S}\|_{\infty} > 8\sigma) < m2^{-47}$

We recall two well-studied lattice problems over rings: RSIS and RLWE.

Definition 2.2 (RSIS$_{m,q,\beta}$ problem [21]). *The RSIS$_{m,q,\beta}$ problem asks given a vector $\mathbf{A} \xleftarrow{\$} \mathcal{R}^{1\times m}_q$ to find a vector $\mathbf{S} \in \mathcal{R}^m_q$ such that $\mathbf{AS} = \mathbf{0} \bmod q$ and $\|\mathbf{S}\| \leq \beta$. The inhomogeneous version of RSIS asks to find $\mathbf{S} \in \mathcal{R}^m_q$ such that $\mathbf{AS} = \mathbf{u}$, and $\|\mathbf{S}\| \leq \beta$ for given uniformly random $\mathbf{A}$ and $\mathbf{u}$.*

Definition 2.3. RLWE$_{k,\chi}$ problem, normal form, cf. [22] *The RLWE$_{\chi,\mathbf{s}}$ distribution (resp., the RLWE$_\chi$ distribution in the normal form) outputs pairs $(\mathbf{a},\mathbf{b}) \in \mathcal{R}_q \times \mathcal{R}_q$ such that $\mathbf{b} = \mathbf{as} + \mathbf{e}$ for a uniformly random $\mathbf{a}$ from $\mathcal{R}_q$, $\mathbf{s} \in \mathcal{R}_q$ and $\mathbf{e}$ sampled from distribution χ (resp., $\mathbf{a} \xleftarrow{\$} \mathcal{R}_q$, $\mathbf{s}, \mathbf{e} \xleftarrow{\$} \chi$). The RLWE$_{k,\chi}$ decisional problem on ring $\mathcal{R}_q$ with distribution χ is to distinguish whether k pairs $(\mathbf{a}_1,\mathbf{b}_1), \ldots, (\mathbf{a}_k,\mathbf{b}_k)$ were sampled from the RLWE$_\chi$ distribution or from the uniform distribution over $\mathcal{R}^2_q$. The RLWE$_{k,\chi}$ search problem on ring $\mathcal{R}_q$ with distribution χ is given k pairs $(\mathbf{a}_1,\mathbf{b}_1), \ldots, (\mathbf{a}_k,\mathbf{b}_k)$ sampled from the RLWE$_\chi$ distribution, find $\mathbf{s}$.*

Module-RSIS and Module-RLWE [16] are a more general formulation of RSIS and RLWE. *Module-RSIS* asks to find a short vector $\mathbf{S} \in \mathcal{R}^{m_2}_q$ such that $\mathbf{AS} = \mathbf{0}$ given a *matrix* $\mathbf{A} \xleftarrow{\$} \mathcal{R}^{m_1\times m_2}_q$ (the inhomogeneous version is defined analogously). The *Module-RLWE* distribution outputs pairs $(\mathbf{A}, \langle \mathbf{A},\mathbf{S}\rangle + \mathbf{e}) \in \mathcal{R}^k_q \times \mathcal{R}_q$, where the secret $\mathbf{S}$ and the error $\mathbf{e}$ are drawn from $\mathcal{R}^k_q$ and $\mathcal{R}_q$ respectively.

2.2 RLWE Encryption Scheme

Let n be a power of 2, p, and q be two primes such that $q \gg p$, and χ be an error distribution. The RLWE encryption scheme (EParGen, EKeyGen, Enc, Dec) [22] to encrypt a binary message $\mu \in \mathcal{S}_1$ works as follows. On input the security parameter λ, the parameters generation EParGen outputs (n,p,q). The key generator EKeyGen samples $\mathbf{a} \xleftarrow{\$} \mathcal{R}_q$, $\mathbf{s} \xleftarrow{\$} \mathcal{R}_q$ and $\mathbf{d} \leftarrow \chi$, and sets $\mathbf{b} = \mathbf{as} + \mathbf{d} \bmod q$. The encryption key is $epk = (\mathbf{a},\mathbf{b})$, the decryption key is $esk = \mathbf{s}$. On input a message μ, the encryption algorithm Enc generates the ciphertext $(\mathbf{v},\mathbf{w})$ as $\mathbf{v} = p(\mathbf{ar} + \mathbf{e}) \bmod q$, $\mathbf{w} = p(\mathbf{br} + \mathbf{f}) + \mu \bmod q$, where $\mathbf{e},\mathbf{f} \xleftarrow{\$} \chi$ and $\mathbf{r} \xleftarrow{\$} \mathcal{R}_q$. Decryption amounts to computing $(\mathbf{w} - \mathbf{sv} \bmod q) \bmod p$. This encryption scheme is IND-CPA secure under RLWE$_{1,\chi}$, and can be made IND-CCA2 secure combining it with a non-malleable NIZK proof system following Naor-Yung construction [25]. In our instantiation we choose the error distribution χ to be a Gaussian distribution with standard deviation $s_{RLWE} = \omega(\sqrt{\log q})$ (cf. Theorem 1 in [10]).

We remark that this encryption scheme encrypts plaintexts that are polynomials of degree n with binary coefficients. In case it would be necessary to encrypt a bit string $\vec{b} = (b_1, \ldots, b_k)$, we assume the encryption algorithm first converts it to an element of $\mathcal{S}_1$ (or more than one, if $k > n$) by setting $b_i = 0$ for $k < i \leq n$ and constructing the polynomial $\mathbf{b} = \sum_{i=1}^{n} b_i x^{i-1}$ (the case $k > n$ is analogous).

2.3   Boyen's Signature on Ideal Lattices

A digital signature scheme is composed by 4 PPT algorithms (SParGen, SKeyGen, Sign, SVerify). Existential unforgeability against adaptive chosen-message attacks (*eu-acma*) requires that the adversary should not be able to forge a signature on some message μ^* of her choice, even if she has access to a signing oracle. In this section we describe the variant of Boyen's signature [9] by Micciancio and Peikert [23], adapted to have security based on hardness assumptions on ideal lattices. Such variant has been claimed to be secure since long time, but, to the best of our knowledge, this is the first time in which a security proof is given explicitly (cf. the full version of this paper). In particular, we prove the signature secure when defined over the $(2n)$-th cyclotomic ring.

Theorem 2.4 (Trapdoor generation, from [23]). *Let $\mathcal{R}_q$ be a power of 2 cyclotomic ring and set parameters $m = 2$, $k = \lceil \log q \rceil$, $\bar{m} = m + k$. There exists an algorithm GenTrap that outputs a vector $\bar{\mathbf{A}} \in \mathcal{R}_q^{1 \times \bar{m}}$ and a trapdoor $\mathbf{R} \in \mathcal{R}_q^{m \times k}$ with tag $\mathbf{h} \in \mathcal{R}_q$ such that:*

- $\bar{\mathbf{A}} = [\mathbf{A} | \mathbf{A}\mathbf{R} + h\mathbf{G}]$, *where* $\mathbf{G}$ *is the* gadget matrix, $\mathbf{G} = [1\,2\,4 \ldots 2^{k-1}]$, *and* $\mathbf{A} = [\mathbf{a}|1] \in \mathcal{R}_q^{1 \times 2}$, $\mathbf{a} \xleftarrow{\$} \mathcal{R}_q$.
- $\mathbf{R}$ *is distributed as a Gaussian* $\mathcal{D}_{\mathcal{R},s}^{2 \times k}$ *for some* $s = \alpha q$, *where* $\alpha > 0$ *is a RLWE error term, $\alpha q > \omega(\sqrt{\log n})$ (cf [22, Theorem 2.22]).*
- $\mathbf{h}$ *is an invertible element in* $\mathcal{R}_q$.
- $\bar{\mathbf{A}}$ *is computationally pseudrandom (ignoring the component set to* **1***) under (decisional) RLWE$_D$ where $D = \mathcal{D}_{\mathcal{R},s}$.*

Genise and Micciancio [13] give an optimal sampling algorithm for the previous trapdoor construction.

Theorem 2.5 (Gaussian sampler, adapted from [23] and [13]). *Let $\mathcal{R}_q$, m, k, $\bar{m}$ be as in Theorem 2.4, $\mathbf{G}$ be the gadget matrix $\mathbf{G} = [1\,2\,4 \ldots 2^{k-1}]$, $\mathbf{A} \in \mathcal{R}_q^{1 \times m}$ and $\mathbf{R} \in \mathcal{R}_q^{2 \times k}$ be the output of GenTrap, and $\mathbf{B}$ a vector in $\mathcal{R}_q^{1 \times d}$ for some $d \geq 0$. Then, there is an algorithm that can sample from the distribution $\mathcal{D}_{[\mathbf{A} \mid \mathbf{A}\mathbf{R}+\mathbf{G} \mid \mathbf{B}],\mathbf{u},s}^{\perp}$ for any $s = O(\sqrt{n \log q}) \cdot \omega(\sqrt{\log n})$ for any $\mathbf{u} \in \mathcal{R}_q$ in time $\tilde{O}(n \log q)$ for the offline phase and $\tilde{O}(n^2)$ for the online phase.*

The original signature was proved existentially unforgeable against adaptive chosen-message attacks *eu-acma* under SIS. Micciancio and Peikert proved their variant to be strongly unforgeable against static chosen-message attack (*su-scma*) under SIS with a tighter reduction, and then made it strongly unforgeable against adaptive chosen-message attacks *su-acma* using chameleon hash functions [26]. For our purposes adaptive existential unforgeability is enough, so our aim is to prove the scheme *eu-acma* under RSIS combining the techniques used in the proofs of these two papers.

Parameters. *spar* ← SParGen(1^λ)

Let $\mathbf{f}$ be the $(2n)$-th cyclotomic polynomial, $\mathbf{f} = \mathbf{x}^n + 1$. Construct the polynomial rings $\mathcal{R} = \mathbb{Z}[X]/\langle \mathbf{f} \rangle$ and $\mathcal{R}_q = \mathbb{Z}_q[X]/\langle \mathbf{f} \rangle$. Let $k = \lceil \log_2 q \rceil$, $m = 2$, and $\bar{m} = m + k = 2 + \lceil \log q \rceil$ be the length of the public matrices, and ℓ be the length of the message. Let $s_{ssk} = \sqrt{\log(n^2)} + 1$ and $s_\sigma = \sqrt{n \log n} \cdot \sqrt{\log n^2}$ be the standard deviations of the distributions of the signing key and of the signature respectively (their values are determined following Theorems 2.4 and 2.5 respectively).

Key Generation. (svk, ssk) ← SKeyGen($spar$)

Run the algorithm GenTrap from Theorem 2.4 to get a vector $[\mathbf{A} \mid \mathbf{B}] = [\mathbf{A} \mid \mathbf{AR} + \mathbf{G}]$ and a trapdoor $\mathbf{R}$. The public key is composed by $\ell + 1$ random matrices $\mathbf{A}_0, \ldots, \mathbf{A}_\ell \overset{\$}{\leftarrow} \mathcal{R}_q^{1 \times k}$, a random vector $\mathbf{u} \overset{\$}{\leftarrow} \mathcal{R}_q$ and the vector $[\mathbf{A} \mid \mathbf{B}] \in \mathcal{R}_q^{1 \times \bar{m}}$. i.e., $svk = (\mathbf{A}, \mathbf{B}, \mathbf{A}_0, \ldots, \mathbf{A}_\ell, \mathbf{u})$, and the (secret) signing key is $ssk = \mathbf{R}$. Remark that the probability distribution of $\mathbf{R}$ is $\mathcal{D}_{\mathcal{R}, s_{ssk}}^{2 \times k}$.

Signing. σ ← Sign(μ, ssk)

To sign a message $\mu = (\mu_1, \ldots, \mu_\ell) \in \{0, 1\}^\ell$, the signer constructs a message-dependent public vector $\mathbf{A}_\mu = [\mathbf{A} \mid \mathbf{B} \mid \mathbf{A}_0 + \sum_{i=1}^{\ell} (-1)^{\mu_i} \mathbf{A}_i]$ and then it samples a short vector $\mathbf{S} \in \mathcal{R}_q^{\bar{m}+k}$ running the algorithm SampleD from Theorem 2.5 on input $(\mathbf{A}_\mu, \mathbf{u}, \mathbf{R})$. The algorithm outputs the signature $\sigma = \mathbf{S}$. Remark that the probability distribution of the signature $\mathbf{S}$ is $\mathcal{D}_{\mathbf{A}_\mu, \mathbf{u}, s_\sigma}^\perp$.

Verification. $\{0, 1\}$ ← SVerify(σ, μ, svk)

The verifier checks that the vector $\mathbf{S}$ has small norm, i.e., $\|\mathbf{S}\|_\infty \leq 8 s_\sigma$. Then, he constructs $\mathbf{A}_\mu = [\mathbf{A} \mid \mathbf{B} \mid \mathbf{A}_0 + \sum_{i=1}^{\ell} (-1)^{\mu_i} \mathbf{A}_i]$ and checks that $\mathbf{S}$ satisfies the verification equation, i.e., $\mathbf{A}_\mu \mathbf{S} = \mathbf{u} \mod q$.

Correctness follows from Theorems 2.4 and 2.5 and from Lemma 2.1. We prove the *eu-acma* security of the scheme under RSIS by proving that if there exists a PPT adversary A that can break the signature scheme we can construct an algorithm B that can solve RSIS exploiting A. The proof is obtained combining the message guessing technique in the proof of Theorem 25 in [9] with the proof of Theorem 6.1 in [23] and can be found in the full version.

Theorem 2.6 *(eu-acma security).* *If there exists a PPT adversary* A *that can break the* eu-acma *security of the signature scheme* (SParGen, SKeyGen, Sign, SVerify) *in time* t_A *with probability* ϵ_A *asking* q_A *queries to the signing oracle, then there exists a PPT algorithm* B *that can solve* $RSIS_{\bar{m}+1, q, \beta}$ *for a* *large enough* $\beta = 8s_\sigma + (\ell + 1)kn8s_\sigma$ *exploiting* A *in time* $t_B \sim t_A$ *with probability* $\epsilon_B = \epsilon_A \cdot (1 - \epsilon_{RLWE}) \cdot \frac{1}{q}\left(1 - \frac{q_A}{q}\right)$ *or a PPT algorithm that solves* $RLWE_{(\ell+1)k,\mathcal{U}(S_1)}$ *with probability* ϵ_A *in time* t_A.

2.4   The Aurora Protocol

Aurora is a Interactive Oracle Proof for R1CS relations by Ben-Sasson et al. [5].

Definition 2.7 (R1CS relation). *The relation* $\mathcal{R}_{R1CS}$ *consists of the set of all pairs* $((\mathbb{F}, k, m, n, A, B, C, v), w)$ *where* $\mathbb{F}$ *is a finite field,* k *is the number of inputs,* n *is the number of variables,* m *is the number of constraints,* A, B, C *are matrices in* $\mathbb{F}^{m \times (n+1)}$, $v \in \mathbb{F}^k$, *and* $w \in \mathbb{F}^{n-k}$ *such that* $Az \circ Bz = Cz$ *where* $z = (1, v, w) \in \mathbb{F}^{n+1}$ *and* $\circ$ *denotes entry-wise (Hadamard) product.*

The following theorem summarizes the properties of Aurora when compiled to a SNARK via the transform by Ben-Sasson et al. (cf. Theorem 7.1 in [6]). In the statement below, $N := \max(m, n)$; generally n and m will be of roughly the same magnitude.

Theorem 2.8 (informal, cf. Theorem 1.2 in [5]). *There exists a non-interactive zero-knowledge argument for R1CS that is unconditionally secure in the random oracle model with proof length* $O(\lambda^2 \log^2 N)$ *and one-time simulation soundness error* $2^{-\lambda}$ *against adversaries making at most* 2^λ *queries to the oracle. The prover runs in time* $O_\lambda(N \log N)$ *and the verifier in time* $O_\lambda(N)$.

Remark 2.9 (Simulation soundness). To use the above construction in the Naor–Yung paradigm, as we later do, requires one-time simulation soundness (OTSS). This is shown as follows; we assume some familiarity with [7]. Let π be a proof output by the simulator for a statement x supplied by the adversary. First recall that to achieve adaptive soundness and zero knowledge, the oracle queries of the verifier and honest prover are prefixed with the statement x and a fresh random string $r \in \{0,1\}^\lambda$. Since with high probability no efficient adversary can find $x' \neq x, q, q'$ such that $\rho(x\|r\|q) = \rho(x'\|r\|q')$, if the adversary in the OTSS game chooses an instance different from that of the simulated proof, the success probability of the extractor is affected only by a negligible amount.

Now suppose that an adversary generates a different proof $\pi' \neq \pi$ of the same statement x. In the Aurora IOP, the query locations for the first oracle are a uniformly random subset of $[\ell]$ (where ℓ is the oracle length, $\ell = \Omega(N)$) of size $\Omega(\lambda)$. This is determined by the verifier's final randomness, which in the compiled NIZK depends on all of the Merkle tree roots; these are all included in π. Moreover, these collectively depend on every symbol of π; hence no efficient adversary can find a valid $\pi' \neq \pi$ whose query set is the same as that of π. In particular, the Merkle tree root corresponding to the *first* round has some query in π' which is not in π; since it is infeasible to find an accepting authentication path for this query relative to the root provided by the simulator, the value of this root must differ between π and π'. It follows that, with high probability, the extractor only 'programs' queries which were not already programmed by the simulator, and so one-time simulation soundness holds.

3   NIZKs for Lattices from R1CS

We build the NIZKs from simple, reusable building blocks. When composing these building blocks, it is often necessary to make explicit inputs private. Generally this involves no additional complication; if changes are needed to ensure soundness, we will point them out. When we construct R1CS instances (cf. Definition 2.7), we typically write down a list of variables and constraints, rather than explicitly constructing the matrices.

3.1   Basic Operations

We describe how to express some basic lattice operations in $\mathcal{R}_q$ as arithmetic operations over $\mathbb{F}_q \cong \mathbb{Z}_q$ for prime q.

Representation of Ring Elements. We represent ring elements as vectors in $\mathbb{F}_q^n$ w.r.t. some basis of $\mathcal{R}_q$. Note that regardless of the choice of basis, addition in $\mathcal{R}_q$ corresponds exactly to component-wise addition of vectors. An $\mathcal{R}_q$-element is denoted by a lowercase bold letter (e.g. $\mathbf{a}$) and the corresponding vector in $\mathbb{F}_q^n$ by an arrow (e.g. $\vec{a}$). A vector in $\mathcal{R}_q^m$ is denoted by an uppercase bold letter (e.g. $\mathbf{A}$) and the corresponding matrix in $\mathbb{F}_q^{m \times n}$, whose rows are the coefficients of the elements of the vector, is denoted by an uppercase letter (e.g. A).

Bases. We will use two bases: the coefficient basis and the evaluation or number-theoretic transform (NTT) basis. The NTT basis, which is the discrete Fourier basis over $\mathbb{F}_q$, allows polynomial multiplication to be expressed as pointwise multiplication of vectors. Transforming from the coefficient basis to the NTT basis is a linear transformation $T \in \mathbb{F}_q^{n \times n}$. The choice of basis depends on the type of constraint we wish to check; generally we will represent inputs in the coefficient basis. An issue with the NTT basis is that to multiply ring elements $\mathbf{a}, \mathbf{b} \in \mathcal{R}_q$ naively requires us to compute the degree-$2n$ polynomial $\mathbf{ab} \in \mathbb{F}_q[X]$ and then reduce modulo $X^n + 1$. This would make multiplying ring elements quite expensive. For our choice of $\mathcal{R}_q$, however, so long as q has $2n$-th roots of unity we can employ the *negative wrapped convolution* [20], which is a linear transform T such that if $\vec{a}, \vec{b}, \vec{c}$ represent the coefficients of $\mathbf{a}, \mathbf{b}, \mathbf{c} \in \mathcal{R}_q$ respectively, $T\vec{a} \circ T\vec{b} = T\vec{c}$ if and only if $\mathbf{c} = \mathbf{ab}$ in $\mathcal{R}_q$. From here on, T is the negative wrapped convolution.

Addition and Multiplication. Following the above discussions, addition is (always) componentwise over $\mathbb{F}_q$ and multiplication is componentwise in the NTT basis. Hence to check that $\mathbf{a} + \mathbf{b} = \mathbf{c}$ or $\mathbf{a} \cdot \mathbf{b} = \mathbf{c}$ in $\mathcal{R}_q$ when $\mathbf{a}, \mathbf{b}, \mathbf{c}$ are represented in the coefficient basis as $\vec{a}, \vec{b}, \vec{c}$, we use the constraint systems $\vec{a} + \vec{b} = \vec{c}$ or $T\vec{a} \circ T\vec{b} = T\vec{c}$ respectively. Each of these 'constraints' is a shorthand for a set of n constraints, one for each dimension; i.e., $a_i + b_i = c_i$ for all $i \in [n]$, or $\langle T_i, \vec{a} \rangle \circ \langle T_i, \vec{b} \rangle = \langle T_i, \vec{c} \rangle$ for all $i \in [n]$ where T_i is the i-th row of T.

Decomposition. A simple but very important component of many primitives is computing the subset-sum decomposition of a $\mathbb{Z}_q$-element a with respect to a list of $\mathbb{Z}_q$-elements $(e_1, \ldots, e_\ell)$; that is, finding $b_1, \ldots, b_\ell$ such that $b_i \in \{0, 1\}$ and $\sum_{i=1}^{\ell} b_i e_i = a$. For example, when $e_i = 2^{i-1}$ for each i, this is the bit decomposition of a. The following simple constraint system enforces that $b_1, \ldots, b_\ell$ is the subset-sum decomposition of $a \in \mathbb{F}_q$ with respect to $(e_1, \ldots, e_\ell)$.

$$b_i(1 - b_i) = 0 \quad \forall i \in \{0, \ldots, \ell - 1\} \quad \wedge \quad \sum_{i=0}^{\ell-1} b_i e_i - a = 0$$

For the case of $e_i = 2^{i-1}$ we will use the notation $\vec{b} = \mathsf{BitDec}(a)$ to represent this constraint system. For a vector $\vec{a} \in \mathbb{F}_q^n$ and matrix $B \in \mathbb{F}_q^{n \times \ell}$ we write $B = \mathsf{BitDec}(\vec{a})$ for the constraint system "$B_j = \mathsf{BitDec}(a_j) \quad \forall j \in [k]$", for B_j the j-th row of B.

Proof of Shortness. Showing that $a \in \mathbb{Z}_q$ is bounded by $\beta < (p-1)/2$, i.e. $-\beta < a < \beta$, can be achieved using its decomposition. It was observed in [18] that taking $e_1 = \lceil \beta/2 \rceil, e_2 = \lceil (\beta - b_1)/2 \rceil, \ldots, e_\ell = 1$ for $\ell = \lceil \log \beta \rceil$ yields a set of integers whose subset sums are precisely $\{0, \ldots, \beta - 1\}$. We then have that $|a| < \beta$ if and only if there exist $b_1, \ldots, b_\ell \in \{0, 1\}, c \in \{-1, 1\}$ such that $c \sum_{i=1}^{\ell} b_i e_i = a$. The prover will supply $b_1, \ldots, b_\ell$ as part of the witness. This introduces the following constraints:

$$b_i(1 - b_i) = 0 \quad \forall i \quad \wedge \quad \left(\sum_{i=1}^{\ell} b_i e_i - a \right)\left(\sum_{i=0}^{k-1} b_i e_i + a \right) = 0$$

The number of new variables is k; the number of constraints is $k + 1$. When we describe R1CS instances we will write the above constraint system as "$|a| < \beta$". For $\vec{a} \in \mathbb{Z}_q^n$, we will write "$\|\vec{a}\|_\infty < \beta$" for the constraint system "$|a_i| < \beta \quad \forall i \in [n]$", i.e. n independent copies of the above constraint system, one for each entry of $\vec{a}$.

3.2 Proof of Knowledge of RLWE Secret Key

We give a proof of knowledge for the relation $\mathcal{R} = \{(\mathbf{c}, \mathbf{d}; \mathbf{t}, \mathbf{e}) \in \mathcal{R}_q^4 \; : \; \mathbf{d} = \mathbf{ct} + \mathbf{e} \bmod q \wedge \|\mathbf{e}\|_\infty < \beta\}$. Let $\vec{c}, \vec{d}, \vec{t}, \vec{e} \in \mathbb{F}_q^n$ encode $\mathbf{c}, \mathbf{d}, \mathbf{t}, \mathbf{e}$ in the coefficient basis. The condition is encoded by the following constraint system:

$$T\vec{c} \circ T\vec{t} = T\vec{f} \quad \wedge \quad \vec{f} + \vec{e} = \vec{d} \quad \wedge \quad \|\vec{e}\|_\infty \le \beta$$

where $\vec{f} \in \mathbb{F}_q^n$ should be the coefficient representation of $\mathbf{ct}$. The number of variables and constraints are bounded by $n(\log \beta + 6)$. We write $\mathsf{RLWE}_\beta(\vec{c}, \vec{d}, \vec{t}, \vec{e})$ as shorthand for the above system of constraints. Note that we did not use the fact that the verifier knows $\vec{c}, \vec{d}$; this will allow us to later use the same constraint system when $\vec{c}, \vec{d}$ are also secret. Hence, applying Theorem 2.8 yields the following.

Lemma 3.1. *There is a NIZK proof (SNARK) for the relation* $\mathcal{R}$, *secure and extractable in the random oracle model, with proof length* $O(\lambda^2 \log^2 (n \log \beta) \log q)$.

With our parameters as given in Sect. 5.4, the size of a NIZK for a single proof of knowledge of an RLWE secret key is 72 kB (obtained from our implementation Sect. 4 using libiop). Constraint systems for RSIS, Module-RSIS and Module-RLWE can be derived similarly.

3.3   Proof of Knowledge of Plaintext

We give a proof of knowledge for the relation $\mathcal{R} = \{(\mathbf{a}, \mathbf{b}, \mathbf{v}, \mathbf{w}; \mathbf{e}, \mathbf{f}, \mathbf{r}, \mu) \in \mathcal{R}_q^7 \times \mathcal{S}_1 : \mathbf{v} = p(\mathbf{ar} + \mathbf{e}) \wedge \mathbf{w} = p(\mathbf{br} + \mathbf{f}) + \mu \wedge \|\mathbf{e}\|_\infty, \|\mathbf{f}\|_\infty < \beta\}$. Recall that $\mathcal{S}_1 \subseteq \mathcal{R}_q$ is the set of all polynomials of degree less than n whose coefficients are in $\{0, 1\}$, which is in natural bijection with the set $\{0, 1\}^n$.

Let $\vec{a}, \vec{b}, \vec{v}, \vec{w}, \vec{e}, \vec{f}, \vec{r}, \vec{\mu} \in \mathbb{F}_q^n$ be the coefficient representations of the corresponding ring elements. The condition is encoded by the following constraint system:
$$\mathsf{RLWE}_\beta(\vec{g}, \vec{a}, \vec{r}, \vec{e}) \wedge \mathsf{RLWE}_\beta(\vec{h}, \vec{b}, \vec{r}, \vec{f}) \wedge \vec{w} = p \cdot \vec{g} \wedge \vec{v} = p \cdot \vec{h} + \vec{\mu} \wedge \mu_i(\mu_i - 1) = 0 \ \forall i.$$

The number of variables is $n(2 \log \beta + 10)$; the number of constraints is $n(2 \log \beta + 15)$. This constraint system (repeated twice) is also used to build the NIZK required for the Naor-Yung construction. We write "$\vec{v}, \vec{w} = \mathsf{Enc}_p(\vec{a}, \vec{b}, \vec{r}, \vec{\mu})$" to denote the above system of constraints; $\vec{e}$ and $\vec{f}$ will be fresh variables for each instance of the system. Once again, we do not use the fact that the verifier knows $\vec{a}, \vec{b}, \vec{v}, \vec{w}$, which will be useful later.

To encrypt tn bits, we simply encrypt t n-bit blocks separately. The constraint system is then given by t copies of the above system. We will use the notation $V, W = \mathsf{Enc}_p(\vec{a}, \vec{b}, \vec{r}, \vec{\mu})$ to represent this, where V, W are $n \times k$ matrices whose rows are the encryptions of each n-bit block.

3.4   Proof of Valid Signature

An important component of the group signature scheme is proving knowledge of a message $\mu \in \{0, 1\}^\ell$ together with a Boyen signature on μ (see Sect. 2.3). We first consider a simpler relation, where we prove knowledge of a signature on a publicly-known message. In the Boyen signature scheme, this corresponds to checking an inner product of ring elements, along with a proof of shortness for the signature. This corresponds to checking the relation $\mathcal{R} = \{(\mathbf{A}_\mu, \mathbf{u}; \mathbf{S}) \in (\mathcal{R}_q^{1 \times k} \times \mathcal{R}_q) \times \mathcal{R}_q^k : \mathbf{A}_\mu \mathbf{S} = \mathbf{u} \wedge \|\mathbf{S}\|_\infty < \beta\}$. Let $A, S \in \mathbb{F}_q^{k \times n}$ be the matrices whose rows are the coefficients of the entries of $\mathbf{A}_\mu, \mathbf{S}$, and let $\vec{u} \in \mathbb{F}_q^n$ be the coefficient representation of $\mathbf{u}$. We obtain the following constraint system:

$$TA_i \circ TS_i = TF_i \quad \forall i \in [k], \quad \wedge \quad \sum_{i=1}^k F_i = \vec{u}, \quad \wedge \quad \|S_i\|_\infty < \beta \quad \forall i \in [k]$$

where $F \in \mathbb{F}_q^{k \times n}$, and A_i, S_i, F_i are the i-th rows of the corresponding matrices.

Now we turn to the more complex task of proving knowledge of a (secret) message and a signature on that message. Here the verifier can no longer compute $\mathbf{A}_\mu$ by itself, and so the work must be done in the proof. In particular, we check the following relation.

$$\mathcal{R} = \left\{ \begin{array}{l} ([\mathbf{A} \mid \mathbf{B}], \mathcal{A}, \mathbf{u}; \mu, \mathbf{S}) \in \mathcal{R}_q^{1 \times m} \times \\ \times (\mathcal{R}_q^{1 \times k})^{\ell+1} \times \mathcal{R}_q \times \{0,1\}^\ell \times \mathcal{R}_q^{m+k} \end{array} : \mathbf{A}_\mu \mathbf{S} = \mathbf{u} \wedge \|\mathbf{S}\|_\infty < \beta \right\},$$

where $\mathcal{A} = (\mathbf{A}_0, \ldots, \mathbf{A}_\ell)$ and $\mathbf{A}_\mu = [\mathbf{A} \mid \mathbf{B} \mid \mathbf{A}_0 + \sum_{i=1}^\ell (-1)^{\mu_i} \mathbf{A}_i]$. Let $M \in \mathbb{F}^{m \times n}$ be the matrix whose rows are the coefficients of the entries of $[\mathbf{A} \mid \mathbf{B}]$, and let $A_0, \ldots, A_\ell \in \mathbb{F}^{k \times n}$ be matrices whose rows are the coefficients of the entries of $\mathbf{A}_0, \ldots, \mathbf{A}_\ell$ respectively. Let $\mu' = ((-1)^{\mu_1}, \ldots, (-1)^{\mu_\ell})$ be the string in $\{\pm 1\}^\ell$ corresponding to the message μ. Clearly, the transform from μ to μ' is bijective. Let $A_i' \in \mathbb{F}^{n \times (\ell+1)}$ be such that the j-th column of A_i' is the i-th row of A_j (i.e., the coefficients of the i-th entry of A_j). Observe that $A_i' \cdot (1, \mu')$ is the coefficient representation of the i-th entry of $\mathbf{A}_0 + \sum_{j=1}^\ell \mu_j' \mathbf{A}_j$. Given this, the following constraint system captures the relation we need:

$$TM_i \circ TS_i = TF_i \quad \forall i \in [m], \quad \wedge \quad (TA_i')(1, \mu) \circ TS_{m+i} = TF_{m+i} \quad \forall i \in [k]$$

$$\sum_{i=1}^{k+m} F_i = \vec{u}, \quad \wedge \quad (1 + \mu_i) \cdot (1 - \mu_i) = 0 \quad \forall i \in [\ell], \quad \wedge \quad \|S_i\|_\infty < \beta \quad \forall i \in [m+k]$$

with $F \in \mathbb{F}_q^{(m+k) \times n}$. We will denote the above constraint system by $\mathsf{SVerify}_\beta(M, \mathcal{A}, \vec{u}, S, \mu)$, with $\mathcal{A} = (A_0, \ldots, A_\ell)$. The number of variables and constraints are bounded by $(4 + \log \beta)(m + k)n + k(\max(n, \ell + 1))$.

3.5   Signature Generation

Here we specify the relation whose proof constitutes a signature for our group signature scheme; see Sect. 5.2 for details. We repeat its formal description below.

$$\mathcal{R}_S = \left\{ \begin{array}{l} (\mathbf{A}, \mathbf{B}, \mathcal{A}, \mathbf{u}, (\mathbf{a}_0, \mathbf{b}_0, \mathbf{a}_1, \mathbf{b}_1), \\ (\mathbf{V}_0, \mathbf{W}_0), (\mathbf{V}_1, \mathbf{W}_1); \mathbf{t}, i, \mathbf{c}, \mathbf{d}, \mathbf{e}, \mathbf{S}) \end{array} \text{ s.t. } \begin{array}{l} 1 \leftarrow \mathsf{SVerify}(\mathbf{S}, (\mathbf{c}, \mathbf{d}, i), \mathbf{A}, \mathbf{B}, \mathbf{A}_0, \ldots, \mathbf{A}_\ell, \mathbf{u}) \\ \wedge \; \mathbf{d} = \mathbf{ct} + \mathbf{e} \wedge \|\mathbf{e}\| \leq \beta' \\ \wedge \; (\mathbf{V}_0, \mathbf{W}_0) \leftarrow \mathsf{Enc}(i, \mathbf{c}, \mathbf{d}, (\mathbf{a}_0, \mathbf{b}_0)) \\ \wedge \; (\mathbf{V}_1, \mathbf{W}_1) \leftarrow \mathsf{Enc}(i, \mathbf{c}, \mathbf{d}, (\mathbf{a}_1, \mathbf{b}_1)) \end{array} \right\}$$

We now describe the constraint system which represents this relation. The variables $\vec{c}, \vec{d}, \vec{e}, i, A, B, \mathcal{A}, \vec{u}, S, \vec{a}_0, \vec{a}_1, \vec{b}_0, \vec{b}_1, V_0, W_0, V_1, W_1$ are the coefficient representations of the corresponding variables in the relation. Using the notation defined in the previous subsections, the constraint system is as follows.

$$C = \mathsf{BitDec}(\vec{c}) \quad \wedge \quad D = \mathsf{BitDec}(\vec{d}) \quad \wedge \quad \vec{i} = \mathsf{BitDec}(i) \quad \wedge$$

$$\mathsf{SVerify}_\beta([A|B], \mathcal{A}, \vec{u}, S, (C, D, \vec{i})) \quad \wedge \quad \mathsf{RLWE}_{\beta'}(\vec{c}, \vec{d}, \vec{e}), \quad \wedge$$

$$V_0, W_0 = \mathsf{Enc}_p(\vec{a}_0, \vec{b}_0, \vec{r}, (C, D, \vec{i})) \quad \wedge \quad V_1, W_1 = \mathsf{Enc}_p(\vec{a}_1, \vec{b}_1, \vec{r}, (C, D, \vec{i}))$$

The number of variables and constraints are bounded by $(4 + \log \beta)(m + k)n + 2kn \log q + 5n \log \beta + 30n + 6$. With our parameters this yields approximately 10 million variables and constraints. By applying the proof system of [5], we obtain the following lemma

Lemma 3.2. *There is a NIZK proof (SNARK) for the relation $\mathcal{R}_S$, secure and extractable in the random oracle model, with proof length $O(\log^2\left((m+k)n\log\beta + n^2\log q\right)\log q)$.*

3.6   Proof of Valid Decryption

The relation $\mathcal{R} = \{(\mathbf{v}, \mathbf{w}, \mu, \mathbf{a}, \mathbf{b}; \mathbf{s}, \mathbf{e}) : (\mathbf{w} - \mathbf{sv}) \bmod p = \mu \wedge \mathbf{b} = \mathbf{as} + \mathbf{e} \wedge \|\mathbf{s}\|_\infty, \|\mathbf{e}\|_\infty \leq \beta\}$, captures the statement that the prover knows the RLWE secret key corresponding to a given public key, and that a given ciphertext decrypts to a given message under this key. The constraint system is as follows.

$$\mathsf{RLWE}_\beta(\vec{a}, \vec{b}, \vec{s}, \vec{e}) \quad \wedge \quad T\vec{w} - T\vec{s} \circ T\vec{v} = T(\vec{\mu} + p\vec{h}) \quad \wedge \quad \|\vec{h}\|_\infty < (q-1)/2p$$

The final constraint ensures that $\vec{\mu} + p\vec{h}$ does not 'wrap around' modulo q. Since $\vec{v}, \vec{w}$ are public, the verifier can incorporate them into the constraint system. The number of variables and constraints is bounded by $n(\log\beta + \log(q/p) + 5)$.

3.7   Parameter Choices

In this section we discuss how the parameter choices in Sect. 5.4 relate to the relations described in the above sections, and the resulting constraint system sizes given by our implementation (Sect. 4). Throughout we let q be a prime with $\log_2 q \approx 65$, and $\mathcal{R}_q = \mathbb{F}_q/\langle X^n + 1\rangle$ with $n = 1024$. We have $\log\beta = 10$.

Proof of Knowledge of RLWE Secret Key. Our implementation yields a constraint system with 16,383 variables and 15,361 constraints for the parameters specified. The resulting proof is 72 kB in size, and is produced in roughly 40 seconds on a consumer laptop (MacBook Pro).

Proof of Knowledge of Plaintext. Our implementation yields a constraint system with 32,769 variables and 29,696 constraints for the parameters specified. The resulting proof is 87 kB in size, and is produced in roughly three minutes.

Proof of Valid Signature. Here $k = \bar{m} = 67$, $m = 2\bar{m} = 134$. Proving knowledge of a message $\mu \in \{0, 1\}^\ell$ and signature on μ yields at most $3\times10^6 + 67\ell$ constraints, for $\ell > n$. Our message size is $\ell = 2nk + \log N$, where N is the number of users in the system; we obtain roughly $12 \times 10^6 + 67\log N$ constraints. Since the number of users will always be bounded by (say) 2^{40}, the number of constraints is bounded by 12 million.

Our implementation yields a constraint system of 2,663,451 variables and 2,530,330 constraints. This is too large to produce a proof for on our Google Cloud instance, but extrapolating from known proof sizes we expect this to be at most 150 kB.

Signature Generation. Our implementation yields a constraint system with 10,196,994 variables and 10,460,226 constraints. This is too large to produce a proof for, but extrapolating from known proof sizes we expect at most 250 kB.

4   Implementation

The implementation was written in C++, primarily using the following libraries:

- `libff` (https://github.com/scipr-lab/libfff)
- `libiop` (https://github.com/scipr-lab/libiop)

`libff` is a C++ implementation of finite fields, and libiop includes a C++ implementation of the Aurora IOP and SNARK. The implementation took advantage of the `libiop`-provided APIs to construct the R1CS encodings of the various relations detailed in Sect. 3. Once these R1CS constraint systems were constructed, `libiop` was used to construct the Aurora IOPs, which where then compiled to zkSNARKs. Finally, the proof size of these SNARKs was measured directly.

`libiop` does not currently provide primitives to organize very large constraint systems as in this paper. To prevent the constraint systems from getting unwieldy, an additional class `ring_poly` was created to represent ring elements Sect. 3.1 as vectors of R1CS variables. This class also contains an implementation of the negative wrapped convolution (along with its inverse), which was tested by comparing with multiplication of polynomials in the 'long-form' method. In addition, now polynomial multiplication using the negative wrapped convolution could be represented as a basic constraint and be composed as part of a larger constraint system. Similarly, bit decompositions and proofs of shortness were also represented as basic constraints.

Mirroring the definition of the relations themselves, the implementations for Lemmas 3.1, 3.2 were composed by referencing the relevant smaller relations.

Several small utilites were also created in order to compute the parameters `libff` requires for the specific prime fields used in this paper, and to generate other prime fields to test how proof sizes varied with number of bits of the underlying prime field.

The constraint systems were compiled and run on a consumer-grade 2016 Macbook Pro, when running the prover and verifier could fit in memory. For the larger constraint systems such as for Lemma 3.2, a Google Cloud large-memory compute instance was used to finish constructing the proofs.

5   Group Signatures

We present a dynamic group signature $\mathsf{GS} = (\mathsf{GKg}, \mathsf{UKg}, \mathsf{Join}, \mathsf{Iss}, \mathsf{GSign}, \mathsf{GVerify}, \mathsf{GOpen}, \mathsf{GJudge})$ that supports N users and guarantees non-frameability in the ROM under post-quantum assumptions. Being *dynamic* means that users can join at any time during the lifespan of the group. Our construction follows the framework by Bellare, Shi and Zhang [4] and is built from a lattice-based hash-and-sign signature $(\mathsf{SParGen}, \mathsf{SKeyGen}, \mathsf{Sign}, \mathsf{SVerify})$ (cf. Sect. 2.3), SNARKs (P, V), a post-quantum one-time signature scheme $(\mathsf{OTSGen}, \mathsf{OTSSign}, \mathsf{OTSVf})$ (e.g., Lamport's signature scheme with key length 2λ bits) and a CCA2-secure encryption scheme $(\mathsf{EParGen}, \mathsf{EKeyGen}, \mathsf{Enc}, \mathsf{Dec})$ (the RLWE encryption scheme [22] made CCA2-secure via the Naor-Yung paradigm [25], cf. Sect. 2.2). Correctness of our construction trivially follows from the correctness of the building blocks. Security can be proved along the lines of the proofs in [4]. Proofs can be found in the full version.

5.1   Key Generation and Joining Protocol

Let N be the maximum number of users supported by the scheme. We assume there exists a publicly available list **upk** containing the personal (OTS) verification keys of the users, i.e., $\mathbf{upk}[i] = vk_i$.

GKg: A trusted third party generates the parameters $spar \leftarrow \mathsf{SParGen}(1^\lambda)$ and $epar \leftarrow \mathsf{EParGen}(1^\lambda)$. The error distribution of the RLWE encryption scheme is a Gaussian distribution with standard deviation $\sigma_{RLWE} = 2\sqrt{\log q}$. Then it sets $\ell = 2n\lceil \log q \rceil + \lceil \log N \rceil$, and checks that $q \geq 4p\sqrt{\log q \log n}\sqrt{64 \log q + n}$. If that's not the case, it aborts and restarts the parameter generation. It generates the group manager's secret signing key $T_\mathbf{A}$ with corresponding public key $(\mathbf{A}, \mathbf{B}, \mathbf{A}_0, \ldots, \mathbf{A}_\ell, \mathbf{u})$ running the key generation algorithm $\mathsf{SKeyGen}$ of the signature scheme. Finally, it generates the opener's keys by first generating two pairs of encryption and decryption keys of the encryption scheme, $((\mathbf{a}_i, \mathbf{b}_i), \mathbf{s}_i) \leftarrow \mathsf{EKeyGen}(epar)$ for $i = 0, 1$, and then setting $opk = (\mathbf{a}_0, \mathbf{b}_0, \mathbf{a}_1, \mathbf{b}_1)$ and $osk = \mathbf{s}_0$; $\mathbf{s}_1$ is discarded. Recall that the RLWE error distribution χ is set to be a discrete Gaussian with standard deviation s_{RLWE}. By Lemma 2.1 an element $\mathbf{e} \xleftarrow{\$} \chi$ has norm bounded by $B_I = 8s_{RLWE}$.

UKg: The i-th user generates her OTS keys running $(sk_i, vk_i) \leftarrow \mathsf{OTSGen}(1^\lambda)$. The verification key vk_i is added as the i-th entry to the public list **upk**. The keys of the user are $(usk_i, upk_i) = (sk_i, vk_i)$.

Join and Iss: The joining protocol is composed by a pair of algorithms (Join, Iss) run by the user and the group manager respectively, as showed in Fig. 1.

– The user starts by running Join on input her key pair $((\mathbf{c}_i, \mathbf{d}_i), \mathbf{t}_i)$. The algorithm ends outputting $(\mathbf{c}_i, \mathbf{d}_i, \sigma_i, vk_i)$ to M along with a proof Π_i that the user knows $\mathbf{t}_i, \mathbf{e}_i$, i.e., a proof that $(\mathbf{c}_i, \mathbf{d}_i)$ is a RLWE pair. The signature is generated running $\mathsf{OTSSign}((\mathbf{c}_i, \mathbf{d}_i), sk_i)$, while the proof is generated running $\mathsf{P}_I(\mathbf{c}_i, \mathbf{d}_i; \mathbf{t}_i, \mathbf{e}_i)$ that is the prover algorithm of a SNARK $(\mathsf{P}_I, \mathsf{V}_I)$ for the following relation:

$$\mathcal{R}_I = \{(\mathbf{c}_i, \mathbf{d}_i; \mathbf{t}_i, \mathbf{e}_i) \in \mathcal{R}_q^4 \; : \; \mathbf{d}_i = \mathbf{c}_i \mathbf{t}_i + \mathbf{e}_i \bmod q \; \wedge \; \|\mathbf{e}_i\|_\infty \leq \beta'\}$$

where β' is an upper bound on the absolute value of the coefficients of $\mathbf{e}_i$ computed in the parameters generation phase.

- M runs $V_I(\mathbf{c}_i, \mathbf{d}_i, \Pi_i)$ and $\mathsf{OTSVf}(\sigma_i, (\mathbf{c}_i, \mathbf{d}_i), vk_i)$. If any of them outputs 0, the group manager aborts. Otherwise, he signs $(\mathbf{c}_i, \mathbf{d}_i, i)$ using the signature scheme, i.e., he generates $\mathbf{S}_i$ with small norm such that $[\mathbf{A} \mid \mathbf{B} \mid \mathbf{A}_0 + \sum_{j=1}^{\ell}(-1)^{\mu_j}\mathbf{A}_j]\mathbf{S}_i = \mathbf{u} \bmod q$ where $\mu = (\mu_1, \ldots, \mu_\ell)$ is the binary expansion of $(\mathbf{c}_i, \mathbf{d}_i, i)$. Then, M sends $\mathbf{S}_i$ to U_i.
- the user verifies that $\mathbf{S}_i$ is a valid signature on $(\mathbf{c}_i, \mathbf{d}_i, i)$. If this is the case, she sends *accept* to the issuer, and sets her signing key to be $(\mathbf{t}_i, \mathbf{c}_i, \mathbf{d}_i, i, \mathbf{S}_i)$. Otherwise, she aborts.
- on input *accept*, the issuer stores in the list $\mathsf{l}[i] = (\mathbf{c}_i, \mathbf{d}_i, \sigma_i)$ and concludes the protocol.

5.2 Signing Algorithm

The signature algorithm is shown in Fig. 2.

To produce a valid signature, a user has to prove that she has a valid credential. This means she has to prove that she has a signature by M on her user public key and group identity $(\mathbf{c}_i, \mathbf{d}_i, i)$. Moreover, to allow the opener to output a proof of honest opening, it is necessary that he can extract $\mathbf{c}_i$ and $\mathbf{d}_i$ from the signature. Hence, the user attaches to the NIZK proof also two encryptions $(\mathbf{V}_0, \mathbf{W}_0), (\mathbf{V}_1, \mathbf{W}_1)$ of the user's identity i and of the RLWE sample $(\mathbf{c}_i, \mathbf{d}_i)$

$U_i \ (usk_i = \mathbf{t}_i)$		M $(\mathbf{T}_\mathbf{A})$
$\mathbf{c}_i \xleftarrow{\$} \mathcal{R}_q,\ \mathbf{t}_i \xleftarrow{\$} \mathcal{R}_q,\ \mathbf{e} \xleftarrow{\$} \chi$		
$\mathbf{d}_i = \mathbf{c}_i \mathbf{t}_i + \mathbf{e}_i \bmod q$		
$\Pi_i \leftarrow \mathsf{P}_I(\mathbf{c}_i, \mathbf{d}_i; \mathbf{t}_i, \mathbf{e}_i)$		
$\sigma_i \leftarrow \mathsf{OTSSign}(\mathsf{BitD}(\mathbf{c}_i, \mathbf{d}_i), sk_i)$	$\xrightarrow{\ \mathbf{c}_i, \mathbf{d}_i, \Pi_i, \sigma_i, vk_i\ }$	
		If $1 \leftarrow V_I(\mathbf{c}_i, \mathbf{d}_i, \Pi_i)$
		and $1 \leftarrow \mathsf{OTSVf}(\sigma_i, (\mathbf{c}_i, \mathbf{d}_i), vk_i)$:
		$\mu \leftarrow \mathsf{BitD}(\mathbf{c}_i, \mathbf{d}_i, i)$
		$\mathbf{S}_i \leftarrow \mathsf{Sign}(\mathbf{T}_\mathbf{A}, \mu)$
	$\xleftarrow{\ \ \mathbf{S}_i\ \ }$	
If $1 \leftarrow \mathsf{SVerify}(\mathbf{S}_i, \mu, \mathbf{A})$:		
	$\xrightarrow{\ \ accept\ \ }$	
		$\mathsf{l}[i] \leftarrow (\mathbf{c}_i, \mathbf{d}_i, \sigma_i)$
Output $gsk_i = (\mathbf{c}_i, \mathbf{d}_i, \mathbf{t}_i, i, \mathbf{S}_i)$.		

Fig. 1. Joining protocol.

$\mathsf{GSign}(gsk_i, gpk, opk, \mu)$
$\quad$ Parse $gsk_i = (\mathbf{c}_i, \mathbf{d}_i, \mathbf{t}_i, i, \mathbf{S}_i)$ and $opk = (\mathbf{a}_0, \mathbf{b}_0, \mathbf{a}_1, \mathbf{b}_1)$
$\quad$ For $b = 0, 1 \ (\mathbf{V}_i, \mathbf{W}_i) \leftarrow \mathsf{Enc}(\mathsf{BitD}(\mathbf{c}_i, \mathbf{d}_i, i), (\mathbf{a}_b, \mathbf{b}_b))$
$\quad$ $\Pi_S \leftarrow \mathsf{P}_S(\mu; gpk, opk, (\mathbf{V}_0, \mathbf{W}_0), (\mathbf{V}_1, \mathbf{W}_1); \mathbf{t}_i, i, \mathbf{c}_i, \mathbf{d}_i, \mathbf{e}_i, \mathbf{S}_i)$
$\quad$ Return $\sigma = (\Pi_S, \mathbf{V}_0, \mathbf{W}_0, \mathbf{V}_1, \mathbf{W}_1)$.

Fig. 2. Signing algorithm

w.r.t the two RLWE encryption keys in the opener public key. Remark that this does not compromise the user, as the opener never gets the user's secret key nor the user's signing key. To guarantee that the user is not cheating by encrypting a fake credential or by encrypting different plaintexts in the two ciphertexts, the user has to prove that the two ciphertexts encrypt the same $(i, \mathbf{c}_i, \mathbf{d}_i)$ on which she proved she has a credential. The relation becomes:

$$\mathcal{R}_S = \left\{ \begin{array}{l} (\mathbf{A}, \mathbf{B}, \mathbf{A}_0, \ldots, \mathbf{A}_\ell, \mathbf{u}, \\ opk, (\mathbf{V}_0, \mathbf{W}_0), \\ (\mathbf{V}_1, \mathbf{W}_1); \\ \mathbf{t}_i, i, \mathbf{c}_i, \mathbf{d}_i, \mathbf{e}_i, \mathbf{S}_i) \end{array} : \begin{array}{l} 1 \leftarrow \mathsf{SVerify}(\mathbf{S}_i, \mathsf{BitD}(i, \mathbf{c}_i, \mathbf{d}_i), \mathbf{A}, \mathbf{B}, \mathbf{A}_0, \ldots, \mathbf{A}_\ell, \mathbf{u}) \\ \wedge\ \mathbf{d}_i = \mathbf{c}_i \mathbf{t}_i + \mathbf{e}_i\ \wedge\ \|\mathbf{e}_i\| \le \beta' \\ \wedge\ (\mathbf{V}_0, \mathbf{W}_0) \leftarrow \mathsf{Enc}(\mathsf{BitD}(i, \mathbf{c}_i, \mathbf{d}_i), (\mathbf{a}_0, \mathbf{b}_0)) \\ \wedge\ (\mathbf{V}_1, \mathbf{W}_1) \leftarrow \mathsf{Enc}(\mathsf{BitD}(i, \mathbf{c}_i, \mathbf{d}_i), (\mathbf{a}_1, \mathbf{b}_1)) \end{array} \right\} \quad (1)$$

and $(\mathsf{P}_S, \mathsf{V}_S)$ is a non-interactive SNARK for $\mathcal{R}_S$ (cf. Sect. 3.5). The user outputs the signature $\sigma = (\mathbf{V}_0, \mathbf{W}_0, \mathbf{V}_1, \mathbf{W}_1, \Pi_S)$.

5.3 Signature Verification, Opening, and the Judge Algorithm

To *verify* a signature σ on a message μ, the algorithm $\mathsf{GVerify}$ checks Π_S by outputting what $\mathsf{V}_S(\Pi_S, \mu, \mathbf{A}, \mathbf{B}, \mathbf{A}_0, \ldots, \mathbf{A}_\ell, \mathbf{u}, opk, (\mathbf{V}_0, \mathbf{W}_0, \mathbf{V}_1, \mathbf{W}_1))$ outputs.

The *opener* first runs $\mathsf{GVerify}$ on the signature. If $\mathsf{GVerify}$ returns 0 the opener outputs $(0, \epsilon)$. Otherwise he decrypts the ciphertext $(\mathbf{V}_0, \mathbf{W}_0)$ using his secret key $\mathbf{s}_0$ to recover the identity i and public key $(\mathbf{c}'_i, \mathbf{d}'_i)$ of the signer using his secret key $\mathbf{s}$. Then, to prove that the user's identity he extracted is valid, he recovers the i-th entry of the list $\mathsf{l}[i] = (\mathbf{c}_i, \mathbf{d}_i, \sigma_i)$ and checks that $(\mathbf{c}'_i, \mathbf{d}'_i) = (\mathbf{c}_i, \mathbf{d}_i)$. If that is true, he outputs $\mathsf{l}[i]$ along the $(\mathbf{c}'_i, \mathbf{d}'_i)$ he recovered from the signature. Finally, the opener produces a proof that the opening procedure was performed honestly using the decryption key osk corresponding to the opener's public key opk, i.e., he outputs a proof Π_O for the following relation:

$$\mathcal{R}_O = \left\{ \begin{array}{l} (\mathbf{V}_0, \mathbf{W}_0, i, \mathbf{c}'_i, \mathbf{d}'_i, \\ \mathbf{a}_0, \mathbf{b}_0; \mathbf{s}_0, \mathbf{e}_0) \end{array} : (\mathbf{W}_0 - \mathbf{s}_0 \mathbf{V}_0) \bmod p = \begin{pmatrix} \hat{i} \\ \hat{\mathbf{c}}'_i \\ \hat{\mathbf{d}}'_i \end{pmatrix} \wedge \begin{array}{l} \mathbf{b}_0 = \mathbf{a}_0 \mathbf{s}_0 + \mathbf{e}_0 \bmod q \\ \|\mathbf{s}_0\|_\infty, \|\mathbf{e}_0\|_\infty \le \beta' \end{array} \right\}, \quad (2)$$

where $\hat{i}, \hat{\mathbf{c}}'_i, \hat{\mathbf{d}}'_i$ are the binary polynomials obtained from the binary expansions of $i, \mathbf{c}'_i, \mathbf{d}'_i$. If every check and the decryption go through, the output of the opener is $(i, \tau) = (i, (\mathbf{c}'_i, \mathbf{d}'_i, \mathbf{c}_i, \mathbf{d}_i, \sigma_i, \Pi_O))$. Otherwise, the opener outputs $(i, \tau) = (0, \epsilon)$.

The *Judge* algorithm verifies the opener claims of having opened correctly a signature. Hence, it has to verify Π_O and that the decrypted public key, the entry in the list and the certified public key of the user coincides. It takes as input $(gpk, \sigma, \mu, (i, \tau))$, i.e., the group public key, the signature $\sigma = (\Pi_S, (\mathbf{V}_0, \mathbf{W}_0, \mathbf{V}_1, \mathbf{W}_1))$ and the respective message μ, and the output of the opener $(i, \tau) = (i, (\mathbf{c}'_i, \mathbf{d}'_i, \mathbf{c}_i, \mathbf{d}_i, \sigma_i, \Pi_O))$. It recovers the public key upk_i of user i from the public list, and outputs 1 if all of the following conditions hold:

- $(i, \tau) \ne (0, \epsilon)$
- $1 \leftarrow \mathsf{GVerify}(\sigma, \mu, gpk)$
- $(\mathbf{c}, \mathbf{d}) = (\mathbf{c}', \mathbf{d}')$
- $1 \leftarrow \mathsf{V}_O(\Pi_O, \mathbf{V}_0, \mathbf{W}_0, i, \mathbf{c}'_i, \mathbf{d}'_i, \mathbf{a}_0, \mathbf{b}_0)$
- $1 \leftarrow \mathsf{OTSVf}(\sigma_i, (\mathbf{c}_i, \mathbf{d}_i), vk_i)$.

Otherwise, the algorithm outputs 0.

5.4   Correctness, Security and Parameters

Correctness follows from the correctness of the building blocks. Our group signature guarantees anonymity, traceability and non-frameability, meaning that it protects also against a corrupted group manager trying to frame a honest user. The proof of the following statements can be found in the full version of the paper.

Theorem 5.1 (Anonymity). *The group signature scheme* GS *is anonymous in the Random Oracle Model under the zero-knowledge and simulation soundness property of the NIZK proof system and under the IND-CPA security of the encryption scheme.*

Theorem 5.2 (Traceability). *The group signature scheme* GS *satisfies traceability in the Random Oracle Model if the signature scheme is eu-acma secure and the proof system is a sound argument of knowledge.*

Theorem 5.3 (Non-Frameability). *The group signature scheme* GS *satisfies non-frameability in the Random Oracle Model if the proof system is a zero-knowledge argument of knowledge, the OTS is a OTS, and* $RLWE_{1,\mathcal{U}(\mathcal{S}_1)}$ *is hard.*

We compute parameters for $\lambda \geq 128$ bits of security in the "paranoid" framework of Alkim et al. [1], that in particular requires $\delta \leq 1.00255$. We intend "security" here as the claim that the underlying hardness assumptions are hard to solve for a quantum computer. We choose as ring the polynomial ring $\mathcal{R}_q$ defined by $n = 2^{10}$ and a prime $2^{64} < q < 2^{65}$. Such choice of degree guarantees that the set $\mathcal{S}_1$ contains more than 2^{256} elements, hence finding the user's secret $\mathbf{t}_i$ through a brute-force attack is not possible. The number N of supported users is 2^{26}. For technical reasons, Aurora requires that $\mathbb{F}_q$ has a large power-of-2 multiplicative subgroup, and so we choose q accordingly (most choices of q satisfy this requirement). This implies that the unforgeability of the signature scheme is based on a $RSIS_{d,\beta}$ instance where $d = 68$ and $\beta \leq 2^{46}$, and on a $RLWE_{l,\chi}$ instance with $l < 2^{25}$. To estimate their hardness, we use the root Hermite factor δ (cf. [24]), and we obtained a $\delta_{RSIS} \leq 1.00062$ and $\delta_{RLWE} \leq 1.00001$.

We now compute the length of the keys and of a signature output by the group signature. An element in $\mathcal{R}_q$ can be stored in $nk \leq 8.32$ KB. The opener's secret key is composed by one ring element, hence it can be stored in 8.32 KB, while the opener's public key in 33.28 KB (as it is composed by 4 ring elements).

The group manager's public key requires a bit of care. Indeed, the key $(\mathbf{A}, \mathbf{B}, \mathbf{A}_0, \ldots, \mathbf{A}_\ell, \mathbf{u})$ includes $\mathbf{A} = [\mathbf{a}, 1]$, $\mathbf{B} \in \mathcal{R}_q^{1 \times \bar{m}}$ that are generated with the trapdoor (cf. Sect. 2.3), ℓ random vectors with $\bar{m} = 67$ components in $\mathcal{R}_q$, where $\ell = 2nk + \lceil \log N \rceil$, and a random element $\mathbf{u} \in \mathcal{R}_q$. Storing these would require $nk \cdot (1 + \bar{m} + \bar{m} \cdot \ell + 1) = 2^{10} \cdot 65 \cdot (1 + 67 + 67 \cdot 2^{18} + 1) = 146$ GB, and it is clearly infeasible. Instead, the issuer can send a condensed (pseudorandom) representation of the random elements $\mathbf{A}_0, \ldots, \mathbf{A}_\ell, \mathbf{u}$, having considerably smaller size. The size of the public key then becomes the size of such a representation plus $(\bar{m} + 1)nk \leq 0.57$ MB.

The group manager's secret key is the trapdoor $\mathbf{T_A}$, that has components with coefficients smaller than $8s_{ssk} = 8\sqrt{\log(n^2)} + 1$ (cf Lemma 2.1 and Theorem 2.4). Hence the size of $\mathbf{T_A}$ is $2kn\log(8s_{ssk}) \leq 91$ KB.

At the end of the joining phase the user obtains the credential $(\mathbf{c}_i, \mathbf{d}_i, \mathbf{t}_i, i, \mathbf{S}_i)$, where the vector $\mathbf{S}_i$ is composed by $2\bar{m}+2$ ring elements with coefficients smaller than $8s_\sigma = 8\sqrt{n\log n \log n^2}$ (cf. Sect. 2.3). Hence it has size $3nk + \lceil \log N \rceil + (2\bar{m} + 2)n\log(8\sqrt{n\log n} \cdot \log n^2) \leq 231$ KB. The secret signing key of the OTS can be discarded after the joining phase.

Finally, a signature is composed by the NIZK proof Π_S, and 4 vectors of elements in the ring. The proof length is around 250 KB (estimate from [5]). The vectors $\mathbf{V}_0, \mathbf{W}_0, \mathbf{V}_1, \mathbf{W}_1$ are the encryptions of two ring elements $(\mathbf{c}_i, \mathbf{d}_i)$ and a number $i < N$. As the encryption algorithm converts them into polynomials in $\mathcal{S}_1$ whose coefficients are the bits of their binary expansions, each vector is composed by $\lceil (2nk + \lceil \log N \rceil)/n \rceil = 2k + \lceil \lceil \log N \rceil / n \rceil$ elements in $\mathcal{R}_q$, hence $(\mathbf{V}_0, \mathbf{W}_0, \mathbf{V}_1, \mathbf{W}_1)$ has size $(2k + \lceil \lceil \log N \rceil / n \rceil) \cdot nk \leq (2 \cdot 65 + \lceil 26 \cdot 2^{-10} \rceil) \cdot 2^{10} \cdot 65 = 131 \cdot 1024 \cdot 65 = 1.09$ MB. Hence a signature is roughly 1.34 MB long.

To compare our scheme with previous ones (such as del Pino et al. [12] or Boschini et al. [8]), we compute the length of the signature for the case in which the group manager is always honest. For our group signature this essentially means that it is enough that during issuance the user gets a signature by the group manager on the user identity i. Hence, opening only requires the signature to contain an encryption of the user's identity i, whose bit decomposition can be encoded as one element of $\mathcal{S}_1$. Therefore, the vectors $\mathbf{V}_0, \mathbf{W}_0, \mathbf{V}_1, \mathbf{W}_1$ actually are just ring elements, hence the size of the signature is at most $250 + 4 \cdot 2^{10} \cdot 65 \leq 300$ KB (obviously, the size of the proof should shrink too, as the number of variables is smaller, but we mean this number as a rough upper bound).

References

1. Alkim, E., Ducas, L., Pöppelmann, T., Schwabe, P.: Post-quantum key exchange - a new hope. In: 25th USENIX Security Symposium, USENIX Security 16, Austin, TX, USA, 10–12 August 2016, pp. 327–343 (2016)
2. Banaszczyk, W.: New bounds in some transference theorems in the geometry of numbers. Math. Ann. **296**(1), 625–635 (1993)
3. Baum, C., Bootle, J., Cerulli, A., del Pino, R., Groth, J., Lyubashevsky, V.: Sublinear lattice-based zero-knowledge arguments for arithmetic circuits. In: Shacham, H., Boldyreva, A. (eds.) CRYPTO 2018, Part II. LNCS, vol. 10992, pp. 669–699. Springer, Cham (2018). https://doi.org/10.1007/978-3-319-96881-0_23
4. Bellare, M., Shi, H., Zhang, C.: Foundations of group signatures: the case of dynamic groups. In: Menezes, A. (ed.) CT-RSA 2005. LNCS, vol. 3376, pp. 136–153. Springer, Heidelberg (2005). https://doi.org/10.1007/978-3-540-30574-3_11
5. Ben-Sasson, E., Chiesa, A., Riabzev, M., Spooner, N., Virza, M., Ward, N.P.: Aurora: transparent succinct arguments for R1CS. IACR Cryptology ePrint Archive, 2018:828 (2018)
6. Ben-Sasson, E., Chiesa, A., Spooner, N.: Interactive oracle proofs. IACR Cryptology ePrint Archive 2016:116 (2016)

7. Ben-Sasson, E., Chiesa, A., Spooner, N.: Interactive oracle proofs. In: Hirt, M., Smith, A. (eds.) TCC 2016, Part II. LNCS, vol. 9986, pp. 31–60. Springer, Heidelberg (2016). https://doi.org/10.1007/978-3-662-53644-5_2

8. Boschini, C., Camenisch, J., Neven, G.: Floppy-sized group signatures from lattices. In: Preneel, B., Vercauteren, F. (eds.) ACNS 2018. LNCS, vol. 10892, pp. 163–182. Springer, Cham (2018). https://doi.org/10.1007/978-3-319-93387-0_9

9. Boyen, X.: Lattice mixing and vanishing trapdoors: a framework for fully secure short signatures and more. In: Nguyen, P.Q., Pointcheval, D. (eds.) PKC 2010. LNCS, vol. 6056, pp. 499–517. Springer, Heidelberg (2010). https://doi.org/10.1007/978-3-642-13013-7_29

10. Brakerski, Z., Vaikuntanathan, V.: Fully homomorphic encryption from ring-LWE and security for key dependent messages. In: Rogaway, P. (ed.) CRYPTO 2011. LNCS, vol. 6841, pp. 505–524. Springer, Heidelberg (2011). https://doi.org/10.1007/978-3-642-22792-9_29

11. Chiesa, A., Manohar, P., Spooner, N.: Succinct arguments in the quantum random oracle model. In: Hofheinz, D., Rosen, A. (eds.) TCC 2019, Part II. LNCS, vol. 11892, pp. 1–29. Springer, Cham (2019). https://doi.org/10.1007/978-3-030-36033-7_1

12. del Pino, R., Lyubashevsky, V., Seiler, G.: Lattice-based group signatures and zero-knowledge proofs of automorphism stability. In: Lie, D., Mannan, M., Backes, M., Wang, X.F. (eds.) ACM CCS 2018, pp. 574–591. ACM Press, New York (2018)

13. Genise, N., Micciancio, D.: Faster Gaussian sampling for trapdoor lattices with arbitrary modulus. In: Nielsen, J.B., Rijmen, V. (eds.) EUROCRYPT 2018, Part I. LNCS, vol. 10820, pp. 174–203. Springer, Cham (2018). https://doi.org/10.1007/978-3-319-78381-9_7

14. Gennaro, R., Minelli, M., Nitulescu, A., Orrù, M.: Lattice-based zk-SNARKs from square span programs. In: Lie, D., Mannan, M., Backes, M., Wang, X.F. (eds.) ACM CCS 2018, pp. 556–573. ACM Press, New York (2018)

15. Katsumata, S., Yamada, S.: Group signatures without NIZK: from lattices in the standard model. In: Ishai, Y., Rijmen, V. (eds.) EUROCRYPT 2019, Part III. LNCS, vol. 11478, pp. 312–344. Springer, Cham (2019). https://doi.org/10.1007/978-3-030-17659-4_11

16. Langlois, A., Stehlé, D.: Worst-case to average-case reductions for module lattices. Des. Codes Crypt. **75**(3), 565–599 (2014). https://doi.org/10.1007/s10623-014-9938-4

17. Libert, B., Ling, S., Nguyen, K., Wang, H.: Lattice-based zero-knowledge arguments for integer relations. In: Shacham, H., Boldyreva, A. (eds.) CRYPTO 2018, Part II. LNCS, vol. 10992, pp. 700–732. Springer, Cham (2018). https://doi.org/10.1007/978-3-319-96881-0_24

18. Ling, S., Nguyen, K., Stehlé, D., Wang, H.: Improved zero-knowledge proofs of knowledge for the ISIS problem, and applications. In: Kurosawa, K., Hanaoka, G. (eds.) PKC 2013. LNCS, vol. 7778, pp. 107–124. Springer, Heidelberg (2013). https://doi.org/10.1007/978-3-642-36362-7_8

19. Lyubashevsky, V.: Lattice signatures without trapdoors. In: Pointcheval, D., Johansson, T. (eds.) EUROCRYPT 2012. LNCS, vol. 7237, pp. 738–755. Springer, Heidelberg (2012). https://doi.org/10.1007/978-3-642-29011-4_43

20. Lyubashevsky, V., Micciancio, D., Peikert, C., Rosen, A.: SWIFFT: a modest proposal for FFT hashing. In: Nyberg, K. (ed.) FSE 2008. LNCS, vol. 5086, pp. 54–72. Springer, Heidelberg (2008). https://doi.org/10.1007/978-3-540-71039-4_4

21. Lyubashevsky, V., Peikert, C., Regev, O.: On ideal lattices and learning with errors over rings. In: Gilbert, H. (ed.) EUROCRYPT 2010. LNCS, vol. 6110, pp. 1–23. Springer, Heidelberg (2010). https://doi.org/10.1007/978-3-642-13190-5_1

22. Lyubashevsky, V., Peikert, C., Regev, O.: A toolkit for ring-LWE cryptography. In: Johansson, T., Nguyen, P.Q. (eds.) EUROCRYPT 2013. LNCS, vol. 7881, pp. 35–54. Springer, Heidelberg (2013). https://doi.org/10.1007/978-3-642-38348-9_3

23. Micciancio, D., Peikert, C.: Trapdoors for lattices: simpler, tighter, faster, smaller. In: Pointcheval, D., Johansson, T. (eds.) EUROCRYPT 2012. LNCS, vol. 7237, pp. 700–718. Springer, Heidelberg (2012). https://doi.org/10.1007/978-3-642-29011-4_41

24. Micciancio, D., Regev, O.: Lattice-based cryptography. In: Bernstein, D.J., Buchmann, J., Dahmen, E. (eds.) Post-Quantum Cryptography, pp. 147–191. Springer, Heidelberg (2009). https://doi.org/10.1007/978-3-540-88702-7_5

25. Naor, M., Yung, M.: Public-key cryptosystems provably secure against chosen ciphertext attacks. In: 22nd ACM STOC, pp. 427–437. ACM Press, May 1990

26. Shamir, A., Tauman, Y.: Improved online/offline signature schemes. In: Kilian, J. (ed.) CRYPTO 2001. LNCS, vol. 2139, pp. 355–367. Springer, Heidelberg (2001). https://doi.org/10.1007/3-540-44647-8_21

Short Zero-Knowledge Proof of Knowledge for Lattice-Based Commitment

Yang Tao[1,2(✉)], Xi Wang[1,2], and Rui Zhang[1,2(✉)]

[1] State Key Laboratory of Information Security (SKLOIS),
Institute of Information Engineering (IIE), Chinese Academy of Sciences (CAS),
Beijing, China
{taoyang,wangxi2,r-zhang}@iie.ac.cn
[2] School of Cyber Security, University of Chinese Academy of Sciences,
Beijing, China

Abstract. Commitment scheme, together with zero-knowledge proof, is a fundamental tool for cryptographic design. Recently, Baum et al. proposed a commitment scheme (BDLOP), which is by far the most efficient lattice-based one and has been applied on several latest constructions of zero-knowledge proofs. In this paper, we propose a more efficient zero-knowledge proof of knowledge for BDLOP commitment opening with a shorter proof. There are a few technical challenges, and we develop some new techniques: First, we make an adaption of BDLOP commitment by evaluating the opening with the singular value rather than ℓ_2 norm in order to get compact parameters. Then, we try to use the bimodal Gaussian technique to minimize the size of the proof. Finally, utilizing a modulus-switch technique, we can retain the size of the commitment.

Keywords: Lattice-based commitment · Zero-knowledge proof of knowledge · Bimodal Gaussian

1 Introduction

Commitment scheme [6] is a fundamental tool for the cryptographic protocols, which allows a committer to commit to a receiver a message m and reveals it later. A commitment is secure, if it is both hiding and binding. The former means that a commitment c reveals no information about the committed message before the open phase, while the latter means that c should not be opened to two different messages. In theory, the existence of commitment can be based on the existence of one-way functions [15,22]. However, such a generic construction is quite inefficient, and several commitment schemes [11,14,23] from number theory assumptions offer the efficiency. There are numerous applications for commitments, such as coin-flipping over telephone [6], contract signing [13], electronic voting [9] and so on. When applied as a building block in a high-level protocol, a commitment is usually combined with a zero-knowledge proof of knowledge (of the opening) against malicious adversaries.

© Springer Nature Switzerland AG 2020
J. Ding and J.-P. Tillich (Eds.): PQCrypto 2020, LNCS 12100, pp. 268–283, 2020.
https://doi.org/10.1007/978-3-030-44223-1_15

1.1 Lattice-Based Commitment

Lattice-based cryptography has attracted much attention due to its quantum resistance and rich functionalities. Several work has focused on the lattice-based commitment with a zero-knowledge proof of knowledge (Σ-protocol). In 2008, Kawachi et al. [17] presented a string commitment based on the short integer solution (SIS) assumption, whose message space is restricted to short vectors. Hereafter, Jain et al. [16] proposed a commitment scheme based on the learning parity with noise (LPN) assumption. Xie et al. [25] constructed a commitment scheme based on the ring learning with errors (RLWE), together with a Σ-protocol. However, both the zero-knowledge proofs of [16] and [25] have knowledge error of $\frac{2}{3}$ in one run and it needs many iterations for zero-knowledge protocols to achieve a negligible knowledge error. Then, Benhamouda et al. [4] improved the efficiency of Σ-protocol by reducing the knowledge error to $\frac{1}{2n}$. Furthermore, Benhamouda et al. [5] relaxed the requirements on a valid opening of a commitment and proposed a commitment based on the RLWE assumption.

A Nontrivial Problem Remains. Recently, Baum et al. [3] constructed a more efficient commitment (BDLOP commitment), based on the module-SIS (MSIS) and module-LWE (MLWE) assumptions[1], associated with a zero-knowledge proof of knowledge of commitment opening, which is basically a Σ-protocol of [18]. It adopted a Gaussian variant as the randomness and utilized the rejection sampling in case of transcript leakage. BDLOP commitment has been by far the most efficient known scheme and was applied in the latest construction of the lattice-based exact zero-knowledge proofs [7,26]. Compression technique [2] was also mentioned in [3] to achieve a smaller proof, which makes the verifier check an approximate equality.

However, it seems uneasy to balance the proof size, abort probability and security with concrete parameters, since compression technique [2] brings another abort condition which affects the verification. A proof size reduction by such compression technique may be at the cost of a large abort probability or a lower security level, thus not easy to work. To remark, after a careful calculation of the method stated in [3], we conclude that under the parameters of [3], the proof size drops from 6.6 KB to 4.4 KB, but the non-abort probability is approximately 3.7×10^{-4}! Obviously, this is unacceptable. More detailed discussions are given in Appendix A.

To summarize, BDLOP commitment is useful but it seems nontrivial to have a more efficient lattice-based commitment (cf. BDLOP) with a shorter proof size. In this paper, we investigate this problem.

1.2 Our Treatment

Inspired by a bimodal Gaussian technique [12] that brings a better approximation in the rejection sampling and smaller Gaussian parameters, thus a smaller

---

[1] It degenerates to RSIS and RLWE when $n = 1$.

signature size, it seems easy to obtain a shorter proof without sacrificing the non-abort probability and security. However, this is actually not straightforward, and we elaborate the reasons below.

One may think that if adapting the bimodal Gaussian technique to BDLOP commitment and evaluating the opening with the singular value rather than ℓ_2 norm, it will be possible to minimize the proof size. However, such optimizations cannot be applied to [3] directly, since bimodal Gaussian technique requires modulus $2q$ while the commitment needs modulus exactly to be q. A trivial solution is to expand the commitment modulus to $2q$, however, such approach inevitably results in a larger commitment. Hence, in order to retain the commitment size, we utilize a modulus-switch technique. Concretely, we make a pre-procession procedure to lift the modulus of the public key and commitment when performing the protocol, while in the security proof, we transform the modulus from $2q$ to q by modulus reduction. When considering different security levels, our protocol is more efficient than [3] under the concrete parameters.

2   Preliminary

In this section, we review some useful notations, definitions and facts.

Notations. Denote the real numbers by $\mathbb{R}$ and integers by $\mathbb{Z}$. For any integer q, identify $\mathbb{Z}_q$ with the interval $[-\frac{q}{2}, \frac{q}{2}) \cap \mathbb{Z}$. Vectors are assumed to be in column form. Denote column vectors with lower-case bold letters (e.g. $\mathbf{x}$) and matrices by boldface capital letters (e.g. $\mathbf{A}$). Denote the matrix $[\mathbf{A}_1|\mathbf{A}_2]$ as the matrix concatenating matrices $\mathbf{A}_1$ and $\mathbf{A}_2$. If S is a set, $U(S)$ denotes the uniform distribution over S and $s \leftarrow S$ denotes choosing s uniformly from S. A function $negl(n) : \mathbb{R}_{\geq 0} \to \mathbb{R}_{\geq 0}$ is negligible if $negl(n) < 1/poly(n)$ for $n > n_0$ (n_0 is a constant). For a matrix $\mathbf{R} \in \mathbb{R}^{l \times t}$, the largest singular value of $\mathbf{R}$ is defined as $s_1(\mathbf{R}) = \max_{\|\mathbf{u}\|_2 = 1} \|\mathbf{R}\mathbf{u}\|_2$.

Lemma 1 (Rejection Sampling Lemma, Lemma 4.7 of [18]). Let f, g be probability distributions with property that $\exists M \in \mathbb{R}^+$, such that $\Pr_{z \leftarrow f}[Mg(z) \geq f(z)] \geq 1 - \varepsilon$, then the distribution of the output of the following algorithm $\mathcal{A}$:

1: $z \leftarrow g$
2: output z with probability $\min\{\frac{f(z)}{Mg(z)}, 1\}$

is within statistical distance $\frac{\varepsilon}{M}$ of the distribution of the following algorithm $\mathcal{F}$:

1: $z \leftarrow f$
2: output z with probability $\frac{1}{M}$

Moreover, the probability that $\mathcal{A}$ outputs something is at least $\frac{1-\varepsilon}{M}$.

2.1 Ring, Lattices and Gaussians

Ring. We consider the ring $\mathcal{R} = \mathbb{Z}[x]/(x^N + 1)$ for N a power of 2 and $\mathcal{R}_q = \mathbb{Z}_q[x]/(x^N + 1)$ for some integer q. Each element of $\mathcal{R}$ written as a lower-case bold letter has a polynomial representation of degree $N - 1$ with coefficients in $\mathbb{Z}$. There is a coefficient embedding $\phi : \mathcal{R} \to \mathbb{Z}^N$, mapping as $\phi(\mathbf{a}) = (a_0, a_1, \cdots, a_{N-1})^t \in \mathbb{Z}^N$ with $\mathbf{a} = a_0 + a_1 x + \cdots + a_{N-1} x^{N-1} \in \mathcal{R}$. We define the ℓ_p-norm of $\mathbf{a}$ as $\|\mathbf{a}\|_p = (\sum_i |a_i|^p)^{\frac{1}{p}}$ with $p \in \mathbb{Z}^+$ and its ℓ_∞-norm as $\|\mathbf{a}\|_\infty = \max_i |a_i|$ for $\mathbf{a} \in \mathcal{R}$. Besides, we can also view $\mathcal{R}$ as the subring of anti-circulant matrices in $\mathbb{Z}^{N \times N}$ by viewing the element $\mathbf{a} \in \mathcal{R}$ as $\mathrm{rot}(\mathbf{a}) = [\phi(\mathbf{a})| \cdots |\phi(\mathbf{a}x^{i-1})| \cdots |\phi(\mathbf{a}x^{N-1})]$. For $\forall \mathbf{x} = [\mathbf{x}_1| \cdots |\mathbf{x}_d] \in \mathcal{R}^{1 \times d}$, $\mathrm{rot}(\mathbf{x}) = [\mathrm{rot}(\mathbf{x}_1)| \cdots |\mathrm{rot}(\mathbf{x}_d)] \in \mathbb{Z}^{N \times dN}$. More generally, we define the largest singular value $s_1(\mathbf{x})$ for $\mathbf{x} \in \mathcal{R}^{l \times d}$ as $s_1(\mathrm{rot}(\mathbf{x}))$. The following lemma shows, for a particular prime q, all elements with small norms are invertible in $\mathcal{R}_q$.

Lemma 2 ([19], Corollary 1.2). Let $N \geq d > 1$ be powers of 2 and $q = 2d + 1 \bmod 4d$ be a prime. Then $x^N + 1$ factors into d irreducible polynomials $x^{N/d} - r_j \bmod q$ and any $\mathbf{y} \in \mathcal{R}_q \setminus \{0\}$ that satisfies $\|\mathbf{y}\|_\infty < \frac{1}{\sqrt{d}} \cdot q^{1/d}$ or $\|\mathbf{y}\|_2 < q^{1/d}$ is invertible in $\mathcal{R}_q$. Particularly, we choose $d = 2$ in this paper.

Lattices. An n-dimension (full-rank) lattice $\Lambda \subseteq \mathbb{R}^n$ is a set of all integer linear combinations of some set of independent basis vectors $\mathbf{B} = \{\mathbf{b}_1, \ldots, \mathbf{b}_n\} \subseteq \mathbb{R}^n$, $\Lambda = \mathcal{L}(\mathbf{B}) = \{\sum_{i=1}^n z_i \mathbf{b}_i | z_i \in \mathbb{Z}\}$. The dual lattice of $\Lambda \subseteq \mathbb{R}^n$ is defined as $\Lambda^* = \{\mathbf{x} \in \mathbb{R}^n | \langle \Lambda, \mathbf{x} \rangle \subseteq \mathbb{Z}\}$. For integers $n \geq 1$, $q \geq 2$ and $\mathbf{A} \in \mathbb{Z}_q^{n \times m}$, an m-dimensional lattice is defined as $\Lambda^\perp(\mathbf{A}) = \{\mathbf{x} \in \mathbb{Z}^m | \mathbf{A}\mathbf{x} = \mathbf{0} \in \mathbb{Z}_q^n\} \subseteq \mathbb{Z}^m$. For any $\mathbf{y}$ in the subgroup of $\mathbb{Z}_q^n$, we also define the coset $\Lambda_\mathbf{y}^\perp(\mathbf{A}) = \{\mathbf{x} \in \mathbb{Z}^m | \mathbf{A}\mathbf{x} = \mathbf{y} \bmod q\} = \Lambda^\perp(\mathbf{A}) + \bar{\mathbf{x}}$, where $\bar{\mathbf{x}} \in \mathbb{Z}^m$ is an arbitrary solution to $\mathbf{A}\bar{\mathbf{x}} = \mathbf{y}$. For $\Lambda = \mathcal{L}(\mathbf{B})$, let $\widetilde{\mathbf{B}}$ denote the Gram-Schmidt orthogonalization of $\mathbf{B}$, and $\|\widetilde{\mathbf{B}}\|_2$ is the length of the longest vector in it.

Gaussian Measures. Let Λ be a lattice in $\mathbb{Z}^n$. For any vector $\mathbf{c} \in \mathbb{R}^n$ and parameter $\sigma > 0$, the n-dimensional Gaussian function $\rho_{\sigma,\mathbf{c}} : \mathbb{R}^n \to (0, 1]$ is defined as $\rho_{\sigma,\mathbf{c}}(\mathbf{x}) := (\frac{1}{\sqrt{2\pi}\sigma})^n \exp(-\|\mathbf{x} - \mathbf{c}\|_2^2/2\sigma^2)$. The discrete Gaussian distribution over Λ with parameter σ and center $\mathbf{c}$ (abbreviated as $D_{\Lambda,\sigma,\mathbf{c}}$) is defined as $\forall \mathbf{y} \in \Lambda, D_{\Lambda,\sigma,\mathbf{c}}(\mathbf{y}) := \frac{\rho_{\sigma,\mathbf{c}}(\mathbf{y})}{\rho_{\sigma,\mathbf{c}}(\Lambda)}$, where $\rho_{\sigma,\mathbf{c}}(\Lambda) = \sum_{\mathbf{y} \in \Lambda} \rho_{\sigma,\mathbf{c}}(\mathbf{y})$. When $\mathbf{c} = \mathbf{0}$, we write ρ_σ and $D_{\Lambda,\sigma}$ for short. Below we list some properties of the discrete Gaussian distribution.

Lemma 3 (ℓ_2 norm, [18]). For any $\eta_1 > 0$, $\Pr[\|\mathbf{z}\|_2 > \eta_1 \sigma \sqrt{m} | \mathbf{z} \leftarrow D_{\mathbb{Z}^m, \sigma}] < \eta_1^m e^{\frac{m}{2}(1-\eta_1^2)}$. In this paper, we choose $\eta_1 = 2$.

Lemma 4 (ℓ_∞ norm, [18]). For any $\tau > 0$, $\Pr[|z| > \tau \sigma | z \leftarrow D_{\mathbb{Z}, \sigma}] \leq 2e^{\frac{-\tau^2}{2}}$.

2.2 Subgaussian and Random Matrices

For $\delta > 0$, a random variable X over $\mathbb{R}$ is δ-subgaussian with parameter $s > 0$ if for all $t \in \mathbb{R}$, the (scaled) moment-generating function satisfies $\mathbb{E}[\exp(2\pi t X)] \leq \exp(\delta) \cdot \exp(\pi s^2 t^2)$. Any B-bounded centered random variable X (i.e. $\mathbb{E}[X] = 0$ and $|X| \leq B$ always) is 0-subgaussian with parameter $B\sqrt{2\pi}$. More generally, a random matrix $\mathbf{X}$ is δ-subgaussian of parameter s if all its one-dimensional marginals $\mathbf{u}^t \mathbf{X} \mathbf{v}$ for unit vectors $\mathbf{u}, \mathbf{v}$ are δ-subgaussian of parameter s. The concatenation of independent δ_i-subgaussian vectors with common parameter s, is $(\sum \delta_i)$-subgaussian with parameter s.

Lemma 5 (Singular Value, [20,24]). Let $\mathbf{X} \in \mathbb{R}^{n \times m}$ be a δ-subgaussian random matrix with parameter s. There exists a universal constant $C > 0$ such that for any $t \geq 0$, we have $s_1(\mathbf{X}) \leq C \cdot s \cdot (\sqrt{m} + \sqrt{n} + t)^2$ except with probability at most $2\exp(\delta)\exp(-\pi t^2)$.

2.3 Hard Problems

The centered binomial distribution $\mathcal{S}_\eta$ [8] for some positive integer η is defined as follows. Sample $(a_1, \cdots, a_\eta, b_1, \cdots, b_\eta) \leftarrow \{0,1\}^{2\eta}$ and output $\sum_{i=1}^{\eta}(a_i - b_i)$. If $\mathbf{v}$ is an element of $\mathcal{R}$, denote $\mathbf{v} \leftarrow \mathcal{S}_\eta$ as $\mathbf{v} \in \mathcal{R}$ generated from a distribution where each of its coefficients is generated according to $\mathcal{S}_\eta$. A $k \times m$ matrix of polynomials $\mathbf{V} \in \mathcal{R}^{k \times m}$ is generated according to the distribution $\mathcal{S}_\eta^{k \times m}$, if each element in $\mathbf{V}$ is from $\mathcal{S}_\eta$. Especially for $m = 1$, we write $\mathcal{S}_\eta^k$ for short. Below we review the RLWE and RSIS problems.

Definition 1 (RLWE). The RLWE distribution over $\mathcal{R}_q^l \times \mathcal{R}_q$ is a distribution of $(\mathbf{a}, \mathbf{b})$, where $\mathbf{a} \leftarrow \mathcal{R}_q^l$ and $\mathbf{b} = \mathbf{a}^t \mathbf{s} + \mathbf{e}$ with $\mathbf{s} \leftarrow \mathcal{S}_\eta^l$ and $\mathbf{e} \leftarrow \mathcal{S}_\eta$. The search RLWE problem consists in recovering $\mathbf{s}$ from polynomially many samples chosen from the RLWE distribution. The decision RLWE problem is to distinguish the RLWE distribution from the uniform distribution $U(\mathcal{R}_q^l \times \mathcal{R}_q)$. We write $\mathrm{RLWE}_{N,l,q,\eta}$ for short.

Definition 2 (Inhomogeneous RSIS). The inhomogeneous RSIS problem is to find a short non-zero preimage $\mathbf{x}$ satisfying $\mathbf{A}\mathbf{x} = \mathbf{t} \bmod q$ and $\|\mathbf{x}\|_2 \leq B$, where $\mathbf{A} \leftarrow \mathcal{R}_q^{1 \times l}$ and $\mathbf{t} \leftarrow \mathcal{R}_q$. Especially, for $\mathbf{t} = \mathbf{0}$, we denote such problem as $\mathrm{RSIS}_{N,l,q,B}$.

2.4 Commitment and Zero-Knowledge Proofs

A commitment scheme contains three algorithms: KeyGen, Com and Ver.

- The key generation algorithm KeyGen: Taking as input 1^λ, it outputs a public parameter PK containing a definition of the message space $\mathcal{M}$.

---

[2] We choose $C = \frac{1}{\sqrt{2\pi}}$ empirically. Besides, for $\delta = 0$ and $t = 5$, the above probability is approximate 2^{-112}.

- The commitment algorithm Com: Taking as input the public parameter PK, a message $x \in \mathcal{M}$, it outputs a commitment/opening pair (c, r).
- The verification algorithm Ver: Taking as input the public parameter PK, a message $x \in \mathcal{M}$, a commitment c and an opening r, it outputs a bit $b \in \{0, 1\}$.

A commitment is correct if $\Pr[\text{Ver}(\text{PK}, m, c, r) = 1 | \text{PK} \leftarrow \text{KeyGen}(1^\lambda), m \in \mathcal{M}, (c, r) \leftarrow \text{Com}(\text{PK}, m)] = 1 - negl(\lambda)$. There are two security notions for a commitment—hiding and binding. A commitment scheme is hiding if for all PPT algorithms $\mathcal{A}$,

$$\Pr\left[b' = b \middle| \begin{array}{l} \text{PK} \leftarrow \text{KeyGen}(1^\lambda); x_0, x_1 \leftarrow \mathcal{A}(\text{PK}); b \leftarrow \{0, 1\}; \\ (c, r) \leftarrow \text{Com}(\text{PK}, x_b); b' \leftarrow \mathcal{A}(c) \end{array}\right] \leq \frac{1}{2} + negl(\lambda),$$

where the probability is taken over the randomness of KeyGen, Com and $\mathcal{A}$. Similarly, a commitment scheme is binding if for all PPT algorithms $\mathcal{A}$,

$$\Pr\left[\begin{array}{l} (x, x', r, r', c) \leftarrow \mathcal{A}(\text{PK}), s.t. \ x \neq x' \\ \text{and } \text{Ver}(\text{PK}, x, c, r) = \text{Ver}(\text{PK}, x', c, r') = 1 \end{array} \middle| \text{PK} \leftarrow \text{KeyGen}(1^\lambda)\right] \leq negl(\lambda),$$

where the probability is taken over the randomness of KeyGen and $\mathcal{A}$.

Zero-Knowledge Proof and Σ-Protocol. A zero-knowledge proof of knowledge is an interactive protocol between a prover $\mathcal{P}$ and a verifier $\mathcal{V}$. The prover holds some secret information and convinces the verifier to accept that he knows the secret but without revealing any other information. It is well-known that Σ-protocol is a proof of knowledge [10]. In this section, we adopt the definition of Σ-protocol and tailor it to the setting of a commitment opening.

Definition 3. Let Π be a two-party protocol between $\mathcal{P}$ and $\mathcal{V}$, where $\mathcal{V}$ is a polynomial-time algorithm. Assume $\text{PK} \leftarrow \text{KeyGen}(1^\lambda), x \in \mathcal{M}, (c, r) \leftarrow \text{Com}(\text{PK}, x)$, and $\mathcal{C}$ is a challenge space. Then a protocol Π is a Σ-protocol if it satisfies the following conditions:

- Three-Move Form: Π has the following form.
  1. $\mathcal{P}$ sends $\mathcal{V}$ a commitment t.
  2. $\mathcal{V}$ samples a random challenge $d \leftarrow \mathcal{C}$ and sends it to $\mathcal{P}$.
  3. $\mathcal{P}$ returns a response s to $\mathcal{V}$.
- Completeness: If $\mathcal{P}$ on input (PK, c, x, r) and $\mathcal{V}$ on input (PK, c) follow the protocol honestly, then $\mathcal{V}$ outputs 1 except with negligible probability.
- Special Soundness: Given a pair of accepting transcripts (t, d_1, s_1) and (t, d_2, s_2) satisfying $d_1 \neq d_2$, there exists a PPT algorithm $\mathcal{E}$, which can extract a valid opening (x', r') of c such that $\text{Ver}(\text{PK}, x', c, r') = 1$.
- Honest-Verifier Zero-Knowledge: There exists a PPT algorithm $\mathcal{S}$ whose output distribution on input (PK, c) is indistinguishable from the transcript of Π generated by the real protocol.

3   Modifying BDLOP Commitment

In this section, we present an adaption of the BDLOP commitment [3] for compact parameters. There are two adjustments. First, we extend the additional element $\mathbf{f}^3$ in the opening to a wider range. Then, we apply the singular value to evaluate the openings instead of ℓ_2 norm.

- KeyGen: Create the public key $\mathbf{A}_1 \in \mathcal{R}_q^{l \times k}$ and $\mathbf{A}_2 \in \mathcal{R}_q^{l \times k}$ as $\mathbf{A}_1 = [\mathbf{1}|\mathbf{A}_1']$ and $\mathbf{A}_2 = [\mathbf{0}^{l \times 1}|\mathbf{I}_l|\mathbf{A}_2']$, where $\mathbf{A}_1' \leftarrow \mathcal{R}_q^{1 \times (k-1)}$, $\mathbf{A}_2' \leftarrow \mathcal{R}_q^{l \times (k-l-1)}$ and $\mathbf{I}_l$ is an $l \times l$ identity matrix. It outputs $\mathsf{PK} = \{\mathbf{A}_1, \mathbf{A}_2\}$.
- Com: The message space is $\mathcal{R}_q^l$. Taking as input a message $\mathbf{x} \in \mathcal{R}_q^l$ and a randomness $\mathbf{r} \leftarrow \mathcal{S}_\beta^k$, where $\mathcal{S}_\beta^k$ is a centered binomial distribution for integer β over $\mathcal{R}^k$, it outputs $(\mathbf{c}, \mathbf{r})$ with

$$\mathbf{c} := \begin{pmatrix} \mathbf{c}_1 \\ \mathbf{c}_2 \end{pmatrix} = \begin{pmatrix} \mathbf{A}_1 \\ \mathbf{A}_2 \end{pmatrix} \mathbf{r} + \begin{pmatrix} \mathbf{0} \\ \mathbf{x} \end{pmatrix}. \tag{1}$$

- Ver: A valid opening of a commitment $\mathbf{c} = \begin{pmatrix} \mathbf{c}_1 \\ \mathbf{c}_2 \end{pmatrix}$ is a 3-tuple $(\mathbf{x}, \mathbf{r}, \mathbf{f})$ with

$\mathbf{x} \leftarrow \mathcal{R}_q^l$, $\mathbf{r} = \begin{pmatrix} r_1 \\ ... \\ r_k \end{pmatrix} \in \mathcal{R}_q^k$ and $\mathbf{f} \in S_f$, where $S_f = \{\mathbf{f} \in \mathcal{R}|\mathbf{f}$ is invertible in $\mathcal{R}_q$ and $\|\mathbf{f}\|_2 \le B_f^2\}$ with some constant B_f^2. The verifier returns 1 if it satisfies

$$\mathbf{f} \begin{pmatrix} \mathbf{c}_1 \\ \mathbf{c}_2 \end{pmatrix} = \begin{pmatrix} \mathbf{A}_1 \\ \mathbf{A}_2 \end{pmatrix} \mathbf{r} + \mathbf{f} \begin{pmatrix} \mathbf{0} \\ \mathbf{x} \end{pmatrix},$$

and $s_1(\mathbf{r}) \le \frac{\sigma_1}{\sqrt{\pi}}(\sqrt{kN} + \sqrt{N} + 5)$.

Since these adjustments don't affect the commit phase, the hiding property is exact as [3]. It suffices to present a security proof for the binding property.

Lemma 6 (hiding property). Assuming there is an algorithm $\mathcal{A}$ with advantage ϵ in breaking the hiding property of the above commitment, there is an algorithm $\mathcal{A}'$ solving the $\mathrm{RLWE}_{N,k-l-1,q,\beta}$ problem with advantage ϵ.

Lemma 7 (binding property). If there is an algorithm $\mathcal{A}$ breaking the binding property of the above commitment with advantage ϵ, then there is an algorithm $\mathcal{A}'$ solving the $\mathrm{RSIS}_{N,k,q,B}$ problem with advantage ϵ, where $B = \frac{2\sigma_1}{\sqrt{\pi}}(\sqrt{kN} + \sqrt{N} + 5) \cdot B_f^2$.

---

[3] Since there is no efficient zero-knowledge proofs that can prove knowledge of the message and randomness in the commit phase, some additional element $\mathbf{f}$ is applied for a relaxed opening, which makes the zero-knowledge proof can prove something weaker. Such property is also used in [5] and [3].

Proof (Lemma 7). Given $\mathbf{A}_1 = [\mathbf{1}|\mathbf{A}_1']$ with $\mathbf{A}_1' \leftarrow \mathcal{R}_q^{1 \times (k-1)}$ as an instance of $\mathrm{RSIS}_{N,k,q,B}$, we construct an algorithm $\mathcal{A}'$ to solve the $\mathrm{RSIS}_{N,k,q,B}$ as follows. First, $\mathcal{A}'$ generates a matrix $\mathbf{A}_2 = [\mathbf{0}^{l \times 1}|\mathbf{I}_l|\mathbf{A}_2']$ with $\mathbf{A}_2' \leftarrow \mathcal{R}_q^{l \times (k-l-1)}$ and sends $\mathbf{A}_1, \mathbf{A}_2$ as the public key to an adversary $\mathcal{A}$. If $\mathcal{A}$ attacks the binding property successfully, he can return a commitment $\begin{pmatrix} \mathbf{c}_1 \\ \mathbf{c}_2 \end{pmatrix}$ and its two valid openings $(\mathbf{x}, \mathbf{r}, \mathbf{f})$ and $(\mathbf{x}', \mathbf{r}', \mathbf{f}')$ with $\mathbf{x} \neq \mathbf{x}'$ satisfying

$$\mathbf{f}\begin{pmatrix} \mathbf{c}_1 \\ \mathbf{c}_2 \end{pmatrix} = \begin{pmatrix} \mathbf{A}_1 \\ \mathbf{A}_2 \end{pmatrix}\mathbf{r} + \mathbf{f}\begin{pmatrix} \mathbf{0} \\ \mathbf{x} \end{pmatrix}, \tag{2}$$

$$\mathbf{f}'\begin{pmatrix} \mathbf{c}_1 \\ \mathbf{c}_2 \end{pmatrix} = \begin{pmatrix} \mathbf{A}_1 \\ \mathbf{A}_2 \end{pmatrix}\mathbf{r}' + \mathbf{f}'\begin{pmatrix} \mathbf{0} \\ \mathbf{x}' \end{pmatrix}. \tag{3}$$

where $\mathbf{f}, \mathbf{f}' \in S_f$ and $s_1(\mathbf{r}), s_1(\mathbf{r}') \leq \frac{\sigma_1}{\sqrt{\pi}}(\sqrt{kN} + \sqrt{N} + 5)$.

After multiplying Eq. (2) with $\mathbf{f}'$ and Eq. (3) with $\mathbf{f}$ and subtracting, we have

$$\mathbf{A}_1(\mathbf{f}'\mathbf{r} - \mathbf{f}\mathbf{r}') = \mathbf{0}, \tag{4}$$

$$\mathbf{A}_2(\mathbf{f}'\mathbf{r} - \mathbf{f}\mathbf{r}') + \mathbf{f}\mathbf{f}'(\mathbf{x} - \mathbf{x}') = \mathbf{0}^l. \tag{5}$$

Since $\mathbf{f}, \mathbf{f}' \in S_f$ and $\mathbf{x} \neq \mathbf{x}'$, it implies that $\mathbf{f}\mathbf{f}'(\mathbf{x} - \mathbf{x}') \neq \mathbf{0}^l$ and $\mathbf{f}'\mathbf{r} - \mathbf{f}\mathbf{r}' \neq \mathbf{0}^k$. Notice that $\|\mathbf{f}\mathbf{r}'\|_2 \leq s_1(\mathbf{r}')\|\mathbf{f}\|_2 \leq \frac{\sigma_1}{\sqrt{\pi}}(\sqrt{kN} + \sqrt{N} + 5) \cdot B_f^2$, so is $\mathbf{f}'\mathbf{r}$. Then, we have $\|\mathbf{f}'\mathbf{r} - \mathbf{f}\mathbf{r}'\|_2 \leq \frac{2\sigma_1}{\sqrt{\pi}}(\sqrt{kN} + \sqrt{N} + 5) \cdot B_f^2$. Finally, $\mathcal{A}'$ outputs $\mathbf{f}'\mathbf{r} - \mathbf{f}\mathbf{r}'$ as a valid solution of $\mathrm{RSIS}_{N,k,q,B}$ problem.

4   Short Zero-Knowledge Proof of Knowledge of Opening

In this section, we optimize the zero-knowledge proof of knowledge of BDLOP commitment opening with a shorter proof by bimodal Gaussian technique [12], which requires a modulus $2q$ while it is q in the commitment. Thus, we apply a modulus-switch technique containing two phases—up phase and down phase.

– Up phase: Taking as input an arbitrary matrix $\mathbf{A} \in \mathcal{R}_q^{n \times m}$, it outputs a matrix $\mathbf{A}' \in \mathcal{R}_{2q}^{n \times m}$ satisfying $\mathbf{A}' = 2\mathbf{A}$.
– Down phase: Taking as input an arbitrary matrix $\mathbf{B}' \in \mathcal{R}_{2q}^{n \times m}$, it outputs a matrix $\mathbf{B} \in \mathcal{R}_q^{n \times m}$ with $\mathbf{B} = \mathbf{B}' \bmod q$.

4.1   Protocol

In order to handle the inconsistent modulus, there is a pre-processing procedure in our protocol to lift the modulus from q to $2q$. The challenge set $\mathcal{C} = \{\mathbf{c} \in \mathcal{R}_{2q} \mid \mathbf{c} = \sum_{i=0}^{N-1} c_i x^i$ with $c_i \in \{0, 1\}$ and $\|\mathbf{c}\|_1 = \kappa\}$. Our interactive protocol $\varPi$ is Table 1.

Table 1. Zero-knowledge proof of knowledge of commitment opening

Protocol Π

Public Key: $\mathbf{A}_1 \in \mathcal{R}_q^{1 \times k}$ and $\mathbf{A}_2 \in \mathcal{R}_q^{l \times k}$

Prover's Information: $\mathbf{r} = \begin{pmatrix} \mathbf{r}_1 \\ \dots \\ \mathbf{r}_k \end{pmatrix} \leftarrow \mathcal{S}_\beta^k$ with $\beta = 1$

Commitment: $\mathbf{c} = \begin{pmatrix} \mathbf{c}_1 \\ \mathbf{c}_2 \end{pmatrix} \in \mathcal{R}_q \times \mathcal{R}_q^l$

Pre-Processing: Lift $\mathbf{A}_1$ and $\mathbf{c}_1$ to $\widetilde{\mathbf{A}}_1 = 2\mathbf{A}_1$ and $\widetilde{\mathbf{c}}_1 = 2\mathbf{c}_1$ respectively as in the up phase. Output $\widetilde{\mathbf{A}}_1 \in \mathcal{R}_{2q}^{1 \times k}$ and $\widetilde{\mathbf{c}}_1 \in \mathcal{R}_{2q}$.

Prover $\mathcal{P}$	Verifier $\mathcal{V}$

Sample $\mathbf{y}_1 \leftarrow D_{\mathcal{R}^k, \sigma_1}, \mathbf{y}_2 \leftarrow D_{\mathcal{R}, \sigma_2}$;
Set $\bar{\mathbf{A}} = [\widetilde{\mathbf{A}}_1 | q - \widetilde{\mathbf{c}}_1] \in \mathcal{R}_{2q}^{1 \times (k+1)}$;
Compute $\mathbf{t} = \bar{\mathbf{A}} \begin{pmatrix} \mathbf{y}_1 \\ \mathbf{y}_2 \end{pmatrix} \in \mathcal{R}_{2q}$.

$$\xrightarrow{\quad \mathbf{t} \quad}$$

Choose $\mathbf{d} \leftarrow \mathcal{C}$.

$$\xleftarrow{\quad \mathbf{d} \quad}$$

Choose $b \leftarrow \{0, 1\}$;
Set $\mathbf{s} = \begin{pmatrix} \mathbf{s}_1 \\ \mathbf{s}_2 \end{pmatrix} = \begin{pmatrix} \mathbf{r} \\ 1 \end{pmatrix} \mathbf{d}$;
$\mathbf{z} = \begin{pmatrix} \mathbf{z}_1 \\ \mathbf{z}_2 \end{pmatrix} = \begin{pmatrix} \mathbf{y}_1 \\ \mathbf{y}_2 \end{pmatrix} + (-1)^b \mathbf{s}$;
Abort with probability $1 -$
$\min\{\dfrac{1}{M \exp(-\frac{\|\mathbf{s}_1\|_2^2}{2\sigma_1^2}) \exp(-\frac{\|\mathbf{s}_2\|_2^2}{2\sigma_2^2}) \cosh(\frac{\langle \mathbf{z}_1, \mathbf{s}_1 \rangle}{\sigma_1^2} + \frac{\langle \mathbf{z}_2, \mathbf{s}_2 \rangle}{\sigma_2^2})}, 1\}.$

$$\xrightarrow{\quad \mathbf{z} \quad}$$

Recover $\bar{\mathbf{A}} = [\widetilde{\mathbf{A}}_1 | q - \widetilde{\mathbf{c}}_1] \in \mathcal{R}_{2q}^{1 \times (k+1)}$;
Write $\mathbf{z} = \begin{pmatrix} \mathbf{z}_1 \\ \mathbf{z}_2 \end{pmatrix} \in \mathcal{R}_q^k \times \mathcal{R}_q$;
Accept iff $\bar{\mathbf{A}}\mathbf{z} = \mathbf{t} + q\mathbf{d} \bmod 2q$ and
$\|\mathbf{z}_1\|_2 \le 2\sigma_1\sqrt{kN}, \|\mathbf{z}_2\|_2 \le 2\sigma_2\sqrt{N}$, and $\|\mathbf{z}\|_\infty < \frac{q}{4}$.

Theorem 1. *Let prime $q = 5 \bmod 8$, $\sqrt{q} > 4\sigma_2\sqrt{N}$, $\frac{q}{4} > \max\{\tau\sigma_1, \tau\sigma_2\}$ with some $\tau > 0$. Set $B_f^2 = 4\sigma_2\sqrt{N}$. Assuming $RSIS_{N,k,q,4\sigma_1\sqrt{kN}}$ problem is hard, the protocol Π is a Σ-protocol and has the following properties.*

- *Completeness: When Π does not abort, the verifier accepts the prover with overwhelming probability. Besides, the abort probability is approximately $1 - \frac{1}{M}$ with M some positive real number.*

- *Special Soundness: Given a commitment $\mathbf{c} = \begin{pmatrix} \mathbf{c}_1 \\ \mathbf{c}_2 \end{pmatrix}$ and two valid transcripts $(\mathbf{t}, \mathbf{d}, \mathbf{z}), (\mathbf{t}, \mathbf{d}', \mathbf{z}')$, where $\mathbf{d} \neq \mathbf{d}'$, we can extract a valid opening $(\mathbf{x}, \mathbf{r}, \mathbf{f})$ of commitment $\mathbf{c}$ with $s_1(\mathbf{r}) \le \frac{\sigma_1}{\sqrt{\pi}}(\sqrt{kN} + \sqrt{N} + 5)$ and $\mathbf{f} \in S_f$.*

- *Honest-Verifier Zero-Knowledge: There is a simulator $\mathcal{S}$ whose output distribution is indistinguishable from the non-aborting transcripts of Π with an honest verifier.*

Proof. Our proof consists of three parts. For the special soundness, we utilize the modulus-switch technique from $2q$ to q as the down phase proceeds. The details are given as follows.

Completeness: For any challenge $\mathbf{d} \in \mathcal{C}$, we have $\bar{\mathbf{A}}\mathbf{z} = \mathbf{t} + (-1)^b q\mathbf{d}$ due to $\tilde{\mathbf{c}}_1 = 2\mathbf{c}_1 = 2\mathbf{A}_1\mathbf{r} = \tilde{\mathbf{A}}_1\mathbf{r} \bmod 2q$ and $\bar{\mathbf{A}}\begin{pmatrix}\mathbf{r}\\1\end{pmatrix} = q \bmod 2q$. Thus, $\bar{\mathbf{A}}\mathbf{z} = \mathbf{t} + q\mathbf{d} \bmod 2q$ holds for any $b \in \{0,1\}$. By rejection sampling, the final distributions of $\mathbf{z}_1$ and $\mathbf{z}_2$ are $D_{\mathcal{R}^k,\sigma_1}$ and $D_{\mathcal{R},\sigma_2}$ respectively, and the abort probability of the protocol Π is approximately $1 - \frac{1}{M}$. When Π is not abort, an honest prover can return a correct answer given any challenge $\mathbf{d}$. For an honest verifier, $\|\mathbf{z}_1\|_2 \leq 2\sigma_1\sqrt{kN}$ and $\|\mathbf{z}_2\|_2 \leq 2\sigma_2\sqrt{N}$ hold except with negligible probability by Lemma 3. Besides, we can assume the coefficients of $\mathbf{z}_1$ and $\mathbf{z}_2$ are smaller than $\tau\sigma_1$ and $\tau\sigma_2$ due to Lemma 4, thus it yields $\|\mathbf{z}\|_\infty < \frac{q}{4}$ except with negligible probability.

Special Soundness: Given two valid transcripts $(\mathbf{t}, \mathbf{d}, \mathbf{z})$ and $(\mathbf{t}, \mathbf{d}', \mathbf{z}')$, we recover $\bar{\mathbf{A}} = [\tilde{\mathbf{A}}_1 | q - \tilde{\mathbf{c}}_1] \in \mathcal{R}_{2q}^{1\times(k+1)}$ and obtain

$$\bar{\mathbf{A}}\mathbf{z} = \mathbf{t} + q\mathbf{d} \bmod 2q \tag{6}$$

$$\bar{\mathbf{A}}\mathbf{z}' = \mathbf{t} + q\mathbf{d}' \bmod 2q \tag{7}$$

From (6) and (7), it yields

$$\bar{\mathbf{A}}(\mathbf{z} - \mathbf{z}') = q(\mathbf{d} - \mathbf{d}') \bmod 2q. \tag{8}$$

Since $\mathbf{d} \neq \mathbf{d}' \in \mathcal{C}$, we have $\bar{\mathbf{A}}(\mathbf{z} - \mathbf{z}') \neq \mathbf{0} \bmod 2q$, thus $\mathbf{z} - \mathbf{z}' \neq \mathbf{0}^{k+1} \bmod 2q$. Notice $\|\mathbf{z}\|_\infty, \|\mathbf{z}'\|_\infty \leq \frac{q}{4}$, it yields $\mathbf{z} \neq \mathbf{z}'$. Write $\mathbf{z} - \mathbf{z}' = \begin{pmatrix}\mathbf{z}_1 - \mathbf{z}_1'\\\mathbf{z}_2 - \mathbf{z}_2'\end{pmatrix}$ with $\mathbf{z}_1 - \mathbf{z}_1' \in \mathcal{R}^k$ and $\mathbf{z}_2 - \mathbf{z}_2' \in \mathcal{R}$. According to (8), it implies $\bar{\mathbf{A}}(\mathbf{z} - \mathbf{z}') = \mathbf{0} \bmod q$, i.e.

$$\tilde{\mathbf{A}}_1(\mathbf{z}_1 - \mathbf{z}_1') + (q - \tilde{\mathbf{c}}_1)(\mathbf{z}_2 - \mathbf{z}_2') = \mathbf{0} \bmod q. \tag{9}$$

Notice that $\tilde{\mathbf{c}}_1 = 2\mathbf{c}_1$ and $\tilde{\mathbf{A}}_1 = 2\mathbf{A}_1$. We can transform the operations in $\mathcal{R}_{2q}$ to that in $\mathcal{R}_q$ as the down phase and derive $2\mathbf{A}_1(\mathbf{z}_1 - \mathbf{z}_1') = 2\mathbf{c}_1(\mathbf{z}_2' - \mathbf{z}_2) \bmod q$. Since $\gcd(2, q) = 1$, we have 2 is an invertible element of $\mathcal{R}_q$ and

$$\mathbf{A}_1(\mathbf{z}_1 - \mathbf{z}_1') = \mathbf{c}_1(\mathbf{z}_2' - \mathbf{z}_2) \bmod q. \tag{10}$$

Now we claim that $\mathbf{z}_2' - \mathbf{z}_2 \neq \mathbf{0}$. Otherwise, it implies $\mathbf{z}_1 - \mathbf{z}_1' \neq \mathbf{0}^k$ due to $\mathbf{z} \neq \mathbf{z}'$ and $\mathbf{A}_1(\mathbf{z}_1 - \mathbf{z}_1') = \mathbf{0} \bmod q$. Besides, $\|\mathbf{z}_1 - \mathbf{z}_1'\|_2 \leq 4\sigma_1\sqrt{kN}$ holds, and it is a valid solution of $\text{RSIS}_{N,k,q,4\sigma_1\sqrt{kN}}$ problem, which contradicts to the RSIS assumption. Therefore, we set $\mathbf{f} = \mathbf{z}_2' - \mathbf{z}_2$, which satisfies $\|\mathbf{f}\|_2 \leq 4\sigma_2\sqrt{N} < \sqrt{q}$ and $\mathbf{f}$ is invertible by Lemma 2.1, thus belonging to S_f.

Finally, let $\mathbf{r} = \mathbf{z}_1 - \mathbf{z}_1'$ and $\mathbf{x} = \mathbf{c}_2 - \mathbf{f}^{-1}\mathbf{A}_2\mathbf{r} \bmod q$. Then, it is obvious that $\begin{pmatrix} \mathbf{A}_1 \\ \mathbf{A}_2 \end{pmatrix} \mathbf{r} + \mathbf{f} \begin{pmatrix} \mathbf{0} \\ \mathbf{x} \end{pmatrix} = \mathbf{f} \begin{pmatrix} \mathbf{c}_1 \\ \mathbf{c}_2 \end{pmatrix}$ holds. Notice that $\mathbf{z}_1$ and $\mathbf{z}_1'$ are independent Gaussian variants with parameter σ_1. Then, it yields $s_1(\mathbf{r}) \leq \frac{\sigma_1}{\sqrt{\pi}}(\sqrt{kN}+\sqrt{N}+5)$ due to Lemma 5 by viewing $\mathbf{r} = \mathbf{z}_1 - \mathbf{z}_1'$ as a Gaussian variant with parameter $\sqrt{2}\sigma_1$. Therefore, $(\mathbf{x}, \mathbf{r}, \mathbf{f})$ is a valid opening of commitment $\mathbf{c}$.

<u>*Honest-Verifier Zero-Knowledge*</u>: Notice that real transcripts will be non-abort with probability $1 - \frac{1}{M}$ approximately. Thus, the simulator $\mathcal{S}$ should abort with probability $\frac{1}{M}$. For non-aborting transcripts, we define $\mathcal{S}$ as follows. It samples $\mathbf{d} \leftarrow \mathcal{C}$, $\mathbf{z}_1 \leftarrow D_{\mathcal{R}^k, \sigma_1}$ and $\mathbf{z}_2 \leftarrow D_{\mathcal{R}, \sigma_2}$. Set $\bar{\mathbf{A}} = [\widetilde{\mathbf{A}}_1 | \, q - \widetilde{\mathbf{c}}_1] \in \mathcal{R}_{2q}^{1 \times (k+1)}$ and $\mathbf{t} = \bar{\mathbf{A}}\mathbf{z} - q\mathbf{d} \bmod 2q$ with $\mathbf{z} = \begin{pmatrix} \mathbf{z}_1 \\ \mathbf{z}_2 \end{pmatrix}$. Then, $\mathcal{S}$ outputs $(\mathbf{t}, \mathbf{d}, \mathbf{z})$. The distribution of $(\mathbf{t}, \mathbf{d}, \mathbf{z})$ and the real transcripts are indistinguishable by rejection sampling. Thus, the output distribution of $\mathcal{S}$ is indistinguishable from the real non-aborting transcript. $\qquad\qquad\qquad\qquad\qquad\qquad\qquad\qquad\qquad\qquad\qquad\qquad\Box$

4.2 Instantiation

We choose parameters according to the requirements of Lemmas 6 and 7 and Theorem 1, i.e. considering the hardness of $\text{RSIS}_{N,k,q,\frac{2\sigma_1}{\sqrt{\pi}}(\sqrt{kN}+\sqrt{N}+5)\cdot B_f^2}$, $\text{RSIS}_{N,k,q,4\sigma_1\sqrt{kN}}$, and $\text{RLWE}_{N,k-l-1,q,1}$. Notice $\text{RSIS}_{N,k,q,4\sigma_1\sqrt{kN}}$ is harder than $\text{RSIS}_{N,k,q,\frac{2\sigma_1}{\sqrt{\pi}}(\sqrt{kN}+\sqrt{N}+5)\cdot B_f^2}$, thus it suffices to evaluate the intractability of $\text{RLWE}_{N,k-l-1,q,1}$ and $\text{RSIS}_{N,k,q,\frac{2\sigma_1}{\sqrt{\pi}}(\sqrt{kN}+\sqrt{N}+5)\cdot B_f^2}$.

Since there is no better attacks of RLWE/RSIS known than plain LWE/SIS, we analyze the security of RLWE and RSIS by using the attacks against LWE and SIS. For simplicity, we use the Hermite factor approach to analyze the hardness of these problems. Concretely, we evaluate the SIS problem with sublattice attack[4] and utilize the software LWE-Estimator [1] presented by Albrecht, Player and Scott to analyze the hardness of the LWE problem.

On the other hand, Gaussian parameters σ_1 and σ_2 make a crucial impact on the proof size and abort probability. Since $\|\mathbf{dr}\|_2 \leq s_1(\mathbf{r})\|\mathbf{d}\|_2$ and $\mathbf{r} \in \mathcal{S}_1^k$ is 1-bounded centered random variable in the commit phase, we have $\|\mathbf{dr}\|_2 \leq (\sqrt{kN} + \sqrt{N} + 5)\sqrt{\kappa}$ by Lemma 5. We choose $\sigma_1 = 0.7 \max_{\mathbf{d}, \mathbf{r}} \|\mathbf{dr}\|_2$ and $\sigma_2 = \|\mathbf{d}\|_2 = \sqrt{\kappa}$. Then, the repetition M is approximate 4.6.

We propose concrete parameters for the non-interactive version of the protocol Π. In the non-interactive protocol, the proof consists of $(\mathbf{d}, \mathbf{z})$ with $\mathbf{z} = \begin{pmatrix} \mathbf{z}_1 \\ \mathbf{z}_2 \end{pmatrix}$ a non-sphere Gaussian variant. Since coefficients of $\mathbf{z}_1$ and $\mathbf{z}_2$ are smaller than $\tau\sigma_1$ and $\tau\sigma_2$, the proof size is approximately $Nk \log(\tau\sigma_1) + N \log(\tau\sigma_2)$. Besides, the size of commitment is $N(l+1) \log q$. Table 2 gives parameter sets under different security levels. The scheme with parameters from Set I, Set II and Set

---

[4] In [21], one should only use $d = \sqrt{\frac{N \log q}{\log \delta}}$ columns and zero out the others, which results in a short vector with length as $\min\{q, q^{\frac{N}{d}} \delta^d\} = \min\{q, q^{\frac{2N}{d}}\}$.

III can achieve a weak security ($\approx$100-bit security), medium security ($\approx$128-bit security) and high security ($\approx$256-bit security) respectively. In comparison with [3], our protocol can obtain a shorter proof at the same security level.

Table 2. Parameters for our protocol

Parameters	Set I-Ours	Set I-[3]	Set II-Ours	Set II-[3]*	Set III-Ours	Set III-[3]*
N	1024	1024	1024	1024	2048	2048
q	$\approx 2^{32}$	$\approx 2^{32}$	$\approx 2^{32}$	$\approx 2^{32}$	$\approx 2^{32}$	$\approx 2^{32}$
κ	44	36	44	36	36	32
k	3	3	4	4	4	4
l	1	1	1	1	1	1
σ_1	430	≈ 27000	469	≈ 27000	592	≈ 32000
σ_2	7	–	7	–	6	–
B_f^2	896	–	896	–	1087	–
τ	6	6	6	6	18	18
δ_{RSIS}	≈ 1.0034	≈ 1.0035	≈ 1.0034	≈ 1.0035	≈ 1.0019	≈ 1.0020
δ_{RLWE}	≈ 1.0055	≈ 1.0055	≈ 1.0029	≈ 1.0029	≈ 1.0015	≈ 1.0015
|com|	8.10 KB	8.10 KB	8.10 KB	8.10 KB	16 KB	16 KB
|proof|	4.93 KB	6.60 KB	6.34 KB	8.65 KB	15.07 KB	19.13 KB

We denote Set I-[3] as the parameters chosen in [3] and also select parameters for [3] as Set II-[3]* and Set III-[3]* following the original strategy in [3] when considering comparisons under a higher security level. We also denote root Hermite factor of RSIS and RLWE as δ_{RSIS} and δ_{RLWE}. The sizes of commitment and proof are denoted as \|com\| and \|proof\| respectively.

Acknowledgement. The authors would like to thank the anonymous reviewers for their valuable comments. This work was partially supported by National Natural Science Foundation of China (Nos. 61772520, 61632020, 61472416, 61802392, 61972094), Key Research and Development Project of Zhejiang Province (Nos. 2017C01062, 2020C01078), Beijing Municipal Science and Technology Project (Grant Nos. Z191100007119007, Z191100007119002).

A Discussion on Protocol of [3] with Compression Technique

The proof $\mathbf{z}$ of zero-knowledge proof of opening in [3] contains two part: $\mathbf{z}^{(1)}$ corresponds to the proof that gets multiplied by the identity matrix of public matrix $\mathbf{A}_1$ and $\mathbf{z}^{(2)}$ corresponds to the proof that gets multiplied by $\mathbf{A}_1'$. The compression technique [2] is to discard $\mathbf{z}^{(1)}$ totally and the verifier merely checks an approximate equality, i.e. an equality of high-order part.

For an inter x with $x = \lceil x \rceil_\gamma \cdot 2^\gamma + [x]_\gamma$, we denote $\lceil x \rceil_\gamma$ as the high-order bits and $[x]_\gamma = x \bmod 2^\gamma$ as the low-order γ bits. The challenge space is $\mathcal{C}' = \{\mathbf{d} \in \mathcal{R}_q | \|\mathbf{d}\|_\infty = 1, \|\mathbf{d}\|_1 = \kappa\}$. The improved protocol Π_{com} of [3] with compression technique [2] is given in Table 3, which satisfies the property of completeness, special soundness and honest-verifier zero-knowledge. Since honest-verifier zero-knowledge property is not affected and will hold as [3] has shown, we only discuss the completeness and special soundness of Π_{com}.

Completeness: It is guaranteed by $\mathbf{A}_1' \mathbf{z} - \mathbf{dc}_1 = \mathbf{t} - \mathbf{dr}_1$ and $[\mathbf{t} - \mathbf{dr}_1]_\gamma = \lceil \mathbf{t} \rceil_\gamma$ when $[\mathbf{t} - \mathbf{dr}_1]_\gamma < \frac{\gamma}{2} - \max_{\mathbf{d},\mathbf{r}_1} \|\mathbf{dr}_1\|_2$ holds, which brings an additional abort condition. Thus, adopting an wide-accepted assumption that the low-order bits are uniformly distributed modulo γ, the non-abort probability is approximately $\left(\frac{2(\frac{\gamma}{2} - \max_{\mathbf{d},\mathbf{r}_1} \|\mathbf{dr}_1\|_2) - 1}{\gamma}\right)^N$, which means the larger γ is, the larger non-abort probability we can get.

Table 3. Improved zero-knowledge proof of knowledge in [3].

<u>Protocol Π_{com}</u>

Public Key: $\mathbf{A}_1 = [\mathbf{1}|\mathbf{A}_1']$ with $\mathbf{A}_1' \leftarrow \mathcal{R}_q^{1\times(k-1)}$ and $\mathbf{A}_2 \in \mathcal{R}_q^{l\times k}$

Prover's Information: $\mathbf{r} = \begin{pmatrix} \mathbf{r}_1 \\ \mathbf{r}_2 \end{pmatrix} \in \mathcal{S}_\beta^k$ with $\mathbf{r}_1 \in \mathcal{S}_\beta$, $\mathbf{r}_2 \in \mathcal{S}_\beta^{k-1}$ and $\beta = 1$

Commitment: $\mathbf{c} = \begin{pmatrix} \mathbf{c}_1 \\ \mathbf{c}_2 \end{pmatrix} \in \mathcal{R}_q \times \mathcal{R}_q^l$ as in (1)

Prover $\mathcal{P}$		Verifier $\mathcal{V}$

Sample $\mathbf{y} \leftarrow D_{\mathcal{R}^{k-1},\sigma}$;
Compute $\mathbf{t} = \mathbf{A}_1' \mathbf{y}$.

$\xrightarrow{\quad \mathbf{t} \quad}$

Choose $\mathbf{d} \leftarrow \mathcal{C}'$.

$\xleftarrow{\quad \mathbf{d} \quad}$

Compute $\mathbf{z} = \mathbf{y} + \mathbf{dr}_2$;
Abort if
$[\mathbf{t} - \mathbf{dr}_1]_\gamma \geq \frac{\gamma}{2} - \max_{\mathbf{d},\mathbf{r}_1} \|\mathbf{dr}_1\|_2$.
Otherwise, abort with probability
$1 - \min\{\frac{1}{M} \exp(\frac{-2\langle \mathbf{z},\mathbf{dr}_2\rangle + \|\mathbf{dr}_2\|_2^2}{2\sigma^2}), 1\}$.

$\xrightarrow{\quad \mathbf{z} \quad}$

Write $\mathbf{z} = \begin{pmatrix} \mathbf{z}_1 \\ \cdots \\ \mathbf{z}_{k-1} \end{pmatrix}$;

Accept iff
$\forall i, \|\mathbf{z}_i\|_2 \leq 2\sigma\sqrt{N}$ and
$\lceil \mathbf{A}_1' \mathbf{z} - \mathbf{dc}_1 \rceil_\gamma = \lceil \mathbf{t} \rceil_\gamma$.

Special Soundness: Given a commitment $\mathbf{c}$ and two valid transcripts $(\mathbf{t}, \mathbf{d}, \mathbf{z})$, $(\mathbf{t}, \mathbf{d}', \mathbf{z}')$, we can extract a valid opening of commitment $\mathbf{c}$ as follows.

$$\lceil \mathbf{A}'_1 \mathbf{z} - \mathbf{dc}_1 \rceil_\gamma = \lceil \mathbf{t} \rceil_\gamma \tag{11}$$

$$\lceil \mathbf{A}'_1 \mathbf{z}' - \mathbf{d}' \mathbf{c}_1 \rceil_\gamma = \lceil \mathbf{t} \rceil_\gamma \tag{12}$$

Therefore, there exist two low-order term $\mathbf{e}, \mathbf{e}'$ with $\|\mathbf{e}\|_\infty, \|\mathbf{e}'\|_\infty \leq \frac{\gamma}{2}$, such that

$$\mathbf{A}'_1 \mathbf{z} - \mathbf{dc}_1 = \lceil \mathbf{t} \rceil_\gamma \cdot 2^\gamma + \mathbf{e} \tag{13}$$

$$\mathbf{A}'_1 \mathbf{z}' - \mathbf{d}' \mathbf{c}_1 = \lceil \mathbf{t} \rceil_\gamma \cdot 2^\gamma + \mathbf{e}' \tag{14}$$

From Eqs. (13) and (14), we obtain

$$\mathbf{A}'_1 (\mathbf{z} - \mathbf{z}') - (\mathbf{d} - \mathbf{d}') \mathbf{c}_1 = \mathbf{e} - \mathbf{e}', \tag{15}$$

and it yields

$$\mathbf{A}_1 \begin{pmatrix} \mathbf{e} - \mathbf{e}' \\ \mathbf{z} - \mathbf{z}' \end{pmatrix} = (\mathbf{d} - \mathbf{d}') \mathbf{c}_1 \tag{16}$$

Notice that $\|\mathbf{e} - \mathbf{e}'\|_\infty \leq \gamma$. Assuming $\gamma \leq 4\sigma$, we have $\|\mathbf{e} - \mathbf{e}'\|_2 \leq 4\sigma\sqrt{N}$. Set $\mathbf{f} = \mathbf{d} - \mathbf{d}'$, $\mathbf{r} = \begin{pmatrix} \mathbf{e} - \mathbf{e}' \\ \mathbf{z} - \mathbf{z}' \end{pmatrix}$ and $\mathbf{x} = \mathbf{c}_2 - \mathbf{f}^{-1} \mathbf{A}_2 \mathbf{r}$. Then $(\mathbf{x}, \mathbf{r}, \mathbf{f})$ is a valid opening[5] of commitment $\mathbf{c}$ in [3].

Now we claim there is a trade-off between the reduced proof size, non-abort probability and security for Π_{com}. When instantiating the protocol Π_{com}, we have to consider the non-abort probability $(\frac{2(\frac{\gamma}{2} - \max_{\mathbf{d}, \mathbf{r}_1} \|\mathbf{dr}_1\|_2) - 1}{\gamma})^N$ for completeness and condition $\gamma \leq 4\sigma$ for special soundness. An observation is that the non-abort probability is 3.7×10^{-4} with $\sigma \approx 27000$ and $\gamma \approx 108000$ under the parameter in [3] (Set I-[3] in Table 2). Thus, it is inevitable to expand σ for a practical non-abort probability. If we choose the non-abort probability $(\frac{2(\frac{\gamma}{2} - \max_{\mathbf{d}, \mathbf{r}_1} \|\mathbf{dr}_1\|_2) - 1}{\gamma})^N \approx 0.3$, then Gaussian parameter σ should be $6.3\times$ larger than before, which may result in a weaker SIS problem. In fact, the root Hermite factor of SIS increases to 1.0047, though the proof size can be reduced to 5KB under the expanded σ. Thus, it seems such improvement with compression technique is possible but at the cost of low non-abort probability or security.

---

[5] In [3], a valid opening of commitment $\mathbf{c} = \begin{pmatrix} \mathbf{c}_1 \\ \mathbf{c}_2 \end{pmatrix}$ is a 3-tuple $(\mathbf{x}, \mathbf{r}, \mathbf{f})$ with $\mathbf{r} = \begin{pmatrix} \mathbf{r}_1 \\ \cdots \\ \mathbf{r}_k \end{pmatrix} \in \mathcal{R}_q^k$ and $\mathbf{f} \in \bar{\mathcal{C}}'$, where $\bar{\mathcal{C}}'$ is a set of differences $\mathcal{C}' - \mathcal{C}'$ excluding $\mathbf{0}$. The verifier checks that $\mathbf{f} \begin{pmatrix} \mathbf{c}_1 \\ \mathbf{c}_2 \end{pmatrix} = \begin{pmatrix} \mathbf{A}_1 \\ \mathbf{A}_2 \end{pmatrix} \mathbf{r} + \mathbf{f} \begin{pmatrix} \mathbf{0} \\ \mathbf{x} \end{pmatrix}$, and that for all i, $\|\mathbf{r}_i\|_2 \leq 4\sigma\sqrt{N}$.

References

1. Albrecht, M.R., Player, R., Scott, S.: On the concrete hardness of learning with errors. J. Math. Cryptol. **9**(3), 169–203 (2015)
2. Bai, S., Galbraith, S.D.: An improved compression technique for signatures based on learning with errors. In: Benaloh, J. (ed.) CT-RSA 2014. LNCS, vol. 8366, pp. 28–47. Springer, Cham (2014). https://doi.org/10.1007/978-3-319-04852-9_2
3. Baum, C., Damgård, I., Lyubashevsky, V., Oechsner, S., Peikert, C.: More efficient commitments from structured lattice assumptions. In: Catalano, D., De Prisco, R. (eds.) SCN 2018. LNCS, vol. 11035, pp. 368–385. Springer, Cham (2018). https://doi.org/10.1007/978-3-319-98113-0_20
4. Benhamouda, F., Camenisch, J., Krenn, S., Lyubashevsky, V., Neven, G.: Better zero-knowledge proofs for lattice encryption and their application to group signatures. In: Sarkar, P., Iwata, T. (eds.) ASIACRYPT 2014. LNCS, vol. 8873, pp. 551–572. Springer, Heidelberg (2014). https://doi.org/10.1007/978-3-662-45611-8_29
5. Benhamouda, F., Krenn, S., Lyubashevsky, V., Pietrzak, K.: Efficient zero-knowledge proofs for commitments from learning with errors over rings. In: Pernul, G., Ryan, P.Y.A., Weippl, E. (eds.) ESORICS 2015. LNCS, vol. 9326, pp. 305–325. Springer, Cham (2015). https://doi.org/10.1007/978-3-319-24174-6_16
6. Blum, M.: Coin flipping by telephone - a protocol for solving impossible problems. In: COMPCON 1982, pp. 133–137. IEEE Computer Society (1982)
7. Bootle, J., Lyubashevsky, V., Seiler, G.: Algebraic techniques for short(er) exact lattice-based zero-knowledge proofs. In: Boldyreva, A., Micciancio, D. (eds.) CRYPTO 2019. LNCS, vol. 11692, pp. 176–202. Springer, Cham (2019). https://doi.org/10.1007/978-3-030-26948-7_7
8. Bos, J.W., et al.: CRYSTALS - Kyber: a CCA-secure module-lattice-based KEM. In: 2018 IEEE European Symposium on Security and Privacy, EuroS&P, pp. 353–367. IEEE (2018)
9. Cramer, R., Franklin, M., Schoenmakers, B., Yung, M.: Multi-authority secret-ballot elections with linear work. In: Maurer, U. (ed.) EUROCRYPT 1996. LNCS, vol. 1070, pp. 72–83. Springer, Heidelberg (1996). https://doi.org/10.1007/3-540-68339-9_7
10. Damgård, I.: On Sigma-Protocols. Lectures on Cryptologic Protocol Theory, Faculty of Science, University of Aarhus (2010)
11. Damgård, I., Fujisaki, E.: A statistically-hiding integer commitment scheme based on groups with hidden order. In: Zheng, Y. (ed.) ASIACRYPT 2002. LNCS, vol. 2501, pp. 125–142. Springer, Heidelberg (2002). https://doi.org/10.1007/3-540-36178-2_8
12. Ducas, L., Durmus, A., Lepoint, T., Lyubashevsky, V.: Lattice signatures and bimodal Gaussians. In: Canetti, R., Garay, J.A. (eds.) CRYPTO 2013. LNCS, vol. 8042, pp. 40–56. Springer, Heidelberg (2013). https://doi.org/10.1007/978-3-642-40041-4_3
13. Even, S., Goldreich, O., Lempel, A.: A randomized protocol for signing contracts. Commun. ACM **28**(6), 637–647 (1985)
14. Fujisaki, E., Okamoto, T.: Statistical zero knowledge protocols to prove modular polynomial relations. In: Kaliski, B.S. (ed.) CRYPTO 1997. LNCS, vol. 1294, pp. 16–30. Springer, Heidelberg (1997). https://doi.org/10.1007/BFb0052225
15. Haitner, I., Reingold, O.: Statistically-hiding commitment from any one-way function. In: Johnson, D.S., Feige, U. (eds.) Proceedings of the 39th Annual ACM Symposium on Theory of Computing, pp. 1–10. ACM (2007)

16. Jain, A., Krenn, S., Pietrzak, K., Tentes, A.: Commitments and efficient zero-knowledge proofs from learning parity with noise. In: Wang, X., Sako, K. (eds.) ASIACRYPT 2012. LNCS, vol. 7658, pp. 663–680. Springer, Heidelberg (2012). https://doi.org/10.1007/978-3-642-34961-4_40

17. Kawachi, A., Tanaka, K., Xagawa, K.: Concurrently secure identification schemes based on the worst-case hardness of lattice problems. In: Pieprzyk, J. (ed.) ASIACRYPT 2008. LNCS, vol. 5350, pp. 372–389. Springer, Heidelberg (2008). https://doi.org/10.1007/978-3-540-89255-7_23

18. Lyubashevsky, V.: Lattice signatures without trapdoors. In: Pointcheval, D., Johansson, T. (eds.) EUROCRYPT 2012. LNCS, vol. 7237, pp. 738–755. Springer, Heidelberg (2012). https://doi.org/10.1007/978-3-642-29011-4_43

19. Lyubashevsky, V., Seiler, G.: Short, invertible elements in partially splitting cyclotomic rings and applications to lattice-based zero-knowledge proofs. In: Nielsen, J.B., Rijmen, V. (eds.) EUROCRYPT 2018. LNCS, vol. 10820, pp. 204–224. Springer, Cham (2018). https://doi.org/10.1007/978-3-319-78381-9_8

20. Micciancio, D., Peikert, C.: Trapdoors for lattices: simpler, tighter, faster, smaller. In: Pointcheval, D., Johansson, T. (eds.) EUROCRYPT 2012. LNCS, vol. 7237, pp. 700–718. Springer, Heidelberg (2012). https://doi.org/10.1007/978-3-642-29011-4_41

21. Micciancio, D., Regev, O.: Lattice-based cryptography. In: Bernstein, D.J., Buchmann, J., Dahmen, E. (eds.) Post-Quantum Cryptography, pp. 147–191. Springer, Heidelberg (2009). https://doi.org/10.1007/978-3-540-88702-7_5

22. Naor, M.: Bit commitment using pseudo-randomness. In: Brassard, G. (ed.) CRYPTO 1989. LNCS, vol. 435, pp. 128–136. Springer, New York (1990). https://doi.org/10.1007/0-387-34805-0_13

23. Pedersen, T.P.: Non-interactive and information-theoretic secure verifiable secret sharing. In: Feigenbaum, J. (ed.) CRYPTO 1991. LNCS, vol. 576, pp. 129–140. Springer, Heidelberg (1992). https://doi.org/10.1007/3-540-46766-1_9

24. Vershynin, R.: Introduction to the non-asymptotic analysis of random matrices. CoRR abs/1011.3027 (2010)

25. Xie, X., Xue, R., Wang, M.: Zero knowledge proofs from ring-LWE. In: Abdalla, M., Nita-Rotaru, C., Dahab, R. (eds.) CANS 2013. LNCS, vol. 8257, pp. 57–73. Springer, Cham (2013). https://doi.org/10.1007/978-3-319-02937-5_4

26. Yang, R., Au, M.H., Zhang, Z., Xu, Q., Yu, Z., Whyte, W.: Efficient lattice-based zero-knowledge arguments with standard soundness: construction and applications. In: Boldyreva, A., Micciancio, D. (eds.) CRYPTO 2019. LNCS, vol. 11692, pp. 147–175. Springer, Cham (2019). https://doi.org/10.1007/978-3-030-26948-7_6

COSAC: COmpact and Scalable Arbitrary-Centered Discrete Gaussian Sampling over Integers

Raymond K. Zhao[✉], Ron Steinfeld, and Amin Sakzad

Faculty of Information Technology, Monash University, Melbourne, Australia
{raymond.zhao,ron.steinfeld,amin.sakzad}@monash.edu

Abstract. The arbitrary-centered discrete Gaussian sampler is a fundamental subroutine in implementing lattice trapdoor sampling algorithms. However, existing approaches typically rely on either a fast implementation of another discrete Gaussian sampler or pre-computations with regards to some specific discrete Gaussian distributions with fixed centers and standard deviations. These approaches may only support sampling from standard deviations within a limited range, or cannot efficiently sample from arbitrary standard deviations determined on-the-fly at run-time.

In this paper, we propose a compact and scalable rejection sampling algorithm by sampling from a continuous normal distribution and performing rejection sampling on rounded samples. Our scheme does not require pre-computations related to any specific discrete Gaussian distributions. Our scheme can sample from both arbitrary centers and arbitrary standard deviations determined on-the-fly at run-time. In addition, we show that our scheme only requires a low number of trials close to 2 per sample on average, and our scheme maintains good performance when scaling up the standard deviation. We also provide a concrete error analysis of our scheme based on the Rényi divergence. We implement our sampler and analyse its performance in terms of storage and speed compared to previous results. Our sampler's running time is center-independent and is therefore applicable to implementation of convolution-style lattice trapdoor sampling and identity-based encryption resistant against timing side-channel attacks.

Keywords: Lattice-based crypto · Discrete Gaussian sampling · Implementation · Efficiency

1 Introduction

The arbitrary-centered discrete Gaussian sampling algorithm is an important subroutine in implementing lattice trapdoor samplers, which is a fundamental tool employed by lattice-based cryptography applications such as digital signature [20] and identity-based encryption (IBE) [3,7]. However, previous works

© Springer Nature Switzerland AG 2020
J. Ding and J.-P. Tillich (Eds.): PQCrypto 2020, LNCS 12100, pp. 284–303, 2020.
https://doi.org/10.1007/978-3-030-44223-1_16

focused more on optimising the lattice trapdoor sampling algorithms, but the implementation details of the arbitrary-centered discrete Gaussian sampling were not well addressed. Typically, arbitrary-centered discrete Gaussian sampling approaches need to perform either rejection sampling [5,8,12,20,21] or precomputations related to some specific discrete Gaussian distributions [14,15,17]. However, both types of methods have issues in the implementation: rejection sampling based methods are either slow due to the large number of trials per sample on average (typically, about 8–10) [8], requiring high precision arithmetic for cryptography applications [12], or relying on a fast implementation of another discrete Gaussian sampler [5,20,21]. On the other hand, pre-computation based methods consume at least few kilobytes (KB) of memory to store the tables and have the following limitations: the pre-computation table size in [14,15] grows significantly when scaling up the standard deviation and this approach cannot support arbitrary standard deviations determined on-the-fly at run-time, while it is unclear how to efficiently implement the offline phase in [17] if the full algorithm needs to be executed during the run-time.

Recently the rounded Gaussian sampling (i.e. sampling from a continuous normal distribution and rounding the samples) was adapted by lattice-based digital signatures [11,25]. Compared with a previous discrete Gaussian sampling algorithm [6], the rounded Gaussian sampler in [11] showed impressive performance with regards to the running speed and can be implemented in constant-time. The implementation in [11] is also notably simple (within less than 40 lines of C++ source code). However, since it is unclear whether a rounded Gaussian distribution can be directly adapted to implement a lattice trapdoor, another interesting question is: can one employ the existing efficient (rounded) continuous Gaussian distribution sampling techniques to implement an arbitrary-centered discrete Gaussian sampler?

1.1   Contribution

In this paper, we introduce a novel arbitrary-centered discrete Gaussian sampling algorithm over integers by generalising ideas from [4]. Our scheme samples from a continuous normal distribution and performs rejection sampling on rounded samples by adapting techniques from [11,25]. Compared to previous arbitrary-centered discrete Gaussian sampling techniques, our scheme has the following advantages:

- Our sampling algorithm does not require any pre-computations related to a specific discrete Gaussian distribution or a specific standard deviation, and both the center and the standard deviation can be arbitrary determined on-the-fly at run-time.
- In addition, we show in Sect. 4 that our sampling method only requires a low number of trials close to 2 per sample on average compared to about 8–10 on average in the rejection sampling with regards to a uniform distribution, and the rejection rate of our algorithm decreases when scaling up σ. Therefore, our sampling algorithm is not limited to small σ and can be adapted to sample from larger σ without affecting the efficiency.

- Since sampling from a continuous normal distribution is a well-studied topic [22] and the sampling algorithms are implemented in many existing software libraries (including the C++11 STL) and hardware devices, one can easily implement our scheme by employing existing tools.
- We provide a center-independent run-time implementation of our algorithm without timing leakage of the center and it can be adapted to achieve timing resistant implementation of convolution-style lattice trapdoor sampler [16,18] and IBE [3].

2 Preliminaries

Let $\rho_{c,\sigma}(x) = \exp\left(-(x-c)^2/(2\sigma^2)\right)$ be the (continuous) Gaussian function with center c and standard deviation σ. We denote the continuous Gaussian (normal) distribution with center c and standard deviation σ by $\mathcal{N}(c,\sigma^2)$, which has the probability density function $\rho_{c,\sigma}(x)/(\sigma\sqrt{2\pi})$. We denote the discrete Gaussian distribution on integer lattices with center c and standard deviation σ by: $\mathcal{D}_{c,\sigma}(x) = \rho_{c,\sigma}(x)/S$, where $S = \rho_{c,\sigma}(\mathbb{Z}) = \sum_{k\in\mathbb{Z}}\rho_{c,\sigma}(k)$ is the normalisation factor. We omit the center in notations (i.e. $\rho_\sigma(x)$ and $\mathcal{D}_\sigma(x)$) if the center is zero. In addition, we denote the uniform distribution on set S by $\mathcal{U}(S)$. Sampling from a distribution $\mathcal{P}$ is denoted by $x \hookleftarrow \mathcal{P}$. We define $\lfloor x \rceil$ as the nearest integer to $x \in \mathbb{R}$. We denote $\mathbb{Z}^+$ as the integer set $\{1,\ldots,\infty\}$ and $\mathbb{Z}^-$ as the integer set $\{-\infty,\ldots,-1\}$, respectively. Also, for a lattice Λ and any $\epsilon \in \mathbb{R}^+$, we denote the smoothing parameter $\eta_\epsilon(\Lambda)$ as the smallest $s \in \mathbb{R}^+$ such that $\rho_{1/(s\sqrt{2\pi})}(\Lambda^*\setminus\{\mathbf{0}\}) \le \epsilon$, where Λ^* is the dual lattice of Λ: $\Lambda^* = \{\mathbf{w}\in\mathbb{R}^n : \forall \mathbf{x}\in\Lambda, \mathbf{x}\cdot\mathbf{w}\in\mathbb{Z}\}$ [18]. An upper bound on $\eta_\epsilon(\mathbb{Z})$ is given by [18]: $\eta_\epsilon(\mathbb{Z}) \le \sqrt{\ln(2+2/\epsilon)/\pi}$.

Theorem 1 (Adapted from [18], Lemma 2.4). *For any $\epsilon \in (0,1)$ and $c \in \mathbb{R}$, if $\sigma \ge \eta_\epsilon(\mathbb{Z})$, then $\rho_{c,\sigma}(\mathbb{Z}) = \left[\frac{1-\epsilon}{1+\epsilon},1\right]\cdot\rho_\sigma(\mathbb{Z})$, and $\rho_\sigma(\mathbb{Z})$ is approximately $\int_{-\infty}^\infty \rho_\sigma(x)\,dx = \sigma\sqrt{2\pi}$.*

Definition 1 (Relative Error). *For two distributions $\mathcal{P}$ and $\mathcal{Q}$ such that $\mathrm{Supp}(\mathcal{P}) = \mathrm{Supp}(\mathcal{Q})$, the relative error between $\mathcal{P}$ and $\mathcal{Q}$ is defined as: $\Delta(\mathcal{P}\|\mathcal{Q}) = \max_{x\in\mathrm{Supp}(\mathcal{P})}\frac{|\mathcal{P}(x)-\mathcal{Q}(x)|}{\mathcal{Q}(x)}$.*

Definition 2 (Rényi Divergence [2,19]). *For two discrete distributions $\mathcal{P}$ and $\mathcal{Q}$ such that $\mathrm{Supp}(\mathcal{P}) \subseteq \mathrm{Supp}(\mathcal{Q})$, the Rényi divergence (RD) of order $\alpha \in (1,+\infty)$ is defined as: $R_\alpha(\mathcal{P}\|\mathcal{Q}) = \left(\sum_{x\in\mathrm{Supp}(\mathcal{P})}\frac{\mathcal{P}(x)^\alpha}{\mathcal{Q}(x)^{\alpha-1}}\right)^{\frac{1}{\alpha-1}}$.*

Theorem 2 (Relative Error Bound, Adapted from [19], Lemma 3 and Eq. 4). *For two distributions $\mathcal{P}$ and $\mathcal{Q}$ such that $\mathrm{Supp}(\mathcal{P}) = \mathrm{Supp}(\mathcal{Q})$, we have: $R_\alpha(\mathcal{P}\|\mathcal{Q}) \le \left(1+\frac{\alpha(\alpha-1)\cdot(\Delta(\mathcal{P}\|\mathcal{Q}))^2}{2(1-\Delta(\mathcal{P}\|\mathcal{Q}))^{\alpha+1}}\right)^{\frac{1}{\alpha-1}}$. The right-hand side is asymptotically equivalent to $1 + \alpha\cdot(\Delta(\mathcal{P}\|\mathcal{Q}))^2/2$ as $\Delta(\mathcal{P}\|\mathcal{Q}) \to 0$. In addition,* *if a cryptographic search problem using M independent samples from $\mathcal{Q}$ is $(\lambda + 1)$-bit secure, then the same problem sampling from $\mathcal{P}$ will be λ-bit secure if $R_{2\lambda}(\mathcal{P}\|\mathcal{Q}) \leq 1 + 1/(4M)$.*

3 Previous Work

3.1 Rejection Sampling

The classic rejection sampling algorithm [8,23] can sample from an arbitrary-centered discrete Gaussian distribution. To sample from $\mathcal{D}_{c,\sigma}$, one can sample $x \hookleftarrow \mathcal{U}([c - \tau\sigma, c + \tau\sigma] \cap \mathbb{Z})$ and accept x with probability $\rho_{c,\sigma}(x)$ as the output, where τ is the tail-cut factor (typically, about 10–12). However, this method is slow as the number of trials is $2\tau/\sqrt{2\pi}$ on average (about 8–10 for typical τ). Recently an algorithm sampling exactly from $\mathcal{D}_{c,\sigma}$ without floating-point arithmetic was presented by [12], which also has a lower rejection rate compared to the classic rejection sampling algorithm. However, this algorithm relies on high precision integer arithmetic to satisfy the precision requirements in cryptography applications.

To reduce the rejection rate, recent works performed rejection sampling with regards to some distributions much closer to $\mathcal{D}_{c,\sigma}$ compared to a uniform distribution: The Falcon signature [20] and its constant-time variant [21] adapted a rejection sampling method with regards to bimodal Gaussians: to sample from $\mathcal{D}_{c,\sigma}$ where $c \in [0,1]$, one can choose some $\sigma' \geq \sigma$ and sample $x \hookleftarrow \mathcal{D}_{\sigma'}^{+}$ (i.e. the discrete Gaussian distribution $\mathcal{D}_{\sigma'}$ restricted to the domain $\mathbb{Z}^{+} \cup \{0\}$). The algorithm computes $x' = b + (2b - 1) \cdot x$ where $b \hookleftarrow \mathcal{U}(\{0,1\})$. The authors of [20,21] showed that x' has a bimodal Gaussian distribution close to the target distribution. The algorithm then accepts x' with probability $C(\sigma) \cdot \exp\left(\frac{x^2}{2\sigma'^2} - \frac{(x'-c)^2}{2\sigma^2}\right)$ as the output, where the scaling factor $C(\sigma) = \min(\sigma)/\sigma$ when sampling from multiple σ. This scheme has the average acceptance rate $C(\sigma) \cdot \rho_{c,\sigma}(\mathbb{Z}) / (2\rho_{\sigma'}(\mathbb{Z}^{+}))$, which is proportional to $\min(\sigma)/\sigma'$ [20,21]. However, if the application needs to sample from different σ, the acceptance probability is high only when $\min(\sigma)$ and $\max(\sigma)$ are sufficiently close. This is not an issue in the Falcon signature, since the parameters in Falcon implies σ' is very close to $\max(\sigma)$ and $\min(\sigma)/\max(\sigma) \approx 0.73$ [21]. However, if the gap between $\min(\sigma)$ and $\max(\sigma)$ is large, since $\sigma' \geq \max(\sigma)$, this algorithm might have a low acceptance rate.[1]

A recent work [5] extended the binary sampling algorithm from the BLISS signature [6] to support non-zero arbitrary centers. For any center $c \in \mathbb{R}$, sampling from $\mathcal{D}_{c,\sigma}$ is equivalent to sampling from $\mathcal{D}_{c_F,\sigma} + \lfloor c \rfloor$, where $c_F = c - \lfloor c \rfloor \in [0,1)$ is the fractional part of c. In addition, for $c_F \in [1/2, 1)$, sampling from $\mathcal{D}_{c_F,\sigma}$ is equivalent to sampling from $1 - \mathcal{D}_{c'_F,\sigma}$ where $c'_F = 1 - c_F \in (0, 1/2]$. A modified binary sampling scheme [5] can then be adapted to sample from $\mathcal{D}_{c'_F,\sigma}$

---

[1] One may employ different implementations for different σ, similar to the implementation of Falcon.

with any $c_F' \in (0, 1/2]$, in which the average number of trials is upper-bounded by: $\frac{\sigma^2}{\sigma_0 \sigma - \sigma_0^2} \cdot \frac{\rho_{\sigma_0}(\mathbb{Z}^+)}{\sigma\sqrt{\pi/2}-1}$, where $\sigma_0 = \sqrt{1/(2\ln 2)}$ is a fixed parameter used by the binary sampling algorithm [5,6] and $\sigma = k\sigma_0$ for some $k \in \mathbb{Z}^+$. This upper-bound is about 1.47 for large σ [5].

3.2   TwinCDT

The authors of [14,15] suggested a variant of the Cumulative Distribution Table (CDT) method [4] with multiple pre-computed tables. These algorithms will have two phases: online and offline. To be more specific, for $c \in [0, 1)$, during the offline phase, the algorithm pre-computes multiple CDT of $\mathcal{D}_{i/n,\sigma}$, where $i \in \{0, \ldots, n-1\}$ and $n \in \mathbb{Z}^+$ is sufficiently large. During the online phase, the algorithm picks a sample generated from either $\mathcal{D}_{\lfloor n(c-\lfloor c \rfloor) \rfloor/n,\sigma}$ or $\mathcal{D}_{\lceil n(c-\lfloor c \rfloor) \rceil/n,\sigma}$ as the output. Although the algorithm is very fast compared to other approaches, however, σ is fixed during the offline computation and thus this algorithm cannot support sampling from $\mathcal{D}_{c,\sigma}$ with both arbitrary c and σ determined on-the-fly at run-time. Another issue is that the pre-computation table size grows significantly when scaling up σ (see Table 2 in Sect. 5) and therefore the algorithm is not scalable.

3.3   Convolution

A recursive convolution sampling scheme for $\mathcal{D}_{c,\sigma}$ was presented in [17] as follows: suppose the center c has k fractional bits. Let $\sigma_0 = \sigma/\sqrt{\sum_{i=0}^{k-1} 2^{-2i}}$. One can sample $x_k \hookleftarrow \mathcal{D}_{c_k,\sigma_0}$ where $c_k = 2^{k-1} \cdot c$, then use $y_k = 2^{-k+1} \cdot x_k$ to round c to a new center $c' = c - y_k$ with $k' = k - 1$ fractional bits. Set $c = c'$ and $k = k'$ in the next iteration until $k = 0$, and $\sum_{i=1}^{k} y_i$ will be a sample distributed as $\mathcal{D}_{c,\sigma}$. The authors of [17] separated this algorithm into an online phase and an offline phase, where the offline phase will generate samples x_i in batch and the online phase will compute the linear combinations of x_i for $i \in \{1, \ldots, k\}$. The online phase is very fast and can be implemented in constant-time. However, for implementations where both sampling from $\mathcal{D}_{c_i,\sigma_0}$ and computing the linear combinations need to be carried during the run-time, it is unclear how to efficiently implement the $\mathcal{D}_{c_i,\sigma_0}$ sampling algorithm in constant-time (which is another discrete Gaussian sampler supporting a small amount of centers c_i). The offline batch sampler also consumes significant amount of memory (see Table 2 in Sect. 5).

4   Proposed Algorithm

In the textbook [4], the author defined a variant of the discrete Gaussian distribution as $\Pr[X = z] = c \cdot \exp\left(-(|z| + 1/2)^2 / (2\sigma^2)\right)$, where $z \in \mathbb{Z}$ and c is the normalisation constant, i.e. $\Pr[X = z] \propto \rho_{-1/2,\sigma}(z)$ for $z \geq 0$ and

---

Algorithm 1. Rejection sampler adapted from [4], pg. 117, ch. 3

Input: Standard deviation $\sigma \in \mathbb{R}^+$.
Output: A sample z distributed as $\Pr[X = z] = c \cdot \exp\left(-\left(|z| + 1/2\right)^2 / \left(2\sigma^2\right)\right)$.
  1: **function** SAMPLER(σ)
  2:     Sample $x \hookleftarrow \mathcal{N}\left(0, \sigma^2\right)$.
  3:     Sample $r \hookleftarrow \mathcal{U}\left([0, 1)\right)$.
  4:     Let $Y = \left(\lfloor|x|\rfloor + 1/2\right)^2 - x^2$.
  5:     **if** $r < \exp\left(-Y/\left(2\sigma^2\right)\right)$ **then**
  6:         Let $z = \lfloor x \rfloor$.
  7:     **else**
  8:             **goto** 2.
  9:     **end if**
 10:     **return** z.
 11: **end function**

$\Pr[X = z] \propto \rho_{1/2,\sigma}(z)$ for $z < 0$. A rejection sampling algorithm (see Algorithm 1) was provided by [4] with rejection probability less than $(2/\sigma) \cdot \sqrt{2/\pi}$ for such a distribution, which is fast for large σ (see Appendix B for the proof).

Here we generalise Algorithm 1 to sample from $\mathcal{D}_{c,\sigma}(z)$. By removing the absolute value and replacing the fixed center $-1/2$ with a generic center c in Algorithm 1, we observe that $Y' = \left(\lfloor x \rfloor + c\right)^2 - x^2 \geq 0$ when $(c \geq 1/2, x \geq 0)$ or $(c \leq -1/2, x < 0)$. Therefore, we can replace Y with Y' and perform a similar rejection sampling to Algorithm 1 when sampling from $\mathcal{D}_{c,\sigma}(z)$ for some c and $z = \lfloor x \rfloor$. To extend Algorithm 1 to support all $c \in \mathbb{R}$ and $z \in \mathbb{Z}$, we first compute $c_I = \lfloor c \rfloor$ and $c_F = c_I - c$, where $c_F \in [-1/2, 1/2]$. Then we can sample from $\mathcal{D}_{-c_F,\sigma}$ instead, since $\mathcal{D}_{c,\sigma} = \mathcal{D}_{-c_F,\sigma} + c_I$. To sample from $\mathcal{D}_{-c_F,\sigma}$ for all $c_F \in [-1/2, 1/2]$, we shift the center of the underlying continuous normal distribution, i.e. sampling $y \hookleftarrow \mathcal{N}\left(\pm 1, \sigma^2\right)$, and perform a rejection sampling over $z = \lfloor y \rceil$ with acceptance rate $\exp\left(-Y''/\left(2\sigma^2\right)\right)$ where $Y'' = \left(\lfloor y \rceil + c_F\right)^2 - (y \mp 1)^2$ (we also need to ensure $Y'' \geq 0$ before performing this rejection sampling). The sampling algorithm for $\mathcal{D}_{-c_F,\sigma}$ is presented in Algorithm 2. Note that the output of Algorithm 2 is restricted to the domain $\mathbb{Z} \setminus \{0\}$. Therefore, the algorithm needs to output 0 with probability $\mathcal{D}_{-c_F,\sigma}(0)$. We present the full algorithm in Algorithm 3. Since both Algorithm 2 and Algorithm 3 do not require precomputations related to σ, our scheme can support arbitrary standard deviations determined on-the-fly at run-time in addition to arbitrary centers.

Theorem 3. *The output z sampled by Algorithm 2 is distributed as $\mathcal{D}_{-c_F,\sigma}\left(\mathbb{Z} \setminus \{0\}\right)$. The output of Algorithm 3 is distributed as $\mathcal{D}_{c,\sigma}(\mathbb{Z})$.*

Proof. When $b = 0$, y is distributed as $\mathcal{N}\left(-1, \sigma^2\right)$. For step 11 in Algorithm 2, we have $Y_1 = \left(\lfloor y \rceil + c_F\right)^2 - (y + 1)^2 \geq 0$ for any $c_F \in [-1/2, 1/2]$ when $y \leq -1/2$. Therefore, the rejection condition $\exp\left(-Y_1/\left(2\sigma^2\right)\right) \in (0, 1]$. Let $z_0 = \lfloor y \rceil$. We have the output distribution:

Algorithm 2. $\mathcal{D}_{-c_F,\sigma}(\mathbb{Z} \setminus \{0\})$ sampler

---

Input: Center $c_F \in [-1/2, 1/2]$. Standard deviation $\sigma \in \mathbb{R}^+$.
Output: A sample z distributed as $\mathcal{D}_{-c_F,\sigma}$ restricted to the domain $\mathbb{Z} \setminus \{0\}$.
1: **function** ROUNDINGSAMPLER(c_F, σ)
2:     Sample $x \hookleftarrow \mathcal{N}(0,1)$.
3:     Sample $b \hookleftarrow \mathcal{U}(\{0,1\})$.
4:     **if** $b = 0$ **then**
5:         Let $y = \sigma \cdot x - 1$.
6:         **if** $y > -1/2$ **then**
7:             **goto** 2.
8:         **end if**
9:         Sample $r \hookleftarrow \mathcal{U}([0,1))$.
10:         Let $Y_1 = (\lfloor y \rfloor + c_F)^2 - (y+1)^2$.
11:         **if** $r < \exp\left(-Y_1/\left(2\sigma^2\right)\right)$ **then**
12:             Let $z = \lfloor y \rfloor$.
13:         **else**
14:             **goto** 2.
15:         **end if**
16:     **else**
17:         Let $y = \sigma \cdot x + 1$.
18:         **if** $y < 1/2$ **then**
19:             **goto** 2.
20:         **end if**
21:         Sample $r \hookleftarrow \mathcal{U}([0,1))$.
22:         Let $Y_2 = (\lfloor y \rfloor + c_F)^2 - (y-1)^2$.
23:         **if** $r < \exp\left(-Y_2/\left(2\sigma^2\right)\right)$ **then**
24:             Let $z = \lfloor y \rfloor$.
25:         **else**
26:             **goto** 2.
27:         **end if**
28:     **end if**
29:     **return** z.
30: **end function**

$$\Pr[z = z_0] \propto \int_{z_0-1/2}^{z_0+1/2} \exp\left(-\frac{(y+1)^2}{2\sigma^2}\right) \cdot \exp\left(-\frac{(z_0+c_F)^2 - (y+1)^2}{2\sigma^2}\right) dy$$

$$= \int_{z_0-1/2}^{z_0+1/2} \exp\left(-\frac{(z_0+c_F)^2}{2\sigma^2}\right) dy = \rho_{-c_F,\sigma}(z_0). \tag{1}$$

In this case, the distribution of $z = z_0$ is $\mathcal{D}_{-c_F,\sigma}$ restricted to the domain $\mathbb{Z}^-$ (due to the rejection of y to $(-\infty, -1/2]$).

Similarly, when $b = 1$, y is distributed as $\mathcal{N}(1, \sigma^2)$. For step 23 in Algorithm 2, we have $Y_2 = (\lfloor y \rfloor + c_F)^2 - (y-1)^2 \geq 0$ for any $c_F \in [-1/2, 1/2]$ when $y \geq 1/2$. Therefore, the rejection condition $\exp\left(-Y_2/\left(2\sigma^2\right)\right) \in (0, 1]$. Let $z_0 = \lfloor y \rfloor$.

Algorithm 3. $\mathcal{D}_{c,\sigma}(\mathbb{Z})$ sampler

Input: Center $c \in \mathbb{R}$. Standard deviation $\sigma \in \mathbb{R}^+$. Normalisation factor $S = \rho_{c,\sigma}(\mathbb{Z}) \approx \sigma\sqrt{2\pi}$.

Output: A sample distributed as $\mathcal{D}_{c,\sigma}(\mathbb{Z})$.

1: **function** ROUNDINGSAMPLERFULL(c, σ)
2:     Let $c_I = \lfloor c \rceil$ and $c_F = c_I - c$.
3:     Sample $r \hookleftarrow \mathcal{U}([0, 1))$.
4:     **if** $r < \exp\left(-c_F^2/(2\sigma^2)\right)/S$ **then**
5:        Let $z' = 0$.
6:     **else**
7:        Let $z' = $ RoundingSampler(c_F, σ).
8:     **end if**
9:     **return** $z' + c_I$.
10: **end function**

We have the output distribution:

$$\Pr[z = z_0] \propto \int_{z_0 - 1/2}^{z_0 + 1/2} \exp\left(-\frac{(y-1)^2}{2\sigma^2}\right) \cdot \exp\left(-\frac{(z_0 + c_F)^2 - (y-1)^2}{2\sigma^2}\right) dy$$

$$= \int_{z_0 - 1/2}^{z_0 + 1/2} \exp\left(-\frac{(z_0 + c_F)^2}{2\sigma^2}\right) dy = \rho_{-c_F, \sigma}(z_0). \tag{2}$$

In this case, the distribution of $z = z_0$ is $\mathcal{D}_{-c_F, \sigma}$ restricted to the domain $\mathbb{Z}^+$ (due to the rejection of y to $[1/2, \infty)$). Therefore, the output z in Algorithm 2 is distributed as $\mathcal{D}_{-c_F, \sigma}$ restricted to the domain $\mathbb{Z} \setminus \{0\}$.

In Algorithm 3, the probability $\Pr[z' = 0] = \exp\left(-c_F^2/(2\sigma^2)\right)/S = \mathcal{D}_{-c_F, \sigma}(0)$. Therefore, variable z' is distributed as $\mathcal{D}_{-c_F, \sigma}(\mathbb{Z})$. Since $c = c_I - c_F$, we have the output $z' + c_I$ distributed as $\mathcal{D}_{c,\sigma}(\mathbb{Z})$.

$\square$

To prove the rejection rate of Algorithm 2, we need the following lemma:

Lemma 1. *For any $\epsilon \in (0, 1)$ and $c \in [-1/2, 1/2]$, if $\sigma \geq \eta_\epsilon(\mathbb{Z})$, then both $\rho_{c,\sigma}(\mathbb{Z}^-)$ and $\rho_{c,\sigma}(\mathbb{Z}^+)$ have the lower bound: $\frac{1}{2} \cdot \frac{1-\epsilon}{1+\epsilon} \cdot \rho_\sigma(\mathbb{Z}) - 1$.*

Proof. When $c \in [-1/2, 1/2]$, for $\rho_{c,\sigma}(\mathbb{Z}^-)$, we have:

$$\rho_{c,\sigma}(\mathbb{Z}) = \rho_{c,\sigma}(\mathbb{Z}^+) + \rho_{c,\sigma}(\mathbb{Z}^- \cup \{0\}) \leq 2\rho_{c,\sigma}(\mathbb{Z}^- \cup \{0\}) = 2\rho_{c,\sigma}(\mathbb{Z}^-) + 2\rho_{c,\sigma}(0).$$

Therefore,

$$\rho_{c,\sigma}(\mathbb{Z}^-) \geq \frac{1}{2} \cdot \rho_{c,\sigma}(\mathbb{Z}) - \rho_{c,\sigma}(0)$$

$$\geq \frac{1}{2} \cdot \frac{1-\epsilon}{1+\epsilon} \cdot \rho_\sigma(\mathbb{Z}) - \rho_{c,\sigma}(0) \quad \text{(By Theorem 1).}$$

We have $\rho_\sigma(0) \geq \rho_{c,\sigma}(0)$ for $c \in [-1/2, 1/2]$. Therefore,

$$\rho_{c,\sigma}(\mathbb{Z}^-) \geq \frac{1}{2} \cdot \frac{1-\epsilon}{1+\epsilon} \cdot \rho_\sigma(\mathbb{Z}) - 1.$$

Similarly, when $c \in [-1/2, 1/2]$, for $\rho_{c,\sigma}(\mathbb{Z}^+)$, we have:

$$\rho_{c,\sigma}(\mathbb{Z}) = \rho_{c,\sigma}(\mathbb{Z}^-) + \rho_{c,\sigma}(\mathbb{Z}^+ \cup \{0\}) \leq 2\rho_{c,\sigma}(\mathbb{Z}^+ \cup \{0\}) = 2\rho_{c,\sigma}(\mathbb{Z}^+) + 2\rho_{c,\sigma}(0).$$

Therefore, since $c \in [-1/2, 1/2]$, we have:

$$
\begin{aligned}
\rho_{c,\sigma}(\mathbb{Z}^+) &\geq \frac{1}{2} \cdot \rho_{c,\sigma}(\mathbb{Z}) - \rho_{c,\sigma}(0) \\
&\geq \frac{1}{2} \cdot \frac{1-\epsilon}{1+\epsilon} \cdot \rho_\sigma(\mathbb{Z}) - \rho_{c,\sigma}(0) \quad \text{(By Theorem 1)} \\
&\geq \frac{1}{2} \cdot \frac{1-\epsilon}{1+\epsilon} \cdot \rho_\sigma(\mathbb{Z}) - 1 \quad (\rho_\sigma(0) \geq \rho_{c,\sigma}(0) \text{ when } c \in [-1/2, 1/2]).
\end{aligned}
$$

□

Theorem 4. *For $\sigma \geq \eta_\epsilon(\mathbb{Z})$, the expected number of trials M in Algorithm 2 has the upper bound: $M \leq 2 \cdot \frac{1+\epsilon}{1-\epsilon} \cdot \frac{\sigma\sqrt{2\pi}}{\sigma\sqrt{2\pi}-1-2\cdot\frac{1+\epsilon}{1-\epsilon}}$. If σ is much greater than $\left(1+2\cdot\frac{1+\epsilon}{1-\epsilon}\right)/\sqrt{2\pi}$, then $M \leq 2 \cdot (1 + O(\epsilon) + O(1/\sigma))$.*

Proof. By Theorem 3, when $b = 0$, we have the output probability density function $f(y) = \rho_{-c_F,\sigma}(\lfloor y \rceil)/\rho_{-c_F,\sigma}(\mathbb{Z}^-)$ and the input probability density function $g(y) = \rho_{-1,\sigma}(y)/(\sigma\sqrt{2\pi})$. The expected number of trials can be written as:

$$M = \max \frac{f(y)}{g(y)} = \max \left(\frac{\rho_{-c_F,\sigma}(\lfloor y \rceil)}{\rho_{-1,\sigma}(y)} \cdot \frac{\sigma\sqrt{2\pi}}{\rho_{-c_F,\sigma}(\mathbb{Z}^-)} \right).$$

We have:

$$\frac{\rho_{-c_F,\sigma}(\lfloor y \rceil)}{\rho_{-1,\sigma}(y)} = \frac{\exp\left(-\frac{(\lfloor y \rceil + c_F)^2}{2\sigma^2}\right)}{\exp\left(-\frac{(y+1)^2}{2\sigma^2}\right)} = \exp\left(-\frac{(\lfloor y \rceil + c_F)^2 - (y+1)^2}{2\sigma^2}\right) \leq 1.$$

Therefore,

$$M \leq \frac{\sigma\sqrt{2\pi}}{\rho_{-c_F,\sigma}(\mathbb{Z}^-)} \leq 2 \cdot \frac{1+\epsilon}{1-\epsilon} \cdot \frac{\sigma\sqrt{2\pi}}{\rho_\sigma(\mathbb{Z}) - 2 \cdot \frac{1+\epsilon}{1-\epsilon}} \leq 2 \cdot \frac{1+\epsilon}{1-\epsilon} \cdot \frac{\sigma\sqrt{2\pi}}{\sigma\sqrt{2\pi} - 1 - 2 \cdot \frac{1+\epsilon}{1-\epsilon}},$$

where the second inequality follows from Lemma 1, and the third inequality follows from $\rho_\sigma(\mathbb{Z}) = \rho_\sigma(\mathbb{Z}^- \cup \{0\}) + \rho_\sigma(\mathbb{Z}^+ \cup \{0\}) - 1$ and the sum-integral comparison: $\rho_\sigma(\mathbb{Z}^- \cup \{0\}) \geq \int_{-\infty}^{0} \rho_\sigma(x)\,dx = \sigma\sqrt{\pi/2}$ and $\rho_\sigma(\mathbb{Z}^+ \cup \{0\}) \geq \int_{0}^{\infty} \rho_\sigma(x)\,dx = \sigma\sqrt{\pi/2}$.

Similarly, when $b = 1$, we have the output probability density function $f(y) = \rho_{-c_F,\sigma}(\lfloor y \rceil)/\rho_{-c_F,\sigma}(\mathbb{Z}^+)$ and the input probability density function $g(y) = \rho_{1,\sigma}(y)/(\sigma\sqrt{2\pi})$. The expected number of trials can be written as:

$$M = \max \frac{f(y)}{g(y)} = \max\left(\frac{\rho_{-c_F,\sigma}(\lfloor y \rceil)}{\rho_{1,\sigma}(y)} \cdot \frac{\sigma\sqrt{2\pi}}{\rho_{-c_F,\sigma}(\mathbb{Z}^+)}\right).$$

We have:

$$\frac{\rho_{-c_F,\sigma}(\lfloor y \rceil)}{\rho_{1,\sigma}(y)} = \frac{\exp\left(-\frac{(\lfloor y \rceil+c_F)^2}{2\sigma^2}\right)}{\exp\left(-\frac{(y-1)^2}{2\sigma^2}\right)} = \exp\left(-\frac{(\lfloor y \rceil + c_F)^2 - (y-1)^2}{2\sigma^2}\right) \le 1.$$

Therefore,

$$M \le \frac{\sigma\sqrt{2\pi}}{\rho_{-c_F,\sigma}(\mathbb{Z}^+)} \le 2 \cdot \frac{1+\epsilon}{1-\epsilon} \cdot \frac{\sigma\sqrt{2\pi}}{\rho_\sigma(\mathbb{Z}) - 2 \cdot \frac{1+\epsilon}{1-\epsilon}} \le 2 \cdot \frac{1+\epsilon}{1-\epsilon} \cdot \frac{\sigma\sqrt{2\pi}}{\sigma\sqrt{2\pi} - 1 - 2 \cdot \frac{1+\epsilon}{1-\epsilon}},$$

where the second inequality follows from Lemma 1, and the third inequality follows from $\rho_\sigma(\mathbb{Z}) \ge \sigma\sqrt{2\pi} - 1$.

When σ is much greater than $\left(1 + 2 \cdot \frac{1+\epsilon}{1-\epsilon}\right)/\sqrt{2\pi}$, $\sigma\sqrt{2\pi}$ is much greater than $1 + 2 \cdot \frac{1+\epsilon}{1-\epsilon}$. Thus,

$$M \le 2 \cdot \frac{1+\epsilon}{1-\epsilon} \cdot \frac{\sigma\sqrt{2\pi}}{\sigma\sqrt{2\pi} - 1 - 2 \cdot \frac{1+\epsilon}{1-\epsilon}} \le 2 \cdot (1 + O(\epsilon) + O(1/\sigma)).$$

$\square$

4.1   Accuracy Analysis

We now analyse the relative error of Algorithm 2 here. Let the absolute error of the continuous Gaussian sample x be e_x: $x' = x + e$, where x' is the actual sample, x is the ideal sample, and the error $|e| \le e_x$. We denote the actual distribution by $\mathcal{P}_{actual}$ and the ideal distribution by $\mathcal{P}_{ideal}$. Since the variable y might be rounded to an incorrect integer due to the error from x when y is close to the boundaries $z_0 \pm 1/2$ [11], we have:

$$\Delta(\mathcal{P}_{actual}\|\mathcal{P}_{ideal}) = \max\left|\frac{\mathcal{P}_{actual}}{\mathcal{P}_{ideal}} - 1\right|$$

$$= \max_{z_0}\left|\frac{\int_{z_0-1/2-\sigma e_x}^{z_0+1/2+\sigma e_x} \exp\left(-\frac{(z_0+c_F)^2}{2\sigma^2}\right)dy}{\rho_{-c_F,\sigma}(z_0)} - 1\right| \quad \text{(by (1), (2), and } y = \sigma x \pm 1\text{)}$$

$$= \max_{z_0}\left|\frac{(1+2\sigma e_x) \cdot \rho_{-c_F,\sigma}(z_0)}{\rho_{-c_F,\sigma}(z_0)} - 1\right| = 2\sigma e_x.$$

By Theorem 2, for λ-bit security, we need:

$$R_{2\lambda}\left(\mathcal{P}_{\text{actual}}||\mathcal{P}_{\text{ideal}}\right) \leq 1 + \frac{1}{4M} \implies 1 + 2\lambda \cdot \frac{\left(\Delta\left(\mathcal{P}_{\text{actual}}||\mathcal{P}_{\text{ideal}}\right)\right)^2}{2} \leq 1 + \frac{1}{4M}$$

$$\implies e_x \leq \frac{1}{4\sigma\sqrt{\lambda M}}.$$

Note that both $\mathcal{P}_{\text{actual}}$ and $\mathcal{P}_{\text{ideal}}$ have the same normalisation factor, since $\mathcal{P}_{\text{actual}}$ is obtained by the imperfect continuous Gaussian distribution with the rounding error contributed to the interval of the integral [11].

5   Evaluation

Side-channel Resistance Our implementation is not fully constant-time because the rejection rate may still reveal σ due to Theorem 4. However, since the rejection rate is independent of the center, our implementation can achieve fully constant-time with respect to the secret if σ is public. The σ in convolution-style lattice trapdoor samplers [16,18] is typically a public constant, but σ in GPV-style sampler [10] depends on the secret. Note that the IBE implementation in [3] adapted a variant of [16], but it appears that the implementation source code[2] of [3] used a different distribution and the side-channel resistance perspective is unclear. Our sampling algorithm can be applied in the IBE implementation of [3] to give a fully constant-time IBE implementation.

We perform benchmarks of Algorithm 3 with fixed σ and random arbitrary centers. We employ the Box-Muller continuous Gaussian sampler [11,25] implemented by using the VCL library [9], which provides $e_x \leq 2^{-48}$ [11]. To compare with [15], we select $\sigma = \{2, 4, 8, 16, 32\}$, and to compare with [17], we choose $\sigma = 2^{15}$. In addition, we also compare with variants [5,26] of the binary sampling algorithm [6] for additional $\sigma = \{2^{17}, 2^{20}\}$. From the error analysis in Sect. 4.1, for given e_x and λ, $M \leq \frac{1}{16\lambda e_x^2 \sigma^2}$. For $\sigma \in [2, 2^{20}]$ and $\lambda = 128$, we have $M \leq 2^{45}$. We adapt techniques similar to [26] to avoid high precision arithmetic (see Appendix A for details) and the scheme[3] is implemented by using the double precision i.e. $\delta_f = 52$. We also compute the normalisation factor S in double precision. We use the AES256 counter mode with hardware AES instructions (AES-NI) to generate the randomness in our implementations. We provide both the non-constant time reference implementation and the center-independent run-time implementation. We take care of all the branches for the center-independent run-time implementation by adapting constant-time selection techniques [1]. For the non-constant time reference implementation (the "Ref." column in Table 1), we use the $\exp(x)$ from the C library, which provides about 50-bit precision [20], while for the center-independent run-time implementation (the "Center-independent" column in Table 1), we adapt the techniques from [26] with about 45-bit precision. From the precision analysis in [19,26], the

---

[2] https://github.com/lbibe/code.
[3] Our implementation is available at https://github.com/raykzhao/gaussian_ac.

Table 1. Number of samples per second for our scheme with fixed σ at 4.2 GHz (with $\lambda = 128$).

σ	Ref. ($\times 10^6$)	Center-independent ($\times 10^6$)
2	10.33 ± 0.18	8.96 ± 0.16
4	11.57 ± 0.18	10.87 ± 0.15
8	11.95 ± 0.17	11.61 ± 0.13
16	12.14 ± 0.16	12.00 ± 0.12
32	12.19 ± 0.15	12.21 ± 0.11
2^{15}	11.70 ± 0.13	11.57 ± 0.09
2^{17}	11.20 ± 0.14	11.63 ± 0.10
2^{20}	11.17 ± 0.13	11.28 ± 0.09

above precisions (including the precision of S) are sufficient for $\lambda = 128$ and $M \leq 2^{45}$.

The benchmark is carried on as follows: we use g++ 9.1.1 to compile our implementations with the compiling options -O3 -march=native enabled. The benchmark is running on an Intel i7-7700K CPU at 4.2 GHz, with the Hyperthreading and the Turbo Boost disabled. We generate 1024 samples (with a random arbitrary center per sample) for 1000 times and measure the consumed CPU cycles, with the exception that we fix $c = 0$ and compare our center-independent run-time implementation with [26], since the scheme in [26] is essentially a constant-time zero-centered discrete Gaussian sampler. Then we convert the CPU cycles to the average number of samples per second for the comparison purpose with previous works.

The benchmark results of our scheme are shown in Table 1 (in the format of mean $\pm$ standard deviation). We also summarise the performance of previous works in Table 2, and show the comparison with [26] in Table 3 when $c = 0$. Since previous works [5,15,17] measured the number of generated samples per second running on CPUs with different frequencies, we scale all the numbers to be based on 4.2 GHz. In addition, since some previous works [15,17] require pre-computations to implement the sampling schemes, we summarise the pre-computation memory storage consumptions in Table 2. Because the TwinCDT method [15] provided different tradeoffs between the running speed and the pre-computation storage consumption, we show all 3 different sampling speeds and the corresponding pre-computation storage consumptions for each σ from [15]. Note that although our sampling scheme does not require pre-computations, however, the $\exp(x)$ implementation typically consumes a small amount of memory to store the coefficients of the polynomial approximation. For example, the polynomial approximation of the $\exp(x)$ in our center-independent run-time implementation (adapted from [26]) has degree 10 with double precision coefficients, and therefore it consumes $(10 + 1) \cdot 8 = 88$ bytes.

Table 2. Summary of previous works for fixed σ at 4.2 GHz (with $\lambda = 128$).

σ	Num. of samples ($\times 10^6$/sec)	Pre-computation storage (KB)
2 [15]	51.01/62.45/76.43	1.4/4.6/46
4 [15]	45.50/56.44/69.09	1.9/6.3/63
8 [15]	37.70/53.31/63.51	3/10/100
16 [15]	31.29/37.63/52.29	5.2/17/172
32 [15]	34.38/39.76/42.60	9.5/32/318
2^{15} [17]	≈ 12.35 (online)[b], 1.78 (online+offline)[a]	$2^{5.4}$[a]
4–2^{20} [5]	≈ 16.3	–[c]

[a]The online+offline benchmark result is obtained and scaled from the variant implemented by [5].
[b]The result in [17] is based on the authors' reference implementation, which is not claimed to be optimal [24].
[c]The base sampler and the Bernoulli sampler may require pre-computations depending on the implementation techniques.

Table 3. Number of samples per second compared with [26] for fixed σ and $c = 0$ at 4.2 GHz (with $\lambda = 128$).

σ	Our Scheme ($\times 10^6$/sec)	[26] ($\times 10^6$/sec)
2	9.44	19.87
4	11.10	19.04
8	12.08	19.04
16	12.63	18.62
32	12.93	18.80
2^{15}	12.67	18.36
2^{17}	12.67	18.90
2^{20}	13.04	18.70

From Table 1, our scheme has good performance for both small and large σ (11.53×10^6 samples per second for the non-constant time reference implementation and 11.27×10^6 samples per second for the center-independent run-time implementation on average). In particular, our scheme has better performance for large σ since the number of trials becomes lower by Theorem 4. Note that the amount of randomness required by the comparison steps in Appendix A will significantly increase for very small or very large σ. Therefore, our implementation consumes different amount of randomness in comparison steps for each σ based on Appendix A, and the performance for some larger σ is slightly slower than smaller σ in Table 1 due to the increased amount of randomness required. The overhead introduced by the center-independent run-time implementation is at most 13.33% in our benchmarks. Note that the overhead of the center-independent run-time implementation is smaller for large σ due to the lower probability of outputting $z' = 0$ in Algorithm 3.

For $\sigma \in [2, 32]$, although the TwinCDT method [15] is 2.5x–7.3x faster than our non-constant time reference implementation, however, this method requires a pre-computation with at least 1.4 KB memory consumption to store the CDT, while our scheme only requires at most several hundred bytes if considering all the polynomial approximation coefficients (including those functions used by the Box-Muller continuous Gaussian sampler). When scaling up σ, the TwinCDT method [15] also costs much larger amount of memory (the pre-computation storage size increases by a factor of 6.7–6.9 when σ changes from 2 to 32), and the performance becomes significantly worse (the number of samples per second decreases by 32.6–44.3% when σ changes from 2 to 32). In contrary, the pre-computation storage of our scheme is independent of σ and only relies on the precision requirements. Our scheme is also scalable and maintains good performance even for large $\sigma = 2^{15}$. In addition, for applications sampling from various σ such as [7], one sampler subroutine implemented by using our scheme is able to serve all σ since the implementation does not require any pre-computations depending on σ, while the TwinCDT method [15] needs to pre-compute a different CDT for each σ.

Compared with [17] for $\sigma = 2^{15}$, if we measure both the online and offline phase running speed in total, our center-independent run-time implementation achieves better performance in terms of both timing (6.5x faster) and pre-computation storage (the implementation in [17] requires about 42 KB to implement the Knuth-Yao [13] offline batch sampler).[4] The online-phase only running speed in [17] is slightly (1.07x) faster than our scheme. On the other hand, our scheme requires no offline pre-computations related to a specific discrete Gaussian distribution. In addition, our scheme can also be accelerated if we generate all the continuous Gaussian samples during the offline phase and only perform the rejection during the online phase. In this case, our center-independent run-time implementation generates 13.73×10^6 samples per second during the online phase, which is 1.11x faster than [17].

For the comparison with variants of the binary sampling algorithm, in Table 2, our non-constant time reference implementation is about 28.2% slower than [5] for $\sigma \in [4, 2^{20}]$ with arbitrary centers, and from Table 3, our center-independent run-time implementation is 30.3%–52.5% slower than [26] when $c = 0$ and $\sigma \in [2, 2^{20}]$. However, the scheme in [26] does not support an arbitrary center, while the side-channel resistance perspective of [5] is unclear. We expect that our implementation can achieve at most about 73.5% of the running speed of [5,26] on average for large σ, since both binary sampling variants [5,26] require less than 1.47 trials per sample on average, while the average number of trials per sample is close to 2 in our scheme for large σ.

---

[4] Here we compare the performance with our center-independent run-time implementation because the implementation in [17] is constant-time.

6 Conclusion

In conclusion, we generalise the idea from [4] and present a compact and scalable arbitrary-centered discrete Gaussian sampling scheme over integers. Our scheme performs rejection sampling on rounded samples from a continuous normal distribution, which does not rely on any discrete Gaussian sampling implementations. We show that our scheme maintains good performance for $\sigma \in \left[2, 2^{20}\right]$ and needs no pre-computations related to any specific σ, which is suitable to implement applications that requires sampling from multiple different σ. In addition, we provide concrete rejection rate and error analysis of our scheme.

The performance of our scheme heavily relies on the underlying continuous Gaussian sampling algorithm. However, the Box-Muller sampler [11,25] employed in our implementation does not have the fastest sampling speed compared to other algorithms according to a survey [22]. The main reason behind the choice of the continuous Gaussian sampler in our implementation is because the Box-Muller sampler is very simple to implement in constant-time [11]. If the side-channel perspective is not a concern, one may employ other more efficient non-constant time algorithms from the survey [22] to achieve a faster implementation of our scheme.

Acknowledgments. Ron Steinfeld was supported in part by ARC Discovery Project grant DP180102199.

A Precision Analysis

To avoid sampling a uniformly random real r with high absolute precisions at rejection steps 11 and 23 in Algorithm 2, and step 4 in Algorithm 3, we adapt the comparison approach similar to [26]. Assume an IEEE-754 floating-point value $f \in (0, 1)$ with $(\delta_f + 1)$-bit precision is represented by $f = \left(1 + mantissa \cdot 2^{-\delta_f}\right) \cdot 2^{exponent}$, where integer $mantissa$ has δ_f bits and $exponent \in \mathbb{Z}^-$. To check $r < f$, one can sample $r_m \hookleftarrow \mathcal{U}\left(\{0,1\}^{\delta_f + 1}\right)$, $r_e \hookleftarrow \mathcal{U}\left(\{0,1\}^l\right)$, and check $r_m < mantissa + 2^{\delta_f}$ and $r_e < 2^{l + exponent + 1}$ instead for some l such that $l + exponent + 1 \geq 0$.

Here we analyse the precision requirement of r_e. We have the following theorem for the worst-case acceptance rate in Algorithm 2:

Theorem 5. *Assume $x \in [-\tau, \tau]$ and $y \in [-\tau\sigma - 1, \tau\sigma + 1]$. In worst case, step 11 in Algorithm 2 has the acceptance rate:*

$$p_1 \geq \exp\left(-\frac{(-2\tau\sigma + c_F - 3/2)(c_F - 3/2)}{2\sigma^2}\right),$$

and step 23 in Algorithm 2 has the acceptance rate:

$$p_2 \geq \exp\left(-\frac{(2\tau\sigma + c_F + 3/2)(c_F + 3/2)}{2\sigma^2}\right).$$

Proof. For $b = 0$ and $y \leq -1/2$, we have the acceptance rate $p_1 = \exp\left(-Y_1/\left(2\sigma^2\right)\right)$ at step 11 in Algorithm 2 where:

$$
\begin{aligned}
Y_1 &= \left(\lfloor y \rfloor + c_F\right)^2 - (y+1)^2 \\
&= (y + \delta + c_F)^2 - (y+1)^2 \quad (\lfloor y \rfloor = y + \delta \text{ where } \delta \in [-1/2, 1/2]) \\
&= (2y + \delta + c_F + 1)(\delta + c_F - 1) \\
&\leq (-2\tau\sigma + c_F - 3/2)(c_F - 3/2). \quad (\text{when } \delta = -1/2 \text{ and } y = -\tau\sigma - 1)
\end{aligned}
$$

Similarly, for $b = 1$ and $y \geq 1/2$, we have the acceptance rate $p_2 = \exp\left(-Y_2/\left(2\sigma^2\right)\right)$ at step 23 in Algorithm 2 where:

$$
\begin{aligned}
Y_2 &= \left(\lfloor y \rfloor + c_F\right)^2 - (y-1)^2 \\
&= (y + \delta + c_F)^2 - (y-1)^2 \quad (\lfloor y \rfloor = y + \delta \text{ where } \delta \in [-1/2, 1/2]) \\
&= (2y + \delta + c_F - 1)(\delta + c_F + 1) \\
&\leq (2\tau\sigma + c_F + 3/2)(c_F + 3/2). \quad (\text{when } \delta = 1/2 \text{ and } y = \tau\sigma + 1)
\end{aligned}
$$

$\square$

Let $\Delta \leq 1/2$ be the maximum relative error of the right hand side computations at rejection steps 11 and 23 in Algorithm 2, and step 4 in Algorithm 3. For $\exp\left(-Y_1/\left(2\sigma^2\right)\right)$ at step 11 in Algorithm 2, we have:

$$
\begin{aligned}
exponent_1 &\geq \left\lfloor \log_2\left((1-\Delta) \cdot \exp\left(-\frac{Y_1}{2\sigma^2}\right)\right) \right\rfloor \\
&\geq \left\lfloor -1 - \frac{(-2\tau\sigma + c_F - 3/2)(c_F - 3/2)}{2\sigma^2} \cdot \log_2 e \right\rfloor \quad (\text{by Thm. 5 and } \Delta \leq 1/2) \\
&\geq \left\lfloor -1 - \frac{2\tau\sigma + 2}{\sigma^2} \cdot \log_2 e \right\rfloor. \quad (\text{when } c_F = -1/2)
\end{aligned}
$$

Similarly, for $\exp\left(-Y_2/\left(2\sigma^2\right)\right)$ at step 23 in Algorithm 2, we have:

$$
\begin{aligned}
exponent_2 &\geq \left\lfloor \log_2\left((1-\Delta) \cdot \exp\left(-\frac{Y_2}{2\sigma^2}\right)\right) \right\rfloor \\
&\geq \left\lfloor -1 - \frac{(2\tau\sigma + c_F + 3/2)(c_F + 3/2)}{2\sigma^2} \cdot \log_2 e \right\rfloor \quad (\text{by Thm. 5 and } \Delta \leq 1/2) \\
&\geq \left\lfloor -1 - \frac{2\tau\sigma + 2}{\sigma^2} \cdot \log_2 e \right\rfloor. \quad (\text{when } c_F = 1/2)
\end{aligned}
$$

For $\exp\left(-c_F^2/\left(2\sigma^2\right)\right)/S$ at step 4 in Algorithm 3, we have:

$$
\begin{aligned}
exponent_3 &\geq \left\lfloor \log_2\left((1-\Delta) \cdot \exp\left(-\frac{c_F^2}{2\sigma^2}\right)/S\right) \right\rfloor \\
&\geq \left\lfloor -1 - \frac{1}{8\sigma^2} \cdot \log_2 e - \log_2\left(\sigma\sqrt{2\pi}\right) \right\rfloor. \quad (\text{when } c_F = \pm 1/2 \text{ and } \Delta \leq 1/2)
\end{aligned}
$$

Therefore, we have:

$$exponent \geq \min\left\{ \left\lfloor -1 - \frac{2\tau\sigma + 2}{\sigma^2} \cdot \log_2 e \right\rfloor, \left\lfloor -1 - \frac{1}{8\sigma^2} \cdot \log_2 e - \log_2\left(\sigma\sqrt{2\pi}\right) \right\rfloor \right\}.$$

Since the probability $\Pr\left[-\tau \leq x \leq \tau\right] = \mathrm{erf}\left(\tau/\sqrt{2}\right)$ for $x \hookleftarrow \mathcal{N}(0,1)$, to ensure $1 - \Pr\left[-\tau \leq x \leq \tau\right] \leq 2^{-\lambda}$, we need $\tau \geq \sqrt{2} \cdot \mathrm{erf}^{-1}\left(1 - 2^{-\lambda}\right)$. Therefore, for $\lambda = 128$ and $\sigma \in \left[2, 2^{20}\right]$, we have $\tau \geq 13.11$, $exponent \geq -23$, and thus $l \geq 22$, i.e. r_e needs to have at least 22 bits.

B   Proof of Algorithm 1

Since Algorithm 1 was an exercise in [4] without solutions, here we provide a brief proof of Algorithm 1.

Normalisation Factor. By definition, we have the normalisation factor:

$$\frac{1}{c} = \sum_{k\in\mathbb{Z}} \exp\left(-\frac{(|k| + 1/2)^2}{2\sigma^2}\right)$$

$$= \sum_{k\in\mathbb{Z}^-} \exp\left(-\frac{(k - 1/2)^2}{2\sigma^2}\right) + \exp\left(-\frac{1}{8\sigma^2}\right) + \sum_{k\in\mathbb{Z}^+} \exp\left(-\frac{(k + 1/2)^2}{2\sigma^2}\right)$$

$$= \rho_{1/2,\sigma}\left(\mathbb{Z}^-\right) + \rho_{-1/2,\sigma}\left(\mathbb{Z}^+\right) + \exp\left(-\frac{1}{8\sigma^2}\right)$$

$$\geq \frac{1 - \epsilon}{1 + \epsilon} \cdot \rho_\sigma\left(\mathbb{Z}\right) + \exp\left(-\frac{1}{8\sigma^2}\right) - 2. \quad \text{(By Lemma 1)}$$

Correctness. Let $z_0 = \lfloor x \rceil$. We have $Y = (|z_0| + 1/2)^2 - x^2 \geq 0$ for any $x \in \mathbb{R}$. Therefore, the rejection condition $\exp\left(-Y/\left(2\sigma^2\right)\right) \in (0, 1]$. We have the output distribution:

$$\Pr\left[z = z_0\right] \propto \int_{z_0 - 1/2}^{z_0 + 1/2} \exp\left(-\frac{x^2}{2\sigma^2}\right) \cdot \exp\left(-\frac{(|z_0| + 1/2)^2 - x^2}{2\sigma^2}\right) dx$$

$$= \int_{z_0 - 1/2}^{z_0 + 1/2} \exp\left(-\frac{(|z_0| + 1/2)^2}{2\sigma^2}\right) dx = \exp\left(-\frac{(|z_0| + 1/2)^2}{2\sigma^2}\right).$$

Rejection Rate. By definition, we have the output probability density function $f(x) = c \cdot \exp\left(-\frac{(\lfloor |x| \rceil + 1/2)^2}{2\sigma^2}\right)$ and the input probability density function $g(x) = \rho_\sigma\left(x\right) / \left(\sigma\sqrt{2\pi}\right)$. The expected number of trials can be written as:

$$M = \max \frac{f(x)}{g(x)} = \max\left(\frac{\exp\left(-\frac{(\lfloor |x| \rceil + 1/2)^2}{2\sigma^2}\right)}{\rho_\sigma\left(x\right)} \cdot \frac{\sigma\sqrt{2\pi}}{1/c}\right).$$

We have:

$$\frac{\exp\left(-\frac{(\lfloor|x|\rceil+1/2)^2}{2\sigma^2}\right)}{\rho_\sigma(x)} = \frac{\exp\left(-\frac{(\lfloor|x|\rceil+1/2)^2}{2\sigma^2}\right)}{\exp\left(-\frac{x^2}{2\sigma^2}\right)} = \exp\left(-\frac{(\lfloor|x|\rceil+1/2)^2 - x^2}{2\sigma^2}\right) \le 1.$$

Therefore,

$$M \le \frac{\sigma\sqrt{2\pi}}{1/c} \le \frac{\sigma\sqrt{2\pi}}{\frac{1-\epsilon}{1+\epsilon}\cdot\rho_\sigma(\mathbb{Z}) + \exp\left(-\frac{1}{8\sigma^2}\right) - 2}$$

$$\le \frac{\sigma\sqrt{2\pi}}{\frac{1-\epsilon}{1+\epsilon}\cdot\left(\sigma\sqrt{2\pi}-1\right) + \exp\left(-\frac{1}{8\sigma^2}\right) - 2},$$

where the second inequality follows from the inequality of $1/c$ and the third inequality follows from the fact that $\rho_\sigma(\mathbb{Z}) \ge \sigma\sqrt{2\pi} - 1$. Thus, we have the rejection probability:

$$1 - \frac{1}{M} \le \frac{\left(1 - \frac{1-\epsilon}{1+\epsilon}\right)\cdot\sigma\sqrt{2\pi} + \frac{1-\epsilon}{1+\epsilon} - \exp\left(-\frac{1}{8\sigma^2}\right) + 2}{\sigma\sqrt{2\pi}} \approx \frac{3 - \exp\left(-\frac{1}{8\sigma^2}\right)}{\sigma\sqrt{2\pi}} \le \frac{2}{\sigma}\sqrt{\frac{2}{\pi}},$$

when ϵ is small.

References

1. Aumasson, J.P.: Guidelines for low-level cryptography software (2019). https://github.com/veorq/cryptocoding. Accessed 28 Jan 2020
2. Bai, S., Langlois, A., Lepoint, T., Stehlé, D., Steinfeld, R.: Improved security proofs in lattice-based cryptography: using the Rényi divergence rather than the statistical distance. In: Iwata, T., Cheon, J.H. (eds.) ASIACRYPT 2015. LNCS, vol. 9452, pp. 3–24. Springer, Heidelberg (2015). https://doi.org/10.1007/978-3-662-48797-6_1
3. Bert, P., Fouque, P.-A., Roux-Langlois, A., Sabt, M.: Practical implementation of ring-SIS/LWE based signature and IBE. In: Lange, T., Steinwandt, R. (eds.) PQCrypto 2018. LNCS, vol. 10786, pp. 271–291. Springer, Cham (2018). https://doi.org/10.1007/978-3-319-79063-3_13
4. Devroye, L.: Non-Uniform Random Variate Generation. Springer, New York (1986). https://doi.org/10.1007/978-1-4613-8643-8
5. Du, Y., Wei, B., Zhang, H.: A rejection sampling algorithm for off-centered discrete Gaussian distributions over the integers. Sci. China Inf. Sci. **62**(3), 39103:1–39103:3 (2019)
6. Ducas, L., Durmus, A., Lepoint, T., Lyubashevsky, V.: Lattice signatures and bimodal Gaussians. In: Canetti, R., Garay, J.A. (eds.) CRYPTO 2013. LNCS, vol. 8042, pp. 40–56. Springer, Heidelberg (2013). https://doi.org/10.1007/978-3-642-40041-4_3
7. Ducas, L., Lyubashevsky, V., Prest, T.: Efficient identity-based encryption over NTRU lattices. In: Sarkar, P., Iwata, T. (eds.) ASIACRYPT 2014. LNCS, vol. 8874, pp. 22–41. Springer, Heidelberg (2014). https://doi.org/10.1007/978-3-662-45608-8_2

8. Ducas, L., Nguyen, P.Q.: Faster gaussian lattice sampling using lazy floating-point arithmetic. In: Wang, X., Sako, K. (eds.) ASIACRYPT 2012. LNCS, vol. 7658, pp. 415–432. Springer, Heidelberg (2012). https://doi.org/10.1007/978-3-642-34961-4_26

9. Fog, A.: VCL C++ vector class library. www.agner.org/optimize/vectorclass.pdf. Accessed 01 Aug 2019

10. Gentry, C., Peikert, C., Vaikuntanathan, V.: Trapdoors for hard lattices and new cryptographic constructions. In: STOC, pp. 197–206. ACM (2008)

11. Hülsing, A., Lange, T., Smeets, K.: Rounded Gaussians. In: Abdalla, M., Dahab, R. (eds.) PKC 2018. LNCS, vol. 10770, pp. 728–757. Springer, Cham (2018). https://doi.org/10.1007/978-3-319-76581-5_25

12. Karney, C.F.F.: Sampling exactly from the normal distribution. ACM Trans. Math. Softw. **42**(1), 3:1–3:14 (2016)

13. Knuth, D., Yao, A.: Algorithms and Complexity: New Directions and Recent Results, chap. The complexity of nonuniform random number generation. Academic Press, Cambridge (1976)

14. Aguilar-Melchor, C., Albrecht, M.R., Ricosset, T.: Sampling from arbitrary centered discrete gaussians for lattice-based cryptography. In: Gollmann, D., Miyaji, A., Kikuchi, H. (eds.) ACNS 2017. LNCS, vol. 10355, pp. 3–19. Springer, Cham (2017). https://doi.org/10.1007/978-3-319-61204-1_1

15. Melchor, C.A., Ricosset, T.: CDT-based Gaussian sampling: From multi to double precision. IEEE Trans. Comput. **67**(11), 1610–1621 (2018)

16. Micciancio, D., Peikert, C.: Trapdoors for lattices: simpler, tighter, faster, smaller. In: Pointcheval, D., Johansson, T. (eds.) EUROCRYPT 2012. LNCS, vol. 7237, pp. 700–718. Springer, Heidelberg (2012). https://doi.org/10.1007/978-3-642-29011-4_41

17. Micciancio, D., Walter, M.: Gaussian sampling over the integers: efficient, generic, constant-time. In: Katz, J., Shacham, H. (eds.) CRYPTO 2017. LNCS, vol. 10402, pp. 455–485. Springer, Cham (2017). https://doi.org/10.1007/978-3-319-63715-0_16

18. Peikert, C.: An efficient and parallel Gaussian sampler for lattices. In: Rabin, T. (ed.) CRYPTO 2010. LNCS, vol. 6223, pp. 80–97. Springer, Heidelberg (2010). https://doi.org/10.1007/978-3-642-14623-7_5

19. Prest, T.: Sharper bounds in lattice-based cryptography using the Rényi divergence. In: Takagi, T., Peyrin, T. (eds.) ASIACRYPT 2017. LNCS, vol. 10624, pp. 347–374. Springer, Cham (2017). https://doi.org/10.1007/978-3-319-70694-8_13

20. Prest, T., et al.: Falcon: fast-fourier lattice-based compact signatures over NTRU. https://falcon-sign.info/ (2017). Accessed 31 Oct 2018

21. Prest, T., Ricosset, T., Rossi, M.: Simple, fast and constant-time Gaussian sampling over the integers for Falcon. In: Second PQC Standardization Conference. https://csrc.nist.gov/CSRC/media/Events/Second-PQC-Standardization-Conference/documents/accepted-papers/rossi-simple-fast-constant.pdf (2019). Accessed 13 Aug 2019

22. Thomas, D.B., Luk, W., Leong, P.H.W., Villasenor, J.D.: Gaussian random number generators. ACM Comput. Surv. **39**(4), 11 (2007)

23. von Neumann, J.: Various techniques used in connection with random digits. In: Householder, A., Forsythe, G., Germond, H. (eds.) Monte Carlo Method, pp. 36–38 (1951). National Bureau of Standards Applied Mathematics Series, 12, Washington, D.C.: U.S. Government Printing Office

24. Walter, M.: Private communication (2020). Accessed 29 Jan 2020

25. Zhang, Z., Chen, C., Hoffstein, J., Whyte, W.: NIST PQ submission: pqNTRUSign a modular lattice signature scheme (2017). https://www.onboardsecurity.com/nist-post-quantum-crypto-submission. Accessed 01 Aug 2019
26. Zhao, R.K., Steinfeld, R., Sakzad, A.: FACCT: fast, compact, and constant-time discrete Gaussian sampler over integers. IEEE Trans. Comput. **69**(1), 126–137 (2020)

Multivariate Cryptography

Combinatorial Rank Attacks Against the Rectangular Simple Matrix Encryption Scheme

Daniel Apon[1], Dustin Moody[1], Ray Perlner[1], Daniel Smith-Tone[1,2(✉)], and Javier Verbel[3]

[1] National Institute of Standards and Technology, Gaithersburg, USA
[2] University of Louisville, Louisville, USA
{daniel.apon,dustin.moody,ray.perlner,daniel.smith}@nist.gov
[3] Universidad Nacional de Colombia, Bogotá, Colombia
javerbel@unal.edu.co

Abstract. In 2013, Tao et al. introduced the ABC Simple Matrix Scheme for Encryption, a multivariate public key encryption scheme. The scheme boasts great efficiency in encryption and decryption, though it suffers from very large public keys. It was quickly noted that the original proposal, utilizing square matrices, suffered from a very bad decryption failure rate. As a consequence, the designers later published updated parameters, replacing the square matrices with rectangular matrices and altering other parameters to avoid the cryptanalysis of the original scheme presented in 2014 by Moody et al.

In this work we show that making the matrices rectangular, while decreasing the decryption failure rate, actually, and ironically, diminishes security. We show that the combinatorial rank methods employed in the original attack of Moody et al. can be enhanced by the same added degrees of freedom that reduce the decryption failure rate. Moreover, and quite interestingly, if the decryption failure rate is still reasonably high, as exhibited by the proposed parameters, we are able to mount a reaction attack to further enhance the combinatorial rank methods. To our knowledge this is the first instance of a reaction attack creating a significant advantage in this context.

Keywords: Multivariate cryptography · Simple Matrix · Encryption · MinRank

1 Introduction

Since the discovery by Shor in the 1990s, cf. [26], of polynomial-time quantum algorithms for computing discrete logarithms and factoring integers the proverbial clock has been ticking on our current public key infrastructure. In reaction to this discovery and the continual advancement of quantum computing technologies, a large community has emerged dedicated to the development and deployment of cryptosystems that are immune to the exponential speedups quantum computers

This is a U.S. government work and not under copyright protection in the U.S.;
foreign copyright protection may apply 2020
J. Ding and J.-P. Tillich (Eds.): PQCrypto 2020, LNCS 12100, pp. 307–322, 2020.
https://doi.org/10.1007/978-3-030-44223-1_17

promise for our current standards. More recently, the National Institute of Standards and Technology (NIST) has begun directing a process to reveal which of the many new options for post-quantum public key cryptography are suitable for widespread use.

One family of candidate schemes relies on the known difficulty of solving large systems of nonlinear equations. These multivariate public key cryptosystems are inspired by computational problems that have been studied by algebraic geometers for several decades. Still, even in the past two decades this field of study has changed dramatically.

When multivariate public key cryptography was still early in its community building phase, a great many schemes were proposed and subsequently attacked. Notable examples of this phenomenon include C^*, HFE, STS, Oil-Vinegar, PMI and SFLASH, see [6,8–10,14,19–22,25,32].

While multivariate cryptography has seen some lasting success with digital signatures, see, for example, [2,4,5,12,23], multivariate encryption seems to be particularly challenging. In the last several years there have been many new proposals inspired by the notion that it may be easier to create a secure injective multivariate function if the codomain is larger than the domain. Such schemes include ZHFE, Extension Field Cancellation (EFC), SRP, HFERP, EFLASH and the Simple Matrix Encryption Scheme, see [3,7,11,28–30,34]. Of these, many have since endured attacks either outright breaking the scheme or affecting parameters, see [1,15–17,24,27].

In this work we present a new attack on the rectangular variant of the Simple Matrix Encryption Scheme, see [30]. This version of the Simple Matrix Encryption Scheme was designed to repair the problems that the original scheme, see [29], had with decryption failures and to choose large enough fields to avoid the attack of [15]. Our new attack is still a MinRank method, but one that exploits the rectangular structure, showing that the new parameterization is actually less secure than the square variant.

In an interesting twist, we also develop a reaction attack based on the decryption failures that the scheme is designed to minimize. This method further boosts the performance of the MinRank step by a factor related to the field size. With these attacks we break all of the published parameter sets at the most efficient field size of 2^8, the only parameters for which performance data were offered.

The article is organized as follows. In Sect. 2, we present the Simple Matrix Scheme. We next review the MinRank attack techniques using properties of the differential that was used against the original square variant of the Simple Matrix scheme. In the subsequent section, we present the improvement obtained in attacking the rectangular variant. Next, in Sect. 5, we present the reaction attack and discuss its affect on key recovery. We then present a thorough complexity analysis including our experimental data verifying our claimed complexity. Finally, we conclude noting the effect this attack has on the status of multivariate encryption.

2   ABC Simple Matrix Scheme

The ABC Simple Matrix Encryption Scheme was introduced in [29] by Tao et al. This scheme was designed with a new guiding principle in mind: make the codomain much larger than the domain. The motivation for this notion comes from the fact that there is a much richer space of injective functions with a large codomain than the space of bijective functions; thus, it may be easier to hide the types of properties we use to efficiently invert nonlinear functions such as low rank or low degree in this larger context. In this section we present the scheme and its functionality.

For clarity of exposition, we establish our notational standard. Throughout this text bold font will indicate a matrix or vector, e.g. $\mathbf{T}$ or $\mathbf{z}$, while regular fonts indicate functions (possibly with outputs considered as matrices) or field elements.

2.1   ABC Public Key Generation

Let $\mathbb{F}$ be a finite field with q elements. Let s be a positive integer and let $n = s^2$. Let $\mathbb{F}[\mathbf{x}]$ be the polynomial ring over $\mathbb{F}$ in the variables $\mathbf{x} = \begin{bmatrix} x_1 \cdots x_n \end{bmatrix}$.

The public key will be a system of $m = 2n = 2s^2$ (for our purposes homogeneous) quadratic formulae in $\mathbb{F}[\mathbf{x}]$. The public key will ultimately be generated by the standard isomorphism construction $P = T \circ F \circ U$ where T and U are invertible linear transformations of the appropriate dimensions, and F is a specially structured system of quadratic polynomials. The remainder of this section is devoted to the construction of F. (In general the scheme can and does use rectangular matrices, but for the ease of writing this note, we will assume that the matrices are square for now.)

Define the matrix

$$\mathbf{A} = \begin{bmatrix} x_1 & \cdots & x_s \\ x_{s+1} & \cdots & x_{2s} \\ \vdots & \ddots & \vdots \\ x_{s^2-s+1} & \cdots & x_{s^2} \end{bmatrix}.$$

Further define the $s \times s$ matrices of $\mathbb{F}[\mathbf{x}]$ linear forms $\mathbf{B} = \begin{bmatrix} b_{ij} \end{bmatrix}$ and $\mathbf{C} = \begin{bmatrix} c_{ij} \end{bmatrix}$.

From these matrices one can construct the matrices $\mathbf{E}_1 = \mathbf{AB}$ and $\mathbf{E}_2 = \mathbf{AC}$. Then we construct a system of m polynomials by concatenating the vectorizations of these two products: $F = Vec(\mathbf{E}_1) \| Vec(\mathbf{E}_2)$. The public key is then $P = T \circ F \circ U$. (Note that we can eliminate U by replacing $\mathbf{A}$ with random linear forms.)

In the rectangular version of this scheme we replace $\mathbf{A}$ by a similar $r \times s$ version (and we can make the matrices $\mathbf{B}$ and $\mathbf{C}$ of size $s \times u$ and $s \times v$, respectively) where the algebra still works the same.

2.2   Encryption and Decryption

Encryption is accomplished by evaluating the public key at a plaintext value encoded as a vector $\mathbf{x}$. One computes $P(\mathbf{x}) = \mathbf{y}$.

Decryption is accomplished by inverting each of the components of the public key. One first sets $\mathbf{v} = T^{-1}(\mathbf{y})$. Then $\mathbf{v}$ can be split in half producing $\mathbf{v}_1$ and $\mathbf{v}_2$. Each of these can be parsed as a matrix by inverting the vectorization operator $\mathbf{E}_1 = Mat(\mathbf{v}_1)$ and $\mathbf{E}_2 = Mat(\mathbf{v}_2)$.

We note that we can consider this pair of matrices as values derived from functions on either the inputs $\mathbf{x}$ or the outputs $\mathbf{y}$. The legitimate user knows both of these representations. We will abuse notation slightly and denote these functions as $E_1(\mathbf{u})$, $E_1(\mathbf{v})$, $E_2(\mathbf{u})$ and $E_2(\mathbf{v})$, where $\mathbf{v} = F(\mathbf{u})$ (and we use similar notation for functions of $\mathbf{u}$ representing the matrices $\mathbf{A}$, $\mathbf{B}$ and $\mathbf{C}$. Thus, we have computed $\mathbf{E}_1 = E_1(\mathbf{v})$ and $\mathbf{E}_2 = E_2(\mathbf{v})$. These values must be equal to $E_i(\mathbf{u})$. For both values of i, the function involves a left product by the square matrix $A(\mathbf{u})$. We construct a matrix $\mathbf{W}$ of new variables w_i for $0 < i \leq s^2$. We suppose that the correct assignment of values in $A(\mathbf{u})$ produces a matrix with a left inverse, so the correct assignment of variables w_i produces a valid left inverse. Then we have

$$\mathbf{W}\mathbf{E}_1 = \mathbf{W}E_1(\mathbf{u}) = \mathbf{W}A(\mathbf{u})B(\mathbf{u}) = B(\mathbf{u}),$$

and similarly for $\mathbf{E}_2$. Since the legitimate user knows the linear forms b_{ij} and c_{ij}, this setup provides a system of $m = 2s^2$ equations in the $s^2 + s^2$ variables w_i and u_i. Via Gaussian elimination, the w_i variables can be eliminated and values for u_i can be recovered.

Once $\mathbf{u}$ is recovered, one applies the inverse of U to this quantity to recover $\mathbf{x}$, the plaintext.

3   Previous Cryptanalysis

In this section, we summarize the technique from [15] recovering a secret key in the square case, that is when $r = s$, via MinRank informed by differential invariant structure. For convenience, we present the relevant definitions we will use in Sect. 4, possibly generalized to the rectangular setting.

The main object used in the attack from [15] is the discrete differential of the public key.

Definition 1. Let $F : \mathbb{F}^n \to \mathbb{F}^m$. The *discrete differential* of F is a bivariate analogue of the discrete derivative; it is given by the normalized difference

$$DF(\mathbf{a}, \mathbf{x}) = F(\mathbf{a} + \mathbf{x}) - F(\mathbf{a}) - F(\mathbf{x}) + F(\mathbf{0}).$$

DF is a vector-valued function since the output is in $\mathbb{F}^m$. Since DF is bilinear, we can think of each coordinate DF_i as a matrix. We can then consider properties of these matrices as linear operators. In particular, we can consider rank and perform a MinRank attack.

Definition 2. The *MinRank* (q, n, m, r) Problem is the task of finding a linear combination over $\mathbb{F}_q$ of m matrices, $\mathbf{DQ}_i$, of size $n \times n$ such that the resulting rank is at most r.

Although there are many different techniques for solving MinRank, the most relevant technique here is known as *linear algebra search*. One attempts to guess $\ell = \lceil \frac{m}{n} \rceil$ vectors that lie in the kernel of the same map. Since matrices with low rank have more linearly independent vectors in their kernels, the distribution of maps whose kernels contain these vectors is skewed toward lower rank maps. Therefore, to solve MinRank, one guesses ℓ vectors $\mathbf{x}_i$, sets up the linear system

$$\sum_{i=1}^{m} \tau_i \mathbf{DQ}_i \mathbf{x}_j = \mathbf{0},$$

for $j = 1, \ldots, \ell$, solves for τ_i and computes the rank of $\sum_{i=1}^{m} \tau_i \mathbf{DQ}_i$. If the rank is at or below the target rank then the attack has succeeded. Otherwise another set of vectors is chosen and the process continues.

In [15], the attack is formulated in the language of differential invariants.

Definition 3. A *subspace differential invariant* of a vector-valued map F is a triple of vector spaces (X, V, W) such that $X \subseteq \mathbb{F}^m$, and $V, W \subseteq \mathbb{F}^n$ satisfying $(\mathbf{x} \cdot DF)V \subseteq W$ for all $\mathbf{x} \in X$ where $dim(W) \le dim(V)$.

In other words, a subspace differential invariant is a subspace X of the span of the DF_i along with a subspace that is mapped linearly by every map in X into another subspace of no larger dimension. The definition is supposed to capture the idea of a subspace of the span of F acting like a linear map on a subspace of the domain of F.

Differential invariants are related to low rank, but not equivalent. They are useful at providing an algebraic condition on interlinked kernels, that is, when there are very many maps in the span of F that have low rank and share a large common subspace in their kernels, see [33]. In such a case, the invariant structure provides a tiny and insignificant savings in some linear algebra steps after the hard MinRank step of the attack is complete. The main value of the idea lies in providing algebraic tools for determining whether an interlinked kernel structure is present in a map.

Considering the Simple Matrix Scheme, there are maps in the span of the public maps that correspond to products of the first row of $\mathbf{A}$ and linear combinations of the columns of $\mathbf{B}$ and $\mathbf{C}$. The differential of this type of map has the following structure, where gray indicates possibly nonzero coefficients.

This map is clearly of low rank, probably $2s$, and illustrates a differential invariant because a column vector with zeros in the top s entries is mapped by this matrix to a vector with zeros in everything except the top s entries. Also, it is important to note that there is an entire $u + v$ dimensional subspace of the public key corresponding to the X in Definition 3 that produces differentials of this shape which we call a band space. There is nothing special about the first row. We could use anything in the rowspace of $\mathbf{A}$ and express our differential as above in the appropriate basis. This motivates the following definition modified from [15, Definition 4]:

Definition 4. Fix an arbitrary vector $\mathbf{v}$ in the rowspace of $\mathbf{A}$, i.e. $\mathbf{v} = \sum_{d=1}^{r} \lambda_d \mathbf{A}_d$ where $\mathbf{A}_d$ is the dth row of $\mathbf{A}$. The $u + v$ dimensional space of quadratic forms $\mathcal{B}_v$ given by the span of the columns of $\mathbf{vB}$ and $\mathbf{vC}$ is called the generalized band-space generated by $\mathbf{v}$.

Thus, recovery of an equivalent private key is accomplished by discovering r linearly independent band spaces in the span of the public key. Since these maps all share the property that they are of rank $2s$, the band spaces can be recovered with a MinRank attack.

Due to the differential invariant structure, it is shown in [15] that there is a significant speed-up in the standard linear algebra search variant of MinRank. The attack proceeds by finding $\lceil \frac{m}{n} \rceil$ vectors in the kernel of the same band space map.

A series of statements about such maps are proven in [15] in the square case revealing the complexity of the MinRank step of the attack.

Definition 5. Let $u_1, \ldots, u_{rs}$ be the components of $\mathbf{Ux}$ and fix an arbitrary vector $\mathbf{v}$ in the rowspace of $\mathbf{A}$, i.e. $\mathbf{v} = \sum_{d=1}^{r} \lambda_d \mathbf{A}_d$ where $\mathbf{A}_d$ is the dth row of $\mathbf{A}$. An rs-dimensional vector, $\mathbf{x}$ is in the band kernel generated by $\mathbf{v}$, denoted $\mathcal{B}_\mathbf{v}$ if and only if $\sum_{d=1}^{r} \lambda_d u_{ds+k} = 0$ for $k = 1, \ldots, s$.

As shown in [15] membership in the band kernel requires that s linear forms vanish; the probability of this occurrence is q^{-s}. They then show that given two maps in the same band kernel, the probability that they are in the kernel of the same band space map is q^{-1}. Therefore the complexity of searching for a second vector given one vector in a band kernel is q^{s+1}. Since $\mathbf{A}$ is singular with probability approximately q^{-1} for sufficiently large q, the total probability of randomly selecting two vectors that are simultaneously in the kernel of the same band space map is q^{-s-2}.

While in [15] it was noted that there are some dependencies in the linear systems resulting in the need to search through a nontrivial space in the case that the characteristic is 2 or 3, it was discovered in [17] that we can add constraints to the system reducing the dimension and eliminating the search. Therefore the complexity of searching for a band space map is the same for all fields. The techniques in [17] can also be adapted to require only 2 band space maps for key recovery, the second of which can be found more cheaply by reusing one of the vectors used to find the first band space map. Since we have to compute the rank of an $n \times n$ matrix for each guess, the complexity of the attack is $\mathcal{O}(n^\omega q^{s+2})$ including the linear algebra overhead.

4   Combinatorial Key Recovery, the Rectangular Case

The change from square instances of the Simple Matrix scheme to rectangular instances was proposed in [30] as a way of improving efficiency by having smaller fields while maintaining a low decryption failure rate. Still requiring a left inverse of $\mathbf{A}$, the proposal requires that $r > s$. Notice, however, that this implies that there is a nontrivial left kernel of $A(\mathbf{x})$ for any vector $\mathbf{x}$!

Specifically, notice that since there are more rows than columns in $\mathbf{A}$ for the new parameters, there is always a linear combination of the rows producing the zero vector for any input. Thus, there is no search through plaintexts to find a vector in some band kernel.

In fact, the situation is worse. Note that any plaintext $\mathbf{x}$ is guaranteed to produce an $\mathbf{A}$ for which there are $r - s$ linearly independent combinations of row vectors producing zero. Therefore $\mathbf{x}$ is in very many distinct band spaces. This fact reduces the complexity of finding a second vector in the band kernel considerably, as we now show.

4.1   The Probability of Choosing a Second Band Kernel Vector

A vector $\mathbf{u} = (u_1, u_2, \ldots, u_{rs})$ belongs to a band kernel $\mathcal{B}_{\mathbf{v}}$ if there is a nonzero vector $\mathbf{v} \in \mathbb{F}^r$ such that for $i = 1, \ldots, s$

$$\mathbf{v} \cdot \mathbf{u}_i = 0, \text{ where } \mathbf{u}_i = (u_i, u_{r+i}, \ldots, u_{((r-1)s+i)}).$$

That is, each subvector $\mathbf{u}_i$ belongs to the orthogonal space $\langle \mathbf{v} \rangle^{\perp}$.

Since the space $\langle \mathbf{v} \rangle^{\perp}$ has dimension $r - 1$, membership of each subvector in this space can be modeled as the satisfaction of one linear relation; therefore, there are a total of s linear constraints on $\mathbf{u}$ defining membership in the $\mathcal{B}_{\mathbf{v}}$. Thus, for any uniformly chosen vector $\mathbf{u} \in \mathbb{F}^{rs}$ we have

$$Pr\left(\mathbf{u} \in \mathcal{B}_{\mathbf{v}}\right) = q^{-s}.$$

Now consider a vector $\mathbf{w} \in \mathbb{F}^r$ linearly independent with $\mathbf{v}$. The dimension of the orthogonal space $(\mathbf{w} \oplus \mathbf{v})^{\perp}$ is $r - 2$. Thus by the same reasoning as above,

$$Pr\left(\mathbf{u} \in \mathcal{B}_{\mathbf{w}} \cap \mathcal{B}_{\mathbf{v}}\right) = q^{-2s}.$$

In the case $r = s + 1$, we are assured that a plaintext $\mathbf{x}$ gives us $\mathbf{u} \in \mathcal{B}_{\mathbf{v}}$, where $\mathbf{u} = U\mathbf{x}$. Therefore membership of a second vector in the same band kernel occurs with probability q^{-s}, and the complexity of finding the second vector is q^s.

In the case that $r > s + 1$, for each plaintext $\mathbf{x}$ we are guaranteed that there are $r - s$ linearly independent vectors $\mathbf{v}_1, \ldots, \mathbf{v}_{r-s}$ such that $\mathbf{u} \in \mathcal{B}_{\mathbf{v}_i}$. Therefore $\mathbf{u}$ belongs to

$$\ell = \frac{q^{r-s} - 1}{q - 1} = q^{r-s-1} + q^{r-s-2} + \cdots + q + 1$$

distinct band kernels. Let them be $\mathcal{B}_{v_1}, \mathcal{B}_{v_2}, \ldots, \mathcal{B}_{v_\ell}$. Here it might be the case that $\mathcal{B}_{v_i} \cap \mathcal{B}_{v_j} \neq \mathcal{B}_{v_s} \cap \mathcal{B}_{v_k}$, but all the intersections have the same dimension $rs - 2s$. So, the probability $\mathbf{u}$, chosen at random, belongs to one of them is roughly

$$Pr\left(\mathbf{u} \in \bigcup_{k=1}^{\ell} \mathcal{B}_{v_k}\right) \approx \frac{(\sum_{i=0}^{r-s-1} q^i)q^{rs-s} - (\sum_{i=0}^{r-s-1} q^i)q^{rs-2s}}{q^{rs}}$$

$$\approx q^{r-2s-1} - q^{2(r-2s-1)}$$

$$\approx q^{r-2s-1}.$$

Thus, the complexity of finding a second band kernel vector is roughly q^{2s+1-r}.

4.2   The Effect of $u + v > 2s$

A further effect of the rectangular augmentation of the Simple Matrix Scheme is that it requires the number of columns of the matrices $\mathbf{B}$ and $\mathbf{C}$ to be increased for efficiency. We therefore find that all of the proposed parameters with $q < 2^{32}$ have $u + v \geq 2s + 4$.

Theorem 1. *If $\mathbf{x}_1$ and $\mathbf{x}_2$ fall within the band kernel $\mathcal{B}_\mathbf{v}$, then they are both in the kernel of some generalized band-space differential $\mathbf{DQ} = \sum_{Q_i \in \mathcal{B}_\mathbf{v}} \tau_i \mathbf{DQ}_i$ with probability approximately q^{-1} if $u + v = 2s$ and probability 1 if $u + v > 2s$. Further, if $u + v > 2s$ then there exists, with probability 1, some $(u + v - 2s)$-dimensional subspace of $\mathcal{B}_\mathbf{v}$, all elements of which have both vectors in their kernel.*

Proof. There are two cases: (i) $u + v = 2s$ and (ii) $u + v > 2s$. The first case follows exactly from [15, Theorem 2]. The second case is new, so we focus on this second case in what follows. This will be quite similar to the original proof, but we include the full details for the reader.

A $\mathbf{DQ}$ meeting the above condition exists iff there is a nontrivial solution to the following system of equations

$$\sum_{Q_i \in \mathcal{B}_v} \tau_i \mathbf{DQ}_i {\mathbf{x}_1}^T = 0$$

$$\sum_{Q_i \in \mathcal{B}_v} \tau_i \mathbf{DQ}_i {\mathbf{x}_2}^T = 0. \tag{1}$$

Expressed in a basis where the first s basis vectors are chosen to be outside the band kernel, and the remaining $n - s$ basis vectors are chosen from within the band kernel, the band-space differentials take the form:

$$\mathbf{DQ}_i = \left[\begin{array}{c|c} \mathbf{S}_i & \mathbf{R}_i \\ \hline \mathbf{R}_i^T & 0 \end{array}\right], \tag{2}$$

where R_i is a random $s \times n-s$ matrix and S_i is a random symmetric $s \times s$ matrix. Likewise $\mathbf{x_1}$ and $\mathbf{x_2}$ take the form $(0 | \ \mathbf{x_k}\ )$. Thus removing the redundant degrees of freedom we have the system of $2s$ equations in $u + v$ variables:

$$\sum_{i=1}^{u+v} \tau_i \mathbf{R}_i \mathbf{x_1}^T = 0$$

$$\sum_{i=1}^{u+v} \tau_i \mathbf{R}_i \mathbf{x_2}^T = 0. \tag{3}$$

This has a nontrivial solution precisely when the following matrix has a nontrivial right kernel:

$$\begin{bmatrix} \mathbf{R}_1\mathbf{x_1}^T & \mathbf{R}_2\mathbf{x_1}^T & \cdots & \mathbf{R}_{u+v}\mathbf{x_1}^T \\ \hline \mathbf{R}_1\mathbf{x_2}^T & \mathbf{R}_2\mathbf{x_2}^T & \cdots & \mathbf{R}_{u+v}\mathbf{x_2}^T \end{bmatrix} \tag{4}$$

By the assumption that $u + v > 2s$, this matrix has more columns than rows, and therefore must have a nontrivial right kernel with probability 1. Moreover, with probability 1, this right kernel has dimension at least $u + v - 2s$. Therefore, any differential produced by taking the direct product of $(Q_1, ..., Q_{u+v})$, where $Q_1, ..., Q_{u+v}$ are the generators of $\mathcal{B}_v$, and a right kernel vector of the aforementioned matrix will have both $\mathbf{x}_1$ and $\mathbf{x}_2$ in its kernel.

4.3 Controlling the Ratio $\frac{m}{n}$.

The new parameters presented in [30] added another feature to Simple Matrix: the ability to decouple the number of variables n from the size rs of the matrix $\mathbf{A}$. The authors want to ensure that the number of equations is not significantly more than twice the number of variables so that the first fall degree of the system is not diminished.

In all but the case of $q = 2^8$, the authors of [30] propose parameters with $m = 2n$. In the case of $q = 2^8$, however, the relationship is more complicated. All parameters in this case are functions of s. Specifically, $r = s + 3$, $u = v = s + 4$, $n = s(s + 8)$ and $m = 2(s + 3)(s + 4)$. Therefore $m - 2n = 24 - 2s$.

For small s, this change poses a challenge to the linear algebra search Min-Rank method. The reason is that choosing merely two kernel vectors results in a system that is underdetermined, and since the size of the field is still fairly large $q = 2^8$, it is very costly to search through the solution space. On the other hand, if we increase the number of kernel vectors we guess to three, we have an additional factor of q^s in our complexity estimate.

Luckily, there is an easy way to handle this issue. We simply ignore some of the public differentials. Consider the effect of removing a of the public equations on the MinRank attack. If $a \geq m - 2n$, then we need to only consider $\lceil \frac{m-a}{n} \rceil = 2$ kernel vectors. Since the expected dimension of the intersection of any band space, which is of dimension $u + v$, and the span of the $m - a$ remaining public maps is $(u+v) + (m-a) - m = u + v - a$, we can apply Theorem 1 with $u + v - a$ in place of $u + v$. We have now shown the following:

Corollary 1. *Consider the public key P with a equations removed. Let $\widehat{\mathcal{B}}_{\mathbf{v}}$ be the intersection of the band space $\mathcal{B}_{\mathbf{v}}$ and the remaining public maps. If $\mathbf{x}_1, \mathbf{x}_2 \in \mathcal{B}_{\mathbf{v}}$, then there exists a band-space differential $\mathbf{DQ} = \sum_{Q_i \in \widehat{\mathcal{B}}_{\mathbf{v}}} \tau_i \mathbf{DQ}_i$ whose kernel contains both $\mathbf{x}_1$ and $\mathbf{x}_2$ with probability approximately q^{-1} if $u + v - a = 2s$ and probability 1 if $u + v - a > 2s$. Further, if $u + v - a > 2s$ then there exists, with probability 1, some $(u + v - a - 2s)$-dimensional subspace of $\widehat{\mathcal{B}}_{\mathbf{v}}$, all elements of which have both vectors in their kernel.*

Considering the parameters from [30], we see that the largest value of a required to produce a fully determined MinRank system with two kernel vectors is in the case that $s = 8$ producing $a = m - 2n = 24 - 2s = 8$. In this same set of parameters $u = v = s + 4$ so that $u + v = 2s + 8$. Therefore, Corollary 1 applies.

5   Improvements from a Reaction Attack

As noted in [30], the original proposal of the square version of Simple Matrix, cf. [29], did not properly address decryption failures. To maintain performance and avoid the attack from [15], the rectangular scheme was introduced with many possible field sizes. Still, the proposed parameters only made decryption failures less common but not essentially impossible. The smallest decryption failure rate for parameters in [30] is 2^{-64} and the only parameters with sufficiently good performance to advertise had decryption failure rates of 2^{-32}.

These augmentations addressed decryption failures out of precaution, but had no claim of how such failures could be used to undermine the scheme. In this section we develop an enhancement of our combinatorial key recovery from the previous section utilizing these decryption failures. To our knowledge, this is the first example of a key recovery reaction attack against a multivariate scheme in this context.

5.1   Decryption Failures in the Simple Matrix Scheme

As described in Sect. 2.2, the decryption algorithm of Simple Matrix assumes that the matrix $A(\mathbf{u})$ has a left inverse. This property is exactly the same assumption in the more general case of rectangular matrices as well. The failure of $A(\mathbf{u})$ to be full rank makes the decryption algorithm fail, producing decryption failures. One could imagine guessing which rows of $\mathbf{WA}$ could be made into elementary basis vectors trying to recover linear relations on the values of $\mathbf{u}$ to recover a quadratic system in fewer variables which may produce an unique preimage, but this is costly in performance and still allows an adversary to detect when $A(\mathbf{u})$ is not of full rank.

If we consider $\mathbf{A}$ to be rectangular, say $r \times s$, then we need the number of rows r to be greater than or equal to s. Then we may still have a left inverse $\mathbf{W}$, an $s \times r$ matrix satisfying $\mathbf{WA} = \mathbf{I}_s$. The probability of the existence of at least one such $\mathbf{W}$ is the same as the probability that the rows of $\mathbf{A}$ span $\mathbb{F}^s$. Thus

$$Pr(\text{Rank}(\mathbf{A}) < s) = 1 - \prod_{i=r-s+1}^{r} (1 - q^{-i}) \approx q^{s-r-1}.$$

Notice that decryption failure reveals precise information about the internal state of the decryption algorithm. Specifically, the quantity $A(\mathbf{u})$ where $\mathbf{u} = U(\mathbf{x})$ is not of full rank. Even for very large q, one requires a disparity in the values r and s to make the decryption failure rate very low. Even for the parameters proposed having the smallest decryption failure rate, $q = 2^{32}$ and $r = s + 1$, the probability of decryption failure is 2^{-64} and 2^{64} decryption queries on average are needed to detect a decryption failure.

5.2   The Reaction Attack

Consider, for a moment, the square case of the Simple Matrix Scheme, that is, when $r = s$. In the search process, you try to find two vectors $\mathbf{x}_1$ and $\mathbf{x}_2$ that are simultaneously in the kernel of the same linear combination of the public differentials. For the search to succeed in finding a band map you need three events to simultaneously occur: (P_1) $\mathbf{x}_i$ to be in the band kernel of a band space; (P_2) $\mathbf{x}_{3-i}$ to be in the band kernel of the same band space; and, (P_3) for them to both be in the kernel of the same band space map.

The probability of these events occurring simultaneously is then

$$Pr(P_1 \wedge P_2 \wedge P_3) = Pr(P_1)Pr(P_2|P_1)Pr(P_3|P_1 \wedge P_2) = q^{-1} \cdot q^{-s} \cdot q^{-1} = q^{-s-2}.$$

So, it takes q^{s+2} guesses in expectation to succeed in finding two such vectors and thereby recover a band space.

Notice that decryption failure occurs when the matrix $\mathbf{A}$ is singular, which is exactly the condition for membership in some band kernel. Thus, the first vector lying in a band kernel need not be found by search. If you already have access to a decryption failure producing plaintext, then the first condition is satisfied saving a factor of q in complexity at the cost of q decryption queries. So this component of q is now, in some sense, additive instead of multiplicative in the complexity analysis of the attack. Therefore, if the decryption failure rate is sufficiently low, a reaction attack can be employed.

We find that decryption failures provide a similar advantage in the rectangular case as well. When $r > s$, a decryption failure $\mathbf{x}$ assures the existence of $r - s + 1$ linearly independent vectors $v_1, \ldots, v_{r-s+1} \in \mathbb{F}^r$ such that $\mathbf{u} \in \mathcal{B}_{v_1} \cap \cdots \cap \mathcal{B}_{v_{r-s+1}}$, where $\mathbf{u} = U\mathbf{x}$. Thus we know for sure there are

$$\ell = \frac{q^{r-s+1} - 1}{q - 1} = q^{r-s} + q^{r-s-1} + \cdots + q + 1$$

distinct band kernel spaces in which $\mathbf{u}$ belongs. Let them be $\mathcal{B}_{v_1}, \mathcal{B}_{v_2}, \ldots, \mathcal{B}_{v_\ell}$. Here it might be the case that $\mathcal{B}_{v_i} \cap \mathcal{B}_{v_j} \neq \mathcal{B}_{v_s} \cap \mathcal{B}_{v_k}$, but all the intersection have the same dimension $rs - 2s$. So, the probability that $\mathbf{u}$, chosen at random, belongs to one of them is roughly

$$Pr\left(\mathbf{u} \in \bigcup_{k=1}^{\ell} \mathcal{B}_{v_k}\right) \approx \frac{\left(\sum_{i=0}^{r-s} q^i\right)q^{rs-s} - \binom{\sum_{i=0}^{r-s} q^i}{2}q^{rs-2s}}{q^{rs}}$$

$$\approx q^{r-2s} - q^{2(r-2s)}$$

$$\approx q^{r-2s}.$$

6   Complexity

Noting that there is statistically no difference between using the input transformation U and choosing $\mathbf{A}$ to consist of random linear forms, we note that full key extraction including the input and output transformations proceeds as in [17]. Since this last part occurs after the recovery of the band spaces, it is of additive complexity. Therefore the complexity of the attack is equivalent to the MinRank step plus some additive overhead.

Recovering a band space then requires q^{2s+1-r} iterations of solving a linear system of size n and rank calculations on a matrix of size n. (Note that in this case, finding the second map from the same band space is cheaper by a factor of q.) Thus the complexity of the combinatorial key recovery is $\mathcal{O}(n^\omega q^{2s+1-r})$, where ω is the linear algebra constant. We note that in practice that assuming ω takes a value of approximately 2.8 results in a big-oh constant of less than one.

In the case of the reaction attack, recovering two maps from a band space requires only $2q^{2s-r}$ iterations of system solving and rank calculations. Therefore, for the reaction attack, the complexity is $\mathcal{O}(n^\omega q^{2s-r})$. The actual complexity in field operations for completing the attacks are listed in Table 3.

Using SAGE[1] [31], we performed some minrank computations on small scale variants of the ABC scheme. The computations were done on a computer with a 64 bit quad-core Intel i7 processor, with clock cycle 2.8 GHz. We were interested in verifying our complexity estimates on the most costly step in the attack, the MinRank instance, rather than the full attack on the scheme. Given as input the finite field size q, and the scheme parameter s, we computed the average number of vectors $\mathbf{x}$ required to be sampled in order to recover a matrix of rank $2s$. For our first experiment we set our parameters to $u = v = s + 1$, $r = s + 2$, and $n = ru = (s+1)(s+2)$. Our results are provided in Table 1.

For higher values of q and s the computations took too long to produce sufficiently many data points and obtain meaningful results with SAGE. Our analysis predicted the number of vectors needed would be on the order of $\text{Exp} = (q-1)q^{s-3}$. Table 1 shows the comparison between our experiments and the expected value. We only used a small number of trials, particularly for the higher values of s listed for each q.

---

[1] Any mention of commercial products does not indicate endorsement by NIST.

We also ran another experiment exhibiting the behavior of the attack when $2n > m$. We used $u = v = s + 1$, $r = s + 2$, and $n = ru - 1 = s^2 + 3s + 1$. We then threw away two of the equations generated. Our analysis predicted the number of trials required to be roughly $(q-1)q^{s-2}$. The resulting data are given in Table 2. The expected number of trials was Exp=$(q-1)q^{s-2}$.

Table 1. Average number of vectors needed for the rank to fall to $2s$. This experiment used $u = v = s + 1$, $r = s + 2$, and $n = ru = (s+1)(s+2)$.

	$s = 3$	Exp	$s = 4$	Exp	$s = 5$	Exp	$s = 6$	Exp	$s = 7$	Exp
$q = 2$	1.8	1	3.0	2	4.7	4	6.6	8	15.8	16
$q = 3$	2.5	2	6.6	6	19.1	18	53.1	54	173	162
$q = 4$	3.1	3	11.9	12	47.6	48	189.0	192		
$q = 5$	4.3	4	20.6	20	99.4	100	520.8	500		
$q = 7$	6.5	6	40.6	42	281.4	284	1873	1988		
$q = 8$	8	7	62.8	56	444.2	448				
$q = 11$	9.8	10	113.6	110	1318.8	1210				
$q = 13$	11.7	12	157.7	156	2026.7	2028				

Table 2. Average number of vectors needed for the rank to fall to $2s$. This experiment used $u = v = s + 1$, $r = s + 2$, and $n = ru - 1 = s^2 + 3s + 1$, and did not use two of the equations generated.

	$s = 3$	Exp	$s = 4$	Exp	$s = 5$	Exp	$s = 6$	Exp
$q = 2$	1.9	2	4.4	4	7	8	14.5	16
$q = 3$	5.9	6	16.3	18	47	54	138.9	162
$q = 5$	17.9	20	86.2	100	500.3	500	2137.3	2500
$q = 7$	36.6	35	277.7	245	2092.3	1715		
$q = 11$	100.4	110	1175	1210				
$q = 13$	148.3	156	1855.4	2028				

Table 3. Complexity of our Combinatorial MinRank and Reaction attacks against $q = 2^8$ parameters of the ABC Simple Matrix Encryption Scheme.

Scheme	Sec. Level	a	Comb. Att. Comp	React. Att. Comp
ABC$(2^8, 11, 8, 12, 12, 264, 128)$	80	8	$2^{75.6}$	$2^{67.6}$
ABC$(2^8, 12, 9, 13, 13, 312, 153)$	90	6	$2^{76.3}$	$2^{68.3}$
ABC$(2^8, 13, 10, 14, 14, 364, 180)$	100	4	$2^{85.0}$	$2^{77.0}$

7   Conclusion

The rectangular version of the Simple Matrix Encryption Scheme is needed to avoid a high decryption failure rate and known attacks. From the analysis made in this paper, we conclude that the security of this version is actually worse than that of the square version. Furthermore, we showed that decryption failures are actually still exploitable in a concrete reaction attack that clearly undermines the security claims of the scheme.

It is interesting to consider the historical difficulty of achieving secure multivariate public key encryption. Even using the relatively new approach of defining public keys with vastly larger codomains—a change which on the surface would seem to allow much greater freedom in selecting secure injective functions—we observe that essentially none of the recent such proposals have attained their claimed level of security after scrutiny. Perhaps there is a fundamental barrier ensuring that any efficiently invertible function must have some exploitable property, such as low rank, preventing the advantage of privileged information of the legitimate user from dramatically separating the complexity of that efficient inversion from the adversary's task. It seems that multivariate encryption is an area still in need of significant development.

References

1. Cabarcas, D., Smith-Tone, D., Verbel, J.A.: Key recovery attack for ZHFE. In: Lange, T., Takagi, T. [13], pp. 289–308 (2017)
2. Cartor, R., Smith-Tone, D.: An updated security analysis of PFLASH. In: Lange, T., Takagi, T. [13], pp. 241–254 (2017)
3. Cartor, R., Smith-Tone, D.: EFLASH: a new multivariate encryption scheme. In: Cid, C., Jacobson Jr., M. (eds.) Selected Areas in Cryptography - SAC 2018. LNCS, vol. 11349, pp. 281–299. Springer, Cham (2018). https://doi.org/10.1007/978-3-030-10970-7_13
4. Chen, M.-S., Yang, B.-Y., Smith-Tone, D.: Pflash - secure asymmetric signatures on smart cards. In: Lightweight Cryptography Workshop 2015 (2015). http://csrc.nist.gov/groups/ST/lwc-workshop2015/papers/session3-smith-tone-paper.pdf
5. Ding, J., Schmidt, D.: Rainbow, a new multivariable polynomial signature scheme. In: Ioannidis, J., Keromytis, A., Yung, M. (eds.) ACNS 2005. LNCS, vol. 3531, pp. 164–175. Springer, Heidelberg (2005). https://doi.org/10.1007/11496137_12
6. Ding, J.: A new variant of the matsumoto-imai cryptosystem through perturbation. In: Bao, F., Deng, R., Zhou, J. (eds.) PKC 2004. LNCS, vol. 2947, pp. 305–318. Springer, Heidelberg (2004). https://doi.org/10.1007/978-3-540-24632-9_22
7. Ding, J., Petzoldt, A., Wang, L.: The cubic Simple Matrix encryption scheme. In: Mosca, M. [18], pp. 76–87 (2014)
8. Dubois, V., Fouque, P.-A., Stern, J.: Cryptanalysis of SFLASH with slightly modified parameters. In: Naor, M. (ed.) EUROCRYPT 2007. LNCS, vol. 4515, pp. 264–275. Springer, Heidelberg (2007). https://doi.org/10.1007/978-3-540-72540-4_15
9. Faugère, J.-C., Joux, A.: Algebraic cryptanalysis of hidden field equation (HFE) cryptosystems using Gröbner bases. In: Boneh, D. (ed.) CRYPTO 2003. LNCS, vol. 2729, pp. 44–60. Springer, Heidelberg (2003). https://doi.org/10.1007/978-3-540-45146-4_3

10. Fouque, P.-A., Granboulan, L., Stern, J.: Differential cryptanalysis for multivariate schemes. In: Cramer, R. (ed.) EUROCRYPT 2005. LNCS, vol. 3494, pp. 341–353. Springer, Heidelberg (2005). https://doi.org/10.1007/11426639_20
11. Ikematsu, Y., Perlner, R., Smith-Tone, D., Takagi, T., Vates, J.: HFERP - a new multivariate encryption scheme. In: Lange, T., Steinwandt, R. (eds.) PQCrypto 2018. LNCS, vol. 10786, pp. 396–416. Springer, Cham (2018). https://doi.org/10.1007/978-3-319-79063-3_19
12. Kipnis, A., Patarin, J., Goubin, L.: Unbalanced oil and vinegar signature schemes. In: Stern, J. (ed.) EUROCRYPT 1999. LNCS, vol. 1592, pp. 206–222. Springer, Heidelberg (1999). https://doi.org/10.1007/3-540-48910-X_15
13. Lange, T., Takagi, T. (eds.): PQCrypto 2017. LNCS, vol. 10346. Springer, Cham (2017). https://doi.org/10.1007/978-3-319-59879-6
14. Matsumoto, T., Imai, H.: Public quadratic polynomial-tuples for efficient signature-verification and message-encryption. In: Barstow, D., et al. (eds.) EUROCRYPT 1988. LNCS, vol. 330, pp. 419–453. Springer, Heidelberg (1988). https://doi.org/10.1007/3-540-45961-8_39
15. Moody, D., Perlner, R., Smith-Tone, D.: An asymptotically optimal structural attack on the ABC multivariate encryption scheme. In: Mosca, M. [18], pp. 180–196 (2014)
16. Moody, D., Perlner, R., Smith-Tone, D.: Key recovery attack on the cubic ABC Simple Matrix multivariate encryption scheme. In: Avanzi, R., Heys, H. (eds.) SAC 2016. LNCS, vol. 10532, pp. 543–558. Springer, Cham (2017). https://doi.org/10.1007/978-3-319-69453-5_29
17. Moody, D., Perlner, R., Smith-Tone, D.: Improved attacks for characteristic-2 parameters of the cubic ABC Simple Matrix encryption scheme. In: Lange, T., Takagi, T. [13], pp. 255–271 (2017)
18. Mosca, M. (ed.): PQCrypto 2014. LNCS, vol. 8772. Springer, Cham (2014). https://doi.org/10.1007/978-3-319-11659-4
19. Patarin, J.: The oil and vinegar signature scheme. In: Dagstuhl Workshop on Cryptography, September 1997 (1997)
20. Patarin, J., Courtois, N., Goubin, L.: FLASH, a fast multivariate signature algorithm. In: Naccache, D. (ed.) CT-RSA 2001. LNCS, vol. 2020, pp. 298–307. Springer, Heidelberg (2001). https://doi.org/10.1007/3-540-45353-9_22
21. Patarin, J.: Cryptanalysis of the matsumoto and imai public key scheme of Eurocrypt'88. In: Coppersmith, D. (ed.) CRYPTO 1995. LNCS, vol. 963, pp. 248–261. Springer, Heidelberg (1995). https://doi.org/10.1007/3-540-44750-4_20
22. Patarin, J.: Hidden Fields Equations (HFE) and Isomorphisms of Polynomials (IP): two new families of asymmetric algorithms. In: Maurer, U. (ed.) EUROCRYPT 1996. LNCS, vol. 1070, pp. 33–48. Springer, Heidelberg (1996). https://doi.org/10.1007/3-540-68339-9_4
23. Patarin, J., Courtois, N., Goubin, L.: QUARTZ, 128-bit long digital signatures. In: Naccache, D. (ed.) CT-RSA 2001. LNCS, vol. 2020, pp. 282–297. Springer, Heidelberg (2001). https://doi.org/10.1007/3-540-45353-9_21
24. Perlner, R., Petzoldt, A., Smith-Tone, D.: Total break of the SRP encryption scheme. In: Adams, C., Camenisch, J. (eds.) SAC 2017. LNCS, vol. 10719, pp. 355–373. Springer, Cham (2018). https://doi.org/10.1007/978-3-319-72565-9_18
25. Kipnis, A., Shamir, A.: Cryptanalysis of the oil and vinegar signature scheme. In: Krawczyk, H. (ed.) CRYPTO 1998. LNCS, vol. 1462, pp. 257–266. Springer, Heidelberg (1998). https://doi.org/10.1007/BFb0055733
26. Shor, P.W.: Polynomial-time algorithms for prime factorization and discrete logarithms on a quantum computer. SIAM J. Sci. Stat. Comp. **26**, 1484 (1997)

27. Smith-Tone, D., Verbel, J.: A key recovery attack for the extension field cancellation encryption scheme. In: concurrent submission to PQCrypto 2020 (2020)
28. Szepieniec, A., Ding, J., Preneel, B.: Extension field cancellation: a new central trapdoor for multivariate quadratic systems. In: Takagi, T. (ed.) PQCrypto 2016. LNCS, vol. 9606, pp. 182–196. Springer, Cham (2016). https://doi.org/10.1007/978-3-319-29360-8_12
29. Tao, C., Diene, A., Tang, S., Ding, J.: Simple Matrix scheme for encryption. In: Gaborit, P. (ed.) PQCrypto 2013. LNCS, vol. 7932, pp. 231–242. Springer, Heidelberg (2013). https://doi.org/10.1007/978-3-642-38616-9_16
30. Tao, C., Xiang, H., Petzoldt, A., Ding, J.: Simple Matrix - a multivariate public key cryptosystem (MPKC) for encryption. Finite Fields Appl. **35**, 352–368 (2015)
31. The Sage Developers. SageMath, the Sage Mathematics Software System (Version 8.7) (2019). https://www.sagemath.org
32. Wolf, C., Braeken, A., Preneel, B.: On the security of stepwise triangular systems. Des. Codes Cryptogr. **40**(3), 285–302 (2006)
33. Yang, B.-Y., Chen, J.-M.: Building secure tame-like multivariate public-key cryptosystems: the new TTS. In: Boyd, C., González Nieto, J.M. (eds.) ACISP 2005. LNCS, vol. 3574, pp. 518–531. Springer, Heidelberg (2005). https://doi.org/10.1007/11506157_43
34. Yasuda, T., Sakurai, K.: A multivariate encryption scheme with rainbow. In: Qing, S., Okamoto, E., Kim, K., Liu, D. (eds.) ICICS 2015. LNCS, vol. 9543, pp. 236–251. Springer, Cham (2016). https://doi.org/10.1007/978-3-319-29814-6_19

A Structural Attack on
Block-Anti-Circulant UOV at SAC 2019

Hiroki Furue[1]([⊠]), Koha Kinjo[2], Yasuhiko Ikematsu[3], Yacheng Wang[1],
and Tsuyoshi Takagi[1]

[1] The University of Tokyo, Tokyo, Japan
{hiroki_furue,yacheng_wang,takagi}@mist.i.u-tokyo.ac.jp
[2] NTT Secure Platform Laboratories, Tokyo, Japan
koha.kinjo.xs@hco.ntt.co.jp
[3] Kyushu University, Fukuoka, Japan
ikematsu@imi.kyushu-u.ac.jp

Abstract. At SAC 2019, Szepieniec and Preneel proposed a new variant of the Unbalanced Oil and Vinegar signature scheme (UOV) called block-anti-circulant UOV (BAC-UOV). In this scheme, the matrices representing the quadratic parts of the public key are designed to be block-anti-circulant matrices, which drastically reduces its public key size compared to UOV that originally has a relatively large public key size.

In this paper, we show that this block-anti-circulant property enables us to do a special linear transformation on variables in the public key polynomials. By executing the UOV attack on quadratic terms in partial variables of the resulting polynomial system, we obtain a polynomial system with less quadratic terms, which can be algebraically solved faster than the plain direct attack. Our proposed attack reduces the bit complexity of breaking BAC-UOV by about 20% compared with the previously known attacks. For example, the complexity of our proposed attack on 147-bit BAC-UOV parameter (claimed security level II in NIST PQC project by its authors) can be reduced only to 119 bits.

Keywords: Post-quantum cryptography · Multivariate cryptography · Unbalanced Oil and Vinegar · Circulant matrix

1 Introduction

Multivariate quadratic polynomials problem over a finite field ($\mathcal{MQ}$-problem) is known to be NP-complete [14] and considered having no advantage of solving using quantum computers. Multivariate public key cryptography, whose security is based on the difficulty of solving this $\mathcal{MQ}$-problem, is considered as one of the candidates for the post-quantum cryptography.

The Unbalanced Oil and Vinegar signature scheme (UOV) [16], as one of the multivariate signature schemes, has withstood various attacks and remained secure for twenty years, which is why it has been highly thought of and considered as one of the securest multivariate signature schemes. Additionally, to avoid

© Springer Nature Switzerland AG 2020
J. Ding and J.-P. Tillich (Eds.): PQCrypto 2020, LNCS 12100, pp. 323–339, 2020.
https://doi.org/10.1007/978-3-030-44223-1_18

the drawback of having a huge public key size, a multi-layered UOV, called Rainbow [9], is proposed and has entered the second round of NIST post-quantum standardization project [18].

Even though UOV generates small signatures, its downside of using very large public keys challenges its practical use. Hence, a great deal of research has endeavored to shorten the public key size of UOV. As an example, the Lifted Unbalanced Oil and Vinegar (LUOV) [5], proposed as one of the variants of UOV, uses polynomials over a small field as its public key, whereas the signature space and message space are defined over an extension field. LUOV was also submitted to NIST post-quantum standardization project [18], and entered the second round of screening. However, Ding et al. [11] recently proposed a new attack on LUOV, that renders a modification on the secure parameters of LUOV.

In order to shorten the public key size, Petzoldt [20] proposed a variant of UOV by introducing a circulant structure into the matrices associated to the public key. Namely, the variant is constructed so that a part of the Macaulay matrix, whose each row consists of the coefficients of each polynomial in the public key, is designed to be a circulant matrix. Here, a circulant matrix is a matrix whose each row vector is rotated one element to the right relative to the preceding row vector (see Subsect. 3.1 for the details). Such a circulant structure can be used to reduce the public key size since a circulant matrix can be recovered from its first row vector. In [19], Peng and Tang proposed another variant of UOV by introducing the circulant structure in generating a signature. This scheme [19] has a very short secret key and can generate signatures very efficiently since the inverse matrix of a circulant matrix can be calculated faster than that of a random matrix. However, Hashimoto [15] has shown that this scheme is not secure against the UOV attack [17].

At SAC 2019, Szepieniec and Preneel [21] proposed a new variant of UOV called block-anti-circulant UOV (BAC-UOV). In this scheme, the matrices representing the quadratic part of polynomials of the public key are block-anti-circulant matrices (block matrices whose every block is an anti-circulant matrix where each row vector is rotated one element to the left relative to the preceding row vector). See Subsect. 3.1 for block-anti-circulant matrices. By using this construction, they succeed in reducing the public key size, because every block of a block-anti-circulant matrix can be represented by using its first row. Additionally, by combining the block-anti-circulant construction with other compression techniques such as the field lifting used in LUOV [5], the public key size of BAC-UOV decreases by about 30–40% compared with LUOV, and the signature size of BAC-UOV also slightly decreases compared with LUOV.

Our Contribution. In this paper, we propose a new attack against the BAC-UOV scheme, that is composed of three steps.

First, we utilize the property of an anti-circulant matrix that the sum of the elements of one row is the same as those of other rows. By using this property, we can transform a block-anti-circulant matrix into the following form:

$$
\begin{array}{|c|c|}
\hline
A & 0 \\
\hline
0 & B \\
\hline
\end{array}
\tag{1}
$$

where A and B are an $N \times N$ matrix and an $(\ell - 1)N \times (\ell - 1)N$ matrix, respectively. The matrices associated with the quadratic forms of the public key polynomials can all be transformed into the form of (1) by multiplying a special invertible matrix shown in Subsect. 4.1 on the right and its transpose on the left. Second, we execute the UOV attack [17] on the upper-left $N \times N$ submatrices of the obtained matrices, which only requires very little complexity, and we can change those submatrices into the form of the matrix representing the quadratic parts of the central map of UOV. By this operation, we can reduce the number of variables that appear in the quadratic terms of the public key polynomials. Finally, we execute the direct attack on the transformed polynomial system.

From our analysis, the complexity of our attack decreases by about 20% compared with the best existing attack on UOV. As a result, we consider that the secure parameters of BAC-UOV need to be modified.

Our paper is organized as follows. In Sect. 2, we explain the UOV scheme and two existing attacks on UOV, which are the direct attack and the UOV attack. Section 3 explains about BAC-UOV. In Sect. 4, we give the details of our proposed attack and estimate its complexity. We conclude the paper in Sect. 5.

2   Unbalanced Oil and Vinegar Signature Scheme

In this section, we first explain the $\mathcal{MQ}$-problem and general signature schemes that are based on the $\mathcal{MQ}$-problem. Next, we give the structure of the Unbalanced Oil and Vinegar signature scheme (UOV) [16]. Subsequently, we describe two attacks on UOV, which are the direct attack and the UOV attack [17], since our attack in this paper is proposed by using these two attacks.

2.1   Multivariate Signature Scheme

Let $\mathbb{F}_q$ be a finite field with q elements and n and m be two positive integers. Given a system of quadratic polynomials $\mathcal{P} = (p_1(x_1, \ldots, x_n), \ldots, p_m(x_1, \ldots, x_n))$ in n variables over $\mathbb{F}_q$ and $\mathbf{y} \in \mathbb{F}_q^m$, the problem of finding $\mathbf{x} \in \mathbb{F}_q^n$ such that $\mathcal{P}(\mathbf{x}) = \mathbf{y}$ is called the $\mathcal{MQ}$-problem and denoted by $\mathcal{MQ}(q, n, m)$. Garey and Johnson [14] showed that the $\mathcal{MQ}$-problem is NP-complete when $n \approx m$. Besides, quantum algorithms for solving this problem in polynomial time has not been proposed. Therefore, $\mathcal{MQ}$-problem is considered to have the potential to resist quantum computer attacks.

Now, we briefly explain the structure of general multivariate signature schemes. First, we generate an easily invertible map $\mathcal{F} = (f_1, \ldots, f_o) : \mathbb{F}_q^n \to \mathbb{F}_q^m$, called a *central map*, such that each f_i is a quadratic polynomial. This $\mathcal{F}$ is constructed to be easily invertible. Next, randomly chose two invertible affine maps T and S in order to hide the structure $\mathcal{F}$. Then the public key $\mathcal{P}$ is given as a polynomial map as follows:

$$\mathcal{P} = T \circ \mathcal{F} \circ S. \tag{2}$$

The secret key consists of T, $\mathcal{F}$ and S. The signature generation is done as follows: Let $\mathbf{m} \in \mathbb{F}_q^m$ be a message to be signed. Compute $\mathbf{m}_1 = T^{-1}(\mathbf{m})$ and find a solution $\mathbf{m}_2$ to the equation $\mathcal{F}(\mathbf{x}) = \mathbf{m}_1$. Then $\mathbf{s} = S^{-1}(\mathbf{m}_2) \in \mathbb{F}_q^n$ is the message $\mathbf{m}$. The verification process is done by confirming whether $\mathcal{P}(\mathbf{s}) = \mathbf{m}$ or not.

2.2   Description of UOV

Let v, o be two positive integers and $n = v + o$ and we assume that $v > o$. For n variables $x_1, \ldots, x_n$ over $\mathbb{F}_q$, we call $x_1, \ldots, x_v$ *vinegar variables* and $x_{v+1}, \ldots, x_n$ *oil variables*.

Now we construct a central map $\mathcal{F} = (f_1, \ldots, f_o)$ such that each f_i is a quadratic polynomial of the following form

$$f_i(x_1, \ldots, x_n) = \sum_{j=1}^{v} \sum_{k=1}^{n} \alpha_{i,j,k} x_j x_k + \sum_{j=1}^{n} \beta_{i,j} x_j + \gamma_i. \tag{3}$$

Here $\alpha_{i,j,k}$, $\beta_{i,k}$ and γ_k are chosen randomly from $\mathbb{F}_q$. Then, the public key map $\mathcal{P}$ is constructed by $\mathcal{P} = \mathcal{F} \circ S$ since T of (2) does not affect to hide the structure of (3). The secret key consists of $\mathcal{F}$ and S.

Subsequently, we explain the way of inverting the central map $\mathcal{F}$. When we solve $\mathcal{F}(x_1, \ldots, x_n) = (m_1, \ldots, m_o)$ for $(x_1, \ldots, x_n) \in \mathbb{F}_q^n$, where $(m_1, \ldots, m_o) \in \mathbb{F}_q^o$, we firstly choose random values $a_1, \ldots, a_v$ in $\mathbb{F}_q$. Then we find a solution $b_1, \ldots, b_o$ for the equation $\mathcal{F}(a_1, \ldots, a_v, x_{v+1}, \ldots, x_n) = (m_1, \ldots, m_o)$, since this is a linear system of o equations in o variables $x_{v+1}, \ldots, x_n$. If there is no solution to the equation, we choose new random values $a_1', \ldots, a_v'$ and repeat the previous procedure. By using this way, we can execute the signing process explained in Subsect. 2.1.

Let $n \times n$ matrices F_i and P_i ($i = 1, \ldots, o$) be the matrices representing the quadratic parts of f_i and p_i ($i = 1, \ldots, o$) respectively, and an $n \times n$ matrix S be the matrix representing S. Then, F_i are of the form

$$\begin{pmatrix} *_{v \times v} & *_{v \times o} \\ *_{o \times v} & 0_{o \times o} \end{pmatrix}, \tag{4}$$

because of (3) and we have $P_i = S^\top F_i S$ from the definition.

2.3   Direct Attack

Given a quadratic polynomial system $\mathcal{P} = (p_1, \ldots, p_m)$ in n variables over $\mathbb{F}_q$ and $\mathbf{m} \in \mathbb{F}_q^m$, the direct attack algebraically solves the system $\mathcal{P}(\mathbf{x}) = \mathbf{m}$. When $n > m$, the polynomial system is called underdetermined. There usually exist many solutions for underdetermined systems, and $n-m$ variables can be specified with random values when only one or a few solutions are needed.

One of the best-known approaches for algebraically solving the $\mathcal{MQ}$-problem is the hybrid approach [4], which randomly guesses k ($k = 0, \ldots, n$) variables before computing a Gröbner basis [6], and the guessing terminates when the correct values are chosen. Some of the well-known algorithm for computing Gröbner bases include F4 [12], F5 [13], and XL [7]. The complexity of this approach by a quantum adversary is estimated to be

$$\min_k \left\{ O \left(q^{k/2} \binom{n-k+2}{2} \binom{d_{reg}+n-k}{n-k}^2 \right) \right\}, \tag{5}$$

where d_{reg} is the *degree of regularity*, which is the highest polynomial degree appeared during a Gröbner basis computation for the components of the highest degree (quadratic) of these polynomials. When $n \leq m$ (so-called overdetermined system), for a certain class of polynomial systems called *semi-regular systems* [1–3], their d_{reg} can be estimated by the degree of the first non-positive term in the following series [3]:

$$\frac{\left(1 - z^2\right)^m}{\left(1 - z\right)^n}.$$

Empirically, a random polynomial system with very high probability is a semi-regular system, and hence the aforementioned formula can be used to estimate its degree of regularity.

2.4   UOV Attack

While the direct attack algebraically finds a signature $\mathbf{s}$ from the equation $\mathcal{P}(\mathbf{x}) = \mathbf{m}$, the UOV attack [17] finds a linear map $\mathcal{S}' : \mathbb{F}_q^n \to \mathbb{F}_q^n$ such that every component of $\mathcal{F}' := \mathcal{P} \circ \mathcal{S}'^{-1}$ has the form of (3). Such an $\mathcal{S}'$ is called an *equivalent key*.

In the UOV attack, we find the subspace $\mathcal{S}^{-1}(\mathcal{O})$ of $\mathbb{F}_q^n$, where $\mathcal{O}$ is the oil subspace defined as follows:

$$\mathcal{O} := \{(0, \ldots, 0, \alpha_1, \ldots, \alpha_o)^\top \mid \alpha_i \in \mathbb{F}_q\}.$$

This subspace $\mathcal{S}^{-1}(\mathcal{O})$ can induce an equivalent key by using the fact that for $\mathbf{y}, \mathbf{z} \in \mathcal{S}^{-1}(\mathcal{O})$, $\mathbf{y}^\top P_i \mathbf{z} = 0$ ($i = 1, \ldots, o$). Let L be an invertible $n \times n$ matrix whose right o columns are basis vectors of $\mathcal{S}^{-1}(\mathcal{O})$. Then the linear map $\mathcal{L}$ corresponding to L is an equivalent key. To obtain $\mathcal{S}^{-1}(\mathcal{O})$, in the UOV attack, we choose two invertible matrices W_i, W_j from the set of linear combinations of $P_1, \ldots, P_o$ defined in Subsect. 2.2. Then, we can probabilistically recover a part of the subspace $\mathcal{S}^{-1}(\mathcal{O})$ by computing the invariant subspace of $W_i^{-1} W_j$. The complexity of this attack by a quantum adversary is estimated to be $O(q^{\frac{v-o}{2}})$ [16].

3 Block-Anti-Circulant UOV

In this section, we first recall the definition of block-anti-circulant matrices. Next, we describe the construction of block-anti-circulant UOV (BAC-UOV) [21]. Also, we explain the way of using the Chinese remainder theorem when attacking BAC-UOV analyzed in [21], and the parameter sets.

3.1 Circulant Matrix

A circulant matrix is a matrix whose each row vector is rotated one element to the right relative to the preceding row vector. On the other hand, an anti-circulant matrix is a matrix whose each row vector is rotated one element to the left relative to the preceding row vector. A circulant matrix X and an anti-circulant matrix Y with size ℓ are of the following form:

$$X = \begin{pmatrix} a_0 & a_1 & \cdots & a_{\ell-2} & a_{\ell-1} \\ a_{\ell-1} & a_0 & \cdots & a_{\ell-3} & a_{\ell-2} \\ \vdots & \vdots & \ddots & \vdots & \vdots \\ a_2 & a_3 & \cdots & a_0 & a_1 \\ a_1 & a_2 & \cdots & a_{\ell-1} & a_0 \end{pmatrix}, Y = \begin{pmatrix} a_0 & a_1 & \cdots & a_{\ell-2} & a_{\ell-1} \\ a_1 & a_2 & \cdots & a_{\ell-1} & a_0 \\ \vdots & \vdots & \ddots & \vdots & \vdots \\ a_{\ell-2} & a_{\ell-1} & \cdots & a_{\ell-4} & a_{\ell-3} \\ a_{\ell-1} & a_0 & \cdots & a_{\ell-3} & a_{\ell-2} \end{pmatrix}. \quad (6)$$

In addition, a matrix is called a block-circulant matrix or a block-anti-circulant matrix with block size ℓ if every square block is an $\ell \times \ell$ circulant matrix or anti-circulant matrix (see the Appendix for examples with $\ell = 4$). For a block-circulant matrix A and a block-anti-circulant matrix B, the products AB and BA become block-anti-circulant matrices.

3.2 Description of BAC-UOV

Let V, O, ℓ be three positive integers. We set $v = V\ell, o = O\ell$ and $N = V + O$.

A central quadratic map $\mathcal{F} = (f_1, \ldots, f_o)$ and an affine map $\mathcal{S}$ are used as a private key for BAC-UOV. The matrices $F_1, \ldots, F_o$ representing the quadratic part of $f_1, \ldots, f_o$ are set to be block-anti-circulant matrices with block size ℓ and the matrix S representing the affine map $\mathcal{S}$ is set to be a block-circulant matrix with block size ℓ. A public key $\mathcal{P} = (p_1, \ldots, p_o)$ is generated by computing $\mathcal{F} \circ \mathcal{S}$, and the matrices $P_1, \ldots P_o$ representing quadratic parts of $p_1, \ldots, p_o$ are block-anti-circulant matrices satisfying $P_i = S^\top F_i S$ for $i = 1, \ldots, o$.

Due to the block-anti-circulant construction, these matrices P_i, F_i and S can be represented by using only the first row of every block. Therefore, these matrices can be represented by using only $N^2\ell$ elements as opposed to the highly redundant $n^2 = N^2\ell^2$ elements associated with an explicit representation. This makes the size of the public key shorter compared to the original UOV.

3.3 BAC-UOV with Chinese Remainder Theorem

In [21], they consider an attack using the Chinese Remainder Theorem (CRT) in the security analysis of BAC-UOV.

An $\ell \times \ell$ circulant matrix X in (6) can be represented by an element of the quotient ring $\mathbb{F}_q[x]/\langle x^\ell - 1 \rangle$, such as $f_X(x) := a_0 + a_1 x + \cdots + a_{\ell-1} x^{\ell-1}$. Then we can say that for two circulant matrices A, B, we have $f_{AB}(x) = f_A(x) f_B(x)$, which means we can compute the multiplication of circulant matrices in $\mathbb{F}_q[x]/\langle x^\ell - 1 \rangle$. Also for anti-circulant matrices, we can make use of the quotient ring because the left or right multiplication by the 90° rotation matrix changes a circulant matrix into an anti-circulant matrix. In addition, arithmetic in the quotient ring can be accelerated using CRT and the decomposition $\mathbb{F}_q[x]/\langle x^\ell - 1 \rangle \cong \mathbb{F}_q[x]/\langle f_0(x) \rangle \oplus \cdots \oplus \mathbb{F}_q[x]/\langle f_t(x) \rangle$, where $\prod_{i=0}^t f_i(x) = x^\ell - 1$.

This technique can be used for the UOV attack [17] and the UOV reconciliation attack [10] because these attacks are executed on the matrices representing the public key. When we estimate the complexity of these attacks, we consider only the largest component ring in the direct sum, which is associated with the irreducible factor of $x^\ell - 1$ that has the largest degree. Therefore, in [21] they choose the block size ℓ such that $1 + x + \cdots + x^{\ell-1}$ is irreducible. This technique actually changes the complexity of UOV attack into $O(q^{\frac{\ell-1}{\ell} \frac{v-o}{2}})$ from $O(q^{\frac{v-o}{2}})$.

3.4 Security Parameters for BAC-UOV

Besides the direct attack in Subsect. 2.3, we also consider a technique for reducing the number of equations in the system $\mathcal{MQ}(q, n, m)$ for $n > m$ proposed by Thomae and Wolf [22]. In this technique, we assume that the characteristic of the finite field $\mathbb{F}_q$ is 2, that is, q is a power of 2. For the $n \times n$ matrices P_i representing the quadratic parts of p_i, the technique chooses a new matrix S' such that $S'^\top P_i S'$ ($i = 1, \ldots, \alpha$) become diagonal for their first m variables where $\alpha = \lfloor \frac{n}{m} \rfloor - 1$. Then we can reduce $(\alpha + (n - m))$ variables and α equations from the system $\mathcal{MQ}(q, n, m)$. Therefore, the system is changed from $\mathcal{MQ}(q, n, m)$ into $\mathcal{MQ}(q, m - \alpha, m - \alpha)$. See [22] for more details.

Thomae and Wolf's technique [22] can be fully applied only for systems that are over fields of even characteristics. However, Thomae and Wolf show that a part of the technique can be applied to odd characteristic case and empirically makes the direct attack faster on systems over finite fields of odd characteristic. Therefore, from a security perspective, it is not extreme that we consider the technique [22] can be applied to odd characteristic case. In fact, the authors of BAC-UOV [21] adopted this thought, which is confirmed via the code to measure the complexity of the direct attack (see https://github.com/aszepieniec/bacuov for the author's code). Note that even if we can not use this technique for BAC-UOV, our attack is still valid (see Remark 2 for more details).

Table 1 shows the parameter sets of BAC-UOV for the security level II, IV and V in NIST PQC project, proposed in [21]. These parameter sets are determined by considering existing attacks with CRT explained in Subsect. 3.3 and the technique proposed by Thomae and Wolf [22]. Besides, in terms of signature

Table 1. A signature and a public key of BAC-UOV (r denotes the degree of field lifting, * shows that the attack uses the technique of CRT)

Security level	Parameters (q, V, O, ℓ, r)	$\lvert pk \rvert$	$\lvert sig \rvert$	Direct attack (bit)	*UOV attack (bit)	*Reconciliation attack (bit)
NIST II	$(3, 56, 8, 7, 12)$	3.45 kB	1.31 kB	**147**	228	149
NIST IV	$(3, 84, 11, 7, 16)$	8.69 kB	2.60 kB	**210**	346	212
NIST V	$(3, 104, 14, 7, 16)$	17.6 kB	2.42 kB	266	427	**257**

and public key size, they use several compression techniques such as Petzoldt's compression technique [20], field lifting [5] and irredundant S [8]. As a result, BAC-UOV makes the signature and public key shorter comparing with LUOV. Though Ding et al. [11] proposed an attack on LUOV, an estimation of Ding et al.'s attack is not applied yet to the parameter sets listed in Table 1, since this attack is proposed after these parameter sets are determined.

4   Our Proposed Attack

In this section, we propose a new attack on the block-anti-circulant UOV [21]. In this attack, after we change the block-anti-circulant matrices obtained from the public key into block-diagonal matrices, we apply the UOV attack [16] and the direct attack. We also estimate the complexity of our attack in this section.

4.1   Linear Transformations on the Public Key

First, we consider the case of $q \mid \ell$, where q is the order of the finite field and ℓ is the block size. Then, we can easily transform an $n \times n$ block-anti-circulant matrix into a matrix of form (4) by using the vector with ℓ consecutive same elements such as $(\underbrace{0, \ldots, 0}_{\alpha\ell}, \underbrace{1, \ldots, 1}_{\ell}, \underbrace{0, \ldots, 0}_{\beta\ell})$ $(0 \le \alpha \le n/\ell - 1, \alpha + \beta = n/\ell - 1)$. This is because for an $\ell \times \ell$ anti-circulant matrix Y, we have $(1, \ldots, 1) Y (1, \ldots, 1)^\top = 0$ since $q \mid \ell$. By using this property, we can easily obtain an equivalent key. In fact, a parameter set with $q \mid \ell$ is not chosen in [21].

Next, we consider the case of $q \nmid \ell$. We define an $\ell \times \ell$ matrix L_ℓ such that $(L_\ell)_{1i} = (L_\ell)_{j1} = 1\ (1 \le i, j \le \ell)$, $(L_\ell)_{ii} = -1\ (2 \le i \le \ell)$ and the other elements equal to 0, namely,

$$L_\ell := \ell \left\{ \begin{pmatrix} \overbrace{\begin{matrix} 1 & 1 & \cdots & 1 \\ 1 & -1 & & \\ \vdots & & \ddots & \\ 1 & & & -1 \end{matrix}}^{\ell} \end{pmatrix} \right. .$$

This matrix is invertible since $q \nmid \ell$. Then, for an $\ell \times \ell$ anti-circulant matrix Y, we have:

$$L_\ell Y L_\ell = \begin{pmatrix} * & 0_{1 \times (\ell-1)} \\ 0_{(\ell-1) \times 1} & *_{(\ell-1) \times (\ell-1)} \end{pmatrix}. \tag{7}$$

This is because for the first column of L_ℓ, we have $Y(1, \ldots, 1)^\top = \alpha(1, \ldots, 1)^\top$ with some $\alpha \in \mathbb{F}_q$ and the other columns of L_ℓ are orthogonal to $(1, \ldots, 1)^\top$.

Let $L_\ell^{(N)}$ be an $n \times n$ $(n = N\ell)$ block diagonal matrix such that every diagonal submatrix is L_ℓ:

$$L_\ell^{(N)} = \begin{pmatrix} \overbrace{L_\ell}^{\ell \times N} & & \\ & \ddots & \\ & & L_\ell \end{pmatrix}.$$

Then, for an $n \times n$ block-anti-circulant matrix Z with block size ℓ, we have $L_\ell^{(N)} Z L_\ell^{(N)}$ becomes a block matrix whose every block is in the form of (7):

$$L_\ell^{(N)} Z L_\ell^{(N)} = \begin{pmatrix} \begin{array}{cc|c} * & 0_{1 \times (\ell-1)} & \\ 0_{(\ell-1) \times 1} & *_{(\ell-1) \times (\ell-1)} & \cdots \\ \vdots & & \ddots \\ \hline * & 0_{1 \times (\ell-1)} & \\ 0_{(\ell-1) \times 1} & *_{(\ell-1) \times (\ell-1)} & \cdots \end{array} \begin{array}{cc} * & 0_{1 \times (\ell-1)} \\ 0_{(\ell-1) \times 1} & *_{(\ell-1) \times (\ell-1)} \\ \vdots \\ * & 0_{1 \times (\ell-1)} \\ 0_{(\ell-1) \times 1} & *_{(\ell-1) \times (\ell-1)} \end{array} \end{pmatrix}.$$

There exists a matrix L' such that

$$L'^\top L_\ell^{(N)} Z L_\ell^{(N)} L' = \begin{pmatrix} *_{N \times N} & 0_{N \times (\ell-1)N} \\ 0_{(\ell-1)N \times N} & *_{(\ell-1)N \times (\ell-1)N} \end{pmatrix}. \tag{8}$$

Such an L' is given as a permutation matrix.

Set $L := L_\ell^{(N)} L'$. We execute the transformation using L on the matrices P_i $(i = 1, \ldots, o)$ representing the quadratic parts of the public key. Then $L^\top P_i L$ $(i = 1, \ldots, o)$ become the special matrix of form (8).

4.2 The UOV Attack on the Transformed Public Key

We use the UOV attack [17] on $L^\top P_i L$ $(i = 1, \ldots, o)$.

Now we consider the matrices obtained by the UOV attack on $L^\top P_i L$ for $i = 1, \ldots, o$. The matrix $L^\top P_i L$ can be represented by $(L^{-1} S L)^\top (L^\top F_i L)(L^{-1} S L)$. Then this $L^\top F_i L$ is in the form of the following:

$$\begin{pmatrix} \begin{array}{cc|c} *_{V \times V} & *_{V \times O} & \\ *_{O \times V} & 0_{O \times O} & 0_{N \times (\ell-1)N} \\ \hline & & *_{(\ell-1)V \times (\ell-1)V} & *_{(\ell-1)V \times (\ell-1)O} \\ 0_{(\ell-1)N \times N} & & *_{(\ell-1)O \times (\ell-1)V} & 0_{(\ell-1)O \times (\ell-1)O} \end{array} \end{pmatrix}, \tag{9}$$

and $L^{-1}SL$ is in the form of (8). Therefore, the matrices obtained by using the UOV attack on $L^\top P_i L$ is in the form of (9).

By this fact, the complexity of the UOV attack on the $N \times N$ and $(\ell-1)N \times (\ell-1)N$ submatrices is $O(q^{\frac{\ell-1}{\ell}\frac{v-o}{2}})$. However, this complexity is the same as the complexity of the UOV attack with CRT in Subsect. 3.3. Therefore, this method does not affect the security of BAC-UOV.

However, we can execute the UOV attack only on the upper-left $N \times N$ submatrices of $L^\top P_i L$ $(i = 1, \ldots, o)$ with a small complexity $O(q^{\frac{1}{\ell}\frac{v-o}{2}})$. Then after executing this attack, we can obtain o matrices that are in the following form:

$$\begin{pmatrix} \begin{array}{c|c} *_{V\times V} & *_{V\times O} \\ \hline *_{O\times V} & 0_{O\times O} \end{array} & 0_{N\times(\ell-1)N} \\ \hline 0_{(\ell-1)N\times N} & *_{(\ell-1)N\times(\ell-1)N} \end{pmatrix}. \tag{10}$$

4.3 Completing Our Attack with Direct Attack

We execute the direct attack in Subsect. 2.3 on the polynomial system represented by the matrices of form (10). The basic idea of this subsection is to obtain quadratic polynomials represented by the following matrix:

$$\begin{pmatrix} 0_{O\times O} & 0_{O\times(\ell-1)N} \\ \hline 0_{(\ell-1)N\times O} & *_{(\ell-1)N\times(\ell-1)N} \end{pmatrix}, \tag{11}$$

by fixing the first V variables to random values in polynomial system represented by the matrices of form (10). Then we can reduce the number of variables appeared in quadratic terms of the polynomials. Therefore this attack can be executed in a smaller complexity.

The first O variables in the system represented by (11) does not appear in quadratic terms, but they appear in linear terms. By applying Gaussian elimination on the O variables, we obtain O equations with $(O+(\ell-1)N)$ variables and $((\ell-1)O)$ equations with only other $((\ell-1)N)$ variables. Then, we execute the direct attack on the system with $((\ell-1)N)$ variables and $((\ell-1)O)$ equations. After that, we obtain a solution for the first O variables by using the remaining O equations and the obtained answer by executing the direct attack.

In addition, we use the reducing technique proposed by [22] for the system with $((\ell-1)N)$ variables and $((\ell-1)O)$ equations as stated in Subsect. 3.4. Let $\alpha := \lfloor \frac{(\ell-1)N}{(\ell-1)O} \rfloor - 1 = \lfloor \frac{V}{O} \rfloor$, then we can reduce α equations. We can also choose first V values in (10) such that the coefficients of x_{V+1} equal to 0 in all o equations when $V \geq o = O \times \ell$ (in [21] they use such a condition when $q = 3$). Finally, we can solve a quadratic system with $((\ell-1)O - \alpha)$ variables and $((\ell-1)O - \alpha + 1)$ equations.

Table 2. Comparison existing attacks and our proposed attack on BAC-UOV

Security level	Parameters (q, V, O, ℓ, r)	Security parameter in [21]	Our proposed attack
NIST II	$(3, 56, 8, 7, 12)$	2^{147}	$\mathbf{2^{119}}$
NIST IV	$(3, 84, 11, 7, 16)$	2^{210}	$\mathbf{2^{171}}$
NIST V	$(3, 104, 14, 7, 16)$	2^{257}	$\mathbf{2^{219}}$

4.4 Complexity Analysis

Now, we estimate the complexity of our attack on BAC-UOV with the level II parameter, $(q, V, O, \ell, r) = (3, 56, 8, 7, 12)$, which is determined so that the complexity of every existing attack is larger than 146 bits in Table 1. Then, the matrices P_i $(i = 1, \ldots, 56)$ representing quadratic parts of the public key of BAC-UOV are 448×448 block-anti-circulant matrices with block size $\ell = 7$. First, we execute the linear transformation explained in Subsect. 4.1 on $P_1, \ldots, P_{56}$ which is changed to the form of (8). This step costs polynomial time. Second, the UOV attack on the upper-left 64×64 submatrices is executed with 38-bit complexity (estimated by $q^{\frac{v-o}{2}}$), which is much smaller than the security parameter of 146 bits. Then, $P_1, \ldots, P_{56}$ are changed to the form of (10) in Subsect. 4.2. Finally, we can change the solving $\mathcal{MQ}$-problem into $\mathcal{MQ}(3^{12}, 41, 42)$ from $\mathcal{MQ}(3^{12}, 49, 49)$ by the discussion in Subsect. 4.3. The complexity of the direct attack on $\mathcal{MQ}(3^{12}, 41, 42)$ is estimated to be 119 bits by the formula (5), while the complexity of the direct attack on $\mathcal{MQ}(3^{12}, 49, 49)$ is 147 bits.

Table 2 compares the complexity of the best existing attack and our proposed attack by a quantum adversary for each parameter set. The security level of BAC-UOV decreases from 210 bits to 171 bits for the level IV parameter and decreases from 257 bits to 219 bits for the level V parameter. Table 2 shows that our proposed attack reduces the security level by about 20% compared with the previously known attacks for each parameter set.

Remark 1. BAC-UOV was proposed before Ding et al. [11] presented a new attack on LUOV using field lifting at Second PQC Standardization Conference 2019. Therefore, the parameter sets in Table 1 do not consider Ding et al.'s attack.

We stress that BAC-UOV also utilizes the technique of the field lifting used in LUOV. Therefore, Ding et al's attack on LUOV is also applicable to BAC-UOV, and results in a lower bit complexity required for breaking BAC-UOV. In terms of our proposed attack, it is possible to apply both our attack and Ding et al.'s attack on BAC-UOV. It means that our attack can further reduce the bit complexity required for breaking BAC-UOV using Ding et al.'s attack together.

Remark 2. As explained in Subsect. 3.4, we estimate the complexity of our proposed attack coupling with the technique proposed by Thomae and Wolf [22].

However, in this remark, we discuss the complexity of our attack and existing attacks without using Thomae and Wolf's technique. When we do not utilize Thomae and Wolf's technique for the direct attack, the complexity of the direct attack becomes larger than that of the reconciliation attack for each parameter set. Therefore, without using Thomae and Wolf's technique, the best existing attack is the reconciliation attack. On the other hand, the complexities of our proposed attack without using Thomae and Wolf's technique are 137 bits, 188 bits and 237 bits for the security level II, IV and V, respectively. From the complexity of the reconciliation attack in Table 1, we remark that our proposed attack reduces the bit complexity of breaking BAC-UOV by about 10% even if we can not use Thomae and Wolf's technique.

5   Conclusion

In this paper, we proposed a new attack on BAC-UOV, which is a variant of UOV using the structure of block-anti-circulant matrices. This attack first changes matrices representing the public key into block-diagonal matrices, then applies the UOV attack on the smaller block submatrices. The resulting matrices correspond to a polynomial system with quadratic terms in less variables, which can be solved algebraically with less complexity than simply applying the direct attack on the public key polynomials of BAC-UOV. As a result, our proposed attack reduces the bit complexity of breaking BAC-UOV by about 20% compared with the previously known attacks. By this analysis, we conclude that the originally proposed secure parameters for BAC-UOV fail in achieving the claimed security levels. Note that since our proposed attack relies on the property of an anti-circulant matrix, it does not affect the security of the original UOV and Rainbow.

The compression technique of using block-anti-circulant can also be applied to Rainbow (BAC-Rainbow), and our proposed attack is expected to be applicable on BAC-Rainbow as well, but we leave how our attack affects the security of BAC-Rainbow as future work.

Acknowledgments. This work was supported by JST CREST Grant Number JPMJCR14D6, JSPS KAKENHI Grant Number 19K20266, and 18J20866.

Appendix: Toy Example

We show a toy example of the proposed attack on BAC-UOV ($q = 3, V = 3, O = 2, \ell = 4$).

1. Generating a BAC-UOV Public Key

- Private Key Generation

The matrix representing the linear map $\mathcal{S} : \mathbb{F}_3^{20} \to \mathbb{F}_3^{20}$ is generated as

```
1 0 0 0 0 0 0 0 0 0 0 0 2 1 1 2 0 2 1 1
0 1 0 0 0 0 0 0 0 0 0 0 2 2 1 1 1 0 2 1
0 0 1 0 0 0 0 0 0 0 0 0 1 2 2 1 1 1 0 2
0 0 0 1 0 0 0 0 0 0 0 0 1 1 2 2 2 1 1 0
0 0 0 0 1 0 0 0 0 0 0 0 0 1 1 0 2 1 2 0
0 0 0 0 0 1 0 0 0 0 0 0 0 0 1 1 0 2 1 2
0 0 0 0 0 0 1 0 0 0 0 0 1 0 0 1 2 0 2 1
0 0 0 0 0 0 0 1 0 0 0 0 1 1 0 0 1 2 0 2
0 0 0 0 0 0 0 0 1 0 0 0 2 0 2 1 0 2 0 0
0 0 0 0 0 0 0 0 0 1 0 0 1 2 0 2 0 0 2 0
0 0 0 0 0 0 0 0 0 0 1 0 2 1 2 0 0 0 2 0
0 0 0 0 0 0 0 0 0 0 0 1 0 2 1 2 2 0 0 0
0 0 0 0 0 0 0 0 0 0 0 0 1 0 0 0 0 0 0 0
0 0 0 0 0 0 0 0 0 0 0 0 0 1 0 0 0 0 0 0
0 0 0 0 0 0 0 0 0 0 0 0 0 0 1 0 0 0 0 0
0 0 0 0 0 0 0 0 0 0 0 0 0 0 0 1 0 0 0 0
0 0 0 0 0 0 0 0 0 0 0 0 0 0 0 0 1 0 0 0
0 0 0 0 0 0 0 0 0 0 0 0 0 0 0 0 0 1 0 0
0 0 0 0 0 0 0 0 0 0 0 0 0 0 0 0 0 0 1 0
0 0 0 0 0 0 0 0 0 0 0 0 0 0 0 0 0 0 0 1
```

,

and the matrices associated to the quadratic form of the central map $\mathcal{F} = (f_1, \ldots, f_8) : \mathbb{F}_3^{20} \to \mathbb{F}_3^8$ are generated to be

```
0 2 2 2 1 2 2 0 2 0 2 2 1 1 0 1 0 0 1 2
2 2 2 0 2 2 0 1 0 2 2 2 1 0 1 1 0 1 2 0
2 2 0 2 2 0 1 2 2 2 2 0 0 1 1 1 1 2 0 0
2 0 2 2 0 1 2 2 2 2 0 2 1 1 1 0 2 0 0 1
1 2 2 0 0 2 1 1 1 0 0 1 0 2 0 0 1 1 0 1
2 2 0 1 2 1 1 0 0 0 1 1 2 0 0 0 1 0 1 1
2 0 1 2 1 1 0 2 0 1 1 0 0 0 0 2 0 1 1 1
0 1 2 2 1 0 2 1 1 1 0 0 0 0 2 0 1 1 1 0
2 0 2 2 1 0 0 1 0 1 2 1 0 0 1 2 0 1 1 1
0 2 2 0 0 1 1 1 2 1 0 1 1 2 0 0 1 1 0 1
2 2 0 1 1 0 0 1 0 1 2 2 0 0 1 1 0 1 1
1 1 0 1 0 2 0 0 0 0 1 2 0 0 0 0 0 0 0 0
1 0 1 1 2 0 0 0 0 1 2 0 0 0 0 0 0 0 0 0
0 1 1 1 0 0 0 2 1 2 0 0 0 0 0 0 0 0 0 0
1 1 1 0 0 0 2 0 2 0 0 1 0 0 0 0 0 0 0 0
0 0 1 2 1 1 0 1 0 1 1 1 0 0 0 0 0 0 0 0
0 1 2 0 1 0 1 1 1 1 1 0 0 0 0 0 0 0 0 0
1 2 0 0 1 1 1 1 1 0 1 0 0 1 0 0 0 0 0 0
2 0 0 1 1 1 1 0 1 0 1 1 0 0 0 0 0 0 0 0
2 0 0 1 1 1 1 0 1 0 1 1 0 0 0 0 0 0 0 0
```
, . . . ,
```
2 0 2 2 0 0 0 2 0 1 0 1 1 2 1 0 1 1 0 1
0 2 2 2 0 0 2 0 1 0 1 0 2 1 0 1 1 0 1 1
2 2 2 0 0 0 1 0 1 1 0 1 0 1 2 0 1 1 1
2 2 0 2 2 0 0 0 1 0 1 0 0 1 2 1 1 1 1 0
0 0 0 2 2 0 0 2 2 0 1 0 1 0 0 0 2 0 1 0 0
0 0 2 0 0 0 2 2 0 1 0 2 0 0 2 1 1 0 0 0
0 2 0 0 0 2 2 0 1 0 2 0 0 2 1 0 0 0 0 1
2 0 0 0 2 2 0 0 0 2 0 1 2 1 0 0 0 0 1 0
0 1 0 1 2 0 1 0 2 1 0 0 0 0 1 0 1 2 0 0
1 0 1 0 0 1 0 2 1 0 0 2 0 1 0 0 2 0 0 1
0 1 0 1 1 0 2 0 0 0 2 1 1 0 0 0 0 0 1 2
1 0 1 0 0 2 0 1 0 2 1 0 0 0 0 1 0 1 2 0
1 2 1 0 1 0 0 2 0 0 1 0 0 0 0 0 0 0 0 0
2 1 0 1 0 0 1 0 0 0 0 0 0 0 0 0 0 0 0 0
1 0 1 2 0 2 1 0 1 0 0 0 0 0 0 0 0 0 0 0
0 1 2 1 2 1 0 0 0 0 0 1 0 0 0 0 0 0 0 0
1 1 0 1 0 1 0 0 1 2 0 0 0 0 0 0 0 0 0 0
1 0 1 1 1 0 0 0 2 0 0 1 0 0 0 0 0 0 0 0
0 1 1 1 0 0 0 1 0 0 1 2 0 0 0 0 0 0 0 0
1 1 1 0 0 0 1 0 0 1 2 0 0 0 0 0 0 0 0 0
```
.

- Public Key Generation

From $\mathcal{S}$ and $\mathcal{F}$, we can obtain a public key $\mathcal{P} = (p_1, \ldots, p_8) : \mathbb{F}_3^{20} \to \mathbb{F}_3^8$ for BAC-UOV, and the matrices associated to their quadratic forms are

$$
\begin{pmatrix}
0\,2\,2\,2\,1\,2\,2\,0\,2\,0\,2\,2\,1\,0\,2\,1\,0\,1\,0\,0 \\
2\,2\,2\,0\,2\,2\,0\,1\,0\,2\,2\,2\,0\,2\,1\,1\,1\,0\,0\,0 \\
2\,2\,0\,2\,2\,0\,1\,2\,2\,2\,2\,0\,2\,1\,1\,0\,0\,0\,0\,1 \\
2\,0\,2\,2\,0\,1\,2\,2\,2\,2\,0\,2\,1\,1\,0\,2\,0\,0\,1\,0 \\
1\,2\,2\,0\,0\,2\,1\,1\,1\,0\,0\,1\,0\,2\,0\,0\,1\,1\,0\,0 \\
2\,2\,0\,1\,2\,1\,1\,0\,0\,0\,1\,1\,2\,0\,0\,0\,1\,0\,0\,1 \\
2\,0\,1\,2\,1\,1\,1\,0\,2\,0\,1\,1\,0\,0\,0\,0\,2\,0\,0\,1\,1 \\
0\,1\,2\,2\,1\,0\,2\,1\,1\,1\,0\,0\,0\,0\,2\,0\,0\,1\,1\,0 \\
2\,0\,2\,2\,1\,0\,0\,1\,0\,1\,2\,1\,2\,1\,2\,1\,2\,0\,0\,1 \\
0\,2\,2\,2\,0\,0\,1\,1\,1\,2\,1\,0\,1\,2\,1\,2\,0\,0\,1\,2 \\
2\,2\,2\,0\,0\,1\,1\,0\,2\,1\,0\,1\,2\,1\,2\,1\,0\,1\,2\,0 \\
2\,2\,0\,2\,1\,1\,0\,0\,1\,0\,1\,2\,1\,2\,1\,2\,1\,2\,0\,0 \\
1\,0\,2\,1\,0\,2\,0\,0\,2\,1\,2\,1\,0\,0\,1\,1\,1\,0\,2\,2 \\
0\,2\,1\,1\,2\,0\,0\,0\,1\,2\,1\,2\,0\,1\,1\,0\,0\,2\,2\,1 \\
2\,1\,1\,0\,0\,0\,0\,2\,2\,1\,2\,1\,1\,1\,0\,0\,2\,2\,1\,0 \\
1\,1\,0\,2\,0\,0\,2\,0\,1\,2\,1\,2\,1\,0\,0\,0\,1\,2\,0\,2 \\
0\,1\,0\,0\,1\,1\,0\,0\,2\,0\,0\,1\,1\,0\,2\,2\,0\,0\,0\,2 \\
1\,0\,0\,0\,1\,0\,0\,1\,0\,0\,1\,2\,0\,2\,2\,1\,0\,0\,2\,0 \\
0\,0\,0\,1\,0\,0\,1\,1\,0\,1\,2\,0\,2\,2\,1\,0\,0\,2\,0\,0 \\
0\,0\,1\,0\,0\,1\,1\,0\,1\,2\,0\,0\,2\,1\,0\,2\,2\,0\,0\,0
\end{pmatrix}, \ldots, \begin{pmatrix}
2\,0\,2\,2\,0\,0\,0\,2\,0\,1\,0\,1\,0\,1\,0\,2\,2\,1\,0\,2 \\
0\,2\,2\,2\,0\,0\,2\,0\,1\,0\,1\,0\,1\,0\,2\,0\,1\,0\,2\,2 \\
2\,2\,2\,0\,0\,2\,0\,0\,0\,1\,0\,1\,0\,2\,0\,1\,0\,2\,2\,1 \\
2\,2\,0\,2\,2\,0\,0\,0\,1\,0\,1\,0\,2\,0\,1\,0\,2\,2\,1\,0 \\
0\,0\,0\,2\,2\,0\,0\,2\,2\,0\,1\,0\,2\,1\,0\,2\,1\,1\,0\,0 \\
0\,0\,2\,0\,0\,0\,2\,2\,0\,1\,0\,2\,1\,0\,2\,2\,1\,0\,0\,1 \\
0\,2\,0\,0\,0\,2\,2\,0\,1\,0\,2\,0\,0\,2\,2\,1\,0\,0\,1\,1 \\
2\,0\,0\,0\,2\,2\,0\,0\,0\,2\,0\,1\,2\,2\,1\,0\,0\,1\,1\,0 \\
0\,1\,0\,1\,2\,0\,1\,0\,2\,1\,0\,0\,0\,1\,1\,2\,1\,0\,2\,2 \\
1\,0\,1\,0\,0\,1\,0\,2\,1\,0\,0\,2\,1\,1\,2\,0\,0\,2\,2\,1 \\
0\,1\,0\,1\,1\,0\,2\,0\,0\,0\,2\,1\,1\,2\,0\,1\,2\,2\,1\,0 \\
1\,0\,1\,0\,0\,2\,0\,1\,0\,2\,1\,0\,2\,0\,1\,1\,2\,1\,0\,2 \\
0\,1\,0\,2\,2\,1\,0\,2\,0\,1\,1\,2\,2\,2\,2\,2\,0\,0\,0\,2 \\
1\,0\,2\,0\,1\,0\,2\,2\,1\,1\,2\,0\,2\,2\,2\,2\,0\,0\,2\,0 \\
0\,2\,0\,1\,0\,2\,2\,1\,1\,2\,0\,1\,2\,2\,2\,2\,0\,2\,0\,0 \\
2\,0\,1\,0\,2\,2\,1\,0\,2\,0\,1\,1\,2\,2\,2\,2\,0\,0\,0\,0 \\
2\,1\,0\,2\,1\,1\,0\,0\,1\,0\,2\,2\,0\,0\,2\,2\,0\,0\,1 \\
1\,0\,2\,2\,1\,0\,0\,1\,0\,2\,2\,1\,0\,0\,2\,0\,0\,0\,1\,2 \\
0\,2\,2\,1\,0\,0\,1\,1\,2\,2\,1\,0\,0\,2\,0\,0\,0\,1\,2\,0 \\
2\,2\,1\,0\,0\,1\,1\,0\,2\,1\,0\,2\,2\,0\,0\,0\,1\,2\,0\,0
\end{pmatrix}.
$$

2. Our Proposed Attack

We first apply a linear transformation represented by $L_4^{(5)}$ and a permutation on the public key $\mathcal{P} = (p_1, \ldots, p_n)$, which is explained in Subsect. 4.1. $L_4^{(5)}$ and the matrices representing the permutation, respectively, are

$$
\begin{pmatrix}
1\,1\,1\,1\,0\,0\,0\,0\,0\,0\,0\,0\,0\,0\,0\,0\,0\,0\,0\,0 \\
1\,2\,0\,0\,0\,0\,0\,0\,0\,0\,0\,0\,0\,0\,0\,0\,0\,0\,0\,0 \\
1\,0\,2\,0\,0\,0\,0\,0\,0\,0\,0\,0\,0\,0\,0\,0\,0\,0\,0\,0 \\
1\,0\,0\,2\,0\,0\,0\,0\,0\,0\,0\,0\,0\,0\,0\,0\,0\,0\,0\,0 \\
0\,0\,0\,0\,1\,1\,1\,1\,0\,0\,0\,0\,0\,0\,0\,0\,0\,0\,0\,0 \\
0\,0\,0\,0\,1\,2\,0\,0\,0\,0\,0\,0\,0\,0\,0\,0\,0\,0\,0\,0 \\
0\,0\,0\,0\,1\,0\,2\,0\,0\,0\,0\,0\,0\,0\,0\,0\,0\,0\,0\,0 \\
0\,0\,0\,0\,1\,0\,0\,2\,0\,0\,0\,0\,0\,0\,0\,0\,0\,0\,0\,0 \\
0\,0\,0\,0\,0\,0\,0\,0\,1\,1\,1\,1\,0\,0\,0\,0\,0\,0\,0\,0 \\
0\,0\,0\,0\,0\,0\,0\,0\,1\,2\,0\,0\,0\,0\,0\,0\,0\,0\,0\,0 \\
0\,0\,0\,0\,0\,0\,0\,0\,1\,0\,2\,0\,0\,0\,0\,0\,0\,0\,0\,0 \\
0\,0\,0\,0\,0\,0\,0\,0\,1\,0\,0\,2\,0\,0\,0\,0\,0\,0\,0\,0 \\
0\,0\,0\,0\,0\,0\,0\,0\,0\,0\,0\,0\,1\,1\,1\,1\,0\,0\,0\,0 \\
0\,0\,0\,0\,0\,0\,0\,0\,0\,0\,0\,0\,1\,2\,0\,0\,0\,0\,0\,0 \\
0\,0\,0\,0\,0\,0\,0\,0\,0\,0\,0\,0\,1\,0\,2\,0\,0\,0\,0\,0 \\
0\,0\,0\,0\,0\,0\,0\,0\,0\,0\,0\,0\,1\,0\,0\,2\,0\,0\,0\,0 \\
0\,0\,0\,0\,0\,0\,0\,0\,0\,0\,0\,0\,0\,0\,0\,0\,1\,1\,1\,1 \\
0\,0\,0\,0\,0\,0\,0\,0\,0\,0\,0\,0\,0\,0\,0\,0\,1\,2\,0\,0 \\
0\,0\,0\,0\,0\,0\,0\,0\,0\,0\,0\,0\,0\,0\,0\,0\,1\,0\,2\,0 \\
0\,0\,0\,0\,0\,0\,0\,0\,0\,0\,0\,0\,0\,0\,0\,0\,1\,0\,0\,2
\end{pmatrix}, \begin{pmatrix}
1\,0\,0\,0\,0\,0\,0\,0\,0\,0\,0\,0\,0\,0\,0\,0\,0\,0\,0\,0 \\
0\,0\,0\,0\,1\,0\,0\,0\,0\,0\,0\,0\,0\,0\,0\,0\,0\,0\,0\,0 \\
0\,0\,0\,0\,0\,1\,0\,0\,0\,0\,0\,0\,0\,0\,0\,0\,0\,0\,0\,0 \\
0\,0\,0\,0\,0\,0\,0\,1\,0\,0\,0\,0\,0\,0\,0\,0\,0\,0\,0\,0 \\
0\,1\,0\,0\,0\,0\,0\,0\,0\,0\,0\,0\,0\,0\,0\,0\,0\,0\,0\,0 \\
0\,0\,0\,0\,0\,0\,0\,0\,1\,0\,0\,0\,0\,0\,0\,0\,0\,0\,0\,0 \\
0\,0\,0\,0\,0\,0\,0\,0\,0\,1\,0\,0\,0\,0\,0\,0\,0\,0\,0\,0 \\
0\,0\,0\,0\,0\,0\,0\,0\,0\,0\,1\,0\,0\,0\,0\,0\,0\,0\,0\,0 \\
0\,0\,1\,0\,0\,0\,0\,0\,0\,0\,0\,0\,0\,0\,0\,0\,0\,0\,0\,0 \\
0\,0\,0\,0\,0\,0\,0\,0\,0\,0\,0\,1\,0\,0\,0\,0\,0\,0\,0\,0 \\
0\,0\,0\,0\,0\,0\,0\,0\,0\,0\,0\,0\,1\,0\,0\,0\,0\,0\,0\,0 \\
0\,0\,0\,0\,0\,0\,0\,0\,0\,0\,0\,0\,0\,1\,0\,0\,0\,0\,0\,0 \\
0\,0\,0\,1\,0\,0\,0\,0\,0\,0\,0\,0\,0\,0\,0\,0\,0\,0\,0\,0 \\
0\,0\,0\,0\,0\,0\,0\,0\,0\,0\,0\,0\,0\,0\,1\,0\,0\,0\,0\,0 \\
0\,0\,0\,0\,0\,0\,0\,0\,0\,0\,0\,0\,0\,0\,0\,1\,0\,0\,0\,0 \\
0\,0\,0\,0\,0\,0\,0\,0\,0\,0\,0\,0\,0\,0\,0\,0\,1\,0\,0\,0 \\
0\,0\,0\,1\,0\,0\,0\,0\,0\,0\,0\,0\,0\,0\,0\,0\,0\,0\,0\,0 \\
0\,0\,0\,0\,0\,0\,0\,0\,0\,0\,0\,0\,0\,0\,0\,0\,0\,1\,0\,0 \\
0\,0\,0\,0\,0\,0\,0\,0\,0\,0\,0\,0\,0\,0\,0\,0\,0\,0\,1\,0 \\
0\,0\,0\,0\,0\,0\,0\,0\,0\,0\,0\,0\,0\,0\,0\,0\,0\,0\,0\,1
\end{pmatrix}.
$$

Then we construct a linear transformation $\mathcal{L}$ by composing these two transformations. The matrices associated to the quadratic forms of the resulting polynomial system $\mathcal{P} \circ \mathcal{L} = (p'_1, \ldots, p'_8) : \mathbb{F}_3^{20} \to \mathbb{F}_3^8$ are in the form of (8):

$$\begin{pmatrix} 0 & 2 & 0 & 1 & 1 & 0 & 0 & 0 & 0 & 0 & 0 & 0 & 0 & 0 & 0 & 0 & 0 & 0 & 0 & 0 \\ 2 & 1 & 2 & 2 & 2 & 0 & 0 & 0 & 0 & 0 & 0 & 0 & 0 & 0 & 0 & 0 & 0 & 0 & 0 & 0 \\ 0 & 2 & 1 & 0 & 0 & 0 & 0 & 0 & 0 & 0 & 0 & 0 & 0 & 0 & 0 & 0 & 0 & 0 & 0 & 0 \\ 1 & 2 & 0 & 2 & 2 & 0 & 0 & 0 & 0 & 0 & 0 & 0 & 0 & 0 & 0 & 0 & 0 & 0 & 0 & 0 \\ 1 & 2 & 0 & 2 & 2 & 0 & 0 & 0 & 0 & 0 & 0 & 0 & 0 & 0 & 0 & 0 & 0 & 0 & 0 & 0 \\ 0 & 0 & 0 & 0 & 0 & 1 & 1 & 2 & 2 & 0 & 0 & 1 & 2 & 2 & 0 & 0 & 1 & 1 & 2 & 2 \\ 0 & 0 & 0 & 0 & 0 & 1 & 2 & 1 & 0 & 1 & 1 & 2 & 0 & 1 & 0 & 1 & 1 & 2 & 0 & 1 \\ 0 & 0 & 0 & 0 & 0 & 2 & 1 & 1 & 0 & 1 & 0 & 2 & 1 & 0 & 1 & 1 & 1 & 2 & 1 & 0 \\ 0 & 0 & 0 & 0 & 0 & 2 & 0 & 0 & 0 & 1 & 0 & 1 & 2 & 1 & 2 & 1 & 1 & 2 & 0 & 1 \\ 0 & 0 & 0 & 0 & 0 & 0 & 1 & 1 & 1 & 1 & 0 & 2 & 2 & 0 & 1 & 0 & 2 & 0 & 2 & 2 \\ 0 & 0 & 0 & 0 & 0 & 0 & 1 & 0 & 0 & 0 & 2 & 1 & 0 & 2 & 1 & 2 & 0 & 1 & 2 & 1 \\ 0 & 0 & 0 & 0 & 0 & 1 & 2 & 2 & 1 & 2 & 1 & 0 & 1 & 1 & 2 & 0 & 2 & 2 & 0 & 0 \\ 0 & 0 & 0 & 0 & 0 & 2 & 0 & 1 & 2 & 2 & 0 & 1 & 2 & 1 & 0 & 0 & 0 & 0 & 1 & 1 \\ 0 & 0 & 0 & 0 & 0 & 2 & 1 & 0 & 1 & 0 & 2 & 1 & 1 & 0 & 2 & 0 & 2 & 0 & 1 & 0 \\ 0 & 0 & 0 & 0 & 0 & 0 & 0 & 1 & 2 & 1 & 1 & 2 & 0 & 2 & 1 & 0 & 2 & 0 & 1 & 0 \\ 0 & 0 & 0 & 0 & 0 & 0 & 1 & 1 & 1 & 0 & 2 & 0 & 0 & 0 & 0 & 1 & 1 & 1 & 1 & 0 \\ 0 & 0 & 0 & 0 & 0 & 1 & 1 & 1 & 1 & 2 & 0 & 2 & 0 & 2 & 2 & 1 & 2 & 0 & 0 & 2 \\ 0 & 0 & 0 & 0 & 0 & 1 & 2 & 2 & 2 & 0 & 1 & 2 & 0 & 0 & 0 & 1 & 0 & 0 & 2 & 1 \\ 0 & 0 & 0 & 0 & 0 & 2 & 0 & 1 & 0 & 2 & 2 & 0 & 1 & 1 & 1 & 1 & 0 & 2 & 0 & 1 \\ 0 & 0 & 0 & 0 & 0 & 2 & 1 & 0 & 1 & 2 & 1 & 0 & 1 & 0 & 0 & 0 & 2 & 1 & 1 & 2 \end{pmatrix}, \dots, \begin{pmatrix} 0 & 2 & 2 & 0 & 2 & 0 & 0 & 0 & 0 & 0 & 0 & 0 & 0 & 0 & 0 & 0 & 0 & 0 & 0 & 0 \\ 2 & 1 & 0 & 2 & 2 & 0 & 0 & 0 & 0 & 0 & 0 & 0 & 0 & 0 & 0 & 0 & 0 & 0 & 0 & 0 \\ 2 & 0 & 0 & 1 & 2 & 0 & 0 & 0 & 0 & 0 & 0 & 0 & 0 & 0 & 0 & 0 & 0 & 0 & 0 & 0 \\ 0 & 2 & 1 & 2 & 2 & 0 & 0 & 0 & 0 & 0 & 0 & 0 & 0 & 0 & 0 & 0 & 0 & 0 & 0 & 0 \\ 2 & 2 & 2 & 2 & 0 & 0 & 0 & 0 & 0 & 0 & 0 & 0 & 0 & 0 & 0 & 0 & 0 & 0 & 0 & 0 \\ 0 & 0 & 0 & 0 & 0 & 1 & 2 & 2 & 0 & 2 & 1 & 1 & 0 & 1 & 1 & 1 & 0 & 0 & 0 & 1 \\ 0 & 0 & 0 & 0 & 0 & 2 & 0 & 1 & 2 & 0 & 1 & 0 & 0 & 0 & 1 & 0 & 2 & 0 & 1 & 1 \\ 0 & 0 & 0 & 0 & 0 & 2 & 1 & 0 & 1 & 1 & 2 & 1 & 0 & 1 & 0 & 2 & 2 & 1 & 1 & 1 \\ 0 & 0 & 0 & 0 & 0 & 0 & 2 & 1 & 2 & 1 & 2 & 0 & 1 & 1 & 0 & 0 & 1 & 2 & 0 & 1 \\ 0 & 0 & 0 & 0 & 0 & 2 & 0 & 1 & 1 & 1 & 0 & 1 & 2 & 1 & 0 & 1 & 1 & 0 & 2 & 2 \\ 0 & 0 & 0 & 0 & 0 & 1 & 1 & 2 & 2 & 0 & 1 & 1 & 1 & 0 & 1 & 1 & 1 & 1 & 2 & 1 \\ 0 & 0 & 0 & 0 & 0 & 1 & 0 & 1 & 0 & 1 & 1 & 0 & 1 & 0 & 2 & 0 & 0 & 0 & 1 & 0 \\ 0 & 0 & 0 & 0 & 0 & 0 & 0 & 0 & 1 & 2 & 1 & 1 & 1 & 0 & 0 & 1 & 1 & 1 & 1 & 0 \\ 0 & 0 & 0 & 0 & 0 & 1 & 0 & 1 & 1 & 1 & 0 & 0 & 0 & 2 & 0 & 1 & 0 & 0 & 0 & 2 \\ 0 & 0 & 0 & 0 & 0 & 1 & 1 & 0 & 0 & 0 & 1 & 2 & 0 & 0 & 0 & 0 & 0 & 0 & 2 & 1 \\ 0 & 0 & 0 & 0 & 0 & 1 & 0 & 2 & 0 & 1 & 1 & 0 & 1 & 1 & 0 & 0 & 0 & 2 & 0 & 1 \\ 0 & 0 & 0 & 0 & 0 & 0 & 2 & 2 & 1 & 1 & 1 & 0 & 1 & 0 & 0 & 0 & 0 & 1 & 1 & 2 \\ 0 & 0 & 0 & 0 & 0 & 0 & 0 & 1 & 2 & 0 & 1 & 0 & 1 & 0 & 0 & 2 & 1 & 2 & 0 & 0 \\ 0 & 0 & 0 & 0 & 0 & 0 & 1 & 1 & 0 & 2 & 2 & 1 & 1 & 0 & 2 & 0 & 1 & 0 & 1 & 1 \\ 0 & 0 & 0 & 0 & 0 & 1 & 1 & 1 & 1 & 2 & 1 & 0 & 0 & 2 & 1 & 1 & 2 & 0 & 1 & 0 \end{pmatrix}.$$

Then by just applying the UOV attack on the smaller upper left submatrices of those above matrices like Sect. 4.2, we obtain a linear transformation $\mathcal{L}' : \mathbb{F}_3^{20} \to \mathbb{F}_3^{20}$, whose linear representation is

$$\begin{pmatrix} 1 & 0 & 0 & 0 & 1 & 0 & 0 & 0 & 0 & 0 & 0 & 0 & 0 & 0 & 0 & 0 & 0 & 0 & 0 & 0 \\ 0 & 1 & 0 & 2 & 2 & 0 & 0 & 0 & 0 & 0 & 0 & 0 & 0 & 0 & 0 & 0 & 0 & 0 & 0 & 0 \\ 0 & 0 & 1 & 2 & 2 & 0 & 0 & 0 & 0 & 0 & 0 & 0 & 0 & 0 & 0 & 0 & 0 & 0 & 0 & 0 \\ 1 & 0 & 0 & 1 & 2 & 0 & 0 & 0 & 0 & 0 & 0 & 0 & 0 & 0 & 0 & 0 & 0 & 0 & 0 & 0 \\ 0 & 1 & 1 & 1 & 0 & 0 & 0 & 0 & 0 & 0 & 0 & 0 & 0 & 0 & 0 & 0 & 0 & 0 & 0 & 0 \\ 0 & 0 & 0 & 0 & 0 & 1 & 0 & 0 & 0 & 0 & 0 & 0 & 0 & 0 & 0 & 0 & 0 & 0 & 0 & 0 \\ 0 & 0 & 0 & 0 & 0 & 0 & 1 & 0 & 0 & 0 & 0 & 0 & 0 & 0 & 0 & 0 & 0 & 0 & 0 & 0 \\ 0 & 0 & 0 & 0 & 0 & 0 & 0 & 1 & 0 & 0 & 0 & 0 & 0 & 0 & 0 & 0 & 0 & 0 & 0 & 0 \\ 0 & 0 & 0 & 0 & 0 & 0 & 0 & 0 & 1 & 0 & 0 & 0 & 0 & 0 & 0 & 0 & 0 & 0 & 0 & 0 \\ 0 & 0 & 0 & 0 & 0 & 0 & 0 & 0 & 0 & 1 & 0 & 0 & 0 & 0 & 0 & 0 & 0 & 0 & 0 & 0 \\ 0 & 0 & 0 & 0 & 0 & 0 & 0 & 0 & 0 & 0 & 1 & 0 & 0 & 0 & 0 & 0 & 0 & 0 & 0 & 0 \\ 0 & 0 & 0 & 0 & 0 & 0 & 0 & 0 & 0 & 0 & 0 & 1 & 0 & 0 & 0 & 0 & 0 & 0 & 0 & 0 \\ 0 & 0 & 0 & 0 & 0 & 0 & 0 & 0 & 0 & 0 & 0 & 0 & 1 & 0 & 0 & 0 & 0 & 0 & 0 & 0 \\ 0 & 0 & 0 & 0 & 0 & 0 & 0 & 0 & 0 & 0 & 0 & 0 & 0 & 1 & 0 & 0 & 0 & 0 & 0 & 0 \\ 0 & 0 & 0 & 0 & 0 & 0 & 0 & 0 & 0 & 0 & 0 & 0 & 0 & 0 & 1 & 0 & 0 & 0 & 0 & 0 \\ 0 & 0 & 0 & 0 & 0 & 0 & 0 & 0 & 0 & 0 & 0 & 0 & 0 & 0 & 0 & 1 & 0 & 0 & 0 & 0 \\ 0 & 0 & 0 & 0 & 0 & 0 & 0 & 0 & 0 & 0 & 0 & 0 & 0 & 0 & 0 & 0 & 1 & 0 & 0 & 0 \\ 0 & 0 & 0 & 0 & 0 & 0 & 0 & 0 & 0 & 0 & 0 & 0 & 0 & 0 & 0 & 0 & 0 & 1 & 0 & 0 \\ 0 & 0 & 0 & 0 & 0 & 0 & 0 & 0 & 0 & 0 & 0 & 0 & 0 & 0 & 0 & 0 & 0 & 0 & 1 & 0 \\ 0 & 0 & 0 & 0 & 0 & 0 & 0 & 0 & 0 & 0 & 0 & 0 & 0 & 0 & 0 & 0 & 0 & 0 & 0 & 1 \end{pmatrix},$$

and with this transformation, we obtain a new polynomial system $\mathcal{P} \circ \mathcal{L} \circ \mathcal{L}' = (p_1'', \ldots, p_8'')$, where its matrices associated to its quadratic terms are given by

$$
\begin{pmatrix}
1 & 1 & 0 & 1 & 1 & 0 & 0 & 0 & 0 & 0 & 0 & 0 & 0 & 0 & 0 & 0 & 0 & 0 & 0 & 0 \\
1 & 1 & 0 & 0 & 0 & 0 & 0 & 0 & 0 & 0 & 0 & 0 & 0 & 0 & 0 & 0 & 0 & 0 & 0 & 0 \\
0 & 0 & 0 & 1 & 1 & 0 & 0 & 0 & 0 & 0 & 0 & 0 & 0 & 0 & 0 & 0 & 0 & 0 & 0 & 0 \\
1 & 0 & 1 & 0 & 0 & 0 & 0 & 0 & 0 & 0 & 0 & 0 & 0 & 0 & 0 & 0 & 0 & 0 & 0 & 0 \\
1 & 0 & 1 & 0 & 0 & 0 & 0 & 0 & 0 & 0 & 0 & 0 & 0 & 0 & 0 & 0 & 0 & 0 & 0 & 0 \\
0 & 0 & 0 & 0 & 0 & 1 & 1 & 2 & 2 & 0 & 0 & 1 & 2 & 2 & 0 & 0 & 1 & 1 & 2 & 2 \\
0 & 0 & 0 & 0 & 0 & 1 & 2 & 1 & 0 & 1 & 1 & 2 & 0 & 1 & 0 & 1 & 1 & 2 & 0 & 1 \\
0 & 0 & 0 & 0 & 0 & 2 & 1 & 1 & 0 & 1 & 0 & 2 & 1 & 0 & 1 & 1 & 1 & 2 & 1 & 0 \\
0 & 0 & 0 & 0 & 0 & 2 & 0 & 0 & 0 & 1 & 0 & 1 & 2 & 1 & 2 & 1 & 1 & 2 & 0 & 1 \\
0 & 0 & 0 & 0 & 0 & 0 & 1 & 1 & 1 & 1 & 0 & 2 & 2 & 0 & 2 & 0 & 2 & 0 & 2 & 2 \\
0 & 0 & 0 & 0 & 0 & 0 & 1 & 0 & 0 & 0 & 2 & 1 & 0 & 2 & 1 & 2 & 0 & 1 & 2 & 1 \\
0 & 0 & 0 & 0 & 0 & 1 & 2 & 2 & 1 & 2 & 1 & 0 & 1 & 1 & 2 & 0 & 2 & 2 & 0 & 0 \\
0 & 0 & 0 & 0 & 0 & 2 & 0 & 1 & 2 & 2 & 0 & 1 & 2 & 1 & 0 & 0 & 0 & 0 & 1 & 1 \\
0 & 0 & 0 & 0 & 0 & 2 & 1 & 0 & 1 & 0 & 2 & 1 & 1 & 0 & 2 & 0 & 2 & 0 & 1 & 0 \\
0 & 0 & 0 & 0 & 0 & 0 & 0 & 1 & 2 & 1 & 1 & 2 & 0 & 2 & 1 & 0 & 2 & 0 & 1 & 0 \\
0 & 0 & 0 & 0 & 0 & 1 & 1 & 1 & 1 & 2 & 0 & 2 & 0 & 2 & 2 & 1 & 1 & 1 & 1 & 0 \\
0 & 0 & 0 & 0 & 0 & 1 & 2 & 2 & 2 & 0 & 1 & 2 & 0 & 0 & 0 & 1 & 0 & 0 & 2 & 1 \\
0 & 0 & 0 & 0 & 0 & 2 & 0 & 1 & 0 & 2 & 2 & 0 & 1 & 1 & 1 & 1 & 0 & 2 & 0 & 1 \\
0 & 0 & 0 & 0 & 0 & 2 & 1 & 0 & 1 & 2 & 2 & 0 & 1 & 1 & 1 & 0 & 2 & 0 & 1 \\
0 & 0 & 0 & 0 & 0 & 2 & 1 & 0 & 1 & 2 & 1 & 0 & 1 & 0 & 0 & 0 & 2 & 1 & 1 & 2
\end{pmatrix}, \ldots,
\begin{pmatrix}
1 & 0 & 0 & 2 & 1 & 0 & 0 & 0 & 0 & 0 & 0 & 0 & 0 & 0 & 0 & 0 & 0 & 0 & 0 & 0 \\
0 & 2 & 2 & 1 & 1 & 0 & 0 & 0 & 0 & 0 & 0 & 0 & 0 & 0 & 0 & 0 & 0 & 0 & 0 & 0 \\
0 & 2 & 0 & 0 & 2 & 0 & 0 & 0 & 0 & 0 & 0 & 0 & 0 & 0 & 0 & 0 & 0 & 0 & 0 & 0 \\
2 & 1 & 0 & 0 & 0 & 0 & 0 & 0 & 0 & 0 & 0 & 0 & 0 & 0 & 0 & 0 & 0 & 0 & 0 & 0 \\
1 & 1 & 2 & 0 & 0 & 0 & 0 & 0 & 0 & 0 & 0 & 0 & 0 & 0 & 0 & 0 & 0 & 0 & 0 & 0 \\
0 & 0 & 0 & 0 & 0 & 1 & 2 & 2 & 0 & 2 & 1 & 1 & 0 & 1 & 1 & 1 & 0 & 0 & 0 & 1 \\
0 & 0 & 0 & 0 & 0 & 2 & 0 & 1 & 2 & 0 & 1 & 0 & 0 & 0 & 1 & 0 & 2 & 0 & 1 & 1 \\
0 & 0 & 0 & 0 & 0 & 2 & 1 & 0 & 1 & 1 & 2 & 1 & 0 & 1 & 0 & 2 & 2 & 1 & 1 & 1 \\
0 & 0 & 0 & 0 & 0 & 0 & 2 & 1 & 2 & 1 & 2 & 0 & 1 & 1 & 0 & 0 & 1 & 2 & 0 & 1 \\
0 & 0 & 0 & 0 & 0 & 2 & 0 & 1 & 1 & 1 & 0 & 1 & 2 & 1 & 0 & 1 & 1 & 0 & 2 & 2 \\
0 & 0 & 0 & 0 & 0 & 1 & 1 & 2 & 2 & 0 & 1 & 1 & 1 & 0 & 1 & 1 & 1 & 1 & 2 & 1 \\
0 & 0 & 0 & 0 & 0 & 1 & 0 & 1 & 0 & 1 & 1 & 0 & 1 & 0 & 2 & 0 & 0 & 0 & 1 & 0 \\
0 & 0 & 0 & 0 & 0 & 0 & 0 & 0 & 1 & 2 & 1 & 1 & 1 & 0 & 0 & 1 & 1 & 1 & 1 & 0 \\
0 & 0 & 0 & 0 & 0 & 1 & 0 & 1 & 1 & 1 & 0 & 0 & 0 & 2 & 0 & 1 & 0 & 0 & 0 & 2 \\
0 & 0 & 0 & 0 & 0 & 1 & 1 & 0 & 0 & 0 & 1 & 2 & 0 & 0 & 0 & 2 & 0 & 0 & 2 & 1 \\
0 & 0 & 0 & 0 & 0 & 1 & 0 & 2 & 0 & 1 & 1 & 0 & 1 & 1 & 0 & 0 & 0 & 2 & 0 & 1 \\
0 & 0 & 0 & 0 & 0 & 0 & 2 & 2 & 1 & 1 & 1 & 0 & 1 & 0 & 0 & 0 & 0 & 1 & 1 & 2 \\
0 & 0 & 0 & 0 & 0 & 0 & 0 & 1 & 2 & 0 & 1 & 0 & 1 & 0 & 0 & 2 & 1 & 2 & 0 & 0 \\
0 & 0 & 0 & 0 & 0 & 0 & 1 & 1 & 0 & 2 & 2 & 1 & 1 & 0 & 2 & 0 & 1 & 0 & 1 & 1 \\
0 & 0 & 0 & 0 & 0 & 1 & 1 & 1 & 1 & 2 & 1 & 0 & 0 & 2 & 1 & 1 & 2 & 0 & 1 & 0
\end{pmatrix},
$$

which are in the form of (10).

Then, in the polynomial system $\mathcal{P} \circ \mathcal{L} \circ \mathcal{L}'(x_1, \ldots, x_{20})$, by fixing x_1, x_2, x_3 randomly, x_4, x_5 disappear from the quadratic parts. This reduces the complexity of the direct attack.

References

1. Bardet, M.: Étude des systèms algébriques surdéterminés. Applications aux codes correcteurs et à la cryptographie. Ph.D. thesis, Université Pierre et Marie Curie-Paris VI (2004)
2. Bardet, M., Faugère, J.-C., Salvy, B.: Complexity of Gröbner basis computation for semi-regular overdetermined sequences over $\mathbb{F}_2$ with solutions in $\mathbb{F}_2$. Research Report, INRIA (2003)
3. Bardet, M., Faugère, J.-C., Salvy, B., Yang, B.-Y.: Asymptotic behavior of the index of regularity of quadratic semi-regular polynomial systems. In: 8th International Symposium on Effective Methods in Algebraic Geometry (2005)
4. Bettale, L., Faugère, J.-C., Perret, L.: Hybrid approach for solving multivariate systems over finite fields. J. Math. Cryptol. **3**, 177–197 (2009)
5. Beullens, W., Preneel, B., Szepieniec, A., Vercauteren, F.: LUOV, signature scheme proposal for NIST PQC project. NIST PQC submission, imec-COSIC KU Leuven (2019)
6. Buchberger, B.: Ein Algorithmus zum Auffinden der Basiselemente des Restklassenringes nach einem nulldimensionalen Polynomideal. Ph.D. thesis, Universität Innsbruck (1965)
7. Courtois, N., Klimov, A., Patarin, J., Shamir, A.: Efficient algorithms for solving overdefined systems of multivariate polynomial equations. In: Preneel, B. (ed.) EUROCRYPT 2000. LNCS, vol. 1807, pp. 392–407. Springer, Heidelberg (2000). https://doi.org/10.1007/3-540-45539-6_27
8. Czypek, P., Heyse, S., Thomae, E.: Efficient implementations of MQPKS on constrained devices. In: Prouff, E., Schaumont, P. (eds.) CHES 2012. LNCS, vol. 7428, pp. 374–389. Springer, Heidelberg (2012). https://doi.org/10.1007/978-3-642-33027-8_22

9. Ding, J., Schmidt, D.: Rainbow, a new multivariable polynomial signature scheme. In: Ioannidis, J., Keromytis, A., Yung, M. (eds.) ACNS 2005. LNCS, vol. 3531, pp. 164–175. Springer, Heidelberg (2005). https://doi.org/10.1007/11496137_12

10. Ding, J., Yang, B.-Y., Chen, C.-H.O., Chen, M.-S., Cheng, C.-M.: New differential-algebraic attacks and reparametrization of rainbow. In: Bellovin, S.M., Gennaro, R., Keromytis, A., Yung, M. (eds.) ACNS 2008. LNCS, vol. 5037, pp. 242–257. Springer, Heidelberg (2008). https://doi.org/10.1007/978-3-540-68914-0_15

11. Ding, J., Zhang, Z., Deaton, J., Schmidt, K., Vishakha, F.N.U.: New attacks on lifted unbalanced oil vinegar. In: Second PQC Standardization Conference 2019. National Institute of Standards and Technology (2019)

12. Faugère, J.-C.: A new efficient algorithm for computing Gröbner bases (F4). J. Pure Appl. Algebra **139**(1–3), 61–88 (1999)

13. Faugère, J.-C.: A new efficient algorithm for computing Gröbner bases without reduction to zero (F5). In: ISSAC 2002, pp. 75–83. ACM (2002)

14. Garey, M.-R., Johnson, D.-S.: Computers and Intractability: A Guide to the Theory of NP-Completeness. W. H. Freeman, New York (1979)

15. Hashimoto, Y.: Key recovery attack on circulant UOV/rainbow. JSIAM Lett. **11**, 45–48 (2019)

16. Kipnis, A., Patarin, J., Goubin, L.: Unbalanced oil and vinegar signature schemes. In: Stern, J. (ed.) EUROCRYPT 1999. LNCS, vol. 1592, pp. 206–222. Springer, Heidelberg (1999). https://doi.org/10.1007/3-540-48910-X_15

17. Kipnis, A., Shamir, A.: Cryptanalysis of the oil and vinegar signature scheme. In: Krawczyk, H. (ed.) CRYPTO 1998. LNCS, vol. 1462, pp. 257–266. Springer, Heidelberg (1998). https://doi.org/10.1007/BFb0055733

18. NIST: Post-quantum cryptography, Round 2 submission (2019). https://csrc.nist.gov/Projects/Post-Quantum-Cryptography/Round-2-Submissions

19. Peng, Z., Tang, S.: Circulant UOV: a new UOV variant with shorter private key and faster signature generation. TIIS **12**(3), 1376–1395 (2018)

20. Petzoldt, A., Buchmann, J. A.: A multivariate signature scheme with an almost cyclic public key. IACR Cryptology ePrint Archive 2009, 440. http://eprint.iacr.org/2009/440 (2009)

21. Szepieniec, A., Preneel, B.: Block-anti-circulant unbalanced oil and vinegar. In: Paterson, K.G., Stebila, D. (eds.) SAC 2019. LNCS, vol. 11959, pp. 574–588. Springer, Cham (2020). https://doi.org/10.1007/978-3-030-38471-5_23

22. Thomae, E., Wolf, C.: Solving underdetermined systems of multivariate quadratic equations revisited. In: Fischlin, M., Buchmann, J., Manulis, M. (eds.) PKC 2012. LNCS, vol. 7293, pp. 156–171. Springer, Heidelberg (2012). https://doi.org/10.1007/978-3-642-30057-8_10

Generalization of Isomorphism of Polynomials with Two Secrets and Its Application to Public Key Encryption

Bagus Santoso[✉]

University of Electro-Communications,
1-5-1 Chofugaoka, Chofu, Tokyo 182-8585, Japan
santoso.bagus@uec.ac.jp

Abstract. Most of the public key encryption (PKE) schemes based on multivariate quadratic polynomials rely on Hidden Field Equation (HFE) paradigm. However, most of HFE based schemes have been broken in only several years just after their introduction. In this paper, we propose an alternative paradigm for constructing PKE based on multivariate quadratic polynomials. At the heart of our proposal is a new family of computational problems based on the generalization of Isomorphism of Polynomials with Two Secrets (IP2S) problem. The main computational problem in the new family is proven as hard as the original IP2S problem and is more robust, in the sense that we can associate it with circulant matrices as solutions without degrading its computational hardness too much, in contrast to the original IP2S problem which immediately becomes easy as soon as it is associated with circulant matrices. By associating it to circulant matrices, we obtain a Diffie-Hellman like structure which allows us to have an El-Gamal like PKE scheme.

Keywords: Multivariate quadratic polynomials · Isomorphism of polynomials · Public-key encryption

1 Introduction

The public key encryption (PKE) schemes based on the family of multivariate quadratic polynomials (MQ) are mostly relying on *Hidden Field Equation* (HFE) structure introduced by Patarin [10]. However, the weakness of HFE structure has been well exploited in the literatures [2,5,9] and most of the PKE schemes based on MQ have been broken within several years after they were just introduced.

Beside HFE, Patarin et al. [10,11] also introduced several other families of MQ based computational problems. One of them is the problem of *Isomorphism of Polynomials with Two Secrets (IP2S)* or *Quadratic Maps Linear Equivalence (QMLE)*, which is defined as follows: given two collections of multivariate quadratic polynomials of n variables $\mathbf{f}$, $\mathbf{g}$, find invertible linear maps S, T such that $\mathbf{g} = T \circ \mathbf{f} \circ S$ holds if there are any. So far up to this moment, for more than

© Springer Nature Switzerland AG 2020
J. Ding and J.-P. Tillich (Eds.): PQCrypto 2020, LNCS 12100, pp. 340–359, 2020.
https://doi.org/10.1007/978-3-030-44223-1_19

two decades since its introduction, in the case when $\mathbf{f}$ is homogeneous, i.e., $\mathbf{f}$ contains only terms with total degree of two, the best complexity to solve IP2S is $O(2^{n/2})$, which is derived by Bouillaguet et al. [3]. Since IP2S is devoid of any algebraic structure which is exploitable by quantum algorithms known so far, IP2S has been considered as a candidate for post-quantum cryptography, especially in the scope of authentication and digital signatures [13,14].

Motivation and Challenge. In the early stage of our research, we discover that the IP2S problem associated with circulant matrices as the solutions can provide us with a Diffie-Hellman (DH) like algebraic structure. We illustrate this in the following Fig. 1.

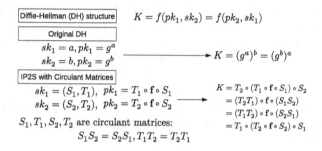

Fig. 1. DH like structure using IP2S with circulant matrices.

It is easy to see that such structure can be used for constructing El-Gamal like PKE scheme. However, we discover that one can efficiently solve IP2S problem in practice when it is associated with circulant matrices as the solutions.

As an illustration, let $\mathbf{f}, \mathbf{g}$ be collections of m quadratic polynomials with n variables satisfying $\mathbf{g} = T \circ \mathbf{f} \circ S$, where S and T are invertible linear maps. Let $(\mathbf{f}, \mathbf{g})$ be a problem instance of IP2S problem. Note that here S and T can be represented as an n-square matrix and an m-square matrix respectively. In the original case where there is no other condition on S and T, it is easy to see that the number of unknowns is $(n^2 + m^2)$. However, in the case that S and T are circulant matrices, S and T are representable by only n and m values respectively and thus the number of unknowns becomes only $(n + m)$. On the other hand, Faugère et al. [6] and Plût et al. [12] have shown that from the relation $\mathbf{g} = T \circ \mathbf{f} \circ S$, we can construct a system of equations consisting of around $mn(n + 1)/2$ independent quadratic polynomials with high probability. In [4], Courtois et al. have shown that if $\bar{\ell} \geq \varepsilon \rho^2$ holds for some constant $\varepsilon > 0$ where $\bar{\ell}$ is the number of independent quadratic polynomials and ρ is the number of unknowns, then by using their proposed *relinearization* algorithm, one can find the unknowns with polynomial complexity, i.e., approximately $\rho^{O(1/\sqrt{\varepsilon})}$. Thus, following this, for IP2S with S and T as circulant matrices, we have the inequations below which hold for some $\varepsilon > 0$ and $m \geq 1$.

$$\frac{mn(n+1)}{2} \geq \varepsilon(m+n)^2 \quad \Leftrightarrow \quad n^2\left(\frac{m}{2}-\varepsilon\right) \geq \varepsilon m^2 + \left(\varepsilon - \frac{1}{4}\right)2mn. \quad (1)$$

It is common to set $m \leq n$ in practice for IP2S [3,6,11]. And it is easy to see that Eq. (1) holds for $\varepsilon = 1/4$ and $m \in [1,n]$. Thus, based on [4], we can say that solving IP2S for the case that S and T are circulant matrices is easy in practice. Therefore, we need to find another way of using IP2S to obtain DH like algebraic structure such that we do not degrade the complexity of the underlying problem.

Overview of Our Strategy. The main cause of the degradation of the complexity of IP2S with circulant matrices shown above is the lack number of unknowns. In order to overcome this, we try to find a way to modify IP2S problem such that we can increase the number of unknowns. We start from our (failed) first idea which is described as follows. Let us have k instances of IP2S problem with circulant matrices as follows: $\mathbf{g}_i = T_i \circ \mathbf{f}_i \circ S_i$ for $i \in [1,k]$ where $\mathbf{f}_i, \mathbf{g}_i$ are collections of m quadratic polynomials with n variables, S_i and T_i are n-square circulant matrices and m-square circulant matrices respectively. Now let us have a new computational problem which requires us to find the solutions of k instances of IP2S problem *simultaneously*. According to [6,12], we may have a total of around $\frac{mn(n+1)}{2} \times k$ independent quadratic polynomials and $(m+n) \times k$ unknowns. Thus, we obtain the inequation which is analogous to Eq. (1) as follows:

$$\frac{mn(n+1)}{2} \times k \geq \varepsilon((m+n) \times k)^2 = \varepsilon(m+n)^2 k^2$$

$$\Leftrightarrow \qquad n^2\left(\frac{m}{2}-(\varepsilon k)\right) \geq (\varepsilon k)m^2 + \left((\varepsilon k) - \frac{1}{4}\right)2mn. \quad (2)$$

It is easy to see that in order to guarantee that Eq. (2) holds for any $m \leq n$, $\varepsilon = 1/4$ is not sufficient if $k > 1$. If we set $\varepsilon = \frac{1}{4k}$, then this new computational problem using algorithm in [4] is approximately $(m+n)^{2\sqrt{k}}$. And if we let $k = \mathcal{O}(n)$, then clearly that the complexity of the algorithm become exponential. Hence, based on this, at first glance, one may argue that the new computational problem is harder than the original IP2S with circulant matrices.

However, we should note here that the above argument is actually false! The reason is that in practice, we can find the solutions of k instances of IP2S problems with circulant matrices *simultaneously* by solving each instance *separately* one by one! Hence, the actual complexity of solving the new computational problem is actually only $k(m+n)^2$. The lesson we got here is that unless we can prevent anyone to solve the problems separately, although we increase the number of the instances, it will not leverage the complexity significantly.

In order to prevent anyone to solve the problems separately, in our next idea, we define a new computational problem such that instead of giving $\{\mathbf{g}_i\}_{i=1}^k$, we give $\mathbf{g}$ as input, where $\mathbf{g} = \sum_{i=1}^k \mathbf{g}_i = \sum_{i=1}^k T_i \circ \mathbf{f}_i \circ S_i$. Using this equation (on $\mathbf{g}$) as input, we prevent anyone to solve the instances separately and also reduces the number of quadratic polynomials simultaneously. However, this modification makes us lose the DH like structure! Roughly said, the most formidable hurdle here is that since each $\mathbf{f}_i$ represents quadratic polynomials, it is hard to represent $\sum_{i=1}^{k} T_i \circ \mathbf{f}_i \circ S_i$ using only simple matrix multiplications and additions. Fortunately, we discover a method to regain DH like structure by constructing $(k-1)$ additional equations in a specific way as additional inputs to the computational problem. We construct the equations for the inputs in a specific way such that not only that we regain DH like structure, but also we control the total number of quadratic polynomials such that one can only obtain approximately $mn(n+1)/2$ from each equation and thus approximately $mn(n+1)/2 \times k$ from the whole system.

Main Results. Based on the idea explained above, we define a generalization of IP2S problem which gives us more freedom in controlling the number of unknowns and based on it, we propose a new computational problem which we call as the *Blockwise Isomorphism of Polynomials (BIP)* problem. We prove that BIP problem is at least as hard as IP2S problem by showing that any instance of IP2S problem is equivalent to a specific instance of BIP problem.

The most important feature of the BIP problem is that we can associate it with circulant matrices as the solutions <u>without</u> degrading its complexity too much, while still preserving the original property of IP2S when associated with circulant matrices, i.e., DH like algebraic structure. Based on computational problems derived from BIP problem associated with circulant matrices, we propose a new public key encryption scheme with similar structure to the El-Gamal encryption.

In this paper, we also list several candidates of secure parameters for 128-bit and 256-bit security to guarantee the hardness of the BIP problem associated with circulant matrices in practice. The parameters are calculated by relying on rough complexity estimations of: (1) a heuristic theoretical algorithm to solve the BIP problem derived from the attack algorithm for solving IP2S proposed by Bouillaguet [3], and (2) a Gröbner Bases attack on solving BIP problem associated with circulant matrices which treats the problem instance as the equations and the solutions (circulant matrices) as the unknowns.

Limitation and Open Problems. In this paper, we have provided a theoretical result that the BIP problem is as hard as the original IP2S problem. However, the theoretical hardness of BIP problem when we limit the solutions to only circulant matrices remains as an open problem. Since we generally take a safety side in deriving the security parameters, the recommended security parameters listed in this paper are still quite large compared to other post-quantum encryption schemes based on HFE, lattice, or isogeny. Whether one can propose a smaller parameters with a more rigorous argument is an interesting open problem. Also, we have not managed to perform analysis on the hardness of BPI problem and our proposed public key encryption scheme against equivalent keys attack in the same manner as the work by Wolf and Preneel in [17]. We leave this as an open problem.

Related Works. The complexity of solving IP2S depends very much on the type of polynomial **f**. For the case when **f** is inhomogeneous, i.e., **f** contains terms with total degree less than two, it has been shown by Faugère and Perret in [6] that the complexity is polynomial. However, for the case when **f** is homogeneous, i.e., **f** contains only terms with total degree of two, the best complexity is $O(2^{n/2})$ [3]. Since IP2S with homogeneous **f** is supposed to preserve the hardness against quantum adversaries, IP2S with homogeneous **f** has been used in several post-quantum cryptographic protocols such as public key identification scheme [13] and signature scheme [14]. Independently, Wang et al. [16] proposed a similar paradigm of constructing PKE scheme using a DH like algebraic structure derived from associating circulant matrices to another computational problem related to IP2S, i.e. Morphism of Polynomials problem [11]. However, it suffers from the same degradation of complexity as our first attempt of creating DH like structure using IP2S and circulant matrices shown in the subsection "Motivation and Challenge" above, i.e., the total number of unknown is only $(m+n)$, while one can obtain a system of equations with around $mn(n+1)/2$ independent quadratic polynomials. Chen et al. [8] proposed an attack algorithm which exploits the vulnerability and shown that they can efficiently break the computational problems proposed in [16] in practice even when using the parameters recommended in [16].

2   Preliminaries

Notations Related to Multivariate Polynomials and Matrices. Let $q \in \mathbb{N}$ be a prime number. Unless noted otherwise, any algebraic element mentioned in this paper is an element in the field $\mathbb{F}_q$ and any algebraic structure defined in this paper is defined over $\mathbb{F}_q$. A quadratic polynomial $f \in \mathbb{F}_q[\chi_1, \ldots, \chi_n]$ is called *homogeneous* if the simplest form of f can be written as follows: $f(\chi_1, \ldots, \chi_n) = \sum_{i,j \in [1,n], i \geq j} \alpha_{i,j} \chi_i \chi_j$. An alternative notation for n-square matrix A is $(a_{i,j})_{i,j \in [1,n]}$, where $a_{i,j}$ is the element of matrix in i-th row and j-th column. Let $\mathbb{M}_n$ denote the set of all n-square matrices and $\mathbb{GL}_n$ denote the set of all invertible n-square matrices. Also, we let 0_n denote the n-square zero matrix.

We put the complexity related notations on Appendix A.

Definition 1 (Multivariate Quadratic Polynomials (MQ) Family).
A Multivariate Quadratic Polynomials (MQ) family, denoted by notation $\mathcal{MQ}(n,m)$, is a family of sets of functions defined as follows.

$$\mathcal{MQ}(n,m) := \left\{ (f_1(\chi), \ldots, f_m(\chi)) \,\middle|\, \begin{array}{l} f_k(\chi) = \sum_{i,j} \alpha_{k,i,j} \chi_i \chi_j + \sum_i \beta_{k,i} \chi_i + \gamma_k \\ \alpha_{k,i,j}, \beta_{k,i}, \gamma_k \in \mathbb{F}_q \text{ for } k \in [1,m] \end{array} \right\},$$

where $\chi = (\chi_1, \ldots, \chi_n), \chi_i \in \mathbb{F}_q$ for $i \in [1,n]$. Any $\mathbf{f} = (f_1, \ldots, f_m) \in \mathcal{MQ}(n,m)$ is said to be homogeneous *if all $f_1, \ldots, f_m$ are homogeneous.*

Remark 1. For simplicity, we call any $\mathbf{f} \in \mathcal{MQ}(n, m)$ as an MQ function. Unless noted otherwise, any quadratic polynomial considered in this paper is homogeneous and we assume that any MQ function in this paper is homogeneous.

The following problem is introduced by Patarin et al. in [11].

Definition 2 (Isomorphism of Polynomials with Two Secrets (IP2S) Problem). *The problem of* Isomorphism Polynomials of Two Secrets (IP2S) *is parameterized with* $n, m \in \mathbb{N}$ *and defined as follows: given* $\mathbf{f}, \mathbf{g} \in \mathcal{MQ}(n, m)$, *find invertible linear maps* $S \in \mathbb{GL}_n$ *and* $T = (t_{i,j})_{i,j \in [1,m]} \in \mathbb{GL}_m$ *such that the following holds.*

$$\mathbf{g} = T \circ \mathbf{f} \circ S. \tag{3}$$

In other words, for all $i \in [1, m]$, *the following holds.*

$$g_i = \sum_{j \in [1,m]} t_{i,j} f_j \circ S, \tag{4}$$

where $\mathbf{f} = (f_1, \ldots, f_m)$ *and* $\mathbf{g} = (g_1, \ldots, g_m)$.

Definition 3 (Isomorphism of Polynomials). *Any two MQ functions* $\mathbf{f}, \mathbf{g} \in \mathcal{MQ}(n, m)$ *are said to be isomorphic if there are invertible linear maps* $S \in \mathbb{GL}_n$ *and* $T = (t_{i,j})_{i,j \in [1,m]} \in \mathbb{GL}_m$ *such that the following holds.*

$$\mathbf{g} = T \circ \mathbf{f} \circ S. \tag{5}$$

3 Generalization of Isomorphism of Polynomials

In this section, we introduce the generalization of IP2S problem into computational problems associated to matrices with blockwise structure as the solutions.

3.1 Basic Idea

Let us revisit Eq. (4) in Definition 2. One can clearly see that although we have m quadratic polynomials inside $\mathbf{f}$, i.e., $f_1, \ldots, f_m$, all of them are associated to only one matrix S in all definitions of $g_1, \ldots, g_m$. Our intuition is that, if we can associate $f_1, \ldots, f_m$ with not only one matrix, but several different matrices, we might be able to obtain a more general computational problem with a greater freedom on adjusting the complexity.

3.2 Blockwise Isomorphism of Polynomials

Definition 4. *Let* $\mathbb{GL}(n, k)$ *denote all* $n \times k$-*square matrices with the same properties and structures as the following matrix* $V \in (\mathbb{GL}_n \cup \{0_n\})^{k \times k}$:

$$V = \begin{bmatrix} V_{[1]} & V_{[2]} & \cdots & V_{[k]} \\ V_{[k]} & V_{[1]} & \cdots & V_{[k-1]} \\ \vdots & \ddots & \ddots & \vdots \\ V_{[2]} & \cdots & V_{[k]} & V_{[1]} \end{bmatrix},$$

where for $i \in [1,k]$, $V_{[i]}$ is an n-square invertible or zero matrix, i.e., $V_{[i]} \in \mathbb{GL}_n \cup \{0_n\}$.

Definition 5 (Blockwise Isomorphism of Polynomials). *Consider two MQ functions $\mathbf{f},\mathbf{g} \in \mathcal{MQ}(n, m \times k)$ and let denote $\mathbf{f}_{[j]} = (f_{1+(j-1)m}, f_{2+(j-1)m}, \ldots, f_{jm})$ and $\mathbf{g}_{[\tau]} = (g_{1+(\tau-1)m}, \ldots, g_{\tau m})$ for any $j, \tau \in [1,k]$. We say that $\mathbf{f}$ and $\mathbf{g}$ are k-blockwise isomorphic if there exist $T \in \mathbb{GL}(m, k)$ and $S \in \mathbb{GL}(n, k)$ such that the following for all $\tau \in [1,k]$:*

$$\mathbf{g}_{[\tau]} = \sum_{j \in [1,k]} T_{[(k-\tau+j) \bmod k+1]} \circ \mathbf{f}_{[j]} \circ S_{[(k-\tau+j) \bmod k+1]}. \tag{6}$$

As an illustration, for $k = 3$, we can write Eq. (6) can be written as follows.

$$\begin{bmatrix} \mathbf{g}_{[1]} \\ \mathbf{g}_{[2]} \\ \mathbf{g}_{[3]} \end{bmatrix} = \begin{bmatrix} T_{[1]} \circ \mathbf{f}_{[1]} \circ S_{[1]} + T_{[2]} \circ \mathbf{f}_{[2]} \circ S_{[2]} + T_{[3]} \circ \mathbf{f}_{[3]} \circ S_{[3]} \\ T_{[3]} \circ \mathbf{f}_{[1]} \circ S_{[3]} + T_{[1]} \circ \mathbf{f}_{[2]} \circ S_{[1]} + T_{[2]} \circ \mathbf{f}_{[3]} \circ S_{[2]} \\ T_{[2]} \circ \mathbf{f}_{[1]} \circ S_{[2]} + T_{[3]} \circ \mathbf{f}_{[2]} \circ S_{[3]} + T_{[1]} \circ \mathbf{f}_{[3]} \circ S_{[1]} \end{bmatrix},$$

where $\mathbf{f}_{[1]} = (f_1, \ldots, f_m)$, $\mathbf{g}_{[1]} = (g_1, \ldots, g_m)$, $\mathbf{f}_{[2]} = (f_{m+1}, \ldots, f_{2m})$, $\mathbf{g}_{[2]} = (g_{m+1}, \ldots, g_{2m})$, $\mathbf{f}_{[3]} = (f_{2m+1}, \ldots, f_{3m})$, $\mathbf{g}_{[3]} = (g_{2m+1}, \ldots, g_{3m})$.

Definition 6 (Blockwise Isomorphism of Polynomials (BIP) Problem). *The problem of Blockwise Isomorphism of Polynomials is parameterized with $n, m, k \in \mathbb{N}$ and associated with $\mathbb{S} \subseteq \mathbb{GL}(n, k)$, $\mathbb{T} \subseteq \mathbb{GL}(m, k)$, and defined as follows: given $\mathbf{f}, \mathbf{g} \in \mathcal{MQ}(n, m \times k)$, find $S \in \mathbb{S}$ and $T \in \mathbb{T}$ such that the following holds for all $\tau \in [1,k]$:*

$$\mathbf{g}_{[\tau]} = \sum_{j \in [1,k]} T_{[(k-\tau+j) \bmod k+1]} \circ \mathbf{f}_{[j]} \circ S_{[(k-\tau+j) \bmod k+1]}, \tag{7}$$

where $\mathbf{f}_{[j]} = (f_{1+(j-1)m}, f_{2+(j-1)m}, \ldots, f_{jm})$ and $\mathbf{g}_{[\tau]} = (g_{1+(\tau-1)m}, \ldots, g_{\tau m})$.

The following theorem says that our new BIP problem is as hard as the original IP2S problem. The full proof is shown in Appendix B.

Theorem 1. *BIP problem parameterized with $n, m, k \in \mathbb{N}$ and associated with $\mathbb{S} := \mathbb{GL}(n, k)$ and $\mathbb{T} := \mathbb{GL}(m, k)$ is at least as hard as IP2S problem parameterized with n, m.*

3.3 Blockwise Isomorphism of Polynomials with Circulant Matrices

Here, we will show that BIP with circulant matrices allows us to have a Diffie-Hellman (DH) like algebraic structure. For convenience and readability, we introduce new notations and an operator.

Definition 7. *A circulant n-square matrix $A = (a_{i,j})_{i,j \in [1,n]}$ is an n-square matrix which has property that $a_{1,j} = a_{i,j+i-1 \bmod n}$ holds for $i, j \in [1,n]$. Let $\mathbb{Circ}_n$ denote the set of all circulant n-square matrices. Let $\mathbb{CGL}(n, k)$ denote all*

$n \times k$-*square matrices with the same properties and structures as the following matrix* $C \in ((\mathbb{C}\mathrm{irc}_n \cap \mathbb{GL}_n) \cup \{0_n\})^{k \times k}$:

$$
C = \begin{bmatrix} C_{[1]} & C_{[2]} & \cdots & C_{[k]} \\ C_{[k]} & C_{[1]} & \cdots & C_{[k-1]} \\ \vdots & \ddots & \ddots & \vdots \\ C_{[2]} & \cdots & C_{[k]} & C_{[1]} \end{bmatrix},
$$

where for $i \in [1, k]$, $C_{[i]}$ *is an n-square invertible circulant or zero matrix, i.e.,* $C_{[i]} \in (\mathbb{C}\mathrm{irc}_n \cap \mathbb{GL}_n) \cup \{0_n\}$.

Definition 8. *Let* $T \in \mathbb{CGL}(m, k)$ *and* $S \in \mathbb{CGL}(n, k)$. *We define the following.*

$$
\varpi(T, S) := \begin{bmatrix} (T_{[1]}, S_{[1]}) & \cdots & & & (T_{[k]}, S_{[k]}) \\ (T_{[k]}, S_{[k]}) & \ddots & & \cdots & (T_{[k-1]}, S_{[k-1]}) \\ \vdots & & \ddots & & \vdots \\ (T_{[2]}, S_{[2]}) & \cdots & (T_{[k]}, S_{[k]}) & (T_{[1]}, S_{[1]}) \end{bmatrix}.
$$

Also, we define the set $\Psi_{[n,m,k]}$ *as follows.*

$$
\Psi_{[n,m,k]} := \left\{ \varpi(T, S) \middle| T \in \mathbb{CGL}(m, k), S \in \mathbb{CGL}(n, k) \right\}.
$$

For any $\psi \in \Psi_{[n,m,k]}$, $\psi_{i,j}$ *denotes the element at i-th row and j-th column in matrix* ψ.

In Appendix D, we show a special property satisfied by any $\psi \in \Psi_{[n,m,k]}$ derived from its circulant structure.

Definition 9 (Operators $*$ and $\boxplus$). *Let* $\mathbf{u} \in \mathcal{MQ}(n, m)$ *and* $\mu := (A, B)$, *where* $A \in \mathbb{GL}_m \cup \{0_m\}$ *and* $B \in \mathbb{GL}_n \cup \{0_n\}$. *We define the operator $*$ as follows.*

$$
\mu * \mathbf{u} := A \circ \mathbf{u} \circ B.
$$

Let $\mathbf{f} \in \mathcal{MQ}(n, m \times k)$ *and* $\psi \in \Psi_{[n,m,k]}$. *We define the operator $\boxplus$ as follows.*

$$
\psi \boxplus \mathbf{f} := \begin{bmatrix} \sum_{j=1}^{k} \psi_{1,j} * \mathbf{f}_{[j]} \\ \vdots \\ \sum_{j=1}^{k} \psi_{i,j} * \mathbf{f}_{[j]} \\ \vdots \\ \sum_{j=1}^{k} \psi_{k,j} * \mathbf{f}_{[j]} \end{bmatrix}.
$$

The following lemma states that we can obtain a Diffie-Hellman (DH) like algebraic structure from blockwise isomorphism of polynomials with circulant matrices.

Lemma 1 (DH like Structure). *Let* $\mathbf{f} \in \mathcal{MQ}(n, m \times k)$ *and* $\psi, \varphi \in \Psi_{[n,m,k]}$. *Then, the following holds.*

$$
\varphi \boxplus (\psi \boxplus \mathbf{f}) = \psi \boxplus (\varphi \boxplus \mathbf{f}).
$$

The proof of Lemma 1 is given in Appendix E.

3.4 Computational Problems from Blockwise Isomorphism of Polynomials with Circulant Matrices

Below, we represent the new computational problems based on blockwise isomorphism of polynomials with circulant matrices.

Definition 10 (BIP with Circulant Matrices (BIPC)). *The problem of Blockwise Isomorphism of Polynomials with Circulant Matrices (BIPC) is parameterized with $n, m, k \in \mathbb{N}$ and defined as follows: given $\mathbf{f}, \mathbf{g} \in \mathcal{MQ}(n, m \times k)$, find $\Upsilon \in \Psi_{[n,m,k]}$ such that the following holds:*

$$\mathbf{g} = \Upsilon \boxplus \mathbf{f}.$$

Next, based on Definition 10, we derive the following computational problem in the similar spirit as Computational Diffie-Hellman problem. We will use the hardness of this problem to prove the security of PKE scheme in later section.

Definition 11 (Computational Diffie-Hellman for BIPC). *The problem of Computational Diffie Hellman for BIPC (CDH-BIPC) is parameterized with $n, m,\ k \in \mathbb{N}$ and defined as follows: given $\mathbf{f}^{(1)}, \mathbf{f}^{(2)}, \mathbf{g}^{(1)} \in \mathcal{MQ}(n, m \times k)$ such that the following holds for some $\Upsilon \in \Psi_{[n,m,k]}$:*

$$\mathbf{g}^{(1)} = \Upsilon \boxplus \mathbf{f}^{(1)},$$

find $\mathbf{g}^{(2)} \in \mathcal{MQ}(n, m \times k)$ such that the following holds:

$$\mathbf{g}^{(2)} = \Upsilon \boxplus \mathbf{f}^{(2)}.$$

4 El-Gamal Like Public Key Encryption Scheme Based on Blockwise Circulant Matrices

In this section, we will show a construction of an El-Gamal like public key encryption scheme based on the DH like algebraic structure shown in Lemma 1.

4.1 Description of the Scheme

We describe our proposed scheme as follows.

- Public parameters: $\ell, n, m, k \in \mathbb{N}$, an encoding function $e : \{0,1\}^{\ell} \to \mathcal{MQ}(n, m \times k)$ and a decoding function $d : \mathcal{MQ}(n, m \times k) \to \{0,1\}^{\ell}$ such that for any $\nu \in \{0,1\}^{\ell}$: $\nu = d(e(\nu))$ holds and for any $\mathbf{x} \in \mathcal{MQ}(n, m \times k)$: $e(d(\mathbf{x})) = \mathbf{x}$ holds.
- Secret Key: $\Upsilon \in \Psi_{[n,m,k]}$.
- Public Key: $\mathbf{g}, \mathbf{f} \in \mathcal{MQ}(n, m \times k)$ such that $\mathbf{g} = \Upsilon \boxplus \mathbf{f}$.
- Encryption: to encrypt a message plaintext $\nu \in \{0,1\}^{\ell}$, one chooses a random $\psi \in \Psi_{[n,m,k]}$ and computes:

$$\mathbf{c}_0 \leftarrow \psi \boxplus \mathbf{f}, \qquad \mathbf{c}_1 \leftarrow e(\nu) + \psi \boxplus \mathbf{g}.$$

The ciphertext is $\mathbf{c} = (\mathbf{c}_0, \mathbf{c}_1)$.

– Decryption: to decrypt a ciphertext $\mathbf{c} = (\mathbf{c}_0, \mathbf{c}_1)$, given the secret key $\varUpsilon \in \varPsi_{[n,m,k]}$, one computes:

$$\nu \leftarrow \mathsf{d}(\mathbf{c}_1 - \varUpsilon \boxtimes \mathbf{c}_0).$$

The decryption result is ν.

Theorem 2 (Correctness). *The decryption process of above encryption produces the correct plaintext when the ciphertext is correctly constructed.*

Proof. If the ciphertext $\mathbf{c} = (\mathbf{c}_0, \mathbf{c}_1)$ is correctly constructed, the followings hold for some $\psi \in \varPsi_{[n,m,k]}$:

$$\mathbf{c}_0 = \psi \boxtimes \mathbf{f}, \qquad \mathbf{c}_1 = \mathsf{e}(\nu) + \psi \boxtimes \mathbf{g}, \tag{8}$$

where ν is the plaintext. Then, in the decryption process, we obtain the following equations.

$$\mathbf{c}_1 - \varUpsilon \boxtimes \mathbf{c}_0 = \mathsf{e}(\nu) + \psi \boxtimes \mathbf{g} - \varUpsilon \boxtimes (\psi \boxtimes \mathbf{f}) = \mathsf{e}(\nu) + \psi \boxtimes (\varUpsilon \boxtimes \mathbf{f}) - \varUpsilon \boxtimes (\psi \boxtimes \mathbf{f})$$
$$\overset{(a)}{=} \mathsf{e}(\nu) + \psi \boxtimes (\varUpsilon \boxtimes \mathbf{f}) - \psi \boxtimes (\varUpsilon \boxtimes \mathbf{f}) = \mathsf{e}(\nu).$$

The transformation to (a) is performed based on the property shown in Lemma 1. Hence, $\mathsf{d}(\mathbf{c}_1 - \varUpsilon \boxtimes \mathbf{c}_0) = \mathsf{d}(\mathsf{e}(\nu)) = \nu$ holds. This ends the proof.

In Appendix C, we prove that the PKE scheme described above is secure against one-way under chosen plaintext attack (OW-CPA) by assuming that CDH-BIPC is hard.

4.2 Extension to Security Against Chosen Ciphertext Attacks

In practice, it is much preferable that a public key encryption scheme satisfies at least IND-CCA (indistinguishability under chosen ciphertext attacks) security. One can transform our proposed encryption scheme into the one with IND-CCA security using a variant of Fujisaki-Okamoto transformation developed by Hoefheinz et al. [7].

5 Complexity of Breaking BIP with Circulant Matrices

For simplicity, here we assume the binary field case, i.e., $q = 2$. We estimate the hardness of BIP with circulant matrices (BIPC) based on two attacks: (1) the attack on IP2S problem with homogeneous instances proposed by Bouillaguet et al. [3], and (2) algebraic attack by solving a system of multivariate quadratic equations with the elements of the solutions matrices of BIP as the unknowns, where the equations are formed by the terms of MQ functions in the problem instances.

5.1   Evaluation Based on the Attack by Bouillaguet et al. [3]

Overview. The core of the attack in [3] is an algorithm for solving IP2S problem which we summarize as follows.

(1) Given the instance $(\mathbf{f}, \mathbf{g})$ of IP2S, we find a pair of vectors $\alpha, \beta \in \mathbb{F}_q^{n \times 1}$ such that $\widetilde{S}^{-1}\alpha = \beta$ holds when $\mathbf{g} = \widetilde{T} \circ \mathbf{f} \circ \widetilde{S}$ holds, where $\widetilde{T}, \widetilde{S}$ are the solutions of IP2S. In [3], Bouillaguet et al. shows how to obtain such α, β by combining a graph-theoretic method and a special hashing using *canonical labeling of graph*. In brief, Bouillaguet et al. construct a hash function H such that if $H(\alpha) = H(\beta)$, then $\widetilde{S}^{-1}\alpha = \beta$ holds with very high probability. The complexity of evaluating H once is $\approx n^5$. And in order to get collision with sufficiently high probability, based on birthday paradox, Bouillaguet et al. construct two hash tables, each with size of $2^{n/2}$. Hence, the total complexity of finding α, β such that $\widetilde{S}^{-1}\alpha = \beta$ holds is $\approx 2 \times n^5 \times 2^{n/2} = O(n^5 2^{n/2})$.

(2) Let define $\mathbf{f}'(\chi) := \mathbf{f}(\chi + \alpha)$, $\mathbf{g}'(\chi) := \mathbf{g}(\chi + \beta)$ using α, β found in step (1). Thus, the followings holds.

$$\widetilde{T} \circ \mathbf{f}' \circ \widetilde{S}(\chi) = \widetilde{T} \circ \mathbf{f}'(\widetilde{S}(\chi)) = \widetilde{T} \circ \mathbf{f}(\widetilde{S}(\chi) + \alpha) = \widetilde{T} \circ \mathbf{f}(\widetilde{S}\chi + \widetilde{S}\beta))$$
$$= \widetilde{T} \circ \mathbf{f}(\widetilde{S}(\chi + \beta)) = \widetilde{T} \circ \mathbf{f} \circ \widetilde{S}(\chi + \beta) = \mathbf{g}(\chi + \beta) = \mathbf{g}'.$$

One can see that the IP2S problem with the original instance $(\mathbf{f}, \mathbf{g})$ and the one with another instance $(\mathbf{f}', \mathbf{g}')$ have the same solution. However, although the original $\mathbf{f}$ is homogeneous, $\mathbf{f}'$ is *inhomogeneous* (no longer homogeneous) and thus we can solve it easily using the procedure in [6]. More precisely, we can input $(\mathbf{f}', \mathbf{g}')$ into the algorithm proposed in [6] which solves IP2S problem with inhomogeneous instances in polynomial time. At the heart of the algorithm are the monomials with degree one in the inhomogeneous problem instance $(\mathbf{f}', \mathbf{g}')$ which form linear equations that reduce the computational complexity of solving the system of $m \times n^2/2$ multivariate quadratic equations with $n^2 + m^2$ unknowns which is generated by $\widetilde{T}^{-1} \circ \mathbf{g}' = \mathbf{f}' \circ \widetilde{S}$.

Now, let $\mathbf{f}, \mathbf{g} \in \mathcal{MQ}(n, m \times k)$ be the problem instance of BIPC. Without loss of generality, let us focus on $\mathbf{g}_{[1]}$. Assuming that the problem has solutions, the following holds for some $T \in \mathbb{CGL}(m, k)$ and $S \in \mathbb{CGL}(n, k)$:

$$\mathbf{g}_{[1]} = \sum_{j \in [1,k]} T_{[j]} \circ \mathbf{f}_{[j]} \circ S_{[j]} \tag{9}$$

Without loss of generality, assume that we successfully find $\alpha_1, \alpha_2, \ldots, \alpha_k, \beta$ such that $S_{[j]}\beta = \alpha_j$ for $j \in [1, k]$. Let define $\mathbf{f}'_{[j]}(\chi) := \mathbf{f}_{[j]}(\chi + \alpha_j)$ for $j \in [1, k]$ and $\mathbf{g}'(\chi) := \mathbf{g}_{[1]}(\chi + \beta)$. Thus, it is easy to see that the following holds.

$$\mathbf{g}' = \sum_{j \in [1,k]} T_{[j]} \circ \mathbf{f}'_{[j]} \circ S_{[j]}. \tag{10}$$

This means that if we can find α_j, β such that $S_{[j]}^{-1}\alpha_j = \beta$ for any of $j \in [1, k]$, we can transform the problem instance into another problem instance consisting of inhomogeneous MQ functions which have the same solutions.

In [3], it is shown that we can see the problem of finding α, β such that $\widetilde{S}^{-1}\alpha = \beta$ is similar to finding a single collision for a special hash function associated with $\widetilde{S}^{-1}$. Here, in a rough way, we see the problem of finding $\alpha_1, \ldots, \alpha_k, \beta$ such that $S_{[j]}^{-1}\alpha_j = \beta$ for all $j \in [1, k]$ as similar to finding simultaneous k collisions of k special hash functions associated with $S_{[j]}^{-1}$, for $j \in [1, k]$.

It is stated in [3] that the complexity of finding a single collision for such special hash function is $\approx 2 \times n^5 2^{n/2}$, where the constant "2" is the number of necessary hash tables, n^5 is the complexity of computing one hash value and $2^{n/2}$ is the necessary size of each hash table to apply the birthday paradox. Using a similar analogy, we estimate that if we want to find k collisions, we will need k hash tables, and we also estimate that based on Suzuki et al. [15], the necessary size of each hash table to apply the birthday paradox for k collisions is $\approx k/e \times 2^{nk/(k+1)}$, where e is the mathematical constant representing the base of natural logarithm, i.e., $e \approx 2.71828$. Thus, we estimate that the total complexity of finding simultaneous k collisions for the special hash function is $\approx k \times n^5 \times k/e \times 2^{nk/(k+1)} \leq k^2/2 \times n^5 2^{nk/(k+1)}$.

Finally, in order to derive a conservative estimation of the security parameters, we take an optimistic approach (from adversary point of view) by assuming that the following holds.

Assumption 1. *There exists an efficient method to "move" the T part from the right hand side to the left hand side of Eq. (10). such that we can use the procedure in [6] to find T and S efficiently.*

5.2   Evaluation Based on Gröbner Bases Attack [1]

Next, we will analyze the complexity of solving BIPC problem with algebraic attacks using Gröbner bases. Similarly, in order to derive a conservative estimation of the security parameters, we take an optimistic approach (from adversary point of view) by assuming that the following holds.

Assumption 2. *There exists an efficient method to "move" the T part from the right hand side to the left hand side of Eq. (7).*

Thus, we can treat the solving of BIPC problem as solving a system of multivariate quadratic polynomials. The number of unknowns is $(n+m) \times k$ and the number of equations is at most $n^2/2 \times mk$. Let v be the number of unknowns and w be the number of equations. According to [1], if w/v^2 tends to 0, the asymptotic complexity of solving this system is approximately $2^{v^2/(8w) \times \log(w/v)}$.

Here $w/v^2 = 1/2 \times n^2mk/((n+m)k)^2 < m/(2k)$ and let assume that m/k tends to 0 asymptotically, i.e., k is much larger than m. Thus, we can compute $v^2/(8w) \times \log(w/v) > (nk)^2/(8/2 \times n^2mk) \times \log(nm) = k\log(nm)/(4m)$. And we obtain the complexity of solving BIPC using algebraic attacks using Gröbner bases as $\approx 2^{k\log(nm)/(4m)}$.

5.3   Conservative Recommended Parameters

By combining the estimated complexity of the attacks shown in previous subsections, we recommend the following parameters to guarantee the hardness of BIPC problem for 128-bit and 256-bit security.

Table 1. Recommended security parameters (1 B = 8 bits)

Bit security	n	m	k	Size of problem instances $(\mathbf{f}, \mathbf{g})\ (= n^2 m k)$		Size of solutions $(S, T)\ (= (n + m)k)$	
128	84	2	140	1,975,680 bits	(246,960 B)	12,040 bits	(1,505 B)
256	206	2	236	20,029,792 bits	(2,503,724 B)	49,088 bits	(6,136 B)

Note that the size of problem instances and the size of solutions are the size of public keys and the size of secret keys in the proposed public key encryption scheme respectively.

5.4   Alternative Parameters

Note that parameters recommended above are based on the assumption that Assumptions 1 and 2 hold such that the adversary can solve BIPC using the similar method as solving a particular system of multivariate quadratic polynomials. Here we assume that Assumption 1 does not hold and only Assumption 2 holds, so that the adversary can only solve BIPC directly using Gröbner bases as described in Sect. 5.2. We derive security parameters for this scenario as follows.

Table 2. Alternative security parameters (1 B = 8 bits)

Bit security	n	m	k	Size of problem instances $(\mathbf{f}, \mathbf{g})\ (= n^2 m k)$		Size of solutions $(S, T)\ (= (n + m)k)$	
128	16	2	205	104,960 bits	(13,120 B)	3,690 bits	(462 B)
256	16	2	410	209,920 bits	(26,240 B)	7,380 bits	(923 B)

5.5   Aggressive Variants with Smaller Parameters

The size of problem instance of BIPC is basically the size of the public key and the ciphertext of the encryption scheme based on BIPC. The parameters shown in Table 1 might be too large for practical uses. Here we propose two variants of BIPC, where the sizes of the instances are much smaller compared to the ones proposed in previous subsection (Table 1).

Variant 1 (extremely aggressive): $\mathbf{f} \in \mathcal{MQ}(n, m \times k)$ is such that $\mathbf{f}_{[1]} = \mathbf{f}_{[2]} = \cdots = \mathbf{f}_{[k]}$ holds. Automatically $\mathbf{g}_{[1]} = \mathbf{g}_{[2]} = \cdots = \mathbf{g}_{[k]}$ holds. Thus, we only need to define $\mathbf{f}_{[1]}$ and $\mathbf{g}_{[1]}$ (Table 3).

Table 3. Security parameters for variant 1 (1 B = 8 bits)

Bit security	n	m	k	Size of problem instances $(\mathbf{f}, \mathbf{g})$ $(= n^2 m)$		Size of solutions (S, T) $(= (n+m)k)$	
128	84	2	140	14,112 bits	(1,764 B)	12,040 bits	(1,505 B)
256	206	2	236	84,872 bits	(10,609 B)	49,088 bits	(6,136 B)

Variant 2 (moderately aggressive): $\mathbf{f} \in \mathcal{MQ}(n, m \times k)$ is such that $\mathbf{f}_{[1]} = \mathbf{f}_{[2j'-1]}$, $\mathbf{f}_{[2]} = \cdots = \mathbf{f}_{[2j']}$ hold for $j' \in [1, k/2]$ when k is even, or $\mathbf{f}_{[1]} = \mathbf{f}_{[2j'+1]}, \mathbf{f}_{[2]} = \cdots = \mathbf{f}_{[2j']}$ hold for $j' \in [1, \lfloor k/2 \rfloor]$ when k is odd. Automatically $\mathbf{g}_{[1]} = \mathbf{g}_{[2j'-1]}, \mathbf{g}_{[2]} = \cdots = \mathbf{g}_{[2j']}$ hold for $j' \in [1, k/2]$ when k is even, or $\mathbf{g}_{[1]} = \mathbf{g}_{[2j'+1]}, \mathbf{g}_{[2]} = \cdots = \mathbf{g}_{[2j']}$ hold for $j' \in [1, \lfloor k/2 \rfloor]$ when k is odd. Thus, we only need to define $\mathbf{f}_{[1]}, \mathbf{f}_{[2]}$ and $\mathbf{g}_{[1]}, \mathbf{g}_{[2]}$ (Table 4).

Table 4. Security parameters for variant 2 (1 B = 8 bits)

Bit security	n	m	k	Size of problem instances $(\mathbf{f}, \mathbf{g})$ $(= n^2 m \times 2)$		Size of solutions (S, T) $(= (n+m)k)$	
128	84	2	140	28,224 bits	(3,528 B)	12,040 bits	(1,505 B)
256	206	2	236	169,744 bits	(21,218 B)	49,088 bits	(6,136 B)

Above aggressive parameters are derived from the conservative parameters shown in Table 1. One can easily derive the aggressive parameters in a similar way from the alternative parameters shown in Table 2.

Note 1. Since the number of equations to hold is significantly decreasing in the aggressive variants, intuitively the aggressive variants are more susceptible to equivalent keys attacks. We leave the complexity analysis of BIPC against equivalent keys attacks as an open problem.

Acknowledgement. We would like to express our gratitude to the anonymous reviewers for the constructive comments and advices which have contributed in improving this paper. This work is supported by JSPS Kiban (B) 18H01438 and JPSPS Kiban(C) 18K11292.

A   General Notations Related to Complexity

Let $\lambda \in \mathbb{N}$ be the general security parameter in this paper. Unless noted otherwise, any algorithm in this paper is probabilistic with running time polynomial in λ. The notation $a \leftarrow b$ denotes the assignment of value b into variable a. We say that a function $f(\lambda)$ is negligible if for every $\eta > 0$ there exists a λ_η such that $f(\lambda) < 1/\lambda_\eta$ for all $\lambda > \lambda_\eta$. An algorithm is said to solve a computational task *efficiently* if the probability that it solves the task within time polynomial in λ is not negligible. A task or a computational problem is said to be hard if there exists no algorithm solves the task/problem efficiently.

B   Proof of Theorem 1

Let us be given $\overline{\mathbf{f}}, \overline{\mathbf{g}} \in \mathcal{MQ}(n, m)$ as the instance of IP2S problem defined in Definition 2. Since the lemma holds trivially when $\overline{\mathbf{f}} = \mathbf{0}$ (zero polynomials) or $\overline{\mathbf{g}} = \mathbf{0}$, we are left to prove the case when $\overline{\mathbf{f}} \neq \mathbf{0}$ and $\overline{\mathbf{g}} \neq \mathbf{0}$. Hence, from hereafter we assume that $\overline{\mathbf{f}} \neq \mathbf{0}$ and $\overline{\mathbf{g}} \neq \mathbf{0}$. Next, we construct $\mathbf{f}, \mathbf{g} \in \mathcal{MQ}(n, m \times k)$ as follows. Let $\mathbf{f}_{[1]} = \overline{\mathbf{f}}$, $\mathbf{g}_{[1]} = \overline{\mathbf{g}}$, and $\mathbf{f}_{[\tau]}, \mathbf{g}_{[\tau]} = \mathbf{0}$ for all $\tau \in [2, k]$. In order to complete the proof, we show that the following claim holds.

Claim. $(\overline{\mathbf{f}}, \overline{\mathbf{g}})$ is an instance of IP2S with solutions if and only if $(\mathbf{f}, \mathbf{g})$ is an instance of BIP with solutions.

In order to prove the above claim, first, we prove the "if" part. If the pair $(\mathbf{f}, \mathbf{g})$ is an instance of BIP with solution, then, there exist $S \in \mathbb{GL}(n, k), T \in \mathbb{GL}(m, k)$ such that the following holds.

$$\mathbf{g}_{[1]} = T_{[1]} \circ \mathbf{f}_{[1]} \circ S_{[1]}, \tag{11}$$
$$\forall \tau \in [2, k]:$$
$$\mathbf{0} = T_{[(k-\tau+1) \bmod k+1]} \circ \mathbf{f}_{[1]} \circ S_{[(k-\tau+1) \bmod k+1]}. \tag{12}$$

It is clear that neither $T_{[1]}$ nor $S_{[1]}$ is a zero matrix since by the assumption, neither $\mathbf{g}_{[1]}$ nor $\mathbf{f}_{[1]}$ is a zero polynomial. Therefore, $T_{[1]}$ and $S_{[1]}$ must be invertible matrices, i.e., $T_{[1]} \in \mathbb{GL}_m$, $S_{[1]} \in \mathbb{GL}_n$. Hence, $T_{[1]}$ and $S_{[1]}$ are the solutions for IP2S problem with instance $(\overline{\mathbf{f}}, \overline{\mathbf{g}})$.

Next, we prove the "only if" part. Now, we assume that $(\overline{\mathbf{f}}, \overline{\mathbf{g}})$ is an instance of IP2S with solutions, but $(\mathbf{f}, \mathbf{g})$ is an instance of BIP without any solution. Let $\overline{T} \in \mathbb{GL}_m$ and $\overline{S} \in \mathbb{GL}_n$ be the solutions of $(\overline{\mathbf{f}}, \overline{\mathbf{g}})$ such that $\overline{\mathbf{g}} = \overline{T} \circ \overline{\mathbf{f}} \circ \overline{S}$ holds. Now remind that $\mathbf{f}_{[1]} = \overline{\mathbf{f}}$, $\mathbf{g}_{[1]} = \overline{\mathbf{g}}$, and $\mathbf{f}_{[\tau]}, \mathbf{g}_{[\tau]} = \mathbf{0}$ for $\tau \in [2, k]$ hold by our setting and it is easy to see that we can construct $S \in \mathbb{GL}(n, k), T \in \mathbb{GL}(m, k)$ such that Eqs. (11) and (12) hold by setting $T_{[1]} = \overline{T}$, $S_{[1]} = \overline{S}$, and $T_{[\tau]} = 0_m$, $S_{[\tau]} = 0_n$ for all $\tau \in [2, k]$. This means that $(\mathbf{f}, \mathbf{g})$ is an instance of BIP with solutions and contradicts our assumption. Hence, we have proven the "only if" part of the claim.

Finally, it should be noted that if $(\overline{\mathbf{f}}, \overline{\mathbf{g}})$ is an IP2S problem instance with solution, then we can always extract the solution by using an algorithm $\mathcal{B}$ which solves BIP and setting the input to $\mathcal{B}$ as $(\mathbf{f}, \mathbf{g})$ where $\mathbf{f}_{[1]} = \overline{\mathbf{f}}$, $\mathbf{g}_{[1]} = \overline{\mathbf{g}}$, and $\mathbf{f}_{[\tau]}, \mathbf{g}_{[\tau]} = \mathbf{0}$ for all $\tau \in [2, k]$ as shown above. One can easily see that this statement holds based on the proof of the "if" part of the claim above. This ends the proof of Theorem 1. $\qquad\Box$

C   Security Against Chosen Plaintext Attacks

Here we show that the public key encryption scheme described in Sect. 4.1 is secure against one way under chosen plaintext attack (OW-CPA).

Definition 12. (One Wayness against Chosen Plaintext Attack (OW-CPA)). *Let* PKE *be a public-key encryption scheme. Consider the following one way against chosen plaintext attack (OW-CPA) game, played between a challenger* $\mathcal{B}$ *and an adversary* $\mathcal{A}$:

1. $\mathcal{B}$ *generates a public key/secret key pair, and gives the public key to* $\mathcal{A}$.
2. $\mathcal{A}$ *makes encryption queries, which each is the message* ν *to encryption oracle* Enc *provided by* $\mathcal{B}$. *For each encryption query,* $\mathcal{B}$ *perform the encryption step using the public key and sends back a valid ciphertext* $\mathbf{c}$ *to* $\mathcal{A}$.
3. $\mathcal{B}$ *sends a ciphertext* c' *to* $\mathcal{A}$, *and* $\mathcal{A}$ *outputs* ν'.

The adversary $\mathcal{A}$ *is said to win if* ν' *is a valid decryption of* c'. PKE *is said to be OW-CPA secure if there is no* $\mathcal{A}$ *which wins the above game efficiently.*

Theorem 3. *If there exists an adversary* $\mathcal{A}$ *wins OW-CPA game in the public key encryption scheme described in Sect. 4.1 efficiently, then there exists an algorithm* $\mathcal{B}$ *which solves CDH-BIPC efficiently.*

Proof. We construct the algorithm $\mathcal{B}$ using oracle access to $\mathcal{A}$. The procedure of $\mathcal{B}$ is as follows.

(1) Given input $\mathbf{f}^{(1)}, \mathbf{f}^{(2)}, \mathbf{g}^{(1)} \in \mathcal{MQ}_{[k]}(n, m)$ as the instance of CDH-BIPC, $\mathcal{B}$ input $\mathbf{g}^{(1)}, \mathbf{f}^{(1)}$ as the public key into $\mathcal{A}$. Since $(\mathbf{f}^{(1)}, \mathbf{f}^{(2)}, \mathbf{g}^{(1)})$ is an instance of CDH-BIPC, $\mathbf{g}^{(1)} = \Upsilon \boxplus \mathbf{f}^{(1)}$ holds for some $\Upsilon \in \Psi_{[n,m,k]}$, and thus $(\mathbf{g}^{(1)}, \mathbf{f}^{(1)})$ is a valid public key pair.
(2) $\mathcal{B}$ easily simulates the encryption oracle Enc using $\mathbf{g}^{(1)}, \mathbf{f}^{(1)}$ as the public key by executing the encryption procedure shown in Sect. 4.1.
(3) $\mathcal{B}$ sets $\mathbf{c}'_0 = \mathbf{f}^{(2)}$ and selects randomly $\mathbf{c}'_1$ from $\mathcal{MQ}_{[k]}(n, m)$.
(4) $\mathcal{B}$ sends $(\mathbf{c}'_0, \mathbf{c}'_1)$ to $\mathcal{A}$ and $\mathcal{A}$ outputs ν'.

By assumption $\mathcal{A}$ will output a valid decryption. Hence, we have $\mathbf{c}'_1 = \mathsf{e}(\nu') + \Upsilon \boxplus \mathbf{c}'_0 = \mathsf{e}(\nu') + \Upsilon \boxplus \mathbf{f}^{(2)}$. Finally, $\mathcal{B}$ sets $\mathbf{g}^{(2)} := \mathbf{c}'_1 - \mathsf{e}(\nu') = \Upsilon \boxplus \mathbf{f}^{(2)}$ and output $\mathbf{g}^{(2)}$ as the solution of CDH-BIPC problem with instance $(\mathbf{f}^{(1)}, \mathbf{f}^{(2)}, \mathbf{g}^{(1)})$. This ends the proof of Theorem 3.

D   Special Property of $\Psi_{[n,m,k]}$

Since any $\psi \in \Psi_{[n,m,k]}$ can be seen as a matrix with circulant structure, it is easy to see that the following property holds.

Property 1. Let $\psi \in \Psi_{[n,m,k]}$. Let define as follows.

$$\psi_{0,0} := \psi_{k,k},$$
$$\psi_{i,0} := \psi_{i,k} \qquad \text{for any } i \in [1,k],$$
$$\psi_{0,j} := \psi_{k,j} \qquad \text{for any } j \in [1,k].$$

Then, the followings hold for any $\tau \in [1,k]$.

$$\psi_{\tau,j} = \psi_{i,(i+j-\tau) \bmod k} \qquad \text{for any } i,j \in [1,k], \tag{13}$$

where $a \bmod k$ is always set to non-negative value for any $a \in \mathbb{Z}$.[1]

E   Proof of Lemma 1

In this section, we will prove Lemma 1. First, as preparation, we introduce the following lemma.

Lemma 2. *Let* $\mathbf{u}, \mathbf{w} \in \mathcal{MQ}(n,m)$ *and* $\mu_1, \mu_2 \in ((\mathbb{C}irc_m \cap \mathbb{GL}_m) \cup \{0_m\})$ $\times ((\mathbb{C}irc_n \cap \mathbb{GL}_n) \cup \{0_n\})$. *And let define* $\mu_1 := (A_1, B_1)$ *and* $\mu_2 := (A_2, B_2)$. *Then, the following properties hold.*

– *Distributive property:*

$$\mu_1 * (\mathbf{u} + \mathbf{w}) = \mu_1 * \mathbf{u} + \mu_1 * \mathbf{w}. \tag{14}$$

– *Commutative property:*

$$\mu_2 * (\mu_1 * \mathbf{u}) = \mu_1 * (\mu_2 * \mathbf{u}). \tag{15}$$

We put the proof of Lemma 2 in Appendix F.

In order to prove Lemma 1, it is sufficient for us to prove that the following holds for any $\tau \in [1,k]$.

$$(\varphi \boxtimes (\psi \boxtimes \mathbf{f}))_{[\tau]} = (\psi \boxtimes (\varphi \boxtimes \mathbf{f}))_{[\tau]} \tag{16}$$

Since here we need to use Property 1 shown in Appendix D, let us define the followings.

$$\psi_{0,0} := \psi_{k,k}, \qquad \varphi_{0,0} := \varphi_{k,k}, \tag{17}$$
$$\psi_{i,0} := \psi_{i,k}, \qquad \varphi_{i,0} := \varphi_{i,k} \qquad \text{for any } i \in [1,k], \tag{18}$$
$$\psi_{0,j} := \psi_{k,j}, \qquad \varphi_{0,j} := \varphi_{k,j} \qquad \text{for any } j \in [1,k]. \tag{19}$$

---

[1] For any $a \geq 0$, $a \bmod k = a - \alpha \times k$, where α is the largest integer such that $\alpha \times k \leq a$ holds, and for any $a < 0$, $a \bmod k = \alpha \times k + a$, where α is the smallest integer such that $\alpha \times k + a > 0$.

Now, let us expand the Eq. (16).

$$(\varphi \boxast (\psi \boxast \mathbf{f}))_{[\tau]}$$

$$= \sum_{i=1}^{k} \varphi_{\tau,i} * \left(\sum_{j=1}^{\tau} \psi_{i,j} * \mathbf{f}_{[j]} \right)$$

$$\overset{(a)}{=} \sum_{i=1}^{k} \sum_{j=1}^{k} \varphi_{\tau,i} * \left(\psi_{i,j} * \mathbf{f}_{[j]} \right)$$

$$\overset{(b)}{=} \sum_{i=1}^{k} \sum_{j=1}^{k} \psi_{i,j} * \left(\varphi_{\tau,i} * \mathbf{f}_{[j]} \right)$$

$$\overset{(c)}{=} \sum_{i=1}^{k} \sum_{j=1}^{k} \psi_{\tau,(\tau+j-i) \bmod k} * \left(\varphi_{\tau,i} * \mathbf{f}_{[j]} \right)$$

$$\overset{(d)}{=} \sum_{i=1}^{k} \sum_{j=1}^{k} \psi_{\tau,(\tau+j-i) \bmod k} * \left(\varphi_{(\tau+j-i) \bmod k,((\tau+j-i)+i-\tau) \bmod k} * \mathbf{f}_{[j]} \right)$$

$$= \sum_{i=1}^{k} \sum_{j=1}^{k} \psi_{\tau,(\tau+j-i) \bmod k} * \left(\varphi_{(\tau+j-i) \bmod k,j \bmod k} * \mathbf{f}_{[j]} \right)$$

$$= \sum_{i=1}^{k} \sum_{j=1}^{k} \psi_{\tau,(\tau+j-i) \bmod k} * \left(\varphi_{(\tau+j-i) \bmod k,j} * \mathbf{f}_{[j]} \right)$$

$$= \sum_{j=1}^{k} \sum_{i=1}^{k} \psi_{\tau,(\tau+j-i) \bmod k} * \left(\varphi_{(\tau+j-i) \bmod k,j} * \mathbf{f}_{[j]} \right), \tag{20}$$

where:

- Step (a) is due to the distributive property in Lemma 2,
- Step (b) is due to the commutative property in Lemma 2,
- Step (c) is due to the Property 1 applied to $\psi_{i,j}$,
- Step (d) is due to the Property 1 applied to $\varphi_{\tau,i}$,

and by defining $i' := (\tau + j - i) \bmod k$, we obtain as follows:

$$\text{Eq. (20)} = \sum_{j=1}^{k} \sum_{i'=0}^{k-1} \psi_{\tau,i'} * \left(\varphi_{i',j} * \mathbf{f}_{[j]} \right)$$

$$\overset{(e)}{=} \sum_{j=1}^{k} \sum_{i'=1}^{k} \psi_{\tau,i'} * \left(\varphi_{i',j} * \mathbf{f}_{[j]} \right)$$

$$= \sum_{i'=1}^{k} \sum_{j=1}^{k} \psi_{\tau,i'} * \left(\varphi_{i',j} * \mathbf{f}_{[j]} \right)$$

$$\overset{(f)}{=} \sum_{i'=1}^{k} \psi_{\tau,i'} * \sum_{j=1}^{k} \left(\varphi_{i',j} * \mathbf{f}_{[j]} \right)$$

$$= \left(\psi \boxplus (\varphi \boxplus \mathbf{f}) \right)_{[\tau]}, \tag{21}$$

where:

- Step (e) is due to the definitions in Eqs. (17), (18) and (19),
- Step (f) is due to the distributive property in Lemma 2.

This ends the proof of Lemma 1.   □

F   Proof of Lemma 2

First let us prove Eq. (14).

$$\mu_1 * (\mathbf{u} + \mathbf{w}) = A_1 \circ (\mathbf{u} + \mathbf{w}) \circ B_1 = A_1 \circ (\mathbf{u} \circ B_1 + \mathbf{w} \circ B_1)$$
$$= A_1 \circ \mathbf{u} \circ B_1 + A_1 \circ \mathbf{w} \circ B_1 = \mu_1 * \mathbf{u} + \mu_1 * \mathbf{w}.$$

Next, let us prove Eq. (15). Recall that since $\mu_1, \mu_2 \in ((\mathbb{C}\mathrm{irc}_m \cap \mathbb{GL}_m) \cup \{0_m\}) \times ((\mathbb{C}\mathrm{irc}_n \cap \mathbb{GL}_n) \cup \{0_n\})$, the following matrices are circulant matrices: A_1, A_2, B_1, B_2. Thus, the followings hold: $A_1 A_2 = A_2 A_1$ and $B_1 B_2 = B_2 B_1$. Hence, we obtain as follows.

$$\mu_2 * (\mu_1 * \mathbf{u}) = A_2 \circ (A_1 \circ \mathbf{u} \circ B_1) \circ B_2 = (A_2 A_1) \circ \mathbf{u} \circ (B_1 B_2)$$
$$= (A_1 A_2) \circ \mathbf{u} \circ (B_2 B_1) = A_1 \circ (A_2 \circ \mathbf{u} \circ B_2) \circ B_1 = \mu_1 * (\mu_2 * \mathbf{u}).$$

This ends the proof of Lemma 2.

References

1. Bardet, M., Faugére, J.-C., Salvy, B.: Complexity of Gröbner basis computation for semi-regular overdetermined sequences over $\mathbb{F}_2$ with solutions in $\mathbb{F}_2$, Institut National de Recherche en Informatique et en Automatique (INRIA), techreport 5049 (2003). https://hal.inria.fr/inria-00071534/PS/RR-5049.ps
2. Bettale, L., Faugère, J., Perret, L.: Cryptanalysis of HFE, multi-HFE and variants for odd and even characteristic. Des. Codes Cryptogr. 69(1), 1–52 (2013). https://doi.org/10.1007/s10623-012-9617-2
3. Bouillaguet, C., Fouque, P.-A., Véber, A.: Graph-theoretic algorithms for the "Isomorphism of Polynomials" Problem. In: Johansson, T., Nguyen, P.Q. (eds.) EUROCRYPT 2013. LNCS, vol. 7881, pp. 211–227. Springer, Heidelberg (2013). https://doi.org/10.1007/978-3-642-38348-9_13
4. Courtois, N., Klimov, A., Patarin, J., Shamir, A.: Efficient algorithms for solving overdefined systems of multivariate polynomial equations. In: Preneel, B. (ed.) EUROCRYPT 2000. LNCS, vol. 1807, pp. 392–407. Springer, Heidelberg (2000). https://doi.org/10.1007/3-540-45539-6_27

5. Faugère, J.-C., Joux, A.: Algebraic cryptanalysis of hidden field equation (HFE) cryptosystems using Gröbner bases. In: Boneh, D. (ed.) CRYPTO 2003. LNCS, vol. 2729, pp. 44–60. Springer, Heidelberg (2003). https://doi.org/10.1007/978-3-540-45146-4_3
6. Faugère, J.-C., Perret, L.: Polynomial equivalence problems: algorithmic and theoretical aspects. In: Vaudenay, S. (ed.) EUROCRYPT 2006. LNCS, vol. 4004, pp. 30–47. Springer, Heidelberg (2006). https://doi.org/10.1007/11761679_3
7. Hofheinz, D., Hövelmanns, K., Kiltz, E.: A modular analysis of the Fujisaki-Okamoto transformation. In: Kalai, Y., Reyzin, L. (eds.) TCC 2017. LNCS, vol. 10677, pp. 341–371. Springer, Cham (2017). https://doi.org/10.1007/978-3-319-70500-2_12
8. Chen, J., Tan, C.H., Li, X.: Practical cryptanalysis of a public key cryptosystem based on the morphism of polynomials problem. Tsinghua Sci. Technol. 23(6), 671–679 (2018)
9. Kipnis, A., Shamir, A.: Cryptanalysis of the HFE public key cryptosystem by relinearization. In: Wiener, M. (ed.) CRYPTO 1999. LNCS, vol. 1666, pp. 19–30. Springer, Heidelberg (1999). https://doi.org/10.1007/3-540-48405-1_2
10. Patarin, J.: Hidden fields equations (HFE) and isomorphisms of polynomials (IP): two new families of asymmetric algorithms. In: Maurer, U. (ed.) EUROCRYPT 1996. LNCS, vol. 1070, pp. 33–48. Springer, Heidelberg (1996). https://doi.org/10.1007/3-540-68339-9_4
11. Patarin, J., Goubin, L., Courtois, N.: Improved algorithms for isomorphisms of polynomials. In: Nyberg, K. (ed.) EUROCRYPT 1998. LNCS, vol. 1403, pp. 184–200. Springer, Heidelberg (1998). https://doi.org/10.1007/BFb0054126
12. Plût, J., Fouque, P.-A., Macario-Rat, G.: Solving the "isomorphism of polynomials with two secrets" problem for all pairs of quadratic forms (2014). http://arxiv.org/abs/1406.3163
13. Santoso, B.: Reviving identification scheme based on isomorphism of polynomials with two secrets: a refined theoretical and practical analysis. IEICE Trans. 101-A(5), 787–798 (2018)
14. Santoso, B., Su, C.: Provable secure post-quantum signature scheme based on isomorphism of polynomials in quantum random oracle model. In: Okamoto, T., Yu, Y., Au, M.H., Li, Y. (eds.) ProvSec 2017. LNCS, vol. 10592, pp. 271–284. Springer, Cham (2017). https://doi.org/10.1007/978-3-319-68637-0_17
15. Suzuki, K., Tonien, D., Kurosawa, K., Toyota, K.: Birthday paradox for multi-collisions. In: Rhee, M.S., Lee, B. (eds.) ICISC 2006. LNCS, vol. 4296, pp. 29–40. Springer, Heidelberg (2006). https://doi.org/10.1007/11927587_5
16. Wang, H., Zhang, H., Mao, S., Wu, W., Zhang, L.: New public-key cryptosystem based on the morphism of polynomials problem. Tsinghua Sci. Technol. 21(3), 302–311 (2016)
17. Wolf, C., Preneel, B.: Equivalent keys in multivariate uadratic public key systems. J. Math. Cryptol. 4(4), 375–415 (2011)

Practical Cryptanalysis of k-ary C^*

Daniel Smith-Tone[1,2]([envelope])

[1] Department of Mathematics, University of Louisville, Louisville, KY, USA
`daniel.smith@nist.gov`
[2] National Institute of Standards and Technology, Gaithersburg, MD, USA

Abstract. Recently, an article by Felke appeared in Cryptography and Communications discussing the security of biquadratic C^* and a further generalization, k-ary C^*. The article derives lower bounds for the complexity of an algebraic attack, directly inverting the public key, under an assumption that the first-fall degree is a good approximation of the solving degree, an assumption that the paper notes requires "greater justification and clarification."

In this work, we provide a practical attack breaking all k-ary C^* schemes. The attack is based on differential techniques and requires nothing but the ability to evaluate the public key and solve linear systems. In particular, the attack breaks the parameters provided in CryptoChallenge 11 by constructing and solving linear systems of moderate size in a few minutes.

Keywords: Multivariate cryptography · k-ary C^* · Differential attack

1 Introduction

Massively multivariate public key cryptography was first introduced outside of Japan in the EuroCrypt'88 paper by Matsumoto and Imai, see [1], that presented what has become known as the C^* cryptosystem. After Shor discovered polynomial-time factoring and discrete logarithm quantum algorithms, see [2], schemes based on different problems, and in particular on NP-hard problems such as that of solving multivariate nonlinear systems, became much more interesting to cryptographers. Now with the ongoing post-quantum standardization effort by the National Institute of Standards and Technology (NIST), see [3], such multivariate schemes are now being considered for practical widespread use.

In [4], Patarin broke the original C^* scheme with an attack based on linearization equations. At around this time, in the late'90s, there was an explosion of research in multivariate cryptography. Numerous schemes were introduced and cryptanalyzed, see, for example, [5–11].

In 2005, Dobbertin et al. present a cryptographic challenge based on the idea of C^*. The scheme is called a biquadratic C^* and has a massive public key of

J. Ding and J.-P. Tillich (Eds.): PQCrypto 2020, LNCS 12100, pp. 360–380, 2020.
https://doi.org/10.1007/978-3-030-44223-1_20

quartic polynomials. Like C^*, biquadratic C^* is derived from a power function, but with an exponent of Hamming weight four in its q-ary expansion, where q is the size of the public finite field. Naturally, this construction can be generalized to a k-ary C^* in which the q-ary expansion of the exponent of the private power function has Hamming weight k.

This more general k-ary C^* is analyzed by Felke in [12], where he derives lower bounds for the first-fall degree of the public key under direct attacks via Gröbner bases. Although we should note that in the practical setting that the first-fall degree is dependent on both the polynomial system and the Gröbner basis algorithm (consider for example a user's freedom to choose a selection function in F4), Felke's result relates to the algebraic first fall degree and thus implies a lower bound in the complexity of solving such a system with *any* Gröbner basis algorithm. As noted in [12], the complexity estimates of the direct attack on k-ary C^* derived therein depend on an assumption that the first-fall degree is equal to the solving degree, an assumption which is not always true.

In this work, we provide an efficient cryptanalysis of k-ary C^* and some modest generalizations. This attack is based on a property of the differential of a power function that the author derived over ten years ago, see [13]. The attack reduces the task of deriving a decryption key to that of solving systems of linear equations. In particular, for the CryptoChallenge 11, see [14], one evaluation of the public key, the calculation of the differential of two public equations and the solution of two linear systems of size 627 and 625, respectively, are sufficient to completely break the scheme. The complexity for an optimized implementation for these parameters is roughly 2^{38} operations over GF(16). We implemented the attack using crude and simple symbolic algebra techniques and, after a few minutes of sloppily gathering coefficients, solved the linear system and broke the proposed parameters in an instant. In the most general case, the complexity of the optimized attack is $\mathcal{O}\left(n^2\binom{n}{k}^2\right)$. Using the full formula for this estimate produces an upper bound of 2^{68} operations over $GF(16)$ even for the "secure" biquadratic scheme proposed in [12].

These newer high degree versions of the C^* scheme proposed in [12] echo several other attempts in recent years proposing schemes with cubic public keys, using cubic polynomials for inversion or offering evidence for security based on the analysis of cubic polynomials, see, for example, [15, 16]. What we are learning, however, is that there is no enhancement in security achieved by going to a higher degree, see [17, 18]. Thus, of independent interest is our theoretical framework for analyzing our attack on k-ary C^* which together with [19] indicate that the same constructions we use for measuring security in the quadratic setting generalize to higher degrees.

This article is organized as follows. In Sect. 2, we introduce the k-ary version of C^*. We then briefly review the cryptanalytic history of C^* and its principal variants. Next, in Sect. 4, we motivate our approach in higher degrees by developing an original cryptanalysis of C^*. In the following section, we derive a practical attack on k-ary C^* breaking the scheme in a few minutes. In Sect. 6, we derive the complexity of the attack and conclude that all proposed parameter sets are broken. Due to space restrictions, the theoretical constructions characterizing all maps having these differential properties are relegated to Appendices B and C.

2 k-ary C^*

Let $\mathbb{F}_q$ be a finite field with q elements. Consider $\mathbb{K}$, a degree n extension of $\mathbb{F}_q$. Fix an $\mathbb{F}_q$-vector space isomorphism $\phi : \mathbb{F}_q^n \to \mathbb{K}$. Then for any univariate map $f : \mathbb{K} \to \mathbb{K}$ we can construct the vector-valued map $F : \mathbb{F}_q^n \to \mathbb{F}_q^n$ defined by $F = \phi^{-1} \circ f \circ \phi$. Since any multivariate function on a finite field is a polynomial, each coordinate of F is a polynomial in its n inputs.

To hide the structure of an efficiently invertible univariate map it is necessary to randomize the input and output bases of the representation of $\mathbb{K}$ as a commutative $\mathbb{F}_q$-algebra. Thus the public key P is related to the private map F by an isomorphism (T, U) where T and U are $\mathbb{F}_q$-affine maps of dimension n. Thus the entire construction is given by Fig. 1.

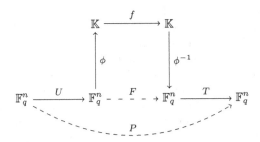

Fig. 1. The structure of big field public key cryptosystems.

As defined in [14], a k-ary C^* map is an univariate function $f : \mathbb{K} \to \mathbb{K}$ of the form $f(x) = x^e$, where the q-ary expansion of e is binary having Hamming weight k and e is coprime with $|\mathbb{K}^*|$. Notice that

$$x^e = x^{q^{a_1} + \cdots + q^{a_k}} = \prod_{i=1}^{k} x^{q^{a_i}},$$

and since the Frobenius automorphisms are $\mathbb{F}_q$-linear, $F = \phi^{-1} \circ f \circ \phi$ is of $\mathbb{F}_q$-degree k.

3 Previous Cryptanalyses of C^* and Variants

In [4], Patarin breaks the original C^* scheme by deriving the so-called linearization equations. He noticed that given a C^* map of the form $f(x) = x^{q^\theta + 1}$, we obtain the bilinear relation $uf(u)^{q^\theta} = u^{q^{2\theta}} f(u)$. That is, if we let $v = f(u)$, then we obtain a bilinear relation between u and v. Since u and v are related to the plaintext and ciphertext of the public key system via the maps U and T, respectively, we have a bilinear relation between plaintext and ciphertext. A simple analysis shows that even in the most fortuitous case, the adversary can reduce the dimension of the possible preimage space by a factor of three, thus rendering C^* too inefficient for practical use.

As a method of repairing the scheme, it was suggested in [8] to remove some of the public equations. The technique avoids the linearization equations attack since the bilinear relation between plaintext and ciphertext pairs for C^* is explicitly given by

$$\phi(\mathbf{Ux})\phi(\mathbf{T}^{-1}\mathbf{y})^{q^\theta} = \phi(\mathbf{Ux})^{q^{2\theta}}\phi(\mathbf{T}^{-1}\mathbf{y}).$$

This idea eventually evolved in to the SFLASH digital signature scheme of [9].

In [20], an attack that completely breaks SFLASH is presented. The attack uses the discrete differential of the public key. Given a function $G : A \to A$, on some additive group A, the discrete differential is defined by

$$DG(a, x) = G(a + x) - G(a) - G(x) + G(0).$$

The attack proceeds by way of a symmetric relation satisfied by a C^* monomial map $f(x) = x^{q^\theta + 1}$. Specifically,

$$Df(\sigma a, x) + Df(a, \sigma x) = (\sigma^{q^\theta} + \sigma)Df(a, x).$$

This property is inherited by the public key $P = \Pi \circ T \circ F \circ U$ in the form:

$$D\left[\Pi \circ P\right](\mathbf{N}_\sigma \mathbf{a}, \mathbf{x}) + D\left[\Pi \circ P\right](\mathbf{a}, \mathbf{N}_\sigma \mathbf{x}) = \Pi \circ \Lambda_\sigma \circ DP(\mathbf{a}, \mathbf{x}), \qquad (1)$$

where $\mathbf{N}_\sigma = \mathbf{U}^{-1}\mathbf{M}_\sigma \mathbf{U}$, $\mathbf{M}_\sigma$ is a left multiplication representation of $\sigma \in \mathbb{K}$, Π is the projection onto the first $n - a$ coordinates, and Λ_σ is linear depending on σ. (Here and throughout Roman typeface denotes a function or field element while bold typeface denotes a– possibly corresponding– vector or matrix.)

For any validly formed $\mathbf{N}_\sigma$, Eq. 1 guarantees that the left-hand side is a linear combination of the differential coordinate forms without equations removed. Thus, Eq. (1) provides a criterion for finding such an $\mathbf{N}_\sigma$. Specifically, if we insist that a few coordinates of the left-hand side of Eq. (1) are in the span of the known differential coordinate forms, then it is likely that $\mathbf{N}_\sigma$ is a multiplication. In this way, one can recover such a multiplication. Once found, $P \circ N_\sigma$ provides new linearly independent equations that can be added to the original public key to recreate a compatible C^* public key. At this point, Patarin's original linearization equations attack can be used to break the scheme.

4   A Different Cryptanalysis of C^*

The attack of [20] inspires a new idea for attacking the original C^* directly. The idea is to interpret the map recovered via the differential symmetry technique as a multiplication map under a different basis, one parameterized by U. Using this map one may recover a representation of $\mathbb{K}$ as an $\mathbb{F}_q$-algebra. Then one uses this information along with the public key to recover another representation of $\mathbb{K}$ as an $\mathbb{F}_q$-algebra, this time parameterized by T. Then one can view the public key as a power function between these two representations. Once the function is known, a single input-output pair can be used to construct an efficient inverse function.

4.1   Alternate Decryption Key Recovery

Suppose that we have a nontrivial solution $\mathbf{N}_\sigma$ of Eq. 1. Then necessarily,

$$
\begin{aligned}
P \circ N_\sigma &= T \circ F \circ M_\sigma \circ U \\
&= T \circ M_{f(\sigma)} \circ F \circ U \\
&= \left(T \circ M_{f(\sigma)} \circ T^{-1} \right) \circ T \circ F \circ U \\
&= Z_{f(\sigma)} \circ P.
\end{aligned}
$$

Thus P translates right composition of multiplications in the basis U^{-1} into left composition of multiplications in the basis T.

Given such a matrix $\mathbf{N}_\sigma$, we compute $\mathbf{Z}_{f(\sigma)}$, and by guessing f (since there are fewer than n possibilities), we may recover the corresponding pair $(\mathbf{N}_{f(\sigma)}, \mathbf{Z}_{f(\sigma)})$. Naturally, if we have guessed f, then we can raise $\mathbf{Z}_{f(\sigma)}$ to the appropriate power to similarly recover $\mathbf{Z}_\sigma$. Either way, with probability $\frac{\varphi(q^n-1)}{q^n-q}$, where φ is the Euler totient function, σ is a generator of $\mathbb{K}^*$ and thus $f(\sigma)$ is also a generator. So we may form a basis for the two representations of $\mathbb{K}$ as $\mathbb{F}_q$-algebras by computing $\{\mathbf{I}, \mathbf{N}_\sigma, \mathbf{N}_\sigma^2, \ldots, \mathbf{N}_\sigma^{n-1}\}$ and $\{\mathbf{I}, \mathbf{Z}_\sigma, \mathbf{Z}_\sigma^2, \ldots, \mathbf{Z}_\sigma^{n-1}\}$.

Now, given a single input output pair $\mathbf{y}_0 = P(\mathbf{x}_0)$, we can decrypt any message $\mathbf{y} = P(\mathbf{x})$ by first finding the appropriate multiplication $\mathbf{Z}_\tau$ such that $\mathbf{Z}_\tau \mathbf{y}_0 = \mathbf{y}$. Given the representation of $\mathbf{Z}_\tau$ over its basis,

$$
\mathbf{Z}_\tau = \sum_{i=0}^{n-1} \lambda_i \mathbf{Z}_\sigma^i,
$$

we construct

$$
\mathbf{N}_\tau = \sum_{i=0}^{n-1} \lambda_i \mathbf{N}_\sigma^i.
$$

Then, by construction, we have that

$$
\begin{aligned}
\mathbf{y} = \mathbf{Z}_\tau \mathbf{y}_0 &= Z_\tau \circ P(\mathbf{x}_0) \\
&= T \circ M_\tau \circ T^{-1} \circ T \circ F \circ U(\mathbf{x}_0) \\
&= T \circ M_\tau \circ F \circ U(\mathbf{x}_0) \\
&= T \circ F \circ M_{f^{-1}(\tau)} \circ U(\mathbf{x}_0) \\
&= T \circ F \circ U \circ U^{-1} \circ M_{f^{-1}(\tau)} \circ U(\mathbf{x}_0) \\
&= P \circ N_{f^{-1}(\tau)}(\mathbf{x}_0).
\end{aligned}
$$

Thus $P^{-1}(\mathbf{y}) = \mathbf{x} = \mathbf{N}_{f^{-1}(\tau)}\mathbf{x}_0$. To find $\mathbf{N}_{f^{-1}(\tau)}$, we simply find $he = 1$ modulo $|\mathbb{K}^*|$, and compute $\mathbf{N}_\tau^h = \mathbf{N}_{f^{-1}(\tau)}$.

Thus, the key step in breaking C^* in this manner is a solution of Eq. (1) in the case that Π is the identity map. We generically have no extraneous solutions as long as $3\theta \neq n$ as proven in [21].

This method provides a distinct cryptanalysis of C^* involving only solving linear systems. The technique is quite efficient, and provides a new signing key that is different from the original signing key and the one derived with the linearization equations attack.

These computational techniques are described in more detail in Algorithm 1 in Appendix A. One should note that the random selection in step 6 is selecting from exactly an n-dimensional $\mathbb{F}_q$-vector space of solutions corresponding to the "multiplication maps" of the form $\mathbf{N}_\sigma$ as proven in [21]. This step can be modified to assure that a nontrivial solution is obtained.

4.2   Full Key Decomposition

One may extend the attack further to recover a private key of the form (T', U')— recall that f was already guessed. We consider the decomposition in stages. First, we derive linear maps $(\widehat{T}, \widehat{U})$ such that $\widehat{T}^{-1} \circ P \circ \widehat{U}^{-1}$ is multiplicative. Once obtained, a single input/output pair for this map is computed and used to anchor this multiplicative function to f and ultimately to derive equivalent maps (T', U').

Having recovered the maps $\mathbf{N}_\sigma$ and $\mathbf{Z}_{f(\sigma)}$, we consider the relations

$$\mathbf{N}_\sigma = \mathbf{U}^{-1}\mathbf{M}_\sigma\mathbf{U} \text{ and } \mathbf{Z}_{f(\sigma)} = \mathbf{T}\mathbf{M}_{f(\sigma)}\mathbf{T}^{-1}.$$

Clearly, the minimal polynomial $\min(\mathbf{N}_\sigma) = \min(\mathbf{M}_\sigma)$ which is the same as the minimal polynomial of σ or any of its conjugates. In particular, under the action of $\mathbb{K}^* \rtimes \mathrm{Gal}_{\mathbb{F}_q}(\mathbb{K}) \hookrightarrow GL_n(\mathbb{F}_q)$ by conjugation, the orbit of $\mathbf{M}_\sigma$ is

$$\{\mathbf{M}_\tau : \phi(\sigma) = \tau \text{ for some } \phi \in \mathrm{Gal}_{\mathbb{F}_q}(\mathbb{K})\}.$$

Thus the stabilizer corresponds to the subgroup isomorphic to $\mathbb{K}^*$.

We directly solve the linear system

$$\widehat{\mathbf{U}}\mathbf{N}_\sigma = \mathbf{M}_\tau\widehat{\mathbf{U}},$$

in the unknown coefficients of $\widehat{\mathbf{U}}$ for some τ a root of $\min(\mathbf{N}_\sigma)$. Since the action of $\mathbb{K}^* \rtimes \mathrm{Gal}_{\mathbb{F}_q}(\mathbb{K})$ on the image of $\mathbb{K}$ in $GL_n(\mathbb{F}_q)$ is transitive and since the choice of τ in general fixes the automorphism, there are usually n degrees of freedom in $\widehat{\mathbf{U}}$. We similarly solve the linear system

$$\mathbf{Z}_{f(\sigma)}\widehat{\mathbf{T}} = \widehat{\mathbf{T}}\mathbf{M}_{f(\tau)},$$

with the same τ as the first step, again with n degrees of freedom, usually.

Next, we construct the augmented key $\widehat{P} = \widehat{T}^{-1} \circ P \circ \widehat{U}^{-1}$. Notice that

$$
\begin{aligned}
\widehat{P} \circ M_\tau &= \widehat{T}^{-1} \circ T \circ F \circ U \circ \widehat{U}^{-1} \circ M_\tau \\
&= \widehat{T}^{-1} \circ T \circ F \circ M_\sigma \circ U \circ \widehat{U}^{-1} \\
&= \widehat{T}^{-1} \circ T \circ M_{f(\sigma)} \circ F \circ U \circ \widehat{U}^{-1} \\
&= M_{f(\tau)} \circ \widehat{T}^{-1} \circ T \circ F \circ U \circ \widehat{U}^{-1},
\end{aligned}
$$

where σ is a conjugate of τ. Thus $\widehat{P}$ is an isomorphic copy of the public key that is multiplicative.

Finally, we fix an arbitrary input/output pair $\mathbf{y}' = \widehat{P}(\mathbf{x}')$. We can now directly compute a decomposition of the public key as $T' = \widehat{T} \circ M_{y'}$, $U' = M_{x'}^{-1} \circ \widehat{U}$, and of course f which was guessed before. Note that if $\mathbf{y} = P(\mathbf{x})$, then $\widehat{T}^{-1}\mathbf{y}$ can be viewed as the output of $\widehat{P}$ with input $\widehat{U}(\mathbf{x})$. So we may use the same trick from Subsect. 4.1 to find a preimage of $\widehat{T}^{-1}\mathbf{y}$ under $\widehat{P}$. Specifically, this involves dividing by $y' = \phi(\mathbf{y}')$ (multiplying on the left by $\mathbf{M}_{y'}^{-1}$), inverting F and multiplying by x' (that is, $\mathbf{M}_{x'}$). At this point we have obtained $\widehat{U}\mathbf{x}$, so inversion is completed by the application of $\widehat{U}^{-1}$. More explicitly, observe that

$$
\begin{aligned}
&\left(\widehat{T} \circ M_{y'}\right) \circ \widehat{T}^{-1} \circ T \circ F \circ U \circ \widehat{U}^{-1} \circ \left(M_{x'}^{-1} \circ \widehat{U}\right) \\
&\quad = \left(\widehat{T} \circ M_{y'}\right) \circ \widehat{T}^{-1} \circ T \circ F \circ M_{\overline{x'}^{-1}} \circ U \circ \left(\widehat{U}^{-1} \circ \widehat{U}\right) \\
&\quad = \left(\widehat{T} \circ M_{y'}\right) \circ \widehat{T}^{-1} \circ T \circ M_{\overline{f(x')}^{-1}} \circ F \circ U \\
&\quad = \widehat{T} \circ \left(M_{y'} \circ M_{f(x')^{-1}}\right) \circ \widehat{T}^{-1} \circ T \circ F \circ U \\
&\quad = \left(\widehat{T} \circ \widehat{T}^{-1}\right) \circ T \circ F \circ U \\
&\quad = T \circ F \circ U.
\end{aligned}
$$

5   Cryptanalysis of k-ary C^*

We now prove for any k that k-ary C^* has a differential symmetry. Moreover, multiplication maps are the only maps inducing symmetry in this way, assuring that once the symmetric equations are solved that a multiplication map has been found. We then use this fact to construct an attack analogous to that of Sect. 4.

We first define the rth discrete differential.

Definition 1. *Let A be an additive group. The rth discrete differential of a map $F : A \to A$ is defined as*

$$
D^r F(x_0, \ldots, x_r) = \begin{cases} F & \text{if } r = 0 \\ \begin{aligned} &D^{r-1}F(x_0 + x_1, x_2, \ldots, x_r) \\ -&D^{r-1}F(x_0, x_2, \ldots, x_r) \\ -&D^{r-1}F(x_1, x_2, \ldots, x_r) \\ +&D^{r-1}F(0, x_2, \ldots, x_r) \end{aligned} & \text{otherwise.} \end{cases}
$$

We note explicitly that since the discrete differential operator D is symmetric, when given a symmetric multivariate function $G(a, \ldots, b)$, we have that $D_a G(x, a, \ldots, b) = D_b G(a, \ldots, b, x)$ and is symmetric; that is, the same function is obtained when taking the differential with respect to any variable. Thus all higher order differentials are the same regardless of the sequence of variables with respect to which the differentials are taken and the rth differential is well-defined.

Theorem 1. *Let $f : \mathbb{K} \to \mathbb{K}$ be the k-ary C^* map $f(x) = x^{q^{i_1} + \cdots + q^{i_k}}$. Then f satisfies the differential symmetry*

$$\sum_{j=1}^{k} D^{k-1} f(\sigma^{\delta_{j,1}} x_1, \ldots, \sigma^{\delta_{j,k}} x_k) = \left(\sum_{j=1}^{k} \sigma^{q^{i_j}}\right) D^{k-1} f(x_1, \ldots, x_k), \qquad (2)$$

where $\delta_{r,s}$ is the Kronecker delta function.

Proof. By calculation, $D^{k-1} f(x_1, \ldots, x_k)$ is $\mathbb{F}_q$-multilinear and so every monomial summand is of the form

$$x^\alpha = x_1^{q^{\alpha_1}} x_2^{q^{\alpha_2}} \cdots x_k^{q^{\alpha_k}},$$

for some α, a permutation of $(i_1, \ldots, i_k)$. Each summand of the left hand side of Eq. (2) contains exactly one term of the form $\sigma^{q^{\alpha_i}} x^\alpha$ and the contribution of each differential is distinct. Thus, the sum of the x^α terms of the left hand side of Eq. (2) is $(\sum_{j=1}^{k} \sigma^{q^{i_j}}) x^\alpha$ for every α. Summing over all possible α and factoring out $(\sum_{j=1}^{k} \sigma^{q^{i_j}})$, we obtain the result.

Thus, k-ary C^* monomial maps satisfy the same multiplicative symmetry that C^* monomial maps exhibit. The key here seems to be that these maps are multiplicative, and the multiplicative symmetry is the manifestation of that property in the differential. By an argument analogous to that in [21], it can be shown that if $\mathbf{L}$ induces a differential symmetry with a k-ary C^* map, then $\phi(\mathbf{Lx}) = \sigma(\phi(\mathbf{x}))$ for some $\sigma \in \mathbb{K}$. See Appendix B for details.

Now we may implement an attack of the exact same manner as that of Sect. 4. The main difference is that we must compute a higher order differential and guess an encryption exponent of a different form. For all of the details, see Algorithm 2 in Appendix A.

6   Complexity

Even a direct symbolic approach to implementing the attack of Sect. 5 is sufficient to break the parameters of CryptoChallenge11 from [14]. Specifically, using symbolic algebra, we broke the biquadratic C^* with parameters $q = 16$, $n = 25$ and $e = 1 + q + q^3 + q^{12}$ with a straightforward MAGMA[1] implementation with symbolic algebra, in 593.25 s using 3.9 GB of memory, see [22].

---

[1] Any mention of commercial products does not indicate endorsement by NIST.

The implementation is not at all optimized, as it is not necessary to make a complex implementation to break the full-sized parameters. The implementation uses symbolic algebra over a polynomial ring over a polynomial ring over a polynomial ring over $\mathbb{F}$! We did, however, incorporate some of the trivial to implement optimization techniques we now present. An optimized implementation will make use of the fact that the symmetry relations derived to effect the attack are linear in the coefficients of the public key; thus, with some engineering, the entire attack can be reduced to a few operations on some matrices of moderate size. We describe this technique in more detail at the end of the section.

First, the linear system

$$\sum_{i=1}^{k} D^{k-1} P(\mathbf{N}_\sigma^{\delta_{i,1}} \mathbf{x}_1, \ldots, \mathbf{N}_\sigma^{\delta_{i,k}} \mathbf{x}_k) = \mathbf{\Lambda}_\sigma D^{k-1} P(\mathbf{x}_1, \ldots, \mathbf{x}_k), \tag{3}$$

where $\delta_{i,j}$ is the Kronecker delta, is massively redundant. The system is dramatically overdefined typically even when one coordinate of the left-hand side is used.

Each monomial $x_{1,i_1} \cdots x_{k,i_k}$ with the i_j pairwise distinct in each coordinate of $D^{k-1}P$ produces an equation. Thus the entire linear system in Eq. (3) is $n\binom{n}{k}$ equations in the $2n^2$ unknown coordinates of $\mathbf{N}_\sigma$ and $\mathbf{\Lambda}_\sigma$.

Since we are only interested in solving for $\mathbf{N}_\sigma$, we can reduce this system dramatically by considering fewer coordinates of the left-hand side. The resulting system will use a corresponding number of rows of the matrix Λ_σ, so fewer variables are required as well. We may choose r coordinates to recover $r\binom{n}{k}$ equations in $n^2 + rn$ unknowns. Clearly, the system is fully determined with 3 coordinates when $k = 2$ and $n \geq 9$ or with even a single coordinate when $k > 3$ and $n > 10$, for example. In particular, the large values of k make the system more overdetermined when even a single coordinate on the left hand side is considered.

We can improve the complexity even further by not considering all of the coordinates of $D^{k-1}P$ on the right-hand side of Eq. (3). As in the attack on SFLASH of [20], we may consider an analysis of the number of linear maps whose symmetric action on the first r coordinates of the differential map it into the span of the first s coordinates of $D^{k-1}P$.

Fix an arbitrary matrix $\mathbf{M}$ and consider the expression

$$\widetilde{\mathbf{M}}_i = \sum_{j=1}^{k} D^{k-1} P_i(\mathbf{M}^{\delta_{j,1}} \mathbf{x}_1, \ldots, \mathbf{M}^{\delta_{j,k}} \mathbf{x}_k), \text{ for } i \in \{1, \ldots, r\},$$

which can be viewed as an r-tuple of symmetric k-tensors. The span of all such symmetric k-tensors $\mathcal{S}$, under the heuristic that P_i is random, q and n are sufficiently large and $k > 2$, has dimension rn^2, that is, r times the dimension of $\mathcal{M}_{n \times n}(\mathbb{F}_q)$. The first s coordinates of $D^{k-1}P$ generate an s-dimensional space V_s of k-tensors. We note explicitly that since each multiplication of the form $\mathbf{N}_\sigma$

produces k-tensors that are guaranteed to be in V_n that V_n, and therefore V_s is contained in $\mathcal{S}$.

Membership of each coordinate of $\widetilde{\mathbf{M}}$ in V_s requires the satisfaction of $n^2 - s$ linear equations. Thus the membership of all coordinates of $\widetilde{\mathbf{M}}$ in V_s requires the satisfaction of $r(n^2 - s)$ linear equations. This analysis thus suggests that it is unlikely for all coordinates of $\widetilde{\mathbf{M}}$ to be in V_s for random $\mathbf{M}$ as soon as $r > 1$.

On the other hand, if $\mathbf{M}$ is already a multiplication map of the form $\mathbf{N}_\sigma$ then $\widetilde{\mathbf{M}}$ is already guaranteed to be in V_n. Moreover, the condition that each of the first r coordinates of $\widetilde{\mathbf{M}}$ is in V_s is satisfied explicitly under the appropriate change of basis by the preimage of $\mathrm{Span}(1, \alpha^{-1}, \ldots, \alpha^{1-s})$ under the linear map $x \mapsto x^{q^{a_1}} + x^{q^{a_2}} + \cdots + x^{q^{a_k}}$ if $r \leq s$. In particular, if $r = s$ we obtain an s-dimensional space of multiplications.

Considering the above analysis, we expect for $k > 2$ and n sufficiently large that choosing the first two coordinates of the left-hand side of Eq. (3) to be in the span of the first two coordinates of the right-hand side provides enough relations to produce a 2-dimensional subspace consisting entirely of maps of the form of $\mathbf{N}_\sigma$. Our experiments confirm that this approach works. Table 1 provides performance numbers for this attack using $r = s = 2$ for biquadratic C^* instances.

Table 1. The performance of a simple Magma implementation of the above attack against biquadratic C^* over GF(16) using $r = 2$ coordinates of the left-hand side and the span of $s = 2$ coordinates of the right-hand side of Eq. (3). The last column is the performance in breaking CryptoChallenge11 from [14].

n	9	11	13	15	25
(s)	0.9	2.88	8.04	21.3	593.25
(MB)	22.6	46.71	85.99	287.63	3883.34

We note a couple of properties of this attack. Since the symmetric relations of Eq. 3 are linear in the highest degree terms of the public key, there exists a massive binary matrix that produces the symmetric relations from the public coefficients. In the symbolic implementation above, almost all of the time was spent recovering these linear equations, with all of the overhead of the polynomial rings with hundreds of variables, before they were nearly instantly solved.

To make the attack more efficient, one can note that the differential symmetric equations are linear functions of the coefficients of the public key. Thus one may construct a linear function to derive the relations directly from the public key coefficients. We derive this function in the $k = 2$ case. The general case is similar and quite tedious to build.

Note that

$$DP_l(\mathbf{Ma}, \mathbf{x}) + DP_l(\mathbf{a}, \mathbf{Mx})$$

$$= \sum_{i<j} c_{ijl} \left[\sum_{k=1}^{n} m_{ik} a_k x_j + \sum_{k=1}^{n} m_{jk} a_i x_k + \sum_{k=1}^{n} m_{jk} a_k x_i + \sum_{k=1}^{n} m_{ik} a_j x_k \right]$$

$$= \sum_{k=1}^{n} \sum_{j=2}^{n} \sum_{i<j} c_{ijl} m_{ik} a_k x_j + \sum_{k=1}^{n} \sum_{i=1}^{n-1} \sum_{i<j} c_{ijl} m_{jk} a_i x_k$$

$$+ \sum_{k=1}^{n} \sum_{i=1}^{n-1} \sum_{i<j} c_{ijl} m_{jk} a_k x_i + \sum_{k=1}^{n} \sum_{j=2}^{n} \sum_{i<j} m_{ik} a_j x_k.$$

Collecting coefficients of $a_r x_s$ we obtain

$$[a_r x_s] = \sum_{i<s} c_{isl} m_{ir} + \sum_{r<i} c_{ril} m_{is} + \sum_{s<i} c_{sil} m_{ir} + \sum_{i<r} c_{irl} m_{is}.$$

We form a matrix $\mathcal{A}_l$ whose rows are indexed by (r, s) with $r < s$ and whose columns are indexed by (u, v) with $1 \leq u, v \leq n$.

$$\mathcal{A}_{l,(r,s),(u,v)} = \begin{cases} c_{usl} & \text{if } u < s \text{ and } v = r \\ c_{url} & \text{if } u < r \text{ and } v = s \\ c_{rul} & \text{if } r < u \text{ and } v = s \\ c_{sul} & \text{if } s < u \text{ and } v = r \\ 0 & \text{otherwise.} \end{cases}$$

From this expression, we may derive as many as n matrices of size $\binom{n}{2} \times n^2 \binom{n}{2}$ which can be multiplied on the left by the vector of cross term coefficients of each public formula to produce row vectors of $\mathcal{A}_l$. Each row of $\mathcal{A}_l$ now represents the coefficients of m_{ij} occurring in the left-hand side of coordinate l of Eq. (3). In a similar way we can construct additional matrices generating the right-hand side of the relations from the public coefficients and horizontally join the result to $\mathcal{A}_l$. Elements in the nullspace of this matrix then correspond to matrices $\mathbf{M}$ satisfying Eq. (3).

Considering the more general case of k-ary C^*, for $k > 2$, we may limit the number of matrices above to 2 for each of the left and right-hand sides. Then deriving the symmetry relations requires linear algebra on matrices of size $n^2 \binom{n}{k}$, and solving the system requires finding a kernel vector for a matrix of size $2n^2 \binom{n}{k} \times (n^2 + 4)$. Note that a nontrivial kernel vector exists when the rank of this matrix is bounded by $n^2 + 3$, and in this case we can find a vector with high probability by only considering $\mathcal{O}\left(n^2\right)$ rows. Thus the complexity for the entire recovery of the multiplication map is

$$2n^2 \binom{n}{k}^2 + \mathcal{O}\left(n^2\right)\left(n^2 + 4\right) = \mathcal{O}\left(n^2 \binom{n}{k}^2\right),$$

ignoring sparse optimizations. For CryptoChallenge11, this quantity is upper bounded by 2^{38}, which is far superior to the symbolic implementation described and executed above. For the "secure" variant of biquadratic C^* recently proposed in [12], the formula above provides an upper bound of 2^{68}, far less than the claimed security bound of 80 bits.

7   Conclusion

Although C^* has been the foundation of one of the main approaches to multivariate public key cryptography in the last decades, it has also been a source of failure for many constructions based too directly on it, see, for example, [23]. The k-ary generalization of C^* falls into this category as well. While the differential relations are more cumbersome to derive in the k-tensor space than for the original C^*, the extent of the symmetry inherent to the central map makes it easy to derive the polynomially sized overdetermined linear system required to break the scheme.

Some of the major accomplishments of multivariate cryptography in the twenty-first century are derivations of proofs that certain modifications of schemes preclude certain classes of attacks. For C^* variants, one may provably prevent an attack recovering a differential symmetry on the public key by using nontrivial projections on both the input variables and the output polynomials, see [21,24]. It is an interesting theoretical question as to whether the same result can be derived in the k-ary case. Clearly, the attack presented here can be used to recover a full rank scheme from a minus modified one and break it similarly to SFLASH. While the projection modifier removes this symmetry, it is an open question as to whether a projected k-ary C^{*-} scheme can be secure.

A   Algorithms

Algorithm 1: Decrypt* C^*

Input : public key P, ciphertext $y = P(x)$
Output: plaintext x such that $P(x) = y$

1 $x_0 \xleftarrow{\$} \mathbb{F}_q^n$;
2 $y_0 \longleftarrow P(x_0)$;
3 $DP(a,x) \longleftarrow P(a+x) - P(a) - P(x) + P(0)$;
4 $N_\sigma \longleftarrow$ Matrix$([[r_1,\ldots,r_n],\ldots,[r_{n^2-n+1},\ldots,r_{n^2}]])$;
5 $\Lambda_\sigma \longleftarrow$ Matrix$([[s_1,\ldots,s_n],\ldots,[s_{n^2-n+1},\ldots,s_{n^2}]])$;
6 $v \xleftarrow{\$}$ LinearSolve$(DP(N_\sigma a, x) + DP(a, N_\sigma x) = \Lambda_\sigma DP(a,x))$;
7 $N_\sigma \longleftarrow$ Eval$(N_\sigma, [v[i]: i \in [1..n^2]])$;
8 $Z_{f(\sigma)} \longleftarrow$ Matrix$([[r_1,\ldots,r_n],\ldots,[r_{n^2-n+1},\ldots,r_{n^2}]])$;
9 $w \longleftarrow$ LinearSolve$(Z_{f(\sigma)} \circ P = P \circ N_\sigma)$;
10 $Z_{f(\sigma)} \longleftarrow$ Eval$(Z_{f(\sigma)}, w)$;
11 **for** e in $[1+q^1,\ldots,1+q^{n-1}]$ st $(e, q^n - 1) = 1$ **do**
12 | $h \longleftarrow$ InverseMod$(e, q^n - 1)$;
13 | $Z_\sigma \longleftarrow Z_{f(\sigma)}^h$;
14 | $\lambda \longleftarrow$ LinearSolve$(\sum_{i=1}^n \lambda_i Z_\sigma^{i-1} y_0 = y)$;
15 | $N_\tau \longleftarrow \sum_{i=1}^n \lambda_i N_\sigma^{i-1}$;
16 | $N_{f^{-1}(\tau)} \longleftarrow N_\tau^h$;
17 | $x_{cand} \longleftarrow N_{f^{-1}(\tau)} x_0$;
18 | **if** $y == P(x_{cand})$ **then**
19 | | **return** x_{cand}
20 | **end**
21 **end**

Algorithm 2: Decrypt* k-ary C^*

Input : public key P, ciphertext $y = P(x)$
Output: plaintext x such that $P(x) = y$

1 $x_0 \xleftarrow{\$} \mathbb{F}_q^n$;
2 $y_0 \longleftarrow P(x_0)$;
3 $D^{k-1}P(a,x) \longleftarrow$ Differential$(P, k\text{-}1)$;
4 $N_\sigma \longleftarrow$ Matrix$([[r_1,\ldots,r_n],\ldots,[r_{n^2-n+1},\ldots,r_{n^2}]])$;
5 $\Lambda_\sigma \longleftarrow$ Matrix$([[s_1,\ldots,s_n],\ldots,[s_{n^2-n+1},\ldots,s_{n^2}]])$;
6 $v \xleftarrow{\$}$ LinearSolve$(\sum_{j=1}^k D^{k-1}P(N_\sigma^{\delta_{j,1}} x_1,\ldots,N_\sigma^{\delta_{j,k}} x_k) = \Lambda_\sigma D^{k-1}P(a,x))$;
7 $N_\sigma \longleftarrow$ Eval$(N_\sigma, [v[i]: i \in [1..n^2]])$;
8 $Z_{f(\sigma)} \longleftarrow$ Matrix$([[r_1,\ldots,r_n],\ldots,[r_{n^2-n+1},\ldots,r_{n^2}]])$;
9 $w \longleftarrow$ LinearSolve$(Z_{f(\sigma)} \circ P = P \circ N_\sigma)$;
10 $Z_{f(\sigma)} \longleftarrow$ Eval$(Z_{f(\sigma)}, w)$;
11 **for** e of binary q-weight k st $(e, q^n - 1) = 1$ **do**
12 | $h \longleftarrow$ InverseMod$(e, q^n - 1)$;
13 | $Z_\sigma \longleftarrow Z_{f(\sigma)}^h$;
14 | $\lambda \longleftarrow$ LinearSolve$(\sum_{i=1}^n \lambda_i Z_\sigma^{i-1} y_0 = y)$;
15 | $N_\tau \longleftarrow \sum_{i=1}^n \lambda_i N_\sigma^{i-1}$;
16 | $N_{f^{-1}(\tau)} \longleftarrow N_\tau^h$;
17 | $x_{cand} \longleftarrow N_{f^{-1}(\tau)} x_0$;
18 | **if** $y == P(x_{cand})$ **then**
19 | | **return** x_{cand}
20 | **end**
21 **end**

B   The Multiplicative Symmetry

We first derive a modest generalization of [24, Theorem 1].

Lemma 1. *Let $\mathbb{K}$ be an extension of $\mathbb{F}$, $f : \mathbb{K}^r \to \mathbb{K}$ be a polynomial, and $g : \mathbb{K}^r \to \mathbb{K}$ be a monomial summand of f. If f is $\mathbb{F}$-multilinear, then g is $\mathbb{F}$-multilinear.*

Proof. Since the discrete differential operator D is linear, we may take the differential with respect to an arbitrary variable, x_d, and obtain

$$0 = D_{x_d} f = \sum_i D_{x_d} g_i = \sum_i c_i \sum_{j=1}^{\alpha_{i,d}-1} \binom{\alpha_{i,d}}{j} a^j x_1^{\alpha_{i,1}} \cdots x_d^{\alpha_{i,d}-j} \cdots x_r^{\alpha_{i,r}},$$

where the binomial coefficients are computed modulo $char(\mathbb{K})$. Since necessarily the multidegree of each g_i is unique, the multidegree of every summand is unique. Therefore, we find that $D_{x_d} g_i = 0$ for all i. Therefore, since all c_i are nonzero and the monomials x^α, $\alpha = (\alpha_1, \ldots, \alpha_r)$, are linearly independent in $\mathbb{K}[a, x_1 \ldots, x_r]$, we have that for all d and i that $char(\mathbb{K})$ divides $\alpha_{i,d}$. Thus by the binomial theorem, every summand g_i of f is $\mathbb{F}$-additive.

Since f is $\mathbb{F}$-multilinear, $f(x_1, \ldots, ax_d, \ldots, x_r) = af(x_1, \ldots, x_r)$ for all d, for all $a \in \mathbb{F}$ and for all x. Again, by the independence of the monomials x^α, the monomial summand g_i must satisfy $g_i(x_1, \ldots, ax_d, \ldots, x_r) = ag_i(x_1, \ldots, x_r)$, and thus g_i is $\mathbb{F}$-linear. As a bonus, considering the exponent of a in this expression shows that $\alpha_{i,d}$ is a multiple of q, the order of $\mathbb{F}$, for all i and d.

The usefulness of this result lies in its corollary.

Corollary 1. *Let $f : \mathbb{K} \to \mathbb{K}$ be a polynomial, and let $g : \mathbb{K} \to \mathbb{K}$ be a monomial summand of f. If $D^n f$ is multilinear, then $D^n g$ is multilinear.*

For simplicity of notation and consistency with previous work, see [24], we call the polynomial in σ on the right hand side of Eq. 2 the *separation polynomial*.

Lemma 2. *Let $g : \mathbb{K} \to \mathbb{K}$ be a monomial function. Then g has the multiplicative symmetry. Furthermore, two monomial functions g_1 and g_2 share the same separation polynomial if and only if $g_1 = cg_2$ for some constant c.*

Proof. Note that the proof of Theorem 1 applies to any monomial. Further notice that the separation polynomial is of the form

$$p(\sigma) = \sum_{i=1}^{r} \sigma^{q^{\alpha_i}},$$

where $g(x) = cx^\alpha = cx_1^{\alpha_1} \cdots x_r^{\alpha_r}$. Clearly the sum of the exponents in p is the multidegree of g, and thus any two monomials g_1 and g_2 sharing the same separation polynomial have the same multidegree, and $g_1 = cg_2$.

Now we can classify all field maps with the general multiplicative symmetry.

Theorem 2. *A function $f : \mathbb{K} \to \mathbb{K}$ has the multiplicative symmetry if and only if it has a unique summand of maximum q-weight.*

Proof. ($\Leftarrow$) Suppose that f has a unique summand, g, of maximum q-weight k. Given any other monomial summand, h, we have the q-weight condition:

$$
\begin{array}{ccccccccc}
wt(x,g) & \xrightarrow{D} & wt(x,Dg) & \xrightarrow{D} & \cdots & \xrightarrow{D} & wt(x,D^{k-1}g) = 1 & \xrightarrow{D} & wt(x,D^k g) = 0 \\
\Big\downarrow{\scriptstyle >} & & \Big\downarrow{\scriptstyle >} & & & & \Big\downarrow{\scriptstyle >} & & \\
wt(x,h) & \xrightarrow{D} & wt(x,Dh) & \xrightarrow{D} & \cdots & \xrightarrow{\quad D \quad} & 0 & &
\end{array}
$$

where $wt(x,j)$ is the q-weight of x in j. Thus $D^{k-1}f = D^{k-1}g$, and f has the multiplicative symmetry with the same separation polynomial as g.

($\Rightarrow$) Suppose, by way of contradiction, that f has the multiplicative symmetry and has r distinct monomial summands, g_m, of maximum q-weight k. Then we have

$$
D^k f = \sum_{m=1}^{r} D^k g_m. \tag{4}
$$

By Lemma 2, each monomial summand has a unique separation polynomial, p_{g_m}. Let p_f represent the separation polynomial of f. Since f has the multiplicative symmetry, we have:

$$
\sum_{i=0}^{k} D^k f(\sigma^{\delta_{0i}} x_0, \ldots, \sigma^{\delta_{ki}} x_k) = p_f(\sigma) D^k f(x_0, \ldots, x_k)
$$
$$
= p_f(\sigma) \sum_{m=1}^{r} D^k g_m(x_0, \ldots, x_k). \tag{5}
$$

On the other hand,

$$
\sum_{i=0}^{k} D^k f(\sigma^{\delta_{0i}} x_0, \ldots, \sigma^{\delta_{ki}} x_k) = \sum_{m=1}^{r} \sum_{i=0}^{k} g_m(\sigma^{\delta_{0i}} x_0, \ldots, \sigma^{\delta_{ki}} x_k)
$$
$$
= \sum_{m=1}^{r} p_{g_m}(\sigma) D^k g_m(x_0, \ldots, x_k). \tag{6}
$$

Taking the difference of (5) and (6), we obtain:

$$
\sum_{m=1}^{r} (p_f - p_{g_m})(\sigma) D^k g_m(x_0, \ldots, x_k) = 0, \tag{7}
$$

for all $(\sigma, x_0, \ldots, x_k) \in \mathbb{K}^{k+2}$. From Lemma 2, we know that each $D^k g_m$ is a complete symmetric multilinear function, therefore we can rewrite:

$$
\sum_{m=1}^{r} c_m (p_f - p_{g_m})(\sigma) \sum_{\alpha} x_0^{q^{\alpha_0}} \cdots x_k^{q^{\alpha_k}} = 0. \tag{8}
$$

Again, since the monomials x^α are linearly independent in $\mathbb{K}[x_0, \ldots, x_k]$, for any arbitrary fixed $\sigma \in \mathbb{K}$, we obtain:

$$c_m(p_f - p_{g_m})(\sigma) = 0, \tag{9}$$

for all $1 \le m \le r$. Since $c_m \ne 0$ for each m, and σ is arbitrary, we have that $p_f = p_{g_m}$ for all m. Since the g_m are distinct, by Lemma 2, r is zero or one. Thus, f has a unique monomial summand of maximum weight.

Again, it seems that the multiplicative symmetry is the differential manifestation of the fact that f, restricted to its highest weight terms is, up to a constant factor, multiplicative.

C   The Effect of Projection

Projection proved to be effective, in the quadratic case, in eliminating the symmetry which weakened C^{*-}. We can still prove an analogue of that result in this more general setting.

Theorem 3. *Let M be an $\mathbb{F}_q$-affine transformation and let $f : \mathbb{K} \to \mathbb{K}$ have the multiplicative symmetry. The composition $f \circ M$ has the multiplicative symmetry if and only if M is a translation of a linear monomial map, i.e. $M(x) = cx^{q^i} + d$ for some $i < n$.*

Proof. As in [24, Theorem 3], it suffices to consider linear maps. In addition, since all monomials, except that of weight k, disappear in $D^{k-1}f$ along with the fact that $D^{k-1}(cf) = cD^{k-1}f$, it suffices to analyze the case when $f(x) = x^{\sum_{i=0}^{k-1} q^{\alpha_i}}$. In particular, we can even insist that $\alpha_0 = 0$, since M composed with the factor $x^{q^{\alpha_0}}$ remains a monomial function of the same weight.

($\Leftarrow$) Suppose M is a linear monomial map, $M(x) = c_M x^{q^i}$ for some $i < n$. Now, $f \circ M(x)$ is still a monomial of the same weight, since the composition simply changes the exponents of q in the power of x. Thus, as a consequence of Theorem 2, $f \circ M$ has the multiplicative symmetry.

($\Rightarrow$) Let $\hat{f} = f \circ M$. Since every $\mathbb{F}_q$-linear transformation, M, can be written $M = \sum_{i=0}^{n-1} c_i x^{q^i}$, we have the following:

$$\begin{aligned}
\hat{f}(x) &= f \circ M(x) \\
&= f \circ \sum_{i=0}^{n-1} c_i x^{q^i} \\
&= \left(\sum_{i=0}^{n-1} c_i x^{q^i} \right)^{\sum_{j=0}^{k-1} q^{\alpha_j}} \\
&= \sum_{i_0, \ldots, i_{k-1} < n} c_{i_0} c_{i_1 - \alpha_1}^{q^{\alpha_1}} \cdots c_{i_{k-1} - \alpha_{k-1}}^{q^{\alpha_{k-1}}} x^{\sum_{j=0}^{k-1} q^{i_j}}.
\end{aligned} \tag{10}$$

Assuming that $\hat{f}$ has the multiplicative symmetry, since all terms have the same weight, only one of the above coefficients is nonzero. Suppose, by way of contradiction, that M has at least two nonzero coefficients, $c_{k_1} \neq c_{k_2}$.

Setting $i_0 = k_1$, and $i_j = k_1 + \alpha_j$, we can see that the coefficient on the right side of (10) is $c_{k_1}^{\sum_{i=0}^{k-1} q^{\alpha_i}}$, and therefore this term is nonzero.

On the other hand, we can set $i_0 = k_2$ and $i_j = k_1 + \alpha_j$, and we have another nonzero term. Since, $\hat{f}$ has only one nonzero term in the expression, these two nonzero terms must have x occurring with the same power, and we therefore have $k_1 + \sum_{j=1}^{k-1} q^{k_1 + \alpha_j} = k_2 + \sum_{j=1}^{k-1} q^{k_1 + \alpha_j}$. Hence, $k_1 = k_2$, a contradiction, and M must be an univariate linear monomial map.

Projection, therefore, removes the multiplicative symmetry from any field map.

D   Toy Example

To illustrate the attack, we present a key recovery for a small instance of 4-ary C^*. We simplify the exposition by considering a homogeneous key.

Let $q = 16$ and let a be a generator of $\mathbb{F}_q^*$. We select the degree $n = 9$ irreducible $g(x) = x^9 + ax^8 + a^2x^7 + x^6 + a^{12}x^5 + a^7x^4 + a^{10}x^3 + a^{14}x^2 + a^2x + a^8$ and construct $\mathbb{K} = \mathbb{F}_q[x]/\langle g(x)\rangle$. Let $b \in \mathbb{K}$ be a fixed root of this irreducible polynomial.

We choose the exponent $q^3 + q^2 + q + 1$ and compute the multiplicative inverse $h = 18.324.145.204$ modulo $|\mathbb{K}^*|$. We then fix the 4-ary C^* monomial map $f(x) = x^{q^3+q^2+q+1}$. We further randomly select two invertible $\mathbb{F}_q$-linear maps U and T given by the matrices

$$U = \begin{bmatrix} 1 & a^{13} & a^5 & a^8 & a^{10} & a^6 & 1 & a^{13} & a^{10} \\ a^5 & 1 & 1 & a^5 & a^6 & 0 & a^5 & a^{10} & 1 \\ a^{12} & a^8 & a^6 & a^{11} & a^7 & a & a^7 & a^8 & a^{11} \\ a^{14} & a^7 & a^2 & 1 & a & a^8 & 0 & a & a^5 \\ a & a^5 & a^4 & a^{10} & a^9 & a^{13} & a^{14} & a^{12} & a^{12} \\ a^{11} & a^3 & a^{11} & a^4 & a^6 & a^7 & a^7 & a^3 & a^7 \\ a^{11} & a^5 & a^{11} & a^{12} & a^{12} & a^{11} & a^6 & a^{11} & a^2 \\ a & a & a^7 & a^{14} & a^6 & a^3 & a^3 & a^{13} & a^6 \\ a^{10} & a & a^{13} & a^9 & a^4 & a^7 & a^{13} & a^{14} & a^{11} \end{bmatrix} \quad T = \begin{bmatrix} a^{12} & 1 & a^{13} & a & a^8 & a^{12} & a^4 & a^{10} & a^{14} \\ 0 & 1 & a^8 & a^{13} & a^{12} & a^4 & a^{11} & a^7 & a^6 \\ a^{11} & a^6 & a^{13} & a^{14} & a^6 & a^5 & a^4 & a^{14} & a^8 \\ a^9 & a^{13} & 0 & a & a^3 & a^7 & a^3 & a^{14} & a^5 \\ a^{12} & a^{12} & a^8 & a^{11} & a^3 & a^6 & a^3 & a^{10} & a^{11} \\ a^4 & a^{11} & a & a^{11} & a^{10} & a & a^{12} & a^{13} & a^9 \\ a^{10} & a^{13} & a^3 & a & a & a^4 & a^{14} & 1 & a^{11} & 0 \\ a^9 & a^{11} & 1 & a^3 & a^{12} & a^4 & a^{14} & a^{10} & a^8 \\ a^9 & a & a^{14} & a^3 & 0 & a^{12} & a^3 & a^8 & a^6 \end{bmatrix}$$

The composition $T \circ \phi^{-1} \circ f \circ \phi \circ U$ then produces a quartic public key of 9 equations in 9 variables.

D.1   Key Recovery

The recovery of an equivalent private key proceeds in three steps. First, we use the differential to recover a linear operator corresponding to a masked multiplication by an extension field element. We then use this map to recover a vector-valued function equivalent to f. Finally, we recover linear input and output transformations such that the composition of all of these maps is equal to the public key.

We construct the polynomial ring $\mathbb{F}_q[T]$ with $T = \{t_1, \ldots, t_{n^2}\}$ and collect the variables into the matrix $\mathbf{N}_\sigma$. Then we solve the linear system

$$\sum_{i=1}^{4} D^3 P(\mathbf{N}_\sigma^{\delta_{i,1}} \mathbf{x}_1, \ldots, \mathbf{N}_\sigma^{\delta_{i,4}} \mathbf{x}_4) = \Lambda_{\mathbf{N}_\sigma} D^3 P(\mathbf{x}_1, \ldots, \mathbf{x}_4)$$

for $\mathbf{N}_\sigma$ by imposing the constraints that the first two coordinates of the left hand side are in the span of $D^3 P(\mathbf{x}_1, \ldots, \mathbf{x}_4)$. There is a two dimensional subspace of solutions from which we choose the random solution

$$\mathbf{N}_\sigma = \begin{bmatrix} a^{14} & a^9 & a^{10} & a^6 & a^7 & a^8 & a^{13} & a^{10} & a^{12} \\ a^{10} & a & a^7 & a^3 & a^2 & a^2 & a^{14} & a^4 & a^{11} \\ a^{14} & a^{12} & a^{12} & a & a^{12} & a^5 & a & a^6 & 1 \\ a^{12} & a^3 & a^{10} & a^4 & a^{12} & a^6 & 0 & a^4 & a^7 \\ a^3 & a^{14} & a^{10} & 0 & a & a^5 & a^{13} & 0 & a^4 \\ a^9 & a^8 & a^{10} & a^{12} & a^6 & a^2 & a^{14} & a^{11} & a^3 \\ a^6 & a^{11} & a^3 & a^7 & a^2 & a^{14} & a^9 & 0 & a^5 \\ a^8 & 0 & a^6 & a^7 & a^{13} & 0 & a^{10} & a^{10} & a^{11} \\ a^9 & a^{10} & a^7 & 1 & a^{14} & 1 & a^2 & 1 & 0 \end{bmatrix}.$$

From this matrix we solve the equation $Z_{f(\sigma)} \circ P = P \circ N_\sigma$ linearly for $Z_{f(\sigma)}$, recovering in matrix form

$$\mathbf{Z}_{f(\sigma)} = \begin{bmatrix} a^8 & a & 0 & a & a^{11} & 0 & 0 & a & a^{14} \\ a^4 & a^7 & a^7 & a^{14} & a^{13} & 0 & a^{11} & 0 & a^{14} \\ a^7 & a^{11} & a^8 & a^{13} & a^2 & a & a^{12} & 1 & a \\ a & a^{12} & a^{13} & a^8 & a^2 & a^{10} & a & 0 & a^9 \\ a^3 & a^4 & a^{14} & a^6 & a^6 & a^6 & a^{13} & a^6 & a^5 \\ a^3 & a^{11} & a^{11} & a^{14} & a^6 & a^9 & a^2 & a^{10} & a^{11} \\ a^{13} & a^4 & a^{13} & a^{10} & a^7 & a^{14} & a^{11} & 1 & 0 \\ 0 & 0 & 1 & 0 & a^6 & a^{13} & a^2 & a^8 & a^{12} \\ a^6 & 0 & a^3 & 1 & a^{10} & a^{11} & a^8 & a^6 & 0 \end{bmatrix}.$$

We next recover a random root of the minimal polynomial of $\mathbf{N}_\sigma$,

$$\tau = ab^8 + b^7 + a^{12}b^6 + a^7b^5 + a^3b^4 + a^3b^3 + b^2 + a^2b + a^8,$$

and solve the linear systems

$$\widehat{\mathbf{U}}\mathbf{N}_\sigma = \mathbf{M}_\tau\widehat{\mathbf{U}} \quad \text{and} \quad \mathbf{Z}_{f(\sigma)}\widehat{\mathbf{T}} = \widehat{\mathbf{T}}\mathbf{M}_{f(\tau)},$$

where $\mathbf{M}_\tau$ and $\mathbf{M}_{f(\tau)}$ are the left multiplication matrices for τ and $f(\tau)$, respectively. We recover the two matrices

$$
\widehat{\mathbf{U}} = \begin{bmatrix}
a^7 & 0 & a^5 & a^3 & a^8 & a^6 & a^{14} & a^{12} & a^{10} \\
1 & a^{10} & a^3 & a & a^{11} & a^3 & a^6 & a^{12} & a^{10} \\
a^{10} & a^{11} & a^5 & a^{11} & a^8 & a^{13} & 1 & a^4 & a^3 \\
a^{12} & a^5 & a^4 & a^7 & a^4 & a^5 & a^6 & a & a^{11} \\
a^5 & a^{11} & a^{13} & a^5 & a^4 & a^8 & a & a^{13} & a \\
0 & a^8 & a^{12} & a^{12} & a & a^{13} & a^6 & a^5 & 1 \\
a^{14} & a^9 & a^{10} & a^7 & a^6 & a^3 & a^7 & a^8 & a \\
a^3 & a^{11} & a^{11} & a^{13} & a^3 & a^{10} & a^{10} & a^{13} & a^{11} \\
1 & a^3 & a^9 & a^{13} & a^4 & 1 & a^3 & a^{14} & a^9
\end{bmatrix}, \widehat{\mathbf{T}} = \begin{bmatrix}
a^{12} & 0 & a^2 & a^{10} & a^6 & a^6 & a^{10} & 0 & a^{14} \\
a^6 & a^{12} & a^2 & a^{14} & 1 & 0 & a^8 & a^6 & a \\
a^{14} & a^8 & a^{13} & a^4 & a^5 & a^9 & a^{13} & a & a^7 \\
a^3 & 0 & a^{10} & a^{11} & 0 & a^2 & a^{11} & a^{14} & a^6 \\
1 & a & a^7 & 0 & a^5 & a^5 & a^2 & a^3 & a^7 \\
a & a^{14} & a^2 & a^{11} & a^5 & a^2 & 1 & 1 & a^{10} \\
a & a^{10} & a^7 & a^{13} & a^{14} & 0 & a^6 & a^3 & 1 \\
a^{13} & a^{12} & a & a^3 & a^{11} & a^9 & a^{12} & 0 & a^5 \\
a^{10} & a^4 & a^6 & a^8 & a^{10} & a^5 & a^{10} & a^4 & a^{11}
\end{bmatrix}.
$$

We construct $\widehat{F} = \widehat{T}^{-1} \circ P \circ \widehat{U}^{-1}$, which is not only isomorphic to F but also multiplicative. Finally, we randomly select $\mathbf{x}' = \begin{bmatrix} a^2 & a^8 & a^2 & a^{10} & a^{14} & a^6 & a^2 & 1 & a \end{bmatrix}$, set $\mathbf{y}' = \widehat{F}(\mathbf{x}')$, and compute $\mathbf{U}' = \mathbf{M}_{\mathbf{x}'}^{-1}\widehat{\mathbf{U}}$ and $\mathbf{T}' = \widehat{\mathbf{T}}\mathbf{M}_{\mathbf{y}'}$ recovering

$$
\mathbf{U}' = \begin{bmatrix}
a^{12} & a^9 & a^3 & a^4 & a^2 & a^{11} & a^9 & a^{11} & a^{11} \\
a & a^{12} & a^9 & a^{11} & a^{10} & a^5 & a^7 & a^7 & a^2 \\
a^7 & a^{13} & a^{11} & a & a^4 & 1 & a^{10} & a^{10} & a^2 \\
a^{10} & a^{10} & a^3 & a^9 & a^{10} & a^5 & a & a^3 & a^7 \\
a^5 & a^4 & a^3 & 0 & a^4 & a & a^{11} & a & a^{13} \\
a^{13} & a^8 & a^2 & a^5 & a^6 & 1 & a & a^{13} & a^{10} \\
1 & a^{11} & a^7 & a^{11} & a^{10} & a^6 & a & a^9 & a^{11} \\
a^7 & a^9 & a^9 & 1 & a^3 & a^9 & a^2 & a^{14} & a \\
a^{13} & a & a^{10} & a^7 & a^2 & a^4 & a^5 & a^3 & a^{12}
\end{bmatrix}, \mathbf{T}' = \begin{bmatrix}
a^5 & a^{14} & 0 & a^{10} & a^{10} & a^2 & a^9 & 0 & 0 \\
a & a^{10} & a^{13} & a^{10} & a^6 & a^{11} & a^9 & a & a^{12} \\
a^2 & a^3 & 1 & a^{14} & a^{13} & a^3 & a^4 & a^6 & a^7 \\
a^{14} & a^6 & a^8 & a^{14} & a^4 & a^8 & a^{14} & a^4 & a^{13} \\
a^{10} & 0 & a^{12} & a^5 & 0 & a^{13} & a^5 & a^7 & a^2 \\
0 & a^{10} & a^2 & a^9 & a^7 & a^6 & a^{11} & 0 & a^7 \\
a^{11} & a^{13} & a^{11} & a^{10} & 0 & a^8 & a & a^4 & 1 \\
a^{11} & 0 & a^6 & 1 & a^9 & a^{13} & a^6 & a^4 & a \\
a^{10} & a^{14} & a^5 & a^5 & 1 & a^6 & a^3 & a^5 & a^{10}
\end{bmatrix}.
$$

The public key now satisfies $P = T' \circ \widehat{F} \circ U'$.

References

1. Matsumoto, T., Imai, H.: Public quadratic polynomial-tuples for efficient signature-verification and message-encryption. In: Barstow, D., et al. (eds.) EUROCRYPT 1988. LNCS, vol. 330, pp. 419–453. Springer, Heidelberg (1988). https://doi.org/10.1007/3-540-45961-8_39

2. Shor, P.W.: Polynomial-time algorithms for prime factorization and discrete logarithms on a quantum computer. SIAM J. Sci. Stat. Comput. **26**, 1484 (1997)

3. Group, C.T.: Submission requirements and evaluation criteria for the post-quantum cryptography standardization process. NIST CSRC (2016). http://csrc.nist.gov/groups/ST/post-quantum-crypto/documents/call-for-proposals-final-dec-2016.pdf

4. Patarin, J.: Cryptanalysis of the matsumoto and imai public key scheme of Eurocrypt'88. In: Coppersmith, D. (ed.) CRYPTO 1995. LNCS, vol. 963, pp. 248–261. Springer, Heidelberg (1995). https://doi.org/10.1007/3-540-44750-4_20

5. Patarin, J.: The oil and vinegar algorithm for signatures. Presented at the Dagstuhl Workshop on Cryptography (1997)

6. Kipnis, A., Patarin, J., Goubin, L.: Unbalanced oil and vinegar signature schemes. In: Stern, J. (ed.) EUROCRYPT 1999. LNCS, vol. 1592, pp. 206–222. Springer, Heidelberg (1999). https://doi.org/10.1007/3-540-48910-X_15

7. Patarin, J.: Hidden fields equations (HFE) and isomorphisms of polynomials (IP): two new families of asymmetric algorithms. In: Maurer, U. (ed.) EUROCRYPT 1996. LNCS, vol. 1070, pp. 33–48. Springer, Heidelberg (1996). https://doi.org/10.1007/3-540-68339-9_4

8. Patarin, J., Goubin, L., Courtois, N.: C^*_{-+} and HM: variations around two schemes of T. Matsumoto and H. Imai. In: Ohta, K., Pei, D. (eds.) ASIACRYPT 1998. LNCS, vol. 1514, pp. 35–50. Springer, Heidelberg (1998). https://doi.org/10.1007/3-540-49649-1_4

9. Patarin, J., Courtois, N., Goubin, L.: FLASH, a fast multivariate signature algorithm. In: Naccache, D. (ed.) CT-RSA 2001. LNCS, vol. 2020, pp. 298–307. Springer, Heidelberg (2001). https://doi.org/10.1007/3-540-45353-9_22

10. Kipnis, A., Shamir, A.: Cryptanalysis of the HFE public key cryptosystem by relinearization. In: Wiener, M. (ed.) CRYPTO 1999. LNCS, vol. 1666, pp. 19–30. Springer, Heidelberg (1999). https://doi.org/10.1007/3-540-48405-1_2

11. Faugère, J.-C., Joux, A.: Algebraic cryptanalysis of hidden field equation (HFE) cryptosystems using Gröbner bases. In: Boneh, D. (ed.) CRYPTO 2003. LNCS, vol. 2729, pp. 44–60. Springer, Heidelberg (2003). https://doi.org/10.1007/978-3-540-45146-4_3

12. Felke, P.: On the security of biquadratic C^* public-key cryptosystems and its generalizations. Cryptogr. Commun. **11**(3), 427–442 (2018). https://doi.org/10.1007/s12095-018-0337-y

13. Smith-Tone, D.: Multivariate Cryptography. ProQuest (2010)

14. Dobbertin, H., Faugère, J., Felke, P.: Mystery twister crypto challenge 11 (2005). https://www-polsys.lip6.fr/jcf/Papers/CC11_twister.pdf

15. Ding, J., Petzoldt, A., Wang, L.: The cubic simple matrix encryption scheme. [25], pp. 76–87

16. Porras, J., Baena, J., Ding, J.: ZHFE, a new multivariate public key encryption scheme. [25], pp. 229–245

17. Cabarcas, D., Smith-Tone, D., Verbel, J.A.: Key recovery attack for ZHFE. In: Lange, T., Takagi, T. (eds.) PQCrypto 2017. LNCS, vol. 10346, pp. 289–308. Springer, Cham (2017). https://doi.org/10.1007/978-3-319-59879-6_17

18. Moody, D., Perlner, R., Smith-Tone, D.: Key recovery attack on the cubic ABC simple matrix multivariate encryption scheme. In: Avanzi, R., Heys, H. (eds.) SAC 2016. LNCS, vol. 10532, pp. 543–558. Springer, Cham (2017). https://doi.org/10.1007/978-3-319-69453-5_29

19. Baena, J., Cabarcas, D., Escudero, D.E., Khathuria, K., Verbel, J.: Rank analysis of cubic multivariate cryptosystems. In: Lange, T., Steinwandt, R. (eds.) PQCrypto 2018. LNCS, vol. 10786, pp. 355–374. Springer, Cham (2018). https://doi.org/10.1007/978-3-319-79063-3_17

20. Dubois, V., Fouque, P.-A., Shamir, A., Stern, J.: Practical cryptanalysis of SFLASH. In: Menezes, A. (ed.) CRYPTO 2007. LNCS, vol. 4622, pp. 1–12. Springer, Heidelberg (2007). https://doi.org/10.1007/978-3-540-74143-5_1

21. Smith-Tone, D.: On the differential security of multivariate public key cryptosystems. In: Yang, B.-Y. (ed.) PQCrypto 2011. LNCS, vol. 7071, pp. 130–142. Springer, Heidelberg (2011). https://doi.org/10.1007/978-3-642-25405-5_9

22. Bosma, W., Cannon, J., Playoust, C.: The Magma algebra system. I. The user language. J. Symb. Comput. **24**, 235–265 (1997). Computational algebra and number theory, London (1993)

23. Ding, J.: A new variant of the Matsumoto-Imai cryptosystem through perturbation. In: Bao, F., Deng, R., Zhou, J. (eds.) PKC 2004. LNCS, vol. 2947, pp. 305–318. Springer, Heidelberg (2004). https://doi.org/10.1007/978-3-540-24632-9_22

24. Smith-Tone, D.: Properties of the discrete differential with cryptographic applications. In: Sendrier, N. (ed.) PQCrypto 2010. LNCS, vol. 6061, pp. 1–12. Springer, Heidelberg (2010). https://doi.org/10.1007/978-3-642-12929-2_1
25. Mosca, M. (ed.): PQCrypto 2014. LNCS, vol. 8772. Springer, Cham (2014). https://doi.org/10.1007/978-3-319-11659-4

A Rank Attack Against Extension Field Cancellation

Daniel Smith-Tone[1,2]($\boxtimes$) and Javier Verbel[3]

[1] National Institute of Standards and Technology, Gaithersburg, USA
daniel.smith@nist.gov
[2] University of Louisville, Louisville, USA
[3] Universidad Nacional de Colombia, Bogotá, Colombia
javerbel@unal.edu.co

Abstract. Extension Field Cancellation (EFC) is a multivariate-based primitive for encryption proposed by Szepieniec, Ding and Preneel in 2016. They claim to provide 80 bits of security for all the proposed variants and parameters. In this paper, we develop a rigorous security analysis and show that none of the proposed variants archive the claimed security levels. While the Joux-Vitse algorithm can perform message recovery on the variants $\mathrm{EFC}_p^-(2, 83, 10)$ and $\mathrm{EFC}_{pt^2}^-(2, 83, 8)$ in less than 2^{80} bit operations, we offer a new key recovery technique based on MinRank that can break the last proposed variant $\mathrm{EFC}_p^-(3, 59, 6)$ with complexity 2^{73}. We also introduce a new technique based on a *spectral decomposition* with respect to a subfield to recover the first half of the isomorphism of polynomials in $\mathrm{EFC}_p^-(q, n, a)$, when $a = 0, 1$. This technique is of independent interest.

Keywords: Multivariate cryptography · EFC · Discrete differential · MinRank

1 Introduction

In the last few years we have seen more focus in cryptography shift towards the development and analysis of post-quantum cryptosystems. Such systems do not rely on the common constructions involving factoring and computing discrete logarithms that are rendered insecure by Shor's algorithm, see [33]. This shift in focus is due to a combination of factors including the ongoing standardization efforts of the European Telecommunications Standards Institute (ETSI) and the National Institute of Standards and Technology (NIST) as well as an increase in attention and investment from large industry players.

Several subdisciplines have emerged in the field of post-quantum cryptography that seem particularly suited to various security applications. The most

J. Verbel—This work was performed with the support of the University of Louisville facilities.

J. Ding and J.-P. Tillich (Eds.): PQCrypto 2020, LNCS 12100, pp. 381–401, 2020.
https://doi.org/10.1007/978-3-030-44223-1_21

developed of these areas include code-based, lattice-base, and multivariate cryptography as well as isogeny-based key exchange and hash-based signatures. Each of these arenas has strengths and weaknesses in terms of theory and performance.

One of these areas, multivariate cryptography, seems particularly well-suited for digital signatures. There are several schemes with a fairly long and fairly stable history, see, for example, [6,8,9,22,30]. In contrast, multivariate encryption schemes have a much shorter life expectancy. Several of the earlier schemes were broken with practical attacks, including, for example, cryptosystems such as C^*, HFE, STS and PMI, see [10,15,17,28,41].

In the last five years or so a new methodology has begun to be used for constructing multivariate encryption schemes. While the earlier cryptosystems tried to use maps that were nearly permutations, in the sense that it is difficult to find collisions or an element in the codomain that is not in the range, this newer class of cryptosystem attempts to created efficiently invertible maps merely under the condition that they are statistically injective. Since there is much more freedom in accomplishing this task by making the codomain much larger than the domain, the hope is that we can find a family of such functions providing security and efficiency.

Several schemes have been proposed following this paradigm including the Simple Matrix Encryption Scheme, ZHFE, SRP, HFERP, EFLASH and Extension Field Cancellation (EFC), see [7,12,20,35–37,42]. Unfortunately a few of these have fallen victim to attacks that either break the scheme or make it require reparameterization, see [1,5,24–26,31]. Thus we are left to wonder whether multivariate schemes are suitable for encryption.

In this article we strike another blow to multivariate encryption. We show that none of the parameters proposed for EFC in [35] are secure.

While the claims of 80-bit security for the characteristic 2 parameters of EFC were dubious even considering known techniques at the time, we now have solid evidence that the Joux-Vitse algorithm, see [21], can break the characteristic 2 parameters of EFC in well less than 2^{80} bit operations, cf. [27, Section 5.2].

Our main contribution is the development of a new Minrank attack on the EFC encryption scheme. While the characteristic 2 parameters broken by Joux-Vitse have sufficiently high rank, we are able to break the odd characteristic parameters convincingly. This advancement is due to a careful derivation of the Q-rank of the public key (the minimum rank as a quadratic form over the extension field in the span of the public key) as well as in large part to the advancement in techniques recently accomplished in [39]. We are able to show that the rank of the public key is $2\lceil \frac{a+1}{2} \rceil$ and, in conjunction with new techniques for solving Minrank, that the complexity of the Minrank attack on EFC is much smaller than expected.

In addition, we introduce a new cryptanalysis technique of independent interest. We call this technique subfield spectral decomposition because it uses the spectral decomposition of an operator derived from the public key, which is linear over an extension field, to apply a function linear over the subfield to the operator revealing its special structure. The technique seems useful in deriving maps over an extension field of a particular shape in contexts where there is not enough information to derive them linearly.

The paper is organized as follows. In Sect. 2, we establish notation and introduce EFC. In the following section we introduce the Minrank problem, a modeling of the problem and the concept of superdetermined instances. In Sect. 4, we present a new rank analysis showing that EFC has low rank. We next present our complete key recovery technique. Then, in Sect. 6, we derive a complexity estimate for our attack, showing that EFC does not achieve its claimed security levels. Finally we conclude, reflecting on the status of multivariate encryption.

2 Preliminaries

Let $\mathbb{F}_q$ be a field with q elements, $\mathbb{F}^n$ and $\mathbb{F}_q^{n \times n}$ the sets of row vectors and of square matrices over $\mathbb{F}_q$ of size n, respectively. Throughout the article $\mathbb{E}$ denotes a degree n extension field of $\mathbb{F}_q$, and $\varphi : \mathbb{F}_q^n \to \mathbb{E}$ the natural vector space isomorphism.

Suppose $g(x) \in \mathbb{F}_q[x]$ is the irreducible polynomial of degree n such that $\mathbb{E} \cong \mathbb{F}_q(x)/\langle g(x) \rangle$. Given a root $b \in \mathbb{E}$ of $g(x)$, the following matrix

$$\mathbf{M} = \begin{pmatrix} 1 & 1 & \cdots & 1 \\ b & b^q & \cdots & b^{q^{n-1}} \\ b^2 & b^{2q} & \cdots & b^{2q^{n-1}} \\ \vdots & & \ddots & \vdots \\ b^{n-1} & b^{(n-1)q} & \cdots & b^{(n-1)q^{n-1}} \end{pmatrix}$$

is invertible, and can be used to compute and to invert the map φ. Given $A \in \mathbb{E}$ we have $\varphi^{-1}(A) = \left(A, A^q, \ldots, A^{q^{n-1}} \right) \mathbf{M}^{-1}$, and for any $\mathbf{a} = (a_1, a_2, \ldots, a_n) \in \mathbb{F}_q^n$ we have $\varphi(\mathbf{a}) = a_1 + a_2 b + \cdots + a_n b^{n-1}$, which is the first coordinate of the vector $\mathbf{aM}$.

2.1 The Basic EFC Encryption Scheme

In this section we describe the basic version of the Extension Field Cancellation encryption scheme of [35].

Suppose $\mathbf{A} \in \mathbb{F}_q^{n \times n}$ is a random matrix and $\mathbf{x} = (x_1, x_2, \ldots, x_n)$ are variables over $\mathbb{F}_q$. Let $\alpha : \mathbb{F}_q^n \to \mathbb{E}$ be the linear map given by $\alpha(\mathbf{x}) = \varphi(\mathbf{xA})$, and $\alpha_m \in \mathbb{F}_q^{n \times n}$ be the matrix representing the map $\mathbf{a} \mapsto \varphi^{-1}(\alpha(\mathbf{x})\varphi(\mathbf{a}))$ in the standard basis.

The central map in basic EFC is given by the following function

$$\mathcal{F} : \mathbb{F}_q^n \to \mathbb{F}_q^{2n} : \mathbf{x} \mapsto (\mathbf{x} \cdot \alpha_m(\mathbf{x}), \mathbf{x} \cdot \beta_m(\mathbf{x})),$$

where similarly β_m is the $\mathbb{F}_q$-linear map representing multiplication by $\beta(\mathbf{x})$, and $\beta(\mathbf{x}) = \varphi(\mathbf{xB})$ for a given matrix $\mathbf{B} \in \mathbb{F}_q^{n \times n}$.

Given an image $(\mathbf{d}_1, \mathbf{d}_2)$ of $\mathcal{F}$, we can find a preimage $\mathbf{x}_0$ by solving for $\mathbf{x}$ the following system of n linear equations

$$\mathbf{d}_1 \beta_m(\mathbf{x}) - \mathbf{d}_2 \alpha_m(\mathbf{x}) = \mathbf{0}. \tag{1}$$

Hence the complexity of decryption is at most $O\left(n^{2.8}\right)$ $\mathbb{F}_q$ operations.

The public key in the basic version of EFC is a sequence of $2n$ quadratic polynomials in n variables given by

$$P(\mathbf{x}) = T \circ \mathcal{F} \circ U(\mathbf{x}),$$

where $T : \mathbb{F}_q^{2n} \to \mathbb{F}_q^{2n}$, $U : \mathbb{F}_q^n \to \mathbb{F}_q^n$ are invertible affine maps. The private key is the tuple of matrices over $\mathbb{F}_q$ given by $(\alpha_m(\mathbf{x}), \beta_m(\mathbf{x}), T, U)$.

As described in the original paper, the basic EFC is insecure. We can efficiently perform several attacks, such as a linearization attack [29], a Minrank attack [23] and a direct algebraic attack. Thus some modifications are applied to the basic version to boost the security of EFC while keeping good levels of efficiency. For space reasons, we discuss these modifications in Appendix A.

3   Minrank

In this section we introduce the well-known Minrank problem. We define a particular kind of Minrank instance typically arising in multivariate cryptography. A particular feature of these instances is that the given matrices are restricted to be over the base field $\mathbb{F}_q$, while the solution coefficients are allowed to be in the extension field $\mathbb{E}$.

Definition 1 (Minrank Problem). *Given an integer r and a set of m square matrices $M_1, M_2, \ldots, M_m \in \mathbb{F}_q^{n \times n}$. Find a nonzero vector $(x_1, x_2, \ldots, x_m) \in \mathbb{E}^m$ satisfying*

$$\mathsf{Rank}\left(\sum_{i=1}^{m} x_i M_i\right) \le r.$$

The hardness of this problem has a direct implication in the security of many multivariate and code-based schemes [2,5,18,19,23,38]. Nowdays the most efficient models to solve the Minrank problem are known as: minors modeling [16], linear algebra search [3,19], and KS modeling [23]. Here we introduce only KS modeling because it provides the best complexity against Minrank problem instances arising in this context, see [39].

3.1   KS Modeling

The KS model was introduced by Kipnis and Shamir in [23]. The technique exploits the fact that a low rank matrix must have a high dimensional right kernel. We may generically apply the following assumption: there is a Minrank solution $(a_1, a_2, \ldots, a_m) \in \mathbb{E}^m$ such that the column space of the resulting linear combination is generated by its r rightmost columns. Thus such a solution can be found by solving the following system of bilinear equations

$$
\left(\sum_{i=1}^{m} x_i \mathbf{M}_i\right)
\begin{pmatrix}
1 & 0 & \cdots & & 0 \\
0 & 1 & \cdots & & 0 \\
 & & \ddots & & \\
0 & 0 & \cdots & & 1 \\
k_1 & k_{r+1} & \cdots & k_{r(\kappa-1)+1} \\
k_2 & k_{r+2} & \cdots & k_{r(\kappa-1)+1)} \\
 & & \ddots & & \\
k_r & k_{2r} & \cdots & & k_{r\kappa}
\end{pmatrix}
= \mathbf{0},
\tag{2}
$$

where $\kappa = n - r$. The k_i variables are called *kernel variables* and x_i variables are called *linear variables*. We refer to the two matrices on the left hand side of Eq. (2) as the *target matrix* and the *kernel matrix*, respectively.

3.2   Superdetermined Instances

A square Minrank instance with m matrices of size $n \times n$ and target rank r is called *superdetemined* if $m < n \cdot r$. The complexity of solving superdetermined instances is studied by Verbel et al. in [39]. There it is shown that one may use fewer variables in the KS modeling and solve it using an XL-like algorithm that only multiplies by kernel variables. When the instances are chosen uniformly at random, only $\frac{m}{n-r} < \kappa < n-r$ column vectors of the kernel matrix are required to expect non-spurious solutions. Furthermore, everytime $\kappa \geq d_{KS} + 1$, the first fall degree of such systems is bounded by $d_{KS} + 2$, where

$$
d_{KS} = \min\left\{ d \mid n\binom{r}{d} > m\binom{r}{d+1} \right\}.
$$

Here we use the first fall degree as our estimation of the solving degree, which is the maximum degree required in the Gröbner basis computation. We expect that as long as the system is overdetermined and generic enough, the solving degree is in general no more than one more than the first degree fall, see [39].

Hence, to solve superdetermined instances of the Minrank problem, we need only solve a sparse linear system involving a matrix over $\mathbb{F}_q$ of size

$$
O\left(m\binom{r\kappa + d_{KS}}{d_{KS} + 1}\right) \times O\left(m\binom{r\kappa + d_{KS}}{d_{KS} + 1}\right),
$$

with at most $m(r+1)$ nonzero entries in each row. Sparse systems of linear equations of the form $\mathbf{xA} = \mathbf{b}$, where $\mathbf{A} \in \mathbb{F}_q^{r_a \times c_a}$ and $\mathbf{b} \in \mathbb{F}_q^{r_a}$, can be solved by using Wiedemann's algorithm [40]. Provided that a solution exists, this algorithm finds a solution by performing an expected number of $O\left(n_0(\omega + n_1 \log_2 n_1) \log n_1\right)$ multiplications in $\mathbb{F}_q$, where ω is the number of nonzero entries in $\mathbf{A}$, where

$n_0 = \min\{r_a, c_a\}$ and where $n_1 = \max\{r_a, c_a\}$, see [40, Section IV]. Consequently, the complexity of solving superdetermined Minrank instances is given by

$$O\left(m^3(r+1)\binom{r\kappa + d_{KS}}{d_{KS}+1}^2\right),$$

where $\kappa \geq \min\left\{\frac{m}{n-r}, d_{KS}+1\right\}$ is the number of vectors involved in the KS modeling; see [39] for more details.

4 Rank Analysis

In this section, we derive the rank of the public key of the basic EFC scheme as well as the modified versions EFC^- and EFC_p^-.

4.1 Rank of Basic EFC

Recall that the core function in basic EFC is the concatenation of two maps $\mathbf{x}\alpha_m(\mathbf{x})$ and $\mathbf{x}\beta_m(\mathbf{x})$, where $\alpha_m(\mathbf{x})$ and $\beta_m(\mathbf{x})$ are both matrices $\mathbb{F}_q^{n\times n}$ representing the multiplication by $\alpha(\mathbf{x})$ and $\beta(\mathbf{x})$, respectively.

First, note that the map $\alpha(\mathbf{x}) = \varphi(\mathbf{x}A)$ can be written as $\sum_{j=0}^{n-1} a_j X^{q^j}$, where $X = \varphi(\mathbf{x})$ and $a_j \in \mathbb{E}$ for $j = 0, 1, \ldots, n-1$. Similarly, $\beta(\mathbf{x}) = \sum_{j=0}^{n-1} b_j X^{q^j}$. Thus the public key in the basic version of EFC is the sequence of polynomials given by the following composition

$$P(\mathbf{x}) = T \circ \varphi_2^{-1} \circ (\mathcal{F}_1, \mathcal{F}_2) \circ \varphi \circ U(\mathbf{x}),$$

where $\mathcal{F}_1(X) = \sum_{j=0}^{n-1} a_j X^{q^j+1}$ and $\mathcal{F}_2(X) = \sum_{j=0}^{n-1} b_j X^{q^j+1}$ are functions in $\mathbb{E}$, where $\varphi_2^{-1}(X_0, X_1) = (\varphi^{-1}(X_0), \varphi^{-1}(X_1))$, and where φ, T and U are as before.

Over a field $\mathbb{E}$ of odd characteristic, the map $\mathcal{F}_1$ is represented by the rank 2 symmetric matrix $\mathbf{F}_1 \in \mathbb{E}^{n\times n}$ such that $\mathbf{F}_1[1,1] = a_0$, and for $j = 1, \ldots, n-1$, we have $\mathbf{F}_1[j+1,1] = \mathbf{F}_1[1,j+1] = a_j/2$. Similarly, the map $\mathcal{F}_2$ is represented by a rank 2 symmetric matrix $\mathbf{F}_2 \in \mathbb{E}^{n\times n}$. (In the characteristic 2 case, we use the symmetric representation, $\mathbf{F}_1[1,1] = 0$ and $\mathbf{F}_1[j+1,1] = \mathbf{F}_1[1,j+1] = a_j$ for $j \in \{1, \ldots, n-1\}$, as first suggested in [23].)

For $i = 1, 2$ and $j = 0, \ldots, n-1$, the j-th *Frobenius power* of $\mathcal{F}_i$ is the polynomial $\mathcal{F}_i^{q^j}$. Analogous to the previous discussion, in any characteristic, the map $\mathcal{F}_i^{q^j}$ can be represented by a rank 2 symmetric matrix in $\mathbb{E}^{n\times n}$. We denote the matrix representing the Frobenius power $\mathcal{F}_i^{q^j}$ by $\mathbf{F}_i^{*j}$.[1]

---

[1] In block form $(\mathbf{P}_1, \ldots, \mathbf{P}_{2n}) = (\mathbf{G}_1, \ldots, \mathbf{G}_n, \mathbf{G}_1', \ldots, \mathbf{G}_n')\left[\left(\left[\mathbf{I}_2 \otimes \mathbf{M}^{-1}\right]\mathbf{T}\right) \otimes \mathbf{I}_n\right]$, where $\otimes$ denotes the Kronecker product; i.e., $\mathbf{P}_i = \sum_{k=1}^n (s_k \mathbf{G}_k + t_k \mathbf{G}_k')$ for $i = 1, \ldots, 2n$, where $(s_1, \ldots, s_n, t_1, \ldots, t_n)^\top$ is the i-th column of $\left[\mathbf{I}_2 \otimes \mathbf{M}^{-1}\right]\mathbf{T}$.

For simplicity suppose that both T and U are homogeneous linear maps and let $\mathbf{T}$ and $\mathbf{U}$ denote the matrices representing T and U, respectively. Reasoning as in the proof of [5, Theorem 1], we have

$$(\mathbf{P}_1, \dots, \mathbf{P}_{2n}) = (\mathbf{G}_1, \dots, \mathbf{G}_n, \mathbf{G}_1', \dots, \mathbf{G}_n') \left[\mathbf{I}_2 \otimes \mathbf{M}^{-1}\right] \mathbf{T}, \tag{3}$$

where $\mathbf{G}_{j+1} = \mathbf{W}\mathbf{F}_1^{*j}\mathbf{W}^\top$, $\mathbf{G}_{j+1}' = \mathbf{W}\mathbf{F}_2^{*j}\mathbf{W}^\top$ for $j = 0, \dots, n-1$ and $\mathbf{W} = \mathbf{U}\mathbf{M}$. Thus for any column $(r_1, r_2, \dots, r_{2n})^\top$ of $\mathbf{T}^{-1}\left[\mathbf{I}_2 \otimes \mathbf{M}\right]$ we have

$$\mathrm{Rank}\left(\sum_{i=1}^{2n} r_i \mathbf{P}_i\right) \le 2. \tag{4}$$

That is, for each basic EFC public key, there is a linear combination of the matrices in the public key having rank less than or equal to 2.

4.2 Rank Analysis for EFC_p^-

In this section we show the existence of at least one rank $2 \lceil \frac{a+1}{2} \rceil$ matrix in the span of any set of symmetric matrices representing the polynomials in a $\mathrm{EFC}_p^-(q, n, a)$ public key. We first show this holds for any $\mathrm{EFC}^-(q, n, a)$ public key, and then we show this holds even if we add the projection modifier.

An $\mathrm{EFC}^-(q, n, a)$ public key $P_a = (p_1, p_2, \dots, p_{2n-a})$ is the output of the minus modifier applied to the basic EFC public key $P = (p_1, p_2, \dots, p_{2n})$. By Eq. (3) we have

$$(\mathbf{P}_1, \dots, \mathbf{P}_{2n}) = (\mathbf{G}_1, \dots, \mathbf{G}_n, \mathbf{G}_1', \dots, \mathbf{G}_n') \mathbf{R}_a, \tag{5}$$

where $\mathbf{G}_{j+1} = \mathbf{W}\mathbf{F}_1^{*j}\mathbf{W}^\top$ and $\mathbf{G}_{j+1}' = \mathbf{W}\mathbf{F}_2^{*j}\mathbf{W}^\top$ for $j = 0, \dots, n-1$, $\mathbf{R}_a$ is the submatrix of $\left[\mathbf{I}_2 \otimes \mathbf{M}^{-1}\right]\mathbf{T}$ formed by its first $2n - a$ columns.

Let $a_2 = \lceil \frac{a}{2} \rceil$ and let $a_1 = a - a_2$. If the $(2n - a) \times (2n - a)$ submatrix $\mathbf{R}'$ of $\mathbf{R}_a$ consisting of rows $n - a_1 + 1$ through n and $2n - a_2 + 1$ through $2n$ is invertible, then there is a sequence of column operations $E_1, E_2, \dots, E_\ell$ such that when applied to $\mathbf{R}_a$ we obtain a matrix of the form

$$\tilde{\mathbf{R}}_a = \left(\begin{array}{c|c} \mathbf{C} & \\ \hline \begin{array}{c} \mathbf{I}_{n-a_1} \\ \hline \mathbf{D} \end{array} & \mathbf{0}_{(n-a_1)\times(n-a_2)} \\ \hline \mathbf{0}_{(n-a_2)\times(n-a_1)} & \mathbf{I}_{n-a_2} \end{array}\right),$$

where $\mathbf{0}_{e \times t}$ denotes a zero matrix of size $e \times t$ and $\mathbf{C}, \mathbf{D}$ are matrices over $\mathbb{E}$ of size $a_1 \times (2n - a)$ and $a_2 \times (2n - a)$, respectively.

The matrix $\mathbf{R}'$ is derived from the product of the $(2n - a) \times 2n$ submatrix $\mathbf{M}'$ of $\left[\mathbf{I}_2 \otimes \mathbf{M}^{-1}\right]$ consisting of rows $n - a_1 + 1$ through n and $2n - a_2 + 1$ through $2n$ with the submatrix $\mathbf{T}'$ consisting of the first $2n - a$ columns of $\mathbf{T}$. Thus $\mathbf{R}'$ is invertible if the right kernel of $\mathbf{M}'$ intersects the column space of $\mathbf{T}'$ trivially. Random subspaces of $\mathbb{E}^{2n}$ of dimension a and $2n - a$ intersect trivially with high probability; given the extra constraint that there is a basis for the column space of $\mathbf{T}'$ whose components lie in $\mathbb{F}_q$, we thus conclude that $\mathbf{R}'$ is invertible with probability close to 1.

Let $\mathbf{E}_1, \mathbf{E}_2, \ldots, \mathbf{E}_\ell$ be the matrices representing the column operations needed to convert $\mathbf{R}_a$ into $\tilde{\mathbf{R}}_a$. If $\mathbf{E} = \mathbf{E}_1 \cdot \mathbf{E}_2 \cdots \mathbf{E}_\ell$, then by Eq. (5) we have

$$(\mathbf{P}_1, \mathbf{P}_2, \ldots, \mathbf{P}_{2n-a})\, \mathbf{E} = (\mathbf{G}_1, \ldots, \mathbf{G}_n, \mathbf{G}'_1, \ldots, \mathbf{G}'_n)\, \tilde{\mathbf{R}}_a.$$

If $(\gamma_1, \gamma_2, \ldots, \gamma_{2n-a})^\top$ denotes the first column in $\mathbf{E}$, then the following equation holds

$$\sum_{i=1}^{2n-a} \gamma_i \mathbf{P}_i = \mathbf{W} \left(\sum_{i=1}^{a_1} c_{1i} \mathbf{F}_1^{*(i-1)} + \mathbf{F}_1^{*a_1} + \sum_{i=1}^{a_2} d_{1i} \mathbf{F}_2^{*(i-1)} \right) \mathbf{W}^\top. \tag{6}$$

And denoting by $(\rho_1, \rho_2, \ldots, \rho_{2n-a})^\top$ the $(n - a_1 + 1)$-th column in $\mathbf{E}$, we have

$$\sum_{i=1}^{2n-a} \rho_i \mathbf{P}_i = \mathbf{W} \left(\sum_{i=1}^{a_1} c_{ki} \mathbf{F}_1^{*(i-1)} + \sum_{i=1}^{a_2} d_{ki} \mathbf{F}_2^{*(i-1)} + \mathbf{F}_2^{*a_2} \right) \mathbf{W}^\top, \tag{7}$$

where $k = n - a_1 + 1$.

Notice that the matrix from Eq. (6) has rank at most $2(a_1 + 1)$ and matrix from Eq. (7) has rank at most $2(a_2 + 1)$. Thus, when the number of removed equations a is even, both matrices have rank $a + 2$. On the other hand, if a is odd, matrix in Eq. (6) has rank $2\lceil \frac{a}{2} \rceil$ and matrix in Eq. (7) has rank $2\lceil \frac{a}{2} \rceil + 2$.

It is clear that the projection modifier does not affect the shape of the basic EFC central maps $\mathcal{F}_1$ and $\mathcal{F}_2$. Thus, projection has no effect on the previous analysis. At this point we have proven the following two theorems. In both theorems we assume q is odd.

Theorem 1. *Suppose $P_1, P_2, \ldots, P_{2n-a}$ are symmetric matrices representing the public quadratic forms of $EFC_p^-(q, n, a)$. Then there exists a nonzero vector $(s_1, s_2, \ldots, s_{2n-a}) \in \mathbb{E}^{2n-a}$ such that*

$$\text{Rank}\left(\sum_{i=1}^{2n-a} s_i P_i \right) \leq 2\left\lceil \frac{a+1}{2} \right\rceil. \tag{8}$$

Theorem 2. *Provided that the parameter a in $EFC_p^-(q, n, a)$ is even, for any sequence $(P_1, P_2, \ldots, P_{2n-a})$ of symmetric matrices representing the public quadratic forms of $EFC_p^-(q, n, a)$, there exist at least two linearly independent vectors $(s_1, s_2, \ldots, s_{2n-a})$, $(s'_1, s'_2, \ldots, s'_{2n-a}) \in \mathbb{E}^{2n-a}$ satisfying Eq. (8).*

5   Full Key Recovery Attack

In this section we demonstrate a full key recovery attack on the $\widehat{EFC}_p^-$ encryption scheme. Similar to previous Minrank attacks [5,23,32,38], given an $\widehat{EFC}_p^-$ public key P, we aim to recover an equivalent key $(T', \mathcal{F}'_1, \mathcal{F}'_2, U')$ satisfying

$$P(\mathbf{x}) = T' \circ \varphi_2^{-1} \circ (\mathcal{F}'_1, \mathcal{F}'_2) \circ \varphi \circ U'(\mathbf{x}).$$

Thoughout the following we abuse language stating that we are recovering the maps $(T, \mathcal{F}_1, \mathcal{F}_2, U)$.

5.1   Recovering First Half of T

By Theorem 1, given an EFC_p^- public key P, the Minrank problem involving the $2n - a$ public matrices and target rank $2\lceil\frac{a+1}{2}\rceil$ has at least one solution. To recover the first half of T, we solve this Minrank problem and we obtain a solution vector $\mathbf{s} \in \mathbb{E}^{2n-a}$. We expand this vector to a vector $\mathbf{t} \in \mathbb{E}^{2n}$ by right concatenation of a randomly chosen elements from $\mathbb{E}$. A matrix representing the first part of our hidden linear map T is then given by $\mathbf{T}_1\mathbf{M}^{-1}$, where $\mathbf{T}_1 \in \mathbb{E}^{2n \times n}$ is the matrix with columns $\mathbf{t}^{(0)}, \ldots, \mathbf{t}^{(n-1)}$, respectively, where $\mathbf{t}^{(i)}$ is the vector $\mathbf{t}$ with all its coordinates raised to the power q^i.

5.2   Recovering U

The step of recovering U varies depending whether $r > 2$ or $r = 2$. In the former case we use a standard technique for such a purpose [2,5,32]. For the latter case we use the new subfield spectral decomposition technique, see Sect. 5.3.

For $r > 2$, after finding a Minrank solution $s = (s_1, s_2 \ldots, s_{2n-a}) \in \mathbb{E}^{2n-a}$ we can build a rank r matrix $\mathbf{L}_1$ given by

$$\mathbf{L}_1 = \sum_{i=1}^{2n-a} s_i \mathbf{P}_i,$$

where $\mathbf{P}_1, \mathbf{P}_2, \ldots, \mathbf{P}_{2n-a}$ are the symmetric matrices representing the polynomials in the EFC_p^- public key P. This matrix has the form of Eq. (6) with probability almost 1. Thus, the first $\frac{r}{2}$ columns $\mathbf{w} = \mathbf{w}^{(0)}, \mathbf{w}^{(1)}, \ldots, \mathbf{w}^{(\frac{r}{2})}$ of the matrix $\mathbf{W}$ belong to the image of $\mathbf{L}_1$. Consequently, by the symmetry of $\mathbf{L}_1$, for $i = 1, 2, \ldots, \frac{r}{2} - 1$ we have $\mathbf{w}^{(i)}\mathbf{K} = \mathbf{0}$, where $\mathbf{K}$ is the right kernel matrix of $\mathbf{L}_1$. In other words, $\mathbf{w}$ is a solution of the system of linear equations $\mathbf{w}\mathbf{K}^{q^{n-i}} = \mathbf{0}$ for any $i = 0, 1, \ldots \frac{r}{2}$. That system of linear equations has $\frac{r}{2}(n - r)$ equations and n variables. As long as $r > 2$ and n is large enough, by solving such a system of linear equations, we can recover $\mathbf{w}$, and thus recover $\mathbf{W}$ and U.

5.3   Spectral Decomposition

In the case that the target rank in a Minrank instance is $r = 2$, i.e. when $a = 0$ or $a = 1$, the system of linear equations defining the first column of the matrix $\mathbf{W}$ is underdefined. In this scenario, we have to consider additional algebraic relations to recover an appropriate basis.

To this end, we develop a technique we call *subfield spectral decomposition*. The spectral decomposition of a linear operator is a very useful tool from the roots of functional calculus, providing a canonical way of generating from the operator new operators with desired properties. In our context, we want to transform a linear operator $\mathbf{L}$ into another operator $\mathbf{F}_1'$ having a special structure, with the added restriction that $\mathbf{F}_1'$ is an $\mathbb{F}_q$-linear function of $\mathbf{L}$. Since any $\mathbb{F}_q$-linear map on $\mathbb{E}^n$ can be represented as a matrix of the form $\mathbf{W} = \mathbf{UM}$, the task of constructing such a $\mathbf{F}_1'$ is equivalent to finding the first column of $\mathbf{W}$.

Given our rank 2 symmetric matrix $\mathbf{L}$, we must show that the first column vector, $\mathbf{w}$, of $\mathbf{W} = \begin{bmatrix} \mathbf{w}^{(0)\top} & \mathbf{w}^{(1)\top} & \cdots & \mathbf{w}^{(n-1)\top} \end{bmatrix}$ is in the span of the nonzero eigenvectors of $\mathbf{L}$. First, note that we expect any Minrank solution to be of the form, $\mathbf{L} = \mathbf{WFW}^\top$, where $\mathbf{F}$ is a symmetric matrix having the shape

$$\mathbf{F} := \begin{bmatrix} a_0 & a_1 & \cdots & a_{n-1} \\ a_1 & 0 & \cdots & 0 \\ \vdots & \vdots & \ddots & \vdots \\ a_{n-1} & 0 & \cdots & 0 \end{bmatrix}.$$

Consider the product

$$\mathbf{WF} = \begin{bmatrix} \sum_{i=0}^{n-1} a_i \mathbf{w}^{(i)\top} & a_1 \mathbf{w}^{(0)\top} & a_2 \mathbf{w}^{(0)\top} & \cdots & a_{n-1} \mathbf{w}^{(0)\top} \end{bmatrix}.$$

For a $\mathbf{v} \in \mathbb{E}^n$, the product $\mathbf{vL}$ corresponds to taking $\mathbf{v}$ times the above matrix and then times $\mathbf{W}^\top$. First we compute $\mathbf{v}$ times the above matrix.

$$\mathbf{vWF} = \begin{bmatrix} \sum_{i=0}^{n-1} a_i \mathbf{vw}^{(i)\top} & a_1 \mathbf{vw}^{(0)\top} & a_2 \mathbf{vw}^{(0)\top} & \cdots & a_{n-1} \mathbf{vw}^{(0)\top} \end{bmatrix}.$$
$$= \begin{bmatrix} \sum_{i=0}^{n-1} a_i \left\langle \mathbf{v}, \mathbf{w}^{(i)} \right\rangle & a_1 \left\langle \mathbf{v}, \mathbf{w}^{(0)} \right\rangle & a_2 \left\langle \mathbf{v}, \mathbf{w}^{(0)} \right\rangle & \cdots & a_{n-1} \left\langle \mathbf{v}, \mathbf{w}^{(0)} \right\rangle \end{bmatrix}$$
$$= \begin{bmatrix} \sum_{i=0}^{n-1} a_i \left\langle \mathbf{v}, \mathbf{w}^{(i)} \right\rangle & 0 & 0 & \cdots & 0 \end{bmatrix} + \left\langle \mathbf{v}, \mathbf{w}^{(0)} \right\rangle \begin{bmatrix} 0 & a_1 & a_2 & \cdots & a_{n-1} \end{bmatrix}.$$

Next, we take this vector and multiply on the right by $\mathbf{W}^\top$ to recover $\mathbf{vL}$. The entire product produces

$$\mathbf{vL} = \left(\sum_{i=0}^{n-1} a_i \left\langle \mathbf{v}, \mathbf{w}^{(i)} \right\rangle \right) \mathbf{w}^{(0)} + \left\langle \mathbf{v}, \mathbf{w}^{(0)} \right\rangle \sum_{i=1}^{n-1} a_i \mathbf{w}^{(i)}. \tag{9}$$

Consider the case that $\mathbf{v}$ is an eigenvector of $\mathbf{L}$. In this case, the right hand side of Eq. (9) is equal to $\lambda_v \mathbf{v}$ for some λ_v in $\mathbb{E}$. Thus if $\lambda_v \neq 0$,

$$\mathbf{v} = \lambda_v^{-1} \left(\sum_{i=0}^{n-1} a_i \left\langle \mathbf{v}, \mathbf{w}^{(i)} \right\rangle \right) \mathbf{w}^{(0)} + \lambda_v^{-1} \left\langle \mathbf{v}, \mathbf{w}^{(0)} \right\rangle \sum_{i=1}^{n-1} a_i \mathbf{w}^{(i)}.$$

It is clear that any such $\mathbf{v}$ is in the span of the two vectors $\mathbf{w}^{(0)}$ and $\sum_{i=1}^{n-1} a_i \mathbf{w}^{(i)}$. Therefore if we have two linearly independent eigenvectors of $\mathbf{L}$ corresponding to nonzero eigenvalues, we recover two necessarily linearly independent linear combinations of these two vectors, and therefore there is a linear combination of the two eigenvectors producing $\mathbf{w} = \mathbf{w}^{(0)}$.

Next, take Eq. (9) and multiply on the right by $\mathbf{v}^\top$. We obtain

$$\mathbf{vLv}^\top = \left(\sum_{i=0}^{n-1} a_i \left\langle \mathbf{v}, \mathbf{w}^{(i)} \right\rangle \right) \left\langle \mathbf{v}, \mathbf{w}^{(0)} \right\rangle + \left\langle \mathbf{v}, \mathbf{w}^{(0)} \right\rangle \sum_{i=1}^{n-1} a_i \left\langle \mathbf{v}, \mathbf{w}^{(i)} \right\rangle. \tag{10}$$

Equation (10) implies two additional facts. First, we learn that $\langle \mathbf{v}, \mathbf{w}^{(0)} \rangle$ is a factor of every coefficient of $\mathbf{v}\mathbf{L}\mathbf{v}^\top$; thus any vector $\mathbf{v}$ that is not in the kernel of $\mathbf{L}$ and is orthogonal to $\mathbf{w}^{(0)}$ is a non-trivial solution of the equation

$$\mathbf{v}\mathbf{L}\mathbf{v}^\top = 0 \tag{11}$$

in *any* characteristic as long as $a_0 \neq 0$. (In the characteristic 2 case, if $a_0 = 0$ every vector $\mathbf{v}$ is a trivial solution.) Moreover, since the rank of $\mathbf{L}$ is two, there is a 1-dimensional solution space of such vectors $\mathbf{v}$. Second, we note that such solutions, being orthogonal to $\mathbf{w}^{(0)}$, satisfy $\mathbf{v}\mathbf{L} = a\mathbf{w}$, where

$$a = \sum_{i=1}^{n-1} a_i \left\langle \mathbf{v}, \mathbf{w}^{(i)} \right\rangle,$$

by Eq. (9). Therefore, once such a vector $\mathbf{v}$ is found, we can recover equivalent matrices for $\mathbf{W}$ and $\mathbf{U}$. Thus, to recover the map U we solve Eq. (11) using the spectral decomposition of some matrix congruent over $\mathbb{F}_q$ to $\mathbf{L}$.

We are attempting to find a vector $\mathbf{w}$ with which we can build an $\mathbb{F}_q$-linear map, so we do not rely on the spectral decomposition of $\mathbf{L}$ over an algebraic closure of $\mathbb{E}$; instead, we require that the eigenvalues of $\mathbf{L}$ lie in $\mathbb{E}$. If $\mathbf{L}$ does not have two distinct nonzero eigenvalues in $\mathbb{E}$, we keep choosing random matrices in $\mathbf{S} \in \mathbb{F}_q^{n \times n}$ until $\mathbf{S}^\top \mathbf{L}\mathbf{S}$ has two distinct eigenvalues. The map $\mathbf{L}$ has such eigenvalues when its minimal polynomial splits in $\mathbb{E}$. Under the heuristic that the minimal polynomials of $\mathbb{F}_q$-congruent symmetric matrices are random subject to the singularity constraint, $\mathbf{L}$ has two distinct nonzero eigenvalues with probability roughly $\frac{1}{r!}$. We have verified this estimate for small r experimentally.

Assume that $\mathbf{L}$ has two distinct nonzero eigenvalues λ_1, λ_2. Let $\mathbf{v}_1$ and $\mathbf{v}_2$ be the eigenvectors corresponding to λ_1 and λ_2, respectively. We find a solution to Eq. (11) by computing

$$\begin{aligned}
0 &= (x\mathbf{v}_1 + \mathbf{v}_2)\, \mathbf{L}\, (x\mathbf{v}_1 + \mathbf{v}_2)^\top \\
&= (x\mathbf{v}_1 + \mathbf{v}_2)\, (\lambda_1 \mathbf{v}_1^\top \mathbf{v}_1 + \lambda_2 \mathbf{v}_2^\top \mathbf{v}_2)\, (x\mathbf{v}_1 + \mathbf{v}_2)^\top \\
&= \lambda_1 x^2 \|\mathbf{v}_1\|^4 + \lambda_2 \|\mathbf{v}_2\|^4.
\end{aligned}$$

Solutions of the above univariate equation are given by

$$x = \pm \left(\frac{-\lambda_2}{\lambda_1} \right)^{\frac{1}{2}} \frac{\|\mathbf{v}_2\|^2}{\|\mathbf{v}_1\|^2}. \tag{12}$$

Finally, we construct $\mathbf{w} = (x\mathbf{v}_1 + \mathbf{v}_2)\mathbf{L}$, recover $\mathbf{W}$ and an equivalent $\mathbf{U}$.

5.4   Recovering Second Half of T:

After recovering the hidden map U, compute

$$\mathbf{W}^{-1}\mathbf{P}(\mathbf{W}^{-1})^\top = \left(\mathbf{W}^{-1}\mathbf{P}_1(\mathbf{W}^{-1})^\top, \ldots, \mathbf{W}^{-1}\mathbf{P}_{2n-a}(\mathbf{W}^{-1})^\top \right)$$

with $\mathbf{W} = \mathbf{UM}$. A second linearly independent solution of the Minrank problem can be found by solving the following system of linear equations:

$$Sub_{a_2 \times a_2} \left(\sum_{i=1}^{2n-a} x_i \mathbf{P}_i \right) = \mathbf{0}_{(n-a_2) \times (n-a_2)},$$

where for $\mathbf{A} \in \mathbb{E}^{n \times n}$, the notation $Sub_{i,j}(\mathbf{A})$ denotes the lower right submatrix of A of size $(n-i) \times (n-j)$ starting in the coordinate $(i+1, j+1)$.

After solving the aforementioned linear system, we recover the second half of $\mathbf{T}$ as in Subsect. 5.1. We then compute a second low rank map $\mathbf{F}_2'$.

5.5   Recovering Central Maps

At this point we have recovered maps $U', T', \mathcal{F}_1', \mathcal{F}_2'$ such that

$$P = T' \circ \varphi_2^{-1} \circ (\mathcal{F}_1', \mathcal{F}_2') \circ \varphi \circ U'.$$

By Eqs. (6) and (7), the central polynomials $\mathcal{F}_1', \mathcal{F}_2'$ have the following form:

$$\mathcal{F}_1' = \sum_{i=1}^{a_1} c_{1i} \mathcal{F}_1^{q^{i-1}} + \mathcal{F}_1^{q^{a_1}} + \sum_{i=1}^{a_2} d_{1i} \mathcal{F}_2^{q^{i-1}}, \tag{13}$$

$$\mathcal{F}_2' = \sum_{i=1}^{a_1} c_{2i} \mathcal{F}_1^{q^{i-1}} + \sum_{i=1}^{a_2} d_{2i} \mathcal{F}_2^{q^{i-1}} + \mathcal{F}_2^{q^{a_2}}, \tag{14}$$

where $\mathcal{F}_1, \mathcal{F}_2$ are the original central polynomials. Thus, there are $2n$ variables defining $\mathcal{F}_1$ and $\mathcal{F}_2$

$$\mathbf{F}_1 = \begin{pmatrix} x_1 & x_2 & \cdots & x_n \\ x_2 & 0 & \cdots & 0 \\ & \vdots & \ddots & \vdots \\ x_n & 0 & \cdots & 0 \end{pmatrix}, \quad \mathbf{F}_2 = \begin{pmatrix} x_{n+1} & x_{n+2} & \cdots & x_{2n} \\ x_{n+2} & 0 & \cdots & 0 \\ & \vdots & \ddots & \vdots \\ x_{2n} & 0 & \cdots & 0 \end{pmatrix}.$$

In addition, $x_{1,1}, \ldots, x_{1,a_1}, x_{2,1}, \ldots, x_{2,a_1}, y_{1,1}, \ldots, y_{1,a_2}, y_{2,1}, \ldots, y_{2,a_2}$ form an additional $2a_1 + 2a_2$ variables defining $\mathcal{F}_1'$ and $\mathcal{F}_2'$. Thus, we obtain

$$\mathbf{F}_1' = \mathbf{F}_1^{*a_1} + \sum_{i=1}^{a_1} x_{1,i} \mathbf{F}_1^{*(i-1)} + \sum_{j=1}^{a_2} y_{1,j} \mathbf{F}_2^{*(j-1)}$$

$$\mathbf{F}_2' = \mathbf{F}_2^{*a_2} + \sum_{i=1}^{a_1} x_{2,i} \mathbf{F}_1^{*(i-1)} + \sum_{j=1}^{a_2} y_{2,j} \mathbf{F}_2^{*(j-1)}.$$

Each entry of the matrices $\mathbf{F}_1', \mathbf{F}_2'$ produces an equation in $2n + a_1 + a_2$ variables where $2n$ of the variables are raised either to the power q^{a_2} or q^{a_1} and $a = a_1 + a_2$ of the variables occur linearly. (Since $\mathbf{F}_1'$ and $\mathbf{F}_2'$ are symmetric matrices these systems contain $\frac{n(n+1)}{2}$ equations each.) These systems of equations are bilinear when expressed over $\mathbb{F}_q$ and are easily solvable. Experimentally, we have found such systems to be efficiently solvable even over $\mathbb{E}$ for full sized parameters due to their structure.

By solving these systems we can recover polynomials $\tilde{\mathcal{F}}_1$ and $\tilde{\mathcal{F}}_2$ and recover linear maps $\phi_{1,1}(X) = \sum_{i=1}^{a_1} \tilde{c}_{1i} X^{q^{i-1}} + X^{q^{a_1}}$, $\phi_{2,1}(X) = \sum_{i=1}^{a_1} \tilde{c}_{2i} X^{q^{i-1}}$, $\phi_{1,2}(Y) = \sum_{j=1}^{a_2} \tilde{d}_{1j} Y^{q^{j-1}} + Y^{q^{a_2}}$, and $\phi_{2,2}(Y) = \sum_{j=1}^{a_2} \tilde{d}_{2j} Y^{q^{j-1}}$ such that

$$\begin{pmatrix} \mathcal{F}_1' \\ \mathcal{F}_2' \end{pmatrix} = \begin{pmatrix} \phi_{1,1} & \phi_{1,2} \\ \phi_{2,1} & \phi_{1,2} \end{pmatrix} \begin{pmatrix} \tilde{\mathcal{F}}_1 \\ \tilde{\mathcal{F}}_2 \end{pmatrix}.$$

6   Key Recovery Complexity

As described in Sect. 5 we can perform a key recovery attack on EFC_p^- by way of a Minrank calculation with some additional overhead. This section describes the complexity of such an attack for the proposed parameters.

There are two steps in the key recovery attack in which nonlinear systems are solved. The first such system is the Minrank instance itself; the second system occurs in the recovery of the central polynomials of the form (13) and (14). Experimentally, we have verified that the latter system is quite easy to solve, requiring only a few seconds of calculation for the proposed parameters even when expressed over $\mathbb{E}$. Therefore, the complexity of the full key recovery is dominated by the complexity of solving one instance of the Minrank problem. As described in Sect. 5, once the Minrank problem has been solved, a second solution can be found efficiently via the solution of a system of linear equations.

The Minrank instance involves $2n - a$ matrices of size $n \times n$ over $\mathbb{F}_q$. The solution vectors are in $\mathbb{E}^{2n-a}$ and the target rank is $2\lceil \frac{a+1}{2} \rceil$. If $a \geq 2$, the target rank is always greater than 2. Thus all Minrank instances coming from EFC public keys are superdetermined (See Sect. 3.2).

For the set of parameters $q = 3$, $n = 59$ and $a = 6$ in the modified version EFC_p^- we obtain from Eq. (8) a target rank of 8, and compute $d_{KS} = 5$, see [39, Section 5]. We may choose $\kappa = 6$ deriving a complexity of about 2^{73}.

We ran proof-of-concept experiments of the key recovery using the MAGMA Computer Algebra System[2] see [4]. Running our non-optimized code we perform a complete key recovery on an $\mathrm{EFC}^-(3, 10, 3)$ instance. The running time was widely dominated by the first Minrank part, taking 212810 seconds to complete and having a solving degree of 5, as predicted.

Using our complexity estimation to compute a set of parameters achieving 128-bit security, we find that the most efficient scheme with $q = 3$ requires $a = 12$ and $n = 149$, resulting in a scheme approximately 12000 times slower than the original parameters.

---

[2] Any mention of commercial products does not indicate endorsement by NIST.

7 Conclusion

Again, we find ourselves learning of new attacks that affect our understanding of security for multivariate encryption schemes. It is striking to note that with the exception of schemes proposed within the last two years, as of the writing of this article, none of the prominent multivariate encryption schemes listed in the introduction have succeeded in attaining the claimed security level.

Also interesting is the fact that yet another scheme has fallen victim to Minrank methods. On one hand, it is alarming that so fundamental a computational problem on which so much of post-quantum cryptography is built is seeing such rapid improvement. Minrank is becoming a mass-murderer of cryptographic schemes. On the other hand, perhaps it is reassuring that in more recent years there are fewer schemes failing against ad hoc attacks. Perhaps we are developing to the point in multivariate cryptography that we are avoiding the numerous pitfalls of developing an efficient, secure scheme, as long as we are careful about rank.

Acknowledgements. The author Javier Verbel is supported by "Fondo Nacional de Financiamiento para la Ciencia, la Tecnología y la Innovación Francisco José de Caldas", Colciencias (Colombia). Some of the experiments were conducted on the Gauss Server, financed by "Proyecto Plan 150×150 Fomento de la cultura de evaluación continua a través del apoyo a planes de mejoramiento de los programas curriculares".

The authors would also like to thank the program committee and reviewers for their many valuable comments contributing to the quality of this manuscript.

A Modifiers

To protect against linearization equations, Minrank, and direct algebraic attacks the basic EFC scheme is modified. Here we present these modifiers.

A.1 Minus Modifier

This modifier can be seen as a function parameterized by an integer a. It takes as input a sequence of polynomials $(p_1(\mathbf{x}), p_2(\mathbf{x}), \ldots, p_\ell(\mathbf{x}))$ and outputs the sequence $(p_1(\mathbf{x}), p_2(\mathbf{x}), \ldots, p_{\ell-a}(\mathbf{x})$. It is well known that this modification either avoids or increases the complexity some of the aforementioned attacks [11,13, 32,38]. As usual, the minus modification of EFC is denoted by EFC$^-$.

The efficiency of EFC is strongly affected by this modifier. In particular, Eq. (1) cannot be directly used for decryption for the modified scheme. Instead, we need to guess the vector in $\mathbb{F}_q^a$ which corresponds to the output of the missed polynomials $(p_{\ell-a+1}(\mathbf{x}_0), p_{\ell-a+2}(\mathbf{x}_0) \ldots, p_\ell(\mathbf{x}_0))$. The expected complexity of decryption becomes $O\left(q^a n^{2.8}\right)$ multiplications over $\mathbb{F}_q$.

A.2 Projection Modifier

There is another style of attack that can undermine the minus modifier. These are the well known differential attacks [14,34]. To avoid these attacks, a kind of projection is applied inside of the central maps $\mathcal{F}_1$, $\mathcal{F}_2$. More precisely, instead of choosing completely at random matrices A, B, those are chosen randomly under the constraint of having rank $n-1$. The designers also insist for n to be a prime number, and that the kernels of A B have not nontrivial intersection. The symbol EFC_p is used to denote a projected scheme.

A.3 Frobenius Tail Modifier

This modifier works over characteristic 2 of 3. In the characteristic two case, the central map is defined from $\mathbb{E}$ to $\mathbb{E}^2$ as follows

$$X \mapsto \begin{pmatrix} \alpha(X)X + \beta(X)^3 \\ \beta(X)X + \alpha(X)^3 \end{pmatrix},$$

where $\alpha(X)$ and $\beta(X)$ are $\mathbb{F}_q$-linear maps. (The construction for characteristic 3 is similar using the square instead of the cube.) For decryption details see [35]. Schemes employing this modifier are denoted EFC_{t^2} or EFC_{t^3}.

B Toy Example

To illustrate the attack, we present the recovery of an equivalent private key for an instance of EFC over a small odd prime field.

B.1 Key Generation

Let $q = 3$, $d = n = 7$, and $a = 1$. Let $\mathbb{K} = \mathbb{F}_q[x]/\langle x^7 - x^2 + 1\rangle = \mathbb{F}_q(b)$, where b is a root of this irreducible polynomial.

We randomly select two $\mathbb{F}_q$-linear maps $\alpha(X)$ and $\beta(X)$ and construct $F_1(X) = X \cdot \alpha(X)$ and $F_2(X) = X \cdot \beta(X)$. Explicitly, as quadratic forms on $\mathbb{E}$, we have:

$$F_1 = \begin{bmatrix} b^{1267} & b^{398} & b^{1100} & b^{1036} & b^{1905} & b^{521} & b^{1334} \\ b^{398} & 0 & 0 & 0 & 0 & 0 & 0 \\ b^{1100} & 0 & 0 & 0 & 0 & 0 & 0 \\ b^{1036} & 0 & 0 & 0 & 0 & 0 & 0 \\ b^{1905} & 0 & 0 & 0 & 0 & 0 & 0 \\ b^{521} & 0 & 0 & 0 & 0 & 0 & 0 \\ b^{1334} & 0 & 0 & 0 & 0 & 0 & 0 \end{bmatrix},$$

$$F_2 = \begin{bmatrix} b^{1818} & b^{842} & b^{1991} & b^{1157} & b^{380} & b^{596} & b^{895} \\ b^{842} & 0 & 0 & 0 & 0 & 0 & 0 \\ b^{1991} & 0 & 0 & 0 & 0 & 0 & 0 \\ b^{1157} & 0 & 0 & 0 & 0 & 0 & 0 \\ b^{380} & 0 & 0 & 0 & 0 & 0 & 0 \\ b^{596} & 0 & 0 & 0 & 0 & 0 & 0 \\ b^{895} & 0 & 0 & 0 & 0 & 0 & 0 \end{bmatrix}$$

We further select two invertible $\mathbb{F}_q$-linear transformations T and U:

$$
T = \begin{bmatrix}
0\,2\,1\,2\,0\,2\,2\,1\,0\,2\,2\,0\,1\,2 \\
1\,1\,1\,0\,1\,1\,1\,2\,1\,0\,0\,2\,1 \\
2\,0\,0\,1\,1\,1\,2\,2\,0\,1\,1\,1\,1\,0 \\
0\,2\,0\,2\,2\,1\,0\,2\,0\,2\,1\,1\,2\,2 \\
1\,1\,0\,1\,0\,1\,1\,2\,1\,1\,2\,0\,1\,0 \\
1\,1\,2\,0\,0\,2\,1\,0\,1\,0\,1\,0\,0\,1 \\
0\,2\,0\,1\,1\,0\,0\,2\,0\,1\,1\,1\,1\,0 \\
1\,1\,2\,1\,0\,1\,0\,0\,2\,2\,0\,1\,0\,1 \\
0\,1\,1\,0\,0\,1\,0\,1\,0\,1\,0\,0\,0\,0 \\
1\,2\,1\,0\,2\,2\,0\,0\,0\,1\,1\,1\,2\,2 \\
1\,0\,1\,0\,1\,2\,0\,2\,0\,1\,0\,1\,1\,2 \\
0\,2\,2\,2\,0\,1\,2\,1\,0\,2\,0\,0\,0\,1 \\
0\,0\,1\,2\,0\,1\,0\,0\,1\,2\,1\,1\,1\,2 \\
1\,2\,1\,2\,0\,2\,1\,2\,2\,0\,0\,0\,1\,0
\end{bmatrix}, U = \begin{bmatrix}
1\,2\,0\,1\,0\,1\,0 \\
0\,0\,1\,0\,2\,1\,2 \\
2\,0\,2\,2\,2\,0\,0 \\
1\,0\,1\,0\,1\,1\,1 \\
1\,0\,0\,0\,2\,1\,0 \\
1\,0\,0\,0\,0\,0\,2 \\
0\,1\,2\,1\,1\,2\,2
\end{bmatrix}.
$$

We then fix $\Pi : \mathbb{F}_q^{2n} \to \mathbb{F}_q^{2n-1}$, the projection onto the first $2n-1$ coordinates. The public key, $\mathcal{P} = \Pi \circ T \circ \varphi_2^{-1} \circ (\mathcal{F}_1\ \mathcal{F}_2)^\top \circ \varphi \circ U$ is then computed as a collection of quadratic forms, $\mathbf{P}_i$ for $i = 0, \ldots, 12$, following Eq. (3).

B.2   Recovering an Equivalent Key

The first step in key recovery is solving a Minrank instance on the public key with target rank 2. As proven in Theorem 1, a solution to the Minrank instance exists with high probability. There are $n = 7$ solutions; specifically, the solutions are the Frobenius powers of the coordinates of

$$
\mathbf{s} = \begin{pmatrix} 1 & b^{873} & b^{1492} & b^{1983} & b^{899} & b^{359} & b^{1463} & b^{2062} & b^{1982} & b^{689} & b^{422} & b^{665} & b^{1371} \end{pmatrix}.
$$

The matrix $\mathbf{L}_1 = \sum_{i=0}^{12} s_i \mathbf{P}_i$ has rank 2 as required. We concatenate a random value to $\mathbf{s}$ to produce a vector $\mathbf{t}_1 \in \mathbb{E}^{2n}$ and to give it the correct dimension to represent an $\mathbb{F}_q$-linear transformation from $\mathbb{K}^2 \to \mathbb{K}$. The linear transformation producing this low rank matrix from the public key is then given by:

$$
\mathbf{T}_1 = \begin{bmatrix} \mathbf{t}_1^\top & \mathbf{t}_1^{(q)\top} & \cdots & \mathbf{t}_1^{(q^{n-1})\top} \end{bmatrix}.
$$

We next compute the spectral decomposition $\mathbf{Q}\mathbf{D}\mathbf{Q}^\top$ of $\mathbf{L}_1$. As noted in Sect. 5.3, over $\mathbb{F}_q$ there is a degree of freedom in choosing $\mathbf{w}$ in the column space of $\mathbf{Q}$ with the property that $\mathbf{W} = \begin{bmatrix} \mathbf{w} & \mathbf{w}^q & \cdots & \mathbf{w}^{q^{n-1}} \end{bmatrix}$ produces $\mathbf{W}^{-1}\mathbf{L}_1\mathbf{W}^{-\top}$ of the appropriate shape. We obtain $\mathbf{w} = \begin{bmatrix} b^{1199} & b^{586} & b^{358} & b^{2144} & b^{553} & b^{199} & b^{400} \end{bmatrix}$, revealing the input transformation:

$$\mathbf{U}' = \begin{bmatrix} 0 & 0 & 0 & 1 & 2 & 2 & 1 \\ 0 & 2 & 1 & 0 & 1 & 1 & 0 \\ 0 & 1 & 0 & 0 & 2 & 2 & 1 \\ 2 & 1 & 1 & 1 & 0 & 2 & 0 \\ 1 & 2 & 0 & 1 & 2 & 1 & 2 \\ 2 & 2 & 0 & 1 & 1 & 0 & 0 \\ 2 & 2 & 0 & 2 & 0 & 2 & 2 \end{bmatrix},$$

and producing the first recovered central map:

$$\mathbf{F}'_1 = \begin{bmatrix} b^{1182} & b^{1997} & b^{274} & b^{994} & b^{1902} & b^{253} & b^{652} \\ b^{1997} & 0 & 0 & 0 & 0 & 0 & 0 \\ b^{274} & 0 & 0 & 0 & 0 & 0 & 0 \\ b^{994} & 0 & 0 & 0 & 0 & 0 & 0 \\ b^{1902} & 0 & 0 & 0 & 0 & 0 & 0 \\ b^{253} & 0 & 0 & 0 & 0 & 0 & 0 \\ b^{652} & 0 & 0 & 0 & 0 & 0 & 0 \end{bmatrix}.$$

Transforming the public key $\mathcal{P}' = \mathcal{P} \circ U'^{-1}$, we recover a linear combination of the public matrices over $\mathbb{K}$ of the form of a central map composed with a projection. We find that the nonlinear equations defining this relationship are already in the ideal generated by the linear equations, so this step requires only the solution of a linear system. Appending an additional random coefficient to this linear combination, we obtain:

$$\mathbf{t}_2 = \begin{pmatrix} b^{569} & b^{1471} & b^{31} & b^{1373} & b^{613} & b^{1670} & b^{698} & b^{1749} & b^{1445} & b^{400} & b^{239} & b^{1441} & b^{1598} & b^{1127} \end{pmatrix}.$$

and build $\mathbf{T}_2 = \begin{bmatrix} \mathbf{t}_2^\mathsf{T} & \mathbf{t}_2^{(q)\mathsf{T}} & \cdots & \mathbf{t}_2^{(q^{n-1})\mathsf{T}} \end{bmatrix}$, from which, in conjunction with $\mathbf{T}_1$, we recover an equivalent output transformation:

$$\mathbf{T}'^{-1} = \begin{bmatrix} \mathbf{T}_1 \mathbf{M}^{-1} & \mathbf{T}_2 \mathbf{M}^{-1} \end{bmatrix} = \begin{bmatrix} 1 & 0 & 0 & 0 & 0 & 0 & 0 & 2 & 2 & 2 & 2 & 2 & 1 \\ 0 & 1 & 2 & 2 & 0 & 0 & 2 & 1 & 0 & 2 & 1 & 1 & 2 & 1 \\ 1 & 1 & 1 & 0 & 1 & 1 & 2 & 0 & 0 & 1 & 1 & 1 & 2 & 1 \\ 2 & 2 & 2 & 0 & 0 & 2 & 0 & 2 & 0 & 2 & 1 & 2 & 1 & 1 \\ 1 & 0 & 0 & 2 & 1 & 1 & 1 & 2 & 2 & 1 & 0 & 0 & 0 & 1 \\ 2 & 0 & 2 & 0 & 0 & 2 & 2 & 1 & 2 & 2 & 0 & 2 & 0 & 0 \\ 2 & 2 & 2 & 2 & 0 & 1 & 1 & 0 & 1 & 1 & 1 & 1 & 2 & 0 \\ 1 & 2 & 1 & 0 & 2 & 0 & 1 & 2 & 2 & 0 & 2 & 2 & 1 & 0 \\ 2 & 1 & 0 & 0 & 2 & 0 & 1 & 0 & 0 & 1 & 0 & 1 & 2 & 0 \\ 0 & 2 & 1 & 2 & 1 & 2 & 2 & 2 & 2 & 0 & 2 & 0 & 2 & 2 \\ 1 & 0 & 0 & 2 & 1 & 0 & 2 & 2 & 1 & 0 & 0 & 1 & 2 & 2 \\ 1 & 2 & 2 & 0 & 0 & 0 & 2 & 2 & 2 & 0 & 0 & 0 & 2 & 0 \\ 1 & 1 & 2 & 1 & 1 & 1 & 0 & 0 & 1 & 0 & 2 & 2 & 2 & 2 \\ 2 & 0 & 2 & 1 & 0 & 2 & 0 & 1 & 2 & 0 & 1 & 2 & 2 & 2 \end{bmatrix}.$$

Furthermore, the recovered map:

$$\mathbf{L}_2 = \begin{bmatrix} b^{863} & b^{260} & b^{889} & b^{2123} & b^{265} & b^{1375} & b^{375} \\ b^{260} & b^{1730} & b^{1077} & b^{1808} & b^{1138} & b^{2122} & b^{1080} \\ b^{889} & b^{1077} & 0 & 0 & 0 & 0 & 0 \\ b^{2123} & b^{1808} & 0 & 0 & 0 & 0 & 0 \\ b^{265} & b^{1138} & 0 & 0 & 0 & 0 & 0 \\ b^{1375} & b^{2122} & 0 & 0 & 0 & 0 & 0 \\ b^{375} & b^{1080} & 0 & 0 & 0 & 0 & 0 \end{bmatrix}$$

is decomposed into the composition of the central map:

$$\mathbf{F}_2' = \begin{bmatrix} b^{863} & b^{1374} & b^{889} & b^{2123} & b^{265} & b^{1375} & b^{375} \\ b^{1374} & 0 & 0 & 0 & 0 & 0 & 0 \\ b^{889} & 0 & 0 & 0 & 0 & 0 & 0 \\ b^{2123} & 0 & 0 & 0 & 0 & 0 & 0 \\ b^{265} & 0 & 0 & 0 & 0 & 0 & 0 \\ b^{1375} & 0 & 0 & 0 & 0 & 0 & 0 \\ b^{375} & 0 & 0 & 0 & 0 & 0 & 0 \end{bmatrix}$$

and the projection

$$\Pi'(X) = X + b^{1327}X^q.$$

We then find that the public key satisfies $\mathcal{P} = \Pi \circ T' \circ [\mathrm{Id}\ \Pi'] \circ [F_1'\ F_2']^\top \circ U'$, where Π is the minus modifier.

References

1. Apon, D., Moody, D., Perlner, R., Smith-Tone, D., Verbel, J.: Combinatorial rank attacks against the rectangular simple matrix encryption scheme. Concurrent Submission to PQCrypto 2020 (2020)
2. Bettale, L., Faugère, J.-C., Perret, L.: Cryptanalysis of HFE, multi-HFE and variants for odd and even characteristic. Des. Codes Crypt. **69**(1), 1–52 (2013)
3. Billet, O., Gilbert, H.: Cryptanalysis of rainbow. In: De Prisco, R., Yung, M. (eds.) SCN 2006. LNCS, vol. 4116, pp. 336–347. Springer, Heidelberg (2006). https://doi.org/10.1007/11832072_23
4. Bosma, W., Cannon, J., Playoust, C.: The Magma algebra system I: the user language. J. Symb. Comput. **24**(3–4), 235–265 (1997)
5. Cabarcas, D., Smith-Tone, D., Verbel, J.A.: Key recovery attack for ZHFE. In: Lange, T., Takagi, T. (eds.) PQCrypto 2017. LNCS, vol. 10346, pp. 289–308. Springer, Cham (2017). https://doi.org/10.1007/978-3-319-59879-6_17
6. Cartor, R., Smith-Tone, D.: An updated security analysis of PFLASH. In: Lange, T., Takagi, T. (eds.) PQCrypto 2017. LNCS, vol. 10346, pp. 241–254. Springer, Cham (2017). https://doi.org/10.1007/978-3-319-59879-6_14
7. Cartor, R., Smith-Tone, D.: EFLASH: a new multivariate encryption scheme. In: Cid, C., Jacobson Jr., M. (eds.) Selected Areas in Cryptography - SAC 2018, pp. 281–299. Springer, Heidelberg (2018). https://doi.org/10.1007/978-3-030-10970-7_13. 25th International Conference, Calgary, AB, Canada, August 15–17, 2018, Revised Selected Papers

8. Chen, M.-S., Yang, B.-Y., Smith-Tone, D.: PFLASH - secure asymmetric signatures on smart cards. Lightweight cryptography workshop 2015 (2015). http://csrc.nist. gov/groups/ST/lwc-workshop2015/papers/session3-smith-tone-paper.pdf

9. Ding, J., Schmidt, D.: Rainbow, a new multivariable polynomial signature scheme. In: Ioannidis, J., Keromytis, A., Yung, M. (eds.) ACNS 2005. LNCS, vol. 3531, pp. 164–175. Springer, Heidelberg (2005). https://doi.org/10.1007/11496137_12

10. Ding, J.: A new variant of the Matsumoto-Imai cryptosystem through perturbation. In: Bao, F., Deng, R., Zhou, J. (eds.) PKC 2004. LNCS, vol. 2947, pp. 305–318. Springer, Heidelberg (2004). https://doi.org/10.1007/978-3-540-24632-9_22

11. Ding, J., Kleinjung, T.: Degree of regularity for HFE. Cryptology ePrint archive, report 2011/570 (2011)

12. Ding, J., Petzoldt, A., Wang, L.: The cubic simple matrix encryption scheme. In: Mosca, M. (ed.) PQCrypto 2014. LNCS, vol. 8772, pp. 76–87. Springer, Cham (2014). https://doi.org/10.1007/978-3-319-11659-4_5

13. Ding, J., Yang, B.-Y.: Degree of regularity for HFEv and HFEv-. In: Gaborit, P. (ed.) PQCrypto 2013. LNCS, vol. 7932, pp. 52–66. Springer, Heidelberg (2013). https://doi.org/10.1007/978-3-642-38616-9_4

14. Dubois, V., Fouque, P.-A., Shamir, A., Stern, J.: Practical cryptanalysis of SFLASH. In: Menezes, A. (ed.) CRYPTO 2007. LNCS, vol. 4622, pp. 1–12. Springer, Heidelberg (2007). https://doi.org/10.1007/978-3-540-74143-5_1

15. Faugère, J.-C., Joux, A.: Algebraic cryptanalysis of hidden field equation (HFE) cryptosystems using Gröbner bases. In: Boneh, D. (ed.) CRYPTO 2003. LNCS, vol. 2729, pp. 44–60. Springer, Heidelberg (2003). https://doi.org/10.1007/978-3-540-45146-4_3

16. Faugère, J.-C., El Din, M.S., Spaenlehauer, P.-J.: Computing loci of rank defects of linear matrices using Gröbner bases and applications to cryptology. In: Symbolic and Algebraic Computation, International Symposium, ISSAC 2010, Munich, Germany, 25–28 July 2010, Proceedings, pp. 257–264 (2010)

17. Fouque, P.-A., Granboulan, L., Stern, J.: Differential cryptanalysis for multivariate schemes. In: Cramer, R. (ed.) EUROCRYPT 2005. LNCS, vol. 3494, pp. 341–353. Springer, Heidelberg (2005). https://doi.org/10.1007/11426639_20

18. Gaborit, P., Ruatta, O., Schrek, J.: On the complexity of the rank syndrome decoding problem. IEEE Trans. Inf. Theory 62(2), 1006–1019 (2016)

19. Goubin, L., Courtois, N.T.: Cryptanalysis of the TTM cryptosystem. In: Okamoto, T. (ed.) ASIACRYPT 2000. LNCS, vol. 1976, pp. 44–57. Springer, Heidelberg (2000). https://doi.org/10.1007/3-540-44448-3_4

20. Ikematsu, Y., Perlner, R., Smith-Tone, D., Takagi, T., Vates, J.: HFERP - a new multivariate encryption scheme. In: Lange, T., Steinwandt, R. (eds.) PQCrypto 2018. LNCS, vol. 10786, pp. 396–416. Springer, Cham (2018). https://doi.org/10. 1007/978-3-319-79063-3_19

21. Joux, A., Vitse, V.: A crossbred algorithm for solving Boolean polynomial systems. In: Kaczorowski, J., Pieprzyk, J., Pomykała, J. (eds.) NuTMiC 2017. LNCS, vol. 10737, pp. 3–21. Springer, Cham (2018). https://doi.org/10.1007/978-3-319-76620-1_1

22. Kipnis, A., Patarin, J., Goubin, L.: Unbalanced oil and vinegar signature schemes. In: Stern, J. (ed.) EUROCRYPT 1999. LNCS, vol. 1592, pp. 206–222. Springer, Heidelberg (1999). https://doi.org/10.1007/3-540-48910-X_15

23. Kipnis, A., Shamir, A.: Cryptanalysis of the HFE public key cryptosystem by relinearization. In: Wiener, M. (ed.) CRYPTO 1999. LNCS, vol. 1666, pp. 19–30. Springer, Heidelberg (1999). https://doi.org/10.1007/3-540-48405-1_2

24. Moody, D., Perlner, R., Smith-Tone, D.: An asymptotically optimal structural attack on the ABC multivariate encryption scheme. In: Mosca, M. (ed.) PQCrypto 2014. LNCS, vol. 8772, pp. 180–196. Springer, Cham (2014). https://doi.org/10.1007/978-3-319-11659-4_11

25. Moody, D., Perlner, R., Smith-Tone, D.: Key recovery attack on the cubic ABC simple matrix multivariate encryption scheme. In: Avanzi, R., Heys, H. (eds.) SAC 2016. LNCS, vol. 10532, pp. 543–558. Springer, Cham (2017). https://doi.org/10.1007/978-3-319-69453-5_29

26. Moody, D., Perlner, R., Smith-Tone, D.: Improved attacks for characteristic-2 parameters of the cubic ABC simple matrix encryption scheme. In: Lange, T., Takagi, T. (eds.) PQCrypto 2017. LNCS, vol. 10346, pp. 255–271. Springer, Cham (2017). https://doi.org/10.1007/978-3-319-59879-6_15

27. Niederhagen, R., Ning, K.-C., Yang, B.-Y.: Implementing Joux-Vitse's crossbred algorithm for solving $\mathcal{MQ}$ systems over $\mathbb{F}_2$ on GPUs. In: Lange, T., Steinwandt, R. (eds.) PQCrypto 2018. LNCS, vol. 10786, pp. 121–141. Springer, Cham (2018). https://doi.org/10.1007/978-3-319-79063-3_6

28. Patarin, J.: Hidden fields equations (HFE) and isomorphisms of polynomials (IP): two new families of asymmetric algorithms. In: Maurer, U. (ed.) EUROCRYPT 1996. LNCS, vol. 1070, pp. 33–48. Springer, Heidelberg (1996). https://doi.org/10.1007/3-540-68339-9_4

29. Patarin, J.: Cryptanalysis of the Matsumoto and Imai public key scheme of Eurocrypt 1998. Des. Codes Cryptogr. **20**, 175–209 (2000)

30. Patarin, J., Courtois, N., Goubin, L.: QUARTZ, 128-bit long digital signatures. In: Naccache, D. (ed.) CT-RSA 2001. LNCS, vol. 2020, pp. 282–297. Springer, Heidelberg (2001). https://doi.org/10.1007/3-540-45353-9_21

31. Perlner, R., Petzoldt, A., Smith-Tone, D.: Total break of the SRP encryption scheme. In: Adams, C., Camenisch, J. (eds.) SAC 2017. LNCS, vol. 10719, pp. 355–373. Springer, Cham (2018). https://doi.org/10.1007/978-3-319-72565-9_18

32. Petzoldt, A., Chen, M.-S., Yang, B.-Y., Tao, C., Ding, J.: Design principles for HFEv-based multivariate signature schemes. In: Iwata, T., Cheon, J.H. (eds.) ASIACRYPT 2015. LNCS, vol. 9452, pp. 311–334. Springer, Heidelberg (2015). https://doi.org/10.1007/978-3-662-48797-6_14

33. Shor, P.W.: Polynomial-time algorithms for prime factorization and discrete logarithms on a quantum computer. SIAM J. Comput. **26**(5), 1484–1509 (1997)

34. Smith-Tone, D.: Properties of the discrete differential with cryptographic applications. In: Sendrier, N. (ed.) PQCrypto 2010. LNCS, vol. 6061, pp. 1–12. Springer, Heidelberg (2010). https://doi.org/10.1007/978-3-642-12929-2_1

35. Szepieniec, A., Ding, J., Preneel, B.: Extension field cancellation: a new central trapdoor for multivariate quadratic systems. In: Takagi, T. (ed.) PQCrypto 2016. LNCS, vol. 9606, pp. 182–196. Springer, Cham (2016). https://doi.org/10.1007/978-3-319-29360-8_12

36. Tao, C., Diene, A., Tang, S., Ding, J.: Simple matrix scheme for encryption. In: Gaborit, P. (ed.) PQCrypto 2013. LNCS, vol. 7932, pp. 231–242. Springer, Heidelberg (2013). https://doi.org/10.1007/978-3-642-38616-9_16

37. Tao, C., Xiang, H., Petzoldt, A., Ding, J.: Simple matrix - a multivariate public key cryptosystem (MPKC) for encryption. Finite Fields Appl. **35**, 352–368 (2015)

38. Vates, J., Smith-Tone, D.: Key recovery attack for all parameters of HFE-. In: Lange, T., Takagi, T. (eds.) PQCrypto 2017. LNCS, vol. 10346, pp. 272–288. Springer, Cham (2017). https://doi.org/10.1007/978-3-319-59879-6_16

39. Verbel, J., Baena, J., Cabarcas, D., Perlner, R., Smith-Tone, D.: On the complexity of "Superdetermined" Minrank instances. In: Ding, J., Steinwandt, R. (eds.) PQCrypto 2019. LNCS, vol. 11505, pp. 167–186. Springer, Cham (2019). https://doi.org/10.1007/978-3-030-25510-7_10
40. Wiedemann, D.: Solving sparse linear equations over finite fields. IEEE Trans. Inf. Theory **32**(1), 54–62 (1986)
41. Wolf, C., Braeken, A., Preneel, B.: On the security of stepwise triangular systems. Des. Codes Cryptogr. **40**(3), 285–302 (2006)
42. Yasuda, T., Sakurai, K.: a multivariate encryption scheme with rainbow. In: Qing, S., Okamoto, E., Kim, K., Liu, D. (eds.) ICICS 2015. LNCS, vol. 9543, pp. 236–251. Springer, Cham (2016). https://doi.org/10.1007/978-3-319-29814-6_19

Multivariate Encryption Schemes Based on Polynomial Equations over Real Numbers

Takanori Yasuda[1(✉)], Yacheng Wang[2], and Tsuyoshi Takagi[2]

[1] Okayama University of Science, Okayama, Japan
tyasuda@bme.ous.ac.jp
[2] Department of Mathematical Informatics, University of Tokyo, Tokyo, Japan
{yacheng_wang,takagi}@mist.i.u-tokyo.ac.jp

Abstract. The MQ problem, an NP-complete problem, is related to the security of Multivariate Public Key Cryptography (MPKC). Its variant, the constrained MQ problem, was first considered in constructing secure multivariate encryption schemes using the *pq*-method proposed at ProvSec2018. In this paper, we propose an encryption scheme named PERN, whose key space completely includes that of the *pq*-method. The decryption of PERN uses methods of solving nonlinear equations over the real numbers, which is different from the decryption of the existing encryption schemes in MPKC. The construction of PERN is fairly flexible, which enables us to construct a multivariate encryption scheme, whose public key consists of multivariate polynomials of degree 2, 3 or higher degrees while constraining its public key to a reasonable size.

Keywords: Multivariate Public Key Cryptosystems · Constrained MQ problem · MQ problem · Nonlinear equations · Post-quantum cryptography

1 Introduction

Multivariate Public Key Cryptography (MPKC) [8], which is a candidate for post-quantum cryptography, uses multivariate polynomial systems as its public key, and in most cases, its security is based on the difficulty of solving a set of multivariate polynomials. This problem of solving a set of multivariate polynomials is called the MP problem as follows.

MP problem: For a prime number q and positive integers m, n, let $\mathcal{F}(\mathbf{x})$ be a polynomial system of m polynomials over a finite field $\mathbb{F}_q$ in n variables $\mathbf{x} = (x_1, \ldots, x_n)$. Then, find $\mathbf{x}_0 \in \mathbb{F}_q^n$ such that $\mathcal{F}(\mathbf{x}_0) = \mathbf{0}$.

The constrained MP problem is derived from the MP problem.

Constrained MP problem: For a prime number q and positive integers m, n, L, let $\mathcal{F}(\mathbf{x})$ be a polynomial system of m polynomials over $\mathbb{F}_q$ in n variables $\mathbf{x} = (x_1, \ldots, x_n)$. Then, find $\mathbf{x}_0 = (x_{0,1}, \ldots, x_{0,n}) \in \mathbb{Z}^n$ such that $\mathcal{F}(\mathbf{x}_0) = \mathbf{0}$ and $-\frac{L}{2} < x_{0,i} \leq \frac{L}{2}$ $(i = 1, \ldots, n)$.

© Springer Nature Switzerland AG 2020
J. Ding and J.-P. Tillich (Eds.): PQCrypto 2020, LNCS 12100, pp. 402–421, 2020.
https://doi.org/10.1007/978-3-030-44223-1_22

When only quadratic polynomials are used in the (constrained) MP problem, the problem is called the (constrained) MQ problem. At ProvSec2018, Yasuda [37] introduced the constrained MQ problem for the first time, and proposed a method called the pq-method for constructing multivariate encryption schemes whose security is mainly based on the difficulty of solving the constrained MQ problem. The constrained MP problem is also related to the SIS problem. In fact, the SSNE Problem [30] derived from the SIS problem is very similar to the constrained MP problem.

As MPKC encryption schemes, Simple Matrix Scheme [31], EFC [29], and HFERP [16] are known. A detailed cryptanalysis for HFERP is not yet done since it was recently proposed. For Simple Matrix Scheme and EFC, critical attacks have not been reported, but they require using very large parameters, which sacrifices the performance of encryption and decryption. Because of such circumstances, developing new encryption schemes in MPKC becomes an important problem.

One reason that accounts for the difficulty of designing a secure MPKC encryption scheme is the difficulty of constructing trapdoor one-way functions given by injective polynomial maps. However, by adding a restriction on the definition range of a polynomial map, the map can easily become injective. Consequently, it is easy to construct an injective trapdoor one-way function with a constrained polynomial map, and this function can be used to construct MPKC encryption schemes whose security is based on the difficulty of solving the constrained MP problem.

Most of the MPKC encryption schemes uses a bipolar structure. The key generation of a multivariate encryption scheme with the bipolar structure is described as follows.

1. Choose an injective multivariate polynomial map $G(\mathbf{x}) : \mathbb{F}_q^n \to \mathbb{F}_q^m$ whose inverse can be computed efficiently.
2. Choose randomly affine isomorphisms S, T on $\mathbb{F}_q^n, \mathbb{F}_q^m$, respectively.
3. Compute $F(\mathbf{x}) = T \circ G(\mathbf{x}) \circ S : \mathbb{F}_q^n \to \mathbb{F}_q^m$.

$F(\mathbf{x})$ is used as a public key, and the secret key consists of $G(\mathbf{x}), T$ and S. $G(\mathbf{x})$ is called the central map of this scheme. Encryption and decryption processes are described as follows.

Encryption: For a plaintext $\mathbf{m} \in \mathbb{F}_q^n$, compute $\mathbf{c} = F(\mathbf{m})$. $\mathbf{c}$ is a ciphertext.
Decryption: For a ciphertext $\mathbf{c} \in \mathbb{F}_q^m$, compute (1) $\mathbf{b}_1 = T^{-1}(\mathbf{c})$, (2) $\mathbf{b}_2 = G^{-1}(\mathbf{b}_1)$, (3) $\mathbf{m}' = S^{-1}(\mathbf{b}_2)$ in this order. $\mathbf{m}'$ coincides with the plaintext $\mathbf{m}$.

The security of the schemes using the bipolar structure is based on the difficulty of solving the (usual) MP problem. If we want to change this security assumption to the constrained MP problem, the map $G(\mathbf{x}) : \mathbb{F}_q^n \to \mathbb{F}_q^m$ should be changed to a constrained polynomial map $G(\mathbf{x}) : \mathcal{I} \to \mathbb{F}_q^m$ where $\mathcal{I}$ is a proper subset of $\mathbb{F}_q^n$ and $\mathbf{m}$ should be chosen from $\mathcal{I}$. Here, $G(\mathbf{x})$ is sufficient to be injective on $\mathcal{I}$. Note that the definition range of $F(\mathbf{x})$ is $S^{-1}(\mathcal{I})$. The pq-method also uses the bipolar structure. (However, S is restricted as $\mathcal{I} = S^{-1}(\mathcal{I})$.)

The construction of $G(\mathbf{x})$ in the pq-method is as follows. First, we construct a central map $G_0(\mathbf{x})$ of an (previously proposed) encryption scheme (e.g. the Matsumoto-Imai scheme [22]) over $\mathbb{F}_p$, where p is enough smaller than q. $G_0(\mathbf{x})$ is then lifted into a polynomial map $\Phi(\mathbf{x})$ with integer coefficients. Next, prepare a certain polynomial map $\Psi_R(\mathbf{x})$ with integer coefficients, $G(\mathbf{x})$ is defined by $G(\mathbf{x}) = \Phi(\mathbf{x}) + \Psi_R(\mathbf{x})$. ($\Psi_R(\mathbf{x})$ is a polynomial map appended to enhance security) In the decryption algorithm of the pq-method, the computation of $\mathbf{b}_2 = G^{-1}(\mathbf{b}_1)$ is done as follows: From $\mathbf{b}_1 = G(\mathbf{b}_2) = \Phi(\mathbf{b}_2) + \Psi_R(\mathbf{b}_2)$, the part $\Psi_R(\mathbf{b}_2)$ can be eliminated due to its special design in the pq-method. After that, $\mathbf{b}_2$ can be obtained by inverting $G_0(\mathbf{x})$. We can say that the pq-method is a modifier that changes encryption schemes in MPKC over $\mathbb{F}_p$ to encryption schemes over $\mathbb{F}_q$. However, the pq-method requires a constraint on the domain of $G(\mathbf{x})$. Due to this constraint, $G(\mathbf{x})$ can become injective. By the existence of the constraint, the security of the pq-method is related to the constrained MQ problem.

In this paper, we propose a new multivariate encryption scheme called PERN (Polynomial Equations over the Real Numbers), whose security is mainly based on the difficulty of solving the constrained MP problem. PERN resembles the pq-method, but PERN does not use a central map of a previously proposed encryption scheme for the construction of $G(\mathbf{x})$. As a $\Phi(\mathbf{x})$, we can choose any polynomial map with small integer coefficients. This implies that the key space of PERN completely includes that of the pq-method. In the decryption of PERN, we need to solve a system of $2n$ equations in n variables with integer coefficients. To solve such a system, we use techniques of solving a system of nonlinear equations over the real numbers, and the fact that its solution has integer components. Since these techniques of solving a system of nonlinear equations over the real numbers are applicable to polynomial systems of any degree, $\Phi(\mathbf{x})$ (and $\Psi_R(\mathbf{x})$) can be chosen with any degree in principle. For the first time, techniques for solving the system of nonlinear equations over the real numbers are used for the decryption in MPKC (Table 1).

Table 1. Different solvers used in the decryption of MPKCs

Tool	Representative schemes
Power operator	C^* [22], Square [6]
Linear equation solver over $\mathbb{F}_q$	Rainbow [9], ABC [31]
Univariate equation solver over $\mathbb{F}_q$	HFE [26], Gui [27]
Multivariate equation solver over $\mathbb{F}_q$	Multi-HFE [4]
Nonlinear equation solver over $\mathbb{R}$	Proposed scheme

In the proposed scheme, the affine isomorphism S is fixed to be an identity map. Therefore, the set of monomials appearing in $G(\mathbf{x})$ and $F(\mathbf{x})$ can be adjusted freely. This means that the key length can also be adjusted freely.

Hence, we do not need to restrict the degree of polynomials to 2 or 3 due to the key length considerations as in the previous MPKC schemes. As another advantage of the proposed scheme, the complexity of the Gröbner basis attack can be maximized. However, if the number of monomials appearing in $G(\mathbf{x})$ and $F(\mathbf{x})$ is too few, the complexity of the Gröbner basis attack decreases and the attack against the inhomogeneous SIS problem works effectively on the proposed scheme. Moreover, it may increase the number of equivalent keys. Therefore, the proposed scheme should take a large number of monomials.

2   Trapdoor Functions by Multivariate Polynomials with Integer Coefficients

For a positive integer l, we denote the least non-negative remainder of an integer a by $a \bmod l$, and the least absolute remainder of a by $\mathrm{lift}_l(a)$. For $a \in \mathbb{Z}/l\mathbb{Z}$, $a \bmod l$ and $\mathrm{lift}_l(a)$ are defined similarly. I_l is defined by $I_l = (-l/2, l/2] \cap \mathbb{Z}$, then $a \bmod l \in [0, l-1]$ and $\mathrm{lift}_l(a) \in I_l$.

Let $x_1, \ldots, x_n$ be n independent variables and $\mathbf{x} = (x_1, \ldots, x_n)$. Let

$$\Phi(\mathbf{x}) = (\phi_1(\mathbf{x}), \ldots, \phi_n(\mathbf{x})) \in \mathbb{Z}[\mathbf{x}]^n, \quad \Psi(\mathbf{x}) = (\psi_1(\mathbf{x}), \ldots, \psi_n(\mathbf{x})) \in \mathbb{Z}[\mathbf{x}]^n$$

be two polynomial systems with integer coefficients of which absolute values are small. Let L be an odd positive number, and M_Φ, M_Ψ be positive integers such that

$$M_\Phi \geq \max_{i=1,\ldots,n} \left\{ |\phi_i(\tilde{\mathbf{d}})| \mid \tilde{\mathbf{d}} \in I_L^n \right\}, \quad M_\Psi \geq \max_{i=1,\ldots,n} \left\{ |\psi_i(\tilde{\mathbf{d}})| \mid \tilde{\mathbf{d}} \in I_L^n \right\}. \quad (1)$$

For example, if $\phi_i^{\mathrm{abs}}(\mathbf{x})$ $(i = 1, \ldots, n)$ are polynomials whose coefficients are given by the absolute value of the corresponding coefficients of $\phi_i(\mathbf{x})$, then

$$M_\Phi = \max_{i=1,\ldots,n} \left\{ \phi_i^{\mathrm{abs}} \left(\frac{L-1}{2} \right) \right\}$$

satisfies (1). This is similar for M_Ψ.

Taking a (large) prime number q, we choose positive integers $r_1, \ldots, r_n$ $(< q)$ such that

$$2M_\Phi < \min_{k=1,\ldots,2M_\Psi} \left\{ |\mathrm{lift}_q(r_i k)| \right\} \quad (i = 1, \ldots, n) \quad (2)$$

and define $\Lambda_i = \{ \mathrm{lift}_q(r_i k) \mid k = 0, \pm 1, \pm 2, \ldots, \pm M_\Psi \}$. The existence of such r_i relies on q being sufficiently large. In fact, $q > 4M_\Phi M_\Psi$ is necessary. Moreover, $r_i > 2M_\Phi$ is also needed.

From (2), for $i = 1, \ldots, n$, we have

$$|\mathrm{lift}_q(\lambda - \lambda')| > 2M_\Phi \quad (\forall \lambda, \lambda' \in \Lambda_i \ (\lambda \neq \lambda')). \quad (3)$$

In fact, for $\lambda = r_i k, \lambda' = r_i k' \in \Lambda_i$, from $|k - k'| < 2M_\Psi$,

$$|\mathrm{lift}_q(\lambda - \lambda')| = |\mathrm{lift}_q(r_i(k - k'))| = |\mathrm{lift}_q(r_i|k - k'|)| > 2M_\Phi.$$

We define polynomial systems,

$$\Psi_R(\mathbf{x}) = (r_1\psi_1(\mathbf{x}), \ldots, r_n\psi_n(\mathbf{x})) \in \mathbb{Z}[\mathbf{x}]^n.$$
$$G(\mathbf{x}) = (g_1(\mathbf{x}), \ldots, g_n(\mathbf{x})) = (\varPhi(\mathbf{x}) + \Psi_R(\mathbf{x})) \bmod q \in \mathbb{F}_q[\mathbf{x}]^n.$$

Then, $G(\mathbf{x})$ can be regarded as a map $G : \mathbb{Z}^n \to \mathbb{F}_q^n$. Regarding the relation between $\varPhi$, Ψ and G, we have the following lemma.

Lemma 1. *For* $\tilde{\mathbf{d}} \in I_L^n$, *let* $\mathbf{c} = (c_1, \ldots, c_n) = G(\tilde{\mathbf{d}}) \in \mathbb{F}_q^n$. *Then, for* $i = 1, \ldots, n$, *there is a unique* $\lambda_i \in \Lambda_i$ *such that* $|\mathrm{lift}_q(c_i - \lambda_i)| < M_\varPhi$. *Moreover, when we write* $\tilde{a}_i = \mathrm{lift}_q(c_i - \lambda_i)$, $\tilde{b}_i = \mathrm{lift}_q(\lambda_i/r_i \bmod q)$ $(i = 1, \ldots, n)$,

$$\varPhi(\tilde{\mathbf{d}}) = (\tilde{a}_1, \ldots, \tilde{a}_n), \quad \Psi(\tilde{\mathbf{d}}) = (\tilde{b}_1, \ldots, \tilde{b}_n).$$

From this lemma, we know for any $\mathbf{c} = (c_1, \ldots, c_n) \in G(I_L^n)(\subset \mathbb{F}_q^n)$, the following holds:

$\tilde{\mathbf{d}} \in I_L^n$ is a solution of $G(\mathbf{x}) = \mathbf{c}$.
$\Leftrightarrow \tilde{\mathbf{d}}$ is a solution of the system of (constrained) nonlinear equations with integer coefficients, $\varPhi(\mathbf{x}) = (\tilde{a}_1, \ldots, \tilde{a}_n)$, $\Psi(\mathbf{x}) = (\tilde{b}_1, \ldots, \tilde{b}_n)$ appeared in Lemma 1.

From the above, an algorithm for computing $G^{-1}(\mathbf{c}) \in I_L^n$ is obtained as follows.

1. For all $i = 1, \ldots, n$, find $\tilde{b}_i \in \{0, \pm 1, \pm 2, \ldots, \pm M_\Psi\}$ such that $|\mathrm{lift}_q(c_i - r_i\tilde{b}_i)| < M_\varPhi$, and set $\tilde{a}_i = \mathrm{lift}_q(c_i - r_i\tilde{b}_i) \in \mathbb{Z}$.
2. Solve the system of constrained nonlinear equations with integer coefficients,

$$\varPhi(\mathbf{x}) = (\tilde{a}_1, \ldots, \tilde{a}_n), \quad \Psi(\mathbf{x}) = (\tilde{b}_1, \ldots, \tilde{b}_n),$$

and output a solution $\tilde{\mathbf{d}} \in I_L^n$.

3   Encryption Scheme PERN

3.1   Key Generation, Encryption and Decryption

Let E be a finite subset of $(\mathbb{Z}_{\geq 0})^n$. For $\mathbf{e} = (e_1, \ldots, e_n) \in E$, $\mathbf{x}^{\mathbf{e}}$ denotes the monomial $x_1^{e_1} \cdots x_n^{e_n}$. We define

$$\mathbb{Z}[\mathbf{x}]_E := \mathrm{Span}_{\mathbb{Z}}\{\mathbf{x}^{\mathbf{e}} \mid \mathbf{e} \in E\}(\subset \mathbb{Z}[\mathbf{x}]),$$
$$\mathbb{F}_q[\mathbf{x}]_E := \mathrm{Span}_{\mathbb{F}_q}\{\mathbf{x}^{\mathbf{e}} \mid \mathbf{e} \in E\}(\subset \mathbb{F}_q[\mathbf{x}]).$$

$\varPhi(\mathbf{x}), \Psi(\mathbf{x})$ appeared in the previous section are chosen as $\varPhi(\mathbf{x}), \Psi(\mathbf{x}) \in (\mathbb{Z}[\mathbf{x}]_E)^n$. Then, we construct $G(\mathbf{x})$ in the same way as shown in the previous section.

The new encryption scheme, PERN makes use of $G(\mathbf{x})$ as a trapdoor function. Choose a random affine isomorphism T on $\mathbb{F}_q^n$, then $F(\mathbf{x}) = T \circ G(\mathbf{x})$ is the public key of PERN.

- **Key Generation Algorithm**

Let L, L_G be odd positive integers, n a positive integer, and E a finite subset of $(\mathbb{Z}_{\geq 0})^n$.

1. Randomly choose multivariate polynomial systems $\Phi(\mathbf{x}), \Psi(\mathbf{x}) = (\psi_1(\mathbf{x}), \ldots, \psi_n(\mathbf{x})) \in (\mathbb{Z}[\mathbf{x}]_E)^n$ whose all coefficients belong to I_{L_G}.

2. Compute M_Φ, M_Ψ satisfying (1), and choose an odd prime number q such that $q > 4M_\Phi M_\Psi$.

3. Choose positive integers $(M_\Phi <) r_1, \ldots, r_n (< q)$ such that

$$2M_\Phi < \min_{k=1,\ldots,2M_\Psi} \{|\mathrm{lift}_q(r_i k)|\} \quad (i = 1, \ldots, n).$$

If such $r_1, \ldots, r_n$ can not be found, go back to Step 2 and reselect q.

4. Compute $\Psi_R(\mathbf{x}) = (r_1 \psi_1(\mathbf{x}), \ldots, r_n \psi_n(\mathbf{x})) \in (\mathbb{Z}[\mathbf{x}]_E)^n$, and

$$G(\mathbf{x}) = (g_1(\mathbf{x}), \ldots, g_n(\mathbf{x})) = (\Phi(\mathbf{x}) + \Psi_R(\mathbf{x})) \bmod q \in (\mathbb{F}_q[\mathbf{x}]_E)^n.$$

5. Choose an affine isomorphism T on $\mathbb{F}_q^n$.

6. Compute $F(\mathbf{x}) = T \circ G(\mathbf{x}) \in (\mathbb{F}_q[\mathbf{x}]_E)^n$.

The secret key is $\Phi(\mathbf{x}), \Psi(\mathbf{x}), \{r_1, \ldots, r_n\}, T$, and the public key is $F(\mathbf{x})$.

- **Encryption Algorithm**

Let $\mathbf{m} \in I_L^n$ be a plaintext.

1. Compute $\mathbf{c} = F(\mathbf{m}) \in \mathbb{F}_q^n$.

Then, $\mathbf{c}$ is the ciphertext corresponding to $\mathbf{m}$.

- **Decryption Algorithm**

Let $\mathbf{c} \in \mathbb{F}_q^n$ be a ciphertext.

1. Compute $\mathbf{c}' = (c_1', \ldots, c_n') = T^{-1}(\mathbf{c})$.

2. For all $i = 1, \ldots, n$, find $\tilde{b}_i \in \{0, \pm 1, \pm 2, \ldots, \pm M_\Psi\}$ satisfying $|\mathrm{lift}_q(c_i' - r_i \tilde{b}_i)| < M_\Phi$ and compute $\tilde{a}_i = \mathrm{lift}_q(c_i' - r_i \tilde{b}_i) \in \mathbb{Z}$.

3. Solve the nonlinear equation system with a box constraint I_L^n,

$$\Phi(\mathbf{x}) = (\tilde{a}_1, \ldots, \tilde{a}_n), \ \Psi(\mathbf{x}) = (\tilde{b}_1, \ldots, \tilde{b}_n).$$

The solution is denoted by $\mathbf{m}' \in I_L^n$.

Then, $\mathbf{m}'$ coincides with the plaintext $\mathbf{m}$.

4   Solving Constrained Nonlinear System with Integer Coefficients

In this section, we consider methods for solving the constrained nonlinear equation system with integer coefficients,

$$\Phi(\mathbf{x}) = (\tilde{a}_1, \ldots, \tilde{a}_n), \ \Psi(\mathbf{x}) = (\tilde{b}_1, \ldots, \tilde{b}_n) \tag{4}$$

appeared in Step 3 of the decryption algorithm. We define $H(\mathbf{x}) : \mathbb{R}^n \to \mathbb{R}^{2n}$ by

$$H(\mathbf{x}) = (h_1(\mathbf{x}), h_2(\mathbf{x}), \dots, h_{2n}(\mathbf{x})) = (\Phi(\mathbf{x}) - (\tilde{a}_1, \dots, \tilde{a}_n)) \,\|\, (\Psi(\mathbf{x}) - (\tilde{b}_1, \dots, \tilde{b}_n)),$$

then the Eq. (4) is equivalent to the equation $H(\mathbf{x}) = \mathbf{0}$.

From the structure of the proposed scheme, we know the plaintext $\mathbf{m}$ is a solution of $H(\mathbf{x}) = \mathbf{0}$.

Let us discuss whether there are other solutions of $H(\mathbf{x}) = \mathbf{0}$ in the definition range $\mathbb{R}^n$ or not. Since the coefficients of $\Phi(\mathbf{x}), \Psi(\mathbf{x})$ are chosen randomly, and by Bézout's theorem, there is a subset S of $\{1, 2, \dots, 2n\}$ of cardinality n such that the number of the rational points of the variety defined by the ideal $I_S = (h_k(\mathbf{x}) \mid k \in S) \subset \mathbb{R}[\mathbf{x}]$ is less than or equal to $\prod_{k \in S} \deg h_k(\mathbf{x})$ (Bézout's bound). $\mathbf{m}$ is one of such rational points, and the chances of existing other rational points satisfying $h_k(\mathbf{x}) = 0$ for $k \in \{1, 2, \dots, 2n\} \setminus S$ are really low. In fact, in our actual experiments of 1000 trials with different parameters presented in Table 4, we had always only obtained one rational point. Therefore, we can assume that

the system $H(\mathbf{x}) = \mathbf{0}$ has only one solution in $\mathbb{R}^n$.

As explained above, if we obtain a solution of the system $H(\mathbf{x}) = \mathbf{0}$ of unconstrained nonlinear equations with real coefficients, it coincides with the plaintext $\mathbf{m}$. Moreover, from the fact that $\mathbf{m}$ has integer components, if we obtain an approximate solution whose component-wise errors from $\mathbf{m}$ are within less than 0.5, its component-wise rounding to integers becomes the exact solution of the system.

To compute an approximate solution of $H(\mathbf{x}) = \mathbf{0}$, we define

$$\theta(\mathbf{x}) = \frac{1}{2}\|H(\mathbf{x})\|_2^2 = \frac{1}{2}(h_1^2(\mathbf{x}) + h_2^2(\mathbf{x}) + \cdots + h_{2n}^2(\mathbf{x})),$$

and consider the least square problem, i.e. to solve the optimization problem of $\theta(\mathbf{x})$. The line search method is known as a method to solve optimization problems. The line search method uses a point sequence $\mathbf{x}_1, \mathbf{x}_2, \dots (\in \mathbb{R}^n)$ with a cluster point. $\mathbf{x}_{k+1}$ is given by the previous term $\mathbf{x}_k$ as

$$\mathbf{x}_{k+1} = \mathbf{x}_k + t_k \mathbf{d}_k,$$

where $\mathbf{d}_k (\in \mathbb{R}^n)$ is called a search direction, and $t_k (\in \mathbb{R})$ is called a step size. $\mathbf{d}_k$ is chosen to be a decent direction, i.e. $\mathbf{d}_k$ satisfies

$$(\nabla \theta(\mathbf{x}_k) \mathbf{d}_k^{\mathsf{T}}) = H(\mathbf{x}_k) J_H(\mathbf{x}_k) \mathbf{d}_k^{\mathsf{T}} < 0.$$

Here, $J_H(\mathbf{x}_k)$ is the Jacobi matrix $\left(\frac{\partial}{\partial x_j} h_i(\mathbf{x})\right) (\in \mathbb{R}^{2n \times n})$ of $H(\mathbf{x})$. $t_k \in (0, 1)$ is chosen to satisfy the Armijo condition: for an $\alpha \in (0, 1)$,

$$\theta(\mathbf{x}_k + t_k \mathbf{d}_k) - \theta(\mathbf{x}_k) \le \alpha t_k H(\mathbf{x}_k) J_H(\mathbf{x}_k) \mathbf{d}_k^{\mathsf{T}}.$$

Then, the sequence $\{\mathbf{x}_k\}$ is globally convergent to a cluster point $\mathbf{x}^*$, and $\mathbf{x}^*$ becomes a stationary point, i.e. it satisfies

$$\nabla\theta(\mathbf{x}^*) = H(\mathbf{x}^*)J_H(\mathbf{x}^*) = \mathbf{0}. \tag{5}$$

We may assume that the rank of $J_H(\mathbf{x}^*)$ is n, hence the dimension of $\ker J_H(\mathbf{x}^*)$ is n. (5) implies that $H(\mathbf{x}^*) \in \ker J_H(\mathbf{x}^*)$, but does not mean $H(\mathbf{x}^*) = \mathbf{0}$ generally. Accordingly, by reselect a sequence $\{\mathbf{x}_k\}$ over and over again until $H(\mathbf{x}^*) = \mathbf{0}$ is satisfied, we eventually obtain a (approximate) solution of $H(\mathbf{x}) = \mathbf{0}$.

Several methods for selecting a search direction have been proposed, and the difference of those methods results in different properties of convergence and efficiency of solving. In this paper, the following 4 line search methods are considered.

1. Steepest decent method
2. Levenberg-Marquardt method
3. Quasi-Newton method
4. Newton method (for optimization problems)

In the steepest decent method, the search direction is chosen by $\mathbf{d}_k = -\nabla\theta(\mathbf{x}_k)$, and in the Levenberg-Marquardt Method,

$$\mathbf{d}_k = -\nabla\theta(\mathbf{x}_k)(J_H(\mathbf{x}_k)^\mathsf{T} J_H(\mathbf{x}_k) + w_k I_n)^{-1}.$$

Here, $w_1, w_2, \ldots$ are a sequence of non-negative real numbers converging to 0, and have the effect of making $J_H(\mathbf{x}_k)^\mathsf{T} J_H(\mathbf{x}_k) + w_k I_n$ a positive definite symmetric matrix. Now, because $J_H(\mathbf{x}_k)$ is a $(2n, n)$-matrix, we can assume that $J_H(\mathbf{x}_k)^\mathsf{T} J_H(\mathbf{x}_k)$ is always a positive definite symmetric matrix, therefore we can take $w_k = 0$. In the quasi-Newton method, a sequence $\{B_k\}$ of matrices are used,

$$\mathbf{d}_k = -\nabla\theta(\mathbf{x}_k)B_k.$$

B_{k+1} is defined by the BFGS update,

$$B_{k+1} = B_k - \frac{\mathbf{s}_k^\mathsf{T} \mathbf{y}_k B_k + (\mathbf{y}_k B_k)^\mathsf{T} \mathbf{s}_k}{(\mathbf{s}_k, \mathbf{y}_k)} + \left(1 + \frac{(\mathbf{y}_k, B_k \mathbf{y}_k)}{(\mathbf{s}_k, \mathbf{y}_k)}\right) \frac{\mathbf{s}_k^\mathsf{T} \mathbf{s}_k}{(\mathbf{s}_k, \mathbf{y}_k)}.$$

Here, $\mathbf{s}_k = \mathbf{x}_{k+1} - \mathbf{x}_k$, $\mathbf{y}_k = \nabla\theta(\mathbf{x}_{k+1}) - \nabla\theta(\mathbf{x}_k)$, and $(\cdot, \cdot)$ denotes the usual inner form. B_1 is defined by $(J_H(\mathbf{x}_1)^\mathsf{T} J_H(\mathbf{x}_1))^{-1}$. In the Newton method (for optimization problems), we take $\mathbf{d}_k = -\nabla\theta(\mathbf{x}_k)(\nabla^2\theta(\mathbf{x}_k))^{-1}$ where $\nabla^2\theta(\mathbf{x})$ is the Hessian matrix of $\theta(\mathbf{x})$.

For the steepest decent method, the Levenberg-Marquardt method and quasi-Newton method, it is known that $\mathbf{d}_k$ is a decent direction. For the Newton method, generally, $\mathbf{d}_k$ is not a decent direction, but we have checked that it is a decent direction in our experiment. Table 2 compares the performance of 4 line search methods. $H(\mathbf{x})$ consists of quadratic polynomials and all solutions are contained in $[-5, 5] \cap \mathbb{Z} = I_{11}$. We experimented 1,000 times for

$n = 30, 40, 50$ with each method. In the table, "time" represents the average time (unit: milli seconds) of solving, "♯ seq" represents the average number of sequences up to reaching the solution $\mathbf{m}$, and "♯ terms" represents the average number of the terms up to reaching a stationary point $\mathbf{x}^*$ for a sequence. Table 2 shows remarkable feature of each method, and overall, the most efficient solving algorithm is the Levenberg-Marquardt method, so that we adopted the Levenberg-Marquardt method in the decryption of the proposed scheme. The algorithm of the Levenberg-Marquardt method is as follows. $\|\cdot\|_\infty$ represents the maximum of the absolute values of the components of a vector, and (2-6) judges whether a sequence gets close enough to a stationary point or not. round($\mathbf{x}_0$) represents the component-wise rounding $\mathbf{x}_0$ to integers.

Table 2. Comparison of algorithms for solving $H(\mathbf{x}) = 0$

Method	$n = 30$			$n = 40$			$n = 50$		
	Time (ms)	♯ seq	♯ terms	Time (ms)	♯ seq	♯ terms	Time (ms)	♯ seq	♯ terms
SD	170.07	1.75	80.70	426.95	1.72	84.92	1202.48	1.79	91.51
L-M	4.12	2.03	14.15	10.87	2.16	15.83	25.36	2.12	17.58
Q-N	23.01	2.09	48.70	75.25	1.99	60.27	232.19	2.13	68.10
Newton	553.28	126.76	6.41	2005.96	198.57	6.93	6068.22	248.05	7.39

Levenberg-Marquardt Method

[**Input**] $H(\mathbf{x})$, an odd number $L \in \mathbb{Z}_{>0}$, $\alpha, \beta, \gamma \in (0,1)$.
[**Output**] A (constrained) solution of $H(\mathbf{x}) = 0$ with integer components.

1. Choose $\mathbf{x}_0 \in [-(L-1)/2, (L-1)/2]^n$ in the range of real numbers randomly.
2. Repeat (2-1)–(2-6):
    2-1. Compute $\mathbf{e} = -H(\mathbf{x}_0)J_H(\mathbf{x}_0)$.
    2-2. Compute $S = J_H(\mathbf{x}_0)^\mathsf{T} J_H(\mathbf{x}_0)$.
    2-3. Solve the linear equation $\mathbf{x}\, S = \mathbf{e}$, its solution is denoted by $\mathbf{d}_0$.
    2-4. Compute the minimal non-negative integer l satisfying the following condition, and set $t_0 = \beta^l$:
    $$\theta(\mathbf{x}_0 + \beta^l \mathbf{d}_0) - \theta(\mathbf{x}_0) \le -\alpha\beta^l \mathbf{e}\, \mathbf{d}_0^\mathsf{T}.$$
    2-5. $\mathbf{x}_0 \leftarrow \mathbf{x}_0 + t_0 \mathbf{d}_0$.
    2-6. If $\|t_0\mathbf{d}_0\|_\infty < \gamma$ then finish the loop, and move to 3.
3. $\tilde{\mathbf{x}}_0 \leftarrow$ round($\mathbf{x}_0$).
4. If $H(\tilde{\mathbf{x}}_0) = 0$ then output $\tilde{\mathbf{x}}_0$, otherwise go back to 1.

The algorithms of the steepest decent method, quasi-Newton method and Newton method are described in the appendix.

Remark 1. The 4 methods explained as above have the only difference of taking the search direction $\mathbf{d}_k$, and other parts is common. In these methods, for any $\mathbf{x}_k$, $H(\mathbf{x}_k + \mathbf{d})$ is approximated by quadratic polynomials

$$m_{\mathbf{x}_k}(\mathbf{d}) = H(\mathbf{x}_0) + \mathbf{d}\,\nabla H(\mathbf{x}_k) + \frac{1}{2}\mathbf{d}\, A_k \mathbf{d}^\mathsf{T} \quad (A_k \in \mathbb{R}^{n\times n}),$$

$\mathbf{d}_k$ is chosen by the solution $\mathbf{d}$ of the (unconstrained) optimization problem of $m_{\mathbf{x}_k}(\mathbf{d})$. For the steepest decent method, $A_k = I_n$ is taken, for the Levenberg-Marquardt method, $A_k = J_H(\mathbf{x}_0)^\top J_H(\mathbf{x}_0)$, for the quasi-Newton method, $A_k = B_k^{-1}$, for Newton method, $A_k = \nabla^2\theta(\mathbf{x}_k)$ are taken, respectively.

5   Security Analysis of the Proposed Scheme

The security of the proposed scheme is mainly based on the difficulty of solving the constrained MP problem.

Constrained MP problem: For positive integers m, n, L, let $\mathcal{F}(\mathbf{x})$ be a polynomial system which consists of m polynomials over $\mathbb{F}_q$ in variables $\mathbf{x} = (x_1, \ldots, x_n)$. Then, find $\mathbf{x}_0 \in I_L^n$ such that $\mathcal{F}(\mathbf{x}_0) = \mathbf{0}$.

In this section, fixing a ciphertext $\mathbf{c} \in \mathbb{F}_q^n$, we consider a polynomial system $\mathcal{F}(\mathbf{x}) = F(\mathbf{x}) - \mathbf{c}$ for a public key $F(\mathbf{x})$ constructed by the proposed scheme. With this $\mathcal{F}(\mathbf{x})$, by solving the constrained MP problem, the plaintext corresponding to $\mathbf{c}$ is obtained.

5.1   Constrained MP Problem

For $\mathcal{F}(\mathbf{x}) = (\hat{f}_1(\mathbf{x}), \ldots, \hat{f}_n(\mathbf{x}))$, each component $\hat{f}_i(\mathbf{x})$ has $s = \sharp E$ monomials. (If E does not include the constant term, $s = \sharp E + 1$.) Determining an order of these monomials, a vector $\mathbf{a}_i \in \mathbb{Z}^s$ is defined as the vector of coefficients lifted to integers from the coefficients of $\hat{f}_i(\mathbf{x})$. The q-ary lattice generated by $\mathbf{a}_1, \ldots, \mathbf{a}_n$ is denoted by $\mathcal{A}$. We assume that by solving the Shortest Independent Vector Problem (SIVP) for $\mathcal{A}$, n linearly independent short vectors $\mathbf{b}_1, \ldots, \mathbf{b}_n \in \mathbb{Z}^s$ in $\mathcal{A}$ are obtained. The polynomial over $\mathbb{Z}$ corresponding to the vector $\mathbf{b}_i$ is denoted by $\hat{h}_i(\mathbf{x})$, and let $\mathcal{H}(\mathbf{x}) = (\hat{h}_1(\mathbf{x}), \ldots, \hat{h}_n(\mathbf{x}))$. Then, the problem solving the equation $\mathcal{F}(\mathbf{x}) = \mathbf{0}$ is reduced to the problem solving the equation $\mathcal{H}(\mathbf{x}) \equiv \mathbf{0} \bmod q$. Here, let us assume that for a solution $\mathbf{x}_0$ of the constrained MP problem,

$$|\hat{h}_i(\mathbf{x}_0)| < \frac{q-1}{2} \quad (i = 1, \ldots, n) \tag{6}$$

is satisfied. Beware that $\mathbf{x}_0$ is not only a solution of $\mathcal{H}(\mathbf{x}) \equiv \mathbf{0} \bmod q$, but also a solution of the equation over $\mathbb{Z}$, $\mathcal{H}(\mathbf{x}) = \mathbf{0}$. Therefore, $\mathbf{x}_0$ can be obtained by solving the equation over $\mathbb{Z}$. Solving the equation $\mathcal{H}(\mathbf{x}) = \mathbf{0}$ is efficiently carried out by combining techniques to solve approximately nonlinear equations over the real numbers with the fact that $\mathbf{x}_0$ has integer components. The approximate solution of $\mathcal{H}(\mathbf{x}) = \mathbf{0}$ can be obtained by, for example, the solving method of the (constrained) optimization problem (least square problem) of the function $\|\mathcal{H}(\mathbf{x})\|_2^2$ where $\|\cdot\|_2$ is the usual Euclid norm [5,25].

First, let us consider the possibility that $\mathcal{H}(\mathbf{x})$ satisfies (6) for a general constrained MP problem. Since $\mathrm{vol}(\mathcal{A}) = q^{s-n}$, by the Gaussian heuristic [24], it is expected that

$$\|\mathbf{b}_i\|_2 \approx \sqrt{\frac{s}{2\pi e}} q^{1-\frac{n}{s}} \quad (i = 1, \ldots, n).$$

Here, e is Napier's constant. Simply, assuming that $\sqrt{\frac{s}{2\pi e}}$ components of $\mathbf{b}_i$ are close to q, the probability satisfying (6) is negligible if s is sufficiently large.

Next, consider the case of the constrained MP problem obtained by the proposed scheme. $\Phi(\mathbf{x}), \Psi(\mathbf{x})$ have small coefficients, but, the distribution of $r_1, \ldots, r_n$ is close to the uniformly distribution on $[2M_\Phi, q - 2M_\Phi - 1]$. Therefore, taking account of the definition of $G(\mathbf{x})$, any coefficient of components of $G(\mathbf{x})$ behaves as chosen randomly in $[M_\Phi, q - M_\Phi - 1]$. Since M_Φ is small enough compared to q, similarly for general constrained MP problem, the probability satisfying (6) must be negligible. The above argument implies that the part $\Psi_R(\mathbf{x})$ is indispensable in the definition of $G(\mathbf{x})$.

5.2 Attack Against Inhomogeneous SIS Problem

For $\mathbf{e} \in E$, $v_{\mathbf{e}}$ denotes the row vector enumerating the coefficients with respect to $\mathbf{x}^{\mathbf{e}}$ of components of $F(\mathbf{x}) = (f_1(\mathbf{x}), \ldots, f_n(\mathbf{x}))$. Taking an order on E, a matrix $A \in \mathbb{F}_q^{n \times \sharp E}$ is defined by the matrix enumerating the column vector $v_{\mathbf{e}}$ ($\mathbf{e} \in E$). Then, for a solution $\mathbf{x}_0 \in I_L^n$ of the constrained MP problem, $\mathbf{w}_0 = (\mathbf{x}_0^{\mathbf{e}})_{\mathbf{e} \in E} \in \mathbb{Z}^{\sharp E}$ is a solution of the linear equation,

$$A\mathbf{w} = \mathbf{c}, \tag{7}$$

and $\mathbf{w}_0$ has a considerably smaller Euclid norm among solutions of the linear equation. This means that $\mathbf{w}_0$ is a solution of the inhomogeneous SIS problem obtained from (7). Therefore, we can consider the attack as follows: First, we gather solutions of the inhomogeneous SIS problem obtained from (7). Next, we search $\mathbf{w}_0$ in the set of the solutions. The inhomogeneous SIS problem is changed to the SVP for a lattice $\mathcal{B}$ of dimension $\sharp E + 1$ (or $\sharp E$), where the co-volume of $\mathcal{B}$, $\mathrm{vol}(\mathcal{B}) = q^n$.

Theorem 1 ([15]). *For an m-dimensional lattice $\mathcal{L}$, we define*

$$N_{\mathcal{L}}(r) = \sharp\{v \in \mathcal{L} \mid \|v\|_2 \leq r\}.$$

If $m \geq 5$, then we have

$$N_{\mathcal{L}}(r) = \frac{V_m}{\mathrm{vol}(\mathcal{L})} r^m + \mathcal{O}(r^{m-2}).$$

Here, V_m is the volume of the unit sphere of $\mathbb{R}^m$.

From this theorem, the number of elements of $\mathcal{B}$ whose Euclid norm is almost same as r is close to

$$\frac{d}{dr}\left(\frac{V_m}{\mathrm{vol}(\mathcal{L})} r^m\right) \cdot 1 = \frac{m V_m}{\mathrm{vol}(\mathcal{L})} r^{m-1}.$$

Going back to our setting, the number of elements of $\mathcal{B}$ whose Euclid norm is almost same as $\|\mathbf{w}_0\|_2$ is about

$$\frac{b\,V_b\,\|\mathbf{w}_0\|_2^{b-1}}{q^n} = \frac{\pi^{\frac{b}{2}}\,b\,\|\mathbf{w}_0\|_2^{b-1}}{\Gamma(\frac{b}{2}+1)\,q^n} \approx \left(\frac{2\pi e}{b}\right)^{\frac{b}{2}}\frac{b\,\|\mathbf{w}_0\|_2^{b-1}}{\sqrt{b\pi}\,q^n} \quad (b=\dim\mathcal{B}=\sharp E+1 \text{ or } \sharp E).$$

Since the solution of the constrained MP problem is unique, the complexity of the attack is the same as this value. Moreover, if a large scale quantum computer is available, the complexity is the 1/2-th power of this value by the Grover's algorithm.

5.3 Key Recovery Attack

Once the linear transformation part of the affine transformation T is known, $G(\mathbf{x})$ is also known from the public key, and $r_1,\ldots,r_n$, $\Phi(\mathbf{x}),\Psi(\mathbf{x})$ can be computed easily from $G(\mathbf{x})$, thus, the secret information which is necessary for decryption is obtained entirely. Therefore, let us consider an attack discovering the linear transformation part T_1 of T.

An adversary who knows r_j for some j can compute the j-th row vector of T_1^{-1} by the following procedure.

1. Choose an integer t such that $n < t \le \sharp E$, and choose a (ordered) subset M of E with cardinality t.
2. For $F(\mathbf{x}) = (f_1(\mathbf{x}),\ldots,f_n(\mathbf{x}))$ and $i = 1,\ldots,n$, compute a vector $\mathbf{a}_i \in \mathbb{Z}^t$ of coefficients lifted to integers from coefficients of $f_i(\mathbf{x})$ with respect to M. The q-ary lattice of $\mathbb{Z}^t$ generated by $\mathbf{a}_1,\ldots,\mathbf{a}_n$ is denoted by $\mathcal{A}$.
3. Choose $\mathbf{b} = (b_1,\ldots,b_s) \in I_{L_G}^t$ randomly.
4. Compute the vector $\mathbf{a}$ in $\mathcal{A}$ closest to $r_j\mathbf{b}$. If $\|r_j\mathbf{b} - \mathbf{a}\|_\infty < L/2$ is satisfied, output the coefficient vector $(c_1,\ldots,c_n)$ of the linear combination $\mathbf{a} = c_1\mathbf{a}_1 + \cdots + c_n\mathbf{a}_n$, and terminate. Otherwise, go back to Step 3.

Since $\mathbf{b}$ satisfying the inequality in Step 4 exists uniquely, even if the cost for searching the closest vector is estimated as 1, the complexity of the above algorithm becomes $\mathcal{O}(L_G^t)$, which in particular, is larger than $\mathcal{O}(L_G^n)$.

Moreover, the above attack can exchange the roll of $\Phi(\mathbf{x})$ and $\Psi(\mathbf{x})$. Namely, if the above algorithm is changed by $r_i \to 1/r_i$, it works as an attack. The complexity of this attack is also $\mathcal{O}(L_G^t)(> \mathcal{O}(L_G^n))$. If the Grover's algorithm is available, the complexity is $\mathcal{O}(L_G^{\frac{t}{2}})(> \mathcal{O}(L_G^{\frac{n}{2}}))$.

5.4 Exhaustive Search

For a ciphertext $\mathbf{c}$, the complexity of finding the solution of $F(\mathbf{x}) = \mathbf{c}$ by the exhaustive search is $\mathcal{O}(L^n)$. In the case of using the Grover's algorithm, the complexity is $\mathcal{O}(L^{\frac{n}{2}})$.

5.5   Algebraic Attack

The algebraic attack uses algebraic equation solver like XL [36] and Gröbner basis technique [12,13] for solving the usual MP problem. The complexity of the algebraic attack is estimated by the complexity of the hybrid approach [1] of computing a Gröbner basis and exhaustive search. In the process of exhaustive search in [1], all elements in a finite field are substituted for several variables, but, in the proposed scheme, the finite field must be changed into I_L. A solution $\mathbf{x}_0$ of $\mathcal{F} = (\hat{f}_1(\mathbf{x}), \ldots, \hat{f}_n(\mathbf{x})) = \mathbf{0}$ in I_L^n is also a zero point of

$$\hat{g}_j(\mathbf{x}) = \prod_{-\frac{L-1}{2} \le a \le \frac{L-1}{2}} (x_j - a) \qquad (j = 1, 2, \ldots, n). \tag{8}$$

Therefore, the ideal we should consider is

$$I = \langle \hat{f}_1(\mathbf{x}), \ldots, \hat{f}_n(\mathbf{x}), \hat{g}_1(\mathbf{x}), \ldots, \hat{g}_n(\mathbf{x}) \rangle.$$

For $k = 0, 1, \ldots, n$, we randomly choose $(v_{n-k+1}, v_{n-k+2}, \ldots, v_n) \in I_p^{\ k}$. We denote the polynomial system in $n - k$ variables obtained by substituting $(x_{n-k+1}, \ldots, x_n) = (v_{n-k+1}, \ldots, v_n)$ for $\mathcal{F}(\mathbf{x})$ by $\mathcal{F}_k(\mathbf{x}^{(k)})$. Here, $\mathbf{x}^{(k)} = (x_1, \ldots, x_{n-k})$. Note that $\mathcal{F}_0(\mathbf{x}^{(0)})$ is the same as $\mathcal{F}(\mathbf{x})$.

For $\mathcal{F}_k(\mathbf{x}^{(k)}) = (\hat{f}_1(\mathbf{x}^{(k)}), \ldots, \hat{f}_n(\mathbf{x}^{(k)}))$, the homogeneous part of $\hat{f}_i(\mathbf{x}^{(k)})$ of the maximal degree $(i = 1, \ldots, n)$ is denoted by $\hat{f}_i^h(\mathbf{x}^{(k)})$, and the homogeneous ideal $J^{(k)}$ of $\mathbb{F}_q[\mathbf{x}^{(k)}]$ is defined by

$$J^{(k)} = \langle \hat{f}_1^h(\mathbf{x}^{(k)}), \ldots, \hat{f}_n^h(\mathbf{x}^{(k)}) \rangle.$$

For $d \ge 0$, let $\mathbb{F}_q[\mathbf{x}^{(k)}]_d$ denote the subspace of $\mathbb{F}_q[\mathbf{x}^{(k)}]$ consisting of homogeneous polynomials of degree d, and $J_d^{(k)} = J^{(k)} \cap \mathbb{F}_q[\mathbf{x}^{(k)}]_d$. The Hilbert series of the quotient ring $\mathbb{F}_q[\mathbf{x}^{(k)}]/J^{(k)}$ is defined by

$$\mathrm{HS}_{\mathbb{F}_q[\mathbf{x}^{(k)}]/J^{(k)}}(t) = \sum_{d=0}^{\infty} \dim_{\mathbb{F}_q}(\mathbb{F}_q[\mathbf{x}^{(k)}]_d/J_d^{(k)}) t^d \in \mathbb{Z}[[t]].$$

If the Krull-dimension of $J^{(k)}$ is zero, $\mathrm{HS}_{\mathbb{F}_q[\mathbf{x}^{(k)}]/J^{(k)}}(t)$ becomes a polynomial. Then, the degree of regularity, $d_{\mathrm{reg}}(k)$ is defined by $d_{\mathrm{reg}}(k) = \deg(\mathrm{HS}_{\mathbb{F}_q[\mathbf{x}^{(k)}]/J^{(k)}}(t)) + 1$. For any $S(t) \in \mathbb{Z}[[t]]$, the power series obtained by truncating $S(t)$ at its first non positive coefficient is denoted by $[S(t)]_+ \in \mathbb{Z}_{>0}[[t]]$. If

$$\mathrm{HS}_{\mathbb{F}_q[\mathbf{x}^{(k)}]/J^{(k)}}(t) = \left[\frac{(1-t^L)^{n-k} \prod_{i=1}^n (1-t^{d_i})}{(1-t)^{n-k}} \right]_+ \tag{9}$$

is satisfied, it is said that $\mathcal{F}_k(\mathbf{x}^{(k)})$ is semi-regular. Here, d_i is the total degree of $\hat{f}_i(\mathbf{x})$.

Remark 2. Taking the result in [35] into consideration, for most of random systems, the right hand side of (9) may seem to be equal to

$$\left[\frac{(1-t^L)^{n-k} \cdot \prod_{i=1}^{n}(1-t^{d_i})}{(1-t)^{n-k} \cdot (1-t^{d_i L})^n} \right]_+ ,$$

but, actually, the part $(1 - t^{d_i L})^n$ is not needed. This is because, different from the case of the usual MP problem considered in [35], in the constrained MP problem, $f_i(\mathbf{x})^L - f_i(\mathbf{x}) = 0$ $(i = 1, 2, \ldots, n)$ (or this analogue) does not hold.

The complexity of the Gröbner basis computation for $J^{(k)}$ is described by

$$\mathcal{O}\left(\binom{n - k + d_{\mathrm{reg}}(k) - 1}{d_{\mathrm{reg}}(k)}^{\omega} \right). \tag{10}$$

Here, $2 \le \omega \le 3$ is the linear algebra constant of solving a linear system. From (10), the complexity of the hybrid attack is described as follows [1]:

$$\min_{0 \le k \le n} \mathcal{O}\left(L^k \binom{n - k + d_{\mathrm{reg}}(k) - 1}{d_{\mathrm{reg}}(k)}^{\omega} \right). \tag{11}$$

If the Grover's algorithm is used for searching elements for substitution, the complexity is changed to

$$\min_{0 \le k \le n} \mathcal{O}\left(L^{\frac{k}{2}} \binom{n - k + d_{\mathrm{reg}}(k) - 1}{d_{\mathrm{reg}}(k)}^{\omega} \right). \tag{12}$$

From randomness of the coefficients of $\Phi(\mathbf{x}), \Psi(\mathbf{x})$, and taking Fröberg conjecture [14] into consideration, it is expected that $J^{(k)}$ is semi-regular. In fact, for $n = 3, 4, \ldots, 15$, we confirmed that $J^{(k)}$ is semi-regular experimentally. Our experiment used Magma. Based on the experiment result, we assume that any $\mathcal{F}_k(\mathbf{x}^{(k)})$ is semi-regular (in particular, for estimation of security parameters).

Remark 3. In the case of that $\mathcal{F}_k(\mathbf{x}^{(k)})$ is semi-regular, the degree of regularity can be computed by using (9). Moreover, in this case, it is expected that the first fall degree $d_{\mathrm{FF}}(k)$ [10] coincides with the degree of regularity. In general, the complexity of the Gröbner basis computation for $J^{(k)}$ is also expressed by

$$\mathcal{O}\left(\binom{n - k + d_{\mathrm{FF}}(k) - 1}{d_{\mathrm{FF}}(k)}^{\omega} \right). \tag{13}$$

If $d_{\mathrm{reg}}(k) = d_{\mathrm{FF}}(k)$, the complexity (13) is equal to the complexity (10). Therefore, in the estimation of security parameters, we use the complexity (11), (12) with $\omega = 2$.

Remark 4. In the security analysis of the *pq*-method in [37], the algebraic attack does not consider the polynomial (8) as one of generators of an ideal, but, this polynomial should be considered.

6   Security Parameters and Implementation

As a set of monomials E used to design the proposed scheme, we take $E = E_{\leq 2} = \{\mathbf{e} \in (\mathbb{Z}_{\geq 0})^n \mid \deg \mathbf{e} \leq 2\}$. Here, $\deg(e_1, \ldots, e_n) = \sum_{i=1}^{n} e_i$, i.e. $E_{\leq 2}$ corresponds to the whole monomials of degree less than or equal to 2. Table 3 shows the security parameters of (n, L, L_G) estimated based on the security analysis in Sect. 5. Secure parameters are estimated considering attacks on classical computers and quantum computers.

Table 3. Security parameter (n, L, L_G)

Security level	Classical attack only	Quantum attack
128 bits	$(65, 7, 5)$	$(80, 15, 11)$
192 bits	$(100, 7, 5)$	$(122, 15, 9)$
256 bits	$(135, 7, 5)$	$(166, 15, 9)$

Tables 4 and 5 show performance result of PERN with an implementation using Intel Core i7-6700, 3.4 GHz. Our implementation used C++ programming language with g++ compiler. $|q|_2$ represents the average of the bit length of q. Key gen., enc. and dec. represent the average time of key generation, encryption and decryption (unit: milli seconds). And SK and PK represent the secret key length and public key length (unit: kilobytes). $\|\mathbf{w}_0\|_2$ represents the minimal integer of $\|\mathbf{w}_0\|_2$ appeared in the analysis in Sect. 5.2 to maintain the corresponding security level. Moreover, in Table 5, $\|\mathbf{w}_0\|_2$ is estimated considering the Grover's algorithm.

Table 4. Performance of PERN with parameters for classical attacks)

(n, L, L_G)	Level	$|q|_2$	Key gen. (ms)	Enc. (ms)	Dec. (ms)	SK (kB)	PK (kB)	$\|\mathbf{w}_0\|_2$
$(65, 7, 5)$	128	31.58	44.62	0.24	56.03	125	575	23
$(100, 7, 5)$	192	34.01	225.01	1.01	285.01	429	2,189	29
$(135, 7, 5)$	256	35.71	843.73	3.51	914.06	1,026	5,659	35

6.1   Implementation for Higher Degrees

For non-negative integers a, b, we define $E_{a,b} = \{a\,\mathbf{e}_i + b\,\mathbf{e}_j \in (\mathbb{Z}_{\geq 0})^n \mid 1 \leq i, j \leq n\}$ where $\mathbf{e}_i$ is the i-th fundamental vector. We implemented the PERN with $E' = E_{2,1} \sqcup E_{\leq 2}$ and $E'' = E_{3,1} \sqcup E_{\leq 2}$ as E. The case of E' uses cubic polynomials, and the case of E'' uses quartic polynomials. For the fixed parameter (n, L, L_G), it is expected that the PERN with E' or E'' is more secure than the PERN with $E_{\leq 2}$, but whether this is true or not is a future study issue, a performance comparison of PERN for $E = 2, E', E''$ under $(n, L, LG) = (65, 7, 5)$ is shown in Table 6.

Table 5. Performance of PERN (with parameters for quantum attacks)

(n, L, L_G)	Level	$|q|_2$	Key gen. (ms)	Enc. (ms)	Dec. (ms)	SK (kB)	PK (kB)	$\|w_0\|_2$
(80, 15, 11)	128	39.99	477.53	0.71	185.18	298	1,328	30
(122, 15, 9)	192	41.79	1499.66	1.87	828.81	1,009	4,884	35
(166, 15, 9)	256	43.55	4369.40	6.47	2526.77	2,481	12,807	43

Table 6. Comparison of PERN for $E_{\leq 2}$, E', E'' $((n, L, L_G) = (65, 7, 5))$

E	Level	$|q|_2$	Key gen. (ms)	Enc. (ms)	Dec. (ms)	SK(kB)	PK(kB)
$E_{\leq 2}$	128	31.58	44.62	0.24	56.03	125	575
E'	-	37.27	237.29	0.54	302.83	128	665
E''	-	41.33	404.61	0.76	529.17	130	737

7 Conclusion

We proposed an encryption scheme called PERN whose security was mainly based on the constrained MP problem. The proposed scheme is flexible to use multivariate polynomials of any degree in its public key. And this public key polynomial system is semi-regular, which indicates the proposed scheme is strong against the algebraic attack.

For inverting the central polynomial map during the decryption process of the proposed scheme, methods for solving nonlinear equations over the real numbers are used, which is used for the first time in MPKC. In this paper, the line search method is used as a solving method for nonlinear equations. However, for solving unconstrained nonlinear equations, there are several solving techniques such as the trust region method [7,11,19–21,34,38]. Moreover, the solving method for constrained nonlinear equations can be related to the decryption of the proposed scheme, and in particular, for the case of the box constraint as I_L^n, there are many research results [2,3,17,18,23,28,32,33]. We, therefore, would like to work on efficient algorithms for solving nonlinear equations from now on to improve the decryption efficiency of the proposed scheme.

Acknowledgement. This work was supported by JSPS Grant-in-Aid for Scientific Research(C) with KAKENHI Grant Number JP17K00197, JSPS Grand-in-Aid for JSPS Fellows with KAKENHI Grant Number JP18J20866 and JST CREST Grant Number JPMJCR14D6.

A Solving Algorithms of Nonlinear Equations Except For the Levenberg-Marquardt Method

Steepest Decent Method

[Input] $H(\mathbf{x})$, an odd number $L \in \mathbb{Z}_{>0}$, $\alpha, \beta, \gamma \in (0,1)$.
[Output] A (constrained) solution of $H(\mathbf{x}) = \mathbf{0}$ with integer components.

1. Choose $\mathbf{x}_0 \in [-(L-1)/2, (L-1)/2]^n$ in the range of real numbers randomly.
2. Repeat (2-1)–(2-4):
   2-1. Compute $\mathbf{d}_0 = -H(\mathbf{x}_0)J_H(\mathbf{x}_0)$.
   2-2. Compute the minimal non-negative integer l satisfying the following condition, and set $t_0 = \beta^l$.

$$\theta(\mathbf{x}_0 + \beta^l \mathbf{d}_0) - \theta(\mathbf{x}_0) \leq -\alpha\beta^l \|\mathbf{d}_0\|_2^2.$$

   2-3. $\mathbf{x}_0 \leftarrow \mathbf{x}_0 + t_0 \mathbf{d}_0$.
   2-4. If $\|t_0 \mathbf{d}_0\|_\infty < \gamma$ then finish the loop, and move to 3.
3. $\tilde{\mathbf{x}}_0 \leftarrow \text{round}(\mathbf{x}_0)$.
4. If $H(\tilde{\mathbf{x}}_0) = \mathbf{0}$ then output $\tilde{\mathbf{x}}_0$, otherwise go back to 1.

Quasi-Newton Method

[Input] $H(\mathbf{x})$, an odd number $L \in \mathbb{Z}_{>0}$, $\alpha, \beta, \gamma \in (0,1)$.
[Output] A (constrained) solution of $H(\mathbf{x}) = \mathbf{0}$ with integer components.

1. Choose $\mathbf{x}_0 \in [-(L-1)/2, (L-1)/2]^n$ in the range of real numbers randomly.
2. Compute $\mathbf{e}_1 = -H(\mathbf{x}_0)J_H(\mathbf{x}_0)$.
3. Compute $B = (J_H(\mathbf{x}_0)^\mathsf{T} J_H(\mathbf{x}_0))^{-1}$.
4. Repeat (4-1)–(4-8):
   4-1. Compute $\mathbf{d}_0 = \mathbf{e}_1 B$.
   4-2. Compute the minimal non-negative integer l satisfying the following condition, and set $t_0 = \beta^l$.

$$\theta(\mathbf{x}_0 + \beta^l \mathbf{d}_0) - \theta(\mathbf{x}_0) \leq -\alpha\beta^l \mathbf{e}_1 \mathbf{d}_0^\mathsf{T}.$$

   4-3. $\mathbf{s}_0 = t_0 \mathbf{d}_0$, $\mathbf{x}_0 \leftarrow \mathbf{x}_0 + \mathbf{s}_0$.
   4-4. If $\|\mathbf{s}_0\|_\infty < \gamma$ then finish the loop, and move to 5.
   4-5. $\mathbf{e}_2 \leftarrow \mathbf{e}_1$.
   4-6. Compute $\mathbf{e}_1 = -H(\mathbf{x}_0)J_H(\mathbf{x}_0)$.
   4-7. $\mathbf{y}_0 = \mathbf{e}_1 - \mathbf{e}_2$.
   4-8. $B \leftarrow B - \frac{\mathbf{s}_0^\mathsf{T} \cdot \mathbf{y}_0 B + (\mathbf{y}_0 B)^\mathsf{T} \cdot \mathbf{s}_0}{(\mathbf{s}_0, \mathbf{y}_0)} + \left(1 + \frac{(\mathbf{y}_0, B\mathbf{y}_0)}{(\mathbf{s}_0, \mathbf{y}_0)}\right) \frac{\mathbf{s}_0^\mathsf{T} \cdot \mathbf{s}_0}{(\mathbf{s}_0, \mathbf{y}_0)}$.
5. $\tilde{\mathbf{x}}_0 \leftarrow \text{round}(\mathbf{x}_0)$.
6. If $H(\tilde{\mathbf{x}}_0) = \mathbf{0}$ then output $\tilde{\mathbf{x}}_0$, otherwise go back to 1.

Newton Method

[Input] $H(\mathbf{x})$, an odd number $L \in \mathbb{Z}_{>0}$, $\alpha, \beta, \gamma \in (0,1)$.
[Output] A (constrained) solution of $H(\mathbf{x}) = \mathbf{0}$ with integer components.

1. Choose $\mathbf{x}_0 \in [-(L-1)/2, (L-1)/2]^n$ in the range of real numbers randomly.
2. Repeat (2-1)–(2-6):
   2-1. Compute $\mathbf{e} = -H(\mathbf{x}_0)J_H(\mathbf{x}_0)$.
   2-2. Compute the Hessian matrix $S = \nabla^2 \theta(\mathbf{x}_0)$.
   2-3. Solve the linear equation $\mathbf{x}\,S = \mathbf{e}$ in the range of real numbers, its solution is denoted by $\mathbf{d}_0$.
   2-4. Compute the minimal non-negative integer l satisfying the following condition, and set $t_0 = \beta^l$.

$$\theta(\mathbf{x}_0 + \beta^l \mathbf{d}_0) - \theta(\mathbf{x}_0) \le -\alpha\beta^l \mathbf{e}\,\mathbf{d}_0^{\mathsf{T}}.$$

   2-5. $\mathbf{x}_0 \leftarrow \mathbf{x}_0 + t_0 \mathbf{d}_0$.
   2-6. If $\|t_0 \mathbf{d}_0\|_\infty < \gamma$ then finish the loop, and move to 3.
3. $\tilde{\mathbf{x}}_0 \leftarrow \mathrm{round}(\mathbf{x}_0)$.
4. If $H(\tilde{\mathbf{x}}_0) = \mathbf{0}$ then output $\tilde{\mathbf{x}}_0$, otherwise go back to 1.

References

1. Bettale, L., Faugère, J.-C., Perret, L.: Hybrid approach for solving multivariate systems over finite fields. J. Math. Cryptol. **3**(3), 177–197 (2009)
2. Bellavia, S., Macconi, M., Morini, B.: An affine scaling trust-region approach to bound-constrained nonlinear systems. Appl. Numer. Math. **44**, 257–280 (2003)
3. Bellavia, S., Morini, B.: An interior global method for nonlinear systems with simple bounds. Optim. Methods Softw. **20**, 1–22 (2005)
4. Bettale, L., Faugère, J.-C., Perret, L.: Cryptanalysis of multivariate and odd-characteristic HFE variants. In: Catalano, D., Fazio, N., Gennaro, R., Nicolosi, A. (eds.) PKC 2011. LNCS, vol. 6571, pp. 441–458. Springer, Heidelberg (2011). https://doi.org/10.1007/978-3-642-19379-8_27
5. Bertsekas, D.P.: Nonlinear Programming, 3rd edn. Athena Scientific, Nashua (2016)
6. Clough, C., Baena, J., Ding, J., Yang, B.-Y., Chen, M.: Square, a new multivariate encryption scheme. In: Fischlin, M. (ed.) CT-RSA 2009. LNCS, vol. 5473, pp. 252–264. Springer, Heidelberg (2009). https://doi.org/10.1007/978-3-642-00862-7_17
7. Dennis, J.E., Schnabel, R.B.: Numerical Methods for Unconstrained Optimization and Nonlinear Equations. Prentice-Hall, Englewood Cliffs (1983)
8. Ding, J., Gower, J.E., Schmidt, D.S.: Multivariate Public Key Cryptosystems, Advances in Information Security, vol. 25. Springer, Heidelberg (2006). https://doi.org/10.1007/978-0-387-36946-4
9. Ding, J., Schmidt, D.: Rainbow, a new multivariable polynomial signature scheme. In: Ioannidis, J., Keromytis, A., Yung, M. (eds.) ACNS 2005. LNCS, vol. 3531, pp. 164–175. Springer, Heidelberg (2005). https://doi.org/10.1007/11496137_12
10. Dubois, V., Gama, N.: The degree of regularity of HFE systems. In: Abe, M. (ed.) ASIACRYPT 2010. LNCS, vol. 6477, pp. 557–576. Springer, Heidelberg (2010). https://doi.org/10.1007/978-3-642-17373-8_32
11. Fan, J.Y., Pan, Y.X.: On the quadratic convergence of the Levenberg-Marquardt method without nonsingularity assumption. Computing **74**, 23–39 (2005)
12. Faugère, J.-C.: A new efficient algorithm for computing Gröbner bases (F4). J. Pure Appl. Algebra **139**, 61–88 (1999)

13. Faugère, J.-C.: A new efficient algorithm for computing Gröbner bases without reduction to zero (F5). In: Proceedings of ISSAC 2002, pp. 75–83. ACM Press (2002)
14. Fröberg, R.: An inequality for Hilbert series of graded algebras. Mathematica Scandinavia **56**, 117–144 (1985)
15. Götze, F.: Lattice point problems and value of quadratic forms. Invent. math. **157**, 195–226 (2004)
16. Ikematsu, Y., Perlner, R., Smith-Tone, D., Takagi, T., Vates, J.: HFERP - a new multivariate encryption scheme. In: Lange, T., Steinwandt, R. (eds.) PQCrypto 2018. LNCS, vol. 10786, pp. 396–416. Springer, Cham (2018). https://doi.org/10.1007/978-3-319-79063-3_19
17. Kanzow, C.: An active-set type newton method for constrained nonlinear systems. In: Complementarity: Applications, Algorithms and Extensions, pp. 179–200. Kluwer Academic (2001)
18. Kanzow, C., Yamashita, N., Fukushima, M.: Levenberg-Marquardt methods with strong local convergence properties for solving nonlinear equations with convex constraints. J. Comput. Appl. Math. **172**(2), 375–397 (2004)
19. Kelly, C.T.: Iterative Methods for Linear and Nonlinear Equations. SIAM, Philadelphia (1995)
20. Levenberg, K.: A method for the solution of certain nonlinear problems in least square. Quart. Appl. Math. **2**, 164–166 (1944)
21. Marquardt, D.W.: An algorithm for least-square estimation on nonlinear problems. SIAM J. Appl. Math. **11**, 431–441 (1963)
22. Matsumoto, T., Imai, H.: Public quadratic polynomial-tuples for efficient signature-verification and message-encryption. In: Barstow, D., et al. (eds.) EUROCRYPT 1988. LNCS, vol. 330, pp. 419–453. Springer, Heidelberg (1988). https://doi.org/10.1007/3-540-45961-8_39
23. Monteiro, R.D.C., Pang, J.S.: A potential reduction Newton method for constrained equations. SIAM J. Optim. **9**, 729–754 (1999)
24. Nguyen, P.Q.: Hermite's constant and lattice algorithms. In: Nguyen, P., Vallée, B. (eds.) The LLL Algorithm: Survey and Applications, pp. 19–69. Springer, Heidelberg (2009). https://doi.org/10.1007/978-3-642-02295-1_2
25. Nocedal, J., Wright, S.J.: Numerical Optimization, 2nd edn. Springer, Heidelberg (2006). https://doi.org/10.1007/978-0-387-40065-5
26. Patarin, J.: Hidden fields equations (HFE) and isomorphisms of polynomials (IP): two new families of asymmetric algorithms. In: Maurer, U. (ed.) EUROCRYPT 1996. LNCS, vol. 1070, pp. 33–48. Springer, Heidelberg (1996). https://doi.org/10.1007/3-540-68339-9_4
27. Petzoldt, A., Chen, M.-S., Yang, B.-Y., Tao, C., Ding, J.: Design principles for HFEv- based multivariate signature schemes. In: Iwata, T., Cheon, J.H. (eds.) ASIACRYPT 2015. LNCS, vol. 9452, pp. 311–334. Springer, Heidelberg (2015). https://doi.org/10.1007/978-3-662-48797-6_14
28. Qi, L., Tong, X.J., Li, D.H.: An active-set projected trust region algorithm for box constrained nonsmooth equations. J. Optim. Theor. Appl. **120**, 601–649 (2004)
29. Szepieniec, A., Ding, J., Preneel, B.: Extension field cancellation: a new central trapdoor for multivariate quadratic systems. In: Takagi, T. (ed.) PQCrypto 2016. LNCS, vol. 9606, pp. 182–196. Springer, Cham (2016). https://doi.org/10.1007/978-3-319-29360-8_12
30. Szepieniec, A., Preneel, B.: Short solutions to nonlinear systems of equations. Cryptology ePrint archive: report 2017/1175. https://eprint.iacr.org/2017/1175

31. Tao, C., Diene, A., Tang, S., Ding, J.: Simple matrix scheme for encryption. In: Gaborit, P. (ed.) PQCrypto 2013. LNCS, vol. 7932, pp. 231–242. Springer, Heidelberg (2013). https://doi.org/10.1007/978-3-642-38616-9_16

32. Ulbrich, M.: Nonmonotone trust-region methods for vound-constrained semismooth equations with applications to nonlinear mixed complementarity problems. SIAM J. Optim. **11**, 889–917 (2001)

33. Wang, T., Monteiro, R.D.C., Pang, J.S.: An interior point potential reduction method for constrained equations. Math. Program. **74**, 159–195 (1996)

34. Yamashita, N., Fukushima, M.: On the rate of convergence of the LM method. In: Alefeld, G., Chen, X. (eds.) Computing Supplementa, vol. 15, pp. 237–249. Springer, Heidelberg (2001). https://doi.org/10.1007/978-3-7091-6217-0_18

35. Yang, B.-Y., Chen, J.-M.: Theoretical analysis of XL over small fields. In: Wang, H., Pieprzyk, J., Varadharajan, V. (eds.) ACISP 2004. LNCS, vol. 3108, pp. 277–288. Springer, Heidelberg (2004). https://doi.org/10.1007/978-3-540-27800-9_24

36. Yang, B.-Y., Chen, J.-M.: All in the XL family: theory and practice. In: Park, C., Chee, S. (eds.) ICISC 2004. LNCS, vol. 3506, pp. 67–86. Springer, Heidelberg (2005). https://doi.org/10.1007/11496618_7

37. Yasuda, T.: Multivariate encryption schemes based on the constrained MQ problem. In: Baek, J., Susilo, W., Kim, J. (eds.) ProvSec 2018. LNCS, vol. 11192, pp. 129–146. Springer, Cham (2018). https://doi.org/10.1007/978-3-030-01446-9_8

38. Yuan, Y.X.: Recent advances in numerical methods for nonlinear equations and nonlinear least squares. Numer. Algebra Control Optim. **1**, 15–34 (2011)

Quantum Algorithms

Improved Quantum Circuits for Elliptic Curve Discrete Logarithms

Thomas Häner[1], Samuel Jaques[2(✉)], Michael Naehrig[3], Martin Roetteler[1], and Mathias Soeken[1]

[1] Microsoft Quantum, Redmond, WA, USA
[2] Department of Materials, University of Oxford, Oxford, UK
samuel.jaques@materials.ox.ac.uk
[3] Microsoft Research, Redmond, WA, USA

Abstract. We present improved quantum circuits for elliptic curve scalar multiplication, the most costly component in Shor's algorithm to compute discrete logarithms in elliptic curve groups. We optimize low-level components such as reversible integer and modular arithmetic through windowing techniques and more adaptive placement of uncomputing steps, and improve over previous quantum circuits for modular inversion by reformulating the binary Euclidean algorithm. Overall, we obtain an affine Weierstrass point addition circuit that has lower depth and uses fewer T gates than previous circuits. While previous work mostly focuses on minimizing the total number of qubits, we present various trade-offs between different cost metrics including the number of qubits, circuit depth and T-gate count. Finally, we provide a full implementation of point addition in the Q# quantum programming language that allows unit tests and automatic quantum resource estimation for all components.

Keywords: Quantum cryptanalysis · Elliptic curve cryptography · Discrete logarithm problem · Shor's algorithm · Resource estimates

1 Introduction

Shor's algorithm [26, 27] solves the discrete logarithm problem for finite abelian groups with only polynomial cost. When run on a large-scale, fault-tolerant quantum computer, its variant for elliptic-curve groups could efficiently break elliptic curve cryptography with parameters that are widely used and far out of reach of current classical adversaries.

Barring the efficient classical post-processing of the measured data, Shor's quantum algorithm consists of three steps: first, a superposition of exponents is created, then those exponents control the evaluation of a group exponentiation,

S. Jaques—Partially supported by the University of Oxford Clarendon fund.
Most of this work was done by Samuel Jaques, while he was an intern at Microsoft Research.

© Springer Nature Switzerland AG 2020
J. Ding and J.-P. Tillich (Eds.): PQCrypto 2020, LNCS 12100, pp. 425–444, 2020.
https://doi.org/10.1007/978-3-030-44223-1_23

and finally a quantum Fourier transform is applied to the exponent register, which is then measured. The group operations in the exponentiation must be computed in superposition and this is by far the most expensive step of the algorithm. Thus, the precise cost of Shor's algorithm depends on a detailed resource estimation for implementing the group operation on a quantum computer. For solving the elliptic curve discrete logarithm problem (ECDLP), the relevant operation is the repeated controlled addition of classical elliptic curve points to an accumulator point in a quantum register.

The first detailed discussion of the elliptic curve case was given by Proos and Zalka in [23]. Based on this work, Roetteler et al. [24] (hereinafter referred to as RNSL) presented explicit quantum circuits for point addition and all its components and automatically derive their resource estimates from a concrete implementation. Both papers focus on minimizing the number of qubits required to run the algorithm, since its polynomial runtime implies that it will run fast once an adversary has enough qubits to do so. They count the required number of *logical* qubits. For example, RNSL estimate that Shor's algorithm needs 2330 logical qubits to attack a 256-bit elliptic curve. Under plausible assumptions about physical error rates, this could translate into $6.77 \cdot 10^7$ physical qubits [11]. But the number of logical qubits is not the only important cost metric, and one might prioritize others such as circuit depth, the total number of gates, or the total number of likely expensive gates such as the Toffoli gate or the T gate.

Our goal in this work is not only to improve the circuits proposed by RNSL [24], but also to explore different trade-offs favoring different cost metrics. To this end, we provide resource estimates for point addition circuits optimized for depth, T gate count, and width, respectively. We also report on initial experiments with automatic optimization for T-depth and T gate count. By using the automatic compilation techniques presented in [18], we find low T-depth and low T-count circuits for a modular multiplication component and show significant improvements compared to their manually designed counterparts, however, at a very high cost to the number of qubits.

Beyond alternative choices for low-level arithmetic components, we also improve the higher-level structure of RNSL's circuit. While many components stay the same, the most dramatic improvements come from windowing techniques similar to those proposed by Gidney and Ekerå in [14] and a better memory management via *pebbling*. For example, instead of copying out the result in an out-of-place circuit that uses Bennett's method for embedding an irreversible function in a reversible computation, the result can be used for the next operation before it is uncomputed. This technique does not treat modular operations merely as black boxes, but can adaptively reduce the cost of the higher-level circuit they are used in. Along with a reformulation of the binary extended Euclidean algorithm, it significantly reduces costs for the modular inversion circuit.

One of our main contributions is a modular, testable library[1] of functions for elliptic curve arithmetic in the Q# programming language for quantum

---

[1] Our code will be released under an open source license.

computing [28]. These incorporate different possible choices for subroutines like addition and modular multiplication. Besides enabling unit testing for all components, the Q# development environment allows automated resource estimation.

We strictly improve RNSL's estimates under all metrics. For example, for solving the ECDLP on a 256-bit elliptic curve, we reduce the number of qubits from 2338 to 2124, improve the T-count by a factor of 119 and the T-depth by a factor of 54. Under a different trade-off optimizing for depth, our circuit costs 2^{33} T gates with T-depth of 2^{25} and 2871 qubits. Compared to RNSL, this is a factor 6000 reduction in T-depth with only a 22% increase in width.

Extrapolating analogous values, breaking RSA-3072 would cost 2^{34} T gates and 9287 logical qubits [14]. This suggests that, at similar classical security levels, elliptic curve cryptography is less secure than RSA against a quantum attack.

2   Preliminaries

This section only gives a very brief discussion of the basic concepts used in this work. For a more detailed introduction to quantum computing, we refer to [22], for Shor's algorithm see [26] and [27] and for its ECDLP variant [23] and [24].

Quantum Computing. A quantum computer acts on *quantum states* by applying quantum gates to its qubits. A quantum state is denoted by $|x\rangle$ for some label x. We work entirely with computational basis states, so x is always a bit string. As the fundamental gate set we use the Clifford+T gate set and assume that the T gate is by far the most expensive, including measurements. This is a plausible assumption because, in a quantum computer using a surface code for error correction, T gates consume special states which require many qubits and many surface code cycles to produce, and surface codes require frequent measurements for all gates [10]. A quantum algorithm is described by a sequence of gates in the form of a quantum circuit. We use standard quantum circuit diagrams. For circuit design and testing, we use circuits built from NOT, CNOT and Toffoli gates as those can be simulated efficiently at scale on classical inputs [24]. However, for cost estimation, we use decompositions over the Clifford+T gate set, such as the ones introduced in [1,12,25].

Shor's Algorithm for the ECDLP. Let an instance of the ECDLP be given by two $\mathbb{F}_p$-rational points $P, Q \in E(\mathbb{F}_p)$ on an elliptic curve E over a finite field of large characteristic p such that $\mathrm{ord}(P) = r$, $Q \in \langle P \rangle$. The problem is to find the unique integer $m \in \{1, \ldots, r\}$ such that $Q = mP$. Shor's algorithm applies a Hadamard transform to two registers with $n+1$ qubits initialized to $|0\rangle$ to create the state $\frac{1}{2^{n+1}} \sum_{k,\ell=0}^{2^{n+1}-1} |k\rangle |\ell\rangle$. Next, the state $\frac{1}{2^{n+1}} \sum_{k,\ell=0}^{2^{n+1}-1} |k\rangle |\ell\rangle |kP + \ell Q\rangle$ is computed using the elliptic curve group law. A quantum Fourier transform $\mathrm{QFT}_{2^{n+1}}$ on $n+1$ qubits is applied to both $|k\rangle$ and $|\ell\rangle$ and the $2(n+1)$ qubits in $|k\rangle |\ell\rangle$ are measured. Classical post-processing then yields the discrete logarithm m. We assume that the algorithm is modified using the semiclassical Fourier transform method [15], which means that a small number of qubits can be re-used to act as the $2n+2$ qubits for $|k\rangle |\ell\rangle$. RNSL use only one qubit for this [24], but we use more than one to allow windowed arithmetic (see Sect. 5.1). The most cost-intensive part is the double-scalar multiplication to compute $|kP + \ell Q\rangle$.

Functions as Quantum Circuits. The elliptic curve group law is built from various classical functions that operate on bit strings of varying lengths n. For any function f, we use U_f to denote a quantum circuit that computes f.

We often want U_f to compute f *in-place*, meaning it has the action $U_f :$ $|x\rangle \mapsto |f(x)\rangle$ on inputs $x \in \{0,1\}^n$. If U_f is built out of Clifford+T gates, each gate is easy to invert; thus, an in-place circuit U_f automatically yields an in-place circuit $U_f^\dagger$ that computes f^{-1}. As quantum circuits need to be reversible, an in-place circuit is not always possible, e.g. if f is not injective.

When an in-place circuit is not possible, U_f needs to implement f *out-of-place* as $|x\rangle |0\rangle^n \mapsto |x\rangle |f(x)\rangle$. Some circuits might require a number m of *auxiliary qubits*, such that $U_f : |x\rangle |0\rangle^n |0\rangle^m \mapsto |x\rangle |f(x)\rangle |g(x)\rangle$, where g is some function of the input. The auxiliary qubits are entangled with the other registers, and g must be *uncomputed* before the end of the computation to restore them to their original state. In our circuit diagrams, white triangles indicate such outputs.

If it is too costly to compute $g(x)$ from x and $f(x)$, one can use a method due to Bennett [4] to clean any auxiliary qubits. By adding another n-qubit register, the output $f(x)$ is "copied" to that register using CNOT gates. Then, the inverse $U_f^\dagger$ is applied. This trick roughly doubles the cost to reversibly compute f.

In a sequence of out-of-place circuits, uncomputing early steps prevents us from uncomputing later steps. To make the full algorithm work, we either need to keep intermediate steps at the cost of an increasing number of qubits or recompute them repeatedly at the cost of additional gates. This is an instance of a general problem known as a *pebbling game*.

Controlled Circuits. As larger circuits are composed from smaller ones, the smaller circuit often needs to be controlled with a single qubit. We can "promote" each Clifford+T gate in the smaller circuit into a controlled variant, which is expensive, e.g., for CNOT and Toffoli gates. Thus, we want to optimize which gates we control. For example, a circuit using Bennett's trick can be controlled by changing only the middle CNOT gates into Toffoli gates. For other circuits, we design controlled versions as needed.

3   Components

Design Strategies. A full cost estimate of Shor's algorithm requires estimates at all layers of the architecture, including error correction, layout, and possibly architecture design. We focus only on the logical layer, and provide circuits that operate on abstracted logical qubits. From this level we cannot decide which design choices will be optimal. A shallower circuit with more logical qubits would have smaller error correction overhead and could have fewer physical qubits.

Thus, we provide different approaches and tradeoffs. We measure the T-depth, T-count, depth including all gates, and total number of qubits used ("width"). We focus on three strategies, favouring depth, T-count, or width. We could instead make different choices for each sub-circuit of Shor's algorithm, resulting in a large parameter space for potential optimization. Since we wrote Q# functions for all circuits, future work could combine different choices for each step.

Toffoli and AND Gates. As RNSL explain in the introduction of [24], circuits expressed as Toffoli gate networks can be implemented exactly over the Clifford+T gate set and can be classically simulated and tested. Therefore, we designed our circuits using the same approach. Toffoli gates are the only source of T-gates in such a circuit. In many instances, we know that the output qubit is in the $|0\rangle$ state and we can use a dedicated AND circuit with a lower T-count instead. We use an AND gate design which combines Jones' and Selinger's AND gates [16,25]. It uses 4 T gates, while a Toffoli gate uses 7, and the inverse AND† uses no T gates while Toffoli† uses 7. AND gates use 1 auxiliary qubit for T-depth 1; Toffoli gates can use 4 auxiliary qubits for T-depth 1 or none for T-depth 3, see [1].

Integer Addition. The adder of lowest known T-count is Gidney's modification of the Cuccaro et al. adder [8] (hereinafter called the CDKMG adder), which uses only $4n$ T gates to add two n-bit numbers, but uses n auxiliary qubits [12]. The adder of lowest known T-depth is the carry lookahead adder of Draper et al. [9] (hereinafter the DKRS adder), with logarithmic depth but $2n - O(n)$ auxiliary qubits. The adder of lowest width is due to Takahashi et al. [29] (hereinafter the TTK adder), which computes in-place using no auxiliary qubits. RNSL used the TTK adder. The DKRS adder uses $10n$ Toffoli gates, but of these, $4n$ can be replaced with an AND or AND† gate.

We provide new methods for controlling the addition circuits. The DKRS adder uses a circuit to propagate carries, which is uncomputed. These gates do not need to be controlled. The remaining gates which must be promoted to controlled versions are all CNOT gates, leading to only a slight increase in the T-count. To control the CDKMG adder, we promote two CNOT gates per bit to Toffoli gates, as Fig. 2a shows, and we change the final CNOT for the carry qubit to a Toffoli gate. Unfortunately, for both addition circuits, the new Toffoli gates cannot be replaced with AND gates.

Constant Addition. When tackling an ECDLP instance, the prime modulus is a classically known integer, and we need a circuit to add it to integers encoded in quantum registers. The simplest method allocates a new quantum register, inputs the integer into the quantum register, runs any quantum addition circuit, then uncomputes the integer from the quantum register to free the qubits. This simple method is easy to control. Only copying the integer into the quantum register is controlled, and then an uncontrolled addition is used, as shown in Fig. 1a. Copying an integer uses only X gates, so a controlled copy operation only uses CNOT gates, giving the same T-cost as uncontrolled quantum addition. We use this strategy with the CDKMG and TTK adders.

An alternative is to "curry" the quantum addition circuit. In the DKRS adder, the qubits of one of the two inputs are only used as controls for CNOT and Toffoli gates. We can replace these with X and CNOT gates which are conditionally applied according to the bits of the classical integer. A controlled classical addition with this method needs to control the entire curried circuit (Fig. 1b), but we found that this is the most efficient approach with the DKRS adder.

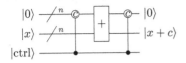

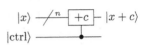

(a) Copying the classical constant c is controlled, followed by uncontrolled addition.

(b) The addition circuit is curried for the constant c, then the full circuit is controlled.

Fig. 1. Two methods for controlling addition by a constant c.

Comparing Integers. An addition circuit immediately gives a comparator by the one's complement trick. For integers x and y represented in binary, if we let x' denote the one's complement (all bits flipped), then $(x'+y)' = x-y$. If $y > x$, then $x - y < 0$ and the leading bit of $(x'+y)'$ will be 1. Thus, to construct a comparator, we simply flip all bits in x, compute the first half of an addition circuit, copy out the carry, then uncompute the addition circuit. With a control, we only need to control the final copy of the carry bit. We use this technique for comparators based on the previous adders. DKRS provide a comparator which we did not use for ease of implementation.

Fan-Out and Fan-In of Control Qubits. When a single qubit controls multiple parallel gates, they must be performed sequentially. To avoid this increase in depth, we opt to allocate extra qubits and fan-out the control [21] to these qubits using CNOTs. Then these qubits can control all the gates in parallel before we clear them again. For n simultaneous controlled gates, this requires n auxiliary qubits and at most $4n$ CNOT gates in depth $\lceil \lg n \rceil$, but no T gates. Our low-width optimization does not do this.

The fanned-out auxiliary control qubits could be retained to control many gates, depending on the application. Because the Q# language allocates qubits in a stack, this is often difficult. A function that allocates clean auxiliary qubits must restore them to the $|0\rangle$ state before returning. Because of this difficulty and the low gate cost of fan-out, we do not make such optimizations.

To control a single gate with the logical AND of n qubits requires a fan-in of control qubits. For low width, we use Barrenco et al.'s method [3], as RNSL did. This performs a multi-AND in-place but with $8n$ Toffoli gates and linear depth. If we instead allocate $n-1$ auxiliary qubits and "compress" the controls with a tree of AND gates, it requires only $n-1$ AND gates and AND-depth $\lceil \lg n \rceil$.

4   Modular Arithmetic

Because modular reduction is irreversible, we cannot design an in-place circuit which maps x to $x \bmod N$ without auxiliary qubits to represent the quotient $\lfloor x/N \rfloor$. Any algorithm for modular arithmetic that uses many modular reductions thus creates significant qubit overhead. Instead, we design bespoke circuits for each operation. Primarily, we follow RNSL [24]. We find that working in Montgomery representation [20] has the lowest costs. For an odd modulus p with $n = \lceil \lg p \rceil$, the Montgomery representation of an integer x is $x2^n \bmod p$.

We use the modular addition circuit from RNSL. Addition in Montgomery representation is the same as in standard representation. For controlled modular addition, we only need to control two operations (Fig. 2b). This automatically gives us modular addition by a constant, by replacing the quantum-quantum addition and comparison circuits by their quantum-classical counterparts.

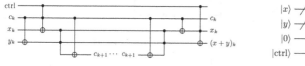

(a) Addition block from [12], with controls.   (b) Controlled modular addition.

Fig. 2. Efficient controlled addition.

4.1   Multiplication and Squaring

RNSL provide two circuits each for multiplication and squaring. We use the one that operates on n-bit integers in Montgomery form with $2n$ additions and n halvings, and justify this choice in Appendix A.1. This circuit is a direct translation of classical Montgomery multiplication.

Windowed Arithmetic. Windowed multiplication, such as [13], is not directly possible in our setting because we multiply two quantum integers, but we can adapt some of these techniques to our setting. When computing $x \cdot y$, the Montgomery multiplier uses the ith bit of $|x\rangle$ to control an addition of $|y\rangle$ to the output register. It then copies the lowest bit of the output to an auxiliary register $|m\rangle$ and uses this bit to control addition of the modulus p. This ensures that the sum is even, and so we rotate the register to divide by 2.

When using a window of size k, the integer x is split into k-bit words $x_{(1)}, \ldots, x_{(n/k)}$, analogous to classical interleaved radix-2^k Montgomery multiplication. The k-bit value $x_{(i)}$ is multiplied with y, adding the $(n+k)$-bit result to the output register. To add a suitable multiple of p to the output to set the k least significant bits to 0, these k bits are copied to an auxiliary register m_i. The multiple $t_{m_i} p$ such that $t_{m_i} p + m_i \equiv 0 \mod 2^k$ can be looked up from a classically pre-computed table T, where $T[m_i] = t_{m_i} p$ for $t_{m_i} \equiv p^{-1} m_i \mod 2^k$.

We use the bits in m_i as an address for a sequential quantum look-up [2], writing the resulting $(n+k)$-bit integer $t_{m_i} p$ into an auxiliary register. Then an uncontrolled addition of $t_{m_i} p$ into the output register clears the bottom k bits, so we can cyclically rotate by k bits. Figure 3 illustrates this process.

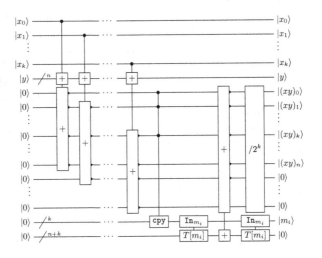

Fig. 3. Circuit for a single window of windowed add-and-halve multiplication. The cpy gate copies k bits with k CNOT gates. The gate $\mathtt{In}_{m_i}$ performs a quantum table lookup of $T[m_i]$, where T is the table described in the text. The circuit in this figure is repeated $\lceil n/k \rceil$ times, with a final modular correction step, to perform a single modular multiplication.

Pebbling. Given integers x, y, and z, one method to compute $xy + z$ in place is to first compute xy in an auxiliary register, then to add it to the register containing z, and finally to uncompute xy. This works for any generic multiplication circuit, but at the cost of two multiplications.

The circuit we use requires the Bennett method, and we replace its CNOT step with an addition. This is just a pebbling technique [5]; we are keeping the auxiliary qubits until we have finished the next computation (an addition) before uncomputing them. The cost of this multiply-then-add is just the sum of the costs of a multiplication and an addition, rather than twice the cost of a multiplication and an addition.

In particular, RNSL treat their squaring circuit as a black box in the full elliptic curve addition circuit. The computed square is only needed for one subtraction before it must be uncomputed; therefore we can use this multiply-then-add trick. Figure 4 shows how this saves almost half the gate cost and depth of the squaring, as well as saving an auxiliary register.

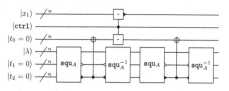

(a) Original circuit [24] with squ circuit expanded, squ$_A$ produces dirty auxiliary qubits in $|t_1\rangle$.

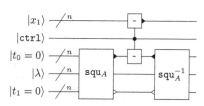

(b) More efficient version.

Fig. 4. Improvement to the squaring circuit from [24] in the context of elliptic curve point addition.

Automatic Optimization. The multiply-then-add operation is a very costly component in the point addition circuit. We explore what is possible when reducing its T-depth and T-gate count. Appendix D shows the results for a compilation using the method from [18] after automatic optimization [30] of a logic network generated from the operation. We achieve extremely low T-depth and T-count, but the number of logical qubits increases significantly. We leave further exploration of such techniques for future work.

4.2 Modular Inversion

Modular inversion uses variants of the extended Euclidean algorithm (EEA). The EEA repeatedly divides integers. For two n-bit integers, we might expect each division requires $O(n^2)$ operations and, in the worst case, we need $O(n)$ divisions. In practice the complexity is smaller, because the complexity of the divisions becomes smaller in the course of the algorithm. Unfortunately, to exploit this fact, the circuit must be *dynamic*: The number of divisions and the circuit for each division depend on the inputs. We cannot build such a quantum circuit, since we cannot observe the input (it may be in superposition).

We considered several approaches, but found that RNSL's circuit is the best. Appendix A.2 details our reasoning. However, we found several improvements to it. Their circuit models an algorithm of Kaliski [17], which applies a round operation (Fig. 6a) for up to $2n$ iterations. Conditional logic selects one of four different cases that can occur in each round. As a quantum circuit, this requires applying all four possible rounds, each with a different control. Figure 6b shows our alternative formulation based on swaps.

Figure 5a shows the round operation of RNSL's quantum circuit implementation of Kaliski's algorithm. This circuit repeats the controlled additions, doublings, and halvings, with different registers playing the role of input or output. Our method (Fig. 5b) performs each of these operations once, using controlled swaps to arrange inputs and outputs for the respective case. The lower auxiliary bit and $|m_i\rangle$ uniquely specify the round and we use these bits to control a swap. A controlled n-bit swap is approximately the same cost as a controlled n-bit cyclic shift.

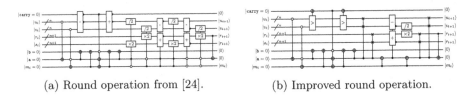

(a) Round operation from [24].   (b) Improved round operation.

Fig. 5. Improvement to the round operation in the binary extended Euclidean algorithm from [24] addressing the different cases by controlled swaps.

Correcting Pseudo-Inverses in Parallel. Classically, the Kaliski algorithm uses only k rounds, with $n \leq k \leq 2n$ for n-bit integers. RNSL's quantum circuit executes $2n$ rounds, controlled in such a way that only k actually modify the input. This produces an auxiliary qubit counter with a value of $2n - k$ and a pseudo-inverse output of $x^{-1}2^{-n+k} \bmod p$ for an input x. We want to output the Montgomery inverse $x^{-1}2^n \bmod p$, which requires correcting the pseudo-inverse.

Instead of a separate doubling circuit like the one RNSL use, we add a doubling operation to each division round. After copying out the pseudo-inverse, during the subsequent uncomputation we use the same control that the round operation uses: in each of the $2n$ rounds, either we double the output register or perform a division round. These can be done in parallel, which improves the depth without increasing the total gate count. The result is that we compute $2n - k$ doublings, exactly what is needed to correct the pseudo-inverse.

Modular Division. In elliptic curve point addition, the inversion is only necessary to compute a division. To divide an integer x by y modulo a prime p, RNSL first invert y in an auxiliary register, perform the multiplication by the result, then invert y again to uncompute the auxiliary qubits as shown in Fig. 7a.

Because the inversion uses Bennett's method, we pebble in the same way as the multiply-then-add circuit. To save qubits, we notice that after the inversion, three registers contain known values of 0, 1, and the modulus p. We can clear these auxiliary qubits with at most $3n$ parallel X gates, then re-use them for

(a) Kaliski's algorithm	(b) Equivalent formulation

1: **if** u odd and v even **then**
2:     $v \leftarrow v/2$
3:     $r \leftarrow 2r$
4: **else if** u even and v odd **then**
5:     $u \leftarrow u/2$
6:     $s \leftarrow 2s$
7: **else if** u odd and v odd and
     $u > v$ **then**
8:     $u \leftarrow (u - v)/2$
9:     $r \leftarrow r + s$
10:     $s \leftarrow 2s$
11: **else if** u odd and v odd and
     $v \geq u$ **then**
12:     $v \leftarrow (v - u)/2$
13:     $s \leftarrow r + s$
14:     $r \leftarrow 2r$
15: **end if**
	1: $b_{swap} \leftarrow$ `false`
	2: **if** u even and v odd, or u and
	     v both odd and $u > v$ **then**
	3: **swap** u and v
	4: **swap** r and s
	5: $b_{swap} \leftarrow$ `true`
	6: **end if**
	7: **if** u odd and v odd **then**
	8: $v \leftarrow v - u$
	9: $s \leftarrow r + s$
	10: **end if**
	11: $v \leftarrow v/2$
	12: $r \leftarrow 2r$
	13: **if** b_{swap} **then**
	14: **swap** u and v
	15: **swap** r and s
	16: **end if**

Fig. 6. Kaliski's algorithm, and an equivalent formulation based on swaps.

modular multiplication. Denoting the inverse and multiplication operations with auxiliary qubits by $\mathtt{inv}_A$ and $\mathtt{mul}_A$, respectively, Fig. 7b depicts a full modular division. The pseudo-inverse correction is compatible with modular division.

5   Elliptic Curves

Elliptic curve arithmetic has been heavily optimized for *classical* computers, but because Shor's algorithm requires unique representations of points and in-place point addition, few of these optimizations apply. We find affine Weierstrass coordinates to be the most efficient method; Appendix A.4 explains this choice in more detail.

Affine Weierstrass coordinates are one of the conceptually simplest methods, and RNSL use them for their circuit. We assume the elliptic curve equation has the form $E : y^2 = x^3 + ax + b$ with $a, b \in \mathbb{F}_p$ and we represent points by pairs (x, y) that satisfy this equation. Combining RNSL's circuit with the optimizations from this paper, we obtain a circuit with a total cost of 2 divisions, 2 multiplications, 1 squaring, and 9 additions.

The simple formulas with affine coordinates are naturally in-place. The general concept is the same as in [24]. The original x and y coordinates are replaced by multiplying and adding to them, and once we have, we can use the new coordinates to uncompute the slope. This also means that the circuit produces incorrect outputs if P or Q is the point at infinity or if $P = \pm Q$, because in these

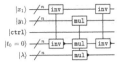

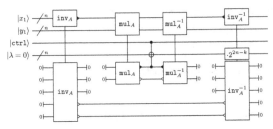

(a) Inversion steps in elliptic curve point addition from [24]. Auxiliary qubits are not shown. Each inv block represents inv$_A$, copying out, then inv$_A^{-1}$ (with the same pattern for mul). Thus, this circuit contains 4 inv$_A$ steps and 2 mul$_A$ steps.

(b) More efficient modular division. o⊢ depicts initializing an auxiliary qubit to zero, and ⊣o depicts removing an auxiliary qubit known to be zero. The doubling of the output λ in the last step corrects the pseudo-inverse output.

Fig. 7. Improvement to the modular division circuit from [24] by clearing and re-using auxiliary qubits before the full uncomputation.

cases the slope does not exist. Proos and Zalka [23] and RNSL [24] both argue that these exceptional cases only slightly distort the desired quantum state in Shor's algorithm and their influence is negligible.

5.1   Windowed Arithmetic

Shor's algorithm uses $2n$ qubits as control qubits, half of which control circuits that add P, $2P$, $4P$, etc.; the other half control addition of Q, $2Q$, etc. The points are added to a single quantum register which we call the *accumulator*. This process requires $2n$ point additions. We instead use a windowed approach, analogous to ubiquitous classical pre-computation techniques and similar to the techniques used for RSA in [14]. Other classical pre-computation strategies are less effective, as Appendix A.5 discusses.

For windowed scalar multiplication, we use the index as an address for a sequential quantum look-up, which loads a superposition of points $\mathcal{O}, P, 2P, 3P, \ldots, (2^{\ell} - 1)P$ into an auxiliary register which we call the *cache*. For elliptic curves, this requires us to switch from a circuit adding a classical point to a circuit adding two quantum points, but this has little effect on the cost. The depth and T-count of the look-up are exponential in the window size ℓ, but we save ℓ point additions.

Signed Addition. We can save a factor of 2 in windowing by using one qubit to control the sign of $P = (x, y)$ and only using $\ell - 1$ for the look-up (Fig. 8). Since $-P = (x, -y)$, the extra qubit only needs to control a cheap modular negation. This changes the indexing slightly. Our original windowed circuit took an address register $|b\rangle$ and an input register $|R\rangle$, and produced $|b\rangle\,|[b]P + R\rangle$. Using the top bit $b_{\ell-1}$ of $b = b_{\ell-1}2^{\ell-1} + b'$ as a sign and looking up $b'P$ if $b_{\ell-1} = 1$ and $(2^{\ell-1} - b')P$ and negating it if $b_{\ell-1} = 0$, we can implement the operation

$$\sum_{b\in\{0,1\}^\ell} |b\rangle\,|R\rangle \mapsto \sum_{b\in\{0,1\}^\ell} |b\rangle\,\big|[b - 2^{\ell-1}]P + R\big\rangle . \qquad (1)$$

Thus, we get an offset in each round, but since the offset is constant, it has no effect on the final phase estimation.

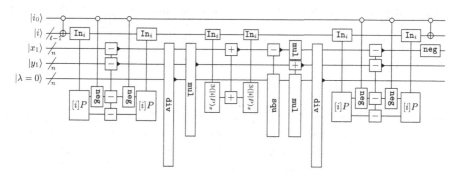

Fig. 8. Signed windowed elliptic curve addition, with ℓ address qubits. In_i is the indexing half of the look-up gate, which writes the classical data shown into the output registers. The width of the circuits is proportional to the number of auxiliary qubits used.

6 Results

We present quantum resource estimates for Shor's algorithm based on our cost estimates for windowed elliptic curve point addition. We optimized for three different cost metrics: either minimizing circuit width (the total number of logical qubits), the total number of T gates in the circuit, or total circuit depth. Window sizes above 18 were too large to simulate, so we extrapolated from the costs for smaller lookup tables. With Q#, we calculated the cost of a point addition on the three NIST curves [31] P256, P384 and P521, using 8-bit look-ups, then subtracted the cost of six 8-bit look-ups and added the cost of six ℓ-bit look-ups to get the cost of point addition with an ℓ-bit window. We multiplied this cost by the number of windows dividing $2n$ to get the full cost of Shor's algorithm for ECDLP. From this we selected optimal window sizes. We can use n instead of $n+1$ because the order of each NIST curve is less than its modulus [31].

Table 1 shows our results together with those of RNSL [24] for comparison. Their circuits use fewer than 2 Toffoli gates per time step on average, so we assume that with 8 extra qubits (c.f. Sect. 3) they can use Toffoli gates of T-depth 1. Our optimization for the number of qubits is shown in the row labeled *Low W*. Since RNSL optimize for the same metric, those results allow a direct comparison. We were able to improve on RNSL's circuit in all metrics. For P256, we reduce the number of logical qubits from 2338 to 2124, while reducing the T-depth and T-count by factors of 54 and 119, respectively.

Additionally, we report more significant improvements over RNSL's work in depth and T-count when optimizing for those. For 521-bit moduli, the improvement is a factor of 13,792 in depth for an increase of 22% in qubits, or a 463 factor reduction in T-gates for a 12% increase in qubits.

Table 1. Resource estimates for Shor's full algorithm to compute the ECDLP. RNSL results are taken from [24]. Rows labeled Low W/Low T/ Low D show estimates for circuits minimizing width, T gate count and total depth, respectively.

Circuit	Window size	Gates Cliffords	Measure	T	Total	Depth T	All gates	Width Qubits
256-bit modulus								
RNSL	–	–	–	$1.60 \cdot 2^{39}$	–	$1.69 \cdot 2^{36}$	–	2338
Low W	19	$1.32 \cdot 2^{34}$	$1.76 \cdot 2^{26}$	$1.72 \cdot 2^{32}$	$1.45 \cdot 2^{35}$	$1.98 \cdot 2^{30}$	$1.89 \cdot 2^{32}$	2124
Low T	19	$1.75 \cdot 2^{33}$	$1.95 \cdot 2^{27}$	$1.08 \cdot 2^{31}$	$1.80 \cdot 2^{34}$	$1.44 \cdot 2^{29}$	$1.85 \cdot 2^{31}$	2619
Low D	15	$1.04 \cdot 2^{34}$	$1.61 \cdot 2^{28}$	$1.34 \cdot 2^{32}$	$1.40 \cdot 2^{34}$	$1.12 \cdot 2^{24}$	$1.40 \cdot 2^{27}$	2871
384-bit modulus								
RNSL	–	–	–	$1.44 \cdot 2^{41}$	–	$1.51 \cdot 2^{38}$	–	3492
Low W	21	$1.46 \cdot 2^{36}$	$1.23 \cdot 2^{29}$	$1.51 \cdot 2^{34}$	$1.57 \cdot 2^{37}$	$1.68 \cdot 2^{32}$	$1.77 \cdot 2^{34}$	3151
Low T	19	$1.05 \cdot 2^{35}$	$1.28 \cdot 2^{29}$	$1.74 \cdot 2^{32}$	$1.10 \cdot 2^{36}$	$1.21 \cdot 2^{31}$	$1.31 \cdot 2^{33}$	3901
Low D	15	$1.73 \cdot 2^{35}$	$1.34 \cdot 2^{30}$	$1.13 \cdot 2^{34}$	$1.17 \cdot 2^{36}$	$1.23 \cdot 2^{25}$	$1.48 \cdot 2^{28}$	4278
521-bit modulus								
RNSL	–	–	–	$1.81 \cdot 2^{42}$	–	$1.91 \cdot 2^{39}$	–	4727
Low W	22	$1.85 \cdot 2^{37}$	$1.59 \cdot 2^{30}$	$1.82 \cdot 2^{35}$	$1.98 \cdot 2^{38}$	$1.99 \cdot 2^{33}$	$1.09 \cdot 2^{36}$	4258
Low T	20	$1.45 \cdot 2^{35}$	$1.49 \cdot 2^{30}$	$1.00 \cdot 2^{34}$	$1.57 \cdot 2^{36}$	$1.40 \cdot 2^{32}$	$1.54 \cdot 2^{34}$	5273
Low D	15	$1.10 \cdot 2^{37}$	$1.70 \cdot 2^{31}$	$1.43 \cdot 2^{35}$	$1.48 \cdot 2^{37}$	$1.13 \cdot 2^{26}$	$1.27 \cdot 2^{29}$	5789

Acknowledgements. We thank Dan Bernstein, Martin Ekerå, Iggy van Hoof, and Tanja Lange for helpful suggestions about elliptic curve arithmetic. We thank Martin Albrecht for lending computing power to run resource estimates.

A   Alternative Approaches

A.1   Modular Multiplication

RNSL provide two circuits for modular multiplication. The first is the one proposed by Proos and Zalka [23], which uses a double-and-add approach, where doubling and addition are both modular operations modulo p. The other is reversible Montgomery multiplication, which uses an add-and-halve approach and works in Montgomery form. The primary motivation for considering Montgomery multiplication instead of the straightforward double-and-add method is that modular reduction is achieved by suitable additions to clear lower order bits and divisions by 2 (i.e. bit rotations) as part of the whole circuit, not delegated to the addition and halving circuits. This results in simpler operations per bit.

However, Montgomery multiplication has the downside that it entangles with a register of auxiliary qubits which must be cleared. In our case, at every point in an elliptic curve point addition, we have enough spare auxiliary qubits for this. Overall, it is cheaper, even with the Bennett method, and especially with the multiply-then-add technique of Sect. 4.1.

A.2   Modular Inversion

Proos and Zalka [23] (PZ) gave an approach to modular inversion based on precise control of a bit-shift division operation, with asymptotic complexity of $O(n^2)$. There are $O(n)$ iterations of a *round*. Each round implements conditional logic by computing state qubits, then using those state qubits to control some operations on the integer registers.

RNSL use a similar round-based construction, which implements a reversible binary extended Euclidean algorithm. As with multiplication, the primary difference between the PZ division and the RNSL division is that PZ's is based on doubling and integer long division, while RNSL's is based on halving and binary operations. The PZ inversion leaves only $O(\lg n)$ auxiliary qubits, while RNSL creates $2n + O(\lg n)$ auxiliary qubits, but PZ has a higher depth and gate cost.

Naively, the PZ approach uses $5n$ qubits, though they show that, with fidelity loss on the order of $O(n^{-3})$ per round, they require only $2n + 8\sqrt{n} + O(\log n)$ qubits. The RNSL approach uses $6n$ qubits. We choose to use the RNSL algorithm. It is exactly correct, so it can be used for higher depth algorithms, and the total T-cost and depth are less than half of the PZ approach.

A.3   Recursive GCD Algorithms

There are several sub-quadratic GCD algorithms (such as [7]). These work by defining a series of 2×2 matrices T_n such that $T_n T_{n-1} \cdots T_1(u, v)^T$ will map integers u and v to the nth step of the Euclidean algorithm. These can be computed and multiplied together recursively.

Adapted to quantum circuits, these approaches require quantum matrix multiplication. We could find no efficient method to do this in-place, meaning that each recursive call would require a new set of auxiliary qubits to store the matrix output. This would quickly overwhelm our qubit budget. The base case of [7] is nearly identical to our approach for a single round.

One of the primary advantages of [7] is that the recursive process allows much of the arithmetic to be done with small integers which fit into the registers of classical CPUs. All the qubits in our model of a quantum computer are identical, so it has no caching or register issues. If quantum technologies arise with different kinds of qubits (perhaps a "memory" with higher coherence times but lower gate fidelity), then recursive GCD algorithms should be revisited. It is also possible that the specific structure of the matrices in this approach permit an easy, in-place multiplication circuit. We leave this to future work.

A.4   Alternate Curve Representations

Projective Coordinates. Projective coordinates use equivalence classes $(X : Y : Z)$ of triples (X, Y, Z) to represent an elliptic curve point, where $(X_1, Y_1, Z_1) \sim (X_2, Y_2, Z_2)$ iff there is some non-zero constant c such that $X_1 = cX_2$, $Y_1 = cY_2$, and $Z_1 = cZ_2$. These can be used with many different families of curves. Projective coordinates lend themselves to efficient, inversion-free arithmetic, which is appealing for classical computers.

Projective coordinates do not give a *unique* representation of each point, which Shor's algorithm requires to ensure history independence and thus proper interference of states in superposition. Dividing by the Z coordinate produces a unique representation but requires an expensive division. It is an open problem to provide a unique projective representation with division-free arithmetic.

Another issue is that the classical elliptic curve formulas, naively adapted to quantum circuits, operate out-of-place. An out-of-place addition circuit is easy to adapt into an in-place addition circuit. If we can construct a circuit U_{+Q} to add a point Q, we can construct a circuit U_{-Q}, and we can construct an in-place point addition by writing $P + Q$ into another register, then subtracting Q from $P + Q$ to clear the input. This doubles the cost of point addition.

This technique requires a unique representation. If $(P + Q) - Q$ does not have the same representation as P, we cannot cancel them out. Thus, for any current algorithm to compute addition with projective coordinates with cost C, we can transform it to a quantum-suitable in-place version with cost $2C + 2D$, where D is the cost of division. The division creates a unique representation.

According to the Explicit Formulas Database [6], the lowest-cost addition uses 6 squares and/or multiplications. With the required reductions, the total cost is 12 squares/multiplications and 2 divisions, much higher than affine Weierstrass coordinates. Thus, we choose not to use projective coordinates in this work.

A.5   Precomputation

Precomputed tables of certain powers of the base element can speed up exponentiations. The "comb" method is a standard technique used for elliptic curve scalar multiplication. To multiply a point P by a scalar k, we divide k into $k_1 + 2k_2 + \cdots + 2^\ell k_\ell$ for some ℓ, with the property that k_j contains bits of k in positions congruent to j modulo ℓ (each k_j looks like a comb of bits). We then precompute a table of all multiples of P by scalars of the form $b_0 + b_1 2^\ell + b_2 2^{2\ell} \ldots$, with $b_i \in \{0, 1\}$. By the definition of k_j, each $k_j P$ is a precomputed point in this table for all j. Thus, we can compute kP by using k_j to look up elements of the table, adding them to a running total, and doubling the running total.

The advantage of the comb technique is that it saves precomputation. We only precompute one table and use it for the entire computation. Unfortunately for the quantum case, precomputation is essentially free because it is entirely classical, but look-ups are expensive. The comb technique does not reduce the number of table look-ups, since we must do a separate look-up for each index k_j.

Further, efficient in-place point doubling is unlikely, since it implies efficient in-place point halving. Thus, doubling points in the comb would require some pebbling technique which would likely add significant depth or width costs.

B   Modular Division and Addition

For elliptic curve addition, we only need to divide integers and copy the result to a blank output, but other applications may wish to construct a circuit that, given registers containing x, y, and z, will compute $yx^{-1} + z$.

We might simply invert, multiply, and then add the output of the multiplication instead of copying. However, doubling the output to correct the pseudo-inverse while uncomputing will also multiply z by a factor of 2^{2n-k}. To correct for this, we can repeatedly halve z during the *forward* computation of the modular inverse. This means that while we compute the modular inverse, we control a modular halving of the register containing z by the counter, which will halve z exactly $2n - k$ times. Then we multiply the pseudo-inverse by y and add the result to the register with z, producing the state $\left| x^{-1}2^{2n-k} \bmod p \right\rangle \left| y2^n \bmod p \right\rangle \left| z2^{2n-k} + x^{-1}y2^{2n-k} \bmod p \right\rangle$. From here, if we perform controlled modular doublings of the register containing z as we uncompute the inversion circuit, this will correct both z and the pseudo-inverse of x, producing the desired output.

C   Analysis of Windowed Arithmetic

A quantum look-up to N elements requires $4N$ T-gates [2]. To optimize window costs, we balance this cost against the operations we save.

Multiplication. Section 4.1 describes a single windowed multiplication round. For n-bit integers with window size k, repeating this round $\lceil n/k \rceil$ times performs the full multiplication. Since the quantum look-up will cost $4 \cdot 2^k$ T gates [2] and uncontrolled $n + k$-bit addition costs $O(n + k)$ T gates, we expect the optimal window size to be approximately $k = O(\lg n)$. The total multiplication cost is still $O(n^2)$ because we only window addition by p, not addition of the quantum register y. Compared to un-windowed add-and-halve multiplication, windowing should save a factor of roughly $\frac{1}{2} + O(\frac{1}{\lg n})$. Similar reasoning suggests savings of $\frac{1}{2} + O(\frac{1}{\lg \lg n})$ in depth.

Numerical estimates show a window size of $k \approx 0.7 \lg n + 0.5$ optimizes T-count, and $1.97 \lg \lg n - 1.11$ optimizes T-depth. At the scale we estimate, this is only noticeable in the leading coefficient of the cost. We found a 22% reduction in T-depth at 384 bits, for example.

Windowing adds a significant cost of roughly $n + k$ auxiliary qubits, but the full elliptic curve point addition circuit has enough unused auxiliary qubits during any multiplication that this does not make a difference.

Point Addition. Windowing requires 2 extra registers as the cache to load the precomputed points. We use the components of the second point three times during point addition. We could perform the look-up once and keep the values, increasing total circuit width by two registers. Alternatively, we can fit the look-ups within the existing space. At every point where x_2 or y_2 are added, the circuit has spare auxiliary qubits available. Thus, we can perform the look-up, add the point to the quantum register, then uncompute the quantum look-up to free the qubits for the expensive modular division. This requires us six look-ups (including uncomputing) rather than just two, but uses no extra registers.

With a window size of ℓ, including sign bit, each look-up costs $4 \cdot 2^{\ell-1}$ T gates and T-depth. The windowing saves us $\ell - 1$ point additions. If point addition costs A T gates, we would expect $\ell \approx \lg(A/24)$ to be the optimal value, leading to a factor ℓ reduction in T-gate cost.

D   Automatic Compilation for Aggressive T-Count and T-Depth Reduction

In this section, we motivate automatic compilation methods to drastically reduce the T-count and the T-depth if we allow a significant increase in circuit width.

The modular multiplication followed by an addition is one of the most costly operations in the overall algorithm. It is implemented as a unitary $U : |x\rangle|y\rangle|z\rangle|0\rangle \mapsto |x\rangle|y\rangle|(xy + z) \bmod p\rangle|0\rangle$ that adds the result of the multiplication of two numbers x and y onto a third number z, all in Montgomery form with bit-width n and modulus p. We apply the following procedure to automatically obtain a quantum circuit for this operation:

1. We generate logic networks over the gate basis $\{\text{AND}, \text{XOR}, \text{INV}\}$, called Xor-And-inverter Graphs (XAGs), for the functions $xy \bmod p$, $(x+y) \bmod p$, and $(x - y) \bmod p$, where x and y are integers in Montgomery form.
2. We apply the logic optimization method described in [30] to minimize the number of AND gates in the XAGs.
3. The optimized XAGs are then translated into out-of-place quantum circuits using the method in [18], which requires 4 T gates for each AND gate in the XAG. Optimizing these circuits for depth requires roughly 2 qubits for each AND gate in the XAG, by using the AND gate construction from Sect. 3.

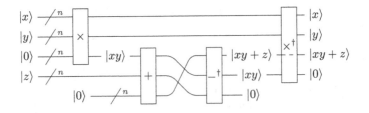

Fig. 9. Quantum circuit that implements $xy+z \bmod p$, using out-of-place constructions for modular multiplication, modular addition, and modular subtraction.

4. The automatically generated unitaries are composed as described in Fig. 9, which uses a technique similar to that described in Appendix A.4 to turn the out-of-place addition and subtraction into an in-place addition.

Table 2. Comparison of resource costs between a manual and automatic construction to implement $|xy + z \bmod p\rangle$.

Bit-width	Manual construction			Automatic construction		
	T-count	T-depth	Width	T-count	T-depth	Width
256	8,176,739	50,253	2,319	1,576,296	1,542	394,588
384	18,322,671	76,125	3,470	3,550,552	2,310	888,408
521	33,751,240	137,183	4,702	6,535,384	3,132	1,634,890

Table 2 lists the resource costs in terms of T-count, T-depth, and circuit width, for both the manual construction and the automatic construction. Several factors of reduction in T-count and T-depth are possible, while the increase in the number of qubits is significant. However, such a design point can be of high interest, in particular when combined with automatic quantum memory strategies, e.g., pebbling [19], that can find intermediate trade-off points that lie in between the manual and automatic construction.

References

1. Amy, M., Maslov, D., Mosca, M., Roetteler, M.: A meet-in-the-middle algorithm for fast synthesis of depth-optimal quantum circuits. IEEE Trans. Comput. Aided Des. Integr. Circuits Syst. **32**(6), 818–830 (2013)
2. Babbush, R., et al.: Encoding electronic spectra in quantum circuits with linear T complexity. Phys. Rev. X **8**(4), 041015 (2018). arXiv: quant-ph/1805.03662
3. Barenco, A., et al.: Elementary gates for quantum computation. Phys. Rev. A **52**(5), 3457–3467 (1995). arXiv: quant-ph/9503016
4. Bennett, C.H.: Logical reversibility of computation. IBM J. Res. Dev. **17**(6), 525–532 (1973)
5. Bennett, C.H.: Time/space trade-offs for reversible computation. SIAM J. Comput. **18**(4), 766–776 (1989)
6. Bernstein, D.J., Lange, T.: (2007). https://www.hyperelliptic.org/EFD
7. Bernstein, D.J., Yang, B.-Y.: Fast constant-time GCD computation and modular inversion. IACR Trans. Cryptogr. Hardw. Embed. Syst. **2019**(3), 340–398 (2019)
8. Cuccaro, S.A., Draper, T.G., Kutin, S.A., Moulton, D.P.: A new quantum ripple-carry addition circuit (2004). arXiv:quant-ph/0410184
9. Draper, T.G., Kutin, S.A., Rains, E.M., Svore, K.M.: A logarithmic-depth quantum carry-lookahead adder, June 2004. arXiv: quant-ph/0406142
10. Fowler, A.G., Mariantoni, M., Martinis, J.M., Cleland, A.N.: Surface codes: towards practical large-scale quantum computation. Phys. Rev. A **86**, 032324 (2012)

11. Gheorghiu, V., Mosca, M.: Benchmarking the quantum cryptanalysis of symmetric, public-key and hash-based cryptographic schemes (2019)
12. Gidney, C.: Halving the cost of quantum addition. Quantum **2**, 74 (2018)
13. Gidney, C.: Windowed quantum arithmetic (2019). arXiv: quant-ph/1905.07682
14. Gidney, C., Ekerå, M.: How to factor 2048 bit RSA integers in 8 hours using 20 million noisy qubits, May 2019. arXiv: quant-ph/1905.09749
15. Griffiths, R., Niu, C.-S.: Semiclassical Fourier transform for quantum computation. Phys. Rev. Lett. **76**(17), 3228–3231 (1996)
16. Jones, C.: Low-overhead constructions for the fault-tolerant Toffoli gate. Phys. Rev. A **87**(2), 022328 (2013)
17. Kaliski, B.S.: The Montgomery inverse and its applications. IEEE Trans. Comput. **44**(8), 1064–1065 (1995)
18. Meuli, G., Soeken, M., Campbell, E., Roetteler, M., De Micheli, G.: The role of multiplicative complexity in compiling low T-count oracle circuits (2019). arXiv: quant-ph/1908.01609
19. Meuli, G., Soeken, M., Roetteler, M., Bjørner, N., De Micheli, G.: Reversible pebbling game for quantum memory management. In: Design, Automation & Test in Europe Conference, pp. 288–291 (2019)
20. Montgomery, P.L.: Modular multiplication without trial division. Math. Comput. **44**(170), 519–521 (1985)
21. Moore, C.: Quantum circuits: fanout, parity, and counting (1999). arXiv: quant-ph/9903046
22. Nielsen, M.A., Chuang, I.L.: Quantum Computation and Quantum Information. Cambridge University Press, Cambridge (2000)
23. Proos, J., Zalka, C.: Shor's discrete logarithm quantum algorithm for elliptic curves, January 2003. arXiv: quant-ph/0301141
24. Roetteler, M., Naehrig, M., Svore, K.M., Lauter, K.: Quantum resource estimates for computing elliptic curve discrete logarithms. In: Takagi, T., Peyrin, T. (eds.) ASIACRYPT 2017. LNCS, vol. 10625, pp. 241–270. Springer, Cham (2017). https://doi.org/10.1007/978-3-319-70697-9_9
25. Selinger, P.: Quantum circuits of T-depth one. Phys. Rev. A **87**(4), 042302 (2013). arXiv: 1210.0974
26. Shor, P.W.: Algorithms for quantum computation: discrete logarithms and factoring. In: FOCS 1994, pp. 124–134 (1994)
27. Shor, P.W.: Polynomial-time algorithms for prime factorization and discrete logarithms on a quantum computer. SIAM J. Comput. **26**(5), 1484–1509 (1997)
28. Svore, K.M., et al.: Q#: enabling scalable quantum computing and development with a high-level DSL. In: RWDSL@CGO 2018 (2018)
29. Takahashi, Y., Tani, S., Kunihiro, N.: Quantum addition circuits and unbounded fan-out. Quantum Inf. Comput. **10**, 10 (2009)
30. Testa, E., Soeken, M., Amarù, L.G., De Micheli, G.: Reducing the multiplicative complexity in logic networks for cryptography and security applications. In: Design Automation Conference, p. 74 (2019)
31. U.S. Department of Commerce/National Institute of Standards and Technology. Digital signature standard (DSS). FIPS-186-4 (2013). http://nvlpubs.nist.gov/nistpubs/FIPS/NIST.FIPS.186-4.pdf

The Power of Few Qubits and Collisions – Subset Sum Below Grover's Bound

Alexander Helm[✉] and Alexander May

Ruhr-University Bochum, Bochum, Germany
{alexander.helm,alex.may}@rub.de

Abstract. Let $a_1, \ldots a_n, t$ be a solvable subset sum instance, i.e. there exists a subset of the a_i that sums to t. Such a subset can be found with Grover search in time $2^{\frac{n}{2}}$, the square root of the search space, using only $\mathcal{O}(n)$ qubits. The only quantum algorithms that beat Grover's square root bound – such as the Left-Right-Split algorithm of Brassard, Hoyer, Tapp – either use an exponential amount of qubits or an exponential amount of expensive classical memory with quantum random access (QRAM). We propose the first subset sum quantum algorithms that breaks the square root Grover bound with linear many qubits and without QRAM. Building on the representation technique and the quantum collision finding algorithm from Chailloux, Naya-Plasencia and Schrottenloher (CNS), we obtain a quantum algorithm with time $2^{0.48n}$.

Using the Schroeppel-Shamir list construction technique, we further improve downto run time $2^{0.43n}$. The price that we have to pay for beating the square root bound is that as opposed to Grover search our algorithms require classical memory, but no QRAM, i.e. we get a time/memory/qubit tradeoff. Thus, our algorithms have to be compared to purely classical time/memory subset sum trade-offs such as those of Howgrave-Graham and Joux. Our quantum algorithms improve on these purely classical algorithms for all memory complexities $M < 2^{0.2n}$. As an example, for memory $2^{0.1n}$ we obtain run time $2^{0.47n}$ as opposed to $2^{0.63n}$ for the best classical algorithm.

Keywords: Quantum algorithms · Amplitude amplification · Representation technique · Subset sum · Collision finding

1 Introduction

Although there is remarkable progress in the development of quantum computing devices, in the medium-term we will implement our quantum algorithms with a very limited number of qubits. Thus, it is of great importance both from a theoretical and practical perspective to develop algorithms that run with small quantum memory consumption, say polynomial or even linear.

A. Helm—Founded by NRW Research Training Group SecHuman.

A. May—Funded by DFG under Germany's Excellence Strategy - EXC 2092 CASA - 390781972.

© Springer Nature Switzerland AG 2020
J. Ding and J.-P. Tillich (Eds.): PQCrypto 2020, LNCS 12100, pp. 445–460, 2020.
https://doi.org/10.1007/978-3-030-44223-1_24

A prominent candidate for sharpening our algorithmic tools is the random subset sum problem, which lies at the heart of many post-quantum hardness assumptions such as SIS [Reg09]. Random subset sum instances consist of randomly chosen $a_1, \ldots, a_n \in \mathbb{Z}_{2^n}$, and a t that is the sum of a subset of a_i's modulo 2^n.

Classically, random subset sum instances can be solved with *polynomial memory* using collision finding and the representation technique [HGJ10] in time $2^{0.65n}$ [BCJ11, EM19], and without memory restrictions in time and space $2^{0.29n}$ [BCJ11]. There exist various time/memory tradeoffs in between [HGJ10, BCJ11, DDKS12, DEM19].

Quantumly, random subset sum can be solved with $\mathcal{O}(n)$ qubits in time $2^{n/2}$ using Grover search [Gro96]. The Left-Right-Split algorithm of Brassard, Hoyer and Tapp [BHT98, BJLM13] solves subset sum in time $2^{n/3}$ using $\mathcal{O}(n)$ many qubits, but also using $2^{n/3}$ classical memory with quantum random access (QRAM). However, QRAM is believed to be expensive to realize in practice [GR04]. The currently best time bound of $2^{0.23n}$ for subset sum is achieved by using a quantum random walk technique on the Becker-Coron-Joux algorithm [HM18]. However, this quantum walk algorithm also requires $2^{0.23n}$ many qubits, and therefore is practically completely unattainable.

In this paper, we want to focus on subset sum algorithms with a linear amount of qubits and without using QRAM. Our central research question is whether we can beat the Grover square root bound $2^{n/2}$ in our setting. Notice that our setting is motivated by the research direction initiated by Chailloux, Naya-Plasencia and Schrottenloher [CNPS17]. The authors of [CNPS17] developed a hash collision algorithm (called CNS) for hash functions $\{0,1\}^* \rightarrow \{0,1\}^n$ with run time $2^{2/5n}$ using $2^{1/5n}$ classical memory (without QRAM) and $\mathcal{O}(n)$ qubits.

Our Contribution. Since the best classical polynomial memory algorithms for subset sum also use collision finding, we take CNS quantum collision finding as our starting point. Combining CNS with the representation technique, we achieve a first quantum subset sum algorithm with run time $2^{0.48n}$ and classical memory $2^{0.24n}$. While this already breaks Grover's bound using only $\mathcal{O}(n)$ many qubits, our first algorithm is still a bit unsatisfactory. Namely, there exist purely classical subset sum algorithms that with the same memory $2^{0.24n}$ achieve run time only $2^{0.39n}$, without using any qubits. Thus, our first algorithm does not improve on the known classical subset sum landscape.

Based on our first CNS adaption, we develop a second subset sum quantum algorithm using Schroeppel-Shamir list construction [SS81]. With $\mathcal{O}(n)$ qubits, our new construction achieves a time/memory tradeoff with

$$\text{time } T = \frac{2^{0.5n}}{M^{0.25}} \quad \text{for any classical memory } M \leq 2^{0.28n}.$$

The resulting tradeoff line is depicted in Fig. 1 as 2nd algorithm. Notice that for maximal memory $2^{0.28n}$ we go downto $2^{0.43n}$. As desired, our algorithm achieves Grover complexity $2^{n/2}$ when we use no memory. Moreover for any additional memory, we go below the Grover bound, see the red area in Fig. 1. In comparison to purely classical time-memory tradeoffs, we improve for any memory $M \leq 2^{n/5}$, see the shaded area in Fig. 1. Thus, our relatively moderate $\mathcal{O}(n)$ qubit memory provides speedups in a relatively large parameter space.

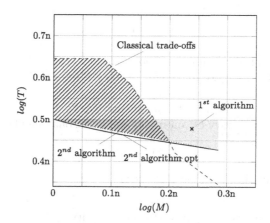

Fig. 1. Comparison of our results and the previous best classical trade-offs for subset sum. (Color figure online)

We further optimize our second algorithm, resulting in the slightly improved convex curve denoted in Fig. 1 by 2nd algorithm opt.

Our paper is organized as follows. In Sect. 2 we recall the CNS quantum collision finding algorithm [CNPS17]. We develop our first subset sum algorithm based on collision finding in Sect. 3. The second subset sum algorithm, that achieves a linear time-memory tradeoff, is described in Sect. 4. In Sect. 4.1 we further optimize our second quantum subset sum algorithm.

2 Quantum Collision Finding

Let us briefly define some preliminaries and recall the CNS collision finding algorithm [CNPS17].

We consider random subset sum instances defined as follows.

Definition 1 (Random Subset Sum). *Let* $\mathbf{a}$ *be chosen uniformly at random from* $(\mathbb{Z}_{2^n})^n$. *For a random* $\mathbf{e} \in \{0,1\}^n$ *with Hamming weight* $\mathrm{wt}(\mathbf{e}) = \frac{n}{2}$ *we define* $t = \langle \mathbf{a}, \mathbf{e} \rangle = \sum_{i=1}^{n} a_i e_i \mod 2^n$. *Then* $(\mathbf{a}, t) \in (\mathbb{Z}_{2^n})^{n+1}$ *is called a* random subset sum instance *and any* $\mathbf{e}' \in \{0,1\}^n$ *with* $\langle \mathbf{a}, \mathbf{e}' \rangle = t$ *is called a* solution.

By Definition 1, every random subset sum instance has at least one solution and with high probability at most poly(n) many solutions. For ease of notation we assume, that we have a unique solution $\mathbf{e}$, which is the worst-case for our algorithms. Any $(\mathbf{x_1}, \ldots, \mathbf{x_k}) \in \{-1, 0, 1\}^n$ with $\mathbf{e} = \sum_{i=1}^{k} \mathbf{x_i}$ is called a *representation* of $\mathbf{e}$.

By $H(\cdot)$ we denote the binary entropy function $H(\alpha) := -\alpha \log \alpha - (1 - \alpha) \log(1 - \alpha)$ for $\alpha \in [0, 1]$, where $0 \cdot \log 0 := 0$. We use Stirling's formula to approximate binomial coefficients by the entropy function, as

$$\binom{n}{m} = \tilde{\Theta}\left(2^{H(\frac{m}{n})n}\right),$$

where the soft-Oh notion suppresses polynomial factors. We also round upwards for ease of notation, e.g. we have $n2^{n/3} = \tilde{\mathcal{O}}(2^{n/3}) \le 2^{0.34n}$ for sufficiently large n.

Let $\mathcal{A}$ be an algorithm that implements $f : \mathbb{F}_2^n \to \mathbb{F}_2^m$ within runtime t_f. Then the quantum unitary O_f on $n + m$ and additional ancilla qubits defined as

$$O_f(|\mathbf{x}\rangle \, |\mathbf{y}\rangle) := |\mathbf{x}\rangle \, |\mathbf{y} \oplus f(\mathbf{x})\rangle$$

can be implemented in runtime $T_f = \mathcal{O}(t_f)$.

Set-Membership Oracle [CNPS17]**:** Let $|\phi\rangle = \sum_i |\mathbf{x_i}\rangle$ be a quantum superposition, where each $\mathbf{x_i} \in \mathbb{F}_2^n$ has non-zero amplitude. Let $L \subseteq \mathbb{F}_2^n$ define a list. Notice that by definition, L does not contain an element twice.

We want to know which of the vectors $\mathbf{x_i}$ of $|\phi\rangle$ are in L. To this end, define the characteristic function

$$f_L : \mathbb{F}_2^n \to \mathbb{F}_2, \quad \mathbf{x} \mapsto \begin{cases} 1 & \text{if } \mathbf{x} \in L \\ 0 & \text{else} \end{cases}.$$

Then the quantum set-membership oracle for L with operator

$$O_{f_L}(|\phi\rangle \, |0\rangle) := \sum_i |\mathbf{x_i}\rangle \, |f_L(\mathbf{x_i})\rangle \tag{1}$$

can be computed in time $T_{f_L} = \mathcal{O}(n \cdot |L|)$ with $2n + 1$ qubits.

Amplitude Amplification [BHMT02]**:** Let $\mathcal{A}$ be a quantum algorithm that works with no measurements and produces a uniformly distributed superposition $|\phi\rangle = \sum_{\mathbf{x} \in \mathcal{X}} |\mathbf{x}\rangle$ for some set $\mathcal{X} \subseteq \mathbb{F}_2^n$ in runtime $T_{\mathcal{A}}$. Let $f : \mathbb{F}_2^n \to \mathbb{F}_2$ be a function with quantum unitary O_f on $n + 1$ and additional ancilla qubits that has runtime T_f.

Let us define the set $\mathcal{X}_f := \{\mathbf{x} \in \mathcal{X} \mid f(\mathbf{x}) = 1\}$. Thus a random $x \in \mathcal{X}$ evaluates to $f(\mathbf{x}) = 1$ with probability $p = \frac{|\mathcal{X}_f|}{|\mathcal{X}|}$. Then there exists a quantum algorithm, called *amplitude amplification*, that outputs an element $\mathbf{x} \in \mathcal{X}$ with $f(\mathbf{x}) = 1$ by sending $\mathcal{O}(\sqrt{p^{-1}})$ many queries to $\mathcal{A}, \mathcal{A}^{-1}, O_f$ and O_f^{-1} and finally measures.

We call $\mathcal{A}$ the setup and f the oracle function of amplitude amplification and set $T_{Setup} = T_{\mathcal{A}}$. The total runtime of amplitude amplification is given by

$$T = \tilde{\mathcal{O}}\left((T_{Setup} + T_f) \cdot \sqrt{p^{-1}}\right). \tag{2}$$

Amplitude amplification is a generalization of Grover search [Gro96]. Notice that in the Grover setting we have $\mathcal{X} = \mathbb{F}_2^n$ and $\mathcal{A}$ consists of a Hadamard operation on each qubit, which can be done efficiently in time $T_{Setup} = \mathcal{O}(1)$.

Remark 1. For the setup $\mathcal{A}$ we may use Grover search without final measurement. If we use as Grover oracle the characteristic function $g(\mathbf{x}) = 1 \Leftrightarrow \mathbf{x} \in \mathcal{X} \subseteq \mathbb{F}_2^n$ of $\mathcal{X}$, we achieve the desired uniform superposition $|\phi\rangle = \sum_{\mathbf{x} \in \mathcal{X}} |\mathbf{x}\rangle$. A random $\mathbf{x} \in \mathbb{F}_2^n$ evaluates to $g(\mathbf{x}) = 1$ with probability $p = \frac{|\mathcal{X}|}{|\mathbb{F}_2^n|}$. This implies $T_{Setup} = \tilde{\mathcal{O}}\left(T_g \cdot \sqrt{p^{-1}}\right)$.

CNS Quantum Collision Finding [CNPS17]. Let us slightly adapt CNS quantum collision finding to our needs. Instead of finding a collision for a random function $h \colon \mathbb{F}_2^n \to \mathbb{F}_2^n$ we use two random functions $h_i \colon S_i \to \mathbb{F}_2^n$ for $i = 1, 2$ with arbitrary domains S_1, S_2 satisfying $|S_1| \leq 2^n$. We denote the set of collisions between h_1 and h_2 by

$$C = \{(\mathbf{x_c}, \mathbf{x}_q) \in S_1 \times S_2 \mid h_1(\mathbf{x_c}) = h_2(\mathbf{x_q})\} \text{ with } |C| = R.$$

Let $(\mathbf{x_c}, \mathbf{x}_q) \in C$. We call $\mathbf{x_c}$ the *classical half* and $\mathbf{x_q}$ the *quantum half* of a collision, since we store $\mathbf{x_c}$ classically and compute $\mathbf{x_q}$ in quantum superposition.

Correctness. The CNS algorithm (see Algorithm 0) finds a collision $(\mathbf{x_c}, \mathbf{x}_q) \in C$ with only $\mathcal{O}(n)$ qubits in a two step process, see also Fig. 2. First one constructs a classically stored list L that contains candidates for the classical half $\mathbf{x_c}$ of a collision. The second step is an amplitude amplification that quantumly enumerates in superposition potential quantum halves $\mathbf{x_q}$ of a collision. We find matching halves by using the quantum set-membership oracle for L.

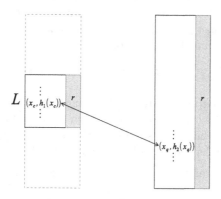

Fig. 2. Main idea of CNS quantum collision finding (Algorithm 0).

Algorithm 0: QUANTUM COLLISION FINDING

Input   : $h_i \colon S_i \to \mathbb{F}_2^n$ for $i = 1, 2$
Output   : $(\mathbf{x}_c, \mathbf{x}_q) \in S_1 \times S_2$ with $h_1(\mathbf{x}_c) = h_2(\mathbf{x}_q)$
Parameters: Optimize r, ℓ.
1. Let $S_r^{h_i} := \{\mathbf{x} \in S_i \mid h_i(\mathbf{x}) = 0 \bmod 2^r\}$ for $i = 1, 2$.
    Construct, element-wise via Grover search, a sorted (by second entry) list

$$L = \{(\mathbf{x}_c, h_1(\mathbf{x}_c)) \in S_r^{h_1} \times \mathbb{F}_2^n\} \text{ with } |L| = 2^\ell.$$

2. Perform amplitude amplification with the following Setup and Oracle.

(i) Setup: Construct

$$|\phi_r\rangle := \frac{1}{\sqrt{|S_r^{h_2}|}} \sum_{\mathbf{x}_q \in S_r^{h_2}} |\mathbf{x}_q, h_2(\mathbf{x}_q)\rangle \, |0\rangle .$$

(ii) Oracle: Set-Membership-Oracle $O_{f_L^h}$

$$O_{f_L^h}(|\phi_r\rangle) = \frac{1}{\sqrt{|S_r^{h_2}|}} \sum_{\mathbf{x}_q \in S_r^{h_2}} |\mathbf{x}_q, h_2(\mathbf{x}_q)\rangle \, |f_L^h(\mathbf{x}_q)\rangle .$$

Amplitude amplification eventually outputs some $|(\mathbf{x}_q, h_2(\mathbf{x}_q))\rangle\, |1\rangle$.

3. For the quantum half $\mathbf{x}_q$ search for the classic half $\mathbf{x}_c \in L$ with $h_1(\mathbf{x}_c) = h_2(\mathbf{x}_q)$.

In more detail, we construct a sorted (by second entry) list

$$L = \{(\mathbf{x_c}, h_1(\mathbf{x_c})) \mid h_1(\mathbf{x_c}) = 0 \bmod 2^r\} \subseteq S_1 \times \mathbb{F}_2^n,$$

where each element of L is constructed via Grover search. Since we fix r bits in L, on expectation $\frac{|S_1|}{2^r}$ elements of S_1 fulfill restriction $h_1(\mathbf{x_c}) = 0 \bmod 2^r$, and $h_1(\mathbf{x_c})$ can take at most 2^{n-r} different values. Since elements in L are different and $|S_1| \leq 2^n$, we obtain the restriction

$$\log L = \ell \leq \min\{\log |S_1| - r, n - r\} = \log |S_1| - r.$$

Furthermore we want to guarantee that on expectation L contains at least one element $\mathbf{x_c}$ that can be completed to a collision $(\mathbf{x_c}, \mathbf{x_q})$. In other words, we need an $\mathbf{x_c} \in L$ such that there exists an $\mathbf{x_q}$ with $(\mathbf{x_c}, \mathbf{x_q}) \in C$, $|C| = R$. A random $\mathbf{x_c} \in S_1$ can be completed to a collision with probability $\frac{R}{|S_1|}$. Thus, L should contain at least $\frac{|S_1|}{R}$ many elements, leading to the condition

$$\log |S_1| - \log R \leq \ell \leq \log |S_1| - r. \tag{3}$$

From (3) we obtain

$$0 \leq r \leq \log R. \tag{4}$$

For amplitude amplification we define the oracle function

$$f_L^h(\mathbf{x}_q) := \begin{cases} 1 & \text{if } \exists(\mathbf{x}_c, h_1(\mathbf{x}_c)) \in L \text{ with } h_1(\mathbf{x}_c) = h_2(\mathbf{x}_q) \\ 0 & \text{else} \end{cases}.$$

Then the set-membership oracle for L, defined for a single $\mathbf{x}_q$, becomes

$$O_{f_L^h}(|\mathbf{x}_q, h_2(\mathbf{x}_q)\rangle |0\rangle) := |\mathbf{x}_q, h_2(\mathbf{x}_q)\rangle |f_L^h(\mathbf{x}_q)\rangle.$$

Runtime. Let $|L| = 2^\ell$. By the randomness of h_1, every $\mathbf{x}_c \in S_1$ satisfies the restriction $h_1(\mathbf{x}_c) = 0 \bmod 2^r$ with probability $p = 2^{-r}$. Thus the runtime of the first step is

$$T_1 = \tilde{\Theta}\left(|L| \cdot \sqrt{p^{-1}}\right) = \tilde{\Theta}\left(2^\ell \cdot 2^{\frac{r}{2}}\right). \tag{5}$$

In the second step of Algorithm 0 we create a superposition over the set $S_r^{h_2} := \{\mathbf{x}_q \in S_2 \mid h_2(\mathbf{x}_q) = 0 \bmod 2^r\}$, as described in Remark 1. By the randomness of h_2, every $\mathbf{x}_q \in S$ satisfies the restriction $h_2(\mathbf{x}_q) = 0 \bmod 2^r$ with probability $p = 2^{-r}$. Hence the setup runtime of amplitude amplification is

$$T_{Setup} = \tilde{\mathcal{O}}\left(\sqrt{p^{-1}}\right) = \tilde{\mathcal{O}}\left(2^{\frac{r}{2}}\right).$$

As described before, the quantum set-membership oracle for L requires time

$$T_{f_L^h} = \tilde{\mathcal{O}}(|L|) = \tilde{\mathcal{O}}(2^\ell).$$

Recall that a random element $\mathbf{x}_c \in S_1$ can be completed to a collision $(\mathbf{x}_c, \mathbf{x}_q)$ with probability $\frac{R}{|S_1|}$. Notice that this probability is unchanged if we choose a random $\mathbf{x}_c \in S_r^{h_1}$ as in Algorithm 0. Therefore, we expect in total $|L| \cdot \frac{R}{|S_1|}$ many collisions between L and the set $S_r^{h_2}$ constructed in superposition. Thus, every $\mathbf{x}_q \in S_r^{h_2}$ evaluates to $f_L^h(\mathbf{x}_q) = 1$ with probability

$$p = \frac{|L|R}{|S_r^{h_2}||S_1|} = \frac{|L|R2^r}{|S_1||S_2|}.$$

Using (2), we obtain for the second step (amplitude amplification) runtime

$$T_2 = \tilde{\mathcal{O}}\left(\left(T_{Setup} + T_{f_L^h}\right) \cdot \sqrt{p^{-1}}\right) = \tilde{\mathcal{O}}\left(\left(2^{\frac{r}{2}} + 2^\ell\right) \cdot \sqrt{\frac{|S_1||S_2|}{|L|R2^r}}\right)$$

$$= \tilde{\mathcal{O}}\left(\left(2^{-\frac{\ell}{2}} + 2^{\frac{\ell-r}{2}}\right)\frac{|S_1|^{\frac{1}{2}}|S_2|^{\frac{1}{2}}}{|R|^{\frac{1}{2}}}\right). \tag{6}$$

Since L is sorted, the third step of Algorithm 0 runs in time $\mathcal{O}(\ell)$. In total, we obtain runtime

$$T = \tilde{\mathcal{O}}\left(\max\{T_1, T_2\}\right). \tag{7}$$

3   Subset Sum via Quantum Collision Finding

Let $\mathbf{e}$ be a unique solution for a random subset sum instance from Definition 1. Let $(\mathbf{x_c}, \mathbf{x_q}) \in \{-1, 0, 1\}^n$ be a representation of $\mathbf{e}$, i.e. $\mathbf{e} = \mathbf{x_c} + \mathbf{x_q}$. Then $\langle \mathbf{a}, \mathbf{e} \rangle = t$ which implies

$$\langle \mathbf{a}, \mathbf{x_c} \rangle = t - \langle \mathbf{a}, \mathbf{x_q} \rangle. \tag{8}$$

Let $S_i \subseteq \{-1, 0, 1\}^n$ for $i = 1, 2$. We define two functions $\Sigma_i : S_i \to \mathbb{Z}_{2^n}$, $i = 1, 2$, with

$$\Sigma_1 : \mathbf{x} \mapsto \langle \mathbf{a}, \mathbf{x} \rangle \text{ and } \Sigma_2 : \mathbf{x} \mapsto t - \langle \mathbf{a}, \mathbf{x} \rangle. \tag{9}$$

Then every representation $(\mathbf{x_c}, \mathbf{x_q})$ of $\mathbf{e}$ is a collision of Σ_1, Σ_2, i.e. $\Sigma_1(\mathbf{x_c}) = \Sigma_2(\mathbf{x_q})$. However, the converse is not true.

Let $(\mathbf{x_c}, \mathbf{x_q}) \in \{-1, 0, 1\}^{2n}$ be a collision of Σ_1, Σ_2. Then by construction $(\mathbf{x_c}, \mathbf{x_q})$ fulfills Eq. (8) and therefore satisfies the subset sum identity $\langle \mathbf{a}, \mathbf{x_c} + \mathbf{x_q} \rangle = t$. However, in general we have $\mathbf{x_c} + \mathbf{x_q} \in \{-2, \dots, 2\}^n$. Therefore, $(\mathbf{x_c}, \mathbf{x_q})$ is a representation of the unique solution $\mathbf{e}$ iff $\mathbf{x_c} + \mathbf{x_q} \in \{0, 1\}^n$.

Definition 2. *Let $(\mathbf{x_c}, \mathbf{x_q}) \in \{0, 1, -1\}^{2n}$ be a collision of Σ_1, Σ_2. We call $(\mathbf{x_c}, \mathbf{x_q})$ consistent iff $\mathbf{x_c} + \mathbf{x_q} \in \{0, 1\}^n$.*

Hence solving subset sum is equivalent to finding a consistent collision $(\mathbf{x_c}, \mathbf{x_q})$. Moreover, the representations of $\mathbf{e}$ are exactly the consistent collisions of Σ_1, Σ_2. Remark 2 follows.

Remark 2. The number R of representations of the solution $\mathbf{e}$ is equal to the number of consistent collisions of Σ_1, Σ_2.

Remark 3. Notice that our hash function Σ_1 is linear, i.e.

$$\Sigma_1(\mathbf{x} + \mathbf{y}) = \langle \mathbf{a}, \mathbf{x} + \mathbf{y} \rangle = \langle \mathbf{a}, \mathbf{x} \rangle + \langle \mathbf{a}, \mathbf{y} \rangle = \Sigma_1(\mathbf{x}) + \Sigma_1(\mathbf{y}).$$

We use this linearity for our improved algorithm in Sect. 4.

It remains to define good representations $(\mathbf{x_c}, \mathbf{x_q})$ of $\mathbf{e}$. Let us start for didactical reasons with a natural, unique representation of $\mathbf{e}$ that fails to beat Grover's square root bound.

Unique Representation. Let us define

$$S_1 = \{0, 1\}^{n/2} \times 0^{n/2} \text{ and } S_2 = 0^{n/2} \times \{0, 1\}^{n/2}.$$

Then every $\mathbf{e}$ has a unique representation in $S_1 \times S_2$. This implies that Σ_1, Σ_2 have a single collision, i.e. $R = 1$. Condition (3) implies

$$\ell \geq \log |S_1| - \log R = \frac{n}{2}.$$

From Eq. (5) we have $T_1 = \Omega(2^{\frac{n}{2}})$, which implies that we cannot beat Grover's bound.

More Representations. Let $0 \leq \alpha \leq 1/4$. For $i = 1, 2$ we define

$$S_i = \{\mathbf{x} \in \{-1, 0, 1\}^n \mid \mathbf{x} \text{ contains } \left(\frac{1}{4} + \alpha\right) n \text{ many 1's and } \alpha n \text{ many } (-1)\text{'s}\}$$

(10)

with size

$$|S_1| = |S_2| = \binom{n}{(\frac{1}{4} + \alpha)n, \alpha n}.$$

By the choice of S_1, S_2 every 1-entry of the solution $\mathbf{e}$ can be represented as $1 + 0$ and $0 + 1$ and every 0-entry can be represented as $0 + 0$, $1 + (-1)$ and $(-1) + 1$. Thus the number of representations is

$$R = \binom{\frac{n}{2}}{\frac{n}{4}} \binom{\frac{n}{2}}{\alpha n, \alpha n}.$$

Quantum Collision Finding for Subset Sum. Let us adapt the CNS quantum collision finding (Algorithm 0) to our subset sum setting, resulting in Algorithm 1.

Algorithm 1: QUANTUM SUBSET SUM COLLISION FINDING

Input   : $(\mathbf{a}, t) \in (\mathbb{Z}_{2^n})^{n+1}$
Output   : $\mathbf{e} \in \{0, 1\}^n$
Parameters: Optimize r, ℓ, α as $r = 0.4784n$, $\ell = 0.2392n$, $\alpha = 0.0175$.
1. Let $S_r^{\Sigma_i} := \{\mathbf{x} \in S_i \mid \Sigma_i(\mathbf{x}) = 0 \bmod 2^r\}$ for $i = 1, 2$.
   Construct, element-wise via Grover search, a sorted (by second entry) list

$$L = \{(\mathbf{x}_c, \Sigma_1(\mathbf{x}_c)) \in S_r^{\Sigma_1} \times \mathbb{Z}_{2^n}\} \text{ with } |L| = 2^\ell.$$

2. Perform amplitude amplification with the following Setup and Oracle.
   (i) Setup: Construct

$$|\phi_r\rangle := \frac{1}{\sqrt{|S_r^{\Sigma_2}|}} \sum_{\mathbf{x}_q \in S_r^{\Sigma_2}} |\mathbf{x}_q, \Sigma_2(\mathbf{x}_q)\rangle |0\rangle.$$

   (ii) Oracle: Set-Membership-Oracle $O_{f_L^\Sigma}$

$$O_{f_L^\Sigma}(|\phi_r\rangle) = \frac{1}{\sqrt{|S_r^{\Sigma_2}|}} \sum_{\mathbf{x}_q \in S_r^{\Sigma_2}} |\mathbf{x}_q, \Sigma_2(\mathbf{x}_q)\rangle |f_L^\Sigma(\mathbf{x}_q)\rangle.$$

   Amplitude amplification eventually outputs some $|(\mathbf{x}_q, \Sigma_2(\mathbf{x}_q))\rangle |1\rangle$.

3. For the quantum half $\mathbf{x}_q$ search for the classic half $\mathbf{x}_c \in L$ with
   $\Sigma_1(\mathbf{x}_c) = \Sigma_2(\mathbf{x}_q)$ and $\mathbf{x}_c + \mathbf{x}_q \in \{0, 1\}^n$.

We instantiate the hash functions by Σ_1, Σ_2 from Eq. (9), where S_1, S_2 are defined via (10).

In addition, we have to slightly modify the quantum set-membership oracle, because we have to check for consistency of collisions (Definition 2). Let us define the oracle function

$$f_L^{\Sigma}(\mathbf{x}_q) := \begin{cases} 1 & \text{if } \exists (\mathbf{x}_c, \Sigma_1(\mathbf{x}_c)) \in L \text{ with } \Sigma_1(\mathbf{x}_c) = \Sigma_2(\mathbf{x}_q) \wedge \mathbf{x}_c + \mathbf{x}_q \in \{0,1\}^n \\ 0 & \text{else} \end{cases}.$$

Then our quantum set-membership oracle for L, defined for a single $\mathbf{x}_q$, becomes

$$O_{f_L^{\Sigma}}(|\mathbf{x}_q, \Sigma_2(\mathbf{x}_q)\rangle |0\rangle) := |\mathbf{x}_q, \Sigma_2(\mathbf{x}_q)\rangle |f_L^{\Sigma}(\mathbf{x}_q)\rangle. \tag{11}$$

The set-membership oracle can be realized in time $T_{f_L^{\Sigma}} = \tilde{\mathcal{O}}(|L|)$.

Theorem 1. *Algorithm 1 solves random subset sum instances* $(\mathbf{a}, t) \in (\mathbb{Z}_{2^n})^{n+1}$ *in expected time* $T = 2^{0.4785n}$ *using* $\mathcal{O}(n)$ *qubits and memory* $M = 2^{0.2392n}$.

Proof. Our parameter choice $\alpha = 0.0175 \leq \frac{1}{4}$ determines the values of $|S_1|, |S_2|$ and R as

$$|S_1| = |S_2| = \binom{n}{(\frac{1}{4} + \alpha)n, \alpha n} = \tilde{\mathcal{O}}(2^{0.9569n}),$$

$$R = \binom{\frac{n}{2}}{\frac{n}{4}} \binom{\frac{n}{2}}{\alpha n, \alpha n} = \tilde{\mathcal{O}}(2^{0.7177n}).$$

Moreover, we easily check that our optimized parameter choice $\alpha = 0.0175$, $r = 0.4784n$ and $\ell = 0.2392n$ fulfills restrictions (3) and (4):

$$\log |S_1| - \log R = 0.2392n \leq \ell \leq 0.4785n = \log |S_1| - r,$$

$$0 \leq r \leq 0.7177n = \log R.$$

Using Eqs. (5) and (6), we obtain runtimes

$$T_1 = \mathcal{O}\left(2^{\ell} \cdot 2^{\frac{r}{2}}\right) = \tilde{\mathcal{O}}(2^{0.4784n}),$$

$$T_2 = \tilde{\mathcal{O}}\left(\frac{|S_1|^{\frac{1}{2}}|S_2|^{\frac{1}{2}}}{|R|^{\frac{1}{2}}}2^{-\frac{\ell}{2}} + \frac{|S_1|^{\frac{1}{2}}|S_2|^{\frac{1}{2}}}{|R|^{\frac{1}{2}}}2^{\frac{\ell-r}{2}}\right) = \tilde{\mathcal{O}}(2^{0.47845n} + 2^{0.47845n}).$$

Thus, by Eq. (7) Algorithm 1 has total runtime

$$T = \tilde{\mathcal{O}}\left(\max\{T_1, T_2\}\right) = \tilde{\mathcal{O}}(2^{0.47845n}) \leq 2^{0.4785n}.$$

The memory complexity is determined by the size of L as

$$M = \tilde{\mathcal{O}}(|L|) = \tilde{\mathcal{O}}(2^{\ell}) = \tilde{\mathcal{O}}(2^{0.2392n}) \leq 2^{0.2392n}.$$

The application of Grover search and amplitude amplification both require only $\mathcal{O}(n)$ many qubits. □

While Theorem 1 beats Grover's bound using only $\mathcal{O}(n)$ qubits and no QRAM, it does not improve over purely classical time/memory tradeoffs, see Fig. 1.

4   Using a Classical Algorithm for List Construction

While Algorithm 1 is a direct adaptation of CNS quantum collision finding, it ignores special properties of the subset sum setting. E.g. in step 1 of Algorithm 1 we are building a classical list L, where r bits of the hash function evaluation $\Sigma_1(x)$ are fixed to zero. Each list element is constructed one by one using Grover search, resulting in total runtime $|L| \cdot 2^{r/2}$ for step 1.

However, quantum algorithms like Grover Search are not optimal in finding many solutions to a problem, and Grover search does not take advantage of the linearity of hash function Σ_1 (see Remark 3). We improve the step 1 list construction by using the classical Schroeppel-Shamir algorithm [SS81]. We also tried other more advanced classical list constructions for L such as BCJ [BCJ11], but could not further improve over Schroeppel-Shamir.

To make optimal use of the representation technique, we also have to redefine our search spaces.

Tunable Representations. Let $0 \leq c \leq 1$. We define the following sets

$$T(c) := \left\{ \mathbf{x} \in \{-1,0,1\}^{cn} \;\middle|\; \begin{array}{c} \mathbf{x} \text{ contains } (1/4 + \alpha)\, cn \text{ many 1's} \\ \text{and } \alpha cn \text{ many } (-1)\text{'s} \end{array} \right\},$$

$$B(c) := \left\{ \mathbf{x} \in \{0,1\}^{cn} \;\middle|\; \mathbf{x} \text{ contains } \frac{1}{2}cn \text{ many 1's} \right\}.$$

Let $0 \leq c_1 \leq 1$. We set our search spaces as

$$S_1 = T(c_1) \times 0^{(1-c_1)n},$$
$$S_2 = T(c_1) \times B(1 - c_1).$$

Therefore, we obtain in S_1, S_2 an overlapping part of length $c_1 n$, and an additional length $(1 - c_1)n$ search space for the quantum part, see also Fig. 3. In the additional search space $\mathbf{x}_q$ has relative weight $1/2$. In the overlapping part both $\mathbf{x}_c, \mathbf{x}_q$ have relatively (to the length $c_1 n$) $(1/4 + \alpha)$ many 1-entries and α many (-1)-entries.

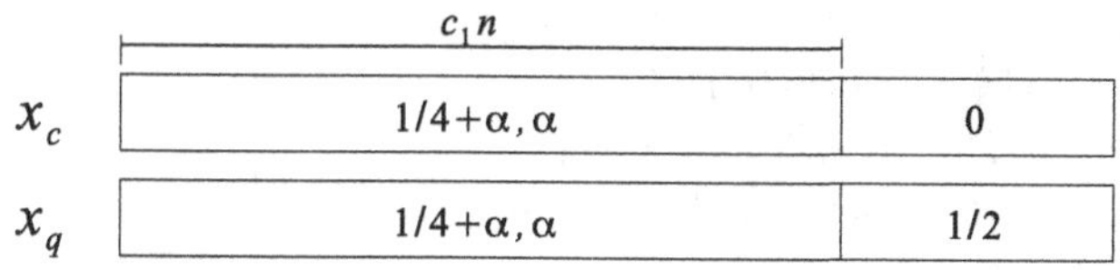

	$c_1 n$		
$\mathbf{x}_c$	$1/4+\alpha, \alpha$		0
$\mathbf{x}_q$	$1/4+\alpha, \alpha$		1/2

Fig. 3. Visualization of search spaces S_1, S_2.

Thus S_1 and S_2 have sizes

$$|S_1| = |T(c_1)| = \binom{c_1 n}{(\frac{1}{4} + \alpha)c_1 n, \alpha c_1 n},$$

$$|S_2| = |T(c_1)| \cdot |B(1 - c_1)| = \binom{c_1 n}{(\frac{1}{4} + \alpha)c_1 n, \alpha c_1 n}\binom{(1 - c_1)n}{\frac{1}{2}(1 - c_1)n},$$

and the number of representations is

$$R = \binom{\frac{1}{2}c_1 n}{\frac{1}{4}c_1 n}\binom{\frac{1}{2}c_1 n}{\alpha c_1 n, \alpha c_1 n}.$$

Constructing L via Schroeppel-Shamir. Our hash functions Σ_1, Σ_2 from (9) remain unchanged. We have to compute

$$L = \{(\mathbf{x}_c, \Sigma_1(\mathbf{x}_c)) \in S_1 \times \mathbb{Z}_{2^n} \mid \Sigma_1(\mathbf{x}_c) = 0 \bmod 2^r\}.$$

We expect that L has size $\frac{|S_1|}{2^r}$. By Definition 1 of our random subset sum instances, it is not hard to show that by a Chernoff bound with overwhelming probability $|L|$ deviates from its expectation by at most a logarithmic factor. Hence, in the following we set $|L| = \tilde{O}(\frac{|S_1|}{2^r})$.

L can be computed with the Schroeppel-Shamir algorithm in time

$$T_1 = \tilde{O}\left(\max\left\{|S_1|^{\frac{1}{2}}, |L|\right\}\right) = \tilde{O}\left(\max\left\{|S_1|^{\frac{1}{2}}, \frac{|S_1|}{2^r}\right\}\right) \tag{12}$$

using classical memory $M = \tilde{O}(\max\left\{|S_1|^{\frac{1}{4}}, \frac{|S_1|}{2^r}\right\})$.

Our modifications result in Algorithm 2.

Theorem 2. *Algorithm 2 solves random subset sum instances $(\mathbf{a}, t) \in (\mathbb{Z}_{2^n})^{n+1}$ by using only $O(n)$ qubits in expected runtime*

$$T = \tilde{O}\left(\frac{2^{0.5n}}{M^{0.2532}}\right) \quad \text{for any classical memory } M \leq 2^{0.2852n}.$$

Proof. Our parameter choice $\alpha = 0.0042 \leq \frac{1}{4}$ determines the values of $|S_1|, |S_2|$ and R as a function of $0 \leq c_1 \leq 1$ as

$$|S_1| = \binom{c_1 n}{(\frac{1}{4} + \alpha)c_1 n, \alpha c_1 n} = \tilde{O}(2^{0.8556 c_1 n}),$$

$$|S_2| = \binom{(1 - c_1)n}{\frac{1}{2}(1 - c_1)n}\binom{c_1 n}{(\frac{1}{4} + \alpha)c_1 n, \alpha c_1 n} = \tilde{O}(2^{(1 - 0.1444 c_1)n}),$$

$$R = \binom{\frac{1}{2}c_1 n}{\frac{1}{4}c_1 n}\binom{\frac{1}{2}c_1 n}{\alpha c_1 n, \alpha c_1 n} = \tilde{O}(2^{0.5704 c_1 n}).$$

From Eq. (12) and $r = \log R$, Schroeppel-Shamir runs in time

$$T_1 = \tilde{O}\left(\max\left\{|S_1|^{\frac{1}{2}}, \frac{|S_1|}{2^r}\right\}\right) \leq \max\left\{2^{0.4278 c_1 n}, 2^{0.2852 c_1 n}\right\} = 2^{0.4278 c_1 n},$$

Algorithm 2: QUANTUM SUBSET SUM COLLISION FINDING II

Input   : $(\mathbf{a}, t) \in (\mathbb{Z}_{2^n})^{n+1}$
Output   : $\mathbf{e} \in \{0,1\}^n$
Parameters: Optimize r, α as $r = \log R$, $\alpha = 0.0042$ and $0 \le c_1 \le 1$.
1. Let $S_r^{\Sigma_i} := \{\mathbf{x} \in S_i \mid \Sigma_i(\mathbf{x}) = 0 \bmod 2^r\}$ for $i = 1, 2$.
   Construct, via Schroeppel-Shamir algorithm, a sorted (by second entry) list

$$L = \{(\mathbf{x}_c, \Sigma_1(\mathbf{x}_c)) \in S_r^{\Sigma_1} \times \mathbb{Z}_{2^n}\} \text{ with } |L| = 2^\ell.$$

2. Perform amplitude amplification with the following Setup and Oracle.
   (i) Setup: Construct

$$|\phi_r\rangle := \frac{1}{\sqrt{|S_r^{\Sigma_2}|}} \sum_{\mathbf{x}_q \in S_r^{\Sigma_2}} |\mathbf{x}_q, \Sigma_2(\mathbf{x}_q)\rangle |0\rangle.$$

   (ii) Oracle: Set-Membership-Oracle $O_{f_L^{\Sigma}}$

$$O_{f_L^{\Sigma}}(|\phi_r\rangle) = \frac{1}{\sqrt{|S_r^{\Sigma_2}|}} \sum_{\mathbf{x}_q \in S_r^{\Sigma_2}} |\mathbf{x}_q, \Sigma_2(\mathbf{x}_q)\rangle |f_L^{\Sigma}(\mathbf{x}_q)\rangle.$$

   Amplitude amplification eventually outputs some $|(\mathbf{x}_q, \Sigma_2(\mathbf{x}_q))\rangle |1\rangle$.

3. For the quantum half $\mathbf{x}_q$ search for the classic half $\mathbf{x}_c \in L$ with
   $\Sigma_1(\mathbf{x}_c) = \Sigma_2(\mathbf{x}_q)$ and $\mathbf{x}_c + \mathbf{x}_q \in \{0,1\}^n$.

using classical memory

$$M = \tilde{\mathcal{O}} \left(\max \left\{ |S_1|^{\frac{1}{4}}, \frac{|S_1|}{2^r} \right\} \right) \le \max \left\{ 2^{0.2139 c_1 n}, 2^{0.2852 c_1 n} \right\} = 2^{0.2852 c_1 n}. \quad (13)$$

Algorithm 2's amplitude amplification operates on $\mathcal{O}(n)$ qubits without classical memory.

Using Eq. (6) and $\ell = \log |S_1| - r$, amplitude amplification runs in expected time

$$T_2 = \tilde{\mathcal{O}} \left(\left(2^{-\frac{\ell}{2}} + 2^{\frac{\ell-r}{2}} \right) \frac{|S_1|^{\frac{1}{2}} |S_2|^{\frac{1}{2}}}{|R|^{\frac{1}{2}}} \right) = \tilde{\mathcal{O}} \left(|S_2|^{\frac{1}{2}} + \frac{|S_1||S_2|^{\frac{1}{2}}}{R^{\frac{3}{2}}} \right)$$

$$= \tilde{\mathcal{O}} \left(2^{(0.5 - 0.0722 c_1)n} + 2^{(0.5 - 0.0722 c_1)n} \right) = \tilde{\mathcal{O}} \left(2^{(0.5 - 0.0722 c_1)n} \right).$$

Thus by (7) the total expected runtime is

$$T = \tilde{\mathcal{O}} \left(\max \{ T_1, T_2 \} \right) = \tilde{\mathcal{O}} \left(\max \left\{ 2^{0.4278 c_1 n}, 2^{(0.5 - 0.0722 c_1)n} \right\} \right)$$

$$= \tilde{\mathcal{O}} \left(2^{(0.5 - 0.0722 c_1)n} \right).$$

Using $2^{-c_1 n} \leq M^{-\frac{1}{0.2852}}$ from Eq. 13, we achieve the desired trade-off

$$T = \tilde{\mathcal{O}}\left(\frac{2^{0.5n}}{M^{0.2532}}\right) \quad \text{for } M \leq 2^{0.2852n}.$$

$\square$

Theorem 2 provides a time-memory-tradeoff between runtime and classical memory while using only $\mathcal{O}(n)$ qubits. Note that any classical memory consumption helps us to beat Grover's square root bound. We compare to purely classical time/memory tradeoffs in Fig. 4. Notice that our quantum algorithm beats any classical algorithm in the memory regime $M \leq 2^{n/5}$.

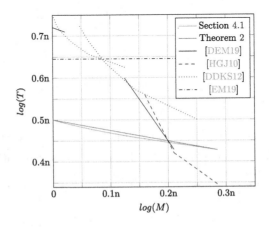

Fig. 4. Comparison of our small qubit algorithm with purely classical time/memory tradeoffs.

4.1 Optimization of Algorithm 2

We further improve on the analysis of Algorithm 2 by elaborating on the representations, the algorithm itself remains unchanged.

More Tunable Representations. Let $0 \leq z \leq 1/2$ and $c, d \in [0, 1]$ with $c + d \geq 1$. We define the following sets

$$T(c, d, z) := \left\{ \mathbf{x} \in \{-1, 0, 1\}^{(c+d-1)n} \,\middle|\, \begin{array}{l} \mathbf{x} \text{ contains } (z + \alpha)(c + d - 1)n \text{ many 1's} \\ \text{and } \alpha(c + d - 1)n \text{ many } (-1)\text{'s} \end{array} \right\},$$

$$B(c) = \left\{ \mathbf{x} \in \{0, 1\}^{cn} \,\middle|\, \mathbf{x} \text{ contains } \frac{1}{2}cn \text{ many 1's} \right\}.$$

We set our search spaces as

$$S_1 = B(1 - c_2) \times T(c_1, c_2, z) \times 0^{(1-c_1)n},$$
$$S_2 = 0^{(1-c_2)n} \times T\left(c_1, c_2, \frac{1}{2} - z\right) \times B(1 - c_1).$$

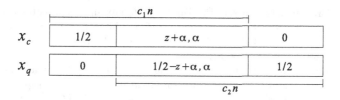

Fig. 5. Visualization of search spaces S_1, S_2.

In Algorithm 2 the parameter $0 \leq z \leq 1/2$ controls the relative weight in the overlapping part, see Fig. 5. The sizes of the search spaces are

$$|S_1| = |B(1 - c_2)| \cdot |T(c_1, c_2, z)|$$
$$= \binom{(1 - c_2)n}{\frac{1}{2}(1 - c_2)n}\binom{(c_1 + c_2 - 1)n}{(z + \alpha)(c_1 + c_2 - 1)n, \alpha(c_1 + c_2 - 1)n},$$
$$|S_2| = |B(1 - c_1)| \cdot |T(c_1, c_2, \frac{1}{2} - z)|$$
$$= \binom{(1 - c_1)n}{\frac{1}{2}(1 - c_1)n}\binom{(c_1 + c_2 - 1)n}{(\frac{1}{2} - z + \alpha)(c_1 + c_2 - 1)n, \alpha(c_1 + c_2 - 1)n},$$

with the number of representations

$$R = \binom{\frac{1}{2}(c_1 + c_2 - 1)n}{z(c_1 + c_2 - 1)n}\binom{\frac{1}{2}(c_1 + c_2 - 1)n}{\alpha(c_1 + c_2 - 1)n, \alpha(c_1 + c_2 - 1)n}.$$

Optimization of c_1, c_2, α and z yields a slight improvement over Theorem 2, as illustrated in Table 1 and Fig. 4.

Table 1. Results of optimization.

	$\log_2(M)/n$	0.00	0.05	0.10	0.15	0.20	0.25	0.285
Optimization	$\log_2(T)/n$	0.500	0.483	0.469	0.456	0.446	0.436	0.428
Theorem 2		0.500	0.487	0.475	0.462	0.449	0.437	0.428

References

[BCJ11] Becker, A., Coron, J.-S., Joux, A.: Improved generic algorithms for hard knapsacks. In: Paterson, K.G. (ed.) EUROCRYPT 2011. LNCS, vol. 6632, pp. 364–385. Springer, Heidelberg (2011). https://doi.org/10.1007/978-3-642-20465-4_21

[BHMT02] Brassard, G., Hoyer, P., Mosca, M., Tapp, A.: Quantum amplitude amplification and estimation. Contemp. Math. **305**, 53–74 (2002)

[BHT98] Brassard, G., Høyer, P., Tapp, A.: Quantum cryptanalysis of hash and claw-free functions. In: Lucchesi, C.L., Moura, A.V. (eds.) LATIN 1998. LNCS, vol. 1380, pp. 163–169. Springer, Heidelberg (1998). https://doi.org/10.1007/BFb0054319

[BJLM13] Bernstein, D.J., Jeffery, S., Lange, T., Meurer, A.: Quantum algorithms for the subset-sum problem. In: Gaborit, P. (ed.) PQCrypto 2013. LNCS, vol. 7932, pp. 16–33. Springer, Heidelberg (2013). https://doi.org/10.1007/978-3-642-38616-9_2

[CNPS17] Chailloux, A., Naya-Plasencia, M., Schrottenloher, A.: An efficient quantum collision search algorithm and implications on symmetric cryptography. In: Takagi, T., Peyrin, T. (eds.) ASIACRYPT 2017. LNCS, vol. 10625, pp. 211–240. Springer, Cham (2017). https://doi.org/10.1007/978-3-319-70697-9_8

[DDKS12] Dinur, I., Dunkelman, O., Keller, N., Shamir, A.: Efficient dissection of composite problems, with applications to cryptanalysis, knapsacks, and combinatorial search problems. In: Safavi-Naini, R., Canetti, R. (eds.) CRYPTO 2012. LNCS, vol. 7417, pp. 719–740. Springer, Heidelberg (2012). https://doi.org/10.1007/978-3-642-32009-5_42

[DEM19] Delaplace, C., Esser, A., May, A.: Improved low-memory subset sum and LPN algorithms via multiple collisions. IACR Cryptology ePrint Archive, 2019:804 (2019)

[EM19] Esser, A., May, A.: Low weight discrete logarithms and subset sum in $2^{0.65n}$ with polynomial memory. Cryptology ePrint Archive, Report 2019/931 (2019). https://eprint.iacr.org/2019/931

[GR04] Grover, L., Rudolph, T.: How significant are the known collision and element distinctness quantum algorithms. Quantum Inf. Comput. 4(3), 201–206 (2004)

[Gro96] Grover, L.K.: A fast quantum mechanical algorithm for database search. In: Proceedings of the Twenty-Eighth Annual ACM Symposium on Theory of computing, pp. 212–219. ACM (1996)

[HGJ10] Howgrave-Graham, N., Joux, A.: New generic algorithms for hard knapsacks. In: Gilbert, H. (ed.) EUROCRYPT 2010. LNCS, vol. 6110, pp. 235–256. Springer, Heidelberg (2010). https://doi.org/10.1007/978-3-642-13190-5_12

[HM18] Helm, A., May, A.: Subset sum quantumly in 1.17^n. In: Jeffery, S. (ed.) 13th Conference on the Theory of Quantum Computation, Communication and Cryptography, TQC 2018, Sydney, Australia, 16–18 July 2018. LIPIcs, vol. 111, pp. 5:1–5:15. Schloss Dagstuhl - Leibniz-Zentrum fuer Informatik (2018)

[Reg09] Regev, O.: On lattices, learning with errors, random linear codes, and cryptography. J. ACM (JACM) 56(6), 34 (2009)

[SS81] Schroeppel, R., Shamir, A.: A t=o($2^{n/2}$), s=o($2^{n/4}$) algorithm for certain NP-complete problems. SIAM J. Comput. 10(3), 456–464 (1981)

On Quantum Distinguishers for Type-3 Generalized Feistel Network Based on Separability

Samir Hodžić[(✉)], Lars Knudsen Ramkilde, and Andreas Brasen Kidmose

DTU Compute, Technical University of Denmark, Kongens Lyngby, Denmark
{saho,lrkn,abki}@dtu.dk

Abstract. In this work, we derive a method for constructing quantum distinguishers for GFNs (Generalized Feistel-like schemes with invertible inner functions and XORs), where for simplicity 4 branches are considered. The construction technique is demonstrated on Type-3 GFN, where some other cyclically inequivalent GFNs are considered as examples. Introducing the property of separability, we observe that finding a suitable partition of input blocks implies that some branches can be represented as a sum of functions with almost disjoint variables, which simplifies the application of Simon's algorithm. However, higher number of rounds in most of the cases have branches which do not satisfy the previous property, and in order to derive a quantum distinguisher for these branches, we employ Simon's and Grover's algorithm in combination with a suitable system of equations given in terms of input blocks and inner functions involved in the round function. As a result, we are able to construct a 5-round quantum distinguisher for Type-3 GFNs using only a quantum encryption oracle with query complexity $2^{N/4} \cdot \mathcal{O}(N/4)$, where N size of the input block.

Keywords: Simon's algorithm · Grover's algorithm · Generalized Feistel network · Quantum cryptanalysis

1 Introduction

The interest in post-quantum cryptanalysis of block ciphers has significantly increased in the last decade after Kuwakado and Morii [17] proposed a polynomial time quantum distinguisher for 3-round Feistel Network based on Simon's algorithm [25]. The current state of quantum cryptanalysis of block ciphers encompasses several approaches which range from quantifying the known classical attacks, to applying the quantum algorithms which result in significant reduction of attack complexities, such as Simon's and Grover's [11] algorithms. In various settings, these two algorithms have been utilized in many recent works [3–6,8–10,12,14–17,19,21,23,24,27]. In general, the overall attention of researchers has been further motivated by total/partial breaks of several ciphers (or proofs that certain schemes provide much less security than expected) such

© Springer Nature Switzerland AG 2020
J. Ding and J.-P. Tillich (Eds.): PQCrypto 2020, LNCS 12100, pp. 461–480, 2020.
https://doi.org/10.1007/978-3-030-44223-1_25

as Even-Mansour [18], AEZ cipher [3], LED cipher [27], FX construction [6,19], and certain authenticated encryption schemes [16].

The previous works demonstrate that Simon's and Grover's algorithm can be utilized for key-recovery attacks and construction of quantum distinguishers. The main idea is to construct a function, f, which has a hidden shift, that can be recovered using Simon's algorithm. The shift can then either reveal the secret key or be used to distinguish the cipher from a random permutation. A problem that may arise is that f may have unwanted collisions, however, Kaplan et al. [16] showed this can be solved by performing sufficient measurements.

An interesting application of combining Simon's and Grover's algorithm has been shown in [19] on the FX construction, where G. Leander and A. May showed that key-whitening method does not provide the same increase of the key space as in the classical environment. The combination of these two algorithms has been used in the context of amplitude amplification technique derived by Brassard et al. [7]. The work [19] initialized the series of papers [6,8–10,15] which have been combining Simon's and Grover's algorithm in a similar way, resulting in quantum distinguishers and key recovery attacks.

In this paper, we derive a method for constructing quantum distinguishers based on Simon's/Grover's algorithm for Generalized Feistel networks. Recently, iterated classical Feistel schemes in combination with advanced slide attacks have been analysed in [8]. A distinguisher for 5-round Feistel networks is provided in [10], which is then turned into a key-recovery attack with the Simon/Grover combination. Moving to more general schemes, Dong et al. [9] provides a polynomial time quantum distinguisher for Type-1 GFN with d branches on $2d - 1$ rounds. In the same work, the authors provide a $(2d + 1)$-round polynomial time quantum distinguisher for $2d$-branch Type-2 GFN. Ito and Iwata [15] improved the Type-1 distinguisher to cover $3d - 3$ rounds.

We notice that the previous distinguishers are based on finding a suitable partition of the input block, such that, some branch can be written as a sum of functions with almost disjoint variables. Here, 'almost' means that one of the functions contain one specific variable that is not involved in other functions, and 'disjoint' refers to its suitable placement in the context of Simon's algorithm. We call this property *separability* and refer to Definition 1 for the details. The construction of f, that we use in our work, is based on the concatenation of two suitable functions whose values are obtained by querying the encryption oracle in superposition and truncating the output. Therefore, the attacks belong to the so-called **Q2** attack model. According to Hosoyamada and Sasaki [13, Section 5.2] truncation is possible in the quantum world, i.e., it has been shown that computing a truncated function can be done as efficiently as computing the complete function.

However, the propagation of separability, which we consider in strong and weak settings, is limited throughout the cipher. In order to demonstrate our approach, we analyze the Type-3 GFN [28], which has not been addressed in previous works. We notice that one can consider a specific set of terms which is actually present in almost the whole cipher, which gives rise to a system of equations given in terms of input blocks and inner functions employed in the definition of underlying GFN. The solvability of this system, in combination with Simon's and Grover's algorithm, then implies suitable parameters upon which the distinguisher is constructed. For instance, we show that for 5-round Type-3 GFN one needs $2^n \cdot \mathcal{O}(n)$ query complexity and $2n + 2(2n + 1)(n + 1 + \sqrt{n + 1})$ qubits, in order to extract suitable parameters required for a distinguisher. Here, n is the branch size of a given GFN, since for simplicity we fix the number of branches to be 4 for all GFNs that we consider.

In general, we note that a successful construction of a distinguisher (by our method) highly depends on the solvability of the observed system of equations, along with the employed technique for constructing the Simon's function f. Recall that in our work the concatenation method is used, but other methods can be utilized as well. Further consideration of the presented methods on other GFNs in terms of the design and security, is left as an open problem.

This paper is organized as follows. In Sect. 2 we provide an overview of Simon's and Grover's algorithm (along with the basic notation). In Sect. 3 we demonstrate the presence of the separability property in 3-round Feistel cipher, Type-1 and Type-2 GFNs, which we formalize by considering three different types, namely (semi-) strong and weak separability. In the same section we analyze the Type-3 GFN (precisely, the 4-th branch of 5-th round). In Sect. 4 we employ Simon's and Grover's algorithm to derive necessary parameters that will enable us to construct a quantum distinguisher. Some concluding remarks are given in Sect. 5.

2 Preliminaries

The vector space $\mathbb{F}_2^n$ is the space of all n-tuples $x = (x_1, \ldots, x_n)$, where $x_i \in \mathbb{F}_2$. For $x = (x_1, \ldots, x_n)$ and $y = (y_1, \ldots, y_n)$ in $\mathbb{F}_2^n$, the usual scalar (or dot) product over $\mathbb{F}_2$ is defined as $x \cdot y = x_1 y_1 \oplus \cdots \oplus x_n y_n$, where by '$\oplus$' we denote the modulo 2 computation in $\mathbb{F}_2^n$. A qubit is a superposition of the classical basis states, $|0\rangle$ and $|1\rangle$, i.e. $\mu |0\rangle + \nu |1\rangle$ $(\mu, \nu \in \mathbb{C})$ with $|\mu|^2 + |\nu|^2 = 1$, which represents the normalization condition. A quantum register is a collection of n qubits, and formally we denote it as $|x\rangle = |c_1\rangle \otimes \ldots \otimes |c_n\rangle$, where $c_i \in \mathbb{F}_2$ (and thus $x \in \mathbb{F}_2^n$). The process of measuring a quantum state, say $|\vartheta\rangle$ (which is a superposition of classical states $|x\rangle$, $x \in \mathbb{F}_2^n$) is a non-reversible physical process in which we collapse the state $|\vartheta\rangle$ into a classical state.

Since all computations in the quantum circuit are done in the Hilbert space, it is necessary that any operator (and every single gate) implemented in the quantum environment is invertible. To implement a function $f : \mathbb{F}_2^n \to \mathbb{F}_2^z$ quantumly, one uses an ancilla register (i.e., a register with auxiliary qubits), say y, as

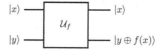

Here, $\mathcal{U}_f$ denotes the quantum oracle (as unitary operator) that provides the values of the function f. If $|y\rangle$ is the all-zero register of size τ, then the oracle $\mathcal{U}_f$ actually provides the mapping $|x\rangle \rightarrow |f(x)\rangle$, where the output $|x\rangle$ after the evaluation of $\mathcal{U}_f$ is simply neglected.

In relation to quantum algorithms described later on, we will use the Hadamard transform $H^{\otimes n}$, $n \geq 1$ (also known as the Sylvester-Hadamard matrix), which is defined recursively as

$$H^{\otimes 1} = 2^{-1/2} \begin{pmatrix} 1 & 1 \\ 1 & -1 \end{pmatrix}; \quad H^{\otimes n} = 2^{-1/2} \begin{pmatrix} H^{\otimes(n-1)} & H^{\otimes(n-1)} \\ H^{\otimes(n-1)} & -H^{\otimes(n-1)} \end{pmatrix}.$$

Throughout the article, by $|0\rangle$ we will denote the all-zero quantum register whose size will be clear from the context. Throughout the work we will use the following notation related to GFNs.

Notations

x_j^{r-1} the input of j-th branch in r-th round, $r \geq 1$, $j \geq 1$.

$x_j^0 = x_j$ the input to j-th branch (first round). At some places x_j denote input variables to a function, which is clear from the context.

$F_i^r = F_i^r(k_r, \cdot)$ the inner function (in the round function) at r-th round of a GFN, which involves the secret round key k_r.

$F_i = F_i^1$ the inner functions in the first round. Only in relation (5), F^j denotes a single inner function (in the round function) which involves a secret round key.

$RF_r^{(t)}$ the function which denotes the t-th branch at r-th round of a GFN.

2.1 A Brief Overview of Simon's and Grover's Algorithm

Simon's algorithm [25] solves the following problem in polynomial time.

Simon's Problem: Given a function $f : \mathbb{F}_2^n \rightarrow \mathbb{F}_2^\tau$ ($\tau \geq 1$) and the promise that there exists a vector $s \in \mathbb{F}_2^n$ such that for all $(x, y) \in \mathbb{F}_2^n \times \mathbb{F}_2^n$ it holds that

$$f(x) = f(y) \Leftrightarrow x \oplus y \in \{0, s\}, \tag{1}$$

the goal is to find s.

The property (1) means that for an arbitrary vector $x \in \mathbb{F}_2^n$ the value $f(x)$ will repeat *only* when the input x is shifted by s (the case when $y = x$ is trivial). The value s is called the *shift* or the *period*. Classically, one can find s in time complexity $\mathcal{O}(2^{n/2})$. However, with the following quantum algorithm it is possible to solve this problem with quantum complexity $\mathcal{O}(n)$.

Simon's Algorithm [25]:

(1) Prepare the state $2^{-n/2}\sum_{x\in\mathbb{F}_2^n}|x\rangle\,|0\rangle$, where the second all-zero register is of size τ ($x\in\mathbb{F}_2^n$).
(2) Apply the operator $\mathcal{U}_f$ which implements the function $f:\mathbb{F}_2^n\to\mathbb{F}_2^\tau$ in order to obtain the state $2^{-n/2}\sum_{x\in\mathbb{F}_2^n}|x\rangle\,|f(x)\rangle$.
(3) Measuring the second register (the one with values of f), the previous state is collapsed to $|\Omega_a|^{-1/2}\sum_{x\in\Omega_a}|x\rangle$, where $\Omega_a=\{x\in\mathbb{F}_2^n:f(x)=a\}$, for some $a\in Im(f)$.
(4) Apply the Hadamard transform $H^{\otimes n}$ to the state $|\Omega_a|^{-1/2}\sum_{x\in\Omega_a}|x\rangle$ in order to obtain $|\varphi\rangle=|\Omega_a|^{-1/2}2^{-n/2}\sum_{y\in\mathbb{F}_2^n}\sum_{x\in\Omega_a}(-1)^{x\cdot y}|y\rangle$.
(5) Measure the state $|\varphi\rangle$:
    (i) If f does not have any period, the output of the measurement are random values $y\in\mathbb{F}_2^n$.
    (ii) If f has a period s, the output of measurement are vectors y which are strictly orthogonal to s, since the amplitudes of y are given by $2^{-(n+1)/2}\sum_{x\in\Omega_a}(-1)^{x\cdot y}=2^{-(n+1)/2}[(-1)^{x'\cdot y}+(-1)^{(x'\oplus s)\cdot y}]$, where we use the assumption that $\Omega_a=\{x',x'\oplus s\}$ ($x'\in\mathbb{F}_2^n,f(x')=f(x'\oplus s)=a$), for any $a\in\mathbb{F}_2^n$.
(6) If f has a period, repeat the previous steps until one collects $n-1$ linearly independent vectors y_i. Then, solve the homogeneous system of equations $y_i\cdot s=0$ (for collected values y_i) in order to extract the unique period s.

Throughout the paper, a Simon's function f will be constructed using the well-known concatenation technique which is given as follows.

Proposition 1. *Let the function $f:\mathbb{F}_2\times\mathbb{F}_2^n\to\mathbb{F}_2^n$ be defined as*

$$f(b,x)=\begin{cases}g(x),\,b=0\\h(x),\,b=1\end{cases},\qquad(2)$$

where $g,h:\mathbb{F}_2^n\to\mathbb{F}_2^n$. Then:

(i) If s is a period of both g and h, then $f(b,x\oplus s)=f(b,x)$ holds for all $(b,x)\in\mathbb{F}_2\times\mathbb{F}_2^n$, i.e., f has period $(0,s)\in\mathbb{F}_2\times\mathbb{F}_2^n$.
(ii) If $h(x\oplus s)=g(x)$ holds for all $x\in\mathbb{F}_2^n$, then f has period $(1,s)\in\mathbb{F}_2\times\mathbb{F}_2^n$.

Remark 1. Note that using the same computation as in the proof of Lemma 1 in [17], one can show that if $g(x)$ and $h(x)=g(x\oplus s)$ are permutations in Proposition 1-(ii), then the period $(1,s)$ of f is unique.

Example 1. [17] analyses the distinguishability of 3-round Feistel cipher (Fig. 1), and in Sect. III-A the function $f:\mathbb{F}_2\times\mathbb{F}_2^n\to\mathbb{F}_2^n$ is defined by

$$f(b,x)=\begin{cases}F_2(x\oplus F_1(\alpha))\oplus(\alpha\oplus\beta),\,b=0\\F_2(x\oplus F_1(\beta))\oplus(\alpha\oplus\beta),\,b=1\end{cases},\qquad(3)$$

where $\alpha,\beta\in\mathbb{F}_2^n$ are different fixed vectors, where the restrictions of the function $f(b,x)$ are utilizing the second branch $y_1=x_0\oplus F_2(x_1\oplus F_1(x_0))$.

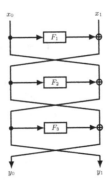

Fig. 1. The 3-round Feistel network with keyed inner functions F_i.

Denoting by $g(x) = f(0, x)$ and $h(x) = f(1, x)$, it is easily verified that $h(x \oplus (F_1(\alpha) \oplus F_1(\beta))) = g(x)$, and thus f has the shift $(1, s) = (1, F_1(\alpha) \oplus F_1(\beta)) \in \mathbb{F}_2 \times \mathbb{F}_2^n$, and thus this construction corresponds to the case (ii) of Proposition 1.

Remark 2. Note that several works use the idea of Proposition 1 to construct the Simon's function f, e.g. [8,16,27]. On the other hand, there are constructions which are not based on the concatenation method, such as the analysis of the Even-Mansour and LRW ciphers in [16].

Another quantum algorithm that will be used in our work is Grover's algorithm [11] which finds a target vector in a given set of vectors, without assuming any structure on the set. Formally, the following problem is considered.

Grover's Problem: Let X denote the search set whose elements are represented on $\lceil \log_2 |X| \rceil$ qubits, such that the superposition $\sum_{x \in X} |x\rangle$ is computable in $\mathcal{O}(1)$. Given oracle access to a function $\mathcal{B} : X \to \mathbb{F}_2$, called the classifier, find $x \in X$ such that $\mathcal{B}(x) = 1$.

If there are 2^u preimages of 1, then the procedure of the Grover's algorithm is based on applying approximately $\sqrt{|X|/2^u}$ times the operator Q (which queries $\mathcal{U}_\mathcal{B}$ as a subroutine), in order to amplify the target amplitudes towards the preimages of 1. If $\mathcal{B}$ has a value 1 only at one vector x, then Grover's algorithm runs in time $\mathcal{O}(\sqrt{|X|})$.

Our method of constructing a quantum distinguisher for GFNs will be based on the combination of Simon's and Grover's algorithm (similarly to [9,10,19]) in framework of the following result derived by Brassard et al. [7].

Theorem 1. [7] *Let $\mathcal{A}$ be any quantum algorithm on q qubits that uses no measurement. Let $\mathcal{B} : \mathbb{F}_2^q \to \mathbb{F}_2$ be a function that classifies outcomes of $\mathcal{A}$ as good or bad. Let $p > 0$ be the initial success probability that a measurement of $\mathcal{A}|0\rangle$ is good. Set $t = \lceil \frac{\pi}{4\theta} \rceil$, where is defined via $\sin^2(\theta) = p$. Moreover, define the unitary operator $Q = -\mathcal{A}S_0\mathcal{A}^{-1}S_\mathcal{B}$, where the operator $S_\mathcal{B}$ changes the sign of the good state*

$$|x\rangle \rightarrow \begin{cases} -|x\rangle, & \text{if } \mathcal{B}(x) = 1 \\ |x\rangle, & \text{if } \mathcal{B}(x) = 0 \end{cases},$$

while S_0 changes the sign of the amplitude only for the zero state $|0\rangle$. Then after the computation of $Q^t A |0\rangle$, a measurement yields good with probability at least $\max\{p, 1-p\}$.

3 Analysis of GFNs

In this section, we present a new approach for constructing distinquishers for GFNs. In Sect. 3.1 we illustrate the main idea behind the quantum distinguishers constructed for Type-1 and Type-2 GFNs. Introducing the property of separability, which is the main focus of our approach, in Sect. 3.2 we analyze the Type-3 scheme with 4 branches. Later on in Sect. 4 we present our approach in full detail.

3.1 On Quantum Distinquishers for Type-1 and Type-2 GFN

Recall that quantum distinquishers for classical 3-round Feistel network were presented in [17], and for Type-1/Type-2 GFNs have been constructed in [9, 15] (see also [8,10,14]). In this section we discuss the main idea behind the distinguishers on these schemes.

Let us consider the classical 3-round Feistel network (Fig. 1), denoted by $FN_3(x_0, x_1) = (y_0, y_1)$, where y_0 and y_1 are given by

$$\begin{cases} y_0 = x_1 \oplus F_1(x_0) \oplus F_3(x_0 \oplus F_2(x_1 \oplus F_1(x_0))), \\ y_1 = x_0 \oplus F_2(x_1 \oplus F_1(x_0)). \end{cases} \tag{4}$$

As shown in [17], by fixing the input x_0 two times, first by α and then by β, then using the right branch of FN_3 one can construct a function $f : \mathbb{F}_2 \times \mathbb{F}_2^n \rightarrow \mathbb{F}_2^n$ as in (3), and consequently verify that $f(b, x) = f(b \oplus 1, x \oplus s)$ holds, where $s = F_1(\alpha) \oplus F_1(\beta)$. Moreover, they showed that $(1, s)$ is the only non-trivial period of f. Since this is highly unlikely to hold for a random permutation (FN_3 is proved to be indistinguishable from a random permutation in classical environment under exponential number of queries), this automatically provides a quantum distinguisher which is based on Simon's algorithm.

Similarly, for d-branch Type-1 GFN (CAST256-like scheme), whose r-th round function is given by Fig. 2, where x_j^{r-1} is j-th branch in the input for r-th round, one can construct the function $f : \mathbb{F}_2 \times \mathbb{F}_2^n \rightarrow \mathbb{F}_2^n$ [9] by

$$f : (b, x) \rightarrow \alpha_b \oplus x_1^{2d-1} = F^d(h(\alpha_b) \oplus x), \tag{5}$$

where $(x_0^{2d-1}, \ldots, x_{d-1}^{2d-1}) = E_k(\alpha_b, x)$ and

$$h(\alpha_b) = F^{d-1}(F^{d-2}(\ldots (F^2(F^1(\alpha_b) \oplus x_1^0) \oplus x_2^0) \ldots \oplus x_{d-3}^0) \oplus x_{d-2}^0),$$

with blocks $x_0^0, \ldots, x_{d-2}^0$ taken to be constants and $x_{d-1}^0 = x$. It is not difficult to see that the period of the function f is given by $(1, s) = (1, h(\alpha_0) \oplus h(\alpha_1)) \in$

$\mathbb{F}_2 \times \mathbb{F}_2^n$, which provides the quantum distinguisher for $2d - 1$ rounds based on Simon's algorithm. In a similar way, in [9] the distinguisher of Type-2 GFN (RC6/CLEFIA-like scheme) for $2d + 1$ rounds has been provided for $2d$ branches.

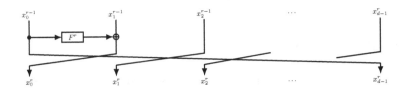

Fig. 2. The round function of Type-1 GFN with d branches involving keyed function F^r.

An improvement of the distinguisher (5) has been given in [15], where the same idea of fixing suitable inputs results in a periodic function f has been applied to $(3d - 3)$ and $(d^2 - d + 1)$-round Type-1 GFN.

In general, our main observation on previously mentioned distinguishers is that the construction of the Simon's function f is based on the property that we call *separability*, which is defined as follows.

Definition 1. *Let $RF_r^{(t)} : (x_0, \ldots, x_{d-1}) \in \mathbb{F}_2^{dn} \rightarrow \mathbb{F}_2^n$ denotes the t-th branch at round r of a given GFN. In addition, assume that the input plaintext $(x_0, \ldots, x_{d-1})$ can be written with disjoint variables as $(x_0, \ldots, x_{d-1}) = (x, y, z) \in \mathbb{F}_2^{e_1} \times \mathbb{F}_2^{e_2} \times \mathbb{F}_2^{e_3}$ $(e_1 + e_2 + e_3 = dn, e_1 \geq 1)$. Then:*

(i) *The GFN satisfies the* **strong separability** *property if $RF_r^{(t)}(x_0, \ldots, x_{d-1})$ can be represented as*

$$RF_r^{(t)}(x_0, \ldots, x_{d-1}) = RF_r^{(t)}(x, y, z) = \lambda(y, z) \oplus G(x \oplus H(y, z)),$$

where λ is a known function (i.e., implementable by adversary[1]).

(ii) *The GFN satisfies the* **semi-strong separability** *property if*

$$RF_r^{(t)}(x_0, \ldots, x_{d-1}) = RF_r^{(t)}(x, y, z) = y \oplus \lambda(z) \oplus G(x \oplus H(y), z),$$

where λ is not available (to be implemented or queried).

(iii) *The GFN satisfies the* **weak separability** *property if $RF_r^{(t)}(x, y, z) = \lambda(y, z) \oplus G(x \oplus H(y, z), y, z)$ and λ eventually is not available (e.g. due to involvement of secret keys, or non-existence of the oracle to provide its values).*

In all three cases, $G, H : \mathbb{F}_2^n \rightarrow \mathbb{F}_2^n$ are some vectorial functions such that G depends on the whole term '$x \oplus H(\cdot)$' (i.e., x is appearing only in the term '$x \oplus H(\cdot)$' and nowhere else outside of this term), the function $H(\cdot)$ depends on variables y and/or z only (depending on the case), but not on x.

---

[1] Or due to existence of an oracle to provide its values, and being available to be queried by any inputs.

Remark 3. Note that in general, we are not necessarily limited to only three disjoint variables x, y, z, but more can be employed. It just appears that the separability of many GFNs schemes is captured by Definition 1 which uses three disjoint variables.

To provide more clarification, we remark the following points:

- In the case of FN_3 (construction (3)), we notice that the variable $x = x_1$ is appearing only in the term '$x_1 \oplus F_1(x_0)$' and nowhere else outside of this term. Here we consider that $(x_0, x_1) = (y, x)$ and $H(y) = F_1(y)$. Considering y_1 in relation (4), we see that FN_3 satisfies the strong separability, since $y = x_0$ is appearing in $H(y)$ and also outside of it as a summand (where $G = F_2$ and λ is the identity mapping in variable y only).
- In (5) we have that the input block $x_d^0 = x$ is appearing only in the term '$x \oplus h(x_1^0, \ldots, x_{d-1}^0) = x \oplus H(y)$', i.e., it is not involved in the definition of the function H, nor in any other term outside of this one.

In general, if a given GFN satisfies the strong or semi-strong separability property, then one can always construct a Simon's function directly by querying the quantum encryption oracle with suitable constant/variable input blocks x, y, z and applying Proposition 1-(ii). We have the following results.

Proposition 2. *Let* $RF_r^{(t)} : (x_0, \ldots, x_{d-1}) \in \mathbb{F}_2^{dn} \to \mathbb{F}_2^n$ $(x_i \in \mathbb{F}_2^n)$ *denotes the output of the t-th branch at round r of a given GFN, which satisfies the semi-strong separability, that is* $RF_r^{(t)}(x_0, \ldots, x_{d-1}) = RF_r^{(t)}(x, y, z) = y \oplus \lambda(z) \oplus G(x \oplus H(y), z)$, *for some functions* $G, H, \lambda : \mathbb{F}_2^n \to \mathbb{F}_2^n$ *(λ is not available to the adversary). Then the Simon's function* $f : \mathbb{F}_2 \times \mathbb{F}_2^n$ *defined by*

$$f(b, x) = \begin{cases} \alpha_1 \oplus RF_r^{(t)}(x, \alpha_0, \beta) & b = 0 \\ \alpha_0 \oplus RF_r^{(t)}(x, \alpha_1, \beta) & b = 1 \end{cases},$$

has the period $(1, s) = (1, H(\alpha_0) \oplus H(\alpha_1))$, *were* α_b *and* β *are fixed and known.*

Proposition 3. *Let* $RF_r^{(t)} : (x_0, \ldots, x_{d-1}) \in \mathbb{F}_2^{dn} \to \mathbb{F}_2^n$ $(x_i \in \mathbb{F}_2^n)$ *denotes the output of the t-th branch at round r of a given GFN, which satisfies the strong separability, that is* $RF_r^{(t)}(x_0, \ldots, x_{d-1}) = RF_r^{(t)}(x, y, z) = \lambda(y, z) \oplus G(x \oplus H(y, z))$, *for some functions* $G, H, \lambda : \mathbb{F}_2^n \to \mathbb{F}_2^n$ *(λ is available to the adversary). Then the Simon's function* $f : \mathbb{F}_2 \times \mathbb{F}_2^n$ *defined by*

$$f(b, x) = \begin{cases} \lambda(\alpha_1, \beta) \oplus RF_r^{(t)}(x, \alpha_0, \beta) & b = 0 \\ \lambda(\alpha_0, \beta) \oplus RF_r^{(t)}(x, \alpha_1, \beta) & b = 1 \end{cases},$$

has the period $(1, s) = (1, H(\alpha_0, \beta) \oplus H(\alpha_1, \beta))$, *were* α_b *and* β *are fixed and known.*

Recall that $RF_r^{(t)}(\alpha_b, x)$ are obtained by querying and truncating the encryption oracle $\mathcal{U}_{GFN}$, and thus we assume that f can be implemented. Note that in the context of [6] and the asymmetric-query approach (related to **Q2** attack model), we are not able to reduce the query complexity, since our function f is using the quantum encryption oracle $\mathcal{U}_{GFN}$ for both restrictions of the function $f(b, x)$.

Remark 4. Proposition 3 shows that semi-strong separability is in fact strong separability (regardless of whether λ is known or not in the representation of $RF_r^{(t)}$). Essentially, this is due to the fact that the functions H and λ are disjoint variable functions, i.e., they do not depend on same variables.

In the next subsection we analyze the Type-3 GFN and present the main idea of our approach (which is further described in details in Sect. 4) that applies to certain rounds which satisfy the weak separability property.

3.2 On Separability of the Type-3 GFN

In general, one can notice that for all GFNs provided on [2, Figure 3] (and other schemes that one can find, for instance in [1,22]) the weak separability property is appearing after several initial rounds only, and thus makes the application of Simon's algorithm very difficult. In what follows, we consider 4 rounds of the so-called Type-3 scheme which satisfies the weak separability property, and we demonstrate a new approach that potentially allows us to analyze a somewhat increased number of rounds (at some branches).

Recall that the Type-3 GFN is given by Fig. 3, where the round function of Type-3 GFN (shortly RF) is defined as

$$RF : (x_0, \ldots, x_3) \rightarrow (x_1 \oplus F_1^r(x_0), x_2 \oplus F_2^r(x_1), x_3 \oplus F_3^r(x_2), x_0), \qquad (6)$$

where $x_i \in \mathbb{F}_2^n$ and $F_i^r : \mathbb{F}_2^n \rightarrow \mathbb{F}_2^n$.

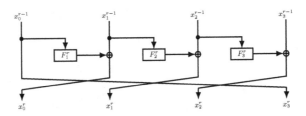

Fig. 3. The round function of Type-3 GFN.

Notice that, if we consider the 4-th branch of 4-round Type-3 (shortly GFN_3), which is given by

$$RF_4^{(4)}(x_0, \ldots, x_3) = x_3 \oplus \underbrace{F_1^3(x_2 \oplus F_1^2(x_1 \oplus F_1(x_0)) \oplus F_2(x_1)) \oplus F_2^2(x_2 \oplus F_2(x_1)) \oplus F_3(x_2)}_{\text{Does not involve } x_3},$$

then it actually satisfies the strong separability. This observation allows that we fix blocks (x_0, x_1, x_2) to be constants, say to take two arbitrary (different) values $\alpha_0 = (\alpha_0^{(0)}, \alpha_1^{(0)}, \alpha_2^{(0)})$, $\alpha_1 = (\alpha_0^{(1)}, \alpha_1^{(1)}, \alpha_2^{(1)}) \in \mathbb{F}_2^{3n}$, and set $x_3 = x$. This way (having an encryption oracle), we can construct the functions $g_0(x) =$

$RF_4^{(4)}(\alpha_0, x)$ and $g_1(x) = RF_4^{(4)}(\alpha_1, x)$ and consequently the function $f : \mathbb{F}_2 \times \mathbb{F}_2^n \to \mathbb{F}_2^n$ defined by

$$f(b, x) = \begin{cases} g_0(x), & b = 0 \\ g_1(x), & b = 1 \end{cases}, \tag{7}$$

is a periodic function in vector $(1, s) = (1, H(\alpha_0) \oplus H(\alpha_1))$, where $H(x_0, x_2, x_3) = x_3 \oplus RF_4^{(4)}(x_0, \dots, x_3)$. Note that the periodicity follows from Proposition 1-(ii), since $g_0(x \oplus s) = g_1(x)$ holds for all $x \in \mathbb{F}_2^n$. Thus we obtain a quantum distinguisher for 4 rounds of GFN_3 with polynomial-time complexity, due to the possibility of applying Simon's algorithm directly. In general, at some other branches of RF_4 one can apply the same idea by utilizing some other suitable inputs.

Remark 5. Note that in the case of Type-3 GFN with d-branches, we have that the branch $RF_d^{(d)}(x_0, \dots, x_{d-1})$ can be written as $RF_d^{(d)}(x_0, \dots, x_{d-1}) = x_{d-1} \oplus G(x_0, \dots, x_{d-2})$, for some function G given in terms of inner functions F_i^r, where $i, r \in \{1, \dots, d-1\}$. This means that $RF_d^{(d)}$ satisfies the strong separability, and thus one can construct Simon's function f similarly as in (7) providing the attack complexity $\mathcal{O}(n)$.

Attacking More Rounds: If we consider the GFN_3 with many rounds (say ≥ 5), then we are facing the weak separability property. Let us consider the 5-round (4-th branch), which is given by

$$\begin{aligned} RF_5^{(4)}(x_0, \dots, x_3) &= x_0 \oplus F_3^2(x_3 \oplus F_3(x_2)) \oplus F_2^3[x_3 \oplus F_3(x_2) \oplus F_2^2(x_2 \oplus F_2(x_1))] \\ &\oplus F_1^4[x_3 \oplus F_3(x_2) \oplus F_1^3(x_2 \oplus F_2(x_1) \oplus F_1^2(x_1 \oplus F_1(x_0))) \quad (8) \\ &\oplus F_2^2(x_2 \oplus F_2(x_1))]. \end{aligned}$$

Note that other branches of the 5-th round are even more complex. In this case we do not have the separability of input blocks x_i, since all of them appear at many places. However, the main idea is to notice a "term" which has a potential to be periodic, as for instance "$x_3 \oplus F_3(x_2)$". The choice of this term is motivated by the fact that input block x_3 in round function RF is not input of any inner function F_i^r.

Let us fix $x_3 = x$ to be a variable, and let $(x_0, x_1, x_2) = (\alpha^{(0)}, \alpha^{(1)}, \alpha^{(2)})$ be a constant vector from $\mathbb{F}_2^{3n}$. Now, if in the place of x_2 we consider two values, say $\alpha_0^{(2)}$ and $\alpha_1^{(2)}$, then in the form of $RF_5^{(4)}(\alpha^{(0)}, \alpha^{(1)}, \alpha^{(2)}, x)$ the value $\alpha_0^{(2)}$ will appear in the term "$x \oplus F_3(\alpha_0^{(2)})$", and it will appear at other places as well.

Considering the fixed inputs, we have

$$\begin{aligned} RF_5^{(4)}(\alpha_0, \boldsymbol{x}) &= \alpha^{(0)} \oplus F_3^2(\boldsymbol{x} \oplus \boldsymbol{F_3(\alpha_0^{(2)})}) \oplus F_2^3[\boldsymbol{x} \oplus \boldsymbol{F_3(\alpha_0^{(2)})} \oplus F_2^2(\alpha_0^{(2)} \oplus F_2(\alpha^{(1)}))] \\ &\oplus F_1^4[\boldsymbol{x} \oplus \boldsymbol{F_3(\alpha_0^{(2)})} \oplus F_1^3(\alpha_0^{(2)} \oplus F_2(\alpha^{(1)}) \oplus F_1^2(\alpha^{(1)} \oplus F_1(\alpha^{(0)}))) \\ &\oplus F_2^2(\alpha_0^{(2)} \oplus F_2(\alpha^{(1)}))]. \end{aligned}$$

where $\alpha_0 = (\alpha^{(0)}, \alpha^{(1)}, \alpha_0^{(2)})$. In general, the function $RF_5^{(4)}(\alpha_0, \boldsymbol{x})$ can be written in terms of some function $G : \mathbb{F}_2^n \to \mathbb{F}_2^n$ as

$$g_{00}(x) = RF_5^{(4)}(\alpha_0, \boldsymbol{x}) = G(\boldsymbol{x} \oplus \boldsymbol{F_3}(\boldsymbol{\alpha_0^{(2)}}), \alpha^{(0)}, \alpha^{(1)}, \alpha_0^{(2)}),$$

which is shortly denoted by $g_{00}(x)$ with respect to variable x, where the index '00' stands for the index of $\alpha_0^{(2)}$ that is appearing inside $F_3(\cdot)$ and outside of it.

Remark 6. Note that we here do not consider that any part of $RF_5^{(4)}$ represents a function λ, since it does not make much difference in the case of weak separability (considering also the definition of the round function RF given by (6)).

At this step, we cannot point out some value $s \in \mathbb{F}_2^n$ which will enable us to construct a periodic function by concatenating two functions (and thus applying Proposition 1), since the variable $\alpha_b^{(2)}$ ($b = 0, 1$) is appearing at other places outside '$x \oplus F_3(\alpha_b^{(2)})$' as well. Since one may consider $s = F_3(\alpha_0^{(2)}) \oplus F_3(\alpha_1^{(2)})$ (which is not known due to the secret key k_3), we have that

$$g_{00}(x \oplus s) = RF_5^{(4)}(\alpha_0, \boldsymbol{x} \oplus \boldsymbol{s}) = G(\boldsymbol{x} \oplus \boldsymbol{F_3}(\boldsymbol{\alpha_1^{(2)}}), \alpha^{(0)}, \alpha^{(1)}, \alpha_0^{(2)}).$$

In order to construct a periodic function f, it is convenient to query the function $RF_5^{(4)}(x_0, x_1, x_2, x_3)$ with suitable inputs such that the obtained function matches the function $g_{10}(x) = g_{00}(x \oplus s)$.

Considering the function $RF_5^{(4)}(x_0, x_1, x_2, x_3)$ (relation (8)), we notice that the terms $x_3 \oplus F_3(x_2)$, $x_2 \oplus F_2(x_1)$, and $x_1 \oplus F_1(x_0)$ are related such that they have maximally one common variable. Namely, $x_3 \oplus F_3(x_2)$ and $x_2 \oplus F_2(x_1)$ have x_2 in common, $x_2 \oplus F_2(x_1)$ and $x_1 \oplus F_1(x_0)$ have x_1 in common. Since in our functions $g_{00}(x)$ and $g_{10}(x)$ we are fixing the term $x_3 \oplus F_3(x_2) = x \oplus F_3(\alpha_b^{(2)})$ ($b = 0, 1$), if we then query the encryption oracle with parameters $(\beta, \gamma, \alpha_1^{(2)}, x)$, where $\alpha_1^{(2)}$ is an arbitrary fixed value, we have

$$RF_5^{(4)}(\beta, \gamma, \alpha_1^{(2)}, x) = G(\boldsymbol{x} \oplus \boldsymbol{F_3}(\boldsymbol{\alpha_1^{(2)}}), \beta, \gamma, \alpha_1^{(2)})$$

Due to the structure of the function $RF_5^{(4)}$ in (8) it is not difficult to see that if for fixed vectors $\alpha^{(1)}$ and $\alpha_1^{(2)}$ it holds that

$$\begin{cases} \alpha_1^{(2)} \oplus F_2(\gamma) = \alpha_0^{(2)} \oplus F_2(\alpha^{(1)}) \\ \gamma \oplus F_1(\beta) = \alpha^{(1)} \oplus F_1(\alpha^{(0)}) \end{cases}, \tag{9}$$

then

$$(\alpha^{(0)} \oplus \beta) \oplus RF_5^{(4)}(\beta, \gamma, \alpha_1^{(2)}, x) = G(\boldsymbol{x} \oplus \boldsymbol{F_3}(\boldsymbol{\alpha_1^{(2)}}), \alpha^{(0)}, \alpha^{(1)}, \alpha_0^{(2)})$$
$$= g_{10}(x). \tag{10}$$

In (10), $G(\boldsymbol{x} \oplus \boldsymbol{F_3}(\boldsymbol{\alpha_1^{(2)}}), \alpha^{(0)}, \alpha^{(1)}, \alpha_0^{(2)})$ is denoted by g_{10}, since we have $\alpha_1^{(2)}$ inside $F_3(\cdot)$, and $\alpha_0^{(2)}$ outside of the term $x \oplus F_3(\alpha_1^{(2)})$. Once we find the vectors

β and γ for which (9) holds, the Simon's function f is constructed as

$$f(b, x) = \begin{cases} g_{00}(x), & b = 0 \\ g_{10}(x) = g_{00}(x \oplus s), & b = 1. \end{cases} \tag{11}$$

which has the period $(1, s) = (1, F_3(\alpha_0^{(2)}) \oplus F_3(\alpha_1^{(2)}))$, extractable with Simon's algorithm in time $\mathcal{O}(n)$.

Assuming that F_1 and F_2 are invertible mappings, from (9) we have that

$$\begin{cases} \gamma = F_2^{-1}(\alpha_0^{(2)} \oplus \alpha_1^{(2)} \oplus F_2(\alpha^{(1)})) \\ \beta = F_1^{-1}(\alpha^{(1)} \oplus F_1(\alpha^{(0)}) \oplus \gamma) \end{cases}, \tag{12}$$

which means that system (9) has a unique solution pair (β, γ), where β depends on γ.

Remark 7. It is important to note that the assumption on invertibility of F_i implies that the period $(1, s)$ of f given by (11), is unique (Remark 1). More importantly, for fixed $\alpha^{(0)}, \alpha^{(1)}, \alpha_b^{(2)}$ ($b = 0, 1$), the solution pair (β, γ) actually *guarantees* that the construction of f given by (11) has a non-zero period.

From the aspect of periodicity of f, which is imposed by solving the system (9), we note that (9) may have more solution pairs (β, γ), since all these pairs are involved in the function g_{10} and considered to be a valid pairs as long as it holds that $g_{10}(x) = g_{00}(x \oplus s)$ for all $x \in \mathbb{F}_2^n$. Hence, the solution (12) ensures the periodicity of f, but does not describe all solution pairs (β, γ) that impose the periodicity of f.

Since oracles for F_1 and F_2 may not be available (due to unknown keys k_1, k_2), we are unable to compute γ and β directly. Now, our approach (further analysed in Sect. 4) is based on combining the Simon's and Grover's algorithm [19] (see also [9,10]).

Remark 8. For the Type-3 GFN with d-branches, the branch $RF_{d+1}^{(d)}(x_0, \ldots, x_{d-1})$ can be written as $RF_{d+1}^{(d)}(x_0, \ldots, x_{d-1}) = x_0 \oplus G(x_{d-1} \oplus F_{d-1}(x_{d-2}), x_0, \ldots, x_{d-2})$, for some function G given in terms of inner functions F_i^r, where $i \in \{1, \ldots, d-1\}$ and $r \in \{1, \ldots, d\}$. Since $RF_{d+1}^{(d)}$ satisfies the weak separability, by choosing suitable inputs x_i (as constants or variables) one can apply the Simon-Grover algorithm presented in Sect. 4 (similarly as for $RF_5^{(4)}$). In this case, the underlying system of equations is larger and its solvability can be deduced by using the same arguments as for (9). Note that the attack complexity, with respect to the combination of Simon's and Grover's algorithm, would depend on how many constant and variables x_i have been chosen.

4   Combining Simon's and Grover's Algorithm

The exhaustive search for pairs (β, γ) that provide the periodicity of f, given by (11), is highly inefficient (for larger n). In this section we combine Simon's and Grover's algorithm in order to find such pairs, where the main focus is the strong scenario which assumes the randomness of inner functions F_i^r (denoted as **CASE I**). We also discuss the weakened scenario (denoted as **CASE II**) in which there may exist many (β, γ) which result in periodicity of f in s which are not necessarily of the form $s = F_3(\alpha_0^{(2)}) \oplus F_3(\alpha_1^{(2)})$. In terms of the Simon-Grover algorithm this scenario has even smaller complexity, since in this case the underlying classifier $\mathcal{B}$ has larger preimage set (good inputs) of the output value 1 (as described in Sect. 2.1, in the part related to Grover's algorithm).

Recall that as a part of Grover's algorithm, we will have to define the classifier $\mathcal{B}$. For this purpose we will use the function $f : \mathbb{F}_2^{2n+(n+1)} \rightarrow \mathbb{F}_2^n$, which is defined as

$$f(\beta, \gamma, b, x) = \begin{cases} g_{00}(x) = RF_5^{(4)}(\alpha^{(0)}, \alpha^{(1)}, \alpha_0^{(2)}, x), & b = 0 \\ g_{10}(x) = (\alpha^{(0)} \oplus \beta) \oplus RF_5^{(4)}(\beta, \gamma, \alpha_1^{(2)}, x), & b = 1 \end{cases}, \quad (13)$$

where the values of $g_{00}(x)$ we directly take from the truncated encryption oracle $\mathcal{U}_{GFN_3}$, in which the keys involved in F_i^r are known to the oracle. On the other hand, the values of $g_{10}(x)$ also use $\mathcal{U}_{GFN_3}$, with additional inputs γ and β, where vectors $\alpha^{(0)}, \alpha^{(1)}, \alpha_b^{(2)}$ ($b = 0, 1$) are known and fixed in advance.

Now, let us define the function $\xi : (\mathbb{F}_2^n)^2 \times (\mathbb{F}_2^{n+1})^\ell \rightarrow \mathbb{F}_2^{\ell n}$ by

$$\xi : (\beta, \gamma, y_1, \ldots, y_\ell) \rightarrow f(\beta, \gamma, y_1) || \cdots || f(\beta, \gamma, y_\ell),$$

where the parameter ℓ ($\approx \mathcal{O}(n)$) implements the parallelized application of Simon's algorithm [19]. Denoting by $\mathcal{U}_\xi$ the quantum oracle defined by

$$\mathcal{U}_\xi : (\beta, \gamma, y_1, \ldots, y_\ell, \mathbf{0}, \ldots, \mathbf{0}) \rightarrow |\beta, \gamma, y_1, \ldots, y_\ell, \xi(\beta, \gamma, y_1, \ldots, y_\ell)\rangle,$$

where $\mathbf{0}$ is the all-zero quantum state of length n, then we define:

The Quantum Algorithm $\mathcal{A}$:

(1) Prepare the initial all-zero state $|\mathbf{0}\rangle$ of size $(2n + \ell(n+1) + \ell n)$.
(2) Apply the Hadamard transform $H^{\otimes(2n+\ell(n+1))}$ (on the first $\upsilon = 2n + \ell(n+1)$ qubits) and the operator $\mathcal{U}_\xi$ in order to obtain the state

$$2^{-\upsilon/2} \sum_{\substack{\beta, \gamma \in \mathbb{F}_2^n, \\ y_1, \ldots, y_\ell \in \mathbb{F}_2^{n+1}}} |\beta, \gamma\rangle |y_1\rangle \cdots |y_1\rangle |\xi(\beta, \gamma, y_1, \ldots, y_\ell)\rangle.$$

(3) Apply the Hadamard transform to states $|y_1\rangle \cdots |y_\ell\rangle$, to get the state

$$|\varphi\rangle = 2^{-\frac{\upsilon+(n+1)\ell}{2}} \sum_{\substack{\beta, \gamma \in \mathbb{F}_2^n, \\ u_1, \ldots, u_\ell \in \mathbb{F}_2^{n+1}, y_1, \ldots, y_\ell \in \mathbb{F}_2^{n+1}}} |\beta, \gamma\rangle (-1)^{u_1 \cdot y_1} |u_1\rangle \cdots (-1)^{u_\ell \cdot y_\ell} |u_\ell\rangle |\xi(\beta, \gamma, y_1, \ldots, y_\ell)\rangle.$$

At this moment, we are not doing any measurement on $|\varphi\rangle$, since we need to apply Grover's algorithm in addition. Now, we define:

The Classifier $\mathcal{B} : (\beta, \gamma, u_1, \ldots, u_\ell) \in \mathbb{F}_2^{2n+\ell(n+1)} \to \mathbb{F}_2$

(1) If dimension of the linear span of $u_1, \ldots, u_\ell \in \mathbb{F}_2^{n+1}$ is not equal to n, i.e., $dim(\langle u_1, \ldots, u_\ell \rangle) \neq n$, then we set $\mathcal{B}(\beta, \gamma, u_1, \ldots, u_\ell) = 0$. Otherwise, use [19, Lemma 2] to compute a candidate period $s' \in \mathbb{F}_2^{n+1}$.
(2) Then, check whether $f(\beta, \gamma, y) = f(\beta, \gamma, y \oplus s')$ holds for some amount of (randomly) provided y. If all equalities hold, then the output of $\mathcal{B}$ is 1, otherwise 0.

Remark 9. Notice that the definition of the classifier $\mathcal{B}$ actually implements the idea of Simon's algorithm, by finding a test period s' in the first step, and testing it then in the second step.

Thus, we say that a state $(\beta, \gamma, u_1, \ldots, u_\ell)$ is good if and only if $\mathcal{B}(\beta, \gamma, u_1, \ldots, u_\ell) = 1$, that is, when both tests (1) and (2) are satisfied. The classifier $\mathcal{B}$ partitions the state $|\varphi\rangle$ into a good and bad spaces $|\varphi_0\rangle$ and $|\varphi_1\rangle$ respectively, as $|\varphi\rangle = |\varphi_0\rangle + |\varphi_1\rangle$. Here $|\varphi_0\rangle$ and $|\varphi_1\rangle$ denote the projection onto the good and bad subspace respectively. In order to discuss the probability p of obtaining a good state (after measuring the state $|\varphi\rangle$), we distinguish the following cases:

CASE I: Let us assume that F_i^r behave as pseudo-random permutations. Then with very high probability we are expecting that not many pairs (β, γ), different than those given by (12), are implying the periodicity of the function f. This expectation is partly supported in a weak setting presented in Appendix - Table 1, in which we set that $F_i^r(x) = S(x \oplus k_i^r)$, $x \in \mathbb{F}_2^n$, where S is the S-box used in TWINE [26] ($n = 4$) and SMS4 [20] ($n = 8$). Even in these weak settings, the experiments indicate that periodicity of f in $s = F_3(\alpha_0^{(2)}) \oplus F_3(\alpha_1^{(2)})$ is mainly related to existence of two pairs (β, γ). Formally, we have the following result which is quite similar to [19, Lemma 5], where a short proof is provided for self-completeness.

Lemma 1. *Let $\sigma = (\beta', \gamma', u_1, \ldots, u_\ell)$ be an observed state. If a candidate pair (β', γ') is given by $(\beta', \gamma') = (\beta, \gamma)$, where (β, γ) is given by (12), then $\mathcal{B}(\sigma) = 1$ holds with probability at least $\frac{1}{5}$. On contrary, assume that probability of (β, γ) to be a wrong pair, that is when $(\beta', \gamma') \neq (\beta, \gamma)$ is not given by (12), is upper bounded by 2^{-z} with $z > 2n - 4$ (based on the pseudorandomness of F_i^r). If the output of $\mathcal{B}$ is equal to 1, then $(\beta', \gamma') = (\beta, \gamma)$ holds probability $> 1 - \frac{1}{2^{z-2n+4}}$.*

Proof. Using the same arguments as in the first part of the proof of [19, Lemma 5], one obtains that $p_0 = Pr[\mathcal{B}(\sigma) = 1 | \beta' = \beta, \gamma' = \gamma] \geq \frac{1}{5}$. Regarding the second part, let $\sigma = (\beta', \gamma', y_1, \ldots, y_\ell)$ be an input for which it holds that $\mathcal{B}(\sigma) = 1$. Assume that probability of the pair (β', γ') to be a wrong one (that is $(\beta', \gamma') \neq (\beta, \gamma)$) is upper bounded by $q = 2^{-z}$, where $z > 2n - 4$. Here by a wrong pair we mean that at least one of the keys $\beta', \gamma' \in \mathbb{F}_2^n$ is not correct. By law of total probability, it is not difficult to see that $Pr[\mathcal{B}(\sigma) = 1] \leq 2^{-2n} \cdot p_0 + 2^{-n-z+1} + 2^{-z}$, which consequently (using the first part of the proof) gives that

$$Pr[\beta' = \beta, \gamma' = \gamma | \mathcal{B}(\sigma) = 1] \geq 1 - \frac{2^{2n-z+4} - 2^{2(2n-z+4)}}{1 - 2^{2(2n-z+4)}}.$$

Note that the previous two inequalities are obtained using the same computational steps as in [19, Lemma 5]. Assuming that $\nu = z - 2n + 4 > 0$ (i.e., $z > 2n - 4$), we have that $\frac{2^{-\nu} - 2^{-2\nu}}{1 - 2^{-2\nu}} < \frac{1}{2^\nu}$, which consequently (by $-\nu = 2n - z - 4$) gives $Pr[\beta' = \beta, \gamma' = \gamma | \mathcal{B}(\sigma) = 1] \geq 1 - \frac{2^{2n-z-4} - 2^{2(2n-z-4)}}{1 - 2^{2(2n-z-4)}} > 1 - \frac{1}{2^{z-2n+4}}$.   □

Consequently, by law of total probability the value p (without loss of generality) is estimated as

$$p = Pr[\|\beta', \gamma', u_1, \ldots, u_\ell\rangle \text{ is good}]$$
$$\approx Pr[(\beta', \gamma') = (\beta, \gamma)] \cdot Pr[\mathcal{B}(\beta', \gamma', u_1, \ldots, u_\ell) = 1 | (\beta', \gamma') = (\beta, \gamma)] \approx 2^{-2n},$$

where (β, γ) are given by (12). Let us consider the second part of definition of $\mathcal{B}$, where we observe ρ randomly taken vectors $y \in \mathbb{F}_2^n$ and $s' = (c, \bar{s}) \in \mathbb{F}_2 \times \mathbb{F}_2^n$ as some candidate period. If $c = 0$ and $y = (0, x)$, then testing the equality $f(\beta, \gamma, y) = f(\beta, \gamma, y \oplus s')$ is equivalent to $g_{00}(x) = g_{00}(x \oplus \bar{s})$, which is highly unlikely if we assume that F_i^r are random permutations (or if we assume that $RF_r^{(t)}$ behaves as a random permutation for considered number of rounds). Let us consider the case when $g_{00}(x) = g_{10}(x \oplus \bar{s})$, where $g_{00}(x)$ are values coming from $\mathcal{U}_{GFN_3}$ (involving all correct keys) and g_{10} takes the candidate values β, γ as inputs (by design (13)). Then it is reasonable to assume that the probability of satisfying $g_{00}(x) = g_{10}(x \oplus \bar{s})$ (for many random inputs x) with respect to β, γ is equal to $2^{-\varepsilon}$, for sufficiently large ε.

Consequently, the probability of guessing a right pair (β, γ), for which all ρ equalities $g_{00}(x) = g_{10}(x \oplus \bar{s})$ hold, is given by $2^{-\rho \cdot \varepsilon}$, and thus the value z from Lemma 1 is taken to be $z = \rho \cdot \varepsilon$. Thus, we simply observe $\rho = \lceil \frac{2n-4}{\varepsilon} \rceil$ vectors y in order to ensure a high probability of having correct β, γ, if we observe an input $\sigma = (\beta, \gamma, y_1, \ldots, y_\ell)$ for which $\mathcal{B}(\sigma) = 1$. For instance, if $\varepsilon = 2$ (which is very low considering our assumptions), then $\rho = \lceil n - 2 \rceil$, which is always possible.

Hence, $\mathcal{B}$ defines a unitary operator $S_\mathcal{B}$ that changes the signs of states as

$$S_\mathcal{B} : \sigma = |\beta, \gamma, u_1, \ldots, u_\ell\rangle \rightarrow \begin{cases} -|\beta, \gamma, u_1, \ldots, u_\ell\rangle, & \mathcal{B}(\sigma) = 1 \\ |\beta, \gamma, u_1, \ldots, u_\ell\rangle, & \mathcal{B}(\sigma) = 0 \end{cases}.$$

The application of Grover's algorithm is realized by applying the operator $\mathcal{Q} = -\mathcal{A}S_0\mathcal{A}^{-1}S_\mathcal{B}$ consecutively t times to the state $|\varphi\rangle = \mathcal{A}|0\rangle$. Thus, measuring the state $\mathcal{Q}^t \mathcal{A}|0\rangle$ we obtain a good state with probability p_{good}, which is estimated as follows.

By Theorem 1, we have $\sin^2(\theta) = p = \langle \varphi_1 | \varphi_1 \rangle$ which implies $\theta \approx \arcsin(\sqrt{p}) \approx 2^{-n}$. Therefore, the number of iterations (by Theorem 1) given by $t = \lceil \frac{\pi}{4\theta} \rceil = \lceil \frac{\pi}{4 \cdot 2^{-n}} \rceil \approx 2^n$ is sufficient to result in angle $\pi/2$ between the resulting state $\mathcal{Q}^t \mathcal{A}|0\rangle$ and the bad subspace. Consequently, the success probability $p_{good} = 1 - 2^{-n}$ is very close to 1 for somewhat larger n.

CASE II: The experiments considered in weak settings given in Appendix - Sect. A.1 indicate that it may be the case that for various periods $s \in \mathbb{F}_2^n$ there may exist pairs (β, γ) (used as inputs in g_{10}) which imply the periodicity of f. By testing the periodicity for all vectors $s \in \mathbb{F}_2^n$, for the TWINE S-box on average we find 3 vectors s for which there exist two pairs of (β, γ) such that f (given by (11)) is periodic. In rare cases, for certain key sets taken randomly for 5 rounds, we may have that for almost all $s \in \mathbb{F}_2^4$ (TWINE S-box is of size 4) one finds at least two pairs of (β, γ) giving the periodicity of f.

If the underlying GFN has this property (at observed branch), i.e., that there exist different periods s which are ensured with more pairs (β, γ), then the classifier $\mathcal{B}$ has the initial probability p much larger than 2^{-2n}, and consequently, the final query complexity is significantly less than $2^n \cdot \mathcal{O}(n)$. In this context, it is important to emphasize that a good outcome $(\beta, \gamma, u_1, \ldots, u_\ell)$ is useful as long as its values β, γ which imply the periodicity of f (where clearly the corresponding period can be computed from vectors $u_1, \ldots, u_\ell$). Also, the probability p_{good} of obtaining this outcome is still satisfying, since the space φ_1 is larger. Note that by [7, Theorem 3], one can still run the Grover's algorithm even when the value p is not known in advance, where due to existence of many periods and corresponding pairs (β, γ), our algorithm will not run forever, but it will be significantly faster than $2^n \cdot \mathcal{O}(n)$.

To Summarize: Considering the strong scenario (when F_i^r are pseudorandom permutations), the overall procedure of obtaining a pair $(\beta, \gamma) \in \mathbb{F}_2^{2n}$ for $RF_5^{(4)}$: $\mathbb{F}_2^{4n} \to \mathbb{F}_2^n$ requires $2n + \ell(2n + 1) = 2n + 2(2n + 1)(n + 1 + \sqrt{n+1})$ qubits and approximatively $2^n \cdot \mathcal{O}(n)$ quantum queries, where the value $\ell = 2(n + 1 + \sqrt{n+1})$ is chosen according to [19, Lemma 4] (for vectors $y_i \in \mathbb{F}_2^{n+1}$ in the algorithm $\mathcal{A}$). In addition, a good outcome provides also a set of vectors $y_1, \ldots, y_\ell$ which we can use to find a period $s = F_3(\alpha_0^{(2)}) \oplus F_3(\alpha_1^{(2)})$ with very high probability, as discussed earlier. In the weak scenario (when different periods are possible with many (β, γ) pairs), the query complexity tends to be lower, which clearly depends on the observed GFN.

5   Conclusions

For the classical environment, many works have been devoted to improve the diffusion properties of GFN, since they depend on inner round functions. However, in the quantum environment the cryptanalytic methods are taking different direction, in which the quantum algorithms (such as Simon's, Grover's, and others) are playing an important role (for which in many cases the inner functions are not important that much). The method presented in this work focuses on two elements, namely a suitable construction of a Simon's function and collection of a specific equations in terms of inner functions (with suitably fixed inputs). We show that the solvability of the system of collected equations may imply a construction of a quantum distinguisher for (almost) any number of rounds if the considered system has solutions. Unfortunately, our method (being generic) does not run in polynomial time, but in exchange indicates on which specific inner round functions the security may rely. As an interesting research direction, we leave our method for further investigation in the context of: other (cyclically inequivalent) GFNs used in some well-known block ciphers, GFNs with non-binary group operations, unbalanced GFN, design criterions, combination with other attacks, and so on.

Acknowledgment. S. Hodžic and L. R. Knudsen are supported by a grant from the Independent Research Fund Denmark for Technology and Production, grant no. 8022-00348A.

A   Appendix

A.1   Experimental Results Related to System (9)

In Table 1 we consider the number of pairs (β, γ) which are implying the periodicity of f exactly in $s = F_3(\alpha_0^{(2)}) \oplus F_3(\alpha_1^{(2)})$, where f is given by (11) as

$$f(b,x) = \begin{cases} g_{00}(x) = RF_5^{(4)}(\alpha^{(0)}, \alpha^{(1)}, \alpha_0^{(2)}, x), & b = 0, \\ g_{10}(x) = (\alpha^{(0)} \oplus \beta) \oplus RF_5^{(4)}(\beta, \gamma, \alpha_1^{(2)}, x), & b = 1. \end{cases} \quad (14)$$

We take that F_i^r are defined by $F_i^r(x) = S(x \oplus k_i^r)$, $x \in \mathbb{F}_2^n$, with S being the S-box used in TWINE [26] ($n = 4$) and SMS4 [20] ($n = 8$). Since we are considering only 5 rounds, the keys supplied to inner functions F_i^r are taken to be arbitrary, and thus we are considering in total $5 \times 3 = 15$ random keys (effectively it is needed 4×3, since $RF_4^{(1)} = RF_5^{(4)}$). In addition, with respect to these random sets of keys, we are also taking random quadruples $(\alpha^{(0)}, \alpha^{(1)}, \alpha_0^{(2)}, \alpha_0^{(2)})$.

Table 1. The number of pairs (β, γ) that imply a periodic function f given by (14).

S-box	Number of random quadruples $(\alpha^{(0)}, \alpha^{(1)}, \alpha_0^{(2)}, \alpha_0^{(2)})$	Number of key sets for the first 5 rounds	Number of pairs (β, γ) which imply periodicity of f in s
TWINE cipher ($n = 4$)	10	10	2
SMS4 cipher ($n = 8$)	10	10	2

We notice that for different random key sets, one may obtain the same pairs of (β, γ), or eventually the first/second values are equal. Unfortunately, we did not find why in almost all cases one obtains exactly 2 different pairs of (β, γ). In rare cases, for the TWINE S-box, for certain instances of keys and quadruples $(\alpha^{(0)}, \alpha^{(1)}, \alpha_0^{(2)}, \alpha_0^{(2)})$ there exist 16 pairs (β, γ) which imply periodicity of f. However, recall that this is a weak setting of the inner functions F_i^r considered only on 5 rounds (if one would relate these to the presence of weak keys).

References

1. Berger, T.P., Minier, M., Thomas, G.: Extended generalized feistel networks using matrix representation. In: Lange, T., Lauter, K., Lisoněk, P. (eds.) SAC 2013. LNCS, vol. 8282, pp. 289–305. Springer, Heidelberg (2014). https://doi.org/10.1007/978-3-662-43414-7_15
2. Bogdanov, A., Shibutani, K.: Generalized Feistel networks revisited. Des. Codes Crypt. **66**(1–3), 75–97 (2013)
3. Bonnetain, X.: Quantum key-recovery on full AEZ. In: Adams, C., Camenisch, J. (eds.) SAC 2017. LNCS, vol. 10719, pp. 394–406. Springer, Cham (2018). https://doi.org/10.1007/978-3-319-72565-9_20
4. Bonnetain, X., Naya-Plasencia, M.: Hidden shift quantum cryptanalysis and implications. In: Peyrin, T., Galbraith, S. (eds.) ASIACRYPT 2018. LNCS, vol. 11272, pp. 560–592. Springer, Cham (2018). https://doi.org/10.1007/978-3-030-03326-2_19
5. Bonnetain, X., Naya-Plasencia, M., Schrottenloher, A.: On quantum slide attacks. In: Paterson, K.G., Stebila, D. (eds.) SAC 2019. LNCS, vol. 11959, pp. 492–519. Springer, Cham (2020). https://doi.org/10.1007/978-3-030-38471-5_20
6. Bonnetain, X., Hosoyamada, A., Naya-Plasencia, M., Sasaki, Y., Schrottenloher, A.: Quantum attacks without superposition queries: the offline Simon's algorithm. In: Galbraith, S.D., Moriai, S. (eds.) ASIACRYPT 2019. LNCS, vol. 11921, pp. 552–583. Springer, Cham (2019). https://doi.org/10.1007/978-3-030-34578-5_20
7. Brassard, G., Høyer, P., Mosca, M., Tapp, A.: Quantum amplitude amplification and estimation. Quant. Comput. Inf. (Washington, DC, 2000) Contemp. Math. **305**, 53–74 (2002)
8. Dong, X., Dong, B., Wang, X.: Quantum attacks on some Feistel block ciphers. IACR Cryptology ePrint Archive (2018). https://eprint.iacr.org/2018/504.pdf
9. Dong, X., Li, Z., Wang, X.: Quantum cryptanalysis on some generalized Feistel schemes. Sci. China Inf. Sci. **62**, 22501 (2019)
10. Dong, X., Wang, X.: Quantum key-recovery attack on Feistel structures. Sci. China Inf. Sci. **61**, 102501 (2019)
11. Grover, L.K.: A fast quantum mechanical algorithm for database search. In: Proceedings of the Twenty-Eighth Annual ACM Symposium on Theory of Computing, Philadelphia, Pennsylvania, USA, 22–24 May, pp. 212–219 (1996)
12. Hosoyamada, A., Aoki, K.: On quantum related-key attacks on iterated Even-Mansour ciphers. In: Obana, S., Chida, K. (eds.) IWSEC 2017. LNCS, vol. 10418, pp. 3–18. Springer, Cham (2017). https://doi.org/10.1007/978-3-319-64200-0_1
13. Hosoyamada, A., Sasaki, Y.: Quantum Demiric-Selçuk meet-in-the-middle attacks: applications to 6-round generic Feistel constructions. In: Catalano, D., De Prisco, R. (eds.) SCN 2018. LNCS, vol. 11035, pp. 386–403. Springer, Cham (2018). https://doi.org/10.1007/978-3-319-98113-0_21
14. Ito, G., Hosoyamada, A., Matsumoto, R., Sasaki, Y., Iwata, T.: Quantum chosen-ciphertext attacks against Feistel ciphers. In: Matsui, M. (ed.) CT-RSA 2019. LNCS, vol. 11405, pp. 391–411. Springer, Cham (2019). https://doi.org/10.1007/978-3-030-12612-4_20
15. Ito, G., Iwata, T.: Quantum distinguishing attacks against Type-1 generalized Feistel ciphers. IACR Cryptology ePrint Archive (2019). https://eprint.iacr.org/2019/327.pdf

16. Kaplan, M., Leurent, G., Leverrier, A.,   Naya-Plasencia, M.: Breaking symmetric cryptosystems using quantum period finding. In: Robshaw, M., Katz, J. (eds.) CRYPTO 2016. LNCS, vol. 9815, pp. 207–237. Springer, Heidelberg (2016). https://doi.org/10.1007/978-3-662-53008-5_8

17. Kuwakado, H., Morii, M.: Quantum distinguisher between the 3-round Feistel cipher and the random permutation. In: IEEE International Symposium on Information Theory (2010). https://doi.org/10.1109/ISIT.2010.5513654

18. Kuwakado, H., Morii, M.: Security on the quantum-type Even-Mansour cipher. In: International Symposium on Information Theory and its Applications, 28–31 October, Honolulu, HI, USA (2012)

19. Leander, G., May, A.: Grover meets Simon – quantumly attacking the FX-construction. In: Takagi, T., Peyrin, T. (eds.) ASIACRYPT 2017. LNCS, vol. 10625, pp. 161–178. Springer, Cham (2017). https://doi.org/10.1007/978-3-319-70697-9_6

20. Liu, F., et al.: Analysis of the SMS4 block cipher. In: Pieprzyk, J., Ghodosi, H., Dawson, E. (eds.) ACISP 2007. LNCS, vol. 4586, pp. 158–170. Springer, Heidelberg (2007). https://doi.org/10.1007/978-3-540-73458-1_13

21. Ni, B., Ito, G., Dong, X., Iwata, T.: Quantum attacks against type-1 generalized Feistel ciphers and applications to CAST-256. In: Hao, F., Ruj, S., Sen Gupta, S. (eds.) INDOCRYPT 2019. LNCS, vol. 11898, pp. 433–455. Springer, Cham (2019). https://doi.org/10.1007/978-3-030-35423-7_22

22. Nyberg, K.: Generalized Feistel networks. In: Kim, K., Matsumoto, T. (eds.) ASIACRYPT 1996. LNCS, vol. 1163, pp. 91–104. Springer, Heidelberg (1996). https://doi.org/10.1007/BFb0034838

23. Röetteler, M., Steinwandt, R.: A note on quantum related-key attacks. Inf. Process. Lett. **115**(1), 40–44 (2015)

24. Santoli, T., Schaffner, C.: Using Simon's algorithm to attack symmetric-key cryptographic primitives. Quant. Inf. Comput. **17**(1–2), 65–78 (2017)

25. Simon, D.R.: On the power of quantum computation. SIAM J. Comput. **26**(5), 1474–1483 (1997)

26. Suzaki, T., Minematsu, K., Morioka, S., Kobayashi, E.: *TWINE*: a lightweight block cipher for multiple platforms. In: Knudsen, L.R., Wu, H. (eds.) SAC 2012. LNCS, vol. 7707, pp. 339–354. Springer, Heidelberg (2013). https://doi.org/10.1007/978-3-642-35999-6_22

27. Xu, L., Guo, J., Cui, J., Li, M.: Key-recovery attacks on LED-like block ciphers. Tsinghua Sci. Technol. **24**(5), 585–595 (2019)

28. Zheng, Y., Matsumoto, T., Imai, H.: On the construction of block ciphers provably secure and not relying on any unproved hypotheses. In: Brassard, G. (ed.) CRYPTO 1989. LNCS, vol. 435, pp. 461–480. Springer, New York (1990). https://doi.org/10.1007/0-387-34805-0_42

Security Proofs

Many a Mickle Makes a Muckle: A Framework for Provably Quantum-Secure Hybrid Key Exchange

Benjamin Dowling[1]([envelope]), Torben Brandt Hansen[2], and Kenneth G. Paterson[1]

[1] Department of Computer Science, ETH Zurich, Zürich, Switzerland
{benjamin.dowling,kenny.paterson}@inf.ethz.ch
[2] Information Security Group, Royal Holloway, University of London, Egham, UK
Torben.Hansen.2015@rhul.ac.uk

Abstract. Hybrid Authenticated Key Exchange (AKE) protocols combine keying material from different sources (post-quantum, classical, and quantum key distribution (QKD)) to build protocols that are resilient to catastrophic failures of the different components. These failures may be due to advances in quantum computing, implementation vulnerabilities, or our evolving understanding of the quantum (and even classical) security of supposedly quantum-secure primitives. This hybrid approach is a prime candidate for initial deployment of post-quantum-secure cryptographic primitives because it hedges against undiscovered weaknesses. We propose a general framework HAKE for analysing the security of such hybrid AKE protocols. HAKE extends the classical Bellare-Rogaway model for AKE security to encompass forward security, post-compromise security, fine-grained compromise of different cryptographic components, and more. We use the framework to provide a security analysis of a new hybrid AKE protocol named Muckle. This protocol operates in one round trip and leverages the pre-established symmetric keys that are inherent to current QKD designs to provide message authentication, avoiding the need to use expensive post-quantum signature schemes. We provide an implementation of our Muckle protocol, instantiating our generic construction with classical and post-quantum Diffie-Hellman-based algorithmic choices. Finally, we report on benchmarking exercises against our implementation, examining its performance in terms of clock cycles, elapsed wall-time, and additional latency in both LAN and WAN settings.

Keywords: Authenticated key exchange · Hybrid key exchange · Provable security · Protocol analysis · Quantum key distribution · Post-compromise security

1 Introduction

NIST's Post Quantum Cryptography (PQC) process has triggered significant effort into the design of new post-quantum public key algorithms that can eventually be used to replace existing algorithms in protocols such as IPsec and

© Springer Nature Switzerland AG 2020
J. Ding and J.-P. Tillich (Eds.): PQCrypto 2020, LNCS 12100, pp. 483–502, 2020.
https://doi.org/10.1007/978-3-030-44223-1_26

TLS. Indeed, NIST's 2017 call received 69 complete submissions in various categories. However, much less attention has been paid on how to securely integrate these new algorithms into applications, and to assessing the impact they will have on the performance of real-world network protocols. A key issue is that the new algorithms are relatively immature, and our understanding of their security is still evolving. NIST lacked confidence in 13 of the original submissions [22]; meanwhile Albrecht et al. [4] highlight how poor our current understanding is of how to assess the cost of lattice attacks. During the cryptographic interregnum, sensitive data is still at risk from attackers who are willing to record and store network traffic for later cryptanalysis. One response to this uncertainty is to quickly roll out post-quantum secure algorithms in protocols like TLS. For example, in 2016 Google carried out an experiment in which they deployed the NewHope lattice-based scheme [5] in Chrome and in Google servers [13], and in 2019 Cloudflare and Google jointly carried out similar experiments [20]. These tests adopted hybrid approaches, combining post-quantum schemes with forward-secure key exchange mechanisms, namely Elliptic Curve Diffie Hellman Ephemeral (ECDHE). Adopting a hybrid approach hedges against security vulnerabilities in the post-quantum algorithm (fundamental as well as implementation-related) whilst providing security against quantum adversaries. While discussions have started [27], at this point no formal standardisation has begun integrating post-quantum algorithms into secure Internet protocols, a few unadopted IETF drafts notwithstanding [25,29]. Standardisation will inevitably be needed, and we anticipate that a hybrid approach will be used. But first the community needs to research (a) how to build and analyse hybrid protocols, and (b) how to assure the security of their post-quantum components. The former is the main focus of this work, while the latter falls under the aegis of the NIST PQC process.

Quantum Key Distribution (QKD) is often promoted as an alternate solution to the threat posed by large-scale quantum computers, and has some attractive features: when well-implemented, it can offer unconditional security, it is also increasingly well-integrated with standard optical communications and electronics systems, with small package sizes and high raw bit rates, cf. [26]. However, the achievable bit rate does not yet practically allow the use of QKD keying material in a one-time-pad encryption system, so while the keying material may be unconditionally secure, no practical overall secure communications system relying on QKD is (to date). Moreover, QKD is fundamentally range limited (in the absence of quantum repeaters) and so cannot offer true end-to-end security in wide-area networks. Furthermore the technology is still quite immature, and vulnerable to various implementation attacks ("quantum hacking"), cf. [18,28]. Even the physical basis of QKD has been questioned [10,30]. Despite this, QKD may still usefully augment existing technologies in point-to-point applications, such as intra or inter data-centre communications or in metropolitan networks. Given this context, we should consider the possibility of incorporating QKD-based keying material into our hybrid protocol designs, resulting in three sources of keying material to combine: classically-secure (e.g. ECDHE), post-quantum secure (e.g. NewHope, SIDH, or another NIST candidate), and QKD-based. Having established this context, we can now begin to describe our contributions.

1.1   Our Contributions

The HAKE Security Framework: We introduce a flexible framework for capturing and analysing Hybrid Authenticated Key Exchange (AKE) protocols that combine a wide variety of symmetric and asymmetric primitives. The HAKE framework is the result of heavily modifying the classic Bellare-Rogaway [7] model for AKE, incorporating security notions such as perfect forward secrecy and post-compromise security (referring to the ability of a key exchange protocol to recover security in the event of a catastrophic compromise of all its secrets) and smoothly caters for different strengths of adversary (quantum or even classical). It features a particularly simple and novel abstraction of QKD protocols to allow them to be modelled in a standard computational setting: pairs of parties are given private access to a shared source of secret random bits.

The Muckle AKE Protocol: To exercise the HAKE framework, we also present the Muckle AKE protocol,[1] its security analysis, details of a working software implementation of Muckle, and benchmarking results. Muckle securely combines keying material obtained from a quantum key distribution (QKD) protocol with that from a post-quantum-secure key encapsulation mechanism (KEM) and a classically-secure KEM. Muckle is a one-round (1-RTT) protocol which exploits the presence of a QKD component to simplify the authentication of protocol messages. Specifically, QKD protocols typically assume the presence of an initial or pre-shared key (PSK) between the pair of communicating parties. This is used to bootstrap an authenticated channel for exchanging basis measurement information.[2] Muckle's design assumes the presence of a second PSK (since the cost of establishing two such keys is not any greater in practice than the cost of establishing just one), and uses it as the basis for authenticating its protocol messages via MACs. Muckle evolves this key and associated state, using outputs from the various KEM primitives as well as the QKD itself.

Benchmarking Muckle: We instantiate and implement Muckle in 'C' (which we denote C-Muckle) and benchmarked it in different network settings, selecting specific schemes in order to fix a concrete design. We profile the cost of the underlying C-Muckle functions in terms of the median execution wall-time and clock cycle counts. We also contrast the wall-time profiling of C-Muckle functions when it runs over a LAN with the same profiling when it is run between London and Paris (approximately 500 km, somewhat more than the current maximum range of single-hop QKD systems). These experiments are done without a real QKD system, which is simulated via access to a file of keying material.

---

[1] The name Muckle derives from the traditional English phrase "Many a mickle makes a muckle": many small things can add up to make a big thing.

[2] As a side-note, this is why QKD in this normal form does not solve the key distribution problem, but only the key expansion problem.

Security Analysis of Muckle: Finally, we demonstrate that Muckle achieves AKE security as defined by our HAKE framework. This allows us to make security statements about Muckle in the presence of quantum adversaries (assuming post-quantum variants of standard cryptographic assumptions), or under the catastrophic failure of all but one of its distinct components. The latter includes scenarios where, for example, all public key cryptography evaporates (and only Muckle's QKD component remains secure). It also includes the situation where the QKD component turns out to be badly engineered and therefore insecure and where the classical component becomes vulnerable to a quantum computer, but where its post-quantum counterpart remains secure.

1.2   Related Work

While the analysis of "fully classical" hybrid schemes have appeared in the past (for instance, work on combining multiple public-key encryption schemes [31]), little work has been done on combining post-quantum and classical cryptographic primitives. Bindel et al. [12] examine a variety of hybrid digital signature schemes in quantum and post-quantum settings. They also formalise the notion of *separability*, which captures the ability of an attacker to separate the hybrid scheme into its individual cryptographic components. Bindel et al. [11] is most closely related to our work, considering hybrid key exchange in a similar setting to our own, but is focussed on quantum-secure KEM combiners. Their setting and security model are less general than ours in some regards (our HAKE framework can accommodate KEMs, theirs is limited to KEMs), but considers a hierarchy of attackers depending on quantum-computing capability and quantum access to the protocol participants. In addition, their compromise paradigm is less fine-grained, considering only the compromise of long-term and session keys. Complementing our approach, Mosca et al. [23] analyse the security of the QKD protocol BB84 [8], using an AKE security model in the tradition of Bellare-Rogaway to formalise the protocol in their notation. They prove the security of BB84 in this security model, and their notions of keys output by the QKD protocol match our assumptions. The concept of *breakdown resilience* was introduced by Brendel et al. [14]; this concept considers the effect on overall protocol security of failures of individual cryptographic components. They also extend Bellare-Rogaway security models by providing an interface for an attacker to break individual cryptographic components, similar to our approach of providing specific key exposure oracles. There have been a couple of recent IETF drafts [25, 29] describing hybrid approaches for TLS 1.3, but without any accompanying formal security analysis as far as we are aware.

2   The Muckle Protocol

Here we introduce the Muckle hybrid key exchange protocol; see Fig. 1 for an overview. At a high-level, Muckle simultaneously executes post-quantum and classical key encapsulation primitives, and draws key material from a QKD protocol, represented abstractly in the protocol as a shared array of bits into which

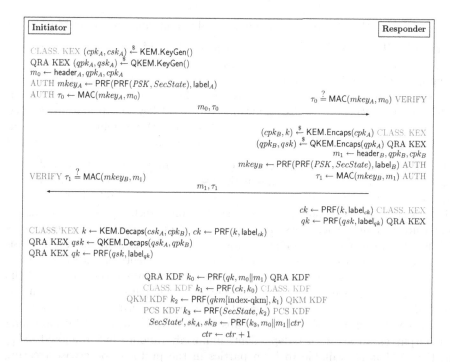

Fig. 1. A single stage of the Muckle protocol.

the two parties can index. The three distinct types of key material are used as inputs to a sequence of key derivation steps that we refer to as the Muckle key schedule. The design of the Muckle key schedule allows us to prove that the session keys produced by Muckle are resilient to vulnerabilities in the underlying QKD or key exchange primitives. Muckle is a multi-stage protocol, where the initiator and responder repeatedly run the single stage shown in Fig. 1, updating the session keys sk_A, sk_B and the secret, shared state $SecState$ of the protocol at each stage. We highlight the key features of Muckle below:

- One round trip (1-RTT) to establish post-quantum-secure session keys.
- Multi-stage design and the inclusion of an updating secret state ($SecState$) allows Muckle to achieve post-compromise security, i.e. recover security after full compromise attacks (under certain restrictions, see Sect. 4).
- Hybrid key exchange approach allows Muckle to be secure against classical adversaries even if the QKD and post-quantum components fail.
- Use of symmetric cryptography (of an appropriate key-length) allows Muckle to achieve post-quantum authentication without the use of computationally-expensive and bandwidth-intensive post-quantum signatures.
- Modular design allows implementers to easily replace underlying key exchange primitives if vulnerabilities are discovered.
- Key confirmation and full message transcript agreement of previous stages are provided in successive stages via the computation of authentication keys.

We expand on these below, and explain the different components of Muckle.

Message Structure: There are four elements to a Muckle message: a header (referred to in Fig. 1 as header$_A$ and header$_B$), containing message identifiers, cryptographic primitive identifiers and party identifiers; a classical ephemeral key encapsulation, (which we instantiate with elliptic-curve-based Diffie-Hellman (ECDH) in C-Muckle); a post-quantum ephemeral key encapsulation, (which we instantiate with Supersingular Isogeny-based Diffie-Hellman (SIDH) in C-Muckle); and a MAC tag computed over the message.

QKD: Muckle assumes that a QKD scheme is running between pairs of communicating parties. QKD schemes make use of classically-authenticated communication channels, and such channels are (in practice) built using symmetric keys (though they could use other cryptographic techniques, such as digital signatures). Thus, Muckle assumes the presence of pre-shared symmetric keys (PSKs) between pairs of communicating parties. Likewise, this makes it possible to assume the existence of pre-established party identifiers in the protocol. Theses two value allow us to achieve post-quantum-secure authentication of the Muckle messages without incurring the significant computational or communication overhead that would be associated with a post-quantum signature scheme.

In our description of Muckle, we abstract the QKD protocol by modelling its output as an array of independent, uniformly-random bits (denoted $qsk[\cdot]$ in Fig. 1) that is available to both parties in the protocol, otherwise treating the QKD component as a black box. Thus, we assume that the QKD system is implemented perfectly. This significantly simplifies our security analysis task, since it avoids the need for us to integrate existing QKD security models with our HAKE security framework. However, this is an idealisation that we plan to relax in future work, see Sect. 6 for more discussion. The pre-shared key is denoted PSK in Fig. 1, and is 256 bits in size. The party identifiers are 32-byte strings (they do not appear explicitly in Fig. 1, but instead are implicit in label$_A$ and label$_B$).

Authentication: MAC tag computations use freshly-generated keys ($mkey_A$, $mkey_B$) for each new stage. Specifically, $mkey_A \leftarrow \mathsf{PRF}(\mathsf{PRF}(PSK, SecState),$ label$_A$), and $mkey_B \leftarrow \mathsf{PRF}(\mathsf{PRF}(PSK, SecState), $label$_B)$. Note that $SecState$ is updated with each new stage, and thus $mkey_A$ and $mkey_B$ are similarly fresh.

Key Schedule: The key schedule is run after the initiator and responder have sent and received their respective messages. The straightforward iterative design simplifies the analysis of the protocol. Each step takes as input some key material and a chaining key, and outputs a new chaining key used in the next iteration, seen in the KDF steps at the bottom of Fig. 1. We also include a counter ctr (a 256-bit integer) in the final PRF computation; ctr is incremented after each stage.

State Update: The secret state $SecState$ is updated at the end of a Muckle stage (initialised as a constant, public value in the first stage), when the session keys are computed. Specifically, $SecState, sk_A, sk_B \leftarrow \mathsf{PRF}(k_3, m_0\|m_1\|ctr)$, taking as input the final chain key k_3 from the key schedule, and the concatenation of the message transcript and counter: $m_0 \| m_1 \| ctr$. Thus, consecutive Muckle stages provide implicit key confirmation (since in order to derive the same $SecState$, protocol participants must also derive the same session keys sk_A, sk_B) of previous stages, as well as full message transcript agreement of previous stages.

Post-Compromise Security (PCS): At a high-level, PCS is the ability of a key exchange protocol to recover security when an attacker has compromised all secrets of a session, if the attacker becomes passive in a later protocol execution. Our Muckle design achieves PCS by virtue of the inclusion of the secret state $SecState$ in the MAC computations and in the derivation of the session keys.

3   Instantiation and Implementation of Muckle

This section describes our reference implementation of Muckle in 'C', which we denote C-Muckle [2]. C-Muckle follows the same governing design principles as Muckle, favouring simplicity and verifiability. As a result, we optimise for readability and reproducibility and sacrifice features such as fully performance-optimised code. C-Muckle targets 128-bit post-quantum security. To instantiate C-Muckle, we have made the following choice of parameters and cryptographic algorithms: For the classically-secure KEM, we use elliptic-curve Diffie-Hellman key exchange using the elliptic curve curve25519 [9], and for the post-quantum-secure KEM, we chose supersingular isogeny Diffie-Hellman key exchange using field arithmetic over the prime p503, construction and parameters by Costello et al. [16]. The pseudo-random function is instantiated by the key derivation scheme HDKF [19] using 256-bit keys, and similarly the message authentication code is instantiated by HMAC [6] using 256-bit keys. For details about the C-Muckle message format, refer to the full version.

Dependencies: To provide support for the chosen cryptographic components C-Muckle relies upon two libraries: mbedtls [1] version 2.13.0 and PQCrypto-SIDH [3] version 3. The former is used to support the ECDHE, PRF, and MAC cryptographic components as well as random number generation, while the latter is used to support SIDH.

QKD Bits: Currently, our software implementation of C-Muckle does not engage with real QKD devices. The process of obtaining the bits produced by a QKD protocol is therefore emulated. We provide two distinct methods for doing this. The first method is to store a static array of bits in the source code. During an execution, bits are read from the array depending on an index. The second method reads from a file, with bits similarly read from the file depending on an index. In both cases the bits should be uniformly random. The method of emulation can be changed during compile-time. Currently, C-Muckle defaults to using the static array method. These methods are solely implemented for experimental use and should not be used in any production system. C-Muckle is designed to allow easy switching to a method that provides true access to QKD key material.

3.1 Performance Study

Here we profile and discuss the performance of C-Muckle. Our experiments aim at conveying the cryptographic costs associated with the different components of Muckle, as well as the total cost of executing a complete run of the protocol. To achieve this, we benchmark different parts of C-Muckle as well as the core cryptographic API calls made to external libraries.

Methodology: We measure the performance of C-Muckle using two metrics: clock cycles and wall-time. For each metric, a single stage execution of C-Muckle is measured and recorded. The cost of lower layer functions responsible for performing cryptographic operations is also measured and separately recorded. Below we list these functions and describe the cryptographic operation they each perform:

muckle_ecdh_gen(): Generates an ECDHE public key pair.
muckle_ecdh_compute(): Computes the ECDHE secret.
muckle_sidh_gen(): Generates the SIDH public key pair.
muckle_sidh_compute(): Computes the SIDH shared secret.
muckle_read_qkd_keys(): Reads the QKD keying material using a method described above.
muckle_derive_keys(): Derives the secret state and session keys according to the key schedule defined in Sect. 2.

Note that the functions above perform more than just cryptographic operations. Additional operations include initialisation, copying between buffers, and general glue-code. We further discuss the overhead relative to the cryptographic operations for a subset of these functions.

Our experiments were performed between two Amazon Web Service (AWS) dedicated m5.large EC2 instances in two different availability zones (AZs) in the London Region. Each instance runs lLinux 4.14 with an Intel Xeon Platinum 8175M 2.5 GHz CPU. We chose this relatively short distance between the initiator and responder to remain faithful to the practical restrictions on the deployment of Muckle. The QKD is an inherent part of the protocol, and deployment of a QKD network currently has a maximum distance of approximately 100 km between nodes. For both metrics, the median over 100 samples is reported and each process is pinned to a single CPU.

To contrast running C-Muckle over this short distance with a more typical real-world setting, we performed the same experiment between two m5.large EC2 instances in two different regions, London and Paris, but only measuring the wall-time.

Wall-Time Complete Execution: The complete execution time for a Muckle protocol run between two AZs is approximately 12.9 ms. In comparison, the complete execution time between two regions is 26 ms. The measurement scope is the execution of one entire stage of Muckle, including networking, initialising contexts, running clean up functions and executing general glue-code. By contrast, the round-trip-times for simple pings between two AZs and two regions were 0.745 ms and 8.224 ms.

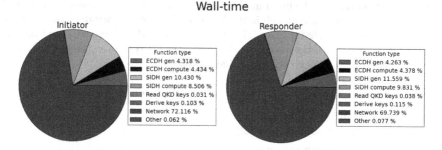

Fig. 2. Results of the wall-time measurement experiment between two AWS EC2 instances in two different regions (London and Paris). The top 6 categories for each chart are functions that correspond to C-Muckle functions described earlier. The network category includes time taken to initialise of the socket, as well as sending and receiving messages. The percentage for the Other category is computed by subtracting the median wall-time for the top 6 functions and the median time for networking from the entire median wall-time of the participant. (**Left**) C-Muckle initiator. (**Right**) C-Muckle responder.

Wall-Time Function Profiling: Figure 3 in Appendix A provides a more granular view of the cost for specific functions in C-Muckle between two AZs. For the initiator, approximately 7.22 ms is spent on various cryptographic function calls, with more than 68% of the 7.22 ms spent performing SIDH-related operations. The same behaviour can be observed for the responder. The relative cost of cryptographic operations in C-Muckle is therefore more than 65% when it is run over the short distances between AZs.

Clock Cycle Function Profiling: Table 1 contains an overview of the measured number of clock cycles for various functions. Each cell contains two functions: the first in each cell is the C-Muckle function described above, while the second is the function from the library dependencies,[3] used to implement the cryptographic operations in the C-Muckle function, i.e. during the execution of e.g. muckle_ecdh_gen() the function mbedtls_ecdh_gen_public() from the mbedtls library will be called. The table highlights the absolute overhead of the cryptographic operations as implemented in C-Muckle compared to the core cryptographic operation supported via one of the two library dependencies. We have excluded the functions muckle_read_qkd_keys() and muckle_derive_keys() because their cost is negligible relative to the total cost of the execution flow in C-Muckle.

The overhead in cryptographic C-Muckle functions relative to the corresponding external library functions is less than 15,000 clock cycles with one spike at 77,000 clock cycles. The overhead is predominately from copying buffers, initialisation and retrieving parameters. The "compute" functions also involve key derivation steps.

---

[3] Either mbedtls or PQCrypto-SIDH.

Table 1. (**Left column**) The first function in each cell is a C-Muckle function described in the text. The second in each cell is the function from the library dependency, used to implement the C-Muckle function. The functions prefixed with mbedtls are from the mbedtls library, otherwise they are from the PQCrypto-SIDH library. (**Right column**) The median number of clock cycles over 100 samples.

Function	Clock cycles
muckle_ecdh_gen()	2,769,893
mbedtls_ecdh_gen_public()	2,768,317
muckle_ecdh_compute()	2,875,367
mbedtls_ecdh_calc_secret()	2,846,614
initiator muckle_sidh_gen()	6,852,319
EphemeralKeyGeneration_A_SIDHp503()	6,775,268
initiator muckle_sidh_compute()	5,630,939
EphemeralSecretAgreement_A_SIDHp503()	5,613,257
responder muckle_sidh_gen()	7,531,586
EphemeralKeyGeneration_B_SIDHp503()	7,526,757
responder muckle_sidh_compute()	6,399,884
EphemeralSecretAgreement_B_SIDHp503()	6,391,934

The number of clock cycles for the ECDHE mbedtls functions using the elliptic curve curve25519, are far from state-of-the-art. For example, Bernstein [9] reports a total of 832,457 clock cycles for both key generation and secret key computation. It should therefore be possible to significantly improve the ECDHE performance in C-Muckle using a different library to mbedtls. However, we have found the mbedtls library to be easier to work with than other available libraries (like OpenSSL).

4   Hybrid Security Framework

Here we introduce our multi-stage hybrid authenticated key exchange (AKE) security framework HAKE for the analysis of our new protocol. HAKE follows the tradition of standard Bellare-Rogaway-based AKE models, and cleanly captures adversaries of differing strength (quantum and classical) via a fine-grained key compromise interface. Specifically, we model quantum adversaries by allowing them to corrupt non-post-quantum key exchange mechanisms (for instance, discrete logarithm-based key exchange algorithms). We highlight that our HAKE framework is flexible, and extends beyond Muckle, as HAKE captures (for example) the use of long-term asymmetric secrets, which are not used within Muckle. This allows HAKE to capture a variety of hybrid schemes, and is not simply to restricted to the use case of Muckle. We explain the HAKE framework in Sect. 4.2, and describe the corruption abilities of the adversary in Sect. 4.3. We then describe cleanness and partnering definitions in Sects. 4.4 and 4.5.

4.1   Secret Key Generation

HAKE addresses secret key generation (the output of a "KeyGen" algorithm) of individual key exchange components explicitly, and categorises them into *long-term* (i.e. generated once and used in every execution of the protocol), and *ephemeral* (i.e. generated on a per-stage basis) secret generation. We further divide these into the following sub-categories:

Post-quantum Asymmetric Secret Generation: The generation of a public-key pair for post-quantum code-based signature schemes is an example of a long-term variant. We denote the algorithm that generates these secrets as LQKeyGen. An algorithm that generates SIDH public-key pairs is an example of an ephemeral variant, which we denote as EQKeyGen.

Classical Asymmetric Secrets: An algorithm that generates long-term RSA public-key pairs for signatures (that do not offer post-quantum security), for example, would be denoted via LCKeyGen. Similarly, the generation of ECDHE public-key pairs would be done via ECKeyGen.

Symmetric Secrets: Long-term preshared secret keys are generated via LSKeyGen, while (for instance), we consider that the ephemeral keying material generated by a quantum key distribution protocol to be captured as a ephemeral symmetric secret generation algorithm, which we denote ESKeyGen.

4.2   Execution Environment

Consider an experiment $\mathsf{Exp}_{\Pi,n_P,n_S,n_T}^{\mathsf{HAKE,clean},\mathcal{A}}(\lambda)$ played between a challenger $\mathcal{C}$ and an adversary $\mathcal{A}$. $\mathcal{C}$ maintains a set of n_P parties $P_1,\ldots,P_{n_P}$ (representing users interacting with each other in protocol executions), each capable of running up to (potentially parallel) n_S sessions of a probabilistic key-exchange protocol Π. Each session can consist of up to n_T consecutive stages, each an execution of the key-exchange protocol Π, represented as a tuple of algorithms $\Pi = (f, \mathsf{EQKeyGen}, \mathsf{ECKeyGen}, \mathsf{ESKeyGen}, \mathsf{LQKeyGen}, \mathsf{LCKeyGen}, \mathsf{LSKeyGen})$. We use π_i^s to refer to both the identifier of the s-th instance of the Π being run by party P_i and the collection of per-session variables maintained for the s-th instance of Π run by P_i, and f is a algorithm capturing the honest execution of the protocol Π by protocol participants. We describe generically these algorithms below:

$\Pi.f(\lambda, \boldsymbol{pk}_i, \boldsymbol{sk}_i, \boldsymbol{pskid}_i, \boldsymbol{psk}_i, \pi, m) \xrightarrow{\$} (m', \pi')$ is a (potentially) probabilistic algorithm that takes a security parameter λ, the set of long-term asymmetric key pairs $\boldsymbol{pk}_i, \boldsymbol{sk}_i$ of the party P_i, a collection of per-session variables π and an arbitrary bit string $m \in \{0,1\}^* \cup \{\emptyset\}$. f outputs a response $m' \in \{0,1\}^* \cup \{\emptyset\}$ and an updated per-session state π', behaving as an honest protocol implementation.

We describe a set of algorithms $\Pi.\mathsf{XYKeyGen}(\lambda) \xrightarrow{\$} (pk, sk)$, where $X \in \{\mathsf{E},\mathsf{L}\}$ and $Y \in \{\mathsf{C},\mathsf{Q}\}$. $\Pi.\mathsf{XYKeyGen}$ is a probabilistic *post-quantum ephemeral* (if $\mathsf{XY} = \mathsf{EQ}$), *post-quantum long-term* (if $\mathsf{XY} = \mathsf{LQ}$), *classic ephemeral* (if $\mathsf{XY} = \mathsf{EC}$), or *classic long-term* (if $\mathsf{XY} = \mathsf{LC}$) asymmetric keygen algorithm, taking a security parameter λ and outputting a public-key/secret-key pair (pk, sk).

We describe a set of algorithms $\Pi.\mathsf{ZSKeyGen}(\lambda) \xrightarrow{\$} (psk, pskid)$, where $Z \in \{E, L\}$. $\Pi.\mathsf{ZSKeyGen}$ is a probabilistic *ephemeral* (if $Z = E$), or *long-term* (if $Z = L$) symmetric key generation algorithm taking as input a security parameter λ and outputting some symmetric keying material and (potentially) a keying material identifier $(psk, pskid)$, (or $(qkm, qkmid)$, respectively).

$\mathcal{C}$ runs $\Pi.\mathsf{LQKeyGen}(\lambda)$, $\Pi.\mathsf{LCKeyGen}(\lambda)$ and $\Pi.\mathsf{LSKeyGen}(\lambda)$ n_P times to generate asymmetric post-quantum and classical key pairs (which we denote with $\boldsymbol{pk_i}, \boldsymbol{sk_i}$) for each party $P_i \in \{P_1, \ldots, P_{n_P}\}$ as well as a symmetric keys and identifier $(\boldsymbol{psk}, \boldsymbol{pskid})$ and delivers all public-keys $\boldsymbol{pk_i}, \boldsymbol{pskid}$ for $i \in \{1, \ldots, n_P\}$ to $\mathcal{A}$. The challenger $\mathcal{C}$ then randomly samples a bit $b \xleftarrow{\$} \{0,1\}$ and interacts with the adversary via the queries listed in Sect. 4.3, also maintaining a set of corruption registers, containing a list of ephemeral and long-term secrets that have been compromised by $\mathcal{A}$ via Reveal, Corrupt and Compromise queries. Eventually, $\mathcal{A}$ terminates and outputs a guess d of the challenger bit b. The adversary wins the HAKE key-indistinguishability experiment if $d = b$, and additionally if the test session π satisfies a cleanness predicate clean, which we discuss in more detail in Sect. 4.5. We give an algorithmic description of this experiment in the full version. Each session maintains a set of per-session variables:

$\rho \in \{\texttt{init}, \texttt{resp}\}$: The role of the party in the current session. Note that parties can be directed to act as init or resp in concurrent or subsequent sessions.

$pid \in \{1, \ldots, n_P, \star\}$: The intended communication partner, represented with $\star$ if unspecified. Note that the identity of the partner session may be set during the protocol execution, in which case pid can be updated once.

$stid \in [n_T]$: The current (or most recently completed) stage of the session.

$\alpha \in \{\texttt{active}, \texttt{accept}, \texttt{reject}, \perp\}$: The status of the session, initialised with $\perp$.

$\mathbf{m}_i[stid] \in \{0,1\}^* \cup \{\perp\}$, where $\mathbf{i} \in \{\mathbf{s}, \mathbf{r}\}$: An array of the concatenation of messages sent (if $\mathbf{i} = \mathbf{s}$) or received (if $\mathbf{i} = \mathbf{r}$) by the session in each stage. Initialised by $\perp$ and indexed by the stage identifier $stid$.

$\mathbf{k}[stid] \in \{0,1\}^* \cup \{\perp\}$: An array of the session keys from each stage, or $\perp$ if no session key has yet been computed. Indexed by the stage identifier $stid$

$\mathbf{exk}[stid] \in \{0,1\}^* \cup \{\perp\}$, where $\mathbf{x} \in \{\mathbf{q}, \mathbf{c}, \mathbf{s}\}$: An array of the *post-quantum ephemeral asymmetric* (if $\mathbf{x} = \mathbf{q}$), *classic ephemeral asymmetric* (if $\mathbf{x} = \mathbf{c}$), or *ephemeral symmetric* (if $\mathbf{x} = \mathbf{s}$) secret keys used by the session in each stage. Initialised by $\perp$ and indexed by the stage identifier $stid$.

$\mathbf{pss}[stid] \in \{0,1\}^* \cup \{\perp\}$: Any per-stage secret state that is established during protocol execution for use in the following stage. Sessions use $\mathbf{pss}[stid - 1]$ during the protocol execution of stage $stid$. Indexed by $stid$.

$\mathbf{st}[stid] \in \{0,1\}^*$: Any additional state used by the session in each stage.

4.3   Adversarial Interaction

Our HAKE framework considers a traditional AKE adversary, in complete control of the communication network, able to modify, inject, delete or delay messages. They are able to compromise several layers of secrets: (a) long-term private keys, allowing our model to capture forward-secrecy notions and quantum adversaries.

(b) ephemeral private keys, modelling the leakage of secrets due to the use of bad randomness generators, or potentially bad cryptographic primitives or quantum adversaries. (c) preshared symmetric keys, modelling the leakage of shared secrets, potentially due to the misuse of the preshared secret by the partner, or the forced later revelation of these keys due to the compromise of partner devices. (d) ephemeral keying material, modelling attacks on the quantum key distribution. For instance, capturing things such as photon splitting attacks. (e) session keys, modelling the leakage of keys by their use in bad cryptographic algorithms. The adversary interacts with the challenger $\mathcal{C}$ via the queries below:

Create$(i, j, role) \rightarrow \{(s), \bot\}$: Allows the adversary $\mathcal{A}$ to initialise a new session owned by party P_i, where the role of the new session is $role$, and intended communication partner party P_j. Note that if $\mathcal{A}$ has already initialised the intended partner session, $\mathcal{A}$ must give the session index r (indicating the intended partner session π_j^r) in order to synchronise ephemeral symmetric keys. If a session π_i^s has already been created, $\mathcal{C}$ returns $\bot$. Otherwise, $\mathcal{C}$ returns (s) to $\mathcal{A}$.

Send$(i, s, m) \rightarrow \{m', \bot\}$: Allows $\mathcal{A}$ to send messages to sessions for protocol execution and receive the output. If the session $\pi_i^s.\alpha \neq$ active, then $\mathcal{C}$ returns $\bot$ to $\mathcal{A}$. Otherwise, $\mathcal{C}$ computes $\Pi.f(\lambda, \boldsymbol{pk}_i, \boldsymbol{sk}_i, \boldsymbol{pskid}_i, \boldsymbol{psk}_i, \pi_i^s, m) \rightarrow (m', \pi_i^{s'})$, sets $\pi_i^s \leftarrow \pi_i^{s'}$, updates transcripts $\pi_i^s.\mathbf{m}_r$, $\pi_i^s.\mathbf{m}_s$ and returns m' to $\mathcal{A}$.

Reveal(i, s, t): Allows $\mathcal{A}$ access to the session keys computed by a session. $\mathcal{C}$ checks if $\pi_i^s.\alpha[t] =$ accept and if so, returns $\pi_i^s.\mathbf{k}[t]$ to $\mathcal{A}$. In addition, the challenger checks if there exists another session π_j^r that $matches$ with π_i^s, and also sets $\mathbf{SK}_j^r[t] \leftarrow$ corrupt. Otherwise, $\mathcal{C}$ returns $\bot$ to $\mathcal{A}$.

Test$(i, s, t) \rightarrow \{k_b, \bot\}$: Allows $\mathcal{A}$ access to a real-or-random session key k_b used in determining the success of $\mathcal{A}$ in the key-indistinguishability game. If a session π_i^s exists such that $\pi_i^s.\alpha =$ accept, then the challenger $\mathcal{C}$ samples a key $k_0 \xleftarrow{\$} \mathcal{D}$ where $\mathcal{D}$ is the distribution of the session key, and sets $k_1 \leftarrow \pi_i^s.\mathbf{k}[t]$. $\mathcal{C}$ then returns k_b (where b is the random bit sampled during set-up) to $\mathcal{A}$. Otherwise $\mathcal{C}$ returns $\bot$ to $\mathcal{A}$.

CorruptXK$(\{i, j\}) \rightarrow \{k_i, \bot\}$: Allows $\mathcal{A}$ access to the secret preshared key $psk_i^j = psk_j^i$ (if X = S), the secret post-quantum long-term key qsk_i (if X = Q) or the secret classical long-term key csk_i (if X = C), generated for the party P_i (and P_j, in the preshared case) prior to protocol execution. If the secret long-term key has already been corrupted previously, then $\mathcal{C}$ returns $\bot$ to $\mathcal{A}$.

CompromiseYK$(i, s, t) \rightarrow \{esk[t], \bot\}$: Allows $\mathcal{A}$ access to the secret ephemeral post-quantum key $\pi_i^s.eqk[t]$ (if Y = Q), the secret ephemeral classical key $\pi_i^s.eck[t]$ (if Y = C), or the secret ephemeral symmetric key $\pi_i^s.esk[t]$ (if Y = S) generated for the session π_i^s prior to protocol execution in stage t. Note that if there exists another session π_j^r such that $\pi_i^s.esk[t] = \pi_j^r.esk[t]$, then that session's ephemeral symmetric key is also considered corrupted. If $\pi_i^s.esk[t]$ has already been corrupted previously, then $\mathcal{C}$ returns $\bot$ to $\mathcal{A}$.

CompromiseSS$(i, s, t) \rightarrow \{pss[t], \bot\}$: Allows the adversary access to the secret per-session state $\pi_i^s.pss[t]$ generated by a session π_i^s during protocol execution. For use in the next stage of the session's protocol execution. Note that if there exists another session π_j^r such that $\pi_i^s.\mathsf{pss}[t] = \pi_j^r.\mathsf{pss}[t']$, then that session's per-stage secret state is also considered corrupted. If $\pi_i^s.\mathsf{pss}[t]$ has already been corrupted previously, then $\mathcal{C}$ returns $\bot$ to $\mathcal{A}$.

4.4 Partnering Definition

To evaluate the secrets that $\mathcal{A}$ can reveal without trivially breaking the security of the protocol, key-exchange models must first define how sessions are *partnered*. Otherwise, $\mathcal{A}$ would simply run a protocol between two sessions, faithfully delivering all messages, Test the first session to receive the real-or-random key, and Reveal the other session's key. If the keys are equal, then the Test key is real, and otherwise the session key has been sampled randomly.

In our work, we use both the matching definition *matching sessions* defined in the original eCK model [21], and *origin sessions*, introduced by Cremers and Feltz [17]. On a high level, π_i^s is an origin session of π_j^r if π_i^s has received the messages that π_j^r sent without modification, even if the reply that π_i^s sent back has not been received by π_j^r. If all messages sent and received by π_i^s and π_j^r are identical, then the sessions *match*.

4.5 Cleanness Predicates

We now define the exact combinations of secrets that an adversary $\mathcal{A}$ is allowed to compromise without trivially breaking a hybrid key exchange protocol. However, we note that the cleanness predicate defined below is specific to Muckle, and the threat model that Muckle intends to defend against. Other predicates, both stronger and weaker, can be constructed.

We wish to capture security against a quantum-equipped adversary, so a successful adversary is allowed to compromise the long-term and ephemeral classical asymmetric secrets without penalty. Since Muckle itself does not use public-key cryptography to authenticate its messages, we allow $\mathcal{A}$ to compromise the long-term asymmetric secrets (however, the challenger $\mathcal{C}$ will respond to CorruptCK and CorruptQK queries with $\bot$).

Since we wish to capture perfect forward secrecy, we allow a successful adversary to have issued a Test query to a session π_i^s owned by a party P_i (with no origin session) that has had its long-term symmetric key compromised previously, as long as the session was completed before the CorruptSK(i,j) query was issued (and $\pi_i^s.pid = j$). In addition, our construction should be post-compromise secure (as explored by Cohn-Gordon et al. [15]), so our cleanness predicate allows an adversary to have compromised *all* ephemeral secrets associated with a particular stage as long as there exists some stage previous that has not had all its ephemeral secrets compromised and the adversary has been passive in all stages between the "Test" stage and the previous "clean" stage.

Coming full circle then, a "clean" stage intuitively is one where the adversary has not compromised *all* of: (a) the ephemeral classic secrets of the Test session and its matching partner in the tested stage (b) the ephemeral post-quantum secrets of the Test session and its matching partner in the tested stage (c) the previous per-stage secrets shared by the Test session and its matching session in the tested stage, and (d) the quantum keying material/ephemeral symmetric secrets shared by the Test session and its matching session in the tested stage.

It may also be desirable to determine the security guarantees that Muckle provides in the event of a new vulnerability discovered in the underlying post-quantum asymmetric key-exchange primitive, or a side-channel attack being discovered in the hardware of the QKD system. In order to capture this scenario, we provide a second cleanness predicate that captures non-quantum-equipped adversaries, which we denote $\mathsf{clean_{cHAKE}}$. It is more-or-less identical to $\mathsf{clean_{qHAKE}}$, but the adversary is allowed to compromise the ephemeral secrets (either symmetric or post-quantum) if they do not additionally compromise classic ephemeral secrets derived during the protocol execution. Now, we formalise the advantage of a QPT algorithm $\mathcal{A}$ in winning the HAKE key indistinguishability experiment in the following way:

Definition 1 (HAKE Key Indistinguishability). *Let Π be a key-exchange protocol, and n_P, n_S, $n_T \in \mathbb{N}$. For a particular given predicate clean, and a QPT algorithm $\mathcal{A}$, we define the advantage of $\mathcal{A}$ in the HAKE key-indistinguishability game to be $\mathsf{Adv}^{\mathsf{HAKE,clean},\mathcal{A}}_{\Pi,n_P,n_S,n_T}(\lambda) = 2 \cdot \left| \Pr\left[\mathsf{Exp}^{\mathsf{HAKE,clean},\mathcal{A}}_{\Pi,n_P,n_S n_T}(\lambda) = 1 \right] - \frac{1}{2} \right|$. We say that Π is post-quantum HAKE-secure if, for all $\mathcal{A}$, $\mathsf{Adv}^{\mathsf{HAKE,clean},\mathcal{A}}_{\Pi,n_P,n_S,n_T}(\lambda)$ is negligible in the security parameter λ.*

5 Security Analysis

This section is dedicated to presenting our main result Theorem 1. Due to space constraints, the full proof and advantage bound can be found in the full version. For our proof, we require post-quantum analogues of various security assumptions. These are mostly identical to classical prf, dual-prf ind-cpa and eufcma assumptions, but require security against all quantum probabilistic polynomial-time algorithms. It is also desirable to assess security of Muckle with respect to classic probabilistic polynomial-time adversaries, and thus we also prove that Muckle is HAKE-secure with cleanness predicate $\mathsf{clean_{cHAKE}}$. Recall that $\mathsf{clean_{cHAKE}}$ used here is a generalisation of $\mathsf{clean_{qHAKE}}$, allowing us to establish key indistinguishability security in the scenario where the classical cryptographic component of Muckle remains secure and uncompromised, even if the post-quantum and QKD components both become insecure.

Theorem 1. *The Muckle key exchange protocol is HAKE-secure with cleanness predicate $\mathsf{clean_{qHAKE}}$ (capturing perfect forward secrecy and post-compromise security) under the qprf, eufqcma, dual-qprf, and qind-cpa assumptions of PRF, MAC, PRF and KEM, respectively. That is, for any QPT algorithm $\mathcal{A}$ against the HAKE key-indistinguishability game $\mathsf{Adv}^{\mathsf{HAKE,clean_{qHAKE}},\mathcal{A}}_{\mathsf{Muckle},n_P,n_S,n_T}(\lambda)$ is negligible in the security parameter λ.*

Proof (Sketch). We begin by dividing the proof into three separate cases where the query Test(i,s,t) has been issued: 1. The session π_i^s (where $\pi_i^s.\rho = \texttt{init}$) has no origin session in stage t. 2. The session π_i^s (where $\pi_i^s.\rho = \texttt{resp}$) has no origin session in stage t. 3. The session π_i^s in stage t has a matching session.

We bound the probability of each case, and show that under certain assumptions, the advantage of $\mathcal{A}$ winning the key-indistinguishability game is negligible.

Cases 1 and 2: Test Session Without Origin Session. We show that $\mathcal{A}$ has negligible change in causing π_i^s to reach an accept state without an origin session. By the cleanness predicate, if π_i^s accepts without an origin session, then $\mathcal{A}$ cannot have exposed the preshared symmetric key between π_i^s and its intended partner, before that point. We first replace the computation of $mkey_B$ with a uniformly random value $\widetilde{mkey_B}$ in stage t of π_i^s. Since $mkey_B = \mathsf{PRF}(PSK, SecState)$ (where $PSK = psk_i^j$ is itself uniformly random and independent), this is a sound replacement. Any $\mathcal{A}$ that can distinguish this change can be turned into an algorithm that breaks the post-quantum PRF assumption. Next, we define an abort event that triggers if π_i^s verifies a MAC tag in stage t successfully. We show that if $\pi_i^s.\alpha[t] \leftarrow \texttt{accept}$ without a matching session, that means that a MAC tag τ was produced that verified correctly, but there existed no matching session that produced τ. Any adversary capable of triggering this abort event can thus break the eufcma security of the MAC scheme.

Case 3: Test Session with Matching Session. Here, we show that if $\mathcal{A}$ that has issued a Test(i,s,t) query to a clean session π_i^s in stage t, then $\mathcal{A}$ has negligible advantage in guessing the test bit b. In what follows, we split our analysis of Case 3 into the following sub-cases, each corresponding to a condition necessary for the cleanness predicate to be upheld by π_i^s in stage t: 3.1 CompromiseQK(i,s,t), CompromiseQK(j,r,t) have not been issued, where π_j^r *matches* π_i^s in stage t; 3.2 CompromiseSK(i,s,t), CompromiseSK(j,r,t) have not been issued, where π_j^r *matches* π_i^s in stage t; 3.3 CompromiseQK(i,s,t'), CompromiseQK(j,r,t') have not been issued, where π_j^r *matches* π_i^s in stages u such that $t' \leq u < t$ and no CompromiseSS(i,s,u), CompromiseSS(j,r,u) queries have been issued; 3.4 CompromiseSK(i,s,t'), CompromiseSK(j,r,t') have not been issued, where π_j^r *matches* π_i^s in stages u such that $t' \leq u < t$ and no CompromiseSS(i,s,u), CompromiseSS(j,r,u) queries have been issued.

It is clear to see that the advantage of $\mathcal{A}$ in Case 3 is bound by the sum of the advantage of $\mathcal{A}$ in all subcases. Due to space restrictions, we only detail the proof sketch of Subcase 3.1. The other subcases follow similar proof strategies.

3.1: CompromiseQK(i,s,t), CompromiseQK(j,r,t) have not been issued, where π_j^r *matches* π_i^s in stage t. We begin by guessing the parties, sessions and stage such that $\mathcal{A}$ issues Test(i,s,t) and π_i^s matches π_j^r (aborting if our guess was incorrect). After, we replace the secret QKEM value qsk with the uniformly random and independent value $\widetilde{qsk}$, by interacting with a ind-cpa QKEM challenger and replacing the qpk_A, qpk_B values sent in m_0 and m_1 respectively with challenge values from the ind-cpa challenger. By the definition of this case, we know that the QKEM values exchanged in m_0 and m_1 were not modified between the sessions. Next, we replace the quantum key qk and the first chaining key k_0 (in the test session and its matching partner) with uniformly random values $\widetilde{qk}$, $\widetilde{k_0}$ from the same distribution. Since $qk = \mathsf{PRF}(\widetilde{qsk}, \mathsf{label}_{qk})$ and $k_0 \leftarrow \mathsf{PRF}(\widetilde{qk}, m_0 \| m_1)$ where $\widetilde{qsk}$, $\widetilde{qk}$ are uniformly random and independent, these are sound replacements. Any algorithm $\mathcal{A}$ that can distinguish these changes can be used to break the post-quantum PRF assumption.

In the next steps, we iteratively replace the second, third and fourth chaining keys $k_1 \leftarrow \mathsf{PRF}(ck, \widetilde{k_0})$, $k_2 = \mathsf{PRF}(qkm, \widetilde{k_1})$, and $k_3 = \mathsf{PRF}(SecState, \widetilde{k_2})$, with uniformly random values $\widetilde{k_1}$, $\widetilde{k_2}$, $\widetilde{k_3}$ from the same distribution. Unlike previous steps, we require a post-quantum dual-prf assumption here, but otherwise these changes proceed identically to the replacement of qsk and qk. Any algorithm $\mathcal{A}$ that can distinguish these changes can be used to break the post-quantum dual-prf assumption.

In this final step, we replace the secret state and session keys $SecState$, sk_A, $sk_B \leftarrow \mathsf{PRF}(\widetilde{k_3}, m_0 \| m_1 \| ctr)$ with uniformly random and independent values $\widetilde{SecState}, \widetilde{sk_A}, \widetilde{sk_B}$. As before, any algorithm $\mathcal{A}$ that can distinguish this change can be used to break the post-quantum PRF assumption.

Since $\widetilde{sk_A}, \widetilde{sk_B}$ are now uniformly random and independent values independent of the protocol flow regardless of the value of the test bit b, $\mathcal{A}$ has no advantage in guessing the test bit.

6 Future Work

Our paper opens up many avenues for future work. First, we have strongly abstracted the QKD component in our framework, treating is as an inexhaustible supply of shared, random bits. Yet there is a fine tradition of developing security proofs for QKD systems based purely on physical models. It is a significant challenge to integrate such approaches in our framework. The work of [24] provides one route forward using Universal Composability. In future QKD systems, the bit-rate of key agreement will exceed that which can be achieved by classical communication, at least over short ranges. This suggests adapting Muckle to allow rapid key refreshing from QKD keying material and slower refreshing from other sources. Our analysis framework could be extended to support such "differential refreshing". But this approach also raises implementation challenges, particularly around key synchronisation, which would need to be carefully addressed in order to avoid DoS and other attacks.

Acknowledgments. The research of Dowling was supported by Innovate UK and EPSRC grant EP/L018543/1 (the EQUIP project). The research of Hansen was supported by the EPSRC and the UK government as part of the Centre for Doctoral Training in Cyber Security at Royal Holloway, University of London (EP/K035584/1). The research of Paterson was supported by Innovate UK and EPSRC grants EP/L018543/1, EP/K035584/1 and EP/M013472/1 and a gift from VMware.

A   Wall-Time Function Profiling in Two Availability Zones

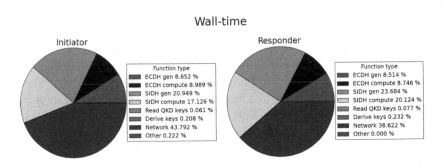

Fig. 3. Results of the wall-time measurement experiment between two AWS EC2 instances in two different availability zones located in the same region (London). Specifically, the chart captures the relative median wall-time spent executing various functions in the C-Muckle execution flow. The top 6 categories for each chart are functions that correspond to C-Muckle functions described in the text. The network category includes time taken to intialise of the socket, as well as sending and receiving messages. The percentage for the Other category is computed by subtracting the median wall-time for the top 6 functions and the median time for networking from the entire median wall-time of the participant. (**Left**) C-Muckle initiator. (**Right**) C-Muckle responder.

References

1. ARM mbed TLS. https://tls.mbed.org/. Accessed 12 Nov 2018
2. C-Muckle source code. https://github.com/himsen/muckle. Accessed 29 Jan 2020
3. Microsoft   PQCrypto-SIDH.   https://github.com/Microsoft/PQCrypto-SIDH. Accessed 12 Nov 2018
4. Albrecht, M.R., et al.: Estimate all the {LWE, NTRU} schemes! In: Catalano, D., De Prisco, R. (eds.) SCN 2018. LNCS, vol. 11035, pp. 351–367. Springer, Cham (2018). https://doi.org/10.1007/978-3-319-98113-0_19
5. Alkim, E., Ducas, L., Pöppelmann, T., Schwabe, P.: Post-quantum key exchange - a new hope. In: Holz, T., Savage, S. (eds.) 25th USENIX Security Symposium, USENIX Security 16, Austin, TX, USA, 10–12 August 2016, pp. 327–343. USENIX Association (2016)
6. Bellare, M., Canetti, R., Krawczyk, H.: Keying hash functions for message authentication. In: Koblitz, N. (ed.) CRYPTO 1996. LNCS, vol. 1109, pp. 1–15. Springer, Heidelberg (1996). https://doi.org/10.1007/3-540-68697-5_1
7. Bellare, M., Rogaway, P.: Entity authentication and key distribution. In: Stinson, D.R. (ed.) CRYPTO 1993. LNCS, vol. 773, pp. 232–249. Springer, Heidelberg (1994). https://doi.org/10.1007/3-540-48329-2_21
8. Bennett, C., Brassard, G.: Quantum cryptography: public key distribution and coin tossing. In: Proceedings of IEEE International Conference on Computers, Systems and Signal Processing, vol. 175, no. P1 (1984)

9. Bernstein, D.J.: Curve25519: new Diffie-Hellman speed records. In: Yung, M., Dodis, Y., Kiayias, A., Malkin, T. (eds.) PKC 2006. LNCS, vol. 3958, pp. 207–228. Springer, Heidelberg (2006). https://doi.org/10.1007/11745853_14
10. Bernstein, D.J.: Is the security of quantum cryptography guaranteed by the laws of physics? CoRR, abs/1803.04520 (2018)
11. Bindel, N., Brendel, J., Fischlin, M., Goncalves, B., Stebila, D.: Hybrid key encapsulation mechanisms and authenticated key exchange. In: Ding, J., Steinwandt, R. (eds.) PQCrypto 2019. LNCS, vol. 11505, pp. 206–226. Springer, Cham (2019). https://doi.org/10.1007/978-3-030-25510-7_12
12. Bindel, N., Herath, U., McKague, M., Stebila, D.: Transitioning to a quantum-resistant public key infrastructure. In: Lange, T., Takagi, T. (eds.) PQCrypto 2017. LNCS, vol. 10346, pp. 384–405. Springer, Cham (2017). https://doi.org/10.1007/978-3-319-59879-6_22
13. Braithwaite, M.: Experimenting with post-quantum cryptography, July 2016. https://security.googleblog.com/2016/07/experimenting-with-post-quantum.html
14. Brendel, J., Fischlin, M., Günther, F.: Breakdown resilience of key exchange protocols: NewHope, TLS 1.3, and Hybrids. In: Sako, K., Schneider, S., Ryan, P.Y.A. (eds.) ESORICS 2019. LNCS, vol. 11736, pp. 521–541. Springer, Cham (2019). https://doi.org/10.1007/978-3-030-29962-0_25
15. Cohn-Gordon, K., Cremers, C.J.F., Garratt, L.: On post-compromise security. In: IEEE 29th Computer Security Foundations Symposium, CSF 2016, Lisbon, Portugal, 27 June–1 July 2016, pp. 164–178. IEEE Computer Society (2016)
16. Costello, C., Longa, P., Naehrig, M.: Efficient algorithms for supersingular isogeny Diffie-Hellman. In: Robshaw, M., Katz, J. (eds.) CRYPTO 2016. LNCS, vol. 9814, pp. 572–601. Springer, Heidelberg (2016). https://doi.org/10.1007/978-3-662-53018-4_21
17. Cremers, C., Feltz, M.: Beyond eCK: perfect forward secrecy under actor compromise and ephemeral-key reveal. In: Foresti, S., Yung, M., Martinelli, F. (eds.) ESORICS 2012. LNCS, vol. 7459, pp. 734–751. Springer, Heidelberg (2012). https://doi.org/10.1007/978-3-642-33167-1_42
18. Huang, A., Sun, S.-H., Liu, Z., Makarov, V.: Quantum key distribution with distinguishable decoy states. Phys. Rev. A **98**, 012330 (2018)
19. Krawczyk, H.: Cryptographic extraction and key derivation: the HKDF scheme. In: Rabin, T. (ed.) CRYPTO 2010. LNCS, vol. 6223, pp. 631–648. Springer, Heidelberg (2010). https://doi.org/10.1007/978-3-642-14623-7_34
20. Kwiatkowski, K., Valenta, L.: The TLS post-quantum experiment, October 2010. https://blog.cloudflare.com/the-tls-post-quantum-experiment
21. Li, J., Kim, K., Zhang, F., Chen, X.: Aggregate proxy signature and verifiably encrypted proxy signature. In: Susilo, W., Liu, J.K., Mu, Y. (eds.) ProvSec 2007. LNCS, vol. 4784, pp. 208–217. Springer, Heidelberg (2007). https://doi.org/10.1007/978-3-540-75670-5_15
22. Moody, D.: What was NIST thinking? Round 2 of the NIST PQC "Competition". Talk at Oxford University (2019)
23. Mosca, M., Stebila, D., Ustaoğlu, B.: Quantum key distribution in the classical authenticated key exchange framework. In: Gaborit, P. (ed.) PQCrypto 2013. LNCS, vol. 7932, pp. 136–154. Springer, Heidelberg (2013). https://doi.org/10.1007/978-3-642-38616-9_9
24. Müller-Quade, J., Renner, R.: Composability in quantum cryptography. CoRR, abs/1006.2215 (2010)
25. Schank, J., Stebila, D.: A Transport Layer Security (TLS) extension for establishing an additional shared secret. IETF Draft (2017)

26. Sibson, P., et al.: Chip-based quantum key distribution. Nat. Commun. **8**, 13984 (2017)

27. Stebila, D., Fluhrer, S., Gueron, S.: Design issues for hybrid key exchange in TLS 1.3. IETF Draft (2019). https://tools.ietf.org/id/draft-stebila-tls-hybrid-design-01.html0

28. Vakhitov, A., Makarov, V., Hjelme, D.R.: Large pulse attack as a method of conventional optical eavesdropping in quantum cryptography. J. Mod. Opt. **48**, 2023 (2001)

29. Whyte, W., Fluhrer, S., Zhang, Z., Garcia-Morchon, O.: Quantum-safe hybrid (QSH) key exchange for transport layer security (TLS) version 1.3. IETF Draft (2017)

30. Yuen, H.P.: Security of quantum key distribution. IEEE Access **4**, 724–749 (2016)

31. Zhang, R., Hanaoka, G., Shikata, J., Imai, H.: On the security of multiple encryption or CCA-security+CCA-security=CCA-security? In: Bao, F., Deng, R., Zhou, J. (eds.) PKC 2004. LNCS, vol. 2947, pp. 360–374. Springer, Heidelberg (2004). https://doi.org/10.1007/978-3-540-24632-9_26

A Note on the Instantiability
of the Quantum Random Oracle

Edward Eaton[1][(✉)] and Fang Song[2]

[1] Cheriton School of Computer Science, University of Waterloo, Waterloo, Canada
eeaton@uwaterloo.ca
[2] Department of Computer Science and Engineering, Texas A&M University,
College Station, USA
fang.song@tamu.edu

Abstract. In a highly influential paper from fifteen years ago [10], Canetti, Goldreich, and Halevi showed a fundamental separation between the Random Oracle Model (ROM) and the standard model. They constructed a signature scheme which can be proven secure in the ROM, but is insecure when instantiated with any hash function (and thus insecure in the standard model). In 2011, Boneh et al. defined the notion of the *Quantum* Random Oracle Model (QROM), where queries to the random oracle may be made in quantum superposition. Because the QROM generalizes the ROM, a proof of security in the QROM is stronger than one in the ROM. This leaves open the possibility that security in the QROM could imply security in the standard model. In this work, we show that this is not the case, and that security in the QROM cannot imply standard-model security. We do this by showing that the original schemes that show a separation between the standard model and the ROM are also secure in the QROM. We consider two schemes that establish such a separation, one with length-restricted messages, and one without, and show both to be secure in the QROM. Our results give further understanding to the landscape of proofs in the ROM versus the QROM or standard model, and point towards the QROM and ROM being much closer to each other than either is to standard model security.

1 Introduction

In this note, we show that there exist digital signature schemes that can be proven secure against any poly-time quantum adversaries in the *quantum random-oracle model* [7], but they can be broken by a *classical* poly-time adversary when the random oracle is instantiated by any poly-time computable hash function family. This extends to the quantum setting the impossibility of instantiating a classical random oracle [3,9,10,17,24,26].

Given the classical result (e.g., [10]) that there exists a secure signature scheme in the random oracle model but insecure under any efficient instantiation, the first doubt to clear up is probably why it does not immediately follow

© Springer Nature Switzerland AG 2020
J. Ding and J.-P. Tillich (Eds.): PQCrypto 2020, LNCS 12100, pp. 503–523, 2020.
https://doi.org/10.1007/978-3-030-44223-1_27

that a *quantum* random oracle cannot be instantiated as well. The reason is that the signature scheme in the classical result may as well get *broken* in the quantum random oracle model. In other words, all one needs to do is to prove quantum security of these classical constructions in the quantum random oracle model. This is exactly what this work does: we show that three examples in the classical setting [9,10,24] can be proven secure in the quantum random oracle model, and hence they demonstrate that the quantum random oracle model is *unsound* in general.

We dive into an overview of the proofs right away, so that those who are familiar with this subject can quickly digest the gist and walk away satisfied (or disappointed). If you are a more patient reader, you can come back here after enjoying the (more conventional) introduction.

Let us first review the classical examples [9,10,24] to be analyzed in the quantum random oracle model, and we present them under a unified framework which we hope will be easy to grasp. They all start with a secure signature scheme Σ and a function F, and Σ is "punctured" so that the signing algorithm would simply reveal the signing key when the function F is "non-random" (e.g., instantiated by a concrete hash function). To break it, an adversary just needs to convince the signing algorithm that F is indeed non-random. Therefore, it boils down to designing a proof system where a prover (adversary in the signature setting) proves "non-randomness" of a given function to a verifier (signing algorithm); whereas if the function is indeed random, no prover can fool the verifier to accept. The natural approach to such a proof system is based off the intuition that it is difficult to *predict* the output of a random oracle on an unknown input. The three classical examples nurture this intuition in two variations: predicting on a *single* input or *multiple* inputs.

1. The basic idea in [10] is to have the prover provide *an* input where the output is predictable and can be efficiently verified by the verifier. For starters, suppose we want to rule out a specific hash function H, then the prover can pick an arbitrary x and the verifier just checks if $F(x) = H(x)$. The verifier always accepts when F is instantiated by H, but accepts only with negligible probability if F is random. This immediately implies that for any function family, in particular the family of *poly-time computable* functions $\mathcal{H} = \{\mathcal{H}_\lambda = \{H_s\}_{s\in\{0,1\}^\lambda}\}$[1], we can construct a signature scheme following the idea above, where a (random) member in $\mathcal{H}$ is chosen as implementation of F, and the signing algorithm reveals the signing key whenever the "non-randomness" verification passes. Note that, nonetheless, the construction depends on the function family, which is *weaker* than the goal of establishing a signature scheme that is secure in the random oracle model, but insecure however when implement it from function family $\mathcal{H}$.

   Diagonalization comes in handy to reverse the quantifiers. The prover will provide a description s of a function H_s, which purportedly describes the

---

[1] We assume a canonical encoding of functions into binary strings, under which s is the description of a function. Complexity is measured under security parameter λ.

function F. Then the verifier runs H_s on s and checks if it matches $F(s)$. Clearly, when F is implemented by a member $H_s \in \mathcal{H}$, the description s is public (i.e., part of the verification key), and it is trivial for the prover to convince the verifier. Nonetheless, if F is a random oracle $\mathcal{O}$, the event $\mathcal{O}(s) = H_s(s)$ occurs only with negligible probability for any s that a prover might provide.

A technicality arises though due to the time complexity for computing $H_s(s)$ for all $\mathcal{H}$. Loosely speaking, we need a universal machine for the family $\mathcal{H}$ that on a description s computes $H_s(\cdot)$. Such a machine exists, but would require slightly super-polynomial time, which makes the verifier (i.e., signing algorithm) inefficient. This final piece of the puzzle is filled by CS-proofs introduced by Micali [25]. A CS-proof allows verifying the computation of a machine M, where the verifier spends significantly less time that the time to run M directly. This naturally applies to the problem here. Instead of running the universal machine to check $H_s(s) = F(s)$ by the verifier, the prover generates a CS-proof on the input $\langle M, s \rangle^F$ (relative to F) certifying the statement $M(s) := H_s(s) = F(s)$, which the verifier can check in poly-time. When $F = \mathcal{O}$ is a random oracle, $\langle M, s \rangle^{\mathcal{O}}$ (relative to $\mathcal{O}$) is almost always a false statement, and the soundness of the CS-proof ensures that verifier will reject with high probability. Micali proved in general the soundness of CS-proofs in the random oracle model (to avoid confusion, in CS-proofs think of an random oracle independent of F).

2. Another strategy for proving "non-randomness", as employed in Maurer *et al.* [24] and Canetti *et al.* [9], is to predict on *multiple* inputs. This offers a direct *information-theoretical* analysis without relying on CS-proofs.

In essence, a prover provides a machine π that allegedly predicts the output of F on sufficiently many inputs, and the verifier can run π and compare with the answers from F. This is easy for the prover when F is instantiated by $\mathcal{F}$ where the description s is given. On the other hand, by tuning the parameters, a counting argument would show that the randomness in a random oracle is overwhelming for any single machine (even inefficient ones!) to predict. Specifically, the "predicting" machine π needs to match with F on $q = 2|\pi| + \lambda$ inputs (i.e., the number of correct predictions has to be significantly more than the length of the description of the machine). Suppose that F is a random oracle $\mathcal{O} \leftarrow \{f : \{0,1\}^* \to \{0,1\}\}$ that outputs one bit (for the sake of simplicity), then for any π the probability that it will match $\mathcal{O}$ on q inputs is at most $2^{-(2|\pi|+\lambda)}$. A union bound on all machines of length n shows that p_n, the probability that some length-n machine is a good predictor, is at most $2^n \cdot 2^{-(2n+\lambda)} = 2^{-n-k}$. Another union bound shows that regardless of their length, no machine can be a good predictor, since $p := \sum_{n=1}^{\infty} p_n = 2^{-\lambda} \sum_n 2^{-n} \leq 2^{-\lambda-1}$ is negligible.

3. Both examples above suffer from an artifact. Namely the signature schemes need to be able to sign *long* messages or otherwise maintain *states* of prior signatures. This is rectified in [9], where a *stateless* scheme that signs only messages of polylogarithmic length is proven secure in the random oracle model but insecure under any instantiation.

At the core of this construction is an *interactive* counterpart of the *non-interactive* proof system in part 2 above. It can be viewed as a *memory* delegation protocol, where a verifier with limited (e.g., poly-logarithmic) memory wants to check if the machine provided by the prover is a good predictor. Roughly speaking, it will execute the machine step by step and use the prover to bookkeep intermediate configurations of the machine. However, the configurations may be too long for the verifier to store and transit to the prover. Instead, the verifier employs a Merkle tree and only communicates an *authentication path* of the configuration with the prover. In particular, the verifier will memorize only a secret authentication key in between subsequent rounds. The security of the "punctured" signature scheme reduces to essentially a stronger *unforgeability* of a valid authentication path in a Merkle tree with respect to a random oracle, which is proven classically.

Proving Security of Separation Examples in QRO. Once the constructions and classical analysis are laid out, proving their security in the quantum random oracle model becomes more or less mechanic, given the techniques developed for QRO so far [1, 2, 15, 30, 31].

1^Q. (Example in [10] with CS-proofs.) Following the classical proof, we first show that the quantum security reduces to one of three cases: (1) hardness of a Grover-type search problem, which ensures that an adversary cannot feed the CS-proof a true statement in the case of a random oracle; (2) security of the original signature scheme; and (3) soundness of CS-proofs against quantum adversaries. A precise query lower bound for the search problem follows by standard techniques. And thanks to a recent work [11], CS-proofs are proven sound against quantum adversaries.

2^Q. (Example in [9, 24] based on information-theoretical analysis.) It is easy to verify that the information-theoretical argument sketched above holds regardless of the kind of adversaries, and as a result the "punctured" signature scheme remains secure in the quantum random oracle model (and against quantum adversaries).

3^Q. (Example in [9] that only needs to sign short messages.) Our proof follows the classical one, where we first carefully verify and lift the reduction to the (stronger) unforgeability of Merkle tree against quantum adversaries, and then prove this property in the quantum random oracle model.

Specifically, we can model the unforgeability game as follows. Think of two correlated random oracles $\mathcal{O} : \{0,1\}^* \to \{0,1\}^{\ell(\lambda)}$ and $\mathcal{O}' := \mathcal{O}(ak, \cdot)$ where ak is a random authentication key kept secret. Given *quantum* access to $\mathcal{O}$ and *classical* access to $\mathcal{O}'$, the adversary needs to come up with an authentication path $(\langle \sigma_1, \ldots, \sigma_d \rangle, \langle (v_{1,0}, v_{1,1}), \ldots, (v_{d,0}, v_{d,1}) \rangle, t)$ where $\sigma_i \in \{0,1\}$, $t = \mathcal{O}'(d, \mathcal{O}(0, v_{1,0}, v_{1,1}))$ and $v_{i,\sigma_i} = \mathcal{O}(i, v_{i+1,0}, v_{i+1,1})$ for every $i = 1, \ldots, d-1$. We prove that this is infeasible by reductions from a randomized decisional search problem and collision finding in random functions [8, 20, 32].

Background and Motivation. The random oracle model, since its introduction [4], has proven a popular methodology for designing cryptographic schemes[2]. Basically a construction is first described and analyzed in an idealized setting where a random function is available as a black-box. To implement it in the real-world, one substitutes a cryptographic hash function for the random oracle. This methodology often leads to much more efficient schemes than alternatives. Examples include digital signatures by the Fiat-Shamir transform [16], hybrid public-key encryption following Fujisaki-Okamoto-type transforms [5], as well as succinct non-interactive zero-knowledge arguments that rise with the trending technology of blockchain and cryptocurrencies [28]. Its popularity is also attributed to the fact that one can often prove security in the random oracle model which is otherwise much more challenging or simply unknown.

It is, however, exactly the latter advantage that stirred considerable debate. *What does a security proof in the random oracle model mean?* To be pragmatic, a random-oracle proof at least serves as a sanity check that rules out inherent design flaws. Indeed, in practice most constructions that are instantiated from ones proven secure in the random oracle model have stood up extensive cryptanalysis. More formal pursuit, however, arrives at an irritating message. There are separation examples which show secure constructions in the random oracle model, but will be trivially broken whatever "nice" functions we use to instantiate the random oracle. Namely, the methodology is *unsound* in general. This does not mean all schemes following this approach are insecure. In fact, some random-oracle scheme can be instantiated under strong but reasonable assumptions and achieve desirable security in the real-world [22]. To say the least, a question mark lingers on schemes developed under this methodology.

Quantum computing adds another layer of complication to the issue here (and the overall landscape of cryptography). Because of the threats to widely deployed cryptosystems [29], a growing effort is undertaken to design and transition to so called *post-quantum cryptography* – a new set of cryptosystems that hopefully resist quantum attacks. In particular, the random oracle model has been re-examined in the presence of quantum adversaries. Since eventually a scheme (designed in RO) will be realized via a cryptographic function, whose specification is known in public, a quantum adversary can in principle construct a coherent quantum circuit that evaluates the hash function in quantum *superposition*. Consequently, when analyzing the scheme in the idealized setting, it seems necessary to grant quantum superposition queries to the random oracle by a quantum adversary. This brings about the quantum random oracle model [7]. The rationale is, very informally, good cryptographic functions are lacking structures for a quantum computer to exploit (aside from generic speedup due to quantum search), and hence realizing a scheme proven secure relative to a quantum random oracle this way is a fine practice.

Formally analyzing security in the quantum random oracle model turns out to be challenging. Many classical proof techniques, such as simulating and

---

[2] According to Google Scholar, [4] has a citation count at 5089 (November 2019), which would be ranked top 20 at a (dated) list of most cited computer science papers [12].

programming a random oracle on-the-fly or recording the queries, seem to fail due to unique features of quantum information. Thanks to a lot of continued effort, in recent years, researchers managed to develop various techniques for reasoning about the quantum random oracle model, and restored the security of many important constructions against quantum adversaries [2,13,15,19,20,30,32,33]. In fact, quantum random oracle model is becoming a booming research topic. To get an idea, as of writing, there are 166 citations in total of [7] and about 90 since 2018, of which about **60** came out since 2019. Also out of the 9 signature scheme submissions that made the second round of the post-quantum cryptography standardization at NIST [27], 5 of them involve the quantum random oracle. This just adds more at stake regarding "what does it mean that a scheme is proven secure in the *quantum* random oracle model?"

How to Interpret This Result? Our work show that in general, security in the quantum random oracle model could be vacuous in a real-world implementation. There seems a dilemma, probably more puzzling than the classical situation. On the one hand, since a quantum adversary is given more power (e.g., quantum computation and superposition access), security in the quantum random oracle provides more justification that the construction is solid. And this indeed explains the difficulty in establishing security in the quantum random oracle. Hence it might occur that security in QRO would be sufficiently strong to imply security in the plain model and rule out separations. Our work nonetheless shows otherwise, and it reveals the other side of the dilemma. Any bit of success in restoring proof techniques in the quantum random oracle model just casts another bit of shadow on this methodology, since the seemingly stronger quantum security does not promise the security of real-world implementations, not even their security against *classical* adversaries only.

On the other hand, many cryptosystems that have been proven secure in the random oracle model have fared well in retrospect [23]. The use of the random oracle model to get a proof can allow for schemes that are simpler and more efficient than those in the standard model. While proofs in the quantum random oracle model appear more difficult, every year new techniques, more general and user-friendly, are developed to establish quantum random oracle model security [13,18,20,33]. This has lead researchers to question what guarantees security in the quantum random oracle provides versus the classical random oracle model. In this line, our results can be taken as further justification that the difference between these models does not appear to be a large one. If one hopes to show that security in the classical and quantum oracle model provide a similar set of assurances, then it seems natural that the same instantiability problems exist in the classical random oracle model as well as the quantum counterpart.

2   Background

2.1   The (Quantum Random) Oracle Model and Notation

The random oracle model, originally devised in [4], replaces a cryptographic hash function with an entirely random oracle. The reduction algorithm is often allowed to manage this oracle, and can perform operations like looking up the queries that the adversary makes to it, or programming the oracle on inputs of interest. Using the random oracle model can often greatly simplify a proof or even enable a proof where otherwise not known or possible.

The intuitive idea behind the soundness of the random oracle methodology is that an adversary interacting with a scheme is unlikely to take advantage of the structure of the hash function. For most cryptographic schemes, even the adversary is likely to treat the hash function as a 'black box', and so by treating it as such, we can derive proofs for schemes that otherwise may not exist.

However, as pointed out in an influential paper by Boneh et al. [7], the random oracle model makes a fundamentally classical assumption about how an adversary interacts with the hash function (or random oracle). If we are concerned about an adversary who has access to a quantum computer, than we can assume that such an adversary is capable of instantiating the hash function on a quantum computer and making queries to it in *superposition*. Such behaviour is excluded by the random oracle model, and so when considering a quantum adversary, a more cautious approach for proofs is to consider the quantum random oracle model.

In the quantum random oracle model, the reduction algorithm still manages the oracle, but now the adversary must be allowed to make a superposition query to this oracle. For an oracle $\mathcal{O} : \mathcal{D} \to \mathcal{R}$, the reduction provides access to a unitary $U_{\mathcal{O}}$ which performs the action

$$U_{\mathcal{O}} : \sum_{x \in \mathcal{D}, y \in \mathcal{R}} \alpha_{x,y} |x\rangle |y\rangle \mapsto \sum_{x \in \mathcal{D}, y \in \mathcal{R}} \alpha_{x,y} |x\rangle |y \oplus \mathcal{O}(x)\rangle,$$

where the input must be a valid quantum state, i.e., the sum of the square amplitudes of the $\alpha_{x,y}$'s must be 1.

For clarity, we will denote a random oracle as $\mathcal{O}$, while actual instantiations of random oracles (e.g., typically hash functions) are denoted H. When describing a scheme where a function may replaced with a random oracle in the proof, or with a hash function in the real world, we will denote this function with F. The security parameter of a scheme is denoted by λ, while the output length of a hash function is denoted n. While we separate these two values for generality and expressiveness, throughout this work it is the case that $\lambda = n$.

2.2   Computationally Sound Proofs

Computationally sound proofs, introduced by Micali in 2000 [25], allow extremely efficient verification of a problem $\mathcal{L}$ with the help of a prover. In our context, CS-proofs are useful for showing the validity of a computation without having to run the computation. Imagine a description of an arbitrary function f, which may take super-polynomial time to run on an input x, but will result in $f(x) = y$. A CS-proof system allows us to generate a proof π that $f(x) = y$. Even though f may take a super-polynomial amount of time to run, the CS-Proof verification system allows a verifier, on input of f, x, y, and π to verify that $f(x) = y$ in only poly-logarithmic time.

For concreteness in our work, a CS-proof system consists of two algorithms: CSProve and CSVerify. Both algorithms implicitly take a security parameter λ. CSProve also takes in a function f and an input x, and returns a value y and a proof π. The CSVerify function takes in a function f, an input x, an output y, and a proof π. It returns either accept or reject, based on the validity of the proof. Crucially, the CSVerify function runs in time poly-log in the security parameter λ, and not in relation to the time it takes f to run.

The correctness property states that for an honestly generated proof π, the CSVerify function will always accept. The soundness property ensures that if $f(x) \neq y$, then it is computationally infeasible to find a proof π that will cause CSVerify(f, x, y, π) to return accept. The soundness of CS-proofs was originally shown in the random oracle model. Very recently, Chiesa et al. [11], proved the soundness of CS-proofs in the quantum random oracle model, which we will rely on in this work.

3   Instantiating Quantum Random Oracles

In this section we define three signature schemes, Σ_1, Σ_2, and Σ_3, such that:

- Σ_1 is secure in the quantum random oracle model, but insecure if that random oracle is instantiated with some specific hash function H.
- Σ_2 is secure in the QROM, but insecure when the random oracle is instantiated with any of a pre-defined set of hash functions $\{H_1, \ldots, H_m\}$.
- Σ_3 is secure in the QROM, but insecure if the random oracle is ever instantiated with *any* polynomial-time function.

These signature schemes lift the results in [10] to the quantum random oracle model. In all cases, the only assumption we require is that we have a signature scheme $\Sigma_0 = (\mathsf{KeyGen}_0, \mathsf{Sign}_0, \mathsf{Vrfy}_0)$ which is existentially unforgeable in the quantum random oracle model. Examples of schemes proven secure in the quantum random oracle model with no additional assumptions include the stateful LMS signatures [14] and the stateless SPHINCS+ framework [6] (both hash-based signatures). If one is willing to accept a computational assumption such as ring-LWE, many other signature schemes, including several of those under consideration in the NIST standardization process serve as examples [21].

3.1   Warm Up—Schemes Σ_1 and Σ_2

The first step in considering the instantiation of a random oracle is to consider instantiation with a single hash function, H. Then we can define the scheme Σ_1 as follows. Clearly this scheme satisfies the correctness property, as Σ_0 does.

This scheme is eu-acma secure in the (quantum) random oracle model, where F is replaced with an oracle $\mathcal{O}$. This is intuitively because in this case, the security reduces to that of Σ_0 unless an adversary is able to find a msg such that $\mathcal{O}(\mathsf{msg}) = H(\mathsf{msg})$ (which occurs for every possible input with uniform and independent probability $1/2^n$).

Signature scheme Σ_1

- $\mathsf{KeyGen}_1(1^\lambda)$: Generate $(pk, sk) \leftarrow \mathsf{KeyGen}_0(1^\lambda)$, and return.
- $\mathsf{Sign}_1(sk, \mathsf{msg})$:
  - Compute $\sigma_0 = \mathsf{Sign}_0(sk, \mathsf{msg})$.
  - Check to see if $F(\mathsf{msg}) = H(\mathsf{msg})$. If so, return $\sigma_1 = \sigma_0 \| sk$.
  - Otherwise, return $\sigma_1 = \sigma_0 \| 0$.
- $\mathsf{Vrfy}_1(pk, \mathsf{msg}, \sigma_1)$:
  - Parse σ_1 as $\sigma_0 \| x$.
  - Run $\mathsf{Vrfy}_0(pk, \mathsf{msg}, \sigma_0)$.

Furthermore, this scheme is *insecure* if it is instantiated with H replacing the random oracle. Then the adversary is able to trivially break security, as the condition $H(\mathsf{msg}) = H(\mathsf{msg})$ is always satisfied and $\sigma_1 = \sigma_0 \| sk$ will be returned for any message.

The next step is considering a finite collection of m hash functions, say $\mathcal{H} = \{H_1, H_2 \ldots, H_m\}$.

Then we can define Σ_2 similarly to Σ_1, but change the condition to first check if $\mathsf{msg} \in \{1, \ldots, m\}$ (in some encoding of the integers 1 through m) and if so, further check if $F(\mathsf{msg}) = H_{\mathsf{msg}}(\mathsf{msg})$.

The analysis in the (quantum) random oracle model is again fairly straightforward. For any random oracle $\mathcal{O}$, the probability that $\mathcal{O}(i)$ matches $H_i(i)$ for any of $i = 1$ to m is at most $m \cdot \frac{1}{2^n}$. When m is small (e.g., polynomially sized in λ), this is small enough that it is likely to not be possible that an adversary can make a query that provides them with sk. Even for a large m, each $i \in \{1, \ldots, m\}$ will have the property that $\mathcal{O}$ and H_i match with probability $1/2^n$, and so an adversary must perform an unstructured search to find such an i. Hence an adversary's ability to break Σ_2 in the (quantum) random oracle model reduces to their ability to break Σ_0.

However, as before, if F is actually replaced by any one of the H_i's, an adversary can easily break the scheme by querying i to the signing oracle.

3.2   Signature Scheme Σ_3

Schemes Σ_1 and Σ_2 are only to gain an intuition for the full result, Σ_3, which is a signature scheme that is secure in the quantum random oracle model, but insecure when the oracle is instantiated with any polynomial-time function as the hash function. Following the strategy for Σ_2, we would like to fix some enumeration of all algorithms that one may use as a hash function, say $\mathcal{H} = \{H_1, H_2, \ldots\}$, with $H_i : \{0,1\}^* \to \{0,1\}^n$. Then as before, we would modify an eu-acma secure scheme Σ_0 to introduce a check in the signing algorithm to interpret msg as a non-negative integer, and check if $F(\mathsf{msg}) = H_{\mathsf{msg}}(\mathsf{msg})$. However, there are several issues that must be resolved to make this fully rigorous. Such a set of functions cannot simply be defined and used in the signature scheme, as the signature scheme requires that on input i, hash function H_i is actually run.

To fix this, we start with an enumeration of *all* algorithms, $\mathcal{A} = \{A_1, A_2, A_3, \dots\}$. We make no assumptions about this enumeration except that we can efficiently swap between the index i and some standard description of A_i. Changing between A_i and i should not be seen as a computational task to carry out, but rather a reinterpretation of the same data. Algorithms are encoded, using some standard encoding depending on the computational model, into bit strings, which can then easily be interpreted as an integer. To think of a construction that achieves this, it is helpful to think of quantum circuits. If we are working with l registers, then we can interpret the index i as a value in $\{0,1\}^*$ which specifies which gates are applied to which registers in what order. From a description of a quantum circuit, it is easy to convert this into a binary string, and then an index, and vice versa. To be reversible and match the format of a hash function, we can then consider all circuits that perform the mapping $|x\rangle|y\rangle \mapsto |x\rangle|y \oplus A_i(x)\rangle$.

Note that not all of these algorithms necessarily run in polynomial-time in the security parameter. It is of course impossible to tell which algorithms will even terminate. We would like to assume that when a random oracle is instantiated, the function it is instantiated with will run in polynomial time in the security parameter. As well, these algorithms do not necessarily have the correct output length of n bits.

To fix this, we modify each algorithm in the following way: For each algorithm, stop after taking $n^{\log n}$ steps, and pad or truncate the output (in an arbitrary way) so that each algorithm always outputs n bits. The value $n^{\log n}$ is chosen so it bounds all polynomial-time algorithms. We enumerate our modified algorithms $\mathcal{H} = \{H_1, H_2, \dots\}$. Notice that any algorithm that is polynomial time, and outputs n bit binary strings is unmodified. So, any function that would be used as a hash function is not affected by this.

We can then make a first attempt at defining Σ_3. Given an eu-acma (in the quantum random oracle model) signature scheme Σ_0 and an enumeration of hash functions $\mathcal{H}$ as described above, we define Σ_3 as follows.

Signature Scheme Σ_3, first attempt

- KeyGen$_3$: The key generation algorithm remains the same as in the original scheme Σ. Run KeyGen$_0(1^\lambda)$ and return (pk, sk).
- Sign$_3$: On input of a message msg, and the secret key sk, do the following:
  - Compute $\sigma_0 \leftarrow$ Sign$_0(sk, \text{msg})$.
  - Interpret msg as a non-negative integer. Compute $H_{\text{msg}}(\text{msg})$.
  - Check to see if $F(\text{msg}) = H_{\text{msg}}(\text{msg})$.
  - If so, return signature $\sigma_3 = \sigma_0||sk$. Otherwise, return $\sigma_3 = \sigma_0||0^{l_{sk}}$.
- Vrfy$_3$: On input of a message msg, a signature σ_3 and a public key pk, we parse σ_3 as $\sigma_0||x$, where x is a (possibly all zero) string of length l_{sk}. Then compute and return Vrfy$_0(pk, \text{msg}, \sigma_0)$.

There is a very noticeable problem in this scheme. We bounded the run time of the H_i's by $n^{\log n}$, in order to make sure that we could leave *every* polynomial-time algorithm unaffected. However, any algorithm A_i that runs in $\geq$ $n^{\log n}$ steps will be modified to run in $n^{\log n}$ steps. If a message msg is signed which corresponds to such an algorithm, the signer will have to evaluate $H_{\mathsf{msg}}(\mathsf{msg})$. This means that the signing algorithm *does not run in polynomial time in the security parameter*, and so it does not fit a valid definition of a signing algorithm.

To resolve this issue, CS-proofs are employed.

Rather than directly checking to see if $F(\mathsf{msg}) = H_{\mathsf{msg}}(\mathsf{msg})$, we can instead accept a CS-proof π that $F(\mathsf{msg}) = H_{\mathsf{msg}}(\mathsf{msg})$. This scheme is still trivial to break when F is instantiated, but we are now guaranteed that the signing algorithm always runs in polynomial time, no matter what is queried.

Signature Scheme Σ_3, correct with CS-proofs

- KeyGen$_3$: The key generation algorithm remains the same as in the original scheme Σ_0. Run KeyGen$_0(1^\lambda)$ and return (pk, sk).
- Sign$_3$: On input of a message msg, and the secret key sk, do the following:
  - Compute $\sigma_0 \leftarrow \mathsf{Sign}_0(sk, \mathsf{msg})$.
  - Using some standard parsing rule, parse msg as $i\|\pi$, an index i and a string π.
  - Run CSVerify to check if π is a CS-proof that $H_i(i) = F(i)$.
  - If so, return signature $\sigma_3 = \sigma_0\|sk$. Otherwise, return $\sigma_3 = \sigma_0\|0^{l_{sk}}$.
- Vrfy$_3$: On input of a message msg, a signature σ_3 and a public key pk, we parse σ_3 as $\sigma_0\|x$, where x is a (possibly trivial) string of length l_{sk}. Then compute and return $\mathsf{Vrfy}_0(pk, \mathsf{msg}, \sigma_0)$.

This allows us to state the main theorem of our paper.

Theorem 1 (Security of Σ_3). *Let $g : \{0,1\}^* \to \{0,1\}$ be a random function such that for each x, $\Pr[g(x) = 1] = \frac{1}{2^n}$ and all outputs of the function are independent.*

Let $\mathcal{Q}$ be a quantum adversary capable of breaking the existential-unforgeability of Σ_3 with probability p in the quantum random oracle model. Then there exists a reduction algorithm $\mathcal{R}$ that, in slightly super-polynomial time, is capable of either breaking Σ_0, breaking the computational soundness of the CS-proof system, or finding an $x \in \{0,1\}^*$ such that $g(x) = 1$.

3.3   Proof of Theorem 1

To prove that Σ_3 is secure in the quantum random oracle model, we reduce its security to the adversary's ability to do one of three things:

- Break signature scheme Σ_0 in the quantum random oracle model in *slightly super-polynomial time*.
- Find a marked item with respect to a random oracle g.
- Break the computational soundness of a CS-proof in the quantum random oracle model.

The reduction algorithm has two main components: How it answers random oracle queries and how it answers signature queries.

For handling a random oracle, we will need to construct a pseudo-random function f that takes in two parameters: x and y. This function must satisfy that $f(x, y)$ is a uniform random element from the set $\{0, 1\}^n \setminus \{y\}$. Such a function can be quickly constructed on a quantum accessible circuit by using $2q$-wise independent hash functions.

Then consider the following oracle:

$$\mathcal{O}(i) = \begin{cases} H_i(i) & \text{if } g(i) = 1 \\ f(i, H_i(i)) & \text{otherwise} \end{cases} \tag{1}$$

By creating the proper quantum-accessible circuits, we can create such a circuit that implements such an oracle in super-polynomial time. We will give the adversary $\mathcal{Q}$ access to this oracle.

We also need to show that the adversary cannot distinguish between this oracle and a truly random oracle. In fact, we can show something stronger than this, that this is in fact a truly random oracle. To see this, take any $y \in \{0, 1\}^n$, and any $i \in \{0, 1\}^*$ and consider $Pr[\mathcal{O}(i) = y]$.

$$\begin{aligned} &\Pr[\mathcal{O}(i) = y] \\ &= \Pr[g(i) = 1] \Pr[\mathcal{O}(i) = y | g(i) = 1] + \Pr[g(i) = 0] \Pr[\mathcal{O}(i) = y | g(i) = 0] \\ &= \frac{1}{2^n} \Pr[\mathcal{O}(i) = y | g(i) = 1] + \frac{2^n - 1}{2^n} \Pr[\mathcal{O}(i) = y | g(i) = 0]. \end{aligned}$$

Then note that

$$\Pr[\mathcal{O}(i) = y | g(i) = 1] = \begin{cases} 1 & \text{if } y = H_i(i) \\ 0 & \text{otherwise} \end{cases}$$

$$\Pr[\mathcal{O}(i) = y | g(i) = 0] = \begin{cases} 0 & \text{if } y = H_i(i) \\ \frac{1}{2^n - 1} & \text{otherwise} \end{cases}$$

In either case, putting these values into the equation gives that $\Pr[\mathcal{O}(i) = y] = \frac{1}{2^n}$. Furthermore, we can see that as long as g and H_i are each $2q$-wise independent, the overall hash function is $2q$-wise independent, and so we have that this gives us an oracle that is indistinguishable from a truly random one, even by a quantum adversary.

We next describe how the reduction algorithm $\mathcal{R}$ handles the signature queries. On input of a query msg, our reduction does the following:

- Parse msg as $i \| \pi$, an index i and a string π.
- Run the CS-verification procedure, with π as the potential proof that $H_i(i) = \mathcal{O}(i)$. If it accepts, check if $H_i(i) = \mathcal{O}(i)$
  - If it is, then by construction, $g(i) = 1$ and we have successfully found such an i, and may stop.
  - If it isn't, then we have a CS-proof of a false fact, and may stop.
- If it did not accept, then query the challenger for a signature on msg under the scheme Sign_0 and return the signature $\sigma_0 \| 0^{l_{sk}}$ to $\mathcal{Q}$.

If we never stop on any signature query, then eventually the adversary would submit a forgery $(\mathsf{msg}^*, \sigma_3^*)$, where msg^* was never submitted to the signing oracle. We may then parse σ_3^* as $\sigma_0^* || x$. If this forgery is accepted by the verification procedure Vrfy_3, then $\mathsf{msg}^*, \sigma_0^*$ will form a forgery with respect to Σ_0.

4 Signing Short Messages

In this section we describe the scheme that appears in [9] and argue that the proof of security that appears in that work translates to the quantum random oracle model. This scheme has the same restrictions as the one that appears in the previous section—we want a scheme that is secure in the quantum random oracle model, but insecure when the scheme is instantiated with any polynomial-time function. At a high level, this is accomplished in the same way as before. The signing algorithm will interpret all submitted messages as a potential description of a hash function, and check to see if this hash function matches the random oracle in such a way that proves that the random oracle is in fact, the hash function. The main distinction is that the signing algorithm will only accept messages of length poly-logarithmic in the security parameter. This means that the usage of CS-proofs is no longer a possibility. To overcome this, the authors of [9] devised a proof system for an NP-language in which the verifier need only accept *multiple, short* messages.

This proof system can then be turned into a signature scheme, and the adversary (who acts as the prover) will submit a proof that the random oracle is not random by making multiple signing queries. At first glance, it may seem that it is not hard to construct a proof system that can take multiple short messages—all we need to do is to take a proof system that requires one, large message and send that message in multiple rounds. However, such a strategy would require the verifier to be *stateful*. The verifier would need to "save" the messages that the prover sends them to be verified against future messages. When translated to the context of a signature scheme, this makes the signer stateful as well. To rule out stateless signature schemes as well, the verifier in the proof system devised in [9] needed to both accept only short messages and be *stateless*.

In this section we show that this proof system remains secure in the quantum random oracle model. To do this, we first restate the proof system as it appears in [9], and then discuss how it is used in a signature scheme similar to Sect. 3. Finally, we show how the security of the system remains unchanged in the quantum random oracle model.

4.1 A Stateless Interactive Proof System with Short Messages

As mentioned, the proof system introduced in [9] is an interactive proof system with the following goals:

- It must only require short messages, so that the signing algorithm only needs to accept short messages.

- It must be stateless so that the signing algorithm also is.
- It must be unconditionally secure in the (quantum) random oracle model, again so that the signature scheme may be as well.

At a high level, these goals are accomplished with the following strategy: the proof that the verifier needs to process is modelled as a Turing machine. The initial state to this Turing machine is "fed" to the verifier, one block at a time. Each time a block of the initial state is fed to the verifier, they authenticate the current configuration, and send an updated tag to the prover. This authentication tag is submitted to the verifier as part of each subsequent update.

Remember however, that the verifier is completely stateless. While we may describe this process as the verifier learning the configuration of the Turing machine, what is really happening is that the verifier is incrementally authenticating each part of the configuration, without ever knowing the whole state.

Once the initial state is "loaded" the prover then proceeds by having the verifier execute the Turing machine, one step at a time. The prover needs to tell the verifier the parts of the machine that they need to know, as well as the authentication tags for those parts. The verifier can then execute one step, update the authentication tags, and send these back to the prover so that they may repeat the process. Since the authentication tags are small (more on this later) and the prover only needs to communicate the parts of the Turing machine that are necessary to execute one step, the communication in each round is small. Because the authentication tags cannot be forged, the only way for the prover to get the Turing machine to be in an accepting state (authenticated by the verifier) is to have to walk the verifier through each step of the computation, having them authenticate the process along the way.

We now expand on this sketch, starting by describing the machine that the verifier will be executing to establish that the oracle is non-random.

Non-randomness machine $M^{\mathcal{O}}(1^k, \pi)$

- Input π is interpreted as a description of a Turing machine. Let $n = |\pi|$.
- For $i \in \{1, \ldots, 2n + k\}$:
  - $y_i = \mathcal{O}(i)$.
  - $z_i = \pi(i)$.
  - If the first bit of y_i and z_i disagree, return *reject*.
- Return *accept*.

The configuration is described in four tapes—the security parameter tape sp, the oracle query tape q, the oracle reply tape r, and the worktape w initially containing π. The security of M when $\mathcal{O}$ is a random oracle is shown in [9].

Lemma 1 ([9], Proposition 2). *If the oracle $\mathcal{O}$ is chosen uniformly, the probability that there exists a description of a Turing machine π such that $M^{\mathcal{O}}(1^k, \pi)$ returns* accept *is less than 2^{-k}.*

Note that this lemma refers to the existence of a Turing machine π. This property holds just as well when $\mathcal{O}$ is quantum-accessible. Also note again that if $\mathcal{O}$ is not a random oracle, and is described by the Turing machine τ, then we can simply set $\pi = \tau$ and have that $M^\tau(1^k, \pi) \to accept$ with certainty.

To iteratively load and run the machine M, we need a mechanism for the verifier to authenticate the current state of the machine, which is described by the four work tapes (sp, q, r, w), the heads of the tapes $h_1, \ldots, h_4$, and the finite control $\mathcal{F}$. These eight values describe entirely the state of the machine M. Using some standard encoding method, they may be encoded as a binary string. It is this string, denoted c that the verifier will be authenticating.

Say the oracle $\mathcal{O}$ returns values in $\{0,1\}^n$. Then we will pad the string c to one of length $n \cdot 2^d$, where d is the smallest positive integer such that $n \cdot 2^d \geq |c|$. This allows us to construct a Merkle tree out of the string c, with the leaf nodes consisting of bit strings of length n, and the tree having height d. The Merkle tree is constructed out of the oracle $\mathcal{O}$ by setting, for level i of the tree, the value of each node to be $\mathcal{O}(i, \mathsf{left}, \mathsf{right})$, where left and right are the values (in $\{0,1\}^n$) of the two nodes in the tree directly below.

Note, in particular, that domain separation is used to separate the different levels, but not for the calculations *within* a level. This is done to speed up the process of creating a Merkle tree when the configuration c is homogeneous. For the parts of the work tapes that entirely blank (as they will be in the initial configuration), when converted into a binary string, and then a Merkle tree, their will be many repeated leaf values, which means that the entire tree can be constructed in time polynomial in the security parameter, k.

The verifier will possess an authentication key ak, which is used to authenticate the root of the Merkle tree as in a MAC scheme. The authentication tag for the tree is computed as $\mathcal{O}(d, ak, \mathsf{root})$. The loading and execution machine then proceeds as follows (Full details of this process are described in [9]).

1. The prover sends a message indicating that they wish to initialize the process. In response, the verifier loads up a blank configuration c in which the tapes are all empty, the heads are at a starting position, and the finite control is empty. They compute the root of the Merkle tree where this blank configuration forms the leaf nodes, and authenticate the root of the tree, sending the authentication tag back to the prover.

2. The prover loads the initial state of the machine M leaf-node-by-leaf-node. For any leaf node i they wish to update, they send a message to the verifier with the position they want to update, the Merkle tree verification path for that leaf node, the new value they want that position to take on, and the authentication tag for the most recent root node. The verifier uses the Merkle tree verification path to reconstruct the root node, which it verifies with the authentication tag and its key ak. Once checked, the verifier produces an authentication tag for the tree with the desired update, by swapping out the leaf node value, computing the new resulting root node (again, by using the Merkle tree verification path) and constructing a tag for the root node.

3. When the initial state of M has been loaded, the prover can then get the verifier to begin executing M. To execute a step of M, the prover must send any leaf nodes involved in one step of the computation (e.g., the leaf node the header is pointed to, the values of the headers) and the Merkle tree verification paths for those leaves, as well as the authentication tag. The verifier computes one step of the Turing machine, recomputes the root node for the new state, and sends the authentication tag for the new state to the prover. If the machine reaches the accepting state, then the verifier accepts the state as valid.

We now proceed to prove a lifting of Proposition 4 in [9] to the quantum random oracle model.

Lemma 2. *Let ak be chosen uniformly at random in $\{0,1\}^n$, then for any prover $\mathcal{P}$ it holds that*

$$\Pr_{\mathcal{O},ak}\left[V^{\mathcal{O}}(1^k, ak) \to \mathsf{accept}\right] \leq O(q^3/2^n) \tag{2}$$

Where q is the number of (quantum) oracle queries made by $\mathcal{P}$.

Proof. As noted in Lemma 1, the probability over the randomness in $\mathcal{O}$ that there exists an accepting machine π is less than 2^{-k}. Assuming there does not exist such a machine, a dishonest prover must somehow manage to trick the verifier into reaching an accepting state. Because an accepting machine cannot be loaded into the configuration, it must be the case that some machine which should not accept was instead loaded, and the execution of this machine is then tampered with by the prover. To tamper with the execution of the machine, the adversary must, at some point, provide the verifier with a leaf node that was not in the configuration that was just authenticated.

In order to load in a falsified leaf node, the adversary must still submit a correct authentication tag. There are two cases: either the associated authentication tag was provided by the verifier, or it was not.

First we consider the case where the authentication tag was provided by the verifier. We consider the first time the adversary submits a leaf node that corresponds to an invalid machine configuration. We know that the authentication tag matches a previously issued one, but the corresponding leaf node was not part of how the previous authentication tag was generated. There are two possibilities for how this may happen. It may be the case that (i) at some point along the verification path we have values left, left$'$, right, right$'$ and i such that $\mathcal{O}(i, \mathsf{left}, \mathsf{right}) = \mathcal{O}(i, \mathsf{left}', \mathsf{right}')$. Of course, at most one of the left and right values can be equal. The other possibility is that (ii) the root values of the resulting Merkle trees are different, but we have a collision in the authentication tag: $\mathcal{O}(d, ak, \mathsf{root}) = \mathcal{O}(d, ak, \mathsf{root}')$.

Because an adversary who is able to break the soundness of the proof system must provide enough classical information to be able to construct a collision in the quantum random oracle $\mathcal{O}$, we can bound the success probability simply by the probability of being able to find such a collision. This can be asymptotically bounded by a $O(q^3/2^n)$ term.

The second case happens when the authentication tag for the invalid machine configuration was never previously issued. This means that the adversary was able to submit a tag t, a value d, and a Merkle tree path that leads to a value root such that $t = \mathcal{O}(d, ak, \text{root})$ when the value t was never before returned by the verifier.

Intuitively, this is a structureless search problem on the part of the adversary: in order to provide a valid authentication tag, they must perform an unstructured search to find the ak value that causes authentication tags to accept. To formally show this, we provide a reduction from an adversary who can create a new authentication tag to one that can distinguish between to functions, g_0 and g_1, both mapping $\{0,1\}^n$ to $\{0,1\}$. The function g_0 simply returns 0 for all inputs x, whereas for g_1 there is precisely one random input on which g_1 will return 1.

We are given quantum access to one of the two functions, g_b, and asked to determine b. To do this, we first construct two independent quantum-accessible random oracles $\mathcal{O}_0$ and $\mathcal{O}_1$. We then construct the oracle $\mathcal{O}$ as follows:

$$\mathcal{O}(d, x, y) = \begin{cases} \mathcal{O}_0(d, x, y) & \text{if } g_b(x) = 0 \\ \mathcal{O}_1(d, y) & \text{if } g_b(x) = 1. \end{cases} \tag{3}$$

Note that since there is at most one x for which $g_b(x) = 1$, $\mathcal{O}$ is itself a random oracle, for anyone who does not have direct access to $\mathcal{O}_0$ and $\mathcal{O}_1$.

When the verifier needs to produce an authentication tag on an input (d, root), this can simply be done by computing $t = \mathcal{O}_1(d, \text{root})$. Then note that these tags will be valid authentication tags with respect to some authentication key only when $b = 1$, in which case the valid authentication tag will be the value x such that $g(x) = 1$.

When $b = 1$, the authentication tags that are issued by the verifier will be correctly correlated with the oracle $\mathcal{O}$, but when $b = 0$, the tags will be entirely uncorrelated with $\mathcal{O}$. In this case, the adversary's ability to produce a forgery is bounded by a simple random guess, which corresponds to a probability of $1/2^n$. This is because in this case the oracle $\mathcal{O}$ can tell the adversary no information about correct authentication tags. To try and guess an authentication tag for a configuration (d, root^*) would mean trying to guess the value of $\mathcal{O}_1(d, \text{root}^*)$ without ever having queried it (and having made no quantum queries to it). Any non-negligible difference in the success probability of the adversary $\mathcal{P}$ can be used in order to determine which function we are dealing with, and thus leads to a determination of the unknown bit b.

The probability of determining such a bit in q queries to g is bounded above by $O(q^2/2^n)$ from known result [20]. Note that each quantum query $\mathcal{P}$ makes to $\mathcal{O}$ corresponds to exactly one quantum query to g_b. Because the other case is bounded by a $O(q^3/2^n)$ term, we can drop this term entirely.

Signature Scheme Σ_4

- KeyGen$_4$: Because the verifier in the interactive proof system requires an authentication key, we sample one as $ak \xleftarrow{\$} \{0,1\}^n$. Obtain $(pk_0, sk_0) \leftarrow$ KeyGen$_0(1^\lambda)$ and return $(pk_4, sk_4) = (pk_0, (sk_0, ak))$.
- Sign$_4$: On input of a message msg, and the secret key $sk_4 = (sk_0, ak)$, do the following:
  - Compute $\sigma_0 \leftarrow$ Sign$_0(sk, \text{msg})$.
  - Using some standard parsing rule, parse msg as an input to the verifier $\mathcal{V}$.
  - Run $\mathcal{V}(ak; \text{msg})$, obtaining output t, and whether the machine M reached the authenticating state.
  - If so, return signature $\sigma_4 = \sigma_0 || sk_0$. Otherwise, return $\sigma_3 = \sigma_0 || t$.
- Vrfy$_4$: On input of a message msg, a signature σ_4 and a public key $pk_4 = pk_0$, we parse σ_4 as $\sigma_0 || x$, where x is some string. Then compute and return Vrfy$_0(pk_0, \text{msg}, \sigma_0)$.

4.2   Signature Scheme Σ_4

With the interactive, stateless, short messaged proof system fleshed out, we can now discuss the signature scheme Σ_4, built out of this proof system.

Theorem 2 (Security of Σ_4). *Let $\mathcal{Q}$ be a quantum adversary capable of breaking the existential-unforgeability of Σ_4 with probability p in the quantum random oracle model, with q queries to the quantum random oracle $\mathcal{O}$. Then there exists a reduction algorithm $\mathcal{R}$ that, with probability (over $\mathcal{R}$ and $\mathcal{O}$) at least $p - O(q^3/2^n)$ is capable of either breaking Σ_0 or finding an $x, x' \in \{0,1\}^*$ such that $\mathcal{O}(x) = \mathcal{O}(x')$.*

Proof. It is easy to see that

$$\Pr[\mathcal{Q} \text{ wins eu-acma} \wedge \nexists \pi : M^{\mathcal{O}}(1^\lambda, \pi) \to \text{accept}] \geq p - 2^{-\lambda},$$

where the probability is taken over the randomness in the oracle $\mathcal{O}$ and the randomness of the adversary, as well as whatever randomness is needed in the signature scheme Σ_0.

There are then two cases: either the adversary submits a signing query that causes the proof system to move into an accepting state, or they do not. If they do, then since we know there is not a π such that $M^{\mathcal{O}}(1^\lambda, \pi)$, the only way for an adversary to do this is to have found a collision in $\mathcal{O}$, which can be found by looking at the (classical) signing queries made by the adversary. We can bound the probability this happens by a $O(q/2^\lambda)$ term. Assuming that the adversary does not submit such a message, then whatever forgery is submitted by the adversary will work as a valid forgery to the signature scheme Σ_0.

Acknowledgments. E.E. acknowledges the support of the Natural Sciences and Engineering Research Council of Canada (NSERC) for grant 401230696. F.S. acknowledges the support by the National Science Foundation.

References

1. Ambainis, A., Hamburg, M., Unruh, D.: Quantum security proofs using semi-classical oracles. In: Boldyreva, A., Micciancio, D. (eds.) CRYPTO 2019. LNCS, vol. 11693, pp. 269–295. Springer, Cham (2019). https://doi.org/10.1007/978-3-030-26951-7_10
2. Ambainis, A., Rosmanis, A., Unruh, D.: Quantum attacks on classical proof systems: the hardness of quantum rewinding. In: 2014 IEEE 55th Annual Symposium on Foundations of Computer Science, pp. 474–483. IEEE (2014)
3. Bellare, M., Boldyreva, A., Palacio, A.: An uninstantiable random-oracle-model scheme for a hybrid-encryption problem. In: Cachin, C., Camenisch, J.L. (eds.) EUROCRYPT 2004. LNCS, vol. 3027, pp. 171–188. Springer, Heidelberg (2004). https://doi.org/10.1007/978-3-540-24676-3_11
4. Bellare, M., Rogaway, P.: Random oracles are practical: a paradigm for designing efficient protocols. In: Proceedings of the 1st ACM Conference on Computer and Communications Security, pp. 62–73. ACM (1993)
5. Bellare, M., Rogaway, P.: Optimal asymmetric encryption. In: De Santis, A. (ed.) EUROCRYPT 1994. LNCS, vol. 950, pp. 92–111. Springer, Heidelberg (1995). https://doi.org/10.1007/BFb0053428
6. Bernstein, D.J., Hülsing, A., Kölbl, S., Niederhagen, R., Rijneveld, J., Schwabe, P.: The SPHINCS$^+$ signature framework. In: Proceedings of the 2019 ACM SIGSAC Conference on Computer and Communications Security, CCS 2019, pp. 2129–2146 (2019)
7. Boneh, D., Dagdelen, Ö., Fischlin, M., Lehmann, A., Schaffner, C., Zhandry, M.: Random oracles in a quantum world. In: Lee, D.H., Wang, X. (eds.) ASIACRYPT 2011. LNCS, vol. 7073, pp. 41–69. Springer, Heidelberg (2011). https://doi.org/10.1007/978-3-642-25385-0_3
8. Boyer, M., Brassard, G., Høyer, P., Tapp, A.: Tight bounds on quantum searching (1996). arXiv:quant-ph/9605034
9. Canetti, R., Goldreich, O., Halevi, S.: On the random-oracle methodology as applied to length-restricted signature schemes. In: Theory of Cryptography Conference, TCC 2004, pp. 40–57 (2004)
10. Canetti, R., Goldreich, O., Halevi, S.: The random oracle methodology, revisited. J. ACM 51(4), 557–594 (2004). A preliminary version appeared in STOC 1998
11. Chiesa, A., Manohar, P., Spooner, N.: Succinct arguments in the quantum random oracle model. Cryptology ePrint Archive, Report 2019/834 (2019). https://eprint.iacr.org/2019/834
12. CiteseerX: Most cited computer science citations (2015). https://citeseerx.ist.psu.edu/stats/citations
13. Don, J., Fehr, S., Majenz, C., Schaffner, C.: Security of the Fiat-Shamir transformation in the quantum random-oracle model. In: Boldyreva, A., Micciancio, D. (eds.) CRYPTO 2019. LNCS, vol. 11693, pp. 356–383. Springer, Cham (2019). https://doi.org/10.1007/978-3-030-26951-7_13
14. Eaton, E.: Leighton-Micali hash-based signatures in the quantum random-oracle model. In: Adams, C., Camenisch, J. (eds.) SAC 2017. LNCS, vol. 10719, pp. 263–280. Springer, Cham (2018). https://doi.org/10.1007/978-3-319-72565-9_13
15. Eaton, E., Song, F.: Making existential-unforgeable signatures strongly unforgeable in the quantum random-oracle model. In: 10th Conference on the Theory of Quantum Computation, Communication and Cryptography, TQC 2015. LIPIcs, vol. 44, pp. 147–162. Schloss Dagstuhl (2015)

16. Fiat, A., Shamir, A.: How to prove yourself: practical solutions to identification and signature problems. In: Odlyzko, A.M. (ed.) CRYPTO 1986. LNCS, vol. 263, pp. 186–194. Springer, Heidelberg (1987). https://doi.org/10.1007/3-540-47721-7_12

17. Goldwasser, S., Kalai, Y.T.: On the (in) security of the Fiat-Shamir paradigm. In: Proceedings of the 44th Annual IEEE Symposium on Foundations of Computer Science, pp. 102–113. IEEE (2003)

18. Hallgren, S., Smith, A., Song, F.: Classical cryptographic protocols in a quantum world. In: Rogaway, P. (ed.) CRYPTO 2011. LNCS, vol. 6841, pp. 411–428. Springer, Heidelberg (2011). https://doi.org/10.1007/978-3-642-22792-9_23

19. Hofheinz, D., Hövelmanns, K., Kiltz, E.: A modular analysis of the Fujisaki-Okamoto transformation. In: Kalai, Y., Reyzin, L. (eds.) TCC 2017. LNCS, vol. 10677, pp. 341–371. Springer, Cham (2017). https://doi.org/10.1007/978-3-319-70500-2_12

20. Hülsing, A., Rijneveld, J., Song, F.: Mitigating multi-target attacks in hash-based signatures. In: Cheng, C.-M., Chung, K.-M., Persiano, G., Yang, B.-Y. (eds.) PKC 2016. LNCS, vol. 9614, pp. 387–416. Springer, Heidelberg (2016). https://doi.org/10.1007/978-3-662-49384-7_15

21. Kiltz, E., Lyubashevsky, V., Schaffner, C.: A concrete treatment of Fiat-Shamir signatures in the quantum random-oracle model. In: Nielsen, J.B., Rijmen, V. (eds.) EUROCRYPT 2018. LNCS, vol. 10822, pp. 552–586. Springer, Cham (2018). https://doi.org/10.1007/978-3-319-78372-7_18

22. Kiltz, E., O'Neill, A., Smith, A.: Instantiability of RSA-OAEP under chosen-plaintext attack. J. Cryptol. 30(3), 889–919 (2017). https://doi.org/10.1007/s00145-016-9238-4

23. Koblitz, N., Menezes, A.J.: The random oracle model: a twenty-year retrospective. Des. Codes Cryptogr. 77(2), 587–610 (2015). https://doi.org/10.1007/s10623-015-0094-2

24. Maurer, U., Renner, R., Holenstein, C.: Indifferentiability, impossibility results on reductions, and applications to the random oracle methodology. In: Naor, M. (ed.) TCC 2004. LNCS, vol. 2951, pp. 21–39. Springer, Heidelberg (2004). https://doi.org/10.1007/978-3-540-24638-1_2

25. Micali, S.: Computationally sound proofs. SIAM J. Comput. 30(4), 1253–1298 (2000)

26. Nielsen, J.B.: Separating random oracle proofs from complexity theoretic proofs: the non-committing encryption case. In: Yung, M. (ed.) CRYPTO 2002. LNCS, vol. 2442, pp. 111–126. Springer, Heidelberg (2002). https://doi.org/10.1007/3-540-45708-9_8

27. NIST: Post-quantum cryptography (2019). https://csrc.nist.gov/Projects/post-quantum-cryptography

28. Ben Sasson, E., et al.: Zerocash: decentralized anonymous payments from bitcoin. In: 2014 IEEE Symposium on Security and Privacy, pp. 459–474. IEEE (2014)

29. Shor, P.W.: Polynomial-time algorithms for prime factorization and discrete logarithms on a quantum computer. SIAM J. Comput. 26(5), 1484–1509 (1997)

30. Unruh, D.: Non-interactive zero-knowledge proofs in the quantum random oracle model. In: Oswald, E., Fischlin, M. (eds.) EUROCRYPT 2015. LNCS, vol. 9057, pp. 755–784. Springer, Heidelberg (2015). https://doi.org/10.1007/978-3-662-46803-6_25

31. Zhandry, M.: How to construct quantum random functions. In: 2012 IEEE 53rd Annual Symposium on Foundations of Computer Science, pp. 679–687. IEEE (2012)

32. Zhandry, M.: A note on the quantum collision and set equality problems. Quantum Inf. Comput. **15**(7–8), 557–567 (2015)

33. Zhandry, M.: How to record quantum queries, and applications to quantum indifferentiability. In: Boldyreva, A., Micciancio, D. (eds.) CRYPTO 2019. LNCS, vol. 11693, pp. 239–268. Springer, Cham (2019). https://doi.org/10.1007/978-3-030-26951-7_9

Collapseability of Tree Hashes

Aldo Gunsing$^{(\boxtimes)}$ and Bart Mennink

Digital Security Group, Radboud University, Nijmegen, The Netherlands
aldo.gunsing@ru.nl, b.mennink@cs.ru.nl

Abstract. One oft-endeavored security property for cryptographic hash functions is collision resistance: it should be computationally infeasible to find distinct inputs x, x' such that $H(x) = H(x')$, where H is the hash function. Unruh (EUROCRYPT 2016) proposed collapseability as its quantum equivalent. The Merkle-Damgård and sponge hashing modes have recently been proven to be collapseable under the assumption that the underlying primitive is collapseable. These modes are inherently sequential. In this work, we investigate collapseability of tree hashing. We first consider fixed length tree hashing modes, and derive conditions under which their collapseability can be reduced to the collapseability of the underlying compression function. Then, we extend the result to two methods for achieving variable length hashing: tree hashing with domain separation between message and chaining value, and tree hashing with length encoding at the end of the tree. The proofs are performed using the collapseability composability framework of Fehr (TCC 2018), that allows us to discard of deeply technical quantum details and to focus on proper composition of the tree hashes from their compression function.

Keywords: Collapseability · Collision resistance · Tree hashing · Composition

1 Introduction

Hash functions are functions that map arbitrarily long strings, or at least very long strings, to a digest of fixed length. Their introduction dates back to the seminal work of Diffie and Hellman [7] in the context of digital signatures. Nowadays, hash function outgrew their original role: they find thousands of applications in cryptography. These applications all require certain security properties of the hash function. One of these properties is collision resistance: it should be computationally infeasible for an attacker to find two distinct messages with the same hash digest. The notion appeared first in Merkle's PhD thesis [9], and is the leading security property when it comes to breaking hash functions. Well-known hash functions MD5 [11] and SHA-1 [12], and many others, are considered insecure mainly because practical collision attacks were mounted on these (cf. Stevens et al. [15] for MD5 and Stevens et al. [14] for SHA-1). However, finding collisions appears not to be a purely academic exercise: in 2012 the Flame

© Springer Nature Switzerland AG 2020
J. Ding and J.-P. Tillich (Eds.): PQCrypto 2020, LNCS 12100, pp. 524–538, 2020.
https://doi.org/10.1007/978-3-030-44223-1_28

virus exploited collisions in MD5 to act as a properly signed Windows Software Update security patch [13].

When we move to the quantum setting, the classical notion of collision resistance is not strong enough. Unruh [17, Theorem 19] (Theorem 22 in the full version) showed that there is a hash function that is collision resistant and thus can safely be used in a classical commitment scheme, but is not secure when the commitment scheme is used in a quantum setting. We can therefore conclude that, even if a hash function is (classically) collision resistant, it behaves unexpectedly when used in a quantum environment. We need a stronger model in favor of collision resistance.

1.1 Collapseability

Unruh [17] presented collapseability as a quantum equivalent of collision resistance of hash functions. Informally, for cryptographic hash functions, collapseability requires an adversary that outputs a hash value together with a superposition of corresponding preimages is not able to tell if the superposition gets measured or not. We revisit collapseability in Sect. 3, and particularly outline the idea as to why this would be the quantum equivalent of collision resistance in Sect. 3.3.

The model of collapseability has gained traction. In a follow-up work, Unruh [16] proved that the Merkle-Damgård hashing mode [6,10] is collapsing if the compression function is. Later, Czajkowski et al. [5] proved collapseability of the sponge construction [1] if the underlying one-way function is (their work combined independent works of Unruh [18] and Czajkowski et al. [4]). These proofs are, however, quite tedious and technically involved. They require the reader to possess a large amount of quantum knowledge.

In [8], Fehr introduced an alternative framework for collapseability. His definition is more algebraic in nature, whereas that of Unruh is more algorithmic. This allowed Fehr to reason about composability of collapseable functions in a neat and compact way. In more detail, Fehr showed that collapseability is closed under certain compositions, all with very concise proofs. These composability properties make it possible to reason about collapseability from a purely classical view, without requiring quantum knowledge. He applied the approach to the Merkle-Damgård and sponge hash construction, proving that they are collapsing if the underlying compression function is. Therewith, he confirmed the correctness of the earlier results in his new framework.

1.2 Our Contribution

We consider collapseability of tree hashing. We will make full use of Fehr's framework [8] in order to argue what conditions a tree hashing mode must meet in order to be collapseable.

First, in Sect. 4 we consider the basic problem of tree hashing for fixed length messages. For messages of a certain fixed length n, we recursively define a tree hash function TH_n. It is defined based on a split function $split(n) \in \{1, \ldots, n-1\}$

that prescribes how the final digest is derived from two tree hashes $TH_{split(n)}$ and $TH_{n-split(n)}$ applied to the first $split(n)$ and last $n - split(n)$ message blocks.

Then, in Sect. 5, we detail how the result can be extended to variable length hashing using domain separation. In this case, it is assumed that processing of message blocks and chaining values is properly domain-separated in the way the mode calls its compression function. One way in doing so is by appending a 0 to message blocks and a 1 to chaining values. Intuitively, this makes it impossible to replace the chaining value of a subtree with a message block with the same value. We prove that the resulting variable length tree hash function is collapsing. This is done by extending trees with 'empty' blocks in such a way that we can reduce collapseability of the variable length mode to that of the fixed length mode.

Finally, in Sect. 6, we consider a second way to turn the fixed length construction into a variable length hashing mode: length encoding. Here, we allow any tree hashing mode, but the block length of the message will be included by using a final compression function call. This approach makes the final compression functions disjoint for different message lengths, and using previous techniques and the composition results of Fehr, we likewise manage to prove collapseability.

All three collapseability results come with a security bound that expresses the adversarial advantage relative to the collapseability of the underlying compression function, as well as with a complexity analysis of the resulting modes.

1.3   Related Work

One might likewise consider quantum indifferentiability of tree hashing in the framework of Zhandry [19]. We remark, however, that in the classical setting indifferentiability implies collision resistance, but not conversely, and for some applications the weaker property of collision resistance is sufficient. A similar remark applies to the quantum setting, i.e., collapseability is sufficient in many applications such as the simple commitment schemes given by Unruh [17]. In such settings, it is senseless to rely on a stronger property with a more complex security proof and a, likely, weaker security bound.

2   Preliminaries

We will use the following compositions of functions.

- For $g : X \to Y$ and $h : W \to Z$, the *concurrent composition* $g \| h : X \times W \to Y \times Z$ is given by $(x, w) \mapsto (g(x), h(w))$.
- For $g : X \to Y$ and $h : Y \to Z$, the *nested (or sequential) composition* $h \circ g : X \to Z$ is given by $x \mapsto h(g(x))$.
- For $g : X \to Y$ and $h : X \to Z$, the *parallel composition* $(g, h) : X \to Y \times Z$ is given by $x \mapsto (g(x), h(x))$.
- For $g : X \to Y$ and $h : W \to Z$, the *disjoint union* $g \sqcup h : X \cup W \to Y \cup Z$ maps $x \in X$ to $g(x)$ and $w \in W$ to $h(w)$. Furthermore, f and g are required to have disjoint domains and images, so $X \cap W = Y \cap Z = \varnothing$.

Furthermore, we write $S_n = 1 + 2 + \cdots + n = n(n+1)/2$ for the sum of positive integers up to n.

2.1 Qubits and Measurements

Classical computers work with classical bits. These bits can be either a 0 or a 1, but not a combination of both. However, quantum computers work with quantum bits (qubits). These qubits can be just a 0 or 1, but can also be in a state which is a combination of both. A qubit that has a single value is denoted by $|0\rangle$ or $|1\rangle$ (pronounced 'ket 0' and 'ket 1'), for 0 and 1 respectively. However, a qubit can also be a linear combination of both, denoted as $\alpha|0\rangle + \beta|1\rangle$ for some $\alpha, \beta \in \mathbb{C}$ such that $|\alpha|^2 + |\beta|^2 = 1$. This is called a superposition. A superposition can also be written in a single ket. For example, we could define the state $|\phi\rangle = \alpha|0\rangle + \beta|1\rangle$. If a qubit is in a superposition, computations on it are applied to all values at the same time. However, we cannot directly measure the coefficients in the states. We have to do a measurement, which destroys the superposition.

Given a qubit $|\phi\rangle = \alpha|0\rangle + \beta|1\rangle$, we can measure it in the standard computational basis $\{|0\rangle, |1\rangle\}$. Then one of the following happens:

- $|\phi\rangle$ collapses to the state $|0\rangle$ with probability $|\alpha|^2$. We get the result '0'.
- $|\phi\rangle$ collapses to the state $|1\rangle$ with probability $|\beta|^2$. We get the result '1'.

Since $|\alpha|^2 + |\beta|^2 = 1$, exactly one of these happens with probability 1.

In addition to single qubit states, there are also states of multiple qubits. In general a quantum state of dimension n has the form

$$\sum_{i \in \{0,1\}^n} \alpha_i |i\rangle,$$

where $\alpha_i \in \mathbb{C}$ and $\sum_i |\alpha_i|^2 = 1$. For example, we can have the 2-dimensional state

$$\frac{1}{\sqrt{2}}\left(|00\rangle + |11\rangle\right).$$

Measurements happen in a similar way to single qubits. When measured in the standard computational basis $\{\,|i\rangle \mid i \in \{0,1\}^n\,\}$, a state $|\phi\rangle = \sum_i \alpha_i |i\rangle$ collapses to the state $|i\rangle$ with probability $|\alpha_i|^2$. We get the result 'i'.

We can also measure in other bases. This can be any orthonormal basis. The measurements happen in the same way as before, but we have to rewrite our state in the new basis. For example, a popular basis is $\{|+\rangle, |-\rangle\}$ given by

$$|\pm\rangle = \frac{1}{\sqrt{2}}\left(|0\rangle \pm |1\rangle\right).$$

If we want to measure $|0\rangle$ in it, we have to rewrite it as

$$|0\rangle = \frac{1}{2}\left(|0\rangle + |1\rangle\right) + \frac{1}{2}\left(|0\rangle - |1\rangle\right) = \frac{1}{\sqrt{2}}|+\rangle + \frac{1}{\sqrt{2}}|-\rangle.$$

This means that the measurement results in either $|+\rangle$ or $|-\rangle$, both with probability $1/2$.

3   Collapseability

Unruh [17] introduced *collapseability* as the quantum version of classical collision resistance. His definition uses an 'algorithmic' view on collapseability. Later, Fehr [8] introduced a new formalism of collapseability. His new definition uses a more 'algebraic' view, which allows for simpler proofs of some composition results. We will mostly use Fehr's formalism to classically prove that certain tree hash functions are collapsing.

Although most proofs become easier with the more 'algebraic' definition, we present the more 'algorithmic' one given in [17] as it is easier to understand.

Definition 1. *Given a (hash) function H, we play the following game. An adversary $\mathcal{A}$ generates a quantum state $|\phi\rangle = \sum_{x \in X} \alpha_x |x\rangle$ such that $H(x) = c$ for all $x \in X$ for some c. Then, one of the following happens:*

1. *The state $|\phi\rangle$ gets measured in the computational basis.*
2. *The state $|\phi\rangle$ is left untouched.*

The adversary $\mathcal{A}$ does not know which one happened, but it tries to determine it. It returns a bit b, indicating which case it thinks has happened. Its advantage is given by

$$\mathrm{cAdv}[H](\mathcal{A}) = \big| \mathbb{P}[b = 1 : \textit{Case (1)}] - \mathbb{P}[b = 1 : \textit{Case (2)}] \big|.$$

In the remaining of this section, we first look at the query complexity of functions in Sect. 3.1. This allows us to give a definition of collapseability that maximizes over adversaries. Then we look at the composability of collapseability in Sect. 3.2. These lemmas allow us to reason classically about the collapsing advantage. Finally, in Sect. 3.3 we explain why collapseability is a stronger notion than collision resistance.

3.1   Complexity

In order to limit the resources of the adversary, we adopt the notion of complexity from Fehr [8]. Given a function f, we assign it a *complexity* $c(f)$, which is a non-negative integer. We usually normalize the complexity of the compression function as 1. We also assume that this abstract notion satisfies some natural properties. Simple functions like constants, copying, deleting, the identity, etc., have zero complexity. Furthermore, we assume that the complexity function behaves well under compositions, so that

$$c(f \| g) \leqslant c(f) + c(g),$$
$$c(g \circ f) \leqslant c(f) + c(g),$$
$$c(f \sqcup g) \leqslant c(f) + c(g).$$

The final inequality is not mentioned in [8]. However, we will need it in our proofs, and it seems natural to assume. If we were to apply the functions just classically, it seems enough to bound $\mathfrak{c}(f \sqcup g)$ by $\max(\mathfrak{c}(f), \mathfrak{c}(g))$, as every application computes either f or g, but not both. However, since we work with qubits, we also have to account for superpositions. If a qubit is in a superposition consisting of inputs from both domains, we have to compute both functions. This means that its complexity can be $\mathfrak{c}(f) + \mathfrak{c}(g)$.

Given the notion of complexity, we can define the advantage we get when we limit the resources of the adversaries.

Definition 2. *The* collapsing advantage *of H with complexity q is given by*

$$\mathrm{cAdv}[H](q) = \max_{\mathcal{A} \in \mathcal{A}(q)} \mathrm{cAdv}[H](\mathcal{A}),$$

where $\mathcal{A}(q)$ are all adversaries with query complexity q.

We also say that a function H is ε-collapsing if $\mathrm{cAdv}[H](q) \leqslant \varepsilon(q)$.

3.2   Composability of Collapseability

The main advantage of the formalism introduced by Fehr is that some composability results have very concise proofs. The following lemmas are taken from Fehr [8].

Lemma 1 (Concurrent composition). *The concurrent composition $g \| h$ satisfies*

$$\mathrm{cAdv}[g \| h] \leqslant \mathrm{cAdv}[g] + \mathrm{cAdv}[h].$$

Lemma 2 (Nested composition). *The nested (or sequential) composition $h \circ g$ satisfies*

$$\mathrm{cAdv}[h \circ g](q) \leqslant \mathrm{cAdv}[g](q + \mathfrak{c}(g)) + \mathrm{cAdv}[h](q + \mathfrak{c}(g)).$$

Lemma 3 (Parallel composition). *The parallel composition (g, h) satisfies*

$$\mathrm{cAdv}[(g, h)] \leqslant \min(\mathrm{cAdv}[g], \mathrm{cAdv}[h]).$$

Lemma 4 (Disjoint union). *The disjoint union $g \sqcup h$ satisfies*

$$\mathrm{cAdv}[g \sqcup h] \leqslant \mathrm{cAdv}[g] + \mathrm{cAdv}[h].$$

3.3   Collapseability Implies Collision Resistance

We show that collapseability is a stronger notion than collision resistance. Our reasoning is similar to the one of Unruh [17, Lemma 22] (Lemma 25 in the full version), but simplified to only require the basic knowledge of qubits and measurements given in Sect. 2.1.

Suppose one can obtain distinct x, x' with $H(x) = H(x')$. We show how such a collision can be used to break the collapseability of H. As the state in the collapsing game, we choose

$$|\phi\rangle = \frac{1}{\sqrt{2}} \left(|x\rangle + |x'\rangle \right).$$

Now $|\phi\rangle$ may or may not get measured in the computational basis. If it gets measured, it either collapses to $|x\rangle$ or to $|x'\rangle$, both with probability $1/2$. If it does not get measured, it stays the same.

In order for adversary $\mathcal{A}$ to differentiate between the two cases, we measure $|\phi\rangle$ in a modified basis. Almost all basis elements stay the same, but we replace $|x\rangle$ and $|x'\rangle$ with

$$|+_{x,x'}\rangle = \frac{1}{\sqrt{2}}\left(|x\rangle + |x'\rangle\right) \text{ and } |-_{x,x'}\rangle = \frac{1}{\sqrt{2}}\left(|x\rangle - |x'\rangle\right).$$

This is still an orthonormal basis. If $|\phi\rangle$ is not measured, it is equal to $|+_{x,x'}\rangle$, hence the result of the measurement is $|+_{x,x'}\rangle$ with probability 1.

However, if $|\phi\rangle$ is measured, it is either $|x\rangle$ or $|x'\rangle$. We rewrite these in the new basis as

$$|x\rangle = \frac{1}{2}\left(|x\rangle + |x'\rangle\right) + \frac{1}{2}\left(|x\rangle - |x'\rangle\right) = \frac{1}{\sqrt{2}}|+_{x,x'}\rangle + \frac{1}{\sqrt{2}}|-_{x,x'}\rangle,$$

$$|x'\rangle = \frac{1}{2}\left(|x\rangle + |x'\rangle\right) - \frac{1}{2}\left(|x\rangle - |x'\rangle\right) = \frac{1}{\sqrt{2}}|+_{x,x'}\rangle - \frac{1}{\sqrt{2}}|-_{x,x'}\rangle.$$

This means that both $|x\rangle$ and $|x'\rangle$ get measured as either $|+_{x,x'}\rangle$ or $|-_{x,x'}\rangle$, both with probability $1/2$.

The adversary thus operates as follows. If it finds $|+_{x,x'}\rangle$, it concludes that $|\phi\rangle$ was not measured, and if it finds $|-_{x,x'}\rangle$, it concludes that $|\phi\rangle$ was measured. Since it gets the case without measurement always right, and it basically guesses in the case with measurement, its advantage is $1/2$. Hence H is not collapsing.

4   Fixed Length Tree Hashing

Fehr [8] showed that some simple hash constructions like Merkle-Damgård can be proven to be collapsing by only using the composition lemmas of Sect. 3.2. This means that the reasoning in the proofs is just classical, as the hash constructions are broken down as the composition of smaller functions for which the composition lemmas apply. The main technicality moved from actually proving collapseability to describing hash functions as clever compositions of collapseable functions. In this work we investigate tree hashes.

We start with tree hashes of fixed length that can only take a fixed number of blocks and for which the structure is the same for all inputs.

Let $f : \{0,1\}^c \times \{0,1\}^c \to \{0,1\}^c$ be a compression function. We define a tree hashing mode by its splitting points, that is a function $split : \mathbb{N}_{\geq 2} \to \mathbb{N}$. Given a message $x_1, \ldots, x_n$ the parts $x_1, \ldots, x_{split(n)}$ and $x_{split(n)+1}, \ldots, x_n$ are hashed separately and compressed with f. No part can be empty, so $1 \leq split(n) \leq n-1$ for all n. An example is displayed in Fig. 1 with a splitting function such that

$$\begin{aligned} split(5) &= 3, \\ split(3) &= 2, \\ split(2) &= 1. \end{aligned} \tag{1}$$

Note that it is irrelevant for this particular tree what value $split(n)$ takes for $n \notin \{2, 3, 5\}$.

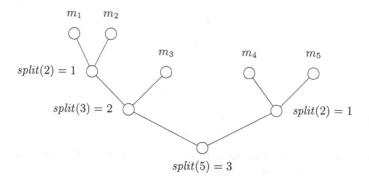

Fig. 1. Tree hash with the split function of (1). The circles with messages m_i represent the message blocks, while the other circles represent calls to the compression function f and their resulting chaining value. The final digest is the result of the compression call of the root.

Likewise, we can express the Merkle-Damgård mode as a tree hash with $split(n) = n - 1$. The example mode of Sakura [2, Section 5.4], which balances the tree very well, can be expressed with $split(n)$ the largest power of 2 smaller than n.

We now define the general tree hashing mode that we will consider in this work.

Definition 3. *Given a compression function* $f : \{0,1\}^c \times \{0,1\}^c \to \{0,1\}^c$ *and a function* $split : \mathbb{N}_{\geq 2} \to \mathbb{N}$, *we recursively define the tree hashes* $TH_n :$ $(\{0,1\}^c)^n \to \{0,1\}^c$ *for* $n \in \mathbb{N}_{\geq 1}$ *as*

$$TH_1(x_1) = x_1,$$
$$TH_n(x_1, \ldots, x_n) = f(TH_k(x_1, \ldots, x_k), TH_{n-k}(x_{k+1}, \ldots, x_n)),$$

where $k = split(n)$. *Note that we can express this definition equivalently using the composition functions defined in Sect. 3.2 as follows:*

$$TH_1 = \mathrm{id},$$
$$TH_n = f \circ (TH_k \| TH_{n-k}).$$

The function TH_n calls the compression function $n - 1$ times. As we normalize the complexity of f as $\mathfrak{c}(f) = 1$, we would expect the complexity of TH_n to be $n - 1$. This is indeed the case.

Lemma 5. *If* f *has complexity* $\mathfrak{c}(f) = 1$, *then* $\mathfrak{c}(TH_n) \leq n - 1$ *for all* n.

Proof. We use strong induction to n. Since we assume the identity has 0 complexity, we get

$$\mathfrak{c}(TH_1) = \mathfrak{c}(\mathrm{id}) = 0.$$

For $n > 1$ we have $TH_n = f \circ (TH_k \| TH_{n-k})$, which means, using the composition properties of the complexity function (See Sect. 3.1), that

$$\begin{aligned}
\mathfrak{c}(TH_n) &= \mathfrak{c}(f \circ (TH_k \| TH_{n-k})) \\
&\leqslant \mathfrak{c}(f) + \mathfrak{c}(TH_k) + \mathfrak{c}(TH_{n-k}) \\
&\leqslant 1 + (k-1) + (n-k-1) = n-1.
\end{aligned}$$
$\square$

We now look at the collapseability of TH_n. As it only accepts a fixed number of blocks, we find that it is collapsing regardless of the *split* function used.

Proposition 1. *If f has complexity $\mathfrak{c}(f) = 1$ and is ε-collapsing, then TH_n is collapsing for all n with advantage*

$$\mathrm{cAdv}[TH_n](q) \leqslant (n-1) \cdot \varepsilon(q + S_{n-2}).$$

Proof. We use strong induction to n. Since the identity has an advantage of 0, we get

$$\mathrm{cAdv}[TH_1](q) = 0.$$

For $n > 1$ we have $TH_n = f \circ (TH_k \| TH_{n-k})$, which means, using nested composition and the fact $\mathfrak{c}(TH_m) = m - 1$ (Lemma 5), that

$$\begin{aligned}
\mathrm{cAdv}[TH_n](q) &\leqslant \mathrm{cAdv}[f]\,(q + \mathfrak{c}\,(TH_k \| TH_{n-k})) \\
&\quad + \mathrm{cAdv}[TH_k \| TH_{n-k}]\,(q + \mathfrak{c}\,(TH_k \| TH_{n-k})) \\
&\leqslant \varepsilon(q + n - 2) + \mathrm{cAdv}[TH_k \| TH_{n-k}](q + n - 2).
\end{aligned}$$

Using concurrent composition and the induction hypothesis, we find that

$$\begin{aligned}
\mathrm{cAdv}[TH_k \| TH_{n-k}](q + n - 2) &\leqslant \mathrm{cAdv}[TH_k](q + n - 2) \\
&\quad + \mathrm{cAdv}[TH_{n-k}](q + n - 2) \\
&\leqslant (k-1) \cdot \varepsilon(q + n - 2 + S_{k-2}) \\
&\quad + (n - k - 1) \cdot \varepsilon(q + n - 2 + S_{n-k-2}).
\end{aligned}$$

Since k and $n - k$ are strictly smaller than n, we have that $n - 2 + S_{k-2}$ and $n - 2 + S_{n-k-2}$ are less or equal to S_{n-2}, which means that

$$\begin{aligned}
\mathrm{cAdv}[TH_k \| TH_{n-k}](q + n - 2) &\leqslant (k-1) \cdot \varepsilon(q + S_{n-2}) \\
&\quad + (n - k - 1) \cdot \varepsilon(q + S_{n-2}) \\
&= (n-2) \cdot \varepsilon(q + S_{n-2}).
\end{aligned}$$

Putting these together, and using that $n - 2 \leqslant S_{n-2}$, we get that

$$\begin{aligned}
\mathrm{cAdv}[TH_n](q) &\leqslant \varepsilon(q + n - 2) + (n-2) \cdot \varepsilon(q + S_{n-2}) \\
&\leqslant (n-1) \cdot \varepsilon(q + S_{n-2}).
\end{aligned}$$
$\square$

5   Variable Length Using Domain Separation

We have seen that any binary tree hash of fixed length is collapsing. However, a hash function has to be able to hash inputs of varying lengths. We cannot just use the tree hash corresponding to the input we got, as this leads to collisions. For example, suppose that we have a big tree hash. We can replace two leaves, that get compressed together to a chaining value CV, by just a single leaf with CV as the message. This is a collision, as the resulting digests of both trees are the same.

One solution to this problem is using domain separation between the message blocks and the chaining values. For example, all message blocks can end with a 0, while the chaining values all end with a 1. We see that this requirement arises naturally when we apply a similar idea as Fehr [8]. He proves Merkle-Damgård secure by limiting the block size of the input to some L. Every smaller message is expanded to a message of size L by prepending 'empty' blocks $\perp$. Then the compression function is modified to also take these 'empty' blocks as input and ignore them. We use a similar strategy where we embed a smaller tree in a larger tree and fill the extra leaves with these 'empty' blocks.

To do so, we define the mapping $\mathrm{Extend}[U](T)$ which takes an unlabeled binary tree U and a labeled binary tree T, such that T is a subtree of U. This means that every node in T has to be a node in U as well, and not a leaf. Then $\mathrm{Extend}[U](T)$ outputs a labeled binary tree with the same structure as U, but with labels based on T. Every leaf of T with value m is mapped to its part in U, with the label m on the leftmost leaf, and the label $\perp$ on all the other leaves. An example is displayed in Fig. 2.

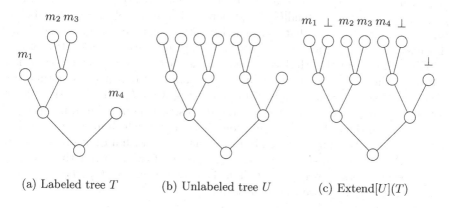

(a) Labeled tree T (b) Unlabeled tree U (c) $\mathrm{Extend}[U](T)$

Fig. 2. Extending a tree. The tree T has to be a subtree of U.

More formally, assume that the tree hashing mode uses domain separation: input blocks can be differentiated from the chaining values. This means that we can identify two disjoint sets $M \subseteq \{0,1\}^c$ and $C = \{0,1\}^c \setminus M$ that cover all message block values and chaining values, respectively. Next, we define three different types of tree hashing modes, with different types of output: a message block in M, a chaining value in C or either one in $\{0,1\}^c$. These functions are defined as $TH_n^M : M_n \to M$, $TH_n^C : C_n \to C$, and $TH_n^X : X_n \to \{0,1\}^c$, where the domains are recursively defined as

$$M_n = M \times \{\bot\}^{n-1},$$
$$C_1 = \varnothing,$$
$$C_n = X_k \times X_{n-k},$$
$$X_n = M_n \sqcup C_n,$$

where $k = split(n)$. Given these domains, we now define the three types of tree hashing modes themselves.

Definition 4. *Given a compression function* $f : \{0,1\}^c \times \{0,1\}^c \to C$ *and a function split* $: \mathbb{N}_{\geq 2} \to \mathbb{N}$, *we recursively define the tree hashes* $TH_n^M : M_n \to M$, $TH_n^C : C_n \to C$ *and* $TH_n^X : X_n \to \{0,1\}^c$ *as*

$$TH_n^M(m, \bot, \ldots, \bot) = m,$$
$$TH_n^C(x_1, \ldots, x_n) = f(TH_k^X(x_1, \ldots, x_k), TH_{n-k}^X(x_{k+1}, \ldots, x_n)),$$
$$TH_n^X = TH_n^M \sqcup TH_n^C,$$

where $k = split(n)$.

Using these functions, we finally define the variable input length function $TH_{\mathrm{dom}}^{\leqslant L} : M^{\leqslant L} \to \{0,1\}^c$ which hashes variable length trees up to length L. Let U, with a size of K blocks, be the smallest tree of which all trees up to length L are a subtree of. $TH_{\mathrm{dom}}^{\leqslant L}$ maps an input $m_1, \ldots, m_n$, to $TH_K^X(x_1, \ldots, x_K)$, where $x_1, \ldots, x_K$ is the tree $\mathrm{Extend}[U](T_n)$, where T_n is the tree of size n with labels of $m_1, \ldots, m_n$. This means that x_i is equal to either some m_j or $\bot$. We can apply this mapping non-ambiguously as every tree up to length L is a subtree of U.

For example, in the Merkle-Damgård construction every tree of size n is a subtree of the tree of size n' if $n \leqslant n'$. This means that U is just the normal tree of size L, hence $K = L$. This is displayed in Fig. 3 for $L = 4$. Note that this is not the case in general. For example in the construction in Sakura, if L is equal to $2^\ell + 1$, then the right branch only contains one leaf, which means that it does not contain the tree for 2^ℓ, which is a full binary tree with a right branch of size $2^{\ell-1}$. However, we can still choose the next power of two as a tree that contains the necessary trees, hence $K \leqslant 2L$. This is displayed in Fig. 4 for $L = 5$.

We are ready to prove the collapseability of $TH_{\mathrm{dom}}^{\leqslant L}$.

Theorem 1. *If* f *has complexity* $\mathfrak{c}(f) = 1$ *and is* ε-*collapsing, then* $TH_{\mathrm{dom}}^{\leqslant L}$ *is collapsing for any* L *with advantage*

$$\mathrm{cAdv}[TH_{\mathrm{dom}}^{\leqslant L}](q) \leqslant (K-1) \cdot \varepsilon(q + S_{K-2}),$$

where K *is the size of the smallest tree of which all the trees up to length* L *are a subtree of. Furthermore, we have that* $L \leqslant K \leqslant S_L$.

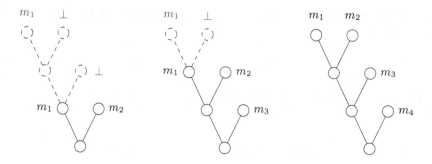

(a) Tree T_2 (solid) and Extend$[U](T_2)$ (dashed).

(b) Tree T_3 (solid) and Extend$[U](T_3)$ (dashed).

(c) Tree T_4, equal to U.

Fig. 3. Hashing variable sized hashes with the Merkle-Damgård mode. U, displayed in Fig. 3c, is the smallest tree structure of which all trees up to length 4 are a subtree of. This tree happens to be the same as the normal Merkle-Damgård construction with $n = 4$.

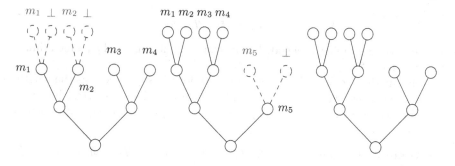

(a) Tree T_4 (solid) and Extend$[U](T_4)$ (dashed).

(b) Tree T_5 (solid) and Extend$[U](T_5)$ (dashed).

(c) Tree U, not equal to any previous tree.

Fig. 4. Hashing variable sized hashes with the example mode of Sakura. The trees up to length 3 are not shown. Tree U, displayed in Fig. 4c, is the smallest tree structure of which all trees up to length 5 are a subtree of. This tree is different from all the constructions up to length 5.

Proof. As the first step, an input $m_1, \ldots, m_n$ is mapped to the extended input $x_1, \ldots, x_K$, on which the tree hash TH_K^X is applied. This mapping is injective, hence 0-collapsing, hence we have to show that

$$\text{cAdv}[TH_K^X](q) \leqslant (K - 1) \cdot \varepsilon(q + S_{K-2}).$$

As TH_n^M is injective, it is 0-collapsing, hence we see that $\text{cAdv}[TH_n^X] = \text{cAdv}[TH_n^C]$ by disjoint union. Furthermore, TH_n^C is defined in almost the same way as TH_n in Definition 3. The only difference is that the recursive call is to TH_k^X instead of itself. However, as the advantage of TH_k^X is the same as that of TH_k^C we can still apply the same proof as in Proposition 1, which gives the desired result.

Furthermore, we look at the value of K, which is the size of the smallest tree U of which all the trees up to length L are a subtree of. First, the tree of size L has to be a subtree of U, which means that its size is at least L, hence $L \leqslant K$. Second, every tree of size n adds at most n leaves to U for all n up to L. This means that its size is at most $1 + 2 + \cdots + L = S_L$, hence $K \leqslant S_L$. □

6   Variable Length Using Length Encoding

We have seen that we can make a variable length tree hash collapsing by using domain separation between the message blocks and the chaining values. However, this method adds some overhead and might not work well with the alignment of the message blocks, as at least a bit has to be added to every block. Another way to allow a variable length input is by using length encoding. Here, the length of the message is used in a final compression call. We define the hash with length encoding $TH_{\text{len}}^{\leqslant L} : (\{0,1\}^c)^{\leqslant L} \to \{0,1\}^c$, which hashes variable length trees up to length L, as

$$TH_{\text{len}}^{\leqslant L}(x_1, \ldots, x_n) = f(\underline{n}, TH_n(x_1, \ldots, x_n)),$$

where $\underline{n}$ is the number n encoded as a binary number in $\{0,1\}^c$, which limits L to be at most 2^c.

This method requires less overhead than domain separation, as the length of the message is added just once. We find that any tree hash with length encoding in a final compression call is collapseable, by applying the composition lemmas on some smaller functions.

Theorem 2. *If f has complexity $\mathsf{c}(f) = 1$ and is ε-collapsing, then $TH_{\text{len}}^{\leqslant L}$ is collapsing for any L with advantage*

$$\mathrm{cAdv}[TH_{\text{len}}^{\leqslant L}](q) \leqslant (S_{L-1} + 1) \cdot \varepsilon(q + (L-1)^2).$$

Proof. Instead of looking at $TH_{\text{len}}^{\leqslant L}$ directly, we build it as the composition of smaller functions. First we define for every $n \in \mathbb{N}$ the function $LTH_n : (\{0,1\}^c)^n \to \{0,1\}^c \times \{0,1\}^c$ as

$$LTH_n(x_1, \ldots, x_n) = (\underline{n}, TH_n(x_1, \ldots, x_n)).$$

Note that we can also write this as $LTH_n = (c_{\underline{n}}, TH_n)$, where $c_{\underline{n}} = x \mapsto \underline{n}$ is the constant function with value $\underline{n}$. By parallel composition we get that

$$\mathrm{cAdv}[LTH_n](q) = \mathrm{cAdv}[TH_n](q) \leqslant (n-1) \cdot \varepsilon(q + S_{n-2}).$$

Let $LTH^{\leqslant L} : (\{0,1\}^c)^{\leqslant L} \to \{0,1\}^c \times \{0,1\}^c$ be

$$LTH^{\leqslant L} = \bigsqcup_{n=1}^{L} LTH_n.$$

Note that the images are disjoint as LTH_n stores $\underline{n}$ in the output, which is different for every n, as long as $L < 2^c$. By disjoint union we get that

$$\mathrm{cAdv}[LTH^{\leqslant L}](q) \leqslant \sum_{n=1}^{L} \mathrm{cAdv}[LTH_n](q)$$
$$\leqslant \sum_{n=1}^{L} (n-1) \cdot \varepsilon(q + S_{n-2})$$
$$\leqslant S_{L-1} \cdot \varepsilon(q + S_{L-2}).$$

For its complexity we have that

$$\mathfrak{c}(LTH^{\leqslant L}) \leqslant \sum_{n=1}^{L} \mathfrak{c}(LTH_n)$$
$$= \sum_{n=1}^{L} \mathfrak{c}(TH_n)$$
$$\leqslant \sum_{n=1}^{L} (n-1)$$
$$= S_{L-1}.$$

Finally we have that $TH_{\mathrm{len}}^{\leqslant L} = f \circ LTH^{\leqslant L}$. Using the facts that $S_{L-1} \leqslant (L-1)^2$ and $S_{L-1} + S_{L-2} = (L-1)^2$ we get

$$\mathrm{cAdv}[TH_{\mathrm{len}}^{\leqslant L}](q) \leqslant \mathrm{cAdv}[f](q + \mathfrak{c}(LTH^{\leqslant L})) + \mathrm{cAdv}[LTH^{\leqslant L}](q + \mathfrak{c}(LTH^{\leqslant L}))$$
$$\leqslant \varepsilon(q + S_{L-1}) + S_{L-1} \cdot \varepsilon(q + S_{L-1} + S_{L-2})$$
$$\leqslant \varepsilon(q + (L-1)^2) + S_{L-1} \cdot \varepsilon(q + (L-1)^2)$$
$$= (S_{L-1} + 1) \cdot \varepsilon(q + (L-1)^2). \qquad \square$$

Acknowledgments. The authors would like to thank Joan Daemen and the anonymous reviewers of PQCrypto for their valuable feedback. Aldo Gunsing is supported by the Netherlands Organisation for Scientific Research (NWO) under TOP grant TOP1.18.002 SCALAR.

References

1. Bertoni, G., Daemen, J., Peeters, M., Van Assche, G.: Sponge functions. In: Ecrypt Hash Workshop, May 2007
2. Bertoni, G., Daemen, J., Peeters, M., Van Assche, G.: Sakura: a flexible coding for tree hashing. In: Boureanu, I., Owesarski, P., Vaudenay, S. (eds.) ACNS 2014. LNCS, vol. 8479, pp. 217–234. Springer, Cham (2014). https://doi.org/10.1007/978-3-319-07536-5_14
3. Brassard, G. (ed.): CRYPTO 1989. LNCS, vol. 435. Springer, New York (1990). https://doi.org/10.1007/0-387-34805-0

4. Czajkowski, J., Groot Bruinderink, L., Hülsing, A., Schaffner, C.: Quantum preimage, 2nd-preimage, and collision resistance of SHA3. Cryptology ePrint Archive, Report 2017/302 (2017)
5. Czajkowski, J., Groot Bruinderink, L., Hülsing, A., Schaffner, C., Unruh, D.: Postquantum security of the sponge construction. In: Lange, T., Steinwandt, R. (eds.) PQCrypto 2018. LNCS, vol. 10786, pp. 185–204. Springer, Cham (2018). https://doi.org/10.1007/978-3-319-79063-3_9
6. Damgård, I.: On the existence of bit commitment schemes and zero-knowledge proofs. In: Brassard [3], pp. 17–27. https://doi.org/10.1007/0-387-34805-0_3
7. Diffie, W., Hellman, M.E.: New directions in cryptography. IEEE Trans. Inf. Theory **22**(6), 644–654 (1976). https://doi.org/10.1109/TIT.1976.1055638
8. Fehr, S.: Classical proofs for the quantum collapsing property of classical hash functions. In: Beimel, A., Dziembowski, S. (eds.) TCC 2018. LNCS, vol. 11240, pp. 315–338. Springer, Cham (2018). https://doi.org/10.1007/978-3-030-03810-6_12
9. Merkle, R.: Secrecy, Authentication, and Public Key Systems. UMI Research Press, Ann Arbor (1979)
10. Merkle, R.C.: One way hash functions and DES. In: Brassard [3], pp. 428–446. https://doi.org/10.1007/0-387-34805-0_40
11. Rivest, R.: The MD5 message-digest algorithm. Request for Comments (RFC) 1321, April 1992. http://tools.ietf.org/html/rfc1321
12. National Institute of Standards and Technology. FIPS 180-4: Secure Hash Standard (SHS). Federal Information Processing Standards Publication 180-4, August 2015
13. Stevens, M.: Counter-cryptanalysis. In: Canetti, R., Garay, J.A. (eds.) CRYPTO 2013. LNCS, vol. 8042, pp. 129–146. Springer, Heidelberg (2013). https://doi.org/10.1007/978-3-642-40041-4_8
14. Stevens, M., Bursztein, E., Karpman, P., Albertini, A., Markov, Y.: The first collision for full SHA-1. In: Katz, J., Shacham, H. (eds.) CRYPTO 2017. LNCS, vol. 10401, pp. 570–596. Springer, Cham (2017). https://doi.org/10.1007/978-3-319-63688-7_19
15. Stevens, M., et al.: Short chosen-prefix collisions for MD5 and the creation of a rogue CA certificate. In: Halevi, S. (ed.) CRYPTO 2009. LNCS, vol. 5677, pp. 55–69. Springer, Heidelberg (2009). https://doi.org/10.1007/978-3-642-03356-8_4
16. Unruh, D.: Collapse-binding quantum commitments without random oracles. In: Cheon, J.H., Takagi, T. (eds.) ASIACRYPT 2016. LNCS, vol. 10032, pp. 166–195. Springer, Heidelberg (2016). https://doi.org/10.1007/978-3-662-53890-6_6
17. Unruh, D.: Computationally binding quantum commitments. In: Fischlin, M., Coron, J.-S. (eds.) EUROCRYPT 2016. LNCS, vol. 9666, pp. 497–527. Springer, Heidelberg (2016). https://doi.org/10.1007/978-3-662-49896-5_18
18. Unruh, D.: Collapsing sponges: post-quantum security of the sponge construction. Cryptology ePrint Archive, Report 2017/282 (2017)
19. Zhandry, M.: How to record quantum queries, and applications to quantum indifferentiability. In: Boldyreva, A., Micciancio, D. (eds.) CRYPTO 2019. LNCS, vol. 11693, pp. 239–268. Springer, Cham (2019). https://doi.org/10.1007/978-3-030-26951-7_9

Encryption Schemes Using Random Oracles: From Classical to Post-Quantum Security

Juliane Krämer and Patrick Struck$^{(\boxtimes)}$

Technische Universität Darmstadt, Darmstadt, Germany
{jkraemer,pstruck}@cdc.tu-darmstadt.de

Abstract. The security proofs of post-quantum cryptographic schemes often consider only classical adversaries. Therefore, whether such schemes are really post-quantum secure remains unknown until the proofs take quantum adversaries into account. Switching to a quantum adversary might require to adapt the security notion. In particular, post-quantum security proofs for schemes which use random oracles have to be in the quantum random oracle model (QROM), while classical security proofs are in the random oracle model (ROM). We remedy this state of affairs by introducing a framework to obtain post-quantum security of public key encryption schemes which use random oracles. We define a class of encryption schemes, called *oracle-simple*, and identify game hops which are used to prove such schemes secure in the ROM. For these game hops, we state both simple and sufficient conditions to validate that a proof also holds in the QROM. The strength of our framework lies in its simplicity, its generality, and its applicability. We demonstrate this by applying it to the code-based encryption scheme ROLLO-II (Round 2 NIST candidate) and the lattice-based encryption scheme LARA (FC 2019). Thereby we prove that both schemes are post-quantum secure, which had not been shown before.

Keywords: QROM · Game-based proofs · Code-based cryptography · Lattice-based cryptography

1 Introduction

Relying on quantum-hard mathematical assumptions is not sufficient to develop cryptographic schemes that withstand attackers with quantum computing power. To truly provide security against quantum adversaries, their quantum computing power has to be considered in the security proof as well. At least three models regarding the quantum computing power of the adversary and the schemes' users are distinguished [13]: classical security, post-quantum security, and quantum security. In classical security proofs no one has quantum computing power. In post-quantum security proofs, by contrast, the adversary has quantum computing power and can thereby deploy quantum computation in its attacks, e.g., by evaluating hash functions in superposition. The users of the cryptographic scheme, however, remain classical. In a world where every party has quantum

© Springer Nature Switzerland AG 2020
J. Ding and J.-P. Tillich (Eds.): PQCrypto 2020, LNCS 12100, pp. 539–558, 2020.
https://doi.org/10.1007/978-3-030-44223-1_29

computing power, quantum security is needed. In this model, for instance, a quantum adversary is able to query a decryption oracle in superposition.

Post-quantum security of schemes is mandatory to be deployed in a world with large quantum computers. Hence, if only classical proofs exist, it has to be evaluated if these translate to a quantum adversary, i.e., whether the classical security can be lifted to post-quantum security. This is not always the case [9,24]. For cryptographic schemes which are proven secure in the random oracle model (ROM), this entails that they have to be proven secure in the quantum random oracle model (QROM) [9]. In this model, the adversary can query the random oracle in superposition. This requires different proof techniques to cope with the additional power of the adversary.

A popular technique to prove security of a cryptographic scheme is to organise the proof as a sequence of games [7,23]. In a game-based proof, the advantage of an adversary $\mathcal{A}$ in a game G_0 can be bound by its advantage to distinguish the real game G_0 from an ideal game G_k in which the adversary has no advantage. To this end, several intermediate games $G_1, \ldots, G_{k-1}$ are constructed between G_0 and G_k so that the change between successive games is small. This makes the advantage to distinguish each pair of consecutive games, i.e., each game hop, easier to analyse and allows to upper bound the overall advantage of $\mathcal{A}$ by the sum of these advantages. To lift a classical game-based proof to post-quantum security, an adversary with quantum computing power has to be considered and the classical games have to be replaced by their corresponding post-quantum versions.

In this work, we study under which conditions security proofs of public key encryption (PKE) schemes can be lifted from the ROM in the QROM. The security notion we are considering is *indistinguishability under chosen-plaintext attacks* (IND-CPA), a basic security notion for PKE schemes. Intuitively, an encryption scheme is IND-CPA-secure if an adversary can not distinguish between the encryption of two adversarial chosen messages. More precisely, we study how classical IND-CPA security proofs in the ROM can be lifted to post-quantum IND-CPA (pq-IND-CPA), where the adversary can query the random oracle in superposition (QROM) [13].

1.1 Our Contribution

The contribution of this work is a method to prove IND-CPA-secure encryption schemes pq-IND-CPA-secure. We define a class of public key encryption schemes, called oracle-simple, and develop a framework to lift the security of such schemes from the ROM to the QROM. To this end, we define two different types of game hops and state simple, easily checkable conditions such that the classical proof can be lifted against quantum adversaries. Each PKE scheme which can be proven IND-CPA-secure in this framework thereby is automatically post-quantum secure. Due to its simplicity we expect the framework to be helpful when designing post-quantum secure encryption schemes. Another important aspect is that our framework is generic and not restricted to a certain family of post-quantum cryptography, e.g., lattice-based cryptography.

We demonstrate the value of our framework by applying it to two public key encryption schemes, which until this work were not known to be post-quantum secure: (1) the code-based encryption scheme ROLLO-II [20] and (2) the lattice-based encryption scheme LARA [4].

Two more schemes which can be proven post-quantum secure using our framework are the code-based encryption scheme BigQuake [5] and the lattice-based encryption scheme LIMA [1][1], both Round 1 NIST candidates. Applying our framework to these schemes is very much akin to the application to ROLLO-II and LARA, which is why we omit it. To the best of our knowledge, our framework covers all random-oracle-based encryption schemes submitted to NIST [1,4,5,20] and, in particular, we are not aware of any random-oracle-based encryption scheme which is not covered by it.

To obtain classical security against chosen-ciphertext attacks (CCA), all these schemes rely on generic transformations like the FO-transformation [12]. The pq-IND-CPA security of the schemes is the final requirement for applying the post-quantum variants of this transformation [15,25], i.e., to gain CCA security against quantum adversaries. More recent results of post-quantum secure FO-transformations [17,22] achieve tighter bounds for CCA security at the cost of an additional property called *disjoint simulatability*. Intuitively, this means that there exists a simulator, knowing merely the public key, that can generate fake ciphertexts that are indistinguishable from real ciphertexts of random messages. Showing this property for the concrete schemes ROLLO-II and LARA is beyond the scope of this work.

1.2   Related Work

Song [24] provides a general framework to lift security reductions. However, the main limitation is that the applicability is restricted to the scenario in which the classical security notion holds true even for quantum adversaries, e.g., in the standard model. This restrains the usage of the framework for any proofs in the ROM, since post-quantum security proofs have to be in the QROM. If the security notion changes towards a quantum adversary, applying the framework requires to come up with a quantum proof. That is, one has to transform a quantum adversary in the QROM into a quantum adversary in the ROM.

For signature schemes, there exist results to obtain post-quantum security in the QROM. Along with the introduction of the QROM, Boneh et al. [9] present the concept of history-free reductions for signature schemes proven secure in the ROM. They show that history-free reductions provide post-quantum security for signature schemes in the QROM. Since the known ROM proofs for Fiat-Shamir signatures are not history-free, several works study their post-quantum security and identify specific properties of Fiat-Shamir signatures such that schemes with these properties are post-quantum secure in the QROM, e.g., [10,11,18,19,27].

---

[1] We note that the IND-CPA security of LIMA can also be proven in the standard model. This makes its pq-IND-CPA security somewhat trivial, as it avoids the main challenge, that is, the switch from the ROM to the QROM.

Others, for instance Alkim et al. [2] for the signature scheme qTESLA, prove post-quantum security directly. Hence, the question whether or not classical security proofs for signature schemes can be lifted to post-quantum security is discussed both with and without random oracles.

For encryption schemes, however, no broad analysis of liftable security proofs in the QROM exists. Zhandry [28] shows that quantum random oracles can be simulated using q-wise independent functions, thereby removing the additional assumption required in the proofs by Boneh et al. [9]. In addition, Zhandry shows how the classical random oracle technique of challenge injection can be restored in the quantum setting using so-called semi-constant distributions. With these results several cryptographic schemes, including identity-based encryption schemes, are proven secure against quantum adversaries. Unruh [26] develops the one-way to hiding (O2H) lemma, another proof technique in the QROM. The O2H lemma is used, for instance, by Targhi and Unruh [25] to prove a slight modification of the FO transformation [12] indistinguishable against chosen-ciphertext attacks in the QROM. Tighter bounds for the O2H lemma have been proposed by Ambainis et al. [3] and Bindel et al. [8] at the cost of a more restricted applicability.

1.3   Organization of the Paper

The rest of this paper is organized as follows. In Sect. 2, we provide the notation and the necessary background on both the quantum random oracle model and security proofs. In Sect. 3, we present our framework and show under which conditions a classical security proof in the ROM can be lifted to the QROM. Finally, we apply our framework to the code-based scheme ROLLO-II and the lattice-based scheme LARA in Sect. 4 and thereby reveal that their IND-CPA security proofs remain valid towards a quantum adversary.

2   Preliminaries

2.1   Notation

For a non-negative integer n we denote the set $\{1, \ldots, n\}$ by $[n]$. The domain and co-domain of a function f are denoted by $\mathsf{Dom}(f)$ and $\mathsf{CoDom}(f)$, respectively. A function f is called negligible if $f(n) < 1/n^c$ for any $c > 0$ and sufficiently large n. For a set $\mathcal{S}$, we write $s \leftarrow_\$ \mathcal{S}$ to denote that a value which is sampled uniformly at random from $\mathcal{S}$ is assigned to s. By $|\mathcal{S}|$ we describe the number of elements in $\mathcal{S}$. We write $\mathcal{A}_z = (\mathcal{M}_z, \mathcal{D}_z)$ to denote an IND-CPA adversary $\mathcal{A}_z$ which consists of two algorithms $\mathcal{M}_z$, the message generator which outputs two messages, and $\mathcal{D}_z$, the distinguisher, which outputs a bit. The subscript z indicates whether the adversary is classical ($z = c$) or quantum ($z = q$). We omit it in the case it is not relevant. It is assumed that $\mathcal{M}_z$ and $\mathcal{D}_z$ share state.

We suppose the reader to be familiar with the fundamental basics of quantum computation, e.g., the ket notation $|\cdot\rangle$ and measurements. For a more thorough discussion of the topic, we refer to [21].

2.2 The Quantum Random Oracle Model

The random oracle model (ROM), formalized by Bellare and Rogaway [6], is a commonly used model to prove cryptographic schemes secure. In the ROM, all parties have access to a random oracle H which, upon being queried on a value x, returns a random value y. Every further query of x, for instance by another party, is answered using the same y as before. When a scheme is proven secure in the ROM, one idealises components like hash functions by a random oracle. Given that the code of a hash function is publicly available, one has to assume that a quantum adversary implements hash functions on its quantum computer, thereby being able to evaluate it in superposition. This assumption gives rise to the quantum random oracle model (QROM), which has been advocated by Boneh et al. [9]. In the QROM, parties which have quantum computing power are allowed to query the random oracle in superposition. In more detail, for a random oracle H, the QROM allows these parties access to the quantum random oracle $|H\rangle$, where $|H\rangle : |x, y\rangle \mapsto |x, y \oplus H(x)\rangle$. To prove a scheme post-quantum secure, the proof should always be in the QROM, as a proof in the ROM would imply the unrealistic expectation that the adversary refrains from implementing a hash function on its quantum computer. We use superscripts to denote oracle access, e.g., $\mathcal{A}^H$ and $\mathcal{A}^{|H\rangle}$ for the ROM and QROM, respectively.

In our proofs we also consider reprogrammed random oracles. For a random oracle H, we denote the random oracle which is reprogrammed on input x to y by $H_{x \to y}$, i.e.,

$$H_{x \to y}(a) = \begin{cases} y & \text{, if } a = x \\ H(a) & \text{, else} \end{cases}.$$

Below we recall some results we use in our framework. We start with the one-way to hiding (O2H) lemma by Unruh [26], albeit using the reformulation by Ambainis et al. [3] adapted to our case.

Lemma 1 (One-way to hiding (O2H) [3]). *Let* G, H: $\mathcal{X} \to \mathcal{Y}$ *be random functions, let z be a random bitstring, and let $\mathcal{S} \subset \mathcal{X}$ be a random set such that $\forall x \notin \mathcal{S}$, $G(x) = H(x)$. $(G, H, \mathcal{S}, z)$ may have arbitrary joint distribution. Furthermore, let $\mathcal{A}_q^{|H\rangle}$ be a quantum oracle algorithm which queries $|H\rangle$ at most q times. Define an oracle algorithm $\mathcal{B}_q^{|H\rangle}$ as follows: Pick $i \leftarrow_\$ [q]$. Run $\mathcal{A}_q^{|H\rangle}(z)$ until just before its i-th query to $|H\rangle$. Measure the query in the computational basis, and output the measurement outcome. Let*

$$P_{left} := \Pr[\mathcal{A}_q^{|H\rangle}(z) \Rightarrow 1]$$
$$P_{right} := \Pr[\mathcal{A}_q^{|G\rangle}(z) \Rightarrow 1]$$
$$P_{guess} := \Pr[x \in \mathcal{S} \mid \mathcal{B}_q^{|H\rangle}(z) \Rightarrow x].$$

Then it holds that

$$|P_{left} - P_{right}| \leq 2q\sqrt{P_{guess}}.$$

The same result holds with $\mathcal{B}_q^{|G\rangle}(z)$ instead of $\mathcal{B}_q^{|H\rangle}(z)$ in the definition of P_{guess}.

Bindel et al. [8] developed another variant of the O2H lemma, called double-sided O2H, which is based on the *compressed oracle framework* by Zhandry [29]. It leads to a tighter bound, namely by dropping the factor q. This comes at the cost of requiring two additional properties. First, the simulator $\mathcal{B}_q$ has to be able to simulate both random oracles and, second, the random oracles have to agree on all but one input. To apply the lemma in this work, we only need to show that the two aforementioned properties are satisfied. For a concrete description of the algorithm $\mathcal{B}_q$, we refer to [8].

Lemma 2 (Double-sided O2H (adapted from [8])). *Let* G, H: $\mathcal{X} \to \mathcal{Y}$ *be random functions, let* z *be a random bitstring, and let* $x_0 \in \mathcal{X}$ *be a random value such that* $\forall x \neq x_0$, $G(x) = H(x)$. *(G, H, x_0, z) may have arbitrary joint distribution. Let* $\mathcal{A}_q^{|H\rangle}$ *be a quantum oracle algorithm. There exists another quantum oracle algorithm* $\mathcal{B}_q^{|G\rangle,|H\rangle}(z)$ *which returns either* x_0 *or a failure symbol* $\perp$. $\mathcal{B}_q$ *runs in about the same amount of time as* $\mathcal{A}_q$, *but when* $\mathcal{A}_q$ *queries* $|H\rangle$, $\mathcal{B}_q$ *queries both* $|G\rangle$ *and* $|H\rangle$. *Let*

$$P_{left} := \Pr[\mathcal{A}_q^{|H\rangle}(z) \Rightarrow 1]$$
$$P_{right} := \Pr[\mathcal{A}_q^{|G\rangle}(z) \Rightarrow 1]$$
$$P_{extract} := \Pr[x = x_0 \,|\, \mathcal{B}_q^{|H\rangle,|G\rangle}(z) \Rightarrow x].$$

Then it holds that

$$|P_{left} - P_{right}| \leq 2\sqrt{P_{extract}} \,.$$

We will use the O2H lemma in the following way. Suppose we have two games G_0 and G_1 which are identical except for the random oracles that the adversary has access to. Namely, in G_0 it has access to $|H\rangle$ while in G_1 it has access to $|H'\rangle$. The advantage of the adversary in distinguishing the games is bound by its advantage in distinguishing the random oracles $|H\rangle$ and $|H'\rangle$, which, in turn, can be bound by the O2H lemma.

Next we state a lemma which bounds the probability of a quantum algorithm in finding marked items in a function. On a high level, a quantum adversary is given superposition access to a function $\mathcal{F}$ which maps a randomly chosen input to 1 (the marked item) while all other inputs are mapped to 0. The goal of the adversary is to find the input that is mapped to 1.

Lemma 3 (adapted from [16]). *Let* $x_0 \leftarrow_\$ \mathcal{X}$ *and* $\mathcal{F} \colon \mathcal{X} \to \{0,1\}$, *such that*

$$\mathcal{F}(x) = \begin{cases} 1 & , \text{ if } x = x_0 \\ 0 & , \text{ else} \end{cases}.$$

Then for any quantum adversary $\mathcal{A}_q$, *making at most* q *(superposition) queries to* $\mathcal{F}$, *it holds that*

$$\Pr[\mathcal{F}(x) = 1 \,|\, \mathcal{A}_q^{|\mathcal{F}\rangle}() \Rightarrow x] \leq \frac{8(q+1)^2}{|\mathcal{X}|} \,.$$

2.3 Security Proofs

We use game-based proofs following [7,23], where an adversary plays a game which eventually outputs a bit indicating whether the adversary has won the game or not. Let G_0, G_1 be games and $\mathcal{A}$ be an adversary. We write $G_0^{\mathcal{A}} \Rightarrow v$ to indicate that the game G_0 outputs v when interacting with $\mathcal{A}$. The *game advantage* between the games G_0 and G_1 is defined as:

$$\mathbf{Adv}\left(G_0^{\mathcal{A}}, G_1^{\mathcal{A}}\right) := \Pr[G_0^{\mathcal{A}} \Rightarrow \mathrm{true}] - \Pr[G_1^{\mathcal{A}} \Rightarrow \mathrm{true}].$$

Whether a game G is in the ROM or the QROM is implicitly defined by the adversary playing the game. That is, $G^{\mathcal{A}_c}$ is in the ROM while $G^{\mathcal{A}_q}$ is in the QROM.

A public key encryption (PKE) scheme $E = (\mathsf{KGen}, \mathsf{Enc}, \mathsf{Dec})$ is a triple of algorithms KGen, Enc, and Dec. KGen outputs a key pair $(\mathsf{pk}, \mathsf{sk})$. The input to Enc is a public key pk and a message m, the output is a ciphertext c. The algorithm Dec, on input a secret key sk and a ciphertext c, outputs a message m. We are interested in PKE schemes which use random oracles. Thus we write Enc^H and Dec^H to denote that both Enc and Dec have oracle access to H.[2]

A basic security notion for encryption schemes is *indistinguishability under chosen plaintext attacks* (IND-CPA) which asks an adversary to distinguish between the encryption of two adversarial chosen messages. Below we formally define the corresponding post-quantum security notion pq-IND-CPA for public key encryption schemes which use random oracles. Note that only the random oracle access changes towards the post-quantum security. Both the inputs and outputs of the adversary (i.e., public key, messages, ciphertexts, and output bit) remain classical in both cases.

Definition 4. *Let* $E = (\mathsf{KGen}, \mathsf{Enc}^H, \mathsf{Dec}^H)$ *be a PKE scheme and let the game* pq-IND-CPA *be defined as in Fig. 1. Then for any adversary* $\mathcal{A}$ *its* pq-IND-CPA *advantages is defined as:*

$$\mathbf{Adv}_E^{\mathsf{pq\text{-}IND\text{-}CPA}}(\mathcal{A}) := 2\Pr\left[\mathsf{pq\text{-}IND\text{-}CPA}^{\mathcal{A}} \Rightarrow \mathrm{true}\right] - 1.$$

We say that $E = (\mathsf{KGen}, \mathsf{Enc}^H, \mathsf{Dec}^H)$ *is* pq-IND-CPA-*secure if* $\mathbf{Adv}_E^{\mathsf{pq\text{-}IND\text{-}CPA}}(\mathcal{A})$ *is negligible. Classical security is defined analogously using game* IND-CPA.

The hardness of a problem P is defined by a game between a challenger and an adversary. In a decisional problem, an adversary obtains a problem instance depending on some secret bit $b \in \{0,1\}$ chosen by the challenger, and is asked to determine b. In a search problem, an adversary obtains a problem instance depending on some secret s chosen by the challenger, and is asked to find s.

---

[2] We do not allow the key generation algorithm access to the random oracle as we are not aware of any scheme which requires it. Besides, proving the resulting game hop would be trivial as in case KGen has access to the random oracle, the adversary gets access to the random oracle only after receiving the public key. Hence, the reduction can trivially reprogram the random oracle unnoticeable for the adversary.

IND-CPA	pq-IND-CPA
$b \leftarrow_\$ \{0,1\}$	$b \leftarrow_\$ \{0,1\}$
$(\mathsf{pk},\mathsf{sk}) \leftarrow_\$ \mathsf{KGen}()$	$(\mathsf{pk},\mathsf{sk}) \leftarrow_\$ \mathsf{KGen}()$
$m_0, m_1 \leftarrow_\$ \mathcal{M}_c^H(\mathsf{pk})$	$m_0, m_1 \leftarrow_\$ \mathcal{M}_q^{|H\rangle}(\mathsf{pk})$
$c \leftarrow_\$ \mathsf{Enc}^H(\mathsf{pk}, m_b)$	$c \leftarrow_\$ \mathsf{Enc}^H(\mathsf{pk}, m_b)$
$b' \leftarrow_\$ \mathcal{D}_c^H(\mathsf{pk}, c)$	$b' \leftarrow_\$ \mathcal{D}_q^{|H\rangle}(\mathsf{pk}, c)$
return $(b' = b)$	**return** $(b' = b)$

Fig. 1. Classical (IND-CPA) and post-quantum (pq-IND-CPA) security games for a public key encryption scheme $\mathrm{E} = (\mathsf{KGen}, \mathsf{Enc}^H, \mathsf{Dec}^H)$ against a classical adversary $\mathcal{A}_c = (\mathcal{M}_c, \mathcal{D}_c)$ and a quantum adversary $\mathcal{A}_q = (\mathcal{M}_q, \mathcal{D}_q)$, respectively, where $\mathcal{M}$ (*message generator*) and $\mathcal{D}$ (*distinguisher*) implicitly share state.

Against quantum adversaries, the games remain the same, i.e., the challenge and the solution remain classical, but the adversary can use local quantum computing power. Similar to the definition above, we write $\mathbf{Adv}^P(\mathcal{A})$ for the advantage of an adversary $\mathcal{A}$ in solving problem P. For a decisional problem, it is understood to be the advantage in solving the problem over guessing. There are also works which analyse problems in the fully quantum setting, where the challenge is quantum (cf. [14]).

3 The pq-IND-CPA Framework

Within this section we develop our framework to lift classical security proofs in the post-quantum setting. To this end, we first define a class of encryption schemes in Sect. 3.1 and identify two types of game hops for this class of encryption schemes in Sect. 3.2. In Sect. 3.3, we show under which conditions the classical proofs for these game hops hold true against quantum adversaries in the QROM.

3.1 Requirements for PKE Schemes

We start by defining so-called *oracle-simple* public key encryption schemes. These are encryption schemes where the encryption algorithm invokes the random oracle exactly once on an input independent of the message and the public key.[3] Below we formally define such schemes.

Definition 5. *Let* $\mathrm{E} = (\mathsf{KGen}, \mathsf{Enc}^H, \mathsf{Dec}^H)$ *be a public key encryption scheme. If there exists an algorithm* Enc-Sub *and a deterministic function* f *which maps*

---

[3] This property is required to get a meaningful bound from applying the one-way to hiding lemma. Since we are not aware of any PKE scheme which does not satisfy this requirement, we do not consider it a restriction.

from some set $\mathcal{R}$ to $\mathsf{Dom}(\mathsf{H})$ such that $\mathsf{Enc}^{\mathsf{H}}$ can be written as in Fig. 2, i.e., it first invokes the random oracle on $\mathsf{f}(r)$ for a random $r \in \mathcal{R}$ to obtain y and then computes the ciphertext using $\mathsf{Enc\text{-}Sub}(\mathsf{pk}, m, r, y)$, then we call E an oracle-simple (public key) encryption scheme with function f.

$$\boxed{\begin{array}{l} \mathsf{Enc}^{\mathsf{H}}(\mathsf{pk}, m) \\ \hline r \leftarrow_{\$} \mathcal{R} \\ x \leftarrow \mathsf{f}(r) \\ y \leftarrow \mathsf{H}(x) \\ c \leftarrow_{\$} \mathsf{Enc\text{-}Sub}(\mathsf{pk}, m, r, y) \\ \textbf{return } c \end{array}}$$

Fig. 2. Algorithm Enc of an oracle-simple encryption scheme using f and $\mathsf{Enc\text{-}Sub}$.

Based on this definition, we can rewrite the IND-CPA and pq-IND-CPA security games for oracle-simple encryption schemes yielding the security games displayed in Fig. 3.

Since our framework is based on oracle-simple encryption schemes, its generality depends on the generality of this class of encryption schemes. Analysing all encryption schemes submitted as Round 1 NIST candidates which use random oracles [1,4,5,20], reveals that all of them are indeed oracle-simple schemes. Note that this analysis is based on the underlying encryption scheme as all candidates use random oracles when applying generic transformations to achieve CCA security. Thus, we see this as a style of notation which greatly simplifies the presentation of our proofs, rather than a restriction of its generality.

3.2   Identification of Game Hops

Within this section we define two different types of game hops which are used to prove security of oracle-simple encryption schemes. Due to the structure of oracle-simple encryption schemes, we can distinguish between game hops for which lifting is rather trivial since they are independent of the random oracle, and game hops which are not independent of the random oracle. We start by defining a Type-I game hop which is independent of the random oracle.

Definition 6. *Let G_i and G_{i+1} be two IND-CPA games (cf. Fig. 3) for an oracle-simple public key encryption scheme $\mathsf{E} = (\mathsf{KGen}, \mathsf{Enc}^{\mathsf{H}}, \mathsf{Dec}^{\mathsf{H}})$. We call the game hop between G_i and G_{i+1} a Type-I game hop if the games only differ in using different algorithms KGen to generate the key pair or different algorithms $\mathsf{Enc\text{-}Sub}$ to generate the ciphertext.*

Next, we define a Type-II game hop which affects the usage of the random oracle while encrypting one of the challenge messages by the adversary.

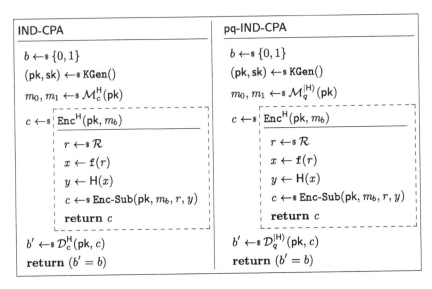

Fig. 3. Security games IND-CPA and pq-IND-CPA for an *oracle-simple* public key encryption scheme $E = (\text{KGen}, \text{Enc}^H, \text{Dec}^H)$ with function f.

Definition 7. *Let G_i and G_{i+1} be two IND-CPA games (cf. Fig. 3) for an oracle-simple public key encryption scheme $E = (\text{KGen}, \text{Enc}^H, \text{Dec}^H)$. We call the game hop between G_i and G_{i+1} a Type-II game hop if their only difference is that game G_i obtains y by invoking H on x while game G_{i+1} samples y uniformly at random from $\text{CoDom}(H)$.*

Having discussed the generality of the class of encryption schemes, the next natural question asks for the generality of the defined game hops. A Type-II game hop is a standard game hop to make the challenge independent of the random oracle, thereby rendering it obsolete for the adversary. As for Type-I game hops, we observe the following. To bound the game advantage, one transforms an adversary that distinguishes the games into an adversary (the reduction) that solves some problem. To achieve this, the game hop has to be connected with the problem instance. Thus the reduction has to feed the problem instance to the adversary. Considering IND-CPA security, its options are fairly limited. Either it feeds it via the inputs to the adversary, that is the public key pk or the ciphertext c, or as a response from the random oracle. The former case is the one we cover with a Type-I game hop. The latter case is not covered, as none of the schemes, that we are aware of, requires such a game hop. Nevertheless, we emphasise that our framework can be easily extended by another type of game hop, if needed. The post-quantum analogue of such a challenge injection in a random oracle response can be achieved using Zhandry's semi-constant distributions [28], where a challenge is injected in a subset of inputs which gives a significant chance that the adversary uses the injected challenge while the probability of detecting the challenge injection remains small enough.

3.3 Lifting Security

Within this section we state the conditions under which a classical security proof holds true in the post-quantum setting. We present one lemma to lift Type-I game hops and two lemmas for lifting Type-II game hops, one being a special case of the other.

The lemma below states that classical reductions from a decisional problem to the game advantage of a Type-I game hop hold true in the post-quantum setting.

Lemma 8. *Let* G_i *and* G_{i+1} *be games such that the game hop between these is a* Type-I *game hop. Suppose there exists a decisional problem* P *which is reduced to the game advantage between the games. Then, for any quantum adversary* $\mathcal{A}_q$, *there exists a quantum adversary* $\mathcal{B}_q$ *against* P *such that*

$$\mathbf{Adv}\left(G_i^{\mathcal{A}_q}, G_{i+1}^{\mathcal{A}_q}\right) \leq \mathbf{Adv}^P(\mathcal{B}_q).$$

Proof. The difference between the games is independent from the random oracle. Hence the same proof holds against quantum adversaries, albeit the adversary $\mathcal{B}_q$ has to simulate a quantum random oracle for the adversary $\mathcal{A}_q$. This can be done using a $2q_H$-wise independent function, where q_H is the number of random oracle queries by $\mathcal{A}_q$ [28]. □

Alternatively, Lemma 8 can be formally proven using the framework by Song [24]. Due to the complex notation used in [24], however, this leads to a rather long and tedious proof.

The following lemma states conditions under which the classical proof for a Type-II game hop holds true against quantum adversaries. Recall that we consider oracle-simple encryption schemes with function f. For an arbitrary function f, we can not argue about the distribution of the value that is queried to the random oracle. This prevents us to use known results like finding marked items in a function, as we do when proving a special case of the lemma.

Lemma 9. *Let* G_i *and* G_{i+1} *be games such that the game hop between these is a* Type-II *game hop. Suppose there exists a search problem* P *which is reduced to the probability that an adversary queries the random oracle on* x. *Then, for any quantum adversary* $\mathcal{A}_q$, *making* q_H *queries to* $|H\rangle$, *there exists a quantum adversary* $\mathcal{C}_q$ *against* P *such that*

$$\mathbf{Adv}\left(G_i^{\mathcal{A}_q}, G_{i+1}^{\mathcal{A}_q}\right) \leq 2q_H\sqrt{\mathbf{Adv}^P(\mathcal{C}_q)}.$$

Proof. We observe that the games G_i and G_{i+1} are perfectly indistinguishable given that $\mathcal{A}$ has no knowledge about the random oracle output on x, that is, $H(x)$. Hence the game advantage can be bound by the knowledge of $\mathcal{A}$ about $H(x)$. For the classical proof in the ROM, this is fairly easy as the only way for the adversary to obtain knowledge about $H(x)$ is to query x. For the post-quantum proof in the QROM, the issue is that, for example, superposition access allows the adversary to trivially get (some) knowledge about $H(x)$ by making an equal superposition query over all possible inputs. If the distribution of x is uniform, this issue can be tackled using existing results on finding marked items in a random function. For oracle-simple encryption schemes, however, the distribution of x depends on the function f. Hence, for an arbitrary function f, we can not argue using the distribution of x.

We tackle this issue as follows. First, we show that the game advantage is bound by the distinguishing advantage between two random oracles, see Eq. (1). This enables us to apply the O2H lemma as the second step, see Eq. (2). In the final step, we bound the resulting term from the O2H lemma using the hardness of P, see Eq. (3).

Recall that the games differ in how the value y (input to Enc-Sub) is generated. In G_i it is the output of the random oracle on input x while it is sampled uniformly at random from $\mathsf{CoDom}(H)$ in G_{i+1}. By the random oracle paradigm, the value y is distributed identically in both games, as is the ciphertext c. Based on this, we conclude that the only inconsistency lies in the random oracle. Namely, querying the random oracle on x yields the same y which is fed as input to Enc-Sub in G_i, while it yields a random value independent of the inputs to Enc-Sub in G_{i+1}. This allows us to see G_{i+1} as G_i, that is $y \leftarrow H(x)$, with the exception that the random oracle H, which $\mathcal{A}$ has access to, is replaced with $H_{x\to\$}$. Based on this thought, it is easy to see that the game advantage is bound by the chance that $\mathcal{A}$ can distinguish between the two random oracles H and $H_{x\to\$}$. The same argument holds for a quantum adversary $\mathcal{A}_q$ except that access to the corresponding quantum random oracles $|H\rangle$ and $|H_{x\to\$}\rangle$ is granted. For ease of notation, we henceforth assume that the random oracle is reprogrammed to $\perp$ instead of a random value. Then it holds that

$$\mathbf{Adv}\left(G_i^{\mathcal{A}_q}, G_{i+1}^{\mathcal{A}_q}\right) \leq \left|\Pr[\mathcal{A}_q^{|H\rangle} \Rightarrow 1] - \Pr[\mathcal{A}_q^{|H_{x\to\perp}\rangle} \Rightarrow 1]\right|. \tag{1}$$

Applying the O2H lemma (cf. Lemma 1) yields that there exists a quantum algorithm $\mathcal{B}_q$ such that

$$\left|\Pr[\mathcal{A}_q^{|H\rangle} \Rightarrow 1] - \Pr[\mathcal{A}_q^{|H_{x\to\perp}\rangle} \Rightarrow 1]\right| \leq 2q_H \sqrt{\Pr[\mathcal{B}_q^{|H\rangle} \Rightarrow x]}. \tag{2}$$

It remains to bound the probability that $\mathcal{B}_q$ outputs x. At this point we use the classical security proof, that is, the problem P is reduced to the probability of querying x. It holds that the solution for P is x or can be derived from it, thus $\mathcal{B}_q$ can be transformed into an adversary $\mathcal{C}_q$ against P. The mere difference is that this adversary $\mathcal{C}_q$ is quantum, as $\mathcal{B}_q$ is quantum. Hence, we conclude with

$$2q\sqrt{\Pr[\mathcal{B}_q^{|H\rangle} \Rightarrow x]} \leq 2q_H \sqrt{\mathbf{Adv}^P(\mathcal{C}_q)}. \tag{3}$$

This proves the claim. □

Finally we prove a special case for Type-II game hops. Here the function f, induced by the oracle-simple encryption scheme, is the identity function.[4]

---

[4] In fact, we could relax the requirement to f being bijective, however, we are not aware of a scheme where f is bijective and not the identity.

In this case we can bound the game advantage using well known results about finding marked items in a function given superposition access to the function. This works because the random oracle is invoked on an input chosen uniformly at random while generating the challenge ciphertext.

Lemma 10. *Let G_i and G_{i+1} be games such that the game hop between these is a Type-II game hop. Suppose the function f, specified by the oracle-simple encryption scheme, is the identity function. Then, for any quantum adversary $\mathcal{A}_q$, making q_H queries to $|H\rangle$, it holds that*

$$\mathbf{Adv}\left(G_i^{\mathcal{A}_q}, G_{i+1}^{\mathcal{A}_q}\right) \leq \frac{6(q_H + 1)}{\sqrt{|\mathsf{Dom}(H)|}} .$$

Proof. Given that f is the identity function, it holds that x is sampled uniformly at random from $\mathsf{Dom}(H)$. This allows us to bound the game advantage by the advantage of an adversary in finding marked items, for which bounds are known. Instead of the plain O2H lemma (cf. Lemma 1), we make use of the double-sided O2H lemma (cf. Lemma 2) to obtain a tighter bound.

Using the same argument from the proof of Lemma 9, we bound the game advantage by bounding the probability of detecting reprogramming of the random oracle, again, for ease of notation, assuming that the random oracle is reprogrammed to $\perp$. Thus it holds that

$$\mathbf{Adv}\left(G_i^{\mathcal{A}_q}, G_{i+1}^{\mathcal{A}_q}\right) \leq \left| \Pr[\mathcal{A}_q^{|H\rangle} \Rightarrow 1] - \Pr[\mathcal{A}_q^{|H_{x \to \perp}\rangle} \Rightarrow 1] \right| .$$

In order to apply the double-sided O2H lemma, two conditions have to be fulfilled. First, the random oracles must agree on all but one input and, second, the simulator $\mathcal{B}_q$ has to be able to simulate both random oracles. The former is fulfilled as the random oracles only differ on input x. The latter is a bit more subtle. The reason is that $\mathcal{B}_q$ has to simulate $|H_{x \to \perp}\rangle$ for an x unknown to $\mathcal{B}_q$, as knowledge of x would trivially allow to find the marked item. We show that this does not pose a hindrance. Let $\mathcal{B}_q$ be an algorithm that has access to a function $\mathcal{F} : \mathsf{Dom}(H) \to \{0,1\}$, such that $\mathcal{F}(x) = 1$ and $\mathcal{F}(a) = 0$ for all $a \neq x$. Consider the mapping $\mathcal{G} : \mathsf{Dom}(H) \times \{0,1\} \to \mathsf{CoDom}(H) \cup \{\perp\}$ such that

$$\mathcal{G}(x, b) = \begin{cases} \perp & , \text{if } b = 1 \\ H(x) & , \text{else} \end{cases} .$$

To simulate the quantum random oracle $|H\rangle$, $\mathcal{B}_q$ simply fixes the last input bit of $\mathcal{G}$ to be 0. To simulate the quantum random oracle $|H_{x \to \perp}\rangle$, $\mathcal{B}_q$ first invokes the function $\mathcal{F}$ on the input and sets the last input bit of $\mathcal{G}$ to the output of $\mathcal{F}$. For the marked item of $\mathcal{F}$, $\mathcal{G}$ will return $\perp$ as the last input bit is 1, while $\mathcal{G}$ returns the output of the random oracle for all non-marked items. This is illustrated in Fig. 4, where we assume that the domain and co-domain of the random oracle can be represented using n and k qubits, respectively.

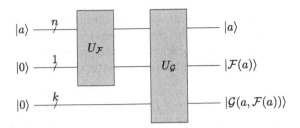

Fig. 4. Simulation of $|H_{x\to\perp}\rangle$ using $\mathcal{F}$ and $\mathcal{G}$.

If the adversary $\mathcal{A}_q$ can detect the reprogramming, then the simulator $\mathcal{B}_q$ can find the marked item in the function $\mathcal{F}$. Hence we conclude with

$$
\begin{aligned}
\mathbf{Adv}\left(\mathsf{G}_i^{\mathcal{A}_q}, \mathsf{G}_{i+1}^{\mathcal{A}_q}\right) &\leq \left|\Pr[\mathcal{A}_q^{|H\rangle} \Rightarrow 1] - \Pr[\mathcal{A}_q^{|H_{x\to\perp}\rangle} \Rightarrow 1]\right| \\
&\overset{\text{(Lemma 2)}}{\leq} 2\sqrt{\Pr[\mathcal{B}_q^{|H\rangle, |H_{x\to\perp}\rangle} \Rightarrow x]} \\
&\overset{\text{(Lemma 3)}}{\leq} 2\sqrt{\frac{8(q_H + 1)^2}{|\mathrm{Dom}(H)|}} \\
&\leq \frac{6(q_H + 1)}{\sqrt{|\mathrm{Dom}(H)|}}
\end{aligned}
$$

which proves the claim. $\qquad\qquad\qquad\qquad\qquad\qquad\qquad\qquad\qquad\qquad\quad\square$

Now we are ready to state our main result, namely the conditions under which our framework lifts the classical security proof of an oracle-simple public key encryption scheme in the post-quantum setting.

Theorem 11. *Let* $\mathrm{E} = (\mathsf{KGen}, \mathsf{Enc}^H, \mathsf{Dec}^H)$ *be an oracle-simple PKE scheme with function* f *according to Definition 5. Suppose there exists a classical security proof using a sequence of games* $\mathsf{G}_0, \ldots, \mathsf{G}_k$, *where* G_0 *is the* IND-CPA *game instantiated with* E *and* G_k *is constructed such that* $\mathbf{Adv}^{\mathsf{G}_k}(\mathcal{A}_c) = 0$. *Let* i *be such that the game hop between* G_{i-1} *and* G_i *is a Type-II game hop. If*

1. *for any* $j \in [k]\backslash\{i\}$, *the game hop between* G_{j-1} *and* G_j *is a Type-I game hop such that a quantum hard (decisional) problem* P_j *is reduced to the game advantage between* G_{j-1} *and* G_j *and*
2. *either some quantum hard (search) problem* P_i *is reduced to the probability of querying* x *or the function* f *is the identity function,*

then E *is* pq-IND-CPA-*secure.*

Proof. The proof follows pretty much from the previous lemmas. For the Type-I game hops, i.e., between G_{j-1} and G_j for $j \in [k]\backslash\{i\}$, we can apply Lemma 8 and conclude that the game advantage is bound by the post-quantum hardness of P_j. Since P_j is a quantum hard problem, this is negligible. For the Type-II game hop, i.e., between G_{i-1} and G_i, we can apply either Lemma 9, using again that P_i is hard for quantum adversaries, or using Lemma 10 if the function f is the identity function. As the game advantage of all game hops is negligible, we conclude that the advantage of any quantum adversary $\mathcal{A}_q$ in game pq-IND-CPA against $E = (\mathsf{KGen}, \mathsf{Enc}^H, \mathsf{Dec}^H)$ is also negligible. Hence, the oracle-simple public key encryption scheme E is pq-IND-CPA-secure.   □

4   Post-Quantum Security of PKE Schemes

We use our framework to lift the classical security of two public key encryption schemes to post-quantum security. In Sect. 4.1 we lift the security for the code-based public key encryption scheme ROLLO-II [20]. The post-quantum security of the lattice-based public key encryption scheme LARA [4] is proven in Sect. 4.2.

4.1   Code-Based Public Key Encryption Scheme ROLLO-II

We start by introducing the notation used in the public key encryption scheme ROLLO-II [20]. The scheme can be written as an oracle-simple encryption scheme with function f, where f maps vectors to their support. The pseudocode is given in Fig. 5.

Throughout, p is a prime and q is some power of p. For an integer k, the finite field that contains q^k elements is $\mathbb{F}_{q^k}$ and the corresponding vector space of dimension n is given by $\mathbb{F}_{q^k}^n$. The set of vectors of length n with rank weight w over the set $\mathbb{F}_{q^k}$ is denoted by $\mathcal{S}_w^n(\mathbb{F}_{q^k})$, where the rank weight of a vector is the rank of a specific matrix associated with that vector (see [20] for more details). Below we define the support of a word.

Definition 12. *Let* $\mathbf{x} = (x_1, \ldots, x_n) \in \mathbb{F}_{q^k}^n$. *The support* E *of* $\mathbf{x}$, *denoted* $\mathsf{Supp}(\mathbf{x})$, *is the* $\mathbb{F}_q$-*subspace of* $\mathbb{F}_{q^k}$ *generated by the* $\mathbf{x}$, *i.e.,* $E = \langle x_1, \ldots, x_n \rangle_{\mathbb{F}_q}$.

Multiplications are considered to be polynomial multiplications, where vectors and polynomials are transformed into one another by taking the vector entries as coefficients and vice versa. In the scheme, d and r are integers while P is an irreducible polynomial over $\mathbb{F}_{q^k}$.

The Ideal-LRPC codes indistinguishability problem, where LRPC stands for *low rank parity check*, asks to distinguish whether a vector $\mathbf{h}$ is sampled uniformly at random or computed as $\mathbf{x}^{-1}\mathbf{y} \bmod P$, for vectors $\mathbf{x}$, $\mathbf{y}$ of small dimension. In the ideal *rank support recovery* (Ideal-RSR) problem, one is given a vector $\mathbf{h}$, a polynomial P, and a syndrome σ, and asked to find a support E containing vectors $\mathbf{e}_1$, $\mathbf{e}_2$ such that $\mathbf{e}_1 + \mathbf{e}_2\mathbf{h} = \sigma \bmod P$.

The theorem below shows that the code-based encryption scheme ROLLO-II is pq-IND-CPA-secure.

Theorem 13. *Assuming the post-quantum hardness of the* Ideal-LRPC *problem and the* Ideal-RSR *problem, the code-based encryption scheme* ROLLO-II, *described in Fig. 5, is* pq-IND-CPA-*secure.*

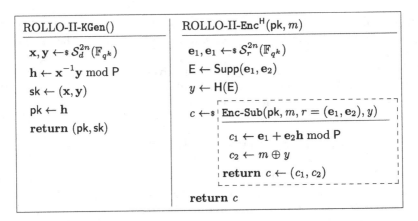

ROLLO-II-KGen()	ROLLO-II-Enc^H(pk, m)

$$\mathbf{x}, \mathbf{y} \leftarrow_{\$} \mathcal{S}_d^{2n}(\mathbb{F}_{q^k})$$

$$\mathbf{h} \leftarrow \mathbf{x}^{-1}\mathbf{y} \bmod P$$

$$\mathrm{sk} \leftarrow (\mathbf{x}, \mathbf{y})$$

$$\mathrm{pk} \leftarrow \mathbf{h}$$

return (pk, sk)

$$\mathbf{e}_1, \mathbf{e}_1 \leftarrow_{\$} \mathcal{S}_r^{2n}(\mathbb{F}_{q^k})$$

$$E \leftarrow \mathsf{Supp}(\mathbf{e}_1, \mathbf{e}_2)$$

$$y \leftarrow \mathsf{H}(E)$$

$$c \leftarrow_{\$} \mathsf{Enc\text{-}Sub}(\mathrm{pk}, m, r = (\mathbf{e}_1, \mathbf{e}_2), y)$$

$\quad\quad c_1 \leftarrow \mathbf{e}_1 + \mathbf{e}_2\mathbf{h} \bmod P$

$\quad\quad c_2 \leftarrow m \oplus y$

$\quad\quad$**return** $c \leftarrow (c_1, c_2)$

return c

Fig. 5. Encryption scheme ROLLO-II written as oracle-simple encryption scheme. Decryption is omitted as it is irrelevant for the IND-CPA security of the scheme.

Proof. The classical IND-CPA security proof of ROLLO-II, given in [20], uses games $G_0, \ldots, G_3$. Except for the first game G_0, we only state the change to its predecessor.

Game G_0: This is the IND-CPA game instantiated with ROLLO-II.
Game G_1: In this game the vector $\mathbf{h}$ is sampled randomly.
Game G_2: The value y is sampled randomly, independent of H.
Game G_3: The value c_2 is sampled randomly.

The game hop between G_1 and G_2 is a Type-II game hop, while all other game hops are Type-I game hops. The classical proof reduces the Ideal-LRPC problem to the game advantage between G_0 and G_1 (Type-I) and the Ideal-RSR problem to the probability of querying the random oracle on $E = \mathsf{Supp}(\mathbf{e}_1, \mathbf{e}_2)$ and thereby also to the game advantage between G_1 and G_2 (Type-II). The game hop between G_2 and G_3 (Type-I) is bound by the problem of distinguishing between a one-time pad encryption and a random ciphertext. Since all these problems are assumed to be hard even for quantum adversaries, Theorem 11 proves the claim. $\qquad \square$

4.2 Lattice-Based Public Key Encryption Scheme LARA

We start by introducing the notation used in the public key encryption scheme LARA [4]. The scheme, written as an oracle-simple encryption scheme, is given in Fig. 6. Throughout this section, q is an integer and n is a power of 2. The polynomial ring $\mathbb{Z}_q[X]/\langle X^n + 1 \rangle$ is denoted by $\mathcal{R}_q$. The decisional learning with errors (DLWE) problem asks to distinguish whether a polynomial z is sampled uniformly at random or generated as $z \leftarrow as + e$, where a is given and s and e are small polynomials which are kept secret.

We refer to [4] for the parameters s, w, p, and r_{sec}, as applying our framework is independent of those. LARA uses the discrete Gaussian distribution which is denoted by $\mathcal{D}_{x,\sigma}$, where x and σ are the support and standard deviation, respectively. Multiplications are considered to be polynomial multiplications. Vectors and polynomials are transformed into one another by setting the coefficients to the vector entries and vice versa. The scheme uses an encoding function Encode which maps messages to polynomials.

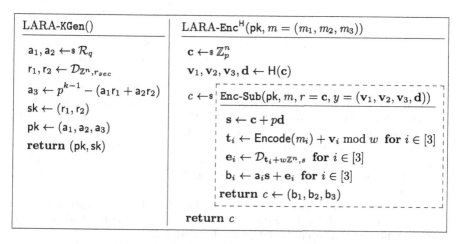

Fig. 6. Encryption scheme LARA written as an oracle-simple encryption scheme. Decryption is omitted as it is irrelevant for the IND-CPA security of the scheme.

The following theorem states that the lattice-based encryption scheme LARA is pq-IND-CPA-secure.

Theorem 14. *Assuming the post-quantum hardness of the* DLWE *problem, the lattice-based encryption scheme LARA, described in Fig. 6, is* pq-IND-CPA-*secure.*

Proof. The classical IND-CPA security proof of LARA, given in [4], uses games $G_0, \ldots, G_4$. Except for game G_0, we only state the change to its predecessor.

GameG_0: This is the IND-CPA game instantiated with LARA.
GameG_1: In this game the polynomial a_3 is sampled randomly.
GameG_2: The vectors v_1, v_2, v_3, d are sampled randomly, independent of H.
GameG_3: The polynomials e_i are sampled according to the distribution $\mathcal{D}_{\mathbb{Z}^n, s}$.
GameG_4: The polynomials b_i are sampled randomly.

The game hop between G_1 and G_2 is a Type-II game hop, while all other game hops are Type-I game hops. The classical proof reduces the DLWE problem (with a different number of samples) to the game advantage between the Type-I game hops. We further observe that the function f is the identity function for LARA. Thus, we can apply Theorem 11 which proves the claim.   □

Acknowledgements. We thank Nina Bindel and Lucas Schabhüser for insightful discussions. We also thank an anonymous reviewer for valuable feedback on an earlier version of this paper. This work was funded by the Deutsche Forschungsgemeinschaft (DFG) – SFB 1119 – 236615297 and by the German Ministry of Education, Research and Technology in the context of the project Aquorypt (grant number 16KIS1022).

References

1. Albrecht, M.R., Orsini, E., Paterson, K.G., Peer, G., Smart, N.P.: Tightly secure Ring-LWE based key encapsulation with short ciphertexts. In: Foley, S.N., Gollmann, D., Snekkenes, E. (eds.) ESORICS 2017. LNCS, vol. 10492, pp. 29–46. Springer, Cham (2017). https://doi.org/10.1007/978-3-319-66402-6_4
2. Alkim, E., et al.: Revisiting TESLA in the quantum random oracle model. In: Lange, T., Takagi, T. (eds.) PQCrypto 2017. LNCS, vol. 10346, pp. 143–162. Springer, Cham (2017). https://doi.org/10.1007/978-3-319-59879-6_9
3. Ambainis, A., Hamburg, M., Unruh, D.: Quantum security proofs using semi-classical oracles. In: Boldyreva, A., Micciancio, D. (eds.) CRYPTO 2019. LNCS, vol. 11693, pp. 269–295. Springer, Cham (2019). https://doi.org/10.1007/978-3-030-26951-7_10
4. El Bansarkhani, R.: LARA: a design concept for lattice-based encryption. In: Goldberg, I., Moore, T. (eds.) FC 2019. LNCS, vol. 11598, pp. 377–395. Springer, Cham (2019). https://doi.org/10.1007/978-3-030-32101-7_23
5. Bardet, M., et al.: Big quake. NIST Round 1 Candidate (2019)
6. Bellare, M., Rogaway, P.: Random oracles are practical: a paradigm for designing efficient protocols. In: Denning, D.E., Pyle, R., Ganesan, R., Sandhu, R.S., Ashby, V. (eds.) ACM CCS 1993, pp. 62–73. ACM Press, November 1993
7. Bellare, M., Rogaway, P.: The security of triple encryption and a framework for code-based game-playing proofs. In: Vaudenay, S. (ed.) EUROCRYPT 2006. LNCS, vol. 4004, pp. 409–426. Springer, Heidelberg (2006). https://doi.org/10.1007/11761679_25
8. Bindel, N., Hamburg, M., Hövelmanns, K., Hülsing, A., Persichetti, E.: Tighter proofs of CCA security in the quantum random oracle model. In: Hofheinz, D., Rosen, A. (eds.) TCC 2019. LNCS, vol. 11892, pp. 61–90. Springer, Cham (2019). https://doi.org/10.1007/978-3-030-36033-7_3
9. Boneh, D., Dagdelen, Ö., Fischlin, M., Lehmann, A., Schaffner, C., Zhandry, M.: Random oracles in a quantum world. In: Lee, D.H., Wang, X. (eds.) ASIACRYPT 2011. LNCS, vol. 7073, pp. 41–69. Springer, Heidelberg (2011). https://doi.org/10.1007/978-3-642-25385-0_3
10. Dagdelen, Ö., Fischlin, M., Gagliardoni, T.: The Fiat–Shamir transformation in a quantum world. In: Sako, K., Sarkar, P. (eds.) ASIACRYPT 2013. LNCS, vol. 8270, pp. 62–81. Springer, Heidelberg (2013). https://doi.org/10.1007/978-3-642-42045-0_4
11. Don, J., Fehr, S., Majenz, C., Schaffner, C.: Security of the Fiat-Shamir transformation in the quantum random-oracle model. In: Boldyreva, A., Micciancio, D. (eds.) CRYPTO 2019. LNCS, vol. 11693, pp. 356–383. Springer, Cham (2019). https://doi.org/10.1007/978-3-030-26951-7_13
12. Fujisaki, E., Okamoto, T.: Secure integration of asymmetric and symmetric encryption schemes. In: Wiener, M. (ed.) CRYPTO 1999. LNCS, vol. 1666, pp. 537–554. Springer, Heidelberg (1999). https://doi.org/10.1007/3-540-48405-1_34

13. Gagliardoni, T.: Quantum security of cryptographic primitives. Ph.D. thesis, Darmstadt University of Technology, Germany (2017)
14. Grilo, A.B., Kerenidis, I., Zijlstra, T.: Learning-with-errors problem is easy with quantum samples. Phys. Rev. A **99**(3), 032314 (2019)
15. Hofheinz, D., Hövelmanns, K., Kiltz, E.: A modular analysis of the Fujisaki-okamoto transformation. In: Kalai, Y., Reyzin, L. (eds.) TCC 2017. LNCS, vol. 10677, pp. 341–371. Springer, Cham (2017). https://doi.org/10.1007/978-3-319-70500-2_12
16. Hülsing, A., Rijneveld, J., Song, F.: Mitigating multi-target attacks in hash-based signatures. In: Cheng, C.-M., Chung, K.-M., Persiano, G., Yang, B.-Y. (eds.) PKC 2016. LNCS, vol. 9614, pp. 387–416. Springer, Heidelberg (2016). https://doi.org/10.1007/978-3-662-49384-7_15
17. Jiang, H., Zhang, Z., Chen, L., Wang, H., Ma, Z.: IND-CCA-secure key encapsulation mechanism in the quantum random oracle model, revisited. In: Shacham, H., Boldyreva, A. (eds.) CRYPTO 2018. LNCS, vol. 10993, pp. 96–125. Springer, Cham (2018). https://doi.org/10.1007/978-3-319-96878-0_4
18. Kiltz, E., Lyubashevsky, V., Schaffner, C.: A concrete treatment of Fiat-Shamir signatures in the quantum random-oracle model. In: Nielsen, J.B., Rijmen, V. (eds.) EUROCRYPT 2018. LNCS, vol. 10822, pp. 552–586. Springer, Cham (2018). https://doi.org/10.1007/978-3-319-78372-7_18
19. Liu, Q., Zhandry, M.: Revisiting post-quantum Fiat-Shamir. In: Boldyreva, A., Micciancio, D. (eds.) CRYPTO 2019. LNCS, vol. 11693, pp. 326–355. Springer, Cham (2019). https://doi.org/10.1007/978-3-030-26951-7_12
20. Melchor, C.A.: Rollo. NIST Round 2 Candidate (2019)
21. Nielsen, M.A., Chuang, I.L.: Quantum Computation and Quantum Information: 10th Anniversary Edition, 10th edn. Cambridge University Press, New York (2011)
22. Saito, T., Xagawa, K., Yamakawa, T.: Tightly-secure key-encapsulation mechanism in the quantum random oracle model. In: Nielsen, J.B., Rijmen, V. (eds.) EUROCRYPT 2018. LNCS, vol. 10822, pp. 520–551. Springer, Cham (2018). https://doi.org/10.1007/978-3-319-78372-7_17
23. Shoup, V.: Sequences of games: a tool for taming complexity in security proofs. Cryptology ePrint Archive, Report 2004/332 (2004). http://eprint.iacr.org/2004/332
24. Song, F.: A note on quantum security for post-quantum cryptography. In: Mosca, M. (ed.) PQCrypto 2014. LNCS, vol. 8772, pp. 246–265. Springer, Cham (2014). https://doi.org/10.1007/978-3-319-11659-4_15
25. Targhi, E.E., Unruh, D.: Post-quantum security of the Fujisaki-Okamoto and OAEP transforms. In: Hirt, M., Smith, A. (eds.) TCC 2016. LNCS, vol. 9986, pp. 192–216. Springer, Heidelberg (2016). https://doi.org/10.1007/978-3-662-53644-5_8
26. Unruh, D.: Revocable quantum timed-release encryption. J. ACM **62**(6), 49:1–49:76 (2015)
27. Unruh, D.: Post-quantum security of Fiat-Shamir. In: Takagi, T., Peyrin, T. (eds.) ASIACRYPT 2017. LNCS, vol. 10624, pp. 65–95. Springer, Cham (2017). https://doi.org/10.1007/978-3-319-70694-8_3
28. Zhandry, M.: Secure identity-based encryption in the quantum random oracle model. In: Safavi-Naini, R., Canetti, R. (eds.) CRYPTO 2012. LNCS, vol. 7417, pp. 758–775. Springer, Heidelberg (2012). https://doi.org/10.1007/978-3-642-32009-5_44

29. Zhandry, M.: How to record quantum queries, and applications to quantum indifferentiability. In: Boldyreva, A., Micciancio, D. (eds.) CRYPTO 2019. LNCS, vol. 11693, pp. 239–268. Springer, Cham (2019). https://doi.org/10.1007/978-3-030-26951-7_9

Author Index